THE CAMBRIDGE HISTORY OF
GAY AND LESBIAN LITERATURE

The Cambridge History of Gay and Lesbian Literature presents a global history of the field. It is an unprecedented summation of critical knowledge on gay and lesbian literature that also addresses the impact of gay and lesbian literature on cognate fields such as comparative literature and postcolonial studies. Covering subjects from Sappho and the Greeks to queer modernism, diasporic literatures, and responses to the AIDS crisis, this volume is grounded in current scholarship. It presents new critical approaches to gay and lesbian literature that will serve the needs of students and specialists alike. Written by leading scholars in the field, *The Cambridge History of Gay and Lesbian Literature* will not only engage readers in contemporary debates but also serve as a definitive reference for gay and lesbian literature for years to come.

E. L. MCCALLUM is associate professor of English at Michigan State University. Her essays have appeared in journals such as *Technoculture, Postmodern Culture, Poetics Today, differences, Arizona Quarterly,* and *Camera Obscura,* as well as in a number of edited collections.

MIKKO TUHKANEN is associate professor of English and Africana studies at Texas A&M University. His essays have appeared in *diacritics, American Literature, GLQ, Modern Fiction Studies,* and *Cultural Critique.*

THE CAMBRIDGE
HISTORY OF
GAY AND LESBIAN LITERATURE

*

Edited by

E. L. MCCALLUM
Michigan State University

MIKKO TUHKANEN
Texas A&M University

CAMBRIDGE
UNIVERSITY PRESS

32 Avenue of the Americas, New York, NY 10013-2473, USA

Cambridge University Press is part of the University of Cambridge.

It furthers the University's mission by disseminating knowledge in the pursuit of education, learning, and research at the highest international levels of excellence.

www.cambridge.org
Information on this title: www.cambridge.org/9781107035218

© E. L. McCallum and Mikko Tuhkanen 2014

First published 2014

Printed in the United States of America

A catalog record for this publication is available from the British Library.

Library of Congress Cataloging in Publication data
The Cambridge history of gay and lesbian literature / edited by
E. L. McCallum, Mikko Tuhkanen.
pages   cm
Includes bibliographical references and index.
ISBN 978-1-107-03521-8 (hardback)
1. Homosexuality in literature.   2. Homosexuality and literature.   3. Gays' writings –
History and criticism.   4. Gays in literature.   5. Homosexuality – History.
I. McCallum, E. L. (Ellen Lee), 1966–   II. Tuhkanen, Mikko, 1967–
PN56.H57C365   2014
809'.8920664–dc23   2014016635

ISBN 978-1-107-03521-8 Hardback

Contents

v

Contents

Contents

Contents

PART VI
GENRES OF THE PRESENT

Contents

Contributors

HARRIETTE ANDREADIS, Texas A&M University
ABDULHAMIT ARVAS, Michigan State University
GERSHUN AVILEZ, Yale University
BRIAN JAMES BAER, Kent State University
THOMAS BAUER, Westfälische Wilhelms-Universität Münster
DAVID BERGMAN, Towson University
BRINDA BOSE, University of Delhi
MICHAEL BRONSKI, Harvard University
STEVEN BRUHM, University of Western Ontario
CHRISTOPHER CASTIGLIA, Pennsylvania State University
MERRILL COLE, Western Illinois University
PETER COVIELLO, Bowdoin College
SARA DANIUS, Södertörn University
TIM DEAN, University at Buffalo (SUNY)
PHILIPPE C. DUBOIS, Bucknell University
CHRIS DUNTON, National University of Lesotho
ELISA GLICK, University of Missouri
JONATHAN GOLDBERG, Emory University
HELENA GURFINKEL, Southern Illinois University, Edwardsville
NEVILLE HOAD, University of Texas, Austin
THOMAS K. HUBBARD, University of Texas, Austin
ANALOUISE KEATING, Texas Women's University
ERIC KEENAGHAN, University at Albany (SUNY)
DAVID DECOSTA LEITAO, San Francisco State University
KARMA LOCHRIE, Indiana University
E. L. MCCALLUM, Michigan State University
LISA O'CONNELL, University of Queensland
DAVID L. ORVIS, Appalachian State University
GEMA PÉREZ-SÁNCHEZ, University of Miami
JAY REED, Brown University
ROBERT REID-PHARR, City University of New York
STEVEN RUSZCZYCKY, University at Buffalo (SUNY)
DARIECK SCOTT, University of California, Berkeley

Contributors

PATRICIA SIEBER, Ohio State University
HUGH STEVENS, University College London
LISA TATONETTI, Kansas State University
OMISE'EKE NATASHA TINSLEY, University of Texas, Austin
ROBERT TOBIN, Clark University
ERIC L. TRIBUNELLA, University of Southern Mississippi
MIKKO TUHKANEN, Texas A&M University
SHERRY VELASCO, University of Southern California
GIOVANNI VITIELLO, University of Naples, "L'Orientale"
SARA WARNER, Cornell University

Acknowledgments

The editors would like to thank our contributors for their excellent scholarship and thoughtful engagement with this project's endeavor not simply to define but to reframe this important area of study. We are immensely grateful to our editorial assistant, Steven Ambrose, whose eye for detail and careful reading were indispensable to bringing this book to completion. We thank as well our editor at Cambridge University Press, Ray Ryan, for his patient and understanding support of this project; his advice and assistance have been invaluable at every stage.

Introduction

E. L. MCCALLUM AND MIKKO TUHKANEN

Is there such a thing as "gay and lesbian literature?" It might seem odd to pose this question at the outset of a collection of essays appearing under this very heading, much less one whose title implicitly asserts that not only does such literature exist but that it has a history. Our view is that all the terms of the title bear equal degrees of skepticism, yet insofar as there is a thing called "literature," or a formation of "history" that charts the evolution of this entity, there could be something that might be called "gay and lesbian" literature. As Barbara Johnson has observed, "it is not simply a question of literature's ability to say or not say the truth of sexuality. For from the moment literature begins to try to set things straight on that score, literature itself becomes inextricable from the sexuality that it seeks to comprehend" (13). As astute a close reader as Johnson would not miss the queer resonances of "to set things straight"; we begin with Johnson's insight in order to signal this volume's intention to undo how literary studies has been set (as) straight.

To peruse the ranks of Cambridge's History of Literature series is to be faced with collections largely organized by nation, period, or genre. By contrast, this volume works across those three major vectors for organizing literary studies. Notwithstanding Queer Nation's campy activist formation in the 1990s, and in line with Lauren Berlant and Elizabeth Freeman's trenchant assessment of the nation paradigm for queer sociopolitical organizing, LGBTQI people hardly constitute a nation. Indeed, as not a few of our contributors point out, the state may attempt to expunge all evidence of same-sex desire, whether in literary or actual practice, in the very name of "nation." Nor does "gay and lesbian" necessarily indicate a period, even though the history of sexuality marks the inception of the term "homosexual" as a particular Western ontological category in the sexual taxonomy of the late nineteenth century. If "gay and lesbian literature" depends on a notion of the homosexual, such literature would be periodized as a peculiarly modern and Western phenomenon. Nor, finally, is "gay and lesbian literature" a genre. Ever since the Sumerian story

I

of *Gilgamesh*, one of the first epics, the expression of same-sex desire has been narrativized, lyricized, dramatized, and chronicled – at times, moreover, bending gender to the point where the sameness of "sex" is itself in question, even if the genre is not. Moreover, within a geographically or historically bounded literary field, "genre" is a multiply significant term that can code class and educational differences as differences of taste. The representation of same-sex desire, however, crosses all literary tastes, from readily accessible pulp fiction to more difficult experimental modernist genre-bending texts and rigorously formal Shakespearean sonnets.

Any attempt to historicize lesbian and gay literature immediately confronts, then, several interlocking difficulties: namely, how do we identify, much less understand, identity categories like "gay" or "lesbian," which are founded on locally contingent sexual practices, networks, and desires? As scholars of sexuality's histories have recurrently told us, we must be wary of simplifying, miscategorizing, and thereby misreading literary and sexual expressions that vary widely across cultures and historical periods. Post-Stonewall anthologies of "gay" or "gay and lesbian" literature have been faulted for uncritically uniting under the banner "gay" such incommensurable figures as the pederast of ancient Greece, the Two-Spirit individual of many indigenous cultures of North America, and the medieval sodomite, among others. The question of whether there can be said to be a "homosexuality" before persons in first-world modern societies began identifying themselves through this term, promoted in nineteenth-century sexology, has been expatiated by cultural and literary scholars for more than twenty years, and our contributors continue this inquiry. As critics who research sexual expression in texts from premodern periods or from non-Western cultures refine and complicate their analyses, they map the continuities and discontinuities of how people in times and places other than the modern West inscribe their sexual identities, practices, and desires through literature. Such research enables us to say, albeit with some degree of caution, that there *is* a literary history of and for sexually marginalized people, and that this literary history must be understood as situated in cultures across the globe and from ancient times to modern.

In a similar way – especially for this set of texts, once they have been identified – the term "literature" itself cannot be taken for granted because the writing of same-sex desire traverses canonical as well as noncanonical or even uncanonizable works – which is to say, writing that exceeds literary boundaries or invents new genres (as Montaigne's essays do, defining *l'amitié* as what can only be explained by "parce que c'était lui, parce que c'était moi"; "because it was he, because it was I"). The literature of same-sex desire includes texts ranging from philosophical dialogues of antiquity, to early modern sonnets, to award-winning twentieth-century novels, to science fictions of future worlds. The recent long century of "homosexuality" has witnessed the emergence of a literary canon that draws its inspiration from expressions and representations of same-sex desires in prior centuries. This canon – or, to put it more accurately, these canons – have greatly influenced how individuals have identified themselves as lesbian or gay. As David Bergman noted some twenty years ago, so many questioning youth come first to acknowledge their desires through their relation to texts rather than people (5–6). Yet the solitary pursuits of the library are indissociable from the pursuit of like-minded others; thus, beyond supporting individuals' identities, gay or lesbian literary canons have served to elaborate a common culture for their respective communities and subcultures. And while these canons have – like any other in the past half century – not stood unchanged or unchallenged, in the several iterations of lists of books every young queer should read persist some literary classics of same-sex desire (Sappho's fragments; Plato's *Symposium*; a number of Shakespeare's sonnets; Whitman's "Calamus" series; Oscar Wilde's oeuvre; Radclyffe Hall's *The Well of Loneliness*; James Baldwin's *Giovanni's Room*; Virginia Woolf's *Mrs. Dalloway*).

Each chapter in this volume implicitly charts the formation, and many seek the de-formation, of such canons. The chapters constitute responses to ongoing debates about gay historiography – how same-sex sexual desires and practices have been culturally and historically configured in a wide range of modes – as well as to the debates about the nature of literature and of literary canons per se, the politics around inclusion and exclusion, or the sensitivity to questions of aesthetics and literary merit versus representational or cultural significance. Our principle for defining the horizon and organization of this volume draws on Wai Chee Dimock's idea of planetary literatures, fields of texts that constitutively cross temporal and geographic boundaries. As Dimock puts it in *Through Other Continents* (2006), this paradigm models how to relinquish the idea of national literature as a bounded entity and replace it with one that consists of "a crisscrossing set of pathways, open-ended and ever multiplying, weaving in and out of other geographies, other languages and cultures" (3). We had asked contributors to bear in mind such traversals of language, culture, and geography as they formulated their chapters because we think that this approach offers a promising way to open up connections even beyond the necessary limits of this volume.

While we aim to keep an eye on the larger literary-historical trends, at the same time we recognize that readers of *The Cambridge History of Gay and*

Lesbian Literature are likely to turn to this volume in search of a particular author – say, Sappho, Lord Byron, Walt Whitman, Marcel Proust, Thomas Mann, Virginia Woolf, Gertrude Stein, James Baldwin, Gloria Anzaldúa – or certain key works. So in addition to the encyclopedic scope of some chapters, we sought to include a few essays that focus narrowly on specific works or authors, providing a keyhole that will open up the discussion to a larger tradition/history in a national, transnational, subcultural, or transcultural context. By including such perspectives, we balance the "planetary" with a much more local approach, helping readers scale their understandings of lesbian and gay literary history at multiple levels: the level of the unique text; of the author's oeuvre; or, in the absence of an author-figure, a constellation of texts that speak to one another in a particular cultural moment (be it lesbian pulp novels or the Elizabethan stage), the region, school, or movement in which certain works are situated (for example, romanticism, modernism, or feminism), or the planetary traversals that lesbian or gay literature traces (say, the elegy, in ancient Greece or the age of AIDS).

As we planned this volume we questioned whether chapters should focus on the works of identifiably gay or lesbian authors (Christopher Marlowe, Audre Lorde, Constantine Cavafy) or on works featuring same-sex eroticism no matter what the orientation of the author. We suggested our contributors not choose between but rather embrace both. Moreover, setting aside the complications of historical apprehension and naming, questions of the "degree" of same-sex interest haunt critical reading and selection: how do we acknowledge and discuss a spectrum of sexuality? If explicitly represented erotic acts and professions of ardor count, how do they compare to the more ambiguous or indirectly represented ranges of sociability, friendship, or even unshared affect (desire, love, obsession, repressed attraction)? To what extent does representation of women's desire – a challenge in patriarchal cultures in the best of times and a long-standing concern of feminist criticism – differ from that of men, which may be under other kinds of pressure – whether to explicitness in phallophilic cultures, or indirection in homophobic ones. In some instances, we disintricated lesbian and gay literary history in separate chapters or threads within chapters, for however interrelated the histories of male and female homosexuality are, there remain distinctions that must not be assimilated into one "homosexual" paradigm. In other instances, we encouraged contributors to work across the traditions of lesbian and gay writing, for the perspectives they share in being sexual minorities or for their common ground in other social and political commitments (to friendship, say, or social justice), or simply to highlight the incommensurability of the comparison.

Although the title claims a focus on *Gay and Lesbian Literature*, a number of our contributors shied from using the eponymous terminology. While this is at minimum an issue of translation – as Patricia Sieber and Giovanni Vitiello show, for instance, in Chinese there are a range of terms that signify same-sex desiring individuals – terminology tends to be an intellectual question deeply imbricated in each chapter's stakes. Even the question of translation is hardly simple. Thomas Bauer's chapter on classical Arabic and Abdulhamit Arvas's chapter on Ottoman literature converge on some similar terms that crossed between Arabic and Turkish languages and marked some shared cultural practices; but as Bauer and Arvas show, these seemingly similar terms take on very distinct cultural valences in their respective contexts. At times, of course, it just makes scholarly sense to avoid "gay" or "lesbian" to discuss the depictions of sexuality, as Karma Lochrie's medieval chapter demonstrates: to use these terms is to impose a modern view of sexuality on a much different cultural world, even if it is the one historically anchoring the Anglophone culture of today. Similarly, Lisa Tatonetti's chapter on Native American literature charts a political nomenclature that signals the recovery of a larger marginalized history of indigenous North Americans.

But even the chapters focusing on the modern West will work among a range of terms, quite often favoring some version of the acronym LGBTQI (lesbian-gay-bisexual-transgender-queer/questioning-intersex) or simply the term "queer," which itself seeks to destabilize and call into question the very possibility of identity categories and concomitant politics (a liberal, entity-based rights system rather than, say, a progressive antidiscriminatory and possibility-generating system). We embrace the range of terms and acronyms offered by the chapters as a key rhetorical move for underscoring the politics of literary canonization and the urgency of literature as a dynamic, world-making force. This is part of our attempt to move away from what Robert Reid-Pharr, in his contribution, calls "the production of tinny, one-dimensional depictions of human possibility that disable us in our efforts to name the complexity of human existence."

With our planetary approach, we thus do not presume a single canon or tradition. Rather, our aim is to provide a composite and dynamic view: how certain texts traverse the distance from one cultural or historical context to implant themselves into another, how certain other texts might remain dominant across centuries even as their significance is reconfigured or revalued by readers, and finally how some texts circulated forcefully in one place or era but have not (yet) been picked up by subsequent moments. Thus, while our trajectory ostensibly moves from ancient times to the present, it is important to recognize how within that order the chapters afford different, lateral, and retrospective movements. Epitomizing this queerly nonlinear history, for example, the very first chapter traces cross-temporal genealogies of Sappho as both a lesbian icon and a writer whose case illustrates the complexities of reading literature outside one's own historical, geographical, and linguistic moment. Because so much of the tradition in what might belatedly be called "gay and lesbian literature" draws on and refers back to antiquity, especially ancient Greece, we felt it important to anchor the volume in classical literature but simultaneously to mark how the return to antiquity varies in later centuries and in different cultural traditions. Other chapters in the section "Reading Ancient and Classical Cultures" trace the importance of such formations as the Platonic dialogues and the Greek pastoral for subsequent eras' expression of same-sex desire. Jay Reed's treatment of the pastoral will resonate with Thomas Hubbard's and Jonathan Goldberg's subsequent attention to this form. These ancient texts provide a paradigmatic case for the accessibility of meaning in writing that is remote from our moment in time, space, and cultural practice, and they illustrate how the movement of poems or dialogues through time and across cultures is affected not only by the material transformation of the text (fragmentation or loss of the physical record) but by the contextual transformation of meaning. Yet a similarly meticulous stance toward texts in a more recent field, like children's literature – which the volume's penultimate chapter explores – yields equally resonant questions about the shifting nature of representation, expression, and identity.

The chapter groupings suggest the importance of same-sex passions' expression to various historical moments, but the sectioning is not neat. The first section includes chapters on founding moments in other major literatures: those in English, Arabic, and Chinese. So while these are not strictly speaking "ancient" in historical terms, these literatures serve, as antiquity does for European culture in general, as the intellectual anchor of cultural identity. Moreover, Karma Lochrie's term "configurations" of sexuality and gender as a way to highlight the difficulty of interpreting same-sex intimacies in a remote period continues to reverberate in later sections and eras. While the chapters in the "Renaissance and Early Modern" section map the configurations of same-sex desire that might be said to be the genealogical forbearers of modern gays and lesbians, these authors also trouble any easy linearity that might be drawn from, say, the libertine to the invert to the homosexual. Both Goldberg and Arvas trace the shifting significance of the expression of same-sex love in canonical literatures, while Sherry Velasco, David Orvis, and Lisa O'Connell examine in the literary traces of what we might think of as queer figures today the complications of claiming early modern subversions of gender and sexuality as gay precursors.

As we move into the "Enlightenment Cultures" section, the authors' attention turns to the affective bonds that undergird the nascent discourses and institutions of the Age of Reason – bonds of nation, friendship, and affection in which same-sex expression plays a significant role. Speaking of the French Revolution and the rise of the modern state, Enlightenment and Rousseau scholar Robert Wokler writes: "In addition to superimposing undivided rule upon its subjects, the genuinely modern state further requires that those who fall under its authority be united themselves – that they form one people, one nation, morally bound together by a common identity" (197). As Peter Coviello suggests, in the early days of the United States such unity coalesced from various forms of intimate affiliation, some of which appear to twentieth- and twenty-first century observers markedly queer. Many of the shifts in the ways that such intimacies signified as the nineteenth century progressed were responses to the discourses and institutions of human sciences, including sexology and racial sciences; hence, Coviello enjoins us to recognize the history of nationhood – the production of its affective collectivity – as coincident with the history of sexuality. It is here that we can discern Eve Kosofsky Sedgwick's continuing importance to LGBTQI scholarship. Sedgwick's early work, particularly in *Between Men: English Literature and Male Homosocial Desire* (1985), famously rendered visible the purloined letter of male same-sex desire – the shifting line between the homosocial and the homosexual – in the most canonical of historical and literary texts. Drawing on the recent "affective turn" in literary scholarship, the chapters in this section seek to access the unspent energies of queer intimacies that the epistemological frames of traditional historiographies tend to render invisible. Where Robert Tobin, Christopher Castiglia, and Peter Coviello track the range and intensity of homo-desiring cadences that, given later twentieth-century shifts in identity formations, were to be silenced, Steven Bruhm and GerShun Avilez attend to literatures that have, albeit for different reasons, more directly problematized sexuality – namely, the Gothic and African American literature.

The section "Queer Modernisms" frames the emergence of a self-consciously defined homosexual culture and its self-consciously experimental literature, but even here, as Sara Danius reminds us in the case of Proust, the resistances to "homosexual" enrich the reading and the writing of these texts. Similarly, Omise'eke Natasha Tinsley reads Caribbean women's expressive histories in line with the affective problematic framed by the "Enlightenment Cultures" section, to seek the frequencies we need to tune into to discern the prolific traces of women-loving women in the archives of transatlantic Caribbean literature. In various ways, Elisa Glick, Merrill Cole, and Helena Gurfinkel's chapters work across national and linguistic boundaries to map the collusion of modern cultural forces in the emergence of queer figures and queer affective flows.

The last two sections focus largely on contemporary literature, understood as the long twentieth century into the present moment. Again, the division is schematic rather than strict. We brought together the chapters in the "Geographies of Same-Sex Desire in the Modern World" section to make manifest the planetary stakes of LGBTQI literature – that it is not some marginal, peculiarly Euro-American phenomenon. The chapters themselves trouble national definitions of literature, whether it be Philippe Dubois's reading of francophone texts from Paris to Quebec to Morocco or Lisa Tatonetti's and Neville Hoad and Chris Dunton's continental vantage that reads across the literatures of a number of nations. Finally, we conclude with a section that uses the commonality of language and period to focus attention on genre. Authors in "Genres of the Present" explore the various ways that modern homosexuality articulated itself in specific ways through poetry, drama, fiction, autobiography, sci-fi/fantasy literatures, pulp fiction and popular culture, children's literature, and the various responses elicited by the AIDS crisis.

As essential to the history of any literature as primary texts are, a thorough literary archive also concerns itself with secondary work – that which elucidates, critiques, interprets, or otherwise comments on the literature itself. Most of our contributors not only reflect the state of the field, glossing how previous scholarship has treated representations of same-sex desire, but, more important, work to engage and redefine the scholarship. That is, the critical task of each essay is twofold: to weigh the various scholarly approaches that have developed in lesbian and gay literary studies (with its necessary links to the fields of historical, sociological, or psychological research); and to contribute to the reconceptualization or elaboration of scholarship. Bearing in mind the "deep time" scale of our planetary approach, we have also encouraged contributors to sustain anachronistic and other critical tensions in order to open up not only the field of "gay and lesbian literature" but also link to other fields – national literatures, bodies of texts understood in terms of temporal, cultural, or geographical boundedness – and their ongoing reconceptualization.

The ethos of our project, then, strives toward opening up categories and establishing interconnections, in agreement with recent trends in literary studies that seek to rearticulate previously bounded entities (for example, "American literature" or "Medieval literature") with neglected genealogies that connect these entities to other traditions across temporal and geographic boundaries. The project conceives of literary history not as a master narrative but along Foucauldian lines as a genealogy, or, to push the planetary metaphor further, as a sampled geology. This collection makes no claim to bring a total view of the possibilities for lesbian and gay literary history; inevitably not all texts or subfields, even quite significant ones, can be included. We hope that the silences, absences, and gaps in the composite picture emerge as productively as do the interconnections among what *is* here.

Because of the unusual breadth of the project and the liveliness of current debates in literary studies about lesbian, gay, and queer historiography, as well as the extension and evolution of literature itself, we are mindful, then, of a certain impossibility that characterizes this project. The task of deciding what to include is necessarily arbitrary, whether at the chapter level or in the book as a whole. Many of our contributors acknowledge this bind by issuing what Darieck Scott, in his chapter, calls "the standard prophylactic": that what follows does not seek coverage but aims at experimenting with useful narratives through which to think about the field's past, present, and future. The range of possible accounts seems infinite, and we make no claims to offering a comprehensive view. If in our conceptualization of the project we are deemed guilty of courting what Hegel calls "bad infinity," we may want to own our badness. For Hegel, true infinity tends toward the synthetic moment of the Absolute, the subsumption of disparate parts into sense-making unity; this has allowed not only him but also later critics, such as Francis Fukuyama, to claim "the end" as their historical moment, as embodied in a given collectivization (say, the nation), political structure (liberal democracy), or socioeconomic system (neoliberal capitalism).

Rather than adopting this teleological movement as history's truth, one might think about a different model of history with some help from Chinua Achebe. In *Things Fall Apart* (1959), Achebe narrates, in what many scholars have considered a tragic mode, the encounter between Igbo culture and European colonizers. He illustrates the various ways this encounter may have taken place by briefly contrasting the actions of Okonkwo, the novel's non-adaptive protagonist, to those of Uchendu, his more thoughtful neighbor. Uchendu addresses a group of villagers debating the appropriate response to the strangers' arrival: "'There is no story that is not true,'" he says, deploying the culture's typically allusive language. "'The world has no end, and what is good among one people is an abomination among others. We have albinos among us. Do you not think that they came to our clan by mistake, that they have strayed from their way to a land where everybody is like them?'" (141).

If the world has no end – if it is infinite – then another name for the processes of disintegration that the title of Achebe's novel evokes is *becoming*, the world's movement toward new constellations. This becoming is not, like the Enlightenment "perfectibility" that Hegel posits, a disinterested process in which the truth of being would irresistibly reveal itself. Rather, as Achebe's narrative too suggests, the stakes – political, ethical, and otherwise – may be enormously high as one chooses among the stories, all "true," clamoring for one's attention. Thus, Uchendu's view bespeaks not "cultural relativism," as the term is pejoratively deployed by contemporary neoconservatives; instead, he promotes a motivated reading of the past that, eschewing the kind of fundamentalism that Okonkwo's fearfully self-defensive postures bespeak, would help one negotiate the unexpectedness arising in the present. Through an ingenious – and, we should note, dangerous – act of storytelling, he invites the tribesmen to reorganize their world by seeing the new ("white men") as part and parcel of that which they already know ("albinos"), but an already-known rendered uncanny. In his story, the albinos – the villagers' neighbors, sisters, brothers – become traces of the unknown in the familiar, requiring a second look, a new reading. Uchendu suggests that the albinos have been inadequately understood, foreign bodies whose familiar strangeness – uncanniness – can help negotiate the disruption that challenges the tribe's knowledge of the world.

Uchendu's deployment of storytelling is analogous to Michel Foucault's advocacy of a genealogical view of history, which he brings to bear particularly in his history of sexuality, a touchstone for many of our contributors. Both Uchendu and Foucault construct motivated narratives that, from the vantage point of an urgent "now," look to history for usable fragments that can be reactivated in the service of present emergencies. Many of the chapters in this volume repeat this gesture, sometimes demonstrating the ways various writers have sought to re-cognize their own uncanny albinos, sometimes themselves performing this act of invocation. Jointly, the chapters affirm futurities undetermined by teleologies: theirs is an open "now" without a resolution – an *Aufhebung* – in sight.

For this reason, our project remains necessarily incomplete, perhaps "badly" infinite. The historical, geographical, and generic range of possible texts and the lability of representations of same-sex desire – whether under the duress of a homophobic context or in the cultural freedom of a homophilic culture – present a plenitudinous store of exemplars to consider, while both the availability of scholars within particular fields to take on writing a chapter and the material limits for production of this book constrain what it is possible to accomplish in this volume. Were time and resources themselves infinite, readers would find included here numerous other chapters. No doubt readers can supply their own lists of single authors whose continuing – or, crucially, potential – importance for LGBTQI imagination would have justified chapter-length studies. Similarly, we would have liked to include substantive explorations of national or regional traditions beyond those we could include here, as well as writing from contemporary non-Western traditions that may be unrecognizable from the epistemological perspectives of homonationalism or the Gay International, to cite Jasbir Puar's and Joseph Massad's terms. Furthermore, if many of our chapters demonstrate the historical and material contingency of "literature" as the primary, canonical genre of LGBTQI expression, the recent emergence of digital communications challenges all such hegemonies. The Internet's proliferation at the end of the twentieth century will have changed drastically the forms of selfhood and connectedness available to queer adolescents, and the incipient history of digital "literatures" remains to be written.

Despite recent scholarship's ambition to trouble such conceptual principles as the Nation, canonicity still exerts an unrelieved – but also, for editors, not unhelpful – pull in organizing the plenitude of literary expression according to genres, historical periods, or political geographies. In a collection such as ours, the decisions over the order of the chapters, or their groupings, more nakedly perform the labor of the canon's production. Yet we hope this explicitness at once suggests the necessary arbitrariness of this work and encourages readers to continue elaborating – un-forming and re-forming – the themes that our editorial and authorial decisions conjure out of the material. We invite readers to tell their own stories – for there is not a genealogy that is not true – from the fragments of infinity coalescing here. In brief – to return to the question from which we began – no, there is no such thing as lesbian and gay literature, only many things that might compose and decompose that entity.

Works Cited

Achebe, Chinua. *Things Fall Apart*. 1959. New York: Anchor, 1994. Print.
Bergman, David. *Gaiety Transfigured: Gay Self-Representation in American Literature*. Madison: U of Wisconsin P, 1991. Print.
Berlant, Lauren and Elizabeth Freeman. "Queer Nationality." *Fear of a Queer Planet: Queer Politics and Social Theory*. Ed. Michael Warner. Minneapolis: U of Minnesota P, 1993. 193–229. Print.
Dimock, Wai Chee. *Through Other Continents: American Literature across Deep Time*. Princeton: Princeton UP, 2006. Print.
Faderman, Lillian. *Surpassing the Love of Men: Romantic Friendship and Love between Women from the Renaissance to the Present*. New York: Morrow, 1981. Print.

Foucault, Michel. "Nietzsche, Genealogy, History." 1971. Trans. Donald F. Brouchard and Sherry Simon. *Essential Works, Vol. 2: Aesthetics, Method, and Epistemology*. Ed. James D. Faubion. New York: New P, 1998. 369–91. Print.

Johnson, Barbara. *The Critical Difference: Essays in the Contemporary Rhetoric of Reading*. 1980. Baltimore: Johns Hopkins UP, 1992. Print.

Massad, Joseph A. *Desiring Arabs*. Chicago: U of Chicago P, 2007. Print.

Puar, Jasbir K. *Terrorist Assemblages: Homonationalism in Queer Times*. Durham: Duke UP, 2007. Print.

Sedgwick, Eve Kosofsky. *Between Men: English Literature and Male Homosocial Desire*. New York: Columbia UP, 1985. Print.

Smith-Rosenberg, Carroll. "The Female World of Love and Ritual: Relations between Women in Nineteenth-Century America." 1975. *Disorderly Conduct: Visions of Gender in Victorian America*. New York: Oxford UP, 1985. 53–76. Print.

Wokler, Robert. *Rousseau, the Age of Enlightenment, and Their Legacies*. Ed. Bryan Garsten. Princeton: Princeton UP, 2012. Print.

PART I

★

READING ANCIENT AND
CLASSICAL CULTURES

I

The Sappho Tradition

HARRIETTE ANDREADIS

ἰόπλοκ᾽ ἄγνα μελλιχόμειδε Σάπφοι
Violet-haired, pure, honey-smiling Sappho
– Alkaios (fr. 384)[1]

Sappho and her island Lesbos are omnipresent in literature about women
loving women, whatever the gender or sexual preference of the writer and
whether or not Sappho and her island are explicitly named.
– Elaine Marks, "Lesbian Intertextuality"

Her body is an apocrypha. She has become a book of tall stories, none of
them written by herself. Her name has passed into history. Her work has
not. Her island is known to millions now, her work is not.
– Jeanette Winterson, *Art and Lies*

For Western culture, and particularly for women, the Greek lyric poet
Sappho – born between ca. 630 and 612 BCE on the island of Lesbos in the
Aegean Sea – has come down to us as the original poet of female desire as well
as the original figure of same-sex female erotics. Yet the evolving history of
her reputation and the recovery of her poems have been fraught with the complexities of informational lacunae and textual instability, so much so that the
myths of Sappho soon overtook Sappho the poet and Sappho the person. In
short, each era has remade Sappho in its own image, a phenomenon Monique
Wittig and Sande Zeig underlined wittily: the entry for Sappho in their *Lesbian
Peoples: Material for a Dictionary* (1979) consists of a blank page to be filled in by
the reader (136).
   Sappho was renowned throughout the ancient world for the unique power
and expressiveness of her lyricism. Her academy for girls is said to have drawn
students to Lesbos from all over Greece, young women to whom she taught
the lyric and choric arts and with whom she was said to have developed erotic as
well as pedagogical relations.[3] Her preeminence in the ancient world of letters
was acknowledged by numerous tributes, not least of which was Aristotle's

(384–322 BCE) remark: "Everybody honors the wise ..., and the Mytilineans honored Sappho although she was a woman" (qtd. in Andreadis, *Sappho* 37). Plato (427?–347? BCE) called her "the Tenth Muse" (qtd. in Andreadis, *Sappho* 38), an epithet that was to become conventionally attached to her name well into the early modern period.

Although her poetry – in the Aeolian dialect – did not survive in any contemporary examples and may not have been recorded during her lifetime, except perhaps as transmitted orally and performatively, it is believed that a papyrus edition of nine books comprising more than five hundred of her poems was preserved in the ancient library in Alexandria and was lost or destroyed about the ninth century CE, during the early Christian era. The apparently sudden disappearance of these nine books of Sappho's poetry may be accounted for by the diminishing status of and scribal familiarity with the Aeolian dialect and by the material shift from papyrus rolls to more long-lasting parchment codex; if, as has been speculated, the books were later preserved on parchment codices in the libraries at Constantinople (which replaced Alexandria as a center of learning), the many depredations that city suffered in all likelihood would have destroyed them. So it was not until the late nineteenth and early twentieth centuries CE (i.e., 1898–1907) that important fragmentary remains of Sappho's poems were recovered from discarded third-century CE papyri in an ancient landfill dump in central Egypt, on the outskirts of the provincial capital city of Oxyrhynchus, providing for the first time material evidence of Sappho's poetic powers (Oxyrhynchus Papyrus 1787). And it was not until a century later, in 2004, that a stunning new recovery of several fragments and a virtually intact poem – only the fourth to have survived almost complete – now known as the Cologne Sappho, was made from an earlier, fragmentary Hellenistic papyrus manuscript used in painted mummy-cartonnage, that is, recycled papyrus used for decorative funerary art as papier-mâché mummy wrapping (Cologne Papyri inv. 21351 and 21376; early third-century BCE, four centuries before the Oxyrhynchus copy).

Until the discoveries at Oxyrhynchus, Sappho's reputation as the preeminent lyric poet of ancient Greece was conveyed secondhand by Roman and then by medieval writers. Until the turn of the twentieth century, then, the basis of her poetic reputation in Western culture was established by two of her poems and a number of fragments transmitted to Renaissance Europe in the works of others. Her two most famous fragments, the *Ode to Aphrodite* (fr. 1)[4] and *Phainetai moi* (Φαίνεταί μοι; *That man seems to me* ...; fr. 31) were transmitted, respectively, by Dionysius of Halicarnassus in his *On Literary Composition* (ca. 30 BCE) and by Longinus in his treatise *On the Sublime* (first century CE). The European recovery of her work was led by the French when in 1566 printer Henri Estienne published these two odes as well as all known fragments. It was thus the French and the English who, during the sixteenth and seventeenth centuries, preserved and translated the available poems and fragments, several poets making her poems their own, so that knowledge of her work survived and was perpetuated into a sort of renaissance in the following centuries.

At the same time, early modern Europe also inherited Ovid's fictionalized Sappho in his epistolary *Heroïdes* (Letter XV in *Letters of the Heroines*) through Giovanni Boccaccio's fourteenth-century *De mulieribus claris* (*Of Famous Women* [1360–74]) and Christine de Pisan's reinvented Sappho in *Le livre de la Cité de dames* (*The Book of the City of Ladies* [1405]) of the early fifteenth century. While both extant Sapphic odes – the *Ode to Aphrodite* and *Phainetai moi* – were known in the Renaissance to address love between women, Sappho was also said to have been enamored of the much younger ferryman Phaon, who abandoned her and on whose account she purportedly gave up both her art and female companions, finally committing suicide by plunging into the sea from the Leucadian cliffs; this fictionalized Sappho elaborated by Ovid originated at least as early as the comic dramatist Menander (fr. 258 K) and was later perpetuated by the numerous English translations and editions of his *Heroïdes* from the sixteenth well into the eighteenth centuries (see Andreadis, *Sappho* 27–53; "Early").

A garbled tradition of "the two Sapphos," made up of extravagant tales that may have originated with a number of Attic comedies,[5] was carried on by tenth-century commentators, particularly the encyclopedic lexicon *Suda*. The two simultaneous yet contradictory fictions of Sappho that prevailed before the Renaissance were a desexualized, chaste Sappho – the Sappho of her contemporary ancients – that coexisted with a second, polymorphously promiscuous Sappho – the Sappho of the Athenians and of Ovid and the Romans. Despite these ambiguities of her sexual reputation – the poet and the whore – Sappho's became the one name associated with female poetic excellence; she was the sole ancient model to whom early modern women writers might compare themselves and to whom they might be compared.

The Sappho who was transmitted from ancient times into the middle of the first millennium CE became a more multi-figured Sappho. The succeeding centuries perpetuated the mental habits of the previous millennia in mythologizing Sappho for their own purposes and to their own ends, but also in complicating and multiplying her representations for a greater variety of uses. The three primary modes of representing Sappho during the early modern period, incorporating the garbled tradition of "the two Sapphos," were repeatedly elaborated and sometimes conflated; Sappho was represented 1) as the first example of female poetic excellence, Plato's "Tenth Muse"; 2) as an early exemplar of the "unnatural" or monstrous sexuality of the tribade[6]; and 3) as a mythologized figure who acts the suicidal abandoned woman in the Ovidian tale of Sappho and Phaon.[7] More recently, since the late twentieth century, we might add a fourth figure of the heroic lesbian exemplar, surely an inverted version of the monstrous tribade: passionate poet and teacher, lover of women, and proto-feminist muse residing on the sacred island of Lesbos.

Sappho and Poetic Excellence

As the exemplar of female poetic excellence, Sappho was known to address love between women in both surviving Sapphic odes – the *Ode to Aphrodite* and *Phainetai moi*, in which the speaker's passion for her beloved is triangulated by a man – as well as to name a number of young women, in addition to her daughter, throughout the fragments. Yet Sappho's preeminence derived both from her innovative choric lyricism – her poems were intended for performance – and from her original description of the physical symptomatology of erotic passion, particularly in fr. 31, *Phainetai moi*. Numerous male poets have emulated her uniquely subjective expression of feeling in fr. 31, eagerly reconfiguring its male-female-female triangulation into a male-female-male configuration. Perhaps the earliest was the Roman Gaius Valerius Catullus's (ca. 84–ca. 54 BCE) famous fifty-first ode to Lesbia, in imitation of fr. 31, which opens "Ille mi par esse deo videtur," and pays homage to his Aeolian predecessor by using her Sapphic meter and by appropriating the physical markers of a helpless passion:

> He seems to me a god, or if
> that's possible, still more divine,
> that other in your company
> who sees and hears
>
> you laughing softly. Sense at once
> is snatched away beholding you,
> and, Lesbia, in my mouth
> there is no voice.
>
> My tongue is quelled, and subtle fire
> flows down my limbs; my ears are filled
> with siren tumult: dark eyes burn
> twice black as night.

Your sloth, Catullus, that's to blame:
excessive sloth that flourishes
in kings and wealthy cities: makes them
desolate.   (130)[8]

Having translated the physical particulars of fr. 31, Catullus makes Sappho's poem his own by turning in a last stanza to admonish himself and to open out its theme with a gesture toward a more expansive political and philosophical arena beyond the personally erotic. Catullus's moralizing turn was to be picked up by some later male poet/translators subtly denigrating the power of a now-heterosexualized erotics. The enduring appeal of Catullus's version is testified to by its having been set to music as recently as 1943 by Carl Orff as part of his *Catulli Carmina*.[9]

Sappho's anatomy of the particularly physical, subjective nuances of erotic passion has proved compelling to writers for several millennia. Her identification of the physical manifestations of passion seems to have been absorbed by and vibrated across transcultural literary wavelengths from ancient into postmodern times. After Catullus, *Phainetai moi* (fr. 31) has been translated, imitated, adapted, paraphrased, and/or transposed into longer works hundreds of times in French and in English from the sixteenth through the eighteenth and nineteenth centuries and into the present.

Following the edition of Henri Estienne, the French were especially prolific in translating Sappho. Among the notable French writers who recreated fr. 31 are Louise Labé (1555); members of La Pléiade, the sixteenth-century group of French Renaissance poets that included Pierre de Ronsard (1560), Rémy Belleau (1528–77; publ. 1556), Jean-Antoine de Baïf (1567), and Joachim du Bellay (ca. 1522–60); and later, Jacques Amyot (1572), François de Malherbe (1607–09), Jean Racine (1677), Anne Le Fèvre Dacier (1681), Baron de Longepierre (1684), Jacques Delille (1788), André Chénier (1762–94; publ. 1819), Alphonse de Lamartine (1823), Emile Deschanel (1847), Philoxène Boyer (1850), Alexandre Dumas (1858), Alexandre Keller (1902), and Maurice Morel (1903).[10] Perhaps not surprisingly, almost all the men among these French poets reconstruct the female same-sex erotics of fr. 31 to express a heterosexually triangulated passion, several with a more or less scolding moralism, à la Catullus. For Louise Labé and Anne Dacier, however, the poem's erotics may have functioned neutrally with regard to sex, suggesting that they themselves may be crossdressing the speaker's voice as male. No doubt the taboo against sexualized writing by literary women would have militated against either a sexualized same-sex triangulation or a more than genteel translation of a heterosexualized triangulation. It was for Madeleine de Scudéry in the seventeenth century to make Sappho permissible as a model for women writers.

While the French led the way in the cultural appropriation of Sappho, fr. 31 has also regularly been translated and refashioned in English by, among many others, Sir Philip Sidney (1554–86), John Addison (1735), Tobias Smollett (1741), George Gordon, Lord Byron (ca. 1820), Alfred, Lord Tennyson (ca. 1850), John Addington Symonds (1883), Bliss Carman (1904), William Carlos Williams (1958), Mary Barnard (1958), Richmond Lattimore (1960), Robert Lowell (1962), and Willis Barnstone (1965 and 1988).[11] Apart from these versions by distinguished poets and classicists, Sappho continues to be translated anew by poets and would-be poets testing their skills.

That most of the writers engaging fr. 31 have been male testifies to the historical marginalization of literary women, to the unequal status of women generally, and – again – almost certainly to the taboo against literary women's production of sexualized writing. In English at least, this pattern has begun to change since Mary Barnard's translation of Sappho's poems in 1958 and the decoupling of the translations from the necessary connection between speaker and love object; that is, the translation of Sappho no longer requires that the female translator / speaker necessarily be identified with Sappho's same-sex desire. In short, the universality of subjectivity and eroticism seems to operate in a transgender fashion.

Two modern translations in English of *Phainetai moi* offer especially effective examples of both the unique poetic passion and the female same-sex erotics that have animated Sappho's voice since ancient times. William Carlos Williams's (1883–1963) spare modernity conveys the essence of the shattering erotic emotions that overwhelm the speaker:

> That man is peer of the gods, who
> face to face sits listening
> to your sweet speech and lovely
> laughter.
>
> It is this that rouses a tumult
> in my breast. At mere sight of you
> my voice falters, my tongue
> is broken.
>
> Straightway, a delicate fire runs in
> my limbs; my eyes
> are blinded and my ears
> thunder.

> Sweat pours out: a trembling hunts
> me down. I grow
> paler than grass and lack little
>   of dying.   (Williams 348)

Anne Carson's more recent translation, presented with facing-page original Greek, adheres more closely to Sappho's word order and includes the last incomplete line, her intent being to "stand out of the way" of Sappho's voice. Carson captures Sappho's famously soaring lyricism here:

> He seems to me equal to gods that man
> Whoever he is who opposite you
> Sits and listens close
>   To your sweet speaking
>
> and lovely laughing – oh it
> puts the heart in my chest on wings
> for when I look at you, even a moment, no speaking
>   is left in me
>
> no: tongue breaks and thin
> fire is racing under skin
> and in eyes no sight and drumming
>   fills ears
>
> and cold sweat holds me and shaking
> grips me all, greener than grass
> I am and dead – or almost
>   I seem to me.
>
> But all is to be dared, because even a person of poverty   (Carson 63)

Apart from the appeal of Sappho's poems to classicists and poets challenging themselves via translation and the use of Aeolian meter, Sappho's representation as an originary poetic figure has captured the imagination of many generations. In looking back to establish a tradition of female poetic excellence, literary women and many men have seen Sappho as an aspirational figure. In the same way that early modern women sought ancient and biblical models of educated women as predecessors, so they looked back for writing women they might emulate. Sappho's status as the first and pre-eminent female poet established her as the ancient model who legitimated the desire to write for early modern women writers: they might compare themselves and each other to her, and they might be compared to her by their male contemporaries. Sappho thus furnished a much-desired anchor for an early modern female literary tradition. In France, Madeleine de Scudéry (1607–1701) presented herself as a second Sappho and composed the first modern biographical fiction of Sappho in which "Sapho" extols women's abilities to encourage them to write.[12] In England, Katherine Philips (1632–64), who emulated Scudéry's literary style and who wrote impassioned poems to her female friends employing the conventions of the ideology of male friendship, was referred to by her male contemporaries – who made certain always to emphasize her exemplary virtue – as "the new Sappho."[13] This encomium was later taken over by English women writers who used it among themselves, so much so that it became almost *de rigueur* in the commendatory poems that introduce work by, for example, poets Anne Killigrew (1660–85),[14] Jane Barker (1652–1732), and Anne Finch, Countess of Winchelsea (1661–1720), and even dramatists Delarivier Manley (ca. 1670–1724), Catharine Trotter (1679–1749), and Mary Pix (1666–1709) used it to laud each other.

Sappho's Transgressive Sexuality

This well-established literary reputation in early modern Europe was regularly shadowed by Sappho's reputedly transgressive sexuality, as is suggested by disclaimers about a female poet's virtue in encomia comparing her to Sappho. The representation of Sappho as an early model for the "unnatural" or monstrous sexuality of the tribade also caused her to become the most prominent exemplar of sexual behaviors between women. Early modern accounts of the clitoris in anatomy and medical texts repeatedly used Sappho to illustrate tribadism and so perpetuated the even earlier biographies that saw her as sexually transgressive: "She has been accused by some of being irregular in her ways and a woman-lover" (Oxyrhynchus papyrus, late second or early third century CE); "She had three companions and friends, Atthis, Telesippa and Megara, and she got a bad name for her impure friendship with them" (the *Suda*, tenth-century Byzantine encyclopedic lexicon of the ancient Mediterranean world) (Campbell 3, 7).[15] As early as the late 1400s, this perspective was disseminated throughout Continental Europe in commentaries on Book XV, the letter of Sappho to Phaon, in a series of Latin and later in English editions of Ovid's *Heroïdes*: "Ovid indicates that her poems were lascivious.... [S]he did not fail to love [her friends] in the manner of a man, but was with other women a tribade, this is abusing them by rubbing, for tribein [Greek] is to rub, which we say according to Juvenal and Martial, and she was named by Horace *mascula Sappho*" (see Andreadis, *Sappho* 28–37, esp. 29–30). In 1653, Thomas Bartholin, the Swedish anatomist, revised, expanded, and translated into English his father's

1633 Latin anatomy of the human body, adding anecdotal embellishments and the example of Sappho to the entry "Of the Clitoris":

> The Greeks call it *clitoris*, others name it *Tentigo*, others the womans Yard or Prick: both because it resembles a Mans Yard, in Situation, Substance, Composition, Repletion, with Spirits and Erection. And Also because it hath somewhat like the Nut and Fore-skin of a Mans Yard, and in some Women it grows as big as the Yard of a man: so that some women abuse the same, and make use thereof in place of a mans Yard, exercising carnal Copulation one with another, and they are termed *Confricatrices* Rubsters. Which lascivious Practice is said to have been invented by Philaenis and Sappho, the Greek Poetress, is reported to have practised the same. And of these I conceive the Apostle Paul speaks in the I. of *Romans 26*. And therefore this part is called *Contemptus virorum* the Contempt of Mankind. (sigs. Z2–Z2ᵛ)

But representations of Sappho's sexual transgressiveness were hardly confined to anatomies and editions of the *Heroïdes*, though they often appeared only in Latin texts accessible primarily to men. The male fascination with a female same-sex erotics can be seen in poet John Donne's (1573–1631) rewriting of Ovid's heroical epistle and adaptation of the Sapphic voice and tropes of the *Phainetai moi* fragment in a philosophical meditation that explores the utopian dynamics of female desire; in "Sapho to Philænis," Donne's Sappho takes pleasure in the physicality of a woman who mirrors her own desires:

> Thy body is a naturall *Paradise*,
>   In whose selfe, unmanur'd, all pleasure lies,
> ....
> And betweene us all sweetnesse may be had;
>   All, all that *Nature* yields, or *Art* can adde.
> My two lips, eyes, thighs, differ from thy two,
>   But so, as thine from one another doe;
> And, oh, no more: the likenesse being such,
>   Why should they not alike in all parts touch?
> Hand to strange hand, lippe to lippe none denies;
>   Why should they brest to brest, or thighs to thighs?
> Likenesse begets such strange selfe flatterie,
>   That touching my selfe, all seemes done to thee.
> My selfe I embrace, and mine owne hands I kisse,
>   And amorously thanke my selfe for this.
> Me, in my glasse, I call thee; But alas,

When I would kisse, teares dimme mine *eyes,* and *glasse.*
O cure this loving madnesse, and restore
  Me to mee; thee, my *halfe,* my *all,* my *more.*
So may thy cheekes red outweare scarlet dye,
  And their white, whitenesse of the *Galaxy,*
So may thy mighty, amazing beauty move
  Envy' in all *women,* and in all *men, love,*
And so be *change,* and *sicknesse,* farre from thee,
  As thou by comming neere, keep'st them from me.   (ll. 35–36, 43–64)

It is this aspect of Sappho's reputation as a tribade, and the male literary fascination with what that might mean both in erotic/sexual terms and in the philosophical implications of the absence of men, that was instrumental in eventually establishing Sappho's later stature in the twentieth century as a kind of lesbian foremother.

Sappho's Abjection and Suicide

The third mode of figuring Sappho, implicit in the fifteenth epistle of Ovid's *Heroïdes,* "Sapho to Phaon," portrays Sappho's abjection: left to her fate by the humiliation and rejection of the younger Phaon, for whom she has abandoned both her art and her female companions, Sappho leaps to her death in the sea. Perhaps jealous of Sappho's reputation as a poet, and certainly misogynistic, Ovid elaborated the brief account of the second Sappho in the *Suda,* itself based on earlier versions by at least one Athenian comedian, to produce a ventriloquized narrative representation of Sappho's anguished lament for her lost art, her female companions, and her youthful male lover that was translated and reproduced in edition after edition of the *Heroïdes* for several centuries.

Beginning with the Latin Venetian editions of 1492 and 1499, and continuing in subsequent Continental editions, Ovid's defamation of Sappho was elaborated and perpetuated by the reproduction of the Latin commentary of one "Domitius," quoted earlier, that conveyed Sappho's tribadism only to underline her abjection by heterosexual passion. This commentary, which describes Sappho's tribadism as both "rubbing" and penetrative ("in the manner of a man"), served the dual purpose of disseminating knowledge of Sappho's tribadism as well as of ensuring an understanding of her inevitable abjection. It opens with remarks that emphasize her attachment to her female companions: "Erynna was the concubine (*concubina*) of Sappho ... [he gives the names of

three of her friends (*amicas*)] who it is said she used libidinously (*ad libidinem*)."
The subsequent references to Latin authors (Juvenal, Martial, and Horace)
as authorities seal Sappho's reputation and set her up nicely for a punishing
abjection. In this way, Sappho's presumed erotic connections with women
were implicated in Ovid's representation of her as driven and destroyed by
an unrequited heterosexual passion. She was punished for her aberrant erotic
tastes as well as for the threatening and dangerous (to men) power of her art.
This construction of her "life" was available to educated sixteenth- and seventeenth-century readers of Latin and continued to be reproduced through
the early modern period in English translations of the *Heroïdes*, though made
rather less explicit by the absence of commentary or an additionally appended
"life" of Sappho, suggesting the translations' appropriateness for reading by
women.[16]

This figure of an abjected Sappho was further carried forward from the
late seventeenth century well into the nineteenth century by the numerous
editions of John Dryden's original 1680 collection of Ovid's epistles, published
by Jacob Tonson and translated by a number of prominent contemporary
literary figures, all men with the exception of Aphra Behn (see Andreadis,
Sappho 28–37; "Early"). While there were other translations, the Dryden /
Tonson collection appears to have been the most popular vernacular edition
of the *Heroïdes*. By moving the Sapphic epistle from its traditional position as
the fifteenth epistle to the opening of the volume, the Dryden / Tonson edition
foregrounded for the entire volume the figure of a humiliated older woman
made abject by her delirious self-abandonment to an overwhelming and passionate infatuation for a beautiful younger man:

> My Muse and Lute can now no longer please,
> They are th' Employments of a mind at ease.
> Wandring from thought to thought I sit alone
> All day, and my once dear Companions shun.
> In vain the Lesbian Maids claim each a part,
> Where thou alone hast ta'en up all the heart.[17]

Not only was Ovid's defamation of Sappho thus perpetuated but, located at
the opening of the volume, it shadowed the entirety of the *Heroïdes*. While
Sappho's heterosexual abjection continued to be depicted in the myth of
Sappho and Phaon, her identification with tribadism in the epistle was gradually suppressed as knowledge of sexual identity formations circulated more
widely and behavioral taboos rose to consciousness.

Sappho as Modern Lesbian Heroine

As we enter the modern period, between the late seventeenth and the mid-nineteenth centuries, a broad range of fictions of Sappho was produced in Continental Europe, particularly in France, Germany, and Italy; these were in addition to the various scholarly translations of the then available – and fragmentary – corpus of Sappho's poetry. These fictions were usually motivated by the various nationalistic, political, and/or scholarly agendas operating at any particular historical moment (see DeJean). As a result, simultaneous, yet contradictory, traditions of Sappho continued to be perpetuated: a desexualized, chaste Sappho coexisted with a second, hetero- or bisexual and promiscuous Sappho, recapitulating yet again, but in a more contemporary key, the earlier garbled tradition of "the two Sapphos," which went back to late tenth-century CE commentators. At the same time, in France, Germaine de Staël (1766–1817) – as had Scudéry before her – kept invigorated, through her own identification with the classical poet, the power of Sappho as a model for women writers.[18]

By the end of the nineteenth century, two important sociocultural developments came together to create the perfect context for continued fictions of Sappho and for her adoption as lesbian patron saint: not only had homosexual identities and the language used to describe them begun to crystallize into their modern form by late mid-century and then solidified by century's end throughout most of Europe, but the stunning discovery of the Oxyrhynchus papyri with their Sappho fragments was made at the turn of the twentieth century. As Sappho's poetry was newly heralded and her reputation overflowed the bounds of purely literary or scholarly venues, her figure began to be absorbed into more popular understandings and so became increasingly attached to female same-sex erotic representations and self-representations.

The language used to describe female sexual identities newly emerging into the public sphere tracks alongside the emergence of the later nineteenth-century sexologists and the invention of the "homosexual" at mid-century in Germany. For example, French dictionaries note the occurrence of *sapphisme* in the sense of "female homosexuality" as early as 1838 and *lesbienne* in the sense of "female homosexual" in 1867. In English, a similar vocabulary for female same-sex sexuality develops somewhat later, probably inspired by French usage, so that by the early twentieth century, it is not unusual to find references to "sapphists" or to "a Sapph" in the writings of Virginia Woolf (1882–1941) and other members of London's sexually and socially progressive Bloomsbury group. A nomenclature derived from representations of Sappho was replacing the language of tribadism by the mid-nineteenth century. Clearly, by the beginning of the twentieth century, the conflation of Sappho and her Aegean island with the rhetoric of emerging modern female same-sex sexual identities and behaviors was complete.

But it was the elaborate hoax Pierre Louÿs created in *Les chansons de Bilitis* (*The Songs of Bilitis*, 1894) – a collection of quasi-pornographic erotic poems purporting to be by one "Bilitis," a contemporary disciple of Sappho's – that initiated the consolidation of Sappho's role in the twentieth century as the classical exemplar of female homosexuality and her subsequent use as a patroness of modernity by lesbians themselves. Natalie Clifford Barney (1876–1972), a wealthy American expatriate in Paris and the center of a well-known lesbian salon, established the basis for the twentieth-century tradition of Sappho as a sort of proto-lesbian foremother. The joint events of Barney's discovery of an edition of Sappho and of Louÿs's fiction of supposedly classic female same-sex eroticism inaugurated the twentieth century's popular understanding of Sappho as lesbian poet. This cult of the modern lesbian Sappho began with Barney's pseudonymous publication of *Cinq petits dialogues grecs* (*Five Small Grecian Dialogues*) in 1902, her influence on her lover Renée Vivien's (pseudonym of Pauline Tarn [1877–1909]) spurious edition of Sappho's poems in 1903, and her integration of what she understood as Sapphic eroticism into her Paris salon, which featured classical costumes, songs, dance, and gestures à la Sappho. Barney, Vivien, and their Paris circle ignored what had been and continue to be the profound ambiguities in what is actually known about Sappho's sexuality to create a figure of erotic obsession and a model for both literary and sociosexual emulation. Their movement produced the cult of Sappho's person that was to be called *Sapho 1900* or *Sapho cent pour cent* (Sappho one hundred percent).

Literary modernists of the earlier twentieth century, both male and female and on both sides of the Atlantic, reevaluated their artistic position in relation to classical writers as they explored experimental modes of expression and invented new approaches to classical myth and legacy. Sappho's lyricism furnished an evocative style for, among others, Americans Amy Lowell (1874–1925) and H. D. (Hilda Doolittle [1886–1961]), as well as Parisian Anna de Noailles (1876–1933) (see Gregory; Clark). More recently, Olga Broumas (1949–) also looks back to Sappho as a poetic and perhaps erotic precursor but, like the earlier modernists, does not emulate classical social mores reinvented à la Barney and her circle.[19] In mid-century America, in less rarefied nonliterary lesbian circles and perhaps seeking to avoid a too-obvious association with Sappho, Del Martin and Phyllis Lyon founded the Daughters of Bilitis (DOB) in 1955, the first lesbian civil and political rights organization in the

United States.[20] *The Ladder*, DOB's newsletter (1956–72), was intended to and did reach a national audience of readers. A "Sapphistries" column of original poetry was included and Sappho herself appeared "in many guises": "She was included . . . as a mythic-historical ancestor and as an honorary member of the readers' and writers' community, while . . . Lesbos was reimagined as a safe place within which this community of lesbians could develop a positive identity" (Valentine 146). The naming of DOB, with its association of the fictitious Bilitis with Sappho, and the ever-present figure of Sappho herself, may be seen to have sealed the connection between lesbian identity and the Greek ancient world in popular culture and for American women.

It is almost certainly the very fragmentary nature of what remains to us of Sappho's life and work, rather than any enterprise of accurate historical reconstruction, that has enabled the invention of elaborate and contradictory Sapphic fictions that serve the purposes of their creators. The figure established at the beginning of the twentieth century to preside over lesbian salons and provide an imprimatur of classical significance and literary / intellectual importance was revivified during the feminist movements of the later twentieth century when women again sought a model they could emulate. By the end of the twentieth century, apart from continued scholarly debates among classicists about the nature of Sappho's poems and sexuality, Sappho continued to be popularly regarded as a cult figure by lesbian women, especially by many lesbian feminists who made – and continue to make – the pilgrimage to Lesbos to partake of the environs inhabited by their putative precursor so many centuries ago.

Among scholars and classicists the conversation about Sappho has been changed considerably by the discovery of the Cologne papyrus fragments in 2004; that conversation promises to continue for many years as more scholars examine the newly recovered fragments and as more information comes to light. It is unlikely, however, that this significant discovery will affect the representations of Sappho held dear by nonacademic lesbians and in the popular imaginary that associates her with a female same-sex erotics, though it cannot but enhance the power of Sappho's poetic voice and her importance as a literary icon. The new poem, frr. 58–59, also known as the "Tithonus Poem," concerns old age rather than the lyric passion for other women that we associate with Sappho's well-known poems and fragments; yet the physical experience of aging is described with the same precision as the effects of erotic thrall in her more generally known works:

> Pursue the violet-laden Muses' handsome gifts,
> my children, and the loud-voiced lyre so dear to song:

But me – my skin which once was soft is withered now
by age, my hair has turned to white which once was black,
my heart has been weighed down, my knees give no support
which once were nimble in the dance like little fawns.
How often I lament these things. But what to do?
No being that is human can escape old age.
For people used to think that Dawn with rosy arms
and loving murmurs took Tithonus[21] fine and young
to reach the edges of the earth; yet still grey age
in time did seize him, though his consort cannot die.

In this restoration and translation of the fragments by M. L. West (see Greene and Skinner 15), Sappho's distinctive lyric voice is clearly recognizable. In addition to perhaps providing the banal autobiographical information that Sappho lived into old age, frr. 58–59 expand her poetic range to embrace a broader understanding of the human experience, thus creating an entirely new dimension of the figure of Sappho to be contemplated, interrogated, and assimilated into previous assumptions about her life and work.

As a cultural figure and icon, then, as well as the poetic standard of lyric poetry, Sappho will continue to evolve in complex and unexpected ways. So, for example, the (postmodern) gay/lesbian/bisexual/transgender women who have adopted Sappho as their personal icon might assimilate the enlarged perspective of this newly discovered Sappho into the figure of erotic foremother that they cherish. While Sappho's future may depend on possible discoveries of still additional fragments,[22] their probable existence leaves us with a state of affairs in which current understandings will resonate in unforeseen ways in cultural contexts yet to emerge. Thus each era will continue to remake Sappho in its own image.

Notes

1. I follow Willis Barnstone, the translator of *Sappho: Lyrics in the Original Greek* (2), in using this line from Sappho's countryman and contemporary Alkaios (Alcaeus) as an epigraph.
2. Lyric, that is, in the strict sense: poetry composed to be sung to the accompaniment of the lyre. It is now widely accepted that the transmission of Sappho's poems/songs took place via oral performance. See Nagy.
3. Some controversy surrounds Sappho's academy. Despite the absence of evidence confirming its existence, it continues to be cited and presumed to have existed.

4. The numerical identifying system used here follows the standard established by Lobel and Page; fragments hereafter will be simply cited as fr. 1, fr. 31, and so forth.

5. At least six (lost) plays by different dramatists featured Sappho since she had become a stock figure on the Athenian stage.

6. *Tribade* and *tribadism*, from the Greek *tribein* (τριβειν), to rub, were the terms used to describe the identity and behavior we would now name as lesbian and lesbianism.

7. In a tradition that humiliated her as it made her heterosexual, Sappho was said, in her desolation, to have abandoned her poetry as well as her female companions before leaping to her death in the sea.

8. D. F. S. Thomson, trans., *Catullus*. Though Catullus wrote a series of poems to "Lesbia," the poetic name referencing Sappho that he assigned to his female lover (usually identified as Clodia Metelli), he also wrote a number of clearly same-sex erotic poems to men.

9. Modern translations of fr. 31 via Catullus continue to proliferate on the Internet, as just a casual search makes clear; easily accessible are Holcombe 4, and several other English versions by A. S. Kline (2001), Clive Brooks (2007), and H. J. Walker (n.d.) as well as the original Latin at www.textetc.com/workshop/wt-catullus-2.html (accessed 13 June 2013).

10. See Brunet for a more complete listing.

11. See www.bopsecrets.org/gateway/passages/sappho.htm (accessed 13 June 2013) for a fuller listing. More translations of Sappho generally are to be found at www.sacred-texts.com/cla/sappho/index.htm, including those by Edwin Marion Cox (1925) and at classicpersuasion.org/pw/sappho/index.htm, "The Divine Sappho" (accessed 28 June 2013).

12. *The Story of Sapho* is a self-contained section from Scudéry's long and popular novel *Artamène ou le Grand Cyrus* (10 vols., 1648–53). See DeJean 60–78, 103–10, for an account of Scudéry's use of the figure of Sappho as a woman writer inaugurating the new genre of the heroic novel. Hinds points out that while a pejorative portrait of Sappho's tribadism was part of legal and medical discourse in France at this time, "the importance of female homosocial relations in fashioning a utopian vision of a heterosexual world" (33) was nevertheless integral to Scudéry's narrative of gender dynamics.

13. See Andreadis, "Sapphic-Platonics"; and *Sappho* 55–150, for the ways Philips's poems as well as the writings of other early modern women writers may be read through the lens of a female same-sex erotics. See also Traub.

14. John Dryden's elegy comparing Killigrew to Sappho is particularly well known.

15. The *Suda* appears to have been responsible for the myth of "the two Sapphos"; a second entry for "the other Sappho" gives the story of the lyre player who drowned herself for love of Phaon. Campbell remarks that this "other

Sappho" "was almost certainly the invention of a scholar who wished to save S.'s reputation" (7).

16. See, for example, the translations of the *Heroïdes* by George Turberville (1567), Wye Saltonstall (1636), and John Sherburne (1639).

17. This original version of Epistle XV in the Dryden / Tonson by Sir Carr Scrope – which was not a complete translation but may rather have been a pastiche of parts of earlier translations – was later (in 1712 and editions thereafter) supplemented by a second, complete translation by Alexander Pope. These versions were both to take on lives of their own and to be reproduced apart from the original collection. See Andreadis, "Early" 409ff.

18. In *The Sappho Companion* (2001), Margaret Reynolds provides an invaluable compendium of primary sources from ancient times to the turn of the twenty-first century, introduced with wit and sharp historical insights; she offers an important selection of visual figures of Sappho in addition to textual representations.

19. The figure of Sappho also appears in several works of the Harlem Renaissance. See Somerville for a reading of the possibly coded, subtextual same-sex eroticism associated with the Sappho character in Pauline Hopkins's novel *Contending Forces* (1900). In the same way, an episode in Claude McKay's novel *Home to Harlem* (1928) in which a character is reading Alphonse Daudet's 1884 novel *Sapho: moeurs parisiennes* – a reimagining of the destructive love of Sappho and Phaon in modern dress – becomes an encoded opportunity for the protagonist's exposure to a positive view of female same-sex desire. For an extensive exploration of this episode in the larger context of the novel, see Maiwald.

20. Jody Valentine provides this statement by one of the founding members of the DOB: "We thought that 'Daughters of Bilitis' would sound like any other women's lodge – you know like the Daughters of the Nile or the DAR" (147).

21. In Greek mythology, Tithonus was granted immortality, but his lover Eos (Aurora) neglected to ask Zeus for eternal youth, with the result that Tithonus continued to age into eternity.

22 In late January 2014, the discovery of two more Sappho poems was announced: Oxford papyrologist Dirk Obbink confirmed the authenticity of a papyrus fragment in the possession of an anonymous private collector. The first, nearly complete poem concerns her brothers Charaxos and Larichos and the second, more fragmented poem, addressed to Aphrodite, is about unrequited love. A preliminary version of Obbink's "Two New Poems by Sappho" is available at www.web.archive.org/ web/ 20140130212614/ http:/ / www.papyrology.ox.ac .uk/ Fragments/ Obbink.Sappho7.draft.pdf (accessed 6 July 2014). While the authenticity of the poems does not appear to be in question, there has been some controversy concerning the provenance of the fragment.

Works Cited

Andreadis, Harriette. "The Early Modern Afterlife of Ovidian Erotics: Dryden's *Heroides*." *Renaissance Studies* 22.3 (2008): 401–16. Print.

"The Sapphic-Platonics of Katherine Philips, 1632–1664." *Signs* 15.1 (1989): 34–60. Print.

Sappho in Early Modern England: Female Same-Sex Literary Erotics, 1550–1714. Chicago: U of Chicago P, 2001. Print.

Bartholin, Thomas. *The Anatomical History of Thomas Bartholinus, Doctor and Kings Professor, Concerning the Lacteal Veins of the Thorax, Observ'd by Him Lately in Man and Beast: Publickly Proposed by Michael Lyserus Answering*. London: Octavian Pulleyn, 1653. Print.

Brunet, Philippe. *L'égal des dieux: cent versions d'un poèm de Sappho*. Paris: Editions Allia, 1998. Print.

Campbell, David A., trans. *Greek Lyric I: Sappho and Alcaeus*. Cambridge: Harvard UP, 1990. Print.

Carson, Anne, trans. *If Not, Winter: Fragments of Sappho*. New York: Vintage, 2003. Print.

Catullus. *Catullus: Edited with a Textual and Interpretive Commentary*. Ed. and trans. D.F.S. Thomson. Toronto: U of Toronto P, 2003. Print.

Clark, Catherine O. "Sapphic Consciousness in H. D. and de Noailles." *CLCWeb: Comparative Literature and Culture* 12.3 (2010): Web. 13 Jan. 2014. <http://docs.lib.purdue.edu/clcweb/vol12/iss3/9>.

DeJean, Joan. *Fictions of Sappho, 1546–1937*. Chicago: U of Chicago P, 1995. Print.

Donne, John. "Sapho to Philænis." *The Poems of John Donne*. Ed. Sir Herbert Grierson. London: Oxford UP, 1960. 111–12. Print.

Estienne, Henri [Henricus Stephanus]. *Carminum poetarum novem, lyricæ poesews [sic] principum fragmenta*. Paris, 1566. Print.

Greene, Ellen, and Marilyn Skinner, eds. *The New Sappho on Old Age: Textual and Philosophical Issues*. Hellenic Studies 38. Center for Hellenic Studies. Cambridge: Harvard UP, 2009. Print.

Gregory, Eileen. "Rose Cut in Rock: Sappho and H. D.'s 'Sea Garden.'" *Contemporary Literature* 27.4 (1986): 525–52. Print.

Hinds, Leonard. "Female Friendship as the Foundation of Love in Madeleine de Scudéry's 'Histoire de Sapho.'" *Journal of Homosexuality* 42.3/4 (2001): 23–35. Print.

Holcombe, Colin John, trans. *Selections from Catullus*. Santiago: Ocaso P, 2010. ebook.

Lobel, Edgar, and Denys Page. *Poetarum Lesbiorum Fragmenta*. Oxford: Oxford UP, 1955. Print.

Maiwald, Michael. "Race, Capitalism, and the Third-Sex Ideal: Claude McKay's *Home to Harlem* and the Legacy of Edward Carpenter." *Modern Fiction Studies* 48.4 (2002): 825–57. Print.

Marks, Elaine. "Lesbian Intertextuality." *Homosexualities and French Literature*. Ed. George Stambolian and Elaine Marks. Ithaca: Cornell UP, 1979. 353–77. Print.

McKay, Claude. *Home to Harlem*. Chatham: Chatham, 1973. Print.

Nagy, Gregory. "The 'New Sappho' Reconsidered in the Light of the Athenian Reception of Sappho." Greene and Skinner 176–99.

Ovid. *Ovid's Epistles Translated by Several Hands*. London: J. Tonson, 1680. Print.

Reynolds, Margaret. *The Sappho Companion*. New York: Palgrave, 2001. Print.

Sappho. *Sappho: A New Translation*. Trans. Mary Barnard. Berkeley: U of California P, 1958. Print.

Sappho: Lyrics in the Original Greek. Trans. Willis Barnstone. New York: New York UP, 1965. Print.

Sappho: Poems, A New Version. Trans. Willis Barnstone. Los Angeles: Green Integer, 1999. Print.

Scudéry, Madeleine de. *The Story of Sapho*. Trans. Karen Newman. Chicago: U of Chicago P, 2003. Print.

Snyder, Jane McIntosh. *Lesbian Desire in the Lyrics of Sappho*. New York: Columbia UP, 1997. Print.

The Woman and the Lyre: Women Writers in Classical Greece and Rome. Carbondale: Southern Illinois UP, 1989. Print.

Somerville, Siobhan. "Passing through the Closet in Pauline Hopkins's *Contending Forces*." *American Literature* 69.1 (1997): 139–66. Print.

"Tithonus Poem." Trans. M. L. West. Green and Skinner 15.

Traub, Valerie. *The Renaissance of Lesbianism in Early Modern England*. Cambridge: Cambridge UP, 2002. Print.

Valentine, Jody. "Lesbians Are from Lesbos: Sappho and Identity Construction in *The Ladder*." *Helios* 35.2 (2008): 143–69. Print.

Williams, William Carlos. *The Collected Poems of William Carlos Williams, Volume II: 1939–1962*. Ed. A. Walton Litz and Christopher J. MacGowan. New York: New Directions, 1986. Print.

Winterson, Jeannette. *Art and Lies: A Piece for Three Voices and a Bawd*. New York: Vintage, 1996. Print.

Wittig, Monique, and Sande Zeig. *Lesbian Peoples: Material for a Dictionary*. New York: Avon, 1979. Print.

2

Plato and the Philosophical Dialogue

DAVID DECOSTA LEITAO

The philosophical dialogues of Plato, especially the *Symposium* and *Phaedrus*, have been enormously influential on modern gay writers. But what does it mean to give these works a place – a privileged, foundational place, even – in a volume dedicated to the history of gay and lesbian literature? We face two difficulties.

The first has to do with the incommensurability between ancient and modern sexual practices and ideologies. It is by now well established that terms like "gay" and even "homosexual" are anachronistic to describe the forms of sexuality we encounter in ancient Greece. The form of same-sex eroticism that was tolerated and, in some circles, even celebrated was the sexual pursuit of adolescent males in their mid- to late teens, termed *paiderastia* by the Greeks, which was not incompatible with a simultaneous interest in girls and women. Ancient Greek sexuality, at least during the classical period, was less concerned with the biological sex of one's partners than with the sexual role (active) that one publicly identified with; an individual's "sexuality" was determined not so much by a deep psychological orientation toward sexual partners of a particular gender or toward sexual acts of a particular sort, but by the extent to which one maintained a degree of self-control in the satisfaction of sexual and other desires, by the ethical "style" one adopted in the living of life (Foucault, *Use*; Halperin, *One* 15–71). It is only with its reception in modern culture, and with the ideological reframing that is an inevitable part of this process, that ancient Greek sexual practice can properly take up its place in the teleology of modern same-sex desire.

The second difficulty is perhaps more surprising: there is considerable uncertainty regarding the function of and attitude toward same-sex eroticism in the philosophical dialogues of Plato. There is no denying that pederastic attractions are alluded to frequently in the works of Plato and other writers of "Socratic dialogues," and are indeed given greater prominence in this genre than in other contemporary genres of literature; this is at least partly a reflection of the fact that the consumers of philosophy as practice and as text were primarily young aristocratic males, who were precisely those who had been socialized to pursue the love of boys and had the leisure to do so.[1] But in Plato, at least, homosocial *erōs* functions as a metaphor for the philosophical pursuit of truth, and it is quite possible that this was its primary or even sole function in the Platonic dialogue. We will see that this link between pederastic desire and philosophical practice was, from the very beginning, to some extent accidental, and what is perhaps most interesting is the way that this accidental marriage was absorbed into philosophical discourse first by Socrates and Plato and subsequently by later thinkers, ancient and modern. And so the Greek philosophical dialogue, and the Platonic dialogue in particular, represents a rather ambiguous model for modern gay literature.

Same-Sex Eroticism in the Platonic Dialogue

Same-sex eroticism is a frequent theme in the dialogues of Plato. References to pederastic attractions are often part of Plato's literary *mise en scène*, especially common in the prologues and epilogues, which frame the philosophical discussion at the heart of each dialogue (Dover, *Greek* 154–55). These casual references are in many cases tied thematically to the philosophical question of the dialogue. The *Lysis*, for example, begins with the young Hippothales's sexual attraction toward the beautiful Lysis, and it is Socrates's claim to instruct Hippothales on the best way to speak to his beloved that motivates the philosophical discussion of friendship that is the focus of the dialogue. Similarly, the *Charmides* begins with Socrates's acknowledgment of the intense attraction he experiences when he catches a glimpse of Charmides's naked body; Socrates's own self-control in the face of the youth's physical beauty becomes the starting point for the dialogue's philosophical investigation into the nature of self-control. Socrates is the prime erotic figure in the Platonic dialogues, either as a lover himself or one expert to advise others about love, clearly a reflection of the teaching of the historical Socrates (see later in this chapter).

But in two dialogues, the *Symposium* and *Phaedrus*, same-sex *erōs* is not just a part of the literary setting, but plays a central role in the philosophical discussion. The *Symposium* is Plato's most famous and most sublime inquiry into the nature of desire. Set at a drinking party to commemorate a victory won by the tragic poet Agathon, it records a series of speeches given by the guests in praise of the god Eros, the personification of sexual love and desire (*erōs*). The speakers focus, at the outset, on the sexual desire elite Greek men frequently experienced in the presence of beautiful youths, but as the speeches progress, the focus shifts toward an increasingly more abstract conception of desire and its objects. Pausanias, for example, distinguishes between ordinary "vulgar" desire (Eros Pandemos), which guides men who pursue women and the less enlightened among those who pursue boys, and a higher "celestial" desire (Eros Ouranios), which, directed exclusively at boys, aims to inculcate virtue. And Aristophanes, the comic playwright, suggests, by means of a myth of human origins apparently invented for the occasion, that *erōs* is about regaining a kind of existential wholeness.

The culmination of the dialogue is the speech of Socrates, who reports what he learned about desire from a priestess named Diotima, a speech that most scholars believe represents the views of Plato himself. According to Diotima, what one really desires is not the physical or even intellectual beauty of an individual youth or indeed of any person whatsoever, but rather permanent possession of the good and the beautiful; the philosophical lover, inspired in the presence of beauty, "gives birth," as it were, to reflections on the nature of beauty and virtue and, in so doing, gains a kind of immortality.[2] The dialogue ends with the entrance of a drunken Alcibiades, who gives a speech in praise not of Eros, but of Socrates, his erstwhile lover, which includes a memorable account of Socrates's refusal to be seduced by Alcibiades's physical charms.

Plato's privileged and indeed foundational place in the prehistory of Western gay literature is due to the influence of the *Symposium* more than any other work. But the presentation of sexual desire that we encounter in this dialogue is ambiguous. Plato appears to be interested not so much to provide a coherent philosophical account of the nature of erotic desire for other people (especially handsome youths), but to show that what we really "desire" as human beings is goodness and ultimately happiness, which come from a deeper, metaphysical understanding of reality. This appears to be the thrust of the so-called ascent passage from the *Symposium*, in which Diotima describes the philosopher's erotic progress as a series of seven graded steps: (1) "first ... he must love (*eran*) one body and in its presence beget beautiful discourses"; (2) "next he must recognize that the beauty in one body is akin to that in another body" and therefore must "become a lover (*erastēs*) of all beautiful bodies"; (3) "thereafter he must realize that the beauty in souls (*psychai*) is more valuable than that in the body" and "it must be sufficient for him to love (*eran*) [sc. a person beautiful in soul] ... and give birth to the sort of beautiful discourses that will make young men better"; (4) thus "he will be compelled to contemplate the beauty in practices and laws and to see that this beauty is all related"; (5) then he must be led "to see the beauty in forms of knowledge"; (6) and then "to turn toward the great sea of beauty" and "to give birth to many beautiful and impressive discourses": (7) "until … he beholds a single knowledge of this sort, which is knowledge of beauty [itself]" (210a–d).³ In the first three steps, individuals are the focus of the philosopher's desire – first it is their bodies, then their souls – and words conventionally used by the Greeks to denote "desire" (*eran, erastēs*) are used to characterize his attraction at these lower steps. But from the fourth step onward, Plato makes no mention of an individual beloved nor uses any Greek word denoting "desire" (Ferrari 258).

There are two possible ways to interpret this fact. One is to conclude that Plato was not interested to provide a theory of personal love: either true philosophical *erōs* requires us, after the third step, to abandon love for individuals in favor of love for beautiful practices and ideas and indeed for beauty in its most abstract form, or, perhaps more likely, one comes to realize, retrospectively, that one was never attracted to the beauty of an individual in the first place, but was attracted to the one beauty reflected (imperfectly) *in the individual* (Moravcsik 291; Vlastos 19–34). It is tempting to conclude that Plato exploits the conventions of pederastic courtship in order to make a contribution not to the philosophy of love but instead to ethics (humans "desire" the good) and epistemology (the way that the philosopher comes to know beauty in the ascent passage is the model for how we come to know anything worth knowing), that Plato's presentation of the *Symposium* as an inquiry into love and desire is an exercise in "bad faith" (Ferrari 248). But this is not the only way to interpret the absence of an individual beloved at the highest levels of the ascent. David Halperin argues that Plato is attempting to provide a theory of human desire, after all, but in terms that are foreign to our lay understanding of what we do when we love other people: one of Plato's insights is that our desire is necessarily mediated by external values, what Plato calls "forms" ("Platonic" 173–76).

But some scholars believe that although Plato is silent on the presence of an individual beloved at the highest steps of the ascent, there are other reasons to believe that personal love was still central to Plato's vision. Anthony Price, for example, argues that the lover's experience at the apex of the ascent, especially his giving birth to beautiful discourses and virtue and his gaining of immortality, can logically be accomplished only in partnership with another person: one gives birth, in effect, to an enlightened way of life *in* the person of the (younger) partner, and it is through him that the lover gains a kind of vicarious immortality (28–34; cf. Reeve 300–01). Other scholars resort to evidence outside the ascent passage. Martha Nussbaum, for example, argues that although Diotima's speech presents one picture of desire, Plato presents a rather different picture in his portrait of the relationship of Alcibiades and

Socrates in the final section of the *Symposium*: in her dialogic reading of the *Symposium*, Alcibiades's account of his personal desire for Socrates as a fully particularized individual is no less important than Diotima's suggestion that all desire is mediated, to some extent, by the external "forms" (157–60, 166–69).

Nussbaum's brilliant and disruptive reading has not, however, been followed by most scholars, who think that the relationship Alcibiades has with Socrates represents not an alternative erotic model for Plato, but the antithesis of the Platonic ideal (Ferrari 261–62; Reeve 297). But there is perhaps another way that Alcibiades's desire for Socrates may be taken as evidence that Plato was interested in actual sexual practice: Alcibiades is the most powerful embodiment of the notion, developed over the course of the *Symposium*, that all men, lovers as well as beloveds, are to be *active* lovers of beauty and the good, a notion that so deftly neutralizes worries about the beloved's sexual *passivity* in traditional pederastic practice that one suspects that Plato intended it to perform just this function (Foucault, *Use* 239–40; Halperin, "Plato" 67; cf. Reeve 297–98).

In the *Phaedrus*, written somewhat later, Plato similarly subordinates *erōs* to ethical and metaphysical concerns. That dialogue features a conversation between Socrates and a young man named Phaedrus, who has become infatuated with an erotic speech written by the Athenian rhetorician Lysias, in which the speaker aims to seduce a beautiful youth with the paradoxical argument that he is not in fact in love with him and thus not subject to the emotional lability or "madness" most Greeks associated with *erōs*, but that his erotic interest is a result of rational calculation. This speech becomes the foil for Socrates, who, in his powerful second speech, presents a paradox of his own: the philosopher's *erōs* is not calculating and rational, as one might expect; it is rather a kind of madness, sent by the gods, that puts him in touch with the immortal "forms," which, in Plato's philosophy, represent the metaphysical reality of the world. Plato's inquiry into the nature of desire is restricted to the first half of the dialogue; the second half takes up the issue of how to use rhetoric in a manner consistent with the methods and values of philosophy.

In the *Phaedrus*, too, there is a whiff of "bad faith." Socrates here places great importance on the relationship between lover and beloved as the ultimate context for the practice of philosophy. But we are as far from the real world of personal love as ever: these relationships are engaged in serious metaphysical work, which unfolds over the long count of eschatological time. It is only after presenting a proof of the immortality of the human soul and an account of how each soul, after multiple incarnations over a period of several thousand years, seeks finally to return to its heavenly home among the gods and "forms" that Socrates describes the nature of erotic madness. He explains that when a man sees a beautiful youth he is reminded of the divine "form" of beauty itself that he saw as a disembodied soul (251a–252b): he feels a quasi-religious ecstasy – the lover's "madness" – and treats his beloved as a god (254e–255a), not fully realizing that what he is in love with is not his beloved's beauty, but the "form" of beauty. The beloved has a similar experience, but less intense, and this shared experience is the basis of the friendship that the two have both during the erotic phase of their affair and afterward, which extends, ideally, to (and perhaps into) their blessed life in the hereafter (256b).

The role Socrates envisions for physical pleasure is inversely related to one's philosophical progress. The man who has forgotten what he saw of the "forms" as a disembodied soul or who has become "corrupted" for some reason does not experience reverence in the presence of his beloved's beauty; he surrenders to pleasure and attempts to "mount [his beloved] like a farm animal" (250e). The man who has a more philosophical disposition, by contrast, is drawn to the more modest pleasure that comes from "touching, kissing, and lying down together" (255e), but he struggles against these feelings. If both lover and beloved resist the temptation, they live a blessed life here on earth and, after death, their souls become winged and float up to the realm of the gods and divine "forms." "But if they turn to a more vulgar and unphilosophical way of life, but nevertheless pursue a life of honor, perhaps while drinking or in some other moment of carelessness, … [they] will make the choice deemed 'blessed' by the masses and will have sex. And once they have had sex, they continue to engage in it, but sparingly, because they are doing something that has not been approved by their whole soul." This pair also spends its life together, but does not enjoy the degree of friendship the philosophical pair does, and when they die, their souls do not sprout wings, though they desire to (255e–256d). We can see a clear hierarchy: the nonphilosophical man seeks penetrative intercourse with his beloved; the man of honor will engage in "touching, kissing, and lying down together," but "sparingly"; the philosophical man will renounce sexual contact altogether and will reap a rich eschatological reward as a result.

The devaluation of sexual pleasure that we encounter in the *Phaedrus* is consistent with what Plato has to say on this topic in other works. In the *Symposium*, there are allusions to physical affection in the earlier speeches of Pausanias and Aristophanes (184c–e, 191e–192a), but Alcibiades's account, toward the end of the dialogue, of his unsuccessful attempt to have sex with Socrates suggests that sexual renunciation is indeed the ideal. And in a few well-known passages from the later *Laws*, written toward the end of Plato's career, a character called the "Athenian," the primary interlocutor in this dialogue, suggests that same-sex intercourse is "contrary to nature" (*para phusin*) and advocates banning it outright from his ideal city (636c–d, 836c, 841d). This has struck some as a remarkable departure from Plato's earlier valorization of same-sex eroticism in the *Symposium* and *Phaedrus*, but these passages from the *Laws* are not as censorious as they might appear. First, Plato uses the word "nature" to characterize those forms of sexual intercourse, in both the human and the animal realm, whose goal is reproduction, and not necessarily to characterize the moral status of one form of sexual activity in comparison to others. Plato implicitly invokes a popular contrast between "nature" and "culture" that had been deployed, for at least a generation, to characterize sex and other types of human behavior (Dover, *Greek* 154; Hubbard, "Paradox" 250–51), and in fact seems to recognize that these kinds of arguments are rhetorically powerful but philosophically suspect (Goldhill 55–56). Second, the "Athenian," probably reflecting the views of Plato himself, is criticizing the tendency of sex-segregated societies such as Sparta and the cities of Crete to promote a form of same-sex eroticism, in men as well as women, that is unabashedly physical in its aim. Which leads to a third point: this kind of carnality, which he diagnoses here as resulting from a "lack of control in the face of pleasure" (636c), is something that Plato eschewed no less consistently earlier in his career, including in the *Symposium* and *Phaedrus* (see earlier in this chapter), and not only in reference to same-sex sexual conduct, but with respect to the indulgence of appetites of all kinds.

But, in the end, Plato's theory of *erōs* is concerned less with the presence or absence of an individual beloved or the presence or absence of physical sex than with the ultimate object of desire, which is the beautiful and the good. Although it may be stimulated initially by a beautiful youth, *erōs* becomes, in Plato's hands, a grand metaphor for the practice of philosophy, a literalization of the Greek word *philosophia*, which means "love of wisdom." Although Plato's exploration of philosophical *erōs* takes place in the context of an aristocratic society that celebrated the courtship of handsome youths, a practice alluded to frequently in the dialogues themselves, Plato's *Symposium* and *Phaedrus* are certainly not the ingenuous celebrations of man-boy love that they were later often taken to be.

Socrates, Socratic Dialogues, and Athenian Civic *Erōs*

We may turn now to a consideration of the larger social and literary context in which Plato's *Symposium* and *Phaedrus*, with their complex reflections on the true object of desire, were produced. There is a tendency, among some scholars and many in the educated public, to assume that Plato's ideas were a natural extension of traditional Greek attitudes, or, more specifically, that Platonic *erōs* represents a philosophical codification of pedagogical protocols that supposedly constituted the *raison d'être* of Greek pederasty. But the evidence, as we shall see, points in a rather different direction.

We may begin with the views of the historical Socrates. Socrates would of course play a privileged role in the reception of Greek philosophical ideas about *erōs* in modern gay literature, but the figure celebrated in those later texts is the Platonic Socrates of the *Symposium* and *Phaedrus*. Our quarry here is the man himself. What we know of the historical Socrates's views of desire comes mostly from works written by his followers – Antisthenes, Aeschines of Sphettus, Phaedo, Euclides, Plato, and Xenophon – which often featured Socrates speaking of his own erotic pursuits or of the nature of love and desire more generally (Kahn 1–35). Of these "Socratic dialogues," the only ones to survive complete are those written by Plato and Xenophon; we will return briefly to Xenophon in the next section. But there survive sufficient fragments of the dialogues of Antisthenes and Aeschines of Sphettus, both most likely written before the great erotic dialogues of Plato (Kahn 29), to give us a sense of the historical Socrates's theory of desire, uncontaminated by later Platonic ideas.

Antisthenes, the oldest pupil of Socrates, wrote two dialogues that addressed the nature and object of *erōs*. In the *Heracles*, a character, probably Socrates himself, suggested that the wise man is "a worthy object of *erōs*," quite likely in the context of a reciprocal friendship with another wise man (Giannantoni fr. 99; cf. Xenophon, *Symposium* 8.3–4). It appears that he, or possibly another character, provided an example from the life of the hero Heracles, who came to the cave of Chiron, a mythical educator of Greek heroes, "out of desire (*erōs*)," presumably out of desire for the person of the wise Chiron or, perhaps more likely, his wisdom (Giannantoni fr. 92).[4] We hear of a beautiful youth whom Heracles encounters there, probably Achilles, who is described as a beauty suitable only for a lover as brave as Heracles (Giannantoni fr. 93), but this youth is probably a foil for the real, ultimate object of Heracles's desire, which is wisdom. In another dialogue, the *Alcibiades*, Antisthenes seems to have explored the theme of *erōs* in the context of the relationship between Socrates and Alcibiades, but the fragments from this work are not sufficient to form an opinion of how Socrates's views of *erōs* were presented.

Aeschines of Sphettus also wrote a dialogue entitled *Alcibiades*, from which substantial quotations survive. Socrates is there presented as a sort of "doctor" of philosophy: whereas regular doctors heal people with the medical skill (*technē*) learned from their teachers, Socrates owes his philosophical healing to a "divine dispensation" (*theia moira*), which works by activating "desire" (*epithumia*) within the patient to acquire the wisdom and virtue necessary for the health of his soul. Both teacher and pupil are motivated by a kind of erotic desire (*erōs*): Socrates is drawn to the beautiful Alcibiades by *erōs* to "make him better," and Alcibiades is caused to feel a kind of desire of his own, in his case desire to acquire virtue and knowledge (Giannantoni fr. 53). This kind of erotic reciprocity is also central to the portrayal of their relationship in a Socratic dialogue entitled *First Alcibiades*, which is attributed to Plato, but perhaps not by him. There Alcibiades is shown not to have the knowledge and virtue that he needs to be a ruler in the city, and vows to "attend upon" Socrates, as pupil to teacher, much as Socrates used to "attend upon" Alcibiades, as lover to beloved. Socrates acknowledges this change of roles: "my desire (*erōs*)," he says, "will hatch a winged desire (*erōs*) in you and be cared for it in return," much as storks are cared for in old age by their offspring (135d–e). Socrates's *erōs* for Alcibiades, in other words, instills in the young man the *erōs* to cultivate his own virtue.

The Socratic dialogues of Antisthenes and Aeschines suggest that the historical Socrates had used *erōs* as a metaphor for the pursuit of virtue and knowledge, and it is likely that this was a specific application of his more general belief that what motivates all human action is "desire" (*erōs*) for the good (Wolfsdorf 29–85). It is difficult to know which aspect of this formulation would have struck the Athenians as more radical: that *erōs* or "desire" is at the root of *everything* that we do or that the object of sexual desire, the desire that most Greeks associated with the word *erōs*, is goodness and not, say, pleasure. The tradition locates much of the historical Socrates's reflection on the nature of desire within the context of his friendship – certainly erotic but perhaps not sexual – with Alcibiades, the handsome politician (Gribble 214–61), but according to Aeschines of Sphettus Socrates was also interested in the operation of *erōs* in the relationship between husband and wife (Giannantoni fr. 70), and indeed in all the ethical choices humans make, in the sexual sphere and elsewhere.

Some scholars have argued that the most natural cultural context in which to understand Socratic (and then Platonic) *erōs* is in a supposed pedagogical function of Greek pederasty (Patzer; Percy), an idea that has enjoyed periodic popularity since the publication of Karl Müller's *Die Dorier* in 1824. But there are two difficulties with the "pedagogy hypothesis." First, the evidence on which it rests is problematic. The evidence for institutionalized pederasty in

Sparta and Crete, for example, comes from the late classical or early Hellenistic period at the earliest, and there is reason to believe that these institutions were reinterpreted at this time in response to synchronic social needs and ideologies (Dodd; Dover, "Greek"); indeed, it is quite likely that these later interpretations are strongly influenced by Platonic ideas about the philosophical function of *erōs*. We face a different kind of problem with use of the archaic poet Theognis: there are indeed verses in the Theognidean corpus that are pederastic and some too that are pedagogical, but very few that are both, and none of these is certainly by Theognis himself.[5] Second, and more troubling, the "pedagogy hypothesis" removes desire from the practice of pederastic courtship (Halperin, *One* 54–61). One can perhaps appreciate the motivation of some to do so. For those unsympathetic to pederasty, the hypothesis shows that Greek men pursued handsome youths not because they were genuinely attracted to them, but in order to discharge some kind of social duty. For those sympathetic, it shows that Greek pederasty was not (just) about sex, but performed an important social function.

A different, and probably more likely, source of inspiration for Socrates's (and later Plato's) conception of *erōs* was an erotic metaphor that was common in Athenian political discourse in the last third of the fifth century, as Athens's radical democracy was at its height (Ludwig; Wohl). There were a number of forms of the metaphor. One could describe the bonds between citizens in terms of *erōs* (Aristotle, *Politics* 1262b8–17) or one could, with Pericles, famously, suggest that citizens should feel *erōs* for the city (*polis*) as a whole (Thucydides 2.43). There were other versions of the civic *erōs* metaphor that aimed to describe the more dysfunctional features of political life in Athens. Politicians competed for the attentions of the people, the democratic rabble, by proclaiming their *erōs* for it: they played the homosexual lover (*erastēs*) to the rabble's beloved (Aristophanes, *Knights* 1340–44). And the people, in turn, could similarly describe their support of their favorite politicians in terms of desire: in 405 BCE, Aristophanes described the city as "longing for" (*pothei*) the popular exiled politician Alcibiades (*Frogs* 1423–25). Indeed, Alcibiades was perhaps the politician most associated with the erotic metaphor: he was the most famous object of the people's desire and he himself experienced a healthy desire for fame and power (Wohl 124–70).

The philosophical conception of *erōs* would represent a reformulation of this civic erotic metaphor. The historical Socrates changed the focus from politics to ethics: *erōs* for the body politic or for its leaders should be redirected toward something higher, notably virtue, wisdom, and goodness. Then Plato put this object of Socratic desire on a metaphysical footing: we desire a pure and highly abstract goodness and beauty that transcend individual good or beautiful persons or things. For Socrates, same-sex eroticism was just one context in which to explore human desire for the good; for Plato, it was consistently the starting point for such explorations. But both men looked far beyond the individual beloved and whatever bodily pleasures he might offer.

Reception of Platonic *Erōs*, in Antiquity and Beyond

Much of the rhetorical and philosophical subtlety of Plato's explorations of *erōs* was lost on later readers in antiquity and beyond. Theirs is a largely deracinated Plato, reduced to a number of memorable images and metaphors: celestial love and spiritual birth, from the *Symposium*, *erōs* as a form of divine madness or inspiration, from the *Phaedrus*. And later readers of the *Symposium* seem comfortable deriving Platonic thought from all the speeches equally and tend to grant no special priority to the words of Socrates and Diotima. The metaphysics of desire and its political genealogy were almost entirely forgotten.

This opportunistic (mis)reading of Platonic *erōs* was well under way already in Plato's own lifetime. Xenophon, a younger contemporary of Plato, wrote a Socratic dialogue entitled *Symposium*, which aimed to correct the views expressed in Plato's dialogue of the same name. Xenophon clearly reads Plato as an apologist for pederasty, who, even as he argues that *erōs* for the soul is superior to that for the body, nevertheless does not rule out more strictly carnal desires. So the focus of the long speech Xenophon puts into the mouth of Socrates (8.6–41) is the importance of chastity in relationships between men and youths. His Socrates has nothing to say of the ultimate metaphysical object of human desire. And whereas Plato had concluded his *Symposium* with the disruptive entry of the beautiful Alcibiades, Xenophon ends his dialogue with an erotic pantomime performed by a male and a female slave, which inspires the married men at the gathering to seek out their wives for love making and the unmarried men to find wives (9.2–7), a clear signal that marital sexuality is the Xenophontic ideal.

Same-sex desire is also explored in two surviving dialogues from the postclassical period, both clearly engaged, to at least some extent polemically, with the erotic dialogues of Plato. The *Erotikos* of Plutarch, written in the late first or early second century CE, is an account of a conversation, held at Thespiae and later on Mount Helicon, by Plutarch and some of his friends on the subject of *erōs*. It invokes Platonic ideas in order to exalt the institution of marriage and ultimately devalue the love of boys (Foucault, *Care* 197, 209). This emphasis on marriage is evident in the double framing of the dialogue: Plutarch and his new wife have come to Thespiae in order to seek the assistance of the god Eros to heal a quarrel between their parents, and the discussion of *erōs* begins in response to the marriage proposal presented by a wealthy widow to a beautiful youth named Bacchon.

The first part of the dialogue is devoted to a debate regarding the merits of boys and women as objects of love, which is occasioned when Bacchon's male lover objects to the widow's proposal of marriage. The advocate for the superiority of male love (750c–751b) makes the explicitly Platonic argument that *erōs* is the force that draws us toward "a talented young soul" and inspires us to bring him "to a state of virtue through friendship (*philia*)." Desire for women is not *erōs*, but mere "lust" (*epithumia*), which is pursued only for pleasure, a formulation of the contrast Pausanias makes in the *Symposium* between "vulgar" and "celestial" love. The advocate for the love of women (751c–752b), by contrast, argues that *erōs* has no value without physical consummation, so that it is precisely the physical pleasure that one is permitted to experience with women that makes them superior objects of desire. Boys must avoid sexual intercourse with their lovers, lest they compromise their masculinity, the view of the philosophers themselves, if we take them at their word. Sexual intercourse between men and boys is "unnatural," the argument from nature now being deployed not with the ambivalence of Plato in the *Laws*, but with the censoriousness more typical of the Stoic diatribe of the early empire.

Plutarch himself, in the final and longest section of the dialogue, makes his own case on behalf of the love of women, but his strategy is to use explicitly Platonic arguments – that *erōs* "leads to virtue and friendship (*philia*)" (758c), that *erōs* represents an "inspired" form of madness (759ab), which enables us to "recollect" true beauty (764e) – to suggest that relationships with women are not only capable of realizing these philosophical ideals but in fact better able to achieve them than relationships between men and youths, precisely because of the role that physical love plays in them.

The other postclassical dialogue devoted to a discussion of sexual desire is the *Erotes* attributed to Lucian of Samosata, written as early as the mid-second century and as late as the early fourth century CE.[6] It features a man named Lycinus recounting to his friend Theomnestus a debate he once heard about the merits of women versus boys as objects of love. What is most interesting about this dialogue is not the specific arguments deployed, which had become traditional by this time, but the response by Lycinus and Theomnestus to them. Lycinus, present at the actual debate, was asked to judge and issued this verdict: "Marriage is a profitable and blessed thing for men when it turns out well, but I think that the love of boys, which courts the pure and just rewards of friendship, is an undertaking for philosophy alone. So let all men get married, but may it be left to wise men alone to love boys. For rarely in women does perfect virtue grow" (51). This judgment in favor of pederasty is far from decisive: it assumes the centrality of marriage as the context in which most men experience desire and praises the philosophical love of boys precisely because of its grand claims to be "pure and just" (Foucault, *Care* 226). And Theomnestus, though he approves of Lycinus's verdict overall, proceeds to puncture these very claims: "Let the ivory-tower types and those who raise the brow of philosophy above their temples herd the ignorant [masses] with the cleverness of their fancy phrases. But Socrates succumbed to *erōs* as much as anyone, and Alcibiades, after he lay down with him under a single cloak, did not rise unassailed. Let there be no doubt of that" (54).

How should we characterize the relation between these two works and the tradition of the Platonic erotic dialogue? Although these later dialogues clearly invoke the Platonic dialogue as their model, there are some important formal differences between them: the Platonic dialogue focuses on the figure of Socrates, who debates with one or more interlocutors and presents clear principles of inquiry and serious philosophical argumentation; neither Plutarch nor the author of *Erotes* presents arguments of a rigorous philosophical nature, though Plutarch himself was steeped in philosophy (mostly Platonic philosophy), and in the *Erotes* there is no single controlling voice that we may identify as the author's. Both Plutarch and the author of *Erotes* make ample use of specific ideas and images from Plato's *Symposium* and *Phaedrus*, but Plato's theory has largely been reduced to the idea that *erōs* promotes virtue and friendship without recourse to sex. Plutarch responds that in relationships with women, one can realize all three: virtue, friendship, and sex. The author of the *Erotes* suggests that if this kind of *erōs* is the ideal (and one believes its commitment to chastity), it is ultimately accessible only to high-minded philosophers.

Representations of Greek sexuality seem to have shifted somewhat since the time of Socrates. Sexuality in this later period is still not a question of exclusive sexual identity. Plutarch and the author of *Erotes* do contrast devotees of boys and those of women, but this does not imply exclusive orientations; indeed, in the *Erotes*, the debate is narrated by one Lycinus, who "inclines" to neither women nor boys, to one Theomnestus, who likes both. These are preferences, not orientations, a phenomenon we see already in the classical period. But the focus of the discourse of sexuality, at least as manifested in high literary genres written by elite men, has changed. Marriage is now the focus of Greek discussions of sexual ethics; pederasty is now more marginalized from these discussions and has become associated, in the popular imagination, with the practitioners of philosophy, an association due, at least in part, to the enormous influence of Plato's *Symposium* and *Phaedrus*.

Platonic *erōs* also inspired numerous gay or proto-gay authors from later centuries. In the interests of space, we may restrict ourselves to brief mention of a few figures from American and British literature in the nineteenth century. Herman Melville, for example, who read Plato first in the translation of Sydenham and Taylor (1804), attempts, in an anonymous review entitled "Hawthorne and his Mosses" (1850), to figure his homosocial relationship with Nathaniel Hawthorne in the language of spiritual pregnancy from Plato's *Symposium*: "I feel that this Hawthorne has dropped germinous seeds into my soul" (250; see Voloshin). Walt Whitman, meanwhile, encountered Plato in the translations published by Bohn from 1848 to 1854. His praise of "manly love" in the "Calamus" poems (1860) has been thought to invoke the arguments of Pausanias and Aristophanes in the *Symposium* that the lover of boys is more masculine than the lover of women (Erkkila 158 n. 46). And in "The Base of All Metaphysics," which was added to the "Calamus" poems in the 1871 edition, Whitman writes: "Yet underneath Socrates [sc. I] clearly see, and underneath Christ the divine I see / The dear love of man for his comrade, the attraction of friend to friend, / Of the well-married husband and wife, of children and parents, / Of city for city, and land for land" (88), suggesting, as indeed Socrates and several other speakers do in Plato's *Symposium*, that male love is one species of a larger, more encompassing, and more abstract love (cf. Erkkila 137).

British writers such as the Uranian poets and Oscar Wilde, meanwhile, came to Plato through the translations and Oxford pedagogy of Benjamin Jowett. The Uranian poets, active from the late 1850s to the early 1930s, explicitly looked to the account of "celestial" or "uranian" *erōs* from Pausanias's speech in the *Symposium* (Dowling 114, 130–36). But many British homosexuals at this time, including some who identified with this movement, felt that "celestial" love left no room for their quite physical sexual needs. And so a pessimistic Lord Alfred Douglas, in his poem entitled "Two Loves," turns Pausanias's contrast between "vulgar" *erōs* and "celestial" *erōs* into one between "true" heterosexual love and the "love that dares not tell its name" (Dowling 143), replicating a heteronormative strategy of which we saw hints already in Plato's ancient critics, Xenophon and Plutarch. But it is Oscar Wilde who engaged most deeply with Plato's discussions of *erōs*. He traces his initiation into Platonic *erōs* to his days as a student at Oxford, which he describes as spent, metaphorically, conversing with Socrates by the river Ilissus (Dowling 117), a reference to the setting of Plato's *Phaedrus*. Wilde clearly saw Platonic *erōs* as a way to understand not only his own sexual feelings, but also his inspiration as an artist (Dowling 119, 124–25, 127). There are times, as in the *Portrait of W.H.* (1889), when he believes that Plato, in the *Symposium*, provides a way to reconcile "intellectual enthusiasm and the physical passion of love" (1174), but in the end, he despairs of this project. So in the epistolary *De Profundis*, published posthumously in 1905, he styles himself the true Platonic "celestial" lover as against the more carnal Douglas (Dowling 147–48) – "I blame myself for allowing an unintellectual friendship, a friendship whose primary aim was not the creation and contemplation of beautiful things, to dominate my life" (874) – in effect playing an exhortatory Socrates to the latter's Alcibiades.

Notes

1. On the association of pederasty in the classical period with the elite, see Hubbard, "Popular."
2. On the pregnancy metaphor in Plato's *Symposium*, see Leitao 182–226.
3. All translations from the Greek are the author's own. The Works Cited lists bilingual editions of the texts of Aristophanes, Aristotle, Athenaeus, Lucian, Plato, Plutarch, Theognis, Thucydides, and Xenophon purely for the convenience of readers with no reading knowledge of ancient Greek.
4. Xenophon (*On Hunting* 12.18–20) says that heroes came to Chiron's cave out of desire (*erōs*) for Virtue, personified as a female goddess. This likely constitutes a polemical response to the homosocial context of Antisthenes's *Heracles* (in Giannantoni).
5. One could argue that lines 237–54, which are almost certainly by Theognis, are both pedagogical and pederastic, but this is far from certain. Classical authors read the relationship between Theognis and Cyrnus, his young addressee, as exhortatory, not erotic: see, e.g., Plato, *Laws* 630a; Xenophon, *Symposium* 2.4. The only pederastic poem Athenaeus (310ab), in the late second or early third century CE, can find in his collection of Theognis's poems is 993–96, which is very likely not by Theognis. The best discussion of which poems in the Theognidean corpus are by Theognis himself is still West 40–64.
6. Many scholars have doubted that the work is by Lucian, but Jope (111–16) has recently made a strong case against the skeptics and thinks it was written by Lucian in the second century CE.

Works Cited

Aristophanes. *The Frogs. Aristophanes: Volume IV.* Ed. and trans. Jeffrey Henderson. Cambridge: Harvard UP, 2002. Print.

The Knights. Aristophanes: Volume I. Ed. and trans. Jeffrey Henderson. Cambridge: Harvard UP, 1998. Print.

Aristotle. *Politics.* Ed. and trans. H. Rackham. Cambridge: Harvard UP, 1932. Print.

Athenaeus. *The Learned Banqueters.* 7 vols. Ed. and trans. S. Douglas Olson. Cambridge: Harvard UP, 2007–12. Print.

Dodd, David. "Athenian Ideas about Cretan Pederasty." *Greek Love Reconsidered.* Ed. Thomas Hubbard. New York: W. Hamilton P, 2000. 33–41. Print.

Dover, Kenneth. *Greek Homosexuality.* 2nd ed. Cambridge: Harvard UP, 1989. Print.

"Greek Homosexuality and Initiation." *The Greeks and Their Legacy.* Vol. 2. Ed. Kenneth Dover. Oxford: Oxford UP, 1988. 115–34. Print.

Dowling, Linda. *Hellenism and Homosexuality in Victorian Oxford.* Ithaca: Cornell UP, 1994. Print.

Erkkila, Betsy. *Walt Whitman's Songs of Male Intimacy and Love: "Live Oak, with Moss" and "Calamus."* Iowa City: U of Iowa P, 2011. Print.

Ferrari, Giovanni. "Platonic Love." *The Cambridge Companion to Plato.* Ed. Richard Kraut. Cambridge: Cambridge UP, 1992. 248–76. Print.

Foucault, Michel. *The Care of the Self: Volume 3 of the History of Sexuality.* Trans. Robert Hurley. New York: Pantheon, 1986. Print.

The Use of Pleasure: Volume 2 of the History of Sexuality. Trans. Robert Hurley. New York: Pantheon, 1985. Print.

Giannantoni, Gabriele. *Socratis et Socraticorum reliquiae.* 4 vols. Naples: Bibliopolis, 1990. Print.

Goldhill, Simon. *Foucault's Virginity: Ancient Erotic Fiction and the History of Sexuality.* Cambridge: Cambridge UP, 1995. Print.

Gribble, David. *Alcibiades and Athens: A Study in Literary Presentation.* Oxford: Clarendon P, 1999. Print.

Halperin, David. *One Hundred Years of Homosexuality, and Other Essays on Greek Love.* New York: Routledge, 1990. Print.

"Plato and Erotic Reciprocity." *Classical Antiquity* 5 (1986): 60–80. Print.

"Platonic *Erōs* and What Men Call Love." *Ancient Philosophy* 5 (1985): 161–204. Print.

Hubbard, Thomas. "The Paradox of 'Natural' Heterosexuality with 'Unnatural' Women." *Classical Bulletin* 102 (2009): 249–58. Print.

"Popular Perceptions of Elite Homosexuality in Classical Athens." *Arion* 6 (1998): 48–78. Print.

Jope, James. "Interpretation and Authenticity of the Lucianic *Erotes*." *Helios* 38 (2011): 103–20. Print.

Kahn, Charles. *Plato and the Socratic Dialogue: The Philosophical Use of a Literary Form.* Cambridge: Cambridge UP, 1996. Print.

Leitao, David. *The Pregnant Male as Myth and Metaphor in Classical Greek Literature.* New York: Cambridge UP, 2012. Print.

Lucian (or Pseudo-Lucian). *Erotes [Amores]. Lucian: Volume VIII.* Ed. and trans. M. D. MacLeod. Cambridge: Harvard UP, 1967. Print.

Ludwig, Paul. *Eros and Polis: Desire and Community in Greek Political Theory.* Cambridge: Cambridge UP, 2002. Print.

Melville, Herman. "Hawthorne and His Mosses." *The Piazza Tales and Other Prose Pieces, 1938–1860.* Ed. Harrison Hayford, Alma A. MacDougall, and G. Thomas Tanselle. Evanston: Northwestern UP, 1987. Print.

Moravcsik, Julius. "Reason and Eros in the 'Ascent'-Passage of the *Symposium*." *Essays in Ancient Greek Philosophy*. Ed. John Anton and George Kustas. Albany: State U of New York P, 1971. 285–302. Print.

Nussbaum, Martha. "The Speech of Alcibiades: A Reading of Plato's *Symposium*." *Philosophy and Literature* 3 (1979): 132–72. Print.

Patzer, Harald. *Die griechische Knabenliebe*. Wiesbaden: Franz Steiner, 1982. Print.

Percy, William. *Pederasty and Pedagogy in Archaic Greece*. Urbana: U of Illinois P, 1996. Print.

Plato. *Laws*. Ed. and trans. R. G. Bury. 2 vols. Cambridge: Harvard UP, 1926. Print.

⸻. *Phaedrus*. *Plato: Volume I*. Ed. and trans. Harold North Fowler. Cambridge: Harvard UP, 1914. Print.

⸻. *Symposium*. *Plato: Volume V*. Ed. and trans. W. R. M. Lamb. Cambridge: Harvard UP, 1925. Print.

Plato (or Pseudo-Plato). *First Alcibiades [Alcibiades I]*. *Plato: Volume XII*. Ed. and trans. W. R. M. Lamb. Cambridge: Harvard UP, 1927. Print.

Plutarch. *Erotikos [Dialogue on Love]*. *Plutarch: Moralia, Volume IX*. Ed. and trans. Edwin L. Minar, F. H. Sandbach, and W. C. Helmbold. Cambridge: Harvard UP, 1961. Print.

Price, Anthony. *Love and Friendship in Plato and Aristotle*. Oxford: Clarendon, 1989. Print.

Reeve, C. D. C. "Plato on Eros and Friendship." *A Companion to Plato*. Ed. Hugh Benson. Malden: Wiley-Blackwell, 2006. 294–307. Print.

Theognis. In *Greek Elegiac Poetry*. Ed. and trans. Douglas Gerber. Cambridge: Harvard UP, 1999. Print.

Thucydides. *History of the Peloponnesian War*. 4 vols. Ed. and trans. C. F. Smith. Cambridge: Harvard UP, 1919–23. Print.

Vlastos, Gregory. *Platonic Studies*. 2nd ed. Princeton: Princeton UP, 1981. Print.

Voloshin, Beverly. "Parables of Creation: Hawthorne, Melville and Plato's *Banquet*." *Leviathan: A Journal of Melville Studies* 13 (2011): 18–29. Print.

West, Martin. *Studies in Greek Elegy and Iambus*. Berlin: de Gruyter, 1974. Print.

Whitman, Walt. "The Base of All Metaphysics." Erkkila 87–88.

Wilde, Oscar. *The Complete Works of Oscar Wilde*. London: Collins, 1966. Print.

Wohl, Victoria. *Love among the Ruins: The Erotics of Democracy in Classical Athens*. Princeton: Princeton UP, 2002. Print.

Wolfsdorf, David. *Trials of Reason: Plato and the Crafting of Philosophy*. Oxford: Oxford UP, 2008. Print.

Xenophon. *On Hunting*. *Xenophon: Volume VII*. Ed. and trans. E. C. Marchant and G. W. Bowersock. Cambridge: Harvard UP, 1968. Print.

⸻. *Symposium*. *Xenophon: Volume IV*. Ed. and trans. E. C. Marchant and O. J. Todd. Cambridge: Harvard UP, 1923. Print.

3

The Pastoral Lament in Ancient Greek and Latin

JAY REED

Before Elegy

A reader of the pastoral lament in European literature – a tradition that includes such exponents as Petrarch, Ronsard, Spenser, and Milton – may be forgiven for assuming that that most idiosyncratic form, in which herdsmen mourn a dead companion or the like, must rest on a foundation of conventions solidly established in a sizeable body of ancient poems. There are, in fact, exactly two in ancient Greek (Theocritus's *Idyll* 1 and the anonymous *Epitaph on Bion*) and a couple more in ancient Latin (Virgil's *Eclogue* 5 and Nemesianus's *Eclogue* 1). It is not until the end of the fifteenth century that a critical mass of pastoral laments permits the real sense of a genre. What this genre makes out of so few and – as we shall see – such disparate poems will be clearer for our casting into relief its difference from the classical poems that it claims to continue; there are rewards for reintegrating the ancient specimens with literature of their own times and permitting their unfamiliar configurations of death, desire, and poetic consciousness to emerge. Our understanding of the modern type can also benefit from a suspension of expectations: "Canonical elegies reveal a heterogeneity and resistance to oppressive normalization" (Zeiger 168). Our criticism tends to lean too heavily on the tradition leading to and from Milton's *Lycidas*. It seems easy to forget, for example, that most European pastoral lament does not mourn a poet; that it does not necessarily envision a consolatory translation to a world beyond; or that for its first century and more, before its sixteenth-century efflorescence, it predominantly mourned women: Petrarch's *Galatea*, Boccaccio's *Olympia*, Boiardo's *Philyroe* and *Nysa*, Pontano's *Ariadna*, Sannazaro's "Mamillia" lament in the *Arcadia* (and this version never disappears, as Marot's *Complainte* on Louise of Savoy or Spenser's "November" eclogue, among others, attest).

Particularly unfamiliar from our standpoint is the ancient poems' apparent disinclination to articulate a relationship between the framing voice and the mourned object. They resist readings for values that critics of the modern elegy readily look for and interrogate: a psychoanalytic "work of mourning" on the part of a poetic "I" responding to and projecting itself into the departed; the inheritance or appropriation of a speaking or poetic voice; an economy of loss and recuperation.

Here I find a heuristic center of this group in the *Epitaph on Bion*, whose speaker, personally mourning his precursor in a thoroughgoing pastoral mimesis, most teasingly fulfills modern expectations of what this kind of poem should be. It is the strongest influence on some of the strongest poems in this tradition – Spenser's *Astrophel* and Shelley's *Adonais* are examples – the ones that most fully escape the category of pastoral lament and reach into others, yet still maintain as their binding force the strange node of tropes that the Greek poem invents. A close reading of the *Epitaph* nevertheless discloses tensions between voice and silence, a reticence concerning the power of poetry that the poem itself would seem to presuppose. The speaker has an uneasy relation to Bion and his poetic world; he keeps warily avoiding the obvious self-comparison in favor of metonymical relationships based on both inheritance and mourning and, more obliquely, forms of desire.

Interpretive problems involve those of terminology and titulature, which deserve clarification. These ancient poems exemplify in different ways the more general category of epicedion (*epikēdeion*, a common enough Greek label for a piece of mourning literature), whose various conventions of lamentation, praise, and consolation they in various measures project or muffle. Our main text's manuscript title, *epitaphios*, is properly used of an oration with like functions delivered "over the grave," and was no doubt given to the poem in a later age by scribes well trained in rhetoric; I use "epitaph" in English to keep present the incongruity and historicity of the Greek title, and call the nameless author-speaker the "Epitaphist." The label "elegy," so obvious in a discussion of the form in modern poetry, wreaks confusion in the context of Greek and Latin, where it is both far broader (counting lamentation among many other themes and discursive modes) and narrower (referring strictly to a distinct metrical form – ancient bucolic is composed almost solely in hexameters, not elegiacs), and I avoid it except when talking about the later tradition. The terms "bucolic" and "pastoral" both derive from Greek and Latin terms amounting to "herdsmanly," and may be used for the same literary phenomena, but I (following David Halperin and others) try to distinguish herdsmanly themes and settings by "pastoral" and to use "bucolic" for the increasingly polythematic ancient genre signaled by formal features. "Idyll" (*eidullion*) is the conventional term for any poem by Theocritus or attributed to him in manuscripts or early printed editions; "eclogue" (*ecloga*) is a poem in the Latin bucolic tradition that begins with Virgil.

The value of these texts for the history of gay literature lies in the way they expose and estrange the ancestry of later articulations of male desire for a male in relation to loss and mourning, that is, of the homoerotic – or, to speak more tentatively, homosocial – constructions that have often been seen to underpin early modern pastoral laments and their successors, all the way up to the poems of mortality that almost, or quite fully, leave the rustic setting and personae behind: Gray's *Elegy*, Shelley's *Adonais*, Arnold's *Thyrsis*, Tennyson's *In Memoriam*, and the AIDS elegies and similar poetry of the late twentieth century. Recent criticism finds, for example, "that the elegy is the poetic form concerned with the erotics of mourning ... [T]he ideology of the elegy form itself functions both to carve out a space for male-male desire at the same time that it reinscribes that desire within the contours of hegemonic cultural practice. In the end, not desire but loss becomes the most recognizable feature of male love" (Haggerty 187). In our four Greek and Latin texts there is almost nothing overtly "gay"; ancient pastoral as a whole, apart from Virgil's "Corydon" eclogue (followed by Nemesianus's fourth), has in fact little homoerotic content. (Among exceptions, the inset songs in *Idyll* 7 and some of Bion's fragments stand out; Bion's interest is perhaps reflected in the Epitaphist's commemoration at line 83 that "he taught the kisses of boys.") Moreover, we are looking at a period when male-male desire was quite differently problematized than in early and later modern Europe, and the liberating space of the countryside, studied for nineteenth- and twentieth-century gay literature by David Shuttleton and others, is not at issue; Corydon's withdrawal to the wildwood to sing, and invitation to Alexis to join him on the farm, mean something different in the *Eclogues* than to modern readers. We should also be aware that whatever post-antique readers seem to find in the contours of the *ancient* pastoral lament, it is not precisely grooves of yearning down which they can pour erotic desire as readily as grief. Rather, as is often the case with Greek and Roman literature, in tracing the difference between ancient and modern versions we are tracing an even more basic misreading, an urge to make explicit a subject position, and a corresponding object, imputed to the ancient texts but, on close inspection, difficult to discern there. Ultimately this small body of precedents to a larger and much later body of literature discloses a process, congenial to queer-theoretical interests, of identity formation against the silences of ancient texts.[1]

"A Beautiful Singer Has Died"

The *Epitaph on Bion* is roughly datable to the early first century BCE. Its author, like those of a number of late bucolic poems in Greek, is unknown; an ascription to Moschus of Syracuse (sometimes still met with in the critical literature) emerges in the late fifteenth century, but the few facts at our disposal are against it (Reed, "Continuity" 209–10). This is not an easy poem to read past its surface, and it so far lacks the detailed commentary that would explicate its linguistic and rhetorical oddities, alleviate its textual corruptions, and elucidate its imagery. English translation tends to reduce to monochrome its iridescent Greek (there are four different verbs for mourning, for example, in the first three lines alone, and the vocabulary of singing similarly effloresces). Part of its difficulty comes from the extravagance of its voice, whose exuberant tropes and opportunistic hyperboles lead to a degree of self-contradiction. Its occasional non sequiturs, its redundancies and backpedaling, may sometimes, of course, be attributable to a poorly copied text (there are frequent corruptions, some not yet corrected to the satisfaction of editors). We might also suspect that phrases borrowed from Bion's own work (we can observe many, and there must be many we cannot recognize) have been integrated awkwardly into the later poem, adding to its difficulty, though this latter possibility might also be treated as the trace of a rhetoric of inclusion, an ostentatiously failed assimilation of mourning self and mourned other.

The opening lines introduce some basic elements: "Moan '*ailina*' with me, O woodlands and Dorian water, and weep, ye rivers, for the lovely [literally "desirable," *himeroenta*] Bion." Immediately we have the lament of nature, Bion as object of mourning and desire (*himeros*) in a fictionalized world, and the obscure interest of the speaker himself. He calls on all the world to mourn – or, from line 23, describes the world as already mourning – the Greek bucolic poet Bion of Smyrna (we possess his *Epitaph on Adonis*, whose own nexus of desire and mourning will be noted later in this chapter, and seventeen excerpts preserved in late Roman-era anthologies). Through line 98 the poem lists grieving natural entities, mythical beings, and urban populations, ending with the speaker himself, who at 99–108 sardonically deplores the ephemerality of "we men of greatness, might, and craft," compared with the perennial life of nature. The next section (109–14) finally gives cryptic information about Bion's death – he took poison! – and the poem ends in an analogy with Orpheus's descent to the Underworld (114–26). Allusions to Bion's poetry (on the Cyclops Polyphemus, Adonis, and Hyacinthus) make him the beloved of the nymph Galatea, of the goddess Aphrodite, and of the god Apollo, setting him on the same narrative level as his creations; the Orpheus myth, too, although clear evidence is lacking, may have been among Bion's subjects. Above all, Bion is pictured as a cowherd, *boutas* – that is, as a character in his own pastoral poetry, which is metonymically characterized, after the characteristic dialect and setting of pastoral poetry since Theocritus, as "Doric" and "Sicilian."

The lament of nature itself – rare in Greek poetry, but prominent in Bion's own *Adonis* and the lament for Daphnis in Theocritus's *Idyll* 1, in addition to the one deeply embedded in *Idyll* 7.74–5 – establishes the dead Bion in his own created world, or more broadly (and by a perhaps slippery synecdoche) in the world of the whole bucolic tradition. The *Epitaph* improvises boldly on the ancient mimetic complex of imitation (*mimēsis*) and emulation (*zēlōsis*), fictionalizing and containing the precursor even as it appropriates his creations. Of modern exemplars, this trope – casting the author in his own fictions and retroactively figuring his poetry as autobiographical – is perhaps most closely followed by Spenser's *Astrophel*, on Philip Sidney, where the dead Astrophel seamlessly becomes the shepherd of both Sidney's and Bion's pastoral as well as a Bionean Adonis, hunting the boar, and the lover of Stella of Sidney's own sonnets. The tradition is longer: Anisio's *Melisaeus* (on Pontano), Sá de Miranda's *Nemoroso* (on Garcilaso de la Vega), and Zanchi's *Damon* (on Castiglione) all mourn their subjects in the guises that they, working in the allegorical tradition of pastoral that came to them through Petrarch, had given themselves in pastoral laments. This masquerade performs a version of the extremely influential identification of poet with poet-herdsman that is already traceable in the ancient criticism of bucolic, perhaps starting with the work of the father and son Artemidorus and Theon of Alexandria a generation or so later than the *Epitaph on Bion*.

Bion is mourned by his characters as if by lovers, and epithets used by the Epitaphist make him "desirable," "beautiful," "lovely," "yearned for" (*himeroenta* [2], *kalos* [7], *erasmios* [20], *tripothate* [51]), potentially troping loss as erotic desire. His absence, though, is expressed by a more indirect series of comparisons and replacements, sometimes proceeding through complicated stages of response, with the Epitaphist telling mourners to tell mourners to mourn. He himself is at the center of the swirl of substitutions, but his own place in this world – whose relationship to the dead Bion he expresses no doubt about – is equivocal. I half-translated the opening, "Moan '*ailina*' with me ..." *Ailina*, from the ritual lamentatory exclamation *ailinon* (here presumably an adverb, "mournfully"), is actually the first word: the speaker seems to begin by mourning, but immediately projects that onto others. "With me" is subtler in Greek: the dative *moi*, insinuating the vaguest sense of interest on the part of the speaker. Aside from his tone of indignant sorrow, the Epitaphist's attitude does not emerge clearly until 93–97, after the roster of cities that mourn Bion more than their own deceased poets: "But I sing a song of Italian grief, I, no stranger to herdsmen's song, but heir to the Doric Muse that you taught your disciples; bestowing that on me, you left your wealth to others, but to me your song." Yet this possibility has already been questioned. In line 12, with Bion "song, too, has died and Doric poetry has been lost." At 21–22 he sings in the Underworld, no longer in the upper world. But at 53–54 Bion's "lips still breathe" and Echo still feeds on his song in the "reeds" (pipes); Pan himself might hesitate to take up Bion's pipe, "lest he take second place" (55–56). This is itself a kind of anti-echo of lines 30–31, where, among the responses of natural features, "among the rocks Echo grieves that she is silent and no longer imitates your lips" (cf. 23) – itself in turn a "correction" of Bion's *Adonis* 38 (where Echo augments the lamentations of natural features), coming between echoes of other tropes from the *Adonis*, weeping springs and wilting flowers. Is this a denial that Bion can be imitated, even while he is being imitated? Is his voice present or gone?

The Epitaphist's next explicit account of himself leads into his final mythological allusion, which recalls lines 14–18 ("the Doric Orpheus has perished," amid geographical recollections of the myth). The last lines of the poem, with their play of diffidence and deferral, repay careful reading:

> But I,
> shedding tears, grieve for your fate. If I could,
> descending to the Underworld – like Orpheus, like Odysseus once,
> like Heracles aforetime – I too perhaps would have gone to the house
> of Pluto to see you and, if you were singing for Pluto,
> to hear what you were singing. But come now, for Persephone
> sing something Sicilian and make sweet herdsman's music.
> She too is Sicilian; she used to play on the shores by Etna,
> and she knows Doric song. Not without reward
> will your singing be, and as before she granted to Orpheus,
> when he sang sweetly, the swift return of Eurydice,
> you also, Bion, she will restore to the hills. But if I too
> could aught avail by piping, I myself would sing before Pluto.   (114–26)

Here is the distant ancestor of the Orpheus motif in modern elegy, a rich and versatile thematic simultaneously embracing poetry, mourning, marriage, and erotic desire (see Boehrer; Zeiger). But compare the coyness of the *Epitaph*'s treatment. The analogy with Orpheus and Eurydice (a myth for which, unfortunately, we have only the most elliptical evidence before this passage, and none that would tell us with certainty whether the story that he ultimately failed to bring her back, first attested in Virgil, was older) emerges obliquely from a catalogue of living visitors to the Underworld that serves a different purpose, to emphasize how sharply the Epitaphist feels the loss of Bion's music. Only in the next lines, it seems, does the further analogy with Orpheus occur to him, and he then urges Bion to combine the roles of Orpheus and Eurydice within himself, to be both subject and object, to redeem himself as the wages of song. When the thought occurs that he himself might perform this task – that Bion might be troped as Eurydice and the speaker (who began his lament of more than one hundred lines by singing Nature into a response) as Orpheus – the poem abruptly ceases.

In refusing, despite the tease, to identify with Orpheus at the end, the Epitaphist declines to cast himself as Bion's lover or to participate in the mimesis enacted by the characters, or in the economy that he projects onto their world. Bion's singing before Persephone "will not be without reward" (*ageraston*), that is, will not fail to secure a *geras*, or meed of honor. This adjective is actually attested in Bion's fragment 6; the Epitaphist's recusal may be built paradoxically of words learned from his master, possibly even from the master's Orpheus – a case somewhat like the echoed (or non-echoed) Echo. At line 22, Bion's absence is strikingly registered by the assertion that he is "singing a Lethaean song" before Pluto – named for the underworldly river Lethe, literally "forgetfulness, oblivion." More than a mere geographical determinant, this sounds like a way of saying that Bion's song is lost: does the epithet not contradict everything a work of the Muses is supposed to do? Yet this very song of commemoration, which in some places sums Bion up and recapitulates and reproduces him, is in other ways a Lethaean song itself, forgetting itself as it goes along feinting and dodging, declining to remember its own tropes. At line 22, perhaps, is the poem's closest and stealthiest assimilation of the dead Bion's song to itself.

The Dolors of Daphnis

The wellspring of all pastoral laments is Theocritus's *Idyll* 1 (early third century BCE), which stands at the head of his collection in modern and, presumably, ancient editions and colors all perceptions of pastoral, lamentatory and otherwise. Even a superficial reading against the *Epitaph* shows the latter's debt in such details as the narratorial refrain (addressed to the Muses of herdsmen) and the mourning of waters, mountains, and animals, as well as other motifs that the later tradition will make deeply familiar. "Where were ye, nymphs, when Daphnis was wasting away [*etaketo*]?" (line 66). Yet *Idyll* 1 is not exactly a lament. It is a conversation between two herdsmen, one of whom (Thyrsis) sings by request the tale of the famous cowherd's death. He seems a distant legend even to the speaking characters, although a familiar enough one that Thyrsis's narrative presents its lineup of speaking deities without commenting on their allusions or motivations, and lets Daphnis answer with equal opacity, although it implies (Hunter 63–68) that he is languishing for love.

Where does this text suggest what exactly is lost with Daphnis, and who misses him? Thyrsis's companion requests "the dolors of Daphnis" (*Daphnidos algea* [19]; note the emphasis on Daphnis's own felt experience) as an object of pleasure – he will reward Thyrsis with an artfully carved cup – and the dialogue never quite lets us see why, beyond qualifying the performance as a "lovely" or "desirable song" (*ephimeron humnon* [61] – the *Epitaph* will introject the quality onto the object of mourning himself, *himeroenta Biōna*, in line 2). The narrative emphatically begins with lines of trademark-like self-advertisement: "Lead, dear Muses, lead the herdsmanly song. Thyrsis from Etna is the singer, and the voice of Thyrsis is sweet." Thyrsis, his companion cajoles, is a past champion in singing contests (24); the poem resists reading laments other than as "forms that are repeated and repeatable" (Kennedy 13). The dialogue that frames the performance carries no trace of active personal mourning for the remote and legendary Daphnis; "[t]he song of Thyrsis," moreover, "is distinguished, as a member of the genre epicedion, by its omission of consolation" (DuQuesnay 25). Most significantly, the object of his characters' mourning is not exactly Daphnis's death, but his dying; he is living until the last four lines, and in fact the bulk of the narrative is given to his own voice and his own self-mourning. (*Idyll* 7.72–7, triply embedded within the song of Lycidas, narrates his love and death more objectively.) Defying the gods of love, expansively bidding nature mourn for himself, Daphnis emphatically refuses to be a wordless Adonis figure, an object.

We have here a case study in the discontinuities and contingencies within a literary tradition. Pastoral, for some reason, seems persistently to attract criticism eager to find an essence for the genre, a comprehensive origin, even a prescription. It is as if the insistence of ancient scholarship on tracing the genre back to the actual performances of herdsmen, programmatically confusing the poetry's internal matter with its external composition (a creative impulse behind the *Epitaph*), must be perpetuated and updated in some slightly more plausible form. But Theocritean bucolic is a confluence of different traditions, made whole only, and barely, by the synopsis performed by the later tradition (see Halperin; Reed, "*Idyll*"). Its most distinctive form would seem to be a conflation of the low, humorous, dramatic "mime" with the more elevated style and meter of *epos* (hexameter poetry): that accounts for the pastoral *Idylls* 1, 3, 4, and 5. Yet that same criterion would include the non-pastoral *Idylls* 2, 10, 14, and 15, and would exclude the vitally influential *Idylls* 7 (the first-person narrative of an encounter with a herdsman-singer) and 11 (on the Cyclops's cure for his love, introduced and concluded by Theocritus in his own persona). The Cyclops poem and the Daphnis one both incorporate myths from choral lyric – where, perhaps, the compelling first-person complaint of each character had constituted an aria – and embed them in different forms, in the first instance framing that complaint within the author's own commentary (addressed to his friend Nicias) and in the second showcasing a narrative (in which a first-person speech is prominent) within mime-like dialogue.

Idyll 1 teases us with the possibility of a metapoetic commentary between the song and its dialogic frame. A hint, perhaps, emerges in the goatherd's encouragement to Thyrsis at 62–63: "Go ahead, good friend, for you will not keep your singing in Hades that brings utter forgetfulness (*Aïdan ge ton eklelathonta*)." This sentiment, which will be interrogated by the *Epitaph*, is only obscurely picked up by Thyrsis's account of Daphnis. Daphnis has no further use for his panpipe (128–30), but he purposes to be, even dead, a retaliatory "grief" to love (103, *algos*, the same word used for his own woes at 19). The elaborate cup that Thyrsis's companion promises him for his song, of course, parallels the song itself – and, within the song, the similarly described panpipe that Daphnis offers Pan. The "singing" of the pine in Thyrsis's opening words (2) is consonant with the narrator's and Daphnis's own conception within the narrative that nature can and should commiserate and mourn. But Daphnis's status as inventor and supreme exponent of herdsman's song (recorded by Diodorus Siculus 4.84), which might enable a mutual commentary on the nature of the characters' (and Theocritus's?) poetry, is muted here, except in his boastful bequeathal of his pipe to Pan and Thyrsis's closing characterization of him as "the man dear to the Muses and not displeasing to the Nymphs" (141).

Virgil's only pastoral lament, *Eclogue* 5 (circa late 40s BCE), is his most straightforward, least extravagant imitation of *Idyll* 1. Here, the herdsmen who speak in the framing dialogue each contribute a song on the death of Daphnis. Mopsus's song tells how deities of the countryside, animals tame and wild, and natural features lament his death; that of Menalcas "raises your Daphnis to the stars," as the singer promises (50–51), reinterpreting a detail from the closing lines of Mopsus's song (an imagined self-epitaph by Daphnis, "famous from here to the stars"): he will become a god, hymned by a nature now in harmony and worshiped forever by country people with libations, song, and dance. This claim of apotheosis is the original of those in later pastoral laments by Petrarch, Marot, Sannazaro, Milton, and many others.

With the *Eclogues* we enter a collection of intricate short poems whose frequent outward resemblance to the herdsman dialogues of Theocritus, and to later Greek bucolic poetry, should not obscure their innovation and acute sensitivity to a vaster cultural tradition. A long-standing interpretation, going back at least to a note by the commentator Servius (circa 400 CE) on line 29, holds that *Eclogue* 5 laments Julius Caesar under the name of Daphnis – an identification that will support a lively tradition of pastoral laments for princes, overtly or under fictional names (starting with Petrarch's *Argus*, for Robert of Naples). Nothing in the poem points specifically to Caesar (see DuQuesnay 30–33; Hubbard 97–98), but the terms in which Daphnis is lamented and praised point unambiguously toward the general discourse aimed at Hellenistic rulers – particularly the Ptolemaic rulers of Egypt – in emulation of whom Roman rulers were increasingly celebrated in this transitional period between the oligarchic Republic and Augustus's autocracy. Daphnis will receive altars; he is like Bacchus and Apollo (29–31, 66; these are respectively the patron gods of Mark Antony and Augustus); he evidently presides over a new age of peace and bounty. The redemptorist discourse of the Hellenistic East will ultimately serve Christian (and mixed Christian-and-classicizing) eschatological ideas in European pastoral, but here – as in *Eclogue* 4, read as "Messianic" in later antiquity and the Middle Ages – it is coopted into a rising vision of the Roman world order, a peculiarly Virgilian one, to be developed further in the *Georgics* and finally perfected in the *Aeneid*, which stealthily assimilates the Roman self to its various ethnic foils and conquered others, even as it subsumes other cultural discourses into its poetic fabric.

Nor does the apotheosis serve a consolatory function, even within Menalcas's song, which bids no woeful shepherds "weep no more" (as *Lycidas* will) and offers its good news not as reassurance to survivors, but as a more or less straightforward hymn to Daphnis. Their Daphnis, unlike the one in Theocritus, is not a legendary figure: the speakers seem to have known him personally ("Daphnis loved me too" [52]; "the guy was worth singing about" [54]). But they affect no personal lamentation; the dramatic premise is that he died a year or more ago (36–39). The framing dialogue is as concerned with poetic competition and practice as in *Idyll* 1; the songs themselves are even less concerned with poetry than that of Thyrsis. In the external dialogue Menalcas calls Daphnis their teacher in song (*magistrum* [48] – assuming the term refers to Daphnis here), like the Bion of the *Epitaph*; within the songs his role as singer is invisible. He is voiceless, except (doubly vicariously) in the inscription that Mopsus's song bids herdsmen set on his grave, in which he declares him-self "Daphnis … keeper of a beautiful flock, myself more beautiful" (in an echo of Daphnis's words at Theocritus 1.120–21, though the boast is only in Virgil, and the repetition of "beautiful" endemic to Bion's *Adonis*).

The vagueness of the relations between each Daphnis, Theocritean and Virgilian, and his narrators may come as a surprise from the standpoint of the modern tradition, where the characters or a narrator normally make the cathexis plain (to pull up one typical, though not canonical, example, consider the opening lines of William Gager's *Daphnis*, on the death of Sidney: "For the shepherd Daphnis, snatched away by a cruel death, the shepherd Meliboeus was shedding tears on the hilltop of Shotover"). Yet it may be that criticism even of *Lycidas* could give more weight to the break between embedded song and frame, to the opacity of the singer's mind when we unexpectedly pull back from within his song to see him "twitch his Mantle blew" and head homeward; for his personal sense of loss and reparation we have only the word of his per-formance. As Eric Smith discovers, in *Lycidas* the "therapy of mourning," the possibility of consolation, "does not receive comment" (13–15).

In the case of the *Epitaph on Bion*, the difference (or, to speak in historical terms, the shift) in narratological structure from Theocritus helps account for many of the interpretive problems in the former: the absence of any frame – in a poem in which an unnamed voice simply launches into its mourning and (unlike Milton's *Lycidas*) never gets framed by an external narrator – helps evade the illogic that poetry has died while poetry is being produced. The mime-like dialogues invented by Theocritus are increasingly framed and embedded, in succeeding generations, in ways that make room for a poetic "I" and problema-tize its relation to its objects, never with more complexity than in the redundant *mise en abyme* of the *Eclogues* (our interest in the dramatic or diegetic structures of these texts should be more than formalist). In executing the opposite move – in dissolving any such frame, and pulling the lament out of any performative context – does the *Epitaph* even count as poetry within its own fiction? What *does* it present itself as? Would it be more profitably read as an internal dialogue, a drift between hypotheses, unmoored by the rhetorical stance that would be established by any real, living addressee or audience? It avoids being pinned down by simply withholding a vantage point outside itself.

Late Bucolic Pharmacology

Bion's own "beautiful Adonis" supplies much of his passive, voiceless persona in the *Epitaph*, but late Greek bucolic in general is obsessed with desire and death. Exemplary is Bion's catalogue of heroic couples in fragment 12, designed to illustrate the beatitude "blessed are those who love when they are desired equally in return," which concludes "blessed was [Achilles] in death since he avenged [Patroclus'] terrible fate." Either by giving Achilles to oblivion or by returning him to Patroclus in the afterlife, the final verse, rereading the *Iliad*, restores symmetry to the "unrequited" love that ensued when Patroclus was killed. Theocritus, whose Thyrsis is so reticent on Daphnis's lovesickness, had provided models for treating *erōs* in *Idyll* 3 (a goatherd increasingly hopelessly serenades the unresponsive, and possibly absent, Amaryllis) and 10 (one reaper advises another on his love), as well as in the characters' songs in 7, and even more powerfully in *Idylls* 2 (a girl casts a spell to bring back her boyfriend) and 11 (the Cyclops and Galatea). Surviving late bucolic expands into a meditation on unreciprocated love in poems that often vary widely from the dialogues or monologues of humble people that we most closely identify with the tradition, but that signal their generic affinities through dialect, metrical style, diction, and verbal reworkings. Together this body of poems, some attributable and many anonymous, engage in competitive economies of desire.

Especially susceptible to revisionary commentary is the Cyclops-and-Galatea theme articulated in *Idyll* 11: that passion instigates poetry and that poetry making, in turn, is the drug (*pharmakon*) that cures passion. In Bion's own treatment of this myth, at least as it is preserved in the four lines of fragment 16, the Cyclops seems to disavow any Theocritean sublimation and intends to go on loving Galatea to the end. In the anonymous *Idyll* 23, the lover of a "cruel boy," rehearsing his own suicide and the boy's response to it in a lengthy address outside the boy's closed door, experimentally replaces poetry with death in the Cyclopian formula – "I go where you have condemned me to, where they say the cure [*pharmakon*] for all lovers is, where oblivion is" – but declares that, nevertheless, even if "I put death to my lips and drain it [*amelxō*], I will not thus extinguish my desire" (23–26). It is doubtless in part this poem's proximity to high camp – from the lover's imperious, scenery-chewing bathos to the boy's icy hauteur toward the corpse on emerging on his way to the baths and his immediate punishment by a falling statue of Eros – that has denied it a more dedicated critical reception ("frigid and improbable," warns A. S. F. Gow in what remains the only full commentary; "the sentiment is sloppy . . . and the poem is the least attractive in the whole Theocritean corpus"); but its extravagance performs perhaps the most creative interrogation of late Greek bucolic's favored themes. The lover's reference to oblivion (*lathos*) – the traditional antithesis to poetry – as the main curative ingredient in death implicitly questions the tradition: if poetry cures love by forgetfulness, does it then not lose its nature as poetry? For he himself is a kind of poet, not only in his scripting of his death, but at 47–48, where, in a passage that seems to have influenced the end of Mopsus's song in *Eclogue* 5, he dictates the epitaph to be inscribed on his tomb. Death is his poetic medium.

Read his argument alongside the desperate Aphrodite's revision of the same thematic in Bion's *Adonis*, especially lines 48–50 (probably the model for *Idyll* 23 rather than vice versa): "Kiss me, until I drain [*amelxō* again] your sweet love [*philtron*] and drink up desire; and I will keep that kiss as if it were Adonis himself, since you, wretch, flee from me" – more literally, "until I milk your sweet love potion." Her escalatingly fervid lamentation – which has been troping Adonis's death in terms of unrequited love, of his "fleeing" from her "pursuit" – at this point might seem to desiderate the internalization of the lamented object, the resistance to the idea of severance from the mourner, that Celeste Schenck finds in elegies by women. We might better call it a parody of that idea of the female poetic mourner: an excessive denial of the possibility of letting go, a catachrestic reduction of the Cyclopian *pharmakon* into love itself. It is with these late bucolic transactions over desire, death, and poetry in mind that we should read the *Epitaph*'s reworking of its Theocritean precedent; the speaker's diffidence about being a lover and a poet seems to toy with, only to disavow, the various quasi-poetic "remedies" for loss that emerge from them (somewhat as the *Epitaph* eschews late bucolic strategies of structuring relations between different voices and vantage points, as we noticed earlier), and mirrors in curiously passive-aggressive form their various Daphnis-like refusals to sublimate.

This tradition is also the immediate Greek background to the *Eclogues*. They are suffused with the pathos of loss (even involving political themes of dispossession in poems 1 and 9), and lamentatory discourse enters *Eclogue* 2, in later times a perennial resource and model for homoerotic poetry, which transforms the Cyclops's complaint into that of the herdsman Corydon, hopeless lover of "beautiful Alexis" (note that the Greek examples we have just discussed also typically make boys the objects of desire). This poem, as *Eclogue* 5.86 claims, is the work of Menalcas himself; he frames Corydon's lament with third-person commentary less in the authorial (even epistolary) manner of Theocritus in the Cyclops idyll than in the narratorial one of *Idyll* 23. The erotic content of Theocritus's *Idyll* 1, Daphnis's languishing, in turn bleeds out of Virgil's more overt, and contained, imitation in *Eclogue* 5 into *Eclogue* 10, which adapts it to the lovelorn soliloquy of Gallus – a real poet and contemporary of Virgil, here both subject and object (when the framing narrator professes love for "his" Gallus). He is compared to Adonis at line 18. "Who would refuse to sing for

Gallus?" (line 3) premonitorily strains into a more purely erotic mode, and lifts to a metapoetic plane, the Bionean narrator's conclusion to a catalogue of natural features mourning in sympathy for Adonis, "For Aphrodite's devastating love who would not have cried 'alas'?" (*Adonis* 39).

In the aftermath of Virgil's variations, late bucolic equations seem to become more insistent in the early modern pastoral laments, and assimilations to love enter in tandem with consolatory tropes. Symptomatic, in the later tradition, is the opening of the *Epitaphium Iolae* of Helius Eobanus Hessus (for Wilhelm II of Hesse), where Meletaerus mistakes the grieving Daphnis's *dolor* for love-pains over a girl. But most telling are poems that begin with lines of third-person narrative specifying the mourner, the mourned, and the circumstances of mourning before quoting the lament (for example, the *Daphnis* of Gager quoted earlier): this is the formula of the Corydon eclogue (as well as of *Idyll* 23), most prominent among whose elegiac descendants are Castiglione's *Alcon* and Milton's *Epitaphium Damonis*, which adopt its form but transfer its tropes from love to death – though reluctantly. Each speaker curiously consoles himself with detailed, self-tormenting memories of what he had planned to talk about with the absent friend who is now permanently gone, compensatory games of *fort/da* that become involuted, temporally multiplex. In *Alcon*, the conversation that would have "been pleasing" concerns each other's past "deep anxieties" and "grievances" (*aerumnasque graves ... damna referre simul, rursusque audire juvabit*; 113–14). And this will amount to "resuming their love" (*repetemus amores*; 115) – there is no more talk of their girlfriends; at 125 the site of this hope-in-memory is none other than the Virgilian site of homoerotic yearning and singing thereon: *formosum hic pastor Corydon cantavit Alexin*. Milton begins his *Epitaphium* by invoking *Himerides nymphae* – conventionally "Sicilian" nymphs, to be sure (in Theocritus 7.75 the Sicilian river Himeras is the site of nature's lament for Daphnis's hopeless love), but suggestive of Greek *himeros*, "desire," with the same root as *himeroenta Biōna*, "desirable Bion," at the close of line 2 of the *Epitaph*. Milton too ends his second line with Bion's name, a third lamented object after Daphnis and Hercules's boyfriend Hylas.

Pastures New

The last ancient pastoral lament, Nemesianus's *Eclogue* 1 (late third century CE), is a dialogue between two herdsmen-singers, Tityrus and Timetas, the former of whom persuades the latter to deliver a song in praise of their deceased elder Meliboeus. Thomas Hubbard (178–80) reads a metapoetic allegory against earlier pastoral here, in which Tityrus (the name was long identified with Virgil as author of the *Eclogues*) defers in singing to Timetas ("honored," a name new to the tradition), whose talent outdoes that of Mopsus (line 16), named like the first speaker in *Eclogue* 5. At first reading, this is a perfectly generic composition, hitting all the correct notes. Here the lamented died full of years and honor. Like the Virgilian Daphnis, he is praised in terms of a good king (though of herdsmen), and is said to have taught herdsmanly song wherewith to "beguile hard cares" (*duras ... fallere curas* [59]). The relationship between the speaking characters and their object is thoroughly explored, with the relevant links – song, praise, herding – laid out systematically. But perhaps this is the achievement of Nemesianus: to make us feel, for the first time in the tradition, that such a lament is a variation on a set of generic conventions, wholly expected, unsurprisingly integrable into the norms of pastoral dialogue, and naturally to be set at the head of a collection of pastorals. He makes his metapoetic statement of a poetic handing down seem the most natural thing in a form that had previously occluded or problematized any sense of it.

Praise of the deceased – *laudes*, the last word of the lament – emerges here as paramount. Praise actually functions in an exchange: Meliboeus, while alive, had extolled the *laudes* of Timetas, according to Tityrus at 18. So finally fame, *fama* (potentially identifiable with poetry itself), and its role in a tradition – the readiest tropes of survival and recuperation – emerge as explicit in pastoral lament. (Fame – of an eternal, inalienable kind – will ultimately blaze forth in Apollo's exhortation to the hesitating singer of Milton's *Lycidas* as the reward for his efforts and self-denial.) The Epitaphist's ambivalence about taking up his "inheritance," on the other hand, together with his flirtations with the possibility of "Lethaean song," is perhaps the primary source of the *Epitaph on Bion*'s influence: a powerful draw on later pastoral laments, particularly the ones that follow the *Epitaph* in lamenting a fellow poet or at least (like *Lycidas*) emphasizing the speaker's poetry, and a driving force in the tradition in which constructions of identification and desire gradually inhere. Put another way: his refusal to show himself doing a "work of mourning" or to take a position in relation to his illustrious precursor is a provocation, a question that challenges the reader to resolve it – and the poet-reader to rephrase and reformulate it as heir himself to the Epitaphist, as to others.

Notes

1. Useful surveys of the tradition of pastoral lament through the early modern period are to be found in Harrison and Leon; Lambert; Grant 306–30; and Pigman 159–60. Editions of the major texts I cite, with translations, can be found

in Harrison and Leon; my citations of the secondary literature will point the way to more recent editions, where they exist, as well as to further critical discussions. The *Epitaph on Bion* still has no fully satisfying scholarly commentary, but that of Mumprecht is of use; for more recent scholarship see the articles by Di Nino; and Kania. My account of the poetics of late Greek bucolic is basically that of Reed, "Continuity" (esp. 225–34). For recent critical work on the tradition of elegy, see the rich accounts in Ramazani; Zeiger; and Kennedy.

Works Cited

Boehrer, Bruce. "'Lycidas': The Pastoral Elegy as Same-Sex Epithalamium." *PMLA* 117 (2002): 222–36. Print.

Castiglione, Baldassare. *Alcon.* Harrison and Leon 112–19.

Di Nino, Margherita Maria. "Le 'verità nascoste': consapevole appartenenza a un genere, autoinvestitura e bugie metapoetiche in [Mosco] III." *Philologus* 153 (2009): 86–108. Print.

DuQuesnay, I. M. "Virgil's Fifth Eclogue." *Proceedings of the Virgil Society* 16 (1976): 18–41. Print.

Gow, A. S. F. *Theocritus: Edited with a Translation and Commentary.* 2 vols. Cambridge: Cambridge UP, 1950. Print.

Grant, W. Leonard. *Neo-Latin Literature and the Pastoral.* Chapel Hill: U of North Carolina P, 1965. Print.

Haggerty, George E. "Desire and Mourning: The Ideology of the Elegy." *Ideology and Form in Eighteenth-Century Literature.* Ed. David H. Richter. Lubbock: Texas Tech UP, 1999. 185–206. Print.

Halperin, David M. *Before Pastoral: Theocritus and the Ancient Tradition of Bucolic Poetry.* New Haven: Yale UP, 1983. Print.

Harrison, Thomas Perrin, Jr. and Harry Joshua Leon, eds. *The Pastoral Elegy: An Anthology.* Austin: U of Texas, 1939. Print.

Hubbard, Thomas K. *The Pipes of Pan: Intertextuality and Literary Filiation in the Pastoral Tradition from Theocritus to Milton.* Ann Arbor: U of Michigan P, 1998. Print.

Hunter, Richard. *Theocritus: A Selection.* Cambridge: Cambridge UP, 1999. Print.

Kania, Raymond. "Orpheus and the Reinvention of Bucolic Poetry." *American Journal of Philology* 133 (2012): 657–85. Print.

Kennedy, David. *Elegy.* New York: Routledge, 2007. Print.

Lambert, Ellen Zetzel. "The Pastoral Elegy from Theocritus to Milton: A Critical Study." Diss. Yale U, 1969. Print.

Mumprecht, Vroni. *Epitaphios Bionos: Text, Übersetzung, Kommentar.* Zürich: Juris, 1964. Print.

Pigman, G. W. III. *Grief and English Renaissance Elegy.* Cambridge: Cambridge UP, 1985. Print.

Ramazani, Jahan. *The Poetry of Mourning: The Modern Elegy from Hardy to Heaney.* Chicago: U of Chicago P, 1994. Print.

Reed, Joseph D. "Continuity and Change in Greek Bucolic between Theocritus and Virgil." *A Companion to Greek and Latin Pastoral.* Ed. Marco Fantuzzi and Theodore D. Papanghelis. Leiden: Brill, 2006. 209–34. Print.

"*Idyll* 6 and the Development of Bucolic after Theocritus." *A Companion to Hellenistic Literature*. Ed. James J. Clauss and Martine Cuypers. Oxford: Wiley-Blackwell, 2010. 238–50. Print.

Schenck, Celeste. "Feminism and Deconstruction: Re-Constructing the Elegy." *Tulsa Studies in Women's Literature* 5 (1986):13–27. Print.

Shuttleton, David. "The Queer Politics of Gay Pastoral." *De-centering Sexualities: Politics and Representations beyond the Metropolis*. Ed. Richard Phillips, Diane Watt, and David Shuttleton. London: Routledge, 2000. 125–46. Print.

Smith, Eric. *By Mourning Tongues: Studies in English Elegy*. Ipswich: Rowman and Littlefield, 1977. Print.

Zeiger, Melissa F. *Beyond Consolation: Death, Sexuality, and the Changing Shapes of Elegy*. Ithaca: Cornell UP, 1997. Print.

4

Roman Prose and Poetry

THOMAS K. HUBBARD

Greek Love through Roman Eyes

In confronting Roman literary sources on any topic, the question of Greek cultural influence becomes inevitable, given the proximity of the two civilizations, the migration of learned Greeks to Rome after the absorption of Greece into the Roman empire in the second century BCE, and the advanced state of Greek literary expression long before anything resembling literature came to exist in Rome. The Greeks themselves regarded the institutions of athletic nudity and pederasty as unique and distinguishing marks of their own cultural superiority over the surrounding *barbaroi*. To the extent that neighboring civilizations, such as the Persians, adopted pederasty, the Greeks saw it as due to their own influence (Herodotus 1.135). It is notable that the primary export market for Greek painted ceramics showing pederastic and homosexual themes in the sixth and fifth centuries BCE was Etruria (Lear and Cantarella 71): a large proportion of our surviving pieces were preserved in Etruscan tombs. What literary information we have about the sexual habits of the Etruscans (cf. Athenaeus 12.517d–f, citing the fourth-century BCE historian Theopompus) paints them as a libertine people who enjoyed the company of boys and youths (*neaniskoi*) as well as women; the popularity of this genre of Attic ceramics suggests an interest in Greek-style pederasty, culturally coded as a foreign importation into Etruscan culture. Within Italy, the Etruscan influence on the budding city-state of Rome was in turn profound; legend attributed Etruscan kings to the Romans as early as the seventh century BCE.

The extent of Greek influence on the Roman practice of homosexuality during the period of our recorded texts has been a matter of controversy, with some historians asserting its pervasiveness (e.g., MacMullen; Verstraete, "Slavery") and others emphasizing indigenous Roman traditions (e.g., Veyne; C. Williams, *Roman* 62–95); a more nuanced middle view focuses specifically on pederasty as a Greek influence (Cantarella 97–101, 219–21). To be sure, there were major differences in the cultural articulation of pederasty: whereas the classical Greek ideal was to court freeborn citizen youths of good family and impart some degree of pedagogical mentorship (see Lear and Cantarella 17–18, 67–78; Percy), the Roman variety was devoid of pedagogical intent and largely confined to relations with attractive young slaves. And whereas Greek sources depict interfemoral intercourse (or mere kissing and fondling) as the most common act of consummation, Roman texts refer to more invasive oral and anal penetration. However, it should be observed that the Greek sources also attest relations with pretty slave boys (as in Anacreon's verse or the anecdotes about Sophocles's attentions to a servant at the dinner hosted by Ion of Chios [Athenaeus 13.603e–604d]), and Aristophanes's comedy certainly implies that such relations in practice featured anal penetration (see esp. *Knights* 1384–86 and *Clouds* 1083–1104 in relation to free youths as well). Moreover, Roman relations with favored male slaves were not necessarily devoid of love and genuine devotion, as we see in Statius's lament for a friend's favorite, dead at fifteen (*Silvae* 2.6), Cicero's amorous verses to his freedman Tiro (Pliny, *Letters* 7.4.3–6), or Trimalchio's being made heir to his former master's fortune (Petronius 75–76). The relevant point is not whether the Romans became acquainted with homosexual pleasures only after their conquest of Greece, but how the practice of pederasty came to be coded and represented in Roman ethical discourse of the second century BCE, when orators like Cato the Elder or Scipio the Younger invoked pederasty as an example of Greek indulgence to which his fellow Romans had become too susceptible (Polybius 31.25.2–5), or even of the first century BCE, when Cicero could link Greek athletic nudity with pederasty as practices that set the Greeks apart from Roman norms (*Tusculan Disputations* 4.70; *Republic* 4.3–4; cf. Plutarch, *Roman Questions* 274d–e). Just as today certain sexual practices might be coded as "French" or "Italian" fashion, as a way of contrasting them with an Anglosphere ethical norm, the "Greek" character of pederasty gave it a certain cachet among the smart set, as well as problematizing it for Roman moral traditionalists.

Some scholars (e.g., Boswell 61–87) have argued that Rome was generally tolerant and accepting of homosexual relations, and others (e.g., Cantarella 97–210; C. Williams, *Roman* 30) that some degree of bisexuality was characteristic of most Roman males: as Craig Williams puts it, "Clearly an assumption prevalent among Romans was that, as a group, men normally experience desire for both female and male bodies, and that any given man might act out those desires with persons of one or the other sex, or both" (*Roman* 30). However, ideological uniformity of moral attitudes was no more likely in a complex civilization like that of Rome than it is in our own culture. The vast majority of Romans owned either no slaves or one or two older slaves (see for instance Catullus's rival Aurelius in poem 24); in their eyes, pretty boy slaves were an upper-class luxury they could never enjoy. Even among the literary and political elite, attitudes were far from uniformly approving. The moralist and censor Cato the Elder doubtless spoke for many in warning that the Republic was destined to fall when a handsome slave boy sold for more than a field (Polybius 31.25.5). Similarly, Gaius Gracchus boasted as a sign of his manly virtue in office that he did not own comely male slaves (Aulus Gellius 15.12.2). Cicero routinely used homosexual liaisons as a topos of defamation against opponents in his political oratory, regardless of whether one adopted the active or passive role (*Against Catiline* 2.8; *For Flaccus* 51; *For Milo* 55; *Philippics* 2.44–45). Sexual excess of any kind was liable to upset Roman concerns about the enervating effect of luxury and soft living, which threatened the traditional virtues of the yeoman farmer-citizen who formed the backbone of Rome's military might.

Of the Greek philosophical schools, Stoicism, with its doctrines of obligation, indifference to suffering, and deference to the demands of Fate, gained the greatest influence among the Roman elite, particularly during the Empire. Despite the sexual libertarianism of earlier Stoics like Chrysippus and Zeno, the Roman version of Stoicism emphasized the central importance of leading a life according to Nature's plan, avoiding excessive dependency on any pleasure or passion. To the Stoic Seneca, artificially prolonging a boy's youthful appearance by depilation or castration was a clear violation of Nature's plan, as were women who attempted to assume men's sexual role and the reverse (*Moral Epistles* 47.7, 95.21, 122.7; cf. Seneca the Elder, *Controversies* 10.4.17). Even more severe was the popular Stoic teacher Musonius Rufus, whose essay "On Sexual Matters" denounced all sex not for purposes of procreation, including even sex with slaves. Within such a restrictive economy of pleasures, homosexuality in general came to be viewed as the act of men who refused to live according to natural design and providence. But other philosophical schools more friendly to same-sex relations, such as the Epicureans and Academics, also had their adherents.

Despite such condemnations, something akin to a homosexual subculture did develop at Rome, as both Amy Richlin ("Not") and Rabun Taylor have persuasively argued. No fewer than three texts refer to scratching one's head with a single finger as a semiotic gesture between homosexual men (Juvenal 9.133; Plutarch, *Caesar* 4, citing Cicero as source; and *Pompey* 48.7). That such coded signals evolved during the late Republic suggests strongly the presence of an underground network with its own conventions and rules, even as wearing a red tie or adopting certain affectations of speech would make homosexuals recognizable to one another in the early twentieth century. Other texts tell us of locations familiar as cruising zones for those seeking manly company – the Tuscan Road (Plautus, *Curculio* 482–84), the banks of the Tiber (Ps.-Virgil, *Catalepton* 13.23–26), or even the public baths (Petronius, *Satyricon* 92). Taylor (328–37) in particular has argued that certain religious cults and festivals, such as the Bacchanalia (famously suppressed in 186 BCE for its sexual license and un-Roman character), the Cotytia, or Eastern ecstatic religions like those of the Magna Mater or the Syrian Goddess, became especially popular meeting places.

Comedy and Mime

The comedies of T. Maccius Plautus (active ca. 200 BCE) provide our earliest literary references to homosexual relations, but none of the plots of his twenty-one extant plays are primarily about erotic relations among men. Largely derived from Greek originals of the late fourth to third centuries and retaining the Greek names and settings, Plautus's plots typically concern romantic escapades of a distinctly heterosexual nature. Populated by stock characters, these comedies often feature one or more clever male slaves who enable the young romantic hero's hijinx, often by manipulating or deceiving older authority figures who act as obstacles. As such, Plautine comedy gives us a not unsympathetic insight into the personal lives of the slave characters from their own point of view.[1]

We find in Plautus's work several allusions to the kind of homosexual demands that masters might make on attractive slave boys. Sometimes these relations are a matter of embarrassment that the slave will admit only reluctantly (like Harpax in *Pseudolus* 1177–82, recalling his long past youth). Yet in the same play another boy expresses the wish that he could be more attractive so as to acquire a lover and benefactor (vv. 767–87); although still small and in fear of the pain that might be occasioned by anal sex, he resolves to bear it if it will help him acquire money. In *The Persian* (284–86), a slave boy named Paegnium (literally, "little plaything") boasts of going to bed with his master, confident that it will lead to his eventual manumission. Although such demands by masters were assumed to be common, it is clear that not all masters would make them: Gripus in *The Rope* (1074–75) declares that his master is enlightened enough not to expect oral service from his slaves. What is clear from the evidence of Plautus, however, is that slaves expected and typically received some compensatory favor from their master if they did provide sexual services; from this perspective, they could regard the master's sexual attentions not as a humiliation, but an opportunity.

Attraction to adult slaves was not unknown, as we see in another slave's interpretation of the overheard interaction between the master and his bailiff in *Casina* (449–66); one may compare Cicero's love poetry addressed to his personal secretary Tiro, whom he had already granted freedom (Pliny, *Letter* 7.4.3–6). However, it was overwhelmingly boys of teenage years or even younger who were preferred. A common comic topos was to compare the respective advantages and disadvantages of boys and women: Diniarchus in *Truculentus* (149–57) compares the two, accusing women of greater insolence, slave boys of more deceit. In the end he concludes that women, like the courtesan's maid Astaphium to whom he speaks, are better because they at least feed themselves with any cash rewards, whereas boys just waste money and then ask for more. Other characters judge differently, like a speaker in Novius's *Comic Encore* (fr. 20–21 Ribbeck), who praises the firmness of pubescent boys' erections, or the satirist Lucilius (fr. 866–67 Marx), who says that boys demand less and do not pose the risk of adultery. More coarsely, Lucilius compares the disadvantages: women cover one's member in blood, boys in shit (fr. 1186 Marx).

Although none of Plautus's plays were specifically homosexual in theme, other comic poets whose work is now lost to us did favor plots grounded in same-sex attraction: the prudish rhetorician Quintilian (10.1.100) censures Afranius for filling his plays with pederastic affairs. Afranius wrote a version of literary comedy similar to that of Plautus and Terence, but set in Italian towns and more redolent of Roman *realia*. Even more explicit are the writers of Atellan farce, a subliterary genre based on even more stereotypical characters set in Italian surroundings. Two authors attempted to elevate this form into a versified and published literary genre in the early first century BCE, L. Pomponius Bononiensis and Novius; of their fragments, a fair number featured explicitly homosexual themes. Pomponius created a whole play featuring a male prostitute as the title character (fr. 148–52 Ribbeck). Another stock character, the glutton Dossenus, had unmistakably homoerotic tastes (fr. 75–76 Ribbeck). Novius speaks of men who depilate their buttocks to continue a passive role even after they have grown hairy (fr. 19 Ribbeck), as well as the aforementioned praise of pubescent boys (fr. 20–21 Ribbeck).

Invective Poetry

Modern readers of the varied poetic corpus of G. Valerius Catullus (84–54 BCE) are often struck by the free employment of sexually explicit language pertaining to both homosexual and heterosexual acts.[2] That some of his poems concern a beloved youth named Juventius has led many to assume that Catullus's own tastes were bisexual in nature. However, a note of caution is in order here. In a vigorous programmatic poem (16), immediately following his first Juventius poem (15), Catullus himself calls attention to the figurative nature of his poetic language and warns critics not to draw conclusions about his personal life from the themes of his poetry:[3]

> *Up yours both, and sucks to the pair of you,*
> Queen Aurelius, Furius the faggot,
> Who dared judge *me* on the basis of my verses –
> *They* may be raunchy: does that make *me* indecent?
> Squeaky-clean, that's what every proper poet's
> *Person* should be, but not his bloody squiblets,
> Which, in the last resort, lack salt and flavor
> If they're *not* raunchy and rather less than decent,
> Just the ticket to work a furious itch up,
> 10   I won't say in boys, but in those hirsute
> Clods incapable of wiggling their hard haunches.
> Just because you've read about my countless thousand
> Kisses and such, you think I'm less than virile?
> *Up yours both, and sucks to the pair of you!*   (1–14)

Other considerations should also promote doubt about any biographical veracity to the poetic speaker's claim to a relationship with Juventius. The name (like that of his equally fictional female beloved Lesbia) is evocative, a clear play on the Latin word for youth (*juventus*). Moreover, epigraphic evidence attests to it as the name of a prominent family in the poet's native Verona (see Ellis 82; and Hubbard, "Catullan" 264 for further sources); while this fact might suggest the reality of the relationship to some, we must remember that Roman custom and law regarded relations with freeborn youths as illicit and degrading.[4] Publication of poetry announcing the young poet's claim of pederastic relations with an immature scion of this prominent clan should rather be interpreted as invective in intent, particularly when we consider poems that attack Juventius for preferring other, less worthy men (e.g., 24, 81, 99) despite his illustrious family pedigree ("Juventius, blossom, best of all your blueblood clan" [24.1–2]).

    I would argue that Catullus's poetry employs homosexual imagery and themes in a manner that reflects scant sympathy for the practice. In a wedding hymn, the poet tells the bridegroom's former boy favorite that it is time for him to retreat (61.119–48). Elsewhere, he equates pederasty with prostitution (e.g., 106, on the boy and the auctioneer). The longest and most complex poem to deal with the topic is the narrative and lament of the young Attis (63), who has castrated himself to serve as a *gallus*, a priest dedicated to the Asian mother goddess Cybele.[5] Although eunuch priests would normally continue to be considered male in gender, Catullus makes a point of changing pronouns to the feminine after Attis's testicular loss. Attis's plaintive lament after his/her transformation recalls the days when he was a beautiful boy in Greece, star of the wrestling schools and pursued by numerous male admirers. This pederastic background is presented as in some sense prefiguring his later emasculation; as such, Catullus's poem conveys the typical Roman revulsion at the idea of respectable citizen boys becoming involved in the type of pederastic relation that would be normative in Greece.

The more explicit sexual language, like that we have seen in poem 16, is always connected with abuse and domination, either on the part of powerful political figures like Memmius (28), Mamurra (29), or Julius Caesar (57), or on the part of Catullus himself toward his rivals Furius and Aurelius (15, 16, 21).[6] We are treated to grotesque scenarios of oral rape in which sex is imagined as a zero-sum game in which one man pleasures himself by inflicting pain and humiliation on another: "I'll serve you a proper mouthful! If you'd just dined when you did it I'd keep silent.... [L]ay off while you decently can, or else you'll come to a messy end, mouth crammed to bursting" (21.8–13).

This imagery of sexual violence shares much with the language of graffiti[7] and another collection of poetry known as the *Priapea*. These anonymous poems, ranging in date from the time of Catullus to the following century, adopt the speaking voice of the ithyphallic scarecrow god Priapus, whose function was to protect gardens and orchards by asserting a vigorous masculine presence capable of raping any thief or intruder, regardless of age or gender.[8]

Augustan Bisexuality

It is in the poetry of the Augustan Golden Age (43 BCE–14 CE) that we come closest to the bisexual indifference characteristic of much Greek erotic poetry. Q. Horatius Flaccus ("Horace," 65–8 BCE) stands out as the most prominent lyric poet of Rome: erotic themes play a major role especially in his *Odes* and earlier *Epodes*. Pervaded by an Epicurean detachment from passion, Horatian lyric deploys a persona willing to take his pleasure equally with girls and boys: in *Epode* 11, when Inachia becomes difficult, he replaces her with Lyciscus. Horace's two most important models, both in metrical form and thematics, were the archaic Lesbian poets Sappho and Alcaeus, the former well known for her female same-sex eroticism, the latter known to Horace as the author of pederastic lyric (*Ode* 1.32.9–12), nearly all of which is now lost. From what we can tell of his work, Alcaeus's pederastic poetry, like Anacreon's, was directed to comely slave boys and set within sympotic contexts, much as we see in Horace's short *Ode* 1.38. Such cultivation of beautiful Greek slave boys was fully in keeping with Roman norms, as we have seen. Paul Hay argues, however, that Horace's work also displays a penchant for praise of athletic ephebes exercising bare-chested on the Campus Martius, images of budding manliness like Sybaris in *Ode* 1.8 or Enipeus in 3.7, both of whom, the poet worries, may allow themselves to become dissipated and effeminized if they devote themselves excessively to the wiles of female lovers (37–48). Similar in character is the young Ligurinus praised in two odes of the encomiastic Book IV (4.1 and 4.10), literary heir of the glorious young athletes whose sex appeal shines in Pindar's victory odes.[9]

Horace's slightly younger contemporary Albius Tibullus (ca. 55–19 BCE) also alternates between male and female love objects. He has left behind a cycle of three long elegies dedicated to a youth named Marathus.[10] Although the name appears to be Greek, Marathus was no slave; if anything, Tibullus adopts the traditional elegiac stance of being a metaphorical slave to his beloved. In the first of these three elegies (1.4), the poet presumes to be a teacher of other would-be pederasts by ventriloquizing the didactic voice of the scarecrow god Priapus, whose own poetic tradition of the *Priapea* boldly asserts a phallic potency to tame both boys and girls who enter his garden. Priapus's pederastic advice clearly portrays the love object as a youth adept in elite pursuits, not unlike Horace's Sybaris, Enipeus, or Ligurinus:

> Give in to whatever your boy wants. Yield to him.
>   Love will often conquer by compliance.
> Accompany him, however long the journey,
>   However parched the fields beneath the dog-star,
> Even if the sky is edged with rust-red lace-work,
>   A rainbow warning of the coming storm.
> If he wants to cleave the dark waves in a small craft,
>   Hold the oar yourself, and drive him on.
> Don't shrink from undergoing strenuous labor,
>   Or wearing out your still uncallused hands.
> If he should want to trap game in the wooded vales,
>   Oblige him: sling the net across your shoulder.
> If he wants to spar, you'll take the sword up lightly,
>   And often leave an opening for him.   (1.4.39–52)

Hunting, sailing, sword fighting, athletics, and horse riding are all a gentleman's pursuits, not those of a servile *puer delicatus*. The relationship here is presented as very much in the style of classical Greek pederasty as recorded in the verse of Theognis or the dialogues of Plato and Xenophon: a relationship between class equals in which the younger partner is inculcated in the arts of elite manhood.[11] Borrowing motifs from a variety of archaic Greek and Hellenistic texts, as well as Catullus's Attis poem, Priapus exhorts boys to appreciate the wisdom of poets and reject the allure of those who would attract them with more meretricious incentives.

The lover's pedagogical mentorship of Marathus is extended in the next elegy (1.8), where the lover presumes benevolent superintendence of Marathus's own pursuit of a female beloved named Pholoe. Greek pederasty in its ideal form functioned as a kind of sexual preparation of boys of good class for the role of becoming lovers themselves, whether of other boys or of young women, either courtesans like Pholoe or future wives. As we have seen, this is quite some distance from the normative Roman model of homosexual relations with slaves based on monetary rewards. However, the lover's presumed benevolence in lecturing both Marathus and Pholoe is unmasked at the end of the poem as *Schadenfreude* at seeing the once haughty and love-spurning Marathus himself reduced to the status of helpless lover:

> Marathus himself once trifled with heartsick men
> > Not knowing that a god would take revenge.
> More than once, they say, he laughed at his victim's tears,
> > Prolonged his longing with contrived delays;
> Now he can't stand disdainfulness, and disapproves
> > Of the severity of bolted doors.
> Payback awaits, unless you give up your pride.
> > You'll wish that prayer could call back this lost day.
>
> (1.8.71–78)

The poet's affectation of indulgence at the beginning of the poem now comes closer to the jealous concern of Horace over Lydia's enervating influence on Sybaris or Asterie's on Enipeus.

The bisexual love triangle becomes even more complex in the third and final elegy (1.9). Not only does the poetic lover have to endure Marathus pursuing a courtesan, but perhaps to pay for her favors Marathus now prostitutes himself to an older and richer male admirer. In revenge, the poet prays that his older rival's wife will in turn pursue other men, as payback assumes yet another form.

Without question the most important Augustan poet, particularly in terms of later influence and reputation, was Virgil (P. Vergilius Maro, 70–19 BCE).

Donatus's biography of Virgil (*Life of Virgil* 9), perhaps derived from the work of Suetonius, claims that the poet's own preference was for educated slave boys, at least one of whom was a gift from his early patron Asinius Pollio; some critics, however, have been at pains to deny any credibility to this account (see Jenkyns 6–13). Boys certainly appear side by side with girls as objects of sexual pursuit in Virgil's earliest poetic collection, the pastoral *Eclogues* (see 3.64–83, 7.53–67, 8.17–109, 10.37–41). These relations, although imagined among rustic shepherds, follow the idealizing Greek model rather than common Roman practice, in that they occur among class equals, feature love gifts, and display a pedagogical dimension. This is emphatically the case in the collection's most extended portrayal of erotic passion in *Eclogue* 2: the hopelessly unrefined Corydon attempts to seduce the city-slave Alexis with promises of showing him how to hunt, herd, and play the rustic panpipe. Corydon's failure exudes all the pathos of unrequited love for a younger partner that we typically find in Greek pederastic lyric.[12]

In Virgil's great Roman national epic, the *Aeneid*, we also see an idealized version of Greek pederasty as an older man's mentorship of his younger partner. Apollo taught the Trojan Iapyx the art of medicine to reward his brief intimacy with the god (12.391–94). More important to the epic's plot is the relationship of Nisus and Euryalus, characterized as *pio amore* (5.296), which can be translated either as "dutiful love" or "chaste love" (with Platonic implications). We first meet them at the funeral games celebrated in honor of Aeneas's late father, Anchises (5.293–344), where Nisus fouls another runner to enable his young beloved to win, thereby creating a dispute that Aeneas can only settle by giving every runner a prize. Later in Book 9, they volunteer to sneak through enemy lines to carry a vital message from Aeneas's son, who is away on a diplomatic mission. However, they quickly lose sight of that objective out of eagerness to impress each other by needlessly killing a sleeping contingent of Rutulians. When Euryalus is detected and captured, Nisus sacrifices himself in a hopeless attempt to free his boyfriend, rather than completing the mission on his own. Although cloaked in the heroic ideals of mutual sacrifice associated with Achilles and Patroclus, the Sacred Band of Thebes, or Phaedrus's army of lovers in Plato's *Symposium*, their romantic frivolity ultimately proves ill at home amid the serious business of establishing the Roman state.[13]

More ambiguous and coded is the relationship of the hero Aeneas with his young Latin protégé Pallas (8.104–25, 8.514–19, 8.587–91, 10.362–542; see Putnam), which is clearly modeled on that of Achilles and Patroclus in the *Iliad*. However, like the Homeric epic, the relationship is left implied rather than explicit, somewhere vaguely on the continuum between homosocial and homosexual.

The last great Augustan poet, Ovid (P. Ovidius Naso, 43 BCE–17 CE), moved away from such idealizing representations toward a more ironic inflection of earlier Augustan literary conventions; his attitude and style were even more self-consciously Hellenistic than were his predecessors'. In his spoof didactic poem, the *Art of Love* (2.683–84), he makes his own distaste for pederasty clear; later in the same poem (3.437–38) he ridicules effeminate husbands who maintain soft skin to attract other men. His sweeping mythological epic *Metamorphoses* groups together three pederastic stories (Cyparissus, Ganymede, and Hyacinthus), all appearing as digressions within the story of the heroically faithful lover Orpheus, who braved the Underworld to rescue his beloved wife, only to turn to pederasty as an alternative to women after he fails in that quest (10.78–219). All three of these mythological affairs turn out to be failures of the classical Greek paradigm, in that none of the youths succeed by maturing into adult citizens.[14] At the end of Book 9, immediately prior to the Orpheus episode, Ovid relates a tale of love between two girls, Iphis and Ianthe (9.669–797), that comes to a happy ending only by divine grace allowing the threatened lesbian marriage to become heterosexualized through the transgendering of the transvestite (born a girl, but raised a boy) Iphis (see Pintabone). With Ovid we see an end to the liberal Augustan recuperation of pederasty; in his work, heterosexuality, however scandal prone, reasserts its normative character vigorously.

Imperial Satire

The literature of the first century and early second century CE, often referred to as "Silver Latin," further exhibits a turn toward satire that we have already noticed in the work of Ovid. Amid the excess, corruption, vast disparities in wealth, and political instability of a period that saw no fewer than a dozen emperors, many of them anxious to discredit the authority of their predecessors, and that saw men rise from the lowliest origins to positions of prominence in the Roman state, it was, as Juvenal averred, "difficult not to write satire" (1.30). This tendency manifests itself even in normally sober prose genres such as philosophy and historiography. L. Annaeus Seneca (ca. 1–65 CE), former tutor and advisor to the young emperor Nero, spent his retirement composing scientific and moral treatises, among which we find mordant portraits of male slaves compelled by rich masters to extend their youthful appearance through painful castration or hair removal (*Moral Epistles* 47.7, 122.7), mannish women who penetrate men (*Moral Epistles* 95.21), or the rich degenerate who lines his bedroom with distorting mirrors so as to exaggerate the size of the sexual organs that penetrate his every bodily orifice (*Natural Questions* 1.16). To the Stoic sage, all such ambitions are examples of vain attempts to rebel against our natural endowments and limitations. Similarly, the imperial biographer G. Suetonius Tranquillus (ca. 100 CE) relishes littering his accounts with gossip about the bizarre sexual performances imputed to various emperors: Tiberius swimming naked among his "minnows" (young boys who swam around him and under him, attempting to lick or nibble his genitals) or the spectacle-obsessed Nero engaging in mock weddings with his castrated slave boy Sporus or his more manly ex-gladiator freedman Doryphorus (*Tiberius* 43–44; *Nero* 28–29).[15]

Two poets are worthy of note as chroniclers of gay extravagance, the witty epigrammatist M. Valerius Martialis ("Martial," ca. 40–104 CE) and the satirist D. Junius Juvenalis ("Juvenal," ca. 120 CE). Martial reveals himself as a poet of conservative bisexual tastes consistent with common practice among the Roman elite.[16] His homosexual interests are largely confined to slave boys,[17] although at least two erotic poems (2.55, 8.46) may be addressed to free boys, and the ideal boyfriend is one of free and manly disposition, like the former beloved of his acquaintance Flaccus:

> And let him often force me when I don't want to, and deny me when I do,
> > Let him often act more like a free man than his master;
> And let him fear boys, and often shut out girls;
> > A man to the rest, let him be a boy to me alone.   (4.42.11–14)

12.96 warns a woman not to be jealous of her husband's attentions to slave boys, advising that they can offer delights she cannot or would not.

However, Martial is full of scorn for men who are sexually compulsive and passive: men with worn-out assholes (6.37), plowed like a field (12.16), passive even with boys (3.71), or willing to spend on male prostitutes before feeding their empty bellies (2.51). Particularly worthy of scorn are hypocrites who attempt to laugh off the charge (2.28) or cloak themselves under the pretense of being active pederasts when their interests are really more on the receiving end (11.88). Such inversions of traditional active-passive hierarchies disturb Martial's sense of order, as do prostitutes who cater to passive men (6.50, 9.63), pederasts reduced to pursuing women out of penury (6.33, 11.87), women who willingly take up with unmanly men (7.58, 10.40), male favorites who impregnate their patron's wife (6.39), or worst of all, manly (possibly intersexed) women who penetrate other women and even boys (1.90, 7.67, 7.70). Gay marriages, like those of Nero, are an abomination (1.24, 12.42) in which men of masculine appearance and speech take on the role of blushing brides.

Juvenal's satiric world is populated by a similar menagerie of freaks and oddities. The homophobic rant of *Satire* 2 offers a veritable catalogue: hirsute moralists who wear perfume and wiggle their rumps (2.1–21) or wear chiffon dresses and other feminine garb (2.66–116), the wife showered with lavish gifts to purchase her silence about her husband's intimacy with a freedman (2.58–61), and gay marriage (2.117–42).[18] Nor is the satirist's wrath limited to effeminates and sexual passives: at the end of the poem (2.159–70), he worries that Rome is corrupting the virtuous barbarians by reducing so many of them to pleasure-slaves. In this, even the Roman like Martial, who confines his attention to pretty slaves, is complicit.

However, we should be cautious before attributing the sentiments of this diatribe to Juvenal himself. As has often been observed (since Anderson), Juvenal's early satires are spoken from the standpoint of an "angry man" persona who becomes an object of ironic humor just as much as the nominal subject matter of the satire. Part of *Satire* 2 is delivered through the voice of the adulteress (some say courtesan) Laronia, who denounces the hypocrisy of her male rivals. This attack should not be taken at face value, any more than if a modern satirist were to deliver a diatribe on homosexuality through the voice of Rev. Fred Phelps and the choir of the Westboro Baptist Church. *Satire* 9, in contrast, is far more sympathetic and indulgent in its tone and approach, as it presents a conversation between the satirist and an aging, but well-endowed male prostitute named Naevolus, who denounces his rich patron for ingratitude. Not only did Naevolus penetrate his sexually passive patron, but he saved the patron's never-consummated marriage by satisfying his wife as well.

Without question the high point of self-consciously "queer" literature in Rome is the strange prosimetric novel of Petronius, the *Satyricon*. The author is generally identified with the courtier of Nero briefly referenced by the historian Tacitus (*Annals* 16.17–20) as the emperor's "arbiter of elegance," a witty libertine who slept all day and partied all night, but who was nevertheless efficient in his management of affairs. We possess only one complete book and an excerpted version of two others out of a narrative that spanned at least eighteen books. From what survives, the novel appears to invert the conventions of Greek romance novels by centering its narrative not around a chaste, mutually faithful heterosexual couple, but two very unchaste pederastic lovers: the boy Giton and his lover Encolpius (whose name literally means "in the crotch"), an educated but penniless youth who suffers impotence due to a curse of the ithyphallic god Priapus, whose mysteries Encolpius appears to have somehow violated earlier in the novel. Encolpius seeks a cure at the hands of various women, one of whom, named after the witch Circe in Homer's *Odyssey*, tells him that he can only recover his potency by ceasing to sleep with Giton (129.8). As these two principals travel through southern Italy, they encounter a variety of misadventures, swindles, and colorful characters, including Encolpius's well-endowed romantic rival Ascyltos (who shows off his wares to appreciative men in the public baths), the threadbare poetaster Eumolpus (who boasts about his pederastic seduction of a boy under his tutelage),[19] and the upstart billionaire Trimalchio (who started out as the favorite boy slave of a rich nobleman, eventually becoming his heir).[20] The novel satirizes the vulgarity and hypocrisies of its time in an unforgettable, verbally rich style and with a tone that can only be characterized as high camp (Wooten). As such, the work seems designed to please the tastes of the extravagant and amoral court of the later Nero, a Hellenophile emperor of a markedly literary and performative bent (see Bartsch).[21]

Sex in the *Pax Romana*

The second century CE, the period of the so-called *Pax Romana,* was a time of relative political stability and the apogee of Roman prosperity and power. Under the Hellenophile emperor Hadrian (ruling from 117 to 138), pederasty enjoyed almost unprecedented cultural prestige, reflecting the emperor's own tastes. To this period we owe two substantial literary monuments and also a major religious cult, established in honor of the king's Greco-Bithynian beloved, the fair youth Antinous, who died in his prime of a swimming accident in the Nile. After his death in 130, Hadrian founded the city of Antinoopolis at the site of his drowning, as well as shrines and festivals throughout the empire, decorated by statues of an idealized, athletic figure of divinely ephebic beauty, of which we have numerous extant copies, suggesting some longevity to the cult of deified male beauty even beyond Hadrian's time (see Lambert). Also to Hadrian's reign we can date the *Musa Puerilis* by Strato of Sardis, an anthology of Greek pederastic epigrams, often of a very explicit and graphic character, more than one hundred of which were authored by Strato himself.[22]

Equally fascinating, even if originating as a private correspondence, are the letters between the future emperor Marcus Aurelius (121–180) and his tutor M. Cornelius Fronto. A distant relative of Hadrian, Marcus's beauty and talents were from an early age recognized by the emperor, who near the end of his reign commanded his heir Antoninus Pius to adopt him.

The correspondence between Marcus and his tutor begins when the boy is eighteen and Fronto already in his forties, but reveals from the beginning a tone of erotic intimacy in imitation of Alcibiades's or Phaedrus's relation to Socrates: "I am dying so of love for you, and I'm not scared off by this doctrine of yours, and if you're going to be more ripe and ready for others who don't love you, I will still love you as long as I live and breathe.... If that Phaedrus guy of yours ever really existed, if he was ever away from Socrates, Socrates didn't burn more with desire for Phaedrus than I've burned during these days – did I say days? I mean months – for the sight of you" (Letter 3, qtd. in Richlin, *Marcus* 45). This overheated, even extravagant language persists through several of the youthful letters of Marcus. Is it a Platonic literary exercise, evidence of a real infatuation with a man of superior wisdom and experience, a precocious prince playing the manipulative tease to his new teacher, or conventional rhetoric in a style that had become popular under the homophile emperor Hadrian? It does suggest at the very least that such warm language between males was not felt to be inappropriate or scandalous at the time. More interesting still is the deconstruction of the active/passive, older/younger, master/slave, teacher/student, lover/beloved binaries that seem to structure so much Greek and Roman thought about sexual relations between males. Marcus is at once the beautiful youth, the political superior, and the active suitor of his teacher's wisdom, yet he assigns to himself the role of Socrates at the feet of the beautiful young Phaedrus. Only recently properly edited and translated, these letters still remain a fertile field for further literary and philosophical investigation.

Roman literature of the classical period (from roughly 200 BCE to 200 CE) reveals such a diversity of perspectives toward same-sex love and lust that it defies generalization. What can be said is that male homoerotic relations were openly recognized and discussed by a broad range of authors and texts, whether from the standpoint of satire, ridicule, parody, or idealizing adoption of Greek attitudes and customs. Nevertheless, what it reveals of homosexual practice in ancient Rome stands as something distinctly Roman, influenced by but not limited to classical Greek models.

Notes

1. On homosexuality in Plautus, see Cody; and Lilja 15–50, both concluding that the homosexual allusions are primarily Plautine innovations not in his Greek originals; see also Taylor 341–48.
2. On the homoerotic poems of Catullus generally, see Quinn 242–56; Arkins 104–16; Lilja 51–62; W. Fitzgerald 428–41; Hallett 328–33.

3. For various interpretations of this poem specifically, see Kinsey; Sandy; Winter; Rankin; Selden 476–89; Pedrick 182–87. Unless otherwise noted, all translations are from Hubbard, *Homosexuality*.

4. This depends on what we make of the much disputed *lex Scantinia*; see Dalla 71–99; Cantarella 106–19; C. Williams, *Roman* 119–24.

5. On Attis's homosexuality and his aborted ephebic transition, see Skinner, *"Ego"*; Clay. On the cult of the Galli as a homosexual subculture, see Taylor 330–37.

6. On the sexual imagery in Catullus's political invectives, see Skinner, "Parasites."

7. Many fine examples are preserved in the volcanic ruins of Pompeii; see Varone for an edition, Hubbard, *Homosexuality* 422–23 for translations, and C. Williams, "Sexual" for commentary.

8. On homosexual themes in this collection, see Richlin, *Garden* 120–27; and Hallett 333–44. For the best edition, with German translation, see Kytzler and Fischer.

9. See Crotty 92–102; and Hubbard, "Pindar" 260–65. For the most thorough review of the homoerotic side of Horatian lyric, see Hay 37–48.

10. On this cycle of poems, see Wimmel 17–120; Quinn 247–49; McGann; Booth; Verstraete, "Originality."

11. For this perspective on Greek pederasty, see Hubbard, "Athenian."

12. On the homoerotic themes in this poem, see Olliensis 294–97; and Papanghelis 44–50. For its influence on later writers, see Klein. Hubbard sees pederasty as a trope for relationships of poetic influence and succession (*Pipes* 54–68).

13. Nisus and Euryalus have earned much critical comment: Lee (108–13) and Pavlock see their relationship as nonphysical. Makowski ("Nisus") reads it in terms of conventional Greek pederasty. Most critics regard it as detrimental to the Trojan cause (Hornsby; Duckworth; G. J. Fitzgerald; DiCesare 161–66; Cristofoli). However, Lennox and Potz see them as positive paradigms of personal loyalty.

14. For Ovid's ironic treatment of these myths, see Makowski, "Bisexual"; and Janan. Verstraete ("Ovid") has a different reading of the Hyacinthus myth.

15. Little historical credibility need be given to such episodes, which may have their origins in revisionist accounts after the deaths of those emperors; see Krenkel.

16. For homosexual themes in Martial, see Sullivan, "Martial's" and *Martial* 185–210; Garrido-Hory; Richlin, *Garden* 39–44, 129–41; and Obermayer.

17. See 1.46, 1.92, 3.65, 4.7, 5.46, 5.83, 6.34, 7.29, 8.63, 9.56, 9.103, 10.42, 10.98, 11.6, 11.8, 11.26, 11.58, 12.71, 12.75.

18. On this poem, see Braund and Cloud; Konstan; Nappa; and Walters.

19. On the story of the Pergamene boy, see Dimundo, "Socrate" and "Novella"; and Elsner.

20. For differing views concerning Trimalchio's relation to his master and to his own boy favorite, see Bodel, "Trimalchio" and "Trimalchio's"; Pomeroy; and Schievenin. On master-slave relations more generally, see Cervellera.
21. Some critics have nevertheless interpreted the novel as a moralistic indictment of its time: see Highet; and Arrowsmith. For the contrary view, see Walsh; and Gill. Richardson sees the homosexual themes as reflections of contemporary Roman realities. Sullivan (*Satyricon* 232–53) finds pervasive themes of scopophilia and exhibitionism. On Encolpius's impotence, see McMahon.
22. For editions and commentary, see Paduano; and Steinbichler.

Works Cited

Anderson, William S. "Studies in Book I of Juvenal." *Yale Classical Studies* 15 (1957): 31–90. Print.

Arkins, Brian. *Sexuality in Catullus*. Hildesheim: Olms, 1982. Print.

Arrowsmith, William. "Luxury and Death in the Satyricon." *Arion* 5.3 (1966): 304–31. Print.

Bartsch, Shadi. *Actors in the Audience: Theatricality and Doublespeak from Nero to Hadrian*. Cambridge: Harvard UP, 1994. Print.

Bodel, John. "Trimalchio and the Candelabrum." *Classical Philology* 84.3 (1989): 224–31. Print.
"Trimalchio's Coming of Age." *Phoenix* 43.1 (1989): 72–74. Print.

Booth, Joan. "Tibullus 1.8 and 9: A Tale in Two Poems?" *Museum Helveticum* 53 (1996): 232–47. Print.

Boswell, John . *Christianity, Social Tolerance, and Homosexuality*. Chicago: U of Chicago P, 1980. Print.

Braund, S., and Cloud, J. D. "Juvenal: A Diptych." *Liverpool Classical Monthly* 6 (1981): 203–08. Print.

Buffière, Felix. *Eros adolescent: la pédérastie dans la Grèce antique*. Paris: Belles Lettres, 1980. Print.

Cantarella, Eva. *Bisexuality in the Ancient World*. Trans. Cormac Ó Cuilleanáin. New Haven: Yale UP, 1992. Print.

Catullus, C. Valerius. *C. Valerii Catulli Carmina*. Ed. R. A. B. Mynors. Oxford: Oxford UP, 1958. Print.

Cervellera, Maria Antonia. "Omosessualità e ideologia schiavistica in Petronio." *Index* 11 (1982): 221–34. Print.

Clay, Jenny S. "Catullus' 'Attis' and the Black Hunter." *Quaderni Urbinati di Cultura Classica* 50.2 (1995): 143–55. Print.

Cody, Jane M. "The Senex Amator in Plautus' Casina." *Hermes* 104.4 (1976): 453–76. Print.

Cristofoli, Roberto. "Note di lettura agli episodi di Eurialo e Niso." *Giornale Italiano di Filologia* 48 (1996): 261–68. Print.

Crotty, Kevin M. *Song and Action: The Victory Odes of Pindar*. Baltimore: Johns Hopkins UP, 1982. Print.

Dalla, Danilo. *"Ubi Venus mutatur": Omosessualità e diritto nel mondo romano*. Milan: A. Giuffrè, 1987. Print.

DiCesare, Mario A. *The Altar and the City: A Reading of Vergil's Aeneid*. New York: Columbia UP, 1974. Print.

Dimundo, Rosalba. "Da Socrate a Eumolpo: Degradazione di personaggi e delle funzioni nella novella del fanciullo di Pergamo." *Materiali e Discussioni* 10–11 (1983): 255–65. Print.

——. "La novella dell' Efebo di Pergamo: Struttura del racconto." *Semiotica della novella latina: Atti del seminario interdisciplinare "La novella latina"* (Perugia 11–13 Aprile 1986): 83–94. Print.

Duckworth, G. E. "The Significance and Function of Nisus and Euryalus for *Aeneid* IX-XII." *American Journal of Philology* 68 (1967): 129–50. Print.

Ellis, Robinson. *A Commentary on Catullus.* Oxford: Clarendon P, 1889. Print.

Elsner, Jaś. "Seductions of Art: Encolpius and Eumolpus in a Neronian Picture Gallery." *Proceedings of the Cambridge Philological Society* 39 (1994): 30–47. Print.

Fitzgerald, G. J. "Nisus and Euryalus: A Paradigm of Futile Behavior and the Tragedy of Youth." *Cicero and Virgil: Studies in Honour of Harold Hunt.* Ed. John R. C. Martyn. Amsterdam: Hakkert, 1972. 114–37. Print.

Fitzgerald, William. "Catullus and the Reader: The Erotics of Poetry." *Arethusa* 25 (1992): 419–43. Print.

Garrido-Hory, Marguerite. "La vision du dépendent chez Martial à travers les relations sexuelles." *Index* 10 (1981): 298–315.

Gill, Christopher. "The Sexual Episodes in the *Satyricon*." *Classical Philology* 68.3 (1973): 172–85. Print.

Hallett, Judith. P. "*Nec Castrare Velis Meos Libellos:* Sexual and Poetic *Lusus* in Catullus, Martial and the *Carmina Priapea.*" *Satura Lanx: Festschrift für Werner Krenkel zum 70. Geburtstag.* Ed. C. Klodt. Hildesheim: Olms, 1996. 321–44. Print.

Hay, Paul Jerome. "Sexual Personae in Horace's Erotic Poetry." MA Thesis. U of Texas, Austin, 2012. Print.

Highet, Gilbert. "Petronius the Moralist." *Transactions and Proceedings of the American Philological Association* 72 (1941): 176–94. Print.

Horace. *Q. Horatii Flacci Opera.* Ed. D. R. Shackleton Bailey. Stuttgart: Teubner, 1985. Print.

Hornsby, Roger. "The Armor of the Slain." *Philological Quarterly* 45.2 (1966): 347–59. Print.

Hubbard, Thomas. K. "Athenian Pederasty and the Construction of Masculinity." *What Is Masculinity? Historical Dynamics from Antiquity to the Contemporary World.* Ed. John H. Arnold and Sean Brady. Houndmills: Palgrave, 2011. 189–225. Print.

——. "The Catullan *Libelli* Revisited." *Philologus* 149.2 (2005): 253–77. Print.

——. *Homosexuality in Greece and Rome: A Sourcebook of Basic Documents.* Berkeley: U of California P, 2003. Print.

——. "Pindar, Theoxenus, and the Homoerotic Eye." *Arethusa* 35 (2002): 255–96. Print.

——. *The Pipes of Pan: Intertextuality and Literary Filiation in the Pastoral Tradition from Theocritus to Milton.* Ann Arbor: U of Michigan P, 1998. Print.

Janan, Micaela. "The Book of Good Love? Design versus Desire in *Metamorphoses* 10." *Ramus* 17 (1988): 110–37. Print.

Jenkyns, Richard. *Virgil's Experience: Nature and History, Times, Names, and Places.* Oxford UP: Clarendon P, 1998. Print.

Juvenal. *A. Persi Flacci et D. Juni Juvenalis saturae.* Ed. W. V. Clausen. 2nd ed. Oxford UP: E Typographeo Clarendoniano, 1992, Print.

Kinsey, T. E. "Catullus 16." *Latomus* 25.1 (1966): 101–06. Print.

Klein, Theodore M. "The Greek Shepherd in Vergil, Gide, Genet and Barthes." *Helios* 6 (1978): 1–32. Print.

Konstan, David. "Sexuality and Power in Juvenal's Second Satire." *Liverpool Classical Monthly* 18 (1993): 12–14. Print.

Krenkel, Werner. "Sex und politische Biographie." *Wissenschaftliche Zeitschrift der Wilhelm-Pieck-Universität Rostock, Gesellschaftliche und sprachwissenschaftliche Reihe* 29.5 (1980): 65–76. Print.

Kytzler, Bernhard, and Carl Fischer. *Carmina Priapea: Gedichte an den Gartengott.* Munich: Artemis, 1978. Print.

Lambert, Royston. *Beloved and God: The Story of Hadrian and Antinous.* New York: Viking, 1984. Print.

Lear, Andrew, and Eva Cantarella. *Images of Ancient Greek Pederasty: Boys Were Their Gods.* London: Routledge, 2008. Print.

Lee, M. Owen. *Fathers and Sons in Virgil's Aeneid: Tum Genitor Natum.* Albany: State U of New York P, 1979. Print.

Lennox, Peter. G. "Virgil's Night Episode Re-Examined (*Aeneid* IX, 176–449)." *Hermes* 105 (1977): 331–42.

Lilja, Saara. *Homosexuality in Republican and Augustan Rome.* Helsinki: Societas Scientiarum Fennica, 1983. Print.

MacMullen, Ramsay. "Roman Attitudes to Greek Love." *Historia* 31 (1982): 484–502. Print.

Makowski, John. F. "Bisexual Orpheus: Pederasty and Parody in Ovid." *The Classical Journal* 92.1 (1996): 25–38. Print.

"Nisus and Euryalus: A Platonic Relationship." *The Classical Journal* 85.1 (1989): 1–15. Print.

Martial. *M. Valerii Martialis epigrammata.* Ed. D. R. Shackleton Bailey. Stuttgart: Teubner, 1990. Print.

Marx, Fridericus. *C. Lucilii Carminum reliquiae.* Leipzig: Teubner, 1904–05. Print.

McGann, M. J. "The Marathus Elegies of Tibullus." *Aufstieg und Niedergang der römischen Welt* II.30.3 (1983): 1976–99. Print.

McMahon, John M. *Paralysin Cave: Impotence, Perception, and Text in the Satyrica of Petronius.* Leiden: Brill, 1998. Print.

Nappa, Christopher. "*Praetextati Mores:* Juvenal's Second Satire." *Hermes* 126.1 (1998): 90–108. Print.

Obermayer, Hans-Peter. *Martial und der Diskurs über männliche "Homosexualität" in der Literatur der frühen Kaiserzeit.* Tübingen: Narr, 1998.

Olliensis, Ellen. "Sons and Lovers: Sexuality and Gender in Virgil's Poetry." *The Cambridge Companion to Virgil.* Ed. Charles Martindale. Cambridge: Cambridge UP, 1997. 294–311. Print.

Paduano, Guido. *Antologia Palatina: Epigrammi Erotici: Libro V e Libro XII.* Milan: Biblioteca Universale Rizzoli, 1989. Print.

Papanghelis, T. D. "Eros Pastoral and Profane: On Love in Virgil's *Eclogues.*" *Amor: Roma. Love & Latin Literature: Eleven Essays (and One Poem) by Former Research Students Presented to E.J. Kenney on his Seventy-fifth Birthday.* Ed. Susanna M. Braund and Roland Mayer. Cambridge: Cambridge Philosophical Society, 1999. 44–59. Print.

Pavlock, Barbara. "Epic and Tragedy in Vergil's Nisus and Euryalus Episode." *Transactions of the American Philological Association* 115 (1985): 207–24. Print.

Pedrick, Victoria. "The Abusive Address and the Audience in Catullan Poems." *Helios* 20 (1993): 173–96. Print.

Percy, William A. III. *Pederasty and Pedagogy in Archaic Greece*. Urbana: U of Illinois P, 1996. Print.

Petronius. *Petronii Arbitri Satyricon reliquiae*. Ed. Konrad Müller. 4th ed. Leipzig: Teubner, 1995. Print.

Pintabone, Diane. T. "Ovid's Iphis and Ianthe: When Girls Won't Be Girls." *Among Women: From the Homosocial to the Homoerotic in the Ancient World*. Ed. Nancy. S. Rabinowitz and Lisa Auanger. Austin: U of Texas P, 2002. 256–85. Print.

Plautus. *T. Macci Plauti Comoediae*. Ed. W. M. Lindsay. Oxford UP: Clarendon, 1904–05. Print.

Pomeroy, Arthur. J. "Trimalchio as 'Deliciae.'" *Phoenix* 46.1 (1992): 45–53. Print.

Potz, Erich. "*Fortunati ambo*: Funktion und Bedeutung der Nisus/Euryalus Episode in Vergil's *Aeneis*." *Hermes* 121.3 (1993): 325–34. Print.

Putnam, Michael. C. J. "Possessiveness, Sexuality and Heroism in the *Aeneid*." *Vergilius* 31 (1985): 1–21. Print.

Quinn, Kenneth. *Catullus: An Interpretation*. London: Batsford, 1972. Print.

Rankin, H. D. "Poem 16 of Catullus." *Symbolae Osloenses* 51.1 (1976): 87–94. Print.

Ribbeck, Otto. *Scaenicae Romanorum poesis fragmenta*. 3rd ed. Leipzig: Teubner, 1897–98. Print.

Richardson, T. Wade. "Homosexuality in the Satyricon." *Classica et Mediaevalia* 35 (1984): 105–27. Print.

Richlin, Amy. *The Garden of Priapus: Sexuality and Aggression in Roman Humor*. New York: Oxford UP, 1992. Print.

Marcus Aurelius in Love: The Letters of Marcus and Fronto. Chicago: U of Chicago P, 2006. Print.

"Not before Homosexuality: The Materiality of the *Cinaedus* and the Roman Law against Love between Men." *Journal of the History of Sexuality* 3.4 (1993): 523–73. Print.

Sandy, Gerald. N. "Catullus 16." *Phoenix* 25.1 (1971): 51–57. Print.

Schievenin, Romeo. "Trimalcione e il *puer non inspeciosus*." *Bollettino di Studi Latini* 6 (1976): 295–302. Print.

Selden, Daniel. "*Ceveat Lector*: Catullus and the Rhetoric of Performance." *Innovations of Antiquity*. Ed. Ralph Hexter and Daniel Selden. New York: Routledge, 1992. 461–512. Print.

Skinner, Marilyn. B. "*Ego Mulier*: The Construction of Male Sexuality in Catullus." *Helios* 20 (1993): 107–30. Print.

"Parasites and Strange Bedfellows: A Study in Catullus' Political Imagery." *Ramus* 8 (1979): 137–52. Print.

Steinbichler, Walter. *Die Epigramme des Dichters Straton von Sardes: Ein Beitrag zum griechischen paiderotischen Epigramm*. Frankfurt aM: Lang, 1998. Print.

Sullivan, John. P. *Martial, the Unexpected Classic: A Literary and Historical Study*. Cambridge: Cambridge UP, 1991. Print.

"Martial's Sexual Attitudes." *Philologus* 123 (1979): 288–302. Print.

The Satyricon of Petronius: A Literary Study. London: Faber, 1968. Print.

Taylor, Rabun. "Two Pathic Subcultures in Ancient Rome." *Journal of the History of Sexuality* 7 (1997): 319–71. Print.

Tibullus. *Albii Tibulli aliorumque Carmina*. Ed. Georg Luck. 2nd ed. Leipzig: Teubner, 1998. Print.

Varone, Antonio. *Erotica Pompeiana: Iscrizioni d' amore sui muri di Pompei*. Rome: L'Erma di Bretschneider, 1994. Print.

Verstraete, Beert. "The Originality of Tibullus' Marathus Elegies." *Journal of Homosexuality* 49.3/4 (2005) 299–313. Print.

"Ovid on Homosexuality." *Echos du Monde Classique* 19 (1975): 79–83. Print.

"Slavery and the Social Dynamics of Male Homosexual Relations in Ancient Rome." *Journal of Homosexuality* 5 (1980): 227–36. Print.

Veyne, Paul. "Homosexuality in Ancient Rome." *Western Sexuality: Practice and Precept in Past and Present Times*. Ed. Philippe Ariès and André Béjin. Trans. A. Forster. Oxford: Blackwell, 1985. 26–35. Print.

Virgil. *P. Vergilii Maronis Opera*. Ed. R. A. B. Mynors. Oxford UP: Oxford Clarendon P, 1969. Print.

Walsh, P. G. "Was Petronius a Moralist?" *Greece & Rome* 21 (1974): 181–90. Print.

Walters, Jonathan. "Juvenal, Satire 2: Putting Male Sexual Deviants on Show." *Thinking Men: Masculinity and Its Self-Representation in the Classical Tradition*. Ed. Lin Foxhall and John Salmon. London: Routledge, 1998. 148–54. Print.

Williams, Craig A. *Roman Homosexuality: Ideologies of Masculinity in Classical Antiquity*. Oxford: Oxford UP, 1999. Print.

"Sexual Themes in Greek and Latin Graffiti." *A Companion to Greek and Roman Sexualities*. Ed. Thomas K. Hubbard. Malden: Wiley-Blackwell, 2014. 493–508. Print.

Williams, Gordon. "Poetry in the Moral Climate of Augustan Rome." *The Journal of Roman Studies* 52.1/2 (1962): 28–46. Print.

Wimmel, Walter. *Der frühe Tibull*. München: Fink, 1968. Print.

Winter, Thomas Nelson. "Catullus Purified: A Brief History of *Carmen* 16." *Arethusa* 6 (1973): 257–65. Print.

Wooten, C. "Petronius and 'Camp.'" *Helios* 11 (1984): 133–39. Print.

5

Configurations of Gender and Sexuality in Medieval Europe

KARMA LOCHRIE

In the European Middle Ages, a period that spans more than a thousand years (350 CE–1450 CE), gender and sexuality were, in some senses, more complicated than they are today because the epoch lacked modern categories, primarily heterosexuality and homosexuality, that have been so crucial to modern configurations of sex and gender. Reading premodern literature in terms of its genders and sexualities, therefore, requires readers to abandon presumptive modern sexual categories. The ultimate goal of this kind of historical approach to gender and sexuality is, in the words of David Halperin, "to accede, through a calculated encounter with the otherness of the past, to an altered understanding of the present – a sense of our own non-identity to ourselves – and thus to a new experience of ourselves as sites of potential transformation" (15). At the same time, the discovery of historical genders and sexualities offers the possibility of establishing continuities between the past and present that allow for identification and a more nuanced understanding of contemporary categories.

John Boswell was the first medieval historian to transform the study of medieval sexuality and gender by arguing in 1980 that the Christian Middle Ages were not as hostile to homoeroticism as had been previously assumed. In *Christianity, Social Tolerance, and Homosexuality*, Boswell summoned a wealth of historical and literary evidence of homosexuality in the Middle Ages, and in the process, established medieval sexuality as a legitimate area of scholarly study. Queer medievalists in the past twenty years have been theorizing the relationship between modern queer theory and historical inquiry, as well as charting that complex landscape of medieval sexual and gender categories in literature and culture in Britain and on the Continent. Michel Foucault's first volume of the *History of Sexuality* influenced queer scholars to turn away from the search for homosexuality and homosexuals in history toward the search for categories of sexual acts that might not necessarily reproduce modern identity categories. Carolyn Dinshaw, one of the foremost queer scholars in the field of medieval studies, argues for a queer history that would create affective identifications across historical periods between the present queer reader and the past through a concept she calls the "queer touch." Dinshaw also argues for a queer historicity characterized by asynchrony, rather than a historical linearity that sponsors heteronormative history, as a way of reading past sexualities and genders. Another group of scholars, including Mark Jordan and William Burgwinkle, has sought to understand the medieval category of sodomy both in its religious and literary representations in relationship to modern homosexuality. Other scholars, such as Tison Pugh and Anna Klosowka, have sought to revise our readings of some medieval texts in order to pay more attention to the queer possibilities of those texts. Finally, James A. Schultz and the author of this chapter have dismantled heterosexuality itself as a category for understanding the literary phenomenon of courtly love and medieval culture, respectively.[1]

Medieval texts evidence an array of sexualities that simply do not fit into our binary rubric of heterosexual/homosexual. What we think of as heterosexual and normative was shot through with deviance, according to medieval thinking, while what we think of as "homosexual" deviance was indeed condemned, but not because of its errancy from a heterosexual standard. Sodomy as a sin was often regarded alongside such sins as fornication between men and women, making it less a sin of deviance than one among many, heterosexual and homosexual.

We might, in other words, think of medieval gender and sexuality in terms of "configurations" in that sexuality was not for the Middle Ages a category of identity in its own right; instead, sexual identities and behaviors were often complexly implicated in other kinds of identities and behaviors. For example, heresy and sodomy were often linked in theological and political texts; or, the category of Lechery in the Church's canon of the Seven Deadly Sins was considered to be closely related to Gluttony, while sodomy as a subset of this category was explicitly associated with excessive opulence in the form of soft bedding. Medieval gender, too, is embedded in different cultural contexts and discourses, rendering it somewhat unfamiliar to us. The homosocial bonds of chivalry, for example, trump heterosexual prowess in marking masculinity in men in medieval romance. Medieval masculinity could also be compromised by excessive indulgence in heterosexual conquests, often with humorous results. Medieval femininity in women was also a complex, sometimes contradictory, category. Sexually, femininity was defined by the passive position in heterosexual intercourse, and yet, one of the principal medieval associations with femininity was sexual voracity. It is important, therefore, not to assume that medieval sexual or gender categories were identical to our own.

The survey of genders and sexualities that follows is organized around a few configurations found in medieval literary texts. Each subsection will define a configuration and then explore it in a range of medieval texts from England and the Continent. Configurations of gender will be discussed in terms of masculinity and femininity, but those terms will not necessarily line up with our modern understandings of them.

Masculinity and Male Sexuality in the Heroic Mode

Old English literature is not governed by a heterosexual ethos of romantic love. In fact, romantic love figures rarely in literary texts from the formative period of English literature, 600 CE to 1100 CE. In contrast to the romantic love that defines romances of the later Middle Ages, Anglo-Saxon heroic literature featured homosociality between men as its primary mode of interpersonal relationship. The homosociality of Anglo-Saxon heroic culture is not equivalent to homosexuality in that it designates a social, rather than a sexual, relationship. Friendship, patronage, and the lord-retainer bond represent a few of the forms that male homosociality takes. In addition, this homosociality structures the heroic code of masculinity and the power relations of early medieval society, emphasizing loyalty and military achievements as primary elements of its ethos. With a few exceptions, women figure mainly as adjuncts to this homosociality.

Beowulf (ca. eighth to eleventh centuries), the oldest surviving epic in English, may best be remembered by readers for its monsters – Grendel, Grendel's mother, and the dragon. The eponymous hero of the 3,182-line poem travels from his homeland in Scandinavia to Denmark to battle the monster, Grendel, who attacks King Hrothgar's mead hall nightly. The homosocial ties that bind Hrothgar and Beowulf have historical roots, but Beowulf deepens those ties by defeating Grendel and the monster's mother. Hrothgar declares his thanks to Beowulf in a language of parental love:

> "So now, Beowulf,
> I adopt you in my heart as a dear son.
> Nourish and maintain this new connection,
> you noblest of men; there'll be nothing you'll want for,
> no world goods that won't be yours."   (ll. 945–49)

If this homosocial expression of love between king and hero seems elusive to modern readers, it was the stuff of passionate elegy for Old English poets. In the famous tenth-century poem, *The Wanderer*, a retainer laments his exile from his lord and native land as he wanders despairingly over the wintery ocean alone. He dreams of his "goldfriend," the lord who rewarded his service with rare gifts: "It will seem to him in his mind that he is embracing and kissing his liege lord and laying his hands and his head on his knee, as it some times was in the old days when he took part in gift-giving" (112). His tender reminiscence of lying in the lap of his lord is not sexual, but it is as intimate as it is ceremonial, surrounded by the marks of heroic culture – the mead hall, fellow warriors, the sheer revelry of the event.

Beginning in the twelfth century, the literature of romance initiated a new model of heroic masculinity in tandem with the invention of heterosexual courtly love. This new masculinity would become defined in terms of hetero-sexual love as a prerequisite of exemplary knighthood, and at the same time, it would deepen the homosocial bonds of chivalry beyond those exhibited in Anglo-Saxon literature. The co-development of homosociality and passionate attachments between men with the advent of a new literature of heterosexual love might seem paradoxical, but only because of the exclusionary emphases of modern identity categories. The new ethos of courtly love and its code of masculinity emerged alongside the theological conceptualization of sod-omy as a sexual sin primarily involving same-sex acts (Burgwinkle 1–45).[2] What unites the homosociality, even implied homosexuality, of the knights of the medieval romance with a burgeoning literature of heterosexual love unseen before in European literature is the emergent code of elite masculinity. Homosociality – and even its sexual counterpart – were essential components of this new masculinity.

Chivalric homosociality appears most prominently in those romances in which it is tested when it comes into conflict with the knight's duties as a het-erosexual lover. In the fourteenth-century Middle English poem, *Sir Gawain and the Green Knight*, Gawain's search for the Green Knight takes him to the court of Lord Bertilak, who proposes a strange game between the two men: he will go hunting each day for the next three days, while Gawain rests at court. At the end of each day each man will present his winnings from the day to the other as a gift. Over the next three days, Bertilak's wife visits Gawain in his bedroom, flirting with him and goading him to demonstrate his skill at love-talking for which he is renowned. Chivalry demands on the one hand that he courteously reciprocate the lady's love, but on the other, it also requires him to remain loyal to his host, Lord Bertilak. He tries to fulfill both demands by kissing the lady three times on her successive visits without technically violating his obligations to Bertilak (not to seduce his wife). At the end of each day, Bertilak offers up the deer, boar, and fox he has killed in his hunts, and in return, Gawain remits to him the kisses he has received from his wife. The homosexual possibility haunts Gawain's struggle, but in the end, it is the homosocial bond that wins out over his obligations as a knight to the woman who tests him.

Thomas Malory's *Morte D'arthur* (*Death of Arthur;* 1469–70), known to many through Alfred Lord Tennyson's adaptation of that work in *Idylls of the King* (1859), recounts the famous story of the downfall of Arthur's Round Table and the love story of Lancelot and Guinevere, Arthur's queen. Although the love story between Lancelot and Guinevere is central to Malory's work, what is mourned in Malory's text is not so much the tragic love affair but the grand homosocial community identified with King Arthur. As the king himself realizes the inevitable collapse of his great society of knights, he laments, "Wit you well, my heart was never so heavy as it is now. And much more am I worried for my good knights' loss than for the loss of my fair queen; for queens I might have enough, but such a fellowship of good knights shall never be together in no company" (481–82). When King Arthur meets Lancelot for battle "the tears burst out of his eyes, thinking of the great courtesy that was in Sir Lancelot more than in any other man" (488). The height of pathos in Malory's version of the death of Arthur stems more from the damaged bonds of love between men than from the end of the love between Lancelot and Guinevere.

In some medieval romances, an association between chivalric fellowship and sodomy haunts the story. Chrétien de Troyes's *Conte du grail*, or *Story of the Grail* (1180) introduced European culture to the story of the Holy Grail with Perceval as its subject. Chrétien's unfinished text was developed in later continuations of the story, one of which was by Gerbert de Montreuil (1226–30). In this version, there is a famous encounter with the "Siege perilous," or "perilous seat." Perceval arrives at a feast at Arthur's court and is perplexed by the empty seat that all the knights leave at the table. He is unaware that anyone who sits in this particular seat is doomed to disappear into an abyss unless he is that knight who is worthy of the Holy Grail. To everyone's horror, Perceval sits down like a rude guest, the ground opens up, and instead of swallowing up Perceval, it regurgitates six knights. They recount to the assembled court the mysterious chair's significance:

> They immediately told him how they had suffered great pains and said that as for those who are disloyal, who love young men more than young ladies, all

should know that it's a wonder how those men can stand it under the earth, for they will be found burning on the day of judgment. And you should know for sure, that the fairy who gave you this chair did so only so that anyone who is stained with such a vice might know the truth about what recompense awaits him. (qtd. in Burgwinkle 126)

The sin of sodomy seems to arise out of nowhere, like the knights, suggesting that it is the rare knight (Perceval in this case) who is free of the sodomitic sin. This passage should not be interpreted to suggest that sodomy was widespread among medieval knights, but it does implicate knighthood and its homosocial ethos in the sin of sodomy.

The homosocial world of chivalry presents other complex challenges to elite masculinity represented in medieval romance. The *Lais of Marie de France* written in England by a Frenchwoman in the late twelfth century are stories of love involving knights and women, but they do not always follow the typical courtly love narrative: knight falls for lady, knight has to prove himself to her, knight suffers in the process, knight wins her. Sometimes, in fact, the chivalric homosociality proves to be more enduring and more passionate than heterosexual love. *Bisclavret* tells the unusual story of a knight who loves his wife but leaves her once a week for three days to become a werewolf. When his wife discovers his secret, she steals his clothes so that he cannot return to his human state. Condemned to roam the woods as a wolf, Bisclavret is discovered and adopted at court by the king. They sleep together, and their love for each other is apparent to all: "Wherever the King might go, it [the werewolf] never wanted to be left behind. It accompanied him constantly and showed clearly that it loved him" (*Lais* 76). When Bisclavret is finally restored to his human form, the king "ran forward to embrace him, and kissed him many times" (*Lais* 72). What are we to make of this curious story? Is Bisclavret's werewolf aspect a kind of "illicit identity" that is suggestive of a different sexuality (Burgwinkle 168)? Whatever its meaning, it is clear that Marie de France's tale valorizes the king's love for Bisclavret above that of the knight and his wife and a kind of masculinity that is framed in terms of passionate love between men.

What about the knight who is admirable in all respects except that he rejects the love of women? Marie's Guigemar is one such knight whose flaw is widely recognized:

At that time no one could find his equal as a knight, be it in Lorraine, Burgundy, Anjou or Gascony. But Nature had done him such a grievous wrong that he never displayed the slightest interest in love. There was no lady or maiden on earth, however noble or beautiful, who would not have been happy to accept him as her lover, if he had sought her love.... He showed no visible interest in love and was thus considered a lost cause by stranger and friend alike.

(*Lais* 44)

Guigemar's masculinity is attenuated by this one "flaw," which has a sexual valence as well. He is cured of this mysterious flaw, thanks to a magical boat and an unhappily married woman who becomes his lover.

Although sodomy is never explicit in these tales, it is unequivocally an issue in other romances. In Marie de France's *Lanval*, the hero resembles Guigemar in his isolation from women and his otherness: he is a foreigner in Arthur's court who, in spite of his service to the king and his accomplishments as a knight, goes unrewarded and ignored. His abject state is temporarily relieved after a fairy woman appears to him, and they become secret lovers. When Queen Guinevere later professes her own love for Lanval and he rejects her, she accuses him of being one of "those" knights who don't like women: "'Lanval,' she said, 'I well believe that you do not like this kind of pleasure. I have been told often enough that you have no desire for women. You have well-trained young men and enjoy yourself with them'" (*Lais* 76). Her diatribe against his alleged love of men ends with her impugning his masculinity by calling him a "weak little scoundrel." Lanval denies the charge, saying he is ignorant of that "profession." He is later rescued by his fairy lady in a curious reversal of the traditional rescue narratives of romance. Beneath the seeming triumph of heterosexual love, however, Lanval's unorthodox masculinity and sexuality (he can only have love and sex with otherworldly women) remain.

An even more explicit accusation of a knight's sodomitic inclinations is made against Aeneas in the twelfth-century French romance *Eneas*. In this text the mother of Lavinia tries to quell her feelings for Aeneas by accusing him of sodomy in a flurry of crude metaphors:

> He prefers those who trade in flexible rods; he won't eat hens, but really loves the flesh of a cock. He would rather embrace a boy than you or any other woman. He doesn't know how to play with women, and you wouldn't find him hanging around the hole in the gate; but he really goes for the crack of a young man. The Trojans are raised on this. (qtd. in Burgwinkle xi–xii)

The queen's virulent attack on sodomites is mixed with a good measure of xenophobia, as she imputes this "vice" to all Trojans as opposed to her native Lavinians.

Elite masculinity in medieval romances was thus marked significantly by a homosociality that was sometimes seen to blur the lines between sodomite and courtly lover. Masculinity depended on intimate bonds of loyalty and love between men as one of its primary markers. When these bonds came into conflict with a knight's obligations to engage in courtly love, things could become messy, even downright nasty. Nevertheless, it is possible to discern in the presumed heterosexual systems of chivalry and courtly love a homosociality that was vital to the understanding of noble masculinity and love. In addition, this homosociality formed the affective structure of power relations in medieval courtly society, whereby the bonds between men structured the ways power was exercised and exchanged. A variation on this same homosociality can be found in contemporary masculinities, as Eve Kosofsky Sedgwick famously argued in *Between Men*: "In any male-dominated society, there is a special relationship between male homosocial (*including* homosexual) desire and the structures for maintaining and transmitting patriarchal power" (25). Medieval configurations of homosociality in romance, courtly love, and chivalry not only provide a backstory to contemporary configurations of masculinity, but they suggest salient affiliations between past and present in what Sedgwick calls the "immanence of men's same-sex bonds and their prohibitive structuration" (*Epistemology* 15).

Passionate Friendships

The language of medieval friendships was often more passionate and sexually charged by comparison with modern standards. Sherry Velasco and Jonathan Goldberg argue elsewhere in this volume for the crucial importance of same-sex friendships in the early modern period. Same-sex desire in the Middle Ages also appears most often in the context of friendship. Some of the most famous of passionate letters come down to us from the least likely of places, medieval monasteries and convents. Anselm (1033–1109), prior at the abbey of Bec in Normandy before becoming Archbishop of Canterbury, writes to Gilbert Crispin, abbot of Westminster:

> You know how great is the affection that we have experienced – eye to eye, kiss for kiss, embrace for embrace. I experience it all the more now when you, in whom I have had so much pleasure, are irretrievably separated from me.
>
> (Southern 145)

Although Boswell famously credited Anselm with helping to "incorporate expressions of gay feelings" in medieval Catholicism, Anselm's passionate language can also be seen as part of a tradition elevating the "ennobling love" of male friendship above male-female ties dating back to the Greeks (see Boswell

218; and Jaeger, who argues against a sexual interpretation of this idea of spiritual friendship).

English Cistercian Aelred of Rievaulx (1109–66) is generally credited with articulating this idea of passionate (chaste) spiritual friendship for the Middle Ages. In his treatise *On Spiritual Friendship* (1164–67), Aelred "developed a concept of Christian friendship which, in its emphasis on human affection, surpassed any earlier theological statements and explicitly expressed in prose much of the implicit correlation between human and spiritual love long characteristic of clerical love poetry" (Boswell 221–22). As an example of the perfect love of friendship, Aelred adduces the example of Jesus and John:

> It is in fact a great consolation in this life to have someone to whom you can be united in the intimate embrace of the most sacred love; ... in whose delightful company, as in a sweet consoling song, you can take comfort in the midst of sadness; in whose most welcome friendly bosom you can find peace in so many worldly setbacks; ... through whose spiritual kisses – as by some medicine – you are cured of sickness of care and worry; ... with whom you can rest, just the two of you, in the sleep of peace away from the noise of the world, in the embrace of love, in the kiss of unity, with the Holy Spirit flowing over you; to whom you so join and unite yourself that you mix soul with soul, and the two become one ... for some are joined to us more intimately and passionately than others in the lovely bond of spiritual friendship.
>
> (qtd. in Boswell 225–26)

Although not everyone agrees with Boswell that "there can be little question that Aelred was gay," most would acknowledge the powerful homoerotic element of his idea of friendship by today's standards (222).

Medieval religious men were not the only ones given to erotic expressions of same-sex friendship in their letters. Hadewijch was a prominent thirteenth-century Flemish Beguine, that is, a woman who chose to devote her life to poverty and piety in communities with other women without taking the vows of a nun. A mystic as well as a poet, Hadewijch wrote letters to other beguines, one of which describes her special love for a woman named Sara: "Greet Sara also in my behalf, whether I am anything to her or nothing. Could I be fully all that in my love I wish to be for her, I would gladly do so; and I shall do so fully, however she may treat me.... She is well aware, however, that she could be a comfort to me, both in this life of exile and in the other life in bliss" (qtd. in Matter 156). Hadewijch suffers from a love for Sara that resembles courtly love, in which the beloved is indifferent to the lover's suffering. Like Aelred, Hadewijch would mostly likely consider her love for Sara a "spiritual" one, but it has all the rhetorical markings of romantic love, as well.

Another famous mystic, poet, composer, and playwright from Germany, Hildegard of Bingen (1098–1179), wrote a particularly desperate letter to one of her nuns known as Richardis with whom she had been close friends for ten years, but who finally left her community to take up a position as abbess elsewhere. In a letter to Richardis, Hildegard expresses the profound grief of her loss: "Woe is me, mother, woe is me, daughter, why have you forsaken me like an orphan? I so loved the nobility of your character, your wisdom, your chastity, your spirit, and indeed every aspect of your life." Richardis, who was younger than Hildegard, died suddenly at the age of twenty-eight, and her brother wrote Hildegard of the nun's deathbed profession of love for her: "Thus I ask as earnestly as I can, if I have any right to ask, that you love her as much as she loved you, and if she appeared to have any fault – which indeed was mine, not hers – at least have regard for the tears that she shed for your cloister, which many witnessed. And if death had not prevented, she would have come to you as soon as she was able to get permission" (Hildegard 48–49). Hildegard graciously responds, forgiving the brother for his role in Richardis's move to another convent and surrenders Richardis to her own rival, God.

Poetry of Same-Sex Desire

Passionate friendship, as the previous section attests, looks to us very much like sexual desire. Even in a religious culture that strongly condemned sexual acts, poetry of passionate desire between men (and a few women) nevertheless thrived in Latin, the language of the medieval church. An anonymous twelfth-century nun writes to a companion nun, lamenting their separation and urging her return in language that taps conventional idioms of love poetry:

> I find nothing now that I could compare with your love, sweet beyond honey and honeycomb, compared with which the brightness of god and silver is tarnished. What more? In you is all gentleness, all perfection, so my spirit languishes perpetually by your absence. You are devoid of the gall of any faithlessness, you are sweeter than milk and honey, you are peerless among thousands. I love you more than any. You alone are my love and longing, you the sweet cooling of my mind, no joy for me anywhere without you.
>
> (qtd. in Murray 211)

In another poem from the same period, another nun "aches" for her beloved G. to return to her, recalling "the kisses you gave me, / The way you refreshed my little breasts with sweet words. / I would like to die / Since I cannot see you" (Stehling 105). Both poems engage in the conventional idealization of the beloved, but the second poem invests that idealization with a frisson of sensuality.

Marbod of Rennes (ca. 1035–1123), a bishop of Rennes in France, wrote several poems about youthful male beauty. One poem, written from the perspective of an older man to a younger one, issues the kind of warning that poets have directed at female lovers for centuries, known as *carpe diem*, "seize the day" (while you are young):

> This flesh is now so smooth, so milky, so unblemished,
> So good, so handsome, so slippery, so tender.
> Yet the time will come when it will become ugly and rough,
> When this flesh, dear boyish flesh, will become worthless.
>
> (Stehling 33)

Baudri of Bourgueil (1046–1130), a Benedictine monk, also praises a young boy's "delicate cheeks, blond hair, and modest mouth," noting his sweet voice "could be a boy's or a girl's." He delights in how "the touch of your snow-white body sports with my hands," but these expressions of desire turn out to be a prelude to a headlong assault on the boy's disdain and "intractable heart" (Stehling 39, 41).

Medieval Iberia, a heterogeneous culture made up of Muslims, Jews, and Christians in the territories of modern Spain and Portugal, also produced poetry featuring sex between men, but with a difference: some poets used sodomy satirically as a way of demonstrating their own poetic virtuosity. These poems often use sodomy as a form of invective and power play, but at the same time, they complicate the very cultural idioms they employ. In one poem the poet spars with another man who threatens to bring a lawsuit against him by retorting, "If you put it to me, so will I put it to you / that you'll feel it all the way down to your ass" (qtd. in Blackmore 203). The contest is not about who comes out the sodomite, but who is the active agent of the sodomy. Galician poet Pero da Ponte draws a different analogy between poetry and sodomy in which he seems to acknowledge his own sodomitic experience at the same time that he condemns it in others. The poet's craft itself becomes a kind of sodomitic practice.

Strange Desire in Saints' Lives and Mystical Visions

Crossdressing saints were not uncommon among the very popular medieval genre of the saint's life. These narratives were medieval tales of religious superheroes, if you will, who exemplified not only Christian belief and devotion but often a form of political resistance as well. For female saints the gender ideology of the medieval church could be said to have necessitated a gender change. St. Jerome famously wrote: "As long as woman is for birth and children, she is different from man as body is from soul. But when she wishes to serve Christ more than the world, then she will cease to be a woman and will be called a man" (qtd. in Bullough 45). Because the feminine was associated with the body and the worldly obligations of reproduction, the female religious was expected, in effect, to renounce or transcend her own gender to aspire to holiness. Virginity provided a kind of gender transitivity for women in a way that it did not for male saints. Crossdressing female saints, therefore, simply made this ideology more explicit, but at the same time, crossdressing allowed them to be accepted into monasteries or to escape marriage. In the *Life of St. Euphrosine* (*La Vie de Sainte Euphrosine*; ca. 1200), the young girl of the title decides to disguise herself as a man in order to avoid the pressures of suitors and enter a local monastery. Instead of solving her problems, however, this move ends up inflaming all the monks with desire for the "young man," and she takes up a solitary cell for her own and their protection. In another fourteenth-century French text, Marina accedes to her father's wishes that she disguise herself as a monk (Marin) and join a monastery, but when she is accused of making a local woman pregnant as a presumed man, her disguise is thrown into crisis. Only after she dies is the "truth" of her gender discovered. Both saints' lives, along with those of two other crossdressing saints – St. Eugene and St. Pelagia – may be found in William Caxton's 1482 English translation of Jacobus de Voragine's 1275 Latin work, *The Golden Legend, or Lives of the Saints*.[3]

Another area of medieval religious culture where gender and even sexuality sometimes strayed was in the writings of medieval mystics. Mystics were people who experienced visions of God and Christ, which they either wrote down or dictated to others. In their visions of union with Christ, for example, men and women often used highly eroticized language that was not always discreetly heterosexual. The twelfth-century monk Rupert of Deutz describes climbing on an altar to embrace and kiss Christ: "I sensed how pleasing he found this gesture of love, when in the midst of the kissing he opened his mouth, so that I could kiss him the more deeply" (qtd. in Hollywood 373). For other mystics like Catherine of Siena (1347–1380), Christ's body was feminized in her visions, possessed of breasts and a wound that sometimes invited the mystic to enter into it. Catherine describes her own union with the wound of Christ:

He tenderly placed his right hand on her neck, and drew her towards the wound in his side. "Drink, daughter, from my side," he said, "and by that draught your soul shall become enraptured with such delight that your very body, which for my sake you have denied, shall be inundated with its over-flowing goodness." Drawn close in this way to the outlet of the Fountain of Life, she fastened her lips upon that sacred wound, and still more eagerly the mouth of her soul, and there she slaked her thirst.   (qtd. in Lochrie 188)

The overlaying of maternal imagery with erotic language in this passage is heightened by the rendering of Christ's wound as sexual. Catherine of Siena and Rupert of Deutz provide us with just two different examples of how medieval mystical texts often radically altered the standards of gender and sexuality in their visionary experiences of union with Christ.

Perils and Pleasures of the Unspeakable Vice

This final section addresses literary representations of gender transgression and sexual acts (real or implied) between members of the same sex. Although much of this literary evidence seems merely to reinforce religious censure of the sin of sodomy, a vice that was considered to be so powerful that even speaking its name could harm others, it is important to remember that this negative discourse rested alongside the Latin love poems, the romances, and the ideals of friendship. It was not, in other words, the "whole story" of medieval literature on gender and desire.

Dante's *Inferno* (early 1300s) provides one of the most enduring and touching images of the sodomite in hell. In Canto XV Dante meets an old friend and teacher, Brunetto Latini, whose burnt visage makes him nearly unrecognizable. Once Dante recognizes his former teacher, he laments his own memory of the "kind, paternal image of You / when, there in the world, from time to time, / You taught me how man makes himself immortal" (281). When Dante inquires who all these people are with Brunetto, he responds, "In sum, note that all of them were clerics / or great and famous scholars, befouled / in the world above by a single sin" (283). Brunetto's "scorched face" testifies to his own guilt of the same "single sin" of sodomy, but he asks Dante to remember him for his work only as he turns to join the other sodomites.

Peter Damian's *Book of Gomorrah* (1049) is responsible for creating "sodomy" as a sexual category based on his interpretation of the sin of Sodom and Gomorrah as one of sexual acts between men, rather than the sin against hospitality, as it had been traditionally read. A century later in Alan of Lille's *Complaint of Nature* (1160–65), Nature famously describes the horrors of sodomy using a forging metaphor of the hammer and anvil that spins out of his control:

> He (the sodomite) hammers on an anvil which issues no seeds. The very hammer itself shudders in horror of its anvil. He imprints on no matter the stamp of a parent-stem: rather his ploughshare scores a barren strand.   (69)

Alan means for his metaphor to illustrate the proper sexual relations between men and women in which the man (hammer) is active and the woman (anvil) is passive. This has to be one of the most bizarre and incoherent understandings of heterosexual sex ever written, given its emphasis on violence and the absence of penetration as its fundamental component.

Geoffrey Chaucer's character the Pardoner presents one of the most ambiguous and famous of literary representations of a sodomite. In the General Prologue to the *Canterbury Tales* (1390s) a passing remark of Chaucer's about the Pardoner's beardless face is loaded with sexual suggestion: "I believe he was a gelding (castrated male horse) or a mare (female horse)" (34). Scholars have adduced everything from eunuch to feminoid to homosexual to this veiled remark of Chaucer's; the fact that the Pardoner is one of the most corrupt and cynical of all the pilgrims in the *Canterbury Tales* seems to be related somehow to his ambiguous sexual and gender status. Chaucer's contemporary, Giovanni Boccaccio, offers a different sort of portrait in his *Decameron* (1349–52) of a man who is already known for his desire for other men. He decides to marry "to pull the wool over the eyes of his fellow-citizens or to improve the low opinion they had of him, rather than because of any real wish to marry" (Boccaccio 433). When he discovers his wife's lover hiding in their chicken coop, he devises a three-way for all. The story ends with the young man wondering "with which of the pair he had spent the greater part of the night, the wife or the husband" (440).

Explicit references to women desiring other women or engaging in sex with them are fewer in number in medieval literary texts than references to male sodomy. *Le Livre de Manières* by Etienne de Fougères (1173–78) is one of the few. In his effort to capture the horror of two women having sex, he piles on the metaphors to humorous effect:

> They do their jousting act in couples
> and go at it at full tilt;
> at the game of thigh-fencing
> they lewdly share their expenses.

> They're not all from the same mold:
> one lies still and the other makes busy,
> one plays cock and the other the hen
> and each one plays her role.　　　(qtd. in Clark 166–67)

The same issues of gender assignment according to activity or passivity in the sexual act raised by Alan of Lille are implicit here as well.

Not all literary representations of sex between women were so derisive as Etienne de Fougères's women jousting without lances. Two medieval versions of Ovid's tale "Iphis and Ianthe" from the *Metamorphoses* tell the story of a woman raised as a man who becomes betrothed to another woman. In the English version in John Gower's *Confessio Amantis* (*The Lover's Confession*; 1390–92), Iphis is disguised as a male from birth by her mother because her husband had threatened to kill the baby if it was not a boy. Although Ovid's Iphis is aware of the monstrosity of her love for Ianthe, Gower's Iphis is innocent of the "problem" with loving Ianthe. In fact, he suggests that Nature "compels them to practice / That thing which was entirely unknown to them," meaning sex (Gower, bk. 2, ll. 486–87). Only at this point in Gower's story does Nature, taking pity on their "great love," transform Iphis into a man in mid-kiss. The tale's heterosexual resolution, however, does not erase the same-sex desire that inspired it and that Gower presents as innocent and natural. The French version of the story, *Yde et Olive* (fourteenth century), recount's Yde's adoption of the male disguise to escape her father's incestuous love for her.[4] Yde finds herself later in the same predicament as Iphis, and she, too, is finally miraculously re-gendered as a man.

The "Iphis and Ianthe" story compares with the more famous thirteenth-century romance *The Romance of Silence*. This fascinating romance tackles issues of inheritance, the role of nature and nurture in gender development, and desire between women. "Silence" is the name of the main female character, whose parents decide to raise her as a boy in England because the king has forbidden girls to inherit. Her name, therefore, playfully alludes to the gender disguise she maintains throughout the poem. The problems for Silence arise not in the carrying out her chivalric role – she becomes an accomplished knight and minstrel – but in the face of a woman's attraction to her. When she rejects the woman, she is accused of rape, and Merlin finally rescues her by revealing to all that she is a woman, not a man. Silence dons women's clothes and marries the king, and the king lifts restrictions against women inheriting. The gender and sexual "correction" at the end of the story does not necessarily put to rest the issues of gender transitivity and sexual desire it raises.

Interrupting Modern Heterosexuality

The evidence of medieval literature in the area of gender and sexuality is surprisingly diverse and wide-ranging. Although the medieval church played an
important role in developing the gender and sexual ideologies of the Middle
Ages, the literature of the period did not always follow religious scripts.
Homosociality, passionate friendships, erotic poetry, and mystical visions – the
list could continue – constitute only a small part of the evidence for the complex, even sometimes contradictory ways gender and sexuality were understood. Sometimes orthodox, but more often surprisingly imaginative and even
transgressive in their representations of gender and sexuality, medieval texts
offer intriguing insights into the history of gender and sexuality and, at the
same time, that "altered understanding of the present" that Halperin suggests
is one of the aims of studying the past. By calling the historical reach of heteronormativity into question, medieval genders and sexualities intervene in
the conventional wisdom about the presumed longevity of heterosexuality as
a category structuring genders and other sexualities. Medieval romance likewise provides crucial insight into the ways that modern heterosexuality – and
heterosexual romance – are heavily invested in homosocial desire and same-
sex bonds in everything from the Jeff Nichols movie *Mud* (2012), which deploys
a medieval courtly love ideal in the service of Mud's bonding with the young
boy, Ellis, and his father figure, Tom Blankenship, to modern "bromance"
films. The idioms of passionate friendship and mystical desire challenge the
narrowness of modern categories of homosexual and heterosexual, even as
they confound the boundaries of erotic and spiritual attachments. Even some
of the anti-sodomitic writings, which can strike the modern reader as so, well,
medieval (meaning "homophobic" in this case), offer vital object lessons in the
ways gender and sexual categories are often self-contradictory and unstable.
Finally, the evidence of medieval texts urges an expansion of the categories by
which we recognize gender and sexuality, an attention to past differences and
similarities with respect to our own categories, and perhaps, a rethinking of
our present.

Notes

1. Also see Doan; Sautman and Sheingorn; and Burger and Kruger. In addition,
   the historical work of Bullough and Brundage has figured prominently in queer
   scholarship.
2. See also Jordan's account of sodomy's conceptualization in the eleventh
   century.

3. There are many editions of Caxton's translation online, but the only printed edition is by F. S. Ellis.
4. There is not a widely available edition of this story, although summaries of it can be found online. The work with which *Yde et Olive* is associated, *Huon de Bordeaux*, was translated into English in the sixteenth century as *The Boke of Duke Huon of Burdeaux*.

Works Cited

Alan of Lille. *The Plaint of Nature*. Trans. James Sheridan. Toronto: Pontifical Institute of Mediaeval Studies, 1980. Print.

Anselm. *Letters of Saint Anselm of Canterbury*. Trans. Walter Frölich. Kalamazoo: Cistercian, 1988. Print.

Beowulf. Trans. Seamus Heaney. *The Norton Anthology of English Literature, Vol. A: The Middle Ages*. Ed. Alfred David and James Simpson. New York: Norton, 2006. 29–100. Print.

Blackmore, Josiah. "The Poets of Sodom." *Queer Iberia: Sexualities, Cultures, and Crossings from the Middle Ages to the Renaissance*. Durham: Duke UP, 1999. 195–221. Print.

Boccaccio, Giovanni. *The Decameron*. Trans. G. H. McWilliam. New York: Penguin, 1995. Print.

The Boke of Duke Huon of Burdeaux. Ed. Sir Sidney Lee. London: Early English Text Society 1882–83. Print.

Boswell, John. *Christianity, Social Tolerance and Homosexuality: Gay People in Western Europe from the Beginning of the Christian Era to the Fourteenth Century*. Chicago: U of Chicago P, 1981. Print.

Bullough, Vern L. "Transvestism in the Middle Ages." Bullough and Brundage, *Sexual* 43–54.

Bullough, Vern L., and James Brundage, eds. *Handbook of Medieval Sexuality*. New York: Garland, 2000. Print.

Sexual Practices and the Medieval Church. New York: Prometheus, 1982. Print.

Burger, Glenn, and Steven F. Kruger, eds. *Queering the Middle Ages*. Minneapolis: U of Minnesota P, 2001. Print.

Burgwinkle, William. *Sodomy, Masculinity, and Law in Medieval Literature: France and England, 1050–1230*. Cambridge: Cambridge UP, 2004. Print.

Caxton, William. *The Golden Legend, or Lives of the Saints*. Ed. F. S. Ellis. New York: Temple Classics, 1900. Print.

Chaucer, Geoffrey. *The Riverside Chaucer*. 3rd Ed. Ed. Larry D. Benson. Oxford: Oxford UP, 1987. Print.

Clark, Robert L. A. "Jousting without a Lance: The Condemnation of Female Homoeroticism in the *Livre des manières*." Sautman and Sheingorn 143–78.

Dante. *The Inferno*. Trans. Robert Hollander and Jean Hollander. New York: Anchor, 2000. Print.

Dinshaw, Carolyn. *Getting Medieval: Sexualities and Communities, Pre- and Postmodern*. Durham: Duke UP, 1999. Print.

Doan, Laura, ed. *The Lesbian Postmodern*. New York: Columbia UP, 1994. Print.

Foucault, Michel. *The History of Sexuality, Volume 1: An Introduction.* Trans. Robert Hurley. New York: Random House, 1978. Print.

Gower, John. *Confessio Amantis.* Vol. 2. Ed. Russell A. Peck. Kalamazoo: Medieval Institute, 2006. Print.

Halperin, David M. *How to Do the History of Homosexuality.* Chicago: U of Chicago P, 2002. Print.

Hildegard of Bingen. *Personal Correspondence of Hildegard of Bingen.* Trans. Joseph L. Baird. Oxford: Oxford UP, 2006. Print.

Hollywood, Amy. "Feminist Studies." *The Blackwell Companion to Christian Spirituality.* Ed. Arthur Holder. Oxford: Blackwell, 2005. 363–86. Print.

Jaeger, C. Stephen. *Ennobling Love: In Search of a Lost Sensibility.* Philadelphia: U of Pennsylvania P, 1999. Print.

Jordan, Mark D. *The Invention of Sodomy in Christian Theology.* Chicago: U of Chicago P, 1997. Print.

Klosowska, Anna. *Queer Love in the Middle Ages.* New York: Palgrave, 2005. Print.

The Lais of Marie de France. Trans. Glyn S. Burgess and Keith Busby. New York: Penguin, 1986. Print.

Lochrie, Karma. "Mystical Acts, Queer Tendencies." *Constructing Medieval Sexuality.* Ed. Karma Lochrie, Peggy McCracken, and James A. Schultz. Minneapolis: U of Minnesota P, 1997. 180–200. Print.

Malory, Sir Thomas. *Le Morte Darthur: The Winchester Manuscript.* Ed. Helen Cooper. Oxford: Oxford UP, 1998. Print.

Matter, E. Ann. "My Sister, My Spouse: Woman-Identified Women in Medieval Christianity." *The Boswell Thesis: Essays on Christianity, Social Tolerance, and Homosexuality.* Ed. Mathew Kuefler. Chicago: U of Chicago P, 2006. 152–66. Print.

Murray, Jacqueline. "Twice Marginal and Twice Invisible: Lesbianism in the Middle Ages." Bullough and Brundage, *Handbook* 191–222.

Pugh, Tison. *Sexuality and Its Queer Discontents in Middle English Literature.* New York: Palgrave, 2008. Print.

Sautman, Francesca Canade, and Pamela Sheingorn, eds. *Same-Sex Love and Desire among Women in the Middle Ages.* London: Palgrave, 2001. Print.

Schultz, James A. *Courtly Love, the Love of Courtliness, and the History of Sexuality.* Chicago: U of Chicago P, 2006. Print.

Sedgwick, Eve K. *Between Men: English Literature and Male Homosocial Desire.* New York: Columbia UP, 1985. Print.

Epistemology of the Closet. Berkeley: U of California P, 1990. Print.

Silence: A Thirteenth-Century Romance. Ed. and trans. Sarah Roche-Mahdi. East Lansing: Michigan State UP, 1999. Print.

Southern, Richard W. *St. Anselm: A Portrait in a Landscape.* Cambridge: Cambridge UP, 1990. Print.

Stehling, Thomas, trans. *Medieval Latin Poems of Male Love and Friendship.* New York: Garland, 1984. Print.

The Wanderer. The Norton Anthology of English Literature, Vol. A: The Middle Ages. Ed. Alfred David and James Simpson. New York: Norton, 2006. 111–14. Print.

6

Male-Male Love in Classical Arabic Poetry

THOMAS BAUER

Clouds before the Sun: A Late Representative of a Millenary Tradition

rūḥī fidā'u 'idhārin ḥalla wajnata man fāqa l-kawākiba shamsan thumma aqmārā
law-lā l-'idhāru la-mā stā'at lanā muqalun ilā muḥayyāhu bāhī l-ḥusni ibṣārā
ka-sh-shamsi lam tuṭiqi l-abṣāru ru'yatahā law-lā saḥābun laṭīfun ḥawlahā dārā

I would give everything for the sprouting beard that settled on the cheeks of
   one who – being a sun – is superior to stars and even moons.
If it weren't for his beard, our eyes could not look into his face with its radiant beauty,
Just like the sun, which our glances could not bear if fine clouds did not
   surround it.

This epigram of three lines is one of hundreds of thousands of love poems
on young men that were composed in the millennium between 800 and 1800
in Arabic. It is not only in this respect that it is quite an average poem. The
poem presents a beautiful although not very original image of the beloved
making use of time-honored similes. The beloved's face is compared to the
sun – an object of comparison for beautiful faces that was already in use in
the pre-Islamic period. As a sun, it outshines the other celestial bodies – stars
and moons – that are other potential objects of comparison for beautiful men
and women. But then another phenomenon of the sky comes in, and it is a
more original one: the young man's sprouting beard is likened to *clouds*, which
together with the sun, moons, and stars forms what is known in Arabic stylistics as a nice "harmonious choice of images" ("murā'āt an-naẓīr"; Heinrichs
658). It is only thanks to the clouds that we can look into the sun's face. If the
hyperbolic simile that equates the beloved's face with a sun is taken literally,
a simple poetic syllogism proves that the young man's beard is a prerequisite
for looking into his face. Consequently, it is the beard that makes him loveable

in the first place because without looking into his face one could hardly fall in love with him.

The poem belongs to a category that could be called *apologetic beard epigrams*. In these epigrams of mostly two or three lines, a poet apologizes for his beloved's growing beard. Although the apologetic dimension is not very prominent in our sample poem, every reader would have realized that it belongs to this tradition. As such, the poem is not remarkable because there are thousands of epigrams on this subject. What makes it remarkable, however, is the date of its composition. Lebanese poet ʿAbdallaṭīf Fatḥallāh (1766–1844) composed it in the year 1815 (no. 510). This makes it one of the last poems of its kind. A few decades later, a thousand-year history of homoerotic poetry in Arabic would come to an end.

There is no other premodern literature in which homoerotic texts are as numerous and as central as they are in classical Arabic – Persian being the only serious rival. It is therefore impossible to deal with the whole of homoerotic literature in classical Arabic in the course of this chapter, even superficially. Therefore, I will confine myself to presenting the conditions that made an epigram like ʿAbdallaṭīf's possible. The following section will deal with the early history of male-male love poetry in Arabic, followed by a section on the social norms underpinning it. The subject of the *beard*, the central topic of our poem, will be addressed in this context. Another section will deal with the stunning career of erotic epigrams from the Ayyubid period onward, and after a "mystical intermezzo," a final section will ask why ʿAbdallaṭīf's epigram was one of the last of its kind.

Among the subjects that there is not room here to discuss are prose literature, including love stories and prose works in the form of the *maqāma* (rhymed prose with interspersed verse; see Rowson, "Two"), popular literature including poems in the vernacular and stories like those of the *Thousand and One Nights*, and literature on the love between women, which is far less visible than that about men. Love between women did leave its trace in literature. Indeed, one of the legendary Arabic couples of myth (like Laylā and Majnūn) was a female-female pair (Hind bint Nuʿmān, princess of al-Ḥīra, and Zarqāʾ [Amer 18]). Nevertheless female-female love hardly plays a role in love poetry and the reason for that is simple: while women *did* compose poetry, they were not supposed to *publish* it, and those who did were addressing a male audience. Furthermore, I will limit myself to literature in the narrower sense of the word and not take scientific, religious, and legal texts into account.

A Rose on the Cheek: The Evolution of Homoerotic Poetry

Polythematic odes that open with a melancholic reminiscence of a past love affair are among the oldest Arabic poems we know, dating to the sixth century. It is only after the transformation of Arab society in the wake of Islam's advent and the Arab conquests of the seventh century that poems that were exclusively about love started to be composed. In these poems, a love affair was no longer necessarily a thing of the past. Rather the poet could express his persistent love for a woman, a love that could either be unfulfilled (as in most of the poems in a Bedouin context, so-called *'udhrī* [or "chaste"] love) or fulfilled. Poems of the latter variety flourished in the affluent towns of the Hejaz at the end of the century. This new type of love poetry soon became popular in the towns of Syria and Iraq, especially Kufa, Basra, and after its foundation in 762, in Baghdad. The new urban culture of the Abbasid empire, which rose in 749, not only brought about a new literary style, but also an unprecedented flourishing of *ghazal*, "love poetry," which would remain the most popular genre of Arabic poetry for many centuries (see Bauer and Neuwirth). Another innovation came about that would be no less far reaching: for the first time in Arabic love poetry, the beloved did not have to be a female, but could also be a male.

The poet who enabled the breakthrough of homoerotic love poetry was Abū Nuwās, who was born near Ahvaz (in modern-day Iran) around 755 and died in Baghdad ca. 813 (see Wagner). He was not the first poet to compose homoerotic poetry. His teacher and presumed lover Wāliba ibn Hubāb (d. ca. 786) was his forerunner in this regard, but it was Abū Nuwās who became famous and influential beyond compare. He was a prolific author of love poems, which he directed to both women and – the larger part – to male youths. The redactor of Abū Nuwās's *Dīwān* (poetry collection), Abū Bakr aṣ-Ṣūlī (d. ca. 946), distributed Abū Nuwās's love poems between two separate chapters: love poems on female beloveds (*mu'annathāt*) and love poems on male beloveds (*mudhakkarāt*). This distinction has probably been more influential on modern scholarship than it was in Arabic literary history, however. Although almost all poets after Abū Nuwās composed love poems for beloveds of both genders (and a number of poems in which the beloved's gender remains ambiguous), a classification like aṣ-Ṣūlī's was hardly ever applied again.

Abū Nuwās soon became one of the most famous Arabic poets of all time. In addition to love poetry, *khamriyyāt* (sg. *khamriyya*) "wine-poems" were another genre that became closely associated with him (see Kennedy). Abū Nuwās was a pioneer in creating poems in which wine and wine drinking are the sole subject. In many of these poems, erotic, especially homoerotic, scenes between the speaker and a beautiful *sāqī* "cup-bearer" are central. As in homoerotic love poetry, it was again Abū Nuwās who would establish the conventions of wine poetry for centuries to come. No other language can boast of a comparable number of elaborated and highly artistic wine poems as Arabic and Persian, the Islamic prohibition on wine notwithstanding.

In the twentieth century, Abū Nuwās became the most prominent – and in the West most often translated – Arabic poet. The first *khamriyya* in his *Dīwān*, to mention just one poem, has been translated more than thirty times into Western languages (see Wagner). His homoerotic poems were translated less often, but intensely discussed, especially in modern Arab literary criticism. Here discussion evolved around questions such as was Abū Nuwās "homo-sexual" and what psychological reasons could be detected to explain that (see Massad 76–98). Author-centered approaches, however, failed to take notice of the fact that Abū Nuwās's poems would have been forgotten if they had not met with the expectations of a large public. Besides, the almost com-plete neglect of Arabic love poetry produced in the centuries thereafter made "homosexuality" Abū Nuwās's individual "problem" and detracted from the fact that homoerotic love was a favorite poetic subject throughout the subse-quent centuries.

Almost simultaneously with Abū Nuwās homoerotic love poetry became an established genre of "high literature." Wāliba ibn Hubāb's bohemian life-style and literary output were considered provocative and still in Abū Nuwās a libertine attitude is undeniable. But a great many of Abū Nuwās's love poems are simply very beautiful and affecting and there is nothing in them that could be read as a provocation or a conscious violation of norms. The following four-liner is a rather typical example of Abū Nuwās's *ghazal*. The first two lines describe the appearance of a self-confident, coquettish youth, "clad in beauty." The last two lines describe him with the most common images used for beauty, again forming a "harmonious choice of images": A sand-hill (= the backside) upon which a twig (= the elegantly moving upper body) grows, above which the moon (= the face) shines:

wa-'ārī l-wajhi min ḥulali l-'uyūbī   ghadā fī thawbi fattānin rabībī
tafarrada bi-l-jamāli wa-qāla: hādhā   mina d-dunyā wa-ladhdhatihā naṣībī
barāhu llāhu ḥīna barā hilālan   wa-ḥiqfan 'inda munqata'i l-qadībī
fa-yahtazzu l-hilālu 'alā qaḍībin   wa-yahtazzu l-qaḍību 'alā kathībī

When he, brought up in luxury, appeared, his face was naked,
    bare of blemish, while he was clad in clothes of seduction.
He was unique in beauty and said: This is my share of this
    world and its pleasures.
And God, when he created him, created him as a
    moon and a sand dune at the base of a twig.
Now the moon sways on top of a twig, and the
    twig on top of a sand-hill.   (Abū Nuwās 168, no. 32)

Ghazal poets of the ninth and tenth centuries are legion. *Ghazal*, in the main homoerotic, became the most popular genre, rivaled only by the more official and public affair of panegyric poetry. No poet could escape composing *ghazal*, and a number of poets did nothing but (see Bauer, *Liebe*).

Only three poets out of dozens shall be mentioned here. The first is Abū Tammām (ca. 804–45), who became famous as a panegyrist of high-ranking officials and the Abbāsid caliph al-Muʿtaṣim. He was a controversial figure, not because of the content of his poetry, but on account of his daring mannerist style, which inspired Ibn al-Muʿtazz (see later in this chapter) to write a treatise defending him. That treatise became the founding document of Arabic stylistics. Yet Abū Tammām also wrote love poetry, mainly, but not exclusively, homoerotic, which was quoted again and again in Arabic anthologies of the following centuries but completely neglected by Western scholarship until the 1990s. His *ghazal* poems are short (mostly four-liners), elegant, stylistically sophisticated although unmannered, and of great musicality. With Abū Tammām, homoerotic love poetry had definitely reached the rank of established "high literature" without any hint of provocation or contestation of norms.

Poet al-Khubzaruzzī (d. ca. 938), "the rice-bread baker," demonstrates that homoerotic love poetry in the style of Abū Nuwās and Abū Tammām was no longer limited to elite circles but had become part of popular literature. Al-Khubzaruzzī gained more attention for his love poems than his rice-bread. The story goes that the youths of Basra frequented his shop in the hope of catching his eye so that he would portray them in his love poems, which are exclusively homoerotic: "His style is described as simple and unsophisticated, but delicate and effective" (Rowson, "al-Khubzaruzzī" 443).

Both the rice-bread baker and Khālid al-Kātib (d. 876 or 883), a functionary in the Abbasid administration and author of a large number of love poems of four lines (see Arazi), are extraordinary in that they composed love poems that were exclusively homoerotic. Abbāsid prince Ibn al-Muʿtazz, on the other hand, treated both sexes in his *ghazal*, as did the majority of poets subsequently. Born in 861 in the caliphal palace in Samarra, he spent a life dedicated to poetry and literary criticism until he was himself proclaimed caliph in 908 and was murdered the following day. In spite of his premature death, Ibn al-Mu'tazz was not only the founder of the scholarly discipline of Arabic stylistics, he was also the creator of some of the most breathtaking similes and conceits in Arabic poetry. His poetry acquired canonical status.

In the following short *ghazal* poem, the speaker expresses his perplexity about the beloved's beauty in three exclamations. In the first, his cheeks are compared with a rose; in the second, there is no obvious comparison, but the upper body's "bending" and "straightness" strongly suggest the twig image, which is made more powerful as it is not explicitly mentioned. In the third exclamation, the beloved's teeth are compared to pearls. As in the first line, its continuation is not a comparison but describes the effect of the beloved's eyes as "magic." The last line describes the effect of this beauty on the lover: he weeps and is sleepless. It remains open, however, which of the signs of beauty causes which effect. Again the poet prefers allusion to direct expression. A contemporary reader, however, would have known that "pearls" were not only a common object of comparison for teeth, but for tears as well:

> *ayyu wardin fī khaddi dhāka l-ghazāli   ayyu maylin fī qaddihī wa-'tidāli*
> *ayyū durrin idhā tabassama yubdī   -hi wa-siḥrin fī ṭarfihī wa-dalāli*
> *fa-li-hādhā jarat dumū'u jufūnī   wa-li-hādhā ṭālat 'alayya l-layāli*

> What a rose on the cheek of this gazelle! What a bending,
>   what straightness in his stature!
> What pearls does he reveal when he smiles! What magic,
>   what coquetry lies in his glances!
> These make the tears flow from my eyelids, those make
>   the nights pass all too slowly for me!   (qtd. in Bauer, "Arabic")

Donkeys Ridden with Reins: Social Norms

Abū Tammām was not only the author of elegant and sophisticated love poems, but also a series of "beard poems of hardly any literary value," as a near-contemporary critic remarked (see Bauer, *Liebe* 181 fn 88). They are addressed to his beloved 'Abdallāh, who is reviled first for having forsaken Abū Tammām, and second for having grown a beard that even his use of depilatory cream could not hide. The literary value of these verses may indeed be minor, but they are an interesting early testimony of the perception of male-male love relations.

From Abū Tammām's poems and a host of other sources, we learn that in premodern Middle Eastern societies, the social roles of the lover (*muḥibb*) and the beloved (*maḥbūb*) were precisely distinguished. As is common in patriarchal societies, all social roles were defined around the basis of the adult male. At the same time, sexual relations were understood almost exclusively through the axis of penetration (and this is why female-female relations were given comparatively little attention). Consequently, the standard sexuality of an adult male was to be a penetrator. The sex of the penetrated partner did not affect the active partner's reputation. As for the passive partner, her/his passive role was not considered abasing as long as she/he did not occupy the role of an adult male. The outward manifestation of a man's adulthood was his beard. For the average male-male relation this meant that a lover's beloved should be younger and not yet have a full beard. Consequently, love between bearded men was problematic, not on account of homophobia, nor religious reasons, but because it troubled the image of masculinity in the patriarchal worldview: which member of the pair was the lover, in other words, the "real" male, which the beloved?

To avoid ambiguity, the lover was expected to end the affair and transform his love relationship into pure friendship. Perhaps Abū Tammām would have been less harsh with 'Abdallāh if he had acted according to this norm. If he, having already grown a dense beard, would have given up being Abū Tammām's beloved and taken a beloved of his own, his former lover might have been sad, but he would hardly have reacted in such a drastic way. What 'Abdallāh did instead was to abandon Abū Tammām for another *lover*, which not only violated Abū Tammām's feelings of affection, but also social norms. This is how we can understand the poet's harsh reaction, which remains unique in Arabic literary history.

This was not the normal way relationships were to end. Poetry tells a different story. Obviously, the moment the beloved grew a beard regularly caused emotional crises. What if love persisted despite the beard? And, of course, one does not simply grow a beard in a single moment but over some time, a period of ambiguity. Because premodern Islamic culture was, as a rule, rather tolerant of ambiguity, it was this period of the beard growing gradually more dense that became, in the form of *apologetic beard epigrams*, one of the most popular topics in Arabic love poetry (see Bauer, *Kultur*).

Arabic poetry was not the first literary tradition to deal with the topic, however. The Greek poet Straton (probably second century CE) already composed epigrams to apologize for the sprouting beard of his beloved. Despite the beard, says Straton, his beloved is still as charming as ever. The subject of the sprouting beard accompanied the whole history of Arabic homoerotic poetry, from Abū Nuwās (where it played only a marginal role) until the end as is seen in the poem by ʿAbdallaṭīf that began this chapter. In early poems, the line of argument was similar to that of Straton: despite his beard, the beloved is still attractive. Soon Arabic poets learned to argue in a more sophisticated way. The beard was compared with beautiful things, explained by fantastic etiologies and poetic syllogisms: if the moon is beautiful despite its spots, the same is true of a face; the beard is not a beard but, rather, ants that are attracted by the sweet honey of the beloved's saliva; if you settled in a barren country, you would not move away when spring flowers grow, or, as in ʿAbdallaṭīf's epigram, the beard is like clouds thanks to which it becomes possible to look into the sun of the beloved's face. Arabic poets never ran out of new similes and conceits to present the sprouting beard as something beautiful. Shams ad-Dīn an-Nawājī (1386–1455) even compiled a whole volume of beard epigrams entitled *Khalʿ al-ʿidhār fi waṣf al-ʿidhār*: "Throwing off all restraint in describing the sprouting beard." The collection soon became extremely popular but is – unsurprisingly – still only available in manuscript (Bauer, "al-Nawājī" 328–29).

In many *ghazal* poems, the sprouting beard was no longer treated in an apologetic way, but as an undisputed feature of beauty. Love for fully bearded men, however, had no place in *ghazal*, and had to be treated in another genre called *mujūn*, which comprises funny and provocative texts about forbidden pleasures and embarrassing mishaps. Many if not the majority of *mujūn* poems are about sex. A poet may indulge in graphic descriptions of sexual acts, may boast of a conscious violation of social norms, talk about masturbation, or complain about impotence and other problems preventing good sex. Sex relations treated in *mujūn* form could be either hetero- or homosexual. In the Abbasid period, the former predominated, featured, among others, by the most famous *mujūn* poet, Ibn al-Ḥajjāj (d. 1000). As for *mujūn* treating same-sex relations, sex with bearded men recurs often. Popular poet Ibrāhīm al-Miʿmār (d. 1348), a Cairene mason and architect who was famous for his *mujūn*, boasted of his desire for men with all degrees of beard growth:

> *yā lāʾimī fi dhā l-ʿidhāri ftinī*   *hal yurkabu l-jaḥshu bi-lā miqwadih*
> *uḥibbu arbāba l-liḥā shahwatan*   *wa-kullu man liḥyatuhū fi yadih*
>
> You blame me for desiring one whose beard has sprouted.
>   Tell me your verdict: Can a young donkey be ridden without its rein?
> I go crazy for men with full beards; yeah, even those who can
>   grip theirs with their hands!   (qtd. in Bauer, "Dignity")

The Goldsmith's Kiss: Epigrams about a World of Beauty

When Abū Nuwās composed a love poem about a soldier, he was certainly unaware that countless other poems discussing the beloved's profession would follow in subsequent centuries. The first to collect a whole series of poems of this kind was probably the famous *littérateur* Abū Manṣūr ath-Thaʿālibī (961–1038). His *Book of Youths* (*Kitāb al-Ghilmān*) seems to have been lost (see Talib), but his other works preserve many poems of this kind by him and his contemporaries, among them a poem on a beautiful goldsmith by a certain Abū Bakr an-Nasawī, a law scholar:

> *wa-shādinin ṣāʾighin hāma l-fuʾādu bihī   wa-ḥubbuhū fī sawādi l-qalbi qad rasakhā*
> *yā laytanī kuntu minfākhan ʿalā famihī   kay-mā uqabbila fāhu kulla-mā nafakhā*
>
> My heart is passionately in love with a goldsmith fawn.
>   My love for him has taken firm root in the bottom of my heart.
> Oh would that I were the bellows at his mouth, so that I could
>   kiss his lips every time he blows.   (Thaʿālibī 230)

After the Ayyubids came to power in 1169, the center of Arabic literature shifted from Iraq to Syria and Egypt, and in the more bourgeois atmosphere of the cities of the Ayyubid and Mamluk (1250–1517) empires, epigrams became one of the most popular literary forms. In this new urban ambience, epigrams in the vein of the goldsmith poem flourished. In later Persian and Turkish poetry they became known as *shahrāshūb* or *şehrengiz* "upsetting the town" (de Bruijn, "Shahrangīz" 212). Because there is no Arabic term, I will use the Persian *shahrāshūb* for the corresponding phenomenon in Arabic literature. *Shahrāshūb* poems are "based on the representation of the beloved as a youthful artisan or member of another social group having such marked features as to allow a poet to make fanciful allusions to this quality" (de Bruijn, *Of Piety* 7). In Arabic literature from the Ayyubid period onward, poems of the *shahrāshūb* type were often grouped together in larger collections. The author of the earliest collection of this kind that has been preserved is the rather unknown Syrian poet Ibn ash-Sharīf Daftarkhʷān (d. 1257), who composed a thousand and one epigrams on beautiful youths (mostly three-liners) and published them under the title *The Thousand and One Youths* (*Alf ghulām wa-ghulām*). As a sequel to it, he produced another volume on girls, entitled *The Thousand and One Girls* (*Alf jāriya wa-jāriya*), accordingly. Similar collections followed suit, either of a poet's own epigrams or anthologies of epigrams by different poets, most authors confining themselves to a hundred beloveds or to an undefined number. Most authors wrote about both male and female beloveds, and sometimes they did so in two separate sister works.

The central theme is the beloved's profession. *Shahrāshūb* epigrams are consequently an important (and still largely untapped) source for the history of crafts in the Middle East (perhaps even more important for the history of women's labor than for men's). They are not limited to the crafts or professions, though. The most popular anthology of this kind is probably the *Gazelles' Pastures: On Beautiful Youths (Marātiʿ al-ghizlān fī l-ḥisān min al-ghilmān)* by Shams ad-Dīn an-Nawājī (see Bauer, "al-Nawājī" 329). Unlike other authors, an-Nawājī did not compose a counterpart on women. The book, which comprises about two thousand epigrams by different poets mainly from the Ayyubid and Mamluk period, starts with a chapter of epigrams on young men holding positions in the administration, the military, scholarship and education, or a religious office. A large section on beautiful craftsmen follows, in which more than two hundred trades and crafts are represented. A chapter in which wine merchants, cupbearers, gamblers, prisoners, and youths who do something special such as picking apricots or walking in the court of a mosque follows. Another chapter treats the inevitable subject of the beard, augmented by subchapters on moles and other individual characteristics, among them a series of bodily defects such as pockmarks, wounds, a hunchback, blindness, and illness. A selection of epigrams on beloveds who have died concludes the book with a melancholic tone.

A book like this transforms the whole world, despite its shortcomings and defects, into a world of beauty and erotic attraction. Even people who did not match the current ideal of beauty – because they had blue eyes or were lame, one-eyed, or leprous – were presented as charming and lovable creatures (see Richardson). The large number of manuscripts preserved of an-Nawājī's book (which remains nonetheless unpublished) and the sheer number of epigrams composed during these centuries (including Persian and Ottoman-Turkish counterparts) demonstrate the appeal these poems had for a broad public. In their celebration of human beauty and literary ingenuity, they were not meant to be autobiographical, but nevertheless, one notes that judge and religious scholar Ibn Ḥajar al-ʿAsqalānī composed several epigrams on mosque personnel such as lamplighters, whereas architect Ibrāhīm al-Miʿmār paid more attention to stonecutters, as in the following epigram. Here the point of the epigram is rather simple and consists in deploying technical vocabulary. The word *shāqūf*, which is the rhyming word in the second line, is a special term for a stonecutter's sledgehammer:

yā ḥusna ḥajjārin lahū nāzirun safku dami l-ʿushshāqi maʿlūfuh
yafʿalu fī l-aḥshāʾi aḍʿāfa mā yafʿalu fī l-aḥjārī shāqūfuh

Oh beautiful stonecutter whose eyes are used to shed his many lovers' blood!
They do twice as much damage to hearts than his sledgehammer does to stones![1]

These epigrams usually conclude with a punch line related in one or another way to the beloved's profession or another specific trait. In many cases this is a play on words that does not lend itself to translation. In the following epigram, Ibn Nubāta al-Miṣri (1287–1366), considered by many the greatest poet of his time, portrays a bird hunter who robs everyone's sleep. In the poem, the word *karākī* "cranes" can also be interpreted as the word *karā* "sleep" plus the personal pronoun *kī* "your," thus "your sleep":

wa-mūliʿin bi-fikhākhin yamudduhā wa-shibākī
qālat liya l-ʿaynu mādhā yaṣīdu qultu karākī

His passion is setting snares and laying traps.
My eye said to me: What is it he hunts? I answered: *your sleep* / cranes.[2]

A common way of creating such a point that was already in use in Abbasid times was to playfully transfer literary similes into the real world in order to create a paradox based on pseudo-logical argumentation. In the Ayyubid period, poet Ibn Maṭrūḥ (1196–1251) used the common comparisons of temple-curls with scorpions, locks of hair with snakes, and beautiful faces with the moon to wonder whether his beloved, whose beauty is extraterrestrial, could have really been bitten by a snake:

qālū ḥabībuka malsūʿun fa-qultu lahum min ʿaqrabi ṣ-ṣudghi aw min ḥayyati sh-shaʿarī?
fa-qīla bal min afāʿī l-arḍi qultu lahum min ayna tasʿā afāʿī l-arḍi li-l-qamarī?

They said: Your sweetheart has been bitten! I said: By the scorpion of his temple-curl or the snake of his hair?
No, they said, by the vipers of the earth! Oh but how, I replied, could the earthly vipers have ascended to the moon?   (Ibn Maṭrūḥ 84 no. 63).

Epigrams of the *shahrāshūb* type were composed by professional poets and amateurs alike. The final example may be one of the latter. Its author is not known, its point is simple but convincing, and it reveals an interesting attitude toward painting in a society in which images were allegedly prohibited:

ʿalā fī ṣanʿati t-taṣwīri badrun   yuqābilu kulla makhlūqin bi-shibhih
yuṣawwiru kulla mā fī l-arḍi ḥusnan   wa-yuʿjizu an yuṣawwira mithla ḥusnih

A full moon whose skill as a painter has ascended, he provides every creature with its counterpart.
He paints everything on earth with beauty, but he's incapable of painting his own beauty.[3]

Battleground of Hearts and Glances: A Mystical Intermezzo

Arabic poetry began as a purely profane literature in pre-Islamic times and remained one of the most important secular discourses in the Islamic era until the present day. Yet when *taṣawwuf*, Islamic mysticism, emerged, its proponents, the Sufis, felt a need to cast their feelings in a poetic mold. These were feelings of love for God, the overwhelming desire to be near him or even enter metaphysical union, their intoxication when God's presence could be felt, and their pain and feeling of being forsaken when God seemed far. As for the ascetic dimension of Sufism, the genre of ascetic poetry (*zuhd*), developed by poets like Abū l-ʿAtāhiya (748–826), provided a model. For Sufism's ecstatic side, Sufi poets reverted to the forms, ideas, and topoi of love poetry and wine poetry. A large percentage of poems by early Sufi poets like ash-Shiblī (861–945) can be read as mystical poems as well as purely profane love poems. In many later poems, this culture of ambiguity persisted, not least in the case of one the most famous Middle Eastern poets of all time, the Persian Hafez. In Western scholarship, the question of whether his poetry is profane or mystical has been discussed frequently. It appears that in a culture in which ambiguity was tolerated to a high degree, this question was less pressing and it was considered a hallmark of quality if a poem left room for interpretation.

Love poetry in the form of *ghazal* remained the most common form of mystical poetry, and, just as in the profane *ghazal*, the beloved could be either male or female. Ibn al-Fāriḍ (1181–1235) was and is still considered by most critics the greatest mystical poet in Arabic literature. In one of his six *ghazal* poems the beloved is addressed in the feminine and in the remaining five in the masculine. His *jīmiyya* is perhaps the most famous of these. In the first line, the poet complains about being mortally wounded by the beloved's glances. In Emil Homerin's translation it reads:

mā bayna muʿtaraki l-aḥdāqi wa-l-muhajī   anā l-qatīlu bilā ithmin wa-lā ḥarajī

On the battle ground
>   between hearts and glances,
>   I am slain
>   without sin or guilt.   (Homerin 84)

In a series of antitheses we learn of the ethereal nature of the beloved, again in Homerin's translation:

muhajjabin law sarā fī mithli ṭurratihī aghnat -hu ghurratuhū l-gharrā ʿani s-surujī
wa-in ḍalaltu bi-laylin min dhawāʾibihī   ahdā li-ʿaynī l-hudā ṣubḥun mina l-balajī

He is a veiled one;
>   but were he to pass in a darkness
>   black as his forelock,
>   his blazing face would suffice him light.
So if I stray for a night
>   in his black locks,
>   his brow's bright morn
>   will give guidance to my eyes.   (92)

Of course it is problematic to still call this sort of poetry "homoerotic" because the beloved is clearly no longer a *homos* to the lover. But nevertheless, it was the rich tradition of homoerotic poetry in Arabic that inspired Muslim Sufi poets and provided them with the themes, motives, and conceits to formulate their own specific experience. This was not always only poetic: some Sufis even used the practice of "gazing at beardless youths" to stimulate their mystical experience by becoming intoxicated by male beauty, a practice that was highly controversial from the very beginning. In any case, homoeroticism and Sufism remain closely connected in many ways.

An Encounter with Homophobia

For centuries, Arabic poets hailed both male and female beauty, and there can be no doubt that in doing so they met the expectations of their audience, who came from all walks of life. Numerous extraliterary statements corroborate the view that more or less all men in the premodern Middle East felt that young women and young men were equally attractive and that it was quite natural to fall in love with both. Whenever scholars argued about what was natural, it was an adult male's desire to be the passive partner in a male-male relationship that was seen to need an explanation.

Against this background, the question arises whether it is possible to speak about classical Arabic "gay" or "homosexual" literature. Arabic homoerotic literature that was composed from the eighth century onward until the period of colonialism is (1) not the expression of a *minority*, but the mainstream; (2) not a matter of *identity*, for men who fell in love with other men did not consider themselves to be extraordinary, and no one would have claimed a special identity on account of their "sexuality" (a modern Western concept at any rate); and (3) not associated with a *violation of social norms* on account of its being homoerotic, but only if both male partners are old enough to grow beards. Is it conceivable that *gay literature* is compatible with the literary taste of all men (and perhaps also women) who are interested in literature? Can gay literature affirm and accord with the imaginations of the social elite? Or is classical Arabic literature a challenge to the modern Western conception of heterosexuality and homosexuality, which may not be as universal as the modern West believes?

Before we turn to the influence of Western ideas in the nineteenth and twentieth centuries, a few words on religious norms are in order, as it is the religion of Islam that is mostly seen to be responsible for Middle Eastern homophobia today. Quranic references to the story of the people of Lot (which gave rise to the expression *liwāṭ* for anal intercourse) and the reference to a "grave sin" are less than clear. It is quite probable that they do not refer to male-male relations, though they have been commonly interpreted along these lines (see Kugle). The two most authoritative collections of *ḥadīth* (reports of the prophet Muḥammad and his companions) by al-Bukhārī and Muslim do not mention same-sex relations at all. Nonetheless, Islamic law is quite strict about sexual intercourse between people who are not linked either by marriage or concubinage. Vaginal intercourse with women who are neither a man's wives nor his slaves (*zinā*) and anal intercourse with men (*liwāṭ*, a term that is often also used for anal intercourse with a woman) are sanctioned by the most severe punishments, such as stoning to death (see Schmitt). Practical consequences, however, were less drastic. The requirements for applying a death sentence for adultery, fornication, or *liwāṭ* were extremely high. Thus far hardly any instances of adulterers being stoned to death have been recorded and according to our current knowledge, not a single man was convicted for engaging in consensual sex with another man before the twentieth century.

The influence of legal norms on literature was remarkably low. After all, falling in love with a man was not a sin, nor was composing love poetry, at least not according to mainstream society. Even the Quran provided an excellent excuse for poets who composed literature that conflicted with religious norms, saying that poets "do not do what they say" (26: 226). What was originally meant as a reproach could well be taken as an excuse. There were religious scholars who opposed erotic and bacchic poetry, though. They argued that poems of these kinds might incite people to commit sinful acts. However, poets, some of whom were themselves religious scholars, did not care much. The end of a millennium of homoerotic Arabic poetry was brought about not by religious strictures, but by the encounter with Western values and attitudes:

> Indeed, homosexual practices in Egypt came under assault by the spread of European moral, medical and disciplinary concerns. There is some evidence of direct state intervention to suppress homosexual practices in the military and the homoerotic excesses of popular culture. Far more effective in undermining the long history of social acceptance of homosexual practices in Egypt was the rise of new professional and middle classes championing the values of their European counterparts. Homosexual practices would be found incompatible with the "new" or reformed Egyptian "character" upon which the modern Egyptian "nation" was to be constructed.   (Dunne 108)

Colonialism fostered this development, and Islamic revivalism in the twentieth century finally led to the conclusion of an unspoken, unholy alliance between nationalist and allegedly Islamic virtues in the domain of sexuality.

Still there "is much research to be done in assessing the uneven consequences of ... the ways in which largely European normalizing discourses have intersected with, been resisted by and undergone changes through their encounter with indigenous cultural forms and forces" (Dunne 316). In the meantime, studies by Joseph A. Massad and Georg Klauda show convincingly how the introduction of the concept of identitary sexuality and especially the binary construct of homosexuality versus heterosexuality meant a deep incision in the perception of love and sexuality in the Middle East. In this respect, a study of the history of Middle Eastern sex might also have consequences for Western attitudes about sexuality. Contemporary Western experience shows that despite public campaigns and tremendous progress in gay rights, homophobia is by no means about to vanish. In those Middle Eastern societies in which men were supposed to find men and women equally attractive and male-male sex relations were a matter of sin and not identity, homophobic attitudes did not exist. It was only the introduction of the Western concept of the homo-hetero binary that made people in the Middle East feel deeply uncomfortable with homoerotic love. It is only consequent to ask if the same concept could have a similar effect in the West itself.

The effect Western notions had on Arabic literature is all too clear. Around the middle of the nineteenth century, homoerotic poetry vanished almost completely and people started to look at their own literary heritage with mixed feelings. Homoeroticism began to be considered a perversion, and works of classical literature were (and still are) expurgated. Homoerotic literature became, as Khaled El-Rouayheb noted in his magisterial study, an object of shame, and in "1925, a history of Arabic literature designed for use in secondary and higher education in Egypt stated that love poetry of boys was 'a crime against literature and a disgrace to the history of Arabic poetry'" (158).

The existence of a vibrant homoerotic literature played not an unimportant role in establishing a discourse of "decadence" according to which Islamic culture, after an alleged "Golden Age" in the early Middle Ages, went through a process of decline – politically, intellectually, and, of course, morally. Homoerotic poetry was thus seen as a sign of decadence. And because Western scholarship had contributed to the emergence of this perception and cherished it until quite recently, whole genres and periods of classical Arabic literature remained more or less unstudied. Still today, our knowledge of Arabic literature between the Ayyubid period and the onset of modern Arabic literature in the nineteenth century is insular (see Bauer, "Mamluk"). The enormous role played by homoerotic texts is doubtlessly one of the main reasons for this deplorable state of the art.

In modern Arabic literature, the concept of "homosexuality" of the Western episteme was adopted largely in an uncritical way. It is only very recently that Arabic writers and intellectuals try to find a way out of what Khalid Hadeed calls "the epistemic closure" imposed on homosexuality.

Notes

1. Uways al-Ḥamawī, *Sukkardān al-ʿushshāq*, Ms Berlin 8407, fol. 148b.
2. Shams al-Dīn an-Nawājī, *Marātiʿ al-ghizlān*, Ms Istanbul Top Kapu 722, fol. 41b.
3. Uways al-Ḥamawī, *Sukkardān al-ʿushshāq*, Ms Berlin 8407, fol. 148a.

Works Cited

Abū Nuwās. *Dīwān Abī Nuwās al-Ḥasan ibn Hāniʾ al-Ḥakamī*. Vol. 4. Ed. Gregor Schoeler. Wiesbaden: Franz Steiner, 1982. Print.
Amer, Sahar. *Crossing Borders: Love between Women in Medieval French and Arabic Literatures*. Philadelphia: U of Pennsylvania P, 2008. Print.
Arazi, Albert. *Amour divin et amour profane dans l'Islam medieval à travers le Dīwān de Khālid Al-Kātib*. Paris: G.-P. Maisonneuve et Larose, 1990. Print.
Bauer, Thomas. "The Arabic *Ghazal*: Formal and Thematic Aspects of a Problematic Genre." *Ghazal as World Literature II: From a Literary Genre to a Great Tradition. The Ottoman Gazel in Context*. Ed. Angelika Neuwirth et al. Beirut, Würzburg: Ergon, 2006. 3–13. Print.

"Dignity on the Line: Mujūn Epigrams by Ibn Nubāta (686–768/1287–1366) and His Contemporaries." *The Rude, the Bad and the Bawdy: Essays in Honour of Professor Geert Jan van Gelder.* Ed. Adam Talib, Marlé Hammond, and Arie Schippers. Cambridge: Gibb Memorial Trust, 2014. 164–92. Print.

Die Kultur der Ambiguität: Eine andere Geschichte des Islams. Berlin: Verlag der Weltreligionen, 2011. Print.

Liebe und Liebesdichtung in der arabischen Welt des 9. und 10. Jahrhunderts: Eine literatur-und mentalitätsgeschichtliche Studie des arabischen Ġazal, Wiesbaden: Harrassowitz, 1998. Print.

"Mamluk Literature: Misunderstandings and New Approaches." *Mamlūk Studies Review* 9.2 (2005): 105–32. Print.

"al-Nawājī." *Essays in Arabic Literary Biography 1350–1850.* Ed. Joseph E. Lowry and Devin J. Stewart. Wiebaden: Harrassowitz, 2009. 321–31. Print.

Bauer, Thomas, and Angelika Neuwirth, eds. *Ghazal as World Literature I: Transformations of a Literary Genre.* Beirut, Würzburg: Ergon, 2005. Print.

De Bruijn, J. T. P. *Of Piety and Poetry: The Interaction of Religion and Literature in the Life and Works of Hakīm Sanāʾī of Ghazna,* Leiden: Brill, 1983. Print.

"Shahrangīz in Persian." *Encyclopaedia of Islam.* 2nd ed. Vol. 9. Ed. P. J. Bearman et al. Leiden: Brill, 1960–2005. 212. Print.

Dunne, Bruce W. *Sexuality and the "Civilizing Process" in Modern Egypt.* Diss. Georgetown U, 1996. Print.

El-Rouayheb, Khaled. *Before Homosexuality in the Arabic-Islamic World, 1500–1800.* Chicago: U of Chicago P, 2005. Print.

Fathallāh, ʿAbdallatīf. *Dīwān al-Muftī ʿAbdallatīf Fathallāh.* Ed. Zuhayr Fathallāh. Vol 2. Beirut, Wiesbaden: Steiner, 1984. Print.

Hadeed, Khalid. "Homosexuality and Epistemic Closure in Modern Arabic Literature." *International Journal of Middle East Studies* 45 (2013): 271–91. Print.

Heinrichs, Wolfhart. "Rhetorical Figures." Meisami and Starkey 656–62.

Homerin, Th. Emil. *Passion Before Me, My Fate Behind: Ibn al-Fārid and the Poetry of Recollection.* New York: State U of New York P, 2011. Print.

Ibn Matrūh, Jamāl ad-Dīn Yahyā. *Dīwān Ibn Matrūh.* Ed. Husayn Nassār. Cairo: Matbaʿat Dār al-Kutub wa-l-Wathāʾiq al-Qawmiyya, 2004. Print

Kennedy, Philip F. *The Wine Song in Classical Arabic Poetry: Abū Nuwās and the Literary Tradition.* Oxford: Clarendon P, 1997. Print.

Klauda, Georg. *Die Vertreibung aus dem Serail: Europa und die Heteronormalisierung der Islamischen Welt.* Hamburg: Männerschwarm, 2008. Print.

Kugle, Scott Siraj al-Haqq. *Homosexuality in Islam: Critical Reflections on Gay, Lesbian and Transgender Muslims.* Oxford: Oneworld, 2010. Print.

Massad, Joseph A. *Desiring Arabs.* Chicago: U of Chicago P, 2007. Print.

Meisami, Julie Scott, and Paul Starkey, eds. *Encyclopedia of Arabic Literature.* 2 vols. New York: Routledge, 1998. Print.

Richardson, Kristina L. *Difference and Disability in the Medieval Islamic World: Blighted Bodies.* Edinburgh: Edinburgh UP, 2012. Print.

Rowson, Everett K. "al-Khubzaruzzī." Meisami and Starkey 443.

"Two Homoerotic Narratives from Mamlūk Literature." *Homoeroticism in Classical Arabic Literature*. Ed. J. W. Wright Jr. and Everett K. Rowson. New York: Columbia UP, 1997. 158–91. Print.

Schmitt, Arno. "*Liwāṭ* im *fiqh*: Männliche Homosexualität?" *Journal of Arabic and Islamic Studies* 4 (2001–2): 49–110. Print.

Talib, Adam. "Pseudo-Ṯaʿālibī's *Book of Youths*." *Arabica* 59 (2012): 599–649. Print.

Thaʿālibī, Abū Manṣūr. *Tatimmat Yatīmat ad-dahr fī maḥāsin ahl al-ʿaṣr*. Ed. Mufīd Muḥammad Qumayḥa. Beirut: Dār al-Kutub al-ʿIlmiyya, 1983. Print.

Wagner, Ewald. *Abū Nuwās in Übersetzung: Eine Stellensammlung zu Abū Nuwās-Übersetzungen vornehmlich in europäische Sprachen*. Wiesbaden: Harrassowitz, 2012.

Abū Nuwās: Eine Studie zur Arabischen Literatur der frühen ʿAbbāsidenzeit. Wiesbaden: Franz Steiner, 1965. Print.

7

China: Ancient to Modern

GIOVANNI VITIELLO

Since the publication in Hong Kong of the first systematic review of the sources on homosexuality in Chinese culture about thirty years ago, increasingly nuanced work has been done on the history of ideas and practices of same-sex relations, in both the premodern and modern eras.[1] It must be noted right away, however, that the scholarly record to date is severely lopsided toward the study of homosexual relations between men.[2] To be fair, there are some objective reasons for such an imbalance; while we have in fact an extraordinarily rich set of sources on male-male sexual and romantic relations, the record on female homoeroticism (especially for the premodern era) appears to be scant. This is in turn likely due to the fact that, generally speaking, in premodern Chinese culture male homosexuality was deemed a legitimate expression of male eroticism. The traditional notion of *nanse* ("male beauty," or "male sex appeal") was significantly conceived as a counterpart to *nüse* ("female beauty," or "female sex appeal"); the two aesthetic domains represented equivalent, potential objects of a man's sexual desire. According to this configuration of male sexuality, an adult male could thus be stimulated by either female or male beauty (the latter, as we shall soon see, indicating the beauty of a teenager), exclusively by one or more commonly by both, whether in equal or varying degrees. Female-female eroticism, on the other hand, had no formal space in the dominant premodern discourse on sex, which posited the phallus as indispensable to a woman's social and sexual fulfillment. For these reasons, inevitably this chapter will largely focus on male, rather than female homoeroticism.

The other caveat belonging to the beginning of this chapter concerns its chronological scope. In theory I should cover here a history spanning more than two thousand years, but this obviously cannot be accomplished so easily, both because of the uneven amount of extant sources for this very long period, and of the relevant modern research. Here I shall therefore devote most space to the representation of male homoeroticism in the late imperial era (roughly the stretch from the late sixteenth through the nineteenth centuries), both because it is the richest in literary sources on the subject, and because research so far (including my own) has primarily focused on it.

Foundations: Shared Peaches and Cut Sleeves

But before I move to the late imperial period, a review of some of the earliest Chinese sources on male-male relations is in order, especially because they gave rise to a classic lexicon of homosexuality. The expressions "longyang" (from the name of the Lord of Longyang, a male favorite), "shared peach" (*fentao*), and "cut sleeve" (*duanxiu*) are the most prominent of such lexicon, and are still used (at least in written Chinese) to this day. It should be noted that most of the earliest extant records are not "literary" in the strictest sense, in that they come chiefly from historical, and occasionally philosophical works. Indeed, one of the first situations in which the relationship between two men is discussed is the political context involving rulers and their boy favorites, in particular reference to such boys' potentially pernicious influence on their patrons, hence on the welfare of the state. This concerned approach dominates the biographies of the imperial male favorites that early historian Sima Qian (145–85 BCE) included in his *Historical Records* (*Shi ji*), thereby inaugurating a historiographical practice that continued for about a millennium.

The expression "cut sleeve" refers to the story of Dong Xian, the male favorite of Emperor Ai of the Han dynasty (reigning years: 6–1 BCE). From the *Book of the Han* (*Han shu*) we learn that the two of them were one day resting together, the sleeping boy's head lying on the large sleeve of the emperor's robe, when someone came to announce to the emperor that official business was awaiting him. Lest he disturb the boy's sleep, the ruler cut his own sleeve before rising from the bed. This type of ruler is implicitly deemed in danger, on account of his infatuation (whether for a boy or a woman, the gender of the favorite being ultimately irrelevant).

Another example of a ruler's excessive passion for a male favorite is the story of the Lord of Longyang, a king's young lover in the Warring States period (481–221 BCE). One day, while on a boat fishing with him, the boy suddenly begins to cry. To his puzzled king he explains that he had just hooked a big fish, so impressive that he had decided to throw away the smaller fish he had caught before. Then the sudden, tears-inducing realization had dawned on him – What if my lord did the same to me, and discarded me for some new beauty? This particular lord turns out to be moved by the boy's anguish, and thus threatens to kill anyone who will dare present him "beauties" (presumably of either sex) from that moment on.

But not all rulers were so romantically inclined, or so easily moved by a beautiful boy's tears. An example is the story of the "shared peach," hailing from the fourth-century BCE philosophical work *Master Han Fei* (*Han Feizi*). Here the favorite of a duke is at first praised by him even when he transgresses the rules – once by hopping on the duke's chariot in the middle of the night without the proper authorization so as to go and see his sick mother (the duke finds his gesture ardently filial), and once by offering a sweet peach to his lord, having first bitten into it (the duke finds it the moving sign of his devotion). But when the boy's looks begin to fade, the duke's perception of the boy's past deeds dramatically changes as well, and his acts of generosity are now seen as evidence of his lack of respect for authority. It is significant that the ostensible reason given for this duke's change of heart is the fact that the boy's beauty had begun to decline. In addition to a familiar moralistic discourse on the intersection between politics and sex, here we find an indication of the connoisseurial criteria that made the ideal boy favorite, youth being one of the indispensable requirements.[3]

These early records on male favorites naturally inform us only on male homoeroticism among a very narrow segment of Chinese society – the pre-imperial aristocracy and the world of the imperial court. When, however, the topic resurfaces in vernacular fiction from the sixteenth century on, the cast of characters is far more socially variegated, featuring literati and merchants, clerics and actors. From the late Ming period on (roughly from 1580 to the fall of the dynasty in 1644), because of the flourishing of the novel of manners and of pornographic fiction above all, we can rely on an extraordinary wealth of sources on romantic and sexual relations, including those between men (the latter being occasionally even the exclusive focus of a literary work). These sources help in sketching a picture of late imperial attitudes toward sexuality, and clarify the place male homosexuality occupied in it.

Late Imperial Erotic Discourse

One basic assumption about sexuality that emerges from late imperial literary representations is that an adult male could be attracted to women as well as teenage boys, thereby suggesting the notion of a default male bisexuality. A man's more pronounced inclination toward sex with women or boys was deemed natural (in some accounts even innate), and likened to preference in taste for certain foods and fragrances. A number of requirements, however, should in principle be fulfilled for a sexual relationship between men to fall within acceptable, normative behavior. One basic criterion has to do with age: as in ancient Greece or Rome, in premodern China the ideal male object of a man's desire is a teenager, ideally sixteen. The other chief criterion in the protocol of normative homoerotic relations concerns class. The latter determined the distribution of sexual roles between a man and a boy, in that only a boy of debased, or "vile" status (that is, hailing from a family of actors, prostitutes, or other legally discriminated classes) could legitimately play the role of the sexually receptive partner of a socially superior, or "decent" man (see Vitiello *Libertine's* ch. 1).

Rather than exclusive relations between men, most erotic fiction from the late imperial period portrays an adult man interested in both women and boys. This bisexual libertine is typically a brilliant scholar pursuing a bureaucratic career. He is said to have a wife, a number of gorgeous concubines, and to be very attracted to boys as well; in fact, he often keeps company with an attendant boy, or "studio boy" (*shutong*). In addition to being relatively literate – at least compared to the more lowly "porters" (*menzi*), serving in the office of district magistrates – the "studio boy" must of course have good looks, because his duties clearly go beyond the management of stationary and involve pleasing his master sexually as well. The "outer studio" (*waifang*) – located in the area of the house that is reserved to men (as opposed to the women's "inner quarters") is often the theatre of homosexual encounters in late imperial erotic narratives. The classic example comes from the late sixteenth-century novel *The Plum in the Golden Vase* (*Jin Ping Mei*), where the libertine protagonist Ximen Qing – the "master" of a conspicuous harem of six women – makes love to his "studio boy" (appropriately named Shutong – the proper name here is also the generic term) in his "outer studio." As an ideal libertine, Ximen Qing is bisexual, but he rigorously takes the insertive prerogative in his sexual dealings with Shutong; in other words, he is the impenetrable penetrator of women and boys, and embodies a libertine model followed in many other pornographic novels thereafter. In the episode in question, Ximen Qing's sexual encounter with his page provokes the jealousy of his favorite concubine, Pan Jinlian. This points to a recurring motif in late imperial pornography – the competition between the inner quarters and the outer studio and, by extension, between heterosexuality and homosexuality.[4]

To be sure, besides this narrative in which sex with boys and sex with women are seen as equivalent, legitimate options for the fulfillment of a man's sexual desires, other discourses and attendant representations of sex and love between men circulate in late imperial fiction that either disparage it or approach it with an ironic or satirical attitude. For instance, in narratives often involving clerics or travelers homosexuality is presented as an acceptable substitution only in the event of a lack of women. The underlying theory here is that for a man sex with boys is an expedient of last resort, being implicitly deemed inferior to heterosexual sex. In the fiction of Li Yu (1610–ca. 1680), the exclusive romantic attachment between men in particular becomes the target of a biting satire. This notwithstanding, roughly at this same time we also witness the production of exclusively homoerotic literary collections that take love between men very seriously.[5]

Late Ming Homoerotica

Indeed, the late Ming period, a time modern scholars characterize as marked by an obsession with the sentimental, a veritable "cult of love," saw the publication of two collections of novellas on romantic love between men – *Cap and Hairpins (Bian er chai)* and *Fragrant Essences of Spring (Yichun xiangzhi)* – most likely compiled (by the same, pseudonymous author) in the 1630s or 1640s. In the late Ming playwright Tang Xianzu's formulation, love (*qing*) is famously able to cross the boundary between life and death. These two homoerotic collections expand Tang's notion to the extent of causing love to shatter gender (and even class) distinctions as well.[6] In the first story of *Cap and Hairpins*, for example, we witness the love affair of an academician and a student (hence both from a "decent" family), who are reunited in the end after their respective bureaucratic careers and prolific marriages. The second story features two warriors, again both from a respectable class and equally gifted in literary and martial skills; once again here the younger man is moved by his suitor's love to the point of accepting sexual penetration by him. The last two stories focus on male prostitutes, who were, however, forced into indentured condition because of a sudden turn of fortune, having originally been born "decent folk." The narrator allows them to redeem themselves by making them act as romantic heroes, ready to perform any sacrifice in order to reward their male lovers. In all these narratives the discourse on romantic love intersects that on chivalric friendship, suggesting that chivalric values have a significant role in the formation of the romantic ideal in the late Ming, and perhaps might be even said to underlie the romantic ideology of the late imperial period as a whole. Such ideological interconnection in the homoerotic *Cap and Hairpins* is especially natural in that the concept of chivalric friendship is originally gendered, being predicated on a bond between two men, a bond whose chief value is loyalty between peers (*yi*). In other words, an ideology referring to male-male relations – that is, the egalitarian notion of chivalric friendship – is translated and adapted so as to come to constitute a romantic ideal that applies to both heterosexual and homosexual relations (see Vitiello, *Libertine's* ch. 2).

If *Cap and Hairpins* presents a gallery of exemplary boy-lovers, who cannot but be moved by the love of their pursuers and are ready to sacrifice their decent bodies, or even their very lives, for them, its mirror collection *Fragrant Essences of Spring* focuses on disloyal catamites. The first three stories thus present boys who, because they have betrayed a romantic oath or cynically taken advantage of the passion of their pursuers, deserve to be severely punished. The fourth and last of this collection's novellas focuses instead on a case of redemption from sexual dissipation. The story consists of the fantastic dream of an ugly boy, who is allowed to travel oneirically through the landscape of his hidden desires and to finally liberate himself from them. In the course of the dream, he is transformed into a most handsome boy and experiences all sorts of passions and pleasures and their increasingly nightmarish consequences, only then to renounce them all in order to pursue an ascetic life when he wakes up just as beautiful as in his dream. The journey takes the boy to a variety of kingdoms, corresponding to different forms of sexuality. The first of these, the Kingdom of All-Sons, is made out of only men, half of them in drag. Having caught the king's attention, he is named the new queen. Chased by the vengeful deposed queen, he is then forced to run away, and eventually takes refuge in the Kingdom of Holy-*Yin*, a mirror same-sex country where only women live. This country's king also falls in love with our queen (remember that she is still in female attire). Interestingly, though, when "he" discovers that "she" is really a man, all "he" wants is to try heterosexual sex with him (which by now turns out to be quite impractical for the queen, so the king ends up sodomizing him with a dildo). Ultimately, in this narrative, it would appear, everyone wants men, even the female king of the Kingdom of Women (a state made out supposedly of men-hating women). The gap between the two parallel episodes, both involving the boy's becoming a royal spouse, betrays a bias. The representation of male-male sex remains the focus of this erotic story, which occasionally also features heterosexual sex, yet never sex between women. While a kinship between male and female same-sex sexuality is no doubt hinted at here, a hierarchical perspective privileging men and male homosexuality also clearly transpires.[7]

A third late Ming collection, *Forgotten Stories of Catamites* (*Longyang yishi*), focuses instead on the world of male prostitution, providing a ferociously satirical portrait of it. The prostitutes of these twenty stories are usually men who pretend to be teenagers in order to remain in business, and consequently tend to make an excessive use of make-up and display of youthful attire. Such aged boys are seen as grotesque creatures, as equally grotesque are deemed their clients, lampooned for their obsessive desire and lack of proper connoisseurship of male beauty, at a time when, as the narrator says more than once, "men at the sight of boys are like mosquitoes at the sight of blood – beautiful or not, they cannot refrain from stinging them" (Vitiello, "Forgotten" 230). Some of these stories stage a competition between male and female prostitution, a recurring theme especially in late Ming fiction. The rivalry is typically predicated on an acknowledged social phenomenon, that is, the extraordinary popularity of male prostitution in late Ming urban life (a phenomenon confirmed by a variety of nonfictional sources as well, and that has led scholars to speak of a late Ming "fashion" for male prostitutes among the elites).[8] Theories of male and female beauty often extol the superior simplicity of boys as opposed to feminine artificiality (this while at the same time extolling boys' femininity – in other words, praising male femininity above all). An eloquent example is the commentary appended at the end of the chapter on male love in *The Archives of Love* (*Qing shi* [ca. 1630]), where the compiler illustrates the superiority of boy beauty over female beauty by pointing at the more colorful hide and plumage of male specimens in the animal world compared to that of their female counterparts as irrefutable evidence (see Mowry 140–41).

Libertine Sexuality

We have already noted the figure of the libertine as a sexually impenetrable penetrator of women and boys, as exemplified by Ximen Qing of *The Plum in the Golden Vase*. But representations that transgress this general rule also occur. Some pornographic narratives from the second half of the seventeenth century indeed feature a new type of libertine, who can be sexually penetrated without his masculine credentials being compromised. In these narratives the libertine protagonist finds himself in a fixed predicament – he tries to have an affair with a married woman, whose husband happens to be fond of boys. As a result of this dynamic of desires, he reaches his goal of seducing the woman only by becoming the lover of her husband too. The homosexual initiation takes the form of a rape, with the husband taking advantage of the libertine young scholar's intoxicated state. When the latter finally wakes up, understands what has happened, and would like to kill his offender, the wife comes into his room just in time to explain that she has been sent as a reward for his pains. This appeases the insulted decent man, so much so that in some cases the triangular relationship continues beyond the first (rape) night (which is in all cases forgotten).

Indeed, what is especially remarkable in these stories is that this narrative's husband eventually also becomes the most loyal of our libertine hero's friends, typically coming to his rescue in time of danger. In other words, the at first merely sexual relationship between the two men evolves into a profound homosocial bond. At the end of the generic pornographic plot I am describing, when the libertine has now reached all his goals and is surrounded by all his women and children, his friend comes to invite him to join him and another couple of like-minded single men, to roam around together like itinerant holy men. The seductions of male homosociality thus in the end prevail over the bliss of a polygamous heterosexual marriage.

This narrative appears to have undergone further transformation in yet later pornographic fiction. The character of the penetrated libertine eventually disappears in a reverting movement to the more classic notion of the sexually impenetrable bisexual libertine. The homosexual plot is severely curtailed in these later works and the rape scene of earlier narratives (inaugurating the erotic triangle) is significantly replaced by an invitation to form a literary club (hence, no sexual availability is required of the libertine in exchange for another man's wife he will obtain anyway). The representation of homosexuality appears to be increasingly connected with crime, and its practitioners more and more often wear the clothes of rogues and disloyal servants. The protagonist of this type of narrative often shows his overt contempt for homosexual sex and bristles with rage at the faintest hint that he might submit to a receptive sexual relationship with another man (see Vitiello, *Libertine's* ch. 3). It is tempting to see a relationship between the suppression of the homoerotic plot involving a penetrated libertine and the restrictive gender policies implemented under the Yongzheng reign (1723–35), roughly at the same time these literary representations began to circulate. These laws represented a concern for masculinity and its protection, their main aim being the protection of minor boys from rape, even though for the first time they also formally proscribed even consensual relations between men (see Sommer ch. 4).

Critiques of Homoeroticism in Eighteenth-Century Fiction

A discursive orientation more critical of homoeroticism – often related to a larger critique of masculinity – can certainly be detected in eighteenth-century fiction. The 1730s novel *Nonsense* (*Guwang yan*), for example, features a most virtuous, anti-libertine protagonist, caught in a chaotic world where sexual disorder is the ultimate symbol of an approaching political demise. The critique of homosexual indulgence falls within this general moralistic framework, and as such sex between men is placed side by side with the most brutal acts of unfiliality. This said, in the very same novel, a man's infatuation for a mean boy who takes advantage of his feelings only deserves sympathy. Hence, despite its fierce critique of homosexual lust and dissipation, love for a man is still seen as a legitimate romantic predicament in this novel.

An Old Man's Humble Words (*Yesou puyan*), from the mid-eighteenth century, takes a far more radical attitude toward sex between men. Its protagonist is a hyper-masculine Confucian hero who is fanatically devoted to the destruction of all forms of heterodoxy, and has enlisted in his program of moral regeneration the eradication of (male) homosexuality. Accordingly sex between men in the novel appears as the core of a heterodox religious cult. On the day of its main annual celebration (a fanciful "Asshole Festival"), throngs of men and their boy-lovers follow the paraded statue of a god-patriarch of male love; most perversely in our hero's eyes, even female prostitutes take part in the event dressed as boys in the hope of getting some customers. Determined to eradicate this cult, our moralist hero uses the magical powers given him by the City God to shatter the divine statue with the sheer force of his piercing glance. But despite all this, his annihilation project ultimately does not fully succeed. We are in fact told that, after his sabotage, the number of the devotees of this sexual custom had been reduced by half, yet not been altogether eliminated.

Like the pure hero of *Nonsense*, *Humble Words*' protagonist is a Confucian moralist with strong martial inclinations and even magic skills. In other words, both are hybrid heroes, who represent a new model of masculinity alternative to the one embodied by the decadently hyper-literate scholar who is ultimately deemed responsible for the fall of the Ming empire. In a germane (if more pronouncedly satirical) vein, *The Scholars* (*Rulin waishi*), Wu Jingzi's classic novel from the mid-eighteenth century, also ridicules the aestheticizing mannerisms of the literati elite by significantly singling out their obsession for opera's female impersonators. All attuned to a critique of elite, Confucian masculinity, these eighteenth-century novels propose an antidote – a vigorous, literate yet also martial, masculinity that can hardly be reconciled with the decadent pursuit of sensual pleasures, the literati passion for sex with boys being often selected as the most powerful symbol of sexual indulgence and at once of cultural and political decadence.[9]

The *Dream* and Its *Mirror*

This said, in the very same century we actually also encounter fictional treatments of homoerotic romances, indeed in the most famous of that century's novels, *The Red Chamber Dream* (first published in 1792; hereafter *The Dream*). To be sure, *The Dream*'s narrative focuses on a romantic triangle involving the novel's male protagonist Baoyu and his two female cousins, Daiyu and Baochai, the former his most passionate love, the latter his wife-to-be. There is, however, an important homoerotic streak in Baoyu's romantic experience as well, notably emerging in the portrayal of his relationship with Qin Zhong, a boy about his age, equally handsome and refined. From their very first meeting Baoyu and Qin Zhong have fallen into a mutual romantic contemplation. They become inseparable, and soon Qin Zhong is allowed to join Baoyu at his family's school. As the Three Critics of the novel's nineteenth-century canonical commentary observe, Baoyu is made to discover first the pleasures of heterosexuality and then, after he meets Qin Zhong, those of homosexuality as well. It is at the school that most of the homoerotic narrative in the novel is significantly placed. The school is described as a place saturated with homoerotic desires; Baoyu and Qin Zhong are perceived by their classmates as a couple, and on their part they flirt with two other boys, who used to be the lovers of Xue Pan, Baoyu's older cousin who, the narrator informs us, uses the school as his playground to "fish for boyfriends." It is precisely the jealousy of one of Xue Pan's discarded boyfriends that is at the root of a ruckus in the classroom, when he falsely reports to the rest of the class that he has caught Qin Zhong making out with a pretty classmate in the backyard. From this a scandal ensues, in which sex between men is clearly contested as a potential source of shame. The episode, in other words, presents a true scandal, by featuring a "decent" man as a receptive partner in a sexual relationship with another man – what would in theory be unthinkable in terms of late imperial (homo)sexuality, which requires, as we have seen, one of the two partners hailing from "vile" members of society and playing accordingly the receptive sexual role. Yet, the schoolboys are technically all "decent"; worse still, these affairs are encouraged by the relatives of students hailing from less prominent branches of the clan. (Indeed, we are told that one of the boys' mother was only grateful that her son could receive protection from Xue Pan, in implicit exchange for his sexual services.)

Some scholars have downplayed or even ruled out the possibility of Baoyu and Qin Zhong being lovers in the novel (for example, Huang). However, the narrator does everything to expose, if subtly, the sexual relationship between the two boys. This notably happens in the episode in which Qin Zhong is caught by Baoyu while trying to make love to a young nun he is infatuated with in a dark corner of a monastery. Baoyu plays the role of the jealous lover here, and finally leaves him with the playful threat: "Wait until we are both in bed and I'll settle accounts with you then" (Cao and Gao 1: 300). At this point, the apparently amused narrator interjects that he wasn't there and so he can't say exactly how the account was settled. On the other hand, it's clear that the narrator is precisely referring to a sexual settling here, and his claim to ignorance can only function as a reinforcement of the reader's suspicion that indeed sex is the key to interpret Baoyu's playful threat. This said, generally speaking *The Dream* displays a greater emphasis on the sentimental than on the sexual dimension of all erotic relations, including those between men.[10]

The Dream's romantic ideology is borrowed wholesale and actually radicalized by *Precious Mirror for Ranking Flowers* (hereafter *The Mirror*), the 1849 novel centrally concerned with the romantic and erotic interactions between the imperial capital's gentry and the female impersonators (*dan*) they typically patronized.[11] The novel focuses on the love story between an elite man, modeled after Baoyu ("Precious Jade") and thus named Ziyu ("Little Jade"), and Qinyan, an opera actor (hence a "vile" person), whose name recalls that of Qin Zhong, Baoyu's intimate friend in *The Dream*. The novel constitutes one of the first rewritings of *The Dream*; as it happens, a homoerotic one. Here the protagonist's two "significant others" are of different genders. The boy actor is clearly a new version of *The Dream*'s Daiyu, while our new hero's fiancée is modeled after Baochai, and accordingly will in due time become Ziyu's wife. Because in the end the actor is also redeemed from his indentured position and joins Ziyu's household, we understand that the novel has overturned the tragic outcome of *The Dream* by giving Ziyu both his "Daiyu" and his "Baochai," where arguably the boy-actor Qinyan, in addition, also takes care of recuperating the romance between Baoyu and Qin Zhong in *The Dream*.

Compared to its model, romantic love in this novel is radically desexualized; as a result Ziyu and Qinyan's bodies barely, if ever, come into contact. If anything, *The Mirror* pushes even further the notion of "sublime love" that lies at the core of *The Dream*'s romantic ideology (McMahon, "Sublime"). The novel's ending features the reunion of the two "friends" (or perhaps "brothers," given that Qinyan is adopted by Ziyu's father). By now, Ziyu has married a girl who uncannily looks just like Qinyan, and they apparently have a blissful marriage (even though no sex between them is ever described either). The two men spend the whole night talking until they fall asleep close together, and when Ziyu's cousin enters the room in the morning, Qinyan's head is lying on

Ziyu's arm. The image cannot but recall the archetypal story of Dong Xian sleeping with his head reclining on the sleeve of the emperor's robe, which the latter cuts so as not to disturb the boy's sleep. Ziyu's marriage notwithstanding, the final reunion re-inscribes homoeroticism in the equation.

"Modern" Sex

In 1912, the very year of the collapse of the imperial order and the declaration of the Republic of China, an anthology of male-male erotic records culled from historical and literary sources in classical Chinese was published.[12] The collection updated the seventeenth-century chapter on male love in *The Archives of Love* (itself most likely based on a chapter of a sixteenth-century work on romantic tales), thereby attempting to hold together a long-standing literary tradition and the record of an equally long-standing sexual culture. The publication of *The Cut Sleeve*, in this sense, may be seen as signaling the resilience of a traditional sexual ideology that was about to be displaced by a new model of sexuality, through the dissemination, in both academia and the popular press, of Western sexological knowledge. The 1920s and 1930s represent indeed a watershed in terms of the understanding of sexuality in China. No doubt it is too simplistic to speak of a "traditional," autochthonous sexuality in contrast with a "modern" sexuality modeled after the Western one, the task at hand being rather that of historicizing both, hence recording the discursive changes occurring over time, and paying special attention to the relevant processes of negotiation. On the other hand, it is also certainly true that the challenge to all traditional forms of sexual ideology presented by European sexology during the Republican period (coming in a package of overwhelming power, called "modernity") was unprecedented. As a result, for the first time in Chinese history homoerotic relations are seen as the expression of an exclusive, inborn sexual orientation, and not simply as one option for a man to satisfy his desire; at the same time, female-female eroticism is yoked together with male-male eroticism under the new rubric of "homosexuality." The word "homosexuality" itself reflected a radically new understanding of (same-sex) sexuality that required the creation of a Chinese equivalent. The neologism (borrowed from the Japanese) *tongxing'ai* (and its variants *tongxing lian'ai* and *tongxinglian*), meaning literally "same-sex passion," begins to establish itself by the 1930s (see Sang ch. 1; Kang chs. 1 and 2). Western sexology, though, also carries to China its standards of (hetero)sexual health, and its attendant distaste for homosexual deviance, as a form of psychological perversion. Patronizing male entertainers – a feature of traditional male sexuality – suddenly compromises the masculinity of the Chinese nation, at a time when the country is brutally (and, let's note, gender-specifically) diagnosed as "the sick man of Asia." The May Fourth New Culture movement – which in hindsight will be apprehended as the most prominent advocate of China's modernization – eagerly supports free love, but this means, though, freely chosen heterosexual union, in disparaging contrast and to the detriment of the legitimacy of homosexual relations (Sang, introduction). Soon it will become apparent that the erotic ideology that sustained *The Cut Sleeve* anthology was losing its cultural grip.

Modern Chinese literature (by which I mean here mainly that of the Republican period, spanning roughly thirty years from the May Fourth demonstration of 1919 to the founding of the People's Republic of China in 1949) seems barely to skirt the topic of homosexuality. A few writers associated with Shanghai's Creation Society, in particular, deal with the subject with a fairly positive attitude (a trait that is part and parcel of a celebration of desire in its most primal forms, discursively related with the European Decadent movement). Yu Dafu's "Endless Night" ("Mangmang ye") and Ye Dingluo's "Boyfriend" ("Nan pengyou") are examples of such romantic treatments; it must, though, be noted that in both cases the romances are made to dissolve at the onset of adulthood. Guo Moruo too in 1931 published a memoir of his childhood and early youth where he recalled his ardent devotion to a friend – a sentiment that he admits smacks of homosexual love but that he actually considers to be an affection far deeper and more powerful than that. Possibly here Guo is recycling *The Mirror's* notion of sublime love, and perhaps for this reason, by way of contrast, he emphasizes the homoerotic environment of his middle school, where younger boys sleep tightly wrapped in their quilts even in the middle of the hottest and most humid summers, terrified by possible "raids" by older boys, an apparently recurring phenomenon.[13]

As for the more canonical May Fourth writers, their embodying a more "orthodox" modernity has an effect on their more problematic attitude toward homoeroticism as well. It is interesting to note that two of the movement's most representative members, Ba Jin and Lao She, wrote short stories focusing on female impersonators, and both of them displayed a fundamental ambiguity about this character and the unmistakably homoerotic world he stood for as a likely male prostitute, strongly suggesting that such a social persona was destined to disappear in the modern world (while still exhibiting compassion and understanding for him) (see Vitiello, *Libertine's* epilogue). Most telling is Ba Jin's 1950s rewriting of his story "Second Mother" ("Di'er de muqin"), originally published in the early 1930s, to make the crossdressing "mother" of the original story into a biological woman, thereby erasing the queerness of the first version (Wang, "Impersonating").

After the founding of the People's Republic, the subject of same-sex eroticism – in either variant – virtually disappears from Chinese literature on the Mainland. Taiwan's own politically conservative climate (if of a traditionalist, Confucian variety) also stifles the emergence of gay and lesbian-themed literature. For the first Chinese "gay novel," we need to wait until 1983, when Pai Hsien-yung's *Crystal Boys* (*Niezi*), as it is known in English translation (but a more literal translation would be "Cursed Boys"), appears. The novel evokes the gay life in 1960s Taipei gravitating around the New Park, a cruising public park to this day (although it has been partly reclaimed by the city government in a masked anti-gay move; see Martin, *Situating*). Those who frequent it are men who can live out their most intimate selves only under the cover of darkness – as the narrator puts it at the novel's very opening: "There are no days in our kingdom; only nights" (Pai 17).

The 1990s, after martial law was rescinded in 1987, was a period of growth for gay and lesbian political activism in Taiwan, a development signaling Taiwan's ever stronger political links with the United States and its academic and cultural trends. A new generation of gay and lesbian writers also came to age in the middle of the decade – writers such as Chen Xue, Ta-wei Chi, and Lucifer Hong. Chu T'ien-wen's *Notes of a Desolate Man* (*Huangren shouji*), even though its author belongs to the previous generation, also appeared in the 1990s; its critical success helped posit homosexuality in a more central position in the Taiwanese public discourse. No other writer contributed more to this aim, however, than lesbian author Qiu Miaojin. Able to activate both mainstream literary criticism and the lesbian activist movement, her *Crocodile's Journal* (*Eyu shouji*) became an instant cult book, a status reinforced by the author's suicide in Paris in 1996.[14]

As for Mainland China, female homoeroticism has been the object of some scrutiny in 1990s fiction by women writers such as Chen Ran and Lin Bai, if with an intensely paranoid approach (see Sang ch. 6). During the past decade experimental film director Cui Zi'en has seen a few collections of his gay-themed fiction published, but so far the topic has hardly come to the fore on the PRC literary scene, even though a "comrade" (*tongzhi*, the term for "gay" in Chinese since the 1990s) Internet literature has begun to emerge (Cristini). We might recall in this regard that homosexuality was only in 2001 removed from the official list of psychiatric ailments, and only a few years before it had stopped to be prosecuted under the mantle of "hooliganism" (that is, social unrest), when this category was eliminated from the penal code.

While registering this relative lack of gay-themed literature (especially in the PRC), we might also note, on the other hand, that the 1980s and 1990s saw a resurgence of Chinese cinema in which male homosexuality was intriguingly featured as a recurring theme. The choice of visual narratives centered on the theme of male homoeroticism from the part of Chinese directors from Taiwan (Tsai Ming-liang and Ang Lee), the PRC (Chen Kaige and Zhang Yuan), and Hong Kong (Wong Kar-wai) might be seen as representing a reemerging repressed from premodern sexual culture.[15] It stands to reason, after all, that certain traditional (or, at least, late imperial) notions of sexuality survived the introduction of Western sexology in the first decades of the twentieth century, and that they were shared features of the larger Chinese cultural world preceding the different political formations that emerged in the wake of WWII, and are still playing out and competing in the arena of Chinese sexual culture today.

Notes

1. See Xiaomingxiong. The first book-length treatment of the topic in English is Hinsch. The most comprehensive study to date of the sources on the subject is Z. Zhang. For the late imperial period, see Cuncun Wu; and Vitiello, *Libertine's*. For the twentieth century, see Sang; Martin, *Situating*; Sieber; and Kang.
2. On female homoeroticism, see Sang; L. Wu; Martin, *Situating*; as well as Sieber's introduction, *Red*, and her chapter in the present volume. It should be added that most sources on female homoeroticism were authored by men and not by women, and that the topic is not central even to narratives traditionally authored by women, such as prosimetric novels, *tanci xiaoshuo* (L. Wu).
3. On these early records, see the introduction to Vitiello *Libertine's*.
4. See Vitiello *Libertine's* chs. 1 and 3. For a translation of the episode from *The Plum in the Golden Vase*, see Roy chs. 34–35.
5. See Vitiello *Libertine's* ch. 1; and Volpp. For translations of Li Yu's relevant stories, see *Silent* and *Tower*.
6. On these two collections, see Vitiello, "Exemplary," "Fantastic," and *Libertine's*. The first story of *Cap and Hairpins* has been translated into French; see Lévy.
7. On this story, see Vitiello, "Exemplary."
8. See Brook; Vitiello *Libertine's* ch. 1 and passim.
9. On these three novels, see Vitiello *Libertine's* ch. 4. On *An Old Man's Humble Words*, see also McMahon, *Causality*; Epstein; and Huang. On *The Scholars*, see also Huang ch. 3; for a translation of the novel, see Ching-tzu Wu.
10. For a translation of the episodes referred to here, see Cao and Gao chs. 7–9, 15; for a more detailed commentary on them, see Vitiello *Libertine's* ch. 5.

11. On female impersonators at this time, see Cuncun Wu; Goldstein; and Goldman. On actors as male lovers in the seventeenth century, see also Volpp. On *The Mirror*, see also Wang, *Fin-de-Siècle*; Starr; McMahon, *Misers*; and Vitiello, *Libertine's* ch. 5.
12. For a complete translation (into Italian) of *The Cut Sleeve* anthology, see A. Wu; for a translation into English of selected stories, see Mitchell. For a study of the anthology, see Vitiello, "Dragon's."
13. On these stories, see Kang, ch. 3.
14. On these writers, see Sang; Martin *Situating*; and Sieber's chapter in this collection. For English translations of some of their works, see Martin, *Angelwings*; and Chu.
15. See for example Chen's *Farewell My Concubine* (1993), Lee's *Wedding Banquet* (1993), Tsai's *The River* (1996), Y. Zhang's *East Palace, West Palace* (1996), and Wong's *Happy Together* (1997).

Works Cited

Brook, Timothy. *The Confusions of Pleasure: Commerce and Culture in Ming China*. Berkeley: U of California P, 1998. Print.

Cao Xueqin and Gao E. *The Story of the Stone*. [aka *The Red Chamber Dream*.] Vol. 1. Trans. David Hawkes. Harmondsworth: Penguin, 1973. Print.

Chen, Kaige, dir. *Farewell My Concubine [Bawang bie ji]*. Miramax, 1993. Film.

Chu T'ien-wen. *Notes of a Desolate Man*. Trans. Howard Goldblatt and Sylvia Li-chun Lin. New York: Columbia UP, 1999. Print.

Cristini, Remy. "The Rise of Comrade Literature: Development and Significance of a New Chinese Genre." M.A. Thesis, Leiden U, 2005. Print.

Epstein, Maram. *Competing Discourses: Orthodoxy, Authenticity and Engendered Meanings in Late Imperial Chinese Fiction*. Cambridge: Harvard U Asia Center, 2001. Print.

Goldman, Andrea. *Opera and the City: The Politics of Culture in Beijing, 1770–1900*. Stanford: Stanford UP, 2012. Print.

Goldstein, Joshua. *Drama Kings: Players and Publics in the Re-creation of Peking Opera, 1870–1937*. Berkeley: U of California P, 2007. Print.

Hinsch, Bret. *Passions of the Cut Sleeve: The Male Homosexual Tradition in China*. Berkeley: U of California P, 1990. Print.

Huang, Martin. *Desire and Fictional Narrative in Late Imperial China*. Cambridge: Harvard U Asia Center, 2001. Print.

Kang, Wenqing. *Obsession: Male Same-Sex Relations in China, 1900–1950*. Hong Kong: Hong Kong UP, 2009. Print.

Lee, Ang, dir. *Wedding Banquet*. Samuel Goldwyn, 1993. Film.

Lévy, André, trans. *Épingle de femme sous le bonnet viril: Chronique d'un loyal amour*. Paris: Mercure de France, 1997. Print.

Li, Yu. *Silent Operas*. Trans. Patrick Hanan. Hong Kong: Renditions, 1990. Print.

A Tower for the Summer Heat. Trans. Patrick Hanan. New York: Ballantine, 1992. Print.

Martin, Fran. *Situating Sexualities: Queer Representation in Taiwanese Fiction, Film and Public Culture*. Hong Kong: Hong Kong UP, 2003. Print.

trans. *Angelwings: Contemporary Queer Fiction from Taiwan*. Honolulu: U of Hawai'i P, 2003. Print.

McMahon, Keith. *Causality and Containment in Seventeenth-Century Chinese Fiction*. Leiden: Brill, 1988. Print.

Misers, Shrews and Polygamists: Sexuality and Male-Female Relations in Eighteenth-century Chinese Fiction. Durham: Duke UP, 1995. Print.

"Sublime Love and the Ethics of Equality in a Homoerotic Novel of the Nineteenth Century: *Precious Mirror of Boy Actresses*." *Nan Nü* 4.1 (2002): 70–109. Print.

Mitchell, Mark, ed. *The Penguin Book of International Gay Writing*. New York: Viking, 1995. Print.

Mowry, Hua-yuan Li. *Chinese Love Stories from Ch'ing-shih*. Hamden: Archon, 1983. Print.

Pai, Hsien-yung. *Crystal Boys*. Trans. Howard Goldblatt. San Francisco: Gay Sunshine P, 1990. Print.

Roy, David T., trans. *The Plum in the Golden Vase, or Chin P'ing Mei. Volume Two: The Rivals*. Princeton: Princeton UP, 2001. Print.

Sang, Tze-lan. *The Emerging Lesbian: Female Same-Sex Desire in Modern China*. Chicago: U of Chicago P, 2003. Print.

Sieber, Patricia, ed. and intro. *Red Is not the Only Color: Contemporary Chinese Fiction on Love and Sex between Women*. Lanham: Rowman, 2001. Print.

Sommer, Matthew. *Sex, Law, and Society in Late Imperial China*. Stanford: Stanford UP, 2000. Print.

Starr, Chloe. "Shifting Boundaries: Gender in *Pinhua baojian*." *Nan Nü: Men, Women, and Gender in Early and Imperial China* 1.2 (2000): 268–302. Print.

Tsai, Ming-liang, dir. *The River [He liu]*. 1996. Film.

Vitiello, Giovanni. "The Dragon's Whim: Ming and Qing Homoerotic Tales from *The Cut Sleeve*." *T'oung Pao* 78 (1992): 342–72. Print.

"Exemplary Sodomites: Male Homosexuality in Late Ming Fiction." Diss. U of California Berkeley, 1994. Print.

"The Fantastic Journey of an Ugly Boy: Homosexuality and Salvation in Late Ming Pornography." *positions* 4.2 (1996): 291–320. Print.

"The Forgotten Tears of the Lord of Longyang: Late Ming Stories of Male Prostitution and Connoisseurship." *Linked Faiths: Essays on Chinese Religion and Traditional Culture in Honour of Kristofer Schipper*. Ed. Peter Engelfriet and Jan de Mejer. Leiden: Brill, 2000. 227–47. Print.

The Libertine's Friend: Homosexuality and Masculinity in Late Imperial China. Chicago: U of Chicago P, 2011. Print.

Volpp, Sophie. "The Literary Circulation of Actors in Seventeenth-Century China." *Journal of Asian Studies* 61.3 (2002): 949–984. Print.

Wang, David Der-wei. *Fin-de-Siècle Splendor: Repressed Modernities of Late Qing Fiction, 1849–1911*. Stanford: Stanford UP, 1997. Print.

"Impersonating China." *Chinese Literature: Essays, Articles, Reviews* 25 (2003): 133–63. Print.

Wong, Kar-wai, dir. *Happy Together [Chun gwong cha si]*. Golden Harvest, 1997. Film.

Wu, Ameng di. *La manica tagliata*. Trans. Giovanni Vitiello. Palermo: Sellerio, 1990. Print.

Wu, Ching-tzu. *The Scholars*. Trans. Yang Hsien-yi and Gladys Yang. Peking: Foreign Languages P, 1973. Print.

Wu, Cuncun. *Homoerotic Sensibilities in Late Imperial China*. London: Routledge-Curzon, 2004. Print.

Wu, Laura. "Through the Prism of Male Writing: Representation of Lesbian Love in Ming-Qing Literature." *Nan Nü* 4.1 (2002): 1–34. Print.

Xiaomingxiong. *Zhongguo tongxing'ai shilu*. Hong Kong: Fenhong sanjiao chubanshe, 1984. Print.

Zhang, Yuan, dir. *East Palace, West Palace* [*Donggong xigong*]. Strand Releasing, 1996. Film.

Zhang, Zaizhou. *Aimei de licheng: Zhongguo gudai tongxinglian shi*. Zhengzhou: Zhongzhou guji chubanshe, 2001. Print.

PART II

★

RENAISSANCE AND EARLY MODERN

8

From the Pervert, Back to the Beloved: Homosexuality and Ottoman Literary History, 1453–1923

ABDULHAMIT ARVAS

Early modern Ottoman poetry is predominantly about love; and for the most part, both the subject and the object of this love are men. Same-sex male erotic desire from the fifteenth to the eighteenth century is central to various genres from *gazel* (lyric poetry) to *mesnevi* (narrative poem) and shadow theatre, from *şehrengiz* (catalogue of beautiful men) to *tezkire* (biography) and *bahname* (medico-erotic treatise). While the image of the boy as the beloved pervades the early modern literary imagination, a wide array of other male objects of love calls attention to how same-sex desire is a complex phenomenon in early modern representations. Yet, in the nineteenth century, Westernization and the change in social dynamics at home transformed the "queer" paradigm of this literary lineage, and heteronormativity has since then colored the literary imagination, transforming the beloved into the pervert.

The Ottoman Empire includes Turks, Arabs, Greeks, Armenians, Jews, Kurds, and many other ethnicities from various regions; it would, however, be beyond the scope of this chapter to attend here to the distinct qualities of all regions. In this chapter, I specifically focus on the literary production and social context in Istanbul, which is the political heart of the empire as well as the center of literary production from the late fifteenth century onward. Although it is predominantly influenced by Persian and Arabic traditions, Ottoman literature develops in relation to a unique sexual culture with distinct categories and dynamics in Ottoman language and society. We have to think critically about our assumptions in reading this literature. Indeed, a literary history of Ottoman representations of same-sex desire, as well as sexuality in general, needs to account for a history of reconfigured and revalued readings of these texts. So to begin this chapter, I examine recent critical approaches to same-sex eroticism in Ottoman literature and discuss the theoretical problems regarding the history of sexuality and its terminology. I subsequently turn to homoerotic examples in early modern poetry to uncover commonly used homoerotic patterns and to trace their evolution from the fifteenth through the eighteenth century. While same-sex male eroticism is at the center of male-dominant poetry, women poets are also writing in this period, and they raise the question of same-sex female desire, which becomes my focus in the third section. The question of whether a same-sex object of love is superior is also a popular topic of literary disputes. Prose works in the sixteenth and seventeenth centuries particularly proffer such arguments, in the process laying out the nuances of sexual categories in early modernity. After tracing these intricate categories through historical inquiry, I present the nineteenth-century paradigm shift in the final section so as to "denaturalize heterosexuality" as the norm, to use David Halperin's terms (10) – that is, to undo heterosexuality as the unquestioned standard not only in societal discourses in Turkey, but also in scholarship that analyzes representations of same-sex love through naturalized, heteronormative lenses.

The Ottomans, Ottomanists, and Homosexuality

The understanding of homosexuality as an innate perversion and an immoral practice in the nineteenth century, together with the reverberations of Western descriptions of the Ottomans as sodomites, transformed the societal norms and literary representations in late Ottoman culture and continued to develop as the society strove to modernize and Westernize. This transformation also affected literary criticism in the field of Ottoman studies. The great Orientalist E. J. W. Gibb analyzed Ottoman poetry on the grounds of Western morality in his multivolume *A History of Ottoman Poetry* (1900–09). Subsequently, early twentieth-century Turkish scholars followed Gibb, whose work is based on assumptions not unlike those undergirding travel accounts written about the "pervert" Ottomans in Western travelogues from the sixteenth century onward.[1] Gibb and his Turkish adherents generated moralizing interpretations that imposed heteronormative readings on the poems and relied on an ahistorical understanding of homosexuality. Some scholars read the exclusive same-sex expressions and representations in the early modern Ottoman poetry as perversion, while others read it rather in metaphorical or transcendental terms – accepting the convention of same-sex love only without the bodies involved.[2] While some connect it to the availability of boys, others, who try not to be judgmental of these desires, attribute it to gender segregation, implying that same-sex desire was actually a frustrated heterosexuality. On the other hand, some use the gender-neutral nature of the Turkish language as an excuse to claim the beloved is actually a woman while all the indicators evince the opposite.

The first Turkish study fully focused on sexuality in Ottoman literature is *Divan Şiirinde Sapik Sevgi* (*Perverted Love in Divan Poetry*), a non-scholarly work published in 1968 by a journalist, Ismet Zeki Eyuboglu. With an agenda to disparage early modern Ottoman poetry, Eyuboglu discusses the (homo)sexual aspect of Ottoman poetry to justify why it should not be canonized or studied in schools, and why it must be banned, lest it corrupt the Turkish youth (33). Interestingly, his essentialist approach and thesis, which claims gender segregation as the cause of "pervert love," have been accepted as given by some scholars. Echoing Eyuboglu, Kemal Sılay, for example, claims the Islamic practice of gender segregation and women's exclusion from the public sphere as the main reason for the homoerotic and homosexual relations: "In a social environment where pre- and extramarital 'heterosexual interactions' were strictly prohibited, the absence of a *real* woman as *beloved* in poetry is not surprising" (82).[3] Love for young men emerges when the women are absent; it is simply a substitutive, temporary, and situational desire. Sılay anachronistically follows a homo/hetero matrix, and confines same-sex desires and poetic expressions to the marginal sphere of a minority, a group of frustrated heterosexuals.

In contrast to the early criticism, sex and sexuality in Ottoman representation have become a salient scholarly subject only in recent years thanks to literary scholars and historians like Nuran Tezcan, Selim Kuru, Walter Andrews, Mehmet Kalpaklı, and Dror Ze'evi, who have explored the subject with meticulous attention to the social and historical contexts. Kuru's dissertation (2000) was a significant attempt to present a transcription and English translation of Deli Birader Gazali's erotic text. Most important, Andrews and Kalpaklı's groundbreaking book, *The Age of Beloveds*, introduced a wide array of translated literary materials and vigorous analyses, asserting that "for the Ottomans, artistic literature was first and foremost poetry and that nearly all the poetry was love poetry" about the figure of the beloved youth; hence the title, "the age of beloveds" (10). El-Rouayheb's *Before Homosexuality*, and Ze'evi's *Producing Desire* influentially uncovered the history of sexual practices and categories in the early modern Arab-Islamic world and the Ottoman Middle East respectively.

Such work was made possible by Michel Foucault and other social constructivists who investigated the birth of modern homosexuality, and influentially suggested that "the homosexual" as an identity is a modern, bourgeois concept; indeed, Foucault famously declared "the homosexual [became] a species" only in the nineteenth century (43; see also McIntosh; Weeks; and Halperin). Thus, nowhere in the early modern Ottoman texts do we find conceptualizations of homosexual identity, psychosexual orientation, or stable subjectivities. There is not a term equivalent to modern "sexuality" and "homosexual" in Ottoman-Turkish. The word *cinsellik* (sexuality) itself is a twentieth-century innovation in the Turkish language. The Ottomans have categories like *gulampare* (male-lover), *zenpare* (woman-lover), *köçek* (male dancer), *mukhannes* (passive), *guzeshte* (young man with beard), *emred* (beardless youth); yet none of them can be seen as analogous to "the homosexual."

Nor do we find a normative heterosexuality in premodern Ottoman literature. As Valerie Traub attests in her essay on Islamicate sexuality studies, while many scholars eschew the labels gay/lesbian to describe premodern sexualities, "there is a tendency to use the term *heteronormativity* to describe earlier systems of sexuality and gender." The main reason for this is the lack of or little effort in scholarship toward "historicizing *hetero*sexuality" ("Past" 23). Even when critics are careful to highlight the historicity of homosexuality, recent scholarship in Ottoman sexualities inadvertently approaches heterosexuality and heteronormativity as ahistorical categories, failing to acknowledge how certain sexual practices and their representations were marginalized and became aberrant only after the nineteenth century.

Almost all of the works on Ottoman sexuality start with the inquiry: "Why same-sex?" However, posing this question can be a heteronormative move – particularly if the answer to this question collapses sexuality into gender. Although very careful in terms of avoiding essentializing any sexual identities, Andrews and Kalpaklı's vital work, for example, is at times trapped in a heteronormative angle, especially manifest as they constantly try to elucidate why Ottomans preferred same-sex interactions and expressions of love, as if there must have been a good reason to go astray. The reason has to do with gender segregation and availability of men: "When all the world's a stage and women are not allowed on it, then the beloved is always a boy, however dressed" (22). Similarly, Ze'evi, who is also attuned to historicity of sexual identities, and careful not to simplify same-sex desire by referring to gender segregation, still cannot help but declare when it comes to literary representations: "High-culture texts such as Sufi poetry, classical literature, and the theological discussions sometimes *preferred* male homoerotic metaphors to heteroerotic ones, because the introduction of women, in and of itself, was far more sensitive" (143). Irvin C. Schick similarly sees gender segregation and Islam as the "likely" reasons for same-sex love-object preference in Ottoman poetry, while nonetheless comparing it to the oral tradition, which mostly represents cross-sex love relations (90). Such conclusions naturalize heterosexuality while seeking a reason for the widespread fashion and preference of the literary expression of same-sex love.

What's more important for the emerging field of Ottoman sexualities is to generate a history of the ruptures and turns in sexual and moral paradigms, which may provide us the language and tools to better study premodern representations. The widespread representation of same-sex love, the multitudinous nonnormative sexual categories in Ottoman poetry, and the absence of heteronormativity, therefore, urge us to observe when the change in this type of conceptualization of the aforementioned preferences and the poetic convention emerged, and when the expressions of same-sex eroticism were silenced in order to highlight the processes of heteronormativity in the society in which this literature was composed.

Same-Sex Male Desire and Poetry from the Fifteenth to the Eighteenth Century

If your heart is not bound in the knot of his heathen belt
You're no true believer but a lost soul among lovers.
— Mehmed II

Pious one, should you see those Frankish boys but once
You would never cast an eye on the houris in paradise.
— Revani

In early modern Ottoman literature, the *gazel* (lyric poetry) is the prevailing genre of poetry, and the trope of *love for a young boy* features as the hallmark of this poetry. Almost all early modern poets, from the fifteenth-century Sultan Mehmed II, who conquers Constantinople but cannot conquer the heart of a Christian boy in his poems, to the seventeenth-century libertine poet Revani, who never cast his eye on heavenly women after seeing a Christian boy, to the eighteenth-century court poet Nedim, express love through same-sex male object of desire in their *gazels*. I focus here on literary materials that exemplify the portrayal of *the beloved boy*, how the boy and the poem become one for poets, and how poets compete with other poets for boys through their poems.

In celebrating their love for beloved boys in *gazels*, early modern poets often describe their poems as symbolic bodies of their beloveds. The sixteenth century marks the height of this trope. One of the most famous and respected poets of the period, Zati, describes the poem itself as the beloved:

By describing the beloved's ruby [lip], the poem becomes a sweet-spoken
beloved
With sugar-bearing words the poem becomes a sweet, tender beloved ...
Magically, I brought together fire and cotton in one place
"What is this?" I said, and the poem replied "The heart is cotton, the paper
flame."   (95–96)[4]

Similarly, Fevri, who was a slave in his youth and later a well-known poet as
well a law professor, describes his poems as beautiful boys: "Each of Fevri's
couplets is a lovely new-bearded beloved / On each one of whose hands are
written poems" (99). For another famous poet, İshak Çelebi, a scholar and
Islamic judge, "Poem is a jasmine-cheeked, new bearded, matchless beauty /
Heart attracting, well formed, sweet of speech and action," and he writes
poems only when he is in love with a boy: "No matter I renounce poetry time
and again, when I fall in love / With a faint-mustached young lad, helpless, I
must compose a poem" (99).

Gazel is also a medium to attract the beloved. As the famous poet Mesihi
writes, the poet "aims to hunt that gazelle with gazels," and likewise, as Sani
says, "The heart used poetry to bring that gazelle eye thigh-to-thigh / The
gazel is a wealth of capital to the boy-chasing reveler" (92). Not just written
poetry, but also speech links beloved and poem. Zati, for instance, sees Jesus
speaking in the image of the boy:

> Let me say, longing for your lip,
> should you recite a poem,
> O idol, it would bring dead to life
> like the speech of Jesus.   (97)

Early modern poetic form and the homoerotic imagination are, thus,
inseparable.

Gazel did not solely address imaginary young men. In many *gazels*, we
see how poets compete with one another to steal a beautiful man's heart, or
simply a kiss. The beloved boy's name, in these examples, is hardly a secret.
Zati writes poems to his bath boy Nimet, who "stripped us, Oh Zati, he who
shaved us" (101), or publicizes Muharrem, whose mouth's vial makes "[Zati]
lose [his] mind" (103). Similarly, a poet and a judge, Vasfi, who is under the
patronage of the grand vizier Ali Pasha, explicitly declares his love for a janis-
sary named Memi: "Don't praise the sun or moon to me saying they are loved
/ No beauties of this world do I love but Memi Shah" (104). Another boy, Kaya,
was so popular that there were at least fifty-six poems directly addressed to
him.[5] Some young men, furthermore, were so popular in the sixteenth and

seventeenth centuries that certain poetic catalogues – the genre of *şehrengiz* (city-thrillers)⁶ – ubiquitously circulated among people to describe the disposition and physical beauty of these young boys.⁷

Same-sex male desire in poetry becomes the object of criticism with the rise of zealous anti-Sufi movements in the late sixteenth and seventeenth centuries. The homoerotic dynamics, nevertheless, continue in eighteenth-century literature. Poet and man-lover Fazıl Enderuni writes his *Hubanname* (*The Book of Beautiful Men*), cataloguing and praising the features of beautiful men from many countries including Britain, France, and the New World as well as various Eastern regions in this century. In his *Defter-i Aşk* (*The Book of Love*), he poeticizes the four male lovers of his life; and his *Çenginame* (*The Book of Dancers*) includes licentious portraits of boy dancers, *köçeks*.⁸ Similarly, the most famous and celebrated court poet in that century, Nedim, openly writes about boys and men with beards: "I wish there were me, a musician and a river side; and should there be an attractive young man, too" (qtd. in Sılay 97). For Nedim, "compared to a beard, the eyelashes and waist of the beloved, as thin as a hair, have no value," and subsequently, he yearns: "Oh Nedim, hair, beauty spot, eyes, lips, and the lovelocks.... All these have captured you; however, only his beard has captured me!" (100). Nedim's striking and unconventional stress on the beard and hair of the beloved men suggests the possibility of egalitarian same-sex relations besides transgenerational relations. Evidently, the beloved is not a beardless boy in Nedim's poem, as he usually is in sixteenth-century poetry, but an adult man with a beard: "From hair to hair, I consider every part of your body kissable; / Please help me to choose which part of your body you would like me to kiss" (100). In spite of antihomoerotic discourses, the eighteenth-century poets further develop the Sufi tradition and enrich the homoerotic tradition in literature with the image of the beloved as adult man.

Dildo Women, Lesbian Desire, and Women Writers

Same-sex female desire and relations in early modern Ottoman literature is still the *terra incognita* of Ottoman studies. Interestingly, early modern European travelogues appear as a source for critics to uncover same-sex female relations. Sılay, for example, asserts: "Besides veiling, the separation of men and women in daily life and the formation of exclusively male and female groups must have provided some of the required circumstances for the expression of homosexuality in that society. It is well-known that many Westerners who travelled to the lands of the Ottoman Empire mentioned in their letters their observation concerning homosexuality among Ottoman-Turkish men and women" (92). (Female) homosociality brings forth (female) homosexuality, opines Sılay. Similarly Refik Ahmet Sevengil uses these travelogues to claim: "This psychological sickness [lesbianism], which clinical medicine calls 'love between same gender,' was common in the past among women, too. There were such wealthy women who made love to each other in the harems. They had several young and beautiful girls and women in their service in order to satisfy their sexual desires" (qtd. in Sılay 92–93). Sevengil thus distinguishes the women of the "Islamic Middle Eastern Ottomans" from the healthy women of the Europeanized Turkish Republic. Such generalizing readings do not provide us with any textual evidence that can prove the existence in the early modern Ottoman imagination of the notion of "lesbianism" as a psychological disorder or sexual identity deriving from spatial arrangements. The very discourse of the travel writers that interpreted homosociality in the Ottoman Empire as a reason for the lascivious and unrestrained sexuality practiced in certain spaces continues in the frame of such arguments.[9] I must note that, of course, there were same-sex relations between women in the Ottoman era, but same-sex female relations are not represented as explicitly as male ones in the male-dominant Ottoman literature.[10]

Deli Birader Gazali's work, which I analyze in detail in the following section, mentions same-sex female relations and butch/femme sexual roles, albeit from a male point of view for male readers: "In big cities, there are famous *dildo women*. They put on manly clothes, they ride cavalry horses, and they also ride *kochis* [covered wagons] for fun. Rich and noble women invite them to their houses and offer them nice shirts and clothing. These women tie dildos on their waists and grease them with almond oil and then start the job, dildoing the cunt" (qtd. in Kuru, "Scholar" 235).[11] As Andrews and Kalpaklı point out, it is clear that a satisfying sexual relation between two women was unimaginable by the Ottomans, and not even an idea to be entertained: "We have not been able to locate a single instance in the Ottoman legal literature of a woman being accused of illegal or immoral sexual relations with another woman" (172). This silence is to be expected in a society where sex means penetration and dominance. A literary work on sexuality would then represent all kinds of sexual activities, even with animals, yet ignore woman-woman contact because of the nonpenetrative and nonphallic aspect attributed to it. However, as this example shows, Gazali does not reduce penetration to a male activity. Apparently, the dildo woman becomes the very manifestation of the possibility of female-female penetrative sex.

A closer look at the representation of women in writings by women writers may help us avoid phallocentric readings of the representations related to female desire. Known women poets of early modernity such as Mihri Hatun, Zeyneb, Ayşe Hatun, Nisayi of the Royal Harem, and Tuti Hanım may help us revisit the question of same-sex female love. In most of the poems, we cannot clearly say if the gender of the beloved is male or female, while we can infer that the speaker is a woman from the use of a female penname / speaker in the last couplet. Mihri Hatun (d. 1506), an educated and unmarried woman in a male-dominated society, is an interesting case. Considering marriage as a norm for Ottoman women, Mihri's case as a figure resisting marriage opens her work to queer readings. Huriye Reis sees her as a poet subverting the dominant values and norms, and calls her "Sappho of the Ottomans" (156). Yet, Reis, on the other hand, asserts that "her position in her poetry as a lover is not distinguishable from that of a man addressing a woman beloved" (150). Based on this assumption, Reis interprets the speaker in her poems as "he" and the beloved as "she" even though Mihri uses her name as penname (*mahlas*) in the last couplets, leaving no doubt about the speaker's female gender. Another woman poet, Fitnat Hanım of the eighteenth century, addresses the beloved as "faithful" and "cruel," leaving the gender oblique. Likewise Zeyneb Hatun's call blurs the gender of the addressee, while hinting at a female beloved with the use of "veil": "Remove your veil and illuminate the earth and skies" (qtd. in Andrews, et al. 53). Leyla Hanım in the nineteenth century competes with other rivals:

> I see my rival is chasing you – Come lie beside me ...
> Who cares what they say.
> Leyla, indulge in pleasure with your lovely, moon-faced friend;
> Make sure you pass all your day in joy.
> Who cares what they say! (Halman 39)

The androgynous beloved – male or female – is the passive object of the woman lover, which subverts gender / sexual / social roles and opens the poems to further investigation.

Boy-Lovers, Woman-Lovers, and Other Categories

While most of the male poets choose the young man as the object of desire in their works, or female poets such as Zeynep Hatun blur the gender of the beloved, some male poets such as Hayali Bey desire both female and male beloveds, while other poets such as Tacizade Cafer Çelebi exclusively prefer to write about cross-sex love. It is a popular literary dispute among poets whether it is men or women who best represent love.[12] The famous poet Fevri writes: "the man of [true] love doesn't look at the women of this world/ Does an accomplished man conform to one 'deficient in reason and faith?'" (135). Similarly, another famous and influential sixteenth-century poet, Taşlıcalı Yahya Bey, in his own *mesnevi*, *Sah u Geda*, expresses his distaste for traditional narrative poems (*mesnevi*), which use cross-sex love as the basis of their exemplary love stories, such as the widely circulating *Hüsrev u Shirin*, and *Layla vu Mecnun*.

> Those, woman-chasing, lacking taste
> These, suffering, cure-less, and chaste
> What do they know of love's mystery
> Of the rapture of love and its ecstasy.
> A lover true forever tries
> Making sleep unlawful to his eyes
> Let him love bodies like cypress trees
> Suffer, like Job, love's agonies
> Mirror of body and soul let him shine
> As slave to a robust boy repine
> Who grieves the love of a lovely boy
> Never will *Husrev and Shirin* enjoy.   (56)

While love for woman is carnal, love for boys is superior, deeper, and purer, writes Yahya. The male body is a divine reflection; and after enjoying this love for man, the lover will never take pleasure in even the most famous stories featuring cross-sex love stories.

Prominent sixteenth-century scholar, courtier, bathhouse owner, and dervish Deli Birader Gazali provides us with the most obvious one of these disputes in *Dâfi'ü'l-gumûm ve Râfi'ü'l-humûm* (*Repeller of Sorrows and Remover of Cares*). The worthiest love, for Gazali, is the same-sex male love for many reasons: "Beautiful boys are always with you on campaigns. Moreover they don't have any guardians. You can take them into an empty room, or accompany him to a promenade. You can put your arm around him, or pull him into your arms and kiss him. Touching his face with your face, you can suck his lips, or you can get him drunk in your arms. Neither judge nor master would stop you. Is there anything better than this in the world?" (177–78). His erotic prose, written when he was in the court of Prince Korkut, also presents complex and fluid sexual categories and discourses that help us apprehend the sexual culture in the period.

Starting with advice that poses marriage as "the reason for continuity of lineages, and the cause of reproduction; it is the basis of a family stock, and the practice of the prophet," Gazali notes also that marriage keeps one away from masturbation and the reproach of a beloved (158). After presenting marriage as the normative union, he goes on to describe various nonnormative sexual practices: same-sex male contact, bestiality, masturbation, and so on. As for the ideal love, he suggests the beautiful young man as the beloved, after giving a lengthy chapter on a dispute between a *gulampare* (boy-lover) and *zenpare* (woman-lover). Interestingly, women lovers are dressed "lady-like" and their bodies "grow weak and soft" and feminine, while the boy-lovers are masculine and heroic with their manly attire. The object of love, for Gazali, has the power to emasculate or enhance the masculinity of men. Gazali ends the chapter with a *gazel* celebrating anal sex. The chapter is mainly about desire and pleasure: what is the most desirable to penetrate? It compares sexual pleasures – anal and vaginal – while contesting identity categories of *gulampare* and *zenpare*: "ass is like a jasmine faced beauty with rosebud-lips and apple shaped chin and with silver limbs" (174). Male anality is described with exactly the same terms that traditionally characterize a beloved boy. Losing the dispute, the woman-lovers explore pleasures of anal sex on the body of an old catamite, manifesting how fluid these categories are.

Gazali further demonstrates how same-sex male categories may be complex and instable by differentiating various same-sex male preferences. One group loves "fresh" young boys whose

> cocks are sweeter than sugar cane
> Their shit tastier than jelly
> Their small balls are like rock
> And their penises shaped like fresh almonds.   (188)

Sugar cane as an active phallic image, reinforcing "cocks," complicates active / passive roles, making it difficult for readers to make the generalization that the boy is always the penetrated passive one. Another group of men loves *guzeshte* (young men with beards). Lovers of young men, not prepubescent boys, ask if boys are really men, praising love among equals: "Guzeshte beauties are able to appreciate the worth of a lover" and know how to have good sex (190). The final group is lovers of old men who don't like boys or young men with black mustaches but men with white beards: "One loves bearded boys other loves jasmine-faced boys ... / [But] I fell for a white bearded one in order always to be alone with him" (191). However, Gazali pathologizes one type: *mukhannes*, a man with a disease stemming from having a young boy's sperm inside his anus, which irritates and causes the anus to itch, as a result of which he desires to be penetrated for a cure. Interestingly, the only category pathologized among the known categories in medieval Islamicate cultures is *ubna*, which stands for a man who wants to be penetrated.[13] While *ubna* originates from birth, *mukhannes* is what a man may become in case of reversal of positions in same-sex relations. His stigmatization is evidently due, then, to subversion of the hierarchy of the penetrator and the penetrated. A young boy may be penetrated temporarily – it is quite acceptable because of his young age – while an adult man's desire to be penetrated is a taboo, a disease, whether a genetic one or a later affliction. However, as Gazali's explanation reveals, there is always a "risk" for an active man to be penetrated in same-sex relations and to become a *mukhannes* because of the boy's potential for altering roles.

Another prose example evincing fluidity of early modern sexual categories is Nev'izade Atayi's *Heft han* (*The Seven Stories*) (1637), which narrates the story of two friends and lovers, Tayyib and Tahir. They emerge from their stages of *müşteha* (sexually desirable) and *emred* (beardless youth), and make a transition to the status of *levend* (adventurous) lovers.[14] As young adults, they follow boys in taverns, streets, and parks, and spend their nights with other boys in Istanbul.[15] Later in the story, these two friends become captives of two European men, fall in love with their masters, and develop erotic relations with them as submissive beloveds in European gardens. Finally, this strong loyalty to same-sex love unites all four men back in Istanbul, and the two European men convert to Islam. As Atayi's story demonstrates, although there are expected roles for certain ages, the roles are fluid regardless of the expectations. These two unattached young men are active while they are free, but submissive when they are servant to the two Italian men. Mastery and service as well as Christianity and Islam are imagined in this active/passive matrix.

Rather than sexual identities, it is primarily penetration and dominance that determine early modern Ottoman sexual discourse. As Atayi's story shows, the relations are structured in accordance with social roles, and as Gazali's text indicates, the younger party does not have to get pleasure; it is the older man who experiences the erotic satisfaction, while the younger gets gifts, money, praise, assistance, or a poem in return. To borrow Halperin's assertion about the ancient Greeks, "This is sex as hierarchy, not mutuality, sex as something done to someone by someone else, not a common search for shared pleasure or a purely personal, private experience in which larger social identities based on age or social status are submerged or lost" (115). Instead of a strict homo/hetero division, moreover, we see an evaluation of different avenues for sexual pleasures and activities depending on penetration along with a celebration of marriage as an ethical and religious union with a reproductive imperative.

Westernization, Heterosexualization, and the Birth of the Pervert in the Nineteenth Century

The homoerotic nature of Ottoman literature and popular genres started to disappear in the post-Tanzimat era, the second half of the nineteenth century, when, as Ze'evi's impressive work shows, with the influence of Europeanization and the strength of the *ulema* class (scholars of Islamic law), as well as that of certain pashas and intellectuals who were critical of the homoerotic aspect of Sufi traditions, Sufis changed their ceremonies, reducing the staging of boys. The literary materials including homoerotic relations started to be censored and "needless to say, homoerotic love and sex did not disappear, but now any discussion of such themes became shameful" (Ze'evi 97). Not only Sufi texts and practices were controlled in this era, but all textual materials that portrayed sex very explicitly, like dream interpretations, medical and legal texts, and shadow theatres, were silenced. This is manifest in the new literature that emerged in the nineteenth century with new styles in poetry and new genres such as the novel, drama, and short story borrowed from Europe. So, not only are medical, legal, and religious discourses Westernized, but the literary tradition itself has also been revolutionized with new genres, themes, and morality tales.[16]

Cevdet Pasha, a leader of the nineteenth-century reforms, for example, reports in his autobiographical *Maruzat* the striking change taking place in the moral conduct of people in the 1850s, referring to the eradication of same-sex practices: "With the increase of women lovers the number of boy-beloveds decreased and the sodomites seem to have disappeared off the face of the earth. Ever since then the well-known love for and relationships with the young men of Istanbul was transferred to young women as the natural order of things" (qtd. in Ze'evi 164). This is the very adoption of Victorian discourses, implied in Cevdet Pasha's emphasis on "the natural order of things." As Leslie Peirce asserts, "the impact of the West on nineteenth-century Middle Eastern society is undeniable, whether by force of intellectual inspiration and imperialist aura or on the ground in the form of colonial administrators, missionaries, commercial agents, governesses, young Muslims returning from European educations, and so on" (1336). The post-Tanzimat period engenders marriage and family as normative institutions as well as a process of heterosexualization; and accordingly, the literary representations undergo alterations, now promoting heterosexuality. As Deniz Kandiyoti writes, this new sexual discourse used by reformers "attempts to institutionalize monogamous heterosexuality as the normative ideal" (284). In the same period, Fazıl's explicitly homoerotic works from the previous century are banned because of their hostility toward marriage. Heterosexualization, by eradicating homoerotic friendship and the expression of affection, now replaces this once-best love.[17] This process reaches its apogee with the twentieth-century republican discourses of sexuality that attribute hedonism and all nonnormative sexualities to the Ottomans. Yakup Kadri Karaosmanoglu's novel *Sodom ve Gomore* (1928), for example, depicts the Ottoman elite of Istanbul, in the days immediately following World War I, as decadent and hedonistic, with lesbian and gay relations as well as orgies taking place in the last days of the Ottoman Empire – presented as the immoral other to the twentieth-century, Westernized Turkish Republic's men and women.

Although the change in the sexual discourse and the production of sexual identities in Turkey occur around the same time as in Europe, the shift in literary works of the two societies is incommensurable. All *current* queer categories in Turkey – *ibne*, *köçek*, gay, lesbian, *gulampare*, queer – are sociohistorical and contingent productions, and do not originate from the emergence of homosexuality in the nineteenth-century West. While in Europe the older categories of sodomite, catamite, or effeminate man reemerge in the formation of the abnormal, pathologized homosexual identity – "the unrationalized coexistence of different models" in Eve Kosofsky Sedgwick's terms (47) – the Turkish discourses produce homosexuality as a new category blending with and often including the older categories while simultaneously disowning homosexuality as European "immorality." Take, for example, the term *ibne* in modern Turkish, which serves as a derogatory term indicating a man who desires to be penetrated by another man, while at the same time signifying gay men in recent usage. Deriving from the medieval notion of *ubna*, *ibne* uneasily blends sexuality-as-orientation, based on the sexual object-choice, with sexuality-as-hierarchy based on active/passive roles. *Ibne*, therefore, amalgamates an Arabic-originated word and signification (*ubna*/passive) with a European term and connotation (gay/psycho-sexual identity). The deployment of the Western-originated identity categories of gay, lesbian, or homosexual to refer to non-Western queers may lead to the latter's exclusion and oppression as Westernized, immoral perverts by the state and some other political groups. However, carefully studying *older* categories and their historical changes in literature (i.e., *gulampare* [boy-lover], *emred* [boy], *guzeste* [man with beard], *levend* [adventurous young man], *luti* [sodomite], *mukhannes* [passive/bottom], *ubna* [catamite], *köçek* [dancing men], beautiful men, the feminine, the androgynous, the eunuch, the hermaphrodite,[18] or the masculine woman, the unmarried woman, the dildo woman, the intimate friend) will not only limn a strong literary history of and for sexually marginalized people and their expressions of their desires but also help us show the complexities of queer relations and representations. At the same time this cultural history will denaturalize and denarrativize discourses based on patriarchy, homophobia, hatred, and Occidentalism.

Notes

1. From the travel accounts of Nicolay's *The Navigations* (1585), Sandys's *A Relation of a Journey* (1610), Rycaut's *The Present State of the Ottoman Empire* (1668), English writers openly recognized the existence of female same-sex desire / sexual activity and located its center in the Ottoman East, associating it directly with social conditions such as gender segregation thought to be peculiar to Muslims and the Ottomans. Rycaut, for example, connects same-sex practices to gender segregation and interestingly to the Ottomans' misunderstanding of Plato's *Symposium*. For more on early modern travelogues on same-sex relations, see Matar.

2. Abdulbaki Golpınarlı and Atilla Senturk exemplify those views: Golpınarlı declares the Ottomans as perverts, while Senturk ignores the gender of beloved to point out that it is love not the beloved that matters. According to him, all such representations seek a unity with God by divorcing love strictly from sex.

3. We must take into consideration that all kinds of extramarital relations, including cross-sex ones, were sexual crimes. Same-sex male relations were condemned because they were extramarital. Moreover, even with gender segregation it does not follow that cross-sex activities were unavailable; there was access for men to heterosocial spaces through marriage, taverns, brothels, and public places like picnic areas and gardens.

4. Unless otherwise indicated, all references to the translated works are from Andrews and Kalpaklı, with some silent alterations.

5. On naming the beloved in *gazels*, see Kuru, "Naming."

6. *Sehrengiz*, mostly erotic genre of obscenely cataloguing beautiful men of the cities, is borrowed from Persian models, and it evolves to include different countries while the empire expands its boundaries. For more on the genre, see Levend; Stewart-Robinson; Oztekin; Tugcu. On how this genre is transformed into a visual cataloguing by European modernist artists, see Boone.

7. *Bahname* (book of libido) or medico-erotic treatises were famous examples of erotic literature from the thirteenth century onward. See Bardakci for exemplary passages from *Bahnames*. Some other genres to observe such representations are highly obscene shadow theatres (*Karagoz*), jokes (*Nasreddin Hoca*), *mani*, *sarki* (song), *hamamiye* (on bathhouses), and biographies of poets. For an

excellent overview of sexuality and gender in Ottoman-Turkish literature from medieval to contemporary, see Schick.

8. On Fazil Bey and his influence over the queer reorientations in the West, see Boone.

9. For more on the Western travelers' writing on same-sex female relations in Ottoman Turkey, see Traub, *Renaissance* 198–206.

10. On female homoeroticism in the Middle East excluding Turkey, see Malti-Douglas; Habib; Amer.

11. All references to Gazali's work are from Kuru, "Scholar."

12. *Tezkire* (biographies of poets) is another genre where these disputes are stressed. The early modern biographers, like Aşık Çelebi and Latifi, stress the poet's boy-loving or woman-loving disposition when describing a poet, evincing that erotic preference was something worthy to record about poets.

13. On medical categories, see Rosenthal; Nathan. Ze'evi also argues that *ubna* was considered to be originated from the imbalance of semen of the male and the female at the moment of procreation. For more on *ubna* and *mukhannes* as sexual categories, see Ze'evi; El-Rouayheb.

14 For more on these categories and an in-depth analysis of this story, see Andrews and Kalpaklı 59–84.

15. Some spaces are associated with specific sexual activities. While describing social life in sixteenth-century Istanbul, Mustafa Ali Gelibolulu talks about taverns as spaces for same-sex love relations: "Some come to the tavern with their boy lover, they eat and drink, and when evening falls they make their way over to the tavern's private room. According to the demands of their lust, they extract milk from the sugar cane [they achieve orgasm]" (131). Bathhouses, another popular space for erotic contact, appear in Aşık Çelebi and Evliya Çelebi, as well. Aşık Çelebi describes his and other poets' visits to bathhouses to flirt with and watch beautiful young men. Evliya Çelebi, in his travelogue, mentions the erotic atmosphere in the bathhouses and how lovers and beloveds enjoy each other's company in the warm waters. Some of the other sexual spaces are Tophane and Galata taverns such as Efe Meyhanesi and Yani Meyhanesi, the banks of Bosphorus and Marmara, gardens, coffeehouses, picnic areas such as Goksu, or Kagithane. On Aşık Çelebi, who gives us these sixteenth-century poets' biographies, see Aynur and Niyazioglu. On sexualized spaces, see Andrews and Kalpaklı 63–84. On garden as sexual space, see Hamadeh, "Public" and *The City*.

16. What may be called the "modern state" emerges – with notions like *vatan* (motherland), *hurriyet* (liberty), *inkilab* (change), and *milliyet* (nation) – in this era, while, as Andrews and Kalpaklı show, the nascent forms of these may be observed in the sixteenth century. See Ze'evi's excellent overview on medical, religious, and legal changes. Najmabadi's description of nineteenth-century Iran suggests a similar shift. Massad argues that comparable changes take

place in Arab-speaking societies. He suggests Foucauldian arguments should be revisited by considering the emergence of modern Western notions of sexuality with respect to civilization building.

17. By no means do I suggest a total eradication of homosexuality in nineteenth-century literature. Post-Tanzimat homoerotic literature includes the nineteenth-century anonymous *Hançerli Hanım*; Ahmet Rasim's *Ulfet*, which focuses on lesbianism; and Sait Faik of the early republican era. Recent literature has widespread representations of queer sexualities by popular writers such as Atilla Ilhan, Arslan Yuzgun, Murathan Mungan, Kucuk Iskender, Elif Shafak, Orhan Pamuk, Perihan Magden, Selim Ileri, Adalet Agaoglu, Bilge Karasu, Emine Sevgi Ozdamar, Latife Tekin; and film directors such as Fatih Akin, Ferzan Ozpetek, and Kutlug Ataman.

18. For more on eunuchs and hermaphrodites in Islamicate cultures, see Rowson, "Effeminates" and "Gender"; Marmon; Ringrose; Hathaway; and Sanders.

Works Cited

Amer, Sahar. *Crossing Borders: Love between Women in Medieval French and Arabic Literatures.* Philadelphia: U of Pennsylvania P, 2008. Print.

Andrews, Walter, et al., eds. *Ottoman Lyric Poetry: An Anthology.* Seattle: U of Washington P, 2006. Print.

Andrews, Walter G., and Mehmet Kalpaklı. *The Age of Beloveds: Love and the Beloved in Early Modern Ottoman and European Culture and Society.* Durham: Duke UP, 2005. Print.

Aynur, Hatice, and Asli Niyazioglu, ed. *Asik Celebi ve Sairler Tezkiresi Uzerine Yazilar.* Istanbul: Koc, 2011. Print.

Bardakci, Murat. *Osmanli'da Seks.* Istanbul: Inkilap, 2005. Print.

Boone, Joseph. "Modernist Re-Orientations: Imagining Homoerotic Desire in the 'Nearly' Middle East." *Modernism/Modernity* 17.3 (2010): 561–605. Print.

Çelebi, Aşık. *Mesa'iru's-Su'ara.* Ed. Filiz Kilic. Istanbul: Istanbul Arastirmalari Enstitusu, 2010. Print.

Çelebi, Evliya. *Evliya Çelebi Seyahatnamesi.* Istanbul: Yapı Kredi, 2000. Print.

El-Rouayheb, Khaled. *Before Homosexuality in the Arab-Islamic World, 1500–1800.* Chicago: U of Chicago P, 2005. Print.

Eyuboglu, Ismet Zeki. *Divan Şiirinde Sapık Sevgi.* Istanbul: Okat, 1968. Print.

Foucault, Michel. *The History of Sexuality Volume I: An Introduction.* Trans. Robert Hurley. New York: Pantheon, 1978. Print.

Gelibolulu, Mustafa Ali. *The Ottoman Gentleman of the Sixteenth Century: Mustafa Ali's Mevaiddu'n-Nefa'is Fi Kava'idi'l-Mecalis (Tables of Delicacies Concerning the Rules of Social Gatherings).* Trans. Douglas S. Brook. Cambridge: Harvard UP, 2003. Print.

Gibb, E. J. W. *A History of Ottoman Poetry.* 6 vols. London: Luzac, 1900–09.

Golpinarli, Abdulbaki. *Divan Edebiyatı Beyanındadır.* Istanbul: Marmara UP, 1945. Print.

Habib, Samar. *Female Homosexuality in the Middle East: Histories and Representations.* New York: Routledge, 2007. Print.

Halman, Talat S., ed. *Nightingales and Pleasure Gardens: Turkish Love Poems*. Syracuse: Syracuse UP, 2005. Print.

Halperin, David M. *How to Do the History of Homosexuality*. Chicago: U of Chicago P, 2002. Print.

Hamadeh, Shirine. "Public Spaces and the Garden Culture of Istanbul in the Eighteenth Century." *The Early Modern Ottomans: Remapping the Empire*. Ed. Virginia H. Aksan and Daniel Goffman. Cambridge: Cambridge UP, 2007. 277–312. Print.

———. *The City's Pleasure: Istanbul in the Eighteenth Century*. Seattle: U of Washington P, 2008. Print.

Hathaway, Jane. *Beshir Agha: Chief Eunuch of the Ottoman Imperial Harem*. London: Oneworld, 2006. Print.

Kandiyoti, Deniz. "Some Awkward Questions on Women and Modernity in Turkey." *Remaking Women: Feminism and Modernity in the Middle East*. Ed. Lila Abu-Lughod. Princeton: Princeton UP, 1998. 270–87. Print.

Karaosmanoglu, Yakup Kadri. *Sodom ve Gomore*. 1928. Istanbul: Iletisim, 2011. Print.

Kuru, Selim. "Scholar and Author in the Sixteenth-century Ottoman Empire: Deli Birader and His Work *Dâfi'ü'l-gumûm ve Râfi'ü'l-humûm*." Diss. Harvard U, 2000. Print.

———. "Naming the Beloved in Ottoman Turkish Gazel: The Case of Ishak Celebi (d. 1537/8)." *Ghazal as World Literature II. From a Literary Genre to a Great Tradition. The Ottoman Gazel in Context*. ed. Angelika Neuwirth et. al. Beirut: Beiruter Texte und Studien, 2005. 163–73. Print.

Levend, Agah Sirri. *Türk Edebiyatında Şehrengizler ve Şehrengizlerde İstanbul*. İstanbul: Fetih Cemiyeti, 1958. Print.

Malti-Douglas, Fedwa. "Tribadism/Lesbianism and the Sexualized Body in Medieval Arabo-Islamic Narratives." *Same Sex Love and Desire among Women in the Middle Ages*. Ed. Francesca Canade Sautman and Pamela Sheingorn. New York: Palgrave, 2001. 123–41. Print.

Marmon, Shaun. *Eunuchs and Sacred Boundaries in Islamic Society*. New York: Oxford UP, 1995. Print.

Massad, Joseph A. *Desiring Arabs*. Chicago: U of Chicago P, 2007. Print.

Matar, Nabil. *Turks, Moors, and Englishmen in the Age of Discovery*. New York: Columbia UP, 1999. Print.

McIntosh, Mary. "Homosexual Role." *Social Problems* 16.2 (1968): 182–92. Print.

Najmabadi, Afsaneh. *Women with Mustaches and Men without Beards: Gender and Sexual Anxieties of Iranian Modernity*. Berkeley: U of California P, 2005. Print.

Nathan, Bassem. "Medieval Arabic Medical Views on Male Homosexuality." *Journal of Homosexuality* 26.4 (1994): 37–39. Print.

Oztekin, Dilek. "Sehrengizler ve Bursa: Edebiyat ve Escinsel Egilim." *Kuram* 14 (1997): 37–41. Print.

Peirce, Leslie P. "Writing Histories of Sexuality in the Middle East." *American Historical Review* 114.5 (2009): 1325–39. Print.

Reis, Huriye. "Medieval Women, Poetry, and Mihri Hatun." *Sosyal Bilimler Dergisi* 20 (2008): 147–57. Print.

Ringrose, Kathryn M. *The Perfect Servant: Eunuchs and the Social Construction of Gender in Byzantium*. Chicago: U of Chicago P, 2003. Print.

Rosenthal, Franz. "Ar-Razi on the Hidden Illness." *Bulletin of the History of Medicine* 52 (1978): 45–60. Print.

Rowson, Everett K. "The Effeminates of Early Medina." *Journal of the American Oriental Society* III.4 (1991): 671–93. Print.

"Gender Irregularity as Entertainment: Institutionalized Transvestism at the Caliphal Court in Medieval Baghdad." *Gender and Difference in the Middle Ages*. Ed. Sharon Farmer and Carol Braun Pasternack. Minneapolis: U of Minnesota P, 2003. 45–72. Print.

Sanders, Paula. "Gendering the Ungendered Body: Hermaphrodites in Medieval Islamic Law." *Women in Middle Eastern History: Shifting Boundaries in Sex and Gender*. Ed. Nikki R. Keddie and Beth Baron. New Haven: Yale UP, 1991. 74–95. Print.

Schick, Irvin Cemil. "Representation of Gender and Sexuality in Ottoman and Turkish Erotic Literature." *Turkish Studies Association Journal* 28.1–2 (2007): 81–103. Print.

Sedgwick, Eve Kosofsky. *Epistemology of the Closet*. Berkeley: U of California P, 2008. Print.

Senturk, Atilla. "Osmanlı Şiirinde Aşka Dair." *Dogu Batı* 7.26 (2004): 55–68. Print.

Sılay, Kemal. *Nedim and the Poetics of the Ottoman Court: Medieval Inheritance and the Need for Change*. Bloomington: Indiana UP, 1994. Print.

Stewart-Robinson, James. "A Neglected Ottoman Poem: The Sehrengiz." *Studies in Near Eastern Culture and History: In Memory of Ernest T. Abdel-Massih*. Ed. James Bellamy. Ann Arbor: U of Michigan P, 1990. 201–11. Print.

Traub, Valerie. "The Past Is a Foreign Country? The Times and Spaces of Islamicate Sexuality Studies." *Islamicate Sexualities: Translations across Temporal Geographies of Desire*. Ed. K. Babayan and A. Najmabadi. Cambridge: Harvard UP, 2008. 1–40. Print.

The Renaissance of Lesbianism in Early Modern England. Cambridge: Cambridge UP, 2002. Print.

Tugcu, Emine. "Şehrengizler ve Ayine-i Huban-I Bursa:Bursa Şehrengizlerinde Guzeller." Diss. Bilkent U, 2007. Web. 19 Jan. 2014.

Weeks, Jeffrey. *Coming Out: Homosexual Politics in Britain from the Nineteenth Century to the Present*. New York: Quartet, 1977. Print.

Ze'evi, Dror. *Producing Desire: Changing Sexual Discourse in the Ottoman Middle East, 1500–1900*. Berkeley: U of California P, 2006. Print.

9

English Renaissance Literature in the History of Sexuality

JONATHAN GOLDBERG

Literary history usually is told in one of two ways. The first would be as a story of relations among writers, a mode often thought of as old-fashioned and belletristic, although Harold Bloom's *Anxiety of Influence*, which argues that all poets writing after Milton have had to grapple with his insuperable example, could be cited to indicate that this method also can be allied with literary theory. The second would be one that embeds literary history in forms of history thought to be more real; this is currently the prevailing model. It could be exemplified by the 2002 *Cambridge History of Early Modern Literature*, which is organized through large sections named by conventional historical eras (Tudor and Stuart, and the like) and subdivided by categories of social organization (the court, the city); "national identity" is threaded throughout as a unifying topic. What is remarkable about both modes, at least in these examples, is an absence of considerations of gender and sexuality. (Jeffrey Masten, to provide a strong counter-example, has argued for the intimate relationship between textual history – in particular, the history of the book – and questions of gender and sexuality.) Other literary histories cast in one of the two prevailing models likely would support the picture suggested by the opening examples. This chapter is meant to remedy that situation.

The division of literary history into two supposedly opposing practices, and the absence in both of a concern with gender and sexuality, is remarkable (on both counts) in the context of the history of early modern literature. Consider the two major examples of literary history produced in the Elizabethan era, Sir Philip Sidney's *Defence of Poetry* and George Puttenham's *Arte of English Poesie*. Sidney's text might look like an example of the first kind of literary historical endeavor – it places English literature in a long history of literary production tied to the ancients; it is also a work of theory, arguing for the relationship between poetry, history, and philosophy. Yet it also (perhaps centrally) worries the question of poetry precisely in terms of English nationhood. It cannot think these questions without framing them in terms of gender and sexuality. (Is it ever possible, really, to consider national identity without thinking about gender and sexuality?) Sidney is sure – or would like to be sure – that an attachment to poetry, the one he ambivalently professes in his "ink-wasting toy" (74), as he refers to his treatise, is not effeminizing; he is writing in response to a text like Stephen Gosson's *School of Abuse*, which is certain that it is. "I never heard the old song of Percy and Douglas," Sidney insists, "that I found not my heart moved more than with a trumpet" (46). This exemplary masculine response to poetry, as if it surpassed even as it resembles a call to arms, needs to be put beside Sidney's response to the love poetry written by his English contemporaries, which, he writes, "if I were a mistress, would never persuade me they were in love: so coldly they apply fiery speeches" (69–70). Sidney worries that poetry might be effeminizing, but he also imagines himself as an unpersuaded woman reading poems supposedly meant to move a female reader. The prospect of defending poetry as a worthy national endeavor seems caught up in a defense of gender positions difficult to maintain. This dilemma can be understood within the history of sexuality, which reminds us that intense erotic attachment of a man to a woman was thought to carry the danger of turning a man into a woman. (Romeo voices just that worry.) In his *Defence*, Sidney instances Hercules crossdressed by Omphale as the height of risibility (68), only to offer himself in just that position as a critic of the sonnet.

Puttenham's text, as has been noted often, is as much a manual for courtly success – a way through literary production to rise in the world – as it is a technical manual of poetic forms and practices. Everywhere it mixes a study of poetics with a handbook of politics, with an eye always toward Elizabeth I, who is presented as both an exemplary monarch and an exemplary poet. This means for Puttenham as for Sidney that the prospect of male courtly/ poetic enterprise in the service of a female monarch is likely to turn "we men" into "wee men," men into women, as Puttenham punningly puts it in an anecdote I treat at length in *Sodometries*, in which the gendered implication of poetic practice is also one that puts sexuality in question: "*Not weemen, but weemen beare the bell*" is the ambiguous point of a story Puttenham tells about poetic composition and male-female relations; he offers these under the sign of a king's desire and the desires of his courtiers to satisfy the monarch (147). Puttenham's history of English literature often is told in terms of relations between men. For him and for many literary historians since, Wyatt and Surrey initiate the literary history of his period; such pairings can be seen in modern literary histories that find the male couple – Sidney and Spenser, Shakespeare and Marlowe, Donne and Jonson, for example – a way to organize that story.

This is also Bloom's way of imagining the oedipal struggles of strong poets and their followers, a story feminist critics rightly deplored for the exclusion of women. It also is not just a tale of fathers and sons. In the pages that follow, my charge for this chapter is to consider the canon of English Renaissance literature in terms of the history of sexuality as it relates to relations between men. However, as Eve Kosofsky Sedgwick taught us in *Between Men*, relations between men cannot be thought without a woman between; that woman can be, as in the examples from Sidney and Puttenham's literary histories, the figure of a woman who might stand for poetry, for the nation, or for erotic tendencies in men that can move in more than one direction: they can move men toward and toward being women.

Foucault argues in his introductory volume to *The History of Sexuality*, which I take here as my guide to the history of sexuality, that modernity was marked by the notion of sexuality as the imaginary lynchpin securing identity. In *Epistemology of the Closet*, Sedgwick showed how imaginary the supposed dichotomy of straight and gay is in modernity. Early modernity may be early in part because of the ways it anticipates the regimes of modern identity even as it has yet to install them; it looks toward and resembles modernity not least because the modern installation of discrete sexual identity was riddled with ambiguities and ambivalences that secured it only as imaginary. This is a point that Madhavi Menon and I have argued in a jointly written essay. It could be rendered in the style of (French) theory, as Carla Freccero mobilizes it in *Queer/Early/Modern*, where the slashes between these words instigate questions of how discrete or self-identical the terms might be. Thanks to what Freccero posits as "the very impossibility of fully self-present meaning" (29) then or now, securing the difference between straight and gay is fraught even in the sonnet tradition with its supposedly clearly marked male lover and female beloved. But what is the gender of love? Often in these poems he puts in an appearance as the boy Cupid. What happens when a dualism is replaced by triangulation?

The impossibility of the self-identical can be seen in Sidney's less-than-secure masculinity. One can't help wondering what stirrings of the heart he experiences hearing the old ballad that incites the male camaraderie he celebrates, especially when he goes on to say that it would only be heightened if the earlier English poem were "trimmed in the gorgeous eloquence of Pindar" (46); the name of the Greek male poet moves a description more readily associated with female embellishment to the charms of the kind of male heroic verse Sidney would have his contemporaries write. Puttenham equivocates the relations between men and between men and women; this indicates, no doubt, that he writes in a time before sexuality had been attached to the binary of homosexuality and heterosexuality. However, this is not a regime of free love. Puttenham is constantly aware of a line that is drawn – however impossible it may be to maintain or to define – between acceptable relations between men that support social hierarchies and those that do not. The latter get called "sodomy." As Alan Bray showed in his unsurpassed *Homosexuality in Renaissance England*, the difference between acceptable and unacceptable male behavior does not lie in what two men might be doing (being "bedfellows" is the activity that covers both) as much as who the two men are or are thought to be. The "right" men can do together what the wrong ones cannot. "Wrong" means transgressions of boundaries in social position, in religious belief, in modes of national or racialized difference. The English are fond of assuming that all Italians practice sodomy (Nashe's *Unfortunate Traveller* exploits and explodes the stereotype); colonialist texts see sodomy whenever native sexuality is mentioned, without acknowledging how what is seen among others mirrors what can be seen at home.

Wyatt and Surrey in Literary Histories

Let us start our literary history of early modern literature where Puttenham starts his, in the "new company of courtly makers, of whom Sir *Thomas Wyat* th'elder and *Henry* Earle of Surrey were the two chieftaines" (74). Two chieftains: Puttenham's courtiers are soldiers. Historically, there is no evidence of any great intimacy or friendship between Wyatt and Surrey; their names have been linked from the start thanks to Surrey's elegy for Wyatt (as well as several Surrey sonnets in which Wyatt figures). The two writers appeared together significantly in print, in Richard Tottel's 1557 *Miscellany*, although only Surrey's name is advertised on the title page. In the brief literary history he offers for English writers of his own time, Sidney mentions Surrey, finding "in the Earl of Surrey's lyrics many things tasting of noble birth, and worthy of a noble mind" (64). Puttenham quickly recasts his couple in this direction when he says that he finds "litle difference" between Wyatt and Surrey: "their conceits were loftie, their stiles stately, their conveyance cleanely, their termes proper, their meetre sweete and well proportioned" (76). In this lack of difference Wyatt acquires all the qualities associated with Surrey in literary history. One reason for this indistinction lies with Tottel; in his editing of both poets, he made them seem as much like each other as he could, which meant, in effect, as much like Surrey as possible. Making the two one – stately, lofty, clean, and proper – some notable prophylactic activity is involved.

What is involved is most apparent in modern couplings of the two. Although Surrey maintained precedence in this pairing through the opening years of the twentieth century, since then, with few exceptions, their positions have been reversed. Wyatt has been declared the more accomplished poet. *The Norton Anthology of English Literature* summarizes and endorses this estimation when it informs its readers that "[t]hough his historical importance continues to be acknowledged, Surrey's poetry, harmonious, musical, and metrically regular, is now often compared unfavorably to Wyatt's more vigorous, knotty, and idiosyncratic verse" (570). Vigorous Wyatt assumes the mantle of masculinity; about Surrey, we are told that "as a conventional love poet he is not very convincing"; "his verse comes alive when he writes about his deep male friendships or imagines himself in a chorus of women longing for their men or savagely attacks the 'womanish dotage' of an unmanly king" (570). Modern accounts worry that the polish of Surrey's verse covers and obscures an equivocal, less than convincing heterosexuality, which Wyatt's vigor and "knotty" roughness secure. Early moderns favored Surrey for his aristocratic bearing (he came from old aristocratic stock), and seem to moot the questions of sexuality and gender that inflect modern devaluations of his poetry and person.

It would be easy to chalk up the modern estimations of this couple to modern regimes of sexual identity and their enforcement, as well as to aims of modernist poetics, easy too to suppose that in a time before sexuality the homoerotic is untroubling while in modernity it registers as antinormative. Complicating this neat division between now and then in understanding the values of kinds of poetic practice and their relationship to the proprieties of sex and gender is this: the qualities regularly assigned to Wyatt in modern estimations – his vigor, intellectual depth, idiosyncratic personality, emotional rawness – are precisely those that Surrey lauds in his elegy on Wyatt, "W. resteth here, that quick could never rest." Surrey's poem delivers a man of virtue from his rough exceptionality; for Surrey he sums the very quality "of manhodes shape" (l.32). Frederic Tromly has gone so far as to describe Surrey's poem as an act of "fidelity" to Wyatt in which Surrey so completely identifies with Wyatt and writes so much like Wyatt that the effect of the poem is as if Wyatt were writing his own epitaph. Modern critics may seek to rearrange the couple into a manly Wyatt and an effeminate Surrey, but their rearrangement only echoes Surrey's own mode of incorporation and identification. Before one assumes that the early modern assimilation of Wyatt to Surrey was less troubling in a time before homo/hetero difference had become a governing pair of normative terms, it helps to recall the risk in Tottel's endeavor and its endorsement by Sidney and Puttenham: Henry VIII had executed Surrey for treason. (Wyatt had been suspected of being Anne Boleyn's lover, but never was brought to trial.) The coupling of the two under the name of Surrey could also trespass into the dangerous territory marked by the term sodomy; one presumes that the transfer of the aura of long-established nobility to English poetry trumped that troubling past. Trumped it, yet it (or, at any rate, the specter of sodomy) haunts the writing of Sidney and Puttenham, providing another source for ambivalences and hesitations already attached to the over-estimation of male heteroerotic love.

Across time, in literary history, Wyatt and Surrey have unstably changed places with each other. Between them, and in the varied estimations of their verse – its roughness or smoothness, its forthrightness or its grace – the contours of sexuality, and of the history of sexuality, emerge. Where we are now in looking at these matters is compellingly articulated in the challenge to the current version of literary history and its relationship to sexual history offered by Daniel Juan Gil in *Before Intimacy*. Gil treats Wyatt as a strong example of his thesis that sexuality was emerging as a domain unto itself as early as the sixteenth century. Making this claim, Gil is not suggesting that sexuality in early modernity confirms or anticipates some version of the modern rubrics of heterosexuality or homosexuality. For him sexuality arises when desire cannot be accommodated within preexisting social forms of hierarchy and difference. Sexuality as such is socially wrenching and is experienced as a mastering, unaccountable force felt as loss, self-division, and pain. Hence it is not in Wyatt's masculine swagger that Gil locates sexuality in his verse, rather in those moments when he is virtually indistinguishable from Surrey: "Wyatt's poetry celebrates suicidal despair, murderous hatred, fear, and contempt of self and other as the luxuriant signs of a new form of pleasure that combines a profound turn away from others with a brazen disregard for the limits of the self," he argues (26). Gil's characterization of sexuality works a reversal of the usual Wyatt/Surrey pairing without invoking Surrey at all, and thereby without invoking the hetero-homo distinction that has underpinned the comparison. Gil arguably models a kind of queer approach that brings early modernity into proximity with our late modernity.

Spenser and Sidney's Pastoral Relations

It would be possible to follow the English Petrarchan tradition to Shakespeare's sonnets, the majority addressed to a fair young man, the remainder to a so-called dark lady, and to parse the homo-hetero relations entailed. This is the subject of an opening chapter in Sedgwick's *Between Men*, where it receives exemplary treatment, and it is a path Gil pursues as well (he also considers Shakespeare as a playwright). Here, rather than pursuing any single literary form across the period, I would open another itinerary, beginning our literary history of early modernity this time with the only contemporary text Sidney allows into the very brief list that constitutes the history of English literature for him. Immediately after his mention of Surrey, Sidney writes: "The *Shepherds' Calendar* hath much poetry in his eclogues, indeed worthy the reading, if I be not deceived" (64). Sidney does not name the author of *The Shepheardes Calender*, perhaps preserving the anonymity of Spenser's text, which announces the arrival of a "new Poete" (416), but fails to supply his name. In fact the only name on the title page is "M. Philip Sidney" to whom it is *"Entitled"* as someone *"worthy of all titles"* for his "learning and chevalrie." There is therefore a certain element of self-praise and coupling involved in Sidney's nod in Spenser's direction. There also is a demurral – he may be deceived by the text he praises and that praises him. Hence, as Sidney continues writing about *The Shepheardes Calender*, he voices disapproval of its "rustic" language and style. Sidney is thereby marking his social distance, claiming the "titles" Spenser confers on him (in fact, he had yet to receive a knighthood).

Perhaps Sidney also is marking a distance from Spenser in a manner akin to the distance taking marked in the opening *Januarye* eclogue of Spenser's poem, a lament voiced by the poet Colin Clout, one of the stand-ins for the new poet. Eight stanzas into the ten-stanza poem, Colin explains who causes his grief in a very roundabout way; it is Rosalind, not Hobbinol (the shepherd from whom Colin receives gifts, which he passes on to Rosalind), who causes his pain:

> It is not *Hobbinol*, wherefor I plaine,
> Albee my love he seeke with dayly suit:
> His clownish gifts and curtsies I disdaine,
> His kiddes, his cracknelles, and his early fruit.
> Ah foolish *Hobbinoll*, thy gyfts bene vayne:
> *Colin* them gives to *Rosalind* againe.   (55–60)

One unrequited love deserves another. They recirculate. This male lover has all the propriety of classical allusion: Spenser is imitating Virgil's second eclogue. It is apparently so safe to be doing so that the otherwise unidentified editor E.K. (sometimes thought to be Spenser himself) identifies the allusion to Virgil in a footnote. Elsewhere in his glosses E.K. lets readers know that Hobbinoll is to be identified as Gabriel Harvey, an interlocutor of Spenser's, indeed the figure to whom E.K. pens the opening epistle announcing the arrival of the new poet. Yet at the first mention of Hobbinoll as male lover, E.K. supplies a footnote to help the reader parse the relationship. His help is at least as circular as Colin's explanation of the relationship he has to the lover he spurs and the one who spurns him. By way of Hobbinoll, E.K. explains, Colin / Spenser acknowledges "his very speciall and most familiar freend, whom he entirely and extraordinarily beloved." Without missing a beat, E.K. continues: "In thys place seemeth to be some savour of disorderly love, which the learned call paederastice: but it is gathered beside his meaning." So, this special friendship might be seen as "disorderly," or maybe not; it depends on whether what the learned call it is beside the point or is the very point of a distinction to be drawn. E.K. heads in that latter direction, commenting on the propriety of pederasty (Socrates and Alcibiades are among his dubious examples); he concludes that "paederastice" is "much to be preferred before gynerastice." This conclusion only leads E.K. (and his readers) into further contortions in understanding the relations of heteroerotic and homoerotic relations. E.K. closes by assuring us that in so declaring for pederasty and against gynerasty he is not preferring "forbidden and unlawful fleshlinesse" (422–23). It would be difficult to say that this note exactly clarifies the relationship between admirable and deplorable sexual relations between men or between men and women. Colin's relation to Hobbinoll mirrors Rosalind's to him; E.K.'s note replicates the continuum of denial and desire in the poem. Spenser will perfect this mode of writing two ways at once in the allegorical procedures of *The Faerie Queene*, demanding of the reader the ability to move between sameness and difference to a point at which they cannot be distinguished. This sameness, this "homo" realization – as I will suggest further at the end of this chapter, and as I have in *The Seeds of Things* – is crucial to an ultimate understanding of the place of same-sex sex in early modern literature. (This is a point Laurie Shannon has effectively argued as well.)

The round-robin of *Januarye* might replay Sidney's backhanded endorsement and criticism of Spenser's poem. This coupling of Spenser and Sidney (in the mirror of Spenser and Harvey) could provoke the question that the editors of the Variorum edition of *The Works of Edmund Spenser* asked about *Astrophel*, Spenser's belated pastoral elegy for Sir Philip Sidney (it appeared almost a decade after his death): "How intimate was Spenser with Sidney?" (7: 487), they ask. Their answer parallels what we've seen already in the modern reception of Wyatt and Surrey, for the Variorum editors seek to discredit "the legend that Spenser and Sidney were united by 'friendship' in the deepest and tenderest sense of the word," as Alexander Grosart had characterized their relationship in the early 1880s; they distance themselves as well from

E. De Selincourt, editor of the Oxford edition of Spenser's poems, writing in his 1912 introduction to praise Spenser's pastoral lament for Sidney for its "delicate reserve," "a lingering and tender pathos as potent and moving as the direct expression of personal regard" (xiv). De Selincourt, in other words, writing from the vantage point of modern sexual identities regarded Spenser's as a necessarily closeted performance. The Variorum editors, like so many literary historians after them, preferred instead to think of the relationship between Sidney and Spenser as "poetic," not personal, and thus to elide any question of erotics once the answer to the question "how intimate were they?" seems to involve choosing "straight" or "gay" as the answer.

Astrophel hardly answers the question of intimacy between Sidney and Spenser this way. The poem is written in a doubled literary situation of the poem. On the one hand, Sidney is named "Astrophel" in the poem, and the poem includes his beloved "Stella"; Sidney's life is turned into his own literary creation of the Petrarchan couple. However, Spenser's poem is a pastoral elegy that fetches its guiding plot from Bion's "Epitaph on Adonis." This is not the Petrarchan story of thwarted male desire, but its opposite: Adonis refuses Venus, and it is her thwarted desire that provides the male poet with his elegiac voice. Spenser's speaker occupies the position of Venus: does possible male identification with a woman amount to the same thing as male desire for a woman? Almost as soon as the poem opens, Astrophel is described as "the pride of shepheards praise" (l.7) and the object of "rusticke lasses love" (l.8). He is positioned in relationship to both groups – groups separated by gender and, seemingly, by desire. Astrophel also is described enigmatically as "not so happie ... in one thing onely fayling of the best" (ll.11–12). This singular exception could allude to the frustration of his devotion to Stella (he only wins her love in the poem after he has been mortally wounded). It suggests that he is otherwise indifferent to the shepherds and to the lasses who seek his love, something confirmed at the moment when Astrophel repudiates love and hunts the boar that gores him. The poet laments:

> Ah where were ye this while his shepheard peares
> To whom alive was nought so deare as hee:
> And ye faire Mayds the matches of his yeares,
> Which in his grace did boast you most to bee? (ll.127–30)

Astrophel lies dying "[u]npitied, unplayned ... While none is nigh, thine eyelids up to close, / And kisse thy lips like faded leaves of rose" (ll.136, 137–38). Stella then arrives to minister that kiss and to accompany his bier. But the poet is not satisfied that this ends the story. Instead, he exclaims: "The dolefullest beare that ever man did see, / Was *Astrophel*, but dearest unto mee" (ll.149–50).

With this declaration a contention is voiced between the heteroerotic and homoerotic claims on Astrophel. Yet this claim of the man for the man, for male-male love as dearer than male-female love, is voiced by a poet who occupies the position of Bion's Venus. The question of sexuality will not resolve into the modern dichotomy. Indeed, the poem maintains its irresolution even beyond its end, for it is followed by lines said to be spoken by Clorinda, Astrophel's sister. I continue to believe, as I argued in *Sodometries*, that these lines, often retitled as "The Dolefull Lay of Clorinda," are a poem by Mary Sidney. Yet the question of who authored them is complicated by the ways Clorinda echoes the speaker of *Astrophel*. She too claims to be the one most grieved by Sidney's death: "Great losse to all that ever him did see, / Great losse to all, but greatest losse to me" (ll.35–36). If it is difficult to know whether this really is a woman's voice we hear, it is in part because the voice of *Astrophel* is Spenser's voicing of the grief of Venus. Between men there is not always merely a phantasmatic woman. Same-sex and cross-sex desire do not neatly resolve into gendered difference.

Sacred Erotics and Milton's Angels

Surrey's elegy for Wyatt and Spenser's for Sidney suggest that elegy is a form in the period in which male-male desire often is articulated; it would be possible easily to extend this discussion to other examples, as I have done at greater length in "Between Men: Literary History and the Work of Mourning." Certainly Ben Jonson's lament for his "beloved" Shakespeare, as he names him in the title of his elegy for Shakespeare, would need to be mentioned, and not least for its initial worry that in praising his beloved, he might sound a bit too much like a man selling a woman; or Carew's lament for Donne, in which he takes on the role of widowed poetry as his own and yearns to be ravished once again by his dead master. The erotics of Carew's poem remind one, of course, of Donne's own erotics, whether he is attempting seduction or asking to be battered by the three-personed God in his holy sonnet; as Richard Rambuss notes, that poem demands nothing less than a "trinitarian gang bang" (50). In his analysis of "Batter my heart," Rambuss takes this hypermasculinity as his focus, refusing to read Donne, as he often has been read, as taking the position of a woman asking to be raped. For Rambuss, there is no woman in Donne's poem, and Donne is not asking to be a woman when he desires to be ravished. Carew's poem equivocates between wishing to assume the form of masculinity that it associates with Donne's mastery (of poetry, of woman) and wishing to be in the position of the woman so mastered. Thus, even as it praises Donne for performing "holy Rapes" (1.17), it seeks both to force a poem from widowed poetry, and does so in submission to the effect that Donne's poems had on his readers. The latter aim places the elegist in the position of someone who can be like Donne only to the degree that he has been ravished by Donne. As Rambuss suggests, the confluence of religious feeling and sexual experience is writ large across seventeenth-century religious poetry especially in the flaming Richard Crashaw. I've ventured in *Voice Terminal Echo* into similar territory, examining what the title page of *The Temple* calls George Herbert's "pious ejaculations."

Rather than pursuing sacred erotics or going further with the elegiac tradition, I would close by mentioning two elegies by the preeminent religious poet of the period before I conclude this discussion with a consideration of *Paradise Lost*. The elegies I have in mind are the *Epitaphium Damonis*, Milton's elegy for Charles Diodati, his dearest friend from boyhood on, and "Lycidas." In an essay on same-sex sex in "Lycidas," Bruce Boehrer takes as his focus the "unexpressive nuptial song" (1.176) that greets Lycidas; it has its parallel in "Damon's Epitaph," where a bacchic orgiastic thyrsus is waved at the marriage ceremony with which the epitaph ends: "Your noble head bound with a glittering wreath, in your hands the glad branches of the leafy palm, you shall for ever act and act again the immortal nuptials, where song and the lyre, mingled with the blessed dances, wax rapturous, and the joyous revels rage under the thyrsus of Zion" (ll.215–19). Milton transports to the homoerotic world of classical pastoral elegy (on which Spenser also had drawn) a Christian marriage motif. Boehrer suggests that the male-male marriage and male-male intimacy in the poem "does not – at least not entirely – presuppose the essentialized opposition of man to woman" (231). At the very least, a model for male-female relationship and union subtends what the poem offers. Its offer is not simply some heavenly vision of the afterlife either. The poem intently follows the body of Lycidas to a bodily resurrection:

> So sinks the day-star in the ocean bed,
> And yet anon repairs his drooping head . . .
> So Lycidas sunk low, but mounted high,
> Through the dear might of him that walked the waves,
> Where other groves, and other streams along,
> With nectar pure his oozy locks he laves,
> And hears the unexpressive nuptial song.　　　(ll.168–69, 172–76)

The body, restored, is joined to others in a heaven that looks like the pastoral world from which Lycidas was plucked. The marriage may take place in heaven, but Lycidas returns to earth as "genius of the shore" (l.183), a demonic spirit on the way to the angelic embodiment of *Paradise Lost*.

In his epic, however much Milton celebrates the wedded love of Adam and Eve, he also is intent on Adam's relationship with Raphael, and beyond that, a depiction of the sexual relations of angels as a model for human relatedness. God sends Raphael to Adam to converse with him "as friend with friend" (5.229), and he arrives in Eden to enjoy a pastoral moment that lingers through the four central books of *Paradise Lost*. Adam attempts to prolong the visit beyond its purpose – to tell him about Satan's rebellion and the dangers that may lie ahead. He attests to his erotic transportation in this angelic company:

> For while I sit with thee, I seem in heaven,
> And sweeter thy discourse is to my ear
> Than fruits of palm-tree pleasantest to thirst
> And hunger both, from labour, at the hour
> Of sweet repast; they satiate, and soon fill,
> Though pleasant, but thy words with grace divine
> Imbued, bring to their sweetness no satiety.   (8.210–16)

The lines Adam speaks resonate in their use of "sweet" with those Eve directs to Adam in book four in which she uses the word "sweet" over and again to describe how it is being with Adam that makes the world in which she lives sweet: "Sweet is the breath of morn, her rising sweet," the lines begin, and after ringing many changes on the word, she tells Adam that everything so sweet would not be so "without thee sweet" (4.641–56). To Adam's rapt desire for conversation, the angel responds, complimenting what comes from his lips by substituting Adam's lips for his words: "Nor are thy lips ungraceful, sire of men" (8.218). Raphael's compliment echoes the articulation of Eve's desire, just a few lines before, for conversation (in its fullest sense, including physical congress) with Adam: "from his lip / Not words alone pleased her" (8.56–57). Mouths are significant at this moment; Raphael has eaten the food Eve prepared, and has explained that angels are sufficiently embodied to do so, although their heavenly food is ambrosial. This prompts Adam's final question to Raphael: because, for him, the pleasure of embodiment reaches its climax in sex with Eve, do angels also have sex? Raphael blushes in reply, a somatic signal that Milton immediately insists on as "a smile that glowed / Celestial rosy red, love's proper hue" (8.619–20); angelic sex is no more shameful than is the coupling of Adam and Eve. And no less physical: Adam tells Raphael that as soon as Eve was presented to him "to the nuptial bower / I led her blushing" (8.510–11).

Exactly parallel to his explanation of why and how angels eat is Raphael's answer to Adam's question:

> love thou say'st
> Leads up to heaven, is both the way and guide;
> Bear with me then, if lawful I ask;
> Love not the heavenly spirits, and how their love
> Express they, by looks only, or do they mix
> Irradiance, virtual or immediate touch? (8.612–17)

The sex that Raphael describes is, like the eating process, one that makes angelic copulation the fulfillment of human aspiration. It is fitting that the four-book seduction that is the conversation between Adam and Raphael should end with this moment in which Raphael not only insists that Adam's love for Eve should lead him upward, but then holds out for Adam the kind of sex life that angels have with each other: "Whatever pure thou in body enjoy'st / ... we enjoy / In eminence" (8.622–24). The body that impedes is replaced by the possibility of total oneness, total interpenetration possible to the pure body – the body that has attained the materiality meant by spirit, the body as sheer vitality, life.

Raphael's description of angelic sex – "easier than air with air, if spirits embrace, / Total they mix, union of pure with pure / Desiring" (8.626–28) – is undeniably homoerotic. Stunningly, and countervailing every other depiction of heavenly and earthly life in the poem, it is entirely unhierarchical, lacking all signs of difference of degree and gender. This coupling, where no "membrane, joint, or limb" functions as impediment to coition, is also one devoid of "exclusive bars" (8.625); just as earlier Raphael had explained to Adam that the angelic body cannot be harmed because it is "vital in every part" (6.345), and hence is "all heart ..., all head, all eye, all ear, / All intellect, all sense," and entirely freed from any determinate form of limbing (6.350–53), there is no hierarchy in his description of angelic sex. Indeed this sex is not monogamous, nor does it entail some notion of correct "position" or some procreative goal. This form of coupling is entirely perverse. It might echo the scene Spenser offers in book three of *The Faerie Queene*, in the Garden of Adonis, the seed bed of creation that appears figured as the relationship of Adonis restored to Venus, an Adonis also coupled with Cupid (indeed a Cupid joined to Psyche to produce Pleasure as their offspring). As I suggest at length in *The Seeds of Things*, Spenser ultimately moves beyond a model of heterosexual marriage;

so, too, do Milton's angels. Angelic sex looks forward to that time when all will be all, and differences will no longer obtain. This futurity depends on a story of origins: "all" was made first from "one first matter" (5.472), "one almighty is" (5.469) to which all returns. Renaissance homoerotics arises from a belief that sameness not difference is the basis of life.

Setting the course for much of the literary history of early modern litera-ture in the twentieth century, T.S. Eliot, in "The Metaphysical Poets," blamed Milton for a "dissociation of sensibility" (288), which Eliot hoped with the example of Donne before him his own poetry would heal. Eliot's response could be chalked up to a Bloomian anxiety of influence. (Bloom could just as readily be diagnosed as repeating Eliot's modernist stance.) Eliot failed to see that Milton's vision of a return to original sameness had the same goal in mind as he articulated for modernist poets, to overcome the divisions that Milton's Genesis story in the Garden of Eden tells, of man versus woman, of good versus evil. Perhaps Eliot could not countenance this identification because the vision of oneness in Milton is so fully sexualized. Or, perhaps, he saw what Milton was doing, but only could under the conditions that Sedgwick identi-fied in *Epistemology of the Closet*, and thus could not allow himself to see what he saw. After all, in "Tradition and the Individual Talent," the manifesto for Eliot's modernist poetics, among the few examples of precedents Eliot cites is that of Dante at the moment he hails his master, Brunetto Latini. Brunetto is his poetic exemplar, and Dante finds him in the circle of the sodomites. "Siete voi qui, ser Brunetto" (15.30), he asks. Is this where literary history is located?

Works Cited

Bloom, Harold. *The Anxiety of Influence: A Theory of Poetry*. Oxford: Oxford UP, 1973. Print.

Boehrer, Bruce. "'Lycidas': The Pastoral Elegy as Same-Sex Epithalamium." *PMLA* 117.2 (2002): 222–36. Print.

Bray, Alan. *Homosexuality in Renaissance England*. London: Gay Men's P, 1982. Print.

The Cambridge History of Early Modern English Literature. Ed. David Loewenstein and Janel Mueller. Cambridge: Cambridge UP, 2002. Print.

Carew, Thomas. *The Poems*. Ed. Rhodes Dunlap. Oxford: Clarendon, 1949. Print.

Dante, Alighieri. *Inferno*. Ed. and trans. John D. Sinclair: Oxford UP, 1959. Print.

De Selincourt E., and J.C. Smith, eds. *Spenser: Poetical Works*. Oxford: Oxford UP, 1912. Print.

Eliot, T.S. *Selected Essays*. London: Faber, 1932. Print.

Foucault, Michel. *The History of Sexuality: Vol. 1: An Introduction*. Trans. Robert Hurley. New York: Pantheon, 1978. Print.

Freccero, Carla. *Queer/ Early/ Modern*. Durham: Duke UP, 2006. Print.

Gil, Daniel Juan. *Before Intimacy: Asocial Sexuality in Early Modern England*. Minneapolis: U of Minnesota P, 2006. Print.

Goldberg, Jonathan. "Between Men: Literary History and the Work of Mourning." *The Oxford Handbook of the Elegy*. Ed. Karen Weisman. Oxford: Oxford UP, 2010. Print.

The Seeds of Things: Theorizing Sexuality and Materiality in Renaissance Representations. New York: Fordham UP, 2009. Print.

Sodometries: Renaissance Texts, Modern Sexualities. Stanford: Stanford UP, 1992 Print.

Voice Terminal Echo: Postmodernism and English Renaissance Texts. London: Methuen, 1986. Print.

Goldberg, Jonathan, and Madhavi Menon, "Queering History." *PMLA* 120.5 (2005): 1608–17. Print.

Howard, Henry, Earl of Surrey. *Poems*. Ed. Emrys Jones. Oxford: Clarendon, 1964. Print.

Jonson, Ben. *The Complete Poems*. Ed. George Parfitt. New Haven: Yale UP, 1975. Print.

Masten, Jeffrey. *Textual Intercourse: Collaboration, Authorship, and Sexualities in Renaissance England*. Cambridge: Cambridge UP, 1997. Print.

Milton, John. *The Major Works*. Ed. Stephen Orgel and Jonathan Goldberg. Oxford: Oxford UP, 2003. Print.

Nashe, Thomas. *The Unfortunate Traveller and Other Works*. Harmondsworth: Penguin, 1972. Print.

The Norton Anthology of English Literature. New York: W.W. Norton, 2000. Print.

Puttenham, George. *The Arte of English Poesie*. Kent: Kent State UP, 1970. Print.

Rambuss, Richard. *Closet Devotions*. Durham: Duke UP, 1998. Print.

Sedgwick, Eve Kosofsky. *Between Men: English Literature and Male Homosocial Desire*. New York: Columbia UP, 1985. Print.

Epistemology of the Closet. Berkeley: U of California P, 1990. Print.

Shannon, Laurie. "Nature's Bias: Renaissance Homonormativity and Elizabethan Comic Likeness." *Modern Philology* 98.2 (2000): 183–210. Print.

Sovereign Amity: Figures of Friendship in Shakespearean Contexts. Chicago: U of Chicago P, 2002. Print.

Sidney, Sir Philip. *A Defence of Poetry*. Ed. J.A. Van Dorsten. Oxford: Oxford UP, 1966. Print.

Tottel's Miscellany. Ed. Hyder Edward Rollins. Cambridge: Harvard UP, 1965. Print.

Tromly, Fredric B. "Surrey's Fidelity to Wyatt in 'Wyatt Resteth Here.'" *Studies in Philology* 77 (1980): 376–87. Print.

The Works of Edmund Spenser: A Variorum Edition. Baltimore: Johns Hopkins, 1932–57. Print.

How to Spot a Lesbian in the Early Modern Spanish World

SHERRY VELASCO

Evidence and Terminology

Scholars who spend time thinking about and looking for traces of passion between women in the early modern Spanish world are inevitably confronted with a certain degree of hesitation over evidence and terminology. How should we talk about women who loved other women before modernity? Should we avoid the term "lesbian," judging it anachronistic – a modern, albeit unstable concept that implies notions of identity rather than deviant sexual behaviors? Despite efforts to move beyond recurrent debates articulated in terms of acts versus identity, essentialism versus constructionism, and alterity versus continuism, scholars continue to grapple with contested methodologies, periodization, and nomenclature.[1] While the term "lesbian" (and other references to Sappho and Lesbos) was used in the early modern period, there were many descriptors to discuss women who transgressed traditional codes of sexual conduct. Other terms and phrases included tribade, fricatrice, rubster, *Sahacat, somética* or *bujarrona* (female sodomite), *marimacho* (butch), hermaphrodite, *incuba* (partner who lies on top), *succuba* (partner who lies underneath), *subigatrice* (dominator), *virago*, woman with woman, half man-half woman, like man and woman, impossible love, different, not the marrying type, dildo-wearing scoundrel, little cane girls (in reference to the use of a dildo made from cane reeds), and special friendships, among others.

Beyond tackling the vexing challenges of affective taxonomies, scholars of nonnormative sexuality also ponder uncertainties regarding what kinds of texts and artifacts might be included in our body of evidence. Should we focus on identifying and defining specific sex acts or look for the passionate yet "nonphysical" expressions of intimacy that were deemed problematic for some early modern observers yet seemed less scandalous for others? If we expand evidentiary possibilities to consider likeness and resemblance rather than identity, does the welcoming "lesbian-like" approach proposed by

Judith Bennett become too inclusive (see also Faderman 174)? How did others interpret behaviors, decisions, appearance, gossip, public punishment, popular literary and dramatic representations, and other material objects implicated in publicized relationships or encounters that didn't seem to fit into traditional expectations for female sexuality? Should we consider literary, artistic, and dramatic texts/performances separate from the "nonfictional" references in legal, theological, medical, criminal, Inquisitional cases as well as in life narratives, portraits, and letters?

Consider the particularly rich example of the role of Catalina de Erauso in Pérez de Montalbán's 1626 play *The Lieutenant Nun*, which brings to a head questions of women's actual lives, social sanction, and the representation of female same-sex desire. Surely audience members had differing ways of viewing and understanding the performance of their favorite actress Luisa de Robles as she flirted on stage with another woman while playing the role of real-life celebrity Catalina de Erauso. In fact, viewing patterns would have been especially complex given that news of Erauso's attraction to other women was well known when she became a celebrity in the 1620s in Spain, Italy, and the New World. Despite rejecting traditional gender roles and conformist desire (while adhering to expectations of female abstinence from premarital heterosexual relations), Erauso received a soldier's pension from the king in Spain and dispensation from the pope in Rome to continuing living as a man – even with uncontested female anatomy. Therefore, each spectator had to reconcile for himself or herself the apparent contradiction of a lesbian role model – whether on stage, on display in the street, on canvas in a portrait, in news pamphlets, or in novelistic fiction. In other words, early modern individuals came to their own opinions and beliefs based on an interconnected network involving a variety of sources – including news stories, rumors and gossip, entertainment, and public spectacles (both organized and spontaneous).

Once we uncover compelling evidence of women who desired women, we occasionally find other obstacles – such as attempts to suppress, destroy, or tamper with the evidence. Efforts to obstruct and suppress details of same-sex seduction were occasionally played out graphically on the written page. In one seventeenth-century autobiography of a nun from Seville, for example, Ana de Jesús (?–1617) narrates in detail a defining episode from her tortured adolescence, during which a mulatta servant used various romantic, material, and occult ploys to seduce her. The author concludes the dramatic episode by reporting that the "mulatta had been arrested because she had deceived more than fifty young women and had ruined more than thirty XXXX" (Ana de Jesús 27v). The final words are scratched out in the original manuscript, rendering them both illegible and provocative. As we guess at the obstructed information we might assume that the censored words would have implicated the dozens of women who did succumb to the charms of the unnamed lesbian seducer. While in the unpublished manuscript Ana chose to recount the details of the episode at great length – emphasizing her success at rejecting the would-be suitor's advances and material gifts – when her biographer Alejandro de la Madre de Dios wrote his own extended account of her life in 1707, he silenced the homoerotic episode completely. This notable omission reminds us that what is not said can be equally informative when reconstructing a history of lesbian narratives.

As we look at the diverse third-person accounts of women's transgressive desire, we must weigh how these narratives are structured by, tampered with, and filtered through heterobiased individuals and institutions such as the Inquisition, civil courts, medical practitioners, theologians, scientists, artists, writers, witnesses, and other interested parties. The convergence of discourses is key: as Ana de Jesús's example suggests, early modern observers made connections among mulattos, Moors, sodomy, and witchcraft (see Perry). Ana's reference to the mulatta servant's use of magic spells to force an innocent victim into same-sex relations demonstrates the necessity for a nuanced consideration of how other issues such as ethnicity, race, and class also bear on premodern notions of nonconforming desire.

This chapter considers some of the questions that early modern observers were asking about women suspected of loving other women. In other words, what did different groups and individuals want to know about female intimacy and how did they articulate this desire in various contexts? Conversely, what information did they not want revealed and why? What follows proceeds from the traces registered in texts ranging from legislative discourses to medical ones, from theological treatises and religious instruction manuals to astrological guides, to consider the representation of same-sex desire between women across the literature – in the broadest sense – of the day.

Legislating Sex between Women

If we start with the questions that policy makers were asking, we discover that much of the contradictory legal documentation on lesbian relations in the early modern period reflects the double bind of having to define, legislate, investigate, and punish a crime that was believed better left as "peccatum mutum" (a "silent" sin). A lack of consensus regarding what constituted female sodomy and what was mere same-sex pollution both required and extended discussions about specific sex acts between women. Legislators, medical specialists, theologians, and writers engaged in lively cross-disciplinary debates that pondered basic questions such as what women were doing with each other behind closed doors and what those erotic encounters meant for different individuals and institutions.

In an atmosphere of ambiguity, early modern jurists and theologians directed their attention to determining whether one (or both) of the women used an instrument or artificial penis during sexual relations. In the mid-sixteenth century, jurist Antonio Gómez argued that "if any woman acts the part of a man with another woman ... both are said to commit the crime of Sodom against nature and must be punished with the prescribed penalty" (qtd. in Crompton 19). Gómez stipulated that if a woman had sexual relations with another woman by means of any material instrument then they must be burned; on the other hand, if a woman had sexual relations with any woman without a penis substitute then a lighter penalty could be considered. However, as Cristóbal de Chaves's 1585 report on the jails in Seville demonstrates, when female inmates were caught using an artificial penis or "strap-on" dildo, authorities did not assign the death penalty: "And there are many women who want to be more like men than Nature intended. Many women have been punished in the prison for making themselves into 'roosters' with an instrument made into the shape of a penis, which they tied to themselves with straps. Such women are punished with two hundred lashes" (25–26).

Medical and Theological Interventions

While jurists seemed concerned with identifying prosthetic penetrative lesbian practices, the medical community was intent on determining how anatomy impacted classifications of transgressive sex acts between women. In his 1603 gynecological treatise *On the Universal Medical Art of Women*, Rodrigo de Castro described the illicit sexual consequences (such as genital rubbing and the potential for penetration) that can result from an enlarged clitoris: "When it is continually rubbed by clothing, it is stimulated to such a degree that these women, to whom this member gives erections like men, cannot contain themselves, and fling themselves uncontrollably into lovemaking.... [They] are called tribades or 'rubbers'" (qtd. in Borris 141–43; see also Brooten 4n5).

In an attempt to clarify the contradictions, inconsistencies, and confusion regarding exactly what constituted female sodomy and the difference between that and mere pollution, Franciscan theologian Ludovico Maria Sinistrari applied medical treatises on female anatomy to theological treatments of lesbian practices in a section titled "Pecatum Mutum" in his extensive treatise *On Crimes and Punishments* published in 1700. After establishing the anatomical impossibility of injecting seed "into the natural vase" of the woman lying underneath merely by "thrusting at each other" (35), Sinistrari then repudiates the other most common legal/theological theory on sex between women: the use of an instrument ("some tool of glass, wood, leather, or other material, cunningly wrought in the shape of a man's yard; with this tied between her thighs" [37]) determines whether the women have committed sodomy. For there to be true sodomy, in Sinistrari's view, at least one of the women must possess the kind of overdeveloped clitoris described in works such as Rodrigo de Castro's 1603 medical treatise and Thomas Bartholin's mid-seventeenth-century treatise on anatomy (Bartholin 45–46).

Sinistrari's text, then, claims to be an updated manual on women's anatomy and same-sex desire to help confessors face these issues accurately in their own practice. To help avoid embarrassment and confusion, Sinistrari provides appropriate terminology and sample questions that the confessor might ask his female confessants:

> Should a woman then say she was the *incuba* in alike performance, the Confessor might ask her: Did she penetrate with any part of her person into the vase of the *succuba*? ... If she says yes, it is then plain she has committed Sodomy; if she says no, it is but pollution. He might likewise ask the *succuba*: Did the *incuba* penetrate any other way into her vase? And how? According to her answer, he is to form his judgment. (49)

The theologian clarifies that using fingers to penetrate the same-sex partner does not count as female sodomy because they are merely a part of a member, but not a member (49).

While Sinistrari demonizes lesbian acts, he also exposes a partial explanation for why much of the discussion of same-sex practices between women was encoded and encrypted in a mutual process of silent confession. In his explicit description of sex acts between women, Sinistrari accuses other theologians of being ignorant and confused about genital activity between women, yet he also cautions confessors about eliciting too much information: "A modest and prudent confessor does not dare question them farther, or inquire about the circumstances of so foul a deed, especially if the penitents are virgins or unmarried" (49). Confessors were expected to walk a fine line between discovering enough details to distinguish between sodomy and pollution and not soliciting too much information about these carnal encounters.

While some confessors were concerned with specific sex acts, others focused more on the erotic thoughts and fantasies of their confessants. In his 1631 confessional manual published in Lima, Peru, the sample questions Juan Pérez Bocanegra provides for other priests to use during confession are just as concerned with the mindset of women during sexual encounters with other women than with their sexual behavior: "Have you sinned with another woman? With how many women? How many times? When you were doing this abominable sin, were you thinking about married men? Single men? Clergy? Monks? Relatives? Your husband?" (230).

Pérez Bocanegra's manual demonstrates the heterocentric bias that many male authorities revealed when addressing sexual relations between women. Unable to imagine lesbian relations separate from heterosexual fantasy, the ecclesiastic implies that same-sex acts were a substitute for relations with a man, despite the fact that other factors such as frequency (or marital status) might indicate otherwise. Consistent with the medical and legal evidence describing sex acts between women in terms of "like a man with a woman," early modern observers (both male and female) frequently characterized lesbian relations as more heterosexual-like than lesbian-like.

Imagining Lesbian Passion

The role of erotic fantasy is also significant for understanding how witnesses imagined and articulated sexual relations between women. The importance of witness testimony is perhaps nowhere more noteworthy than in the long-term partnership of Inés de Santa Cruz and Catalina Ledesma, who were arrested as *bujarronas* (female sodomites) in 1603 in Salamanca.[2] The high-profile couple became known locally as "the little cane girls" (*las cañitas*) because of their purported use of dildos made of cane reeds.

What emerges from the graphic and detailed testimonies of the seventeen female witnesses and the two defendants is the dramatic story of an ill-fated domestic partnership between two women during the early modern period. According to witnesses and confirmed by the defendants, the relationship between Inés and Catalina involved long-term cohabitation. (Inés testified that they had lived together for eight years.) Many of the neighbors testified that it was common knowledge that Inés and Catalina lived together ("eating at the same table and sleeping in the same bed") and participated in a personal and sexual relationship: "The affection and love shared between the defendants was public knowledge in the neighborhood where they lived and among other people who know them. This explains why they have carnal relations, during which they use an invention shaped like a man's member and made from a cane. One gets on top of the other in order to insert it and commit the sin and crime that everyone knows has caused a scandal" (4v–5r).

While it may have been public knowledge that Inés and Catalina had been lovers for years and were suspected of committing the serious crime of sodomy by using a dildo, the detail with which the numerous female neighbors and witnesses described the couple's sexual activities reveals as much about the collective fantasies regarding sex between women as it does about the eroticism between the defendants. Much of the testimony by the witnesses relies on auditory clues about the women's sexual activities. This listening-centered testimony of the "ear-witnesses" necessitated a significant degree of guesswork regarding the sex acts that might correspond to the noises that the neighboring residents could hear. The plausible narratives were presented as facts and accompanied by the erotic sound effects, creating a synesthetic "visual listening" or "auditory viewing." A servant who worked in the home where the couple lived testified, in what must have been a strikingly "performative" interview, that she had listened very carefully when Inés and Catalina were engaged in sexual relations, and had therefore been able to deduce exactly what they were doing and to reproduce the sounds that the lovers had been making during the night: "The two were together in the carnal act and so she began to listen very carefully and she understood that one was on top of the other. . . . Catalina was underneath and Inés was on top and she heard that they were panting and puffing and breathing heavily – ah, ah, ah – as if they were exhausted in the carnal act, by which she understood clearly that they were having sexual relations" (5r). When the court scribe transposed the sounds of sex ("*ah, ah, ah*") to paper, he provided material evidence for readers who had not overheard the lovers or listened to the witness's auditory imitation of what lesbians *sound like* during moments of passion.

In spite of extensive testimony that confirmed the two women's use of a phallic device when having sexual relations, Inés and Catalina escaped the death penalty during two trials. The seemingly lenient punishment, nonetheless, cannot erase or minimize the compelling details and the evidence of how numerous people (more than a dozen witnesses – many more than normally required for a sodomy conviction – as well as Inés and Catalina themselves) perceived their long-term romantic partnership. In this way, the one hundred folios of documentation of this widely recognized same-sex relationship belie the idea that lesbians were invisible. And while this surprisingly detailed record seeks to establish the nature of their sexual activities, it also documents other revealing details such as conflicts over finances, their deep affection for one another, their verbal and physical fights, violence and jealousy, and other activities ranging from the mundane to the dramatic. During some of the arguments that took place in public, the defendants were overheard insulting each other using terms and expressions such as a "dildo-wearing scoundrel" (*bellaca baldresera*) or "female sodomite" (*somética*) (4). These accusatory insults contrast vividly with the loving terms of endearment ("my love," "my life") that witnesses also overheard the two women call each other.

"Special Friends" in the Convent

Interestingly, Saint Teresa of Avila (considered the most influential and widely read religious woman in early modern Spain and the New World), in accordance with convent rules and regulations, prohibited the nuns under her direction from using these same terms of endearment (specifically "my love," "my life," "my darling"; 78–79). Given the need for discretion (both to curb natural impulses and to avoid scandal), it is not surprising to note how coded some of the language can be in much convent writing when discussing intimacy between nuns. Indeed, when considering the kind of representations in convent narratives that lead some readers to assume that these "special friendships" might be romantic but ultimately "chaste" (i.e., no genital or physical contact), we should keep in mind that narrators (confessors and nuns) were particularly concerned with unwanted controversy for their convent or religious order (as well as not wanting to incite more passion and desire through suggestion).

In fact, even if vigilant nuns had not witnessed such affection between other nuns directly or even heard rumors about such transgressive desire, they could surely read about same-sex attraction in other religious as well as secular texts. For example, Father Bernardino de Villegas's 1635 treatise *The Bride of Christ Instructed by the Life of Saint Lutgarda* develops an extended and detailed description of *amistades particulares* or "special friendships" in the convent through a seven-point test to determine whether a convent friendship is spiritual or carnal. Features of a carnal friendship between two nuns include topics of conversation ("talking about how much they love each other and who loves whom more"); close proximity and demonstrations of attraction ("the affection with which they look at each other: they always want to be together, going around attached to each other, without knowing how to be apart"); the stress, distraction, and concern over the special friend ("the worried thoughts and troubled heart when one doesn't know what the loved one is doing – where she is, with whom she is talking, what is troubling her, if she is sick, if she needs anything"); jealousy, conflict, and exclusivity ("the anxiety about whether someone is going to steal the person she loves, as when she sees her girlfriend looking at another woman; envy if someone else gives her something; jealousy if she is not by her side"); arguments and conflict ("the anger and upset that sometimes exists between nuns who love each other . . . and they end up hating each other with the same passion with which they had loved each other"); gifts and loving expressions ("the little favors and impertinent gifts . . . childish pleasures and baby-talk") as well as the desire to defend the loved one ("the uncontrollable lying that one nun does to cover the misdeeds of the other, each ignoring the other's faults that are offensive to the community") (Villegas 232).

Villegas's treatment of "inappropriate" friendships in the convent differs from many other documents of the era in its persistent focus, not on punishable sex acts, but on the emotional intricacies of an intimate relationship – the day-to-day challenges of a partnership rather than the isolated sexual encounter. In this way, while the author attempts to outline what the nuns should avoid, he pulls back the curtain on a closed community to expose part of the scenario of intimacy in an all-female space. By not focusing explicitly on specific sexual activities, we see a more nuanced picture of affective relationships within a communal living environment. Moreover, we can assume that to do otherwise might have invited unwanted criticism of the spiritual state of the convent.

The seemingly innocent depictions of same-sex love in certain texts (in light of an apparent absence of sexual details) also create an important body of evidence for how women who desired other women were perceived and identified, and in this way suggest that early modern observers were capable of imagining a broad set of identifying characteristics for women believed to enjoy the romantic company of other women. These encoded texts, considered in tandem with the captivating cases against couples such as Inés de Santa Cruz and Catalina Ledesma provide compelling evidence for how long-term or significant relationships between women as well as isolated romantic encounters were imagined, interpreted, and critiqued by acquaintances, neighbors, friends, and family as well as by legal specialists.

Visible Evidence: Looking, Seeing

While auditory evidence was admissible when investigating women suspected of female sodomy in Inquisitional and criminal cases, other verbal and visual texts suggest that to identify a lesbian in the early modern period, *seeing* is believing. Early modern medical wisdom, for example, would have people believe that masculine women such as Queen Christina of Sweden and Catalina de Erauso – two gender-bending celebrities who were rumored to have participated in same-sex love affairs – might be nonconformist because of a prenatal sex mutation.[3] In other words, originally they were to be born male but a sudden change of temperature in the mother's womb caused the external sex organs to turn inward. Best-selling medical authority Juan Huarte de San Juan explains that the female masculinity resulting from a prenatal sex change (and the related deviant sexual behavior) could be confirmed through visual observation: "She is recognized after birth as having a masculine nature, in her speech as well as in all her movements and behavior" (609). Surely when Catalina de Erauso and Queen Christina made public appearances and agreed to sit for multiple portraits, they provided one answer to the enduring question: what does a lesbian look like?

Early modern evidence also reminds us to consider how a lesbian looks – that is, the ways she looks at other women. Mentioned by confessors such as Bernardino Villegas in his 1635 "special friend" test ("the affection with which they look at each other") as well as Mexican cleric Andrés de Borda (who confirmed in his 1708 treatise *Manual for Confessors of Nuns* that looking with desire at a portrait of a former "inappropriate friend" would be sufficient to break a vow of chastity [46v]), the idea that the gaze can be used as evidence of same-sex desire is also dramatized on a secular stage in Cubillo de Aragón's 1637 play *Añasco el de Talavera*. Without relying on the complication of crossdressing to explore same-sex attraction, both the audience and characters on stage are aware that Dionisia is openly in love with Leonor. Not surprisingly, Dionisia's father has difficulty understanding his daughter's nontraditional desires. When he discusses the situation with Leonor, he asks: "So she really loves you?" to which Leonor answers: "So much that she tells me how much she loves me and she stares at me."[4] He responds: "That she stares at you doesn't surprise me, but that she is in love with you, yes." Leonor then points out the importance of visual stimulus for the creation of desire: "Well, whoever is in love started out first by staring." In other words, passion enters through the eyes. Realizing this fact, the beautiful yet manly Dionisia vehemently rejects the gaze of men who are eager to get a glimpse of her, confirming that she is not like other women: "Although I was born a woman, I am different." And while Dionisia attempts to define her passion for Leonor in platonic terms that interpret love between women as more sincere and stable than heterosexual desire, her cousin reminds her that there is also physical pleasure in same-sex relations: "there can also be sin between women; it may be different but a 'prize' nonetheless."

As literary characters were debating the nature of same-sex desire between women, they also voiced disbelief about whether such inclinations were commonplace in the cultural imaginary. In the novella "Love for the Sake of Conquest," included in best-selling author María de Zayas's 1647 collection of short stories *The Disenchantments of Love*, a doubting participant asks, "who ever heard of a woman in love with another woman?" (227), while in a play based on the life of Queen Christina (penned by famed playwright Pedro Calderón de la Barca) one character quips at the close of the performance: "who ever heard of a play ending with a woman marrying a woman?" As these conversations on the stage and fictional page intended to question the nature of same-sex passion, they were frequently couched in humor – whether it be the nervous laughter when confronting taboo desire or the shortsighted conclusion that passion between women was less threatening to the family's reputation than the (potentially) procreative sex outside the sacrament of marriage. Why else, for example, would the patriarch in Zayas's story respond with a lighthearted joke on learning that his daughter's servant and companion Estefanía was in love with her: "'That's splendid,' Don Bernardo responded, 'and we can expect lovely grandchildren from such a chaste love'" (216). And yet despite the moments of comical confusion over women who love other women in prose and theatre, the open discussion of female homoeroticism allowed a space for expressing such intimacy and perhaps contributed to a context in which readers might be less scandalized by the passionate desire for female friends in the verses of celebrated seventeenth-century poets such as Katherine Phillips (who wrote verses such as "For thou art all that I can prize, / My Joy, my Life, my Rest" for her beloved friend Anne Owen [qtd. in Castle 160]) and famed Mexican nun Sor Juana Inés de la Cruz (whose devotion to the Countess of Paredes is expressed in verses such as "Inés, to one thing I aspire, ... to tumble you to bed I can conspire" [qtd. in Castle 177].

Material Artifacts as Evidence

While portraits, appearances, and plays could offer early modern spectators provocative visual evidence of lesbians and their desire, material artifacts could also provide concrete signs of same-sex passion. Surely the ways different observers understood the sight of a woman "hanged with that artifice around her neck with which she had carnally lain with the two women" (as described by one fifteenth-century eyewitness; see Blackmore 218) or the image of long-term partners Inés and Catalina forced to wear the dildos around their necks when they received public lashings for the crime of female sodomy, could have provided lessons on homoerotic desire for curious onlookers.

While phallic devices and overgrown genitals were used as credible evidence of deviant penetrative activities, the location of the sex scene also provided compelling proof of sexual encounters between women. In particular, the bed on which the women were enjoying each other's company could have a lot to say. When Ana Aler and Mariana López were convicted of female sodomy by Inquisitional courts in 1656 (despite the absence of a prosthetic penis among the evidence used against them), witnesses listening to the women's erotic dialogue and peeping at them during sexual relations implicated the mattress involved in their liaisons:

> The defendant [Ana] slept with Mariana, and the witnesses heard them breathing heavily and saying shameful words like a man and a woman would during the carnal act. This occurred twice a night for two months. They slept on a mattress that showed many signs of the emission of semen, yet it had been brand-new when they started to sleep on it. One day [the witnesses] saw them at nine o'clock in the morning in bed about eight feet from their open window; Ana was on top of Mariana, moving back and forth, and Mariana said, "Give it to me, I can't wait any longer." (*Causas* 482v)

The book – as a material object – could be used as a not-so-subtle message about female intimacy. When Colombian nun Francisca Josefa de la Concepción de Castillo (1671–1742) was reading a book about the dangers of illicit friendships in the convent (perhaps Saint Teresa of Avila's *The Way of Perfection*), the nuns who were engaging in such prohibited relations interpreted the possession and display of such a book as a manipulative strategy to attract other nuns' lovers: "If I was reading a book about particular friendships and the damage that they cause, they would say I was just doing it to steal their girlfriends so they would come see me instead" (53). Again, some of the nuns used their beds as dramatic props to signal discord and perhaps betrayal in intimate relations. Reminiscent of the domestic violence documented in the civil case against Inés and Catalina, Francisca Josefa's account exposes the physical mistreatment of some of the nuns involved in sexual relationships: "Their girlfriends would slap them and throw their beds in the middle of the patio" (54).

Religious material artifacts could also be implicated in forbidden sexual encounters. Who could have imagined, for example, that in 1609 a bronze Christ on a crucifix necklace would tattle on two errant nuns engaged in undisclosed activities during a nocturnal tryst? In this case, prioress Ana de San

Agustín (1555–1634) had lent her beloved cross necklace to another nun, who purportedly participated in scandalous activities behind closed doors, thereby inducing the miniature Christ figure to separate himself from the neck of the nun wearing the crucifix to fly through the air back to inform San Agustín on the wayward nuns. Welcoming the floating and visibly shaken Christ in her arms, the prioress asked him why he had come back to her. The miraculous airborne and talking (actually sobbing) crucifix responded: *"Because there they are offending me"* (see Ana de San Agustín; Alonso de San Jerónimo).

Other cases of transgressive desire during the early modern period demonstrate the creative ways some women used the limited resources in their surroundings toward the goal of participating in same-sex relations. In a 1597 Inquisition case from Mallorca, Esperanza Rojas confessed to having created an altar to pray to the devil while she practiced love magic in the hopes that the two women with whom she had already had sexual relations would come back to her and resume the affair.[5] The Inquisitional report describes how she had removed the religious images from her room in a correctional home for wayward women but kept the one that had a figure of the devil at the bottom (perhaps a portrait of Saint Michael treading on Satan). It was understood that in front of the demonic image, she had performed her superstitious prayers and spells. Again, like the cryptic account of the nuns' scandalous activities that made the bronze crucifix flee the scene of the crime, the case report is silent about the specifics of the sexual encounters between Esperanza and her ex-lovers. However, the summary includes great detail about the love magic (transcribing and repeating multiple times the specific spells; describing the intricate hand gestures and accessories involved such as candles, salt, fire, coal, and the visual image of the devil). Interestingly, the Inquisitors do not record having asked questions about the exact nature of the carnal activities among the female residents, despite witness' testimony that while "burning some coals, [Esperanza] would say that she was enflaming the hearts of certain women whom she loved and with whom she had had carnal relations" (249r). Nonetheless, for certain readers, the lesbian desire that motivated these heretical and superstitious practices becomes evidence for the kind of recovery work needed to fill in a more complete picture of the same-sex relationships that were frequently hidden from vigilant eyes.

Identifying or Inventing Lesbians?

There were some cases, beyond Erauso, in which individuals with nonconforming gender/sexuality chose not to live as women, and hence did not necessarily perceive their desire as *homo*erotic. Indeed, some representations and interpretations (such as those that privileged sex-at-birth in transgender, transsexual, or intersex cases) actually created a lesbian figure or identity where the desiring individual might have articulated "his" desire for a woman not as homosexual but heterosexual. One famous example is the self-declared hermaphrodite Elena/Eleno de Céspedes, who in the late sixteenth century married a woman before an old acquaintance denounced "her" to the authorities as a woman pretending to be a man.[6] Despite medical documentation that Céspedes's male member was "normal" – as was determined during physical examinations by respected physicians and urologists prior to the marriage – the alleged penis mysteriously disappeared during the Inquisitional trial. In an attempt to provide material evidence of what was no longer visible or tangible, Céspedes described the appearance, function, and length of the previously existing organ, which was mapped onto the trial manuscript when the court scribe, following Céspedes's verbal sketch, drew a 3 3/4-inch line to represent the size of the purported male member: "as long as this line _____" (qtd. in Soyer 64). Although Céspedes maintained that a sexual identity as a hermaphrodite could not be assessed as monosexed or fixed, and thus there was no guilt of sodomy, lesbianism, desecration of the sacrament of holy matrimony, or demonic intervention, Céspedes was charged by the Inquisition with female sodomy and found guilty of bigamy as well as collusion with the devil.

Anatomy would not necessarily be sufficient to adjudge transgressive desire but had to be supplemented by an appeal to a higher power. Count Froben Christoph von Zimmern included in his 1560s chronicle an account of a servant woman named Greta, who was described as having a manly demeanor and a reputation for courting young women with material gifts. Suspected of being a hermaphrodite or androgyne until a physical examination revealed she was a "true, proper woman" (qtd. in Roper 257), Greta's nonconforming behavior was also linked to astrological influences and occult practices frequently employed to account for same-sex desire (see Puff). While Greta was believed to be "born under an inverted, unnatural constellation" (qtd. in Roper 257), we may recall from our second example how Ana de Jesús characterized the gifts she received from her admirer as being infused with magic spells. Using astrology to explain Greta's passion for women would have conformed to ideas from ancient texts published during the Renaissance. For example, Claudius Ptolemy's *Tetrabiblos* (first published in 1484 and reprinted several times during the sixteenth century), identifies horoscopes that engender various types of tribades: "If likewise Mars or Venus as well, either one or both of them, is made masculine, ... the females are lustful for unnatural congresses, cast inviting glances of the eye, and are what we call *tribades*; for they deal with females and perform the functions of males" (qtd. in Borris 167–68). Along similar lines, Julius Firmicus's *Mathesis* (Learning) proposed that a particular arrangement of planets in masculine signs created viragos, masculine women, and tribades (Borris 171–73).

At times these historical and fictional narratives describe complex personal relationships, occasionally characterizing these women as being a certain "type" as behaving in a manner that would eventually be recognized as divergent lesbian, bisexual, and/or transgender identities that were dependent on conceptions of gender, anatomy, class, race, ethnicity, religion, and empire. And whether the images of lesbian relations were manipulated for sexual titillation, gossipy "outings," or used for legal, medical, or theological classifications, these intersectional discourses offer multifaceted, sometimes contradictory but other times nuanced guides for how to identify the type of woman who desired other women; in other words, how to spot a lesbian in the early modern Spanish empire.

Notes

1. For discussion of the acts paradigm, see Halperin 29, 46, 167; Sedgwick 46–48; and Borris and Rousseau 4. For recent studies on lesbian sexuality in the early modern period see Velasco, *Lesbians*; Traub; Walen; Andreadis; and Brown; as well as anthologies edited by Giffney, Sauer, and Watt; Delgado and Saint-Saens; and Blackmore and Hutcheson.
2. All references to the criminal case of Inés de Santa Cruz and Catalina Ledesma are cited from *Criminal*. See also Monter 316; Garza Carvajal 55.
3. For more on Erauso see Velasco, *Lieutenant*; *Lesbians* 83–89 and Erauso's memoir.
4. All references to *Añasco* are cited from an early printed edition with no page numbers. Unless otherwise noted, all quotations are from act 1.
5. All references to Esperanza de Rojas are cited from *Relación*.
6. For Elena/Eleno de Céspedes see *Tribunal*. See also Burshatin; and Kagan and Dyer.

Works Cited

Alejandro de la Madre de Dios. *La pobre sevillana. Vida de la fiel sierva de Cristo y Venerable Madre Ana de Jesus ... por Alejandro de la Madre de Dios*. Madrid, 1707. Print.
Alonso de San Jerónimo. *Vida virtudes y Milagros de ... Ana de San Agustín, Carmelita descalza ...* Madrid: Francisco Nieto, 1668. Print.

Ana de Jesús. *Vida de la Venerable Ana de Jesús escrita por ella misma*. Biblioteca Nacional, Madrid: Ms. 13.493.

Ana de San Agustín. *Vida, virtudes, y milagros de la prodigiosa virgen y madre Ana de San Agustín, carmelita descalza* ... Madrid: Francisco Nieto, 1668. Print.

Andreadis, Harriette. *Sappho in Early Modern England: Female Same-Sex Literary Erotics 1550–1714*. Chicago: U of Chicago P, 2001. Print.

Bartholin, Thomas. *Bartholinus Anatomy: Made from the precepts of his father, and from the observations of all modern anatomists, together with his own* ... John Streater, 1668. Print.

Bennett, Judith. "'Lesbian-Like' and the Social History of Lesbianism." *Journal of the History of Sexuality* 9 (2000): 1–24. Print.

Blackmore, Josiah. "The Poets of Sodom." Blackmore and Hutcheson 195–221.

Blackmore, Josiah, and Gregory S. Hutcheson, eds. *Queer Iberia: Sexualities, Cultures, and Crossings from the Middle Ages to the Renaissance*. Durham: Duke UP, 1999. Print.

Borda, Andrés de. *Práctica de confesores de monjas* ... Madrid: Francisco de Ribera Calderón, 1708. Print.

Borris, Kenneth, ed. *Same-Sex Desire in the English Renaissance: A Sourcebook of Texts, 1470–1650*. New York: Routledge, 2004.

Borris, Kenneth, and George Rousseau, eds. *The Sciences of Homosexuality in Early Modern Europe*. New York: Routledge, 2008. Print.

Brooten, Bernadette J. *Love between Women: Early Christian Responses to Female Homoeroticism*. Chicago: U of Chicago P, 1996. Print.

Brown, Judith C. *Immodest Acts: The Life of a Lesbian Nun in Renaissance Italy*. New York: Oxford UP, 1986. Print.

Burshatin, Israel. "Written on the Body: Slave or Hermaphrodite in Sixteenth-Century Spain." Blackmore and Hutcheson 420–56.

Calderón de la Barca, Pedro. "Afectos de odio y amor." *Comedias de don Pedro Calderón de la Barca*. BAE Madrid: Rivadeneyra, 1862. 99–122. Print.

Castle, Terry, ed. *The Literature of Lesbianism: A Historical Anthology from Ariosto to Stonewall*. New York: Columbia UP, 2005. Print.

Las causas despachadas en este Sto Ofo de la Inquisición de Aragón este año de 1656. . . Sodomitas. Archivo Histórico Nacional, Madrid: Inquisición., Libro 995, fols. 405–405v; 482–485v (#22–23). Print.

Cháves, Cristóbal de. *Relación de la cárcel de Sevilla*. Madrid: Clásicos El Arbol, 1983. Print.

Criminal Contra {año 1603} Inés Santa Cruz y Catalina Ledesma por prostitutas y bujarronas, cuya operación ejecutaban con una caña en forma de miembro viril. Archivo General de Simancas, Cámara de Castilla, legajo 2557, expediente 9. Print.

Crompton, Louis. "The Myth of Lesbian Impunity: Capital Laws from 1270 to 1791." *Journal of Homosexuality* 6.1–2 (1980–81): 11–25. Print.

Cubillo de Aragón, Alvaro. *Añasco el de Talavera*. [n.p., n.d.] Special Collections and Rare Books, U of Minnesota. Print.

Delgado, María José, and Alain Saint-Saens, eds. *Lesbianism and Homosexuality in Early Modern Spain*. New Orleans: UP of the South, 2000. Print.

Erauso, Catalina de. *Lieutenant Nun: Memoir of a Basque Transvestite in the New World*. Trans. Michele Stepto and Gabriel Stepto. Boston: Beacon P, 1996. Print.

Faderman, Lillian. "A Usable Past?" Giffney, Sauer, and Watt 171–78.

Francisca Josefa de la Concepción de Castillo. *Obras completas de la Madre Francisca Josefa de la Concepción de Castillo*. Ed. Dario Achury Valenzuela. Bogota: Talleres Gráficos del Banco de la República, 1968. Print.

Garza Carvajal, Federico. *Butterflies will Burn: Prosecuting Sodomites in Early Modern Spain and Mexico*. Austin: U of Texas P, 2003. Print.

Giffney, Noreen, Michelle M. Sauer, and Diane Watt, eds. *The Lesbian Premodern*. New York: Palgrave, 2011. Print.

Halperin, David. *How to Do the History of Homosexuality*. Chicago: U of Chicago P, 2002. Print.

Huarte de San Juan, Juan. *Examen de ingenios para las ciencias*. Ed. Guillermo Serés. Madrid: Cátedra, 1989. Print.

Kagan, Richard L., and Abigail Dyer, eds. *Inquisitorial Inquiries: Brief Lives of Secret Jews and Other Heretics*. Baltimore: Johns Hopkins UP, 2004. Print.

Monter, William. *Frontiers of Heresy: The Spanish Inquisition from the Basque Lands to Sicily*. Cambridge: Cambridge UP, 1990. Print.

Pérez, Llorenc, Lleonard Muntaner, and Mateu Colom, eds. *El Tribunal de la Inquisición en Mallorca. Relación de causas de fe 1578–1806*. Palma de Mallorca: Miquel Font, 1986. Print.

Pérez Bocanegra, Juan. *Ritual formulario e institución de curas, para administrar a los naturales de este Reyno. . .* Lima: Geronimo de Contreras, 1631.

Perry, Mary Elizabeth. *The Handless Maiden: Moriscos and the Politics of Religion in Early Modern Spain (Jews, Christians, and Muslims from the Ancient to the Modern World)*. New Jersey: Princeton UP, 2007. Print.

Puff, Helmut. "Toward a Philology of the Premodern Lesbian." Giffney, Sauer, and Watt 145–157.

Relación de las causas que se han despachado en la Inquisición de Mallorca desde 28 de diciembre del año pasado de 1597 hasta 21 de diciembre de 1598. Archivo Histórico Nacional: Inquisición., Libro 860, fs. 248v–249v.

Roper, Lyndal. *The Holy Household: Women and Morals in Reformation Augsburg*. Oxford UP, 1991. Print.

Sedgwick, Eve Kosofsky. *Epistemology of the Closet*. Berkeley and Los Angeles: U of California P, 1990. Print.

Sinistrari, Ludovico Maria. *Peccatum Mutum (The Secret Sin)*. Intro by Rev. Montague Summers. Paris: Collection "Le Ballet de Muses," 1958. Print.

Soyer, François. *Ambiguous Gender in Early Modern Spain and Portugal: Inquisitors, Doctors and the Transgression of Gender Norms*. Leiden: Brill, 2012. Print.

Teresa of Avila. *The Way of Perfection*. Trans and ed. El Allison Peers. New York: Doubleday, 1964. Print.

Traub, Valerie. *The Renaissance of Lesbianism in Early Modern England*. Cambridge: Cambridge UP, 2002. Print.

Tribunal de Toledo: Céspedes, Elena y Eleno de. MS. Archivo Histórico Nacional, Madrid. Inquisición, legajo 234, expediente 24.

Velasco, Sherry. *Lesbians in Early Modern Spain*. Nashville: Vanderbilt UP, 2011. Print.

The Lieutenant Nun: Transgenderism, Lesbian Desire, and Catalina de Erauso. Austin: U of Texas P, 2000. Print.

Villegas, Bernardino de. *La esposa de Cristo instruida con la vida de Santa Lutgarda, virgen, monja de San Bernardo*. Murcia, 1635. Print.

Walen, Denise A. *Constructions of Female Homoeroticism in Early Modern Drama*. New York: Palgrave, 2005. Print.

Zayas, María de. *The Disenchantments of Love. A Translation of the Desengaños amorosos*. Trans. H. Patsy Boyer. Albany: State U of New York P, 1997. Print.

II

Cross-Dressing, Queerness, and the Early Modern Stage

DAVID L. ORVIS

In the opening scene of Christopher Marlowe's *Edward II*, in a passage that has elicited much commentary from queer scholars, the eponymous king's favorite, Gaveston, having just been recalled from exile in France, ponders various entertainments that "may draw the pliant King which way [he] please[s]." In addition to the "Italian masques by night, / Sweet speeches, comedies, and pleasing shows," Gaveston imagines an intricate role play that would require several boys to crossdress:

> And in the day when he shall walk abroad,
> Like sylvan nymphs my pages shall be clad,
> My men like satyrs grazing on the lawns
> Shall with their goat-feet dance an antic hay;
> Sometime a lovely boy in Dian's shape,
> With hair that gilds the water as it glides,
> Crownets of pearl about his naked arms,
> And in his sportful hands an olive tree
> To hide those parts which men delight to see,
> Shall bathe him in a spring; and there hard by,
> One like Actaeon peeping through the grove,
> Shall by the angry goddess be transformed,
> And running in the likeness of an hart,
> By yelping hounds pulled down, shall seem to die. (1.52, 54–69)

Enlisting pages to play the "sylvan nymphs" and "a lovely boy" to play Diana, Gaveston describes a bawdy scene that interweaves male transvestism, male homoerotic desire, voyeurism, exhibitionism, and sadomasochism. Although Gaveston does not say it outright, one assumes Edward will be the one who, perhaps unwittingly, finds himself in the role of "Actaeon peeping through the grove," his punishment for stumbling on the carefully orchestrated scenario of a simulated gang rape where the king will "seem to die." It would be an understatement, I think, to remark that this entertainment confounds distinctions between spectator and spectacle; according to Gaveston, the performance is designed specifically to ambush its audience, although one suspects the king – the Hero to Gaveston's Leander, if Gaveston is to be believed (1.6–9) – will hardly mind.

This titillating monologue is the last we hear of Gaveston's transvestite theatre; as critics have amply demonstrated, in *Edward II* same-sex desire finds its fullest expression not in transvestism but in the imbricated discourses of friendship, favoritism, and sodomy.[1] According to Jonathan Goldberg, the juxtaposition of crossdressing and effeminacy on the one hand and friendship, favoritism, and sodomy on the other is to the point. That is, Marlowe's play conjures up the familiar association of transvestism and homoeroticism only to leave it behind, discarding it for other discourses that militate against heterosexist reinscriptions of same-sex desire (115). In this way, the play resists the heterosexualizing tendency to see male homoerotic bonds as travesties or perversions of the dominant male-female dyad. Yet, as Alan Sinfield points out, this rejection is not wholesale, as the king's relationship with his favorite is at times defined in cross-gender terms. Positing a butch / femme rather than male / female dynamic in play between Edward and Gaveston, Sinfield suggests that their relationship does have some affinities with transvestite logics, anticipating models that have become more familiar in the twentieth century (108–11). The point, I think, is not that crossdressing and cross-gender identification represent the return of some repressed truth about same-sex desire, but rather that transvestism – much like the group sex, voyeurism, exhibitionism, and sadomasochism Gaveston envisages – becomes a site of pleasure for Edward and Gaveston, without (necessarily) becoming constitutive of their relationship. Hence, while it is true, as Goldberg claims, that Gaveston's transvestite theatre need not be taken at face value as same-sex desire's "pathologized truth" (115), and while it is also true, as Goldberg (114–18) and Valerie Traub (*Desire* 117–23) remind us, that to treat crossdressing as the privileged vehicle for homoerotic desire is to confuse gender and sexuality, it does not follow that homoerotic desire cannot be enacted through precisely those practices about which Gaveston fantasizes. For Gaveston at least, transvestism *is* a means for pursuing desire for another man.

Despite, or rather because of, its precarious position in *Edward II*, Gaveston's transvestite theatre represents an important point of departure for a chapter on crossdressing, queerness, and the early modern stage. To adapt a question posed first by Stephen Orgel ("Tobacco") and then by Mario DiGangi ("How") in their germinal work on locating queerness in early modernity, I want to ask, just how queer *was* the transvestite theatre? In the thirty years that have passed since the publication of Alan Bray's landmark book *Homosexuality in Renaissance England*, feminist and queer scholars have asked and answered this question in a variety of ways.[2] My aim here is to take stock of this robust body of scholarship by teasing out some salient trends as they have shaped critical interpretations of three transvestite comedies: William Shakespeare's *Twelfth Night*, John Lyly's *Galatea*, and Thomas Middleton and Thomas Dekker's *The Roaring Girl*. In the space of this chapter, I am concerned primarily with the diverse ways conjunctions of transvestism and homoeroticism obtain both on the early modern stage and in early modern culture more generally. Of course, in order to discern the queerness of the transvestite stage, one must first define "queer" – that deliberate anachronism whose strategic application to premodernity always runs the risk of obfuscating rather than elucidating precisely those discursive formations that most interest lesbian and gay and queer critics.[3] Following Eve Kosofsky Sedgwick, I use the term "queer" to signify an array of social and sexual practices, arrangements, and peoples that, when put into discourse, confront or undermine the (perceived) dominant culture's views on gender and sexuality (5–9). From this vantage, "queer" carries with it deconstructive as well as generative properties, enabling, on the one hand, the dissection and interrogation of dominant ideology, and, on the other, the construction and expression of alternative configurations. In this chapter, then, "queer" will be deployed to designate those conjunctions of crossdressing and same-sex desire that in the process of challenging dominant beliefs and attitudes, imagine alternative arrangements and practices.

The Uses of Crossdressing

Whether these arrangements and practices aspire to coexist with or else oppose the dominant culture – that is, whether they operate as manifestations of oppositional or alternative ideologies, to borrow Raymond Williams's terms (126) – is contingent on numerous variables, some related specifically to the theatres and their conventions, others more broadly to early modern culture. Mary Bly, for instance, has argued that the Whitefriars syndicate, a small boys' company active for about nine months in 1607–08, catered to a specific clientele with particular tastes: "the similarities between five collaboratively written comedies suggest not only that a community of authors who appreciated homoerotic humour existed, but that they wrote their plays with a specific audience in mind. The plays' clever, queer puns implicate the potential for a queer community in 1607–08 London, given that dramatists targeted those cognizant of homoerotic desire" (23–24). The proliferation of puns foregrounding and eroticizing the body of the boy actor beneath women's clothing reveals Whitefriars to be a theatrical community with a keen interest in the homoeroticism activated by and expressed through transvestism. In these plays, "a cross-dressed boy actor is a pun waiting to detonate: an object of desire who *wears* a primary and a secondary script, a skirt with a 'hanger' below" (Bly 13). Bly's case study shows that the homoerotic potential of theatrical transvestism depended at least in part on the kind of theatre one wished to see. If one attended a performance at Whitefriars – indeed, if one knew such a syndicate existed – one would expect a play teeming with bawdy puns about boys portraying the female characters. In this particular context, Lisa Jardine's argument that crossdressed boys were erotic objects for men (I would say for women, too) rings true (*Still* 24) because the puns articulated in Whitefriars plays repeatedly enjoin attendees to speculate on the play-boy's body.

Such was not the case, however, for transvestite theatre as a whole. While transvestism may always already have the capacity to unsettle gender constructs and give voice to diverse erotic desires – a phenomenon Marjorie Garber associates with the "transvestite effect" (36–37) – it was also standard practice in English playhouses even as women appeared onstage in a variety of roles.[4] Critics have adduced numerous examples of early modern playgoers who appear not to have noticed, or if they did found unremarkable, the cross-gender casting that required boy actors to play the roles of women (see Dawson 31–37; McLuskie; and Orgel, *Impersonations* 31–35). Other commentary from the period suggests that while the English stage was, in its European context anyway, unique in casting boys in women's roles, "that very anomaly seems to have been a point of pride" for English dramatists (Rackin, "Shakespeare's" 115).[5] Of course, antitheatrical polemicists fulminated ad nauseum against crossdressing both on and off the early modern stage, citing Deuteronomy 22:5 – "The woman shall not wear that which pertaineth unto the man, neither shall a man put on woman's raiment, for all that do so, *are* abomination unto the LORD thy God" (Geneva Bible) – but the ecclesiastical courts seem not to have been as concerned about the custom as the Williams Prynnes and Philip Stubbeses were.[6] This is not to say crossdressing was never the subject of controversy. The courts did take up some cases, and certain regional shaming rituals did involve crossdressing, but it is not insignificant that while sumptuary laws regulating the clothes people of certain ranks and incomes could wear remained firmly in place for much of the period, these laws had nothing to say about crossdressing (Orgel, *Impersonations* 14).[7] In the eyes of the courts, then, transgressions of class, not gender, were of more concern. Of course, one cannot assume that the court's actions reflect public sentiment, especially when the polemicists' rhetoric is so virulent, but archival research has begun to cast serious doubt on the premium early moderns placed on texts condemning crossdressers as, in the words of *Hic Mulier*, "not half man/half woman, half fish/half flesh, half beast/half Monster, but all Odious, all Devil" (qtd. in Henderson and McManus 266).[8] What is more, the theatres were far from the only space where transvestism was sanctioned; historical documents describe numerous occasions and events where cross-dressing was perfectly acceptable, even celebrated. In light of all this evidence, one begins to wonder whether the transvestite theatre was a manifestation of the Bakhtinian carnivalesque, where the "temporary suspension, both ideal and real, of hierarchical rank created ... a special type of communication impossible of everyday life" (Bakhtin 10), or whether it simply constituted transvestism's most common expression. As recent work has shown, early modern conceptualizations of gender as prosthetic – that is, as shaped by clothes and other accoutrements one might wear – point to a widespread belief in at least some degree of malleability.[9] This belief might help explain why the theatres prospered during the early modern period despite the objections of what appears to have been a rather vocal minority.

In this milieu, transvestism – a fortiori the transvestite theatre – could either buttress the dominant ideology or undermine it. As Garber's notion of the "transvestite effect" indicates, crossdressing always carries with it radical queer potential; however, in a culture that acknowledged the malleability of gender, transvestism might also reinforce its coordinates, allowing for gender performance that falls along a continuum whose poles remain firmly intact. Early modern dramatists were keenly aware of the "transvestite effect," even if they did not call it that. Indeed, scholars have identified more than one hundred characters who crossdress in their respective plays – "eighty-odd female pages and twenty-odd boy brides," to quote Michael Shapiro and Phyllis Rackin ("Boy" 836).[10] If we add to this list those dramatic entertainments that stage plays-within-the-play, we have a substantial body of works that compel spectators to confront gender performance and the desires it incites. Or as Ann Rosalind Jones and Peter Stallybrass put it,

> Are we not ... forced into contradictory attitudes about both sexuality and gender: on the one hand, gender as a set of prosthetic devices, in which case, the gendered body is absorbed into the play of those devices; on the other, gender as "given" marks of the body – the breast, the vagina, the penis – which (however analogous in Galenic medicine) are read as the signs of absolute difference – in which case, sexuality, whether between man and woman, woman and woman, or man and man, tends to be organized through a fixation upon

the supposedly essential features of gender. But on the Renaissance stage, even these "essential" features are located – whether prosthetically or at the level of the imaginary – upon another body, the body of a boy. (214)

Here Jones and Stallybrass are referring specifically to moments when female characters undress, moments that invite playgoers to speculate on the boy actor beneath women's clothing. But I would suggest that a similar rupture occurs whenever a play calls attention to its artifice, employing metatheatrical gestures that activate what Shapiro describes as the spectators' "dual consciousness" – that is, an awareness of the multiple layers of gender performance involved in cross-gender casting (*Gender* 2–3). Although we have no evidence such gender-play provoked the Master of Revels to censor a dramatic work, perhaps because this office was concerned primarily with passages that might offend the monarchy, the configurations we find in plays that flaunt their metatheatricality point to a vested interest in more radical possibilities for gender and sexuality. In what follows, I aim to show how cross-dressing enacts these possibilities. Following Traub, I am interested in plays that "display a homoerotic circulation of desire," where "homoerotic energy is elicited, exchanged, negotiated, and displaced as it confronts the pleasures and anxieties of its meanings in early modern culture" (*Desire* 118). Although homoeroticism is not, nor ever has been, contingent on transvestism, the conjunctions we find in the drama of the period suggest myriad erotic possibilities that were no less intelligible to early modern audiences than to contemporary queer criticism.

Of particular interest to queer scholars is Shakespeare's *Twelfth Night*, a festive comedy where twins become interchangeable objects of desire. As Phyllis Rackin notes, Viola and her brother Sebastian:

> are identical in almost everything that mattered in Shakespeare's time, since their identical birth and parentage serve as surrogates for identical nature, nurture, and social rank. Even their situations in the play are similar, both shipwrecked, both landing in Illyria, both assisted by seamen, so when Viola imitates the "fashion, colour, ornament" of Sebastian's dress to disguise herself as a boy, their identity is complete in everything except sex. To all the other characters the twins are indistinguishable. ("Shakespeare's" 122)

By and large, critics agree that this indistinguishability engenders, and at times confounds, homoerotic and heteroerotic desire. While in Orsino's service, Viola/Cesario pines for the Duke, confessing in soliloquy, "Whoe'er I woo, myself would be his wife" (1.4.42). Although this utterance registers as heterosocial because Viola imagines herself as Orsino's wife, what spectators see is the page Cesario fantasizing about marriage to the Duke. Orsino, for his part, insists he loves Olivia, even as he finds himself drawn to Cesario. Gazing on his page, Orsino observes:

> For they shall yet belie thy happy years
> That say thou art a man; Diana's lip
> Is not more smooth and rubious: thy small pipe
> Is as the maiden's organ, shrill and sound,
> And all is semblative a woman's part.   (1.4.30–34)

Here again homoeroticism and heteroeroticism run together: although Orsino believes the features he blazons are "semblative a woman's part," they belong, too, to Cesario and the boy actor playing Viola. In *Twelfth Night*, the "master's mistress" (5.1.325) is also the "master-mistress" (2) of Sonnet 20. Olivia's attraction to Viola, and later Sebastian, relies on a similar conflation. About the page Cesario, Olivia declares, "Thy tongue, thy face, thy limbs, actions, and spirit / Do give thee five-fold blazon" (1.5.296–97). In confusing Sebastian with Cesario/Viola, Olivia betrays an erotic interest in both. So, too, does Antonio, who risks his life to follow Sebastian, only to be imprisoned for trying to protect Cesario/Viola. As the officers escort him offstage, Antonio, believing he has been arrested trying to save an ungrateful Sebastian, exclaims, "But O how vile an idol proves this god!" (3.4.374). In the play's final scene, Orsino, Olivia, and Antonio all make the same startling discovery: they desire not one person but two. Orsino perceives "[o]ne face, one voice, one habit, and two persons! / A natural perspective, that is, and is not!" (5.1.214–15). Olivia, meanwhile, learns she is, as Sebastian points out, "betroth'd both to a maid and man" (5.1.261). And Antonio, whose "desire, / More sharp than filed steel" (3.3.4–5), sent him after Sebastian, cannot tell the twins apart. Even after Sebastian identifies himself, Antonio asks, in the last speech he will utter, "Which is Sebastian?" (5.1.222). Over the course of the play, then, the inability to distinguish one twin from the other extends to the diverse heteroerotic and homoerotic desires they incite.

Putative Heterosociality

For feminist and queer critics, the important debate is not whether transvestism instantiates homoerotic desire, but rather how this homoerotic desire operates in a play that attempts, or at least gestures toward, heterosocial marital closure. Much of this criticism has emerged in response to Stephen Greenblatt, who claims that in *Twelfth Night*, as in all plays performed on the transvestite stage, "[t]he open secret of identity – that within differentiated individuals is a single structure, identifiably male – is presented literally in the all-male cast" (93). Citing Galen's authority, Greenblatt attributes to the transvestite theatre a "conception of gender that is teleologically male" (88), thus making all forms of eroticism *homo*erotic.[11] Though some critics maintain that *Twelfth Night*'s transvestism does indeed reinforce patriarchy as a structuring principle of early modern society, in that it displaces the female body and renders women and boys equally available erotic objects for men, others have noted a wider circulation of desire made possible by crossdressing, even if this circulation succumbs, finally, to what has been understood to be the play's (heterosocial) marital trajectory.[12] According to Rackin, "*Twelfth Night* does not frame the issue of homoerotic desire as a shocking secret or serious threat." Ultimately, however, the play's "socially desirable resolution" becomes possible "when the existence of the identical opposite-sex twins is revealed – in effect splitting the doubly gendered Cesario into two conveniently sexed bodies" ("Shakespeare's" 122). Likewise, Traub has argued that *Twelfth Night* "explores a diversity of desire, proceeding with erotic plurality as far as it can; then, in the face of anxiety generated by this exploration, it fixes the homoerotic interest onto a marginalized figure" (*Desire* 123). For Traub, Antonio is the scapegoat sacrificed so that two heterosocial couples – Orsino and Viola, Olivia and Sebastian – can be assimilated into the play's marital ending. In this view, the homoerotics of transvestism belong to the middle space of early modern comedy, heteroeroticism and its normalizing social institutions to the conclusion.

This pattern has proved fertile ground for queer readings of transvestite characters and the plays they inhabit. Paradoxically, however, these readings, in assuming the dominance, if not the ineluctability, of marital closure, have reified precisely that normalizing institution that queer criticism aims to interrogate. As Arthur Little has shown, *Twelfth Night* is remarkable in that "it stages the refusal of compulsory heterosexuality to grant space to or even finally acknowledge the possibility of other formal kinship relations" (214). Noting the play's investment in same-sex couples, Little observes that "the sex-gender crossing *acted* out in *Twelfth Night* more importantly *plays* out the precarious yet prevalent place of queer marriage, at least on the romantic comedic stage" (213–14). At play's end, when Orsino invites Cesario to accompany him offstage (5.1.384–85), spectators witness the Duke exit with the male page he plans to marry. In a way, we have returned to Cesario/Viola's admission in 1.4 that he/she hopes to marry to Duke. Calling into question a priori assumptions about the gender dynamics of *Twelfth Night*'s marriages, Little's analysis demonstrates one way of complicating what critics have taken to be the marital arc of early modern comedy.

Yet, while Little opens up further possibilities for marriage, one might also question the teleological reading practices that place undue emphasis on a text's ending. Such readings, suggests Ejner Jensen, obscure "the sources of arresting theatrical pleasure everywhere available in the comedies" (19). Or as James Bromley writes, "In moments of narrative closure, certain affective relations, such as the monogamous couple form, are guaranteed futurity, and, in the process, temporary or situational intimacies are emptied of their value, an emptying reinforced by reading strategies that privilege closure" (19). In the case of *Twelfth Night*, reading strategies that trivialize what Bromley calls "alternate intimacies" attempt to explain away the very relations that introduce Orsino and Olivia to Cesario/Viola and Sebastian. Observing that in the Renaissance the term "fancy" possessed a creative capacity, Bruce Smith argues: "As it happens, what Olivia comes to fancy is the person named Cesario. As does Orsino. The primary focus of fancy in the play is indeed the part-man-part-woman part-child-part-adult part-eunuch-part-sexual-partner whom other characters attempt to fix with various names: 'Cesario,' 'Sebastian,' 'Viola'" ("'His'" 74). Although the identities of the twins are revealed in the play's closing scene, the intimacies that draw Orsino and Olivia to Cesario/Viola and Sebastian constitute the bulk of the dramatic action. To read *Twelfth Night* teleologically, therefore, is difficult not only because spectators tend not to view plays with closure in mind, but also because a play's ending does not represent a disavowal of the events that precede it. In fact, *Twelfth Night* insists on showing us everything *except* the heterosociality it has promised: the marriage between Orsino and Viola is withheld from us, delayed indefinitely as Orsino and Cesario exit the stage together; the marriage between Olivia and Sebastian is staged, but at the time Olivia thought she was marrying Cesario, the youth Orsino befriended and now intends to wed.[13] Shakespeare's refusal to show us the proposed marriages indicates that, in this play, heterosociality, as an organizing principle, is beside the point. In *Twelfth Night*, marriage and the heterosociality it organizes become irrelevant, deployed only to be obviated; in other words, the play articulates what I want to call a nominal or putative heterosociality – a heterosociality-in-name-only. To take this heterosociality seriously, to assume it represents an inevitable end, is to impose on the play a normalizing view that the text itself rejects. It is to the point, I think, that if one wants to imagine heterosocial couplings – Orsino and Viola, Olivia and Sebastian, Sir Toby and Maria – one must look *beyond* Shakespeare's play to a text he chose not to write.

An even more forceful repudiation of heterosociality occurs in Lyly's
Galatea, a play whose influence on Shakespeare is well documented.[14] Perhaps
the most overt representation of female homoerotic desire in early modern
drama, *Galatea* departs from its source – the story of Iphis and Ianthe from
Ovid's *Metamorphoses* – in several crucial respects. In Ovid's tale, Telethusa
raises her daughter Iphis as a boy to prevent her father, Ligdus, from murder-
ing her. (Ligdus wants sons, not daughters.) The plan works surprisingly well
until Ligdus, in the words of Golding's 1567 translation, "did ensure / The
brown Ianthe to her, a wench of look demure / Commended for her favour
and her person more than all / The maids of Phaestus" (9.841–44). Although
Iphis and Ianthe fall in love, the latter ignorant of the former's sex, Telethusa
believes that two girls cannot marry one another, and so she prays to the goddess Isis, who agrees to change the crossdressed Iphis into a boy. This act of
metamorphosis provides a heteroerotic solution to a homoerotic problem:

> Next morrow over all the world did shine with lightsome flame
> When Juno and Dame Venus and Sir Hymen jointly came
> To Iphis' marriage, who, as then transformed to a boy,
> Did take Ianthe to his wife and so her love enjoy.   (9.934–37)

As critics have shown, Lyly's revisions indicate dissatisfaction not just with
Ovid's heteronormative ending but with the very premise that female same-
sex desire poses some kind of problem. In *Galatea*, we find not one cross-
dressed girl but two, both disguised by a father who wishes not to see his
daughter offered up to Neptune as a sacrificial virgin. As Laurie Shannon has
shown, both Ovid and Lyly appeal to the concept of "homonormativity,"
where "[l]ikeness establishes the social aptness of the pairing as well as the
basis of love" ("Nature's" 198; see also Shannon, *Sovereign*). However, whereas
Ovid uses likeness as the grounds on which Ligdus arranges a marriage
between Iphis and Ianthe, Lyly allows likeness to draw Galatea and Phillida
together without patriarchal interference. Indeed, the "bias for likeness" (204)
Shannon ascribes to Nature helps make sense of Lyly's unflattering depictions
of male/female relations: "Each image this play affords of heterosexual mixing involving actual male figures of the dramatis personae pointedly suggests
some inappropriate combination of violence, rapaciousness, impropriety, or
vulgarity" (201). In brief, Lyly inverts Ovid's dilemma: in the story from *The
Metamorphoses*, the problem is that Iphis and Ianthe are a female couple; in
Galatea, it is that marriage involves opposite-sex partners.[15] Indeed, while initially Galatea and Phillida share the belief that their love is heterosocial, this
belief amounts to a running gag reinforced by Lyly's choosing to keep both

characters crossdressed for the play's entirety: whether spectators focus their attention on the male disguises, the female characters, or the boy actors, the dynamic between Galatea and Phillida resists assimilation into fantasies of heterosocial coupling.

Beyond Lesbian Impossibilities

In doubling the number of crossdressed girls, then, Lyly constructs what I am calling putative heterosociality. For Galatea and Phillida, this heterosociality enables the cultivation of female same-sex desire, but not without invoking and confronting a tradition of rendering such desire impossible, a tradition, to borrow Valerie Traub's phrase, of *amor impossibilis*. Linking Galatea and Phillida's intentions to "make much of one another" (3.2.62–63) offstage with Cupid's designs to cause mischief among Diana's nymphs by "so confound[ing] their loves in their own sex that they shall dote in their desires, delight in their affections, and practise only impossibilities" (2.2.7–10), Traub argues that Lyly's play both "reproduces social orthodoxy" and, "by mining a tension between what can and cannot *be practiced*, ... helps to make the impossible intelligible and the unintelligible possible" (*Renaissance* 6). I would extend this argument to suggest that by play's end, the concept of *amor impossibilis* is reduced to caricature. While it remains unclear precisely when Galatea and Phillida figure out one another's identities, at some point one cannot help wondering if the girls' repeated calls for further experimentation aren't merely a pretense for more clandestine fondling. As late as Act 4, Scene 4, Phillida recommends that she and Galatea "wander into these groves till the hour be past" (34–35). And yet, as early as 2.1, they register suspicions about one another's genders. Certainly by 5.3, when Melibeus and Tityrus identify their daughters (who are still dressed as boys), Galatea and Phillida have collected sufficient evidence not to be shocked by the news. Hence, while one could hear genuine dismay in Galatea and Phillida's reactions, one might also see in "Unfortunate Galatea" (5.3.120) and "Accursed Phillida" (5.3.121) a mock surprise aimed at those who insist, despite ample proof to the contrary, that female homoerotic desire is impossible, unthinkable. Those like Neptune, who cannot comprehend love between women because he cannot "imagine a constant faith where there can be no cause of affection" (5.3.140–41). To agree with Neptune is to side with a god who decided only recently it might be prudent to put a moratorium on virgin sacrifices. At this point, *amor impossibilis* seems an antiquated concept, a remnant of the older, patriarchal order.

While it is true, as critics have remarked, that *Galatea* does, in fact, posit a heterosocial marital future for its title character and Phillida, this future never comes to pass; rather, it is postponed indefinitely, committed to the no-place beyond the play's *terminus*. For Rackin, the very prospect of marriage means the play "ends in the abolition of sexual ambiguity" ("Androgyny" 37). However, Rackin also notes that sexual identity in *Galatea* "proves infinitely malleable in the hands of the gods and irrelevant in the eyes of the audience (since we neither know nor care which girl will become a boy)" (30). As it turns out, Galatea and Phillida don't care much either:

Venus:	How say ye, are ye agreed, one to be a boy presently?
Phillida:	I am content, so I may embrace Galatea.
Galatea:	I wish it, so I may enjoy Phillida. (5.3.155–58)

While their fathers do begin to quarrel over whose daughter will be meta-morphosed into a boy, their dispute is left unresolved at the play's conclusion. Venus decrees, "Neither of them shall know whose lot it shall be till they come to the church door. One shall be" (5.3.183–85). Lyly's refusal to disclose any of the particulars contrasts sharply with his Ovidian source, where we see Iphis transformed into a boy and wed to Ianthe in properly heteroso-cial nuptials. For Denise Walen, Lyly's revisions point up the "insignificance" of the sex change (137); for Theodora Jankowski, they "trivializ[e] the whole notion of the traditional patriarchal marriage" (26). Adapting Traub's formu-lation, I would submit that if the play "helps to make the impossible intelligi-ble and the unintelligible possible," it also renders the possible impossible and the intelligible unintelligible. That is, in declining either to stage the nuptial ceremony or provide details that might allow spectators to envisage it, Lyly renders marriage between Galatea and Phillida impossible, unintelligible. Whereas Ovid imposes a heterosocial solution on a problematic female cou-ple, Lyly exposes this solution *as* the problem and then banishes it to a future that will never be.

The Roaring Girl

In Middleton and Dekker's city comedy *The Roaring Girl*, transvestism and homoeroticism challenge marriage and heterosociality in different ways. Set in contemporary London, the play imports a by-then familiar plot of romantic comedy: Sebastian Wengrave and Mary Fitzallard wish to marry, but Sebastian's father, Sir Alexander Wengrave, disapproves, largely because Mary's "dowry of five thousand marks" isn't sufficient (1.1.87). To change his father's mind, Sebastian feigns interest in Moll Cutpurse, the eponymous roar-ing girl, "a creature / So strange in quality, a whole city takes / Note of her name and person" (1.1.98–100). Sebastian's words here are perhaps truer than he knows because Moll's character is based on an actual London woman who dressed in masculine attire and associated with criminals and vagabonds. Not only did Mary Frith, the real Moll Cutpurse, likely attend productions of *The Roaring Girl* at the Fortune Theatre; she also put on her own show at the same playhouse, as the play's epilogue announces (32–35). "In 1611," writes Orgel, "she appeared in a solo performance at the Fortune Theatre, wearing boots, breeches and a sword, singing and accompanying herself on the lute" (*Impersonations* 145). So, even before Moll Cutpurse appears onstage, London playgoers would have known what type of character to expect. At any rate, the plan succeeds: faced with the possibility that his son might marry Moll in an act of "monstrous impudence" (5.2.153), Sir Alexander praises Mary's "virtues, whom I prize now / As dearly as that flesh I call mine own" (5.2.189–90). Of course, as the figure standing in the way of mutual love for purely economic reasons, Sir Alexander fails to qualify as the play's moral compass. What's more, the playwrights make explicit in their prefatory material that Moll, unlike others "of that tribe" of roaring girls, "flies / With wings more lofty" (Prol.16, 25–26). That is, spectators should not expect to see in Moll a character "[t]hat roars at midnight in deep tavern bowls, / That beats the watch, and constables controls" or that "roars i'th'daytime, swears, stabs, gives braves, / Yet sells her soul to the lust of fools and slaves" (Prol.17–20). One could argue that Middleton and Dekker's version "softens and romanticizes her" (Orgel, *Impersonations* 149), disassociating her from many activities she apparently enjoyed. However, as Mary Beth Rose has pointed out, the play also makes the unconventional move of staging a woman who does not use men's clothing *as a disguise* (64–65). In a letter "To the Comic Play-Readers, Venery and Laughter" included in the 1611 quarto, Middleton implicitly defends the choice with an analogy likening fashion to the theatre:

> The fashion of play-making I can properly compare to nothing so naturally as the alteration in apparel: for in the time of the great crop-doublet, your huge bombasted plays, quilted with mighty words to lean purposes, was only then in fashion. And as the doublet fell, neater inventions began to set up. Now in the time of spruceness, our plays follow the niceness of our garments: single plots, quaint conceits, lecherous jests, dressed up in hanging sleeves, and those are fit for the times and the termers. Such a kind of light-colour summer stuff, mingled with diverse colours, you shall find this published comedy, good to keep you in an afternoon from dice, at home in your chambers.... The book I make no question but is fit for many of your companies, as well as the person itself, and may be allowed both galley room at the playhouse, and chamber room at your lodging. (lines 1–19)

Rather in the same way that *Hic Mulier* declares, "Custom is an Idiot" (qtd. in Henderson and McManus 284), Middleton, perhaps responding to Deuteronomy's proscription against crossdressing, claims that clothes, like plays, follow trends, and there is nothing abominable about changing tastes.

This is not to suggest, however, that in *The Roaring Girl* transvestism does nothing to unsettle marital heterosociality. In Middleton's letter, we are also told, "For Venus being a woman passes through the play in doublet and breeches, a brave disguise and a safe one, if the statute untie not her codpiece point." The association of crossdressing with the goddess of love, sex, and fertility is intriguing for several reasons. First, while one might think Middleton is referring to Moll Cutpurse (a point to which I shall return), she is not the only character who dons men's clothes. Mary Fitzallard does, too, and while ostensibly she crossdresses to avoid detection by Sir Alexander, the ruse allows for a homoerotic kiss between Sebastian and the crossdressed Mary, prompting Sebastian to remark, "Methinks a woman's lip tastes well in a doublet" (4.1.47). Curiously, Moll is the one to observe, "How strange this shows, one man to kiss another" (4.1.45). Moll's comment works on multiple levels because the roles of Sebastian and Mary were both played by male actors. More to the point, however, is that spectators watch as one character's attempt at passing becomes another character's newfound fetish.[16] This interaction would indeed seem to exemplify Venus's "pass[ing] through the play in doublet and breeches," engendering desire in Sebastian and anyone else titillated by the kiss.

If Moll is (also) Venus, then Middleton might be employing the image of a transvestite goddess to demarcate a sexuality that remains firmly outside marital heterosociality. In a memorable passage from the play, Moll explains why she has "no humour to marry":

> I love to lie o'both sides o'th'bed myself; and again o'th'other side; a wife you know ought to be obedient, but I fear me I am too headstrong to obey, therefore I'll ne'er go about it.... I have the head now of myself, and am man enough for a woman; marriage is but a chopping and changing, where a maiden loses one head and has a worse i'th'place. (2.2.35–45)

Moll renounces marriage for personal and political reasons: as a patriarchal institution, marriage subordinates woman to man; as a heterosocial institution, it imposes on a couple a particular form of sexuality. As Jean Howard notes, Moll's preference for "both sides o'th'bed" could mean lots of things: "that she likes her independence; perhaps that she likes a certain unspecified variety in sexual partners and practices; perhaps that she likes to be her own

chief source of erotic pleasure" (125). A similar ambiguity marks Moll's assertion that she is "man enough for a woman": does she mean she embodies both
masculine and feminine qualities, or that she imagines another woman as her
ideal partner?

The contours of her desire matter less than her stalwart opposition to marriage and the sexuality it delimits. In the play's final scene, as Sir Alexander rec-
onciles with Sebastian and Mary, Moll suggests that the overbearing father has
misunderstood the trick played on him: "He was in fear his son would marry
me, / But never dreamt that I would ne'er agree" (5.2.213–14). This rejection of
marriage does not ostracize the roaring girl. "Although Moll and her roarer-
companions reject conventional behavior," writes Viviana Comensoli, "they
are never excluded from the reformed society sketched in the denouement;
instead, their presence during the final two scenes provides a compelling alternative to the ideal marriage" ("Play-Making" 251). Although one must always
beware the intentional fallacy, it seems notable that the actual Mary Frith
did in fact wed, albeit under circumstances that are still debated. Recalling
that she attended, maybe even participated in, productions of *The Roaring
Girl*, one wonders whether the playwrights' decision to keep their Moll single
reflects the titular roarer's ideal relationship status. What is patently clear, in
any case, is that for Middleton and Dekker, heterosociality needn't serve as a
pretense for exploring the homoerotic desires enacted and expressed through
transvestism; sometimes when Venus "passes through the play in doublet and
breeches," she is both the means and the ends of desire.

In several respects, Moll's transvestism seems fundamentally different from
the forms of crossdressing we find in *Twelfth Night* and *Galatea*. Unlike Viola
and Galatea and Phillida, Moll does not try to pass as a man. Nor does she
resort to crossdressing to evade danger or become intimate with a man she
hopes to marry. Perhaps most important, she does not perceive herself as the
"poor monster" (2.2.33) Viola sees. I would nonetheless argue that each of
the transvestite characters I have examined in this chapter disrupt heterosociality in similar ways. In *Twelfth Night* and *Galatea*, as in *The Roaring Girl*,
the normalizing institution critics tend to see as reestablishing the dominant
patriarchal order appears not just inefficient but inefficient *by design*. In these
plays, the homoeroticism expressed through transvestism represents not a situational or circumstantial erotics that succumbs, finally, to marital heterosociality; on the contrary, it becomes an intelligible alternative to a heterosocial
order that, as I have been arguing, is never firmly established in the first place.
For all their differences, then, the transvestite figures I have been examining in this chapter all participate in a common project, one shared by recent

queer scholarship – namely, to puncture fantasies of marital and heterosocial hegemony that are as much an invention of modern criticism as they are a product of early modern discourse. Thus, while it might not be possible to say definitively just how queer the transvestite stage was, the fact that cross-gender casting was a theatrical convention does not mean, ipso facto, that it cannot unsettle the dominant ideology and put into discourse identities and relationalities that seem very queer indeed.

Notes

1. On discourses of sodomy and friendship in *Edward II*, see Bray, "Homosexuality"; Bredbeck 56–77; Callaghan, "Terms"; Comensoli, "Homophobia"; Deats 194–200; DiGangi, *Homoerotics* 100–33 and "Marlowe"; Goldberg 114–26; Perry; Smith, *Homosexual* 209–23; Stymeist; and Summers, "Sex."
2. Bray does not take up possible associations between crossdressing and same-sex relationships, but his book continues to be heralded as inaugurating the field of queer early modern studies. On Bray's influence, see Betteridge 4–6; Goldberg; and Greene.
3. On anachronism and/in queer Renaissance studies, see Summers, "Homosexuality."
4. Feminist and queer scholarship has offered an important corrective to the notion of the all-male stage. On women's involvement in the playhouses, see Brown and Parolin; Findlay; McManus; Orgel, *Impersonations* 1–9; Rackin, "Shakespeare's" 114–15; and Tomlinson.
5. On the use of cross-gender casting in theatres outside Europe, see Senelick.
6. Barish demonstrates that anxieties about cross-gender casting are as old as drama itself. On the role these anxieties played in mobilizing antitheatrical polemics written and circulated in early modern England, see Breitenberg 160–62; Howard 93–95; and Levine.
7. For a discussion of what the sumptuary laws did and did not cover, see Hooper. On the ecclesiastical courts' near indifference to crossdressing, see Cressy.
8. *Hic Mulier: Or, The Man-Woman* and *Haec Vir: Or The Womanish-Man* were both published anonymously in 1620 as part of a series of pamphlet wars known collectively as the *Querelle des Femmes*. On the various cultural contexts of these pamphlet wars, see Henderson and McManus 3–130; Lucas; and O'Malley 1–11.
9. My description of gender as "prosthetic" is indebted to Jones and Stallybrass, who describe clothes as prostheses, and Fisher, who examines the ways cultural artifacts such as handkerchiefs and codpieces and body parts such as beards and hair shape gender identity. See also Bailey; Butler, *Bodies* and *Gender*; Orgel, *Impersonations*; and Howard 93–128.
10. Although published in 1915, Freeburg remains the most complete compilation of early modern plays employing female pages and boy brides. As Shapiro

points out, however, "boy bride" is "a term of convenience, for some are nei-ther boys nor brides" (*Gender* 34).

11. On the predominance of the one-sex model in pre-Enlightenment Europe, see Laqueur. See also Park and Nye, who dispute Laqueur's Galenic model, and Schalkwyk, who argues that *Twelfth Night* rejects Galen's misogynistic humoral theory.

12. For readings of transvestism in *Twelfth Night* as buttressing patriarchy, see Callaghan, *Shakespeare* 26–48; Jardine, *Reading* 63–75; Stone 24–42; cf. Casey.

13. On the amity cultivated between Orsino and Viola, see Osborne.

14. On Lyly's influence on Shakespeare, see Bevington; Egan; Mincoff; Rackin, "Androgyny"; Scragg; and Shannon, "Nature's."

15. According to the 1660 Stationers' Register, a play called *Iphis and Iantha, or A Marriage without a Man* was licensed in 1613. Attributed to Shakespeare (prob-ably erroneously), the play is no longer extant; nevertheless, its title suggests yet another way of (not) solving Iphis and Ianthe's dilemma.

16. On the theoretical distinctions between crossdressing, passing, and drag, see Drouin.

Works Cited

Bailey, Amanda. *Flaunting: Style and the Subversive Male Body in Renaissance England*. Toronto: Toronto UP, 2007. Print.

Bakhtin, Mikhail. *Rabelais and His World*. Trans. Hélène Iswolsky. Bloomington: Indiana UP, 1984. Print.

Barish, Jonas. *The Antitheatrical Prejudice*. Berkeley: U of California P, 1981. Print.

Betteridge, Tom. Introduction. *Sodomy in Early Modern Europe*. Ed. Tom Betteridge. Manchester: Manchester UP, 2002. 1–10. Print.

Bevington, David. "'Jack hath not Jill': Failed Courtship in Lyly and Shakespeare." *Shakespeare Survey* 42 (1990): 1–13. Print.

Bly, Mary. *Queer Virgins and Virgin Queans on the Early Modern Stage*. Oxford: Oxford UP, 2000. Print.

Bray, Alan. *Homosexuality in Renaissance England*. London: Gay Men's P, 1982. Print.

——. "Homosexuality and the Signs of Male Friendship in Elizabethan England." *History Workshop Journal* 29 (1990): 1–19. Print.

Bredbeck, Gregory W. *Sodomy and Interpretation: Marlowe to Milton*. Ithaca: Cornell UP, 1991. Print.

Breitenberg, Mark. *Anxious Masculinity in Early Modern England*. Cambridge: Cambridge UP: 1996.

Bromley, James. *Intimacy and Sexuality in the Age of Shakespeare*. Cambridge: Cambridge UP, 2012. Print.

Brown, Pamela Allen, and Peter Parolin, eds. *Women Players in England, 1500–1660*. Studies in Performance and Early Modern Drama. Hampshire: Ashgate, 2008. Print.

Butler, Judith. *Bodies that Matter: On the Discursive Limits of "Sex."* New York: Routledge, 1993. Print.

Gender Trouble: Feminism and the Subversion of Identity. New York: Routledge, 1990. Print.

Callaghan, Dympna. *Shakespeare without Women: Representing Gender and Race on the Renaissance Stage*. London: Routledge, 2000. Print.

"The Terms of Gender: 'Gay' and 'Feminist' *Edward II*." *Feminist Readings of Early Modern Culture: Emerging Subjects*. Ed. Valerie Traub, M. Lindsay Kaplan, and Dympna Callaghan. Cambridge: Cambridge UP, 1996. 275–301. Print.

Casey, Charles. "Gender Trouble in *Twelfth Night*." *Theatre Journal* 49.2 (1997): 121–41.

Comensoli, Viviana. "Homophobia and the Regulation of Desire: A Psychoanalytic Reading of Marlowe's *Edward II*." *Journal of the History of Sexuality* 4.2 (1993): 175–200. Print.

"Play-Making, Domestic Conduct, and the Multiple Plot in *The Roaring Girl*." *Studies in English Literature, 1500–1900* 27.2 (1987): 249–66. Print.

Cressy, David. "Gender Trouble and Cross-Dressing in Early Modern England." *Journal of British Studies* 35.4 (1996): 438–65. Print.

Dawson, Anthony. "Performance and Participation." *The Culture of Playgoing in Shakespeare's England: A Collaborative Debate*. By Anthony B. Dawson and Paul Yachnin. Cambridge: Cambridge UP, 2005. 11–37.

Deats, Sara Munson. *Sex, Gender, and Desire in the Plays of Christopher Marlowe*. Newark: U of Delaware P, 1997. Print.

DiGangi, Mario. *The Homoerotics of Early Modern Drama*. Cambridge: Cambridge UP, 1997. Print.

"How Queer Was the Renaissance?" *Love, Sex, Intimacy and Friendship between Men, 1550–1800*. Ed. Katherine O'Donnell and Michael O'Rourke. New York: Palgrave, 2003. 128–47. Print.

"Marlowe, Queer Studies, and Renaissance Homoeroticism." *Marlowe, History, and Sexuality: New Critical Essays on Christopher Marlowe*. Ed. Paul Whitfield White. New York: AMS P, 1998. 195–212. Print.

Drouin, Jennifer. "Cross-Dressing, Drag, and Passing: Slippages in Shakespearean Comedy." *Shakespeare Re-Dressed: Cross-Gender Casting in Contemporary Performance*. Ed. James Bulman. Cranbury: Associated UP, 2008. 23–56. Print.

Egan, Gabriel. "Leashing in the Dogs of War: The Influence of Lyly's *Campaspe* on Shakespeare's *All's Well That Ends Well*." *English Language Notes* 40.1 (2002): 29–41. Print.

Findlay, Alison. *Playing Spaces in Early Women's Drama*. Cambridge: Cambridge UP, 2006. Print.

Fisher, Will. *Materializing Gender in Early Modern English Literature and Culture*. Cambridge: Cambridge UP, 2010. Print.

Freeburg, Victor O. *Disguise Plots in Elizabethan Drama*. New York: Columbia UP, 1915. Print.

Garber, Marjorie. *Vested Interests: Cross-Dressing and Cultural Anxiety*. New York: Routledge, 1992. Print.

Goldberg, Jonathan. *Sodometries: Renaissance Texts, Modern Sexualities*. Stanford: Stanford UP, 1992. Print.

Greenblatt, Stephen. *Shakespearean Negotiations: The Circulation of Social Energy in Renaissance England*. Chicago: U of Chicago P, 1989. Print.

Greene, Jody, ed. The Work of Friendship: In Memoriam Alan Bray. Spec. issue of GLQ: *A Journal of Lesbian and Gay Studies* 10.3 (2004). Print.

Henderson, Katherine Usher, and Barbara F. McManus. *Half Humankind: Contexts & Texts of the Controversy about Women in England, 1540–1640.* Urbana: U of Illinois P, 1985. Print.

Hooper, Wilfrid. "The Tudor Sumptuary Laws." *English Historical Review* 30 (1915): 433–49. Print.

Howard, Jean. *The Stage and Social Struggle in Early Modern England.* London: Routledge, 1994. Print.

Jankowski, Theodora. *Pure Resistance: Queer Virginity in Early Modern English Drama.* Philadelphia: U of Pennsylvania P, 2000. Print.

Jardine, Lisa. *Reading Shakespeare Historically.* New York: Routledge, 1993. Print.

——. *Still Harping on Daughters: Women and Drama in the Age of Shakespeare.* Tatowa: Barnes & Noble, 1983. Print.

Jensen, Ejner J. *Shakespeare and the Ends of Comedy.* Bloomington: Indiana UP, 1991. Print.

Jones, Ann Rosalind, and Peter Stallybrass. *Renaissance Clothing and the Materials of Memory.* Cambridge: Cambridge UP, 2000. Print.

Laqueur, Thomas. *Making Sex: Body and Gender from the Greeks to Freud.* Cambridge: Harvard UP, 1990. Print.

Levine, Laura. *Men in Women's Clothing: Anti-Theatricality and Effeminization 1579–1642.* Cambridge: Cambridge UP, 1994. Print.

Little, Arthur L. "'A Local Habitation and a Name': Presence, Witnessing, and Queer Marriage in Shakespeare's Romantic Comedies." *Presentism, Gender, and Sexuality in Shakespeare.* Ed. Evelyn Gajowski. New York: Palgrave, 2009. 207–36. Print.

Lucas, R. Valerie. "*Hic Mulier:* The Female Transvestite in Early Modern England." *Renaissance and Reformation* 12 (1988): 65–83. Print.

Lyly, John. "*Galatea*" and "*Midas.*" Ed. George K. Hunter and David Bevington. Manchester: Manchester UP, 2000. Print.

Marlowe, Christopher. *Edward II.* Ed. Martin Wiggins and Robert Lindsey. 2nd ed. London: Black, 1997. Print.

McLuskie, Kathleen. "The Act, the Role, and the Actor: Boy Actresses on the Elizabethan Stage." *New Theatre Quarterly* 3 (1987): 120–30. Print.

McManus, Clare. *Women on the Renaissance Stage: Anna of Denmark and Female Masquing in the Stuart Court (1590–1619).* Manchester: Manchester UP, 2002. Print.

Middleton, Thomas, and Thomas Dekker. *The Roaring Girl.* Ed. Elizabeth Cook. New Mermaids. 2nd ed. London: Black, 1997.

Mincoff, Marco. "Shakespeare and Lyly." *Shakespeare Survey* 14 (1961): 15–24. Print.

O'Malley, Susan Gushee. Introduction. *"Custom Is an Idiot": Jacobean Pamphlet Literature on Women.* Urbana: U of Illinois P, 2004. 1–11. Print.

Orgel, Stephen. *Impersonations: The Performance of Gender in Shakespeare's England.* Cambridge: Cambridge UP, 1996. Print.

——. "Tobacco and Boys: How Queer Was Marlowe?" *GLQ: A Journal of Lesbian and Gay Studies* 6.4 (2000): 555–76. Print.

Osborne, Laurie E. "'The Marriage of True Minds': Amity, Twinning, and Comic Closure in *Twelfth Night.*" Schiffer 99–113.

Ovid. *Metamorphoses.* Trans. Arthur Golding. Ed. Madeleine Forey. Baltimore: Johns Hopkins UP, 2002. Print.

Park, Katherine, and Robert A. Nye. "*Destiny is Anatomy.*" Rev. of *Making Sex: Body and Gender from the Greeks to Freud*, by Thomas Laqueur. *The New Republic* February 18, 1991: 53–57. Print.

Perry, Curtis. "The Politics of Access and Representations of the Sodomite King in Early Modern England." *Renaissance Quarterly* 53.4 (2000): 1054–83. Print.

Rackin, Phyllis. "Androgyny, Mimesis, and the Marriage of the Boy Heroine on the English Renaissance Stage." *PMLA* 102.1 (1987): 29–41. Print.

"Shakespeare's Crossdressing Comedies." *A Companion to Shakespeare's Works, Volume III: The Comedies*. Ed. Richard Dutton and Phyllis Rackin. Malden: Blackwell, 2003. 114–36. Print.

Rose, Mary Beth. *The Expense of the Spirit: Love and Sexuality in English Renaissance Drama*. Ithaca: Cornell UP, 1988. Print.

Schalkwyk, David. "Music, Food, and Love in the Affective Landscapes of *Twelfth Night*." Schiffer 81–98.

Schiffer, James, ed. *Twelfth Night: New Critical Essays*. London: Routledge, 2011. Print.

Scragg, Leah. "Shakespeare, Lyly, and Ovid: The Influence of *Gallathea* on *A Midsummer Night's Dream*." *Shakespeare Survey* 30 (1977): 125–34. Print.

Sedgwick, Eve Kosofsky. *Tendencies*. Durham: Duke UP, 1993. Print.

Senelick, Laurence. *The Changing Room: Sex, Drag and Theatre*. New York: Routledge. 2000. Print.

Shakespeare, William. *Twelfth Night*. Ed. J. M. Lothian and T. W. Craik. London: Arden Shakespeare, 2000. Print.

Shannon, Laurie. "Nature's Bias: Renaissance Homonormativity and Elizabethan Comic Likeness." *Modern Philology* 98 (2000–2001): 183–210. Print.

Sovereign Amity: Figures of Friendship in Shakespearean Contexts. Chicago: U of Chicago P, 2002. Print.

Shapiro, Michael. *Gender in Play on the Shakespearean Stage: Boy Heroines and Female Pages*. Ann Arbor: U of Michigan P, 1994. Print.

Shapiro, Michael, and Phyllis Rackin. "Boy Heroines." *PMLA* 102.5 (1987): 836–38. Print.

Sinfield, Alan. *Shakespeare, Authority, and Sexuality: Unfinished Business in Cultural Materialism*. London: Routledge, 2006. Print.

Smith, Bruce R. "'His Fancy's Queen': Sensing Sexual Strangeness in *Twelfth Night*." Schiffer 65–80.

Homosexual Desire in Shakespeare's England: A Cultural Poetics. Chicago: U of Chicago P, 1991. Print.

Stone, James W. *Crossing Gender in Shakespeare: Feminist Psychoanalysis and the Difference Within*. New York: Routledge, 2010. Print.

Stymeist, David. "Status, Sodomy, and the Theater in Marlowe's *Edward II*." *Studies in English Literature 1500–1900* 44.2 (2004): 233–53. Print.

Summers, Claude J. "Homosexuality and Renaissance Literature, or the Anxieties of Anachronism." *South Central Review* 9.1 (1992): 2–23. Print.

"Sex, Politics, and Self-Realization in *Edward II*." *"A Poet and a Filthy Play-Maker": New Essays on Christopher Marlowe*. Ed. Kenneth Friedenreich, Roma Gill, and Constance B. Kuriyama. New York: AMS, 1988. 221–40. Print.

Tomlinson, Sophie. *Women on Stage in Stuart Drama*. Cambridge: Cambridge UP, 2009. Print.

Traub, Valerie. *Desire and Anxiety: Circulations of Sexuality in Shakespearean Drama*. London: Routledge, 1992. Print.

The Renaissance of Lesbianism in Early Modern England. Cambridge: Cambridge UP, 2002. Print.

Walen, Denise A. *Constructions of Female Homoeroticism in Early Modern Drama*. New York: Palgrave, 2005. Print.

Williams, Raymond. *Marxism and Literature*. New York: Oxford UP, 1977. Print.

12

The Libertine, the Rake, and the Dandy: Personae, Styles, and Affects

LISA O'CONNELL

The parade of sexualized personae that features in this chapter's title carries a history. Libertines, rakes, and dandies are figures that occur in a sequence that begins in the sixteenth century and effectively comes to an end by the twentieth century, although, admittedly, it is a sequence marked by overlaps and ambiguities. And it is a history each of these figures shares with others. They are jostled by less prominent figures with somewhat similar status: fops, macaronis, coxcombs, and coquettes – to select some eighteenth-century "characters" from a survey recently compiled by Elaine McGirr. Libertines, rakes, and dandies are also defined in the public sphere against a more respectable, if less spectacular, suite of types who more securely belong to the approved ethos: the pious Christian, the honest laborer, the connoisseur, the man of feeling, the bluestocking – again to select at random.

It is no coincidence that the spectrum of types evoked here only approximately corresponds to a modern axis of queerness. Certainly the libertine tradition is marked by the practices and pre-formations of homosexuality – sodomy, sapphism, male effeminacy, homosociability, and so forth – and by the discursive idioms of wit, playfulness, and irony that we readily associate with queer sensibility. Yet libertinism is equally characterized by casual misogyny, phallic violence, voyeurism, female passivity, and other hallmarks of a long, historically entrenched heterosexism. So libertines, rakes, and dandies play a significant part in lesbian and gay literary history, but they do so by showing (once again) that that history did not know a hard hetero-homo distinction until comparatively recently. Indeed, it may be that the emergence of that distinction in its modern form marked the end of the older libertine-rake-dandy assemblage that is under discussion here.

Each figure emerges in particular contexts, or, better, at the point of confluence between various social and cultural forces and zones. In their different ways, libertines, rakes, and dandies appear, more particularly, at the intersection of print culture; court and parliamentary politics; the culture of commerce, entertainment, and spectacle (which includes fashion, the theatre, clubs, and pleasure gardens); the moral reform movement; and lived practices of affect, sexuality, courtship, and marriage. They are not "real" figures, which is to say that they are products of a mediatized civic imaginary. Yet they are not *just* imaginary. They also work as models for lived and experienced styles of comportment: some people did indeed live, at least sometimes, as libertines (John Wilmot, Earl of Rochester; John Wilkes), rakes (George Villiers, Duke of Buckingham; Francis Dashwood), or dandies (Beau Brummell; Benjamin Disraeli; Scrope Berdmore Davies). Others lived (and wrote and became famous) not quite as libertines, rakes, or dandies but in the penumbra of the styles and emotional complexes that these personae exemplified – Lord Byron, William Beckford, and Horace Walpole, for instance, all of whom were themselves involved in same-sex affairs and liaisons.

Drawing on a rich body of scholarship, this chapter traces passages from the libertine through the rake and dandy, concentrating on each in turn. It offers an account, too, of the shifts in the confluences that shaped their passage. But some parameters need to be sketched in advance. First, these figures took distinct forms in different national cultures, which also overlapped. This chapter focuses on (metropolitan) England, where, arguably, the libertine, the rake, and the dandy came most vividly to life. In doing so, however, it necessarily passes over the highly influential French tradition – including the aristocratic novels of Crébillon *fils*, Duclos, Prévost, and Laclos, the obscene philosophical writing of Sade, and the proto-modernist poetry of Baudelaire – from which English instantiations of the libertine, the rake, and the dandy drew.[1] Second, because the libertine, the rake, and the dandy all emerge out of complex and extensive flows and patterns, their history does not belong just to social or to cultural or to literary or to secular or to political or to religious history, but to them all. Third, this is a history where gender matters at least as much as sex. While it would be wrong to say that there were no female libertines, rakes, or dandies (the lives and memoirs of Con Phillips, Laetitia Pilkington, Charlotte Charke, and Harriette Wilson immediately come to mind), it is nonetheless true to say that women who engaged in modes of free thought, publicly sexual behavior, or extravagant self-display were routinely castigated as whores. Their relation to the personae of libertinage was therefore rather different to that of their male counterparts (who were, conversely, celebrated as rogues), and this was a difference that helped mark the distinction between masculinity and femininity in general.[2] Fourth, all these types can be further broken down into more specialized figures – the "polite rake," the "extravagant rake," the "Hobbesian libertine," "the philosophical libertine," the *libertin érudit*, and so on.[3] While this chapter does not provide an exhaustive typology of these variations, it does respect their plurality. It also follows recent scholarship that speaks of "libertinage" (rather than "libertinism") as a means of signaling its consideration of a broader and more diffuse range of early modern everyday practices and contexts than those associated with the high libertine or aristocratic sphere of letters alone (Cryle and O'Connell 2–3). Nonetheless, these types belong, or come to belong, to a history mainly of the elite. While laboring libertines and tradesmen dandies, for instance, did exist (often, tellingly, as figures of fun) these were, in general, types marked by class, persons for whom a life of leisure was possible, and for whom the poor could be typically regarded as a reserve of sexual service. And last, the history from the libertine to the dandy is a history through an emergent modernity. These are all figures thrown up by a society moving away from traditional hierarchies and identities, in a process with its own dead ends and new beginnings. Libertinage was contagious in the last decades of the seventeenth century, for instance, but, by 1800, it had all but disappeared. In 1800, however, a new figure – the dandy – was omnipresent in the media, only itself to disappear by about 1900. Whatever else they might represent, these figures bear the imprint of dangerous modern forces – freethinking, sexuality, fashion, and luxury – out of control. They also represented the possibility of new relations between the body and the passions. It is in these terms that they belong to a heterodox modernity unmoored from inherited moral codes. And it is in these terms, too, that they became freighted with new ethical, and sometimes political, resonances.

Libertines

Libertinage has a long and complex history that reaches back into antiquity. In the fifteenth and sixteenth centuries, the category was mainly applied to a kind of writing that already held a firm place in manuscript culture (Moulton 35–69). But it took on new qualities with the introduction of print technology, especially after Italian satirist Pietro Aretino's contributions. Aretino, who from the English perspective labored under the twin disadvantages of being a Catholic (although his writings were on the Index) and a lover of sodomite pleasures, was the author of texts that quickly became famous across Europe, indeed more famous than read because his writings were equally quickly censored. As Ian Moulton observes, "the English figure of Aretino was ... fundamentally contradictory: it offered an enormously attractive precedent for authorial power [and independence], which was at the same time marked as disorderly, effeminate and sodomitical" (120). He became, as it were, the legendary founder of a genre of print about sex that contained a more or less secreted polemical force and that flowed clandestinely across Europe to become a primary source of modern European culture.

This is to say that Aretino, like his supposed English followers such as Thomas Nashe, belonged in part to a long tradition of what James Grantham Turner (after John Evelyn) has called "popular libertinism" (*Libertines* 21). This was a formation that reached back into traditional balladry and long-estab-lished practices of licensed "misrule," which deployed obscenity against estab-lished authority, whether institutional or intellectual. To be sure, print permit-ted this tradition to become, at times, more purposively autoerotic as well, but Aretino belonged primarily to Italian humanism. The poetry that made him notorious, the *Sonetti Lussuriosi,* was originally written around 1523 to accom-pany a series of erotic engravings by Raphael's disciple, Giulio Romano, while his equally famous and influential *Ragionamenti* (1534–36) imitated the ancient Greek text, Lucian's *Dialogues of Whores,* deploying fictional courtesan gossip as a vehicle for savage satirical attacks on clerical corruption, papal politics, and the power struggles of Italian states (Moulton 130–31). In a widely distrib-uted letter in which he defended his writing, Aretino argued, crucially, that sex was natural and universal, insofar as we all owe our very lives to it: "It seems to me that the you-know-what given us by nature for the preservation of the species should be worn as a pendant around our necks or as a badge in our caps, since it is the spring that pours out the flood of humanity" (qtd. in Hunt, "Obscenity" 25). In its appeal to a generalized human nature, in its dismissal of those who connect sexuality to wickedness, sin, or bestiality, this is a humanist move through and through. But in its freedom of thought and its thinking of sex as a model for liberty and political critique, it also exceeds the humanism of its time and anticipates later forms of libertinage.

Following Aretino, a somewhat more specialized genre of erotic writing began to appear in print by the seventeenth century. Breaking with the heri-tage of popular license and protest, it was aimed more narrowly at stimulating readers to share states of sexual arousal enacted and described by fictional char-acters in familiar domestic settings. It typically did so, however, under the guise of a certain pedagogy. The key text here is *L'Escole des filles, ou La Philosophie des dames* (1655), which was published anonymously although reputed to be by Michel Millot. Recounting the story of an innocent young bourgeois woman's sexual education under the tutelage of her older female cousin, it circulated in England by 1680, under the title *The School of Venus,* before being trans-lated again in the mid-eighteenth century. Recognizably within the "whore's dialogue" genre, *L'Escole des filles* follows Lucian and Aretino. Like Aretino, it has a satiric target, this time the "Platonic" salons of Parisian *précieuses*, dedicated to wit, learning, elegance, and elaborate word games. But here satire is secondary, incidental even, to the specific erotic charge created by the ordinariness of the participants and their detailed naturalistic descriptions of the sex acts that give them pleasure – aspects of the text that James Grantham Turner attributes to its distinctive "domestic turn" (*Schooling* 107–08). By promoting and focalizing female sexual pleasure, in particular, the text acquires a powerful capacity to arouse, as Samuel Pepys famously attested in his diary entry of 1668, and with that to address new readerships enabled by commercial print and modeled in large part on the kind of solitary, masturbatory reading experience that Pepys describes.[4]

In the wake of *L'Escole des filles*, a minor industry of erotic publication developed in England (Peakman 22–27). Its leading figure was the notorious Edmund Curll, who continued the libertine tradition of false and misleading imprints, generic admixtures, clandestinity, and piracy (although the 1695 cancelling of the Licensing Act was an important fillip to the business). In this sector of the book trade, women writers were prominent, including Aphra Behn (e.g., *Love-Letters between a Novelman and his Sister* [1684]); Penelope Aubin (e.g., *Life and Amorous Adventures of Lucinda, an English Lady* [1722]); Jane Barker (e.g., *Love's Intrigues* [1713]); Delarivière Manley (e.g., *Secret Memoirs and Manners of Several Persons of Quality, From the New Atlantis* [1709]); and Eliza Haywood (e.g., *Love in Excess* [1719–20]). Addressing the readerships developed by the scandalous book trade, they mixed and compressed established Continental modes of fiction like the Italian *novella* (of which Boccaccio was the most famous practitioner), the French *nouvelle*, and the Spanish *novela exemplare* (of which Cervantes's *Exemplary Novels* was the most famous) into mildly libertine *chroniques scandaleuses* (see Beasley 162; C. Turner 83–102; Wagner 209–16). Out of these confluences the modern novel will be born (Ballaster 7–30; Hunt, "Obscenity" 30–32; Mudge, *Whore's* 121–49).[5]

But around the time that *L'Escole des filles* was published, a very different mode of libertinage was also emerging. It crystallized around the reception of the works and names of Machiavelli but also, more centrally, Thomas Hobbes. This was *not* a form of erotic writing, of course, nor did it have any relation to traditions of licensed misrule and protest. It belonged, rather, to the high philosophical heritage and, in Hobbes's case in particular, to the Epicurean lineage that had brought back into circulation a metaphysical insistence on materialism and atomism; an ethical insistence that the end of the good life was pleasure; the idea that detachment from society was a condition of living well; and a sophisticated skepticism about religious doctrine and rule. In this context, Hobbes and his school, so-called Hobbists, were viewed as libertine first and foremost because they were irreligious.

For Hobbes, human life consists fundamentally of discrete and minute motions or sensations each of which carries a particular charge of pleasure or its absence, pain. As he famously stated the idea in *Leviathan* (1651), "Life itself is but motion" (6: 39), and all states of consciousness, all actions and virtues are to be viewed as the result of particular combinations of such motions or sensations. The intellectual and cultural consequences of Hobbist Epicureanism are tremendous. Human life has no immanent morality; no innate sociability or benevolence adheres to it. It is not driven by rationality but rather by self-preservation. Souls are imaginary phantasms; human beings are more like "thinking machines" than imitations of divinity. Religious revelation has nothing to say to philosophers. Necessity reigns. Nature is not, as it is for Lucretius, for instance, law-bound, but bloody and cruel. And to control human beings understood like this, a form of artificial and absolutist sovereignty is required. Hobbes, the libertine, is the first theorist of modern secular sovereignty. To maintain civil peace, the sovereign must be able to mandate for its subjects whatever religion he or she pleases. It is only in the interiority of their conscience that subjects can believe as they choose. Under this mode of radical Erastianism, reasons of state trump religious faith.[6]

Hobbes tried to overcome the political problems, leading to war, that the Reformation had introduced, that is, the problems following from monarchs and states identifying with different confessions. Against the republicanism and Calvinist theocracy that had emerged during the English civil war, he invented a version of absolutist sovereignty that is independent of divine right. In doing so, however, he cemented a split within the Royalist side to which he belonged, and this split defines the possibilities for English libertinism. Hobbes, of course, supported the Stuart restoration, but because his political theory dispensed with both divine right and the sense that England was providentially bound to Protestantism (as articulated, for instance, by Richard Hooker), his form of royalism made an enemy of another – finally more powerful – faction within the Royalist party, the one linked to the Church of England. These two factions – libertine and Anglican – were connected to their own sites and institutions: the first to the Court and the two public theatres; the second to the Church, of course, but also to the two Houses of Parliament, where churchmen had substantial influence.

From the 1670s onward, this split intensified a moral panic against libertinism and irreligion, especially as Hobbes's separation of the private realm (where freedom of thought was permitted) from the public realm (where it was not permitted) was displaced among extreme Whigs by a Lockean promotion of general toleration of religious belief. Here is Charles Leslie, a nonjuror and leading anti-Lockean Royalist, writing in 1706 after the Glorious Revolution: "The cry of the Men against the *Church*, is carried on by *Deists*, *Socinians*, and all our *Libertines*, who make use of their *Artillery*; and wage War with the *Church* and all *Instituted Religion* upon their very *Principles*, of not being ty'd to any *Church* or *Communion*, but to change at meer Will and Pleasure" (Leslie 6:6). Leslie's High Church Anglican orthodoxy is joined here by another weapon against libertinism: the rhetoric of "courtly reformation" and moral reform, which, as Tony Claydon has argued, became central to legitimations of the state after the constitutional settlement of 1688 (236). For it, obscenity, drunkenness, swearing, promiscuity, and irreligion formed a unified social problem that desperately needed to be controlled to prevent imminent swamping by libertine disorder.

The moral reform movement was initially under the control of religious associations (often led by High Anglicans like Jeremy Collier), but over the next century it mutated, taking on softer forms that were less strictly based on Christian moral codes, and whose modes of dissemination were more various. One, which we can call Addisonian, emphasized benevolence and taste against libertinism (Addison, Shaftesbury, Temple). Another, which we can call Ciceronian, emphasized decorum, prudence, and reputation (Chesterfield). A third, which emerged from the first, we can call sentimentalism. It combined an emphasis on benevolent sympathy and sociability with an (not always wholly unlibertine) acknowledgment of the driving force of corporeality and pleasure (Steele, Richardson, Sterne, and later, female figures like Radcliffe, Inchbald, and Wollstonecraft). Among them, these ideologies of moral reform, drawing on support from religion and the state and calling on the increasing reach of print and the new genres nurtured within print – the periodical essay and the novel, in particular – helped radically to marginalize the kind of libertinism that had developed from Hobbism.

During the Restoration, the figure who came to be regarded as representative of dangerous Royalist libertinism in its least compromised form was courtier and poet John Wilmot, Earl of Rochester (1647–80). He circulated his bawdy poems, some quite consciously in Aretino's lineage, in manuscript form, sometimes leaving them for anyone to pick up in a public room in the Palace of Whitehall. Indeed, as a favorite of the king (despite his sometimes less than respectful behavior to Charles personally), he was positioned at the center of the so-called Court Wits, a circle of literary rakes in Charles's court in the 1660s and 1670s, which included Buckingham, Dorset, Mulgrave, and others (Hume 145). He was also involved in the public theatres, for which he wrote, and which, as we will see, during the 1670s often presented characters based on his life and thought. But more to the point, he was philosophically adept: an attentive reader of Hobbes as well as at least somewhat familiar with Spinoza's work, he took philosophical libertinage further than either of these significant figures, casually articulating a nihilist libertinism in his witty verses, *Upon Nothing* and *A Satyre against Reason and Mankind*. Indeed, Rochester more than anybody combined Aretino and Hobbes's dual legacies. As such he was a particular target of moral reform and was often figured as libertinage's representative. In 1675 he was denounced in these terms in a sermon delivered in front of the king by Latitudinarian churchman Edward Stillingfleet, for instance. And his deathbed conversion to the Anglican Church became a media event, immediately reported by his confessor, Whig Latitudinarian bishop Gilbert Burnet, in a widely distributed pamphlet regarded as a propaganda triumph for the Church.

As has been widely noted, Rochester's libertinism is animated by tension and paradox (see, for instance, Chernaik 1–21; Kramnick 279–80; Sanchez; Weber 91–93). It was expressed, as we have begun to see, across at least two genres: erotic and philosophic. For him, as for Aretino, sex is democratic and natural where "nature" is a concept with ethical and philosophical force. But because it is also a zone where Hobbist necessity is at work, sex and desire are therefore uncontrollable, exposed to failures of will. Rochester's poetry is often about sexual impotence. And sex, for him, is also an arena where reason and benevolence quickly reveal their limits. One of his most famous erotic poems, "A Ramble in St James's Park," invokes the park's foliage, where "Each imitative branch does twine / In some lov'd fold of *Aretine*" (81, lines 21–22), as sheltering a demotic scene of sexual sociability and confusion. This calls forth a language of mock antinomianism:

> And nightly now beneath their shade
> Are Buggeries, Rapes and Incests made:
> Unto this all-sin-sheltring Grove
> Whores of the Bulk, and the Alcove,
> Great Ladies, Chamber Mayds, and Drudges,
> The Ragg picker, and Heiress Trudges
> Carrmen, Divines, Great Lords, and Taylors,
> Prentices, Poets, Pimps, and Gaolers,
> Footmen, Fine Fopps, doe here arrive
> And here promsicuously they sw – ve.   (82, lines 23–32)

In this scene of joyous sinful democratic misrule, the poet finds himself nonetheless ensnared by hatred and revenge. He is jealous of the beautiful Corinna whom he not only desires but to whom he offers "[s]oft kindness" (line 131). But when she rejects him and courts instead three others (an imitative fop who "looks, and lives, and loves by Rote" [line 61], a pretentious "Grays Inn witt" [line 63] and a jejune "Ladyes Eldest son" [line 69]), Rochester's poetic persona turns. He curses Corinna with imaginative erotic cruelty:

> May stinking vapours Choak your womb
> Such as the Men you doat upon;
> May your depraved Appetite
> That cou'd in Whiffling Fools delight
> Begett such Frenzies in your Mind
> You may goe madd for the North wind.
> And fixing all your hopes upont
> To have him bluster in your C – t,
> Turn up your longing Arse to the Air
> And perish in a wild despair.   (85, lines 132–41)

Nature and the demotic are at work here, but it is an obscene nature, ordered not by the regularities and harmonies of divinely ordained law but – at least by implication – by the brutal drives and needs of the Hobbist state of nature that joins the mechanical to the bestial.

Nature thought about like this may cloak misogyny too. Rochester's "Love to a Woman," for instance, renounces heterosexual love *tout court*, declaring:

> Love a Woman! Th'rt an Ass –
> Tis a most insipid passion . . .
> There's a sweet soft Page of mine
> Can doe the Trick worth Forty wenches.   (37, lines 1–2, 15–16)

Here libertinage becomes, primarily, a deployment of pleasurable "tricks" detached from desire itself and that sodomy can best serve. Indeed, in "A Ramble in St James's Park," Rochester's cynicism about women expresses something more resonant: philosophic nihilism. Indeed, Rochester's privileged position in the libertine heritage is based on the fact that he connected libertinism not just to fertility, democracy, and nature, à la Aretino, or to Hobbist irreligion and mechanical pleasure, but also to a paradoxically lively sense of an existential void. The concept of the void was already available within Epicureanism. As Diogenes Laertus famously reported, Epicurus said that the world consisted only of "bodies and the void" (5). But Rochester's void belonged more to his own time. It referred to the finite universe of matter ordered by the principle of sufficient reason. From within Cartesianism, it became usual to think that God was not continually and actively engaged in the world. Rochester takes this thought to its logical extreme by expunging God's presence from the universe completely.[7]

In his *A Satyre Against Reason and Mankind,* for instance, Rochester attacks the notion that man is God's creation – a rational animal, an "Image of the Infinite" (line 77). Instead man is the most violent, proud, and "[b]asest" (line 128) creature of them all with the result that "wisdom" (line 123), wit, and rationality each become happiness's enemies. Admittedly this poem remains within the Epicurean tradition insofar as it also insists that moral prudence and "right reason" (line 99) are required to conserve the capacity for pleasure. But in his last major poem – his "paradoxical encomium" *Upon Nothing* – Rochester goes further. He suggests that the world, in sheltering life and matter, *betrays* a primordial or "primitive" "Nothing" (line 5). Life is a traitor to the ontologically fundamental void, which will, thankfully, be restored by Time. Here, the libertine-Epicurean-misogynist (and sometimes sodomite) celebration of happiness and pleasure drops away and a much darker libertine ethic emerges, one in which the "wicked" (line 27) are wise when they strain to return to nothingness as quickly as they can. In what is arguably a prophetic move, libertinism becomes a philosophy that recommends not just that humans merge into the inhuman, but that life gives way to death as quickly as it can.

Rakes

Although Rochester's writings mainly circulated in coterie circles (an unauthorized publication of his poems appeared after his death in 1680), he was, as we have seen, a notorious figure, and representations of his persona circulated through the quickly developing public sphere. He was the "original" of numerous dramatic characters performed in the new kind of court-licensed theatres that had been established in London after 1660 – for instance, in George Etherege's *The Man of Mode, or Sir Fopping Flutter* (1676) and Aphra Behn's *The Rover* (1677). More particularly, his dashing and extravagant persona helped to shape a new genre that thrived in this setting: the Restoration comedy of manners. Set in a contemporary London (or sometimes in a thinly disguised stand-in for the city) where "manners" consisted mainly of sexualized and confused encounters between different social and moral types, the comedy of manners carried the libertine ethos into new social sectors.

It did so by converting the libertine into the rake. What was the difference between the two personae? The rake, too, was committed to seduction and pleasure and removed from Christian morality. But he was not necessarily bound to the libertine inheritance, either in its Aretino or Hobbist modes. One way of making the distinction would be to say that the rake was attached to a style as much as to an ethos: a nonchalant, worldly style, and at least in plays like Behn's and Etherege's, one tinged by seemingly effortless charm, wit, and irony. And the rake is more concretely bound to particular sites and institutions than the libertine, and especially to a particular moment in the court's recent past – the interregnum period of exile when established ethical models and precedents were not available to it. That seems to be why the Restoration rake is restless, mobile, unmaterialistic, usually owning no estate and not engaged in any particular profession or business. But he remains attached to the military-aristocratic codes of honor and courage, while his easy charisma and witty deportment enable him to mingle effortlessly with all kinds of people.

Indeed, in the Restoration comedy of manners, the rake becomes a narrative agent when he deploys his personal qualities against the other social types (cuckolds, virgins, cits, town ladies, country squires, and maids) that he continually encounters in crowded metropolitan spaces. Of these various types the most important was the fop – represented as an affected, narcissistic, merely fashionable, usually stupid figure who in cases like Etherege's Lord Foppington (in *The Man of Mode*) stands for an effeminate (and perhaps queer) mode of masculinity that possesses none of the cavalier's virile and careless libertine qualities.[8] Beset by pretentious fops, greedy cits, naïve virgins on the marriage market, sexually frustrated widows, and the like, the rake becomes something of a trickster figure too, outwitting those who live by other codes, and in particular the codes of business and finance. But his real enemy (and usually his fate as well) is not a person or type. It is marriage itself. The Restoration rake, however, does not conceive of marriage as we do today. Marriage is not the point of origin for an affectionate family headed toward childrearing and mutual sustenance of moral and productive personalities. Nor is it even the negotiated joining of bloodlines, or of a dowry to an aristocratic name, although, as Robert Hume has noted, enforced marriages and marriages of economic convenience are under particularly heavy critique on the Restoration stage (142). Rather, as the rake's creed would have it, marriage is the ceremonial institutionalization of a love lacking "romantic" intensity thought of in neoplatonic terms as the harmonious merger of two souls.

Let us take as an example Aphra Behn's *The Rover* (1677), an adaptation of Killigrew's *Thomaso, or the Wanderer* (1664) whose main character, Willmore, was indeed reputed to be based on Rochester. The play is quite explicit in its enmity to moral reform, which in its epilogue it sees as wishing to "confine" "monarch wit" to what it calls "dull method" (247). It is set in Catholic Naples during carnival, but this is a Naples that pretty clearly stands for London. Nonetheless the Italian location helps naturalize the character that most marks the play out from other Restoration comedies: the *ingénue*, Hellena. Intended for the convent by her patriarchal brother, Hellena recoils from celibacy and embraces female rakishness instead, committing to "disobedience," "mischief," and reveling in her own "vigour" (159–60). This means that by the play's end, Willmore and Hellena can recognize each other as different from the hypocrites, bumpkins, and self-serving types who surround them, and fall into a perverse form of neoplatonic love. Willmore declares, "thou'rt a brave girl, and I admire thy love and courage," proposing marriage in this ambivalent couplet: "Lead on, no other dangers they can dread, / Who venture in the storms o'th' marriage bed" (246). Here, for a remarkable moment, marriage is reconciled to the rakish-cavalier-libertine ethos. It is a contract between rakes of both genders, each of whom resists reformation, and who will find in marriage a sense of honor and adventure in keeping with their creed.[9]

When the Stuart regime came to an end in 1688, courtly rakishness entered into decline. At that point, the rake began to be associated with old-fashioned absolutism, now routinely parsed as patriarchy and tyranny. Conversely, the moral reform movement, in both its religious and its polite Addisonian and Ciceronian modes, extended its influence. Furthermore, irreligion (which came to be less linked to Hobbes and more to so-called deism as proposed by figures like John Toland) itself went into decline in the 1730s. What, then, happened to the rakes and libertines of eighteenth-century England?

Erotic libertinism in Aretino's lineage can be said to come to an end with John Cleland's 1748–49 novel *Memoirs of a Woman of Pleasure* (which, to note in passing, Bishop of London Thomas Sherwood declared to be partly responsible for the Lisbon earthquake). Calling on contemporary fictional techniques capable of increasingly efficient illusionism or realism, *Fanny Hill* (as the novel became known) was able to establish pornography as an autonomous genre (Mudge, *Whore's* 199–214 and *When Flesh* xxiv; Wagner 6). Importantly, the novel has no recognizable political program, even though Cleland wrote a considerable amount of political journalism first in the Bolingbrokean interest, and then as hired by Lord Bute. It replaces politicized libertinage with a sexual tolerance: in the edition now available through Peter Sabor's editorial labors we can recognize that the novel promotes what Lisa Moore calls a "politics of pleasure" in which, for instance, same-sex sodomy belongs firmly to the repertoire of human sexual behavior (73).[10] In the end, however, Cleland's novel is best understood as a print commodity designed to arouse sexual curiosity and pleasure rather than an expression of sexual pluralism or demotic misrule.

As to rakes: the rake remained a vital character type in both the theatre and the novel up until the end of the eighteenth century. But the mid-eighteenth-century rake is significantly different from the Restoration rake. He typically awaits the reformation that will close his narrative: for instance, the first "modern" novel, Samuel Richardson's *Pamela*, famously tells the story of how a pious servant converts her quasi-aristocratic, rakish master to domestic respectability, and Richardson's *Clarissa* takes this plot line further with its rake character, Lovelace (another imitation of Rochester), who has seduced the heroine and is responsible for her death, himself dying with a quotation from Nicholas Rowe's *The Fair Penitent* on his lips: "let this expiate!" Death here is not the void's victory but morality's payback. Having loomed large in the early novel, rakes come to accede to "minor character" status (to use Alex Woloch's term) so that by Frances Burney's time (she was publishing novels from the 1770s on) they served merely to allow the heroine's virtuous resolve to be revealed. Rakishness appears only residually in Austen, and in Walter Scott it is absent altogether.

But this gradual diminishment of the rake's cultural power enables a new, intra-gender formation to solidify. In *Clarissa*, for instance, the young women – Clarissa herself and her friend, Anna Howe – transform their friendship into an intimacy that is more secure and spontaneous than any that is available to them inside their families or with men. As a number of scholarly works have shown (Donoghue; Moore; Wahl), such spheres of intimacy between women, often sexualized, became quite common in the period. In Sarah Scott's *Millenium Hall* (1762), for instance, women create a refuge from the debased world of rakishness, dedicating themselves to a mode of piety, good works, and self-improvement that can be regarded as exemplary of moral reform. But this utopian space is beset by tonal instability precisely because the women's same-sex community can so easily be regarded as a repetition or imitation of the nunnery with its reputation for clandestine female sexual license and its hallowed place in libertine pornographic writing.[11] In this way, homosocial resistance to libertinage and rakishness threatens to lead to a new implicitly or secretly sexual form of its own. A similar logic besets Maria Edgeworth's 1801 novel, *Belinda*. Here a brash, crossdressed woman and political radical, helpfully named Harriet Freke, mimics the male rake in order to seduce the heroine, Belinda, into friendly intimacy. Relations between women, entered into against the dangers that men imply, repeat the forms they are positioned against.

Homosocial relations with libertine overtones also fueled male political radicalism. Let us take John Wilkes and his circle as an example. Wilkes can be regarded as the first radical politician, where "radical" means something like agitating for legal and constitutional reforms that will restructure social relations. Wilkes can be called that because his campaign – under the popular catch-cry "Wilkes and Liberty" – intended such reform against what it recognized, perhaps for the first time, as systemic inequities and corruption. But Wilkes also belonged to libertine circles. He was a member of an intensely homosocial Hell-Fire Club, led by Sir Francis Dashwood. He was famous for his rakish charisma and charm, without which his political career would have been inconceivable. He formed close bonds with associates, in particular poet Charles Churchill but also with people like Laurence Sterne, with whom he once spent an evening in the company of Parisian prostitutes (During 18). And by the mid-1760s, he had a public reputation as (to cite one phrase used to describe him) "a vigorous and mighty Cunter" (Sainsbury, *John* 90). So "Wilkes and Liberty" meant not just radical reform but connoted the sexual liberty appealing to demotic and natural license familiar from the Aretino culture of obscene misrule. But now it was also bound to close associations between elite men out of which new political formations could be organized in the interests of expressing the popular will.

Wilkes became famous in 1763 when he was arrested for writing a seditious piece in his journal *The North Briton*. That year, too, an obscene poem in the libertine tradition and reputed to be by Wilkes, *An Essay on Woman by Pego Borewell, Esq*, was privately and anonymously published. It was a parody of William Warburton's posthumous edition of Alexander Pope's famous *An Essay on Man* and offered a line-by-line rewriting of both Pope's poem and Warburton's annotations. Wilkes's text blasphemously imitates Pope's poem by turning Pope's "Man" into "prick," and "God" into "cunt," as well as by reducing Pope's theodicy into the triumphant pursuit of promiscuous sexual pleasure, and then, finally, by hinting that, in this world, archbishops and aristocratic politicians engage in sodomy. In these terms, Wilkes's libertine parody rebukes the Whig hegemony that Warburton, a well-known Anglican clergyman and scholar, helped to legitimate. More particularly, *An Essay on Woman* seems to have been driven by Wilkes's animus against Warburton's revision of Pope. In his edition, Warburton had tried to transform Pope's deism into what he called "a real vindication of Providence against *Libertines* and *Atheists*" (qtd. in Sainsbury, "Wilkes" 161).

Threatened with prosecution for publishing the poem, Wilkes fled to France. After five years in exile he returned and was elected to the lower House as the member for the London seat of Middlesex, one of the few electorates where popular will had effective expression. But his legal right to take up the seat was refused. The outrage and the publicity campaign that followed this illegal action by the government energized the movement for constitutional reform that would lead to the various nineteenth-century parliamentary reform bills. It also secured the dissemination of a new, *radical* sense that English society and government were beset not just by vice and irreligion as the moral reform movement had long supposed, but by a systemic failure that allowed the ruling class to run the country in its own interest.

That understanding was expressed in a powerful metaphor in Charles Churchill's verse satire, *The Times* (1764). Churchill, a one-time Anglican clergyman, was the Wilkesite movement's most talented propagandist who himself was something of a libertine and rake. He was perhaps the last genuinely popular Augustan satirist working in the spirit of Rochester, Swift, and Pope. In *The Times*, he names what characterizes the era and its systemic failure, *sodomy*. It is, he writes, an era in which those who claim "the name of PRIVILEGE" need "feel ... no Conscience" and "fear ... no Law" (Churchill 393, lines 75–76). The oligarchy frees itself to betray the tradespeople who are the nation's real support. They grant themselves license to indulge in luxury and cosmopolitanism as well as to advance those imperial adventures that, in Churchill's view, were weakening the state. They are free, too, to abandon morality for money and "Œconomy" (391, line 30). But most of all they are free to commit a cardinal sin, a sin "[a]gainst Nature's plan" (398, line 267), a sin that now "possess[es] the land at large" (398, line 268) – sodomy: "Go where We will, at ev'ry time and place, / SODOM confronts, and stares us in the face" (398, lines 293–94).

Sodomy is not to be taken literally here. Indeed, it can be argued that this is not a homophobic poem, despite its castigation of political enemies – like the bisexual Lord Hervey – as "Vile Pathicks" (405, line 555). To be sure, Churchill's deployment of sexual identity and homophobic rhetoric for political purposes is an instance both of the link between phallic masculinity and radicalism that characterized the Wilkesite movement, as Kathleen Wilson (*Sense* 219ff.) has argued, and of a more generalized tightening of gender identity in the later eighteenth century as described by Dror Wahrman, for instance (40–44). More than this, however, Churchill's sodomy functions, as just noted, as a metaphor for a condition that has not yet been properly theorized, that is, for a systemic social failure that is, however, capable of peaceful, if difficult, political reform by direct appeal to the popular will. Metaphor, then, is necessary to Wilkesite politics because neither the theory nor the practice of systematic and progressive reform is yet open to articulation. And "sodomy" is, of course, a metaphor that emerges from libertinage's past – it contains an obscene rebuke to, and insult of, the powers that be. Yet in this instance it also directs libertine license against libertinage itself by evoking an internal division inside the world of fucking, pricks, and cunts. Here, sex between men, anal sex, is cast as *unnatural* as it wasn't for Rochester or, more arguably, even for Cleland. Sodomy transgresses that natural – if liberating – law that implicitly sanctions radical reform.

In making this move, Churchill inadvertently signals the weakness of libertine radicalism because to retain its force libertinism needed to be able to appeal to a strict and intensive antinomianism, inclusive of sodomy. But antinomianism of that kind could never win substantial popular support. So while connections between radical politics, libertine writing, and licentiousness continued until the end of the nineteenth century as Iain McCalman helps show in his *Radical Underworld* (1988), they are gradually submerged into that marginalized world much later vividly evoked in Joseph Conrad's *The Secret Agent* (1907), whose hero, Mr. Verloc, sells porn, condoms, and sex toys in a London shop that also serves as a hangout for terrorists and anarchists.

Dandies

After Wilkes, not only did the world of practical radical activism take other avenues and forms, but the rake's transgressive force, already run down, became further depleted. Rakishness did persist into the Regency period, but it did so only as grafted onto a new figure: the dandy. This particular conjuncture is somewhat surprising because the Regency dandy can be best considered as an heir to the fop, and the fop, as we have seen, was the rake's other in the Restoration period. Ellen Moers has argued that the dandy is one of those rare cultural formations with a precise point of origin: the appearance of Beau Brummell as a figure of fashion and celebrity in the nineteenth century's first decade (*Dandy* 17–39). But it is possible to regard Brummell himself as a new kind of fop: a normalized, socially powerful one. Like the fop, he was supremely interested in fashion and self-display. Like the fop, he rejected masculine styles based on manliness per se. Like the fop, too, he had no relation to production; he was essentially a consumer. Unlike the fop, however, Brummell's dandy was an originator and an arbitrator of style with a distinctive ethos. That was an ethos of risk taking (gambling was central to dandy culture), sartorial meticulousness, and an intolerance of ordinariness. Qualities like these conferred on the dandy what we might now call a Byronic aura and became the basis of the rejection of mass industrialization, vulgarity, and bourgeois conformity that were the hallmarks of the dandy aestheticism of later figures such as Baudelaire, Huysmans, and Wilde. This is to say that the dandy, at least in his purest form, was a hybridization of the fop, libertine, and rake, who retained certain connections to the powerful cultural and ethical resonances that had long attended these figures.

That said, the dandy, unlike the Wilkesite libertine, for instance, was all but programmatically detached from politics, indeed from any form of social or communal engagement, and so from the old Aretino lineage. Nor is there in the dandy figure the slightest whiff of misrule or of obscenity as a democratic riposte to hierarchy and order. This means that a figure like Byron, who came closest to joining these various traditions, cannot make them cohere. He was, after all, culturally associated with dandyism; involved in a politics of liberation (most prominently for Greek emancipation); both sexually heterodox and libertine; and he inherited more than a touch of Rochester's nihilism as well. But when he comes to imagine himself publicly, in *Don Juan* (1819), he can do so only in a tongue-in-cheek manner. Don Juan is indeed a libertine, a rake, even something of a dandy. But he is also a joke, or at least a hero of satire (an "epic satire," as Byron said) who is already brushed by obsolescence, as signaled by the arcane verse form – the ottava rima – in which his adventures are described. It is as if, in Don Juan, the parade of types with which this chapter began – the libertine, the rake, and the dandy – comes to fuse, but only under the auspices of an irony through which those types also find their end.

Notes

1. On French libertinage, see Cusset; DeJean; Cryle; and Saint-Amand.
2. Mackie argues that British masculinity in the eighteenth century was increasingly characterized by a slippage between two male types, the rogue (or criminal) and the gentleman, as exemplified by the rake (1–34).
3. For a useful account of the various subtypes of the rake, see Hume 154–67; on the distinction between "Hobbesian" and the "philosophical" libertine (as exemplified by Rochester and Sir William Temple, respectively), see Weber 53–90, 92–129.
4. Pepys's diary entry of February 9, 1668 reads: "We sang till almost night ... and then they parted, and I to my chamber, where I did read through *L'escholle des filles*; a lewd book, but what doth me no wrong to read for information sake (but it did hazer my primick para stand all the while, and una vez to decharger); and after I had done it, I burned it, that it might not be among

my books to my shame" (qtd. in Turner, *Schooling* 223). Moulton usefully contrasts Pepys's encounter with *L'Escole des filles* as it typifies the production and consumption of erotic texts in the late seventeenth-century commercial print marketplace, with the modes of communal reading amongst coteries that generally characterized the circulation of erotica in manuscript form fifty or so years earlier (36–37). On readership, see Turner, who notes that while the text was predominantly purchased and read by men, it belongs to a "pseudo-feminocentric" European libertine tradition that creates a fantasy of female readership on the basis of its representation of women's sexual passion and pleasure (*Schooling* 225, 236). Cryle notes the text's departures from the tropes of female authorship, knowledge, and authority that had characterized earlier erotic narrative: "In *L'Escole des filles* ... [t]he man is visibly first and last, origin and conclusion, and women's knowledge is the instrument of his seductive activity" (25).

5. Ballaster's influential study makes a firm distinction between "male pornography" (in the tradition of Aretino and *L'Escole des filles*), and two streams of feminine writing (the "didactic love fiction" of Aubin, Rowe, Barker, and Davys, on the one hand, and the "amatory fiction" of Behn, Manley, and Haywood, on the other) that underpin the modern English novel (32–35). Mudge, by contrast, argues that pornography and the novel were invented together at the beginning of the eighteenth century. It follows, then, that the amorous prose of early eighteenth-century women authors was "at once proto-literary and proto-pornographic; stand[ing] at the beginning of a process of differentiation" out of which the respectable literary novel had evolved by mid-century (*Whore's* 10). On the simultaneous development of the novel and pornography in the French tradition, see DeJean.

6. This understanding of Hobbes follows that of Carl Schmitt. On Schmitt's interpretation of Hobbes, see Stanton. For an account of Hobbist and Epicurean thinking as they inform Restoration drama, see Chernaik 22–51. Weber's understanding of the "Hobbesian" and "philosophical" libertine relies on a distinction between the two traditions (91–97).

7. On Rochester as an irreligious poet, see Ellenzweig; Trotter; and Manning.

8. For an extended analysis of the fop as the rake's "other," see McGirr 39–51.

9. On the female rake, see Linker; Weber 130–78; and Wilson, "Female."

10. Sabor's unexpurgated edition of Cleland's original text includes a sodomy scene between two young men witnessed by Fanny through a peephole at an inn. It was earlier thought to have been an addition to pirated versions of the text and on these grounds was excluded from standard editions (xxiii). George Haggerty reads the scene as simultaneously one of attraction and repulsion for Fanny (172–77).

11. On the libertine eroticization of institutions of female education and community, see Turner, *Schooling* 225; Peakman 46–48.

Works Cited

Ballaster, Ros. *Seductive Forms: Women's Amatory Fiction from 1684 to 1740*. Oxford: Clarendon, 1992. Print.

Beasley, Jerry C. *Novels of the 1740s*. Athens: U of Georgia P, 1982. Print.

Behn, Alpha. *Oroonoko, The Rover, and Other Works*. Ed. Janet Todd. London: Penguin, 1992. Print.

Burnet, Gilbert. *Some passages of the life and death of the right honourable John earl of Rochester, who died the 26th of July, 1680*. London, 1693. Print.

Chernaik, Warren L. *Sexual Freedom in Restoration Literature*. Cambridge: Cambridge UP, 1995. Print.

Churchill, Charles. *The Poetical Works of Charles Churchill*. Ed. Douglas Grant. Oxford: Clarendon P, 1956. Print.

Claydon, Tony. *William III and the Godly Revolution*. Cambridge: Cambridge UP, 2004. Print.

Cleland, John. *Fanny Hill, or, Memoirs of a Woman of Pleasure*. Ed. Peter Sabor. Oxford: Oxford UP, 1985. Print.

Cryle, Peter. *Geometry in the Boudoir: Configurations of French Erotic Narrative*. Ithaca: Cornell UP, 1994. Print.

Cryle, Peter, and Lisa O'Connell, ed. *Libertine Enlightenment: Sex, Liberty and License in the Eighteenth-century*. Basingstoke: Palgrave, 2004. Print.

Cusset, Catherine, ed. Libertinage and Modernity. Spec. issue of *Yale French Studies* 94 (1998): 1–215. Print.

DeJean, Joan. "The Politics of Pornography: L'Ecole des Filles." Hunt, *Invention* 109–24.

Donoghue, Emma. *Passions between Women: British Lesbian Culture, 1668–1801*. London: Scarlet P, 1993. Print.

During, Simon. "Taking Liberties: Sterne, Wilkes and Warburton." Cryle and O'Connell 15–33.

Epicurus. *The Epicurus Reader: Selected Writings and Testimonials*. Trans. and ed. Brad Inwood and L. P. Gerson. Indianapolis: Hackett, 1994. Print.

Ellenzweig, Sarah. "The Faith of Unbelief: Rochester's *Satyre*, Deism, and Religious Freethinking in Seventeenth-century England." *Journal of British Studies* 44 (2005): 27–45. Print.

Haggerty, George. "Keyhole Testimony: Witnessing Sodomy in the Eighteenth Century." *Eighteenth Century: Theory and Interpretation* 44 (2003): 162–82. Print.

Hobbes, Thomas. *Leviathan*. Ed. Michael Oakeshott. Oxford: Blackwell, 1960. Print.

Hume, Robert D. *The Rakish Stage: Studies in English Drama, 1660–1800*. Carbondale: Southern Illinois UP, 1983. Print.

Hunt, Lynn, ed. *The Invention of Pornography: Obscenity and the Origins of Modernity, 1500–1800*. New York: Zone B, 1993. Print.

"Obscenity and the Origins of Modernity 1500–1800." Hunt, *Invention* 9–48.

Kramnick, Jonathan. "Rochester and the History of Sexuality." *ELH* 69: 2 (2002): 277–301. Print.

Leslie, Charles. *The Theological Works of the Rev. Charles Leslie in Seven Volumes*. Oxford: Oxford UP, 1832. Print.

Linker, Laura. *Dangerous Women, Libertine Epicures, and the Rise of Sensibility, 1670–1730.* Burlington: Ashgate, 2011. Print.

Mackie, Erin. *Rakes, Highwaymen, Pirates: The Making of the Modern Gentleman in the Eighteenth Century.* Baltimore: Johns Hopkins UP, 2009. Print.

Manning, Gillian. "Rochester's *Satyr Against Reason and Mankind* and Contemporary Religious Debate." *Seventeenth Century* 8 (1993): 99–121. Print.

McCalman, Iain. *Radical Underworld: Prophets, Revolutionaries, and Pornographers in London, 1795–1840.* Cambridge: Cambridge UP, 1988. Print.

McGirr, Elaine M. *Eighteenth-Century Characters: A Guide to the Literature of the Age.* London: Palgrave, 2007. Print.

Moers, Ellen. *The Dandy: Brummell to Beerbohm.* Lincoln: U of Nebraska P, 1978. Print.

Moore, Lisa Lynne. *Dangerous Intimacies: Toward a Sapphic History of the British Novel.* Durham: Duke UP, 1997. Print.

Moulton, Ian Frederick. *Before Pornography: Erotic Writing in Early Modern England.* Oxford: Oxford UP, 2000. Print.

Mudge, Bradford Keyes, ed. *When Flesh Becomes Word: An Anthology of Eighteenth-Century Libertine Literature.* Oxford: Oxford UP, 2004. Print.

The Whore's Story: Women, Pornography, and the British Novel, 1684–1830. New York: Oxford UP, 2000. Print.

Peakman, Julie. *Mighty Lewd Books: The Development of Pornography in Eighteenth-Century England.* New York: Palgrave, 2003. Print.

Rochester, John Wilmot, Earl of. *The Poems and Lucina's Rape.* Ed. Keith Walker and Nicholas Fisher. New York: Wiley-Blackwell, 2010. Print.

Sainsbury, John. *John Wilkes: The Lives of a Libertine.* Aldershot: Ashgate, 2006. Print.

"Wilkes and Libertinism." *Studies in Eighteenth-Century Culture* 26 (1998): 151–74. Print.

Saint-Amand, Pierre. *The Libertine's Progress: Seduction in the Eighteenth-century French Novel.* Trans. Jennifer Curtiss Gage. Hanover: U of New England, 1994. Print.

Sanchez, Melissa E. "Libertinism and Romance in Rochester's Poetry." *Eighteenth-century Studies* 38:3 (2005): 441–59. Print.

Schmitt, Carl. *The Leviathan in the State Theory of Thomas Hobbes: Meaning and Failure of a Political Symbol.* Trans. George Schwab and Erna Hilfstein. Chicago: U of Chicago P, 2008. Print.

Stanton, Timothy. "Hobbes and Schmitt." *History of European Ideas* 32.2 (2010): 160–67. Print.

Trotter, David. "Wanton Expressions." *Spirit of Wit: Reconsiderations of Rochester.* Ed. Jeremy Treglown, Oxford: Blackwell, 1982. 111–32. Print.

Turner, Cheryl. *Living by the Pen: Women Writers in the Eighteenth Century.* London: Routledge, 1992. Print.

Turner, James Grantham. *Libertines and Radicals in Early Modern London: Sexuality, Politics, and Literary Culture, 1630–1685.* Cambridge: Cambridge UP, 2002. Print.

Schooling Sex: Libertine Literature and Erotic Education in Italy, France, and England 1534–1685. Oxford: Oxford UP, 2003. Print.

Wagner, Peter. *Eros Revived: Erotica of the Enlightenment in England and America.* London: Secker, 1988. Print.

Wahl, Elizabeth Susan. *Invisible Relations: Representations of Female Intimacy in the Age of Enlightenment.* Stanford: Stanford UP, 1999. Print.

Wahrman, Dror. *The Making of the Modern Self: Identity and Culture in Eighteenth-century England*. New Haven: Yale UP, 2004. Print.

Weber, Harold. *The Restoration Rake-Hero: Transformations in Sexual Understanding in Seventeenth-Century England*. Madison: U of Wisconsin P, 1986. Print.

Wilkes, John. *The Infamous Essay on Woman; or, John Wilkes Seated between Vice and Virtue*. Ed. Adrian Hamilton. London: Deutsch, 1972. Print.

Wilson, Kathleen. "The Female Rake: Gender, Libertinism, and Enlightenment." Cryle and O'Connell 95–111.

The Sense of the People: Politics, Culture and Imperialism in England, 1715–1785. Cambridge: Cambridge UP, 1998. Print.

Woloch, Alex. *The One vs. the Many: Minor Characters and the Space of the Protagonist in the Novel*. Princeton: Princeton UP, 2003. Print.

PART III

★

ENLIGHTENMENT CULTURES

13

Homobonding and the Nation

PETER COVIELLO

Thomas Jefferson has a problem – in fact, several. As he composes the initial draft of what would become a founding document for the nation just then edging itself toward coherence, he must confront dilemmas as delicate as they are seemingly intractable. Some are by now familiar. In detailing the ignominies of the king of England in a series of accusations that escalate in moral gravity, Jefferson ends on a crime not merely procedural, but against what he wishes us to understand as the human as such. "He has waged cruel war against human nature itself," Jefferson asserts, "violating it's [sic] most sacred rights of life and liberty in the persons of a distant people who never offended him, captivating and carrying them into slavery in another hemisphere, or to incur miserable death in their transportation thither."[1] All of this was to be struck out by Congress in its editorial "mutilations," as Jefferson would later ruefully call them. Of course, the slaveholder from Virginia and future president was himself not immune from accusations of a singular hypocrisy in demanding liberty on behalf of a people whose economies depended so greatly on the labor of the enslaved.

But there is another dilemma here as well, one less political and moral than, we might say, conceptual, and complexly temporal. We could put the problem, at its briefest, like this: Jefferson's task is to declare independence on behalf of an entity – a grammatical unit he designates as a "we" – that does not, properly speaking, exist, at least not until *after* the self-creating declaration has been made. What is it that, exactly, grounds Jefferson's use of the first-person plural? By what strategies can he figure, as *already* unified and politically coherent, what was after all an unjoined collection of colonial subjects, by then federated only quite loosely? How, in all, to make claims on behalf of a coherent entity, a *nation*, that the document itself means to pronounce into existence?

Jefferson's approach to the problem is ingenious, and it is revealing. For in the final sections of the initial draft, he speaks up on behalf of a style of coherence that both predates the declaration and, by doing so, underwrites its invocation of unanimity. Turning away from the crimes of the king, Jefferson trains his sights on the British themselves, in an extended passage that was, like the sentences about slavery, destined to be excised:

> Nor have we been wanting in attentions to our British brethren. We have warned them from time to time of attempts by their legislature to extend a jurisdiction over these our states.... [W]e appealed to their native justice and magnanimity, as well as to the ties of our common kindred to disavow these usurpations which were likely to interrupt our connection and correspondence. They too have been deaf to the voice of justice and of consanguinity, and when occasions have been given them, by the regular course of their laws, of removing from their councils the disturbers of our harmony, they have by their free election re-established them in power. At this very time too, they are permitting their chief magistrate to send over not only soldiers of our common blood, but Scotch and foreign mercenaries to invade and deluge us in blood. These facts have given the last stab to agonizing affection, and manly spirit bids us to renounce forever these unfeeling brethren.

It's striking: the Enlightenment tinkerer, who begins the document in the register of perspicuous rationalism ("*When in the course of human events,*" he writes, framing revolutionary rupture as the clockwork unfolding of a mechanistic history), turns here to the language of sentiment and sensibility, condemning the British not chiefly for their tyranny but for their failure of proper feeling. As if the invocation of "unfeeling brethren" and those stabs of "agonizing affection" were not enough, Jefferson ends the paragraph at a pitch wrought up higher still, in what is very nearly the voice of a lovesick ingénue:

> We must endeavor to forget our former love for them, and to hold them as we hold the rest of mankind, enemies in war, in peace friends. We might have been a free and great people together; but a communication of grandeur and of freedom it seems is below their dignity. Be it so, since they will have it: the road to glory & happiness is open to us too. We will tred apart from them, and acquiesce in the necessity which denounces our eternal separation.

Only after these sentences, more melancholy in their aggrievement than awash in revolutionary fervor, does Jefferson's draft at last back away from the passive-voice constructions that have been so much a part of the document's rhetorical strategy (revolution, in the Declaration, *"becomes necessary"*) and move toward decisive and defiant declaration:

> We therefore the representatives of the United States of America in General Congress assembled do, in the name and by authority of the good people of these states, reject and renounce all allegiance and subjection to the kings of

Great Britain and all others who may hereafter claim by, through, or under them; we utterly dissolve all political connection which may have heretofore subsisted between us and the people or parliament of Great Britain; and finally we do assert and declare these colonies to be free and independent states.

The voice that speaks here, with such clarity and force, is of a solidified, unambiguous collectivity: a "we" capable of declaring its independence.

What Jefferson lays out here, in that remarkable turn to the register of affect, feeling, and woundedness, is a style of nationalist imagination that makes perfect sense in the context of revolutionary America – of a nation born in a moment of rupture, and so unable to draw on what Christopher Looby calls the "massive and dense structures of inherited customary practices" that had given shape to extant European nationalisms – but that would also prove splendidly adaptive, for centuries thereafter, to many and disparate populations (14). We could call the social form that issues from this style of imagining an *affect-nation*; and we could think of the fantasy of belonging that stands behind it as the dream of an intimate nationality. As it turns out, just these styles of conceiving nation-ness intimately, and of turning affect into politics, have been much on the minds of scholars in recent years, and have been at the center of some of the finest excavations of feeling in its relation to discourse, authority, and public life. (Such work can be found in a range of important texts: in Ann Cvetkovich's *Mixed Feelings*, Glenn Hendler's *Public Sentiments*, Julia Stern's *The Plight of Feeling*, Dana Nelson's *National Manhood*, Sara Ahmed's *The Cultural Politics of Emotion*, Christopher Castiglia's *Interior States*, Dana Luciano's *Arranging Grief*, and in a series of works by Lauren Berlant, especially *The Queen of America Goes to Washington City* and *The Female Complaint*.) These works form part of what has been named the "affective turn" in cultural criticism, a movement that would be of great importance to queer studies, for reasons we will soon see. Across this scholarship is an interest in the way varying states of affective intensity get transformed, or in some cases resist transformation, into the idioms of political life. So in Jefferson's vision, the American colonies are essentially wounded into collectivity, joined by nothing so much as the grief – the agonizing affection – that traverses them, and united too in their melancholic attachment, their ongoing endeavor to forget *together*. Jefferson imagines a curious kind of specifically affective cohesion for the nation, a species of shared feeling-in-simultaneity – in this case, that feeling is griefstricken-ness – that precedes the formation of the state and, it appears, authorizes it.

We might think here of Benedict Anderson's seminal account of the nation as a variety of "imagined community," distinguished not least, he writes, by "that remarkable confidence of community in anonymity which is the hallmark of the modern nation" (36). For nations born in moments of revolution or rupture, self-consciously dislocated from the traditional forms of nation-ness that might once have obtained, that "confidence of community in anonymity" often takes form as, precisely, an affective reality: a feeling of simultaneous belonging and adhesion, of live present-tense connectedness to others, that somehow transpires even between strangers. This is the dream of the nation as a thing made not by institutions, or laws, or obedience to these, but as a network of relations – even intimate relations – spread out across vast distances.

Intimate Nationality

If this modern imagining of national belonging seems apt for the Age of Revolutions, in which old models of cohesion are being thrown off in the name of liberties newly conceived, it would in the event broach all sorts of difficulties, as well as a great number of terrors. To take only the most prominent example: the vision of nation-ness as a precipitate of anonymous mutual attachment paves the way for the frightening deployment of race in the modern world. It is a deployment that crosses malign and dehumanizing racist caricatures of "Others" – as savage, bestial, indolent, uneducable, less than fully *human* – with new and differently tuned aggrandizements of the race of the home-nation itself, figured now as the concretization of that tie joining together a scattered and mutually anonymous citizenry and binding it into cohesion. Affective visions of national coherence make race into something other, and something more, than an identity, an invidious or aggrandizing distinction. Race comes to emerge, too, as the name for a kind of affiliation: a language with which to describe a species of inborn, embodied connectedness to others. This style of nationalist imagination goes by many names – Reginald Horsman calls it "romantic racial nationalism," although it has also been apprehended as "the nationalization of whiteness" – and marks especially forcefully the nineteenth century, as the imperial ideology of Manifest Destiny travels in ever-widening swaths around the globe.

But nested inside the dream of an affective nationality, and so linked complexly to these larger geopolitical movements, is another kind of drama as well. For to imagine nation-ness as anchored by a particularly vibrant affective connection among the mutually anonymous is to place, at the very center of the nation-form, a quality of bondedness, of *intimacy*, between persons whom a variety of proprieties might otherwise keep separate. What Anderson calls "modern" nationality, that is, carries within it an affective proximity that magnetizes and unsettles the proprietary codes of intimacy itself. "To identify *as*," Eve Kosofsky Sedgwick reminds us, "must always also include multiple processes of identification *with*" (*Epistemology* 61). If this is true of sexual identities (to identify as gay is, Sedgwick suggests, to identify with others who share that designation), it is also true of national affiliations. So to *belong* to the modern nation is to identify as a given nationality but also, complicatingly, *with* a range of others unknown to oneself: to be precipitated, that is, into the whole unruly range of attachments that might travel under the sign of "intimacy," from the most chaste to, perhaps, the most erotically charged. On the scene of an affectively constituted nationality, citizenship itself is a status, to be sure, but it is also, pressingly, a *state of relation* – which, of course, entails all the anxiety, vexation, and unpredictability that relationality brings.

The history of modern nationality, that is to say, unfolds in tandem with transformations in the realm of intimacy and intimate affiliation – with, in short, the history of sexuality. And this is only one of the reasons that the "affective turn" in cultural criticism, with its careful attentiveness to the weaving of feeling in and out of its official forms of codification, would be so energized by queer pursuits and queer studies. What do such queer collisions between affect and politics look like? To take a near example: Walt Whitman's is of course not the only investment in the volatile conjunction of national belonging and sexual exchange, but he does bring to the scene of an erotically charged national feeling a singular clarity. "What is it then between us?" he asks in "Crossing Brooklyn Ferry," of 1856, a poem in which he considers the thronging spaces of urban anonymity, and their almost inconceivable density of carnal possibility, that are so integral to the persona he cultivates at mid-century as America's national bard. The erotic vibrancy of encounters between strangers becomes, in fact, a chief point of fascination, and a central figure, in Whitman's work, especially in the infamous "Calamus" cluster of poems from 1860. There, having "Resolved to sing no songs to-day but those of manly attachment," the poet details, in a succession of lyric vignettes, the desire that kindles between the mutually anonymous men of the city. There, Whitman portrays an America that looks like this:

> Passing stranger! You do not know how longingly I look upon you…
>   You give me the pleasure of your eyes, face, flesh, as we pass,
>   you take of my beard, breast, hands in return.

Or, from "City of Orgies":

> O Manhattan! your frequent and swift flash of eyes offering me love,
> Offering me the response of my own – these repay me
> Lovers, continual lovers, only repay me.

Or from "Whoever You Are Holding Me Now in Hand," where the poet speaks in the voice of his book, held in the hand of his reader:

> Or, if you will, thrusting me beneath your clothing,
> Where I may feel the throbs of your heart or rest upon your hip,
> Carry me when you go forth over land and sea;
> For thus merely touching you is enough is best.

These are only a few of the "Calamus" cluster's characteristic scenes of anonymous eroticized solicitation: in essence of a kind of sexual exchange between strangers.

But these cruisy episodes are not merely demonstrations of an enviable American carnality. Whitman makes clear that they are, to him, *political*, and political in an explicitly nationalist register. "Besides," he writes:

> important as they are in my purpose as emotional expressions for humanity, the special meaning of the "Calamus" cluster of "Leaves of Grass" … mainly resides in its political significance. In my opinion, it is by a fervent, accepted development of comradeship, the beautiful and sane affection of man for man, latent in all young fellows … that the United States of the future, (I cannot too often repeat,) are to be most effectually welded together, intercalated, anneal'd into a living union.

What these passions among the anonymous exemplify – what for him they *are* – are the very bonds of nation-ness. They make legible the affiliative, bodily connectedness, the vitalizing mutuality between strangers, that Whitman understands to constitute nationality as such.

Whitman in this way makes most explicit the quality of intimacy, notably *inclusive* of desire in all its turbulence and adhesive force, that might animate citizenship itself where nation-ness is understood to be rooted less in institutions of governance or obedience to laws than in an affective mutuality transpiring between strangers. He suggests, we might say, just one of the ways even a form as normative and often invidious as the nation might also, in some of its articulations, be queer, or at least available to queer adaptation (which is another way of saying that the normative and nonnormative are not always opposites as much as dialectically entangled counter-images). And Whitman's example allows us clear purchase, too, on the extravagant homoeroticism of the nationalist imagination as it has flourished in many moments, and in many far-flung locales – from idealizations of the dashing Major André in and after the American Revolution to the eroticized *fraternité* of the French Revolution, on outward in varying formations all the way to Queer Nation in its early '90s heyday. Our examples thus far have been European or Eurocentric ones, and this makes sense to the degree that Western imperialism itself did much to solidify the terms in which political groupings could be recognized *as* legitimate, foreclosing the possibility of authority for some forms of sodality (the tribal, say) the better to ratify others (such as the nation-state). But affective conceptions of the nation can play a kind of havoc with the strict identification between "nationness" and political institutionalizations of the nation-state; in this way, they open up nationness itself to queerer inhabitations, some of which would not be amenable to Eurocentric recodification. For to be national, in these affective terms, is to insist on a relation, a bondedness in and through mutual anonymity, in which desire is ever a live and shaping element. As Lauren Berlant and Elizabeth Freeman noted some twenty years ago in an essay called "Queer Nationality," it is no wonder queer people would turn explicitly to the nation-form in a moment of political foment and solidification. The nation, at least in its modern affective modality, has the tumultuous, affiliative force of impassioned intimacy already built into it.

Volatile Intimacies

What Whitman's example, no less than this historically jumbled litany of queered nations, thus recalls to us is the historical fragility – the historicity – of any of these inhabitations of the nation-form. Nation-ness, in other words, is not one thing. If at moments it is a form that underwrites imperial expansion, colonial racism, and every variety of violent dislocation and expropriation, at other junctures, for other populations, claims to nation-ness can provide a bulwark *against* precisely those depredations: imperialism, colonial conquest, dispossession. Much of what Marx has to teach us, in "The Eighteenth Brumaire" and elsewhere, is about exactly this multiplicity: about, that is, the co-presence of seemingly incompatible political imperatives and efficacies that can unfold within a single social form. That form, Marx insists, merely appears uniform, unvarying from place to place, from perspectives that are dematerializing and ultimately dehistoricizing.

Just so, the affective intensities of national belonging that Whitman deploys with such exuberance, in 1860, find themselves subject to different tensions at other moments, often via the anxious proximity of different sorts of *prohibition.* For instance: if, following the conventional wisdom, we take the end of the nineteenth century to be the moment at which homosexuality and heterosexuality most fully emerge in the West as legible and widely circulating identities – when "homosexual" becomes a new category of person, whose sex was seen to anchor a new range of characterizing dispositions, predilections, and determinations – then to the degree that this new erotic dispensation takes hold, to precisely that degree does the scene of national belonging itself become newly, even dangerously volatile. For the national injunction to identify, intimately, with anonymous others cannot help but to run headlong into the new imperative, sharpened by the threat of medical and legal intervention, to keep all attachments to any person of the same sex scrubbed rigorously free of the contaminant of *desire.* Nation citizenship, at such a moment, itself begins to emerge as a spectacularly fraught undertaking: it takes shape as a state of relation balanced on a knife's edge between the compulsory and prohibited. This was one of Sedgwick's most expansively enabling insights in *Between Men,* the book so helped to spark the institutionalization of queer studies by insisting that same-sex intensities of passion and relation were not marginal to but at the defining center of vast swaths of Western culture. Under conditions of patriarchy, Sedgwick argued, intimacies between men are both compulsory and subject to an escalating erotic anxiousness, such that homophobia – the reprobation of certain kinds of same-sex attachment – would come to be an immensely powerful coercive tool. The nation, we might say, is still another scene of enforced identification.

Unsurprisingly, these tensions play out in sometimes dramatically different ways as they unfold across disparate moments and scenes. Sedgwick's work, for instance, begins to suggest to us how men and women might, in their same-sex attachments, find themselves subject to related but differently structured incitements and constraints, which would of course shift and re-form according to the pressures of new moments. For example, the removal of middle-class women from the rigors of public life, which one might imagine would serve to insulate them from such volatilities, in fact provided no such guard against the nation and its instigated scenes of homobonding. On the contrary, the ideology of "separate spheres" potentiates, far more than it chastens, an impassioned bondedness between women. Carroll Smith-Rosenberg famously anatomized "the female world of love and ritual" that obtained for middle-class white women in the latter half of the American nineteenth century – although, as a normative form, its influence could be felt beyond that one demographic – and subsequent scholars like G. J. Barker-Benfield, Kathryn Kent, Valerie Rohy, and Sharon Marcus have shown in rich detail how the compulsory isolation of virtually all attachments within the closed sphere of women could both sponsor and provide a protective carapace of respectability for a great range of passions between women. The sometimes sorrowing, but oftentimes flourishing "uncompanioned" women of Sarah Orne Jewett's fiction could serve as exemplary here, who take their place within an oeuvre fascinated above all by the passionate life that unfolds *away* from the marriage plot and its trajectories and determinations: by, in short, all that women's desire might make and be once unhooked from its territorialization by matrimony.

Still, the escalating volatility that surrounds the intimacies that make up modern nationality is never far off. And we find here, in the *expressions* of that volatility, some insight into the kinds of violence – projective, purgative – that have trailed in the wake of the nation-form. The matter here involves not only the starker forms of homophobia and misogyny to be found in the vicinity of nationalist projects generally, and especially in those in which, say, a putatively "revolutionary" or simply heightened bondedness among vanguard men plays a significant part. It is easy enough to read, for instance, a range of formations of the 1960s Left in just these terms: the more emphatically phobic rhetorical flights of Black Nationalism – especially when conceived as part of a remasculinization of men degraded by Jim Crow racism – can with little enough effort be read as purgative strategies, meant to shield the impassioned fraternity of latter-day revolutionaries from intimations of erotic errancy. And of course Black Nationalists were hardly the only revolutionaries anxious to draw sharp lines, via whatever languages of invidious distinction were to hand, between the radically homosocial and the degenerately homosexual, as any student of the Weathermen, or for that matter of the Lavender Menace, would be quick to remind us.

National Belonging, Racial Belonging

But racial violence itself – not only homophobia, and not only misogyny – unfolds on this terrain as well. As decades of scholarship have made clear, campaigns of racial violence, from eighteenth-century and nineteenth-century Indian killing to twentieth-century technologies of racial terror like lynching, work often as affiliative practices: ways for otherwise disparate populations, in danger perhaps of fraying along the seams of one or several material divides, to reforge a kind of unanimity and coherence under the banner of the nation and its imperatives. But this nationalist regeneration through violence, if it is affiliative in its effects, can be read too as intricately purgative, and not solely in relation to the racial Others against whom the fits of galvanizing violence are likely to be directed. Think, for instance, of Charles Brockden Brown's 1799 novel of the American frontier, *Edgar Huntly, or, Memoirs of a Sleep-Walker*, in which the eponymous hero becomes transformed, over the course of his bewildering adventures in the wilds of Pennsylvania, into a ruthless and extravagantly successful slaughterer of the indigenous populations there. Nothing cures what seems to be for young Edgar Huntly a desperate case of arrested quasi-adolescent development – Edgar is under-employed, unmarried, and exquisitely susceptible to the charismatic power of each of the many men who make up his notably homosocial milieu – as decisively as induction into the ranks of the new nation's improvised militia of Indian killers. Indeed, though those militarized sodalities do not them-selves want for homosocial intensities, the copious blood they shed can be seen as rechristening them in the name of a less anxious and altogether purer, because violent and nominally patriotic, attachment. Violence, we could say, reroutes the homophilic bondings of the nation-form *outward*, making racial terrorism a sanctifying outlet, an alibi of sorts, for the passionate attachment it simultaneously solidifies. In these ways, the racial violence associated with the nation-form and its maintenance finds itself coiled inextricably around the dynamic pressures – pressures of gendered and erotic propriety – gener-ated by a style of cohesion that demands, as a mark of citizenship itself, an openness to the ardor, the intimacy, the dangerous proximities, of national belonging. Indeed, it's with an eye to precisely these kinds of interweavings of sex and geopolitics that Jasbir Puar has encouraged us to think of certain deployments of queer identity and queer affiliation themselves as elements in larger strategies of neoliberal imperialism: to think, that is, of the ways queer politics can decline into what she calls "homonationalism," a making of a sometimes specious sort of unanimity that short-circuits other and more disruptive sorts of affiliation.

Whatever else can be said of the ideal of an intimate nationality, and its entanglement with sexual anxiety and prohibition no less than racial fan-tasy, we know this: that ideal, so resonant in Jefferson's initial draft of the Declaration of Independence, is in the contemporary world far, far from exhausted. Think only of the wholly typical *New York Times* headline marking the anniversary of the attacks on the World Trade Center: "A SINGLE GRIEF KNITS TOGETHER A VAST COUNTRY" (Murphy). Whatever the disori-entations of September 11, 2001 – and there were uncountably many – what issued from it, in these terms, was not a dislocation but a startling *continu-ance* of a venerable, centuries-deep style of nationalist imagining. This is not wholly surprising. We might think of it, indeed, as still another expression of the rise of "neoliberalism," by which critics mean to signify the supersession of political forms, among them "the nation," by the imperatives of global capital, which state institutions are called on more and more nakedly to protect and serve over any other ends. As the escalating global domination of neoliberalism sees to the erosion of the authority and efficacy of the nation-state in its traditional extension; as what political scientists call "trust" in the institutions of governance declines so precipitately as to mark what would seem to be a profound disidentification with the nation-form as embodied in the official practices of the state – as all these diminishments of the reign of the nation-as-institution unfold, a specifically affective sense of belonging and coherence enters the scene as, precisely, a way to *conserve* some semblance of national feeling for populations more and more inured to the charisma of the nation in its more concrete materialization, but desirous still of a scene in which national-like affiliations and self-elaborations might yet be possible. Call it a vestigial nationalism or antistate nationalism, but by whatever name it travels, it is plainly no less fervent, in its contemporary expressions, for the disidentifications that propel it. United, not by untrusted governments, nor cheerfully disparaged institutions, disparate populations cohere into sodality, here in the post-9/11 world, around nothing so much as the grief, the mutual susceptibility to wounding, or loss, or horror in the face of these, that traverses them equally. Mark Seltzer describes this dynamic under the rubric of "wound culture," by which he means to designate those sodalities that gather around spectacles of shattered intimacies, loss of life, mass-mediated tragedy – be it in the form of the cataclysm of September 11, 2001, or the death of Princess Diana, or the vast horror of Japanese tsunamis, or any other suitably massive and media-dispersed scene of woundedness and loss. This is the grammar of much of contemporary national belonging, and the emergence of the age of "terror" has in fact done less to alter than to ratify it, to secure its logics only the more deeply.

Wounding and the Nation

In these ways and others, sex – sexual meaning, its incitements, and its deployments – remains of undiminished importance to the nationalist imagination, even in an era so marked by transnationality, techno-planetary interconnectivity, and the specter of terror. As we have seen, sex has done and yet can do work as an engine for outreaching attachments, filling the space of national feeling with the heat and intensity of desire. But sex is no less useful, too, as a catalyst of a different sort. For what sex can catalyze also, and with singular potency, is, in a word, *trauma*: the evocation of a scene of shock or scandal or loss. Sex, and particularly nonnormative sex or its shadowy prospect, remains a splendidly adaptive vehicle for the conjuring of the sorts of reactive, recoiling horrors that are the mainstay of affective nationalities in their current mood and form. One way to read the increasing prominence of stories of child sexual abuse, for instance, pushes hard against the grain of progress narratives that see in a peaked national sensitivity to such matters only a dawning preventative enlightenment with respect to the grave sexual perils facing young people, and a slow emergence from benighted ignorance or culture-wide self-deceit. The sensational marketability of such stories may also be, rather less happily, a function of the outsized culture-wide hunger for narratives of, precisely, shock and dismay, in the shared and uniform response to which an otherwise sprawlingly heterodox population can feel itself horrified into sodality.

Inasmuch as national belonging is routed through affect, then, and inasmuch as *traumatized* affect works increasingly as a ground note for affiliative fantasies of coherence, sex – that most reliable of traumas – is likely to remain an indispensable element in the grammars of nationalism. Here, too, the note is struck perhaps best by none other than Whitman himself, who in 1889 was speaking not only as a queer radical, but very much as the ardent nationalist he was, when he declared, "Sex sex sex: sex is the root of it all."

Notes

1. All quotations from the *Declaration* are taken from Jefferson's account of it in his *Autobiography*, as reprinted in *Writings* 19–24.

Works Cited

Ahmed, Sara. *The Cultural Politics of Emotion.* New York: Routledge, 2004. Print.

Anderson, Benedict. *Imagined Communities: Reflections on the Origin and Spread of Nationalism.* Revised ed. New York: Verso, 1991. Print.

Barker-Benfield, G. J. *The Horrors of the Half-Known Life: Male Attitudes Toward Women and Sexuality in Nineteenth-Century America.* New York: Harper, 1977. Print.

Berlant, Lauren. *The Female Complaint: The Unfinished Business of Sentimentality in American Culture.* Durham: Duke UP, 2008. Print.

The Queen of America Goes to Washington City: Essays on Sex and Citizenship. Durham: Duke UP, 1997. Print.

Berlant, Lauren, and Elizabeth Freeman. "Queer Nationality." *boundary 2* 19.1 (1992): 149–80. Print.

Brown, Wendy. *States of Injury: Power and Freedom in Late Modernity.* Princeton: Princeton UP, 1995. Print.

Castiglia, Christopher. *Interior States: Institutional Consciousness and the Inner Life of Democracy in the Antebellum United States*. Durham: Duke UP, 2008. Print.

Coviello, Peter. *Intimacy in America: Dreams of Affiliation in Antebellum Literature*. Minneapolis: U Minnesota P, 2005. Print.

"The Sexual Child, or, This American Life." *Raritan* 27.4 (2008): 134–57. Print.

Crain, Caleb. *American Sympathy: Men, Friendship, and Literature in the New Nation*. New Haven: Yale UP, 2001. Print.

Cvetkovich, Ann. *Mixed Feelings: Feminism, Mass Culture, and Victorian Sensationalism*. New Brunswick: Rutgers UP, 1992. Print.

Hendler, Glenn. *Public Sentiments: Structures of Feeling in Nineteenth-Century American Literature*. Chapel Hill: U of North Carolina P, 2001. Print.

Horsman, Reginald. *Race and Manifest Destiny: The Origins of Racial Anglo-Saxonism*. Cambridge: Harvard UP, 1981. Print.

Jefferson, Thomas. *Writings*. Ed. Merrill D. Patterson. New York: Library of America, 1984. Print.

Jewett, Sarah Orne. *The Country of the Pointed Firs*. Ed. Alison Easton. New York: Penguin, 1995. Print.

Kent, Kathryn R. *Making Girls Into Women: American Women's Writing and the Rise of Lesbian Identity*. Durham: Duke UP, 2003. Print.

Looby, Christopher. *Voicing America: Language, Literary Form, and the Origins of the United States*. Chicago: U of Chicago P, 1996. Print.

Luciano, Dana. *Arranging Grief: Sacred Time and the Body in Nineteenth-Century America*. New York: New York UP, 2007. Print.

Marcus, Sharon. *Between Women: Friendship, Desire, and Marriage in Victorian England*. Princeton: Princeton UP, 2007. Print.

Marx, Karl. *Selected Writings*. Ed. Lawrence Simon. New York: Hackett, 1994. Print.

Murphy, Dean E. "A Single Grief Knits Together a Vast Country." *New York Times* 12 Sept. 2002: 1. Print.

Nelson, Dana. *National Manhood: Capitalist Citizenship and the Imagined Fraternity of White Men*. Durham: Duke UP, 1998. Print.

Puar, Jasbir. *Terrorist Assemblages: Homonationalism in Queer Times*. Durham: Duke UP, 2007. Print.

Rohy, Valerie. *Impossible Women: Lesbian Figures and American Fiction*. Ithaca: Cornell UP, 1990. Print.

Sedgwick, Eve Kosofsky. *Between Men: English Literature and Male Homosocial Desire*. New York: Columbia UP, 1985. Print.

Epistemology of the Closet. Berkeley: U California P, 1990. Print.

Seltzer, Mark. *Serial Killers: Life and Death in America's Wound Culture*. New York: Routledge, 1998. Print.

Smith-Rosenberg, Carroll. *Disorderly Conduct: Visions of Gender in Victorian America*. New York: Oxford UP, 1986. Print.

Stern, Julia. *The Plight of Feeling: Sympathy and Dissent in the Early American Novel*. Chicago: U of Chicago P, 1997. Print.

Whitman, Walt. *Leaves of Grass, 1860: The 150th Anniversary Facsimile Edition*. Ed. Jason Stacy. Iowa City: U of Iowa P, 2009. Print.

Poetry and Prose. Ed. Justin Kaplan. New York: Library of America, 1996. Print.

14

Bildung and Sexuality in the Age of Goethe

ROBERT TOBIN

During the lifetime of Johann Wolfgang von Goethe (1749–1832), German-speaking central Europe produced one of the great flowerings of culture in human history. The era's literature, music, philosophy, art, and architecture continue to provoke and entrance. It is less well known that this epoch also conceived sexuality distinctively, not so much out of the legal and medical discourses that would reconfigure sexuality at the end of the nineteenth century, but rather out of anthropological arguments related to race and *Bildung*. The period's neoclassicism, its cult of friendship, and its acknowledgment (or appropriation) of female desire all demonstrate that the age's conception of sexuality must be understood on its own terms to reach a more accurate comprehension of its literary texts.

Despite its centrality to the intellectual and cultural history of the West, the Age of Goethe does not typically figure prominently in lesbian and gay histories. The vocabulary of "homosexuality" did not yet exist – the world had to wait until 1869 for the first appearance in print of a word that combined the Greek prefix *homo* with the Latin root *sexus* and described a person with a sexual orientation toward a member of their own sex. The words *Homosexualität* and *homosexual* (homosexuality and homosexual) debuted in German in Karl Maria Kertbeny's essays arguing for the decriminalization of sodomy in the German penal code (Tobin, "Kertbeny's"). Because the vocabulary was different, the language of erotic love and desire that existed in the late eighteenth and early nineteenth centuries is not immediately legible to the twenty-first-century reader.

Nor does German-speaking central Europe provide evidence of sexual activities between members of the same sex that one finds in other parts of Europe in the eighteenth century. The English "molly houses" – bars where men could meet other men interested in sexual encounters and find a sense of community – seem to have been relatively uncommon in the German-speaking world. One document suggests, however, that there was a similar phenomenon in Berlin: *Briefe über die Galanterien von Berlin auf einer Reise gesammelt von einem österreichischen Offizier* (*Letters on the Gallantries of Berlin, Collected on a Trip by an Austrian Officer*), published in 1782 and attributed to Johann Friedel. In two of the letters, the author asserts that in Berlin there were large groups of men (*warme Brüder* or "warm brothers") who were interested in sex with other men. They formed a recognizable "society of the warm," with their own sense of fashion, their own history, and their own meeting places (Friedel 141–46). Forensic physician Johann Valentin Müller took the account at face value in the chapter on sodomy in his *Entwurf der gerichtlichen Arzneywissenschaft nach juristischen und medicinischen Grundsätzen für Geistliche, Rechtsgelehrte und Aertze* (*Proposal for a Forensic Medical Science according to Legal and Medical Principles for Ministers, Lawyers and Physicians*), citing the *Briefe* when he reported that sodomy was quite common in large cities. In a reference to prostitution, he adds, "in certain public houses, handsome youths suffer the same fate as beautiful women" (1: 133–34).

The accusation that eighteenth-century Berlin was home to sexual affection between men (and the sale thereof) presumably gained traction because of the rumors surrounding Friedrich II, known in English as Frederick the Great. The Prussian king's lifestyle had much more to do with masculinity, militarism, and discipline than the extravagant privilege and principled amorality associated with the libertine, the eighteenth-century aristocratic type whose appetite for sexual transgression often led to sexual activity between members of the same sex. Frederick's life in almost exclusively male surroundings helped foster these stories, as did the king's surprisingly explicit yet casual discussion of historical and literary examples of male-male sexual love – from Plato's account of the pedagogical Eros between Socrates and Alcibiades in the *Symposium* to Virgil's story of the tragic manly love between soldiers Nisus and Euryalus in the *Aeneid* to John's depiction of the tender relationship between Jesus and his beloved disciple in the New Testament. Anton Friedrich Büsching's biography, *Character Friedrichs des Zweytens* (*The Character of Frederick the Second*) reported that the monarch had "a distaste for women and avoided their company," but enjoyed "consorting with men," just as "Socrates loved being with Alcibiades" (22). Frederick's well-known physician Johann Georg Zimmermann defended the monarch in a chapter with the perhaps self-defeating title "On Frederick's Alleged Greek Taste in Love" (85–86).

Penal Histories

As part of these discussions about sexual activities between members of the same sex, the legal system focused on the status of sodomy, responding to secularist theories from the European Enlightenment about the relationship between church and state. In his *Dei delitti et delle penne* (*On Crime and Punishment*) of 1764, Cesare Beccaria had classified sodomy, along with adultery, as a "crime of difficult proof," morally offensive perhaps, but not a legitimate target of legal prosecution by the state. Rather than outright prohibition, Beccaria felt that the government would be wiser to work on policies that lessened the incidence of such offenses. Following the Revolution of 1789, the French penal code of 1791 made no mention of sodomy. Napoleon's penal code of 1810 maintained the decriminalization of all private, consensual, noncommercial sexual acts between adults. As Napoleon conquered much of Europe, he brought with him his secularist legal theories, which were often incorporated into local jurisprudence. Bavaria followed the Napoleonic lead with Paul Anselm Feuerbach's legal reforms of 1813, which insisted that the state had no role enforcing moral strictures affecting only the potential salvation of the individual. For this reason, Bavaria had no sodomy laws at all until the unification of Germany under Prussia in 1871.

The rest of the German-speaking world was considerably more cautious in reforming the sodomy laws, however. In his influential commentary, *Mosaisches Recht* (*Mosaic Law* [first published in 1770–71]), Johann David Michaelis defended the death penalty for sodomy, relying on biopolitical justifications concerning depopulation. He predicted that once a people fell victim to this vice, "the foundation of its future weakness has been laid and after a hundred years it will no longer be a powerful populous nation" (5: 216). Michaelis argued that some cultures were more predisposed to sodomy (such as those in the Mediterranean and the Orient) and therefore needed stricter penalties, which would allow for penalties less severe than the death penalty in countries less predisposed to sodomy (such as those in northern Europe). Prussia ultimately sided with Michaelis and maintained the criminalization of sodomy, while eliminating the death penalty for the act in 1794 (Baumann 37). In the Habsburg Empire, the Enlightened Joseph II had eliminated the death penalty for sodomy in 1787, as part of a general abolition of the death penalty. In a nod to Beccaria, Joseph II also excluded sodomy from the category of "criminal" offenses, and instead listed it as "political," meaning that it was best addressed by proactive "policies" aimed at decreasing its occurrence, rather than punishment (Wachenfeld 24–25). Nonetheless, throughout the Age of Goethe, penalties for sodomy were much more severe in most of the German-speaking world than they were in countries such as France and Italy.

Müller's forensic medical manual of 1796 underscores the increasing importance of medicine in these legal and moral discussions. In contrast to the later nineteenth century, however, eighteenth-century medical sources generally discussed sodomy in terms of its medical *effects* rather than its constitutional *causes*. Müller was typical in framing sodomy as a product of onanism, which he believed was "the primary source from which impure pederasty arises" (1: 141). The analyses did not attempt to determine the medical explanations for a predisposition to onanism and sodomy, but rather to emphasize the deleterious medical consequences of indulging in such sexual vices.

Naturalist and Racial Taxonomies

While the Age of Goethe did not have a vocabulary of "homosexuality," "bisexuality," or "heterosexuality," it did possess an emerging rhetoric of "sexuality." Carl von Linné's taxonomical work focused heavily on the sexual characteristics of plants, resulting in popularizations of his analysis with titles such as *A Dissertation on the Sexes of Plants* (1780) and *Systeme sexuel de végétaux* (1798). These theories provided the basis for an analysis of the "sexuality" of plants, which was still hotly contested in 1820, when August Wilhelm Henschel published *Von der Sexualität der Pflanzen* (*On the Sexuality of Plants*), which attracted the attention of none other than Goethe. In an essay from the same year, Goethe responds to Henschel's new book and discusses his own initial acceptance and subsequent rejection of "das Dogma der Sexualität" ("the dogma of sexuality") (II.6: 187). The "sexuality" of plants referred to their quality of having a sex, being male or female; the meaning remained constant when the word was applied to human beings. In an 1835 article, gynecologist Joseph Hermann Schmidt used *Sexualität* to describe the masculinity or femininity of the individual, insisting that the "concept of sexuality is no longer derived exclusively from the sexual organs, but rather from the entire organism" (166). Nonetheless, because the term was being used to define the qualities of the sexes within the context of discussions about the reproduction of the species, it was not unrelated to questions of sexual orientation – it merely presumed a heterosexual orientation as one of the characteristics of biological sex.

Linné's taxonomy of plants, which relied so heavily on an analysis of their "sexuality," was just one part of his fundamental categorization of the natural world. In the later editions of his *Systemae naturae*, Linné proposed four subcategories of the species *Homo sapiens*: *Americanus*, *Africanus*, *Asiatus*, and *Europeanus*. Following in Linné's footsteps, anthropologists at the University of Göttingen – Christoph Meiners and Johann Friedrich Blumenbach – continued to classify humanity according to race. Like Linné's botanical categories, these speculations on racial difference were intertwined with and helped configure the emerging notion of "sexuality."

Highly decorated professor Christoph Meiners is notorious today for his extensive publications on racial difference, such as his 1785 *Grundriss der Geschichte der Menschheit (Outline of the History of Humanity)* and the four-volume treatise of 1810, *Untersuchungen über die Verschiedenheiten der Menschennaturen (die verschiedenen Menschenarten) (Investigations into the Differences in Human Natures [the Different Human Types])*. As the titles of his books indicate, he believed that the different races had fundamentally different characteristics. A "polygenist" who argued that the races had different origins, he was a seminal figure in the development of European biological racism (Zantop).

In 1775, Meiners also wrote an essay on the male-male love of the Greeks. In "Betrachtungen über die Männerliebe der Griechen, nebst einem Auszug aus dem Gemahle des Plato" ("Observations on the Male Love of the Greeks, along with Excerpts from the Symposium of Plato"), he insisted that the male-male love of the Greeks was originally an outgrowth of the entirely laudable heroic friendships of earliest civilization. He added that it developed and flourished because of the educational system of the Greeks, the gymnasia, where the minds, souls, and bodies of the young men were cultivated in a way that made them nearly irresistible; particularly the practice of nude athletics put men at risk for this behavior. He also noted that the extreme segregation of women from men, particularly in education, was a contributing factor.

Typically scholars do not connect Meiners's work on same-sex desire with his theories on race, but in fact the two are closely related, for the anthropologist embedded his study of male-male desire in a discussion of specific racial differences. He introduced his analysis of Greek male-male love with the claim that the differences between types of men were more significant than the similarities, concluding that "a Newton or a Leibniz is far more distant from a New Caledonian or a Patagonian than the latter are from the animals most closely related to our species" (1: 61). Meiners's explanation of same-sex desire, while it continued to make room for environmental explanations, was thus actually evidence for racial difference. It was not the case that any man who worked with young naked men would begin to desire them sexually, but rather that specific races of people, such as the Greeks, might have an inborn tendency toward sexually desiring members of their own sex. (It is worth recalling here that Michaelis had also presumed that certain races were more inclined to sodomy than others.) From the initial appearance of either category, race and sexuality were intricately intertwined.

Sexuality's *Bildung*

Johann Friedrich Blumenbach, Meiners's colleague and rival at Göttingen, also worked on questions of race, theorizing the categories of "Caucasian," "Ethiopian," "Mongolian," "American," and "Malayan" in works such as *Über die natürlichen Verschiedenheiten im Menschengeschlecht* (*On the Natural Differences in the Human Race*), which appeared in 1798 (Zammito 44–45). Although Blumenbach is responsible for the widespread use of the racial category "Caucasian," he actually opposed Meiners's racist polygenist arguments. Blumenbach's influence on the notion of sexuality is more oblique than Meiners's, but ultimately even more significant (Greif 135). As part of his worldview, Blumenbach developed the notion of the *Bildungstrieb* (developmental drive). In *Über den Bildungstrieb* (*On the Developmental Drive*), which first appeared as a journal article in 1780, Blumenbach argued that "there exists in all living creatures, from men to maggots, and from cedar trees to mold, a particular, inborn, lifelong active drive" (249). This drive, which Blumenbach calls the "Bildungstrieb," ensures that all organisms become that which they are destined to be, with all the specificity (in terms of species or race, for instance) of that being (Richards 18).

The concept of the *Bildungstrieb* relies on the notion of *Bildung*, which is famously difficult to translate. The term, translated as "culture," "cultivation," "education," and "development," with resonances of image (as in *Bild*) and creator (as in *Bildner*), emerged in the Age of Goethe and has become central in the German-speaking world. Johann Gottfried Herder applied it to historical, cultural, and social issues. For Herder's admirer Goethe, the term came to refer also to the personal, psychological development of an individual. The concept of *Bildung*, thus, has two strands: Blumenbach's more biological notion of the development that is predestined by the innate characteristics of a species and Herder's and Goethe's more cultural and social concept of the development that takes place because of one's education, cultivation, and environment. While eighteenth- and early nineteenth-century thinkers were certainly interested in the question of nature versus nurture, the theory of *Bildung* attempted to move beyond those discussions. For the theorist of *Bildung*, the question is not whether a person developed a quality because they were born with that quality or because they learned it. Instead, it is a matter of how one can cultivate someone or something to become that which it was always supposed to be, how one can match the innate qualities with the environmental conditions.

Bildung had immediate application in the emerging analysis of sexuality. Sexuality and *Bildung* come together in Friedrich Wilhelm Basileus Ramdohr's three-volume treatise of 1798, *Venus Urania: Ueber die Natur der Liebe, über ihre Veredlung und Verschönerung (Venus Urania: On the Nature of Love, Its Edification and Beautification)*, which contains lengthy and significant discussions of same-sex desire. (Ramdohr draws his title from the "heavenly" Venus, whom Plato in the *Symposium* associates with male-male love.) In his explanation for the phenomenon of same-sex love, Ramdohr explicitly cites Blumenbach's notion of *Bildung*, describing sexuality as "the developmental force [*Bildungskraft*] of our vegetable organism" (1: 153). His theory that sexual pleasure belongs to the human being's "vegetable" nature is a legacy of Linné's initial discussion of sexuality in the realm of plants.

Heinrich Hössli cements the relationship between sexuality and *Bildung* in his two-volume apology for male-male love, *Eros: Die Männerliebe der Griechen, ihre Beziehung zur Geschichte, Erziehung, Literatur und Gesetzgebung aller Zeiten (Eros: The Male Love of the Greeks, Its Relationship to History, Pedagogy, Literature and Jurisprudence of all Times)*, which was published in 1836 and 1838 in Switzerland. In *Eros*, Hössli clearly relies on Blumenbach's notion of *Bildung* when he declares that "The whole man is in the seed, in the germ, in the embryo" (2: 201). He provides a nice example of the ideals of *Bildung* to harmonize innate characteristics and cultural upbringing when he declares that "we cannot bring anything into it [the seed, germ, embryo], but can only let that which is within him develop and at least not eliminate it, even if much that is in him is not allowed to flourish and is strangled or crippled" (2: 202). Hössli's vision of discovering one's own sexuality and letting it unfold in a way that is harmonious with society clearly draws on the tradition of *Bildung* coming from the scientific tradition of Blumenbach as well as the humanistic tradition of Herder, Schiller, and Goethe (Krah 186).

Sexuality and the Bildungsroman

The Age of Goethe's focus on *Bildung* produced a new genre, identified by Karl Morgenstern as the *Bildungsroman* in his 1819 lecture "Über das Wesen des Bildungsromans" ("On the Essence of the Bildungsroman"), which was published in 1820. The bildungsroman is classically the story of the development or acculturation of (typically) a young man who discovers who he is and how he fits into society. Because the novel has traditionally focused on love and Eros, the bildungsroman made the connection between *Bildung* and sexuality explicit: the protagonist's love life documented his identity and his relationship to society. Although the typical bildungsroman had a relatively heteronormative telos, the presuppositions of *Bildung* implied that every individual had a distinct destiny. Moreover, quite frequently the protagonists of the bildungsroman pass through deep emotional and even erotic relationships with other men.

One of the great bildungsromane of the era that has not generally been read in terms of gay literary history is Wilhelm Heinse's *Ardinghello und die glückseligen Inseln* (*Ardinghello and the Blessed Isles*). This is a shame because the novel brings together, in a paradigmatic way, *Bildung*, sexuality, and radical assertions of individual sexual and political freedom. Published in 1787, *Ardinghello* tells the story of a band of artists and their lovers who travel through Renaissance Italy as they discourse on art, love, and the meaning of life, until they form a utopian community on an island in the Mediterranean. Although not well known in the English-speaking world, the novel was tremendously important for German artists and intellectuals from Herder and Goethe to Richard Wagner and Friedrich Nietzsche.

Clearly conceptualizing *Bildung* in Blumenbach's biological sense, Heinse connects it to the sexual drive in a programmatic sentence: "The developmental power lies in the essence, and is the striving for pleasure" ("Die bildende Kraft liegt in dem Wesen und ist ein Streben nach Genuß"; *Ardinghello* 304). It is worth looking at the German here a little more closely: The *bildende Kraft* (a force that develops or constructs something) is a variant of the *Bildungskraft* (the developmental force) that Ramdohr gets from Blumenbach; its presence in the *Wesen* (essence or being) suggests that it is an essential part of identity; connecting it to the *Streben nach Genuß* (striving for pleasure) links that *Bildung* to a pleasurable experience, which in the context of the novel is clearly sexual. (*Streben* or striving is also the most significant characteristic of Goethe's Faust, associating *Bildung* and sexuality with the human spirit embodied in the Faustian.) Heinse's vision of *Bildung* also replicates the anthropological discussions of race that accompany the theorization of sexuality and the *Bildungstrieb*. Heinse notes in *Ardinghello* that each culture takes pleasure in the specific sounds of its own language: "In general the pleasurability of one sound versus another cannot be determined; it depends on each word itself, its use, and the ear of the people. What sounds strange to us in other nations doesn't sound strange to them" (35). The novel is full of observations about cultural-based differences in aesthetics and taste that are easily applicable to different sexual practices too. So, just as the *bildende Kraft* might lead one *Volk* to find its pleasure in one sound over another, it might also lead that nation to find its pleasure in different forms of sexuality.

Ardinghello provides a useful introduction to a number of the distinctive features of the representation and discussion of sexuality in the writing of the Age of Goethe. To begin with, Heinse relies heavily on ancient Greek and Roman texts to discuss same-sex desire. Anticipating his remarks in *Ardinghello* about the specific pleasure that each culture takes in the sounds of its own language, Heinse writes in a foreword to his 1773 translation of Petronius's *Satyricon*: "Who would prove to the Greeks that the pleasure they take with beautiful Ganymedes should not have delighted them more than the pleasures with their women? Every person carries the measure of his own pleasure in his own breast" ("Vorwort" 20). The argument that everyone has to find his or her own pleasure is central to the notion of *Bildung*. In *Ardinghello*, Heinse continues to sprinkle his prose with many additional signifiers of Greek same-sex love, including a reference to Venus Urania (the same form of Venus under which Ramdohr discusses same-sex love), the beneficial cultural effects of nude exercise in the gymnasia (blamed by Meiners for inciting same-sex desire), Plato's *Symposium* (which seemingly regards sexual love between men as exemplary), and Aristophanes's speech from the *Symposium* about the origins of love (in which Aristophanes memorably divides humanity up into three categories: men looking for men, women looking for women, and men and women looking for each other). Any literate person interested in same-sex desire could find numerous allusions in *Ardinghello*'s classical references.

Classical Influences

Many authors of the Age of Goethe resemble Heinse in their tendency to rely on the classical Greek and Roman canon to discuss attraction between members of the same sex (Tobin, *Warm* 30–34). The primary theoretical discussions of same-sex desire, from Meiners to Ramdohr to Hössli, depend on classical sources for most of their evidence and examples. Christoph Martin Wieland, author of what is often considered the first bildungsroman, *Agathon* (1766), was accused of introducing "Greek love" to German readers in his 1765 poem "Juno and Ganymede," which humorously details the rivalry between the matronly goddess and the young shepherd for Jove's attention (Derks 234). Wieland's *Agathon* documents explicit male-male sex, ranging from the morally objectionable (a priest's efforts at abusing the young hero) to the comical (a sailor's passion for a boy who is actually a girl in disguise) to the laudable (Socrates's love of Alcibiades). Like many authors of the time, Goethe uses the Ganymede myth to discuss masculine desire for another man in his poem "Ganymed" of 1774. He does so with great originality, focusing – perhaps for the first time in the literary history of the West – seriously and sympathetically on the desire of the youthful shepherd, the beloved, rather than on that of Zeus, the lover (Wilson 68–69).

Heinse's friend Friedrich Hölderlin published "Sokrates und Alkibiades" ("Socrates and Alcibiades") in Schiller's *Musenalmanach* in 1797. The poem demonstrates the openness with which a literary artist could discuss male-male erotic desire within a Greek context:

"Warum huldigest du, heiliger Sokrates,
Diesem Jünglinge stets? kennest du Größers nicht?
Warum siehet mit Liebe,
Wie auf Götter, dein Aug' auf ihn?"
Wer das Tiefste gedacht, liebt das Lebendigste,
Hohe Jugend versteht, wer in die Welt geblickt,
Und es neigen die Weisen
Oft am Ende zu Schönem sich.   (Hölderlin 1: 39)
"Why do you worship, holy Socrates,
This young man so? Don't you know anything greater?
Why does your eye look with love
On him, as on the gods?"
Whoever has thought the deepest, loves the liveliest.
He who has seen the world understands high youth
And often the wise bow
In the end to the beautiful.

Interpreters of the poem start with the assumption that the initial questions in the first strophe come from one of Alcibiades's potentially jealous fellow students (Langewand 71–72). Whether this is the case or not, it is clear that the male-male love situation takes place in a pedagogical situation between people of different ages and status in society. Educated Germans were highly aware of the directional nature of Greek love, the distinction between the lover and the beloved. Friedrich Schiller was perhaps particularly interested in publishing Hölderlin's poetic representation of this love, because he himself was working on a play with a similar dynamic, called *Die Malteser* (*The Maltese*). Although Schiller's play centers on medieval Knights Templar, Schiller conceives of their love along Greek lines: "But only one is the lover, the active one; the younger and beloved behaves passively. The lover, however, acts with a blind passion, forgetting the whole world, and verges on the criminal" (3: 173). Despite his somewhat dismissive remarks about Ramdohr (Hull 234), it seems likely that Schiller got many of his ideas about same-sex love from *Venus Urania*.

Later nineteenth- and twentieth-century theorists of homosexuality would find this directional aspect of Greek love entirely foreign, to the point that some would argue that same-sex love among the ancient Greeks had no relation to modern homosexuality. The title of David Halperin's *One Hundred Years of Homosexuality*, for instance, implies that "homosexuality" has only existed since the late nineteenth century and would be an inaccurate signifier of relations between men in ancient Greece. For the Age of Goethe, however, this division between lover and beloved seems to have made intuitive sense. The youthfulness of the beloveds was not particularly surprising to the era's thinkers, who did not recognize the category of "adolescence" (not developed as a technical term until 1904) as an age when people were postpubescent but not ready for sexual activity. Given that various German authors from the time period were in love with very young women (Novalis met Sophie von Kuhn, for instance, when she was twelve and started courting her when she was thirteen), there was not a sense of great surprise about the age difference between lovers and beloveds in the ancient Greek accounts. To take an example from Goethe's *Wilhelm Meisters Lehrjahre* (*Wilhelm Meister's Apprenticeship* [1796–97]), Wilhelm finds it entirely credible that Mignon was the person who crept into his bedroom and spent the night with him after a particularly drunken party. Not only is Mignon described as in her early teens, her sex (or to speak in the language of the late eighteenth century, her "sexuality") is so unclear that neither the characters nor the narrator know initially whether she is a boy or a girl. Wilhelm considers himself entirely capable of having had sex with a youth, and one who might even be male at that. Goethe does not seem to feel any need to explain this as significant, which is itself significant.

Friends and Admirers

A second distinctive aspect of the Age of Goethe's discussion of sexuality is its fervent and sensual depiction of intense physical and emotional friendships between men. More so than England, France, or Holland, German culture was known for its glorification of intense Romantic friendship. Heinse's early supporters, sentimental poet Johann Wilhelm Ludwig Gleim and *Sturm und Drang* author Johann Georg Jacobi, were known for their declarations of love for each other in which they went so far as to announce that they wanted to marry each other (Dietrich 30–33). In *Ardinghello*, Heinse embraces this cult of friendship wholeheartedly. In the opening scene, a handsome stranger rescues the narrator from the waters of Venice. His wet clothes revealingly cling to his tall, well-built, youthful body, his eyes sparkle with light and fire, and a lovely beard surrounds his spell-binding lips. The two embrace passionately, and the narrator's bosom heaves as an ember catches fire within (*Ardinghello* 1). As David Gramling argues, "the erotic voltage of Benedikt and Arnold's first meeting" homoerotically structures the entire novel (30).

In the course of their development, Goethe's male characters also indulge in intense sensual admiration of each other's bodies. Goethe's international best seller of 1772, *Die Leiden des jungen Werthers* (*The Sufferings of Young Werther*), centers on Werther's unhappy love for Lotte, but the epistolary novel's virtually unknown prequel, published in 1796, *Briefe aus der Schweiz* (*Letters from Switzerland*), details the homoerotic experiences of Werther's youth. As in *Ardinghello*, Werther comes to appreciate the beauty of other men while bathing in the nude: "how splendidly my young friend is built! How proportionate are all of his parts! What a fullness of form, what a splendor of youth, what a profit for me to have enriched my imagination with this perfect example of human nature!" (1.19: 213). Goethe similarly waits several decades to reveal a foundational homoerotic episode in the life of his hero Wilhelm Meister. The 1832 sequel to the *Lehrjahre*, *Wilhelm Meisters Wanderjahre* (*Wilhelm Meisters Journeyman Years*), contains a vivid memory from Wilhelm's childhood (related in a letter from Wilhelm to his wife, Natalie), when he fell in love with the fisherman's son. Once again, Cupid strikes when the two youths are bathing: "so beautiful was the human form, of which I never had a concept. He seemed to observe me with the same attentiveness. Quickly clothed, we stood, still undisguised in front of each other, our spirits were attracted to each other, and we swore an eternal friendship amidst the most fiery kisses" (1.25.1: 44). Arguably, Wilhelm's youthful experiences with same-sex love prepare him for the queer family he collects, including the androgynous youth Mignon, the hyperfeminine Philine, and the masculine Therese, as well as the more conventionally femininely ideal Natalie.

In contrast to the triumphant male appreciation of masculine beauty in Heinse's and Goethe's works, Karl Philipp Moritz shows the heartbreaking side of male friendship. The eponymous hero of Karl Philipp Moritz's *Anton Reiser* (1785–90) moves through a series of intense male-male relationships that he calls love and that provoke severe melancholy when they falter. The emotions described in the novel closely resemble the case of male-male love about which Moritz's *Magazin zur Erfahrungsseelenkunde* (*Magazine on Experiential Psychology*) reported very sensitively in 1791; this report is often considered to be among the first efforts to conduct a scientific scholarly investigation of the phenomenon (Moritz 8.2: 6–10). Not only does Moritz show the tragedy of lost male-male friendship, he also describes the failure of *Bildung*. In many ways, *Anton Reiser* is an "anti-bildungsroman" because of the ultimate shattering of its protagonist's hopes, a shattering that could be related to his inability to find the right kind of nurturing for his male-loving nature.

Literary historians typically warn against reading "too much" into these accounts of intense friendship between members of the same sex. As Eve Kosofsky Sedgwick sarcastically observes, it is frequently assumed that "passionate language of same-sex attraction was extremely common during whatever period is under assumption – and therefore must have been completely meaningless" (52). While it would of course be inaccurate to read a modern homosexual or gay identity into these descriptions of eighteenth-century friendship, it is equally false to understand them as heterosexual, as Simon Richter notes: "Against their better knowledge, scholars of German culture have for the last 200 years falsified literary history by assuming, consciously or not, that the complex period known as the Age of Goethe was fundamentally structured along heterosexual lines" (33). In the absence of a clear binary distinction between heterosexuality and homosexuality, one can only say that these declarations of love between men are "not gay" if one also says that they are "not straight." As the Age of Goethe progressed, this blurring of the boundaries became more and more of a problem for society. In fact, precisely those thinkers who, like Ramdohr and Hössli, were most interested in creating a clear-cut identity for men-loving men worked on establishing a distinction between friendship and same-sex love (Tobin, "Love").

In diary entries written in 1816 and 1818 (although not published until the 1890s), poet August von Platen indicates that he sees himself as having a man-loving identity: "But what should make me tremble the most is that my inclinations are far more directed toward my own sex than toward the female sex. Can I change what is not my doing?" (102). Arguably a homosexual *avant la lettre*, Platen struggles with language, attempting to recycle the vocabulary of friendship to articulate his more specific feelings: "Another plan that preoccupies me is writing an extensive treatment of friendship among men, a subject about which I have read much and have also personally experienced and contemplated" (90). By the end of the Age of Goethe, friendship had lost much of its ambiguous quality – but for most of this time period, it included elements of the sensual and the erotic.

Women in the Bildungsroman

Ardinghello couples its depictions of hot and heavy male bonding with accounts of independent women who assert their own female desire, most notably the wealthy and beautiful Fiordimona, who refuses to bind herself with "the indissoluble yoke of marriage." She chooses to remain "unmarried, master of herself, and have her pick of the brave men, for as long as she wants. She lives in society with the wisest, most beautiful, wittiest, most profound people; raises her children with joy, as voluntary children of love" (*Ardinghello* 224). Heinse is not alone in describing strong female desire in the bildungsroman. In Wieland's *Agathon*, the hetaera Danae is generally portrayed quite positively, although she ultimately repents for her sexual life. Goethe's *Wilhelm Meister* is replete with female figures who are capable of powerful desires, from Mignon, who virtually embodies yearning, to Philine, who sees no reason to hide her sexual activities. Even the seemingly austere "Schöne Seele" refers frequently to the men she has loved; in her "Confessions," the "Schöne Seele" describes vividly her discovery of her own naked beauty after one of her lovers has bled all over her: "I may not conceal that, as the blood was being washed from my body, I coincidentally noticed in the mirror for the first time that I could also consider myself beautiful without covering" (1.22: 275). Subsequent Romantic authors are even more committed to depicting strong female desire, in texts such as Friedrich Schlegel's 1797 novel *Lucinde* and Karl Gutzkow's 1835 novel *Wally*.

If there is relatively little documentation of male-male sexual subcultures in the German-speaking world in the Age of Goethe, there is even less regarding female-female ones. Catharina Margarethe Linck was executed in 1721 for impersonating a man and marrying a woman (Faderman 51). In general, the surviving primary evidence of gender insubordination had to do with crossdressing (Krimmer). While this crossdressing did not always overlap with sexual desires for other women, Linck's case shows that at times it did. In his legal studies, Michaelis reports on "lesbian venery" as a consequence of male-male sodomy, which deprives women of men (5: 215). Medical authorities were surprisingly graphic in their concern about the possibilities of "Sapphic" love. In his influential treatise of 1771 on masturbation, Swiss physician Simon André Tissot warns:

> Nature tends to play sometimes, and creates female personages of a sort who, because of the size of their clitoris and out of ignorance about its proper usage, fall into an abuse and want to play the man. Stimulated, they stimulate others and attempt to create hereby for themselves the pleasures of true intercourse. This sort of female personage hates men and is their enemy; they were not unknown to the ancients, who called them "tribades."... [T]hey attributed the establishment of this order to the young Sappho. (39–40)

Müller repeats these ideas:

> there are also female personages in whom the clitoris reaches an unusual size so that it can also take the place of the male member in the degree of its

stiffness. In the olden times, one called such women tribades or fricatrixes, "rubbers," because they allowed themselves to be used by immoral ladies for coitus.... [O]ne called this bestial pleasure lesbian love, after the famous lesbian poet Sappho. (1: 133)

Despite these colorful descriptions, however, there is much less focus on the dangers of female-female sexual desire than there is on male-male desire in the Age of Goethe.

Admittedly, the representation of female desire by male authors of the bildungsroman from Wieland, Heinse, and Goethe to Schlegel and Gutzkow may seem to be more like an appropriation than an acknowledgment. However, the critique and rejection of bourgeois models of femininity at the very moment of the establishment of those models does create an important space for resistance to gender structures that could become oppressive. Moreover, they make possible the emergence of gender inversion theories of same-sex desire. Theorists like Ramdohr and Hössli begin to see some varieties of same-sex love as the products of gender inversion – female souls in male bodies and vice versa. Ramdohr argues that sexual love can take place between two men or two women as long as one of the partners is more masculine and the other more feminine (1: 171). On the frontispiece of the first volume of *Eros*, Hössli explains same-sex desire as the product of a "transmigration of the souls," such that some male bodies have female souls and some female bodies have male souls; he repeats this claim verbatim later in the book (1: 295). While his book is focused almost exclusively on male-male love, the phrasing of this analysis recognizes the power of sensual female desire, and – because it is conceived in terms of gender symmetry – allows for desire between women as well as between men.

Many elements of the thinking about sexuality in the Age of Goethe seem to point in the direction of more modern constructions. The ideology of *Bildung* – of the discovery of the embryonic self and the hopefully harmonious unfolding of that self in society – fits in well with modern notions of "coming out." In fact, the "gay bildungsroman" is a genre so well known that it provokes parodic commentary: "the moist gay bildungsroman, in which some poor soul overcomes obstacles on his way out of the closet to become a better, more honest human being with lots of orgasms" (Ness n. pag.). Blumenbach's understanding of the *Bildungstrieb* anticipates modern science's search for genetic explanations of homosexuality, many of which rely on the same sorts of gender inversion (finding a typically female component in the genetic or hormonal make-up of a male homosexual, and so forth) that Ramdohr and

Hössli began to theorize. While the connection between these eighteenth- and early nineteenth-century theories and those prevalent in the twenty-first century might at times seem tenuous and indirect, it seems certain, at the very least, that the Age of Goethe's conceptualization of sexuality created the intellectual and cultural framework for activists working in the German-language realm such as Karl Maria Kertbeny and Karl Heinrich Ulrichs, for sexologists and psychoanalysts such as Magnus Hirschfeld and Sigmund Freud, as well as for authors from Leopold von Sacher-Masoch to Thomas Mann. Nonetheless, it is equally certain that authors such as Goethe, Heinse, Hölderlin, Moritz, Platen, Schiller, and Wieland were working within their own cultural framework, as they rethought and reconceptualized sexuality.

Works Cited

Baumann, Jürgen. *Paragraph 175: Über die Möglichkeit, die einfache, nichtjugendgefährdende und nichtöffentliche Homosexualität unter Erwachsenen strafffrei zu lassen (zugleich ein Beitrag zur Säkularisierung des Strafrechts)*. Berlin: Luchterhand, 1968. Print.

Blumenbach, Johann Friedrich. "Über den Bildungstrieb (Nisus formativus) und seinen Einfluß auf die Generation und Reproduktion." *Göttingisches Magazin der Wissenschaften und Litteratur* 1.5 (1780): 247–66. Web 22 January 2013 <http://www.ub.uni-bielefeld.de/cgi-bin/neubutton.cgi?pfad=/diglib/aufkl/goettmag/134802&seite=00000255.TIF>.

Büsching, Anton Friedrich. *Character Friedrich des Zweyten, Königs von Preussen*. 2nd ed. Halle: Witwe, 1788. Print.

Derks, Paul. *"Die Schande der heiligen Päderastie"*: *Homosexualität und Öffentlichkeit in der deutschen Literatur 1750–1850*. Berlin: Rosa Winkel, 1990. Print.

Dietrich, Hans [Hans Dietrich Hellbach]. *Die Freundesliebe in der deutschen Literatur*. 1931. Berlin: Rosa Winkel, 1996. Print.

Faderman, Lillian. *Surpassing the Love of Men: Romantic Friendship and Love between Women from the Renaissance to the Present*. New York: Morrow, 1981. Print.

Friedel, Johann. *Briefe über die Galanterien von Berlin auf einer Reise gesammelt von einem österreichischen Offizier*. 1782. Ed. Sonja Schnitzler. Berlin: Eulenspiegel, 1987. Print.

Goethe, Johann Wolfgang von. *Goethes Werke: Herausgegeben im Auftrage der Großherzogin Sophie von Sachsen*. 143 vols. Weimar: Böhlau, 1887–1919. Print.

Gramling, David. "My Ardinghello: Heinse and the Importance of Being Epistolary." *The Germanic Review: Literature, Culture, Theory* 86.1 (2011): 23–36. Print.

Greif, Stefan. "Sexualität im 'Licht des Bildungstriebs': Das Organismusmodell des jungen Schelling und das 'Gesetz der epicurischen Polarität.'" *Sexualität – Recht – Leben: Die Entstehung eines Dispostivs um 1800*. Ed. Maximilian Bergengruen, Johannes. F. Lehmann and Hubert Thüring. Munich: Fink, 2005. 133–51. Print.

Halperin, David. *One Hundred Years of Homosexuality and Other Essays on Greek Love*. New York: Routledge, 1990. Print.

Heinse, Wilhelm. *Ardinghello und die glückseligen Inseln. Kritische Studienausgabe*. Stuttgart: Reclam, 1986. Print.

"Vorwort." Petronius, Begebenheiten des Encolp. Aus dem Satyrikon des Petron übersetzt. 1773. Trans. Wilhelm Heinse. Leipzig: Weigel, 1898. 1–32. Print. Available online at: http:// hdl.handle.net/2027/uc1.loo95801502. Accessed 22 January 2013.

Hölderlin, Friedrich. Werke und Briefe. Ed. Friedrich Beißner and Jochen Schmidt. 3 vols. Frankfurt: Insel, 1969. Print.

Hössli, Heinrich. Eros: Die Männerliebe der Griechen, ihre Beziehungen zur Geschichte, Erziehung, Literatur und Gesetzgebung aller Zeiten. 3 vols. Glarus: n.p., 1836 and St. Gallen: Scheitlin, 1838; Reprint Berlin: Rosa Winkel, 1996. Print.

Hull, Isabel V. Sexuality, State and Civil Society in Germany, 1700–1815. Ithaca: Cornell UP, 1996. Print.

Krah, Hans. "Freundschaft oder Männerliebe?" "Emancipation des Fleisches": Erotik und Sexualität im Vormärz. Ed. Gustav Frank and Detlev Kopp. Bielefeld: Aisthesis, 1999. 185–221. Print.

Krimmer, Elisabeth. In the Company of Men: Cross-Dressed Women around 1800. Detroit: Wayne State UP, 2004. Print.

Langewand, Alfred. "Hölderlins 'Sokrates und Alcibiades' bei Johann Friedrich Herbert." Die aufgegebene Aufklärung: Experimente pädagogischer Vernunft. Ed. Johanna Hopfner and Michael Winkler. Munich: Juventa, 2004. 71–85. Print.

Meiners, Christoph. Vermischte philosophische Schriften. 3 vols. Leipzig: Weygand, 1775. Print.

Michaelis, Johann David. Mosaisches Recht. 2nd ed. Vol. 5. Frankfurt a/M: Garbe, 1780. Google Books. Web. 22 January 2013.

Moritz, Karl Philipp. Das Magazin zur Erfahrungsseelenkunde. Facsimile edition, 1783–92. Ed. Anke Bennholdt-Thomsen and Alfredo Guzzoni. Lindau: Antiqua, 1979. Print.

Müller, Johann Valentin. Entwurf der gerichtlichen Arzneywissenschaft nach juristischen und medicinischen Grundsätzen für Geistliche, Rechtsgelehrte und Aerzte. 3 vols. Frankfurt: Andrea, 1796. Print.

Ness, Patrick. "Hooray for Lesbians." The Guardian. February 21, 2007. Web. 22 January 2013.

Platen, August von. Memorandum meines Lebens. Ed. Gert Mattenklott and Hansgeorg Schmidt-Bergmann. Frankfurt a/M: Insel, 1996. Print.

Ramdohr, Friedrich Wilhelm Basileus. Venus Urania: Ueber die Natur der Liebe, über ihre Veredlung und Verschönerung. 3 vols. Leipzig: Goschen, 1798. Print.

Richards, Robert. "Kant and Blumenbach on the Bildungstrieb: A Historical Misunderstanding." Studies in the History and Philosophy of Biological and Biomedical Sciences 31.1 (2000): 11–32. Print.

Richter, Simon. "Winckelmann's Progeny." Outing Goethe and His Age. Ed. Alice Kuzniar. Stanford: Stanford UP, 1996. 33–46. Print.

Schiller, Friedrich. Sämtliche Werke. 5 vols. Ed. Gerhard Fricke and Herbert G. Göpfert. Munich: Hanser, 1965. Print.

Schmidt, Joseph Hermann. "Ueber die relative Stellung des Oertlichen zum Allgemeinen." Rusts Magazin für die gesammte Heilkunde 45.2 (1835): 163–99. Print.

Sedgwick, Eve Kosofsky. Epistemology of the Closet. Berkeley: U of California P, 1990. Print.

Tissot, Simon-André. Versuch von denen Krankheiten, welche aus der Selbstbefleckung entstehen. Frankfurt: Fleischer, 1771. Print.

Tobin, Robert. "Kertbeny's 'Homosexuality' and the Language of Nationalism." *Genealogies of Identity: Interdisciplinary Readings on Sex and Sexuality*. Ed. Margaret Sönser Breen and Fiona Peters. Amsterdam: Rodopi, 2005. 3–18. Print.

"The Love That Is Called Friendship and the Rise of Sexual Identity." *Literary Paternity, Literary Friendship: Essays in Honor of Stanley Corngold*. Ed. Gerhard Richter. Chapel Hill: U of North Carolina P, 2002. 175–97. Print.

Warm Brothers: Queer Theory and the Age of Goethe. Philadelphia: U of Pennsylvania P, 2000. Print.

Wachenfeld, Friedrich. *Homosexualität und Strafgesetz: Ein Beitrag zur Untersuchung der Reformbedürftigeit des § 175 St.G.B.* Leipzig: Dieterich, 1901. Print.

Wilson, W. Daniel. *Goethe Männer Knaben: Ansichten zur "Homosexualität."* Trans. Angela Steidele. Berlin: Insel, 2012. Print.

Zammito, John H. "Policing Polygeniticism in Germany, 1775: (Kames), Kant and Blumenbach." *The German Discovery of Race*. Ed. Sara Eigen and Mark Joseph Larrimore. Albany: State U of New York P, 2006. 35–54. Print.

Zantop, Susanne. "The Beautiful, the Ugly, and the German: Race, Gender and Nationality in Eighteenth-Century Anthropological Discourse." *Gender and Germanness: Cultural Productions of the Nation*. Ed. Patricia A. Herminghouse and Magda Mueller. London: Berghahn, 1997. 21–30. Print.

Zimmermann, Johann Georg Friedrich. *Fragmente über Friedrich den Großen: zur Geschichte seines Lebens, seiner Regierung, und seines Charakters*. Leipzig: Weidmann, 1790. Print.

15

The Gothic Novel and the Negotiation of Homophobia

STEVEN BRUHM

God Hates Fangs!

– although He does seem partial to puns. The play between "fangs" and "fags" that moves across the opening credits of the HBO television series *True Blood* neatly encapsulates the equation that critics of the "gay and lesbian Gothic" have understood to be present in the genre since its inception in the 1760s: that is, in Eve Kosofsky Sedgwick's often-quoted assertion that "[t]he Gothic novel crystallized for English audiences the terms of a dialectic between homosexuality and homophobia, in which homophobia appeared thematically in paranoid plots" (92). Locating the rise of that paranoid plot within the narratives of three Gothic novelists who were each "in some significant sense homosexual – Beckford notoriously, Lewis probably, Walpole iffily" (92), Sedgwick's *Between Men* itself crystallizes a critical tradition that stretches back at least as far as Montague Summers's reading of Matthew Lewis in *The Gothic Quest* (1938) and that inflects every sustained discussion of homosexuality and the Gothic (at least the male Gothic) of the past three decades. Thus George Haggerty: "The connections between the history of sexuality (and the growth of sexology) and the gothic are not necessarily coincidental. They haunt each other with similarities" (*Queer* 51). Or Paulina Palmer: "The association of the vampire with the period of twilight, since the sunset is supposed to liberate her from her coffin and permit her to venture abroad to stalk her prey, is pertinent in metaphoric terms to the closeted lesbian who, having concealed her sexual orientation during the day, emerges at night to seek romance in the half-lit world of clubs and bars" (102). Or me: "After fifteen years of teaching Gothic literature and queer theory, I have come to regard the phrase 'Gothic sexualities' as self-evident, even somewhat redundant. . . . Sexuality, as it comes to us through a history of Freudian, post-Freudian and queer thought, is nothing short of Gothic in its ability to rupture, fragment, and destroy both the coherence of the individual subject and of the culture in which that subject appears" (Bruhm 93). If Alan Ball's recent *True Blood* can invoke the language of equal rights, of "coming out of the closet" and "assimilating," to refer to vampires instead of – or as well as – queer people, that is because *True Blood* is recycling a centuries-old affiliation between the Gothic and the gay; it can only use parodic humor, rather than the heuristics of urgent discovery, to talk about the Gothic and homophobia.

Yet a narrative like *True Blood* also records a fracture in the Gothic-homosexual-homophobia trajectory that it is my purpose in this chapter to consider. As devotees of the series will know, "gay liberation," along with the American Civil Rights movement, provides the language of the vampires' legitimacy struggles in a post-George W. Bush America, and works to establish what some critics have recently named "queer liberalism," the fully assimilated enjoyment of rights and privileges not just *in spite of,* but sometimes *because of,* claiming a homosexual subject position (Eng, Halberstam, and Munoz 10). But as devotees of the series will also know, the liberation of gays *qua* gays, or lesbians *qua* lesbians, is little in evidence. The benevolent gay vampire Eddie Gauthier of Seasons 1–2 is staked into oblivion; the vicious gay vampire Talbot, lover of the even more vicious and unassimilating Russell Edginton, is staked in Season 3 with Russell to follow shortly thereafter; and while Steve Newlin remains undead and well at the end of Season 5, his combination of perfidy and fundamentalist Christian smarminess assures his gay viewers' disidentification with him and our wish for his death. Things are faring a little better for lesbians: at the end of Season 5 queer vampires Tara and Pam seem to be doing all right, but as we watch their newly found bliss we remember the hypocritical antisex lesbian vampire and head of American Vampire League Nan Flanagan who met the true death in the previous season. What we might see as gay plotlines in *True Blood,* then, are tangential: overall the series built on the rhetoric of gay liberation focuses on heterosexual plots and conventionally straight love triangles in a way that deploys the language of gayness to render gayness irrelevant.

It is this sense of irrelevancy, of occlusion or indirection, by which I want to consider the classic Gothic novel and its negotiations of homophobia. For if homosex is not a central thematic or a representational topos for a twenty-first-century television show, it is even less a representational topos for the eighteenth- and nineteenth-century Gothic novel, at least as far as men are concerned. A genre that is notorious for its presentation of verboten sex acts – voyeurism, rape, incest, sexual torture and bondage, adultery, cuckoldry, "illegitimate" pregnancy – the classic British Gothic, to the best of my knowledge, presents *no* scenes of male-male sodomy, no direct homosexuality that might join the parade of spectacalized perversions or narrative sensationalisms. Nor does it identify a male sodomite as one of myriad religious or judicial trans-gressors, even though such an identification would make for a graphic and predictable scene of phobic punishment. This, to my mind, is a remarkable lacuna, one that cannot be explained with references to literary history or censorship practices. We had seen male-male sex acts earlier in the century, in John Cleland's *Memoirs of a Woman of Pleasure* (1748) and Tobias Smollett's *Adventures of Peregrine Pickle* (1751),[1] and eighteenth-century French pornogra-phy did not stint on the spectacle of male homosexual sex – Sade is enough to cite here (see Hanson, Tuite, and Stoddart) – but no British homophobic Gothic depicts its homo*phobia* with the object lesson of the homo*sexual*. No version of the disgust expressed by Fanny Hill or Peregrine Pickle over the spectacle of the sodomite finds its Gothic equivalent in a genre willing to depict for us the pulverized mass of a Mother Superior's corpse (see Matthew Lewis's *The Monk*) or the teeth marks that lacerate a dead couple's body as, incarcerated and starved, they turn cannibal to prolong their miserable lives (see Robert Maturin's *Melmoth the Wanderer*). The Gothic novel, at least prior to the Stonewall Resistance Riot of 1969, and at least in its male characters, is profoundly reticent about the spectacle of direct homophobia, as reticent as it is about the spectacle of homosexuality. How might we understand this?

Homophobia: The Gothic's Back Side

To approach the dialogue between the structuring principle of homopho-bia in the early Gothic novel and the novel's remarkable silence on the topic of male-male sexual relations, we must return to Sedgwick's formative work in *Between Men*. Like the classic Gothic novel itself, Sedgwick's book is less concerned with a "distinctively ... homosexual experience" than with the "shape of the entire male homosocial spectrum" (90) – although, strangely enough, the "entire homosocial spectrum" here occludes the homosexual in the Gothic, and thus isn't "entire" at all. For Sedgwick, the performative effects of *homophobia* in late eighteenth- and early nineteenth-century British culture would not find their expression in "a comparable body of *homosex-ual* thematics" until the late Victorian Gothic (92; emphasis added), in novels such as Oscar Wilde's *The Picture of Dorian Gray* and Richard Marsh's *The Beetle*. And even in those novels, or in the equally suggestive *Dracula*, male homoeros remains at the level of innuendo, indirection, or threat.[2] In the crit-icism that follows Sedgwick, the early Gothic novel becomes a "homosexual" genre not just because it articulates the place of homophobia in panics among powerful, entitled, fraughtly domesticated white men of the middle classes, but also because it brings together two other richly connotative and resonant forces within readerly practice: the reference to authorial biography where the author's homosexuality appears "only rather sketchily" in the fiction (92) – notoriously, probably, iffily – and the invocation of and transformation by the emerging middle class of a series of tropes (metonyms, to be exact) of what twentieth-century readers will come to regard as unquestionably signifying of homosexuality. I will return momentarily to the question of biography; the metonyms to which I refer are, for Sedgwick as well as for most queer readings of the Gothic, "the feminization of the aristocracy"; the "connois-seurship" and high theatricality of Continental Roman Catholicism (93); the predominance of the "unspeakable" as the crime "'not to be named among Christian men,'" that is, the crime of sodomy (94); the interchangeability or mutual penetration of male psyches; and the geography of the hidden, the rear, the postern, the filthy, the excremental (see Haggerty *Queer*; Showalter). When we would uncover queer men in the classic Gothic novel, we need first beat the metonymic bushes of tropes that conceal them.

The role of metonym as the predominant trope in Gothic representations of homophobia is critically important because, if metonym constitutes the homosexual-homophobic relation in the Gothic, it displaces it at the same time. This constitution via displacement has a material history, and establishes something we might think of as a queer temporality. In *Homographesis* (1994), Lee Edelman returns to Michel Foucault's famous (and now shop-worn) the-sis that, in the nineteenth century, the sodomite moved from being the agent of particular religious and juridical behaviors to the status of "homosexual," a subject, a case history, a "species" (Foucault 43). For Edelman, this move is, among other things, the transformation of rhetorical tropes: the homosexual body as Foucault describes it, Edelman argues, becomes "a visible emblem or metaphor for the 'singular nature' that now defines or identifies a specifically homosexual type of person" (8). But the metaphorical stability arising from such an act of identification – an identification following the grammar "this is that," "this body is that sexuality" – can only be constituted retroactively through a reading (or misreading) of metonym, where a certain set of actions, appearances, or affiliations come to mean in a stable and legible way. What for Foucault becomes a "sexuality" in a historical, juridical, and political sense becomes "sexuality" for Jacques Lacan in the psychoanalytic registers of an hypostatized "desire." As Edelman suggests, sexuality as read through Lacan "comes into existence when desire" – whose chief trope is metonymy, a lead-ing toward or affiliation, rather than an identification with – "is misrecognized or tropologically misinterpreted as a metaphor" (8). Thus, "sexuality cannot be identified with the metonymic without acknowledging that the very act of identification through which it is constituted *as* sexuality is already a positing of its meaning in terms of a metaphoric coherence and necessity" (8). As Lacan would have it, metonymy and its misidentification is what makes possible the stabilizing equations of metaphor, just as for Foucault and Edelman, the metonymic had not only to be in place to produce the metaphoric "homosexual" but it has to be identified in retrospect as having been metonymic, not to the thing itself so much as to an affiliation, an association, a connotation.

What is at stake for Edelman in this rhetorical maneuvering is what I want to bring to the Gothic novel and its alleged negotiations of homophobia. With resounding Foucauldian echoes, Edelman argues that "the historical [nineteenth-century] investiture of sexuality with a metaphoric rather than a metonymic significance made it possible to search for signifiers that would testify to the presence of this newly posited sexual identity or 'essence'" (9). That "search for signifiers" belongs as much to the literary critic as it does to the nineteenth-century physician, pastor, or pedagogue, and its result, I want to suggest, has been to frame in certain ways a Gothic negotiation of homophobia that we might do well to rethink. For if, as Foucault and Edelman suggest, a certain kind of metaphoric retroactivity redoubles upon nodal points of meaning and turns them into metonyms that make "homosexual Gothic" possible – that is, they make homosexuality legible on the Gothic body – then something might be gained in disentangling the homosexual from the paranoid, the metaphor from the metonym, the notorious from the iffy, and to ask again what interventions the Gothic might make in the spectacle of normative sexual relations.

The Monk: Beyond Gay Affirmation

In what follows, then, I want to return to two Gothic narratives from the long nineteenth-century Anglo-Irish tradition: Lewis's 1796 novel *The Monk*, and Sheridan Le Fanu's 1872 novella "Carmilla." I am foregrounding these two works for a number of reasons. First, each has become a lightning rod for thinking about homosexuality and the Gothic. A critical empire has arisen around each work, an empire whose borders and central administration have helped to determine what homophobia might look like in the Gothic. Second, these works divide along gender lines so that a curious homosexual reticence in *The Monk* contrasts sharply with "Carmilla," which all but blatantly presents sex between women. *The Monk*, as Clara Tuite writes, "does not uncover, . . .

does *not* present ... the romance plot of monastic male homoeroticism" (par. 11); "Carmilla," on the other hand, shares with Coleridge's Gothic *Christabel* (1797–1800) sites of lesbian sex that are not just to dream of but to tell. If the classic Gothic could occlude the site of male-male sex, whose presence is detectable only through the rhetorical double-speak of metonymy, the Gothic makes women's same-sex pleasure too legible; it inscribes lesbianism directly on the body. How might this matter in a canon of texts produced in the white, middle-class, Anglo-American tradition that many contemporary queer critics would have us abandon as the work of ethnocentric, Caucasian navel-gazing whose politics can at best be dubious if not downright spurious (see Eng et al.)? I focus on Lewis and Le Fanu here because their critical interplay of metaphor and metonymy produces broader critical practices that we might find useful for thinking about all Gothic texts, all Gothic bodies on display. At a critical moment that has wanted to stabilize and speak from the abjected body and its epistemes, we would do well to remain aware of some dubious metaphoricities.

Given both *The Monk*'s popularity and its rhizomatic sprawl, any attempt at summarizing the plot of the novel or indexing all its queer moments would prove futile. However, one particular narrative thread does mesmerize queer critics: the Ambrosio-Rosario/Matilda story. Ambrosio, the charismatic and pious head of the Church of the Capuchins in Madrid, has befriended a young novice named Rosario, a youth legible to us at first as a closet case: "A sort of mystery enveloped this youth"; "His hatred of society, his profound melancholy ... attracted the notice of the whole fraternity"; "He seemed fearful of being recognized" (66); and of course there is his "respect approaching idolatry" of the monk Ambrosio, whose company he sought "with the most attentive assiduity" and into whose favor he "eagerly seized every means to ingratiate himself" (67). To good effect, too: "Ambrosio on his side did not feel less attracted towards the youth; with him alone did he lay aside his habitual severity. When he spoke to him, he insensibly assumed a tone milder than was usual to him; and no voice sounded so sweet to him as did Rosario's" (67). It is not long, however, before Rosario makes his great confession to his father-confessor: "father! ... I am a woman!" (79). In short time, the two have sex and Matilda – the now unveiled seductress – facilitates for Ambrosio the sexual access to Antonia, a beautiful but naïve maiden whom the monk rapes, kills, and then discovers is his sister. Ambrosio's personal shame in all of this is mitigated only by the fact that Lucifer had stage-managed the whole affair, having the "subordinate but crafty spirit" Matilda assume the guise of the Virgin Mary (361), an image of whom Ambrosio had kept in his cell as a spiritual-cum-erotic aid. At novel's end, Matilda flees the prison of the Inquisition, where she and Ambrosio have been imprisoned (all part of Lucifer's deceptive game) while the monk, having sold his soul to the devil, perishes in a graphic six-day-long torture.

In what remains one of the most sophisticated and enabling readings of this plot trajectory, Tuite argues that it presents, explodes, and then retroactively reconstitutes a homoerotic relationship that is "specifically pedagogical and pederastic, the kind of relationship which Foucault has defined in *The Use of Pleasure* as a characteristic homoerotic relationship between a younger and older man, based on an erotics of restraint, or 'self-denial.' In this erotic economy, whilst desire is repressed or regulated it is still present *as* a specific form of desire" (par. 11). Living in his all-male paradise of subordinate and adoring monks, Ambrosio has in Rosario his "sexual object ... safely repressed" (par. 12), so that the youth's "coming out" as a woman "is in fact not an unveiling but a re-veiling in female costume, one step in an ongoing transvestist game by the Devil" (par. 15). The heterosexual excess that ensues is, for Tuite, made possible by the homoerotic energies established before the unveiling, and retroactively makes of that male bond a sexualized, if unacted on, energy that comes to hold the status of a metonymy for the lustful engagements that follow it (par. 16). For Tuite, this metonymizing then comments on the ways homophobia comes to constitute the precarious life of heterosexuality in the late eighteenth century: "This transvestist-crossing instantiates within the text the structural principle of homosexual panic – a denial of and flight from the blackmailability of homosexual implication, into a parodic version of heterosexual relations, a kind of hyper-heterosexuality" (par. 15).[3] For other critics who follow Sedgwick's model of homosexual paranoia, the unveiling establishes a kind of camp excess that displays in microcosm the novel's larger interest in "'camp,' pastiche, role-playing, excess and androgyny – in other words, with a self-dramatizing self-fashioning" that "insists upon the mobility, and provisionality, of identity," as Robert Miles puts it (45, 53). For Max Fincher, such camp has all the earmarks of an early Judith Butler queer strategy, performing the "'failure' and 'confusion' of the readability and intelligibility of gender 'identity'" so that Matilda's supernaturalism "works as a metaphor for exposing the constructedness of the discourse of naturalized behavior, including sex/gender roles and desires" (par. 3, 7).

True to her reading of Sedgwick, Tuite offers a subtle analysis of how an affectionate, erotic relationship between men comes to be circumscribed by the paranoia of blackmailability and the seeming "protective gesture" of heterosexual or "straight" desire (par. 31), a gesture related directly to identity politics. While such a move has enabled much queer reading of the Gothic, it is, in the case of *The Monk*, a problematic swerve away from what actually happens in the narrative. Tuite's argument that heterosexuality relegates the homosexual to the closet – thus to fears of blackmailability – actually displaces the fear from the site at which it exists: in heterosexual relations. Ambrosio is in danger – of discovery, of disgrace, of immortal perdition – only by virtue of Matilda's presence *as a woman* in the monastery. It is her sex, and not Rosario's purported "sexuality," that renders Ambrosio vulnerable; and his decision to allow Matilda to remain in the convent after she has "come out" is second only in foolishness to his allowing her to inflame his desires for Antonia. The critical sleight-of-hand I'm seeing in such queerings of *The Monk* is further achieved by anachronistic citations of metaphor and metonymy. Writes Tuite: "The text's strategy of Enlightenment exposure and revelation uses heterosexual sex to closet a homosexual metonym," so that the novel enacts "a gesture of *protective* closetting in the wider cultural context of homosexual persecution" (par. 20). Just as the homosexual resonances of all Gothic tropes acquire their homosexual meaning in retrospect – that is, just as homosexuality always comes from behind – so do we see it here, so that homophobia comes to control a scene where it is the destructive force of heterosexuality that is really at stake.[4]

This (mis)reading of homophobia in *The Monk* proceeds from the will to knowledge that critical historicism has produced at least since the 1980s. Miles convincingly notes how biographical concerns have shaped criticism of *The Monk* so that the "open secret" of Lewis's homosexuality compels us to read the novel within the personal and political landscape of sodomy in 1790s Britain. For Miles, this landscape is easy to map, for, like the topology of *Pilgrim's Progress*, it constitutes a series of stable metaphors producing allegory: "For those so minded to read [*The Monk*] as homosexual allegory, Ambrosio's spectacular punishment [in the final pages] takes on the character of a sodomite in the stocks experiencing the rough justice of the crowd" (54). While I agree that the affiliation between this condemned apostate rapist and the persecuted sodomite might tell us something about the public taste for spectacular punishments, I'm less convinced by the ease with which the author's purported "sexuality" anchors the sexual politics of the "homosexual Gothic" as Sedgwick identified it. And there *is* remarkable ease here: George Haggerty claims that "Lewis's repressed Monk becomes the pretext for both sexual fantasy and social retribution. Lewis too *must be playing out the drama* of his worst fears about himself and his place in society" ("Literature" 349, emphasis added)[5]; Jerrold Hogle argues that, "[a]s [Horace] Walpole does in thus tracing and erasing his own sexual preference in and from his book [*The Castle of Otranto*], Lewis both acts out and conceals that kind of desire, flirting with but finally resisting any 'coming out'" (par. 9); William Brewer quotes Lorne Macdonald as arguing that the bloody death of the Prioress is "'the revenge fantasy of a man whose sexuality put him a lifelong risk'" – the "length" of the "life" in question being a whole nineteen years (qtd. in Brewer 136). There is something seductive and enabling about these conclusions, appearing as they do in the bright epistemological glow of New Historicist, gay-affirmative readings, but there is also something profoundly counterintuitive as well. These critics imagine a Gothic novelist's negotiation of homophobia as yet another case study in Foucault's *History of Sexuality*: the confession, the making public of a discursive "truth" about the self, the indulgent pursuit of *"the perpetual spirals of power and pleasure"* in which Lewis teasingly gives us his horrors/fears, his innocence/fantasies, his sufferings, and his damnable desires (Foucault 45). In this reading, Gothic novels are less novels than they are creative autobiographies – and we might pause to wonder whether a subject wishing to confess to a desire that might see him hanged on the morrow would turn to the mode of the Gothic, with its derogatory status of brainless monstrosity, its dubious audience of middle-class women readers, and its laughably formulaic conventions of character appearance and behavior.

Carmilla: Go Forth and Metonymize

If *The Monk* offers its readers a series of anachronistically understood metonyms that can be pressed to cohere in the legible figure of "the homosexual," Le Fanu's "Carmilla" offers a very different experience. As many readers will know, "Carmilla" is the narrative of a young woman named Laura, who lives with her father in a remote castle in the Austrian province of Styria. Her mother having died in Laura's infancy, the protagonist is raised by female attendants, is visited by young ladies from far-neighboring communities, and is only periodically conversant with her benevolent but distant father. At age six, she experiences what she believes is a dream in which a young lady with a "very pretty face" appears at her bedside, places her hands under the coverlet to caress and soothe her, and then crawls into bed with her and pierces her breast before disappearing (277). This dream figure appears to Laura again thirteen years later, as Laura is recovering from the disappointment of learning that the lovely young Bertha Rheinfeldt will not be coming for a visit (because, we will learn, Bertha has been killed by a vampire). The mysterious dream-woman, now flesh and blood, calls herself Carmilla and is left at the castle by her equally mysterious mother. The story then recounts Carmilla's attempts to seduce Laura – into intimacy, into sex, and into death. Laura writes:

> She used to place her pretty arms about my neck, draw me to her, and laying her cheek to mine, murmur with her lips near my ear, "Dearest, your little heart is wounded; think me not cruel because I obey the irresistible law of my strength and weakness; if your dear heart is wounded, my wild heart bleeds with yours. In the rapture of my enormous humiliation I live in your warm life, and you shall die – die, sweetly die – into mine. I cannot help it; as I draw near to you, you, in your turn, will draw near to others, and learn the rapture of that cruelty, which yet is love; so, for a while, seek to know no more of me and mine, but trust me with all your loving spirit." (291)

This deadly sex-talk, we learn, has been Carmilla's modus operandi for destroying other young women, currently and in the historical past. Carmilla is actually the ghostly revenant of Mircalla, countess of the neighboring castle of Karnstein, who, for lo these many, has been performing her lesbian vampiric ways on the young, almost innocent, and almost unwilling women of the land.

As an ur-text of the negotiation of lesbian homophobia in the Anglo-Irish tradition (an honor it shares with *Christabel*), "Carmilla" has a lot to negotiate. The vampire's seductive beauty, her languorous demeanor, her familial vulnerability (like so many Ann Radcliffe heroines, she depends on the kindness of strangers in castles while her parents are either dead or absent) – all these factors have helped us to read Carmilla as a somewhat reluctant villain. As early as 1949, Arthur H. Nethercot argued that Carmilla, like Coleridge's Geraldine, is, "in spite of [her] horrid intentions and conduct, ... by no means consistently unsympathetic" (35). For every part vampire, Carmilla is also part damsel in distress, and for every part distressed damsel, Carmilla is also, for feminist and antihomophobic readers, an agent of sexual liberation. Elizabeth Signorotti, following Sue-Ellen Case, claims that Le Fanu's text holds out the possibility that lesbianism is "healthy and vital" (611), existing as it does in "a province, far removed from England, where women are free to express their sexuality" (628); and Paulina Palmer, following Nina Auerbach, asserts that Carmilla "has the courage to act on her desires and form a relationship that is overtly sexual" (100). This salubrious freedom, courage, and ennobling vitality not only animate Carmilla but infect (Le Fanu's favorite image) the passive and isolated Laura as well: "Despite her long absence" of thirteen years, Carmilla's initial visit and penetration, argues Signorotti, "introduces Laura to the liberating exchange of female sexuality and begins the process of

Laura's ontological shifting" (612). That shifting, according to William Veeder, is toward the utopian goal of self-knowledge, a "complete understanding" (217) of who Laura is and what she wants.

In my reading of *The Monk* and its critics, lines of desirous flight coalesce into a centralizing identity of a Homosexual Author writing his experiences as code within and against a homophobic culture. Antihomophobic critics have read these lines of flight as metonyms-begetting-metaphors, and thus of identity writ large. Something similar happens in "Carmilla," only in reverse. Despite the praise of Carmilla's queerness quoted earlier, her readers, it seems, are as interested in how she *doesn't* signify as lesbian as they are in how she does. While there is nothing very jaw-dropping in Nethercot's conclusion that a thoroughgoing analysis of the Laura-Carmilla relation as lesbian would not be a "true one" (exactly what is "lesbian truth," one wonders, for this critic in 1949?), for later, more liberal critics, lesbianism only makes sense in a larger signifying chain of social and political meanings. Helen Stoddart, one of the tale's most astute and subtle readers, argues that while Carmilla "represents aristocratic female homosexual desire ... the physical nature of the relationship between the narrator and the vampire is a far cry from mutual lesbian desire and can more clearly be seen in this light as a masculine fantasy of and about lesbianism" (32). The heart of this fantasy, she says, is the vampire's attack on "the socio-economic exigencies of a particular late-Victorian, British, bourgeois masculinism" (28). Following Gayatri Spivak, Stoddart locates Carmilla's threat in "the crucial connexions between nineteenth-century literature and the discourse of imperialism which it served," so that Carmilla's lesbianism comes metonymically to encode larger Victorian anxieties about Darwinian evolution, primitivism, and imperialism's "drive" to civilize and subjectivate those still on the periphery of the human:

> In the haunting and persecution of the living [Carmilla] hauls her victims down the Darwinian ladder and back from the subjectivity, which is the end point of this drive [e.g., the drive to civilize and humanize], to a state slippery with wanton degeneration into pre-evolutionary bestiality. So-called civil society cannot expect compliance or respect from those not in the first place "rational" human beings and must be anxious, therefore, to eliminate such aliens from its map. (31–32)

Like Veeder, who argues that the text's lesbianism is a mere occasion for Victorianism's larger concerns regarding repression *tout court* (198), for Stoddart the lesbian makes most sense when she is about something else, about historical, colonial, masculinist pursuits. In these readings, lesbian pleasure in "Carmilla" exists to take us away from lesbian pleasure in "Carmilla," to witness tropologically its insignificance to "larger" questions of the national, the political, and the psychological.

Central to this metonymizing reading of lesbianism in "Carmilla" is the figuration of the vampire as "sterile." In the text's final paragraphs, Baron Vordenburg describes the "birth" of the vampire as occurring in one of two ways: first, "[a] person, more or less wicked, puts an end to himself. A suicide, under certain circumstances, becomes a vampire"; second, "[t]hat spectre visits living people in their slumbers; *they* die, and almost invariably, in the grave, develope into vampires" (338). Stoddart reads this recipe alongside the story's emphasis on the Karnsteins' dead maternal line, Carmilla's (and later Laura's) languorous weakness, and Sedgwick's reflections on the irrelevant, "otiose" quality of the aristocracy, and locates the text's central homophobia in the vampire's inability to contribute to the bourgeois project by bearing children. "She is incapable of reproducing," writes Stoddart: "the vampire's sterile, disembodying liaisons mimetically spread; sterile because, though they involve multiplication of their own kind, within the theme of contagion this is still a form of infection which may never involve reproductive embodiment" (31, 28). Palmer agrees, and more: "the association of the vampire with sterility and death is also, sad to say, applicable from a homophobic point of view to the figure of the lesbian" (102). Of course, both critics know that the vampire *does* reproduce – she makes other vampires – but in Stoddart's estimation, there is nothing life-giving or affirmative about such birthing: the story's lesbianism is "female sexuality, not turned toward itself but turning on itself, and the result is not desire for love but cruelty, possession, contagion, and, potentially, death" (32).[6]

Driving Stakes, and the Stakes of the Drive

"Never [to] involve reproductive embodiment": herein lies the tragedy of the lesbian vampire, just as it constitutes the great human tragedy of Dracula who, according to his wives, has never loved and knows not what love is. Herein lies the association with narcissism and death that, sad to say, still haunts lesbians and gay men in the twenty-first century. (Shall we invoke *True Blood* once again?) But why so sad? Before we see such textual and social homophobia as an attack on our dignity, we might also wonder whether to prefer "sterility" if sterility's opposite – compulsory reproduction – might itself be something that queers want to resist. (Or some do, at any rate.) Indeed, a figure like Carmilla may answer just as richly to Edelman's call for the "queer" *not* to be a metaphor for "embodied reproduction," for social and civil belonging, or for the seamless subjectivity of bourgeois fantasy. Carmilla's purported sterility might instead insist on itself as its own end, or on a figuring of the refusal of reproduction and its attendant normatives – heterosexual monogamy, childbearing, and submission to the call for a better future of civil society. In other words, the sterilely reproductive Carmilla might be a figure for what the queer "ought" to do, according to Edelman: "queerness *should* and *must* redefine such notions as 'civil order' through a rupturing of our foundational faith in the reproduction of futurity" (*No Future* 16–17). Indeed, for Edelman this faith includes the identification and eradication of homophobia by "allowing" homosexuals their "full place" within society, as if such a full place were possible, let alone desirable. Instead, for Edelman the death drive that might characterize an anti-maternal vampire like Carmilla "names what the queer, in the order of the social, is called forth to figure: the negativity opposed to every form of social viability" (9).

The rupturing death drive of which Edelman writes here is similar to that which frames the Gothic's negotiation of homophobia, the same rupturing that might move us beyond "homophobia" – at least provisionally – as the anchoring point for queer readings of the mode. Let us return to Carmilla's pillow talk with Laura, and to that promise of "the rapture of my enormous humiliation" – "the rapture of that cruelty" – "whereby I live in your warm life, and you shall die – die, sweetly die – into mine" (291). This promise that "I would live in you; and you would die for me" comes to Laura as "tumultuous" and death-producing, a seduction into unconsciousness and into "dim thoughts of death" that are "not unwelcome" (300, 292, 307, 307). (And Stoddart ponders long on Laura's attractions to this sexuality and its concomitant refusal of childbearing.) Carmilla's rapture is also a rupture, an "enormous humiliation" of the ego that would otherwise guarantee self-identity and that is here is jubilantly sacrificed in an "unaccountable" jouissance (308). This rapture / rupture is an allegiance to that "irresistible law" of the drive, the drive of sex, which is also the drive of death, the drive to which the queerest of Gothic characters are proudly in thrall. It is the same enthralling drive whose effects Matilda of *The Monk* will describe to Ambrosio as she urges their mutual escape from the prisons of the Inquisition: it is "the power of procuring every bliss which can make [...] life delicious!," the "unrestrained ... gratification of my senses ... indulged even to satiety," the invention of "new pleasures, to revive and stimulate my glutted appetites" (Lewis 353). In a world of moral idealism and socially responsible concerns for human dignity, these imagined pleasures are selfish, murderous, suicidal. But in a world of fantasy, in fictions that might engage a queer reader beset by commands to be otherwise responsible for normative standards, these libidinous promises have more than a little attractiveness. Queer not just for their crossdressing or their lesbian desire, Matilda and Carmilla infect and destroy with the teasing allure of sexuality lived otherwise.

In his analysis of *The Monk*, Peter Brooks notes Tzvetan Todorov's argument that "the fantastic, especially in its diabolical manifestations, is born of the psychological experience of limit situations, extreme moments of desire" (256). That experience of limit situations is, for Brooks, at the heart of Ambrosio's tragedy, as "His tale is one of Eros denied, only to reassert itself with the force of vengeance, to smite him" (257). In his analysis of Sigmund Freud, Leo Bersani argues that such limit situations, such extreme moments of desire, also produce what we call sexuality. For Bersani, sexuality names not an ossified identity or catalogue of preferences but an experience surpassing the boundaries of median stimulation, of shattering the ego that would otherwise delimit us from our sensual surroundings (38–39). It has been my contention in this chapter that the search and rescue mission of detecting gays and lesbians as victims of homophobia in the Gothic has left us trapped in a hermeneutic circle that can only assuredly provide us with what we have been looking for: evidence of phobic persecution. I am suggesting instead that the Gothic propensity to shatter bodies and souls be read alongside the queer propensity to shatter egos and identities that have been sexualized as gay or straight by a culture that fetishizes such identity. In this reading, the "homo" under duress may be less the persecuted or abjected sexual pervert than it is the determined, the stable, the legible self of Western modernity.

Notes

1. Here I part from Miles, who reads heterosexual incest in Lewis as "a cipher for a yet more heinous – within the codes of polite writing, a literally unspeakable – desire" (52), the desire for same-sex pleasure. The eighteenth-century novel *has* spoken this desire at length, and the Gothic novel hardly qualifies as "polite writing." For a discussion of the sodomitic episodes in Smollett and Cleland, see Edelman, *Homographesis* ch. 10.

2. In his crucial study of *Dracula*, Craft notes a similar presence of the homo-erotic encased by the will not to represent the homoerotic. As Dracula creates females as surrogates to perform his own will – a will that involves penetration and ownership of the men in the novel – he fulfills an otherwise "unfulfilled sexual ambition" (Craft 110). "Always postponed and never directly enacted," "Dracula's desire to fuse with a male ... finds evasive fulfillment in an important series of heterosexual displacements.... The novel, nonetheless, does not

dismiss homoerotic desire and threat; rather, it simply continues to diffuse and displace it" (110–11). As with the earlier Gothic fictions I name, this reticence is explained in terms of "the gender-anxious culture" from which the novel arose.

3. Jones makes a similar argument. For her, all Ambrosio's erotic objects are metonyms whose referent is the mother (134).

4. Tuite is specific about Catholicism's affiliation with the homosexual, what Sedgwick delightfully called "the King James Version" (93; qtd. in Tuite par. 22) as one such telling metonym.

5. Haggerty performs a similar lamination of William Beckford's sexual life onto his fiction. Of Gulchenrouz, the child-figure in *Vathek* who closes the novel as innocent as he began, Haggerty writes: "Beckford's lament for his own lost innocence cannot be far from the surface here, nor need we look much further to explain the impetus behind his notorious pederasty" ("Literature" 347–48). In Haggerty's estimation, "*Vathek* becomes in a sense a testimony to the horror with which he contemplated his own internal paradox of innocent love and damning desire or reacted to the social repulsion that greeted publication of his sexual self" (348). "[T]his novel is an elaborate *metaphor* for Beckford's private suffering" (348; emphasis added).

6. So too for Veeder, who argues of Laura's melancholy that her "sexual incompleteness which makes transcendence impossible makes death inevitable" (216).

Works Cited

Bersani, Leo. *The Freudian Body: Psychoanalysis and Art.* New York: Columbia UP, 1986. Print.

Brewer, William D. "Transgendering in Matthew Lewis's *The Monk.*" *Gothic Studies* 6.2 (2004): 192–209. Print.

Brooks, Peter. "Virtue and Terror: *The Monk.*" *ELH* 40.2 (1973): 249–63. Print.

Bruhm, Steven. "Gothic Sexualities." *Teaching the Gothic.* Ed. Anna Powell and Andrew Smith. Houndsmills: Palgrave, 2006. 93–106. Print.

Craft, Christopher. "'Kiss Me with those Red Lips': Gender and Inversion in Bram Stoker's *Dracula.*" *Representations* 8 (1984): 107–33. Print.

Edelman, Lee. *Homographesis: Essays in Gay Literary and Cultural Theory.* New York: Routledge, 1994. Print.

No Future: Queer Theory and the Death Drive. Durham: Duke UP, 2004. Print.

Eng, David L., Judith Halberstam, and José Esteban Munoz. "What's Queer about Queer Studies Now?" *Social Text* 23.3–4 (2005): 1–17. Print.

Fincher, Max. "The Gothic as Camp: Queer Aesthetics in *The Monk.*" *Romanticism on the Net.* 44 (2006): n.pag. *érudit.org.* Web. 18 November 2012.

Foucault, Michel. *The History of Sexuality, Volume I: An Introduction.* Trans. Robert Hurley. New York: Vintage, 1990. Print.

Haggerty, George E. "Literature and Homosexuality in the Late Eighteenth Century: Walpole, Beckford, and Lewis." *Studies in the Novel* 18.4 (1986): 341–52. Print.

Queer Gothic. Urbana: U of Illinois P, 2006. Print.

Hanson, Ellis. "Undead." *Inside/Out: Lesbian Theories, Gay Theories*. Ed. Diana Fuss. New York: Routledge, 1991. 324–40. Print.

Hogle, Jerrold E. "The Ghost of the Counterfeit – and the Closet – in *The Monk*." 1997. *Romanticism on the Net* 8 (1997): n.pag. *érudit.org*. Web. 18 November 2012.

Jones, Wendy. "Stories in Desire in *The Monk*." *ELH* 57.1 (1990): 129–50. Print.

Le Fanu, J. Sheridan. "'Carmilla.'" *Best Ghost Stories of J.S. Le Fanu*. New York: Dover, 1964. 274–339. Print.

Lewis, Matthew Gregory. *The Monk: A Romance*. Ed. D. L. Macdonald and Kathleen Scherf. Peterborough: Broadview P, 2004. Print.

Macdonald, D. Lorne. *Monk Lewis: A Critical Biography*. Toronto: U of Toronto P, 2000. Print.

Miles, Robert. "Anne Radcliffe and Matthew Lewis." *A Companion to the Gothic*. Ed. David Punter. Oxford: Blackwell, 2000. 41–57. Print.

Nethercot, Arthur H. "Coleridge's 'Christabel' and Lefanu's 'Carmilla.'" *Modern Philology* 47.1 (1949): 32–38. Print.

Palmer, Paulina. *Lesbian Gothic: Transgressive Fictions*. London: Cassell, 1999. Print.

Sedgwick, Eve Kosofsky. *Between Men: English Literature and Male Homosocial Desire*. New York: Columbia UP, 1985. Print.

Showalter, Elaine. "Dr. Jekyll's Closet." *Sexual Anarchy: Gender and Culture at the Fin de Siècle*. New York: Penguin, 1990. 105–26. Print.

Signorotti, Elizabeth. "Repossessing the Body: Transgressive Desire in 'Carmilla' and *Dracula*." *Criticism* 38.4 (1996): 607–32. Print.

Stoddart, Helen. "'The Precautions of Nervous People Are Infectious': Sherida le Fanu's Symptomatic Gothic." *The Modern Language Review* 86.1 (1991): 19–34. Print.

True Blood. Dir. Alan Ball et al. Perf. Stephen Moyer, Alexander Skarsgard, and Anna Paquin. 2008–13. DVD.

Tuite, Clara. "Cloistered Closets: Enlightenment Pornography, the Confessional State, Homosexual Persecution in *The Monk*." *Romanticism on the Net*. 8 (1997): n.pag. *érudit.org*. Web. 18 November 2012.

Veeder, William. "Carmilla: The Arts of Repression." *Texas Studies in Literature and Language* 22.2 (1980): 197–223. Print.

16

Same-Sex Friendships and the Rise of Modern Sexualities

CHRISTOPHER CASTIGLIA

The History of Sexuality and the Nineteenth-Century "Homosexual"

A man walks into a department store and is greeted by a handsome salesman. The customer, Al, tells the salesman he's looking for a bed and mattress but can't afford much because his rent is so high. The salesman, Josh, says he's looking for a roommate and proposes that Al move in with him. No need for a bed, he adds, smiling; you can share mine. The two men do share a bed for the next several years and develop the deepest intimacy. When his family pressures Josh to marry, both men are anguished by the separation. Al writes to his beloved Josh nearly every day, telling Josh that if he can hide his aversion until after the wedding, perhaps one day he'll be happy in his marriage. Al begs Josh and his new bride to settle near him, but they don't and the relationship between the two men cools. Al eventually marries, unhappily, and fathers children, but he continues to share his bed with other men when his wife is out of town.

A pretty gay story, except that the scene takes place in the 1830s in Springfield, Illinois. "Al" would become the sixteenth president of the United States and emancipate the slaves while "Josh" would become a Southern plantation owner. The passionate, anguished, affectionate, beseeching letters from Abraham Lincoln to Joshua Speed read like love letters, and love letters they were. But was love between men in the 1830s the same thing it is – or is assumed to be – in the twenty-first century? Does love necessarily involve sex? Do intense passion, sensuality, and affection reveal sexuality? Was the passion between friends a usual stage of development for nineteenth-century American men and women who lived in a largely gender-segregated world that discouraged premarital interaction between the sexes? Was Abraham Lincoln physically attracted to men and if so was his subsequent marriage a sham, the product of internalized shame? On what evidence can we answer these questions? What difference does it make if we *can't* answer them, if love, sex, romance, friendship – the relatively few names we have for the wide range of complex, ambivalent, intense, commonplace, erotic, chaste, short-lived, or long-term relationships we call intimacy – remain as opaque as a culture with an unknown language?

From a contemporary standpoint, quite a few nineteenth-century authors might appear gay or lesbian, including Nathaniel Hawthorne, Sarah Orne Jewett, Walt Whitman, Kate Chopin, Herman Melville, Emily Dickinson, William Dean Howells, and Henry James. Another group of lesser-known authors – Theodore Winthrop, Elizabeth Stoddard, Fitz Hugh Ludlow, Margaret Mussey Sweat, Hannah Crafts, Bayard Taylor, among others – seems downright queer. But what we are seeing when we think we see homosexuality in these writers is far from clear. As Michel Foucault famously asserted in *The History of Sexuality*, the category of the "homosexual" came into existence only at the end of the nineteenth century, long after the lives of most of these authors ("heterosexual" had to wait until the twentieth century to be invented). As homosexuality became a legal, medical, and psychological category, it came to characterize not individual acts (sodomy, for instance), but a type of *personality* – the homosexual – whose sexuality was innate, fundamental, and legible in every aspect of the homosexual's life. This is not to say that people before the 1880s did not have same-sex intimacies – often intense and physical ones – or that people did not perform acts we might today consider "sex" with others of the same gender. It *is* to suggest, however, that the intensities, creativity, rituals, varieties, and rhetoric of nineteenth-century intimacy might prove quite different – perhaps queerer – than our options for intimacy today.

Ralph Waldo Emerson, Masculinity, and Men's Romantic Friendships

In her 1975 essay "The Female World of Love and Ritual," historian Carroll Smith-Rosenberg made available for study one such form of once-common intimacy that is rarely acknowledged today: women's romantic friendships. Studying a range of same-sex female relationships from "the supportive love of sisters, through the enthusiasms of adolescent girls, to sensual avowals of love by mature women" in "a world in which men made but a shadowy appearance" (2), Smith-Rosenberg argues that women's romantic friendships were "both socially acceptable and fully compatible with heterosexual marriage" (8). Living almost entirely within "supportive networks [that] were institutionalized in social conventions or rituals which accompanied virtually every important event in a woman's life," women developed same-sex relationships characterized by "emotional richness" and "devotion to and love of other women" (9). Often physical as well as emotional, "the female world of love and ritual" produced intimacies more flexible, emotional, sensual, and volatile than those usually possible after the "invention" of heterosexuality, when, despite stereotypes of women's natural emotionality, asexuality, and nurturance, such friendships might be perceived as manifestations of an abhorrent sexuality.

For men, the changes wrought on patterns of romantic friendship by an emerging hetero-homosexual binary were arguably more drastic, as Axel Nissen has documented. Whereas men in the first half of the nineteenth century shared friendships every bit as effusively "romantic" as those studied by Smith-Rosenberg, by the end of the century regulated gender codes equated masculinity with competitive individualism and rational practicality, making the loving relationships between men – and the multiple models of manhood they enabled – nearly impossible to maintain. Anxiety over more rigid definitions of manhood led to more definite distinctions between heterosexual and homosexual men, the intimacies and rhetoric of "romantic friendship" becoming the exclusive property of the latter.

How different the case was in the first half of the nineteenth century becomes evident when the renowned philosopher of self-reliance turned his attention to same-sex friendship. In his 1841 essay "Friendship," Ralph Waldo Emerson asks, "What [is] so delicious as a just and firm encounter of two, in a thought, in a feeling?" (116). In a strikingly non-transcendental confession, Emerson reports that a friend is "a great event, and hinders me from sleep" (117), adding, "Everything that is his, – in his name, his form, his dress, books and instruments, – fancy embraces" (117). Given the emotional and imaginative richness friendship engenders, Emerson concluded that "every man passes his life in the search after friendship" (118), which, "like the immortality of the soul, is too good to be believed" (117).

Emerson's meditation makes visible three characteristics of many – though not all – nineteenth-century romantic friendships, traits that distinguish such friendships from modern sexuality. The first is Emerson's focus on *relationships*. Unlike modern sexuality, which is conventionally conceived as an individuating property of a body "oriented" toward other types of bodies, friendship was conceived as a social impulse uniting specific people. One can be "gay" or "lesbian" without other people, but it takes at least two to make a friendship. Second, as Smith-Rosenberg and Nissen note, romantic friendships were marked by a rhetorical intensity, as when Emerson writes of "palpitation which the approach of a stranger causes" (115), of friendship's "delicious torment" (118). Third and most important, there is a visionary cast to many romantic friendships, proclaiming possibilities for what Emerson calls "new worlds of our own creation" (116). Often taking the form of reverie, daydream, or fantasy, these visions show how same-sex friendships motivated writers like Emerson to yearn for new feelings, creativities, and social relationships.

Emily Dickinson's Love Letters and the Anguish of Friendship

Although romantic friendships often took on an idealistic cast, they could also be marked by anguish, loss, and disorientation. Idealism and disappointment, anticipation and apprehension, coexist, generating the emotional and rhetorical excesses that make romantic friendship – like other forms of love – hard to assess by outsiders. Such is the case in one of the best-known nineteenth-century romantic friendships, that between the poet Emily Dickinson and her sister-in-law Susan Gilbert. A letter written on June 11, 1852, from Dickinson to Gilbert is worth quoting at length for the way it typifies such vertiginous alternations in mood. Dickinson writes:

> I have but one thought, Susie, this afternoon of June, and that of you, and I have one prayer, only; dear Susie, that is for you. That you and I in hand as we e'en do in heart, might ramble away as children, among the woods and fields, and forget these many years, and these sorrowing cares, and each become a child again – I would it were so, Susie, and when I look around me and find myself alone, I sigh for you again; little sigh, and vain sigh, which will not bring you home.
>
> I need you more and more, and the great world grows wider, and dear ones fewer and fewer, every day that you stay away – I miss my biggest heart; my own goes wandering round, and calls for Susie – Friends are too dear to sunder, Oh they are far too few, and how soon they will go away where you and I cannot find them, don't let us forget these things, for their remembrance now will save us many an anguish when it is too late to love them! Susie, forgive me Darling, for every word I say – my heart is full of you, none other than you is in my thoughts, yet when I seek to say to you something not for the world, words fail me. If you were here – and Oh that you were, my Susie, we need not talk at all, our eyes would whisper for us, and your hand fast in mine, we would not ask for language – I try to bring you nearer, I chase the weeks away till they are quite departed, and fancy you have come, and I am on my way through the green lane to meet you, and my heart goes scampering so, that I have much ado to bring it back again, and learn it to be patient, till that

dear Susie comes. Three weeks – they can't last always, for surely they must
go with their little brothers and sisters to their long home in the west!   (33)

Dickinson's letter shows how complicated romantic friendships could become
when they were carried out in correspondence, as they often were. Dickinson
asserts a sameness of sentiment between the two women, who share joys
and "sorrowing cares." At the same time, there is an emotional and physical
distance between the friends, evident in Dickinson's plea for Gilbert's forgiveness and her subtle encouragement that Gilbert not forget the value of friendship. Just as letters create the illusion of direct communication even as they
respond to physical distance, so the insistence on shared sentiment is enabled
by a friend's absence because the presence of another's unpredictable, often
inscrutable, and possibly censorious reactions threaten romantic correspondence, in both senses of the term.

Romantic correspondence between friends often proved temporally disorienting as well. Dickinson's letter moves precariously from past to future (and
back), as in lines like "don't let us forget these things, for their remembrance
now will save us many an anguish when it is too late to love them!" Picturing a
future when the present is a remembered past, learning from past experiences
(that are the current present) so as to prevent anguish in the future, which
can be retroactively remedied through remembrance, romantic friends like
Dickinson and Gilbert combine the past of memory with the future of anticipation in order to form a temporal bridge across spaces too far apart.

Romantic Friendship's Racial Politics

Romantic same-sex friendships were often perceived as socially transformative, yet often they strained under the tension between reform and self-inter-
ested prejudice, especially when those friendships formed across the color
line. Racial differences both intensify and undermine friendship's potential
for libratory social change. In his 1948 essay "Come Back to the Raft Ag'in,
Huck Honey," Leslie Fiedler catalogued the many homoerotic friendships in
American literature between men of different races, from James Fennimore
Cooper's Natty Bumppo and Chingachgook to Mark Twain's Huckleberry
Finn and Jim. Those friendships end badly for the men of color (Chingachgook
loses his only son and his tribal lands, while Jim repeatedly suffers on the
Mississippi simply because Huck neglects to inform Jim of his manumis-
sion). Fiedler might have included the friendship in Harriet Beecher Stowe's
Uncle Tom's Cabin between the white slaveholder Augustine St. Clare and two
slaves, Scipio (who nurses St. Clare through a deadly fever but dies himself)

and Tom (who prays for his master's salvation but dies because St. Clare's procrastination results in Tom's sale down river).

Other novels depict interracial romantic friendships that end no less disastrously, although not necessarily for the heroine of color. In Catharine Maria Sedgwick's 1827 *Hope Leslie*, for instance, the romantic friendship between the eponymous heroine and the Indian princess Magawisca terminates with the latter's return to the wilderness, but not before she narrates the wrongs done her people. In Hannah Crafts's *The Bondwoman's Narrative* – one of the few narratives of romantic same-sex friendships penned by an African American – Hannah flees slavery through her friendships with a series of white women who teach her to read, give her money, and enable her escape, and in those friendships the white women suffer (through banishment, lost property, shame, and death), while Hannah achieves freedom. By and large, however, novels featuring cross-racial romantic friendships, the few that exist, prove Foucault's insight that same-sex friendships have the potential to form unexpected alliances (see Foucault, "Friendship"), a potential that made them both a vehicle for reform and an occasion for social prejudice.

One of the most famous cross-racial romantic friendships in nineteenth-century literature also founders between reform and retrenchment. When Ishmael, the narrator of Herman Melville's *Moby-Dick*, attempts to rent a room in the seaport of New Bedford, Massachusetts, he finds the inn full except for a bed he is invited to share with a harpooner, the heathenish and possibly cannibalistic South Pacific islander Queequeg. Ishmael's trepidation deepens when, already undressed and in bed, he sees Queequeg, large and exotically tattooed, enter the darkened room. After much panicked carrying on, Ishmael and Queequeg settle into bed together, the latter enfolding the former in "his bridegroom clasp" (33), leading Ishmael to observe, "you had almost thought I had been his wife" (32). Ishmael acknowledges the unusual occurrence of "hugging a fellow male in that matrimonial sort of style" (33–34), marveling at how quickly Queequeg "take[s] to me quite as naturally and unbiddenly as I to him" (53). But Ishmael resolves to "try a pagan friend," admitting, "I began to feel mysteriously drawn toward him" (53). By the end of their brief stay together at the inn, Queequeg proclaims that "henceforth we were married; meaning, in his country's phrase, that we were bosom friends" (53) and, as Ishmael reports, "in our hearts' honeymoon, lay I and Queequeg – a cosy, loving pair" (54). The end of the episode reforms Ishmael's racial prejudices and his phobia against anonymous intimacy, yet Ishmael's sense of that reform as innocently exotic and his self-satisfaction at overcoming his repulsion disguise – for Ishmael at least – his self-interest (Ishmael gains not only a bed but half Queequeg's savings and a protector aboard the whaling ship). Although the often cross-racial romantic friendships in Melville's fiction exemplify what Richard Chase identified as the "blissful, idyllic, erotic attachment to life and to one's comrades, which is the only promise of happiness" (107), such relationships are often haunted by disappointment, death, betrayal, and abandonment, suggesting friendship's difficulties in maintaining long-term resolutions between reform and convention.

Hawthorne, Melville, Whitman: Friendship's Romantic Canon

Reform becomes the occasion for exploring the possibilities and limitations of friendships between men in Nathaniel Hawthorne's 1852 *The Blithedale Romance*, a fictionalized account of the author's stay at the utopian commune Brook Farm. Hawthorne describes the tumultuous friendship between the foppish Miles Coverdale and the iron-willed reformer Hollingsworth. Despite his austere rectitude, Hollingsworth surprises Coverdale with occasional tenderness, episodes when "his dark, shaggy face looked really beautiful with its expression of thoughtful benevolence" (28). When, soon after his arrival at Blithedale, Coverdale becomes dangerously ill, Hollingsworth serves as his nurse. Although Coverdale contends that men "really have no tenderness," about his friend he finds "something of the woman moulded into the great stalwart frame of Hollingsworth, nor was he ashamed of it, as men often are of what is best in them" (39). As his illness reaches its crisis, Coverdale reports, "I besought Hollingsworth to let nobody else enter the room, but continually to make me sensible of his own presence by a grasp of the hand, a word, a prayer, if he thought good to utter it" (39).

Hawthorne's same-sex friendships generally turn out to be deadly betrayals (Dimmesdale and Chillingworth in *The Scarlet Letter* or Hilda and Miriam in *The Marble Faun*) or tame irrelevancies (Kenyon and Donnatello in *The Marble Faun*). The intimacy between Coverdale and Hollingsworth is neither, although it, too, has no future. Coverdale can imagine his future with Hollingsworth only in death, admitting his regret "that I did not die then, when I had tolerably made up my mind to, for Hollingsworth would have gone with me to the hither verge of life, and have sent his friendly and hopeful accents far over on the other side" (39). Hollingsworth, not Coverdale, dies, however, at least in spirit. When Hollingsworth beseeches Coverdale to join him in his plans to reform prisoners, telling him "'there is not the man in this whole world whom I can love as I could you. Do not forsake me!'" (124), Coverdale refuses.

"Had I but touched his extended hand," he acknowledges, "Hollingsworth's magneticism would perhaps have penetrated me," but instead, he confesses, "I stood aloof" (124). When Hollingsworth asks one last time if Coverdale will be his "friend of friends forever" (125), the consequences of Coverdale's silence produce one of the most heart-wrenching scenes in all of Hawthorne's fiction.

> I never said the word – and certainly can never have it to say hereafter – that cost me a thousandth part so hard an effort as did that one syllable. The heart-pang was not merely figurative, but an absolute torture of the breast. I was gazing steadfastly at Hollingsworth. It seemed to me that it struck him, too, like a bullet. A ghastly paleness – always so terrific on a swarthy face – overspread his features. There was a convulsive movement of his throat, as if he were forcing down some words that struggled and fought for utterance. Whether words of anger, or words of grief, I cannot tell; though many and many a time I have vainly tormented myself with conjecturing which of the two they were. One other appeal to my friendship – such as once, already, Hollingsworth had made, – taking me in the revulsion that followed a strenuous exercise of opposing will, would completely have subdued me. But he left the matter there. "Well!" said he. (126)

In his depiction of the tragic friendship of Coverdale and Hollingsworth Hawthorne may have had in mind the end of his own brief but intense friendship with the equally shaggy and tender Melville. In one November 1851 letter to Hawthorne, Melville responds to Hawthorne's praise for *Moby-Dick*, which Melville dedicated to him.

> Your letter was handed me last night on the road going to Mr. Morewood's, and I read it there. Had I been at home, I would have sat down at once and answered it. In me divine magnanimities are spontaneous and instantaneous – catch them while you can. The world goes round, and the other side comes up. So now I can't write what I felt. But I felt pantheistic then – your heart beat in my ribs and mine in yours, and both in God's. A sense of unspeakable security is in me this moment, on account of your having understood the book. (*Hawthorne* 240)

Proclaiming his friendship "without licentious inclination," Melville asks, "Whence come you, Hawthorne? By what right do you drink from my flagon of life? And when I put it to my lips – lo, they are yours and not mine. I feel that the Godhead is broken up like the bread at the Supper, and that we are the pieces. Hence this infinite fraternity of feeling" (240). The difficulty in maintaining such a fraternity, as I've already suggested, is that feelings rarely correlate across bodies in any but a metaphoric way. When Melville imagines

Hawthorne's presence – their lips joining on the highly allegorical flagon – the unity is imaginary and hence perfect. Real bodies, however, tend to frustrate such fraternal unions, because they are made by divergent and largely unknowable experiences (as suggested by Melville not knowing from whence Hawthorne came) and consequent divergences of desire, as the literature Melville produced after the end of his "romantic friendship" with Hawthorne shows.

Whether or not their romantic friendship was on Hawthorne's mind as he wrote *Blithedale*, it almost certainly was on Melville's when he penned his epic 1876 poem, *Clarel*. When the American Clarel travels to the Holy Land in search of spiritual fulfillment, he finds instead a romantic friendship with Vine, who strikingly resembles Hawthorne. Upon their first encounter, the two "exchanged quick sympathies / Though but in glance," creating an "excess of feeling" (91, 94). Clarel worries whether Vine, taciturn as Hawthorne, will enter "communion true / And close; let go each alien theme; / Give me thyself!" (95), but is ultimately disappointed, as Vine fails to understand Clarel's "thrill / Of personal longing" (226). Caught between his romantic expectations and Vine's responses, Clarel, like Hollingsworth, anguishes:

> After confidings that should wed
> Our souls in one: – Ah, call me *brother!*
> So feminine his passionate mood
> Which, long as hungering unfed,
> All else rejected or withstood.
> Some inkling he let fall. But no: (226–27)

Melville comes close to assigning this failure of romantic friendship to sexual anxiety, as Clarel despairs over the impossibility of physical love between men.

> But for thy fonder dream of love
> In man toward man – the soul's caress –
> The negatives of flesh should prove
> Analogies of non-cordialness
> In spirit. –E'en such conceits could cling
> To Clarel's dream of vain surmise
> And imputation full of sting. (227)

Other poets, however, were more sanguine about the possibilities of physical as well as emotional and spiritual intimacy between male friends. Throughout his poems Walt Whitman "celebrate[s] the need of comrades," proclaiming his release from "the pleasures, profits, conformities, / Which too long I was offering to feed my Soul" once he recognizes that "the Soul of the man I speak for, feeds, rejoices only in comrades" ("In Paths Untrodden"). Accompanied by "he whom I love," the poet is "charged with untold and untellable wisdom – I am silent – I require nothing further" for, he reports, "I am satisfied, / He ahold of my hand has completely satisfied me" ("O the Terrible Question of Appearances"). Although he takes no pleasure in hearing that his "name had been received with plaudits in the capitol," Whitman writes in "When I Heard at the Close of Day" that:

> when I thought how my dear friend, my lover, was on his way coming, O then I was happy;
> O then each breath tasted sweeter – and all that day my food nourished me more – And the beautiful day passed well,
> And the next came with equal joy – And with the next, at evening, came my friend;
>
> And that night, while all was still, I heard the waters roll slowly continually up the shores,
> I heard the hissing rustle of the liquid and sands, as directed to me, whispering, to congratulate me,
> For the one I love most lay sleeping by me under the same cover in the cool night,
> In the stillness, in the autumn moonbeams, his face was inclined toward me,
> And his arm lay lightly around my breast – And that night I was happy.

Popular Fiction's Friendships: Margaret Mussey Sweat

The authors just discussed – Emerson, Dickinson, Hawthorne, Melville, Whitman – show how central romantic friendship was to canonical nineteenth-century American literature. Romantic friendship took its most innovative, intense, and unpredictable forms, however, in popular fiction by authors now – perhaps not coincidentally – mostly unknown. "As with minor literatures," Lauren Berlant observes, "minor intimacies have been forced to develop aesthetics of the extreme" (5–6). Unlike marriage and parenthood, the "minor intimacies" of romantic friendships populate the extreme aesthetics of the nineteenth century's "minor" literature.

In Margaret Jane Mussey Sweat's 1859 epistolary novel, *Ethel's Love-Life*, for example, Ethel's letters to her fiancé, Ernest, depict romantic friendships more erotic, sadomasochistic, secretive, and threatening than those described by Smith-Rosenberg. Ethel is initiated into "the female world of love and ritual" through intense passion and pain that allow her to criticize romantic conventions and to articulate visions of a world tolerant of and conducive to women's intimate relationships. "Women often love each other with as much fervor and excitement as they do men," Ethel reports, and the "emotions awakened heave and swell through the whole being as the tides swell the ocean. Freed from all the grosser elements of passion, as it exists between the sexes," Ethel observes, "it retains its energy, its abandonment, its flush, its eagerness, its palpitations, and its rapture – but all so refined, so glorified, and made delicious and continuous by an ever-recurring giving and receiving from each to each" (82). Women's passionate friendships, Ethel reveals, "are of much more frequent occurrence than the world is aware of" because it "sees only the ordinary appearances of an intimate acquaintanceship, and satisfies itself with a few common-place comments thereon – but the joy and beauty of the tie remain in sweet concealment – silent and inexpressive when careless eyes are upon it, but leaping into the sunlight when free from cold and repelling influences" (83). Ethel knows that her friendships comprise "all its intensity of feeling and all its impetuosity of action" possible only "when the conscious and dissecting powers are in abeyance," leaving the passions to "declare to us their continued dominion" (68–69).

Such romantic friendships are erotic, if not downright kinky. Enjoying the "longing, burning look" (70) of her "stormy, fiery, tempestuous" (69) friend, the "haunting demon Leonora" (92), Ethel reports that Leonora "smothered me with hot kisses" (70) followed by "passionate outpourings of her long pent-up love" (71) before which, Ethel confesses, "I gave myself up with delirious joy" (71). Ethel's friendship with Claudia is just as steamy. Claudia's "serene loftiness" (85) vanishes once Ethel "bend[s] her iron will to my own," enjoying "the loving glance with which she gave her obedience" (88). During Claudia's absence, Ethel believes that "I visit her in the night hours as she visits me – that a wailing cry for the love she has lost sometimes escapes her – that there is an invisible bond which still unites each to the other" (91–92).

Unbreakable "bonds" notwithstanding, unlike the romantic friendships that, according to Smith-Rosenberg, were fully compatible with marriage, Ethel's same-sex passions overshadow and seem opposed to her marriage. Pledging to her fiancé, Ernest, that the "whole of our future shall be consecrated unto noblest uses" (232), Ethel acknowledges that such a future comes only through – and the pun is significant – "earnest labor" (116) because, she admits, the "harness of prescribed routine galls and wearies me" (200). Recognizing that "the natural affections of family and kindred were merely the result of monotonous habit, in which we acquiesced, partly from indolence and partly from fear of finding nothing better if we gave it up" (135), Ethel can imagine "visions of impossible, super-human bliss" (230) in romantic friendships existing outside "a too slavish obedience to that routine developed into wearisome detail of days and hours" (200). For Ethel, who "scorn[s] what the rest of the world seemed to find well enough" (134), visions in which she lives "outside of the laws which governed those about me" (129) are respites from "weary conventionalism" (59), and if Ethel is "still and hushed" as she "brood[s]" over her love for Ernest, still she declares, "I love to wander hither and thither, wherever the whim takes me, in all the other aspects of my life" (199).

And wander she does. Ethel observes, "My twenty years of life must be spread fairly out before me as a chart for study; and the apparent incongruities and contradictions of feeling which marked it must be reconciled and explained to myself, or the future would have no guiding knowledge, no assured path" (113). But Ethel's letters, "wandering away from the little narrative of my external life," frustrate such explanations. Her narrative, "without arrangement and almost without dates" (121), meanders like her dreams and memories. As she warns Ernest, "for one like me, a steady and continuous narrative of incidents is quite out of the question, nor would such a one, however minute in external details, help you to full understanding of myself. I must be fragmentary and irregular in my story, for my life has been episodical and violently contrasted" (42).

The force that most distracts Ethel from the future is, of course, her past. Although she sometimes characterizes her "sad memories" (113) as a "fiend calling up the irrevocable past, with all hidden specters to appal my shrinking sight" (38) and at other moments claims that "all that I now call 'the past'" at present "seems so far away, so mist-like and vague, compared to the sharp-cut and real emotions of the present" (97–98), Ethel, giving her letters over to reminiscence, recognizes, "my mind went backward without reluctance, and memory led me by the hand, a willing visitor, among the chambers of the past" (222). More than transparent recollections, however, Ethel's memories of romantic friendship are, like her "long-continued day-dreams" (127), imaginative departures from proscriptive conventions. Ethel "lay wrapt for hours in dreams" or "aimless reveries" that seem "quite as real as any true and actual experience of the past" (73–74). In her dreams, Ethel reports, "my imagination subdued my reason, my fancy enchained my intellect" and she inhabits "a charmed atmosphere of romance" (18). Only a fanciful "extreme aesthetics" can convey the passion, release, and transport that characterize Sweat's vision of romantic friendship.

Same-Sex Friendship and Subculture:
Theodore Winthrop

As an historical phenomenon, romantic friendship is as difficult to reconcile and explain as Ethel's life narrative. Characteristic features – emotional and rhetorical excess, diffuse sensuality, alternations of joy and despair, presumption of common experience, temporal and narrative disruption, speculative visions – extend to greater or lesser degrees across the range of friendships discussed earlier. Such features make it hard to discern where romantic friendships end and modern sexuality begins. And that is the point. Modern sexuality did not emerge fully formed at a certain historical date with the invention of certain terminologies. Rather, discourses that would eventually cohere into sexual taxonomies were composed, contested, and modified (or abandoned) over the nineteenth and into the twentieth century. Romantic friendships were one such compositional site. Certain features – such as visionary intimacy – were cancelled out by the diagnostic *presence* of modern sexuality. But others survived and developed, and the network of romantic friendships became, over time, the same-sex subcultures inhabited by sexual minorities in the twentieth and twenty-first centuries.

The transformation of romantic friendships into same-sex subculture is central to the work of Theodore Winthrop, whose 1862 novel *Cecil Dreeme* begins with its narrator, Robert Byng, newly returned from Europe, occupying the apartment of Harry Stillfleet, a prototype of what by the late nineteenth century would be called an Aesthete, as personified by Oscar Wilde. Stillfleet's bachelor pad – affectionately named the Rubbish Palace – is crammed with incongruous artworks and relics organized by their owner's quirky aesthetic taste, or what Byng calls "a fine sense of order in the apparent disorder" (51), legible only to those "in the know." There are intimations of camp sensibility in this "theatrical" space that, filled with "uncertified and riotous color" (52), turns rubbish into taste. More important, the Rubbish Palace is "magic, phantasmagorical" (38), exerting a "dreamy influence" (39) that creates a "certain romantic feeing of expectation" (39).

The Rubbish Palace exists, furthermore, within Chrysalis College, described as "unreal and incongruous" (126). As its name suggests, Chrysalis protects and nourishes an inchoate network of unwieldy same-sex intimacies, beginning with Byng and the swarthy and hypnotic Densdeth. Whereas the proto-Aesthete collects and collates art so as to suggest his taste, Densdeth is a dandy who reveals his taste by becoming a living artwork. Possessing a "dark, handsome face" (62) and "a delicate lisp" (74), the "nomad bachelor" (77) is "a little too carefully dressed" with "a conscious air" (29). Like other dandies, Densdeth evinces "perfect sensitiveness and perfect enjoyment" (63) and proclaims, "'I love luxury for its own sake'" (63). Byng admits of Densdeth, "'When his eyes were upon me, I felt something stir in my heart'" (65), awakening "dev- ilish passions," "slumbering lightly, and ready to stir whenever [they] knew a comrade was near" (330). Densdeth is just such a comrade, and Byng readily accepts his "proffered alliance" (66).

Byng's other romantic friendship is with the artist Cecil Dreeme, who is, like Densdeth, "a man of another order, not easy to classify" (138). Like the dreams for which he is named, Cecil is "original, unexpected" (99). When Cecil turns out to be the disguised heiress Clara Denman, however, the dream becomes a nightmare for Byng, who considers his friendships with men "more precious than the love of women" (234–235). Although Clara assures him, "'We shall not be friends the less'" (337), Byng has his doubts, claiming of his friend- ship with Cecil, "This was love, – unforced, self-created, undoubting, com- plete. And now that the friend proved a woman, a great gulf opened between us. Thinking thus, I let fall Cecil's hand, and drew apart a little" (347–48). Even after Clara's revelation, the narrator continues to use the male pseud- onym and the masculine pronoun, perpetuating the visionary friendship with Cecil " – for so I must call him" (338).

Just as important to Byng is preserving Cecil's status as a Dreeme. Although the unwieldy excesses of romantic friendships in the novel appear to be con- tained through Densdeth's death and Cecil's return to Clara, social conven- tions are haunted in *Cecil Dreeme*, as in *Ethel's Love-Life*, by persistent memory and desire, which disrupt and offer alternatives to the normative present. Same-sex romantic friendships in both novels transform social alienation into visions, the opening of imaginative spaces beyond present social imperatives, protected by an aura of imminence that inspires rather than prescribes.

The visionary friendships in *Cecil Dreeme* become inchoate subculture in another of Winthrop's novels, *John Brent*, in which the narrator, Richard Wade, asserts, "there is a small but ancient fraternity in the world, known as the Order of Gentlemen" (101). The men of this Order, although of different clas- ses, nationalities, professions, and religions, share social alienation and a con- sequent sympathy with other outsiders, forming a subculture – an "Order" – whose members recognize each other without explicit tokens of institutional association. "The formulas of the order are not edited," Wade claims,

its passwords are not syllabled; its uniform was never pictured in a fashion- plate, or so described that a snob could go to his tailor, and say, "Make me the habit of a gentleman." But the brothers know each other unerringly wherever they meet be they of the inner shrine, gentlemen heart and life; be they of the outer court, gentlemen in feeling and demeanor.

No disguise delays this recognition. No strangeness of place and circumstances prevents it. The men meet. The magnetism passes between them. All is said without words. Gentlemen know gentlemen by what we name instinct. But observe that this thing, instinct, is character in its finest, keenest, largest, and most concentrated action. It is the spirit's touch. (102–03)

In *John Brent*, Winthrop turns romantic friendships between "brothers and friends" (103) into an incipient subculture that relies not on permanence, written codes, uniforms, mutual disclosure, social reproduction, or abstracted agency, but rather on taste, fruitless effort, improvisation, contingency, and especially romantic same-sex friendships.

Above all, the subcultures emerging in novels like *Cecil Dreeme* and *John Brent* are places of unprecedented and transformative visions that honor the insights gained through suffering rather than promising its eradication. Winthrop's eponymous hero is Wade's "model comrade" (53), described as "delicate, beautiful, dreamy" (41). Brent's painful early life "went near to crush all the innocence, faith, hope, and religion out of my friend's life," Wade reports, yet Brent's heart "was made of stuff that does not know how to break" (41). "Steady disappointment, by and by, informs a man that he is in the wrong place" (9), and Brent's suffering indeed drives him "out of the common paths, to make him a seer instead of a doer" (43). Brent's "very vague" visions are unclear to the reader, but Wade asserts that the seer "must see to the end before he begins to say what he sees," until which time philistines dismiss him as "a purposeless dreamer" (43). Wade himself knows visions are "an innovation, a revolution" (313), an imaginative magnetism that binds survivors into subcultures that honor and inspire in turn more visions, the metaphysical yield of romantic friendship.

Such visions may have disappeared in the splitting of romantic friendship into modern conventions in which the romantic dyadic couple is privileged over a network of friends. As the broad world of same-sex friendships narrowed to what Henry James in his 1886 novel *The Bostonians* called "Boston marriages" or what he might have called "bachelor households" – in which two people of the same gender co-inhabit in long-term relationships tolerated as "open secrets" only as long as they remained private and de-eroticized – the creative possibilities for same-sex sociality beyond the couple did not simply disappear but, as Martha Vicinus shows, continued as romantic relationships that translated friendship into the erotic, economic, and representational ways of life that in the twentieth century became known as "Sapphic" or "lesbian." Moreover, as Winthrop's novels show, romantic friendships gave way to subcultures that took friendship's capacity for forming unpredictable and potentially transformative alliances and opened it into the broad network often loosely referred to as "community." Varieties of gay and lesbian communities retained many of the possibilities for extremely imaginative redefinitions of intimacy, camaraderie, romance, and collective agency that, for Winthrop and Sweat, were intrinsic to same-sex friendship. In the twentieth century, such subcultures became as well key mediums for protection, economic vitality, circulation of information, and proliferations of pleasure. In "coming out" into a more identity-restricted social complex, same-sex friendships might have lost their status as visionary, but they did not necessarily lose their power to inspire imaginings of what "the social" might mean. For as Emerson reminds us, "Friends, such as we desire, are dreams and fables. But a sublime hope cheers ever the faithful heart, that elsewhere, in other regions of the universal power, souls are now acting, enduring and daring, which can love us, and which we can love" (125). The archive of nineteenth-century same-sex friendship reminds us of how fascinating, unwieldy, innovative, and unnerving – how *romantic* – friendships can be.

Works Cited

Berlant, Lauren, "Intimacy: A Special Issue." *Intimacy.* Chicago: U of Chicago P, 2000. 3–8. Print.

Chase, Richard. *The American Novel and Its Tradition.* Baltimore: Johns Hopkins UP, 1957. Print.

Dickinson, Emily. *Open Me Carefully: Emily Dickinson's Intimate Letters to Susan Huntington Dickinson.* Ed. Ellen Louise Hart and Martha Nell Smith. Ashfield: Paris P, 1998. Print.

Emerson, Ralph Waldo. "Friendship." *Collected Essays: The Complete Original First Series.* 1841. Rockville: Arc Manor, 2007. 115–26. Print.

Foucault, Michel. "Friendship as a Way of Life." Trans. John Johnston. *Foucault Live: Interviews 1961–84.* New York: Semiotext(e), 1989. 203–09. Print.

The History of Sexuality, Volume 1: An Introduction. Trans. Robert Hurley. New York: Random House, 1978. Print.

Hawthorne, Nathaniel. *The Blithedale Romance.* 1852. Ed. Seymour Gross. New York: Norton, 1978. Print.

The Hawthorne and Melville Friendship: An Annotated Bibliography, Biographical and Critical Essays, and Correspondence between the Two. Ed. James C. Wilson. Jefferson: McFarland, 1991. Print.

Melville, Herman. *Clarel.* 1876. *The Writings of Herman Melville.* Vol. 12. Ed. Harrison Hayford, Herschel Parker, and G. Thomas Tanselle. Evanston: Northwestern UP, 1984. Print.

Moby-Dick. 1851. Ed. Harrison Hayford and Herschel Parker. New York: Norton, 1967. Print.

Nissen, Axel. *Manly Love: Romantic Friendship in American Fiction*. Chicago: U of Chicago P, 2009. Print.

Smith-Rosenberg, Carroll, "The Female World of Love and Ritual." *Signs* 1.1 (1975): 1–29. Print.

Sweat, Margaret Jane Mussey. *Ethel's Love-Life*. New York: Rudd and Carlton, 1859. Print.

Vicinus, Martha. *Romantic Friends: Women who Loved Women, 1778–1928*. Chicago: U of Chicago P, 2004. Print.

Whitman, Walt. *Leaves of Grass*. 1860. *The Complete Poems*. Ed. Francis Murphy. New York: Penguin, 2005. Print.

Winthrop, Theodore. *Cecil Dreeme*. Boston: Ticknor and Fields, 1862. Print.

John Brent. 1862. Ithaca: Cornell U Library, 2009. Print.

17

African American Writing until 1930

GERSHUN AVILEZ

The African presence in the United States and the construction of American black identity has a history of being sexualized. From this perspective, writing about racialization has often meant writing about sexual relations. Increasingly, scholars have drawn attention not simply to the sexualization of the black body, but also to the historical construction of sexual desire in the writings of African Americans. This chapter explores the representation of same-sex desire as well as the emergence of transgressive ideas about sexuality in these writings. The goal here has less to do with identifying the work of same-sex-desiring artists; instead the focus is on highlighting creative and non-fictional works that contribute to sexuality studies and queer studies. People with same-sex desire created some, but not all, of the texts discussed here.

In this chapter I consider African American writing and cultural expression from the antebellum period until 1930. There are actually three distinct eras contained in this historical range: the antebellum period, the postbellum/turn-of-the-century period, and the Harlem Renaissance. Critics rarely consider all three together. I attend to each separately to draw out the important historical events and artistic strategies that come to define each, while emphasizing salient historical continuities and resonances. This chapter outlines the significance of representations of nonnormative sexuality in African American expressive culture that become the context for late twentieth-century works by self-identified gay and lesbian artists.

The Perverse Erotic Logic of Enslavement

Although not all people of African descent living in the territories of the United States were enslaved, the social logic of enslavement came to inform the understanding and representation of blackness in general. Many of the early narratives that appear make plain how the intimacy surrounding black bodies was nonnormative or, in contemporary parlance, "queer." This opening section tracks the erotic dynamics of U.S. enslavement culture that help to unveil the imagining of all forms of black sexuality during the antebellum period. In his work on early African American literature, Robert Reid-Pharr makes the point that the black enslaved person often emerges in narrative presentations as a "queer animal" because of her "borderline subjectivity" (121). His point is that as legal property the enslaved person occupies a space that marks the boundary between being subject and object. The black writers who document their experiences of enslavement emphasize this vulnerable subject position and make clear that this vulnerability is often framed by sexual or sexualized encounters. Moreover, critical treatments have consistently shown that the logic of enslavement was perverse not simply in the abuse and misuses of power but in the sexual dynamics it encouraged and even required.

The 1829 Supreme Court case *State v. Mann* is an important social document in that it reveals the absolute power that an enslaver was understood as having over the enslaved. In his majority opinion Justice Thomas Ruffin declared: "We cannot allow the right of the master to be brought into discussion in the Courts of Justice. The slave, to remain a slave, must be made sensible, that there is no appeal from his master; that his power is in no instance, usurped; but is conferred by the laws of man at least, if not by the law of God." Importantly, this ostensibly divinely derived authority extended not only to the body's labor but also to the body itself. Recognizing this reality, written texts from the period demonstrate that there is an erotic dimension to such legal decisions.

In addition to establishing an encroaching and invasive racialized system of power, enslavement depended on making the black body into a sexualized spectacle. Public scenes of subjections such as the auction block and punitive whippings carry a sexualized valence. The infamous moment of Aunt Hester's beating by Captain Anthony in Frederick Douglass's 1845 *A Narrative of the Life of Frederick Douglass* stands as only one familiar example of this dynamic. Douglass narrates:

> Before he commenced whipping Aunt Hester, he took her to the kitchen, and stripped her from neck to waist, leaving her neck, shoulders, and back, entirely naked. He then told her to cross her hands, calling her at the same time a d – d b – h. After crossing her hands, he tied them with a strong rope, and led her to a stool under a large hook in the joist, put in for the purpose. He made her get upon the stool, and tied her hands to the hook. She now stood fair for his infernal purpose. Her arms were stretched up at their full length, so that she stood upon the ends of her toes. He then said to her, "Now, you d – d b – h, I'll learn you how to disobey my orders!" and after rolling up his

sleeves, he commenced to lay on the heavy cowskin, and soon the warm, red
blood (amid heart-rending shrieks from her, and horrid oaths from him) came
dripping to the floor.   (4–5)

Such spectacles of punishment become figures of reiterative discursive violence in the texts in which they appear, as both Saidiya Hartman and Fred
Moten argue.[1] The auction block itself as a physical means of commerce
entailed the exhibiting of the black body, the baring of breasts and genitals, as
well as the literal accounting of flesh. In this sense, bodily invasion welcomed
captives into servitude.

Many artists and thinkers responded to these exhibitionist representations
and consequential sexualized understandings of the black body by relying
on modes of silence in framing black sexuality and intimacy. This approach
would later result in what Evelyn Brooks Higginbotham called the "politics
of respectability," to which I will return later. This resistance to talking about
the sexual abuses of enslavement culture manifests itself in Henry Bibbs's
autobiography *Narrative of the Life of Henry Bibb* (1849–50). Frances Smith
Foster details how Bibb implies his wife's rape, but refuses to discuss or even
acknowledge it explicitly; instead the reader encounters silence. The rhetorical moves that constitute this silence around sex occur in many narratives as a
means of self-protection; the silence is a strategic response to the exhibitionist
nature of enslavement culture and people's everyday experiences.

That being said, certain texts do purposefully pierce through this code of
silencing to broadcast the perversity of enslavement, the ubiquity of silence,
and the realities of nonconventional black intimacy. Harriett Jacobs's 1861
autobiography *Incidents in the Life of a Slave Girl*, which she published under
the pseudonym "Linda Brent," details the kinds of sexual abuses by their masters that young female slaves had to face on plantations specifically and in
general regardless of the location. The book also charts the homoerotic, coercive desire of the white mistress in the process of outlining the abuses of the
white master. The mistress Mrs. Flint's insistence on hearing in explicit detail
her husband's sexual abuse of the protagonist functions as a parallel moment
of sexual violation, as Karen Sanchez-Eppler makes evident in her reading.
Aliyyah Abdur-Rahman goes one step further in describing the enforced telling as a scene of violent erotic agency on Mrs. Flint's part and not solely as
an extension of her husband's dominance. In other words, Mrs. Flint takes
pleasure in the recitation and in making the protagonist re-experience the
sexual violence at her hands. Jacobs's book makes clear the sexual vulnerability of the enslaved woman to both male and female abuse, thereby opening possibilities of one means of reading for the homoerotic and sexually

nonconventional within an enslaving culture.[2] Importantly, the homoerotic punishing pleasure is also extended to the male body in Jacobs's text in her discussion of Luke. Luke is a young enslaved man who became "a prey to the vices growing out of the 'patriarchal institution'" (288). He was forced to wait on a bedridden master, who "took into his head the strangest freaks of despotism" (289). Jacobs goes on to explain: "[some] of these freaks were of a nature too filthy to be repeated. When I fled from the house of bondage, I left poor Luke still chained to the bedside of this cruel and disgusting wretch" (289). The fact that Luke is tied to a bed and made subject to such vices and "strangest freaks" suggests the possibility of male rape; his bondage may also entail same-sex sexual violation.

In her well-known essay "Mama's Baby, Papa's Maybe," Hortense Spillers argues that the historical operation of enslavement functioned as a gendering process for the captive body. Narrative writing from the period bears out this point. As explained earlier, the space of the auction block represented a site of scopic sexualization, but it also came to be represented in narratives as a site of un-gendering and re-gendering. Written in response to Harriett Beecher Stowe's best-selling 1852 novel *Uncle Tom's Cabin*, Martin Delany's serialized novel *Blake* (1859–62) offers a view of the auction block that relies on the act of gendering the black body in submission. The protagonist Henry Holland, who becomes a violent and agential subject, is symbolically feminized when put on public display:

> "Come up here my lad!" continued the auctioneer, wielding a long red raw-hide. "Mount this block, stand beside me, an' let's see which is the best look-ing man!" ... "I am offered one thousand dollars; one thousand dollars for the best looking Negro in all Mississippi! If all the Negro boys in the state was as good looking as him, I'd give two thousand dollars for 'em all myself!" This caused another laugh. "Who will give me on thousand five – "
> Just then a shower of rain came on.   (26)

In his treatment of the novel, Reid-Pharr notes the emphasis on physical beauty and desire in this scene of transaction as well as the potent language of "long red rawhide" and "mounting" the auction block. He reads the scene as building in sexual tension that is relieved only by the implied sexual pun of the "coming" of rain. From this perspective, Delany's work demonstrates how mechanisms of enslavement were mechanisms of racialized gender-ing. The diction and imagery make visible the conceptual gendering (not to mention the homoeroticism) that takes place in the context of being made physically vulnerable. More important, this moment indicates how the black body is understood as having a non-stable gendering and possibly as having an inverted gender identification from a heteronormative standpoint.[3]

In addition to demonstrating the attempt to define and delimit black gender identity, other texts also make available nonconventional conceptions of gender on the part of black men and women during this period. The presentation of the black body as a transgressive entity emerges in William and Ellen Craft's escape account *Running a Thousand Miles to Freedom* (1860). In the text, which William narrates, the fair-complexioned Ellen cleverly disguises herself as an invalid white man so that she and her darker husband can travel through slaveholding territory in 1845. This act of racial passing and crossdressing offers to the couple a mobility that makes possible their freedom. The act blurs the line between male and female to traverse state lines. As Barbara McCaskill explains, the Crafts are not the only fugitives who use crossdressing as a means to escape; men and women crossdressed to cross over into freedom. Escaping blacks took advantage of and manipulated assumptions about gender, race, and class in their attempts to flee servitude. Recently, critics such as Ellen Samuels have also made much of Ellen's performance of illness as a component of her crossdressing as a means of thinking about disability at the time period. Ellen's performance has become an important critical means of analyzing black corporeal transgression of the enslavement era. Although the Crafts were able to escape to the North, their freedom was later put in jeopardy because of the Fugitive Slave Act of 1850 – as was the freedom of many black people whether they had been enslaved or not. The Crafts escaped to England and became part of the abolitionist movement there, lecturing about their clever technique. They returned only after the end of the Civil War. For the couple and many others, emancipation offered the possibility in a shift in the social understanding of the black body.

Illicit Postbellum Desires

The end of the Civil War and the legislative acts that followed it promised a radical shift in the social lives and political location of black people in the United States. In this section, I turn to the period following the Civil War through the first decades of the twentieth century to trace how these shifts informed the sexualization of the black body in the social imaginary. The Freedman's Bureau and the Civil Rights Act of 1866 demonstrate the federal government's power to put into place the political machinery to ensure citizenship for a formerly enslaved population. However, these changes to the social sphere did not go unchallenged, and they were ultimately short-lived.

First, there was the retrenchment of the legal framework set in motion by the Compromise of 1877. Following this formal retrenchment, more informal challenges to black political and economic citizenship came to characterize the period after Reconstruction. These legal and social setbacks mark the real shift from the Reconstruction period to the post-Reconstruction/turn-of-the century era, which Rayford Logan calls the "nadir" of U.S. race relations. The period from the 1890s to the 1920s witnessed a large number of lynchings, particularly in the U.S. South. In the last decade of the nineteenth century, Ida B. Wells published two important texts investigating lynching as a social phenomenon: *Southern Horrors* and *The Red Record*; in them she frames the monstrous violence by analyzing white anxieties about black economic and social progress. The allegations of white female rape become for her claims meant to disguise different racialized concerns. Contemporary critics such as Dora Apel have also emphasized the sadistic voyeurism involved in the public mutilation of the black body that lynching entailed.[4]

The particular violence of lynching is an important touchstone in this consideration because of the intensely sexualized nature of the act in many cases. In *Race, Rape, and Lynching*, Sandra Gunning explains that there "was virtually a national obsession with the black male body" during this period that lynching made manifest (4). This obsession was a sexual one and particularly one with a homoerotic valence. With the black body on display in front of a white crowd, the familiar sexual display of the auction block is transmogrified into the public exhibition of the lynching tree in the social imaginary. Lynching as a social formation functions as a sexual spectacle with a homoerotic circuit of violent desire. Nathan Tipton refers to this affective circuit as "the rope and the faggot" of lynching. Trudier Harris discusses how "there is a symbolic transfer of sexual power at the point of the executions. The black man is stripped of his prowess, but the very act of stripping brings symbolic power to the white man. His actions suggest that, subconsciously, he craves the very thing he is forced to destroy" (22). From this perspective, a perverse and repressed desire for the black body – here the male body – can be read as inextricable from the act of violence. As much as these loaded murderous acts give vent to suppressed social desires, they also function as representations of the white male movement from boyhood to manhood. In other words, they are also sexualized sites of gender instruction. This understanding emerges in Sutton Griggs's 1905 novel *The Hindered Hand*, where the experience of having seen a lynching gets connected to adult manhood. The young character Melville Brant complains to his mother: "Every time I tell anything big [his more mature friend Ben] jumps in and tells what he's seen, and that knocks me out. He has seen a whole lot of lynchings" (129). The moment he collects his own piece of charred flesh, he boasts, "Ben Stringer ain't got anything on me now." Harris goes on to insist that this act of one-upmanship illustrates how lynching functions as a cultural rite of initiation and entrée into masculinity in this text. Although it exceeds the purview of the consideration of this chapter, it is worth noting that later twentieth-century writers similarly recognize and explore the psychosexual dynamics of lynching. James Baldwin stands out in this respect. Scenes in his novels *Another Country* (1962) and *Just Above My Head* (1979) and the entirety of the short story "Going to Meet the Man" (1965) revolve around the social implications of the sexual dynamics and how they impact the reading of interracial desire and black masculinity.

To reiterate, the phenomenon of lynching in the United States had much to do with a collective and pervasive anxiety about the new political subject that the formerly enslaved became even if in its enactment such violence functioned as a channel for sadistic desires. In point of fact, because of recurring social violence and the systematic dismantling of legislations, black Americans came to occupy a liminal position in the public sphere. This idea of liminality emerges as one of the dominant modes of representing black identity during the late nineteenth and early twentieth centuries. In fact, W.E.B. Du Bois's conception of "double-consciousness" as well as his contention about the "problem of the twentieth century" being one of the "color line" can be read as elaborations of the idea of black liminality (359). Importantly, this paradigm offered to writers a means for questioning the sexual coordinates of subjectivity as well. Alice Dunbar-Nelson's 1895 short story "Natalie" provides an example: it pivots around a figure that exists between places and races and also demonstrates marked same-sex desire.[5] The title character is referred to as a "tomboy," suggesting her nonconforming gender expression, and she lives along the water's edge and is always connected to the topographical margins and in-between locations. While playing there, she meets another young woman, Olivia. A "close intimacy" develops between the girls as they swim together, take long walks along the shore, sing songs, and exchange kisses. This newfound affection is "strange" but intensely pleasing for Natalie (33). This piece of fiction can be read as primarily reflecting a kind of regional consciousness, specifically the particularities and complexities of racial identity in Louisiana; however, the short story also demonstrates how the racially liminal figure can quickly become a sexually liminal figure as well.

A prominent and recurring expression of this social liminality comes across through the literary motif of passing. The racially passing figure is a key manifestation of an artistic consciousness of social liminality; importantly, the act

of racial passing regularly pushes boundaries of sexuality as well – as Ellen
Craft's performance began to intimate. In other words, the passing novel with
its foregrounding of liminality is an important site for making sense of and
articulating black sexuality. Maurice Wallace makes the case for reading the
passing figure as a queer figure or through a queer frame because of common epistemological parameters. In his thoughtful discussion of Charles
Chesnutt's 1900 passing novel *The House Behind the Cedars*, he contends that
"[the] nonspeech of the homosexual closet is the same dissimulator of race
in the black passing game. This dual heritage suggests that it has not been
merely the queer act of the sociable body Western culture won't tolerate; neither has the occasional fact of that body's blackness been politely embraced"
(115). Wallace argues that the paradigm of the closet obtains through the racial
dynamics of passing. His point is not that passing figures are queer or necessarily have nonnormative sexualities per se, but rather that the analogy between
the two renders black sexual desire nonnormative in effect.

In addition to illustrating the extent to which homophobia and racism
bring about similar circumstances, the move Wallace makes in his reading of
Chesnutt's fiction also signals how the passing figure can become a device for
introducing gender-bending and nonnormative desire. In fact, one comes to
find that the liminal positionality of the black passing figure can make possible
the intertwining of gender inversion and homosexuality. This understanding
is best illustrated in James Weldon Johnson's famous 1912 novel *Autobiography
of an Ex-Colored Man*, which was originally published without an authorial
attribution. In discussing Johnson's novel, Siobhan Somerville argues that
"the representation of the mulatto body [the passing figure in this context] is
mediated by the iconography of gender inversion, and interracial heterosexual desire functions in the text as both an analogy to homosexual object choice
and a screen through which it can be articulated" (112). In other words, the
liminal nature that derives from the passing figure's ability to exist between
racial identities creates possibilities for unsettling gender categories and by
extension sexual identity.

An important work to include in this consideration of the liminal figure
in postbellum and turn-of-the-century work by African Americans is Pauline
Hopkins's 1900 serialized novel *Contending Forces*. Hopkins is an especially
noteworthy figure because she was a prominent and prolific fiction writer,
prose writer, and editor. In *Contending Forces*, her first novel, Hopkins makes
use of the characteristic elements of a passing novel, but the narrative is not
about racial passing; instead Hopkins offers a light-complexioned black character who lies about her background – renaming herself – but not her racial

identity. In part the novel explores the idea of romantic friendship and the power of homosocial intimacy through the character of Sappho Clark, who, while she could, chooses not to pass as white. Hopkins includes a scene of closeted intimacy between the significantly named Sappho and her companion Dora in which female-female desire is displaced onto food in a chapter Hopkins calls "Friendship":

> "your teeth, your beautiful white teeth, where will they be shortly if you persist in eating a pound of bonbons every day? ... "
> [Dora responds,] "I'll eat all the bonbons I want in spite of you, Sappho, and if you don't hurry I'll eat your slice of cream pie, too." At this dire threat there ensued a scramble for the pie, mingled with peals of merry laughter, until all rosy and sparkling, Sappho emerged from the fray with the dish containing her share of the dainty held high in the air. (120)

Somerville finds in this scene of enclosed eating and sharing of affections potential for reading female friendship historically along what Adrienne Rich calls a "lesbian continuum."[6] This understanding of the novel resonates with and extends Lillian Faderman's argument about romantic friendships between women. In this light, *Contending Forces* is valuable in part because it makes possible a reconsideration of representations of black women's intimacy and helps to situate love between women as an important node of black women's history. The novel finds a method for expressing the circuit of desire only hinted at in Dunbar-Nelson's "Natalie." The novel does imagine the possibility of same-sex erotic longing while transferring the desire to the intermediary of food and secreting the expressions away in a closed-off room.

Much of what has been discussed thus far is published material and would be considered "literature." However, in considering the history of U.S. black writing on and about sexuality, it is crucial to consider marginal and unpublished works as well, specifically letters, diaries, and creative work that was drafted but never circulated for publication. These marginal documents often express nonconventional sexual desires and feelings that were not deemed appropriate or suitable for published work. Such self-constraint on the part of black artists illustrates the historical investment in what Evelyn Brooks Higginbotham terms the "politics of respectability." Higginbotham develops this concept to describe the work of women involved in the black Baptist women's movement specifically, but this concept provides a useful hermeneutic for making sense of the artistic and editorial choices made by many black women and men at the end of the nineteenth century and into the twentieth. A discourse of respectability informed much of cultural production that involved representing the race. The concept of the politics of respectability itself reflects the premium placed on uplift ideologies at the time period. Turning attention to work that was effectively outside of the public sphere provides insight on articulations of intimacy. The cache of letters written by Addie Brown to Rebecca Primus between 1854 and 1868 presents an important view of the expression of black female same-sex desire and attachment before, during, and after the Civil War that rarely saw print (see Griffin). This epistolary desire does less to substantiate claims about either woman's identity than it does to archive and show where black same-sex intimacy manifests itself alongside and outside of conventional heterosexual couplings (see Foster). Additionally, Akasha Gloria Hull points to Angelina Weld-Grimké's early twentieth-century manuscript poems and personal letters as later instantiations of the same dynamic. These texts illustrate that same-sex desire may not be unspeakable but may have been effectively unpublishable. However, the tide was turning as the new century progressed.

The Queer Negro

In terms of literary history, the Harlem Renaissance, which spanned the 1920s and spilled over into the 1930s, is understood as having marked a significant shift in black American expressive culture. It is the final component of the discussion in this chapter. The artistic movement known commonly as the "Harlem Renaissance" was called the "Negro Renaissance" during its own time. Regardless of the designation, it is the most well-known and (arguably) most studied period of black American artistic production. It describes the art, activism, and social activities by black Americans attempting to reimagine black identity, undermine white supremacy, and garner recognition of black intellectual and creative ability. In recent years, the Harlem Renaissance has become a crucial site for coming to terms with articulations of black same-sex desire and gender nonconformity in a pre-Stonewall historical context, as the work of critics such as Eric Garber demonstrates. In fact, there has been a veritable explosion in the number of critical works (essays and full-length books) that attend to questions of sexuality and gender expression during the Harlem Renaissance in the past two decades. More important, the recently emerged scholarly paradigms of black queer studies and queer of color critique have created possibilities for rich and suggestive rereadings of familiar and canonical literary texts from the period. From this perspective, the "new" negro touted as the central figure of the Renaissance has come to be understood as a "queer" negro.

A large number of black artists during this period are on record as having had same-sex desires and/or sexual relationships. In fact, the public acknowledgment of such desire was the exception and not the rule. Still, silences and disavowals are understandable and arguably appropriate given the social milieu of the historical moment. More important, they also reflect an investment in the division between the public life of a working author and an individual's private life. However, the works of such artists and their colleagues during the Harlem Renaissance reflect a sustained attention to questioning the normative structures of desire that shape black subjectivity.

The cultural awakening that is the Harlem Renaissance gets connected to modernism and the beginning of a new era, as Houston Baker and James de Jongh make clear. A number of factors contributed to the emergence of this locus of activity: returning black soldiers' frustrations with a Jim Crow society after World War I; the transformation of urban spaces across the nation because of the Great Migration; the increase in popularity of the blues and jazz made possible by advances in the recording industry (see Hutchinson "Introduction"). These significant changes to the social world and public sphere suggest what appears to be a definitive break between the Harlem Renaissance and *fin-de-siècle* U.S. culture and black American cultural production. Nonetheless, it is important to read the Harlem Renaissance as both break with *and* a continuation of the period that immediately precedes it in terms of representations of sexuality and gender expression.

The discussion of sexuality that can be found in some work from the period helps to substantiate the idea of a definite break. The 1926 publication of the literary magazine *FIRE!!* is perhaps the most prominent example. The periodical, which only had one issue, included the work of Aaron Douglas, Zora Neale Hurston, Wallace Thurman, Richard Bruce Nugent, Countee Cullen, Langston Hughes, and Gwendolyn Bennett. The contributions consciously took up controversial topics such as prostitution and same-sex desire. The contributors were primarily younger artists, playfully referred to as the "Niggeratti," who sought to undermine the politics of representation and anxiety about black sexual stereotypes that informed much of the work being published (see Schwarz). Richard Bruce Nugent's contribution to *FIRE!!* is especially important because it is considered to be the first story published by an African American writer that deals explicitly with same-sex desire. One of the goals of the magazine as an artistic project was to upset or refuse moral expectations that shaped earlier work. In other words, its contributors attempted to question the politics of respectability that had informed and continued to inform the work of older artists and thinkers. Indeed, there was genuine generational tension. For example, Alain Locke, editor of the anthology *The New Negro* and mentor to many Renaissance-era writers, criticized the fiction of Wallace Thurman, a key figure of the Niggeratti, as containing merely "prolonged orgies of exhibitionism" (qtd. in Schwarz 35). One might then consider the Harlem Renaissance from the perspective of a generational shift in values, but that reading is not hard and fast. There were actually multiple investments and priorities among artists being expressed simultaneously, and even the younger generation often used similar strategies when it came to questions of gender and sexuality as older writers had employed.

Most of the critical arguments about same-sex desire in the Harlem Renaissance have focused primarily on the work of male writers: Nugent, Wallace Thurman, Langston Hughes, Claude McKay, and to lesser extent Countee Cullen. A. B. Christa Schwarz explains that Countee Cullen and Hughes often used veiled references to same-sex desire or relied on gender-neutral language in their poetry, thereby foregrounding ambiguity in their respective depictions of intimacy. This indeterminacy reflects a purposeful use of linguistic codes that allow for multiple interpretations. Male-male friendship and intimacy is a common motif in the works of several of the writers. For example, the image of "loving comrades" becomes an important figure of same-sex intimacy in McKay's early poetry volumes *Songs of Jamaica* (1912) and *Constab Ballads* (1912) as well as in his novels *Home to Harlem* (1928) and *Banjo* (1929).[7] Thurman's novel *Infants of Spring* (1932) also depicts homosocial companionship but importantly does so across racial lines. There are also more explicit, although minor, representations of pansies or effeminate gay men, some of whom have sexual encounters with more masculine, otherwise heterosexual men. As Thurman's earlier novel, *The Blacker the Berry* (1929), illustrates, most of these characters appear as stereotypes, and this characterization also applies to the occasional representation of lesbian figures as well. There is a marked artistic attraction to the homosocial that becomes evident across these different works. In these texts, the presentation of same-sex intimacy is often crafted around or offered as the backdrop for nuanced exploration of black gender expression, particularly here masculinity.

The emphasis on masculinity does not mean that female same-sex desire was absent. Nella Larsen's fiction has come to be the most significant literary work that deals with such desire – other forms of cultural expression do feature prominently female-female intimacy, and I discuss them later. Larsen published two important novels during this time period: *Quicksand* (1928) and *Passing* (1929). Both books feature a female protagonist "attracted to another woman whose ability to realize the choices that the protagonist can only fantasize about confounds the circuits of desire and identification" in the rest of the narrative (Vogel 95). The subtle attraction in the first novel sets up the more intense and destructive desire in the second. Deborah McDowell argues that in *Passing* there is an awakening of sexual desire of the protagonist Irene for Clare and that this erotic charge represents a confrontation of the "heterosexual priorities ... of bourgeois uplift" (88). The text offers a questioning of the institution of heterosexuality through this attraction even if the novel ends by reaffirming the marital bonds and removing violently the threat of same-sex desire. Larsen provides a different kind of investigation from those that manifest themselves in the work of Thurman, Hughes, or McKay.

Few texts during the era were as widely read or more controversial than *Nigger Heaven* (1926) by Carl van Vechten, a white gay writer, patron, and photographer. Van Vechten was a close friend of Langston Hughes and many other writers and was known to have had relationships with men. His *roman à clef* offers to the reader an insider's perspective on the world of Harlem as well as the lives and foibles of important black artists, intellectuals, and activists of the time period. In the text Harlem often comes across as a site of entertainment and illicit pleasure and black characters are often amusing drifters who seek out and embody this pleasure (see de Jongh). In this sense, the book played into and encouraged the historical interest in exoticism and primitivism during the modernist era (see Bernard). The novel is also important because it is significant to many Renaissance writers – such as Hughes, Hurston, and Thurman – so much so that many scholars understand it to be elemental to the Renaissance itself. The inclusion of Van Vechten in a history of the Harlem Renaissance reveals the importance and accuracy of Henry Louis Gates's often-referenced statement that the Harlem Renaissance was "surely as gay as it was black, *not that it was exclusively either of these*" (233; emphasis added). The recognition of interracial professional and intimate relations has caused critics such as George Hutchinson (*Harlem*) and Emily Bernard to emphasize the interracial dimensions of the period.

Van Vechten's book is also noteworthy in this context because it points to a significant space of art and entertainment during the period: the cabaret. Cabaret and nightlife scenes recur in many of the works from the period, and the scenes often become valuable sites for thinking about sexuality. In point of fact, because of these entertainment spaces Harlem had become an important pleasure center and vice district by the 1920s. The cabaret also functioned as an important site of gay and lesbian subculture in New York City during the Renaissance. The physical space of the cabaret as well as its representation was crucial to the re-articulation of black identity for many artists and performers.

Shane Vogel categorizes these cultural producers as the "Cabaret School," reclaiming what had been at the time denigrating sobriquet. He argues that this school "used the cabaret [and Harlem nightlife in general] to critique the racial and sexual normativity of uplift ideology and to imagine alternative narratives of sexual and racial selfhood" (3). Works such as Larsen's *Quicksand*, Thurmans's *The Blacker the Berry*, and Hughes's poetry situate this illicit entertainment space of the cabaret as one in which nonnormative desires emerge and are dominant. Accordingly, attention to this space of pleasure in literature and performance unveils what contemporary critics would now call a queer artistic tradition.

The move to consider the cabaret as a signature element of Harlem Renaissance theorizing of subjectivity also signals the importance of musical performers and professional actors to gaining an understanding of transgressive conceptions of gender and sexuality. In fact, increasingly performance spaces and theatres are becoming the sites for analyzing the racial *and* sexual complexities of the Harlem era. James F. Wilson demonstrates how performers in musical reviews and cabarets such as Florence Mills and Gladys Bentley often relied on and manipulated gender ambiguity and ambivalence in order to titillate and also to critique traditional modes or conceiving of black identity. An avowed "bulldagger," Bentley crafted gender-questioning performances that resonated with those of blues women singers such as Gertrude "Ma" Rainey and Bessie Smith. In her thorough examination of the blues tradition and black women performers, Angela Davis explains how Rainey and Smith performances employed provocative sexual imagery, including homosexual imagery, in order to challenge "mainstream ideological assumptions regarding women and being in love" (11). Bentley's cultural work creates the opportunity to think explicitly about how performances and performance spaces can function as a critical site for studying black women and nonconventional sexual desire. Related to Bentley's well-known performances, Eric Garber emphasizes the significance of drag balls, which Hughes called "spectacles in color," to the period. Accordingly, public performance spaces have become vital locations for assessing the contestation of sexual boundaries during the Harlem era. That being said, it is also important to note that private parties and "buffet flats" came to function as analogous – or at least connected – spaces to the public one of the cabaret. Many artists would develop songs and performances entertaining at private parties before they debuted them on a public stage. More pertinent to this discussion, private parties were a crucial component of gay and lesbian subculture, as George Chauncey makes clear. They provided opportunities for social and sexual networking. More important, these spaces indicate the necessity of looking beyond printed literature and to different archives in coming to terms with investigations of sexuality during the black artistic renaissance of the 1920s.

In 2008, Richard Bruce Nugent's novel *Gentleman Jigger* was published post-humously. The novel was written between 1928 and 1932 and has many structural and conceptual parallels to Thurman's *Infants of Spring*. In effect, it is a *post-Harlem Renaissance* Harlem Renaissance novel. Nugent's novel offers frank treatments of homosexuality, making the novel a bit more distinct from the works of many of his peers. Given this characteristic, the narrative development of the protagonist could be read as signaling the emergence of a recognizably modern gay voice in the early twentieth century – although published at the end of the century. Notwithstanding this assessment, the novel puts in the foreground a deep investment in what Thomas Wirth calls "sexual hybridity" (ix). Such hybridity functions as the real trademark of the literature and expressive culture of the Harlem era. Nugent, much like his peers, is less interested in articulating what we would now call a gay identity than he is in making visible and at times transgressing the social boundaries defining sexuality and race. Yet, it is through these crossings, these artistic transgressions, that a definite queerness does emerge.

Notes

1. Hartman refuses to replicate the description of Douglass's Aunt Hester in order not to replicate the violence; Moten, on the other hand, insists that simply by citing the text, the violence is manifested and reiterated. This distinction aside, both critics emphasize that the written texts carry traces of the violence of the spectacle.
2. Reid-Pharr similarly discusses the possibility of the homoerotic affiliation in Martin Delany's serial novel *Blake*.
3. Reid-Pharr's understanding of how polymorphous sexuality undergirds these nineteenth-century narratives lends itself to such readings.
4. In addition, Goldsby provides an exhaustive account of the circulation of lynching photographs and picture cards that speaks to this voyeurism in a different way. Apel and Smith similarly examine the politics of spectatorship in relation to circulating images of lynching.
5. By including "Natalie" as the opening selection in their anthology, Weise, Carbado, and McBride suggest that Dunbar-Nelson's story inaugurates a tradition.
6. It is important to note that Rich relies on black women's history in constructing her argument about "the lesbian continuum."
7. Hughes's later work *The Big Sea* (1940) also relies on this imagery.

Works Cited

Abdur-Rahman, Aliyyah. *Against the Closet: Black Political Longing and the Erotics of Race.* Durham: Duke UP, 2012. Print.

Apel, Dora. *Imagery of Lynching: Black Men, White Women, and the Mob.* New Brunswick: Rutgers UP, 2004. Print.

Apel, Dora, and Shawn Michelle Smith. *Lynching Photographs.* Berkeley: U of California P, 2008. Print.

Baker, Houston. *Modernism and the Harlem Renaissance.* Chicago: U of Chicago P, 1989. Print.

Baldwin, James. *Another Country.* New York: Dial, 1962. Print.
  "Going to Meet the Man." *Going to Meet the Man.* 1965. London: Corgi, 1971. 201–21. Print.
  Just Above My Head. New York: Dial, 1979. Print.

Bernard, Emily. *Carl Van Vechten and the Harlem Renaissance: A Portrait in Black and White.* New Haven: Yale UP, 2012. Print.

Chauncey, George. *Gay New York: Gender, Urban Culture, and the Making of the Gay Male World, 1890–1940.* New York: Basic, 1994. Print.

Davis, Angela. *Blues Legacies and Black Feminism: Gertrude "Ma" Rainey, Bessie Smith, and Billie Holliday.* New York: Pantheon, 1998. Print.

De Jongh, James. *Vicious Modernism: Black Harlem and the Literary Imagination.* New York: Cambridge UP, 2009. Print.

Douglass, Frederick. *Narrative of the Life of Frederick Douglass.* 1845. New York: Dover, 1995. Print.

Dunbar-Nelson, Alice. "Natalie." Weise, Carbado, and McBride 28–38. Print.

Du Bois, W.E.B. *The Souls of Black Folk.* 1903. *Writings: The Suppression of the African Slave Trade, The Souls of Black Folk, Dusk of Dawn, Essays and Articles.* Boston: Bedford, 1989. 357–548. Print.

Faderman, Lillian. *Surpassing the Love of Men: Romantic Friendship and Love between Women from the Renaissance to the Present.* New York: Morrow, 1981. Print.

Foster, Frances Smith. *'Til Death or Distance Do Us Part: Marriage and the Making of African America.* New York: Oxford UP, 2010. Print.

Garber, Eric. "A Spectacle in Color: The Lesbian and Gay Subculture in Jazz Age Harlem." *Hidden from History: Reclaiming the Gay and Lesbian Past.* New York. Penguin, 1989. 318–31. Print.

Gates, Henry Louis. "The Black Man's Burden." *Fear of a Queer Planet.* Ed. Michael Warner. Minneapolis: U of Minnesota P, 1993. 230–63. Print.

Goldsby, Jacqueline. *Spectacular Secret: Lynching in American Life and Literature.* Chicago: U of Chicago P, 2006. Print.

Griffin, Farah. *Beloved Sisters and Loving Friends: Letters from Rebecca Primus of Royal Oak, Maryland, and Addie Brown of Hartford, Connecticut, 1854–1868.* New York: Knopf, 1999. Print.

Gunning, Sandra. *Race, Rape, and Lynching: The Red Record of American Literature, 1890–1912.* New York: Oxford, 1996. Print.

Harris, Trudier. *Exorcising Blackness: Historical and Literary Lynching and Burning Rituals.* Bloomington: Indiana UP, 1984. Print.

Hartman, Saidiya. *Scenes of Subjection: Terror, Slavery, and Self-Making in Nineteenth-Century America*. New York: Oxford UP, 1997. Print.

Higginbotham, Evelyn. *Righteous Discontent: The Women's Movement in the Black Baptist Church, 1880–1920*. Cambridge: Harvard UP, 1993. Press.

Hopkins, Pauline. *Contending Forces: A Romance Illustrative of Negro Life North and South*. 1900. New York: Oxford UP, 1988. Print.

Hull, Akaska Gloria. *Color, Sex, and Poetry: Three Women of the Harlem Renaissance*. Bloomington: Indiana UP, 1987. Print.

Hutchinson, George. *Harlem in Black and White*. Cambridge: Harvard UP, 1996. Print.

"Introduction." *The Cambridge Companion to the Harlem Renaissance*. Ed. George Hutchinson. New York: Cambridge, 2007. 1–10. Print.

Jacobs, Harriett. *Incidents in the Life of a Slave Girl*. 1861. New York: Oxford UP, 1988. Print.

Logan, Rayford. *The Negro in American Life and Thought: The Nadir, 1877–1901*. New York: Dial P, 1954. Print.

McCaskill, Barbara. "'Your Very Truly': Ellen Craft – The Fugitive as Text and Artifact." *African American Review* 28.4 (1994): 509–29. Print.

McDowell, Deborah. "'That Nameless . . . Shameless Impulse': Sexuality in Nella Larsen's *Quicksand* and *Passing*." *"The Changing Same": Black Women's Literature, Criticism, and Theory*. Bloomington: Indiana UP, 1995. 78–97. Print.

Moten, Fred. *In the Break: The Aesthetics of the Black Radical Tradition*. Minneapolis: U of Minnesota P, 2003. Print.

Reid-Pharr, Robert. *Conjugal Union: The Body, the House, and the Black American*. New York: Oxford, 1999. Print.

Rich, Adrienne. "Compulsory Heterosexuality and Lesbian Existence." *Blood, Bread, and Poetry: Selected Prose, 1979–1985*. Norton: New York, 1994. Print.

Samuels, Ellen. "'A Complication of Complaints': Untangling Disability, Race, and Gender in William and Ellen Craft's *Running a Thousand Miles to Freedom*." *MELUS* 31.3 (2006): 15–47. Print.

Sanchez-Eppler, Karen. *Touching Liberty: Abolition, Feminism, and the Politics of the Body*. Berkeley: U of California P, 1993. Print.

Schwarz, Christa. *Gay Voices of the Harlem Renaissance*. Bloomington: Indiana UP, 2003. Print.

Somerville, Siobhan. *Queering the Color Line: Race and the Invention of Homosexuality in American Culture*. Durham: Duke UP, 2000. Print.

Spillers, Hortense. "Mama's Baby, Papa's Maybe." *Diacritics* 17.2 (1987): 64–81. Print.

State v. Mann. 13 N.C. 263 (1829). Web. 25 January 2014.

Tipton, Nathan. "Rope and Faggot: The Homoerotics of Lynching in William Faulkner's *Light in August*." *Mississippi Quarterly* 64.3/4 (2011): 369–91. Print.

Vogel, Shane. *The Scene of the Harlem Cabaret: Race, Sexuality, Performance*. Chicago: U of Chicago P, 2009. Print.

Wallace, Maurice. *Constructing the Black Masculine: Identity and Ideality in African American Men's Literature and Culture, 1775–1995*. Durham: Duke UP, 2002. Print.

Wells, Ida B. *The Red Record*. 1895. Southern 73–157.

Southern Horrors. 1892. Southern 49–72.

Southern Horrors and Other Writings: The Anti-Lynching Campaign of Ida B. Wells, 1892–1900. Ed. Jacqueline Jones Royster. New York: Bedford/St. Martin, 1997. Print.

Wilson, James F. *Bulldaggers, Pansies, and Chocolate Babies: Performance, Race, and Sexuality in the Harlem Renaissance.* Ann Arbor: U of Michigan P, 2010. Print.

Wirth, Thomas. "Introduction." *Gentleman Jigger: A Novel of the Harlem Renaissance.* By Richard Bruce Nugent. New York: Da Capo, 2008. x–xviii. Print.

Weise, Don, Devon Carbado, and Dwight McBride, eds. *Black Like Us: A Century of Lesbian, Gay, and Bisexual African American Fiction.* New York: Cleis P, 2011. Print.

PART IV

★

QUEER MODERNISMS

18

Turn-of-the-Century Decadence and Aestheticism

ELISA GLICK

Twentieth-century and twenty-first-century readers often consider decadence an exotic, hothouse bloom that flowered extravagantly and disappeared suddenly around the turn of the century, leaving behind a strange, voluptuous literature surrounded by "the phosphorescence of decay" (Baudelaire, *Painter* 91). For this reason many critics have taken a defensive posture and argued against the notion that decadence was a hermetic and short-lived movement – a minor pit stop on the way between Romanticism and modernism. In fact, fin-de-siècle decadence and aestheticism were avant-garde literary movements; they look forward to modernism both stylistically and thematically (Weir 120). However, decadence was a more pervasive and developed movement than aestheticism, which is why this chapter tends to be weighted toward it. Although the epicenter of the decadent movement is France, decadence was a cosmopolitan, transnational movement, whereas aestheticism was primarily a British school.[1] Nevertheless, there is so much "play" between decadence and aestheticism that the two really cannot be separately delineated; both decadent and aesthetic strategies are elaborations of an essentially modernist project that aims to show how – as Henry James puts it – art makes life.

I want to make it clear from the outset that in this chapter I do not intend to defend or condemn these movements, nor will I make a case for their importance in an LGBTQ literary canon. My discussion begins with the premise that decadence and aestheticism were queer sites of cultural production that helped to define both literary and sexual modernity. I am less interested in telling the histories of these movements and more interested in contributing to a conversation about how the complexities and contradictions of queer modernity are contained within them. I ask, how are queer desires, experiences, and ways of seeing articulated through decadent and aesthetic literatures?

I wish to thank Miranda Mattingly for her excellent research assistance on this project.

The literary traditions of decadence and aestheticism preceded nineteenth-century sexology's creation of the homosexual as an abnormal sexual type and developed their own forms of eroticism that served as a counterdiscourse to the medicalized model. Although not necessarily for the same reasons, both the decadent and the aesthete refused to be a subject of desire as modern sexology and psychiatry defined it.

As many critics have noted, these movements have a more ambivalent relationship to gender ideologies about the "natural" difference between the sexes. In decadence and aestheticism, we see a contradictory tendency to affirm gender polarities and deconstruct them; the figures of the "fatal woman" and the androgyne are paradigmatic of this opposition. Not simply an attempt to scandalize, decadents' rebellion against Victorian sexual conformity sought to fashion a queer way of being in the world, expanding consciousness by embracing the fleeting sensations of life's restless motion. In his 1881 essay about Charles Baudelaire (1821–67), French writer, poet, and critic Paul Bourget (1852–1935) declares: "Literatures of decadent periods ... have no tomorrow. They lead to alterations of vocabulary, subtleties of meaning that make them unintelligible to the generations to come" (130).[2] With this in mind, this chapter does not try to make decadence intelligible for contemporary readers; the focus of the following meditation is not to find out what decadence really was but rather what it is, and can be, for us.

The Work of Decadence

Although a wide range of cultural commentators has viewed decadence and aestheticism as privileged emblems of the fin-de-siècle spirit, both are also elaborations of ideas that first appear much earlier, at the turn of the nineteenth century. For a contemporary such as Max Nordau (1849–1926), "the high priest of the creed of degeneration" (Greenslade 120), decadents like Joris-Karl Huysmans, Paul Verlaine, Algernon Charles Swinburne, Villiers de l'Isle-Adam, Joséphin Péladan, and Barbey d'Aurevilly are the descendants of the Marquis de Sade (1740–1814) and Baudelaire – both satanic worshippers of divine evil. Inflammatory rhetoric aside, Nordau is actually right; the Sadean quest to outrage nature is the kernel for the decadent movement's philosophy.[3] Furthermore, both aestheticism and decadence are represented in the literary periods and movements that followed them. For example, in France, symbolism and surrealism – movements that followed decadence in the late nineteenth and early twentieth centuries – were infused with decadent methods, style, and themes. Internationally, literary decadence was not confined to the fin de siècle but actually "flowered" well into the first decades of the twentieth century.

Decadence is an elusive object of analysis not only because it disrupts historical periodization but also because its strategies are deliberately disorienting. In making this claim, I follow in the footsteps of other critics who have similarly observed that decadence poses conceptual problems because its logic is excessive, contagious, and mobile. To complicate matters, writers and poets who are now closely associated with the decadent movement didn't always embrace it or had an ambivalent relationship to the term "decadent." For example, Arthur Symons (1865–1945), who wrote the influential essay "The Decadent Movement in Literature" (1893), soon renounced the movement he had helped to establish and replaced "decadence" with "Symbolism" in his critical writings such as *The Symbolist Movement in Literature*, which he published in 1899. Across the Channel, Paul Verlaine (1844–96), whose 1883 poem "Langueur" was an early and influential articulation of the new decadent movement – "Je suis l'Empire à la fin de la decadence" ("I am the Empire at the end of decadence"; qtd. in Schoolfield 3, 1) – had left behind the languor and depravity of the Roman Empire by 1889, when Anatole Baju ceased publication of his journal *Le Décadent*.

Decadence was a highly individualistic, if not idiosyncratic, movement with no unifying doctrine, which is why there are so many different definitions of it. It is not my intention to add one more, but I do want to offer some reflections on the work of decadence – not what it is, but what it does. The queer contribution of decadence (about which I will soon have more to say) is its passion for transgressing boundaries, calling categories into question, inverting and/or perverting received ideas. I agree with Liz Constable, Dennis Denisoff, and Matthew Potolsky, the editors of *Perennial Decay* (1999), who argue: "We see this 'perennial decay' of boundaries – the insistence on at once mobilizing and undermining boundaries and differences – as a central quality and effect of decadent writing" (21). But the work of decadence is not only deconstructive. It offers a way of seeing that aims to capture what is both visible and invisible. Like Baudelaire's flâneur, the decadent is also a passionate spectator; his new way of looking is part of a "desperate endeavor to give sensation, to flash the impression of the moment, to preserve the very heat and motion of life" (Symons 102). Despite its enthusiasm for nature (among other distinctions), Pre-Raphaelitism shares with decadence a critique of capitalist modernity; both offer an aesthetic, sensuous antidote to the changes and contradictions of the modern world. Furthermore, even those theorists of decadence who did not emphasize "sense impression" tended to deploy decadence as a rejection of positivism that is decentered, restless, and endlessly open. This is why decadent art and literature is often represented as posing a threat of contagion. Decadence then comes to be seen as a project of heightened self-reflexivity and refinement that seeks to express the inexpressible and contest the illusion of transparency and coherence. Think for example of Bourget's famous description of decadent style:

> A style of decadence is one in which the unity of the book breaks down to make place for the independence of the page, in which the page breaks down to make place for the independence of the sentence and in which the sentence breaks down to make place for the independence of the word.
>
> (qtd. in Dowling, *Language* 133)

Here, decadence is about the fragment (independence of the word) and the disruption of unity that prevails in a universe haunted by the "dark spectre of autonomous language" (Dowling, *Language xiii*). However, this aspect of decadence is not only about the materiality of language and its independent expressive power; it also expresses the perceived social disorder of the fin de siècle.

In an 1891 interview, poet Stéphane Mallarmé (1842–98) links the breakdown of traditional form to social fragmentation, affirming "this incontrovertible notion: that in an unstable society, lacking unity, no stable and definitive art can be created" (Hurt 141). From a Marxist perspective, the focus on fragmentation challenges the false appearance of integration and wholeness in modern commodity culture. I emphasize this critical dimension of decadence because the movement is so frequently described as an individualistic retreat from the social and the political into artifice and spectacle. (A notable exception to this depoliticized reading is provided by Pierre Bourdieu, who characterizes French decadents as committed, politically radical artists who lacked money, social status, and educational capital [67].) In fact, decadence was deeply rooted in the political because it is itself "a method for imagining a community of the future," a kind of queer counterculture (Potolsky 14). The profane illuminations of Arthur Rimbaud (1854–91) demonstrate the ways decadents did not just retreat from society but actively sought to change it.

Nevertheless, decadence is complicit with the objects of its critique. Although it seeks to resist reification by privileging the fragment and protesting against materialism, the decadent movement was a part of the new commodity culture of the fin de siècle even as it rebelled against bourgeois society. For example, when the decadent journal *The Yellow Book* appeared in London in 1894 – shocking the literary establishment with its sexually transgressive content and Aubrey Beardsley's now iconic illustrations – its lurid yellow color advertised an affinity with scandalous French avant-garde fiction published in yellow backs as well as cheap British railway novels, which were also published with garish yellow covers. An unlikely intersection of high and low art, *The Yellow Book* "sought to create a kind of fusion between the contemporary avant-garde and the emergence of mass culture" (Doran 48).[4] Although both decadence and aestheticism share this contradictory relationship to capitalist modernity, it is especially visible in the figure of the decadent dandy, which I will explore in more detail in the final section of this chapter. As critics such as Regenia Gagnier (*Idylls*; "Is Market") and Rhonda Garelick have demon- strated, this relationship to mass culture is at the heart of the decadent dan- dy's engagement with emerging forms of mass media, which played a cru- cial role in making this figure one of our first celebrities. This is particularly true of English dandies like Oscar Wilde (1854–1900) and artist J.M. Whistler (1834–1903), whose dandyism was a strategy of self-advertisement that helped him to succeed in the late Victorian art market (Edwards 18). Although Wilde's success (which surpassed Whistler's) in this arena is sometimes held against him by those who see him as a publicity hound in knee breeches, it's worth remembering that these strategies also helped to bring aestheticism to larger segments of the literary marketplace (Freedman 51).

Aestheticism and Art for Art's Sake

In England the first "wave" of aestheticism begins with Pre-Raphaelitism in the 1850s, but the first English poet to identify publically as an advocate of aestheticism was Algernon Charles Swinburne (1837–1909) (Bell-Villada 83).[5] In 1866, Swinburne created a sensation with the publication of his pur- portedly satanic, perverse, and pagan *Poems and Ballads* (Beckson xxii). Like Baudelaire's *The Flowers of Evil* (*Les Fleurs du mal*; 1861), Swinburne's *Poems and Ballads* exemplifies decadence's valorization of perverse and lesbian eroti- cism. In poems such as the Sapphic "Anactoria," Swinburne uses lesbian love, sadomasochism, and androgynous expressions of "hermaphrodeity" to blend Hellenistic paganism with decadent artifice. In so doing, he reminds us that decadent and aesthetic sexuality is perverse/queer rather than "homosexual." In fact, despite the tendency to associate decadence with debauched hedonists and effeminate sodomites, in decadent literature the ideal of an "aesthetic sex- uality" (to borrow the phrase from Romana Byrne) is really only attained by lesbians and sadomasochists.

Despite the historical importance of Swinburne's work, the text that has come to define aestheticism for us today is Walter Pater's *Studies in the History of the Renaissance* (1873) – later retitled *The Renaissance: Studies in Art and Poetry* – which similarly scandalized the literary world with its hedonism, paganism, and abundant sensuality. *The Renaissance* has a distinct decadent sensibility, which is sometimes overlooked by critics who separate Pater's work from a later, more decadent phase of British aestheticism that emerges at the fin de siècle. Praising *The Renaissance*, Wilde famously said to W.B. Yeats: "It is my golden book. I never travel without it; but it is the very flower of decadence: the last trumpet should have sounded the moment it was written" (qtd. in Beckson xxxii). Pater's valorization of exquisite passions and Hellenic homoeroticism is not, however, about decadent excess; his famous clarion call "to burn always with this hard gem-like flame" articulates a mode of spirituality grounded in the pursuit of beauty and sensations (Pater, *Studies* 120). As Pater (1839–94) demonstrates in *Marius the Epicurean* (1885), the aesthetic is a form of faith, perhaps the only ethical imperative. In his effort to dismantle the mind/body dualism and reunite the spirit and the flesh, Pater underscores the centrality of the body, the queer, desiring subject, and sense perception in aestheticism.[6] Pater's self-enclosed individual subject, who is a "solitary prisoner" of his own dream world, reminds us that his aesthete shares some of the decadent's dilemmas. As Camille Paglia points out, "In Pater, aesthetic perception is at war with its archenemy, female nature" (485). Like the decadent, the aesthete identifies with and disavows the feminine. Although aestheticism offers a more embodied approach than decadence, it isn't necessarily a more materialist one. Pater's male aesthete is a universal subject who is not bounded by time or space; he is therefore free to dematerialize, dissipating his personality "within a broader permeable experience" (Denisoff, "Dissipating" 441).

Paterian aestheticism is notable for its brave celebration of male beauty and same-sex desire, deploying Hellenistic ideals to articulate a new "type" of masculinity that is a part of a transhistorical, homoerotic tradition. In "Diaphaneitè" (1864), Pater's earliest surviving essay, this gossamer figure is recognizable as the emblem of "the love that dare not speak its name":

There are some unworldly types of character which the world is able to estimate. It recognizes certain moral types, or categories, and regards whatever falls within them as having a right to exist. The saint, the artist, even the speculative thinker, out of the world's order as they are, yet work, so far as they work at all, in and by means of the main current of the world's energy. Often it gives them late, or scanty, or mistaken acknowledgment; still it has room for them in its scheme of life, a place made ready for them in its affections.... There is another type of character, which is not broad and general, rare, precious above all to the artist.... It crosses rather than follows the main current of the world's life. The world has no sense fine enough for those evanescent shades, which fill up the blanks between contrasted types of character.... For this nature there is no place ready in its affections. This colourless, unclassified purity of life it can neither use for its service nor contemplate as an ideal. (136)

This queer type who refuses to follow "the main current" of the world is himself exiled from a society that can neither perceive nor appreciate him. As Heather Love observes, "so complete is the world's refusal of him that his only response is to evanesce, to become transparent" (60). Pater's diaphanous ideal should not be equated with the homosexual, a medical category that was not established until the late nineteenth century, nor even seen as an anticipation of it; rather, it is an aesthetic figuration of homoerotically inclined "identity" and sensibility. This "character" is Pater's first attempt to conceptualize a queer masculinity (feminine, androgynous) that departs from traditional Victorian gender norms, provides a new way of seeing (diaphaneity), and opens up a space for male-male desire and intimacy.

Like Pater, Wilde created a counterdiscourse grounded in a Hellenized tradition of male love. Wilde's *The Picture of Dorian Gray* (1890), one of the first attempts to bring male homoeroticism into the English novel (Ellman 318), draws heavily on Paterian aestheticism and celebrates "such love as Michael Angelo had known, and Montaigne, and Winkelmann, and Shakespeare himself" (Wilde, *Picture* 104). In the novel, Wilde uses the Hellenic ideal of spiritual affection between men *against* both the older Christian model of the sodomite and new scientific, pathologizing models of homosexual identity. As Linda Dowling points out, at his trials for committing sodomy and acts of "gross indecency" with men, Wilde ingeniously combined a modern notion of personal identity with ancient Greek ideals of male love, building on Pater's notion of a homoerotic "type" based in aestheticism and spirituality – what we might call a queer art of existence (Dowling, *Hellenism* 2–3). In this way, he challenged sexological theories of homosexuality as unnatural and/or abnormal. Both Wilde and Pater use aesthetic discourses for queer resistance, challenging "the contemporaneous efforts to encode homosexual experience in medical and juridical discourses that in effect deprived homosexuals of their voices at the very moment at which they were finding them" (Dellamora 15).

Keeping this discussion of the sexual politics of aestheticism in mind, I want to conclude this section with some reflections on aestheticism's *bon mot*, "art for art's sake." The phrase *l'art pour l'art* was made famous by Théophile

Gautier in his preface to *Mademoiselle de Maupin* (1835). In England, "art for art's sake" was first used by Swinburne in 1867 (in an essay on William Blake) and by Pater in 1868 in his essay "Poems by William Morris" (Prettejohn 38). Widely regarded as a retreat from the social and moral dimensions of art, art for art's sake actually had various meanings in different contexts. For example, in painting it referred to the movement away from narrative subjects. For writers like Wilde, it was an endorsement for art's "uselessness," its refusal to express anything but itself. But art's autonomy preserves its critical capacity, as aestheticism's critique of Victorian sex/gender norms demonstrates. In his 1929 essay on surrealism, Walter Benjamin speaks of the "obligatory misunderstanding of *l'art pour l'art*. For 'art for art's sake' was scarcely ever to be taken literally; it was almost always a flag under which sailed a cargo that could not be declared because it still lacked a name" (183–84). For Benjamin, the slogan *l'art pour l'art* is about the attempt to isolate art from technology and the commodification of the marketplace. Benjamin links the cult of art to the cult of commodities, arguing that both fail to confront the social relations that undergird nineteenth-century culture. But as Wilde demonstrates in "The Soul of Man under Socialism" (1891), the rise of the doctrine of art for art's sake was a revolt against bourgeois society. As Frederic Jameson asserts, fin-de-siècle aesthetes "deployed beauty as a political weapon against a complacent materialist Victorian bourgeois society and dramatized its negative power as what rebukes power and money, and what generates personal and social transformation in the heart of an ugly industrial society" (134). Nonetheless, the followers of the *l'art pour l'art* movement are caught between embracing the modern notion of art as autonomous and separate from the "real world" and yet wanting to transform the world (challenge materialism), giving a utopian dimension to their project. In other words, they are trapped by the very self-referentiality they championed, perhaps because, ultimately, their aesthetic project of self-actualization has ambitions that are not as strictly individualistic as we have been led to believe.

Decadent Dandies

The dandy is the paradigmatic emblem of fin-de-siècle decadence and aestheticism. Dandyism may appear to be simply a matter of dress and exterior elegance, but for modernity's great dandy theorists, such as Jules Barbey D'Aurevilly (1808–89) and Baudelaire, dandyism is an oppositional way of being. As D'Aurevilly declares in his study of the great English dandy George "Beau" Brummell (1778–1840), dandyism is "the revolt of the individual against the established order, sometimes against nature" (33). Like his predecessor, the Baudelairean dandy, the decadent dandy's pose is taken up by many fin-de-siècle artists and writers because it is a calculated strategy of revenge on conformity, utilitarianism, and "natural" virtue. Although we tend to associate the dandy with luxury, self-indulgence, and excess, dandyism is at heart an ascetic technique "in which a physical form of behavior acts as a route towards the performance of thought" – namely, the determination to fashion oneself as an exquisite originality (Barthes 67). The dandy selfishly cultivates this originality – a badge of intellectual and spiritual distinction that "work and money are unable to bestow" (Baudelaire, *Painter* 28) – as a rebellion against the demands of bourgeois society. This is why, for Baudelaire, the dandy's aristocracy of spirit makes him a hero of modern life – "the last spark of heroism amid decadence" (28–29). However, his heroic revolt against mediocrity and materialism does not transcend the modern world; rather, he exemplifies its contradictions. The Baudelairean dandy exhibits a profound philosophical/spiritual melancholy – ennui, cynicism, and indifference – that is a symptom of the corrupt world he inhabits. Indeed, Baudelaire developed his own style of dandyism distinguished by a devotion to the color black and an "austerity of line" (Moers 272) – a costume that exhibited the idiomatic beauty of a modern world in decline (thus the need for solemnity). The decadent dandy, however, departs somewhat from the solemnity of his predecessor. His outrage at the vulgarity of his age is complicated by an ironic or even playful attitude – a self-conscious awareness that his extreme gestures are excessive, futile, or absurd. Although there was a campiness in dandyism from the start, Wilde and other decadent dandies picked up on this sensibility and amplified it through parodic costuming and posturing, as well as a theatrical cultivation of the unnatural.

Although my focus here is on the decadent dandy and his relationship to queer literature and culture of the fin de siècle, I ask readers to remember that dandyism is not strictly associated with any particular movement, period, or erotic subculture. Dandies have been ambiguous and transgressive figures since their first appearance in early nineteenth-century England and France, but it would be a mistake to read the dandyism of Brummell's era as a form of queer effeminacy or as a cover for homoerotic orientations, desires, or practices. As Alan Sinfield puts it, "Like the rake, the dandy might debauch himself in any direction" (69). Sinfield and Ed Cohen convincingly argue that, after Wilde's 1895 trials for committing sodomy, the effeminate dandy was inextricably linked to the homosexual in the public imagination. Although Wilde's trials thus inaugurate the dandy as an icon of modern queer identity, it is important to remember that the decadent dandy refused to be a subject of desire as modern sexology defined it – that is, primarily in terms of the gender of one's object of desire. The stylized aestheticism of the turn-of-the-century decadent dandy is, among other things, a refusal to inhabit emerging medicopsychiatric categories of homosexuality.[7]

Since its publication in 1884, Joris-Karl Huysmans's *Against Nature* (*A rebours*) has reigned as the "bible of decadence" – a work that could be described without exaggeration as both the genuine first and last word on the subject. Even members of the decadent movement seemed to recognize that, after *A rebours*, there was very little else to say – or do. D'Aurevilly famously declared, "After such a book, the only thing left for the author is to choose between the muzzle of a pistol and the foot of the cross" (qtd. in Huysmans, *Against* 197).[8] I suggest this choice is one reason why the ironic and parodic elements of the movement seem more exaggerated after the publication of *Against Nature*. Huysmans's protagonist, Duc Jean Floressas des Esseintes, articulates the era's most daring synthesis of dandyism and decadence, pushing the figure of the effeminate dandy into the realm of artifice, unbridled perversity, and morbidity – the aesthete *à rebours*. Des Esseintes's world-weary dandy is the anemic solitary descendant of an aristocratic family decimated by inbreeding; nonetheless, his own decline cannot simply be attributed to his degenerate ancestors. His real malady is actually the diseased society he is forced to occupy – a world polluted by mass vulgarity and the "tyranny of commerce" (*Against* 179). Therefore, the decadent hero's weakness and "degeneracy" are not condemned but celebrated as evidence of a spiritual hypersensitivity that produces the artist-aristocrat's anguish in the face of the greed and crude utilitarianism of the modern world. It also produces his paradoxical quest for the seductive poles of civilized refinement and barbaric amorality, which both aim to release the decadent dandy from domestication by bourgeois society.

Worn out by extravagant living and his failing health, Des Esseintes craves solitude and retreats from the city to his secluded new residence, Fontenay-aux-Roses, which he painstakingly creates as a monument to his refined sensorium, a hallucinatory dream world of exotic objects that aims to "substitute the vision of reality for reality itself" (*Against* 20). To cite a particularly famous example of his passion for artifice, his dining room is designed to resemble a ship's cabin (complete with a porthole) and sits inside a giant aquarium filled with mechanical fish and imitation seaweed, providing him with the sights, smells, and sensations of a long voyage without ever having to leave his home. Des Esseintes is such an outlandish character that it may be difficult for contemporary readers to believe that he was modeled on a number of dandies and aesthetes of his day, including Baudelaire, D'Aurevilly, writer and dandy diarist Edmond de Goncourt (1822–96), the so-called mad King Ludwig II of Bavaria (1845–86), and Parisian poet, writer, and dandy Count Robert de Montesquiou-Fezensac (1855–1921). Montesquiou also appears as Marcel Proust's queer aesthete Baron de Charlus in *Remembrance of Things Past* (*À la recherche du temps perdu* [1913–27]). As the story goes, Stéphane Mallarmé (1842–98), whose poetry embodies for Des Esseintes the exquisite decay of language, visited Montesquiou's home in 1883 and described its wondrous objects and *tableaux vivants* to Huysmans. To cite a few examples that would be familiar to readers of *Against Nature*, Montesquiou's home contained the bejeweled shell of a tortoise, a room designed to resemble a monastic cell, another designed as a yacht's cabin, as well as a winter room with a picturesque snow scene containing a sleigh, polar bear rug, and mica-flake snow. King Ludwig II also sought to reshape the world in accordance with his own exacting aesthetic vision. One of his lavish and surreal castles contained a sunken cavern with artificial stalagmites, a waterfall, and a large artificial lake (with waves produced by an underwater machine) where Ludwig would sail in a boat designed to resemble a cockleshell (King 240). Like Huysmans's decadent dandy, the nocturnal, homoerotically inclined king sequestered himself in his gilded rooms and only saw the world during the night. In fact, he created a simulation of the night sky (including an artificial moon) so that day would be transformed into night when he retired in the morning (King 231).[9]

Although fantastic and eccentric, the dandy's project embodies several contradictions that are fundamental to decadent literature. First, the fin-de-siècle dandy has a contradictory relationship to consumerism, mass culture, and even the bourgeoisie he finds so hideous. Huysmans himself worked as a civil servant in the Ministry of the Interior for more than thirty years, making him a part of the era's expanding and increasingly bourgeois state machine (Gill 129–31). In both *Against Nature* and Wilde's *The Picture of Dorian Gray*, we see a tension between the decadent dandy's antibourgeois attitude and his endless appetite for new objects – a hunger that resembles the bourgeois style of consumption he protests against. Despite its critique of materialism, *Against Nature* can only attain its vision of spiritualized aestheticism through "elitist consumption," an exotic and extravagant lifestyle that asserts the decadent dandy's individuality and resistance to the democratization of luxury (see Williams 107–53). Both Huysmans's and Wilde's novels are, to borrow Jennifer Birkett's formulation, hymns to consumption (69). In Wilde's text, his dazzlingly handsome young protagonist falls under the influence of a "poisonous" yellow book (which is easily recognizable as

A rebours) and the equally poisonous dandy Lord Henry, who seduces him with his Paterian philosophy of new hedonism – a passionate search for sensations that culminates, for Dorian, in a frenzied quest for perverse and "sordid" pleasures.[10] Cultivating "the great aristocratic art of doing absolutely nothing" (*Picture* 30), Dorian embraces an aesthetic life of "wanton luxury and gorgeous splendor" that is both an imitation of and homage to Des Esseintes. In his effort to spiritualize his senses, Dorian collects jewels, musical instruments, perfumes, embroideries, and tapestries, seeking, like Des Esseintes, to transcend the commodification of modern life through an aestheticized relationship to objects. This contradictory relationship to consumerism is related to fin-de-siècle aestheticism's simultaneously democratic and elitist relationship to mass culture. Wilde exemplifies this, but both populist and elitist sensibilities played important roles in aestheticism. Susan Sontag famously argues that the dandy is opposed to mass culture, declaring that "camp is the answer to the problem: how to be a dandy in the age of mass culture" (288). The decadent dandy is disdainful of mass culture and yet, as we have seen, dandies are "among the earliest celebrities" (Garelick 11). Figures such as Wilde commodified themselves, using media-oriented strategies to remake the dandy for a mass audience, while also insisting on their superiority to that audience.

Second, Huysmans's decadent dandy embodies a contradiction between premodern authenticity and postmodern simulacra; he combines a nostalgic yearning for the past and its dying traditions with futurist fantasies of technological sublimity. His crowning triumph – "the ultimate deviation from the norm" (*Against* 171) – is his deliverance from the mechanical boredom of eating by taking nourishment through "meals" of peptone enemas. This attempt to dispense with the natural self is an early articulation of the discourse of the posthuman. An essentially prosthetic attitude toward the body, it manifests itself in the decadent's love for artificial copies of the human embodied in mannequins, wax figures, androids, and cyborgs. For example, Rachilde's Jacques in the gender-bending *Monsieur Venus* (1884) is transformed after death into a mechanized wax replica with "adorable" enamel eyes and hair, nails, and teeth taken from his corpse. Another example would be the female android Halady in Villiers de l'Isle-Adam's *Tomorrow's Eve* (*L'Eve futur* [1886]). Created by the dandy-scientist Edison, she is the perfect copy whose glowing, artificial flesh and exquisite workmanship make her "better than real" (60).[11] Huysmans's decadent dandy is similarly seduced by technology (I'm thinking of his preference for the sexy, mechanical beauty of the steam locomotive), while yearning for a world that has not yet been sullied by it.

Third, in *Against Nature* we find a contradiction between Des Esseintes's identification with an aestheticized femininity and his repulsion for women as the embodiment of feminine evil – a contradiction that critics have shown to be pervasive in fin-de-siècle art and literature (see Dijkstra; Felski; Showalter). Although French decadence tended to be more overtly misogynist than English decadence (Schaffer 27), the femme fatale is a truly transnational fin-de-siècle figure. A volatile combination of primitivism and soulless artificiality, she demonstrates the dark side of decadence's affinity for femininity. Along these lines, Rita Felski persuasively argues that Huysmans's *Against Nature*, Leopold von Sacher-Masoch's *Venus in Furs* (1870), and Wilde's *The Picture of Dorian Gray* are examples of the male aesthete / decadent's identification with and appropriation of the feminine – a performance of femininity that is predicated on their horrified "denial and displacement of the sexed female body" (Felski 113). This is not to say that Huysmans's work does not also challenge the gender norms of its day, particularly in its celebration of "bizarre sexual practices and deviant pleasures" (*Against* 8); for example, Des Esseintes's attachment to the decidedly queer circus acrobat Miss Urania detaches gender from sex, making him increasingly feminine as he yearns for this muscular woman who "seemed to make up her mind ... to become a man completely" (*Against* 85). Later, he submits to the "servitude" of a seductive young man, culminating in his greatest passion, which leaves him "painfully fulfilled" – another queer subversion of gender codes (90). Nevertheless, the decadent dandy's effort to conquer nature remains a masculinist gesture, as it is for the Paterian aesthete. As Huysmans's dandy declares:

> Nature has had her day; she has finally exhausted, through the nauseating uniformity of her landscapes and her skies, the sedulous patience of men of refined taste.... [T]here is not one single invention of hers, however subtle or impressive it may be thought to be, that the human spirit cannot create; no forest of Fontainebleau or moonlit scene that cannot be produced with a floodlit stage set; no waterfall that hydraulics cannot imitate so perfectly as to be indistinguishable from the original; no rock that papier-mâché cannot copy; no flower that specious taffetas and delicately painted papers cannot rival! There is no doubt whatever that this eternally self-replicating old fool has now exhausted the good-natured admiration of all true artists, and the moment has come to replace her, as far as that can be achieved, with artifice.
>
> (*Against* 20)

In his contempt for nature's "banality" and "monotony," Des Esseintes's rhetoric sounds a great deal like those turn-of-the-century critics who attacked female artists for their lack of originality and asserted that any aesthetic innovation must be male (Dijkstra 207). Huysmans's dandy is a "true artist," the creator-genius who celebrates artifice as an aesthetic solution to the problem of a feminized nature; furthermore, as Huysmans makes clear elsewhere in the text, nature's deficiencies symbolize not just women's inferiority but their fundamental animality. The figure of Salome, worshipped by Des Esseintes and other actual decadents, is the monstrous extreme of this vision of woman as bestial nature. Describing his hero's fascination with Gustave Moreau's painting *Salome Dancing Before Herod* (1876), Huysmans famously recounts how her sexual power transforms her into a fin-de-siècle Medusa: "the monstrous, indiscriminate, irresponsible, unfeeling Beast who, like the Helen of Antiquity, poisons everything that comes near her, everything that sees her, everything that she touches" (46). A seductive, hysterical goddess of unquenchable perversity, her emasculating power is so great that male transcendence is only possible through her destruction. Wilde, it should be noted, departs from the French tradition and brings more complexity to his dramatic vision of *Salomé* (1891).[12] In his treatment, Salome has more agency than in other accounts (including biblical ones); this is in part because she embodies not just transgressive female desire but decadent, homoerotic, and / or queer desire – decadent aestheticism's rebellion against heteronormativity and sexual asceticism (Cohler 15–21; Gagnier, *Idylls* 137–76). The countercultural sexual politics of fin-de-siècle decadents and dandies has a clear utopian dimension, but it also functions as a containment strategy as it becomes entangled in the movement's battle between "good" and "bad" femininity – good femininity is textualized, aesthetic, and disembodied while bad femininity is natural, embodied, and impure or diseased.

As students of decadence and aestheticism, we must decide: do we put our emphasis on what these movements tried to do or what they failed to do? I hope it is clear by now that I favor the former approach. Decadence's luxurious extravagance refuses the rationalization and utilitarianism of capitalism's restricted economy, producing a convergence of aesthetics and sexuality that is inextricably linked to the market but never fully contained by it. As Theodor Adorno argues, "In a world of brutal and oppressed life, decadence becomes the refuge of a potentially better life by renouncing allegiance to this one and to its culture, its crudeness, and its sublimity" (72). Decadence's negativity is not simply pessimistic or nihilistic; its reified universe contains within it a utopian possibility. The aestheticized, queer ways of seeing, being, and feeling I have discussed in this chapter are embodiments of decadence's regenerative energies. They are evidence that decadence carries with it the aspiration that the world be transformed and reinvigorated, that history would – to borrow Tony Kushner's turn of phrase – crack wide open.

Notes

1. On the transnational and international dimensions of the decadent movement, see Potolsky; Schoolfield. On the difference between English and French decadence, see Weir 61.
2. Bourget's essay "Essai de psychologie contemporaine: Charles Baudelaire" (1881) is one of the first manifestoes of decadence, preceded only by Théophile Gautier's famous preface to the first posthumous edition (1868) of Baudelaire's *Flowers of Evil* (*Fleurs du mal*).
3. On Sade's influence on fin-de-siècle decadence, see Birkett ch. 2; Carter ch. 1; Paglia 247; Praz ch. 3.
4. The decadent journals *The Yellow Book* (1894–7), the overtly homosexual *The Chameleon: A Bazaar of Dangerous and Smiling Chances* (1894), and *The Savoy* (1896) all launched and folded within a four-year period. Although *The Savoy* is typically considered the most decadent and experimental, it is important to note that *The Yellow Book* was more active in contemporary debates about gender. On the sexual politics of 1890s magazines, see Brake, "Aestheticism," "Endgames," and *Subjugated*; Fraser, Johnston, and Green; Hughes; and Ledger.
5. It's worth noting that Swinburne helped to create a female tradition for H.D. and other modernist women poets (expatriate English poet Renée Vivien, for example). For a discussion of Swinburne's relationship to Sappho and later female poets such as H.D., see Laity.
6. See Davis, who argues that Pater seeks to "think" through the body in order to conceptualize "not just the subject of queer desire but also the queer subject of desire" (267).
7. Although I have only been discussing the dandy as a male type, and indeed the scope of the present discussion prevents me from venturing into the terrain of the lesbian dandy (who is more of a modernist figure), I want to acknowledge the importance of decadence and dandyism for female decadents and modernists. Lesbian artists such as Natalie Barney, Romaine Brooks, Radclyffe Hall, and Renée Vivien drew on the traditions of dandyism and decadence "as part of a desire to make a newly emerging lesbian identity publicly visible" (Elliott and Wallace 19). For a more detailed discussion of lesbian dandyism and Sapphic decadence, see Glick.
8. Like many other queer decadents on both sides of the Channel (including Wilde, Verlaine, Beardsley, and Vivien), Huysmans chose the cross, converting to Catholicism in 1892, only a year after the publication of his satanic classic

The Damned (*Là-Bas*), a novel of black magic and demonic homosexuality. On the decadent, homoerotic Catholicism of Huysmans, see Hanson 108–68.

9. Of course, most dandies were not monarchs or even aristocrats. The dandy's "aristocracy" is primarily a spiritual sensibility: "the dandy as a popular phenomenon is middle-class," despite his association with upper-class privilege and aristocratic distinction (Dellamora 198).

10. Lord Henry's "new" hedonism is really an abridged version of Pater's conclusion to *The Renaissance*, which Wilde borrows from quite liberally. Echoing Pater, Wilde explains that the aim of the new hedonism "was to be experience itself, and not the fruits of experience, sweet or bitter as they might be.... [I]t was to teach man to concentrate himself upon the moments of a life that is itself but a moment" (*Picture* 114).

11. On the posthuman dimensions of decadence's disembodied self, particularly in relation to British fin-de-siècle spiritualism, see Denisoff, "'Disembodied.'" For a reading of how the figure of the female android mediates the relationship between decadent dandyism and mass culture, see Garelick ch. 3.

12. Wilde wrote *Salomé* in 1891 in French. In 1892, the play was in rehearsal (with Sarah Bernhardt playing the lead) when it was banned from the English stage because of its supposedly sacrilegious use of biblical characters. It was published in French in 1893 in Paris and London. The English translation of the play appeared in 1894 along with Aubrey Beardsley's iconic illustrations.

Works Cited

Adorno, Theodor. *Prisms*. Trans. Samuel Weber and Shierry Weber. Cambridge: MIT P, 1981. Print.

Baldick, Robert. *The Life of J.K. Huysmans*. Sawtry: Dedalus, 2006. Print.

Barthes, Roland. *The Language of Fashion*. Trans. Andy Stafford. Eds. Andy Stafford and Michael Carter. Oxford: Berg, 2006. Print.

Baudelaire, Charles. *The Flowers of Evil*. Trans. James McGowan. 1861. Oxford: Oxford UP, 1993. Print.

The Painter of Modern Life and Other Essays. Trans. Jonathan Mayne. 2nd ed. London: Phaidon, 1995. Print.

Beckson, Karl, ed. *Aesthetes and Decadents of the 1890s: An Anthology of British Poetry and Prose*. Chicago: Academy Chicago, 1981. Print.

Bell-Villada, Gene H. *Art for Art's Sake and Literary Life: How Politics and Markets Shaped the Ideology and Culture of Aestheticism, 1790–1990*. Lincoln: U of Nebraska P, 1996. Print.

Benjamin, Walter. *Reflections*. Trans. Edmund Jephcott. New York: Schocken, 1986. Print.

Birkett, Jennifer. *The Sins of the Fathers: Decadence in France, 1870–1914*. London: Quartet Books, 1986. Print.

Bourdieu, Pierre. *The Field of Cultural Production: Essays on Art and Literature*. Ed. Randal Johnson. New York: Columbia UP, 1993. Print.

Bourget, Paul. "Baudelaire and the Decadent Movement." *Symbolist Art Theories: A Critical Anthology*. Ed. Henri Dorra. Berkeley: U of California P, 1994. 128–31. Print.

Brake, Laurel. "Aestheticism and Decadence: *The Yellow Book* (1894–7), *The Chameleon* (1894), and *The Savoy* (1896)." *The Oxford Critical and Cultural History of Modernist Magazines: Vol. 1.* Ed. Peter Brooker and Andrew Thacker. Oxford: Oxford UP, 2009. 76–100. Print.

"Endgames: The Politics of *The Yellow Book,* or Decadence, Gender and the New Journalism." *Essays and Studies 1995: The Endings of Epochs.* Ed. Laurel Brake. Woodbridge, Suffolk: D.S. Brewer, 1995. 65–88. Print.

Subjugated Knowledges: Journalism, Gender, and Literature in the Nineteenth Century. New York: New York UP, 1994. Print.

Byrne, Romana. *Aesthetic Sexuality: A Literary History of Sadomasochism.* New York: Bloomsbury, 2013. Print.

Carter, A.E. *The Idea of Decadence in French Literature, 1830–1900.* Toronto: U of Toronto P, 1958. Print.

Cohen, Ed. *Talk on the Wilde Side: Toward a Genealogy of a Discourse on Male Sexualities.* New York: Routledge, 1993. Print.

Cohler, Deborah. *Citizen, Invert, Queer: Lesbianism and War in Early Twentieth-Century Britain.* Minneapolis: U of Minnesota P, 2010. Print.

Constable, Liz, Dennis Denisoff, and Matthew Potolsky, eds. *Perennial Decay: On the Aesthetics and Politics of Decadence.* Philadelphia: U of Pennsylvania P, 1999. Print.

D'Aurevilly, Jules Barbey. *Dandyism.* Trans. Doublas Ainslie. New York: PAJ, 1988. Print.

Davis, Michael F. "Walter Pater's 'Latent Intelligence' and the Conception of Queer Theory." *Walter Pater: Transparencies of Desire.* Ed. Laurel Brake, Lesley Higgins, and Carolyn Williams. Greensboro: ELT Press, 2002. 261–85. Print.

Dellamora, Richard. *Masculine Desire: The Sexual Politics of Victorian Aestheticism.* Chapel Hill: U of North Carolina P, 1990. Print.

Denisoff, Dennis. "'A Disembodied Voice': The Posthuman Formlessness of Decadence." *Decadent Poetics: Literature and Form at the British Fin de Siècle.* Ed. Jason David Hall and Alex Murray. Basingstoke: Palgrave, 2013. 181–200. Print.

"The Dissipating Nature of Decadent Paganism from Pater to Yeats." *Modernism/Modernity* 15.3 (2008): 431–46. Print.

Dijkstra, Bram. *Idols of Perversity: Fantasies of Feminine Evil in Fin-de-Siècle Culture.* New York: Oxford UP, 1986. Print.

Doran, Sabine. *The Culture of Yellow: Or, The Visual Politics of Late Modernity.* New York: Bloomsbury, 2013. Print.

Dowling, Linda. *Language and Decadence in the Victorian Fin de Siècle.* Princeton: Princeton UP, 1986. Print.

Hellenism and Homosexuality in Victorian Oxford. Ithaca: Cornell UP, 1994. Print.

Edwards, Jason. "The Portrait of the Artist as a Young Aesthete: Alfred Gilbert's *Perseus Arming* (1882) and the Question of 'Aesthetic' Sculpture in Late-Victorian Britain." *Sculpture and the Pursuit of a Modern Ideal in Britain, c. 1880–1930.* Ed. David J. Getby. Aldershot: Ashgate, 2004. 11–38. Print.

Elliot, Bridget, and Jo-Ann Wallace. "Fleurs du Mal or Second-Hand Roses?: Natalie Barney, Romaine Brooks, and the 'Originality of the Avant-Garde.'" *Feminist Review* 40 (1992): 6–30. Print.

Ellman, Richard. *Oscar Wilde.* New York: Vintage, 1987. Print.

Felski, Rita. *The Gender of Modernity.* Cambridge: Harvard UP, 1995. Print.

Fraser, Hilary, Judith Johnston, and Stephanie Green. *Gender and the Victorian Periodical.* Cambridge: Cambridge UP, 2003. Print.

Freedman, Jonathan. *Professions of Taste: Henry James, British Aestheticism, and Commodity Culture.* Stanford: Stanford UP, 1990. Print.

Gagnier, Regenia. *Idylls of the Marketplace: Oscar Wilde and the Victorian Public.* Stanford: Stanford UP, 1986. Print.

"Is Market Society the *Fin* of History?" *Cultural Politics at the Fin de Siècle.* Ed. Sally Ledger and Scott McCracken. Cambridge: Cambridge UP, 1995. 290–310. Print.

Garelick, Rhonda. *Rising Star: Dandyism, Gender and Performance in the Fin de Siècle.* Princeton: Princeton UP, 1998. Print.

Gill, Graeme. *Bourgeoisie, State, and Democracy: Russia, Britain, France, Germany, and the USA.* Oxford: Oxford UP, 2008. Print.

Glick, Elisa. *Materializing Queer Desire: Oscar Wilde to Andy Warhol.* Albany: State U of New York P, 2009. Print.

Greenslade, William M. *Degeneration, Culture, and the Novel: 1880–1940.* Cambridge: Cambridge UP, 1994. Print.

Hanson, Ellis. *Decadence and Catholicism.* Cambridge: Harvard UP, 1997. Print.

Hayles, N. Katherine. *How We Became Posthuman: Virtual Bodies in Cybernetics, Literature, and Informatics.* Chicago: U of Chicago P, 1999. Print.

Hughes, Linda K. "Women Poets and Contested Spaces in 'the Yellow Book.'" *Studies in English Literature, 1500–1900* 44.4 (2004): 849–72. Print.

Hurt, Jules. "Interview with Stéphane Mallarmé." *Symbolist Art Theories: A Critical Anthology.* Ed. Henri Dorra. Berkeley: U of California P, 1994. 139–42. Print.

Huysmans, Joris-Karl. *Against Nature: A Rebours.* Trans. Margaret Mauldon. 1884. Oxford: Oxford UP, 1998. Print.

The Damned: Là-Bas. Trans. Terry Hale. London: Penguin, 2001. Print.

Jameson, Frederic. "Transformations of the Image in Postmodernity." *The Cultural Turn: Selected Writings on the Postmodern: 1983–1998.* London: Verso, 1998. 93–135. Print.

King, Greg. *The Mad King: The Life and Times of Ludwig II of Bavaria.* Secaucus: Birch Lane P, 1996. Print.

Laity, Cassandra. "H.D. and A.C. Swinburne: Decadence and Sapphic Modernism." *Lesbian Texts and Contexts: Radical Revisions.* Ed. Karla Jay and Joanne Glasgow. New York: New York UP, 1990. 217–40. Print.

Ledger, Sally. "Wilde Women and the *Yellow Book*: The Sexual Politics of Aestheticism and Decadence." *English Literature in Transition, 1880–1920* 50.1 (2007): 5. Print.

Love, Heather. *Feeling Backward: Loss and the Politics of Queer History.* Cambridge: Harvard UP, 2007. Print.

Moers, Ellen. *The Dandy: Brummell to Beerbohm.* New York: Viking, 1960. Print.

Paglia, Camille. *Sexual Personae: Art and Decadence from Nefertiti to Emily Dickinson.* London: Yale UP, 1990. Print.

Pater, Walter. "Diaphaneitè." *Studies in the History of the Renaissance.* Oxford: Oxford UP, 2010. 136–40. Print.

Marius the Epicurean: His Sensations and Ideas. Kansas City: Valancourt, 2008. Print.

Studies in the History of the Renaissance. Oxford: Oxford UP, 2010. Print.

Potolsky, Matthew. *The Decadent Republic of Letters: Taste, Politics, and Cosmopolitan Community from Baudelaire to Beardsley.* Philadelphia: U of Pennsylvania P, 2012. Print.

Praz, Mario. *The Romantic Agony*. Trans. Angus Davidson. London: Oxford UP, 1970. Print.

Prettejohn, Elizabeth. "Walter Pater and Aesthetic Painting." *After the Pre-Raphaelites: Art and Aestheticism in Victorian England*. Ed. Elizabeth Prettejohn. Manchester: Manchester UP, 1999. 36–58. Print.

Rachilde, *Monsieur Venus*. Trans. Liz Heron. Sawtry: Dedalus, 1992. Print.

Schaffer, Talia. *The Forgotten Female Aesthetes: Literary Culture in Late-Victorian England*. Charlottesville: UP of Virginia, 2000. Print.

Schoolfield, George C. *A Baedeker of Decadence: Charting a Literary Fashion, 1884–1927*. New Haven: Yale UP, 2003. Print.

Showalter, Elaine. *Sexual Anarchy: Gender and Culture at the Fin de Siècle*. New York: Penguin, 1990. Print.

Sinfield, Alan. *The Wilde Century: Effeminacy, Oscar Wilde and the Queer Moment*. New York: Columbia UP, 1994. Print.

Sontag, Susan. "Notes on 'Camp.'" *Against Interpretation and Other Essays*. New York: Picador, 1990. 275–92. Print.

Swinburne, Algernon Charles. *Poems and Ballads & Atalanta in Calydon*. London: Penguin, 2000. Print.

Symons, Arthur. "The Decadent Movement in Literature." *Dramatis Personae*. Indianapolis: Bobbs-Merrill, 1923. 96–117. Print.

Villiers de l'Isle-Adam. *Tomorrow's Eve*. Trans. Robert Martin Adams. Urbana: U of Illinois P, 2001. Print.

Weir, David. *Decadence and the Making of Modernism*. Amherst: U of Massachusetts P, 1995. Print.

Wilde, Oscar. *The Picture of Dorian Gray and Other Writings*. New York: Bantam, 1982. Print.

"The Soul of Man under Socialism." *The Soul of Man and Prison Writings*. Ed. Isobel Murray. Oxford: Oxford UP, 1990. 1–37. Print.

Williams, Rosalind H. *Dream Worlds: Mass Consumption in Late Nineteenth-Century France*. Berkeley: U of California P, 1982. Print.

19

Black Socks, Green Threads: On Proust and the Hermeneutics of Inversion

SARA DANIUS

We all know what Proust's novel is about. A tale of quest and long-delayed discovery, *A la recherche du temps perdu* (1913–27) is an artist's novel where the narrator aspires to become a writer and eventually decides to write ... an artist's novel. It takes him a long time to arrive at that point. We have to read close to three thousand pages of *Remembrance of Things Past* before the narrator finally finds his material – himself and his past life. In the final volume, the grand design becomes apparent.

If we look at Proust's novel from another angle, a different scenario comes into view. We realize that the narrator, as a writer in waiting, must hold back. He must resist. He must delay, postpone, persevere – or else the climax would come early. In volume after volume, he sounds his fears that he'll never succeed at becoming a writer, much less acquire artistic recognition. As he must.

To be sure, some way into the novel he gets a piece of writing accepted for publication in the pages of *Le Figaro*. When he sees it in print, he is ecstatic; after all, it is his debut as writer. Yet his sense of satisfaction recedes quickly, again, as it must – Proust has decided that the protagonist has to wait until the very end, until the hour of redemption is chimed. And when, after three thousand pages, the narrator makes his discovery and the novel reaches its climax, it is immensely satisfying, particularly from a storytelling point of view. We realize just how carefully constructed the narrative architecture is, just as we understand the emphasis on the theme of time and temporality. It is a stroke of genius. All of a sudden things fall into place.

The problem is that the end, no matter how satisfying it is, works a little too well. Of course *Remembrance of Things Past* is more than a novel about a novel. This is banal. The point is a different one: Proust needs this grand superstructure to be able to tell us about the things he really wants to tell us about, namely love, lust, and longing. More than anything else, the novel is an inquiry into the mechanisms of desire.

Yet *Remembrance of Things Past* is primarily associated with Time, Memory, and Aesthetics. Mention Proust, and it's unlikely that the average reader will think of Charlus, the homosexual baron whose destiny is traced in the novel. At one point the narrator comes to witness how Charlus asks to be chained onto a bed at a male brothel in order to be flagellated with a nailed whip. The scene leads to a whole psychology of sadomasochism. Nor will the average reader think of Albertine waltzing slowly with Andrée, chest to chest, hip to hip. And only the odd connoisseur will associate Proust's novel with the sublime fountain in *Cities of the Plain*, recognizing in it a poorly masked metaphor for other, more viscous fluids. In other words, there are the official themes, and then there are the unofficial ones.

The Rhetorical Device of Inversion

Proust's book is inhabited by many books, but the most important one is a vast essay on Eros. He offers us a psychology of attraction, a taxonomy of passion, and an epistemology of desire. His materials are relationships between men and women, as in *Swann in Love*. And between men, as in *Cities of the Plain*. And between women, as in *The Captive*, *The Fugitive*, and elsewhere – about a third of the novel revolves around lesbian love. Proust knew what he was doing: right from the start, he was determined to write about homosexuality – or *sexual inversion*, as he preferred to call it. But even if he knew that it would be a major theme, he realized that the project was a risky one, and so *Remembrance of Things Past* is a little like a Trojan horse.

In 1908, the year when he started work on *Remembrance*, he mentioned his current projects in a letter to a friend. The list was a long one. It included "a study of the aristocracy, a Parisian novel, an essay on Sainte-Beuve and Flaubert, an essay on women." It also included "an essay on pederasty (not easy to publish)" (Proust, *Correspondance* 8: 12–113; see also Compagnon 3: 1198). It has even been suggested that Proust's novel grew out of this essay (Rivers 153). One of Proust's earliest poems carries the title "Pédérastie." An early story, "Avant la nuit" ("Before the Night" [1893]), revolves around the theme of lesbianism and foreshadows *Cities of the Plain* – or, to use the original title, *Sodome et Gomorrhe*. This much is clear: same-sex desire was an integral part of Proust's writing from the very beginning. As early as 1909, he told an editor that homosexuality would be an important theme in the novel he was planning to write, and that one of the main characters would be *homosexuel*; three years later, when he was looking for a publisher for his multivolume novel, he announced – indeed, cautioned – that the work in question would contain "indecent" and "shocking" parts; he also described Baron de Charlus, asserting that he believed that this "virile pederast" was a new kind of literary character (Compagnon 3: 1187–89).

In using the term *sexual inversion*, Proust alluded to a notion that was common enough at the time, namely that homosexual males were "inverted men." It derived from a theory developed in the early 1860s by German lawyer and Latinist Karl Heinrich Ulrichs (1825–95), himself openly gay and generally considered the founder of the homosexual rights movement in Germany (e.g. Bauer 23–30). In his view, homosexuality was inborn; it was not an illness, and could therefore not be "cured." He defined the male homosexual as "the soul of a woman enclosed in the body of a man." Hence the notion of inversion. By the same token, a woman-loving woman was seen as having the soul of a man enclosed in the body of a woman. (The inversion paradigm builds on the idea that same-sex attraction presupposes gender difference; it thus retains a "heterosexual" element.) Moreover, it was Ulrichs who coined the term *Uranier* to denote a male homosexual, or in English, *Uranian*. Psychologically speaking, a homosexual, whether male or female, was a kind of hermaphrodite. In fact, inverts represented a "third sex." Influential sexologist Richard von Krafft-Ebing (1840–1902) was to develop Ulrichs's ideas, especially in *Psychopathia sexualis* (1886); and Magnus Hirschfeld (1868–1935), the physician who founded the Institut für Sexualwissenschaften, helped popularize them. They were all committed to the decriminalization of same-sex acts.

"Inversion," indeed, is a major preoccupation in *Remembrance of Things Past* – just as it is manifest in other writers in the period (Bauer). Yet in Proust inversion is more than a theme. It is part not only of *what* he said but also of *how* he said what he said. In short, inversion is part of the architecture of the novel. Roland Barthes, in an essay from 1971, had something similar in mind when he launched the idea that inversion is a "basic principle" in Proust. Characters, situations, and things turn out to be at one and the same time what they appear to be and their opposite. The ugly, vulgar woman reading a paper on the Balbec train, Barthes notes, is revealed to be ... the princess Sherbatoff; in much the same way Odette, regarded as a superior lady in one milieu, counts for a beast in another, and so on (1221). Barthes discusses sexual inversion only in passing; he is interested in inversion at large. He even goes so far as to say that it is a general law in Proust's novel (1220).

Barthes was right on the mark. Inversion is central. But I'd like to put forward a different idea: inversion serves as a *rhetorical device*. It offered Proust an ingenious mechanism for doing what he wanted to do in approaching the theme of same-sex desire and, equally important, for instructing his readers in the art of reading. At the risk of sounding a little too high-minded, we might call it a *hermeneutics of inversion*. It was part and parcel of the construction of that Trojan horse. As we shall see, it makes itself felt both locally and globally. What is more, the inversion mechanism is responsible for a great deal of comedy. And whenever it makes itself felt, we can be sure that Charlus is very likely to show up too.

Homosexuality's Trials

In turn-of-the-century France, homosexuality was not a criminal offense, to be sure, but it was far from accepted. Homosexuality was felt by many to be a violation of the law of God and the law of Nature, even an affront to the mental health of the nation (Rivers 112–13). Socially speaking, homosexuality could sometimes be tolerated, even accepted, albeit discreetly. In the circles in which Proust moved, especially as a young man, many people understood perfectly well that he had close relationships with men. But he wanted at all costs to avoid being labeled a "homosexual." What was said or understood in private was one thing, what was made public quite another. Honor was at stake. When writer Jean Lorrain, himself a homosexual, published a review article in which he insinuated that the author of *Les Plaisirs et les jours* (*Pleasures and Days* [1896]), namely Marcel Proust, was having an affair with Lucien Daudet, Proust decided to challenge him to a duel. The scene in the forest of Meudon, southwest of Paris, a classic dueling place, was not without its comedy. A homosexual man had accused another homosexual man of being ... homosexual. The pistols were fired in the air; the duel had been fought; Proust's reputation had been cleared (Carter 57–63; White 75–76).

The duel took place in 1897, and Proust probably had good reason to act as he did. Two years before a scandal had erupted: Oscar Wilde had been arrested on charges of "gross indecency" and imprisoned without bail (McKenna 350–97). Within days, the greatest wit of his day had been turned into a social pariah. In Britain, homosexual acts were punishable by law. The trials were monitored by the international press and attracted much public attention, particularly in France, and attitudes toward male homosexuality became harsher.

The Wilde case was certainly not unique. Throughout Europe numerous writers and other public persons were persecuted for their "homosexual" inclinations, for example, Danish author Herman Bang (1857–1912). Bang was pursued by the press as well as by anonymous letter writers, and spent long periods of time abroad (Ahnlund 208–11; Detering 233–83; Müller 39–51).

In 1909, Bang wrote a treatise on male homosexuality together with his German physician. *Gedanken zum Sexualitätsproblem* (*Thoughts on the Problem of Sexuality*) was published posthumously in 1922 – apparently after protests from Bang's family. It's a little-known text, intended as a contribution to German sexology, and the purpose was emancipatory: to argue, once more, that homosexuality is all but a "perversion" and should be decriminalized. The treatise is of particular interest as Bang reflects on the nexus of aesthetics and sexuality. If a writer happens to be homosexual, he writes, he is ideally suited for art. Nature has provided him with a Janus face, thus he is able to inquire into the life of the soul in two ways. He is a man, to be sure, but his psyche is that of a woman ("Er bleibt Mann und fühlt doch mit der Seele einer Frau"; Bang 20).

Bang here alludes to Ulrichs's theory of inversion. He also intimates that a homosexual writer affords a more complete view of the world. It's all due to the invert's Janus-like nature, he suggests. To avoid the "perpetual masquerade," he continues, the homosexual writer is likely to bracket himself and his own feelings, and so naturally turns into an artist, an observer of his fellow beings, even a superior one – because he looks at the world with *four eyes* (20). As we shall see in a moment, Proust too subscribes to the notion of dual vision, a mode of looking at the world made possible by homosexuality, and at the center is the idea of inversion.

A few years after the Oscar Wilde trials, new scandals followed. Sir Hector Archibald Macdonald, a high-ranking officer in the British Army known for his extraordinary courage and patriotism, committed suicide in 1903 after it was made public that he had had sexual relations with men. The press coverage was extensive and continued for months after his death. At roughly the same time, Friedrich Alfred Krupp, a German military man with influential friends, including Kaiser Wilhelm II, also committed suicide – in the wake of virulent press campaigns. In Germany, as in Britain, homosexual acts were punishable by law.

In 1907–09, the Eulenburg affair took place. A top-ranking diplomat, advisor to the emperor, and father of eight, Prince Philipp zu Eulenburg-Hertefeld was accused of homosexuality and tried in court – on evidence that had apparently been fabricated. The affair was politically motivated and quickly turned into a domestic scandal at the very highest level. Although Eulenburg was acquitted, he was persecuted for years. The events attracted a great deal of attention in France, and gave currency to the notion of "the German vice," *le vice allemand* (Compagnon 3: 1196–1202; Rivers 112–30).

Proust used the word "homosexual" only occasionally, and almost never in the novel (Compagnon 3: 1216–18). The term "homosexuality" is relatively recent, coined only in 1869, by Austrian-Hungarian writer Karl Maria Kertbeny, and it was part of the medicalization of sexuality at large (Foucault). Sexuality had become closely linked to notions of individual identity; what people *did* had come to be seen as central to what they *were*. The Eulenburg scandal caused the term to become popularized across Europe. As Antoine Compagnon has pointed out, Proust himself associated the spread of the word *homosexuel* in France with the German trials; besides, he found it "too germanic and pedantic," and preferred "invert" (Compagnon 3: 1202, 1217). At times, Proust used *pédéraste* as a neutral synonym; at other times, he used the word *tante*, old prison slang for "fag." A case in point is the preface to *Cities of the Plain* that depicts how the narrator comes to discover that Baron de Charlus loves men – and is having sex with Jupien, the vest maker. Titled "La Race des Tantes," it quickly turns into a wildly complicated essay on the behavior of men-loving men, complete with sexological reflections. It also contains a brief historicizing account of how homoerotic love has been understood through the ages, taking us back to ancient Greece and so-called Socratic love.

Open Secrets

Homosexuality – male as well as female – is a major subject in *Remembrance of Things Past*. You don't have to be a specialist in hermeneutics to realize this. Still, the common view of the novel tends to concentrate on what Proust has to say about Time, Memory, and Aesthetics. The question of homoerotic love is at best a marginal concern. Why? Given that the novel provoked a great deal of moral debate when it was first published, especially after the appearance of *Cities of the Plain*, it is a peculiar lacuna. The debate continued for years after the last volume was published. Some critics even refused to mention the title of *Sodome et Gomorrhe* – it was simply too indecent (Ahlstedt 72–73). Why has a disproportionate amount of critical attention been devoted to the first and last volumes, and why is the middle part of the novel so little discussed (Bowie, *Freud* 46)? Why, in other words, has the question of homosexuality – literally central to the novel – ended up on the periphery? And why does the tendency persist even today, after decades of critical work on the question of same-sex love in Proust, including its queer aspects?[1]

There are at least three explanations. The first is a banal one. Many readers, no matter how ambitious, give up at an early stage and never get to the important middle volumes – *Cities of the Plain*, *The Captive*, and *The Fugitive*. And even if readers were to take a shortcut and go straight to the closing volume, *Time Regained*, it is likely that, say, the episode about Baron de Charlus at the brothel in that same section will appear as no more than a spicy feature in a novel primarily concerned with the enigmatic mechanisms of human memory.

The second explanation is also rather banal. The usual prejudices have prevented readers from identifying the theme of homosexuality as a major one. It wasn't so very long ago that otherwise liberal-minded scholars took offense when anyone pointed out that Thomas Mann had homosexual inclinations (today scholars have a far more nuanced approach; e.g., Detering 285–334).

The third explanation is a more interesting one: Proust was himself responsible. He wanted it this way. He saw to it that his novel would be read as a work that revolves principally around Time, Memory, and Aesthetics. A particularly instructive example is the circular composition of the novel. It throws a retrospective light over the whole, serving to foreground certain themes and episodes, while making others – for example, the story about Baron de Charlus – seem subordinate.

Yet Charlus may well flash into the present, as though he had just moved out from the wings and positioned himself center stage. For Proust made sure to install a half-hidden, half-exposed interpretive model that encourages a different approach to the text, making it a little easier for the reader to grasp that same-sex desire is in fact one of the novel's central themes. Try double vision, the narrator seems to say. Turn upside down! Read with four eyes!

A case in point is the episode where the narrator describes a conversation he happens to have overheard at a party. Charlus and a small circle of men drawn from the social elite – "two dukes, a distinguished general, a celebrated author, an eminent physician and a great lawyer" – have gathered in a corner and are having a coded conversation about young men. They talk about where they are to be found, about who might be available, and so on. The boys are given feminine pronouns. *She*, it turns out, is a *he*. (3: 244–45, 3: 748).[2]

On the face of it, passages like these are part of Proust's early twentieth-century version of Sodom and Gomorrah, the proverbial cities of the plain whose inhabitants lived unrepentantly in sin. God's anger was so great that he decided to destroy the cities. He rained down burning sulfur, killing the inhabitants, the vegetation, everything. Proust's narrator here emerges as an anthropologist of "vice" – in much the same way as he casts a ruthless eye on the manners of the Parisian aristocracy and those of the bourgeoisie.

But such passages also serve another purpose. They offer a key for understanding a crucial dimension of Proust's novel. They are coded commands to the reader to perform a specific interpretive function: an "inverted" reading or, which ultimately amounts to the same thing, double vision. The reason is simple. Proust's novel both wants and does not want to be about homosexuality. Indeed, it wants to have it both ways, and this, of course, is why the cues are there. If you take the hint, the novel becomes risky. If you don't, it remains innocuous. The most obvious example is that some women in the novel may be seen as masked males, merely passing as women. Matters are, however, complicated. Not all women, not even a majority, can be seen as men – it's enough to think of Odette de Crécy and Oriane de Guermantes.

Throughout the novel, all seven volumes of it, Proust makes sure to provide similar interpretive cues to the understanding of the story. It's a well-known strategy in gay and lesbian literature at large, encouraging something like an allegorical approach. As such, it has been around for a long time, at least since Dante Alighieri's treatise *Il Convivio* (*The Banquet*; 1306–09) – there Dante suggests that vernacular poetry may usefully be understood by way of allegorical interpretation, as practiced in traditional biblical exegesis. The four "senses," furthermore, are inherent in one another; the "literal" level is not a mere vehicle; it's as meaningful as the other levels.

Proust's cues encourage a similar mode of construing textual meaning. Scenes may be interpreted literally and in at least one figurative sense, sometimes two or three. Consider the cues that occur in the episode describing a dinner party at the Verdurins' summer residence on the Normandy coast. The guests are waiting for Charlus and Morel, who happen to be running late. Madame Verdurin cracks a joke: "We're all here now except the young ladies" ("Nous n'attendons plus que ces demoiselles"; 2: 1077, 3: 431). The narrator adds an exclamation mark, meanwhile underscoring that the comment would have greatly surprised Baron de Charlus. Charlus doesn't know that the world knows. Things are evident, but he is oblivious, and happily so.

The larger point is this: right from the beginning Charlus has gone to great lengths to conceal his love for Morel, trying to create a cloak of invisibility, as though Morel was no one in particular, just another fellow being. To the extent that Charlus takes a special interest in him, then, it is because of the music. Indeed, he is interested in Morel as *violinist*, he insists, no more and no less. But his efforts are in vain. Nothing has been said, yet Madame Verdurin and her circle have long since understood the nature of Charlus's emotions; ever so tactfully, she even provides the two men with adjoining rooms on a floor of their own, where they can, as she says, "have a little music." The beauty of it all: that Charlus will continue to believe that his hiding efforts are successful. Music will be had, and everyone's happy – the young ladies, Madame Verdurin, the clan. This is Proust at his comedic best. As so often, the episode offers a comedy of discrepancy, thriving as it does on the gap between disguise and naked truth, between blindness and insight. We could also say: there's insight, but in all the wrong places.

Even so, there is more to the comedy. Passages such as these call attention to the architecture of the novel itself. If we look more closely, we realize that Proust has planted a flag. The young ladies' joke is part of a general interpretive pattern that surfaces at strategic points, serving as hints to that reader who, for some reason or other, may be willing to tune in to an "inverted" mode of reading – to explore, that is, how the literal level invokes the allegorical one, and vice versa. The hints are double-edged: they both cover and uncover, both veil and unveil. In this way Proust manages to craft a story that is risky and harmless, all at the same time.

Fashioning the Narrative

Baron Palamède de Charlus is the novel's great dandy – and surely one of the most complicated and memorable of the three thousand or so characters crowding Proust's literary universe. He is a gloriously self-conscious member of a distinguished aristocratic family, one whose ancestry reaches far back into European history. Proust based a major part of the character of Charlus on Robert de Montesquiou, a society man who once described himself as a "greyhound in a greatcoat." Montesquiou was also a writer, but his works – mostly decadent poems – have long since been forgotten.

Charlus has a literary lineage as well. He alludes to Balzac's homosexual character Vautrin, the escaped convict and mastermind who appears in several novels in the vast cycle *The Human Comedy*. Balzac, in other words, was exemplary – in a number of ways. Not only did he have encyclopedic ambitions that must surely have appealed to Proust – a critic once suggested that if the former was the author of *La Comédie humaine*, then the latter was the author of *La Comédie mondaine* (Ahlstedt 60–61). Balzac was also bold enough to write at length about homosexuals and lesbians, and he did so without ever suggesting that such "sexual deviations" were morally reprehensible (e.g., Muhlstein 63–85). Or as Charlus explains in a lengthy discussion of Balzac with his dull-witted interlocutor, Brichot: "Balzac was acquainted even with those passions which the rest of the world ignores, or studies only to castigate them" (2: 1086, 3: 439). When Proust decided that the introduction to *Cities of the Plain*, that is, *Sodome et Gomorrhe*, would be called "La Race des Tantes," he was alluding to his great predecessor: Balzac was arguably one of the first writers to use the slang word *tante* in a work of serious literature (e.g., Lucey 59–60; see also Proust 3: 1308).

At first Charlus is referred to as a heterosexual man, and virile at that; early in the novel, he is reputed to be the lover of Odette de Crécy. As soon as he enters the action, however, things become more complicated. It's intimated that he's a homosexual, even though it takes a while – a very long while – for the young narrator to understand as much. Like several other characters in the novel, his tastes will be revealed. The narrator himself is presented as a lover of women, as a heterosexual male who, for reasons that remain vague, is determined to study the customs of Sodom and Gomorrah in striking detail. An undeclared fascination – one might even say an inverted one – is at work everywhere.

When Baron de Charlus enters the action of the novel, he is standing out-side the casino in Balbec, a seaside resort on the Normandy coast. The episode occurs in *Within A Budding Grove*. Tall, fattish, sharp, he is a carefully groomed man in his forties. He's got a moss rose in his buttonhole; his suit is *black*, his straw hat is *black*; he has a moustache, of which the narrator says that it's *very black* ("*avec des moustaches très noires*"). He slaps the leg of his trousers with his switch while darting glances all around him.

The young narrator, feeling watched behind his back, turns around – to find that the stranger fixes him with "dilated eyes." He spends hundreds of words describing Charlus's visual behavior, but doesn't understand what's going on – and what's going on is an advanced form of flirtation. In a word, cruising; or as Lawrence Schehr suggests in his analysis of the scene: gaydar (32–37). Such ignorance is punished, it would seem. Shortly afterward, they run into each other on the Balbec beach, and the narrator immediately turns into an object of voluptuous scorn – he's walking about in a bathing suit adorned with *embroidered anchors*. In the world according to Charlus, few things could be more ridiculous.

It's a sizeable loss of prestige for the narrator. But he makes sure to find ways of redeeming himself. He may carry embroidered anchors, but he's got a big novel to write. Every time he gets an opportunity to describe Charlus's exterior, he rises to the occasion. It's a question of distinction. It's as though he's competing with Charlus – and all other scrupulously well-dressed individuals in the novel, in particular Oriane de Guermantes and Odette de Crécy.

Fashion, indeed, is a main thread in Proust. There's also a green thread. It can be detected in the trousers Baron de Charlus is wearing. His entire being exudes a particular kind of restrained elegance, bordering on asceticism. Of what kind? The narrator is as attentive to details as Charlus is meticulous with his appearance. He crafts a description of the baron that, in its accumulation of tell-tale detail, recreates on the stylistic level the very distinction about which it speaks. The action may have come to a halt, but an important subplot is taking shape. We can see before us his discriminating gaze, how it works its way down from the trouser leg to the footgear, inch by inch. Many years later, when the narrator has realized that he will indeed write a novel, his extraordinary observation skills will be transformed into writing, stylish writing:

> I saw that he had changed his clothes. The suit he was wearing was darker even than the other; and no doubt true elegance lies nearer to simplicity than false; but there was something more: from close at hand one felt that if colour was almost entirely absent from these garments it was not because he who had banished it from them was indifferent to it but rather because for some reason he forbade himself the enjoyment of it. And the sobriety which they displayed seemed to be of the kind that comes from obedience to a rule of diet rather than from lack of appetite. A dark green thread harmonised, in the stuff of his trousers, with the stripe on his socks, with a refinement which betrayed the vivacity of a taste that was everywhere else subdued, to which this single concession had been made out of tolerance, while a spot of red on his tie was imperceptible, like a liberty which one dares not take. (1:809, 2:112)

Monsieur Charlus has yet to be formally introduced, but this artfully constructed description of his sartorial preferences, including his subtle skills in chromatic modulation, has already told us a great deal about his character. At the same time, however, the portrait of Charlus is also a means for the narrator to characterize himself. He has a singular eye. He dreams of becoming a writer and wants to produce a work of art, but he fears he will fail utterly. Every sock turns into a promise of maybe. Every dark green thread is a discovery of a potential building block in that vast monument – an artist's novel telling the story of its own coming into being. Charlus's got style, the narrator's got style. Which will have been proved.

Such moments interconnect past, present, and future; and the narrator, as so often in Proust's novel, dissolves into so many scattered temporal versions of himself. Scenes like these prefigure the future of the search, the birth of the writer (Deleuze 3–38, 131–44). But there's more to the casino scene. Otherwise

354

Proust wouldn't be Proust. The young narrator is being watched by Charlus, and meanwhile the older version of the narrator is watching it all. By manipulating the promiscuous temporalities of the narrator, Proust is able to craft a spectacle of same-sex desire in which all is on display – and yet concealed. Things turn out to be at one and the same time what they appear to be and their opposite. It's a little like a three-dimensional postcard. Now you see the motif, now you don't, depending on the perspective you assume. On the face of it, the narrator is saying that he's being stared at, intimating he doesn't understand much. On closer consideration, a rather different story emerges. The innocent heterosexual young man on the scene may be oblivious, at least if we take him at his word, but the older version of the narrator is not: as the protracted meditation on the dark green thread makes clear, his desire-driven interest in Charlus's appearance is no less impassioned than Charlus's interest in the young man. The plurality of the narrator serves the themes of the novel well, in particular the unofficial ones. Between the lines Proust is treading a more dangerous path.

Inverting Reading

Toward the end of the novel, in the final volume, *Time Regained*, Proust's narrator expounds his aesthetic program, spelling out how he conceives of the task of a literary work of art. He has come to realize at this point in the story that he has a vocation. One of the most well-known sections of the novel, this episode is often cited, as the narrator here changes gear and puts into words his theory of art. We hardly notice it, but as soon as we look a little closer we discover that the narrator has eased in exercises in the art of interpretation. As we move into the episode, the narrator emerges from the wings to explain how the mechanism of interpretive inversion can work. It's a little like stereoscopic vision. It sometimes happens that readers see things in the writing that are not quite there, he explains, citing as an example homosexual readers who readily change the gender of the characters. A case in point is when male homosexuals think of female characters as masked men, as women with male faces. Such modes of reading should not be a source of offense, emphasizes the narrator with seeming innocence:

> The writer must not be indignant if the invert [*l'inverti*] who reads his book gives to his heroines a masculine countenance [*visage masculin*]. For only by the indulgence of this slightly aberrant peculiarity can the invert give to what he is reading its full general import. Racine himself was obliged, as a first step towards giving her a universal validity, for a moment to turn the antique

figure of Phèdre into a Jansenist; and if M. de Charlus had not bestowed upon the "traitress" for whom Musset weeps in *La Nuit d'Octobre* or *Le Souvenir* the features of Morel [*le visage de Morel*], he would neither have wept nor have understood, since it was only along this path, narrow and indirect, that he had access to the verities of love. (3: 948–49, 4: 489)

Proust's narrator here articulates the art of reading "homosexually." It's not a partial approach, nor is it a misreading. It's beyond good and evil. It doesn't see less; if anything, it sees more. The "inverted" mode of reading is capable of doing not just one thing but two, and at the same time to boot. It's none other than Charlus who serves as the model for this interpretive theory, the Proustian hermeneutics of inversion. In order to be capable of experiencing the truth in Musset's plays, he has to change the gender of the heroines. Proust's narrator doesn't say it, but what he intimates is this: the interpretive mechanisms may differ, to be sure, but the end is the same – to recognize the truths of love, no matter what one's orientation. It's no coincidence that Charlus returns in these final pages. His fall into social disgrace occurred just a little while ago; and now, at the point at which the novel reaches its long-awaited climax, Baron de Charlus is redeemed, once and for all.

Proust has a reader-friendly approach to the art of hermeneutics. A book is not an expression of the inner life of the author; it is merely an instrument, a humble servant tending to the needs of the reader. It's the reader and nobody else who best understands how the text is to be used:

The writer's work is merely a kind of optical instrument which he offers to the reader to enable him to discern what, without this book, he would perhaps never have perceived in himself. And the recognition by the reader in his own self of what the book says is the proof of its veracity, the contrary also being true, at least to a certain extent, for the difference between the two texts may sometimes be imputed less to the author than to the reader. (3: 949, 4: 489–90)

What is more, there are particular circumstances beyond the author's control, for example, "inversion." It's yet another interpretive clue. Alluding once more to Baron de Charlus, the narrator explains – by way of parenthesis – that the reader may be homosexual:

Besides, the book may be too learned, too obscure for a simple reader, and may therefore present to him a clouded glass through which he cannot read. And other peculiarities [(*comme l'inversion*)] can have the same effect as inversion. In order to read with understanding many readers require to read in their own particular fashion, and the author must not be indignant at this; on the contrary, he must leave the reader all possible liberty, saying to him: "Look for yourself, and try whether you see best with this lens or that one or this other one."

(3: 949, 4: 490)

These lines are also frequently quoted. Critics have paid particular attention to the visual metaphors used by Proust, especially the idea that a work of literature is like an optical instrument – to be used by the reader so that he or she may perceive things that would otherwise have remained invisible (Shattuck).

Yet critics tend to overlook the parenthesis that has been inserted, ever so tactfully, into the last sentence. On the face of it, the passage seems no more than a variation on a familiar theme: the narrator is making aesthetic pronouncements. But as so often, something quite different is afoot. We have seen how the narrator has furnished the novel with coded commands to the reader to perform a specific interpretive function. To understand what the narrator is intimating in this particular passage, all we need to do is apply the recommended reading method. Look the other way round! Read in a double mode! Use four eyes! It's very simple: substitute "the writer" for "the reader," and "reading" for "writing," and Proust's cunning appears in sudden relief:

> And other peculiarities (like inversion) can have the same effect. In order to write with understanding many writers require to write in their own particular fashion, and the reader must not be indignant at this; on the contrary, he must leave the writer all possible liberty.

To put it as simply as possible, it looks as though it is the "writer" who has to grant the "reader" all possible liberty, when in fact it is the narrator who has granted himself all possible liberty. Not only does the passage thematize inversion; it performs the logic itself.

We also realize just how central Baron de Charlus is. In addition to being one of the most interesting characters in the expansive universe emerging in *Remembrance of Things Past*, he plays a special role in the aesthetic program for which the novel serves as a vehicle. Indeed, he figures as an exemplary reader. In the world according to Proust, this is no small matter – reading is a central issue in the novel (Muhlstein 63–85; Watt 17–44).

Female Enigmas

There is a complication, however, and its name is not Sodom but Gomorrah. A striking feature of Proust's novel is perhaps not that it pays a great deal of attention to male homosexuality but rather its passionate interest in lesbianism – besides, many more pages are devoted to the latter than to the former.

A major part of the novel is preoccupied with the narrator's relationship with Albertine, how he falls in love with her; how he courts her; how he discovers her sexual ambiguity; how she inspires the most rampant jealousy in him; how he imagines her relationships with her girlfriends; how she eventually moves in with him in his Paris apartment; how he holds her captive like a precious bird, controlling her every move, meanwhile trying to appease her by giving her a hysterically luxurious collection of Fortuny dresses; how she eventually manages to escape her prison – only to die in an accident a few days later.

Up until the very end of the relationship, the narrator's mind is beset by questions about Albertine. Malcolm Bowie, in his *Freud, Proust, and Lacan*, writes with great force about the middle volumes, arguing that the narrator's jealousy works like an epistemological machine driving much of the plot forward. Has Albertine had sexual connections with women in the past? Is she involved with women lovers now? If not, is she possibly planning to involve herself in such relationships? And equally important: How can I make her speak the truth; and how can I know whether she is telling me the truth? (Bowie, *Freud* 50) The speculative intellect is everywhere hard at work, collecting observations, interpreting signs, evaluating evidence, articulating hypotheses, testing theories, and so on. What these volumes, especially *The Captive*, amount to is not so much a psychology of love; what animates them is the portrait of a scientific mind in process. In short: the representation of a quest for knowledge in its purest form (Bowie, *Freud* 46–65; see also Bersani, *Marcel* 56–97).

Yet for all the achievements of intelligence in these pages, and they are terrifyingly impressive, Albertine cannot be known. Her "truth" is nowhere to be had. She remains an enigma (Bowie, *Freud* 59). With Charlus, the other great "homosexual" character in the novel, things are very different. His "truth" can indeed be known and, above all, seen. He tries to conceal his love for men, but as we have noted, it is there for all to see – and ironically enough, he is gloriously unaware of it. Baron de Charlus is surely the most visible character in the novel, in particular when it comes to the ways he handles his love for men – all the way from the sexual encounter with Jupien in the courtyard to the flagellation scene at the male brothel. Indeed, time and again Charlus is transformed into a theatre of sexual inversion; and the ever-present and ever-ingenious narrator always makes sure to find a peephole – and to describe, in striking detail, what he then sees or hears. This is why Eve Kosofsky Sedgwick speaks of Charlus's "glass closet." Turned into spectacle, Charlus's closet even becomes the "truth" of the "homosexual"; and as such, it runs the risk of blinding the reader to all other forms of homosexual desire in the novel (*Epistemology* 231).

When we take a closer look at Albertine, Andrée, and Gilberte, the little band of young women in bloom first discovered by the narrator on the beach in Balbec, and follow their winding paths throughout the novel, we realize that Proust's lesbians don't fit the inversion model. They are not represented as women with the soul of a man enclosed in the body of a female. They are women, period; and they desire women. Their sexuality is based not on difference (the "heterosexual" model) but on likeness (the "homosexual" model). This is to say that there is no symmetry between Proust's account of men who love men – Charlus, after all, is a Man-Woman, a *tante* – and his treatment of women who love women. Several critics have explored this gulf (Bersani, "Redemption" 416; Ladenson 28–57; Sedgwick, Epistemology 213–51; Silverman 339–88).

But there is more. In Proust's novel, male homosexuality is often represented as a vice, and emphatically so, both in the preface to *Cities of the Plain* and in the narrative action. Lesbianism functions very differently. Albertine's love affairs may cause a great deal of angst in the narrator, sick from jealousy as he often is, but her lesbianism – or anyone else's, for that matter – is not seen as morally reprehensible behavior, as Elisabeth Ladenson has shown. Female homosexuality is represented as – well, perhaps not as a virtue, but it's associated with joy, beauty, play, pleasure, happiness. The contrast is striking. Ladenson even speaks of Proust's *lesbophilia*; in the final analysis, she suggests, it is what makes *Remembrance of Things Past* truly queer.

The Search Is Over

In the final volume, *Time Regained*, the novel eventually reaches its long-awaited climax. Time has passed. Albertine is long since dead; Charlus, for his part, has aged beyond recognition and fallen apart, so much so that he is sometimes an embarrassment to his environment. The narrator is on his way to a Guermantes party. As he enters the courtyard, he stumbles on the uneven paving stones in front of the coach house; and all of a sudden, he recalls a similar experience in the baptistery at St. Marks in Venice many years ago. The past flashes into the present. He is filled with happiness: he captures a "fragment of time in the pure state" (3: 905, 4: 451). The sensation reminds him of the flavor of the madeleine, the sight of the church towers of Martinville, the sounds of the works of Vinteuil. What these sensations have in common is that they release him from fear and intellectual doubts. This time, however, it is once and for all. And so it is that after close to three thousand pages, he comes to understand that his task is to write the very novel that we are about to finish. Speaking of joy and ecstasy, he has discovered his subject matter: himself and his past life. Things have come full circle. The dénouement is in place. The search is over. All that remains to be done is to append a theory of art – and of reading.

Proust's narrator now moves on to his "official" themes – Time, Memory, Aesthetics. Meanwhile, and as he unfolds his aesthetic program with characteristic analytic subtlety, the story about Charlus recedes into the background, as does that about Albertine – as well as the stories about Morel, Jupien, Saint-Loup, Andrée, Gilberte, Mlle Vinteuil. A little while ago, these characters were literally central to the novel; now their destinies begin to seem more peripheral. Relativized by the grand design of the novel, they turn into something like case material, no more, no less. The Trojan horse is almost done.

But as we have seen, Charlus is smuggled back in. He reemerges in the pages where Proust's narrator explains how he conceives of the relation between book and reader. Parenthetically, to be sure – but still. Serving as a coded command to the reader, Charlus works as a subtle yet powerful reminder of Proust's gay science of interpretation, that hermeneutics of inversion whose ingenious mechanisms I have sought to delineate here. As we read Proust's monument to the vicissitudes of human desire, we're asked to look at the world with four eyes. Hence the beauty of Proust's vision. Things turn out to be at one and the same time what they appear to be and their opposite, including the narrator himself.

Notes

1. For example: Bersani, *Marcel* 98–138, "Redemption"; Rivers; Ahlstedt; Bowie, *Freud* 46–65, *Proust* 209–66; Compagnon; Silverman; Sedgwick, *Epistemology* 213–51; Bal 110–36, 218–19; Hartwig 18–101; White; Schehr 13–85; Ladenson 1–9, 131–34; Finch; Eells 11–33; Lucey 193–249; McCrea 157–210; Zoberman; Sollers.
2. Where necessary, references to Proust's novel include the English translation and the French original.

Works Cited

Ahlstedt, Eva. *La Pudeur en Crise. Un aspect de l'accueil d'A la recherche du temps perdu de Marcel Proust, 1913–1930.* Gothenburg: Acta u gothoburgensis, 1985. Print.

Ahnlund, Knut. "Utanför normen. Herman Bang." *Diktarliv i Norden. Litterära essäer,* 145–223. Stockholm: Brombergs, 1981. Print.

Bal, Mieke. *The Mottled Screen: Reading Proust Visually*. Trans. Anna-Louise Milne. Stanford: Stanford UP, 1997. Print.

Bang, Herman. *Gedanken zum Sexualitätsproblem*. Ed. Max Wasbutzki. Bonn: Marcus, 1922. Print.

Barthes, Roland. 1971. "Une idée de recherche." *Oeuvres complètes*. 3 vols. Ed. Eric Marty. Paris: Seuil, 1971. 2:1218–21. Print.

Bauer, Heike. *English Literary Sexology: Translations of Inversion, 1880–1930*. Basingstoke: Palgrave, 2009. Print.

Bersani, Leo. "'The Culture of Redemption': Marcel Proust and Melanie Klein." *Critical Inquiry* 12 (Winter 1986): 399–421. Print.

Marcel Proust: The Fictions of Life and of Art. London: Oxford UP, 1965. Print.

Bowie, Malcolm. *Freud, Proust, and Lacan: Theory as Fiction*. Cambridge: Cambridge UP, 1987. Print.

Proust Among the Stars. London: HarperCollins, 1998. Print.

Carter, William C. *Proust in Love*. New Haven: Yale UP, 2006. Print.

Compagnon, Antoine. "Notice." 1989. *Proust, A la recherche* 3: 1185–261.

Deleuze, Gilles. *Proust & Signs*. Trans. Richard Howard. Minneapolis: U of Minnesota P, 2000. Print.

Detering, Heinrich. *Das offene Geheimnis. Zur literarischen Produktivität eines Tabus von Winckelmann bis zu Thomas Mann*. Göttingen: Wallstein, 1994. Print.

Eells, Emily. *Proust's Cup of Tea: Homoeroticism and Victorian Culture*. Aldershot: Ashgate, 2002. Print.

Finch, Alison. "Love, Sexuality, and Friendship." *The Cambridge Companion to Proust*. Ed. Richard Bales. Cambridge: Cambridge UP, 2001. 168–82. Print.

Foucault, Michel. *The History of Sexuality, Volume 1: An Introduction*. Trans. Robert Hurley. New York: Vintage, 1990. Print.

Hartwig, Ina. *Sexuelle Poetik: Proust, Musil, Genet, Jelinek*. Frankfurt a/M: Fischer, 1998. Print.

Ladenson, Elisabeth. *Proust's Lesbianism*. Ithaca: Cornell UP, 1999. Print.

Lucey, Michael. *Never Say I: Sexuality and the First Person in Colette, Gide, and Proust*. Durham: Duke UP, 2006. Print.

McCrea, Barry. *In the Company of Strangers: Family and Narrative in Dickens, Conan Doyle, Joyce, and Proust*, 157–210. New York: Columbia UP, 2011. Print.

McKenna, Neil. *The Secret Life of Oscar Wilde: An Intimate Biography*. New York: Basic, 2005. Print.

Muhlstein, Anka. *Monsieur Proust's Library*. New York: Other P, 2012. Print.

Müller, Lothar. *Herman Bang*. Berlin: Deutscher Kunstverlag, 2012. Print.

Proust, Marcel. *Correspondance*. 21 vols. Ed. Philip Kolb. Paris: Plon, 1970–93. Print.

A la recherche du temps perdu. 4 vols. Ed. Jean-Yves Tadié et al. Bibliothèque de la Pléiade. Paris: Gallimard, 1987–89. Print.

Remembrance of Things Past. 3 vols. Trans. C.K. Scott Moncrieff and Terence Kilmartin. New York: Vintage, 1982. Print.

Rivers, Julius Edwin. *Proust and the Art of Love: The Aesthetics of Sexuality in the Life, Times, and Art of Marcel Proust*. New York: Columbia UP, 1980. Print.

Schehr, Lawrence. *French Gay Modernism*. Urbana: U of Illinois P, 2004. Print.

Sedgwick, Eve Kosofsky. *Epistemology of the Closet*. Berkeley: U of California P, 1990. Print.

The Weather in Proust. Ed. Jonathan Goldberg. Durham: Duke UP, 2011. Print.

Shattuck, Roger. *Proust's Binoculars*. New York: Vintage, 1967. Print.

Silverman, Kaja. *Male Subjectivity at the Margins*. New York: Routledge, 1992. Print.

Sollers, Philippe. "Sodome contre Gomorrhe." *Marcel Proust*. Spec. issue of *Magazine Littéraire* 13 Feb. 2013: 87–90. Print.

Watt, Adam. *Reading in Proust's A la recherche: "Le délire de la lecture."* Oxford: Oxford UP, 2009. Print.

White, Edmund. *Marcel Proust*. New York: Viking, 1999. Print.

Zoberman, Pierre. "L'inversion comme prisme universel." *Marcel Proust*. Spec. issue of *Magazine Littéraire* 13 Feb. 2013: 81–85. Print.

20

"This Sudden Silence": A Brief History of the Literature of Caribbean Women Who Love Women

OMISE'EKE NATASHA TINSLEY

and look, love, there are no poems to this only
triangles, scraps, prisons of purpled cloth
time begins with these gestures, this
sudden silence needs words instead of whispering
— Dionne Brand, "hard against the soul"

Yes, this sudden silence needs. Reaching across breaks with enjambment, these lines at once caress and rend open silence around desire between Caribbean women; and their publication in Trinidadian Canadian poet Dionne Brand's 1990 collection *No Language is Neutral* marks a sea change in Caribbean women's literature. Buoyed by crucial publications in the late 1980s, the 1990s ushered in an unprecedented storm of writing by Caribbean women who love women – one that has changed the region's literary landscape. Like any other storm, this one crosses all the archipelago's linguistic groupings. Novels by Jamaican diasporic lesbian and queer writers Makeda Silvera, Michelle Cliff, Patricia Powell, and Nalo Hopkinson join poetry and fiction from Trinidadian diasporic writers Cheryl Boyce Taylor, Shani Mootoo, and R. Erica Doyle to mark the Anglophone Caribbean – ironically, often maligned as containing the most homophobic sites in the region – as a powerful source of this movement. Haitian diaspora artists Lenelle Moise and MilDred Gerestant continue oral literary traditions among women who love women with their performance poetry, while Surinamese Dutch novelist Joanna Werners explicitly represents these traditions in her recent fiction. And Dominican novelist and poet Ana Lara, Cuban American novelist and short story writer Achy Obejas, and Cuban short story writer and journalist Marilyn Bobes queer borders between multiple genres as well as languages (Spanish and English). Hasn't Caribbean literature triumphantly arrived at the end of Brand's line, then – lavishing readers with words instead of whispering?

But telling the story in this way calls down a host of problems. On the one hand, it crafts a deceptively simple progress narrative that assumes that this storm of words means that "things are getting better" for women who love women in the Caribbean. In fact, Trinidadian writer Rosamond King – writing her reflections on one of the texts that initiated the boom, Makeda Silvera's classic essay "Man Royals and Sodomites: Some Thoughts on the Invisibility of Afro-Caribbean Lesbians" (1991) – speculates that the marginalization of Caribbean lesbians may have significantly *increased* in the past twenty years (192). And so perhaps the recent literary thunder writes back to new challenges rather than celebrating new gains. On the other hand, narrating Caribbean literature's move from silence to speech about desire between women suggests that these recent publications burst onto the literary scene *out of nowhere*, out of no Caribbean literary tradition – once again positing the region as being "behind" Europe and Euro-America in explorations of sexuality and gender. But there are centuries of representations of women's same-sex desire in the Caribbean, representations that don't necessarily sound like those that emerge from the continents. Yes, there *are* poems to this, including Brand's; and there are triangles, scraps, sudden silences that also speak stormily of the complexities of fixing desire in language.

While Sappho's island became popular as the spatial signifier for female same-sex sexuality in 1870 and in Europe, in Caribbean islands other word-stories circulated before and after that cultural formation. Many women involved in same-sex relationships here have done so openly in the context of working-class Afro-Caribbean traditions like *mati* in Suriname, *zanmi* in Grenada, *kambrada* in Curaçao. These words refer without distinction to female friends and lovers. *Mi mati* is like *my girl* in African American English, maybe *my friend* or maybe *my lover*. *Mati* and *zanmi* particularly are used more frequently in verbal constructions than in nominal ones. You say that women do *mati* work or make *zanmi*, talking about sexuality not as identity but as praxis – a way of becoming that is constantly constructed and reconstructed through daily actions. As the doubly signifying Creole for these practices suggests, *zanmi* love women in a language and culture that at once leave this eroticism unnamed or undifferentiated from other sharings and bend to communicate it without separating *making zanmi* from other aspects of their lives and languages in working-class communities.

You know the noun *lesbian* comes from an island; but east and south of there and sinking deeper, the noun *mati* comes from the middle of the Atlantic Ocean. Derived from Dutch *maat*, *mati* also means *mate* as in shipmate: she who survived the Middle Passage with me. There captive African women created erotic bonds with other women in the sex-segregated holds, resisting commodification of their bought and sold bodies by *feeling for* their co-occupants on these ships.[1] These bonds were expressed in art, in stories that women wrote on their very bodies during the Middle Passage. Anthropologist Gloria Wekker cites a beautiful, wrenching account of a slave ship's arrival in Paramaribo, Suriname, when an eyewitness noted that the female enslaved "had marked each others' heads with different designs, suns, half moons, without the help of a razor, without even soap, only with a piece of glass." She meditates: "Apparently, these shipmates, with their diverse places of origin, languages, and backgrounds, had already been able to find a common idiom with which to encourage themselves and each other. It is worth noting that part of the performance of their subjectivity was beautification" (*Politics* 219). These beautifications represent ephemeral art forms, bodily writings that mark a murky genesis of the literature of Caribbean women who love women, one that can never either be fully brought into words *or* forgotten.

Once arrived in the New World, women in some parts of the Caribbean continued relationships with *mati* in female friendship/kinship networks. As early as 1793, Bryan Edwards remarks: "This is a striking circumstance; the term *shipmate* is understood among [West Indian slaves] as signifying a relationship of the most endearing nature; perhaps as recalling the time when the sufferers were cut off together from their common country and kindred, and awakening reciprocal sympathy from the remembrance of mutual affliction" (94). Two hundred years later, Wekker traces linkages between these shipmate relationships that exist throughout the African diaspora and the socio-sexual practice of *mati* in twentieth-century, working-class Creole communities. And, she concludes, "slave women in other parts of the Caribbean developed comparable forms of relating to each other, pointing to the resiliency of West African cultural heritage" ("What's" 124). We can imagine, too, that these relationships had their own ephemeral art forms, their own triangles and half moons to express common love, loss, and desire.

And there are other traditions of literary expression by Caribbean women who love women that we *know* existed, but that now are so close to being forgotten that they sound like silence, too. Some of these were generated in the context of Carnival, the French Catholic celebration of the approach of Lent that enslaved Africans transculturated to vehicle Yoruba and other West African performance traditions. Creative with culture, these celebrations were also, Rosamond King documents, sites where women expressed creative sexualities through song and other art forms. She cites a description of two all-female bands in Martinique's 1888 Carnival as "feminine associations ... established with a view to pleasure," then quotes at length an 1884 description of female singers in the Trinidad Carnival that complains of bands of female singers "singing at the top of their voices, as if in defiance of the law and all decency." The writer goes on to ask: "Are they not, in the majority of cases, members of bands notoriously formed for immoral purposes, and those practically taught to scorn all that society respects and appreciates, and to indulge in unbridled licentiousness?" (192–93). According to King, these complaints of excessive pleasure and "licentiousness" in all-female groups hint that the women's objectionable promiscuity included same-sex sexuality. And writers' complaints of women singing their pleasure at the top of their lungs suggests that not only were these lovers of women far from silent, but their expressions reached many ears who were unwilling to receive or record them.

In this chapter, I will not pretend to represent these ephemeral texts that no longer exist, much as they command my imagination. Nor will I explore those other, beautiful and easily accessed texts I began by gesturing toward. Instead, I want to focus my considerations of the literature of Caribbean women who love women somewhere between the silenced and the loud-spoken, between the invisible and the high-profile: by offering a close reading of two incandescent, almost-forgotten examples of early twentieth-century Caribbean poetry that I've come to love deeply and learn deeply from. The first is an anonymous song composed by working-class Creole women in Suriname – composed to sing to women lovers and that women have sung from at least 1900 to the present. The second is another poem written to be set to music but never performed, an erotic rondel written in the 1920s by a daughter of a Haitian president and swept into literary corners since its publication. These small texts span a range that speaks the literature of Caribbean women who love women as temporally broad, stretching back before 1900; linguistically broad, moving between multiple Creoles and European languages; and broad in class composition, authored both in communal yards and presidential palaces. A case study of two poems, this is also a case study in reconfiguring the histories we tell of gender and sexuality: a *look*, *love* that questions associations with *Caribbean* and *woman* to imagine both differently, not isolated islands in a sea but a sea of fiery islands.

When a Rose Isn't Always a Rose: Gender and Desire in Paramaribo, 1900

Never enclosed in lesbian salons, from at least the late nineteenth century, *mati* poetry was celebrated as a flower-decorated, sung-and-danced outdoor affair of communal yards and public squares. Here in working-class Paramaribo, Creole (that is, urban black) women in relationships with women engaged in ritual performances that publicized their desires. These performances included lavish birthday parties lovers threw for each other, with songs, dances, and staged fights; and Sunday afternoon weekly *lobisingi*, "love songs" staged in public lots where *mati* chastised misbehaving lovers by singing their wrongs. Songs were accompanied by a crowd, drink, and dance, and ended with dancers lifting their skirts and shouting "Ha! Ha!" (Herskovits, Herskovits, and Kolinski 31). In 1900 Dutch police briefly attempted to shut down all *lobisingi* as public disturbances but quickly realized their attempts were futile. Instead, throughout the twentieth century observers noted overt, uncloseted *mati* expression. Collecting *lobisingi* for their anthology *Creole Drum*, folklorists Jan Voorhoeve and Ursy Lichtveld concluded that "[l]esbian love (*mati*) is more or less institutionalized in Creole society" (18). And as their interest in the *mati* as lyricists suggests, these women were not only public lovers but public artists.

One of the oldest and most popular *lobisingi* proudly shames neglectful lovers by proclaiming singers' "flowerness":

Fa yu kan taki mi no moy? (x 3)	How can you say I'm not fine?
Na tu bromtji meki mi.	It's two flowers that made me.
Rosekunop na mi mama,	Rosebud's my mama,
Stanfaste na mi papa	Everlasting's my daddy.
Fa yu kan taki mi no moy, no moy?	How can you say I'm not fine, not fine?
Na tu bromtji meki mi.	It's two flowers that made me.[2]

Half rose, half *stanfaste*, and every kind of attractive, this *mati* singer proclaims herself to be like no kind of flower *or* woman colonial chronicles ever imagined. The quintessentially European rose and the tropical *stanfaste* are both flowers that appear frequently in *mati* songs. *Rose* images a pretty young woman possessing physical qualities – paleness, softness of skin – that *mati* understand as valuable in European gender systems. Roseness is the kind of colonially, heteropatriarchally invented womanhood that black females weren't supposed to have access to, either as identity or as object of desire. But here working-class Creoles imagine the right to claim roseness for themselves, too – imagine they are also born of and deserve beauty, desirability, softness. This elite model of femininity, long coded as evolutionarily above them, stays metrically, phonetically, and semantically linked to the speaker and to another flower, the *stanfaste*. *Stanfaste*, on the other hand, are flowers of deeper colors and sturdy textures, vehicling qualities valued in the resource-sharing economy of the working class. This flower suggests an Afro-Surinamese gender ideal that privileges qualities associated with *stanfaste*'s name. *Stanfasteness* is steadfastness, loyalty to lovers, family, friends, community; is stand-upness,

staying together, not falling apart; is *ori stan*, the ability to stand ground, persist, take care of business. In effect, *stanfasteness* creates an alternative to hegemonic womanhood, a gender that often has more currency in working-class yards than the rose: "The rose is weak, it falls down," runs another song, "but *stanfaste* stays upright" ("Roos e flaw a de fadon, ma stanfaste dat e tan sidon"; Wekker, *Ik* 62). Singing that she is part rose, part *stanfaste*, a *mati* recognizes that in Creole society not only are *blaka uma* (black women) made rather than born. Their gendered as well as racial identities are made from rule-defying miscegenation among flowers, among gender models. Here difference resides not only *between* identities, between women and men or white and black women. It is also *internal* to Creole gender, which produces crossovers between rose and *stanfaste* that upset and reorder European and tropical ideals of flowers and femininity.

And listen: singing of the two flowers that made her, the performer evokes another kind of hybridity. She's made of flowers, *roos* and *stanfaste*, and flowers generally stand for female sexuality in *mati* symbolic language; but here the two mixing flora are differently gendered, mama and papa. *Mama* and *papa* are not only nouns that suggest feminine-masculine differentiation but are sometimes used as suffixes to create gender markings in Sranan, which, like other Creoles, does not otherwise gender nouns and pronouns. So in the same couplet, these flowers miscegenate and transgender. Echoing the foreplay-ful questions, "Who's your mama? Who's your daddy?," the metaphor of *roos* and *stanfaste* as mother and father evokes the "man" and "woman" roles that *mati* distinguish in sexual relationships. "When two people *mati*, then one plays the man," explains *mati* worker Jet ("Ti toe soema di mattie, dan na wan di pree foe man."; Van Lier 49). The man is the partner who approaches the woman to express sexual interest; lays on top during sex or tells the woman to; has a right to maintain other *mati* while the woman must have only one female lover or risk anger or *lobisingi*; and (when possible) helps with the woman's rent, food, and clothing. As Wekker reports, *mati* consider it "natural" to have a man and a woman in a *mati* relationship (*Ik* 163). So in their symbolic system – in contradistinction to European botany – it becomes ridiculous to deny that rose / *stanfaste*, feminine female / masculine female coupling produces *moy* offspring. How *can* you say I'm not *moy?*: *moy*, a signifier of attractiveness that can be either pretty or handsome, feminine or masculine beauty.

Like this image, *mati* communities are made up of identifications with both female femininity and female masculinity; *mati* are, yes, sometimes men. Yet just as Carnival can be both French and Yoruba, *mati* can and routinely do claim to be both men and women. The movement between man and woman roles may be part of a relationship dynamic. At the beginning of a partnership *mati* may negotiate who will be the man, with some partners switching roles from relationship to relationship (see Van Lier 46–52). Fluctuation between man and woman roles can also be part of navigating multiple contexts. Especially in the early twentieth century, *mati* men as well as women often not only wore dresses but dressed in *par weri* (matching dresses) with lovers to indicate partnership (Wekker, *Ik* 163). So while s/he might be a man with her woman, when s/he went to work, to market, to religious ceremonies a *mati* man might also present as a woman. In fact, all interviewees that I've found insist that *lobisingi* are purely women's affairs and understand themselves and other people in attendance to be women (whether or not they are also men). "This *mati* is something only for women (oema-soema)," a Creole named Wilhelmina declares (Van Lier 48). What Wilhelmina calls *uma-soema* – literally, woman-someone – becomes a term more internally complex than the English-language term *woman* or the Dutch-language *vrouw* in colonial discourses; becomes *roos* and *stanfaste*, *mati* "woman" and "man," expressing Creole gender ideology where *stanfaste*'s being at once a woman and a man is not contradictory. Under slavery, Afro-Caribbeans were told they could have no gender; in *mati* work, Afro-Caribbeans can claim both reimagined womanhood *and* reimagined manhood and refuse to relinquish either.

The "normality" of this gender complexity speaks to the overall complexity of the subject in Afro-Caribbean epistemology. The metaphor that compares *mati* to flowers conveys something more layered and charged than European associations between femininity and decorative delicateness. Here flowers are not inert matter but themselves have multiple levels of consciousness – a life cycle, life force, and the possibility of reincarnation – so when picked for ceremonies one must ask permission. Flowers are like black female bodies in that both are something Europe imagined as dumb matter but that Creoles imagine as wonderfully, electrically, multiply sentient. *Bromtji*/flower is a collective noun whose grammatical singularity signals plurality – the many petals that make a rose or *stanfaste*, the many roses or *stanfaste* that make up a bush, the many lives of each bush. Similarly, what European epistemologies conceive as a single individual is a collective proposition in Sranan. To reference the first person – where English would use *I* or Dutch, *ik* – Sranan speakers use not only *mi* but, metonymically, my body, my soul, my ancestors, my ghost – all composite parts of "me." This speakerly convention reflects that what in Europe would be understood as *the* consciousness is internally multiple. Working together are the *yeye* or soul, made up of a specific manifestation of *srama* (life force); the *dyodyo*, ancestral spirits passed from parent to child; and the *yorka*, the part of individual consciousness that remains after death and reincarnates. The phonetically reduplicating *yeye* and *dyodyo* are themselves a duality composed of a feminine and masculine part: a spiritual mother and father – mama and papa – one feminine and one masculine guiding force.[3]

Everyone, then, is understood to have parts of themselves that are bi-gendered – at once feminine and masculine – and understands themselves in a lifelong process of balancing these elements. As part of this balancing act, feminine or masculine energies may express themselves more strongly at some moments, so that moving between masculine and feminine instantiations of the self is something everyone does. In particular, some guardian spirits – those particularly masculine and/or sexual – can influence females to take female partners and express masculinity. This is why one of Wekker's oldest interviewees – Juliette, a rose in her youth – explains her desire this way: "My soul wouldn't want to be under a man.... Some women are like that.... It's your soul that makes you that way. My soul wanted to be with a woman" (*"Mi yeye no ben wan' de ondro man'* ... Sommige vrouwen zijn so.... Het is je ziel dat je zo maakt. Mijn ziel wilde met een vrouw zijn"; *Ik* 165). And she calls herself and her lovers *women* although one of them was also always the man – because in the complex, hybrid flower that is *yeye*, *dyodyo*, and *yorka*, this multiplicity makes sense. It seems less accurate to say that these are not women, then, than to argue that the Sranan *uma* no longer signifies the same "thing" as *woman* or *vrouw* in imperial gender ideologies. Like *lobisingi* themselves, *uma* becomes a Creole crossover form that takes a Euro-Surinamese song and dance of gender and re-performs it to speak Afro-Surinamese understandings of plural, hybrid selves. These songs drum an example of how Caribbean women theorize on their feet, singing and dancing creative, public reappropriations of flowers and constructs that were meant to stock the colonial garden but grow defiantly *moy* in Paramaribo's yards.

Colorless Flowers, Blue Countries: Re-Shading Racialized Gender in Ida Faubert's Paris

But of course, the rose that is a rose is a rose became a globally renowned signifier of female same-sex desire in a capital across the Atlantic: the City of Light, early twentieth-century Paris Lesbos. Not all of this city's inhabitants were as light as history would remember them, though. Among these was Haitian-born poet Ida Faubert, who, unlike the *mati*, seemed the kind of elite woman writer poised to enter literary history. Shielded from the flowers of public squares, Faubert was raised in closed gardens. Born Ida Salomon in

1882 during her father Lysius's term as president of Haiti, her early childhood was spent in the presidential palace at Turgeau where biographer Madeleine Gardiner imagines her "shielded behind coconut trees with long tresses combed by the wind, banana trees swaying their large fans" (18).[4] After completing schooling in Paris in 1905, Ida returned to Haiti. There she married, published her first poetry, and became a noted society figure at lavish parties and literary gatherings. But, unhappy with the narrowness of the elite and its constrictions on women's behavior, she returned to Paris definitively in 1914, where she divorced her husband and moved to her own apartment. Faubert was redefining herself as a newly independent woman at a time when female same-sex relationships were emerging as an increasingly visible option to compulsory heterosexuality in Paris: when, as French historian Christine Bard notes, "lesbianism enjoys a visibility that accords it a certain legitimacy – people talk of a sapphic fashion" ("le lesbianisme a une visibilité qui lui donne une certaine légitimité – on parle alors de mode saphique."; 6). Literary circles, bars, and dances marked the opening of what Bard describes as *dazzlingly visible* lesbian space in interwar Paris. Faubert moved in these circles, to an extent that remains uncertain. Haitian critics concur on the important personal and literary influence of well-known lesbian writers on Faubert's life and work, including Renée Vivien, Colette, and Anna de Noailles (a poetess nicknamed the *French Sappho*, whom Faubert frequented loyally). Gardiner also notes that Faubert conducted a number of affairs with Parisian acquaintances, but remains vague about the gender (or other) identity of these lovers.

Certainly many women in her milieu were familiar with one of the most well-known lesbian clubs in interwar Paris: le Monocle. Made famous by Brassaï's photographs, this bar owned by Lulu de Montparnasse was space contemporary to *lobisingi* that also celebrated nontraditional genders and sexualities with song, dance, and drink. Featured prominently among these genders was the female masculinity of *la garçonne*, literally "female boy." I started viewing *garçonnes'* photographs when I began research on Faubert and looked through pictures of women of color, Caribbean intellectuals, lesbian clubs to find an image of her. Not only did I never find her picture; I only found two photographs of women of color in lesbian spaces, and none of *garçonnes* of color. The rare photograph that I found of a woman of color in le Monocle was taken by the well-known photographer Brassaï in the 1930s, shortly before Faubert published her erotic poems to women. In his image, club goers gather for the camera in front of an unobtrusive trellis of flowers, a semi-private, self-consciously artificial habitat designed to form a backdrop against which *garçonnes* and *femmes* chose their own poses. *Garçonnes* faced the camera with aristocratic monocles, topcoats, and military uniforms crisply ironed across bound chests, while their *femmes* were draped with evening gowns revealing deep decolletés and setting off deeper lipstick. The gender transgression of not only wearing but being photographed in aristocratic masculine dress and military uniforms playfully, yet seriously claims power for these alternatives to hegemonic femininity and dominant masculinity. The monocles looking back at the camera's lens and the *garçonnes'* direct gaze at viewers challenge who controls visions of female gender and sexuality.

Only one figure looks away from the lens here, the lone woman of color. She neither looks at the camera nor has her body fully in the shot; both in face and body, she is the least visible figure. Most of the chief signifier of her racial difference – the expanse of her dark skin – remains unseeable. Cloaked in a spectacularly feminine, elegantly European dress that befits neither Josephine Baker's exotic femininity nor *la garçonne's* female masculinity, the gender transgression this *femme* seems empowered to perform here is not dressing like a man but dressing like a "modern" European woman. That is, instead of problematizing the normative relationship between (female) sex and (feminine) gender, her queer gender expression problematizes the normative relationship between (white) race and (feminine) gender. The question her dress raises as provocatively as a skirt is not whether a female can be masculine, but whether a black female can be feminine and desirable by European standards. Her belonging to this scene appears contingent on her looking *like* European femininity and looking *at* European masculinity: that is, on her gazing up at a white partner in a faux military uniform. If the viewer turns her or his gaze to these off center figures, we see a woman of color – someone who looks like a colonial subject – remaining literally beneath a partner in uniform – someone who looks like the colonizer. Their poses suggest much about the complicated gender politics of Paris Lesbos: about how, yes, French *garçonnes* disrupted the heteropatriarchal nature of traditional European gender, but without putting pressure on its colonial nature. The trappings of powerful European masculinity aren't erotic for everyone, and perhaps this fetishization of monocles and soldiers' uniforms makes visible something of why Faubert and other women of color are rarely seen in Paris Lesbos.

This is not "really" a picture of Ida Faubert; yet I've come to see it as metaphorically representing her in some way, as visualizing the kind of *étrange* (that is, foreign or queer) femininity she develops in her life and art. Indeed, she dressed much in the style of this Monocle patron; fellow Haitian poet Léon Laleau remembers her as a "grande dame of Haitian society . . . mature, tropical beauty trailed behind her, like the train of a royal robe, a long, trembling wake of admiration" (247).[5] Her poetry, floridly feminine and overflowing with flowers, produces a similar, pointedly artificial high femmeness – yet, like an evening gown, conceals more than it reveals, self-consciously cloaks the speaker's vision of her beloved under flower cover. The poems she writes to other women are slight, sonnets and rondels draped in creeping vines and shrouded in darkness, where racialized gender becomes so hazy it no longer fits into any recognizable uniform; like a photo taken in half light, they blur lines intended to construct both gender and race. As an example of her poetics of the hazy, I want to look at this verse meant to be set to music:

Rondel à Mme R.G.

Avec vos yeux ensorceleurs	With your spellbinding eyes
Dont la sombre beauté nous hante	Whose dark beauty haunts,
Vous avez la grâce attirante	You have the enticing grace
Du plus charmant des oiseleurs	Of the most charming of bird catchers.
Vous ressemblez aux belles fleurs	You're like the beautiful flowers
Des pays bleus où tout enchante	Of those blue countries where all enchants
Avec vos yeux ensorceleurs	With your spellbinding eyes
Dont la sombre beauté nous hante	Whose dark beauty haunts.
Pour calmer toutes les douleurs	To soothe all suffering
Votre voix se fait caressante	Your voice becomes a caress
Et l'on vois croit compatissante ...	People take for compassion ...
Mais vous causez tant de malheurs	But you cause so much heartbreak
Avec vos yeux ensorceleurs!	With your spellbinding eyes!
	(Faubert 84; original ellipsis)

Far from posing for a photograph, this provocatively slight verse seems to perform a disappearing act. The poem takes place *nowhere* – avoiding any setting indoors or out, day or night, Haiti or Paris. This *nowhere* also shows *no body*. The first couplet begins with a focus on the addressee's eyes: bewitching eyes, big eyes whose magic and largeness effect the optical illusion of standing in for the entirety of the desired body, as the description never moves beneath her head. There's no lower body to drape clothes on here, whether military uniforms or evening gowns. Instead the gendered, sexualized, or racialized body refuses to enter the picture; the parts referred to, particularly eyes, are sexually and racially unmarked. Visible signifiers of real places, genders, races, and sexualities evaporate; no recognizable, no fixed place – no country, no structure, no body – materializes as a site to locate racialized gender. While le Monocle patrons rework very specific signifiers of gender and power, this poem sings outside any specificity.

One phrase rhythms the verse: *with your spellbinding eyes*. Moving between these eyes and the speaker's gaze at the addressee, femininity seems locked in a stare with femininity here: the addressee unmistakably grammatically feminized through her appellation as *Madame* and feminine adjective endings, the speakerly voice consistently feminine as well in Faubert's poetry. What kind of magical femininity is bewitching the speaker? Still in the realm of the spectacle, the dark-eyed beauty's gender offers less realness and more complexity than the woman of color's in le Monocle. Her look dances between femininity and masculinity. The first stanza compares the addressee to a *oiseleur* or bird catcher, evoking Guy de Maupassant's poem of the same name, where love is personified as a man shooting arrows into bushes of birds. But in the next line *oiseleur* is rhymed with *belles fleurs* – "beautiful flowers," which, elaborated in Gertrude Stein's roses, Vivien's violets, and de Noaille's well-stocked gardens, planted the poetics of Paris Lesbos with stock floral-cunnic imagery. The addressee's charm also moves between here and there, between Paris and Haiti. The evocation of flowers continues: "You're like the beautiful flowers / Of those blue lands where all enchants / With your spellbinding eyes / Whose dark beauty haunts." Composed in Paris, in the opacity of the addressee's "dark beauty" the poem's vision seems to creep South: the enchantress' round black eyes have the shape and color traditionally associated with Haiti, the black island republic. At the same time, note the (sea-like) blue associated with "lands ... where all enchants" and that the addressee "looks like." This color evokes not only the Caribbean Sea but Faubert's repeated descriptions of Haiti as a *pays bleu*. So this bodyless feminine subject with phallic and cunnic associations, this raceless beauty with black and blueness clinging to her charm, softly blurs the edges of the "real" – blurs the edges of *woman* and *Caribbean*, making them too hazy for any exoticizing gaze to penetrate. This is her magic.

Yet gazing at such complicated, flower- and arrow-decorated femininity, the speaker is not simply seduced by it: she wrestles with its charm, distrusts it from first line to last. *With your spellbinding eyes*: Faubert also often evokes the Afro-Caribbean religion *Vodoun*, and the suggestion of sorcery in the addressee's eyes seems to question what kind of power this *femme* is working with. The repetition of "spellbinding" itself becomes a kind of incantation that perhaps brings on the magical possession of falling into those eyes, perhaps resists it. And while the stuff of gender and race are generally illusory in Faubert's poetry, the gentleness and easy eroticism of femininity becomes particularly suspect here. Drawing blood through the poetics of blue flowers, the last stanza insinuates the cruelty underlying the addressee's power femininity. She seems compassionate, "compatissante...," Faubert writes, ending with ellipses that suggest there's much she's leaving unsaid, "But you cause so much heartbreak/With your spellbinding eyes." Starting with locked eyes and ending with a rhyme pairing *fleurs* and *ensorceleurs* with *malheurs*, this slight poem suggests that it's the power of hegemonic femininity, rather than dominant masculinity, that the elite Haitian poetess has to wrestle with in expressing desire; and that, even queered and abstracted, this femininity continues to be a source of pain to the woman of color. When I call up *women who love women*, as much as I see interlocking flowers, rose and *stanfaste*, black and blue, I see this too: interlocked gazes of desire and struggle electrifying the flow between femininities, *lobisingi*'s chiding of lovers and the wrestling eyes of Faubert's beloved, the endless process of revolutionary love and social critique necessary to any decolonization. This endless process, which can only take place between the publicness of town squares and the placelessness of nowhere.

> You knew the world,
> its weather scraping our skins...
> We should carry you
> to that country you dreamed
> for us, where your liquid voice
> is astonishing.
>
> – Dionne Brand, Inventory

This chapter hasn't been, couldn't be, an inventory of the literature of Caribbean women who love women. Rather, it offers an attempt to carry us to countries dreamed by those come before, to hear the liquidness of their voice. These incandescent moments do as much to make us wonder about what's left in the shadows as they do to illuminate configurations of gender and desire in the path of this lightning. The poetry of the *mati* and Faubert isn't the beginning of the literature of Caribbean women who love women: and I find it crucial to remember where there must have been earlier whispers, earlier unrecovered songs, dances, and stories that reach back to places still unlit. Nor is there any easy line to trace from beginning to end, no uninterrupted movement from *then* to *now*. Brand's poetry echoes that of the *mati* and Faubert without having read these; her voice emerges from so many other histories, from memories of silence as much as those of speech. Our work as readers, I want to suggest, is not to fix an easily traceable history of the literature of Caribbean women who love women – but to listen to what singers, poets, lovers say to us that may not be what we expect to hear. Then every liquid voice, every strike of language and longing will be astonishing.

Notes

1. On this history, see Price and Price, as well as Wekker, *Ik*.
2. Herskovits and Herskovits quote this text (29), as do Voorhoeve and Lichtveld (48). This version comes from a personal communication from Gloria Wekker (August 2001).
3. On the composite parts of the Afro-Surinamese self, see Wooding; Wekker, "What's" 132–33.
4. A fuller sense of the original: "cocotiers à la longue chevelure peignée par le vent, bananiers balançant leurs larges éventails, amandiers chargés de fruits à la pulpe charnue, quénépiers aux grappes smaragdines, manguiers aux senteurs de resine."
5. Again, a fuller sense of the original: "Elle allait d'un cocktail à un té, à une sauterie. Que ce fût à pied, le visage auréolé de son ombrelle aux teintes égayantes et tournantes; que ce fût dans sa voiture tirée par cet allègre cheval souris qui, à la promener, semblait au comble de la fierté; toujours sa grace aduste et tropicale laissait auprès elle, telle la traîne d'une robe de cour, un long sillage de frémissante admiration."

Works Cited

Bard, Christine. *Les Garçonnes: Modes et fantasmes des années folles*. Paris: Flammarion, 1998. Print.

Brand, Dionne. *Inventory*. Toronto: McClelland, 2006. Print.

——. *No Language Is Neutral*. Toronto: Coach House P, 1994. Print.

Edwards, Bryan. *The History, Civil and Commercial, of the British West Indies: With a Continuation to the Present Time*. Vol. 2. New York: AMS P, 1966. Print.

Faubert, Ida. *Coeur des Îles*. Paris: Debresse, 1939. Print.

Gardiner, Madeleine. *Sonate Pour Ida*. Port-au-Prince: Imprimerie Henri Deschamps, 1984. Print.

Herskovits, Melville J., Frances S. Herskovits, and Mieczyslaw Kolinski. *Suriname Folk-Lore*. New York: AMS P, 1969. Print.

King, Rosamond. "More Notes on the Invisibility of Caribbean Lesbians." *Our Caribbean: A Gathering of Lesbian and Gay Writing from the Antilles*. Ed. Thomas Glave. Durham: Duke UP, 2008. 191–96. Print.

Laleau, Léon. "Ida Faubert." *Femmes Haïtiennes*. Ed. Ligue Féminine d'Action Sociale. Port-au-Prince: Imprimerie Henri Deschamps, 1954. 247–52. Print.

Price, Richard, and Sally Price. *Two Evenings in Saramaka*. Chicago: U of Chicago P, 1991. Print.

Van Lier, Rudolf. *Tropische Tribaden: Een Verhandeling Over Homoseksualiteit En Homoseksuele Vrouwen in Suriname*. Dordrecht: Foris, 1986. Print.

Voorhoeve, Jan, and Ursy M. Lichtveld. *Creole Drum: An Anthology of Creole Literature in Surinam*. New Haven: Yale UP, 1975. Print.

Wekker, Gloria. *Ik Ben Een Gouden Munt, Ik Ga Door Vele Handen, Maar Ik Verlies Mijn Waarde Niet: Subjectiviteit En Seksualiteit Van Creoolse Volksklasse Vrouwen in Paramaribo*. Amsterdam: VITA, 1994. Print.

The Politics of Passion: Women's Sexual Culture in the Afro-Surinamese Diaspora. New York: Columbia UP, 2006. Print.

"'What's Identity Got to Do With It?': Rethinking Identity in Light of the *Mati* Work in Suriname." *Female Desires: Same-Sex Relations and Transgender Practices Across Cultures.* Ed. Evelyn Blackwood and Saskia E. Wieringa. New York: Columbia UP, 1999. 119–38. Print.

Wooding, Charles J. "Traditional Healing and Medicine in Winti: A Sociological Interpretation." *Issue: A Quarterly Journal of Africanist Opinion* 9.3 (1979): 35–40. Print.

21

Modernist Poetry

MERRILL COLE

The distinguishing characteristic of literary modernism is difficult form. We can situate queer modernist poetics at the intersection between desire and language, in places where the erotic diverts the ordinary flow of words, deranges normative modes of linguistic comprehension, and speaks in unexpected ways. Since the advent of queer theory, the almost unavoidable model for addressing the homoeroticism of modernist poetry has been Eve Kosofsky Sedgwick's *Epistemology of the Closet*, a study that without any substantial analysis of modernist poems defines literary modernity in terms of deployments of language that work to keep homosexuality secret. Critical readings following Sedgwick's lead often anchor interpretation to the sexuality of the poet. The authorial motive of self-concealment offers a powerful heuristic for deciphering poetic difficulty. It can, however, risk reducing innovative form to the exigencies of the closet, whereby poems become little more than the epiphenomena of personality. Given the impersonal impetus characterizing so much of modernism, personalization can be problematic. Nonetheless, the closet heuristic often functions to bring out and celebrate the queerness of poets who could not make their sexual orientation public, or whose work has been denigrated by homophobic critical interpretation.

Beyond the sexuality of the author, we should pose the question of whether, or to what extent, a poem is "in the closet"; that is to say, how the poem negotiates a modern discursive formation. In Sedgwick's Foucauldian analysis, the closet is both an oppressive mechanism of power and a constitutive aspect of the modern structure of knowledge. It is fundamental to how people read texts, as well as instrumental in the maintenance of control over people. In the latter context, bringing something "out of the closet" can seem a liberatory act, certainly crucial to readers searching for reflections of their own queer identities in modern literature. It is important, nonetheless, to ask whether the project of queer literary criticism should be to construct a canon of lesbian and gay poems, or rather, to reread the sexuality of all modernist poems through a queer optics. The rationale of *The Cambridge History of Gay and Lesbian Literature* leads me to favor the first approach, but I want also to suggest that the boundaries of queer poetic modernism are more fluid than any canonical list could suggest.

At the same time that we attend to the closet, we should consider the discursive formation long governing the articulation of desire in poetry, the sacrificial economy (see Cole, *Other*). The inaugural strategy of Western love poetry, as Jacques Lacan argues in *The Ethics of Psychoanalysis*, is to figure interpersonal relations in the language of Christian devotion, translating the religious asymmetry of lover and beloved into interpersonal terms, in order to reaffirm sacrifice as the proof and substance of love. To consider love in these representational terms, as Western poetry has done since the Troubadours, inevitably entails belatedness, for love is always prior to the poem, existing elsewhere. Traditional mimesis separates the represented from the representation, holding emotion apart from the words used to express it. Mimesis as such, dependent on binary division, tends to confirm the heterosexual paradigm. Much of the difficulty of lesbian and gay modernist poetry derives from its subversion of this representational economy.

Queer approaches to modernist poetry must also examine the homophobia pervading the scene of modernity, affecting the lives of the poets, how they wrote, and how their poems have been received. Homophobic ideology contaminates poems from within and without. From within, economies of concealment can entail poems in strategies of self-abnegation, self-hatred, projection, forced normalization, and denial. The effort to avoid the closet has its own homophobic pitfalls, especially where, universalizing about desire, it refuses to acknowledge that people have sexual orientations. Homophobic criticism, whether based in Marxism or psychoanalysis, the New Criticism or the older historicisms, circumscribes homoerotic poetry in narratives of failure: failure to reach emotional maturity, narcissistic enclosure, the refusal of alterity, the shirking of responsibility. Queer literary criticism confronts and offers alternatives to such reading practices.

The exact chronological and geographical boundaries of modernism and modernity are matters of long-standing critical dispute. This chapter makes no pretense to retheorize them, but rather, works within a widely accepted framework for what constitutes the modernist period, from mid-nineteenth-century France to the beginning of the Second World War. The scope is limited to French, German, and English poetry written in Western Europe and the United States. Because French symbolism has long been seen as the first articulation of poetic modernity, this chapter begins with Charles Baudelaire,

Arthur Rimbaud, and Paul Verlaine, also attending to the French twentieth century's Jean Cocteau. With German modernism, the focus is on Stefan George and Rainer Maria Rilke. Examining the American avatars of what has come to be known as "international" or "high" modernism, this chapter discusses H.D., Ezra Pound, and T.S. Eliot. It considers Hart Crane's reaction to the high modernist aesthetic and Amy Lowell's fraught interaction with it. Two American lesbian poets in Paris, Gertrude Stein and Natalie Barney, are discussed alongside the bisexual Edna St. Vincent Millay. In the 1920s, at the same time that Paris was a lesbian mecca, Harlem arguably became the queer epicenter of the United States. This chapter looks at the Harlem Renaissance poetry of Richard Bruce Nugent, Countee Cullen, and Langston Hughes. Finally, it discusses the British modernism of D.H. Lawrence and W.H. Auden.

France

Perhaps the homoeroticism of modernist poetry begins with an ambivalent cross-gender identification. In "The Paris of the Second Empire in Baudelaire," Walter Benjamin asserts, "[t]he lesbian is the heroine of modernism. In her an erotic ideal of Baudelaire – the woman who bespeaks hardness and mannishness – has combined with a historical ideal, that of greatness in the ancient world. This makes the position of the lesbian in the *Fleurs du mal* unmistakable" (90). Calling forth "la mâle Sapho" ("the male Sappho"; 136) in the poem "Lesbos," first published in 1850, Baudelaire appears to define the lesbian in sexist terms as she who dares counterfeit masculinity.[1] Such a Sappho might be a delightful scandal for the male gaze, more phallic projection than honest other, exemplifying the man-centered androgyny that fascinated nineteenth-century France. However, a "heroine" is someone with whom to identify, a role model, and not just a salacious spectacle. Sappho, poet and creator of new forms of love, serves as the prototype for the French poet, himself aspiring to be another sort of male lesbian. Baudelaire embraces a sacrificial myth, in poses that range from desire to scorn to self-recognition.

The penultimate stanza of the 1857 "Femmes damnées" ("Damned Women") summarizes the lesbians' contradictory allure:

> O vierges, ô demons, ô monstres, ô martyres,
> De la réalité grands esprits contempteurs,
> Chercheuses d'infini, dévotes et satyres,
> Tantôt pleines de cris, tantôt pleines de pleurs. (108)

Virgins, demons, monsters, martyrs, all
great spirits scornful of reality,
saints and satyrs in search of the infinite,
racked with sobs, full of tears.   (130)[2]

In a straightforwardly homophobic sense, lesbianism represents the refusal of reality, a futile revolt against nature, the instantiation of insatiable loss. The original title of *Les Fleurs du mal* was *Les lesbiennes*.

Nostalgia does not so characterize all of the modernist experiment. The effort to articulate desire according to a different economy of signification begins with Arthur Rimbaud. Distinguished critics, including Theodor Adorno, Roland Barthes, and Marjorie Perloff, identify Rimbaud's defiant break with the literary past, including his break with Baudelaire's poetry, as the pivotal moment in the turn to the modern. In his 1870 and 1871 "lettres 'du voyant'" ("Letters of 'the Visionary'"), Rimbaud proclaims, "Je est un autre" ("I is someone else"; 340, 343). Grammatical disruption heralds the transgression of conventional relations: just as Rimbaud requires us to reconceive the connection of subject to verb, so his prose poems in the *Illuminations* dare another conjugation of love.

The prose poem "Antique," like Baudelaire's lesbian poems, uses classical allusion to embody homoerotic desire. The prose poem presents the male physique as an erotic spectacle, challenging the not-to-be-viewed status of conventional masculinity:

Gracieux fils de Pan! Autour de ton front couronné de fleurettes et de baies tes yeux, des boules précieuses, remeunt. Tachées de lies brunes, tes joues se creusent. Tes crocs luisent. Ta poitrine ressemble à une cithare, des tintements circulent dans tes bras blonds. Ton cœur bat dans le ventre où dort le double sexe. Promène-toi, la nuit, en mouvant doucement cette cuisse, cette seconde cuisse et cette jambe de gauche.   (294)

Gracious son of Pan! Around your forehead crowned with flowerets and with laurel, restlessly roll those precious balls, your eyes. Spotted with brown lees, your cheeks are hollow. Your fangs gleam. Your breast is like a lyre, tinklings circulate through your pale arms. Your heart beats in that belly where sleeps the double sex. Walk through the night, gently moving that thigh, that second thigh, and that left leg.   (25)

The satyr's seductive liminality, posed between active desire and passive desirability, maleness and not-necessarily-maleness, music and body, myth and vision, contests the fixity of masculine identity.

However, in *Une saison en enfer* (*A Season in Hell*), Rimbaud condemns himself and his poetry; ridicules his love affair with poet Paul Verlaine; and gestures farewell: "je voudrais me taire" ("I'd rather remain silent"; "Mauvais Sang" 248; "Bad Blood" 11).[3] He confesses, "je suis maudit" ("I am damned"; "Mauvais" 249); and comes to conclude, "je dois enterrer mon imagination et mes souvenirs!" ("I must bury my imagination and my memories!"; "Adieu" 279; "Farewell" 87). Shortly after publishing *Une saison en enfer* in 1873, he abandoned poetry altogether. While the two poets were still together, however, they composed the "Sonnet du Trou du Cul" ("Asshole Sonnet"). Verlaine wrote the quatrains and Rimbaud, the tercets. Densely metaphorical, Verlaine's opening quatrain, like the rest of the sonnet, is sexually graphic:

> Obscur et froncé comme un œillet violet
> Il respire, humblement tapi parmi la mousse
> Humide encor d'amour qui suit la fuite douce
> Des Fesses blanches jusqu'au cœur de son ourlet.   (171)

> Dark and puckered like a purple carnation,
> it breathes out, hiding shyly in the froth,
> still humid, following the love that seeps
> down the white cheeks to the deepest rim.

After Rimbaud's departure, Verlaine reentered the literary closet, alluding to homosexuality without naming it in his 1888 *Les poètes maudits (The Damned Poets)*, where he initiated the critical tradition that has used Rimbaud's final silence and *Une saison en enfer* to signify the visionary's repentance from homosexual transgression against nature, God, or reality.[4] However, Verlaine's posthumously published volume of poems, *Hombres (Men)*, rivals "Sonnet du Trou du Cul" in explicitness, if not in the richness of imagery (see Minahen). Early in his poetic career, and following Baudelaire's lead, Verlaine published *Les Amies (Female Friends)* under a pseudonym. The arguably bisexual poet also composed a companion volume to *Hombres*, entitled *Femmes (Women)*.

The most influential homosexual poet of the French twentieth century is Jean Cocteau, although his influence is not simply a matter of poetry, as the protean artist worked in a wide variety of media, most famously film. Indeed, in an important series of films, the repeated subject is the mythical first poet, Orpheus. Arguably, Cocteau's filmic representations of the poet, or his films as poetry, have overtaken the written poetry; the poetry on the page, though, is worthy of attention. In 1925, Cocteau, mourning the recent death of his lover, Raymond Radiguet, and under the influence of opium, was greeted by an apparition. This apparition, he claimed, dictated "L'ange Heurtebise" ("The Angel Heurtebise"). Perhaps Cocteau's artistic process follows Rimbaud's. Rimbaud couples opium with homoerotic adventure in "Matinée d'ivresse"

("Morning of Drunkenness") and claims that poetry involves "le dérèglement de *tous les sens*" ("the disordering of *all the senses*"; 340; xxvii). The title character of Cocteau's poem, along with the other angel named within it, Cégeste, would be rescripted in the more recondite homoeroticism of the 1949 movie *Orphée*. In "Matinée d'ivresse," the route to love and inspiration is marked by cruelty: the drunk morning "finit par des ange de flamme et de glace!" ("ends with angels of flame and of ice!"; 297; 43). Something similar occurs in the second stanza of Cocteau's poem, although Cocteau displays a camp aesthetic absent in Rimbaud:

> L'ange Heutebise, d'une brutalité
> Incroyable, saute sur moi. De grâce
> Ne saute pas si fort
> Garçon bestial, fleur de haute
> Stature.
> Je m'en suis alité. En voilà,
> Des façons. J'ai l'as; constate.
> L'as-tu?   (65)

> The angel Heurtebise, with an incredible
> Brutality, jumps on me. Please,
> Don't do it so hard
> Bestial boy, high reaching
> Flower.
> I'm confined to bed. Mind your
> Manners. Look: I've got the ace.
> What about you?

In his recent biography of Cocteau, James S. Williams characterizes this poem as an "at once spiritual and violent homoerotic fantasy of possession by a 'heavy male sceptre' ['lourd / Sceptre mâle' (73)], both a violent creative spirit and a young male lover" (134).

Germany

The modernization of German poetry begins in the late nineteenth century, when Stefan George imported French symbolist poetics into the country. Following the lead of his teacher, Stephane Mallarmé, George wrote coterie poetry, an esoteric discourse aimed at the cultivation of an exclusive elite. As Jens Rieckmann observes, the "stylized language" of his poetry is designed "to create barriers for the uninitiated reader" (7). George's poems mask their homoeroticism through classical and Christian allusion. According to Marita

Keilson-Lauritz, love in George's poems, always directed toward men and boys, is "dominated by pain, soreness, and by submission and service" (209). Love is sacrificial. The 1922 "Lobgesang" ("Praise Song") addresses an ambiguous male figure, perhaps human, perhaps a god.[5] The poem begins with a gesture of supplication:

> Du bist mein herr! wenn du auf meinem weg
> Viel-wechselnder gestalt doch gleich erkennbar
> Und schön, erscheinst beug ich vor dir den nacken.

> You are my master! When you appear on the path,
> An ever-changing shape immediately recognizable
> And lovely, I bend my neck before you.[6]

The line between divine visitation and erotic encounter blurs. A submissive positioning procures for the speaker a vision of the master's beauty, in all his naked glory:

> Du trägst nicht waffe mehr noch kleid noch fittich
> Nur einem schmuck: ums haar den dichten kranz.
> Du rührest an – ein duftiger taumeltrank
> Befängt den sinn der deinen odem spürt
> Und jede fiber zuckt von deinem schlag.   (276)

> You don't wear weapons, or wings, or clothes,
> Only one adornment: the garland gathered in your hair.
> Your touch – a shot of frenzy bereaves
> The senses of him who feels your breath
> And his every fiber trembles when you strike.

There is a darker side to such erotic mastery. Although George rejected the Nazis' attempt to position him as a herald of fascism, he, like the Nazis, was an advocate of charismatic, authoritarian male leadership. George's ideal also bears similarity to the hypermasculinity espoused by German homosexual rights activist Adolf Brand (see Keilson-Lauritz, "George's").

If George's erotic entanglement with other men is well documented, no such biographical evidence is available for Rainer Maria Rilke. Yet the receptivity everywhere urged in Rilke's poetry makes homoerotic reading possible. William Waters links misgivings about the frequent second-person address in Rilke's *Die Sonette an Orpheus* (*Sonnets to Orpheus*) to male homosexual panic. Waters finds in the critical tradition "the professional stricture that readers should not get too personally stimulated by the caress of [Rilke's] seductive voice," which "is structurally like, and probably is, prophylaxis against too-great intimacy with the sissy poet" (728).[7] However, in *Sonnets to Orpheus*, as Bernhard Frank points out, Rilke "employs the Greek poet-singer as a symbol of the creative force without reference to his homosexual leanings" (244), such as we find with Cocteau. Frank identifies four Rilke poems that boast homosexual speakers: two concerning Sappho that recall Baudelaire's "Femmes damnées"; one about Antinous, the Greek boy loved by the Roman emperor Hadrian; and one about Jonathan, beloved of the biblical King David. In "Eranna an Sappho" ("Eranna to Sappho"), Eranna tells the poet, "ich zittere wie eine Bitte" ("I tremble like a request"; 26; qtd. in Frank 245; his translation), which signals the receptivity everywhere evident in Rilke's poetry.

United States

It is a critical commonplace that modernist poetry in English begins with Imagism, an early twentieth-century movement that eschewed the discursiveness of Victorian and Edwardian poetry, in favor of what Ezra Pound terms "A Few Don'ts from an Imagiste," "direct treatment of the thing," the removal of superfluous words, and a break from traditional meter. The avatar of Imagism was an American woman poet, Hilda Doolittle. In an encounter that launched her career as a poet and also changed her name, Pound signed her poem "Oread" as "H.D., Imagiste." H.D. had love relationships with both men and women, Pound being one of her earlier romantic entanglements. While she is certainly innovative in the expression of heterosexual desire, H.D. was, as Rachel Blau DuPlessis argues in *The Pink Guitar*, that "transfixed by the psycho-cultural system of romantic love, and she was subject to cycles of seduction and reseduction to male figures throughout her life. Lesbianism *per se* – whether platonic or sexually active – was not for H.D. a sufficient strategy of solution to the cultural problem posed by males" (21).[8] While more substantial lesbian content is to be found in H.D.'s novels – especially *Paint It Today* – a short lyric from the 1921 *Hymen* shows that her poetry does occasionally take a homoerotic turn.[9] In "At Baia," a feminine speaker addresses an implicitly female other:

> Flower sent to flower;
> for white hands, the lesser white,
> less lovely of flower leaf,
>
> or
>
> Lover to lover, no kiss,
> no touch, but forever and ever this.

If the image of a flower greeting a flower suggests an intimate feminine caress, the poem denies physical closeness with "no kiss" and "no touch." The speaker mourns a total separation, "your hands / (that never took mine)" (128).

Although Wayne Koestenbaum reads Ezra Pound and T.S. Eliot's editorial relationship in terms of homosexual panic, Pound's lifelong homophobia is difficult to put aside. It finds perhaps the most resonant articulation in the 1937 Canto XLV, also known as the Usura Canto. At the same time that the canto rails against the practice of usury, a medieval term for the charging of interest on loans, it reopens "The Pact" that Pound had earlier set up with Walt Whitman, condemning both the nineteenth-century poet and his erotic proclivities. The canto ends,

> Usura slayeth the child in the womb
> It stayeth the young man's courting
> It hath brought palsey to bed, lyeth
> between the young bride and her bridegroom
>   CONTRA NATURAM
> They have brought whores for Eleusis
> Corpses are set to banquet
> at behest of usura. *(Cantos* 24)

"[L]yeth / between the young bride and her bridegroom" alludes to a passage from Whitman's "Song of Myself":

> I turn the bridegroom out of bed and stay with the bride myself,
> And tighten her all night to my thighs and lips.
>
> My voice is the wife's voice, the screech by the rail of the stairs,
> They fetch my man's body up dripping and drowned. (691)

All of this is "against nature," a "nature" that the canto implicitly defines as heterosexual matrimony leading to childbirth. The usurer, Robert Casillo writes, is "[a] parasitic and intrusive middleman" who "emerges as the chief obstacle to sexual and economic utopia. He severs the link between lover and beloved, consumer and product.... Because of his greed, hoarding, repression, and antiprocreation, the usurer is linked by Pound with anal retentiveness and sodomy" (127–28).

Pound and his circle aimed a bitter misogyny at Amy Lowell. Pound believed that she hijacked Imagism, which he sarcastically rechristened as "Amygism" (Munich and Bradshaw, introduction; Scott; Bradshaw). Where Pound's approach to poetry is intrinsically elitist, Lowell's, in spite of her wealth and high social standing, is democratic. Lowell's commitment to accessibility, however, did not render her any less experimental than her male modernist peers.

She concealed her lesbian subject matter by removing references to gender in the poems, depending on what Lillian Faderman calls "the reader's habit of taking for granted heterosexuality in the absence of specific evidence to the contrary" (64). In the 1925 poem "In Excelsis," Lowell's speaker exclaims,

> I drink your lips,
> I eat the whiteness of your hands and feet.
> My mouth is open,
> As a new jar I am empty and open.
> Like white water are you who fill the cup of my mouth,
> Like a brook of water thronged with lilies.

Lowell allows the reader to ignore the lesbian insinuations of such lines. Faderman charts how critics, disregarding her lesbianism, received the poems as the output of a frustrated "old maid" (65). If Lowell is a poet celebrating lesbian love, though, she also embraces aspects of the courtly love tradition, as Jaime Hovey argues. Approaching her beloved from a respectful distance in "In Excelsis," the speaker nonetheless manages to touch her: "You are far and sweet as the high clouds. / I dare reach to you, / I dare touch the rim of your brightness" (444).

James E. Miller's *T.S. Eliot's Personal Waste Land* (1977) uses extensive biographical documentation to uncover the homoerotic subtext of Eliot's famous 1922 poem. Attempting to validate the male homoeroticism of *The Waste Land*, Miller overlooks the negative political implications of Eliot's closet.[10] He does not account for the poem's erotics of denial and erasure. Nor can his reading trace the political ramifications of Eliot's circumlocutionary eloquence. Miller posits a single, historical dead man, Jean Verdenal, behind the poem's elaborate rituals of mourning. It is also possible to trace the act of closeting in the composition of *The Waste Land*. Eliot never published "The Death of Saint Narcissus" during his lifetime – he sent the poem to Harriet Monroe at *Poetry*, only quickly to ask her to suppress it – but *The Waste Land* borrows from it. "The Death of St. Narcissus" begins,

> Come under the shadow of this gray rock
> Come in under the shadow of this gray rock,
> And I will show you something different from either
> Your shadow sprawling over the sand at daybreak, or
> Your shadow leaping behind the fire against the red rock:
> I will show you his bloody cloth and limbs
> And the gray shadow on his lips. (95)

The stanza, focusing on the particulars of the male body, makes a voyeuristic promise. This seduction scene reappears in *The Waste Land*, but the saint's concrete embodiment evaporates into a wider context and a heterosexualized meaning:

> Only
> There is a shadow under this red rock,
> (Come in under the shadow of this red rock),
> And I will show you something different from either
> Your shadow at morning striding behind you
> Or your shadow at evening rising to meet you:
> I will show you fear in a handful of dust. (135)

The body is missing, replaced by an allusion to the dust of the Sybil, who appears in The Waste Land's epigraph. Homoeroticism transforms into "fear": the emotion it evokes replaces the former referent. In the transferring of the earlier poem's dead male body into an allusion to a female prophet-figure from Virgil's Aeneid – the work Eliot will later consider absolutely central to the European literary tradition – The Waste Land universalizes. A disembodied and de-eroticized fear dilates into an ahistorical chiding of the human condition.

In the final stanza of the earlier poem, Saint Narcissus ends his journey in masochistic bliss:

> So he became a dancer to God.
> Because his flesh was in love with the burning arrows
> He danced on the hot sand
> Until the arrows came.
> As he embraced them his white skin surrendered itself to the redness of
> blood, and satisfied him.
> Now he is green, dry and stained
> With a shadow in his mouth. (97)

Eliot borrows from the iconography of St. Sebastian, whose martyrdom by arrows has been the subject, since medieval times, of homoerotic depiction. His death is an orgasmic climax. The crucial constraint to such pleasure is that we can only enjoy the male body in the circumstance of its loss. The body disappears in The Waste Land, with perhaps the desexualized, drowned Phlebas the Phoenician, "once handsome and tall as you," its last remainder (143). The indeterminacy of sexual positioning in The Waste Land indicates "the love that dare not speak its name." The gaps and discontinuities of the poem function not only as blank instances of the text's undecidability, or as mimetic indicators of the failure of society's coherence, but also as sites of suppression and disavowal.

In a 1922 letter to Allen Tate, Hart Crane writes of Eliot that, "while I haven't discovered a weak spot yet in his armour, I flatter myself a little lately that I have discovered a safe tangent to strike which, if I can possibly explain the position, – goes through him toward a different goal" (*Letters* 90). In a 1923 letter to Gorham Munson, Crane says, "I take Eliot as a point of departure toward an almost complete reverse in direction" (114). In "Voyages III," speaking as the drowned man – as Phlebas the Phoenician, more or less (see Hammer) – Crane describes a sea passage:

> And so, admitted through black swollen gates
> That must arrest all distance otherwise, –
> Past whirling pillars and lithe pediments,
> Light wrestling there incessantly with light,
> Star kissing star through wave on wave unto
> Your body rocking!
>   and where death, if shed,
> Presumes no carnage, but this single change, –
> Upon the steep floor flung from dawn to dawn
> The silken skilled transmemberment of song.   (36)

Crane's "black swollen gates" admit the reader to the scene of male anal sex. Drowning, death, and orgasm harmonize, a combination anticipated by "sleep, death, desire" in "Voyages II" (35). "The silken skilled transmemberment of song," beyond its implication of masculine orgasm, tells of the sea change from lived experience to poetic word.

Crane develops Rimbaud's strategy of countermimesis, an inversion of the traditional order of representation with the potential to reconfigure how language spells out desire (see Irwin). In figuring suffering as transformative voyage, "Voyages" follows Rimbaud's "Le Bateau ivre" ("The Drunken Boat"). In Rimbaud's poetic process, perhaps best exemplified by the sonnet "Voyelles" ("Vowels"), linguistic play precedes any reference to the external world. Such poetry resembles alchemy, to the extent that it conjures that world out of its novel combinations of sound and concept, much as alchemy aspires through its arcane technology to transmute one thing into another. Rimbaud and Crane's new language reverses the traditional mimetic relationship between referent and sign, the priority of the represented over that which does the representing, upending the hierarchical standard at least as old as Aristotle.

Like Rimbaud and Crane, Gertrude Stein attempts an exit from the poetics of nostalgia dominating the articulation of desire in Western poetry. While some critics see Stein as using linguistic difficulty to disguise lesbian content, others, including me, relate Stein's difficulty to the rigorous compositional demands she places on her writing (see Cole, "Remaking"). *Tender Buttons* and *Lifting Belly* are often celebrated for their articulation of lesbian eroticism, but I will concentrate here on reading the short, rhymically intense 1922 "Susie Asado." It is in the motion of language, and not in description, that the Spanish dancer's character becomes manifest. The Western tradition of poetic praise for women keeps a respectful distance. The lady is elsewhere – lost, unattainable, unapproachable. Stein abolishes this distance. She writes in "Poetry and Grammar" that she feels "the need of making it be a thing that could be named without using its name" (330), and dancing is never designated as such in "Susie Asado." The poem opens by associating Susie Asado with pleasurable consumption:

> Sweet sweet sweet sweet sweet tea.
> Susie Asado.
> Sweet sweet sweet sweet sweet tea.
> Susie Asado.

It is as though the dancer comes to us in sips, suggested both by the repetition of "sweet" and the alliterative insistence of the "s." Susie Asado is an oral enjoyment, a "sweetie," to follow Wendy Steiner (102). "Susie Asado is a told tray sure. / A lean on a shoe this means slips slips hers." Meaning slips as Asado dances; we catch sight of her slippers; and we may glimpse her slip, her or the speaker's more intimate, syncopated meaning. Perhaps the speaker is confident, with "tray sure" a pun on the French "très sur," very surely spoken. Or the speaker hands her to us on a tray. Soon, however, the aplomb seems quite shaken: "This is a please this is a please there are the saids to jelly. There are the wets these say the sets to leave a crown to Incy. / Incy is short for incubus." As "a please" slips into "appease," an attempt at calm, "the saids," perhaps the speaker's words, turn to "jelly." "[T]he wets" follow, perchance alluding to sexual arousal. "[A] crown to Incy" might indicate a circular stain, connecting to the later penitence, "render clean, render clean must." "Incy is short for incubus" is discordant: An "incubus" is a male demon who seduces women in their sleep. This masculine upsurge from the unconscious, nevertheless, does not contradict Stein's often butch self-depictions. After an excited play of "bobbles," small knobs – no doubt, tender buttons – and the thrice stated "a nail," which begins to slip into "anal," the poem returns politely to sipping "[s]weet sweet sweet sweet sweet tea" (362).

Unlike Stein, American poet Natalie Barney composed most of her poetry in French. In *Women of the Left Bank*, Shari Benstock asserts that Barney "consciously chose an outdated form of French prosody in which to declare her commitment to female eroticism" (282). Barney's strategy of deploying conventional poetics to articulate unconventional desire owes a debt to her friend Pierre Louÿs, a French author who claimed his collection of poems, *Les chansons de Bilitis* (*The Songs of Bilitis*), was the translation of a recently discovered ancient Greek lesbian poet (see Benstock; Engelking). If the aim of the collection was to titillate a male audience, it also empowered Barney. The first stanza of "Femme" ("Woman"), in the 1920 *Poems & Poèmes: autres alliances*, exemplifies Barney's forthright approach:

> Femme à la souple charpente.
> Au poitrail courbe, arqué pour
> Les gémissements d'amour.
> Mon désir suivra tes pentes –
> Tes veines, branchages nains –
> Où la courbe rejoint l'angle;
> jambes fermant le triangle
> Du cher coffret féminin.   (1)

> Woman with the supple frame.
> The curved chest, arched for
> Love's moans, my desire
> Follows your slopes –
> Your veins, tiny branches –
> Where the curve meets the angle;
> Legs closing the triangle
> Of the feminine box.

The speaker in no way hides or obscures the object of her desire. Interestingly, in the same volume, Barney's English poems are never so explicit. In her 1910 *Éparpillements*, or *Scatterings*, a collection of epigraphs, she asserts, "La femme: une des portes du merveilleux" ("Woman: one of the doors to the marvelous"; 28).

American poet Edna St. Vincent Millay also relies on traditional verse forms to articulate feminine desire. However, unlike Barney, and in spite of her publicly acknowledged bisexuality, Millay is averse to articulating unambiguous lesbian desire (see Cucinella; Wolfe). The reader tracing lesbian meaning across her lines inevitably comes across a male figure that serves to recontexualize everything. One of the most evocative and sexually ambivalent of her poems is Sonnet VII, from the 1931 *Fatal Interview*. Its first eight lines appear to elaborate a same-sex erotics, spelled out in the Ophelia-like terms of drowning:

Night is my sister, and how deep in love,
How drowned in love and weedily washed ashore,
There to be fretted by the drag and shove
At the tide's edge, I lie – these things and more:
Whose arm alone between me and the sand,
Whose voice alone, whose pitiful breath brought near,
Could thaw these nostrils and unlock this hand,
She could advise you, should you care to hear.

The prostrate speaker seeks the "arm" and "voice" of her "sister." The ambiguous second-person pronoun that appears in the eighth line turns out to be masculine, recoding the poem's eroticism as heterosexual. The man fails to answer the speaker's plea for help:

Small chance, however, in a storm so black,
A man will leave his friendly fire and snug
For a drowned woman's sake, and bring her back
To drip and scatter shells upon the rug.
No one but Night, with tears on her dark face,
Watches beside me in this windy place.   (636)

Anthropomorphized night, which seems at first a female participant, is reduced in the final lines to a mournful spectator of heterosexual love lost. Millay's speaker reproaches her male lover for failing to reciprocate, but she does not break free of heterosexual bonds.

Although, as Henry Louis Gates, Jr. observes in "The Black Man's Burden," the Harlem Renaissance "was surely as gay as it was black" (233), the only openly homosexual participant in the movement was Richard Bruce Nugent, whose erotically explicit prose-poem, "Smoke, Lilies and Jade," distinguished itself as the most censured piece in the one-issue 1926 journal *FIRE!!* It was editor Wallace Thurman's intention to highlight aspects of African American experience that racial propagandists did not want seen, and the experiences embodied in Nugent's poem were beyond what his fellow rebels would dare to publish, even as some of them, including Thurman, enjoyed such homosexual experiences. The contributions of Countee Cullen and Langston Hughes to *FIRE!!* are devoid of homosexual reference. Both poets are more explicit elsewhere, if not nearly so much as Nugent. Yet, as Michael L. Cobb argues, it has been a persistent, homophobic critical strategy to "deemphasize Nugent's literary importance in black letters" (329).

A.B. Christa Schwarz asserts in *Gay Voices of the Harlem Renaissance* that Nugent omits explicit sex scenes from his depictions of same-sex relationships, probably in order to avoid censorship. His homoeroticism, nonetheless, is never concealed, not even when his writing also considers women in erotic terms. "Presenting same-sex-interested men as positive characters and depicting various sexualities," Schwarz writes, "Nugent challenges the boundaries drawn around sexuality by gender norms" (135). In "Smoke, Lilies and Jade," the protagonist, Alex, walking in the dark, meets a man on the street. They go silently together to Alex's apartment:

> no need for words ... they had always known each other .... as they undressed by the blue dawn ... Alex knew he had never seen a more perfect being ... his body was all symmetry and music ... and Alex called him beauty ...   (*FIRE!!* 36; ellipses in original)

After they go to sleep together, Alex has a dream, written like an incantation, that invites the reader's participation:

> he was in a field ... a field of blue smoke and black popp[i]es and red calla lilies ... he was searching ... on his hands and knees ... searching ... among black poppies and red calla lilies ... he was searching pushed aside poppy stems . . and saw two strong white legs ... dancer's legs ... the contours pleased him ...
> (37; ellipses in original)

While, at the end of "Smoke, Lilies and Jade," the speaker expresses desire for a woman named Melva, he never recants his love for the male Beauty. Cobb writes that "the entire story is a collection of phrases divided by ellipses, calling to our attention, as most modernist works do, the form used to express a thought or a feeling, especially [those] that contradict literary convention" (344).[11]

Regarded as the poet laureate by his Harlem Renaissance contemporaries, Countee Cullen has somewhat fallen out of critical favor, a judgment based primarily on the conventional romanticism of his verse, which was lampooned during the Harlem Renaissance by the prescient Wallace Thurman in his novel *Infants of the Spring.*[12] As Schwarz observes, Cullen chose to follow "writers like John Keats, Alfred Tennyson, and A.E. Housman" (48), rather than the jazz rhythms inspiring Hughes and Jean Toomer, or the modernist innovation championed by Hughes, Toomer, and Nugent. Attempting to maintain a respectable public persona, Cullen eschewed explicit sexual description. Expressing homoerotic feeling in code in his private correspondence, he is much more circumspect in his poetry, where we find desire scripted as heterosexual or spelled out in gender-ambiguous terms. "Tableau," from the 1925 collection *Color*, forms somewhat of an exception to this rule. While written

with a structure of deniability, so that any implication of homosexuality can
be denied, the poem celebrates the purity of an interracial, same-sex relationship. In the first stanza, the disrespect of the two boys for social norms can be
read not only as racial, but as sexual transgression:

> Locked arm in arm they cross the way
> The black boy and the white,
> The golden splendor of the day
> The sable pride of night.

In the second stanza, the boys face the dual disapprobation of "dark folk" and
"fair folk," but they continue "[i]n unison to walk." It is left almost entirely to
the reader to imagine what forms their intimacy might take, although Schwarz
suggests a phallic implication in the closing lines: "That lightning brilliant as a
sword / Should blaze the path of thunder" (12).

Any connection between Langston Hughes's poetry and homosexuality
needs to be more tentative than with Cullen, because Hughes carefully evaded
questions of sexual identity throughout his career.[13] This evasion has been a central topic of problematic queer efforts to recuperate him. Schwarz points out
that although he speaks out against the repression of homosexuals in *Montage
of a Dream Deferred* (1955), the scant comments he makes during the Harlem
Renaissance concerning lesbians and gays tend toward the derogatory. Perhaps
the most interestingly ambiguous Harlem Renaissance poem is the 1926 "Joy."
While it seems to offer the opportunity to script its narrative in purely heterosexual terms, the poem's titular female figure never quite descends from
allegory into personhood; and this marks a certain resistance to heterosexual
reinscription:

> I went looking for Joy,
> Slim, dancing Joy,
> Gay, laughing Joy,
> Bright-eyed Joy –
> And I found her
> Driving the butcher's cart
> In the arms of the butcher's boy!
> Such company, such company,
> As keeps this young nymph, Joy!　　　　　(63)

Schwarz suggests that "[t]he presumably male" speaker finds joy "[i]n the
arms of the butcher boy" (75): "Joy" would be then a feminine abstraction that
negotiates a relationship between men and conceals homoerotic desire.

Great Britain

In British author D.H. Lawrence's "Bavarian Gentians" (1930), his last poem, the putatively male speaker identifies himself with the mythological Persephone. This conflation of gender identity reaches its climax in the poem's final lines:

> Persephone herself is but a voice
> or a darkness invisible enfolded in the deeper dark
> of the arms Plutonic, and pierced with the passion of dense gloom,
> among the splendor of torches of darkness, shedding darkness on the
>   lost bride and her groom.
>   (956)

Ironically, perhaps, Persephone, who lost her flowers – indeed, was deflowered – when abducted into the underworld, here retires into an underworld that is itself a flower. Not only is the classical myth revised in the sense of "the passion of the dense gloom," so that it recounts more a sad lovers' rendezvous than a rape, but the speaker himself, to follow Helen Sword, becomes Persephone, "pierced," meeting his male "groom." The bride's gender complicates the poem's theme of deathly phallic dominance, just as the speaker's autonomy disappears: he loses individual identity, personal integrity, and even his visibility to himself (it is, after all, a poem about death). This complicated gesture at once represents yet another male artist's appropriation of the feminine, a pretty poeticization of violence against women, and a peculiar queering of the masculine voice.

The substitution of the speaker for Persephone in "Bavarian Gentians" may exemplify what Gregory Woods terms "the figure of the male bride: the man made fertile by the phallus of another" (132). Woods, however, does not consider the extent to which Lawrence, in such poems as "Eloi, Eloi, Lama Sabachthani?" renders such masculine figures as conflicted, neither homosexual nor heterosexual. Such ambivalence makes the male bride something other than what Woods considers as a shying away from the full articulation of homosexual identity, or the poet's hesitation to depict graphic homosexual acts. The queerness of Lawrence's poetry consists of more than sexual images we can grade according to a scale of homoerotic openness. In the 1929 short lyric "Twilight," no gender designation appears. All eroticism centers on the anus, what Lawrence terms in *Women in Love* "the source of the deepest life-force, the darkest, deepest, strangest life-source of the human body, at the back and base of the loins" (Woods 133). With only six short lines, the poem rather resembles haiku, in that it uses a description of nature to convey intense human emotion:

> Twig light
> thick underdusk
> and a hidden voice like water clucking
> callously continuous.
> While darkness submerges the stones
> and splashes warm between the buttocks. (427)

The poem evokes analingus with a "hidden voice" whose "clucking" is reinforced with the alliteration of "k," "w," and "m" consonants. It also suggests an abandonment, or submersion, of the self – similar to that in "Bavarian Gentians," if less somber. The human subject of the poem, referenced only by "the buttocks," receives warmth or pleasure passively, even as the poem hints at penetration.

W.H. Auden's 1948 "The Platonic Blow" was not published during his lifetime. The poem has recently received attention for its explicit narrative of casual oral sex: "Slipping my lips round the Byzantine dome of the head, / With the tip of my tongue I caressed the sensitive groove. / He thrilled to the trill. 'That's lovely!' he hoarsely said" (n. pag.). Nonetheless, as Richard R. Bozorth observes, the poet's homosexuality "had something of the status of an open secret: known to some readers, to be sure, but either ignored by commentators in print or addressed only by implication or innuendo" ("Auden" 176).[14] In congruence with the high modernist imperative to impersonality, Auden discouraged biographically based readings of his work. Bozorth argues that the last line of Auden's 1929 lyric "This Loved One" references homosexuality as "[a] backward love" (*Auden's* 36). This backwardness is a form of nostalgia: "Auden portrays love as all but irremediably defined by the past" ("Auden" 181).

Auden's perspective on his own sexuality was framed by medicalizing discourses, including psychoanalysis. The 1937 poem "Lullaby" summons the unconscious, what the poem terms "the involuntary powers," to counter the fact that "[b]eauty, midnight, vision dies." Auden's speaker counsels, "[l]et the living creature lie, / Mortal, guilty, but to me / The entirely beautiful." "Lullaby" presents a lover singing to his sleeping beloved. In the absence of gendered pronouns, it is easy to read the relationship in same-sex terms. The best-known lullaby in the English language informs its listeners that the bough will break and the cradle will fall. Similarly, "Lullaby" relates, "Time and fevers burn away / Individual beauty from / Thoughtful children." The approach of sleep ushers in receptivity, although Auden offers no hope that poetry could ever reconcile consciousness and desire. To "the winds of dawn that blow" around his lover's "dreaming head," the speaker urges,

> Such a day of welcome show
> Eye and knocking heart may bless,
> Find our mortal world enough;
> Noons of dryness find you fed
> By the involuntary powers,
> Nights of insult let you pass
> Watched by every human love.   (157–58)

Although "the basic irony" is that "Lullaby" presents "a sincere confession of faithlessness that goes unheard by the beloved," Bozorth finds the poem paradoxically affirming an impossible love ("Auden" 184). To reference Auden as the epitome of modernist antiromanticism has become a critical commonplace. In the love lyrics of the 1930s, he informs us that beauty is temporary; love, transitory; and poetry, no honest protection against their loss. The lyrical eloquence of his denials, though, tells otherwise. Auden makes admission of love through the intricacies of difficult form that define literary modernity.

Notes

1. All Baudelaire citations are from *Oeuvres complètes de Baudelaire*. Except where otherwise noted, the translations are mine.
2. This is Richard Howard's translation, but I have modified the final line.
3. Although a sense of narrative closure leads many critics to assume *Une saison en enfer* was written after the *Illuminations*, the chronology cannot be determined. See Cole, *Other* ch. 2.
4. See Paul Verlaine, "Les poètes maudits: Arthur Rimbaud"; de Gourmont; Fondane; Bousquet; Bonnefoy; and Schmidt.
5. Keilson-Lauritz classifies "Lobgesang" as one of the poems displaying "the fact that a number of explicitly erotic poems in George's work are simply safeguarded by their titles, masked in quasi-religiousity" (*Von der Liebe* 93). She considers the master in "Lobgesang" a mix of Eros and Dionysus (81).
6. My English rendering of George owes a strong debt to Valope and Morwitz's 1943 translation. I have updated the archaizing language and rendered the homoeroticism more explicit.
7. It seems the case that the poet's gender nonconformity is mistaken for homosexuality. In this regard, see Ilett, who reads the poet's boarding school narrative in Sedgwick's terms. For an example of a reading exemplifying the panic of which Waters speaks, see de Man.
8. Chisholm argues that H.D.'s multiple "lesbian liaisons" did not supply the poet with "the necessary literary capital" for her poetry (71).

9. Chisholm defines the poet's first volume, *Sea Garden*, as "erotically animated poems where gender is missing" (70), thus open to lesbian readings.
10. See Cole, *Other* ch. 4 for a full-length reading of *The Waste Land* in terms of three structures of containment, closet, canon, and empire.
11. Cobb, like many other readers, considers "Smoke, Lilies, and Jade" a short story. The ellipses, it seems to me, are one of many reasons to see it as a prose poem (see also Stokes). A number of pieces in Toomer's *Cane* also skirt the boundary between short fiction and poetry.
12. Powers connects the dismissal of Cullen's poetry with his perceived effeminacy. *Infants of the Spring* is *a roman à clef*, DeWitt Clinton standing in for Cullen: "Raymond could not suppress a snort. For DeWitt's few words had given him a vivid mental picture of that poet's creative hours – eyes on a page of Keats, fingers on typewriter, mind frantically conjuring African scenes. And there would of course be a Bible nearby" (Thurman 153–54).
13. Thurman also remarks on this evasiveness through the stand-in character of Tony Crews in *Infants of the Spring*.
14. See Bozorth, *Auden's* for the sole book-length reading of Auden's homosexuality.

Works Cited

Adorno, Theodor. *Aesthetic Theory*. Ed. Gretel Adorno and Rolf Tiedemann. Trans. Robert Hullot-Kentor. Minneapolis: U of Minnesota P, 1997. Print.

Auden, W.H. "Lullaby." 1937. *Collected Poems*. Ed. Edward Mendelson. New York: Vintage, 1991. 157–58. Print.

"The Platonic Blow." *Vulture*. 17 Mar. 2008. Web. 20 Nov. 2012. <http://www.vulture.com/2008/03/how_dirty_is_that_auden_poem_t.html>.

Barney, Natalie Clifford. *Éparpillements*. Paris: Sansot, 1910. Print.

Poems & Poèmes: autres alliances. Paris: Émile-Paul frères, 1920. Print.

Barthes, Roland. *Writing Degree Zero*. Trans. Annette Lavers and Colin Smith. New York: Farrar, 1968. Print.

Baudelaire, Charles. *The Flowers of Evil*. Trans. Richard Howard. Boston: David R. Godine, 1982. Print.

Œuvres complètes de Baudelaire. Ed. Claude Pichois. Paris: Gallimard, 1961. Print.

Benjamin, Walter. *Charles Baudelaire: A Lyric Poet in the Era of High Capitalism*. Trans. Harry Zohn. London: Verso, 1983. Print.

Benstock, Shari. *Women of the Left Bank: Paris, 1900–1940*. Austin: U of Texas P, 1987. Print.

Bonnefoy, Yves. "L'outre-couleur." Guyaux 341–58.

Bousquet, Joë. "Le Rimbaud voyou de Benjamin Fondane." Guyaux 257–61.

Bozorth, Richard R. "Auden: Love, Sexuality, Desire." *The Cambridge Companion to W.H. Auden*. Ed. Stan Smith. Cambridge: Cambridge UP, 2004. 175–87. Print.

Auden's Games of Knowledge: Poetry and the Meanings of Homosexuality. New York: Columbia UP, 2001. Print.

Bradshaw, Melissa. "Remembering Amy Lowell: Embodiment, Obesity, and the Construction of a Persona." Munich and Bradshaw 167–85.

Casillo, Robert. "Troubadour Love and Usury in Ezra Pound's Writings." *Texas Studies in Literature and Language* 20.2 (1985): 125–53. *JSTOR*. Web. 21 Nov. 2012.

Chisholm, Dianne. "Pornopoeia, the Modernist Canon, and the Cultural Capital of Sexual Literacy: The Case of H.D." *Gendered Modernisms: American Women Poets and Their Readers.* Ed. Margaret Dickie and Thomas Travisano. Philadelphia: U of Pennsylvania P, 1996. 69–94. Print.

Cobb, Michael L. "Insolent Racing, Rough Narrative: The Harlem Renaissance's Impolite Queers." *Callaloo* 23.1 (2000): 328–51. *Project Muse.* Web. 6 Oct. 2012.

Cocteau, Jean. *Poèmes: 1916–1955.* Paris: Gallimard, 1956. Print.

Cole, Merrill. *The Other Orpheus: A Poetics of Modern Homosexuality.* New York: Routledge, 2003. Print.

"Remaking Sense: Gertrude Stein and the Names of the Father." *Women's Studies: An Interdisciplinary Journal* 38.1 (2009): 84–99. Print.

Crane, Hart. *Complete Poems of Hart Crane.* Ed. Marc Simon. New York: Liveright, 1993. Print.

The Letters of Hart Crane, 1916–1932. Ed. Brom Weber. New York: Heritage, 1952. Print.

Cucinella, Catherine. "Textual and Corporeal Convergence: Edna. St. Vincent Millay." *Poetics of the Body: Edna St. Vincent Millay, Elizabeth Bishop, Marilyn Chin, and Marilyn Hacker.* New York: Palgrave, 2010. Print.

Cullen, Countee. *Color.* New York: Harper, 1925. Print.

De Gourmont, Remy. "Le plus insupportable voyou." Guyaux 84–86.

de Man, Paul. "Tropes (Rilke)." *Allegories of Reading: Figural Language in Rousseau, Nietzsche, Rilke, and Proust.* New Haven: Yale UP, 1979. 20–56. Print.

DuPlessis, Rachel. *The Pink Guitar: Writing as Feminist Practice.* New York: Routledge, 1990. Print.

Eliot, T.S. *The Waste Land: A Facsimile and Transcript of the Original Drafts Including the Annotations of Ezra Pound.* Ed. Valerie Eliot. New York: Harcourt, 1971. Print.

Engelking, Tama Lea. "Translating the Lesbian Writer: Pierre Louys, Natalie Barney, and 'Girls of the Future Society.'" *South Central Review* 22.3 (2005): 62–77. *Project Muse.* Web. 6 Oct. 2012.

Faderman, Lillian. "'Which, Being Interpreted, Is as May Be, or Otherwise': Ada Dwyer Russell in Amy Lowell's Life and Work." Munich and Bradshaw 59–76.

FIRE!! 1.1 1926. Elizabeth: FIRE!! P, 1982. Print.

Fondane, Benjamin. *Rimbaud le voyou.* Paris: Denoël et Steele, 1933. Print.

Frank, Bernhard. "Homosexual Love in Four Poems by Rilke." *The Gay Academic.* Ed. Louie Crew. Palm Springs: ETC, 1978. 244–51. Print.

Gates, Jr., Henry Louis. "The Black Man's Burden." *Fear of a Queer Planet.* Ed. Michael Warner. Minneapolis: U of Minnesota P, 1993. 230–38. Print.

George, Stefan. *Poems in German and English.* Trans. Carol North Valhope and Ernst Morwitz. New York: Stockten, 1967. Print.

Werke: Ausgabe in zwei Bänden. Ed. Robert Boehringer. Stuttgart: Klett-Cotta, 1984. Print.

Guyaux, André, ed. *Rimbaud: Cahiers de l'Herne.* Paris: l'Herne, 1993. Print.

Hammer, Langdon. *Hart Crane & Allen Tate: Janus-Faced Modernism*. Princeton: Princeton UP, 1993. Print.

H.D. [Hilda Doolittle]. *H.D.: Collected Poems, 1912–1944*. Ed. Louis L. Martz. New York: New Directions, 1983. Print.

Paint It Today. Ed. Cassandra Laity. New York: New York UP, 1992. Print.

Hovey, Jaime. "Lesbian Chivalry in Amy Lowell's *Sword Blades and Poppy Seed*." Munich and Bradshaw 77–89.

Hughes, Langston. *The Collected Poems of Langston Hughes*. Ed. Arnold Rampersad. New York: Vintage, 1995. Print.

Ilett, Darren. "The Poetics of Plausible Deniability in Rainer Maria Rilke's 'Die Turnstunde.'" *Focus on Literature* 13.69 (2006): 69–85. Print.

Irwin, John T. "Hart Crane's 'Logic of Metaphor.'" *Critical Essays on Hart Crane*. Ed. David R. Clark. Boston: G.K. Hall, 1982. 207–20. Print.

Keilson-Lauritz, Marita. "George's Concept of Love and the Gay Emancipation Movement." Rieckmann 207–29.

Von der Liebe die Freundschaft heißt: Zur Homoerotik im Werk Stefan Georges. Berlin: rosa Winkel, 1987. Print.

Koestenbaum, Wayne. "*The Waste Land*: T.S. Eliot's and Ezra Pound's Collaboration of Hysteria." *Double Talk: The Erotics of Male Literary Collaboration*. New York: Routledge, 1989. 112–39. Print.

Lacan, Jacques. *The Seminar of Jacques Lacan: Book VII: The Ethics of Psychoanalysis, 1959–1960*. Ed. Jacques-Alain Miller. Trans. Dennis Porter. New York: Norton, 1992. Print.

Lawrence, D.H. *The Complete Poems of D.H. Lawrence*. Ed. Vivian de Sola Pinto and Warren Roberts. 2 vols. New York: Viking, 1964. Print.

Millay, Edna St. Vincent. *Collected Poems*. Ed. Norma Millay. New York: Harper, 1956. Print.

Miller, James E., Jr. *T.S. Eliot's Personal Waste Land*. University Park: Pennsylvania State UP, 1977. Print.

Minahen, Charles D. "Homosexual Erotic Scripting in Verlaine's *Hombres*." *Articulations of Difference: Gender Studies and Writing in French*. Ed. Dominique D. Fisher and Lawrence R. Schehr. Stanford: Stanford UP, 1997. 119–35. Print.

Munich, Adrienne, and Melissa Bradshaw, eds. *Amy Lowell, American Modern*. New Brunswick: Rutgers UP, 2004. Print.

Perloff, Marjorie. *The Poetics of Indeterminacy: Rimbaud to Cage*. Princeton: Princeton UP, 1981. Print.

Pound, Ezra. "A Few Don'ts by an Imagiste." *Poetry Foundation*. Web. 21 Oct. 2012. <http://www.poetryfoundation.org/journal/article.html?id=335>.

The Cantos of Ezra Pound. New York: New Directions, 1948. Print.

"A Pact." *Personæ*. New York: New Directions, 1971. 89. Print.

Powers, Peter. "'The Singing Man Who Must be Reckoned With': Private Desire and Public Responsibility in the Poetry of Countée Cullen." *African American Review* 34.4 (2000): 661–78. *JSTOR*. Web. 31 Oct. 2012.

Rieckmann, Jens, ed. *A Companion to the Works of Stefan George*. Rochester: Camden, 2005. Print.

Rilke, Rainer Maria. "Eranna an Sappho." *New Poems: A Bilingual Edition*. Trans. Stephen Cohn. Evanston: Northwestern UP, 2000. 24–26. Print.

Die Sonette an Orpheus. Gesammelte Gedichte. Frankfurt a/M: Insel, 1962. 483–527. Print.

Rimbaud, Arthur. *Illuminations and Other Prose Poems.* Trans. Louise Varèse. New York: New Directions, 1946. Print.

Œuvres complètes de Rimbaud. Ed. André Guyaux. Paris: Gallimard, 2009. Print.

A Season in Hell and The Drunken Boat by Arthur Rimbaud. Trans. Louise Varèse. New York: New Directions, 1945. Print.

Schmidt, Paul. "Visions of Violence: Rimbaud and Verlaine." *Homosexualities and French Literature: Cultural Contexts / Critical Texts.* Ed. George Stambolian and Elaine Marks. Ithaca: Cornell UP, 1979. 228–42. Print.

Scott, Bonnie Kime. "Amy Lowell's Letters in the Network of Modernism." Munich and Bradshaw 136–53.

Schwarz, A.B. Christa. *Gay Voices of the Harlem Renaissance.* Bloomington: Indiana UP, 2003. Print.

Sedgwick, Eve Kosofsky. *Epistemology of the Closet.* 2nd ed. Los Angeles: U of California P, 2008. Print.

Stein, Gertrude. "Poetry and Grammar." *Stein: Writings 1932–1946.* Ed. Catharine R. Simpson and Harriet Chessman. New York: Library of America, 1998. 313–36. Print.

"Susie Asado." *Stein: Writings 1903–1932.* Ed. Catherine R. Simpson and Harriet Chessman. New York: Library of America, 1998. 362. Print.

Steiner, Wendy. *Exact Resemblance to Exact Resemblance: The Literary Portraiture of Gertrude Stein.* New Haven: Yale UP, 1978. Print.

Stokes, Mason. "Strange Fruits: Rethinking the Gay Twenties." *Transition* 92 (2002): 56–79. JSTOR. Web. 31 Oct. 2012.

Sword, Helen. "Lawrence's Poetry." *The Cambridge Companion to D.H. Lawrence.* Ed. Anne Fernihough. Cambridge: Cambridge UP, 2001. 119–35. Print.

Thurman, Wallace. *Infants of the Spring.* 1932. Boston: Northeastern UP, 1992. Print.

Toomer, Jean. *Cane.* 1923. New York: Liveright, 1993. Print.

Verlaine, Paul. *Les poètes maudits.* 1888. Whitefish: Kessinger, 2008. Print.

Oeuvres poétiques complètes. Ed. Yves Alain Favre. Paris: R. Laffont, 1992. Print.

Waters, William. "Rilke's Imperatives." *Poetics Today.* 25.4 (2004): 711–30. Print.

Whitman, Walt. *Leaves of Grass and Other Writings.* Ed. Michael Moon. New York: Norton, 2002. Print.

Williams, James S. *Jean Cocteau.* London: Reaktion, 2008. *Project Muse.* Web. 6 Oct. 2012. Print.

Wolfe, Andrea Powell. "Chasing the 'Coloured Phantom': Gender Performance as Revealing and Concealing Modernist Ideology in Millay's Sonnets." *The Journal of American Culture* 32.2 (2009): 155–64. *MLA International Biography.* Web. 16 Nov. 2012.

Woods, Gregory. "D.H. Lawrence." *Articulate Flesh: Male Homo-Eroticism and Modern Poetry.* New Haven: Yale UP, 1987. 125–39. Print.

22

Queer, Cosmopolitan

HELENA GURFINKEL

Queerness and Cosmopolitanism: Defining the Undefinable

If the concept of nationalism emerges in the eighteenth century – as Benedict Anderson notably argues in *Imagined Communities* – the eighteenth century also is widely held by historians to be the time when the middle-class hetero-sexual, monogamous, procreative family ideal, bolstered by the naturalization of the discourse of the separate spheres for men and women, became the fundamental unit of social organization. The secular eighteenth century makes a nation-state, promulgated through literacy and print, a substitute for a shared religious identity.

This notion of a secular, literate nation arises contemporaneously with Immanuel Kant's call for cosmopolitanism as a substitute for a sense of unity provided by world religions and monarchic dynasties. At the same time, sexuality undergoes secularization as well as scientific scrutiny, and the Enlightenment penchant for classification culminates in the late nineteenth century's codification of homosexuality as a pathological identity and the twentieth century's contestation both of that pathologization and identity itself in queer theory. Both separately and combined, queerness and cosmopolitanism combat the assumed naturalness of nation and heterosexuality and expose them as constructs and nonidentities.

When attempting to define queerness – perhaps an ultimately impossible task – one must emphasize its penchant for paradox and its stubborn resistance to definition, or, more precisely, for making such resistance its definition and mission. David Halperin famously writes: "Queer is by definition whatever is at odds with the normal, the legitimate, the dominant. There is nothing in particular to which it necessarily refers. It is an identity without an essence" (62). While not focused on "queer" per se, in *Homos*, Leo Bersani defines homo-ness (as opposed to a Western gay male identity in the twentieth century) as an "anti-identitarian identity" (101). In *Queer Theory: An Introduction*, Annamarie Jagose notes that "queer is unaligned with any specific identity category. . . . Broadly speaking, queer describes those gestures or analytical models which dramatise incoherencies in the allegedly stable relations between chromosomal sex, gender and sexual desire" (3). Queerness "dramatizes," among other things, the fluidity of desire that cannot be pinned down and defined, as well as the impossibility of stable selfhood or sexual identity.

While queerness rejects our attempts to normalize desire, cosmopolitanism communicates the instability of geographic and/or cultural belonging. Through sheer intractability, both concepts render identity fluid and open. Even as writing and thinking about queerness must contend with the paradoxes of an "anti-identitarian identity," or of definition-defying definitions, an attempt to locate cosmopolitanism also encounters, at worst, a roadblock or two. At best, it is doomed to fail. The last two sentences, of course, constitute a paradox. The Greek word "cosmopolitan" ("a citizen of the world"), dating back to the fourth century BC and first used by the Cynic philosophers, is itself paradoxical, as Kwame Anthony Appiah and Julia Prewitt Brown have noted. Appiah writes: "The formulation was meant to be paradoxical, and reflected the general Cynic skepticism toward custom and tradition. A citizen . . . belonged to a particular *polis*, a city to which he or she owed loyalty. The cosmos referred to the world . . . in the sense of the universe" (xiv). Prewitt Brown is seemingly incredulous: "The cosmopolitan says, 'the cosmos is my polis,' the world is my home. Yet how can one feel at home within the vastness of the world, let alone 'fortified' by such an expanse? The idea seems pure puffery" (23).

In "Idea for a Universal History from a Cosmopolitan Perspective" (1784), one of the founding essays of Western cosmopolitanism, Kant observes that a paradoxical "unsocial sociability" characterizes humans: by this "antagonism" he means "their tendency to enter into society, a tendency connected, however, with a constant resistance that continually threatens to break up this society" (6). Appiah's and Prewitt Brown's respective discussions of the paradox of cosmopolitanism echo Kant's thoughts on humans' insistence on simultaneously creating and destroying social frameworks. Ulf Hannerz notes an additional tension that characterizes the existence of the citizen of the world – that of simultaneous mastery and surrender: a cosmopolitan both masters other cultures and surrenders to them, in order to inhabit them fully. Determined not to totalize cosmopolitanism (just as Halperin, Bersani, and Jagose, among others, are determined to keep queerness queerly elusive), Pollock, Bhabha, Breckenridge, and Chakrabarty write: "Cosmopolitanism

... must always escape positive and definite specification, precisely because specifying cosmopolitanism positively and definitely is an uncosmopolitan thing to do" (577). In short, like queerness, cosmopolitanism is challenging to define and ineluctably paradoxical, and, like queerness, it takes a strongly anti-identitarian stance.

By virtue of their shared stubbornness, the two concepts pose a challenge to the twin fictions of nationhood and heteronormativity. In part, they do so through the one aspect of cosmopolitanism on which a number of thinkers agree, and which has also been taken up by queer theorists, most notably, Judith Butler: a hospitable acceptance of the national, ethnic, religious, sexual, and other Others and recognition of their rights. Such acts of acceptance necessitate probing and breaking the rigid boundaries of identity. They can take different shapes but must have an ethical obligation at their core. As a solution to "unsocial sociability," Kant calls for "the achievement of a **civil society** which administers right universally" (8). Kant imagines a concerted effort by nation-states to promote international rights and freedoms for all individuals, regardless of their nationality. Such a key Enlightenment thinker as Voltaire, as well as such Victorian philosophers as Mill and Arnold, insisted on the equal importance of cultures and the importance of being curious about cultures other than one's own.[1]

The catastrophic events of the twentieth century made possible, paradoxically perhaps, the cosmopolitan philosophical imperative of facing and taking a responsibility (economic, moral, legal) for the Other upheld by Emmanuel Levinas, Jacques Derrida, and Butler. In *Precarious Life*, Butler responds to Levinas's plea that "[t]he approach to the face is the most basic mode of responsibility ... the face is the other who asks me not to let him die alone" (qtd. in Butler 131) by suggesting that we "hear the face as it speaks ... to know the precariousness of life that is at stake" (151). The difficulty of defining the cosmopolitan is not, then, a flaw in the Cynics' plan; it is, instead, a necessity, a way to open up the avenues of multiple, sometimes unforeseen modes of coexistence with the Other.

Derrida's "On Cosmopolitanism" focuses on refugee and immigrant rights and, instead of affirming laws and locations, calls for "[e]xperience and experimentation thus. Being on the threshold of these cities [of refuge], of these new cities that would be something other than 'new cities,' a certain idea of cosmopolitanism, *an other*, has not yet arrived, *perhaps*" (421). Accordingly, the queer cosmopolitans considered here both unsettle identitarian certainties *and* model an embrace of the Other, even if this embrace is imperfect, tentative, and impermanent.

Is the embrace physical? Does it follow the call of same-sex desire? These questions are not exactly rhetorical. Sometimes the answer to both is yes, and other times, it is no. Here, though, the possibility of a physical embrace performs the tentative rhetorical gesture of reconciling "queer" with "gay and lesbian," or postmodern, global contingencies of nonidentity with the political exigencies of history and legibility. Again, the situation is rife with contradictions. While Jagose links "queer" with "gay and lesbian" by suggesting that queer theory is a development of gay and lesbian studies, and that the two often coexist at the institutional and curricular levels, she acknowledges that queer theory has met with some resistance because of its very capaciousness and refusal to locate itself in a particular identity, hard won and worn with pride. Similarly, Kevin Ohi contends that "[f]oundational to queer theory (and what separates it from 'gay studies') is an axiom that its analyses extend beyond (indeed must extend beyond) elements of culture where same-sex desire is explicitly at stake" (27). The tension between "lesbian and gay" and "queer" may be impossible, or, in the spirit of queerness, unnecessary to defuse.

The writers discussed here, under the rubric of queer cosmopolitanism, have identified strongly as nonheterosexual and/or participated vocally in movements leading to LGBT legibility and equality, or, in the case of Oscar Wilde, have made these movements possible. Their work contests heteronormativity and at times explicitly includes gay, lesbian, bisexual, or transgender characters. In other words, the definition of "queer" here, insofar as it is possible without committing the sin of essentialism, includes "gay and lesbian" but, like cosmopolitanism, insists on open possibilities, tight knots, and meandering paths when it comes to identity and desire. Simultaneously, these writers are located at crucial historical and intellectual moments – British imperialism, the world wars, the Civil Rights Movement, and the formation of diaspora studies – that required a radical reconsideration of the cosmopolitan principle of coexistence.

(Be)Longing for the Other: Queer Cosmopolitanisms

Oscar Wilde's cosmopolitanism may be defined in a multitude of ways, most of which, although useful, would be more or less obvious: his displacement as an exiled Irishman in England, and an exiled ex-prisoner in France; his ability both to absorb and innovate the narratives of German philosophy, French symbolism and decadence, Pater's aestheticism, the Bible, and classical antiquity.[2]

The urban, sophisticated, aphorism-spouting dandy with a gold-tipped cig-arette who appears in his prose fiction and plays, is also, albeit in a limited way, a familiar visual portrait of a queer cosmopolitan. These examples of Wilde's world citizenships are significant, but a less obvious – and nonbio-graphical – Wildean queer cosmopolitan moment hinges on the idea of a the-atrical performance of identity and, simultaneously, instantiates ethical ways of approaching a national, ethnic, or religious Other.

Early in Wilde's novel *The Picture of Dorian Gray* (1891), a marginal charac-ter, Lady Henry Wotton, makes an important but rarely noticed nod to cos-mopolitanism. She confides in Dorian:

> I have simply worshipped pianists – two at a time, sometimes, Harry tells me.
> I don't know what it is about them. Perhaps it is that they are foreigners. They
> all are, aren't they? Even those that are born in England become foreigners
> after a time, don't they? It is so clever of them, and such a compliment to art.
> Makes it quite cosmopolitan, doesn't it? (34–35)

The neglected wife's ostensibly artless confession centers on the centrality of art to cosmopolitanism and on the concurrently queer ability of both to unsettle the conventional notions of belonging by birth; art invents nationali-ties and recalibrates differences.

An example of queering identity through art and reconsidering the pres-ence of the Other is Dorian's brief infatuation with actress Sibyl Vane. The protagonist falls in love with the androgynously adept performer: "Night after night I go to see her play. One evening she is Rosalind, the next evening she is Imogen. I have seen her die in the gloom of an Italian tomb. . . . I have watched her wandering through the forest of Arden, disguised as a pretty boy in hose and doublet and dainty cap" (38). In this queer romantic encounter, Dorian falls in love with a character on stage, instead of the woman off stage, and out of love when staged passion becomes "reality." Resistance to heteronormativ-ity comes through Dorian's complicated infatuation with Sibyl playing a boy played by a girl playing a boy. Shakespeare provides the queer moment early in the novel, both following the Shakespearean meditation on desire and identity in the story "The Portrait of Mr. W.H." and foreshadowing his famous inclu-sion of Shakespeare in the 1895 trial speech in defense of same-sex love.

As if illustrating Lady Henry's adulation of art's cosmopolitanism, Shakespeare is also responsible for a fleeting but significant moment of con-necting to the Other. Dorian is derisive of "the horrid old Jew" (39), the theatre manager who introduces him to Sibyl, hoping that Dorian is a benevolent theatre critic: "He was a most offensive brute, though he had an extraordinary passion for Shakespeare. He told me once, with an air of pride, that his five bankruptcies were entirely due to 'The Bard,' as he insisted on calling him. He seemed to think it a distinction" (39). Casually contemptuous, Dorian stresses the Jew's vulgarity, the unbearable banality of his use of "the Bard" moniker, and the inevitable and shady embroilment with money ("five bankruptcies"). To this Victorian characterization, itself rather banal, Lord Henry replies: "It was a distinction, my dear Dorian – a great distinction. Most people become bankrupt through having invested too heavily in the prose of life. To have ruined oneself over poetry is an honour" (39). This reply grants dignity and "honor" to the Other by rewriting finance in terms of a literary genre and by creating a cosmopolitan common ground between lovers of art, whose origins and social standing otherwise could not be farther apart.

Wilde's queer cosmopolitanism undermines the normative causality of sex and gender and life and art; it also resists the foundations of imperial national and racial ideologies at the turn of the century. Similarly in spirit, although differently in style, E.M. Forster refuses to abdicate responsibility for the Other immediately before and after World War I, when the nationalist narratives of antagonism verged on hysterical. Forster's refusal of a nationalist narrative that closes cultural and ethical ranks and declares a war against otherness was, like Wilde's, in part personal. Cultural, intellectual, and emotional links to Italy, Greece, Egypt, and India make Forster, like Wilde, a citizen of the world in the accepted sense.

A figure crucial to the shaping of Forster's queer cosmopolitanism, openly homoerotic poet Constantine Cavafy, resided in the Greek quarter of worldly Alexandria, directly above a male brothel. An emblematic cosmopolitan, the civil servant from a prominent Greek family spoke at least three languages and felt equally at home in Hellenism and European modernism and aestheticism. Partly inspired by Cavafy, whom he met while working in Egypt during World War I, Forster embraced various instances of otherness, as well as revised the traditional definitions of family, in his personal life.

His work, in a more subtle fashion, also espouses cosmopolitanism. For instance, *Howards End* (1910) performs a queer cosmopolitan gesture of reconciliation promised in its famous subtitle, "only connect." The Schlegel siblings, Margaret, Helen, and Tibby, epitomize cosmopolitan existence: they are part-German, liberal, highly educated dwellers of Bloomsbury. Their attendance of a performance of Beethoven's Fifth Symphony, "the most sublime noise that has ever penetrated the ear of a man" (25), is perhaps a cosmopolitan statement, one that assumes the existence of a kind of "high" world culture into which the Schlegels have been initiated. More counterintuitively cosmopolitan and queer, however, are the narrator's musings about railway stations that will take Margaret Schlegel, the oldest of the three siblings, to Howards End:

> Like many others who have lived long in a great capital, she had strong feelings about the various railway termini. They are our gates to the glorious and the unknown.... In Paddington all Cornwall is latent and the remoter west; down the inclines of Liverpool Street lie fenlands and the illimitable Broads; Scotland is through the pylons of Euston; Wessex behind the poised chaos of Waterloo. Italians realize this, as is natural; those of them who are so unfortunate as to serve as waiters in Berlin call the Anhalt Bahnhof the Stazione d'Italia, because by it they must return to their homes.... To Margaret ... the station of King's Cross had always suggested Infinity.   (11)

The narrative voice here is worldly; international railway travel and migrant labor prefigure the twentieth-century travails of globalization. The excitement of travel coexists, surprisingly enough, with a longing for home, and both are overwhelmed by a sense of "Infinity" and open possibility (*"experience and experimentation thus"*). It is the tension between the world and home, as well as the interminable journey from the terminus (incidentally – or not – echoing the uncertain origins of Wilde's character Jack Worthing, of *The Importance of Being Earnest*, found in a bag in Victoria Station) that, more pointedly than the references to world-class cities do, communicates the novel's queer cosmopolitan stance against the certainty of origins and destinations.

Howards End, a manor to which Margaret is headed from King's Cross, is not really an end: it is a provisional point of connection between the worldly Schlegels and their Others: the resolutely English, middle-class Wilcoxes and the striving, tragic working-class Basts. The connection here is between the cosmopolitan and the urban and its other, the national, the rural. While, according to most definitions, cosmopolitanism is antinationalist, here the rapprochement is achieved through the merging of the cosmopolitan and the national, which is also the case in the passage on railway stations. The two connect by forming a queer family that inherits the eponymous place. The family consists of the nonprocreative matriarch, Margaret Schlegel (when asked about children, she says, "I am thankful to have none" [239]), married to Henry Wilcox, Margaret's sister, Helen, and Helen's illegitimate child, who inherits the home through a maternal will, rather than the patriarchal imperatives of biology and law.

The cosmopolitanism of Forster's late masterpiece, *A Passage to India* (1924), is more in line with Ulf Hannerz's classic definition as the "willingness to become involved with the Other" (239–40). Set primarily in India and positioned chronologically between the two world wars and at the beginning of the anticolonialist movement, the novel dares to present a queer ethics of cosmopolitanism at a time that demanded explicit commitments and certainly called for clearly articulated, convenient sexual taxonomies. Although supportive of India's anticolonialist struggle, the novel also relies on the restraint of open possibilities in its exploration of the relationship between the Indian Dr. Aziz and Cyril Fielding, his English friend. Forster's characteristic muffled wariness of heterosexual marriage, coupled with the potentiality of attachment between the two male characters, keeps queerness an open secret throughout the novel. At its conclusion,

> Aziz in an awful rage danced this way and that, not knowing what to do, and cried: "Down with the English anyhow.... Clear out you fellows, double quick, I say ... and then" – he rode against him furiously – "and then," he concluded, half kissing him, "you and I shall be friends."
>
> "Why can't we be friends now?" said the other, holding him affectionately. "It's what I want. It's what you want."
>
> But the horses didn't want it ...; the earth didn't want it .... "No, not yet," and the sky said, "No, not there." (322)

"Not yet" and "not there" apply, no doubt, to the Indian-British relations, as well as to the open secret of same-sex passion that will have to wait, until, as another Forster novel, Maurice, puts it in its dedication, "a happier year." The rhetorical possibilities of the ending are produced by a series of unresolved tensions, going "this way and that," between affection and violence, openness and secrecy, desire and enmity, nature and culture, nation and cosmopolitanism. They are queer not only because they have to do with love between men, but also because they refuse, like the King's Cross tracks, a resolution, or an end point, and open up to infinity. The "no" forecloses the connection, while "not yet" and "not there" open it up again tentatively. The ending proffers, in the spirit of Derrida's new cities, potential, yet-to-be-defined forms of postnational cosmopolitanism.

A similar queer cosmopolitan moment in which identitarian indeterminacy and same-sex desire intermingle appears in James Baldwin's *Giovanni's Room* (1956). Although Forster's contemporary, Baldwin is distant from Forster geographically and stylistically, but such difference is precisely the point, for queer cosmopolitanism can offer unexpected modes of connection. Baldwin, an African American writer and a queer cosmopolitan, worked and lived outside of the constraining environment of the pre–Civil Rights United States, in France, Turkey, and Africa, among other places. His 1956 novel is undeniably a staple of the LGBT canon, and his status as a figure central to both the gay and Civil Rights movements is unquestioned. What is significant in the following passage is not its explicit political import, however; on the contrary, it is the resistance of the text to naming desire that, in a Foucauldian fashion, can congeal into an identity, as well as a fragile and violent connection between the first-person narrator and Giovanni, that echo Forster's imperative "only connect ... "³

Against the cosmopolitan backdrop of Paris, Baldwin's American protagonist, David, and Giovanni, an Italian immigrant, banter about the differences between the old world and the new; Giovanni derides America's fondness for "Measure!" (249) and American optimism predicated in a belief in choice ("To *choose*! ... Ah, you are really an American!" [248]). Half-heartedly, David attempts to defend his country of origin. The differences are swept away by the approach of desire, which is as unnamable, untrammeled, and ferociously pleasurable as Aziz's and Fielding's. After the bar banter, David

> could not look at Jacques; which he knew. He stood beside me, smiling at nothing, humming a tune. There was nothing I could say. I did not dare to mention Hella.... I was glad. I was utterly, hopelessly, horribly glad. I knew I could do nothing whatever to stop the ferocious excitement which had burst in me like a storm. I could only drink, in the faint hope that the storm might thus spend itself without doing any more damage to my land. But I was glad.
>
> (254)

Two variously cosmopolitan, queer characters (a privileged white American trying to find himself in Paris and an abjectly displaced immigrant worker who had been banished from his village in Italy) discover desire.

This passage – indeed, the novel as a whole – is queer, in part, because, given the intricate relationship between Baldwin's position as an African American writer, the whiteness of his protagonist, and the double foreignness of Giovanni, it delves into the explosive complexities of what Brent Hayes Edwards calls a "politics of seduction and danger-laden flirtation across the color line and across the sea" (310), thus providing meta-narrative ways of approaching the Other. Within the tradition of American queer expatriate writing, such politics of same-sex interracial desire are also explored, for example, in the identity-testing life and fiction of another New York-born cosmopolitan, Paul Bowles, a resident of Paris and Tangier, disciple of Djuna Barnes and Gertrude Stein, and Baldwin's older contemporary.

More crucially, however, Baldwin's passage is queer because it is as rife with contradictions ("horribly glad"), absences ("could not look," "nothing I could say," "could do nothing") and references to nature, seemingly "unnatural" in an urban setting ("storm," "land") as the conclusion to *A Passage to India*. It accomplishes the same task of a momentary, precarious, to use Butler's adjective, rapprochement with the Other and, simultaneously, of bringing to the fore queer desire by refusing to name it and by replacing it with "nothing."

Both Baldwin and Christopher Isherwood are iconic figures of gay liberation. Isherwood's work is also charged with a task similar to Forster's novels: resistance to the discourses of nationalism, particularly Nazism, on the brink of a war: in Isherwood's case, the Second World War. With his friend, one-time lover, and literary collaborator, poet Wystan Hugh Auden, a transatlantic traveler whose work tirelessly challenged the political and sexual dogmas of his time, Isherwood led an itinerant existence in the 1920s and 1930s. Ultimately, the two writers settled on the opposite coasts of the United States.

Isherwood's memoir, *Christopher and His Kind* (1976), describes the author's travels, as well as his sojourn in Berlin, shortly before and during the early stages of Nazi rule. Portraying a trip to China that Wystan and Christopher took in 1938, on a journalistic assignment, Isherwood writes: "They steamed southward, heading for ... the warm seas sacred to Conrad and to Maugham.... Wystan endured the voyage glumly ...; he disliked being at sea, deplored the tropics, felt uprooted from his chilly beloved North. But Christopher, the place snob, found a new enchantment in each port of call. *He was East of Suez!*" (299). Isherwood's description both alludes subtly to Maugham's queerness and the homosocial seafarers of Conrad's novels and threatens the stability of national identity by exposing it as a construct, rather than a historically determined attachment to a concrete physical space. The passage contrasts Wystan's glum national nostalgia for "his beloved North," awash in natural imagery ("the sea," "the tropics," "uprooted"), with Christopher's delight in travel, expressed in his imaginative "enchantment" and the campy italicized exclamation *"He was East of Suez!"* which renders not only a geographic location but an entire imperial enterprise queerly and self-consciously artificial.

In Berlin, faced with the shared threat of nationalism's ugly culmination, Hitlerism, Isherwood seeks to forge a cosmopolitan alliance with the Other on the brink of destruction:

> But Christopher and the Nazis didn't see eye to eye. The Nazis hated culture itself, because it is essentially international and therefore subversive of nationalism. What they called Nazi culture was a local, perverted, nationalistic cult, by which a few major artists and a few minor ones were honored for their Germanness, not their talent. The rest were condemned as alien and decadent and as representing the culture of the Jews. Christopher himself worshipped culture, but it was a very exclusive religion, to be shared only with fellow artists. (65)

Of note in this passage are the opposition between nationalism and inter-nationalism, culture and ignorance, a strong identification between artists, world-wanderers, queers, aliens, and decadents, at a crucial time in history, and a re-inscription of "perversion." For Isherwood, "perversion" comes to describe hostile philistinism and prejudice. The title of the memoir, published in 1976, as the moment demands, has an identitarian slant: after all, it describes a "kind," or, at times, a "tribe" of people, referring mainly to gay men and lesbians. At this queer cosmopolitan moment, however, along with the re-signification of "perversion," the parameters of the "kind" are redrawn to include intellectual and cultural allegiances and to transcend the needlessly strict identitarian limits of nation, ethnicity, religion, and, yes, sexuality.

Queer and Now: The Cosmopolitan Subject of Color

Cosmopolitanism, insofar as it has stemmed from a particular lineage of Western philosophy, from the Greek Cynics to Kant to Levinas, Derrida, and Butler, has been subjected to critique for the narrowness of its cultural refer-ences and of the place from which the benevolent outreach to the Other takes place. The cosmopolitan described earlier is gay, male, and highly educated, although not necessarily white or European. With the exception of Baldwin, he is committed to the re-inscription and reproduction of Western cultures and artistic expression and uses those to create a common ground with the Other. In the final analysis, too, gay male cosmopolitanism remains within the framework of the nation-state, trying to assimilate the Other within it, instead of destroying its borders altogether.

Wilde, Forster, and Isherwood, in other words, provide a limited set of aes-thetic criteria for an ethical cosmopolitan gesture. As Ackbar Abbas writes, "In the modern era, which corresponded to the economic and political dom-ination of the Western nations, cosmopolitanism meant by and large being versed in Western ways, and the vision of 'one world' culture was only a sometimes unconscious, sometimes unconscionable, euphemism for First World culture" (771). The second half of the twentieth century witnessed the final dissolution of empires, global relocations, and the flows of migrant labor across the Atlantic, as well as from former colonies to former metro-politan capitals. Older diasporas have grown, and new ones have come into being. Defining Western culture as the world culture has become, in such historical circumstances, impossible, and picturing a queer cosmopolitan as an educated gay man residing in a world capital, such as London, Berlin, or Paris, is insufficient.

While the preceding discussion positions writers and their works mostly in a conventional chronological order attached to watershed historical events, I will conclude with an event that is intellectual, rather than historical: the collusion – and collision – of queer and postcolonial theories for the purposes of critique of both nationalism and a narrow definition of cosmopolitanism. Though it retains the same ethical principles, queer diaspora studies, as the product of this collision can properly be called, brings into the fold not the non-European *tout court*, but the dispossessed, the marginalized, the illegal, the silent, the illiterate, the female, and the transgender, and expands the notion of the "world" and "world culture" to include them, all the while remaining committed to delinking sex from gender and, in unison with Eve Kosofsky Sedgwick's now iconic litany of normative family ties in "Queer and Now," to critiquing straight familial arrangements. Queer diasporas come not to replace but to extend the cosmopolitan experience, which, by its very definition, always seeks expansion.

Since the mid-1990s, books, such as Daniel Boyarin's *Unheroic Conduct: The Rise of Heterosexuality and the Invention of the Jewish Man* (1997), Gayatri Gopinath's *Impossible Desires: Queer Diasporas and South Asian Public Cultures* (2005), Martin F. Manalansan's *Global Divas: Filipino Gay Men in the Diaspora* (2003), as well as edited collections, including Cindy Patton and Benigno Sánchez-Eppler's *Queer Diasporas* (2000), John Hawley's *Postcolonial, Queer: Theoretical Intersections* (2001), Eithne Lubhéid and Lionel Cantú's *Queer Migrations: Sexuality, U.S. Citizenship, and Border Crossings* (2005), Jana Evans Braziel and Anita Mannur's *Theorizing Diaspora: A Reader* (2003), to name a few, have helped shape the argument that, while nation is heterosexual, diaspora and migration are queer.

The shapes that family, desire, and gender take in world diasporas undermine the perceived normalcy of procreative heterosexuality, which, in turn, has served as the foundation and guardian of the nation-state. Like queer cosmopolitanism of years past, queer diaspora studies enters into an adversarial relationship with nationalism and is vocally resistant to imperialism. But in addition, the theoretical and literary output by the queers of color introduces experiences of world travelers, who, through multiple cultural and political affiliations and complexity of familial affinities, expand cosmopolitanism beyond the "first world." Similarly to the more canonical gay male texts, such works portray and perform the ethical gesture of approaching and taking responsibility for the Other, but in light of the special focus of queer diaspora studies on rethinking the constructs of family life, the acceptance of the Other is often produced simultaneously with, or as a result of, such resignification of family.

Jackie Kay (Scotland) and Patricia Powell (Jamaica and the United States) continue the line of queer cosmopolitan intellectuals of Caribbean descent, such as Claude McKay and Audre Lorde, who, in their lives and writings, tested and complicated identity at the crossroads of race, class, and sexuality, and lived and worked all over the world, from Morocco to Russia to Germany. But both Kay and Powell also illustrate the intricacies of contemporary queer diasporic critique of color. Kay's 1998 novel *Trumpet* portrays a queer diasporic subject and his queer family. Its protagonist, Joss Moody, is a biologically female biracial Scottish jazz musician who lives as a man. World famous and well traveled, Joss belongs to Africa, Scotland, and the international community of musicians. Family, culture, nation, identity, gender, parenthood, and childhood are the notions that the novel scrutinizes and complicates. The following passage shows Joss performing his experiences and nonidentity on stage:

> So when he takes off he is the whole century galloping to its close. The wide moors. The big mouth. Scotland. Africa. Slavery. Freedom. He is a girl. A man. Everything. Nothing. He is sickness, health. The sun. The moon. Black, white. Nothing weighs him down. Not the past or the future. . . . He just keeps blowing. He is blowing his story. (136)

The relative banality of the relationship between Joss's position as a performer and the performance of gender identity ("a man") aside, this passage, much like Forster's, from *A Passage to India*, is built on irreconcilable oppositions and makes an even more explicit, concerted effort to collapse them. Besides queering Joss Moody's identity, the passage also "worlds" the world, to use Lauren Berlant and Michael Warner's expression, indicating not only that multiple political, racial, national identities coexist in Joss, but that his music is capable of compressing world history into a single explosive performance ("the whole century galloping to its close"). The phrase "he is a girl" is fatal to the sex-gender continuum, and the queer cosmopolitan moment here, like the previous ones, undermines identity.

At the same time, the problematic of cosmopolitan ethics happens in *Trumpet* at the level of the family. Kay's family consists of Joss, a biracial, Scotland-born trans man; his wife Millie, a white Scottish woman who, for the duration of the novel, resists defining her relationship and sexuality as lesbian and protects the privacy of her dead husband from prying tabloid journalists; as well as their adopted biracial son, Colman Moody (formerly William Dunsmore), who negotiates and ultimately accepts his black manhood by struggling with the legacy of his famous father. This family (as, parenthetically, is the Schlegel-Wilcox family in seemingly far-removed *Howards End*) is a far cry from the biological imperatives of heterosexuality or the nation, but the very struggle to create and maintain it is a matter of queer cosmopolitan ethics of accepting and facing the Other.

Patricia Powell similarly limns a contingently queer family born of a diasporic predicament in her 1998 novel *The Pagoda*. The novel, set in nineteenth-century Jamaica, focuses on Lowe, a female Chinese immigrant forced to live as a man because no Chinese women are allowed to live on the island. For years, he maintains a sham marriage and raises his daughter, conceived as a result of rape, as her father. Cecil, the child's biological white father, arranges Lowe's masculinity and marriage.

While Joss's impossible selfhood is all performance, Lowe, a husband, father/mother, and businessman, is the blank screen for other characters' social, racial, and erotic projections:

> Lowe said it again, in a thin, clenched whisper: "Why you couldn't so much as ask me what I want? Eh, why?" Nobody had ever asked him. He had just lived out all their fantasies. There was his father, who used to dress Lowe the same way he dressed himself ... then it was Cecil's fantasies and his grand plans for both Lowe and Miss Sylvie, and now ... Lowe had turned into ... a useless Chinaman. After he had turned concubine to Cecil on board the ship. After he had raised Cecil's daughter. After he had been there, shackled to the shop. (99)

The short passage contains a multitude of identities for Lowe, based on someone else's "fantasies" and "plans." But while Lowe's gender and desire remain – literally – open questions, the titular Pagoda, a Chinese community center in Jamaica which Lowe dreams of building, as well as his queer family – his "wife," the lesbian Miss Sylvie and his daughter, Liz, to whom he is both a father and a mother – remain his reasons for making peace with the new homeland: inhospitable, yet permanent and inhabited by the familiar objects of love and desire.

As a character, Lowe poses questions and shows possibilities for an evolving queer diasporic critique of color. In the past six years, the theories of queer diaspora have been subject to critique. New work has suggested that the link between queerness and diaspora is not automatic, and that more nuanced and inclusive considerations of class and gender are necessary. For example, in *Terrorist Assemblages: Homonationalism in Queer Times* (2007), Jasbir Puar considers the ways "homonationalism" hostile to the Middle Eastern Other props up U.S. national identity. In "Why Queer Diaspora?" (2008), Meg Wesling posits that viewing diaspora exclusively as a queer entity occludes the material realities of the circulation of global labor. Finally, Karen Tongson points to the problem of focusing on urban sophistication and overlooking the complexities of suburban or rural existence. Her *Relocations: Queer Suburban Imaginaries* (2011) zeros in on the suburbs of Southern California and offers the alternative of the suburban "dykeaspora" (47) that inhabits "a site of oscillation ... between spatial and social concepts like provincialism and cosmopolitanism" (83).

Powell's protagonist, Lowe, is a provincial queer, and Tonsgon's trenchant analysis of omission and exclusion is particularly applicable in his case. Although he has crossed the world, he is anything but worldly or educated; being a stowaway constantly subjected to rape and illness hardly qualifies as "well-traveled." Unlike Joss Moody, Lowe is utterly ordinary, outside of the tragically improbable circumstances of his life. Suburban and rural locations, as well as their queer inhabitants lacking in sophistication, unaware of, or uninterested in, the latest fashion trends, and not in possession of a valid passport, are frequently omitted from the critical discourses of cosmopolitanism.

New theories and practices may indeed include post-cosmopolitan queerness and even (after all, Forster already gives us a glimpse of the possibility of facing the Other beyond the city limits in *Howards End* and *A Passage to India*) post-metropolitan cosmopolitanism that, to borrow Tonsgon's term, "relocates" from the *cosmos* to the *polis*. "*Experience and experimentation thus*": patterns of post-cosmopolitan queer existence, which may encompass the city, the suburban sprawl, the backyard, the local park, the makeshift recording studio, and the parking lot, are in the making.

Notes

1. See Appiah's discussion of Voltaire and A. Anderson's discussion of Mill and Arnold.
2. For an excellent analysis of Wilde's cosmopolitanism, see Brown.
3. The reference here is to Michel Foucault's analysis of the science of sexuality.

Works Cited

Abbas, Ackbar. "Cosmopolitan De-scriptions: Shanghai and Hong Kong." *Public Culture* 12.3 (2000): 769–86. Print.

Anderson, Amanda. *The Powers of Distance: Cosmopolitanism and the Cultivation of Detachment.* Princeton: Princeton UP, 2001. Print.

Anderson, Benedict. *Imagined Communities: Reflections on the Origins and Spread of Nationalism.* 1983. London: Verso, 1991. Print.

Appiah, Kwame Anthony. *Cosmopolitanism: Ethics in a World of Strangers.* New York: Norton, 2006. Print.

Baldwin, James. *Giovanni's Room. Early Novels and Stories.* New York: Library of America, 1998. 217–360. Print.

Berlant, Lauren, and Michael Warner. "Sex in Public." *Critical Inquiry* 24.2 (1998): 547–66. Print.

Bersani, Leo. *Homos.* Cambridge: Harvard UP, 1995. Print.

Bowles, Paul. *Collected Stories and Later Writings.* Washington, DC: Library of America, 2002. Print.

Boyarin, Daniel. *Unheroic Conduct: The Rise of Heterosexuality and the Invention of the Jewish Man.* Berkeley: U of California P, 1997. Print.

Braziel, Jana Evans and Anita Mannur, eds. *Theorizing Diaspora: A Reader.* Malden: Blackwell, 2003. Print.

Brown, Julia Prewitt. *Cosmopolitan Criticism: Oscar Wilde's Philosophy of Art.* Charlottesville: U of Virginia P, 1997. Print.

Butler, Judith. *Precarious Life: The Powers of Mourning and Violence.* London: Verso, 2004. Print.

Derrida, Jacques. "On Cosmopolitanism." *The Cosmopolitanism Reader.* Ed. Garret Wallace Brown and David Held. Cambridge: Polity P, 2010. 413–22. Print.

On Cosmopolitanism and Forgiveness. Trans. Mark Dooley and Michael Hughes. New York: Routledge, 2001. Print.

Edwards, Brent Hayes. *The Practice of Diaspora: Literature, Translation, and the Rise of Black Internationalism.* Cambridge: Harvard UP, 2003. Print.

Forster, E.M. *Howards End.* New York: Norton, 1993. Print.

Maurice. New York: Norton, 1993. Print.

A Passage to India. New York: Harcourt, 1924. Print.

Foucault, Michel. *The History of Sexuality, Volume 1: An Introduction.* Trans. Robert Hurley. New York: Vintage, 1990. Print.

Gopinath, Gayatri. *Impossible Desires: Queer Diasporas and South Asian Public Cultures.* Durham: Duke UP, 2005. Print.

Halperin, David. *Saint Foucault: Towards a Gay Hagiography.* Oxford: Oxford UP, 1997. Print.

Hannerz, Ulf. "Cosmopolitans and Locals in World Culture." *Theory, Culture & Society.* 7 (1990): 237–51. Print.

Hawley, John, ed. *Postcolonial, Queer: Theoretical Intersections.* Albany: State U of New York P, 2001. Print.

Isherwood, Christopher. *Christopher and His Kind.* New York: Avon, 1976. Print.

Jagose, Annamarie. *Queer Theory: An Introduction.* New York: New York UP, 1997. Print.

Kant, Immanuel. "Idea of a Universal History from a Cosmopolitan Perspective." *Toward Perpetual Peace and Other Writings on Politics, Peace, and History.* Ed. Pauline Kleingeld. Trans. David L. Colcasure. New Haven: Yale UP, 2006. 3–17. Print.

Kay, Jackie. *Trumpet: A Novel.* New York: Vintage, 1998. Print.

Levinas, Emmanuel. *Otherwise Than Being or beyond Essence*. Trans. Alphonso Lingis. Pittsburgh: Duquesne UP, 1998. Print.

Luibhéid, Eithne, and Lionel Cantú Jr., eds. *Queer Migrations: Sexuality, U.S. Citizenship, and Border Crossings*. Minneapolis: U of Minnesota P, 2005. Print.

Manalansan, Martin F. IV. *Global Divas: Filipino Gay Men in the Diaspora*. Durham: Duke UP, 2003. Print.

Mercer, Kobena. *Exiles, Diasporas, and Strangers*. Cambridge: MIT P, 2008. Print.

Ohi, Kevin. *Henry James and the Queerness of Style*. Minneapolis: U of Minnesota P, 2011. Print.

Patton, Cindy, and Benigno Sánchez-Eppler, eds. *Queer Diasporas*. Durham: Duke UP, 2000. Print.

Pollock, Sheldon, Homi K. Bhabha, Carol A. Breckenridge, and Dipesh Chakrabarty. "Cosmopolitanisms." *Public Culture* 12.3 (2000): 577–90. Print.

Powell, Patricia. *The Pagoda*. New York: Mariner, 1999. Print.

Puar, Jasbir K. *Terrorist Assemblages: Homonationalism in Queer Times*. Durham: Duke UP, 2007. Print.

Sedgwick, Eve Kosofsky. "Queer and Now." *Tendencies*. Durham: Duke UP, 1993. 1–20. Print.

Tongson, Karen. *Relocations: Queer Suburban Imaginaries*. New York: New York UP, 2011. Print.

Wesling, Meg. "Why Queer Diaspora?" *Feminist Review* 90 (2008): 30–47. Print.

Wilde, Oscar. *Collected Works of Oscar Wilde*. Ware: Wordsworth Editions, 1997. Print.

The Importance of Being Earnest. Collected 663–716.

The Picture of Dorian Gray. Collected 1–154.

"The Portrait of Mr. W.H." Collected 219–44.

PART V

GEOGRAPHIES OF SAME-SEX DESIRE IN THE MODERN WORLD

23

Russian Gay and Lesbian Literature

BRIAN JAMES BAER

The history of gay and lesbian literature in Russia is closely tied to the troubled evolution of Russian erotic culture as a whole. Erotic literature developed
relatively late in Russia, hampered by the absence of a broad-based secular
culture before the eighteenth century. Influential cultural movements, such
as the Renaissance with its celebration of the human form, had largely passed
Russia by, and it was in fact illegal for Russian artists to paint nudes well into
the eighteenth century. As Alexei Lalo argues in his study of libertinage in
Russia, "nineteenth-century and modern Russian literature and culture are
characterized by an almost complete absence of vocabulary for dealing with
erotic life within social contexts" (1). This discursive silence had an understandably profound effect on the evolution of gay and lesbian literature.

The enormous gap between the literary culture of Russia's educated elite
and the oral culture of the folk also shaped the evolution of gay literature
in fundamental ways. Until the second half of the nineteenth century, the
two traditions developed along largely separate paths. The language of the
Russian folk as reflected in oral tales and anecdotes was often sexually explicit,
but crude, reflecting a preoccupation with what Mikhail Bakhtin referred to as
"the lower bodily strata." Moreover, the sexual freedom of the Russian peas-
antry and, in particular, the widespread practice of sodomy as documented by
foreign observers in the sixteenth and seventeenth centuries had no corollary
in Russian elite literature, which remained for most of its history silent on the
topic of sex. These general characteristics help to explain some of the unique
features of Russian literary representations of homosexuality, specifically the
persistent association of homosexuality with spirituality, aestheticism, and
asexuality. They also help to explain the significant role translation played in
introducing depictions of same-sex desire into modern Russian literature.

This discursive silence, reinforced in the twentieth century by the Soviet
regime, placed enormous barriers in the path of development of Russian gay
and lesbian culture. Homosexual references were extracted from or altered

in literary works, and the homosexuality of famous historical and cultural figures was denied or dismissed. Many Russian scholars and writers still reject the very idea of gay literature and of homosexuality as a viable interpretive lens through which to study literature. As literary critic Mikhail Zolotonosov expressed it in his review of Kostya Rotikov's "gay" history of St. Petersburg, which appeared in 1997: "There is no such thing as homosexual literature, neither fiction nor folklore, nor any other type, and there cannot be.... [T]here are no means available for the construction of some particular literary form on the part of homosexual authors" (186). Because homosexuality continues to be seen by many as non-Russian, gay and lesbian writers have had to struggle, not only for the right to speak as gay and lesbian individuals, but also for the right to speak as *Russian* gays and lesbians. The relationship of homosexuality to Russian cultural citizenship is a theme that runs throughout the history of Russian gay and lesbian literature.

In the face of this discursive silence, the enormous contribution Western scholars have made to our understanding of Russian gay and lesbian literature over the past thirty-five years cannot be underestimated – Simon Karlinsky's groundbreaking work stands out in this regard. That scholarship, however, was shaped to some degree by the polarized antinomies of Cold War politics and the rigid identity categories promoted by the early gay rights movement. The lifting of censorship restrictions, the opening of archives, and the decentralization of publishing following the fall of the Soviet Union, combined with the growing sophistication of global queer studies, have allowed scholars in both Russia and the West to reevaluate the history of Russian gay and lesbian literature and its contribution to Russian erotic culture.

Gay Poetry in the Golden Age

Simon Karlinsky and others have located the origins of Russian gay literature in the Middle Ages based on accounts of male-male love depicted in the lives of the Orthodox saints, Boris and Gleb, and Moses of Hungary ("Russia's" 1). This brand of historiography, based largely on the unsubstantiated claims of journalist and philosopher Vasilii Rozanov (1856–1919), assumes a willingness to read intense homosocial bonds of another time as homosexual. More reliable evidence suggests that gay literature in Russia has its roots in the late eighteenth and early nineteenth centuries, among the Western-looking Russian elite of the two capitals, St. Petersburg and Moscow.

The first work of gay literature in the Russian language was very likely the translation of Sappho's second ode by Gavril Derzhavin in 1780. Although many translators erased the lesbian thematics of the poem by redefining the lyric voice as masculine, the translations by Derzhavin (1780), Kornei Zhukovskii (1806), and Aleksei Merzliakov (1826) preserved the female gender markers. Original gay-themed literary works appeared in the early nineteenth century during the period commonly referred to as the Golden Age of Russian literature, but these works, largely adaptations, still relied heavily on foreign models. The popularity of ancient Greek culture and contemporary Arabic culture(s) at the time made visible the practice of man-boy love through the lyric poetry it inspired. The first complete edition of the *Greek Anthology*, containing the homoerotic poems collected by Strato of Sardis, was published in 1764, and a collection of Arabic poetry, including several homoerotic works, appeared in French translation in 1819 under the title *Anthologie Arabe: Ou, Choix de poésies arabes inédites, traduites pour la première fois en français* (*Arabic Anthologie: Or, an Unedited Selection of Arabic Poems Translated for the First Time into French*); it was republished in 1828.

Alexander Pushkin (1799–1837), influenced by the vogue for ancient Greek and Arabic poetry, became one of the first Russian writers to experiment with homosexual thematics. Most notable in this regard are his "Podrazhenie Arabskomu" ("An Imitation of the Arabic" [1835]) and the epigrams published in 1836, clearly patterned after ancient Greek verse in both form and content. Pushkin addresses "An Imitation of the Arabic" to a "Sweet lad, tender lad," with whom the lyric subject shares "a sole insurgent fire" (29). That Pushkin is speaking here of homosexuality and not simply of strong homosocial bonds is revealed in the second stanza: "I do not fear the gibes of men." In his Greek-style epigram "On the Statue of a Player at Svaika" Pushkin extols the physical beauty of Russian peasant athletes and does not shy away from physicality, as in the final two lines of the poem: "Here's a fitting companion for you, O Discobulus! Worthy, by my oath, / When sporting's done with, to rest beside you, locked in amicable embrace" (Green 32).

Another source of gay-themed literature was the creation of all-male institutions for the education and training of young boys and men in the late eighteenth and early nineteenth centuries. This created a situation that fostered homosexual relations. It also increased awareness of homosexuality among the Russian elite. Overall, these factors produced a rather tolerant attitude toward homosexuality in elite circles – indeed, several prominent homosexuals in Russian high society of the time led lives that were semi-open, such as Minister of Education Sergei Uvarov (1786–1855), memoirist Filip Vigel' (1786–1856), and Prince M.A. Dondukov-Korsakov (1794–1869), vice president of the Russian Academy of Sciences. Pushkin's humorous references to the homosexuality of his Russian friends and contemporaries reveal an attitude of bemused tolerance.

Those all-male establishments are also responsible for the homoerotic poems of Russia's great Romantic writer Mikhail Iurevich Lermontov (1814–41). Two verses referred to as his Hussar poems, "Ode to the John" ("Oda k nuzhniku" [1834]) and "To Tiessenhausen" ("Tizengauzenu" [1834]), date from his time in the St. Petersburg School of Cavalry Cadets but were first published only in 1879 in Geneva, in a volume entitled *Eros Russe: Russian Erotica Is not for Ladies (Eros Russe. Russkii eros ne dlia dam)*. Lightly pornographic, the first poem recounts how the young cadets would congregate in the lavatory, where they would smoke pipes and have sex with one another: "a kiss resounds through the silence, / And a reddening cock has risen like a hungry tiger; / Now it is being groped by an immodest hand" (Lermontov 37). In the second poem, the poet cautions a charming and popular schoolmate not to make such free use of his powers of sexual attraction for there will come a time when

> All of those who now are begging
> At your feet, stretched on the ground,
> Will not quench your melancholy
> With the sweet dew of a kiss –
> Although then just for a cock's tip
> You would gladly give your life.   (37)

Translation at the time continued to provide a protected venue for the expression of homosexual desire, and it was a venue open to the many members of Russia's elite who were fluent in French and German. Ivan Dmitriev (1760–1837), minister of justice under Alexander I, for example, *queered* his translations of two fables by Lafontaine, while in his original poetry he wore "a heterosexual mask" (Tyulenev 260). In an adaptation based on the poetry of Greek court poet Anacreon entitled "The Pigeon. An Imitation of Anacreon" ("Golubchik. Podrazenie Anakreonu"), the bird (gendered as male in Russian) explains that he is carrying letters from Anacreon to his boy Bathylos, "who attracts all hearts." Not only does he allude to an amorous relationship between the poet and the boy, the bird expresses his own intense feelings for his master (Tyulenev 262). In his translation of two fables by Lafontaine, "Les deux pigeons" ("Two Pigeons") and "Les deux amis" ("Two Friends"), Dmitriev queers the homosocial bonds celebrated in the tales. Dmitriev translates the formal French *vous* with the more familiar Russian *tu*, and where the two pigeons bid each other adieu "in tears" in the French source text, they exchange loving pecks in Dmitriev's version. Similarly, in "Two Friends" Dmitriev introduces physical contact between the two men that is not present in the source (Tyulenev 268). With the tightening of censorship restrictions in the 1840s, however, depictions of sensuality of any kind became more difficult to publish, and "the theme of carnal love disappeared from Russian poetry after Yazykov's and Pushkin's time" (Karlinsky, *Sexual* 213).

Homosexuality and Russian Realism

Although nineteenth-century Russian literature has a reputation for being "chaste," with its authors unwilling and, according to Lalo, unable to render erotic sexual content, homosexuality appears in interesting ways in the works of Russia's three greatest prose authors of that century: Nikolai Gogol, Fyodor Dostoevsky, and Leo Tolstoy. In *The Sexual Labyrinth of Nikolai Gogol* (1976), his revisionist take on Gogol's oeuvre, Karlinsky interpreted the major themes of his fiction against the backdrop of his personal writings and biographical facts as indicating the writer's closeted homosexuality: "An examination of Gogol's homosexual orientation within the context of his biography and writings may provide the missing key to the riddle of his personality" (vii). Among the evidence Karlinsky presented is the fact that Gogol's male characters often express a horror of marriage; his female characters are typically underdeveloped; and all of Gogol's most intense relationships appear to be with male friends. The unmarried Gogol died at the early age of forty-three from the effects of a strict ascetic regime intended to rid him of an unnamed "sin." Through his reinterpretation of Gogol's life and works, Karlinsky was able to place homosexuality at the very center of the Russian literary canon.

The theme of homosexuality in the works of Fyodor Dostoevsky has been explored by a number of Western Slavists. Michael Katz lists eight characters in Dostoevsky's oeuvre whose depiction largely reflects contemporary stereotypes of homosexuals and who express either an attraction to a man or an aversion to women: Petrov and Aley in *Notes from the House of the Dead*, Netochka and Katya in the unfinished novel *Netochka Nezvanova*, Myshkin and Rogozhin in *The Idiot*, Apollon in *Notes from Underground*, and Smerdyakov in *Brothers Karamazov*. Dostoevsky's ambivalence toward homosexuality is suggested by the fact that some of these characters are portrayed in a distinctly positive light and others in a distinctly negative one. American Slavist Susanne Fusso argues in *Discovering Sexuality in Dostoevsky* that homosexuality assumes a compositional function only in *A Raw Youth* (*Podrostok* [1875]) through the main character Arkadii's interaction with male prostitute Petr Trishatov, "a 'pretty boy' dependent on male admirers for nice clothes and pocket money" (43). Most probably based on Dostoevsky's fellow prison inmate Sirotkin, mentioned in his quasi-autobiographical *Notes from the House of the Dead* (*Zapiski iz mertvogo doma* [1862]), Trishatov is treated with compassion by Arkadii, the character "with whom the reader feels the greatest sympathy" (Fusso 53).

Dostoevsky's most famous contemporary, Count Leo Tolstoy (1828–1910), also treated homosexuality in his writings. In his early autobiographical work, *Childhood* (*Detstvo* [1852]), he recounts the intense attraction he felt as a boy toward his friend Seryozha Ivin. That this intense physical and emotional bond was something akin to homosexual desire Tolstoy himself admitted in a diary entry: "I fell in love very often with men. . . . I was falling in love with men before I had a concept of pederasty; but even learning of it, the idea of the possibility of intercourse never entered my head" (Tolstoy 47). Later in life, however, he took a more "jaundiced view of all sexuality" (Moss 42) and of homosexuality in particular. His novel *Anna Karenina* (1874–77) features a homosexual couple whose appearance in the officer's mess inspires the heterosexual Vronsky with disgust.

One of the most overt depictions of homosexuality appeared in the story "Khamid and Manoli: A Cretan Greek Woman's Story about True Events of 1858" ("Khami i Manoli" [1869]) by Konstantin Leontiev (1831–91). Like many other prominent Russian gays of the nineteenth century, Leontiev was religious and politically conservative. By placing his story in a foreign country, Leontiev practiced a common strategy of the time that allowed allusions to homosexuality provided they were disguised in euphemism and Aesopian language and were situated in a far-off land. Leontiev's story takes place on the multicultural island of Crete, where a young and impoverished Greek boy, Manoli, enters into a relationship with a well-off Turk, Hamid, described in rather negative terms as crazy. Told from the point of view of his sister, the story offers little insight into their homosexual relationship, suggesting that Manoli's motivation was material. Moreover, the tale ends tragically for the two homosexual characters. Manoli is executed following his murder of Hamid.

Arguably the greatest contribution to Russian gay literature at the time was the publication in 1879 of the collection *Eros Russe: Russian Erotica Is not for Ladies* in Geneva in a limited print run of only 100. (The phrase "not for ladies" [ne dlia dam] may have been not only a play on the expression "ne dlia pechati" [not for publication] but also an allusion to the volume's homosexual content.) The volume, which included several gay-themed works – Lermontov's three Hussar poems as well as a lengthy pastiche of eighteenth-century French erotica, "The Passage of the Page: A Poem in Two Parts" ("Pokhozhdenie pazha. Poema v dvukh chastiakh" [1879]) – acquired great notoriety. "The Passage of the Page" was attributed to Aleksandr Shenin (1802–55), a librarian and then inspector of classes at the Pavlovsky Cadet Corps who was expelled from the school in 1854 for pederasty and died soon after, bedridden and blind. Based on accounts of Shenin, who is described in the memoirs of his contemporaries as bowlegged and ornery, it may be that he is not the real author of this light, witty, and thoroughly obscene poem. In any case, the poem, which has a total of twenty-four stanzas and is written in unrelenting iambic tetrameter, is a very humorous first-person account of one cadet's initiation into the culture of pederasty at the Cadet Corps. In the opening stanza the lyric subject proclaims:

> I'm sad to leave
> This pink house on Garden Street
> Where every form of vice did grow,
> Which housed our Sodom. (Eros 45)

The poem is accompanied by a short preface in which the author presents Russia as a country particularly accepting of homosexuality: "Pederasty has flourished in Russia from the earliest times. It is well known that Ivan the Terrible, Peter the Great, and Peter II had a propensity for this sin, not to mention the many historical figures and society people who were suspected of it" (154). The author goes on to explain that Russia enforced its antisodomy law less severely than its Western European counterparts and ends the preface with the statement: "Our finest poets – Pushkin, Griboedov, and Lermontov – have written pederastic verse" (154).

Another important event in the development of erotic literature in Russia was the publication of a collection of obscene Russian folk tales collected by A.N. Afanas'ev. Originally censored in Russia, the tales were eventually published in Geneva in 1872, with the help of Alexander Herzen, under the title *Russian Secret Fairy Tales (Russkie zavetnye skazki)*. The bawdy tales included homosexual motifs, but the presentation of sex was crude and tended to separate body and soul, and so made little contribution to the development of high erotic literature. This reflects the findings of scholars, such as Igor Kon and Alexei Lalo, which suggest that Russian elite and folk cultures followed largely separate paths of development, especially where issues of sex were concerned.

In the latter years of the nineteenth century, Russian culture began to turn away from the serious, socially engaged realism of the previous decades. A sophisticated art-for-art's sake aesthetic emerged, presaging the explosion of artistic innovation in the first two decades of the twentieth century, referred to as the Silver Age of Russian literature. The poetry of Aleksei Apukhtin (1840–93) is typical of this time. A friend of composer Pytor Tchaikovsky, Apukhtin did not address gay themes overtly but often left his poems provocatively open to queer readings. For example, the poem "Son" ("The Dream") was about a Petersburg restaurant, "Medved" ("The Bear"), which was a hangout for gays, and the title of his poem "Dorogoi," dedicated to his one-time lover Tchaikovsky, could be pronounced either *dorógoi* (along the road) or *dorogói* (dear; masc.). The following verses can easily be read as a defiant statement of his choice to live as a gay man:

> I do not fear the anger of fate
> Nor the heavy chains, nor the vulgar judgment of people ...
> I would give my whole life for a tender word.
> For a sweet, kind look from pensive eyes!　　　　　　(poem 252)

In this 1876 epigram, as in other lyric poems, such as "In the Theater," Apukhtin goes to rather great lengths to avoid specifying the sex of the addressee. Tchaikovsky set several of Apukhtin's lyrics to music, which became very popular romances.

Homosexuality in the Silver Age

Already by the end of the nineteenth century, almost all the conditions were in place for the emergence of a modern gay and lesbian literary tradition. Rapid industrialization moved masses of Russians from the countryside to the cities, where they lived beyond the supervision of their families and neighbors; in turn, boarding houses for young, single workers appeared in these cities, and features of a gay subculture began to emerge (see Healey 29–49). Moreover, many prominent members of Russian high society, including several grand dukes, carried on rather openly homosexual liaisons and, for the most part, avoided prosecution. In 1905, following the failed workers' revolt, restrictive censorship laws were lifted and questions of gender, sex, and sexuality were for the first time in Russian history discussed with relative freedom in the public sphere (see Engelstein).

　The sources underpinning Russian discourse on homosexuality in the Silver Age were many and varied; some of them were borrowed and adapted from the West while others were more homegrown. Western decadent literature was one important foreign source, as was the emerging field of sexology, as it was developing in Germany, France, and England. Works by leading sexologists such as Richard von Krafft-Ebing, Havelock Ellis, Magnus Hershfeld, Otto Weininger, and, of course, Sigmund Freud were either translated or read in the original, bringing scientific views of gender and sexuality into the Russian public sphere. But there were Russian sources fueling contemporary discourse on sex, as well, such as the Russian religious sects known as the Khlysty, or "Flagellants," and the Skoptsy. Members of the former group were purported to engage in mass orgies and to practice homosexuality, while the latter group promoted self-castration. Moreover, these decades saw a resurgence in religious and mystical philosophy, as exemplified in the writings of Vladimir Soloviev, in which androgyny and homosexuality were used as spiritual tropes. These competing, and to some degree contradictory, models tended to overlap in the popular imagination, and this was reflected in many of the literary representations of homosexuality at that time.

One of the greatest events in the history of Russian gay literature was the publication in 1906 of the novel *Wings*, written by Russian poet and prose writer Mikhail Kuzmin (1872–1936), who was known as the "Russian Wilde." The novel recounts in the form of a bildungsroman the main character Ivan (Vanya) Smurov's symbolic journey toward acceptance of his homosexuality, taking him from St. Petersburg in part one to the Russian countryside in part two and to Italy in part three. And while Kuzmin creates a homosexual character who is largely free of shame, he also follows some of the stereotypes of his day by associating homosexuality with foreignness, as represented by the enigmatic Mr. Stroup, and by the fact that Vanya accepts his homosexuality in Italy, and with aesthetic refinement, as expressed in the "We are Helenes" speech overheard by Vanya in part one. Moreover, the aesthetic focus serves to attenuate any erotic tension in the novel. A *succès-de-scandale* in its time, Kuzmin's novel was only one of many novels that offered new, frank portrayals of sexual desire, such as Mikhail Artsybashev's *Sanin* (1907), Evdokia Nagrodskaia's *The Wrath of Dionysus* (1910), and Anastasiia Verbitskaia's *The Keys to Happiness* (1910–13). Kuzmin also wrote gay-themed short stories, such as "Aunt Sofiia's Sofa" ("Kushetka Teti Soni" [1907]) and "Virginal Victor" ("Devstvennyi Viktor" [1914]). But perhaps Kuzmin's greater contribution to Russian gay and lesbian literature was his poetry.

Kuzmin's poetry is marked by a formal sophistication combined with unabashed sensuality, as in the famous opening lines of his artistic manifesto "The Summer Affair" (1906): "Where shall I find a style to catch a stroll, Chablis on ice, a crisply toasted roll, / The agate succulence of cherries ripe?"

(89). Most of Kuzmin's poetic cycles were inspired by his lover at the time, and, like contemporary homosexual activists in the West, he sought to dignify homosexuality through references to high culture and to ancient Greece and Rome. Antinous, the beautiful companion of the Roman emperor Hadrian, appears throughout Kuzmin's poetic cycle *Alexandrian Songs* (1905–08). Even contemporaries who frowned on the erotic content could not deny the formal sophistication of Kuzmin's verse. The influence of French erotic literature is evident in Kuzmin's most sexually explicit poems contained in the volume *Zanaveshennyi kartinki* (*Covered Pictures*). The slim volume of poems, accompanied by the erotic drawings of Vladimir Somov, was published in Amsterdam in 1920 in a circulation of only 307.

One of Russia's leading Symbolist poets, Viacheslav Ivanov (1866–1945), together with his wife, Lydia Zinovieva-Annibal (1866–1907), hosted an artistic salon in their apartment, which was referred to as "the tower." Open-minded sexually, they were close friends with Kuzmin, who lived with them for several years. A bisexual, Ivanov produced several poems about his homosexual experiences, which were published in his 1911 book of verse, *Cors Ardens*, under the title "Eros." Zinovieva-Annibal made her own contribution to Russian gay literature with her novel *Thirty-Three Freaks* (1907) and her collection of stories *The Tragic Zoo* (1907). But as the titles suggest, these works presented lesbianism in an unflattering light as decadent and perverse. Equally unflattering was the depiction of homosexuality in Fiodor Sologub's novel *Petty Demon* (1907), which features a sadistic schoolmaster who sublimates his pederastic urges by whipping the young boys in his charge. Gay writer Riurik Ivniev's collection of poetry, *Self-Immolation* (1913), also presents homosexual desire in a decadent light.

So central were sexual issues to the public discourse of the time that leading writer and philosopher Vasilii Rozanov (1856–1919) published a treatise devoted exclusively to homosexuality, entitled *People of the Moonlight* (1911). In this work, Rozanov courageously exposes and condemns the sexophobia of Russian Orthodox culture, which was reflected in Tolstoy's promotion of abstinence, even in marriage, and in the bizarre beliefs of the Skoptsy, who practiced self-castration. This disgust with sex, Rozanov argues, is reflected in a loss of virility that is embodied in what he refers to as "spiritual homosexuals." These are men defined not by their attraction to other men but rather by their lack of attraction to women. While he acknowledges the existence of "real" homosexuals, most homosexuals, he suggests, are the products of Russia's sexophobic religious culture. In an attempt to prove that, he makes the argument that the medieval Russian saints Boris, Gleb, and Moses of Hungary were homosexual, based on the expression of mutual love in their vitae. For Rozanov, spiritual homosexuals were a symptom of the decadence of Russian civilization. Despite that, Western scholars have used Rozanov's assertions to suggest that Russia was more gay friendly than the West.

Rozanov's ideas on homosexuality were not as unique as they might at first appear. Evdokia Nagrodskaia (1866–1930), for example, in her sensational novel *The Wrath of Dionysus* (1910), suggests that women with masculine traits are "natural" lesbians while men with feminine traits are "natural" homosexuals. The solution proposed, however, is not that the women should pair up with women and the men with men, but that these natural lesbians should unite with natural homosexuals, which is precisely what happens with the heterosexual couple featured in the novel, Tanya and Ilya. But the passionless union leads Tanya to have an affair with the businessman Stark. Ilya forgives Tanya in the end, admitting that he had taken all the poetry out of her life. Like Rozanov, Nagrodskaia imagines homosexuality in strictly gendered terms, associating it essentially with asexuality.

Two of the most colorful figures of the Silver Age period were undoubtedly Nikolai Kliuev (1884–1937) and Zinaida Gippius (1869–1945). Both were striking examples of life creation, that is, the attempt of artists to merge their life and work. Married to philosopher and writer Dmitrii Merezhkovskii, Gippius was a true gender-bender, often dressing as a man and adopting a male persona in some of her lyric poems. Diana Lewis Burgin contends that Gippius used a male persona "to mask the Lesbian desire of her female self" (185). Unlike the cosmopolitan Gippius, Kliuev came from the provinces from a family that belonged to the Khlysty sect. Even when he moved to St. Petersburg, he continued to dress in peasant garb as a kind of drag. Kliuev was one of several "peasant" poets of the time, but his work was also influenced by the more refined Symbolist poets. Imbued with a robust sensuality, Kliuev's poetry mixes high culture references with peasant motifs, as in the poem "That Fellow with the Green Eyes Smells of Ginger and Mint" (1924). His celebrated collection *Brotherly Songs* (1912) contains a number of homoerotic lyrics. He was the friend, mentor, and probable lover of Sergei Esenin, who dedicated poems to Kliuev. Both Kliuev and Esenin died tragic deaths in the Soviet Union. Esenin committed suicide, leaving a note written in his own blood. Kliuev was exiled to Siberia, where he eventually died. All of Kliuev's unpublished writings, which he had left with an ex-lover, Nikolai Arkhipov, were lost when Arkhipov himself was arrested and sent to the gulag.

The Soviet Period and the Russian Diaspora

Despite the lifting of antisodomy laws following the October Revolution and the anticlerical position of the new Soviet leaders, the cause of homosexual liberation was not embraced by the regime. The last hurrah of gay-themed literature in Soviet Russia was the miraculous publication in 1929 of Kuzmin's collection *The Trout Breaks the Ice.* This was one year after the publication of Konstantin Vaginov's novel *Goat's Song* (1928), which featured the gay character Kostya Rotikov. Lesbian poet and one time lover of Marina Tsvetaeva (1892–1941), Sophia Parnok (1885–1933), also found it increasingly difficult to publish her work in the 1920s. Her first collection of verse, *Poems* (1916), written during her affair with Tsvetaeva, was a positive, nondecadent expression of lesbian desire. She was unable to publish her original work after 1928. Marina Tsvetaeva's poem "Podruga" ("Girlfriend"), inspired by her affair with Parnok, was not published until 1979, in the United States. Poet Riurik Ivniev (1891–1981), too, ceased publishing homoerotic verse in the Soviet period, and his pre-Revolutionary poetry was never republished.

With Stalin's consolidation of power in the late 1920s, the regime began to regulate more strictly what it considered to be "nonnormative" behavior. In 1934, homosexuality was criminalized at the same time that abortion was made illegal. But homosexuality had already disappeared from Russian literature by this time. It would also disappear from the Soviet press and as an object of academic study. Homoerotic references in classical poetry were excised or changed, and Kuzmin's final public reading of his poetry in Leningrad in 1928 was the "last demonstration of Leningrad's homosexuals" (Malmsted and Bogomolov 349).

Unable to publish their own work, writers like Kuzmin and Parnok turned to translation to support themselves, often choosing works through which they might continue to express their aesthetic and thematic concerns. Kuzmin translated Shakespeare's sonnets and Apulieus's *Golden Ass*. One of Kuzmin's intimates, translator Ivan Likhachev (1902–72), who was imprisoned after Kuzmin's death, translated Baudelaire's *Les Fleurs du mal* from memory while in the gulag. The two best-known gay writers of the Soviet period, Evgenii Kharitonov (1941–81) and Gennadii Trifonov (1945–2011), began to write during the Thaw period under Khrushchev. Nevertheless, they were able to circulate their work only in *samizdat*. (The translation of James Baldwin's *Giovanni's Room* by Gennadii Shmakov [1944–88] suffered a similar fate in the 1970s.) Kharitonov's unpublished collection of gay-themed stories, *Under House Arrest*, includes "One Boy's Story: How I Got Like That" and "The Stove," two of his most popular works. Trifonov was arrested and sent to Siberia for his unpublished collection of homoerotic verse entitled *Tblisi by Candlelight*; in 1978 Trifonov sent a courageous letter from prison to the journal *Literaturnaya Gazeta*, defending Italian gay activist Angelo Pezzano and advocating for gay rights. The letter was first published in the United States.

Many other gay, lesbian, and bisexual Russians fled the Soviet Union after the October Revolution and took up residence in various metropolitan centers around the world. Marina Tsvetaeva emigrated to Paris, as did poet Anatolii Steiger (1907–44); poet Valery Pereleshin (1913–92) emigrated first to China, then to Brazil, where he spent the rest of his life. Although the Russian diaspora was only nominally less sexophobic than the Soviet regime, these poets were able to continue working and to find venues in which to publish their work. Pereleshin's magnum opus, *Ariel*, which consists of 169 classical sonnets documenting an epistolary romance Pereleshin had with a man in Moscow, was published in Germany in 1976. Gennadii Shmakov, a translator and balletomane, emigrated to New York City. Shmakov also brought new scholarly attention to the work of Mikhail Kuzmin, who had been all but forgotten in Soviet Russia.

Post-Soviet Russia

The lifting of censorship restrictions, the decriminalization of homosexuality, and the influx of Western NGOs in the early 1990s resulted in new visibility for Russia's sexual minorities and the promise of an LGBT activist movement. All the trappings of an open gay and lesbian subculture appeared in Russia's largest cities: clubs, magazines, publishing houses, and activist organizations. Moreover, the founding of Russia's first gay Web site, gay.ru, gave provincial gays and lesbians access to gay-themed books and journals. Although most of these venues were short-lived and depended on financial support from the West, they nevertheless made possible the publication of works by new Russian gay and lesbian writers and of translations of Western gay literature, as well as the republication of works by Soviet and pre-Revolutionary writers that had been repressed by the regime. Some of the most striking events in post-Soviet publishing involved the publication of overtly gay-themed works, such as Kuzmin's frank and witty diaries (1998, 2000) and Kostya Rotikov's gay "history" of St. Petersburg, *Drugoi Peterburg* (*The Other Petersburg* [1997]). (Kostya Rotikov is the pseudonym of Iurii Piriutko [1946–].) Russia's first anthology of gay literature, *Liubov' bez granits* (*Love without Borders* [1997]) also appeared at this time; it featured Russian writers – Lermontov, Kuzmin,

Zinovieva-Annibal, Ivnev, Esenin, Limonov, and Kharitonov, several of whom were not in fact gay – alongside canonical gay writers of the West, such as Proust, and Michelangelo. Kharitonov's "Listochek" and Rozanov's "Tretii pol" ("The Third Sex") served as introductory essays, while the cover featured a black-and-white reproduction of Russian artist Aleksandr Ivanov's 1822 painting *Two Models*, portraying two provocatively posed male nudes. These works, which were lauded by some and violently denounced by others, represent early attempts by post-Soviet gays and lesbians to reclaim, or queer, their Russian and Soviet past.

As the introductory essays to *Love without Borders* suggest, post-Soviet discourse on homosexuality produced both in the mainstream press and in more restricted gay and lesbian venues was often contradictory and confused. Pre-Revolutionary Russian works appeared alongside new Russian writing and translations of Western works from various periods. Introductions from pre-Revolutionary editions were often republished without dates or commentary. An example of the confusion perpetuated by post-Soviet publishing practices was the translation of American psychologist Alexander Lowen's *Love and Orgasm* that appeared in 1998 in the series Classics of Foreign Psychology. The edition includes no explanatory introduction or any mention of the fact that Lowen's book was originally published in 1965 and reflects now thoroughly discredited views of homosexuality. Similarly, reeditions of the works of Sappho contain essays from the early twentieth century, without the dates, that insist the poet was heterosexual. The critical writings on Kharitonov contained in the historic two-volume Russian edition of his works, *Slezy na tvetakh* (*Tears on Flowers* [1992]), by Glagol Press reflected the Russian intelligentsia's views on homosexuality, which continued to associate homosexuality with suffering, asexuality, and artistic refinement. Writer Viktor Erofeev went so far as to suggest that Kharitonov's homosexuality was just a literary pose.

With the exception of Igor Kon, there were few authoritative scholarly voices in Russia who could make sense of the cacophony of views on homosexuality presented in Russia at that time. To make matters worse, homosexuality became a popular theme in writing by non-gay authors, where it was often used to symbolize the chaos of post-Soviet life. In addition, works of popular psychiatry, such as Dilia Enikeeva's *Sexual Pathology* and *Gays and Lesbians*, presented "nontraditional" love as a trendy, Western-inspired phenomenon and warned of the danger to Russia's youth from semi-hidden gay cabals in the Russian entertainment industry and in the highest political circles.

Early post-Soviet gay and lesbian fiction reflected an enduring ambivalence on the part of Russian gays and lesbians themselves toward homosexuality as a native phenomenon. One of the earliest editions of post-Soviet gay fiction was the collection *Drugoi* (*The Other* [1993]). As the title suggests, all the stories involve romantic encounters with foreign men, reinforcing the popular view that homosexuality was essentially un-Russian. Works by Russian gay writers, such as the novels *Na kogo pokhozh arlekin* (*Who Resembles the Harlequin* [1997]) by Dmitrii Bushuev (1969–) and *I finn* (*And a Finn* [1997]) by Aleksandr Il'ianen, and the drama *Rogatka* (Slingshot, 1989) by Nikolai Koliada (1957–), staged in Russia and the West by openly gay director Roman Viktiuk (1936–), differed little from works by non-gay writers, such as Vasilii Aksyonov's "V raione ploshchadi Diupon" ("Around Dupont Circle" [1996]), Liudmila Ulitskaia's "Golubchik" ("Darling" [2001]), and Ekaterina Kovaleva's *Moi goluboi drug* (*My Gay Friend* [2003]). All of them perpetuated the long-standing association of homosexuality with spirituality, aestheticism, and tragedy. Best-selling author Grigorii Chkhartishvili (pseud. Boris Akunin) published a lengthy work of nonfiction, *The Writer and Suicide*, that included a separate chapter on gay writers because, he asserted, "same sex love, unlike 'normal' love does not hold the promise of a 'happy ending' of the 'they lived happily ever after' variety" (356).

The stereotype of the "spiritual homosexual" has not, however, gone unchallenged. Some very high-profile Russian gay and lesbian writers have rejected the traditional association of homosexuality with spirituality and effete aestheticism. The most visible of these writers is undoubtedly Yaroslav (Slava) Mogutin (1974–), who fashions himself in public and in his poetry collections – *Uprazhneniia dlia iazyika* (*Exercises for the Tongue* [1997]), and *Roman c nemtsem* (*A Romance with a German* [2000]), and *Deklaratsiia nezavisimosti* (*Declaration of Independence* [2004]) – as a defiant, masculine, profoundly sexual rebel. His collection *Termoiadernyi muskul* (*A Thermonuclear Muscle* [2001]) won the prestigious Andrei Bely Prize. Attracted to the poetry and lifestyle of American beat poets, he has translated the works of Alan Ginsberg, William S. Burroughs, and Dennis Cooper into Russian. He was forced to leave Russia in 1995 and was granted asylum in the United States. He now lives in New York. Poet and translator Dmitrii Volchek (1964–), the editor of the influential avant-garde literary magazine *Mitin Zhurnal* (*Mitia's Journal*), has produced several collections of neomodernist poetry, such as *The Talking Tulip* (1992) and *Midday Demon* (1995). Volchek, who shares Mogutin's love of such gay iconoclasts as William S. Burroughs and Jean Genet, was a translator of Burroughs's *Wild Boys* (*Dikie mal'chiki* [2000]), as well as works by Guy Davenport and Paul Bowles, for his publishing house Kolonna. Like Mogutin, Volchek left Russia in the 1990s; he now lives in Prague. Some non-gay-identified writers, like postmodernists

Vladmir Sorokin and Vladmir Pelevin, also introduce an aggressive, unrepentant vision of homosexuality in their works. For them, homosexuality as a motif was part of a broader post-Soviet aesthetic stance that rejected the heteronormativity and sexophobia of official Soviet literature while celebrating a resolutely unedifying form of aesthetic play.

The deep ambivalence toward homosexuality within Russian culture today is reflected in the government's refusal to allow gay pride parades and in new laws to outlaw public discussion of homosexuality, described in legislation as "propaganda." This has made the role of gay writers and publishers, such as Dmitrii Volchek, especially important in circulating gay literature. As a writer, translator, and founder of both Glagol press and the glossy monthly magazine *Kvir (Queer)*, Aleksandr Shatalov (1957–) has also played a very important role in resurrecting Russia's gay past and in making the works of new Russian gay authors and more established foreign gay authors available to Russian readers. Thanks to these publishers, gay writers and translators continue to have a venue for the dissemination of their work.

Despite the general homophobia, gay and lesbian literature in today's Russia is alive and well, as evidenced by a number of talented gay poets who are currently living and writing in Russia. Aleksei Purin (1955–), Aleksandr Anashevich, and Vasilii Chepelev are accomplished poets with very different aesthetics. Dmitry Kuz'min (1968–), grandson of famous literary translator Nina Gul', is one of the most respected poets of his generation, with a reputation that goes well beyond the confines of gay literature. Winner of the Andrei Bely Prize, Kuz'min has been active not only as a poet but also, like Volchek and Shatalov, as a publisher, translator, and promoter of young poets. He founded the journal of young writers *Vavilon* and the gay literary journal *Risk*. Lesbian poets who live and write in Russia include Yashka Kazanova and Faina Grimberg. Queer-friendly women authors who have offered sympathetic portrayals of gays and lesbians include poet Elena Fanailova and prose writer Sonia Adler, whose novel *Ia tebia liubliu, i tozhe net (I Love You, and I Don't* [2004]) offers a touching portrayal of a young Moscow lesbian in a defiant search for love in chat rooms and Internet cafés.

Works Cited

Bakhtin, Mikhail. *Rabelais and His World*. 1965. Trans. Hélène Iswolsky. Bloomington: Indiana UP, 1984. Print.

Burgin, Diana Lewis. "Laid out in Lavender: Perceptions of Lesbian Love in Russian Literature and Criticism of the Silver Age, 1893–1917." *Sexuality and the Body in Russian Culture*. Eds. Jane T. Costlow, Stephanie Sandler, and Judith Vowles. Stanford: Stanford UP, 1993. 177–203. Print.

Chernetsky, Vitaly. "After the House Arrest: Russian Gay Poetry." *Crossing Centuries: The New Generation in Russian Poetry.* Ed. John High. Jersey City: Talisman House, 2000. 315–23. Print.

Chkhartishvili, Grigorii. *Pisatel' i samoubiistvo. [The Writer and Suicide.]* Moscow: Novoe Literaturnoe Obozrenie, 2000. Print.

Engelstein, Laura. *The Keys to Happiness. Sex and the Search for Modernity in Fin-de-Siècle Russia.* Ithaca: Cornell UP, 1992. Print.

Eros Russe. Russkii erot ne dlia dam. [Eros russe. Russian Eros Is Not for Ladies.] 3rd ed. Berkeley: Berkeley Slavic Specialties. 1995. Print.

Fusso, Susanne. *Discovering Sexuality in Dostoevsky.* Evanston: Northwestern UP, 2006. Print.

Green, Michael. "A Pushkin Puzzle." Moss, ed. 30–35.

Healey, Dan. *Homosexual Desire in Revolutionary Russia: The Regulation of Sexual and Gender Dissent.* Chicago: U of Chicago P, 2001. Print.

Karlinsky, Simon. *The Sexual Labyrinth of Nikolai Gogol.* Cambridge: Harvard UP, 1976. Print.

"Russia's Gay Literature and History (11th–20th Centuries)." Gay Sunshine 29–30 (1976): 1–7. Print.

Katz, Michael. "Dostoevskii's Homophilia/Homophobia." *Gender and Sexuality in Russian Civilisation.* Ed. Peter Barta. London: Routledge, 2001. 239–54. Print.

Kuzmin, Michael. "A Summer Affair." Trans. Michael Green. Moss, ed. 89–93.

Lalo, Alexei. *Libertinage in Russian Culture and Literature: A Bio-History of Sexualities at the Threshold of Modernity.* Leiden: Brill, 2011. Print.

Lermontov, Mikhail. "Two Poems." Trans. Vitaly Chernetsky. Moss, ed. 36–37.

Malmsted, John E., and Nikolay Bogomolov. *Mikhail Kuzmin: A Life in Art.* Cambridge: Harvard UP, 1999. Print.

Moss, Kevin. "Leo Tolstoy (1828–1910)." Moss, ed. 42–46.

ed. *Out of the Blue: Russia's Hidden Gay Literature. An Anthology.* San Francisco: Gay Sunshine P, 1997. Print.

Pushkin, Aleksandr. "Imitation of the Arabic." Trans. Michael Green. Moss, ed. 29.

Rozanov, Vasilii. *Liudi lunnogo sveta: Metafizika khristianstva. [People of the Moonlight: The Metaphysics of Christianity.]* St. Petersburg: A.S. Suvorin-Novoe Vremia, 1913. Reprint, Moscow: Druzhba Narodov, 1990. Print.

Shenin, Aleksandr. "Pokhozhdeniia pasha." ["The Passage of the Page."] *Zanaveshennye kartinki. Antologiia russkoi erotiki. [Unveiled Pictures. An Anthology of Russian Erotica.]* Ed. V. Sazhin. St. Petersburg: Amfora, 2002. 149–80. Print.

Tolstoy, Leo. "Pages from Tolstoy's Diaries." Trans. Kevin Moss. Moss, ed. 47.

Tyulenev, Sergey. "Translation as Smuggling." *Thinking through Translation with Metaphors.* Ed. James St. Andre. Manchester: St. Jerome, 2010. 241–74. Print.

Zolotonosov, Mikhail. "Kniga o 'golubom Peterburge' kak fenomen sovremennoi kul'tury." [A Book on "Gay Petersburg" as a Phenomenon of Contemporary Culture.] Novyi mir 5 (1999): 185–91. Print.

24

Spanish Literature in the Long Twentieth Century, 1898–2007

GEMA PÉREZ-SÁNCHEZ

Periods of flourishing and repression of lesbian and gay literature in Spain during the long twentieth century are intimately tied to the country's significant political upheavals and the parallel ebbs and flows between open public discussion and severe censorship of all expressions of sexual desire, but particularly of same-sex sexual practices. In just one century, Spain's political structure moved from the "non-competitive oligarchical monarchy" (Álvarez Junco 71) of King Alfonso XIII of Bourbon (1886–1931) – which included a brief, failed experiment with the "soft" dictatorship of General Miguel Primo de Rivera (1923–30) – to a democratically elected republic (1931–36), through a brutal civil war (1936–39) that led to Francisco Franco's forty-year right-wing dictatorship (1939–75). After much compromise from all political sides, the 1978 democratic constitution paved the way toward an initially fragile yet finally stable parliamentary monarchy (1978–). However, it did not remove the criminalization of homosexuals from the feared 1970 *Ley de Peligrosidad y Rehabilitación Social* (*Law of Social Dangerousness and Rehabilitation*) until 1978 nor the penalties for "public scandal" until 1989, well into the early democracy. Spain's gay and lesbian political journey from timid expression to repression to full legal recognition culminated in 2005, when the country became one of the first nations in the world to legalize same-sex marriage. Further LGBTQ legal rights were achieved in 2007 when *Law 3/2007* allowed transgender citizens to change their gender assignation in the national registry without needing to undergo sex-reassignment surgery and when *Law 52/2007* – *Law by which the Rights of Those Who Suffered Persecution or Violence during the Civil War and the Dictatorship Are Recognized and Expanded* (better known as "Law of Historical Memory") – granted elderly homosexuals who had been imprisoned under the Law of Social Dangerousness and Rehabilitation compensation for their suffering.

Despite these recent milestones, the history of lesbian and gay literature in Spain has not simply followed a linear, teleological progression from pure censorship to open expression. During the early decades of the twentieth century up to the Civil War, there was a recognizable and fairly open gay male cultural milieu that produced popular, marketable works as well as the writings of high literary quality for which the period is known as the Silver Age. However, under Franco's dictatorship, strict censorship of the press, mass media, theatre, and literature drove explicitly homosexual themes underground, as gays and lesbians themselves (or all those accused of being gay or lesbian, regardless of orientation) were actively persecuted as "dangerous subjects" under the aforementioned 1970 law. This period of persecution eased slightly in the late 1960s and early 1970s, facilitating the emergence of the more daring works of elite, bourgeois Catalonian writers and others associated with the *gauche divine* ("the divine left") – such as the Moix siblings (Ana María [1947–] and Terenci [1942–2003]), Jaime Gil de Biedma (1929–90), Uruguayan nationalized Spanish Cristina Peri Rossi (1941–), and self-exiled writer Juan Goytisolo (1931–). These authors paved the way for the younger writers of the democracy.

Another important characteristic of Spanish culture to keep in mind is the profound impact that the nation's primary identity as a Catholic country had on it – and its queer culture – until the early years of the democracy. Whether through reverent, angry, playful, or parodic engagement with Catholic mores, censorship, imagery, and pageantry, many prominent Spanish lesbian and gay authors have defined their works through, against, or with their backs deliberately to the Church, particularly during the Francoist dictatorship and the transition to democracy. The Church's and fascism's legacy of strict gender roles and segregation of the sexes had a profound impact on how all Spanish authors chose to articulate same-sex eroticism and sexuality in their works. For example, Federico García Lorca (1898–1936) embraced the iconography and rituals of the Church in many of his works, such as his overtly homoerotic play *El Público* (*The Audience* [ca. 1930–36]), which includes the character of the crucified *desnudo rojo* ("red nude"), or his most popular collection of poetry, *Romancero Gitano* (*Gypsy Ballads*), where a homoerotic gaze is obviously present in poems dedicated to Saint Michael and Saint Gabriel (*Primer romancero gitano* 143–44). In contemporary works, Eduardo Mendicutti's (1948–) camp novel *Yo no tengo la culpa de haber nacido tan sexy* (*It's Not My Fault that I Was Born So Sexy* [1997]) radically queers the mystical poetic tradition of San Juan de la Cruz and Santa Teresa de Jesús. Likewise, postwar Spanish literature often depicts intense homosocial and occasionally homoerotic bonding in segregated gendered spaces as in Carmen Laforet's (1921–2004) extremely successful bildungsroman *Nada* (*Nothing* [1945]).

Spain's ever-present Catholicism renders the country's LGBTQ literatures different from their Anglo-Saxon and Northern European counterparts. David William Foster has argued that the Church's repression of any form of sexuality that did not conform to the accepted modes of sexual expression – that is, "chastity and marital procreative sex" – had a paradoxical effect: "In Spain, where Catholicism was linked with heterosexuality to a degree it has been in no other country, anti-Catholicism, rebellion, and opposition to authority became similarly linked to homosexuality. After all, if the Catholic Church was against homosexuality, then ... [c]hurch opposition was a powerful endorsement" (1). Hence, the equation of strict heteronormativity with the Church and Francoism has meant that ostensibly heterosexual writers with a politically dissident and anticlerical agenda have chosen on occasion to address homosocial, homosexual, or queer themes in their works. Their treatment of these themes ranges from outright virulent homophobia – as in the work of Pío Baroja (1872–1956) – to complex explorations of homoeroticism, bisexuality, and same-sex sexual desire. For women, what Adrienne Rich terms "the lesbian continuum" can be seen in the case of some works by late-dictatorship, early-democracy feminist writers Carme Riera (1948–), Marina Mayoral (1942–), and Montserrat Roig (1946–91), and, most recently, in the explicitly queer novel *Beatriz y los cuerpos celestes* (*Beatriz and the Heavenly Bodies* [1998]) by Lucía Etxebarria (1966–), which is arguably an explicit, updated retelling of Laforet's *Nada*.[1]

However, the Church and Falangist modes of homoerotism are not the only axes in relation to which gay and lesbian writers produced their works. Alberto Mira has rightly argued that foreign literary influences have marked the production of most gay male Spanish writers. In particular, Oscar Wilde's dandyism, André Gide's homophile vision, and Jean Genet's celebration of criminality have found their correlatives in the work of several Spanish authors, underscoring the cosmopolitanism of Spanish gay writing. Other major coordinates in the development of lesbian and gay Iberian literatures include the ongoing tensions between historical nationalisms (those of Catalonia, the Basque Country, and Galicia, especially, but also of Andalucía and other areas of the nation) and the centralist political privileges that have sought to suppress the diversity of languages spoken in the Iberian Peninsula; the ghosts of postcolonial relations with former Spanish colonies – especially Morocco, Equatorial Guinea, and Latin America – and the influx of new economic immigrants from other parts of the world from the 1990s on, which have led to the emergence of a "literature of immigration" that occasionally includes gay and lesbian themes (almost always tinged with homophobia);

and, finally, the current intense focus of some writers born after the 1950s on recovering the suppressed historical memory of those who lost the Spanish Civil War, were persecuted under Francoism, or contributed to the transition to democracy. All of these axes are variously present in contemporary lesbian and gay Iberian literature.[2] In fact, much of Spain's canonical literature in the long twentieth century has been authored by gays, lesbians, bisexuals, and queers.

Finally, medical, psychological, and endocrinological discourses about gender and sexuality have also influenced Spanish gay and lesbian literary production, especially in the first two-thirds of the century. Mira posits that the formation of particular gay male discursive practices in Spain responds to the emergence in medical and psychological discourses of three distinctive stereotypes of the homosexual: the criminal, the unnatural invert, and the psychologically pathological subject (62). Each of these negative stereotypes corresponds with three literary tendencies or discursive practices, sometimes coexistent in the same author and present throughout the century:

> In the face of the identification between homosexual and criminal we find the decadent-*maudit* model (which values marginality positively); in the face of the tradition that presents the homosexual as an invert and a betrayer of nature emerges the camp model (which questions the essentialism of gender stereotypes); and the homophile model tries to respond to the pressures of the pathologizing gaze. (62)

Besides these three tendencies in gay male Spanish letters, Mira argues that Spain's attitude toward homosexuality follows the global pseudo-scientific, pathologizing, sexological trends also observed in Germany, France, and the Anglo-American world (22). Hence, in spite of the aura of exceptionalism vis-à-vis the rest of Europe that Francisco Franco's dictatorship confers on Spain – as the only post–World War II Western European country where fascism won – the homophobic attitudes in Spain throughout the long twentieth century have very much followed those of other Western nations but were accentuated during the two dictatorships (de Rivera's and Franco's).

In the less repressive moments of the Silver Age and since democracy, one finds an important industry of popular gay and lesbian best-selling authors who write specifically for an LGBTQ audience with the aim of empowering the community through positive narratives of self-affirmation and gay pride. During the early twentieth century, numerous periodical magazines published erotic novellas for mass consumption (see Zubiaurre) in which gay and lesbian characters are on occasion allowed agency, social success, and happiness, at the same time that these characters (both male and female) often react to or conform to the pathologizing discourses about homosexuality of their time. Since the 1990s, mass LGBTQ literature for easy consumption (coming-out narratives as well as detective, mystery, thriller, erotic, and pornographic genre fiction) has proliferated because of the tireless editorial labor of two important gay and lesbian presses: Egales and Odisea. These presses are both supported by brick-and-mortar bookstores in Madrid – Berkana (lesbian-owned) and A Different Life (gay-owned). Also, several literary awards have been created specifically for LGBTQ works, such as Premio Odisea, or, for feminist women writers, the Premio Femenino Singular, by mainstream Catalonian press, Lumen, helmed until her death by bisexual writer Esther Tusquets (1936–2012).

"La Edad de Plata": 1898–1936

The period before the Civil War was marked by a flourishing literary culture so remarkable that critics call it *La Edad de Plata* (the Silver Age), echoing the famed early modern literary apogee of the sixteenth and seventeenth centuries, *La Edad de Oro* (the Golden Age) of Cervantes's *El Quijote*. Although it is one of the most fruitful, diverse, and prolific periods of Spanish literary history, and numerous free-thinking, liberal, secular intellectuals flourished during it, subsequent Francoist literary historiography strongly curtailed rigorous study of this period, leading to oversimplified, sanitized notions of its contributions. Among the most suppressed accomplishments of this period are those of gay and lesbian culture and thought, which must have been accepted "in bohemian environments and artistic and intellectual circles," if one is to judge by the increased presence of homosexuality in literature (Simonis Sampedro 249). Fortunately, through several recent scholarly efforts, a more accurate reflection of what gay and lesbian culture might have really been like in that period has emerged.

The Silver Age encompasses the important literary movements of modernism (both *modernismo* proper and the so-called Generation of '98) and the avant-garde. It also features a small generation of writers and thinkers sometimes called the Generation of 1914, which includes Nobel Prize-winning poet Juan Ramón Jiménez (1881–1958), humorist Ramón Gómez de la Serna (1888–1963), and philosopher José Ortega y Gassett (1883–1955), all of whom published about homosexuality, albeit not always in a positive light (see Mira; Celaya Carrillo; and Foster). The avant-garde is represented both by the historical vanguard writers *sensu proprio* who participated in such poetic movements as *ultraísmo*, *creacionismo*, surrealism, or expressionism, and by the most important group of poets in modern Spanish literature: the Generation of 1927, which included famous gay poets Lorca, Vicente Aleixandre (1898–1984), and Luis Cernuda (1902–63), as well as other lesser-known gay poets and writers suspected of being at the very least "queer," such as Pedro Salinas (1891–1951).

Notable among the historical avant-garde poets is the recently rediscovered Lucía Sánchez Saornil (1895–1970), anarchist lesbian feminist and the only *ultraísta* woman in that vanguard group, whose early works are influenced by *modernista* poets Rubén Darío (1867–1916), Jiménez, and Manuel Machado (1874–1947) and whose later works dramatically shifted to political feminism and anarchy (such as those compiled in *Romancero de mujeres libres* [*Free Women's Ballads* (1937), collected in *Poesía*]). However, her poems from her *ultraísta* period (1919–37) have been the most anthologized.[3] In addition to her poetic activities, she cofounded *Mujer feminista*, a subgroup of the anarchist labor union CNT (Confederación Nacional de Trabajadores [National Workers' Confederation]), and lived with her long-term partner, América Barroso, from 1937 until her death. Her accomplishments, despite her humble class origins, bespeak both her personal courage and the degree of freedom that women had achieved prior to the Civil War.

In spite of her courageous life, Sánchez Saornil had to use the male pseudonym Luciano de San Saor to have her early poetry taken seriously by the male literary establishment. The pseudonym allowed her to compose overtly erotic poems directed to a female beloved (Celma Valero 268), for example, in "Crepúsculo sensual" ("Sensual Twilight"): "roses / throbbed between my open fingers / and it was a throbbing / of warm flesh, / quivering and fragrant flesh. / – Glorious contact / that broke the damn of sweet desires. – / And in such divine / explosion of restlessness / my soul became flesh, too . . ." (Sánchez Saornil 68). Recent critical analyses have emphasized those traits in her *modernista* and *ultraísta* poetry that depart from the traditional conventions of these two movements and suggest a feminist consciousness. When she deploys the dual female images prevalent in male poetic works of the *femme fatale* and the virginal fiancée, Sánchez Saornil critiques male poets for inventing the first stereotype and laments the sexism in the second stereotype for robbing young women of freedom by implying that virgins must wait for the "right" man (Celma Valero 266–70).

The Silver Age is arguably dominated by the group of remarkably talented poets of the Generation of 1927, which included three of the most prominent homosexual writers of the century: Lorca, Cernuda, and closeted Aleixandre (Nobel Prize winner 1977), in addition to the lesser-known Emilio Prados

(1899–1962) – Lorca's lover at one point. The name of the generation in itself is significant for gay and lesbian literary history in that this group of poets gathered to celebrate the tercentenary of the death of baroque poet Luis de Góngora y Argote (1561–1627), who had been accused by his contemporaries of being a sodomite. In fact, the Generation of 1927 was responsible for recovering the work of Góngora and elevating him to the status of mandatory reference both for avant-garde poets and homosexual writers from then on. In this sense, Góngora became a gay literary icon similar to Wilde, Gide, and Genet.

Drama and prose also flourished in this period, starting with the creation of *esperpentos* (a form of the grotesque) by decadent, modernist, heterosexual writer Ramón del Valle-Inclán (1866–1936), who included several queer characters in his works, most notably the protagonist of his *Sonatas* series of novels, the bisexual Marqués de Bradomín, who searches for both kinds of love, "Hebe's and Ganymede's" in his *Sonata de estío* (1903). However, besides the Marquis, most of Valle-Inclán's gay characters are homophobically represented with the aim of satirizing or denigrating them (Oropesa 172). Another significant gay playwright of the period, Nobel Prize-winner Jacinto Benavente (1866–1954), wrote successful bourgeois comedies of manners, and although he publicly maintained an obstinate silence concerning the open secret of his homosexual liaisons with younger men, he dared to publish a series of homoerotic poems and a short story about man-boy love, "Ganímedes" ("Ganymede" [1938]; Mira 70–71). He also subtly addressed homoerotic themes in some of his plays.

Yet the most important gay figure of this period is undoubtedly Andalusian Federico García Lorca – prolific poet, commercially successful playwright, and early martyr for the Republic who was executed in Granada at the beginning of the Civil War by local Falangists and buried in an unidentified mass grave. The recent interest in recovering the historical memory of the Civil War has created a frenzied effort to locate his burial site – an effort repeatedly curtailed by his surviving family members, who have been accused of wanting to keep him in the closet or of having already unburied his body and relocated it to a grave only known to the family. Lorca's reportedly unconsummated yet emotionally passionate relationship with surrealist painter Salvador Dalí (1904–89) has made him a gay icon the world over. Lorca famously confronted, in his "Ode to Walt Whitman" (1933), two ways of being gay: "that of the purist Whitman [and] that of the army of urban and defiled *maricas* [faggots]" (Walsh 263). Thus, Whitman is a "lovely old man" with "thighs as pure as Apollo's" who is an "[e]nemy of the satyr, / enemy of the vine, / and lover of bodies beneath rough cloth" (*Collected* 731). Whitman's venerable example leads the poetic speaker to claim that he does not raise his voice against "the little boy who writes / [his name as a girl's name] on his pillow, / nor against the boy who dresses as a bride / in the darkness of the wardrobe, / nor against the solitary men in casinos / who drink prostitution's water with revulsion, / nor against the men ... / who love other men and burn their lips in silence" (735). Instead, the poet rants "against you, urban faggots, ... / Always against you, who give boys / drops of foul death with bitter poison ... / Let the confused, the pure, / the classical, the celebrated, the supplicants / close the doors of the bacchanal to you" (735–37). Against some homophobic readings of this important poem, John Walsh argues that Lorca lays out a complex "ethic of homosexualities that goes beyond these divisions and layers or boundaries, that creates a disposition that is not constrained in some vertical mold and is ultimately more tolerant" than it may appear after reading the fragmented version of the poem that was released to the general public in 1934 (263).

Lorca's allusions and open representations of homosexual desire are too many to mention here (see Walsh; Mira; Gibson; Sahuquillo), but it is important to remember that his most overtly gay works – the play *El público* (*The Audience*) and the poetic collections, *El divan del Tamarit* (*The Tamarit Divan*) and the *Sonetos del amor oscuro* (*Sonnets of Dark Love*) – were published posthumously during the democratic years because under the dictatorship, Lorca's works were banned until the 1950s and censored until Franco died. In most of Lorca's works, a dense web of poetic images constructs a sometimes cryptic, yet definite universe of homoerotic desire. For example, images of that which is bitter ("lo amargo" in Spanish) and its associated semantic field abound in his poetry (for example, "Dialogue of Amargo" [*Collected* 159–65] or "Ghazal VI of the Bitter Root" [779]) and might be read as variations of the popular saying that homosexuals are "of the bitter peel/shell" ("de la cáscara amarga"; Sahuquillo 132–35). In fact, other Generation of 1927 gay poets, such as Cernuda and Prados, share this imagery that pits "bitterness" against "purity" (134). Ángel Sahuquillo argues that Death is the "underlying secret nexus among the Lorquian symbols of *sailors, the sea, that which is bitter*, and *The Bitter Man* [or *Amargo* as a character]" and sees death "as a symbol of the homosexual act" (135). In *El público*, a brilliant play that performs Lorca's poetics of drama, the "teatro bajo la arena" (theatre under the sand) and the "teatro al aire libre" (theatre in the open air) are pitted against each other as symbols, respectively, of an avant-garde theatrical practice in which, for example, Romeo and Juliet could be played by two men who openly and happily confess their love for each other, and of the conventional, bourgeois, vanilla theatre of playwrights such as Benavente. Addressing issues such as same-sex sadomasochistic love, women's sexual liberation, and the psychologically violent social constraints of "buen gusto" (good taste), *El público* emerges, in spite of its incomplete status, as Lorca's masterpiece.[4]

Besides the poetic giants of the avant-garde and Generation of 1927, the Silver Age witnessed a range of marketable, explicit works such as those by Álvaro Retana (1890–1970), Antonio de Hoyos y Vinent (1885–1940), and Pedro de Répide (1882–1947), and a rapid proliferation of inexpensive, serialized publications that brought popular literary genres – such as the erotic (*sicalíptica*), ghost (*espiritista*), socialist, anticlerical, and mystery novels, among many others – to the mass populace crowding urban centers. Specifically, the daring genre of *sicalipsis*, which would occasionally flirt with the pornographic, would open up a remarkable space for some authors to publish openly gay and lesbian erotic writings, works that became surprisingly popular even among mainstream readers and that give us a glimpse of how gay male urban culture might have really been (happy, thriving) in contrast to the homophobic representations of it as perverse, damned, sad, and criminal (Mira 61). For example, Álvaro Retana's *Las "locas" de postín* (*Elegant Queens* [1919]) and *A Sodoma en tren botijo* (*To Sodoma in a Hick Train* [1933]), recently edited and reissued by contemporary gay writer Luis Antonio de Villena (1951–), are explicit, deliciously camp, and celebratory of gay male life at the same time that the writer cannot avoid representing homosexuals according to the prevalent psychoanalytic and medical theories of the time. Nonetheless, this period also witnessed the first apologia of homosexuality published in Spain, *Homosexualismo creador* (*Creative Homosexualism* [1931]), by Uruguayan diplomat Alberto Nin Frías (1878–1937), which argued for a connection between homosexuality and genius (Mira 85). Men wrote not only about gay male relationships; heterosexual, progressive writer Gómez de la Serna penned *La quinta de Palmyra* (*The Country House of Palmyra* [1923]), where he engages in a "masculine exaltation of lesbianism not only as a sexual option, but as an expression of freedom, of being able to choose one's object of desire" (Castrejón 21).

In addition to the many men, gay and straight, who produced erotic novellas, women also wrote of women's sexual desire in general and female same-sex desire in particular, although almost always within the constraints of a liberal feminist discourse that had painted itself into a corner by using the political and discursive strategy of women's supposed purity as "essentially" asexual mothers (Celaya 50). In this context, the works of notable heterosexual feminist writer Carmen de Burgos (aka "Colombine") (1867–1932) are often ambiguous and contradictory. Although Burgos reportedly socialized with openly gay aristocratic writer Antonio Hoyos y Vinent and his lesbian cousin, Gloria Laguna (Rioyo, qtd. in Celaya 55), and maintained for years a passionate sexual relationship with notorious erotomaniac Gómez de la Serna, she also publicly decried erotic literature, writers, and their female readers (Celaya 49–50). A complex literary and ideological figure (she was one of the first female war correspondents, covering the Spanish-Moroccan War), she published *Ellas y ellos o ellos y ellas* (*Shes and Hes or Hes and Shes* [1916]), an observer's somewhat admiring description of high-society lesbians and gay men in a small, cosmopolitan Madrilenian social group.

Most notably, Ángeles Vicente's (1878–?) erotic novella *Zezé* (1909) is truly a gem of lesbian, feminist eroticism, now widely recognized as the first novel written by a Spanish woman that depicts an explicitly lesbian affair. On a voyage from Argentina to Spain, a cabaret performer, Zezé, narrates her life story to another woman, a writer, openly admitting to sexual liaisons with men and women alike. In addition to describing the protagonist's "sexual perversions," *Zezé* displays a "textual perversion," espousing instead of conventional turn-of-the-century sexual mores a form of feminism that sees lesbian sexuality as an innate tendency in women and encourages the formation of homoerotic bonds between women. Ultimately, the novel seals a feminist, homosocial and, at many points, homoerotic pact between the narrator and Zezé.

The Civil War (1936–1939) and Franco's Dictatorship (1936–1975)

The ideologically diverse and culturally rich Silver Age was promptly curtailed by armed conflict in 1936. During the Civil War, on the Republican side, women acquired many rights and engaged in endeavors previously considered masculine, while men fought at the front. Homosexuality, although still frowned on, particularly among the Communist Party ranks, was acknowledged and permitted. Franco's long dictatorship repressed nonnormative sexualities and halted all gender experimentation. As Mira documents, the most visible homosexual writers from the beginning of the century disappeared rapidly: Hoyos died in jail; Retana was incarcerated several times after the war; Lorca was assassinated in 1936; many more writers (most notably Juan Gil-Albert [1904–93], Cernuda, Répide) exiled themselves; and only Aleixandre and Benavente, both deeply closeted, managed to stay in Spain under Francoism, while Sánchez Saornil and her partner lay low in a small Valencian village (295). Her case highlights how painful and dangerous it must have been for

Republican women and lesbians to live in Spain under the repressive fascist dictatorship.

Insults, silencing, and repression of homosexual experiences marked the existence of gays and lesbians under Francoism. Gay men had to contend with a rabidly homophobic daily discourse. Many critics have documented in great detail the obsession that Francoism had with persecuting homosexuality. Under Franco, writers engaging in homosexual expression were left with only few choices: to court scandal while risking incarceration, to remain in a closeted ghetto (a modality chosen by right-wing gays), to embrace the confines of damaging homophobic stereotypes, or to militate, underground, in left-wing organizations.[5] In the disciplining of homosexual expression, the Church and the psychiatric establishment played key roles and often colluded with each other. Confessions obtained under the cover of the Church's ostensibly confidential sacrament of confession resulted in psychiatric intervention that could lead to internment and electroshock therapies.[6] Internalized homophobia was particularly prevalent in this period, to the extent that even gay writers polarized their representations between stereotypes of the "good" and the "bad" homosexual (Mira 305).

As a recent corrective to this silencing, contemporary writers of historical fiction have recovered in their novels the stories of gay and lesbian survival during and after the war. Furthermore, journalistic writers have also collected the testimonials of gay and lesbian survivors of Francoist persecution in moving volumes. For example, the *Pastora* (the Shepherdess), a Catalonian intersex *maquis* guerrilla fighter, has recently been celebrated in the 2011 Nadal Prize-winning novel, *Donde nadie te encuentre* (*Where No One Can Find You*) by Alicia Giménez Bartlett (1951–), while feminist Madrilenian writer Almudena Grandes (1960–) – author of the popular erotic novel *Las edades de Lulú* (*The Ages of Lulu* [1989]), which includes few lesbian episodes – gives an homage to the quiet, brave lives of anonymous lesbians under Francoism in her monumental work of recovery of historical memories and atrocities of the Civil War, *El corazón helado* (*The Frozen Heart* [2007]). Arturo Arnalte's *Redada de violetas* (*Raiding Queers* [2003]) and Fernando Olmeda's *El látigo y la pluma* (*The Whip and the Swish/Pen* [2004]) collect harrowing testimonials of the experiences of gays and lesbians under Francoism and its prisons.

Paradoxically, the strict censorship laws of the Franco regime challenged the best dissident Spanish writers to develop within a strictly realistic style of narrative a complex system of silences and "unsayings" (heavily inflected by the rhetorical figure of litotes) and to privilege allegorical modes of representation that allowed them to speak the unspeakable and to name the unnamable, whether concerning the repression of dissidents, the hunger suffered by the majority of the population during the 1940s and early 1950s ("los años del hambre"; "the years of hunger"), the oppression of women, or the repression of same-sex desire and eroticism. Thus, alert critics must attend to the clever rhetorical techniques that some writers deployed to negotiate censorship and homophobic insult. Ana María Moix's first novel, *Julia* (1970), deploys a form of "unsaying" (*no decir* in opposition to *callar*, or to remain silent) precisely to name the love that dares not speak its name. Her juggling of voicelessness and muted pointing was a necessity at a time when, as Alfredo Martínez-Expósito reminds us, Francoist censorship laws explicitly forbade the defense of homosexuality (*Escrituras* 155). Moix represents a young woman who descends into suicidal despair because her upper-class Catalonian family cannot recognize that she had been molested and possibly raped as a child by a family friend and because they will not accept her and her brother's homosexuality. Although *Julia* is a powerful indictment of homophobia and sexism, the narrative is also suffocating and full of despair; in this sense, perhaps it is the perfect representation of how gays and lesbians felt under the dictatorship.

If gayness was negatively – yet complexly – represented in these works, lesbianism manifested itself in highly cryptic, heavily encoded narratives by both heterosexual and lesbian writers that required a particular type of *lector entendido* (or "knowing" reader – one who is "family") to decode them (Pérez-Sánchez, *Queer* 35–60). A good example is Laforet's *Nada*. This canonical, realist, postwar novel, winner of the prestigious Nadal Prize, depicts a first-person narrator-observer, Andrea, whose strong homosocial and homoerotic bonding with her higher-class friend Ena – a relationship that most critics insist on interpreting as a nonsexual young adult friendship – can also be read as a lesbian fascination (Amago; Zaviezo).

The towering figure of this period is the dissident, self-exiled writer Juan Goytisolo (1931–). A devotee and friend of Genet, Goytisolo's collected memoirs, *Coto Vedado* (*Forbidden Territory* [1985]) and *En los reinos de Taifa* (*Realms of Strife* [1986]), document his long, painful coming-out process and the shameful pederasty of his grandfather. Goytisolo's most subversive literary achievements in the context of heterosexist Francoist Spain include confessing in his memoirs that his homosexual desire is directed toward rough, hyper-virile, vaguely criminal, Orientalized men, and fictionalizing this desire through the figure of the mythical traitor Count Julián, the medieval Christian governor of Ceuta who supposedly allowed the "invasion" of Spain through the Strait by the Berber, Muslim forces of Tariq ibn Ziyad in 711. Using his signature second-person point of view, Goytisolo describes his first realization of the type of marginal man he desires:

> Raimundo is of average height, athletic build, with muscular legs and arms, unkempt dark brown hair standing on end, hairy-chested, a wild mustache. His face is tough but energetic: his sparkling dark eyes, the whole of his character and physique, radiate powerful animal magnetism. Along with these physical features ... [he] enjoys others that you will eventually learn to discern in the natives of that Sotadic Zone described by Sir Richard Burton, the frontiers of which extend from Tangier to Pakistan: a degree of coarseness in appearance not without charm; instinctive warmth and availability; a proud rejection of the ways and means that open the doors to social climbing in the industrialized countries.... [He] represents absolute marginality.
>
> (*Forbidden* 152–53)

Following Genet's model of criminality and *mauditism*, Goytisolo develops a well-known – yet not unproblematic – model of subversive vindication of homosexual desire and solidarity with Arab, Berber, Palestinian, and Muslim political causes and cultural richness. Thus, in Goytisolo's most celebrated novel of this period, *Don Julián* (*Count Julian* [1970; revised and retitled in 2004]), a nameless Spanish expatriate living in 1960s, post-Spanish Protectorate Morocco narrates – from a split second-person point of view, in several concentric psychological downward spiraling circles – his labyrinthine meanderings through Tangiers. The narrator fantastically embraces the identity of demonized traitor Don Julián – whom he romantically links to a hyper-virile Moroccan man named Tariq, who metamorphoses into the homonymous eighth-century Berber commander – and embarks in a delirious psychological self-doubling, culminating in a series of disturbing sodomitical rapes of himself in the guise of the child Alvarito, "son" of Isabella the Catholic Queen of Spain.

From the Transition to Democracy and *Cambio* (1975–1982) to the Present

Franco died on November 20, 1975, at which point negotiations to avoid bloodshed in transitioning to a democratic regime started. With numerous concessions from the formerly clandestine socialist (PSOE) and communist (PCE) political parties and the willingness among all political persuasions to enter into what has been variously termed "the pact of silence" or "pact of oblivion" – a deliberate amnesia of the atrocities committed by the Francoist side during and after the Civil War in order to avoid bloodshed again – the transition to democracy, via the approval of the 1978 constitution, began in earnest. The transition culminated in the PSOE (Partido Socialista Obrero Español) winning the 1982 elections (the third elections of the democracy) by a landslide, under the banner of "el cambio" – that is, a political change ushered by a younger, more hopeful, and modernized political class. Following the derogation of censorship laws with the passing of the constitution, these years saw three sexual cultural phenomena of importance. The first was the short-lived and eminently heterosexist *destape* porno craze: magazines prominently displayed nude women on their front pages and centerfolds; erotic and pornographic films with "serious" actors proliferated; and frank discussions of sexuality abounded as a demonstration of the newly acquired freedoms of expression and the press. Second, the eagerly awaited derogation in 1978 of the articles in the *Law of Social Dangerousness and Rehabilitation* persecuting homosexuals gave way to a sizeable publication boom of books and films about homosexuality (Martínez-Expósito, *Escrituras* 153–54). Finally, the longer-lasting, more significant, and culturally productive *movida madrileña* – an urban, youth-oriented move to take back the streets after the almost forty years of Francoist repression – emerged in Madrid thanks to the activities of very creative, working-class transgender and gay men from the provinces. Among them, the crucial figure of gay filmmaker Pedro Almodóvar would emerge, as well as many other gay and lesbian visual artists, musicians, and writers.

During this period of transition and expanding cultural possibilities, some of the submerged trends of gay literature from the Silver Age resurfaced. The camp aesthetic that had been so prevalent in Silver Age popular gay writers reemerges with force in the writings of Catalonian Terenci Moix. Moix represents a second phase in the evolution of camp in Spain, one that changes the perspective from which it is enunciated and loses its provocative force, but keeps other elements essential to camp discourse, such as heightened emotions reaching melodramatic levels, representing gender as a performative role, and the affective identification with femininity (Mira 339). Whereas in film, camp and kitsch would be wildly and widely celebrated by Almodóvar, in literature Moix became the iconic gay camp writer and Hollywood cinephile of the last years of Francoism and the transition to democracy, with works such as *El día que murió Marilyn* (*The Day that Marilyn Died* [1984]), *No digas que fue un sueño* (*Don't Say It Was a Dream* [1986]), and, in Catalan, *La caiguda del imperi sodomita i altres contes* (*The Fall of the Sodomite Empire and Other Stories* [1988]), among many others (see Mira 338–49). Moix and Goytisolo belonged to the Catalonian progressive bourgeoisie, but they both rejected and criticized it. In addition, they projected in their writings an idealized, Orientalized vision of Middle Eastern and Maghrebian culture (in the case of Moix, historically removed) as a paradise of male homoeroticism. Both tendencies are highly problematic from a contemporary anti-Orientalizing perspective, although as of yet no other contemporary Spanish gay male writer has emerged to challenge that tendency.

In these early years of the transition the homophile tradition finds its best, yet perhaps most misunderstood, representative in the works of Valencian poet Juan Gil-Albert. A younger member of the Silver Age Generation of 1927 who exiled himself to Mexico after the war, he nevertheless was forced to return to Spain for family reasons in 1947 (Mira 381). As in the case of Aleixandre, Benavente, and Sánchez Saornil, Gil-Albert – who prior to the war was a well-known and somewhat flamboyantly elegant dandy – had to remain silent and keep a discreet lifestyle upon his return to Spain. Like Sánchez Saornil, however, he kept writing for himself and produced many manuscripts that remained unpublished until the dictator died. His most relevant book, *Heraclés: sobre una manera de ser* (*Heracles: About a Way of Being*) – a treatise on homosexuality – had been written in 1955, but was not published until 1975. The asynchronous publication of his works affected their reception, as "the philosophical classicism of Gil-Albert did not mesh well with the new high-sounding vocabulary of historical materialism, Lacan, and Freudian-Marxism" (Mira 381) typical of the years of the transition to democracy. Nonetheless, the work of this sophisticated writer of sublime poetic language merits reconsidering. Most significantly, during the last years of Francoism until his death, Gil-Albert befriended and mentored important younger gay writers, such as poet Jaime Gil de Biedma (1929–90) and Luis Antonio de Villena (1951–), who is still one of Spain's most important contemporary gay voices, winning many national literary awards, including the 1981 National Critics Poetry Award, and who wrote a biography of Gil-Albert.[7]

Although Goytisolo is widely acknowledged as the heir of Genet's antisocial tradition, one might extend the decadent/*maudit* trend to the most recent Generation X writers, who often depict the urban youth world of hard drugs, violence, punk rock, and social alienation, and include queer protagonists in their narratives as a matter of course – albeit not always in the best light. This is the case in the defining work of this generation, *Historias del Kronen* (*Stories from Kronen* [1994]), by José Ángel Mañas (1971–), several novels by Etxebarria, and Juan Bonilla's (1966–) *Los príncipes nubios* (*The Nubian Prince* [2003]) – a cynical, neopicaresque representation of the world of irregular immigration and prostitution where the sexually ambiguous narrator-protagonist is made to pay for his criminal, sexual exploitation of sub-Saharan immigrants through a brutal anal rape. This generation of mainstream writers, although representing many queer characters in their works and thus normalizing homosexuality, often reinscribe homophobic assumptions or use homosexuality as a synecdoche for a general social malaise resulting from Spain's participation in globalization and neoliberalism.

The list of gay writers from the transition and beyond who developed prolific careers and are still active is too extensive to do it justice in this chapter. It includes members of the Royal Academy of Language (Real Academia Española), such as novelist and poet Álvaro Pombo (1939–). Pombo's early works represented characters suffering from internalized homophobia and guilt who tried to negotiate their desires and their Catholic faith. These works garnered him severe criticism from gay activists during the transition.[8] From the 1990s on, however, his ethics and literary approach changed to a more positive representation and self-acceptance of homosexuality. Nevertheless, he has remained critical of normalization and the domestication of gay culture through consumerism. His novel *Contra natura* (2005) proposes two kinds of homosexuals: those who see love "as entertainment" and those who take love "seriously [making] their personal relations their ultimate goal" ("Álvaro Pombo" n.pag.). Other important gay writers of the transition include aesthete, Orientalist poet, essayist, and novelist Antonio Gala (1930–); Valencian Lluís Fernàndez (1945–) author of the camp romp *L'anarquista nu* (*The Naked Anarchist* [1978]); and Alberto Cardín (1948–92), a remarkable anthropologist, writer, and activist, author of the sex-positive *Detrás por delante* (*Behind from the Front* [1986]), whom Mira hails as the most important gay intellectual in Spain in the 1970s (467).

Among the women writers who addressed female homoeroticism and lesbianism during the years of the transition, three emerge as most significant (in addition to Ana María Moix): Carme Riera, Esther Tusquets, and Cristina Peri Rossi. Writing in *mallorquín*, the Balearic dialect of Catalan, literature professor Riera wrote an affecting short story, "Te deix, amor, la mar com a penyora" ("I Leave You, My Love, the Sea as a Token" [1975]), in which she plays with the gender ambiguity of pronouns in Catalan and the heterosexist assumptions of readers to unfold a subtle tale of lost love between two women. The plot hinges on a young narrator's letter to a former lover (her professor), but the gender of the narrator is not revealed until the last paragraph (see Epps). This now-classic work of Spanish lesbian literature has received significant academic attention because of its sophisticated narrative technique (Simonis Sampedro 261). Riera's feminism can be seen in this short story's denunciation of the prejudices that prevent lesbians from living their lives openly, but it remains a representation of lesbian love as tragic and impossible.

In this feminist vein, but with a much clearer denunciation of the stress that a heterosexist society places on lesbian relations, emerges Tusquets's famous trilogy of novels *El mismo mar de todos los veranos* (*The Same Sea as Every Summer* [1978]), *El amor es un juego solitario* (*Love Is a Solitary Game* [1979]), and *Varada tras el último naufragio* (*Stranded* [1980]). With a baroque, syntactically challenging Spanish prose, Tusquets tells with variations and changes in perspective the failed love relationship between a professor (Elia) and her student (Clara) – a relationship triangulated by Elia's husband. This trilogy of novels has been widely studied and much celebrated in academic circles (Pertusa; Molinaro; Castrejón). Castrejón emphasizes Tusquets's new approach to creating explicit descriptions of same-sex lovemaking in sublime literary language, while avoiding the typical heterosexist objectification of the female body and, thus, effectively making lesbian desire visible (43–51).

Also explicitly celebrating the sensuality of female bodies and gender ambiguity, openly lesbian Uruguayan writer Cristina Peri Rossi (now a Spanish citizen and a long-time resident of Barcelona) closes the group of canonical Spanish female writers to have openly addressed gay and lesbian themes in their novels during the democracy. Her remarkable queer novel *Solitario de amor* (*Solitaire of Love* [1988]) and her many works and collections of short stories may be perhaps the most important contribution by a lesbian to the queer Spanish-language literary canon (see Pérez-Sánchez, *Queer*; and Pertusa).

Additional contemporary writers of gay and lesbian themes, too many to include here – such as Leopoldo Alas (1962–2008) and Catalonian poet and novelist Maria-Mercè Marçal (1952–98), author of the exquisite, award-winning novel *La passió segons Renée Vivien* (*Passion according to Renée Vivien* [1995]); *maudit* poet Leopoldo María Panero (1948–); camp humorist Isabel Franc (1955– ; aka Lola Van Guardia); and many other writers – complete a rich and diverse panorama of gay and lesbian literary expression that cannot be adequately explored in this short chapter.

. This long century is bookended by two other important and not unrelated events: by the loss, in 1898, of the last Spanish colonies in Cuba, Puerto Rico, and the Philippines – a loss significantly labeled "el Desastre" (the Disaster) – and by the approval of same-sex marriage (2005) and transgender rights (2007). These latter changes coincide with the increasing presence of economic immigrants – many from former Spanish colonies – in the Peninsula. As the critical analysis of "literature of migration" develops, connections emerge between the Spanish colonial imaginary of the late nineteenth century and contemporary racist and xenophobic anxieties (see Campoy-Cubillo; Flesler; González Alcantud; Majid; Martin-Márquez; Nair; and Pérez-Sánchez, "What"). Intersectional representations of race and sexuality will become even more important as queer critics take on this literature.[9]

In spite of its long periods of sexual repression and homophobic persecution both by a fascist regime and the Catholic Church, Iberia's contemporary gay and lesbian literary output ranks among the best in the world. If we consider this tradition alongside the extremely rich and prolific contributions of queer Spanish American canonical writers, who have contributed works of tremendous importance for world literature (Jorge Luis Borges, Teresa de la Parra, Silvina Ocampo, Gabriela Mistral, José Donoso, Manuel Puig, José Lezama Lima, Salvador Novo, Alejandra Pizarnik, Reinaldo Arenas, Severo Sarduy, Manuel Ramos Otero, Mayra Santos Febres, Mario Bellatin, to name just a few), we can conclude that gay and lesbian literature written in Spanish constitutes a most vital, daring, explicit, and complex corpus. If we expand this rich history further to include contributions in the visual and filmic arts (Dalí, Maruja Mallo, Almodóvar, Guillermo Pérez Villalta, and so forth), then the impact that the Iberian Peninsula has had on Western gay and lesbian culture is staggering.

Notes

1. It is worth noting that none of these writers is Madrilenian or Castilian: Riera and Roig are Catalonian and write in that language; Laforet was Catalonian but wrote in Spanish, as does Mayoral, who is Galician; and Etxebarria is Valencian of Basque descent, although she currently lives in Madrid and has always written in Spanish.

2. The designation "Iberian" in this chapter is meant to include not just Castilian-language works, but also Catalonian, Basque, and Galician ones. I do not address the literature of Portugal, Gibraltar (UK), or Andorra – the other nations that share the Iberian Peninsula – in this chapter, as they lay beyond my expertise.

3. Other important members of the *ultraístas* include Rafael Cansinos-Assens (also a writer of erotic novellas), Guillermo de Torre (theorist of the avant-garde and later apologist of right-wing *falange*), Isaac del Vando-Villar, Pedro Raida, and Argentinean Jorge Luis Borges. Celma Valero argues that Sánchez Saornil's works fell into oblivion partly because of her own personal choice to lead an anonymous life, prioritizing her personal safety and happiness with her partner over publication of her poetry (264). For a former anarchist feminist trying to survive under Francoism, there would have not been any other choice but silence.

4. The most accurate edition of this play in Spanish to date is Antonio Monegal's.
5. Mira identifies three key categories through which to understand how the discourses on homosexuality under Francoism were structured and articulated: "Repression, sublimation, and expression" (290).
6. The film *Electroshock* depicts a real-life case of such collusion between religion and psychiatry with devastating consequences for the protagonist lesbian couple. This film underscores the remarkable fact that such brutal repression of homosexuality was ongoing even under democracy. See Mira (300ff.) for a deeper analysis of such collusion.
7. *"Generación de medio siglo"* ("Generation of 1950") poets include luminaries such as José Ángel Valente, Ángel González, and Francisco Brines.
8. See Martínez-Expósito, *Escrituras* (151–92) for a complex analysis of Pombo's contributions to gay literature.
9. On the confluence of homophobia and racism in Spanish literature about Maghrebian and sub-Saharan African immigration to Spain, see Pérez-Sánchez, "What."

Works Cited

Álvarez Junco, José. "History, Politics, and Culture, 1875–1936." *The Cambridge Companion to Modern Spanish Culture*. Ed. David T. Gies. New York: Cambridge UP, 1999. Print.

"Álvaro Pombo afirma que *Contra natura* es una novela ejemplar." *ABC.es*. 2005. Web.16 Sept. 2013.

Amago, Samuel. "Lesbian Desire and Related Matters in Carmen Laforet's Nada." *Neophilologus*. 86.1 (2002): 65–86. Print.

Arnalte, Arturo. *Redada de violetas: la represión de los homosexuales durante el franquismo*. Madrid: La Esfera de los Libros, 2003. Print.

Bergmann, Emilie, and Paul Julian Smith, eds. *¿Entiendes?: Queer Readings, Hispanic Writings*. Durham: Duke UP, 1995. Print.

Campoy-Cubillo, Adolfo. *Memories of the Maghreb: Transnational Identities in Spanish Cultural Production*. New York: Palgrave, 2012. Print.

Castrejón, María. *... Que me estoy muriendo de agua: Guía de narrativa lésbica española*. Barcelona: Egales, 2008. Print.

Celaya Carrillo, Beatriz. *La mujer deseante: sexualidad femenina en la cultura y novela españolas (1900–1936)*. Newark: Juan de la Cuesta, 2006. Print.

Celma Valero, María Pilar. "Lucía Sánchez Saornil: Una voz 'ultra,' más allá de su condición femenina." *Praestans labore Victor; Homenaje al profesor Víctor García de la Concha*. Ed. Javier San José Lera. Salamanca: Ediciones U de Salamanca, 2005. 263–78. Print.

Electroshock (A Love to Keep). Dir. Juan Carlos Claver. Dacsa Producciones, Kines Producciones, Zip Films, 2006. Film.

Epps, Brad. "Virtual Sexuality: Lesbianism, Loss, and Deliverance in Carme Riera's 'Te deix, amor, la mar com a penyora.'" Bergman and Smith 317–45. Print.

Flesler, Daniela. *The Return of the Moor: Spanish Responses to Contemporary Moroccan Immigration*. West Lafayette: Purdue UP, 2008. Print.

Foster, David William, ed. *Spanish Writers on Gay and Lesbian Themes: A Bio-Critical Sourcebook*. Westport: Greenwood, 1999. Print.

García Lorca, Federico. *Collected Poems: A Bilingual Edition*. Ed. Christopher Maurer. Revised ed. New York: Farrar, 2002. Print.

 Primer romancero Gitano. Llanto por Ignacio Sánchez Mejía. Ed. Miguel García Posada. Madrid: Castalia, 1988. Print.

 El público. El sueño de la vida. Ed. Antonio Monegal. Madrid: Alianza, 2000. Print.

Gibson, Ian. *The Assassination of Federico García Lorca*. London: Penguin, 1983. Print.

 "Caballo azul de mi locura": Lorca y el mundo gay. Barcelona: Planeta, 2009. Print.

 Federico García Lorca: A Life. London: Faber, 1989. Print.

 Lorca-Dalí: El amor que no pudo ser. Barcelona: Plaza, 1999. Print.

Gil-Albert, Juan. *Heraclés: sobre una manera de ser*. Madrid: Betancor, 1975. Print.

Giménez Bartlett, Alicia. *Donde nadie te encuentre*. Barcelona: Destino, 2011. Print.

González Alcantud, José Antonio. *Lo moro: Las lógicas de la derrota y la formación del estereotipo islámico*. Barcelona: Anthropos, 2002. Print.

Goytisolo, Juan. *Forbidden Territory and Realms of Strife: The Memoirs of Juan Goytisolo*. Trans. Peter Bush. New York: Verso, 2003. Print.

 Count Julian (Don Julián). Trans. Helen Lane. Champaign: Dalkey, 2007. Print.

Grandes, Almudena. *The Ages of Lulu*. Trans. Sonia Soto. New York: Seven Stories, 1993. Print.

 The Frozen Heart. Trans. Frank Wynne. London: Orion, 2010. eBook.

Laforet, Carmen. *Nada* (1945). Trans. Edith Grossman. NY: Random, 2007. Print.

Majid, Anouar. *We Are All Moors: Ending Centuries of Crusades against Muslims and Other Minorities*. Minneapolis: U of Minnesota P, 2009. Print.

Martínez-Expósito, Alfredo. *Los escribas furiosos: configuraciones homoeróticas en la narrativa española actual*. New Orleans: UP of the South, 1998. Print.

 Escrituras torcidas: ensayos de crítica "queer." Barcelona: Laertes, 2004. Print.

Martin-Márquez, Susan. *Disorientations: Spanish Colonialism in Africa and the Performance of Identity*. New Haven: Yale UP, 2008. Print.

Mendicutti, Eduardo. *Yo no tengo la culpa de haber nacido tan sexy*. Barcelona: Tusquets, 1997. Print.

Mira, Alberto. *De Sodoma a Chueca: Una historia cultural de la homosexualidad en España en el siglo XX*. Madrid: Egales, 2004. Print.

Moix, Ana María. *Julia*. Barcelona: Seix Barral, 1970. Print.

Moix, Terenci. *La caiguda del imperi sodomita I altres contes*. Barcelona: Edicions 62, 1988. Print.

 El día que murió Marilyn. Barcelona: Plaza, 1984. Print.

 No digas que fue un sueño. Barcelona: Planeta, 1986. Print.

Molinaro, Nina. *Foucault, Feminism, and Power: Reading Esther Tusquets*. Lewisburg: Bucknell UP, 1991. Print.

Nair, Parvati. *Rumbo al norte: Inmigración y movimientos culturales entre el Magreb y España*. Barcelona: Bellaterra, 2006. Print.

Olmeda, Fernando. *El látigo y la pluma: Homosexuales en la España de Franco*. Madrid: Oberón, 2004. Print.

Oropesa, Salvador A. "Valle-Inclán, Ramón María del." Foster 170–72.

Pérez-Sánchez, Gema. *Queer Transitions in Contemporary Spanish Culture: From Franco to "La Movida."* Albany: State U of New York P, 2007. Print.

"What Happens on the Other Side of the Strai(gh)t? Clandestine Migrations and Queer Racialized Desire in Juan Bonilla's Neopicaresque Novel *Los príncipes nubios* (2003)." *Across the Straits: New Visions of Africa in Contemporary Spain*. Ed. Debra Faszer-McMahon and Victoria Ketz. Farnham: Ashgate P, forthcoming 2015. Print.

Peri Rossi, Cristina. *Solitaire of Love*. Trans. Robert S. Rudder and Gloria Arjona. Durham, NC: Duke UP, 2000. Print.

Pertusa Seva, Inmaculada. *La salida del armario: Lecturas desde la otra acera*. Gijón: Llibros del Pexe, 2005. Print.

Retana, Álvaro. *Las "locas" de postín y A Sodoma en tren botijo*. Intro. Luis Antonio de Villena. Madrid: Odisea, 2004. Print.

Riera, Carme. *Te deix, amor, la mar com a penyora*. Barcelona: Laia, 1975. Print.

Sánchez Saornil, Lucía. *Poesía*. Ed. Rosa María Martín Casamitjana. Valencia: Pre-Textos, 1996. Print.

Sauquillo Vázquez, Ángel. *Federico García Lorca y la cultura de la homosexualidad: Lorca, Dalí, Cernuda, Gil-Albert, Prados y la voz silenciada del amor homosexual*. Alicante: Instituto de Cultura Juan Gil-Albert, 1991. Print.

Simonis Sampedro, Angie. "Yo no soy esa que tú te imaginas: representación y discursos lesbianos en la literatura española." *Lesbianas: Discursos y representaciones*. Ed. Raquel Platero. Santa Cruz de Tenerife: Melusina, 2008. 233–79. Print.

Tusquets, Esther. *Con la miel en los labios*. Barcelona: Anagrama, 1997. Print.

Love Is a Solitary Game (El amor es un juego solitario). Trans. Bruce Penman. New York: Riverrun, 1985. Print.

The Same Sea as Every Summer (El mismo mar de todos los veranos). Trans. Margaret E. W. Jones. Lincoln: U of Nebraska P, 1990. Print.

Stranded (Varada tras el último naufragio). Trans. Susan E. Clark. Elmwood Park: Dalkey, 1991. Print.

Vicente García de Elormendi, Ángeles. *Zezé*. 1909. Madrid: Lengua de Trapo, 2005. Print.

Vosburg, Nancy, and Jacky Collins, eds. *Lesbian Realities/Lesbian Fictions in Contemporary Spain*. Lanham: Bucknell UP, 2011. Print.

Walsh, John K. "A Logic in Lorca's 'Ode to Walt Whitman.'" Bergmann and Smith 257–78.

Zaviezo, Gabriela. "Vergüenza y confidencias: estrategias para la construcción del sujeto en *Nada* de Carmen Laforet." *Divirgencias*. Forthcoming.

Zubiaurre, Maite. *Cultures of the Erotic in Spain, 1898–1939*. Nashville: Vanderbilt UP, 2012. Print.

25

French and Francophone Literature

PHILIPPE C. DUBOIS

Same-Sex Politics in French and Francophone Literature

On a cold Sunday in January 2013, more than eight hundred thousand people (according to the organizers) demonstrated in the streets of Paris against an upcoming law proposed by the newly elected socialist government that would give gays and lesbians the right to marry and to adopt. In spite of massive mobilization of conservative forces, and after many vigorous debates, the law was passed and the first officially recognized gay marriage was celebrated on May 29, 2013 in Montpellier. The polemic, however, remains intense and rests mainly on the ensuing redefinition of the sacrosanct institution of the family, and further deliberations are expected on the thorny question of filiation for same-sex couples and their access (or lack of access) to various forms of medically assisted procreation.

Certainly, with this law, the rights extended to same-sex couples go beyond the symbol of marriage and guarantee equal protection for children of homoparental families, access for partners to hospital visitation, inheritance, and so forth. However, because the universalist ideals of the French Republic cannot grant in its public sphere specific rights to particular groups, it is worth noting that this legislation is accordingly referred to as *Mariage pour tous* (*Marriage for All*). Although marriage surely may not be imposed on us all, such an appellation implies, along with the extension of institutional marriage to same-sex couples, the enforcement of a homogeneous view of erotic and romantic relationships in the normative social unit of the couple. The formatting of once-heterogeneous homosexual practices into the most heteronormative of institutions seems to secure the assimilation of homos into homogeneity.

In the meantime in London, the House of Commons in one efficient session also legalized gay marriage in February 2013. The (coincidental) timing of the passing of these legislations goes to show on both sides of the

Channel a certain consensus concerning same-sex issues. Yet it also draws our attention to gender politics similarly organized in both cases around the culturally dominant Anglo American model of civil rights and representations of gay identity. Within such a hegemonic move, the push for "equal rights" favors in fact forms of assimilation that mask issues of discrimination against racially, ethnically, and socioeconomically diverse gays, lesbians, and transpeople. Especially relevant in the French and Francophone contexts, class and immigration questions are equally absent from most public gay discourses; and growing critical attention now focuses on strategies of exclusion that structure current queer politics of visibility in the public sphere. While gay liberalism has accomplished important rights-based goals, a much broader spectrum of queer practices, ideas, and representations at the center of French and Francophone cultural productions needs to be considered.

Keen observers of French-speaking cultures warn against the uncritical transfer to contemporary French and Francophone territories of sexual politics and globalized identities that ignore the localized and cultural specificities governing public and private spheres. In his critical study *Queer French: Globalization, Language, and Sexual Citizenship in France*, Denis M. Provencher problematizes such dynamics. Expanding on that work, Provencher, in his current research on Maghrebi-French men, questions the relevance of identities such as "gay" or "homosexual" to describe same-sex desire for ethnic North Africans negotiating the conservatism of traditional Islam and instances of xenophobia in an urban French context.

Universalizing approaches to same-sex issues not only ignore forms of dissidence, they also put in place hierarchical structures around questions of race, class, gender, ethnicity, age, and nationality that replicate mechanisms of domination. In the French sphere, such processes are compounded by inherited colonial and postcolonial Orientalist narratives, as described by Edward Said. In works by nineteenth-century novelists such as Gérard de Nerval (France, 1808–55) or Pierre Loti (France, 1850–1923), the exoticization of the "other" serves invariably as a point of departure for a journey of sexual self-discovery. Gustave Flaubert (France, 1821–80) himself recounts in his personal correspondence his homosexual experiences while traveling through Egypt; and instances of sexual tourism in the writings of André Gide (France, 1869–1951) while in North Africa (*Si le Grain ne meurt* [1926]) produced and encouraged colonial readings of texts and bodies by heterosexual and homosexual travelers alike. This chapter will draw partly on the intricate relations among canonical French literature and postcolonial writings to articulate some of the lingering effects of Orientalism in contemporary French and Francophone cultures.

Among the many fantasies generated by Orientalist discourses is the space of the *harem*, which in *La fille aux yeux d'or* (1835) by Honoré de Balzac (France, 1799–1850) doubles as a fantasmatic locus of lesbianism in the heart of Paris. Designed as a site of resistance, and therefore a challenge to phallic power, this form of enclosure usually operated narratively as stimulation for heterosexual desire and the ultimate reinforcement of heterosexual domination. In a recent article, however, Gretchen Schultz takes as a starting point the Sapphic figures prominently featured in nineteenth-century French literature, from the poetics of Charles Baudelaire, to the lesser known works of Adolphe Belot, and the naturalist texts of Émile Zola, in order to demonstrate how literature rather than scientific disciplines has impacted the construction of same-sex female eroticism. Schultz tracks instances of this male-authored French literary tradition into 1950s U.S. lesbian pulp fiction designed mostly for the titillation of a male readership, but that also provided for women, she argues, "images and a vocabulary with which to identify their sexual attractions during a time in which there was no public discourse about homosexuality" (193).

While recalling the multiple connections between Orientalism and homosexuality articulated in current literary criticism, this chapter charts postcolonial intersections of race, gender, class, and sexuality in French-speaking cultural sites from Canada, the Caribbean, Paris, the Maghreb, and West Africa. Indeed, in a globalized world where Westerners at home can be in contact with former colonized subjects, as in the case of French suburbs (*banlieues*) turned into the new Orientalist frontier, these spaces contemporize and reinforce some of the stereotypes of violence, poverty, and excessive virility associated with black or Arab males, while revealing in the process old anxieties about Frenchness and whiteness. But cultural productions have also recently pointed to the reworking of these clichés into more critical performances of identities between exoticism and social commentary about relations between white gay subjects and alterity. As I will suggest, a number of contemporary cinematic interpretations provide compelling illustrations of queer reappropriations of such relations. Keeping in mind conservative critiques that essentialize these complex relations as merely racist or exploitative, this analysis will focus on representations of specific differences that enrich homosexual interrelations, while denouncing exclusions and interrogating the validity of hegemonic homo positions.

Because issues of queerness are certainly not a monopoly of Anglo American territory, this chapter identifies localized manifestations of gay, lesbian, and more generally queer voices in contemporary French and Francophone territories, anchored historically and geographically in a range of genres from novels and essays to theatre and the cinema. Specifically, this chapter will address the ways Maghrebin and Caribbean literatures question formulations of nation, patriarchy, and sexuality, and how such dissident queer voices contest the singularity of national origin myths. Because traditions can be challenged in various ways, a short discussion of AIDS narratives will serve to underline the tensions between body as scientific object and body as literary object, while evaluating issues of aesthetics, and their limits, associated with AIDS-related representations.

Finally, I outline, in the context of French queer theory, the specificities of postcolonial and national identity issues as they relate to sexual practices, as well as radical or progressive politics. Therefore, the various transdisciplinary vectors structuring this chapter are inscribed within the transversal nature of homosexual identity categories, as qualified by Michel Foucault (France, 1926–84):

> Homosexuality is an historic occasion to re-open affective and relational virtualities, not so much through the intrinsic qualities of the homosexual, but due to the biases against the position he occupies; in a certain sense diagonal lines that he can trace in the social fabric permit him to make these virtualities visible. (207)

I will consider same-sex desire, and its complex relation to heteronormativity, with the help of reflections drawn from the works of Foucault and Guy Hocquenghem (France, 1946–88), and from a perspective in which sexuality is articulated consistently through disruptive language politics. The goal of this chapter is to outline the contours of post-queer expressions of same-sex erotic desires, romantic relationships, and inventive forms of affective investments, as these have been strategically redefined by women-loving women, lesbians, fags, dykes, gays, sapphists, and queers, as well as those who resist all efforts at naming and those who reject homosexuality as it has been defined in Western terms. In the end, the formation of alternative lines of order resulting from such creative interrelational connections uncovers politics of communication that reorient in compelling ways gay and lesbian literary scholarship.

Homo-Erectus

Giving the legal recognition to same-sex marriages, the new French law points to the intimate connection between homosexual practices and heterocentric views on dominant sexuality, where homosexuality is performed within a reduced range of behaviors dictated by narrow frameworks of heterosexism. If attempting to escape these internalized structures of power is vain, as Foucault tells us, and if sexual liberation only replaces one discourse of domination with another, then it might be productive to substitute the notion of liberation with the concept of freedom of choice to actualize a distinctly gay subjectivity. Not derived from heterosexuality, such subjective space would open possibilities the philosopher describes in an interview: "The problem is not to discover in oneself the truth of sex, but rather to use sexuality henceforth to arrive at a multiplicity of relationships. And no doubt that's the real reason why homosexuality is not a form of desire but something desirable" (204). For Foucault, the obstinate call for external recognition from the homosexual subject should ideally make way for a reflection from within on the creative possibilities of homosexual alliances outside of constraints imposed by heterosexual values. At that moment, heterosexual power structures no longer dictate what constitutes homo-sex; instead sexual organs are reclaimed by the emerging gay discourse to join other body parts reconfigured as organs of pleasure liberated from the *phallic* order, and uncoupled from any reproductive model.

For the late critic Lawrence R. Schehr, who tracked major changes in representations of homosexuality in nineteenth- and twentieth-century French literature, this moment marks an important transition from homosexuality to gayness: "The gay body replaces the object of Gidean pederastic desire, the pure, adolescent ephebe who is neither woman nor man, more different from the lover than he is different from the female beloved. So too does the gay body replace the homosexual body" (151). While Schehr is careful to remind us that the two praxes can coexist, the heterosexually defined homosexual body gives way in the wake of the French gay liberation movement to a gay body refusing secondary status, clamoring for attention in very public ways. A vocal militant and one of the founders of the Front Homosexuel d'Action Révolutionaire (FHAR) in 1971, Hocquenghem seeks to free desire and its organs of pleasure in his novels – such as *L'Amour en relief* (1982) and *Eve* (1987) – and many theoretical writings (for example, *Race d'Ep* [1979] and *Le Gai Voyage* [1980]). Women, ex-colonials, and homosexuals were all originally included in the feminist-inspired liberation movement, which at the time did not uniquely concern gays and lesbians but universalized forms of oppression.

In this context, Jean Genet (France, 1910–86) embodies a particularly salient example of strong political commitment served by poetically graphic language at the antipodes of such contemporary authors as Jean Cocteau (France,

1889–1963). As Edmund White has argued, Genet brought to the literary fore-front marginal characters and lower-class thieves in a conscious response to Marcel Proust's (France, 1871–1922) remembrance of Parisian high society. As early as 1944, in *Notre-Dame-des-Fleurs* (*Our Lady of the Flowers*), Genet chooses to challenge social constraints rather than submit to them and become an impostor. In this sense, he breaks away from extant social constructions of homosexuality and stands as a precursor to the 1971 battle cry from MLF lesbi-ans and FHAR members shouting: "A bas l'homosexualité de papa!" ("Down with Daddy's homosexuality!"). Among the "daddies" in question, the figures of Gide, Proust, and Cocteau loom large.

In their work, the subjective narrator has replaced the omniscient story-teller of the totalizing enterprise of the nineteenth-century realist narrative project, and homosexuality is reinscribed within novel literary devices. The character of Monsieur de Charlus for instance, whom the narrator meets in the second volume of *À la Recherche du temps perdu* (*In Search of Lost Time* [1913–27]), allows Proust to provide the most intricate and dynamic descrip-tion yet of male homosexuality. Indeed, if unable to read Charlus at first, the narrator, Marcel, eventually learns (and the reader along with him) to com-prehend the meaning of the Baron's cruising, thus putting into question sexu-ality, which is henceforth imbued with a sense of fluidity. Two volumes later, Proust famously concludes: "No one was abnormal when homosexuality was the norm" (*Sodome* 422).

At age nineteen, the precocious and versatile Cocteau was exchanging let-ters with Proust, and would soon know artistic recognition in a wide array of genres from poetry and theatre to films, sketches, and ballet. He discovered Genet in 1943 and immediately recognized in his work a new expression of homosexuality.

While the work of these authors made it possible to represent male homo-sexuality and contributed to the construction of a collective memory for homosexuals seeking refuge in literature during the first half of the century, Genet clearly rejects the confessional tone of Gide's *L'Immoraliste* (1902). By dealing with racism, as in *Les Nègres* (1958), or the Algerian revolution, in *Les paravents* (1961), Genet positioned himself politically: he pledged his support to the Black Panther Party and the Palestinian Liberation Organization, asso-ciations that also held an erotic charge for him. In the 1960s and 1970s, colo-nial and postcolonial tensions were reworked through political solidarity with former colonized (although still mostly marginalized) subjects in very physi-cal ways. For example, Hocquenghem tells us, in *La Beauté du métis* (1979), that male members of the FHAR exhibited pride in being "fucked by Arab men" as a form of resistance to racism and a consensual revenge over the colonizing West. The militants' insistence on the active sexual role of Arab men comes as a reaction to the clichés inherited from traditional literary representations, where old white males would have sex with young Arab men. As Schehr succinctly summarizes:

> Hocquenghem may be attracted to Maghrebin men because this marginalized form of desire is acceptable within the structures of heterocratic desire, as Foucault would read it, because the other is believed to be liberated, as Gide would have it, because of the stereotypes of that other as phallic machines, or ... for the "beauty" of the individual. But he may also be attracted to the Maghrebin other, outcast of two societies, because of that sense of solidarity.
>
> (165)

Indeed, Hocquenghem's and Genet's positions as marginalized subjects enable their solidarity with other figures of marginalization around a shared project of political struggle. With Gilles Deleuze and Félix Guattari, Hocquenghem, in Le Désir homosexuel (1972), advocates the "deprivatizing of the anus" as zone of pleasure within an eroticized space of deterritorialized desires, outside of codes imposed by a heterocratic capitalist system preoccupied with perpetuating the phallocentric order. Here, anal penetration does not define exclusively homosexuality but rather an antisocial performance of sexuality containing possibilities of resistance for a wide array of subjects defined as "others" by a system of values invested in the metonymical power of the phallus. While it unchained gay discourse from the dominant heterosexual paradigm, Hocquenghem's theorizing accompanied homosexuality into a postliberation moment that allowed for the critical politicization of literature at a time when the AIDS rhetoric recalled old taboos of exchanged fluids and exposed body parts.

AIDS Body Politics

Hocquenghem-inspired literary productions, such as Renaud Camus's (France, 1946–) Tricks (1978; prefaced by Roland Barthes [France, 1915–80]), provocatively embody the challenge to heterosexual discourse in disconnecting pleasure from the despotic phallus and turning the entire surface of the body into an erogenous zone through mutual frottage, which for Camus resembles "pure homosexuality, the least stained with resemblance to the other love" (Fendre 224). This emphasis on "safer sex" will allow his work to resist the sea change generated by AIDS-related representations of desire and sexuality.

In AIDS narratives by Hervé Guibert (France, 1955–91), including *A l'ami qui ne m'a pas sauvé la vie* (1990), *Le protocole compassionnel* (1991), and *Cytomégalovirus* (1992) – in which the author's seropositivity is presented through a merely rhetorical narrator – as Schehr points out, the body turns into the object of scientific discourse, slowly disintegrating into detailed lists of painfully accurate medical procedures and drug cocktails:

> I had various secondary diseases that Dr. Chandi had treated, often over the phone, one after another: patches of eczema on my shoulder, treated with a 0.1% Locoïd cortisone cream, diarrhea treated with Ercéfuryl 200, one pill every four hours for three days, a doubtful stye treated with Dacrin eye-wash and an Aureomycin cream. (*Ami* 167)

If readers accept, notes Schehr, such a text pushed to its literary limits, they are also forced to contemplate the AIDS body as a "collection of parts" and signs at the limit of the "representable" before its ultimate disintegration into objecthood (170). At this stage, the mirror returns once again to complete the alienation of the sick body, as Yves Navarre (France, 1940–94) writes from Montréal: "If I then shave myself, with the privilege of standing in front of the sink, I cut myself because I no longer dare to look at myself. I am covered with shaving cuts" (99). Post-AIDS representations of the body, desire, and sexuality not only transformed literary aesthetics, but also the tool of yesterday's gay liberation, the penis. Now, at the rank of ordinary organ, the penis disappears along with other body parts except maybe when enveloped into the all-engulfing condom:

> He spread out a rug, and on that rug, aside from his own spread-out body (moreover, pleasing to the eye) a bottle of poppers, rubbers, a tube of lubricant; all quite meticulously aligned, very visible, like in a store window. A good-looking boy, *safe sex*, amyl nitrate, up-to-date technology, all that suits me just fine. (Camus, *Vigiles* 321)

Not only does the autobiographical subject of AIDS narratives challenge literary traditions through its negotiation of tensions between body as scientific versus literary object, it also allows for the formulation of the unspeakable trauma of the AIDS crisis and the creation of an indispensable space for new forms of literature's politicization.

Métissage

In the meantime, across the Atlantic Ocean, contemporaneous literary productions from French-speaking Canada acknowledge the HIV/AIDS health crisis only in passing, and sexual politics are formulated within the context of Québec nationalism through culturally specific linguistic disruptions. The reformulation of sexuality, nation, and patriarchy are examined here through geographically distinct voices mapped out through Québécois, Maghrebin, and Caribbean literatures.

The unique position of Québec as the Francophone province in an otherwise Anglophone Canada favors the intersections of languages, which play an integral part in the representation of Québécois identity politics. The privileged position of the city of Montréal as a diverse, transversal urban space serves for the articulation on stage of such politics – with the 1968 *Les belles-soeurs* by Michel Tremblay (Québec, 1942–) for instance, in which women speak in their native *joual*, the sociolect of the working classes of Montréal. Such a dialectal appropriation of the public stage appeared as something of a revolution, approached by some with contempt and welcomed by others as a liberation. Charles R. Batson describes this as "one century of dominion by people of a different *parlure*, with the play's characters from a Québécois *chez nous* not only speaking about their *consoeurs* and *–frères* but also speaking like them" (161). Tremblay's *La Duchesse de Langeais* (1973) focuses on the love and disillusions of a crossdressing figure from Montréal's theatres. The new centrality accorded to marginal characters gives way to an increasing number of gay-themed productions, from his *Hosanna* (1973) to René-Daniel Dubois's *Being at Home with Claude*, all staging the rich complexity of Québécois identities. In reaction to elites speaking an authoritative form of the French language, the deployment of *joual* in Québécois literature brings a sociocultural authenticity that rewrites official colonizing discourses to include into the Nation dissident narratives of gender, class, and sexuality that resist inherited models of subjectivity.

In the often oppressive enterprise of national construction, dissident voices have denounced acts of repression and exclusion on the part of the Nation by articulating alternative narratives of national origins that are necessarily multiple, heterogeneous, and more inclusive of marginalized subjectivities. This heterogeneity is also sexual, which Jarrod Hayes summarizes as follows:

> When Maghrebin authors formulate representations of homosexuality, sodomy, homoeroticism, lesbianism, cross-dressing, the joys of emasculation, women's resistance, public unveiling, and feminist guerilla warfare, they do not merely challenge sexual taboos, sexual normativity, and patriarchy (which they do); they also reveal the queerness of the Nation. (16)

Maghrebin novelist Assia Djebar (Algeria, 1936–) embodies such a position as she envisions a feminist nation that is also a queer nation. Rejecting male nationalists' accusations of feminism (and homosexuality for that matter) as a tool inherited from colonialist discourse threatening nationalism and Muslim traditions, Djebar rewrites national identity in ways that reinsert marginalized voices in place of the Nation's exclusion of women's struggles and the accomplishments of marginalized subjects. If the veil in novels such as *L'amour, la fantasia* takes on the narrative form of history, *Ombre sultane* portrays an actual unveiling with direct feminist implications when the protagonist, Isma, plays the institution of polygamy to encourage her abusive husband to take a second wife, Hajila, who in turn eludes marriage by escaping into the streets and removing her veil. Thus, by entering the public space, both women challenge the structure of patriarchal marriage that centers the Nation on the family and legitimizes the husband when he rapes his wife. Djebar's queer conception of the *hammam* transforms this traditional space into a healing site for women with homoerotic possibilities, where women can exist aside from men. As in much Maghrebin literature, sexuality in Djebar's work plays an undeniable role as she makes sexuality a political force of opposition to the colonial presence, as well as a threat to male privileges embodied by postindependence and neocolonial social order. Through the unveiling of sexuality as a challenge to hegemonic heterosexuality, women's sexuality functions in similar ways as homosexuality, conceived as a recurrent site of political resistance.

Such is the case also in the works of Rachid Boudjedra (Algeria, 1941–), and in *La répudiation* in particular, about the childhood of the narrator, Rachid, and his inability to comprehend and unveil his brother Zahir's homosexuality. Continuing through North Africa, if Eyet-Chékib Djaziri (Tunisia, 1957–) writes first-person narratives containing significant erotic homosexual encounters, it is Rachid O. (Morocco, 1970–) who established unprecedented connections between homosexuality and the Muslim world as an openly gay Moroccan writer. The autobiographical narrator looks back at his childhood in Morocco to recount candidly and with serenity his experience of homosexuality from a young age. If Rachid O. fits the description of the postcolonial Maghrebin novelist, the French readership of this young gay Moroccan storyteller can easily recall accounts of sexual/textual tourism from authors like Loti or Gide. In the main section entitled "Amours" ("Loves") of his first novel, *L'Enfant ébloui*, Rachid O. recounts to a group of "French-speaking pedophiles" the first love of an adolescent for his Arabic teacher, before he leaves the family home a couple of years later to move in with his thirty-year-older French lover. If the autobiographical subject replaces Western constructions of pedophilia with those of transgenerational love, he is careful not to prescribe the contingencies of his own specific experience as a desirable model. While articulating together erotic and romantic desires, Rachid O. challenges the clichés associated with "Oriental sex" in the Arab-Muslim world; the narrator's sexuality is defined outside of constructions of homosexuality that, relying on binary oppositions, reinforce heterosexual masculinity. Never victimized, the homosexual figures in Rachid O.'s novels, including *Chocolat Chaud*, manage, in fact, a subtle balancing act between Orientalist tropes of homosexuality and the self-actualization of a subject who seeks to enact his own erotic desires and his own sexual subjectivity. Described by novelist Mathieu Lindon as a "pioneer" (99) and compared by critics to Hervé Guibert (Ceccatty n.pag.), the Maghrebin author reveals a vision of both France and homosexuality in calm, appeased, nonmilitant, and yet unprecedented revolutionary terms. Quietly rebellious, Rachid O. reaches out to North African traditions of same-sex love in order to propose a construction of gay identities that are not defined as relations of transgression against institutional models, but rather offered as reconciliation.

As storytellers describing dissident forms of sexuality within the official discourse of the Nation, Maghrebin writers have faced at times uncomfortable situations. Indeed, many nationalists did not hesitate to harshly criticize these authors for such literary acts of public unveiling, to consider them traitors, and even sometimes to question the authenticity of these North African novelists who write in French, for a French readership, and while (in some cases) living in Metropolitan France. If for Rachid O., the return to childhood is expressed as a seemingly peaceful experience, Djebar, on the contrary, sees the choice to write her autobiography in French, a language other than her native tongue, as a way to distance herself from her past, a mechanism she describes as exile. At the same time, such a transversal use of language makes the unveiling possible; the equivocal role of French language as both colonizing and liberating mirrors, in fact, the throes of colonial history and struggles for independence. In both cases, writing their autobiographies in French, the Algerian woman and the young Moroccan gay man seek a return to the roots that resists colonial and postcolonial discourses, while rewriting postindependence homogeneous narratives of the Nation. In the end, these autobiographical subjects do not necessarily reject the notion of the Nation, but rather reconceptualize categories of sexual and national identities as they rewrite them into less oppressive, more heterogeneous narratives composed of a multitude of origins and voices.

In *Moha le fou, Moha le sage* by Tahar Ben Jelloun (Morocco, 1944–), the eponymous character, a madman, takes on the identities of a number of marginalized individuals. The structuring of this polyphonic narrative in multiple

voices represents an exemplary illustration of what Hayes, following the definition proposed by Françoise Lionnet, describes as *métissage*: "If ... identity is
strategy, then *métissage* is the fertile ground of our heterogeneous and heter-
onormous identities as postcolonial subjects" (Lionnet, qtd. in Hayes 50). The
sexual and cultural miscegenation represented by the weaving of heterogeneous voices through *métissage* is to be read as textual and critical strategies for
the construction of postcolonial subjectivities.

The notion of "weaving" itself was originally proposed by Caribbean writer
Édouard Glissant (Martinique, 1928–2011); known for his radical anticolonialist
positions, he writes in *Le Discours antillais* (1981): "The poetics of *métissage* is
exactly that of Relation: nonlinear, nonprophetic, *woven* [*tissé*] from arduous
patience and incomprehensible detours" (251). Inspired in particular by the
works of Franz Fanon, whose theory finds a literary expression in Glissant's
first novel, *La Lézarde* (1958), the author develops a concept of Caribbean solidarity in his writings as political and cultural achievement. This *métissage*
approach to polyphonic narratives ideally corresponds to the diverse environments of the Caribbean, the mélange of races, languages, and cultures that
constitute their specificity.

Thomas Glave, in a gathering of voices entitled *Our Caribbean* (2008), insists
precisely on what makes the plurality as well as the connections between
peoples from so many Caribbeans:

> Our Antilles of Creole and English, Kréyol and French, and Spanish,
> Papiamentu, Dutch. Our many Caribbeans of cricket and *béisbol*, soccer and
> *fútbol*, and Carnival, jouvert, crop-over. Our islands and memories of *zonas
> colonials, ciudades Viejas*, very well-known Soufrière, and Basse-Terre, Grand-
> Terre – all traversed by mountains, rivers, ghosts, *diablesses*, duppies soucoy-
> ants, jumbies, and more.   ("Desire" 3)

Naturally, the polyphonic nature of Caribbean identities is reflected in the
variety of Creole languages that have resisted the violence of the conquer-
ing colonial tongue, all the more authoritative as it also happened to be the
word of the Almighty Father. Mocked as "bastardized" versions of the official
language, Creoles serve nonetheless as powerful signifiers for the complex
variety of sexual identities expressed linguistically through denominations as
diverse as categories themselves: *mati*, or women-loving women in Suriname,
"*zami*, 'that way,' *así*, [or] 'so'" (8). The collection of Caribbean voices gathered by Glave points to those who refuse the terms *gay, lesbian*, or *queer*, perceived as so many forms of enslavement into a colonial ideology that relegates
to others the power of self-naming and reduces to silence the complexities

of same-gender interests. If all Caribbean subjectivities are connected from Fort-de-France to Marie-Galante, to Cayenne, Guyane, and beyond, alternative linguistic and cultural tools provide infinite ways to work toward erotic self-realization and emotional self-inscription, outside of the dialectics of the closet. Such is the case of Audre Lorde (Caribbean-American, 1934–92) and the particular political positioning of her black, female, lesbian body in her essay "Of Generators and Survival," where she discusses her experience in St. Croix after Hurricane Hugo. Her body language reveals that subjectivities go beyond a single-focused perspective to engage in multipronged, interconnected human politics. The articulation of a political project that resists reduction to sameness requires the rich variety of languages, the diversity of words as reflections of sexual and emotional alterities.

Recent histories of liberation movements have emphasized the pioneering role of women in early struggles against forms of colonization and in political resistance to patriarchal oppression. The difficulty for women to access positions of subjects parallels the impossible situation of colonized individuals "othered" by colonial discourses. Female subjects, Luce Irigaray (Belgium, 1930–) reminds us, find themselves in the doubly difficult situation of creating a space for the expression of female subjectivity outside of female-objectifying male constructions by positioning themselves on the other side of the *looking glass* (7–20). Compounding that difficulty is the fact that nationalists not only reject as Western imports all forms of feminism, but government-sanctioned homophobia in parts of Africa simply outlaws same-sex practices, making such violent repression doubly oppressive for women as lesbians and as individuals in a patriarchal system that views them as mothers or grandmothers before allowing any other female identity category.

Yet, following the advice from Joan Nestle in the context of lesbian history to find a balance between "the dangers of romanticizing losses while at the same time aggrandizing little victories" (273), Frieda Ekotto (Cameroon, 1959–) proposes a nuanced approach between the history of oppression and the joyful liberation provided by prospects of resistance. The author of *Portrait d'une jeune artiste de Bona Mbella*, Ekotto is responsible for a series of writings considering "Women Loving Women in Sub-Saharan African Literature." Ekotto suggests an analysis of *Karmen Geï*, in which she reads the erotic film by Joseph Gaï Ramaka as an artifact of modern Senegalese culture to question whether in such a society the sexual taboo of female homosexuality can be overcome ("Erotic"). Following Prosper Mérimée's classic story, the transgressive sexuality deployed by this Senegalese Karmen, and her sexualized body in particular, serves as a site of resistance against postcolonial disciplinary regimes. For instance, in the scene when Karmen sings her way out of prison thanks to a female prison warden she seduces, the female body is represented as a disruptive tool of liberated pleasure. Ekotto also notes that this experimental film marked by the presence of death "relies heavily on musical forms, jump cuts, and spectral images to bring back the ghosts of those who have been *othered* in African society" (78). In the end, Ekotto recognizes in this desiring/desired woman's body emerging forms of sexuality, spirituality, and race subverting the dominant order and reinscribing cultural politics as "queer" through *performative* bodily categories.

Poised to expose the alienation engendered by patriarchal colonial and neo-colonial logics, the embodied reappropriation of erotics reorganizes categories imposed by external discourses of domination. Ekotto's reading clearly demonstrates that the cinematic space provided by Ramaka's film opens new territories for the reevaluation and the repositioning of ideological emphasis in postcolonial cultural productions – a space that transcends issues of morality in order to articulate "ethical calls to action in which difference is mobilized in the service of a progressive political project" ("Erotic" 79). Here, political action is advocated through differentiated forms of erotic, romantic, and emotional relationships. The creative possibilities offered by the inherent heterogeneity of interrelational connections constitute a social and political force, in the way friendship is described by Foucault: "Therefore we have to work at becoming homosexuals and not be obstinate in recognizing that we are. The development toward which the problem of homosexuality tends is the one of friendship" (204). Friendship is to be understood here as one of many infinite possibilities of emotional, romantic, and erotic interconnections. As such, friendship can potentially become the political expression of heterogeneous forms of relationships – a relational heterogeneity gaining increasing social recognition as it circulates ever more widely through networks of representations such as the ones provided in contemporary film. Indeed, as cinematic space creates or reinterprets modes of social, racial, and sexual interconnections, a number of filmmakers provide compelling queer reappropriation of such forms of emotional expressions. A cursory look at such gay *auteurs* will serve to illustrate our final point.

Interrelational Reorientation

Representations from a homoerotic perspective of social and sexual interrelations in the context of ethnic differences have sometimes summoned the Orientalist ghosts of cinematically objectified racial bodies. However, the

hybrid aesthetics of the cinema of Sébastien Lifshitz (France, 1968–), combining documentary style and artistic photography, avoid some of these
Orientalist clichés to portray complex interconnections between race and
sexuality.

As in most of his films, Lifshitz is attentive to some of the urban and
social-class divides permeating gay and lesbian culture. Rarely in contemporary cultural productions are sexual dissidence and social exclusion so
keenly articulated to reveal how black or Arab gay males are only further
marginalized in the difficult alliance between sexual and racial minorities
(Cervulle and Rees-Roberts 95). In *Wild Side* (2004), Lifshitz films the physical
and symbolic violence of racial and social exclusion of three marginalized
heroes (a Russian immigrant without legal papers, a transsexual prostitute,
and a bisexual Arab sex worker), and provides alternative modes of affective
relationships outside of the monogamous couple unit. Most of Lifshitz's
filmography is emblematic of social tensions and cultural anxieties in contemporary France about race, immigration, and sexuality, and particularly
of white middle-class homosexuals holding on tightly to their newfound
privileges. Certainly, a marriage license does not erase the eroticized projections of social and class differences that still mark same-sex relationships in
France today.

In the end, if the exposed anus and penises of yesterday's *Homo Erectus*
have been replaced with the more acceptable attributes of the very marketable *Homo Economicus*, the reconceptualization of interrelational politics
proposes strategies of resistance to ostentatious forms of economic and
social assimilation – a place from which new expressions of queerness can
be articulated. In "Articulating difference," Ekotto takes stock of the impact
of the HIV/AIDS crisis and its *unrepresentable* experience to articulate the
possibilities of reading and writing as acts of witnessing (152). Ekotto is also
careful to emphasize that such acts need to be completed in person with the
empathic presence of the body as a more appropriate response to various
traumas resulting from social oppression. For her, "the traumatic neuroses
of subjects objectified by racism and, I would add, of subjects differently and
concurrently downgraded by sexism, homophobia, and class oppression are
not curable by psychoanalysis treatment alone" (156). Indeed, she proposes
to add to the individual initiative an action at the level of the group that
would create a therapeutic space for political action working toward social
change. Thus, while reminding us that our own oppression should not blind
us to our responsibility in the oppression of others, Ekotto echoes Audre
Lorde when the latter writes, in *Sister Outsider* (1984), that "it is not difference

which immobilizes us but silence" (44), and *"urge[s us] to reach down into that deep place of knowledge inside [ourselves] and touch that terror and loathing of any difference that lives there"* (113). Against univocal positions and categories that shackle and silence subjective alterity, the voicing of differences through polyphonic communication renders possible responsible action and forms of sociability.

The transdisciplinary vectors discussed here situate queer and post-queer productions somewhere between assimilation and radicalism, but within the continuity of Hocquenghem's early admonishing:

> The "heteroclitic" nature of homosexual desire makes it dangerous to the dominant sexuality. Every day a thousand kinds of homosexual behavior challenge the classification one tries to impose on them. The unification of the practices of homosexual desire under the term "homosexuality" is as imaginary as the unification of the component drives in the ego.   (*Désir* 119)

As a product of gay liberalism, "gay marriage" in this case appears as one manifestation of queer life today without representing all of its infinite possibilities. Counter to separatist clichés between lesbians and gay men, post-queer positionings urge us to continue inventing new models of cross-gender collaborations, and vibrant relations across race, class, age, ethnicity, and nationality. Most important, these planetary vectors suggest ways to reimagine our imaginary lives through the elaboration of interrelational politics of sociability that reflect the thriving *mélange* of contemporary French-speaking cultures.

Works Cited

Balzac, Honoré de. *La Fille aux yeux d'or. La Comédie humaine.* Vol. 5. Paris: Gallimard, Bibliothèque de la Pléiade, 1977. 1039–112. Print.

The Girl with the Golden Eyes: History of the Thirteen. Trans. Herbert J. Hunt. New York: Penguin, 1974. 307–91. Print.

Batson, Charles R. "Dis/locating Dominion: *Being at Home with Claude* and Remembering a Queer Montreal." *Contemporary French Civilization* 37.2–3 (2012): 159–75. Print.

Ben Jelloun, Tahar. "Défendre la diversité culturelle du Maghreb." *L'état du Maghreb.* Ed. Yves Lacoste and Camille Lacoste-Dujarin. Paris: La Découverte, 1991. 271–72. Print.

Moha le fou, Moha le sage. Paris: Seuil, 1978. Print.

Boudjedra, Rachid. *La Répudiation.* Paris: Denoël, 1969. Print.

The Repudiation. Trans. Golda Lambrova. Colorado Springs: Three Continents P, 1995. Print.

Camus, Renaud. *Fendre l'air. Journal 1989.* Paris: P.O.L., 1991. Print.

Vigiles. Journal 1987. Paris: P.O.L., 1989. Print.

Cecatty, René de. "Rachid O., le destin d'un écrivain." *Le Monde* April 18, 2003. Web. 31 Jan. 2013.

Cervulle, Maxime, and Nick Rees-Roberts. *Homo Exoticus: Race, classe et critique queer.* Paris: Armand Colin, 2010. Print.

Djebar, Assia. *L'amour, la fantasia.* Paris: Jean-Claude Lattès, 1985. Print.

 Fantasia: An Algerian Cavalcade. Trans. Dorothy S. Blair. Portsmouth: Heinemann, 1993. Print.

 Ombre sultane. Paris: Jean-Claude Lattès, 1987. Print.

 A Sister to Scheherazade. Trans. Dorothy S. Blair. Portsmouth: Heinemann, 1993. Print.

Dubois, René-Daniel. *Being at Home with Claude.* Montréal: Leméac, 1986. Print.

Ekotto Frieda. "Articulating Difference: When I Was Ethnic. A Tribute to Lawrence Schehr." *Contemporary French Civilization* 37.2–3 (2012): 151–57. Print.

 Portrait d'une jeune artiste de Bona Mbella : Roman. L'Harmattan, 2010. Print.

 "The Erotic Tale of Karmen Geï: The Taboo of Female Homosexuality in Senegal." *Sex and the Spirit* 27.1 (2007): 74–80. Print.

Flaubert, Gustave. *Correspondance.* Vol. 1. Paris: Gallimard, Bibliothèque de la Pléiade, 1973. Print.

Foucault, Michel. "Friendship as a Way of Life." *Foucault Live.* Ed. Sylvère Lotringer. Trans. John Johnston. New York: Semiotext(e), 1989. 203–09. Print.

Glave, Thomas. "Desire through the Archipelago." Introduction. Glave, ed. 1–11.

 ed. *Our Caribbean: A Gathering of Lesbian and Gay Writing from the Antilles.* Durham: Duke UP, 2008. Print.

Glissant, Edouard. *Le Discours antillais.* Paris: Seuil, 1981. Print.

Guibert, Hervé W. *A l'Ami qui ne m'a pas sauvé la vie.* Paris: Gallimard, 1990. Print.

Hayes, Jarrod. *Queer Nations: Marginal Sexualities in the Maghreb.* Chicago: U of Chicago P, 2000. Print.

Hocquenghem, Guy. *La Beauté du métis. Réflexions d'un francophobe.* Paris: Éditions Ramsay, 1979. Print.

 Le Désir homosexuel. Paris: Universitaires, 1972. Print.

Irigaray, Luce. *Speculum de l'autre femme.* Paris: Minuit, 1974. Print.

Lindon, Mathieu. *Je vous écris.* Paris: P.O.L., 2004. Print.

Lionnet, Françoise. *Autobiographical Voices: Race, Gender, Self-Portraiture.* Ithaca: Cornell UP, 1989. Print.

Lorde, Audre. "Of Generators and Survival: Hugo Letter (1990)." Glave 232–45.

 Sister Outsider: Essays and Speeches. Trumansburg: Crossing, 1984. Print.

Navarre, Yves. *Ce sont amis que vent emporte.* Paris: Flammarion, 1991. Print.

Nestle, Joan. "I Lift My Eyes to the Hill: The Life of Mabel Hampton as Told by a White Woman." *Queer Representations: Reading Lives, Reading Cultures.* Ed. Martin Duberman. New York: New York UP, 1997. 258–75. Print.

O. Rachid. *Chocolat chaud.* Paris: Gallimard, coll. L'infini, 1998. Print.

 L'enfant ébloui. Paris: Gallimard, coll. Folio, 1999. Print.

Proust, Marcel. *Sodome et Gomorrhe. À la recherche du temps perdu.* Vol. 2. Paris: Gallimard, 1947.

Provencher, Denis. *Queer French: Globalization, Language, and Sexual Citizenship in France.* Burlington: Ashgate, 2007. Print.

Ramaka, Joseph Gaï. Dir. *Karmen Geï*, Sénégal, 2001. Film.

Said, Edward W. *Orientalism*. New York: Vintage, 1979. Print.

Schehr, Lawrence R. *Parts of an Andrology: On Representations of Men's Bodies*. Stanford: Stanford UP, 1997. Print.

Schultz, Gretchen. "Transnationalism and Sexual Identity in Literature: From the French Canon to US Pulp Fiction." *Contemporary French Civilization* 37.2–3 (2012): 193–215. Print.

White, Edmund. *Genet: A Biography*. New York: Knopf, 1993. Print.

26

African Literatures

CHRIS DUNTON AND NEVILLE HOAD

Any discussion of gay and lesbian literature in Africa must begin both with the recognition that, in most countries of the continent, public expression of homophobia is widespread – in many cases backed by repressive legislation – and with an acknowledgment of the contested histories and geographies of the terms themselves. Whilst the constitution of South Africa explicitly affirms the rights of sexual minorities – and indeed was the first constitution in the world to do so (not that this affirmation has provided a comprehensive guarantee against acts of extreme homophobic violence) – throughout much of Africa, LGBTQI-identified people are exposed to contempt and oppression that is often sanctioned by the state. Simultaneously, it should also be noted that there are many African countries without sodomy laws, including Burkina Faso, Central African Republic, Chad, Republic of the Congo, Democratic Republic of the Congo, Egypt, Eritrea, Gabon, Guinea-Bissau, Ivory Coast, Lesotho, Madagascar, Mozambique, Niger, Rwanda, and South Africa. Throughout the continent, care is needed in reading the relation between legal and sociopolitical levels of tolerance and acceptance, but a current trend toward increasing criminalization will create new challenges for African writers wishing to make same-sex identities, practices, desires, and relationships the subject of aesthetic representation.

Although the current wave of criminalizing legislation and the public sentiments they express and foster is a stop-start process, at the time of writing, the trend is toward deepening repression. As Shaun de Waal reports:

> The announcement by Malawi's justice minister [in November 2012] that the country would suspend laws criminalizing gay and lesbian people and activity, pending a parliamentary review, stands out on a continent where gay rights are either ignored or deliberately limited. In February this year the former first lady of Liberia introduced a Bill to the Liberian Parliament that would make homosexuality a first degree felony. Uganda's anti-gay Bill, which has caused controversy since 2009 because it suggests the death penalty

for homosexuality, has been reintroduced to its Parliament.... Last year the Nigerian parliament passed a Bill outlawing gay groups, activism and marriages.... Nigerian senator Baba-Ahmed Yusuf Datti ... said bluntly, "Such elements in society should be killed." (35)

The Nigerian bill was signed into law by Nigerian president Goodluck Jonathan on January 13, 2014. Considerable international pressure, led by British Prime Minister David Cameron and American President Barack Obama and former Secretary of State Hillary Clinton, had been brought to bear in the attempt to halt the final passing of the bill (Nsehe). In a familiar scenario of unintended consequences, Cameron's actions divided the Nigerian human rights community, who had formerly been solidly against the 2006 proposed bill (Ibiwoye). The question of African homophobia/homosexuality is increasingly significant on a global terrain.

The question of exactly how African this homophobia is has been posed in recent years with some force. Kapya Kaoma, in *Colonizing African Values*, has scrupulously documented the role played by U.S.-based evangelicals in the drafting of anti-gay legislation and the attempted redrafting of African constitutions in countries like Uganda, Kenya, and Nigeria. Leading U.S. evangelical Pat Robertson has opened branch offices of his American Center for Law and Justice in Nairobi and Harare, and Scott Lively of Abiding Ministries, instrumental in the drafting of the notorious Ugandan bill, has been forced to back down, saying that while he agrees with the impulse of the bill "it goes too far" (Bennett-Smith, n.pag.). Sectors of an international gay activist public sphere are now making the argument that homophobia rather than homosexuality is the decadent Western import in the current debate.

The terms of this debate about whether homosexuality or homophobia is the inauthentic Western import do little to dislodge questions of homosexuality from rhetorics of national and racial authenticity and may work to occlude African agency – sexual and otherwise. The debate often renders same-sex desiring and practicing Africans as simple stooges or victims of the so-called West. Joel Gustave Nana poignantly invokes a Cameroonian proverb to describe the debate: "When elephants struggle, it is the grass that suffers." African writers of literary texts that broach the topics held under the large umbrella of "homosexuality" have been and continue to be important voices in these ongoing public national and international debates.

In the 1990s, the most widely publicized instances of homophobic discourse and action were generated by the pronouncements of leaders such as Presidents Mugabe and Nujoma of Zimbabwe and Namibia, respectively, who claimed that same-sex sexual activity is a Western phenomenon, an import from the colonial period; that gays and lesbians are worse than pigs and dogs; and that the only defense for their sexual activities is "the white man made me do it." (For documentation of these pronouncements and their accompanying homophobic legislation, see Dunton and Palmberg.)

The fallacies underlying this stand have been exploded in a series of studies by Marc Epprecht, who counters the argument that homosexuality is a malaise imported from the West by revealing indigenous discourses of homosexuality, and who ably demonstrates the multiple ironies with which the scenario of stigmatization and oppression is riddled, not the least of which is the fact that legislation outlawing same-sex sexual activity and the free association of gays and lesbians dates largely from colonial laws such as the British antisodomy statutes. Relatedly, Rudi Bleys, in *The Geography of Perversion*, documents the long European history of the fantasy of Africa as a space free of homosexual persons, acts, and attachments going back at least as far as Edward Gibbon in the eighteenth century.

More recently, the domain of oppression has widened beyond pronouncements from this or that state house. An African bloggers' site notes that many African political and religious leaders in countries such as Ghana, Nigeria, Cameroon, Zambia, Gambia, South Africa, Zimbabwe, Uganda, Malawi, and Botswana have publicly maligned LGBTQI people and in some cases directly incited violence against them while labeling sexual minorities as "un-African." The case study at the heart of the report records that in October 2010 the Ugandan tabloid *Rolling Stone* published the names and photographs of "100 top homos," including gay rights activist David Kato. He and two other activists successfully sued the paper, with the presiding judge noting that "[e]very human being is protected under the African Charter of Peoples and Human Rights and this includes the rights of LGBTQI persons." Kato was murdered in January 2011; previously he had been imprisoned and tortured for his public opposition to an antihomosexuality bill, "proposed in 2009, backed by religious fundamentalists" (Anengiyefa). The various bills proposed across the continent are vague about the explicit censoring of literary representations of same-sex-loving Africans, although it is likely that such literary representations could be restricted under vague and all-encompassing clauses like "publicity and the public show of same-sex amorous relationships" (Same-Sex Marriage Bill).

In parts of contemporary Africa, homophobia is played out in a broader context in which the frank discussion of sex – and especially of transgressive sex – is generally frowned on: witness the hostile reception in many quarters to novels and plays that deal with subjects such as marital rape (Ama Ata Aidoo's *Changes* [1991]), child abuse (Lara Foot Newton's *Tshepang: The Third*

Testament [2005]), or the maladministration of circumcision practices (Thando Mgqolozana's *A Man Who is Not a Man* [2009]). Indeed, a well-known saying relating to the circumcision school could be applied to the field of sexuality in general: "what happens on the mountain stays on the mountain." The historical reasons for this policed reticence around public discussions of sex more generally are contested and have acquired considerable urgency around the HIV/AIDS pandemic ravaging parts of sub-Saharan Africa. Possible reasons might include the missionary education of many African elites in the eras of decolonization and independence, the influence of particularly British customary law, the persistence of indigenous hetero-patriarchy, and the need to respond with narrow notions of respectability to pervasive racist discourses about the sexual lasciviousness of blackness (see Hoad).

In such a context, the dilemma expressed by openly gay South African filmmaker Fanney Tsimang is eminently understandable: "we took a risk to make a gay story. Even e.tv [Zambian television channel] I don't think they were sure they wanted to do that. We tried to tell them that these things are happening in the township and if we don't talk about it, who will talk about it? Who will tell the stories?" (qtd. in Krouse 11).

African writers wishing to bring same-sex sexualities (practices, desires, identities, relationships) into representation have had to respond to this complicated set of contested discourses: the long European history of homosexuality as un-African and its paradoxical fantasy of Africans as polymorphously perverse primitives; the homophobic pronouncements and legislative initiatives of African elites; the ongoing political and economic crises in the reproduction of everyday life under colonialism, postcolonialism, and now globalization that homosexuality can be used to emblematize; as well as the more quotidian difficulties of writing and getting published in countries with small publishing industries, whether tiny ones in African languages (and ones geared toward a school textbook market at that) or ones in the major colonial languages like English or French producing work recognizable to an international audience. Small wonder that during the period 1960–90, the great majority of African plays, novels, and poems that include same-sex sexual activity as part of their subject matter treat this in harshly pejorative terms: as an abnormality or a perversion inflicted on Africans, in one way or another, by Westerners.[1]

Homosexuality and Colonial Allegory

Africa has a vast and wide-ranging corpus of oral poetry and narrative, sometimes referred to as "traditional literature." This term is only meaningful in that the oral corpus has a much longer history than does the written; yet it remains contemporaneous with the latter, constantly finding new subject matter on a continent undergoing convulsive changes, and the oral and written domains synthesize in a number of ways. We have not searched the oral corpus for material relevant to this chapter, but note that oral poetry is able to accommodate homophobic references to same-sex sexuality as readily as the written corpus on which we have focused. This is the case, for instance, in party political songs performed at election rallies, the rhetoric of which combines boast and invective – witness the following onslaught on the political opposition and one of its leaders in a 1983 song from northern Nigeria, translated from the Hausa by William Miles and Lawal Nuhu: "Any NPP stalwart is a dog. As for me, if he dies, / Let him not be buried. . . . Jatau, a slave to / Jews, will teach your children to become effeminate, / To tie cloth wrappers round their hips like Dudu [i.e. a homosexual] / A man of no virility" (Miles 124).

Prior to 1960, there is a fair amount of ethnographic material that engages the questions of same-sex-practicing Africans, but arguably the focus on the literary precludes extensive engagement with it here. Wulf Sach's *Black Hamlet* (1937), set in what was then Southern Rhodesia (now Zimbabwe) and South Africa, bills itself as a psychoanalytic biography, but in 1948 is republished as a "novel" called *Black Anger*. Some critics, including Marc Epprecht, contend that its central protagonist, John Chavafambira, could be read as "gay," although what "gay" can mean for a married Manyika nganga (healer / diviner) in the confines of a rapidly urbanizing Johannesburg in the 1930s is up for grabs. The text documents a historically remarkable, if necessarily massively unequal, interracial friendship between two men, not entirely free of homoerotic charge. Peter Lanham and A.S. Mopeli-Paulus's novel *Blanket Boy's Moon* (1953) contains several coy yet undeniable references to and descriptions of homosexual sex in a variety of social settings from shebeens to prisons to circumcision schools. The central and loosely eponymous protagonist, Monare, a blanket boy from Basotholand – now Lesotho – experiences both homoerotic and heteroerotic attractions, against a backdrop in which African sexual attractions and behaviors are profoundly overdetermined by the experiences of migrant labor, wavering between "traditional" and colonial state power and conflicted religious affiliation.

From the 1950s onward, dozens of novels, short stories, plays, and poems by black Africans appeared in which same-sex sexual activity is depicted as an abnormality – further, whether in the context of depictions of the slave trade or of colonial exploitation, or of the prisons and mine hostels of apartheid South Africa, depicted as a phenomenon alien to Africa and imposed on

Africans by outsiders. This is true not only of texts that explicitly focus on the Western (or, earlier, Arab) entry into Africa – for example, the "cultural nationalist" novels of the 1950s and early 1960s, or work that contests apartheid – but also of work that began to emerge in the mid-1960s and is recognized as a literature of postcolonial disillusionment.

Writing in 1989, Chris Dunton commented:

> What remains conspicuous in all these works is the abstention among African writers, and even among the most searching and responsive of these, from a fully characterized and nonschematic depiction of a homosexual relationship between Africans.... [T]he practice of homosexuality within African society remains an area of experience that has not been granted a history by black African writers, but has been greeted, rather, with a sustained outburst of silence. ("'Wheyting" 445)

In the past two decades, a handful of writers have emerged who have dared to interrupt that silence and whose work we discuss in the last section of this chapter. These include Calixthe Beyala (Cameroon), Frieda Ekotto (Cameroon), K. Sello Duiker (South Africa), and Jude Dibia (Nigeria). In other media, too, the silence has been broken, for example in the Guinean film *Dakan* (1997), a work that, according to the brochure for the Fifth South African Gay and Lesbian Film Festival, "questions the notion that there is a universal gay culture and, more importantly, the notion that homosexuality is un-African." *Woubi Cheri* (1998), a documentary film from Cote d'Ivoire, does similar cultural work.

Prior to this, however, a number of works were published in which the authors' approach to same-sex sexuality is in one way or another more nuanced than in the majority of texts, although this is not so much indicative of a more benign, less denigratory approach to same-sex sexuality on the part of their authors as of an approach to thematic development that presents same-sex sexuality as subject matter pressed into the service of ulterior thematic schema. These works include Ama Ata Aidoo's *Our Sister Killjoy* (Ghana, 1977), Yulisa Amadu Maddy's *No Past, No Present, No Future* (Sierra Leone, 1973), and several others that we now discuss: Yambo Ouologuem's *Bound to Violence* (Mali, 1968), D.N. Malinwa's "Everything Under the Sun" (Tanzania, 1969), Rebeka Njau's *Ripples in the Pool* (Kenya, 1975), Wole Soyinka's *The Interpreters* (Nigeria, 1965), and Thomas Mpoyi-Buatu's *La Re-production* (Democratic Republic of the Congo, 1986). Dunton notes that in a small number of texts published in the period of 1960 to 1990, homosexuality "is treated non-pejoratively and in some cases plays an elaborate and central thematic function" ("'Wheyting'" 428), yet even here "the more responsive and detailed treatments of homosexual relationships … are actually *dependent* upon the pejorative stereotype in the sense that they are only thematically effective when read against this" (444).

Nobel laureate Wole Soyinka's first novel, *The Interpreters* (1965), arguably offers the first sustained depiction of a recognizably homosexual character in African literature in English. In key ways, Soyinka's novel clearly engages the pejorative stereotype of the "homosexual" as un-African. Joe Golder, the African American history professor, part-time singer, and significant member of the Bohemianesque cohort who constitute the social and cultural interpreters in the world of the novel, is referred to as three-quarters white and as "the American." Nevertheless, he also poses for Kola – the painter who is painting portraits of Yoruba divinities – as Erinle, a Yoruba stream god of indistinct and disputed gender; toward the novel's close he is imagined being "baptized" into blackness while singing "Sometimes I feel like a motherless child" by Egbo, the character who voices the most homophobic utterances in the novel. There are clear expressions of homophobic sentiment and ideology in the depiction of Golder, but there are equally powerful representational attempts to assimilate the diasporic homosexual body into imaginings of authentic African blackness.

First published as *Le Devoir de Violence* in 1968 and appearing in English translation in 1971, Yambo Ouologuem's *Bound to Violence* has probably generated more controversy than any other single text by a black African writer. Apart from igniting an extended and complicated debate on charges of plagiarism, the novel was excoriated by many for its squalor and violence, as well as its apparent contempt for the "niggertrash" whose history it depicts, whilst being hailed by others as a subversive, deconstructionist masterpiece (see Wise 1–12). Dunton scrutinizes the question of the novel's depiction of a homosexual relationship ("Representation"), but, as Christopher Wise comments: "there is clearly need for further discussion of Ouologuem's treatment of such themes" (11). We attempt this later in this chapter, acknowledging that *Bound to Violence* remains one of the most important texts in the African literary canon and in postcolonial writing more generally.

For 150 pages, Ouologuem hurls at the reader an unremitting catalogue of horrors. Yet what is even more remarkable than the visceral impact he delivers is his constant foregrounding of the act of representation and, by implication, his subversion of "the relevance of relevance" (Dunton, "Representation" 52). This is achieved in part through his parodic use of pious interjections: "*wassalam!*, God refresh his couch, A prayer for him, *alif lam*, A hymn to it, God save the Queen!, A sob for her, O tempora, o mores …, A tear for him, May God preserve us" – all of these in the first few pages, posing a constant challenge to the reader's sense of the fixity, of the point, of narration. In the same service, it would appear, is the mind-blowing tedium – especially in the section that deals with the French colonization of West Africa, with its collaborators and acts of resistance – of Ouologuem's narration of intrigue and counter-intrigue, accusation and counter-accusation, the sum total of which invites a cynical disregard for what seem to be equally undesirable outcomes.

One of the novel's major characters, Raymond-Spartacus Kassoumi, is dispatched to Paris, the colonial metropolis, to complete his education. At the outset of this episode Ouologuem maintains his sardonic, deconstructionist stance: "The white man had crept into him and this white presence determined even the moves that he, a child of violence, would make against it .... [W]here he should have discovered ... he accepted" (137). There follows Raymond-Spartacus's unwitting incest with his sister in a brothel, the news of the enslavement of his father, and his sister's appalling death, following which Raymond-Spartacus is left with a need "to glut and intoxicate himself with his despair" (148).

It is in this context that he is picked up by a wealthy white businessman who, in the course of a short-lived affair, supports him financially. Raymond-Spartacus recognizes himself initially as being engaged in an act of prostitution – all that he, as a member of the "niggertrash," can expect – yet the course of the affair is traced by Ouologuem with a tenderness, with a total lack of detailing of physical contact, and with a foregrounding of the concept of love that have no precedent in the novel. Lambert, the white man, begins this with his speech of seduction: "'A day freed from anguish by your love and mine.... [T]hat's what I want. Just one day. Would you like that? A day that will save us both'" (153). But the same terms are reciprocated in Ouologuem's account of Raymond-Spartacus's self-recognition: "he knew how much he needed this white man, his warmth, his loneliness, how necessary it was for him to lose himself in his lover" (157). It is possible that here once again Ouologuem is engaged in an act of representation designed to devour its own signifiers, but what strikes one most forcefully – in the context of the (at the time of the novel's composition) almost uniformly denigratory depiction of same-sex sexuality in African literature – is the strategic positioning of the episode: after the horrors that have preceded it, comes *this*.

A text published as early as 1969 – and one that breaks entirely with received wisdom on homosexual relations in Africa – is a short story by Tanzanian writer D.N. Malinwa. The title, "Everything Under the Sun," may be ironic but, if so, this is the only distancing mechanism in the entire text. The editors of the anthology in which the story appeared comment: "There is usually a certain reticence amongst Africans towards the issue of homosexuality. The wicked colonialist ... is widely accredited with having introduced homosexuality on the continent" (Dathorne and Feuser 262). Yet Malinwa's story, a beautifully understated piece, normalizes a homosexual relationship by virtue of having the nature of this slip by as part of the given. Two urban roommates, Meta and Welimo, quarrel over issues that have clearly been simmering for some time: Meta's taking to religion, with the result that he no longer drinks and smokes with his friend, and Welimo's failing to secure a job with the result that he continues to be economically dependent on Meta. In the single piece of action in the story, Meta orders Welimo to move out of their shared room, and then pleads with him to return. At the end, Welimo bares his chest to reveal a tattoo of a crouched black panther (an image the exact nature of which one should perhaps not read too much into), a tattoo identical to Meta's; it becomes clear that not only are the two lovers, but that their love and need for each other are equal. Dathorne and Feuser comment: "What we liked about the story was its simplicity, the absence of condemnation, the regard for the relationship on its own terms" (262).

Thomas Mpoyi-Buatu's 1986 novel *La Re-production* takes the form of a confession by its central character, Kena, who is obsessed by the problem of identity: the development of identity through the matrix of Africa's precolonial value systems and their partial metamorphosis under colonial and postcolonial regimes, and the denial of identity under pressure from orthodoxy. All differences acknowledged, his existential crisis has something in common with that of Raymond-Spartacus in *Bound to Violence* and with that of the hero of Saidou Bokoum's *Chaîne*, a novel discussed in detail by Dunton ("'Wheyting'" 427–28). Bernard Mouralis observes that this is a character whose "marginality appears to reside in a deliberate effort to emancipate himself from accepted moral codes" (19).

Kena's transgressions are corporeal: in Mouralis's words, his sensibility is "nourished by the experience he has of his body, notably in its sexual dimension" (28). Yet, as Mouralis adds, Kena is driven "not by the wish to transgress [hegemonic] values but, much more, by the very conscious aim of effecting their 'transmutation,' rendering possible the establishment of new social forms and a new morality" (31). Kena pursues his goal through both incest and same-sex sexual activity. In a language that is at one and the same time ecstatic and frank in its admission of a loss of nerve, he proclaims: "Re-invest in the legitimacy of the body. Try out multiple paths. Undertake a quest for odours. Male odours.... The practice of 'musexwe' presupposes a heroic abnegation.... The anus offered to all phalluses stiff with desire retracts in agonized pain" (Mpoyi-Buatu 167). In *La Re-production,* same-sex sexual activity as subject matter functions as a kind of conduit through which the novel's thematic material can be forced, and the novel's thematic drive is – as in the novels by Ouologuem and Bokoum – essentially philosophical. It is no matter for surprise that the epigraphs for Mpoyi-Buatu's work are drawn from Nietzsche and Sartre (whose work underpins Bokoum's novel too).

Even in texts that are less audacious – more conventionally structured and narrated – than those by Ouologuem and Mpoyi-Buatu, the way homosexuality as subject matter is integrated into the text's thematic development may depend on one's reading of the narration's focalization, of the relationship between narratorial voice and the perspective of individual characters. This is the case with Rebeka Njau's 1975 novel *Ripples in the Pool.* Here, when a married woman, Selina, seduces a younger woman, Gaciru, the initial response to the affair is located in the domain of the consciousness of Selina's husband, Gikere: "It worried him to see a young girl drawn into an emotional kind of love that was strange for normal human beings" (64). Yet this kind of distancing is partially offset at the end of the novel, when Gaciru leaves Selina and declares: "'Forgive me. I do not want to hurt you.... I love you.... I'm young. I need to be loved in a normal way. But my love for you has not changed'" (141). The least we can say of this is that it appears that narration is not always adequate to the experience of characters who are not capable of grasping their own emotions and life experience.

The Proliferation of Representations

In the past thirty years or so, there has been a marked shift in the treatment of same-sex sexuality in black African literature, as same-sex relationships have been explored with a depth of detail and degree of seriousness that was hardly conceivable before – with, as it were, these relationships being "taken on board" increasingly on their own terms. Sometimes this shift is observable in the output of a single author: contrast the blatant homophobia of some of Tatamkhulu Afrika's early poetry with the elegiac account of a love relationship between two men in his novel *Bitter Eden* (2002). If in decades previously the notion that homosexuality is un-African had been trotted out as a meme, now there are authors prepared openly to challenge this canard.

Although Tatamkhulu Afrika had hitherto passed as white, as a protest against apartheid he had himself reclassified as Malay; he converted to Islam, served in Umkhonto we Sizwe, the military wing of the ANC, and founded the radical antiapartheid group Al-Jihad. During the last years of his life, he lived in near poverty in makeshift accommodations in the Western Cape. It was at this point that he became a full-time writer, publishing eight collections of poetry, two novels, a collection of four novellas, and (posthumously) a large-scale autobiography. In the latter work, *Mr. Chameleon* (2005), he identifies racism as "the overriding preoccupation of my life" (25). This concern is attested to by his courageous stand against apartheid. Even more urgent a preoccupation, however, was with the nature and meaning of masculinity, especially when this is challenged under situations of physical danger or when experiencing homoerotic impulses (see Dunton, "Tatamkhulu").

Two of Afrika's works of most relevance to this chapter are his novella "The Quarry" (in *Tightrope* [1996]) and *Bitter Eden*, both of which explore affective relationships between men that have a strong homoerotic element. Prior to this, references to same-sex sexuality in Afrika's work were plainly homophobic. Witness a number of the poems (Dunton, "Tatamkhulu" 153–55), amongst which is "Gay Samaritans," in which Afrika explores his own coldness toward a gay couple caring for him in hospital: "I ... saw them through / the stone eyes of the straight" (*Turning* 81). In a characteristically contemptuous gesture, he speculates that, years after the encounter, one of them might now be "a raddled courtesan with balls, cornerstanding in Main Road." Yet Afrika does acknowledge the loving charity of the couple toward him and at the end of the poem there is a redemptive recognition: "[I] know a pity and a love / that does not shame me anymore / that is the sweet, astringent gift to me of time" – time being another major preoccupation throughout Afrika's work.

Set largely in prisoner-of-war camps during the Second World War, and evidently closely based on Afrika's own experience (see *Mr. Chameleon* 84), *Bitter Eden* takes this new openness further, tracing the growth of love between the South African narrator, Tom, and a British POW, Danny. At the point at which their relationship comes closest to fulfillment, the emphasis is both on tenderness and on the penis as signifier of desire: Danny explains that his penis "is telling you what you and me always knew" (230). Unsurprisingly, the relationship goes no further, as Tom returns to South Africa and fails to take up Danny's invitation to leave for Britain and to live with him.

The autobiography *Mr. Chameleon*, which can be regarded as a summation of Afrika's work, begins with an account of the adolescent Afrika's fraught sexual awakening and equally fraught relationships with his peer group. Throughout the remainder of this very long work (well over one hundred fifty thousand words), Afrika returns obsessively to the subject of his negotiation of his masculinity and his attitude toward same-sex relations between males: "I fled, though from exactly what I could not guess, my knowledge of homosexuality being about as fuzzy as it was of necrophilia or SM" (47); "Have I just written of Dennis C＿＿ as would a gay man?" (101). Indeed, negotiating a noun can be a problem for Afrika, as it involves questions as to whether male bonding invariably involves homoeroticism, or whether engagement in same-sex sexuality renders one gay or lesbian (the question of categorization being fiercely debated in the African context, for example, in the meetings of LGBTQI support groups): "If that was not friendship, then maybe it was something just as good – or maybe even better, only neither of us could be bothered skewering it with a name" (75).

Especially troublesome to the author are sexual encounters and his turbulent relationship with pop star Paddy Deane, later to provide the model for the young man in "The Quarry." Male-male relationships top the bill in the self-consciousness stakes. Afrika writes of a ride on a shared bicycle: "I was a boy again, lifting a mate after school, and I was the smelling man that to this day judges another by his smell, and he smelt of petrol and sweat and grease and I found all these to be pure and the twilight of an idyll of innocence regained" (158); and of a black Namibian coworker: "I have always felt that using the word 'love' in the context of my relationship with another male reduced the maleness of both of us and it was his maleness that drew me to him in the first place as, hopefully, mine did to him" (266). When same-sex attraction occurs, Afrika describes himself as being "rowelled" by the image of the other man and by the demons of guilt that subsequently plague him (that this word – the original application of which is unpleasant – is a favorite of Afrika's is a marker of the depth of his neurosis).

K. Sello Duiker's career as a writer was meteoric in the sense of being both brilliant and short-lived. Having published two enthusiastically received novels, Duiker committed suicide shortly after his thirtieth birthday (a further work, *The Hidden Star*, for young readers, appeared posthumously). Yet in the words of novelist Siphiwo Mahala, during his brief career "Duiker left an indelible footprint on our consciousness and deserves to be among our heroes" (2011). *thirteen cents* (2000) – Duiker's first work to be published, although written after his major work, *The Quiet Violence of Dreams* (see Mahala) – bears comparison with a work such as Afrika's *Tightrope* in its relentless focusing on its main character's concern with masculinity and maturation. Azure, a thirteen-year-old street kid, lives amongst lowlife characters of all kinds (variously benign and treacherous) and gangsters whose viciousness is boundless. From the beginning to the end of his narrative Azure comments on the world of adults and his own fumbling, violent introduction into this: "I mustn't cry. I must be strong. I must be a man" (24); "That's what they all keep telling me.

Grow up. Fast. Very fast. Lightning speed" (66); "I've done with grown-ups. They are full of shit" (106). Azure's is a life in which affect is virtually absent, but it is not free of sex. Raped by gangsters as a taming exercise, he also trades his body to "moffies" (South African derogatory slang for gay men) in order to live. For the latter he has no feelings whatsoever, either positive or markedly negative; they are merely "tricks" and he is engaged in nothing more than a commercial transaction.

Duiker's second published novel, *The Quiet Violence of Dreams* (2001), is a far longer and more ambitious work than *thirteen cents*. Although a multivocal narrative, it has a central character, Tshepo, who reports more extensively than any of the other voices. In addition, Tshepo's loyal friend, Mmabatho, reports on him from outside and also has her own compelling story to tell about her struggle to find herself, as a woman constantly let down by feckless men. A third voice is that of Tshepo's roommate, Chris, ex-convict and proto-Rasta, who is highly critical of Tshepo's refusal to self-identify on the basis of class and race. The narrative proceeds in three stages. For the first third or so, Tshepo is in a psychiatric hospital, ostensibly on account of cannabis-induced psychosis, although he rejects this as a slack diagnosis. A turning-point comes when Tshepo realizes he is infatuated with Chris ("I shudder to think what he would do if he knew what I thought of him" [168]). This does not work out well. Out of a job (Chris's doing) and excited at the thought of same-sex encounters, Tshepo takes up employment in a massage parlor.

Tshepo's first response to his new life is to tell himself, "You're a slut, a filthy whore" (243). Yet his first encounters with clients leave him untroubled and a fellow worker assures him, "'You know one thing about this job is that you get to the root of your weaknesses and ideas about yourself.'" The man adds: "'Men really haven't been given the chance to explore their sexuality'" (248). In what is a long (close to two hundred thousand words) and capacious novel, there follows an extensive lecture to Tshepo by another colleague who explains that the parlor workers regard themselves as a Gay Brotherhood, in a world being destroyed by the rapacity of male heteros and therefore prime to be taken over by women and gays. A mystic and – very broadly speaking – philosophical strain runs throughout Duiker's work, its terms drawn from myth, the principles of *ubuntu*, Rastafarianism, and end-time assurances.

Self-realization comes to Tshepo in an outstandingly beautiful passage in which a client takes him to the restaurant in which he used to work as a waiter, until Chris beat him up, had him savagely gang raped, and then acquired his job. Having now set Chris up to be humiliated during the meal ordering, he realizes: "I feel hollow and shallow. I was in fact hurting myself and not

Chris. . . . Vengeance is a kind of self-mutilation. . . . I feel no wiser, no bet-ter about myself" (283). Duiker is certainly not inclined to render Tshepo's journey to self-fulfillment free of doubt. Tshepo is anguished to discover that virtually all of his clients are white, although he yearns for love and mutual self-discovery with a black man (331). He is also appalled to discover how racist some South African white gays can be: "With all their moaning, crying and campaigning for equal rights gay men are also . . . bigoted" (417; see also 343). Yet in a deeply moving and expertly plotted episode such as Tshepo's anguish over his treatment of Chris, Duiker's achievement is to construct an imagi-nary in which same-sex sexuality is not only seen as valid in itself for those who live in it, but as a domain that can inform a broader humane outlook. This is an extraordinary break from literary traditions that deny same-sex sexuality as an integral part of a broader humanity.

Duiker's writing can be contextualized further in relation to a body of white South African writing on same-sex sexual relationships and identities. Brenna Munro has analyzed the appearance of legibly lesbian and gay characters in the postapartheid work of South Africa's literary Nobel laureates – Nadine Gordimer and J. M. Coetzee, respectively – arguing for the figure of the queer person as emblematizing the new in the new South Africa (173). Openly gay writers in South African letters include, among others, Hennie Aucamp, Mark Behr, Stephen Gray, Joan Hambidge, Michiel Heyns, Koos Prinsloo, and Marlene van Niekerk. Leloba Molema asserts that Lisa Combrinck's poetry "highlights the great paucity of erotic poetry by and for women in the African literary canon" marking Combrinck's poetry as "nothing short of revolutionary." Matthew Krouse and Kim Berman's important anthology, *The Invisible Ghetto* (1995), marked the first collection of lesbian and gay writing in English from South Africa, after Hennie Aucamp's groundbreaking Afrikaans collection *Wisselstroom: Homoerotiek in die Afrikaanse Verhaalkuns: 'n bloemle-sing* (1990). Shaun de Waal's "A Thousand Forms of Love: Representations of Homosexuality in South African literature" in Mark Gevisser and Edwin Cameron's anthology *Defiant Desire* (1995) provides critical contexts for many of these writers and their predecessors.

Prinsloo's four collections of short stories in Afrikaans document with a kind of bleak, and sometimes hilarious, nihilistic horror the moral bankruptcy of the last years of the apartheid era using explicit representations of taboo forms of sexuality to mock official ideologies of sexual purity and puritan-ism. In *Triomf*, Marlene van Niekerk juxtaposes a loving lesbian couple with a broken and incestuous family as the emblem of apartheid in the eponymous Triomf, the white Johannesburg working-class neighborhood built over the rubble of Sofiatown, the center of Johannesburg black cultural life in the 1940s and 1950s.

Mark Behr's *The Smell of Apples* (1993) culminates with the narrator watching his father rape the former's best friend, while mistaking his father for a visiting Chilean general. Representations of same-sexual activity, desire, or identity often stage more than themselves in the South African literature of the 1980s and '90s, most often racial struggle and shame.

Michiel Heyns's novel, *Lost Ground*, published to widespread acclaim in 2011, partially rewrites these allegorical deployments of sexuality. The narrator, Peter, a freelance journalist, returns to South Africa from London to investigate the murder of his cousin, a story he is convinced will cast light on the social dispensations of the new South Africa. His voyage of discovery requires him to rethink the meaning of passing time, the outcomes of change (post-1994), and questions of identity having to do with race and sexual orientation (he himself has been in a gay relationship with a black man in London, a relationship that has recently floundered). At the heart of this funny and yet desperately sad novel is Peter's re-encounter with a childhood friend, Bennie, and the unarticulated realization by both of them that they have always been in love with each other.

New Openness

Silence, taboo, and gossip are practices that confound the discussion of sexuality in Africa, but these practices may themselves become the subject of discourse, with fruitful, liberating effect. An example is *Dance Me to the End of Time: A Play about Gossip, Silence and HIV & AIDS*, a Theatre for Development project of the National University of Lesotho; through the forum (participatory) theatre approach employed for this project, villages were stimulated into talking openly about not being able to talk, or about talking in ways that were damaging to themselves and others. We conclude this chapter by discussing the work of contemporary African novelists for whom this is a pressing issue: Calixthe Beyala, Jude Dibia, and Frieda Ekotto.

In her 1995 essay *Lettre a mes soeurs occidentals* (*Letter to my Western Sisters*) Calixthe Beyala proclaims: "There are subjects I don't take up with tweezers. Use forceps! I came into the world out of female cack and the whole world is learning who I am: a comical black plum bawling away till I die."[2] Good to her word, it is difficult to think of another Francophone African writer after Yambo Ouologuem whose work has provoked as much controversy as that of Beyala. Just one example: in his review of the book in which Dunton's essay on

Beyala appeared, highly respected Cameroonian scholar Ambroise Kom comments acidly that the essay "gives pause to wonder why [Beyala] could have been chosen to represent African literary Francophony" (220).

Controversy has focused in part on whether Beyala's work can be considered lesbian in orientation. One critic, Richard Bjornson, argues that it is, referring to Beyala's "lesbian approach" to her accounts of relationships between women (420). Beyala herself has stated: "I was not a lesbian and am still not one" (33). And of one of Beyala's more recent novels Sybille N. Nyeck has argued: "When Irene couples with Eva in a homosexual union it is formed to resist the destructive forces that 'suck' the vital energies that empower creativity. . . . [I]t is important to note that *Femme nue femme noire* is not about sexual identities" (n.pag.).

In earlier novels, such as *C'est le soleil qui m'a brûlée* (1988), *Tu t'appelleras Tanga* (1989), and *Assèze l'Africaine* (1994), Beyala repeatedly depicts strong affective relationships between women that may or may not find physical expression. The main thematic dynamic throughout is, however, to construct an alternative to a vehemently rejected patriarchy. In Pius Adesanmi's words, "It is . . . the sheer force of her thematic effusions as well as the unbridled transgressivity of a seemingly irrepressible diction that has confirmed Beyala's reputation as the architect of a post-modern, incendiary feminist discourse aimed at removing the rot of male domination" (203–04). The heroines of Beyala's fiction must find a voice in order to "rediscover woman" (Beyala, *Assèze* 20).

This task of rediscovering woman is taken up in Frieda Ekotto's debut novel *Chuchote Pas Trop* (2001). Ekotto has said that she was unable to find an African publisher for *Chuchotte* on account of its subject matter (Clarke). An indicator of the subversive nature of Ekotto's narrative is the author's interest in the work of Genet, who flaunted both his homosexuality and his criminality, and who opposed the gay rights movement, arguing that homosexuals were criminals and should regard this as a badge of honor (an earlier text by Ekotto is her academic study, *La litterature carcerale et le discours juridique dans l'ouevre de Jean Genet*). The novel, a lyrically rendered bildungsroman, tracks three generations of same-sex loving women. Naminata Diabate argues that it is:

> a narrative about silences, fragments, records, and rediscoveries in which female characters transform their bodies, through spiritual and creative means, into subversive projects against Fulani hetero-patriarchal mechanisms of control. By engaging in taboo sexual practices such as "incest," and intergenerational corporeal intimacy same-sex sexuality, they break the Law of

the Father that unsuccessfully attempts to silence them through institutional regimes of control: female genital surgeries, marital rape, bodily dismemberment, objectification and spectacle.

In interviews, Ekotto has eschewed the terms *lesbian* and *homosexual* to describe her characters, preferring the designation "women-loving women." The uneven import of Eurocentric identitarian categories haunts many of the writers bringing erotic and affective relationships between women and between men into fictional representation.

Jude Dibia's debut novel, *Walking with Shadows* (2005), was hailed as the first Nigerian novel to be gay-themed. Although earlier novels had fielded gay subject matter as important subplot material – Soyinka's *The Interpreters*, for example, and Vintage Promise's novel *In the Middle of the Night*, which features a lesbian relationship – in *Walking with Shadows*, the gay theme is paramount. The Nigerian press, characteristically, had a field day, with much speculation as to whether Dibia himself might be gay.

The plot of *Walking with Shadows* centers on the outing of Adrian by an aggrieved work colleague. Dibia's treatment of Adrian's predicament is generally grim, focusing on the trauma he undergoes when confronted by the horrified reaction to his newly revealed homosexuality by his wife and family, and culminating in a brutal attempt at a "cure" for his "sickness" by an evangelical Christian. But Dibia also introduces characters who live in a stable and fulfilling gay relationship, and in a subplot he focuses on the story of Rotimi, a subordinate of Adrian's. When Rotimi acknowledges that he loves Adrian, Dibia treats the situation with great delicacy:

> Slowly, Rotimi began leaning towards Adrian. At the point when their lips almost touched, Adrian backed away, breaking the spell.
> "Rotimi, stop!" He sighed: "You don't have to do this."
> "I want to, Adrian." (182)

What distinguishes Dibia's novel (and up to a point links him with Beyala) is the candor with which he describes sexual relationships.

Chantal Zabus's recent monograph, *Out in Africa: Same-Sex Desire in Sub-Saharan Literatures & Cultures* (2013), provides the most extensive book-length study of representations of same sex-desire in African literature to date, and marks the emergence of the study of literary representations of such desires as a distinct academic subfield. As a further sign that a new discursive openness may be within grasp, we quote Unoma Azuah, guest editor of an issue of *Qzine* devoted to LGBTQI writing from Africa. Azuah herself is a Nigerian novelist whose work has focused (somewhat in the manner of

Beyala, although less vehemently) on the contestation of patriarchy through strong affective relationships between women (see, for example, her 2005 novel *Sky-High Flames*). In her Editor's Note for *Qzine*, Azuah begins by commenting: "'A word after a word after a word is power,' the Canadian novelist Margaret Atwood has said about the struggle to speak truth to patriarchy. African writers also know this power of words. African literature has been preeminently a 'literature of liberation'" (n.pag.). Like postcolonial liberation in general, LGBTQI liberation is a process of decolonizing the mind. Just as the independence movements had to overcome internalized racism, LGBTQI Africans have to fight a homophobia that presents itself as nativist and patriotic but is actually "a colonial hangover." Azuah concludes by referring to "a rising generation of brave and talented writers [who] will point the way toward a proud, fearless LGBTQI creative expression in Africa." This call is being answered. Kenyan writer Binyavanga Wainaina wrote what he calls the "lost chapter" to his acclaimed 2011 memoir, *One Day I Will Write about This Place*, entitled "I am a homosexual, mum." Leading Nigerian novelist eloquently responded to the passing of the Nigerian criminalization bill in early 2014:

> The new law that criminalizes homosexuality is popular among Nigerians. But it shows a failure of our democracy, because the mark of a true democracy is not in the rule of its majority but in the protection of its minority – otherwise mob justice would be considered democratic. The law is also unconstitutional, ambiguous, and a strange priority in a country with so many real problems. Above all else, however, it is unjust. Even if this was not a country of abysmal electricity supply where university graduates are barely literate and people die of easily-treatable causes and Boko Haram commits casual mass murders, this law would still be unjust. We cannot be a just society unless we are able to accommodate benign difference, accept benign difference, live and let live. We may not understand homosexuality, we may find it personally abhorrent but our response cannot be to criminalize it.

Notes

1. Dozens of examples are included in Vignal and in Dunton, "'Wheyting.'" We wish to observe that the pioneering work here is that of Vignal; Dunton's account constitutes an expansion of Vignal's initiative, only more frequently referenced as it was published in a far more widely disseminated journal than its predecessor.
2. While we have retained the visual image provided by "black plum," the word *prune* might at a pinch be rendered as "nonentity."

Works Cited

Adesanmi, Pius. "The Fire This Time: Discourse of the Body and 'Scrotophobia' in the Works of Calixthe Beyala." *Feminism and Black Women's Creative Writing: Theory, Practice, Criticism.* Ed. Aduke Adebayo. Ibadan: AMD, 1996. 201–19. Print.

Adichie, Chimamanda Ngozi. "Why can't he just be like everyone else." *NewswireNGR* 19 Feb. 2014. Web. 11 July 2014.

Afrika, Tatamkhulu. *Bitter Eden.* London: Arcadia, 2002. Print.

Mr. Chameleon: An Autobiography. Johannesburg: Jacana, 2005. Print.

Tightrope. Cape Town: Mayibuye, 1996. Print.

Turning Points. Cape Town: Mayibuye, 1996. Print.

Aidoo, Ama Ata. *Changes: A Love Story.* New York: Feminist Press CUNY, 1991. Print.

Our Sister Killjoy. London: Longman, 1977. Print.

Anengiyefa. "African Bloggers' Statement on David Kato and Uganda." *Things I Feel Strongly About.* 25 Feb. 2011. Web. 11 Mar. 2013.

Aucamp, Hennie, ed. *Wisselstroom: Homoerotiek in die Afrikaanse Verhaalkuns: 'n bloemlesing.* Cape Town: Human & Rousseau, 1990. Print.

Azuah, Unoma. *Sky-High Flames.* Np: PublishAmerica, 2005. Print.

Azuah, Unoma, and John McAllister. "Editor's Note." *Qzine.* 6 Feb. 2013. Web. 3 Apr. 2013.

Behr, Mark. *The Smell of Apples.* New York: Picador, 1993. Print.

Bennett-Smith, Meredith. "Scott Lively, 'Kill The Gays' Bill Supporter and Evangelist, on Trial for Crimes against Humanity." *Huffington Post* 7 Jan. 2013. Web. 8 Mar. 2013.

Beyala, Calixthe. *Assèze l'Africaine.* Paris: Editions Albin Michel S.A., 1994. Print.

Lettre a mes soeurs occidentales. Paris: Spengler, 1995. Print.

Bjornson, Richard. *The African Quest for Freedom and Identity: Cameroonian Writing and the National Experience.* Bloomington: Indiana UP, 1991. Print.

Bleys, Rudi. *The Geography of Perversion: Male-to-Male Sexual Behavior outside the West and the Ethnographic Imagination 1750–1918.* New York: New York UP, 1995. Print.

Bokoum, Saidou. *Chaîne.* Paris: Denoël, 1974. Print.

Clarke, Nana Ayebia. Letter to Chris Dunton, 10.05.2014. TS.

Combrinck, Lisa. *An Infinite Longing for Love, a Collection of Poetry.* Pretoria: Skotaville Media, 2005. Print.

Dakan. Dir. Mohamed Camara. California Newsreel, 1997. Film.

Dathorne, O.R., and Willfried Feuser, eds. *Africa in Prose.* Harmondsworth: Penguin, 1969. Print.

De Waal, Shaun. "Malawi's Shift on Gays Could Save the Canary." *Mail and Guardian* 9–15 Nov. 2012: 35. Print.

Diabate, Naminata. "Genital Power: Female Sexuality in West African Literature and Film." Diss. U of Texas at Austin, 2011. Print.

Dibia, Jude. *Walking with Shadows.* Lagos: BlackSands, 2005. Print.

Duiker, K. Sello. *The Hidden Star.* Cape Town: Random, 2011. Print.

The Quiet Violence of Dreams. Cape Town: Kwela, 2001. Print.

thirteen cents. Cape Town: David Philip, 2000. Print.

Dunton, Chris. "The Representation of Homosexuality in Ouologuem's *Le devoir de violence.*" *Yambo Ouologuem: Postcolonial Writer, Islamic Militant.* Ed. Christopher Wise. Boulder: Lynne Rienner, 1999. 47–54. Print.

"Tatamkhulu Afrika and the Testing of Masculinity." *Research in African Literatures* 35.1 (2004): 148–61. Print.

"'Wheyting be dat?': The Treatment of Homosexuality in African Literature." *Research in African Literatures* 20.3 (1989): 422–48. Print.

Dunton, Chris, and Mai Palmberg. *Human Rights and Homosexuality in Southern Africa.* Uppsala: Nordiska Afrikainstitutet, 1996. Print.

Ekotto, Frieda. *Chuchote Pas Trop.* Paris: L'Harmattan, 2005. Print.

La litterature carcerale et le discours juridique dans l'oeuvre de Jean Genet. Paris: L'Harmattan, 2001. Print

Epprecht, Marc. *Hungochani: The History of a Dissident Sexuality in Southern Africa.* Montreal: McGill-Queens UP, 2004. Print.

Heterosexual Africa?: The History of an Idea from the Age of Exploration to the Age of AIDS. Athens: Ohio UP, 2008. Print.

Unspoken Facts: A History of Homosexualities in Africa. Harare: GALZ (Gays and Lesbians of Zimbabwe), 2008. Print.

Gevisser, Mark. "SA Leads UN on Gay Rights." *Mail and Guardian* 9–15 March 2012: 7. Print.

Gevisser, Mark, and Edwin Cameron, ed. *Defiant Desire: Gay and Lesbian Lives in South Africa.* New York: Routledge, 1995. Print.

Gray, Stephen. *Time of Our Darkness.* London: Muller, 1998. Print.

Hambidge, Joan. *En skielik is dit aand.* Johannesburg: Protea Boekhuis, 2005. Print.

Palindroom. Cape Town: Genugtig, 2008. Print.

Heyns, Michiel. "Long Perspectives." *Touch: Stories of Contact by South African Writers.* Ed. Karina Magdalena Szczurek. Cape Town: Zebra P, 2009. 193–210. Print.

Lost Ground. Johannesburg and Cape Town: Jonathan Ball, 2011. Print.

Hoad, Neville. *African Intimacies: Race, Homosexuality, and Globalization.* Minneapolis: U of Minnesota P, 2007. Print.

Ibiwoye, Dotun. "Gay Right Controversy: A Gathering Storm over Cameron's Comments." *Vanguard* 23 Nov. 2011. Web. 7 June 2012.

Judge, Melanie. "Prejudice pedaled as tradition." *Mail and Guardian* 7–13 Oct. 2011: 35. Print.

K. Sello Duiker. *Mail and Guardian.* By Chris Dunton. 10–16 August 2001: 6. Print.

Kaoma, Kapya. *Colonizing African Values: How the U.S. Christian Right Is Transforming African Sexual Politics.* Boston: Political Research Associates, 2012. Print.

Kom, Ambroise. Rev. of Derek Wright, ed., *Contemporary African Fiction: Research in African Literatures* 31.2 (2000): 217–21. Print.

Krouse, Matthew. "Ekasi Secrets Laid Bare." *Mail and Guardian.* 23–29 March 2012: 11. Print.

Krouse, Matthew, and Kim Berman, ed. *The Invisible Ghetto: Lesbian and Gay Writing from South Africa.* London: Gay Men's P, 1995. Print.

Lanham, Peter, and A.S. Mopeli-Paulus. *Blanket Boy's Moon.* London: William Collins, 1953. Print.

Maddy, Yulisa Amadu. *No Past, No Present, No Future.* London: Heinemann, 1973. Print.

Mahala, Siphiwo. "Giant in the Making." *Mail and Guardian* 8–14 April 2011: 7. Print.

Malinwa, D.N. 1969. "Everything Under the Sun." Dathorne and Feuser 243–50.

Mgqolozana, Thando. *A Man Who Is Not a Man*. Durban: U of Kwa Zulu-Natal P, 2009. Print.

Miles, William and Lawal Nuhu. "NPN Song" in William Miles. *Elections in Nigeria: A Grassroots Perspective*. Boulder: Lynne Reinner, 1988: 122–28. Print.

Molema, Leloba. Rev. of *An Infinite Longing for Love: A Collection of Poetry*, by Lisa Combrinck. *Feminist Africa* 5 (2005): 153–57. Print.

Mouralis, Bernard. "Un roman super-moral: *La re-production* de Thomas Mpoyi-Buatu." *Présence africaine*. New series 144 (1987): 18–31. Print.

Mpoyi-Buatu, Thomas. *La Re-production*. Paris: L'Harmattan, 1986. Print.

Munro, Brenna M. *South Africa and the Dream of Love to Come: Queer Sexuality and the Struggle for Freedom*. Minneapolis: U of Minnesota P, 2012. Print.

Nana, Joel Gustave. Presentation. The U.S. Religious Right and the Global Export of Homophobia Conference. Council for Global Equality and Human Rights Campaign Religion and Faith program. Washington, DC. Sept. 2012.

Newton, Lara Foot. *Tshepang: The Third Testament*. London: Oberon Modern Plays, 2005. Print.

Njau, Rebeka. *Ripples in the Pool*. London: Heinemann, 1978. Print.

Nsehe, Mfonobong. "Obama Fights Nigerian Anti-Gay Bill 2011, Threatens To Cut Off Aid." Forbes, 9 December 2011. Web. 7 June 2012.

Nyeck, Sybille N. "(Homo)eroticism and Calixthe Beyala." *A Globe of Witnesses* n.d. Web. 13 Nov. 2012.

Ouologuem, Yambo. *Bound to Violence*. Trans. Ralph Manheim. London: Heinemann, 1971. Print.

Prinsloo, Koos. *Jonkmanskas*. Capetown: Tafelberg, 1982. Print.

   Slagplaas. Capetown: Human & Rousseau, 1992. Print.

Sachs, Wulf. *Black Hamlet*. Baltimore: Johns Hopkins UP, 1996. Print.

   Black Anger. New York: Greenwood P Repr., 1968. Print.

Same-Sex Marriage (Prohibition) Bill. Nigerian House of Representatives. 2011. Print.

Soyinka, Wole. *The Interpreters*. London: Duetsch, 1965. Print.

"Uganda Newspaper Published Names/Photos of LGBT Activists and HRDs – Cover Says 'Hang Them.'" *ILGA (International Lesbian and Gay Association)*, 2011. Web. 30 Dec. 2012.

Van Niekerk, Marlene. *Triomf*. Trans. Leon de Kock. Woodstock: Overlook P, 2004. Print.

Vignal, Daniel. "L'homophilie dans le roman négro-africain d'expression anglaise et française." *Peuples noirs, Peuples Africains*. 33 (1983): 63–81. Print.

Wainaina, Binyavanga. "I am a homosexual, mum." *Africa is a country*. 19 Jan. 2014. Web. 11 July 2014.

Wise, Christopher, ed. *Yambo Ouologuem: Postcolonial Writer, Islamic Militant*. Boulder: Lynne Rienner, 1999. Print.

Woubi Cheri. Dir. Phillip Brooks and Laurent Bocahut. California Newsreel, 1998. Film.

Zabus, Chantal. *Out in Africa: Same-Sex Desire in Sub-Saharan Literatures & Cultures*. Rochester: James Currey, 2013. Print.

27

Notes on Queer Politics in South Asia and Its Diaspora

BRINDA BOSE

India emerges as central to the mapping of gay and lesbian cultures in South Asia – in literature and all other forms of creative representation such as art, film, theatre, music, and dance – probably because it occupies a (geo)political centrality in the region. Common lore proposes that India, the land of the famed *Kama Sutra*, transformed into a sexually repressed society under the colonial onslaught of the British, and was unable to revive its innate sense of the sensual when it finally gained political freedom in 1947. Even if this under-standing does not do justice to the complexity of postcolonial inheritances, it is particularly pertinent to fixing a timeline for the history of queer – or same-sex, or LGBT – love on the subcontinent, because all its gay/lesbian/trans-gender wars and victories have ranged around the invidious Section 377 of the Indian Penal Code (IPC).[1] The IPC, after all, was bequeathed on its colony by the British in 1860, and many parts of the Code are still intact in the three nations into which the jewel in the crown eventually splintered: India and Pakistan (West and East) in 1947, and Bangladesh (formerly East Pakistan) in 1971. All histories of South Asian queer literatures, while being traced back to precolonial times, find their watershed years toward the end of the twentieth century when the awareness of rights-based struggles around sexual identities began taking shape. In the past decade and a half, shelves in bookstores have filled with new queer writing in English, a sudden efflorescence for which one might seek political causes.

After a long and arduous battle by LGBT activists in India, aided in sig-nificant measure by a proliferation of creative work that sparked provoca-tive, controversial discussions on alternative sexualities for over more than a decade, the High Court of Delhi in a historic judgment in the Naz Foundation case on July 2, 2009 read down Section 377 and decriminalized homosexual relations between consenting adults. This move was challenged by furious appeals to the Supreme Court of India; on March 27, 2012, the Supreme Court bench reserved verdict on the case but the attorney general finally decided not to file an appeal against the Delhi High Court judgment, stating that Section 377 of the Indian Penal Code, which "criminalises consensual sexual acts of adults in private[,] was imposed upon Indian society due to the moral views of the British rulers" ("Verdict"). Then in a dramatic development on December 11, 2013, a two-member bench of the Supreme Court of India dismissed the July 2009 Delhi High Court reading-down of 377, "re-criminalizing" any kind of "carnal intercourse against the order of nature," thus upholding the Indian Penal Code of 1861 in letter and spirit. The country reacted in shock, terror, rage, and solidarity. The impact of this new milestone on literature and culture remains to be seen.

Creative cultures, as we know, are directly in conversation with the political and social climate of a land, and a leap in political awareness finds multiple, immediate creative expressions. The struggle for the repealing of Section 377 in India, for instance, contrasts with the contemporary story of Nepal, nestled in the Himalayas on the northern borders of the subcontinent. Nepal legalized homosexuality in 2007 when its monarchy was overthrown, and is now looking toward making same-sex marriage legal. It is possible that this tiny country will produce literature in the near future that will reflect the advances it has made on guaranteeing sexual freedoms for its citizens. These different national experiences remind us to bear in mind the obvious pitfalls of assigning a timeline to what Paola Bacchetta calls "agentic positionalities" in "queer representations/effacements" across nations (947–48). The "emergence" in the mid- to late 1990s of the "queer movement" in postcolonial countries has a more complex trajectory than simply its greater visibility in social, cultural, and political contexts.

As these contrasting examples show, it is necessary also to address the vexed subject of geographical boundaries and naming in the South Asian region. We should be aware of the pitfalls of using "South Asia" and "India" interchangeably to talk about the distinct yet deeply intertwined social, cultural, and political histories across this large and fraught landmass. Rohit K. Dasgupta writes of this dilemma when mapping queer archives in South Asia: "The geographical boundaries of any country are marked randomly during different historical periods. The region which we now call South Asia despite its linguistic, cultural and religious differences has enough commonality through its shared literary and cultural traditions to merit being studied under the aegis of a single nation.... The term South Asia is fraught with many problems and covers a larger area which includes Sri Lanka, Nepal, Bhutan and Maldives in addition to [India, Pakistan, and Bangladesh]" (652). We should, in other words, remember what Dasgupta calls "the fluid and shifting nature of the borders in this area and the texts" produced in the region. In tracking literary antecedents, it is particularly important to mark that what we now call "Indian" may historically have belonged to another nation, and that such flags are capriciously ahistorical even when not mischievously incorrect. Keeping in mind, then, that a history of queer writing in South Asia is to be understood as temporally and geographically wider than its "Indian blossoming" in the last decade of the last century, we must appraise what is available to us and then attempt to cast it in more capacious perspectives.

I will here briefly map the terrain of queer cultural productions in India, South Asia, and the South Asian diaspora. Mine is, necessarily, not an exhaustive accounting but gestures toward histories that may be, and should be, explored in more depth. I begin with some examples of ancient texts that have inspired more contemporary commentators on queer desires, before moving to focus on the twentieth century, where not only literary texts but also the visual media – particularly film – have played a crucial role in enabling queer expression.

Autochthonous Homosexuality, Imported Homosexuality

Ruth Vanita points out early in her work on same-sex love in India that although there was no specific term for "queer" – or gay or lesbian – in Indian languages, this did not mean that homosocial, homoerotic, or homosexual behaviors did not exist in South Asia, or that they did not appear in its literatures, prior to such "lifestyle choices" being named in the West. Terms like *sakhi, kothi, panthi*, and *masti* have been identified as Indian equivalents for nonheterosexual loves and intimacies, and their recurrence in a variety of literatures has been accepted as proof that the idea of alternative sexualities found home and voice in Indian creative writing well before their documentation by scholars late in the twentieth century. Debates have continued on whether it is appropriate to use Western terminology and paradigms to understand social phenomena in distinctively locational contexts. For example, queer activist and scholar Dennis Altman has argued that queer theory has remained "Atlantic-centric," but India scholars like Vanita and Saleem Kidwai, among others, have claimed that "queer" is a term that can in retrospect be appropriated to appreciate a common politics of living and writing. Vanita and Kidwai have gone so far as to draw a parallel between ancient Indian thinking and Western queer theory: "In Buddhist and Hindu (and somewhat differently in Jain) traditions, gender itself is questioned. The philosophical basis of this questioning closely resembles the deconstruction of gender in our own times by such thinkers as Monique Wittig and Judith Butler. What these philosophers would call the social construction of gender that only appears to be 'natural,' ancient Indian philosophers call 'illusion' that only appears to be 'real'" (Vanita and Kidwai 22).

Various ancient and medieval South Asian literary traditions have been mined by scholars for expressions of homoerotic love. This excavation starts, most obviously, with the *Kama Sutra*, an ancient Indian Hindu text attributed to the sage Vatsyayana, and dated around the fourth century. The *Kama Sutra* is popularly and globally known as the definitive Indian sex manual but actually appears to have been conceived as a guide to gracious family living that has sensual/sexual pleasure ("Kama") at its heart, while "Sutra" is the thread that holds it together. While often misunderstood to be a book detailing various positions of love making, including same-sex and third-sex practices, it is actually a primer on the art of living in which sexuality plays a significant role. Scholarly work, however, reaches further back to the *Panchatantra*, a collection of fables originally written in Sanskrit between 100 BCE and 500 CE. According to Ana García-Arroyo, "The protagonists are animals that imitate humans in their actions and feelings. The friendship between these creatures is 'odd' as they occur between members of different species.... It is noteworthy to mention that the oddness of friendship and life-defining bonding between animals of different species morally exemplifies the oddness of friendship and love relationships of two people of the same sex, which the social custom attributes to unconventional, degenerate or unnatural behavior" (18). Across Indian literatures – from old Buddhist tales, or a host of mythological and folk stories involving Hindu gods, goddesses, sages, princes, warriors, and commoners, to mystical Islamic Sufi narratives and *ghazals*, or the tradition of Urdu Rekhti poetry in the feminine voice – texts in a range of genres have been read for intense or playful homoerotic sequences. This centuries-long view is substantiated in Vanita and Kidwai's seminal anthology, *Same-Sex Love in India: Readings from Literature and History* (2001), which rocked the literary world with the claim that there is an ancient tradition of homosexual/homosocial love in Indian texts whose long heritage, socially and culturally, continues into the present day. The anthology is the single most important contribution to the history of LGBT literature and culture in the region to date.

Closer to the present, two early twentieth-century texts have drawn the attention of LGBT scholarship. One is the short story collection *Chocolate*, written in 1924 by Pandey Bechain Sharma, who is more commonly known as "Ugra," which Vanita recovered and made available for her LGBT-seeking readership with a comprehensive introduction that puts early twentieth-century gendered writing in perspective. Dasgupta writes of the collection that it "purported to denounce male homosexuality and cast a shadow on the stability of heterosexual manhood. In the words of Ugra, 'Chocolate is the name for those innocent tender and beautiful boys of the country whom society's demons push into the mouth of ruin to quench their own lusts.' ... One of the other things the collection did, was to locate the vice of homosexuality to hybrid Indian-Western elements" (664). Another early text that comes up repeatedly, almost like a touchstone, is a short story in Urdu first published in 1942. Ishmat Chughtai's "Lihaaf" ("The Quilt") is about lesbianism and led to the writer's being brought to trial on charges of obscenity in Lahore (now in Pakistan, then in an undivided India), although the case was dismissed later for lack of evidence against her.

As these debates would indicate, the responses to texts such as *Kama Sutra*, *Chocolate*, and "Lihaaf" evince a strange representational paradox. That is, while the advent of British colonialism is cited in many accounts of queer literatures in India as a historic intervention that arrested the natural flow of life and its narratives of diverse loves and longings, twentieth- and twenty-first-century India largely continues to see homosexuality as a Western import, even though scholarly proof is continuously unearthed that disproves such a notion. On the one hand, colonial management of sexual behavior through Section 377 of the Indian Penal Code is held responsible for the impossibility of attaining same-sex rights in the region, while on the other hand, the political right wing imagines the nation as primordially heterosexual. According to Nivedita Menon, "the heterosexual patriarchal family [is] the cornerstone of the nation" and "any radical transformative politics today must therefore be post-national" (*Sexualities* 38–39).

The latter assumption is best embodied in the meteoric rise of the Hindu right to governmental power in the 1990s, an event that, apart from the repeal of Section 377, fueled the various movements for minority rights in India during the decade. One of the key factors in the construction of a Hindu national identity for the ruling "Hindutva" Bharatiya Janata Party (BJP) was an essentialized understanding of gender roles: on the one hand, the masculinization of the state that valorized aggression and violence for sustaining power, and, on the other, its mythic feminization, deifying aspects of nurture and passivity in conventional family life that its ideal women would exemplify. This perspective rendered all "alternatives" to conservative gender/sex stereotypes unimaginable, and nonnormative sexual behaviors were seen as threatening to the "moral fabric" of the nation. This meant both unconventional (nonconjugal) heterosexual behavior, which was considered destabilizing for the nation built on the edifice of the loyal family, and homosexual behavior, which, as nonprocreative and driven only by sexual pleasure, was considered dangerous to the fragile moral fabric. Interestingly, most of the energies of this moral panic were directed against "unconventional" liaisons between men and women, not homosexual acts.

It may be argued, then, that any foray into writing queer literature constitutes a radical transformative attempt to gesture toward the postnational; this is particularly significant in a political atmosphere that is continually veering rightward, whatever the avowed color and dispensation of the party or coalition currently in power. Since the early 1990s, when India "opened its skies" to a revolution in communication by deciding to participate in the phenomenon of "globalization" through reformed economic policies, increased access to sexually taboo material in the media has been held responsible for a sudden explosion of permissive writing and visual production in the mainstream. Whether the causality, on closer examination, proves quite so neat, it certainly appears that awareness and discussions of alternative sexualities in the urban – especially English-speaking and reading – public domain begins to grow apace from around this time.

Fire and the Contemporary Literature Scene

Apart from the sociopolitical-legal rights movement around Section 377, and the literary quake created by the Vanita and Kidwai collection of Indian writings on same-sex love, the most significant moment in the contemporary history of gay and lesbian cultures in India was sparked by nonresident Indian Deepa Mehta's first Indian-lesbian film, *Fire* (1996; released in India 1998), premised on Chughtai's 1942 short story, "Lihaaf." While it initially slid past the Indian censor board (RSS) with hardly a hiccup, the extreme right wing of the then ruling BJP leapt on the film when it was released in theatres and staged such violent protests that subsequent screenings had to be cancelled and the film returned to the censor board for revaluation. *Fire* was later rereleased with a couple of minor but significant changes, with the intention of diffusing "Hindu" identification of the recalcitrant women protagonists. One alteration was renaming "Sita," the young seducer of her older and more staid sister-in-law Radha, in the film because her name connoted mythic, unadulterated wifely devotion in the Hindu epic *Ramayana*, defiled in Mehta's lesbian recreation. However, what *Fire* unleashed in metropolitan India was a giant homosexual outing in the public domain, in the form of protest rallies and candlelight vigils outside prominent cinema theatres in which unprecedented numbers of queer as well as straight men and women participated. It may be said that a "civil society" movement in support of alternative sexualities was born in India in the wake of the *Fire* controversy in 1998.[2] It may also be speculated that this controversy, having drawn attention to the presence of LGBT people, is to a significant extent actually responsible for the sudden explosion of creative and documentary work around nonnormative sexualities in India and the entire South Asian region.

It may be coincidental that two pioneering anthologies of contemporary gay and lesbian writing were published in India while embers of the *Fire* imbroglio still smoldered brightly. It is certain, however, that protests and counter-protests around the film brought discussions of homosexuality to mainstream newspapers, magazines, and television shows, picking up echoes from theatre, cinema, and literatures in English and the regional languages. In this context, *Facing the Mirror: Lesbian Writing from India*, edited by Ashwini Sukhthankar, and *Yaraana: Gay Writing from India*, by Hoshang Merchant, were companion volumes published in 1999, followed soon in 2001 by the Vanita and Kidwai compendium. Merchant, who put together *Yaraana*, is an established gay poet based in Hyderabad. According to García-Arroyo, "Merchant's poetic world is a homosocial and homoerotic space devoid of homophobia.... [N]o external pressures, fears or dichotomies come to interfere with the centred and not eccentric self of the writer" (116–17). Hoshang is as well known as a gay poet as Mahesh Dattani is respected as a gay playwright, the latter based in the city of Bangalore and visible in directing his own plays around the country. In 2000, Dattani published his *Collected Plays*, which includes his best-known work on homosexuality, *On a Muggy Night in Mumbai*. R. Raj Rao, who teaches at the University of Pune, has written what is seen as the first gay novel in India – *The Boyfriend* (2003) – and has since then become a spokesperson for gay writing from South Asia. Merchant, Dattani, and Rao are identified as writing their personal sexual politics.

The politics of queer literary representation is very much bound up with the issue of language. Because regional languages have limited circulation, larger discussions have almost necessarily been confined to literature in English and in translation – although it has been alleged, and not without value, that same-sex writing in English from the subcontinent suffers from the many ill effects of globalization and is unable to carry or convey the difficulty that actually characterizes the experiences of a marginalized identity: "That smaller, independent publishers in various languages almost do not exist shows that there is almost no attempt at building cultures of literacy and literary expression among communities where such expression barely exists and where such cultures are urgently needed. That most of this writing is in English points to the fact that this 'movement' is still confined to a particular class and is not interested in enabling communities with fraught access to literacy and literary expression," writes Ashley J. Tellis (n.pag.). But in fact it is not true that most of this writing is in English; only the writing that is available to the largest number of us is in English. Small independent publishing in the various languages and dialects of South Asia are of course an endangered species – their very *raison d'être* makes it so – but the texts available in "alternative" sites such as little magazines, pamphlets, pavement pornography, diaries, memoirs, and letters, along with quiet outputs from small independent publishers in all extant regional languages, make up an impressive body of literature.

While the two pioneering anthologies of contemporary, often confessional, gay and lesbian writing from Sukhthankar and Merchant may confirm Tellis's charge that what we receive as queer literature in India is a result of identity politics indulged by a particular (English-educated middle or upper) class, Vanita and Kidwai's collection in itself dramatically challenges this restrictive notion, bringing together texts in a plethora of Indian languages from the ancient Sanskrit and Urdu to the contemporary Hindi, Marathi, Bengali, Tamil, Kannada, Malayalam, and English, texts that gesture toward, or explicitly explore, same-sex love in India over four historical periods from 1500 BCE to the twentieth century. As Rosemary Marangoly George and colleagues suggest, excerpts from Hindu mythological/scriptural texts defy the Hindu right-wing assertion (as manifest in the politically motivated outcry against the film *Fire* in 1998) that "Hindu/Indian traditions and same-sex eroticism are antithetical to each other.... [T]he most pressing issue seems to be the editorial rationale by which a consistent (albeit varyingly represented) theme of emotional attachment between persons of the same sex (as implied in the word 'love') has been traced from disparate written traditions" (9, 10). The academic debates surrounding the rationale for choices apart, the volume is significant because it seems to confirm the argument that same-sex love in some form or other has existed for centuries in the many literatures of India's regional languages. Soon after Vanita and Kidwai's book, Devdutt Pattanaik's *The Man Who Was a Woman and Other Queer Tales from Hindu Lore* (2002) copiously documented Indian folktales, myths, and religious poetry in their homoerotic/sexual content. Five years prior to Vanita and Kidwai, Giti Thadani's *Sakhiyani: Lesbian Desire in Ancient and Modern India* (1996) explored erotic bonding between women in ancient Indian cosmology and mythology. Although it was not the first documentation, then, one may say that Vanita and Kidwai's volume "outed" a long history of gay and lesbian literatures in South Asia in the same way that the film *Fire* first validated LGBT lifestyles in contemporary culture's public – and political – domain.

Diasporic Influence

As the fact that Mehta's *Fire* was first released in North America suggests, the Indian diaspora has been a rich source for the subcontinent's gay and lesbian imagination. More than ten years before *Fire* hit the headlines, a diasporic British-South Asian film out of London had actually captured a great deal of attention for its brave exploration of racism and homophobia in multiethnic England: Hanif Kureishi's screenplay *My Beautiful Laundrette*, brought to the screen by Stephen Frears in 1985. It was this film that paved the way for discussions of creative work about homosexuality in the South Asian diaspora, which included a fairly substantial body of writing toward the end of the twentieth century. One of these diasporic writers is Suniti Namjoshi, whose lesbian identity impelled her to leave India for Canada. The primary genre she writes in, the fable, is a vehicle for carrying her politics of ironic veiling forward. Namjoshi's *Feminist Fables* (1981) is a minor classic among early queer writing in the diaspora. Indo-British diasporic Firdaus Kanga's *Trying to Grow* (1990) is a well-known "coming-out" novel about a Parsi boy with a disability, but it is Sri Lankan-Canadian gay writer Shyam Selvadurai who has garnered the largest readership and a place in the young postcolonial canon with his *Funny Boy* (1994), an autobiographical tale of a young Sri Lankan who flees his country because of the political riots of 1983 but suffers dislocation and homelessness for a variety of reasons, including the fact that he is considered "funny" because he is gay. Among influential writing about the queer South Asian diaspora we also find *A Lotus of Another Color*, edited by Rakesh Ratti, a volume of essays, stories, and poems about the gay and lesbian experience. Published in 1983, Ratti's collection brought together experiences of a larger community named "South Asian," which although varied was often unified in its geopolitical understanding of and resistance to any of its members publicly identifying himself or herself as homosexual.

A case like Vikram Seth's, by far a more internationally acclaimed Indian (diasporic) writer, is more complicated. While Seth only gradually identified as gay, his leadership of intellectuals' campaign demanding the overturning of Section 377 of the Indian Penal Code in 2006 delighted queer rights activists in India, who wished to claim the celebrity writer as one of their own. Indeed, *The Golden Gate* (1986), Seth's quirky and sparkling novel in verse, told a gay tale set in California in which Phil is in love with Ed but is constrained by social and religious beliefs from following his heart and ends up marrying Ed's sister instead. Seth has queer characters in almost all his other work, including his magnum opus, *A Suitable Boy* (1993), in which the gay Mann, writes Leela Gandhi, "finds within the literary culture of Islam a sustaining corpus of same-sex desire, rehearsing, for example, with Saeeda Bai the ghazals of Mir Taqi Mir" (95–96). Writers like Seth and, in India, Vikram Chandra – author of *Love and Longing in Bombay* (1997) – have delineated gay characters without claiming gayness as a personal identity or even making strident political statements.

Challenging Politics in Erotica

Gayatri Gopinath has theorized queer desire, particularly lesbian and diasporic, as "impossible" in her reading of South Asian queer cultures abroad. Much of the impossibility of same-sex desiring appears to be the result of the complex webs of traditions and identities. If the diaspora does not allow for marginal identities, the homeland is generally perceived to be even more constrained by conservative structures of family and community. Erotica circumvents this necessity to name and identify by predicating itself on the private, the secret, the anonymous, and the minimal. The body and its sexual desires are primal and primary, needing no identificatory markings beyond the call for visceral gratification. Arundhati Roy's *The God of Small Things* (1997) constitutes perhaps one of the few significant contributions in Indian English writing that validates the body's transgressive desiring without losing touch with its sheer physicality. Amruta Patil has more recently breached two barriers of respectability in Indian English – content and form – by narrating lesbian love and longing in the graphic novel *Kari* (2008). But erotica has no "respectable" antecedent in the lineage of Indian English writing.

If we see erotica itself as an explosive political intervention in a world of respectable writing, queer erotica is doubly so. It is important to note that many queers who are unambiguous about their gay or lesbian or transgender identity still prefer to write queer tales under pseudonyms or truncated names. One recent example is Meenu and Shruti's *Close, Too Close: The Tranquebar Book of Queer Erotica* (2012); the two published the collection only under their first names, explaining in their self-introduction that *"while the world may have allowed for a South Asian queer erotica anthology to be actually published, it is still not progressive enough for all queer people to feel safe."* While their self-introduction takes on the nature of manifestos, it raises a question about the thin line that anonymity finally treads in the protest politics of identity. Certainly the argument for "solidarity" with unsafe queer lives resonates in the threatening climate of the everyday, but if those who can afford to be identified choose not to be (as those publishing in the niche segment of Indian English, for example), will there ever be the possibility of claiming rights to name oneself?

Other collections take a bolder approach. Ruchir Joshi's *Electric Feather: The Tranquebar Book of Erotic Stories* (2009), and Minal Hajratwala's *Out! Stories from the New Queer India* (2012). Our living myths being literary inheritances, it may be fitting that Parvati Sharma's sparkling early contribution to *Electric Feather* is "The Quilt," a short story that updates Ismat Chugtai's classic by alternating raucous lesbian lovemaking under a quilt with a mock-serious discussion of the original story (174–75). Hajratwala's collection offers queer erotica in urban and urbane Indian English, rather than in the expansive, dispersed Indian vernaculars that boast a long and complex lineage in the cultures of sexuality in India.

Erotica may work against a new politics of respectability that has emerged since the Delhi High Court's judgment in 2009, reading down 377's criminalization of gay sex. Lawyer-activists Lawrence Liang and Siddharth Narrain responded to that "historical" development by connecting the two battles along the axis of breaking prejudice, thereby expanding the space of what is acceptable:

> Constitutions are not merely charters of governance; they are also ethical documents that lay down a collective commitment that members of a community make to a set of principles as well as to each other about the kind of life they wish to pursue. Thus, the political form that we choose to govern our societies is not separable from the way in which we choose to govern ourselves as individuals and in our relation to others.... By locating this commitment in the language of personhood and personal autonomy, the High Court renders the Constitution vulnerable – in the best way possible – to a redefinition of the values of equality and dignity.... The Naz Foundation case is a good instance of how the formidable walls of prejudice that inform most public institutions can be broken down. The next step is to spread the whisper around a bit. By outing sexuality into public discourse in a manner never done before, the Naz Foundation decision is already talking about a revolution.

There may be little to disagree with on the necessity for a constitutional amendment that furthers personal autonomy in sexual behaviors, but we know now that this will not guarantee an epistemic change in social attitudes toward the LGBT community in India. The enemy there – our moral health brigade – is still easily identifiable, however. Potentially more troubling for the whiplash politics of queer erotica is the threat of a post–377 judgment endeavor to steer queer love into grooves of quiet respectability that will then pull the rug out from under the semiotic use of "queering" we depend on. Alain Badiou in his *In Praise of Love* alleges that "liberals and libertarians converge around the idea that love is a futile risk." For Badiou, love becomes caught in a vicious bind of "arrangements" for the delights of consummation and pleasure without passion. He exhorts philosophers to defend love not simply by maintaining its status quo but by "re-inventing" danger: "The world is full of new developments and love must also be something that innovates. Risk and adventure must be re-invented against safety and comfort" (14–15). Perhaps queer erotica in Indian English appropriates for itself that space of risk and adventure in a climate in which gay pride marches are threatening to become genial celebrations rather than assertions of protest at continued discriminations, and lesbian love stories are lapsing quickly into the stuff of chicken soup for the girly romantic soul.

It may be important at this point to think about what such risk taking entails or signifies in the post-377 landscape. Menon, in her recent *Seeing Like a Feminist*, succinctly sketches ground zero: "What is interesting is the general approval for the judgement even in the mainstream – an indicator ... of the successful shifts in common sense effected over a decade of queer interventions at every level." She predicts that, after the repeal of 377:

> the fissures and differences within the movement will become more visible. There are those who are content to be gay or lesbian without fear of opprobrium, and don't want to be political at all; there are queer, politically aware people who are Hindu right-wing or pro-capitalist or anti-reservations; and, of course, there is queer politics that is opposed to all these. This is the moment of coming of age for queer politics, when it encounters searing recognition with which feminism has only recently come to terms, that not all non-heterosexual people are queer, just as not all women are feminist; and not all queer people (nor all politically active women) are Left-oriented or secular.
>
> (*Seeing* 109)

It is perhaps a coming of age that has been valiantly fought for, and even though we know that there will be other queer battles to be lost and won yet, this may be a moment of rest, retrieval, and retribution. But we may believe that it is dangerous to dilute these politics to allow the nonqueer, the nonfeminist, the right wing, or the nonsecular any space at all, and therefore to invest in the need to "queer" what may otherwise turn out to be a politics of validation and victory for the rational. We may then think that this is the moment that needs a series of minor volcanic eruptions in order for us not to become placid, not to rest on partial laurels, not to lose, especially, the essence of what gives sexuality its rawness, vividness, uncertainty, and power – those elements of wonder, astonishment, shock, rage, and passion that make up sexual desire and its visceral pleasures and pain. Perhaps queer erotica charts a route by which queer cultures may be diverted from entering the realms of legitimate, happy love that always runs the danger of becoming apolitical. In its tentative but brave foraying into Indian English writing, moreover, erotica enters a literary territory flagged both for its grand historical narratives and for its small individual battles of postcolonial identity, but very rarely for flagrant – or vagrant – displays of transgressive sexual desire.

Notes

1. Section 377 of the IPC reads: "Whoever voluntarily has carnal intercourse against the order of nature with any man, woman or animal, shall be punished with imprisonment for life, or with imprisonment of either description for term which may extend to ten years, and shall also be liable to fine. Explanation: Penetration is sufficient to constitute the carnal intercourse necessary to the offense described in this section."
2. For analyses of the film and accounts of the events surrounding its release, see Ghosh; John and Niranjana; Kapur; and Bose.

Works Cited

Altman, Dennis. "Global Gaze / Global Gays." *GLQ: A Journal of Lesbian and Gay Studies* 3.4 (1997): 417–36. Print.

Bacchetta, Paola. "Rescaling Transnational 'Queerdom': Lesbian and 'Lesbian' Identitary-Positionalities in Delhi in the 1980s." *Antipode* 34.5 (2002): 947–73. Print.

Badiou, Alain, with Nicolas Truong. *In Praise of Love.* Trans. Peter Bush. London: Serpent's Tail, 2012. Print.

Bose, Brinda. "The Desiring Subject: Female Pleasures and Feminist Resistance in Deepa Mehta's *Fire*." *Indian Journal of Gender Studies* 7 (2000): 249–62. Print.

Chandra, Vikram. *Love and Longing in Bombay: Stories.* Boston: Little, 1997. Print.

Chughtai, Ishmat. *The Quilt: Stories.* London: Penguin, 2011. Print.

Dasgupta, R.K. "Queer Sexuality: A Cultural Narrative of India's Historical Archive." *Rupkatha Journal on Interdisciplinary Studies in Humanities* 3.4 (2011): 651–70. Print.

Dattani, Mahesh. *Collected Plays, Vol. 1.* London: Penguin, 2000. Print.

Frears, Stephen, dir. *My Beautiful Laundrette.* Mainline Pictures, 1985.

Gandhi, Leela. "Loving Well: Homosexuality and Utopian Thought in Post/Colonial India." Vanita, ed. 87–99.

García-Arroyo, Ana. *Alternative Sexualities in India: The Construction of Queer Culture.* Kolkata: Books Way, 2010. Print.

George, Rosemary Marangoly, Indrani Chatterjee, Gayatri Gopinath, C.M. Naim, Geeta Patel, and Ruth Vanita. "Tracking 'Same-Sex Love' from Antiquity to the Present in South Asia." *Gender & History* 14.1 (2002): 7–30. Print.

Ghosh, Shohini. *Fire: A Queer Film Classic*. Arsenal Pulp P, 2010. Print.

Gopinath, Gayatri. *Impossible Desires: Queer Diasporas and South Asian Public Cultures*. Durham: Duke UP, 2005. Print.

Hajratwala, Minal. *Out! Stories from the New Queer India*. Mumbai: Queer Ink, 2012. Print.

John, Mary E., and Tejaswini Niranjana. "Mirror Politics: 'Fire', Hindutva and Indian Culture." *Economic and Political Weekly* 34.10 (1999): 581. Print.

Joshi, Ruchir, ed. *Electric Feather: The Tranquebar Book of Erotic Stories*. Chennai: Tranquebar P, 2009. Print.

Kanga, Firdaus. *Trying to Grow*. London: Bloomsbury, 1990. Print.

Kapur, Ratna. "Too Hot to Handle: The Cultural Politics of Fire." *Feminist Review* 64.1 (1999): 53–64. Print.

Liang, Lawrence, and Siddharth Narrain. "Striving for Magic in a City of Words." *Law Like Love: Queer Perspectives on Law*. Ed. Arvind Narrain and Alok Gupta. New Delhi: Yoda P, 2011. 582–84. Print.

Meenu, and Shruti, eds. *Close, Too Close: The Tranquebar Book of Queer Erotica*. Chennai: Tranquebar P, 2012. Print.

Mehta, Deepa, dir. *Fire*. Zeitgeist Films, 1996.

Menon, Nivedita. *Seeing Like a Feminist*. New Delhi: Zubaan/Penguin, 2012. Print.

    Sexualities. New Delhi: Women Unlimited, 2007. Print.

Merchant, Hoshang, ed. *Yaraana: Gay Writing from India*. London: Penguin, 2000. Print.

Namjoshi, Sumniti. *Feminist Fables*. 1981. Melbourne: Spinifex P, 1993. Print.

Patil, Amruta. *Kari*. New York: HarperCollins, 2008. Print.

Pattanaik, Devdutt. *The Man Who Was a Woman and Other Queer Tales from Hindu Lore*. New York: Harrington Park P, 2002. Print.

Rao, R. Raj. *The Boyfriend*. New Delhi: Penguin, 2003. Print.

Ratti, Rakesh. *A Lotus of Another Color*. Boston: Alyson, 1993. Print.

Roy, Arundhati. *The God of Small Things*. 1997. New York: Random, 2008. Print.

Selvadurai, Shyam. *Funny Boy*. 1994. Orlando: Harvest, 1997.

Seth, Vikram. *The Golden Gate*. 1986. New York: Vintage, 1991. Print.

    A Suitable Boy. 1993. New York: HarperPerennial, 2005. Print.

Sharma, Parvati. "The Quilt." Joshi 172–79.

Sukhthankar, Ashwini, ed. *Facing the Mirror: Lesbian Writing from India*. New Delhi: Penguin, 2000. Print.

Tellis, Ashley J. "Same-Sex Writing: Rotten Fruit from Globalized Soil." *DNA* 5 Aug. 2012. Web. 3 July 2013.

Thadani, Giti. *Sakhiyani: Lesbian Desire in Ancient and Modern India*. London: Cassell, 1996. Print.

"Urga" [Pandey Bechan Sharma]. *Chocolate and Other Writings on Male Homoeroticism*. Trans. Ruth Vanita. Durham: Duke UP, 2009. Print.

Vanita, Ruth, ed. *Queering India: Same-Sex Love and Eroticism in Indian Culture and Society*. New York: Routledge, 2002. Print.

Vanita, Ruth, and Saleem Kidwai, eds. *Same-Sex Love in India: Readings from Literature and History*. New York: Palgrave, 2001. Print.

"Verdict Reserved on Appeals in Gay Sex Case." *The Hindu* 27 Mar. 2012. Web. 3 Oct. 2012.

28

The Crucible of Space, Time, and Words:
Female Same-Sex Subjectivities in Contemporary Chinese-Language Contexts

PATRICIA SIEBER

Chinese literature on female same-sex intimacy complicates the abiding binaries that inform so much contemporary academic writing about queer identity. In the wake of Dennis Altman's influential work on the "neo-liberal imperialism" of "American-style gay identity" (Altman 86–89), every non-Western queer literature runs the danger of being viewed primarily in light of how effectively it opposes cooptation by the dominant mode of queerness. However well intended, Altman's stance threatens to replicate the marginalizing effects of the "center/periphery" structure that it seeks to call into question. However, Western theorists are not alone in structuring their concerns along such profoundly asymmetrical conceptions of cultural contact. Influential Chinese queer theorists such as Hong Kong critic Chou Wah-shan have seized on the idea of a "diversifying rupture" in order to recuperate a nonhomophobic Chinese past with a view toward simultaneously challenging Western colonialism and its legacy of homophobia in the Chinese-speaking world. In this view, far from exporting normative "gayness," the West suppressed locally tolerant practices (Chou 24–26, 42–55).

More recently, in response to viewing "non-Western" queer culture solely as a ground of staging sameness or difference vis-à-vis a hegemonic West, a new generation of scholars has begun to examine the unevenly mediated and multiple intersections among local, regional, and transnational forces at work in different parts of the Chinese-speaking world. On the one hand, such work seeks to attend to the diverse political, economic, and social trajectories of China, Taiwan, Hong Kong, and Singapore in a globalizing world. From this vantage point, "China" cannot be constituted as a totalizing shorthand for a cultural essence or a cultural location, but is always locally provisional and shot through with different transcultural movements (Hu 7–8; Martin, *Situating* 27–33). On the other hand, more recent inquiries are increasingly engaged not only with the local negotiations with Japanese, South East Asian,

European, and U.S. culture, but they have also begun to challenge the axiom of the alleged irrelevance of imperial China as anything other than a stark and largely irrelevant foil for Chinese modernity (Guo 1079–80; Liu and Ding 32–33; Sang 11–12).

In keeping with Kuan-Hsing Chen's call to attend to the force fields of a Chinese cultural matrix in such ways as to make "Asia the method" (252–54), I will examine modern Chinese literary texts on same-sex intimacy not only for their synchronic embeddedness with local, regional, and transnational discourses, but also with regard to the diachronic pressures and possibilities of the discourses on gender within the pre-twentieth-century Chinese cultural repertoire. Despite the ubiquitous belief in an absolute rupture between past and present in the Chinese-speaking world, certain aspects of the imperial past have arguably informed the formation of "modern" Chinese subjects. In particular, as I hope to show, the reproductive imperative of the patriline, the sexualized playsphere of the floating world, and the cultural androgyny of the world of letters have all subtended the formation of modern Chinese same-sex identities. In advancing such a claim, I do not mean to suggest that such a process is unique to a "tradition-bound" China. On the contrary, twentieth-century Chinese discourse has been obsessively future-oriented in the collective quest for national sovereignty, familial modernity, and individual recognition.

As part of reformist aspirations in the early twentieth century, the establishment of universal heteronormativity in the name of love (lian'ai) largely discredited previous, status-specific formulations of "woman," while inaugurating new possibilities and new constraints for constituting female subjectivity. In the interstices of the institutionalization of monogamy abruptly naturalized in the name of national salvation, female same-sex intimacy began to constitute itself as a major discursive phenomenon in Chinese letters. Female-authored literature about same-sex commitments between women explored the tensions among the old imperatives, new institutions, and desires and dwelt at length on the often tortured constitution of socially viable subjects (Barlow 130–51; Sang 15–20). At the same time, such literary portrayals of female same-sex love have been inextricably bound up with how "woman" has been newly and differentially constituted at different historical junctures through the body, physical attributes, comportment, skills, behavior, and/or psychosocial or nationalist values.

In what follows, I will not privilege one type of "female phenomenology" in the interest of determining which of these disrupts heteronormativity most effectively, but rather, I delineate how literary texts constitute "woman/

woman intimacy" in radically different ways depending on how they config-ure "woman" within a given spatiotemporal matrix. Thus, literary accounts address the challenges women with same-sex inclinations faced vis-à-vis the pre-twentieth-century imaginary and apropos of modern heteronormative structures – most notably the reconciliation of respectability with sexuality in general and the simultaneous embodiment as an other's erotic object and as a self-willed subject in particular (Barlow 133). At the same time, fiction also attends to the conflicts between women, who, despite their ostensibly shared interests as "women," operate from radically different, and at times painfully incompatible notions of "woman" (Leung 123–33). Thus, the discussion does not seek to pursue a heroics of lesbian inscriptions reducible to the axes of past or present, local or global, Chinese, Taiwanese, Japanese, or Western, but rather hopes to explore how literature in Chinese depicts constraints, nego-tiations, and improvisations that constitute, in palimpsestic fashion, socially legible, erotically charged intersubjectivity between "women." I will in turn examine five contexts – the theatre, the bar, the school, the movement, and the family together with their associated gender terminologies – in order to pur-sue how same-sex-desiring subjects forge themselves in the crucible of words, space, and time in Chinese-speaking contexts.

The Theatre: Professional Gender

In the Chinese literary imagination, the world of banquets, vocal perfor-mance, and operatic theatre is most reliably associated with the representa-tion of sexuality. While women had served as entertainers at court since time immemorial, the influx of examination candidates into medieval cities precipi-tated the institutionalization of entertainment districts at the heart of Chinese capitals. By the thirteenth century, the Chinese stage became a star vehicle for low-status, high-visibility female performers. Not only did such stars excel in female roles, but they also performed male civil and martial types. Thus, from the inception of full-blown operatic theatre, female cross-gender performance was one of its aesthetic enticements. In some cases, the actresses were known to perform both male and female roles, in others, they specialized in one or the other (Li 48–52). The early sources are silent on whether such male-ori-ented performance became a habituated gender for the performer that carried over into off-stage performance, but we do get a glimpse of how two actresses of a family-based troupe, one specializing in young female roles and the other in young male roles, developed intimate relations with one another in *The Story of the Stone* (*Honglou meng*), the eighteenth-century novel that developed a cult following, particularly among female readers, upon its publication in 1791 (Widmer 139–52). By the late nineteenth century, female performers performed on the public stage, often under the auspices of all-female troupes that came to dominate some of the regional forms of theatre in the twentieth century (Jiang 60–105; Silvio, "Reflexivity"). Importantly, it was the new medium of opera film – first pioneered by Beijing opera reformer and celebrity Mei Lanfang (1894–1961) and popularized in the Mandarin and Cantonese-language cinemas in the 1950s and 1960s – that projected the romance of cross-dressed women and the possibility of multiple identifications among female spectators far beyond the regions where such operas had originated (Martin, *Backward* 1–3).

Among such opera films, *Love Eterne* (1962) occupies a special place in creating a modern iconography of same-sex intimacy. Based on the legend of Liang Shanbo and Zhu Yingtai previously documented in prose, plays, and prosimetric stories, the film dramatized the budding intimacy between cross-dressed Zhu and scholar Liang at a school, while sticking to the unhappy ending of poor Liang's inability to match the marriage offer of a rich dandy. Made in Hong Kong by the Shaw Brothers, an established brand for well-made costume drama with pan-Asian appeal, the film not only became a smash hit among women across the region, but it propelled its cross-dressed actress, Ivy Ling Bo (1939–), to instant and enduring stardom. While many female viewers undoubtedly fantasized about Ling Bo as the incarnation of a softhearted, caring male, for other viewers, the film could enact a same-sex scenario (Kam and Aw 137–43). Such a possibility was made all the more resonant through the film's extended sequences in the school where Liang and Han study together, an institution that, as will be discussed later, figured prominently as a site for same-sex intimacy in Chinese contexts. Situated at the confluence between status-based family pressures, the constraints of female education and ambition, and the floating world of performance, the film – and other successive star vehicles for a cross-dressed Ling Bo – remained a touchstone for a generation of viewers.

While urban Chinese audiences flocked to the movie theatres to enjoy opera film, the live operas also had a devoted following among rural and some urban audiences. Contemporary all-female opera troupes not only dramatize gender in particular ways, but comprise romantic relationship between actresses and, equally important, between actresses and their working-class or rural female fans. At the heart of such relationships are the women who play the role of the "young male scholar" (*xiaosheng*). According to anthropologist Teri Silvio, many forms of reflexivity – narrative, formal, humorous, spectatorial – characterize the performance of Taiwanese opera in Taiwan, but "no character onstage ever makes direct reference to the fact that the male characters are played by actresses" ("Reflexivity" 593). In this world of make-believe, biological sex is not only irrelevant to gender, but more important, the body is not gendered until in motion. Thus, Taiwanese opera relies on comportment (for example, mix of role type, personae, personality, and clothes, certain vocal and personal characteristics) to create the gender of the "young scholar." Hence, unlike drag, there is no truth of the body that is exposed. Furthermore, lesbian sexuality is incidental to the "young scholar" in both senses; it is widely practiced and accepted, but it is not rationalized through the lens of a Freudian psychosexual subjectivity (Silvio, "Reflexivity" 600).

With the lifting of martial law in 1987, local Minnan-speaking island culture, including Taiwanese opera, emerged from the shadows of the previous mainland-Chinese oriented cultural policies of the KMT (Nationalist Party). In the wake of this new cultural orientation, a quest for "localist culture" (*bentu*) gave rise to a new literary movement in search of a Taiwan that was neither "Chinese outpost" nor "Western copy" nor "former Japanese colony" (S. Chang 127–29). Whereas in 1977, Xiao Lihong's (1950–) novel *Osmanthus Alley* (Guihua xiang) had already featured the ambiguous relationship between a Taiwanese opera actress of male roles and a wealthy widow, by 1990, Ling Yan's (1965–) debut novel *The Silent Thrush* (Shisheng Huamei) won a major Taiwanese literary award, the first of three lesbian-themed novels in 1990s Taiwan to garner such public accolades (Lim 240). The novel concerned the fictionalization of the experiences of the author as a middle-class student traveling with a working-class, local, single-sex opera troupe of Hoklo (Fujianese) descent, embodying the tension between the nostalgia for the childhood in an agricultural setting in contrast to the decadence of contemporary industrial, urban life. On the one hand, the novel portrayed lesbian relationships as a natural part of the "local customs" together with other working-class practices (betel nut chewing, gambling, swearing, and so forth). On the other hand, the sexualization of the opera repertoire with its inclusion of pop songs from Japan, Hong Kong, and elsewhere as well as strip shows are presented as a nostalgic critique of the demise of real Taiwan opera under the onslaught of modernity (Silvio, "Lesbianism" 217–19).

Despite the critical acclaim of the novel, the 1992 film version of the novel turned out to be a ruinous box office flop (Silvio, "Lesbianism" 219). Neither the urban working-class lesbians of the world of T-Bars nor the lesbian feminists of the college campuses in Taiwan could very easily relate to the ethnically identified, working-class protagonists of rural Taiwan. Even among urban working-class women, same-sex intimacy was predicated on encodings of female gender substantially different from the professionally feminized student of the world of neo-traditional opera.

The Bar: Physicalized Gender

In 1960s Taipei, as in other parts of Asia, American GI culture intersected with local entertainment practices to create bars and entertainments that catered to so-called T and *po* women. Importantly, neither of these terms mimics Chinese or English exactly, pointing to the confluence of global, regional, and local culture in the constitution of these neologisms. While T is said to derive from the English word "tomboy," *po* derives from one of the colloquial Chinese terms for "wife" (*laopo*). Gay bars for men, in particular, attracted the Minnan-speaking, working-class T women. Such spaces were often the only spaces where the Ts as strongly male-identified women could escape from pervasive harassment on the streets or from arrest under suspicion of being a Communist spy. By 1985, a T and a *po* opened the first dedicated T-bar, Wangyougu (The Reprieve), in one of the red light districts in Taipei to cater to sex workers. This initial opening was followed by the establishment of dozens of other T-Bars in the major cities in Taiwan (Chao, "Global" 378–80). T-bars constitute highly performative spaces where the physicalization of secondary gender and the stylized culture of singing and storytelling converge to produce yet another variant of same-sex intimacy that would find its way into contemporary fiction.

In contrast to the "young scholar" of Chinese opera, T identity is contingent on physical maleness. Ts cut their hair short, wear aftershave, bind their breasts, and wear masculine clothes. Among the older generation of Ts, passing was common, with Ts customarily using male WCs. Among younger Ts, passing is no longer the goal and typically, they are said to use women's restrooms (Chao, "Drink" 191–92). However, in addition to the physical persona, Ts have to embrace certain performative aspects to produce their gender. Not only are they expected to hold their liquor, but they cultivate a persona of having been "abandoned" by a previous *po* to whom they are still devoted, thus exhibiting their capacity for love and fidelity to new *po* prospects. At the same time, such storytelling skills are completed by the ability to sing karaoke love songs drawn from the greater East Asian repertoire featuring devoted male lovers (Chao, "Drink" 193–95). By contrast, the *po* exaggerates aspects of a coquettish femininity in order to establish her *po* identity; she is always under pressure to prove that she is not simply a "woman" but a "femme." In order to stimulate exchanges between the T and *po* clients, T-bars, adopting the model of the Japanese escort bar, offer "young lords" (*shaoye*) and "princesses" (*gong-guan*) (Chao, "Global" 380–82).

In rewriting earlier Taiwanese pulp fiction about mannish tomboys, the literary works by Qiu Miaojin (1969–95) mediated between the world of the bars and the world of lesbian feminists in Taiwan, even if she herself may have felt caught between the strictures of heterosexuality and lesbian feminist ideals (Martin, "Stigmatic" 183). After committing suicide in Paris at the age of twenty-six, Qiu became an instant legend. Both her short fiction and her two semiautobiographical novels, *The Crocodile's Journal* (*Eyuji*, 1994) and the *Montmartre Testament* (*Mengmate yishu*, 1996) featured T/*po* relations. Upon its publication in 1994, *The Crocodile's Journal* became not only an instant classic within lesbian circles, but it posthumously won the *China Times* Honorary Novel Prize. Exploring the tension between wanting to be visible (*xianshen*) and being exposed and exploited by the news media (*puguang*), the novel satirizes Taiwan's media's pursuit of "lesbians" in the allegorical guise of an island-wide "crocodile" fever (Martin, *Situating* 215–35; Sang 261–66), but at the same time, it also probes the T protagonist's conflicted understanding of the heterosexism unleashed against her and of her internalized self-loathing. In contrast to the standard popular narrative of the mannish lesbian seducing a good girl or the T-bar narrative of a fickle *po* abandoning the T, Qiu's T protagonist is loved and seduced by a delicate *po*, but the T decides preemptively to abandon her, only to find out that the *po* later on falls in love with another woman. If the world of T/*po* sensibilities also partially encodes the clash between class-based femininities as examined in other stories by Qiu, it is the modern setting of the school that becomes the privileged middle-class site for the exploration of same-sex intimacy. As such, the same-sex school is the site of the most mainstream of all lesbian representations in twentieth-century Chinese cultural production (Martin, *Backward* 21–26).

The School: Environmental Gender

Schools for girls were a decidedly modern institution. Girls from late imperial gentry families were routinely educated by their mothers and by female tutors and so typically did not attend schools. Thus unlike the case of boys where the *Story of the Stone* tropes the clan school as a site for homosexual, homoerotic, and homophobic bonds between young men, the same-sex school for girls is not imagined as such until the 1920s. Initially, school for girls were set up by

Christian missionaries in the second half of the nineteenth century, but often only poor or orphaned girls attended as well-to-do families continued to educate their daughters at home. By the early twentieth century, however, Liang Qichao (1873–1929), one of China's foremost reformers, had made the public education of women a sine qua non for the development of China as a modern nation. Thus, at the turn of the century, as the curriculum switched from ethics and poetry to foreign language, math, and sciences, public education for girls became more common for women from middle- and upper-class families. Modeled after single-sex institutions in Japan and in Europe, girls' high schools began to attract scores of new students. At the same time, however, early twentieth-century intellectuals also began to translate the European discourse on sexology that both problematized and trivialized the same-sex school as a site for the neologistic affliction of "homosexuality" (*tongxing'ai* or *tongxing lian'ai*) (Sang 102–22).

Several of the well-known women writers of the 1920s explored the bonds between young women, including Lu Yin (1894–1934), Ding Ling (1904–86), and Ling Shuhua (1900–90). Among them, Lu Yin, herself part of a circle of female friends from Beijing Women's Normal College, most consistently examined the tension between female same-sex attachment in one's adolescence and the destructive imperative of heterosexual monogamous marriage in adulthood. Such conflicts were further compounded insofar as love between women was perceived to be compatible with artistic and professional pursuits, whereas marriage with its attendant reproductive imperative often interfered with such ambitions. In the novella *Old Acquaintances by the Seaside* (*Haibin guren* [1923]), Lu Yin depicts a community of women devoted to each other and the pursuit of learning, but dispersed by graduation, marriage, and childrearing. Lu Yin imagines a house that would be home to women engaged in writing and teaching. While no mention of physical intimacy is made in *Old Acquaintances*, another story by Lu Yin, "Lishi's Diary" ("Lishi de riji" [1923]), embraces the neologism "homosexuality" to frame the relationship between two female schoolmates (Sang 133–48). However, as they imagine a future couched in the language of late imperial romance between scholars and beauties, the parents have already married off one of them. The woman left behind and admonished by the newlywed to "abandon homosexuality" dies of melancholy, a common symptom of passionate love in late imperial Chinese literature now newly recoded for same-sex love (Martin, *Backward* 42–43). But before she does so, she describes a dream that, as Tze-lang Sang compellingly argues, can be read as a Freudian displacement of sexual intercourse as a "visit to the Crystal Palace in the stream" (140–41).

In Ling Shuhua's "Once Upon a Time" ("Shuo you zemme yihui shi" [1928]), it is not the Chinese dramatic tradition that mediates middle-class status and physical intimacy, but the school play *Romeo and Juliet*. Interestingly, the whole school is privy to the budding romance between an initially reluctant Juliet and an adoring Romeo. Thus, not only does the story self-consciously stage a female-female gaze, but the classmates readily and jokingly accept the two girls as "husband and wife." Even when they are found in bed together by the warden, they are sent to their rooms without much fuss. When they sleep together in the same bed in plain view of everyone, Juliet is overcome for the first time with an "indescribable sense of well-being" as opposed to her usual feelings of "emptiness, fear, and loneliness" (Ling 188). However, even though the young women are aware of the precedent of the two female school instructors who have chosen to live together, one of the girls is married off by the parents, leaving the other one behind to faint upon hearing the news. If Ling Shuhua's story holds out the happiness of a pair of mature women through the passing mention of two devoted schoolteachers, Ding Ling's short story "Summer Vacation" ("Shujiazhong" [1928]) does away with the utopian nature of such a union. The story mercilessly stages an acute sense of crisis of the subject for "new women" caught between the social dislocation of the old structure of the patriline and the nebulous promise of an "independent existence" heralded by the eponymous name of the school where the story takes place: "Independence Girl School" (Barlow 137–38; Zhu 39–59).

In contemporary Chinese fiction, the school romance continues to be haunted by the relative perfection of the love between the young women and the disappointments of marriage and motherhood. While critically acclaimed PRC novelist Wang Anyi's (1954–) story "Brothers" ("Dixiongmen") ultimately embraces maternal love over sisterly love (136–40), many stories from Taiwan are less sanguine about the enchantments of heterosexual love. "A Story of Spring Butterflies," a famous story by prizewinning author Chu T'ien-hsin (1958–), well known for her explorations of relationships in girls' schools, concludes her mature female protagonist's letter to the intimate female friend of her youth with the following words: "Over the past ten years I've experienced love, been a wife, been a mother; I've experienced every one of life's emotions. I only know that what I felt with you back then is beyond compare" (93). Thus it is perhaps not too surprising that, despite the recurring trope of a passing inclination toward adolescent same-sex romance in fiction, women nowadays who identify as "queer" in Taiwan often credit their high school bonds as a foundational experience for a self-consciously "lesbian" identity that they then further develop through the consumption of literary and academic texts (Hu

45). This highly mediatized form of women-to-women texts has spawned not just the occasional story with a theme of female same-sex romance, but intersects with a vibrant queer scene in Taiwan.

The Movement: Mediatized Gender

From the thirteenth century onward, in the fictional world of scholar-beauty plays and novels, it was customary for men and women to express their erotically charged appreciation for members of the same or the other sex through poetry. In *The Fragrant Companion (Lianxiang ban* [1650s]) by Li Yu (1611–80), one of the most idiosyncratic and widely read literati of the late imperial period, two gentry women fall in love with each other at a temple, but their mutual admiration, although at first mediated through the notion of fragrance – a trope that recurs time and again in contemporary lesbian writing – is confirmed through their appreciation for the literary extension of their "kindred kind," that is, the poems they write (D. Chang 239–57). Female-authored poems similarly conveyed their appreciation of the beauty of women with mildly erotic overtones (Ko 266–74). At the same time, the theme of crossdressing was ubiquitous in female-authored literature of this period. For example, when gentry daughter Ye Xiaowan's (1613–57) mourned the death of her two very talented sisters in the play *The Mandarin Ducks (Yuanyang meng* [ca. 1633]), she imagined the three of them as a group of young sworn literati brothers (Hua 102–09). In Wu Zao's (1799–1862) play *Drinking Wine and Reading "Encountering Sorrow": A Reflection on Disguise (Yinjiu du Lisao tu: Qiaoying* [1825]), the female author pays tribute to a cross-dressed portrait of herself that embodies the literary talent that her worldly self, poet Xie Xucai, aspires to have recognized, but also fantasizes about the comforts of female sexual companionship as a mark of her literary talent (Wu 239–50). In other words, in these works, the forces of what Kang-i Sun Chang has termed "cultural androgyny" (21–31) create an eroticized, but highly cultured space nested in the sphere of print in the interstices between the state and the family (Ko 155–57; Sieber, *Theaters* xviii–xxi). In the world of print, it is possible to construct "our kind" through physical beauty and literary talent across a spectrum of nearly interchangeable gender identities (McMahon 99–115). In other words, poetry could serve as a vehicle to transcend the orthodox strictures of wifely invisibility or the demeaned status of courtesan life and instead inscribe a nonnormative femininity into the notion of a "talented beauty" (*jiaren*), who nevertheless remained socially legible.

When we turn to the late twentieth-century world of the lesbian movement in Asia, the extrafamilial articulation of queer identity is heavily mediated through the consumption of magazines, bulletin posts (BBS), Web sites, and literature. In Taiwan in particular, in the 1990s, new public spaces such as bookstores, cafés, university associations, activist groups, government-sponsored festivals, and online forums have proliferated. Of course, the ground of such a mediatized queer identity is no longer the literatus of yore. Instead, in transculturally complex coinage, the Soviet term "comrade" translated through the founder of the Republic of China, Sun Yatsen, and through common, but disappearing everyday parlance in the PRC, was appropriated by Hong Kong activist Chou Wah-shan in 1989 to denote "gays" and "lesbians" as part of the inaugural Hong Kong lesbian and gay film festival. From there, the term was widely adopted in the Chinese-speaking world. Chou credits the success of his coinage with the integration of a Chinese emphasis on socialized subjectivity with a Western-style individual, yet politicized, sexual identity (1–2). At the same time, its intersubjective dimension combined with the progressive, future-oriented, movement-based, egalitarian rhetoric of the Chinese revolution taps into the powerful "love plus revolution" formula that underwrote the construction of "love" as a modern structure of feeling in China (Lee 256–65). The term unites "kindred spirits" under the aegis of an emancipatory project that can be pursued by individuals, organizations, and the state alike. In an effort to distinguish itself from the PRC, government officials in Taiwan pride themselves on Taiwan's recent development as a focal point for queer activism in Asia with the largest annual and very international *tongzhi* pride parade in the region (Hu 1–2).

Among the writers that emerged amidst this transnationally mediated, but profoundly indigenized queer movement, Hong Ling (1971–) and Chen Xue (1970–) have received the most critical attention. While some critics have identified these writers' embrace of the aesthetic of "queer" (*ku'er*) as a marketing strategy in a crowded literary market (Lim 240), others have argued that their literary works exceeded the existing boundaries of queer writing. In Chen Xue's seminal story "In Search of the Lost Wings of the Angels" (X. Chen 153–68), the protagonist, a university student by the name of Caocao, is raised by a prostitute-mother and enters into a love relationship with A-Su, a prostitute whom she meets in a bar and with whom she proceeds to move in. Previously, Caocao had always destroyed her writing, but with A-Su's encouragement, she continues to write. When A-Su mysteriously disappears, Caocao finds herself in possession of the manuscript of the eponymous story. Caocao's expression of her filial love at her dead mother's grave is not only rewritten as the lesbian love for A-Su, but allows the protagonist to assume a viable subject position (Martin, *Situating* 130).

In terms of the mediatized gender that I explore here, the story opens with the notion that Caocao and A-Su were kindred spirits. Furthermore, in the course of the story, A-Su reminds Caocao that she only had "to write continually, then on paper, you will see me, and you will see yourself.... You must never cease to write" (X. Chen 166). After A-Su's disappearance, the handwritten manuscript of the story remains as the only tangible evidence of their passion, tenderness, and love for each other. Thus, writing, here through a lesbian identification with the maternal, allows for the inscription of a legible lesbian subject (Martin, *Situating* 129–34). In contrast to critics who subsume such queer writing under a normative gender ideology, such works do not, in Fran Martin's words, "simply represent emergent forms of sexual subjectivity, but also enable and produce them" (*Situating* 8). If Chen Xue wills a viable lesbian daughter-cum-subject into existence through queer writing, we observe another form of strategic remembrance among some of the foremost feminist writers of the PRC. With the ascendance of consumerism as a "liberating and objectifying force," the literary landscape of the PRC has been altered rapidly, with many contrary effects among the state, the cultural elite, the mass media, the rising middle class, and the market opening up new spaces for women's writing (L. Wang 168–72).

The Family: Politicized Gender

The abolition of the polygynous household and a range of associated social identities constituted a major site for the institution of Chinese modernity throughout the twentieth century. The legitimacy of new state regimes was consolidated under the new protocol of a monogamous heteronormativity. Such regulations were not simply a matter of "social mores" or "moral regulation," but with the establishment of the PRC, sexual behavior was tied to the notion of the citizen's loyalty to the state. After 1949, sexuality was strictly controlled, with heterosexuality being circumscribed by marriage and all other forms of sexuality becoming not only taboo, but grounds for being singled out as either mentally ill or politically disloyal (Evans 4–10, 189–215).

Only in the 1980s, in the wake of Mao Zedong's death, did literary writings begin to challenge the pervasive puritan rhetoric of a state that had regulated its citizens' private life in schools, neighborhood committees, and work units (*danwei*). Among these, the writings of Lin Bai (1958–) and Chen Ran (1962–) stand out. After establishing her reputation as an avant-garde writer in China in the 1980s, Chen Ran came to international attention through the UN World Congress of Women held in Beijing in 1995. Not only was a film version of one of her stories shown (*Yu wangshi ganbei*/*A Toast to the Past*), but she also published "Breaking Open," a philosophical meditation on the possibility of mature intellectual women who just might choose intimate relations with each other. However, rather than making a case for same-sex intimacy per se, Chen Ran, building on the humanist discourse of the 1980s in China, sought to imagine commitments beyond the constraints of the highly politicized form of normative womanhood tied to familial and natalist objectives. In response to critics who sought to trivialize her landmark coming-of-age novel, *A Private Life* (*Siren shenghuo* [1996]), Chen Ran herself insists on being understood as a "politicized writer" whose methods – lyrical fragmentation, multiple narrative voices, fragments of quotidian life, highly symptomatic memories tied to high-profile political events such as the Tian'anmen Square student protests, creative concepts such as the undefinable "Lady Zero," and multivalent symbols such as the mirror – are meant to fracture and undermine the grand socialist narratives of the past (Schaffer and Song 162–63; L. Wang 179–86; Zheng 59–60).

Similarly resistant to the notion of being characterized as a writer of "private novels" (*sixiaoshuo*), Lin Bai strategically "misremembers" the revolutionary past in order to call into question political common sense about both history and women's place in it. When she completed her first novel, *A Self at War* (*Yigeren de zhanzheng*), she first published it in serialized form (1993) and then in book form (1994). Packaged with a lurid cover image, the book attracted unwelcome attention from reviewers affiliated with the official censorship bureau who denounced the work as "pornographic" and "obscene." Other male-authored novels with numerous heterosexual scenes had gotten past the censors without incident, but Lin's novel, while containing very little sex, opened and closed with an autoerotic scene, featured homoerotic scenes between women, and contained only one scene of pleasurable heterosexual sex told from a male vantage point. At the same time, the 1994 edition sold in the tens of thousands of copies, forming a part of a broader trend to turn an array of what were routinely termed "women's fictional exposés" (*nüxing sixiaoshuo*) into fodder for male voyeurs (Sang 175–81).

Just as Chen Ran imagined a happy maternal, literary, and erotic relationship with her narrator's neighbor, widow He, in *A Private Life*, Lin focused on the unmarried teacher, Mei Ju, as an object of her erotic fantasies in *A Self at War* (L. Wang 197–99). In other words, while neither of the two writers claims to have had sexual relationships with women, they turn same-sex bonds with women of "suspect sexualities" (widows, virgins, dancers, and maids, among others) into beacons of erotic and emotional fulfillment (Evans 189–91). Thus, the new family order that their stories envision is designed to disrupt the unitary, exclusive, and pervasive frame of heterosexual monogamy within the official political discourse. Accordingly, rather than merely rewriting their own family history, Lin and Chen take aim at the institutionalized amnesia vis-à-vis the revolutionary and the prerevolutionary past that may harbor alternatives to the constraints of an unhappy, but state-mandated heterosexuality (Lin 83–109). Rather than producing "personal writing" (*gerenhua xiezuo*), they have deployed the private to incubate a newly politicized gender in the "modern Chinese woman" (*nüxing*).

The Mirage of Same-Sex Desire

In this chapter, I have strenuously resisted the temptation to write a stable, adequately gendered, psychosexually inscribed, and culturally unitary "lesbian subject" into being. In refusing such a sweeping genealogy either to critique a grand narrative of heteronormativity or to construct a genealogy of same-sex desire, I hope to have gone beyond pointing to the common gloss of differentially gendered phenomenologies as "neologisms" within a modern Chinese context. Instead, in attending to the specific sites of production of new and old signs such as "young scholar" (*xiaosheng*), "homosexual" (*tongxing lian'ai*), "T/po" or "comrade" (*tongzhi*), or "modern woman" (*nüxing*), I meant to treat them, in Tani Barlow's parlance, as diverse instantiations of "catachresis," that is, as "normalizing strategies which often appear as a subject form" (32). Thus, the subjects that we encounter in Chinese-speaking settings cannot be subsumed under a single, stable denominator of "woman," let alone a "woman-identified woman." Insofar as Altman and Chou posit continuous gay subjects either across a U.S.-centric globe or across a transhistorical construct of "China," they both obscure the diversity of same-sex inscriptions within a single language tradition. My microanalysis of differently weighted gender typologies may do little to stabilize an East/West binary in an effort to generate symbolic capital for one or the other. But if we want to expand on the scholarship of same-sex desire in the Chinese archive we must not subordinate our terms to the exigencies of "same as/different from"; close readings offer a provisional vantage point from which to begin to loosen the vice grip of naturalized subjectivities around the world.

Works Cited

Altman, Dennis. "Rupture or Continuity? The Internationalization of Gay Identities." *Social Text* 48 (1996): 77–94. *JSTOR*. Web. 5 Dec. 2012.

Barlow, Tani E. *The Question of Women in Chinese Feminism*. Durham: Duke UP, 2004. Print.

Chang, Dongshin. "'Xiang Yong' (Poems on Fragrance): A Translation of a Scene from *Lianxiang ban* (The Fragrant Companion)." *CHINOPERL Papers* 30 (2011): 239–57. Print.

Chang, Kang-i Sun. "Ming-Qing Women Poets and Cultural Androgyny." *Feminism/Femininity in Chinese Literature*. Ed. Peng-hsiang Chen and Whitney Crothers Dilley. New York: Rodopi, 2002. 21–31. Print.

Chang, Sung-sheng Yvonne. *Literary Culture in Taiwan: Martial to Market Law*. New York: Columbia UP, 2004. Print.

Chao, Antonia Y. "Drink, Stories, Penis, and Breasts: Lesbian Tomboys in Taiwan from the 1960s to 1990s." *Journal of Homosexuality* 40.3–4 (2001): 185–209. Taylor & Francis Online. Web. 10 Jan. 2013.

——. "Global Metaphors and Local Strategies in the Construction of Taiwan's Lesbian Identities." *Culture, Health & Sexuality* 2:4 (2000): 377–90. *JSTOR*. Web. 12 Jan. 2013.

Chen, Kuan-Hsing. *Asia as Method: Toward Deimperialization*. Durham: Duke UP, 2010. Print.

Chen, Ran. *A Private Life*. Trans. John Howard-Gibbon. New York: Columbia UP, 2004. Print.

——. "Breaking Open." Trans. Paola Zamperini. Sieber, ed. 49–71.

——. "Sunshine between the Lips." Trans. Howard Goldblatt. *Chairman Mao Would Not Be Amused: Fiction from Today's China*. Ed. Howard Goldblatt. New York: Grove P, 1995. 112–29. Print.

Chen, Xue. "In Search of the List Wings of the Angels." Trans. Patricia Sieber. Sieber, ed. 153–68.

Chou, Wah-shan. *Tongzhi: Politics of Same-Sex Eroticism*. New York: Haworth, 2000. Print.

Chu, T'ien-hsin. "A Story of Spring Butterflies." Martin, ed. *Angelwings* 75–94.

Evans, Harriet. *Women and Sexuality in China: Female Gender and Sexuality since 1949*. New York: Continuum, 1997. Print.

Guo, Jie. "Where Past Meets Present: The Emergence of Gay Identity in Pai Hsien-yung's *Niezi*." *MLN* 126.5 (2011): 1049–82. Print.

Hu, Yu-Ying. "Gender, Transnational Culture, and New Media: Enacting Female Queer Sexuality in Taiwan." Diss. Indiana U, 2011. ProQuest. 22 Jan. 2013.

Hua, Wei. *Ming Qing funü zhi xiqu zhuangzuo yu piping* (A Critical Study of the Plays by Women from the Ming and the Qing periods). Taipei: Academica Sinica, 2003. Print.

Jiang, Jin. *Women Playing Men: Yue Opera and Social Change in Twentieth-Century China*. Seattle: U of Washington P, 2009. Print.

Kam, Tan See, and Annette Aw. "*Love Eterne*: Almost a (Heterosexual) Love Story." *Chinese Films in Focus: 25 New Takes*. Ed. Chris Berry. London: British Film Institute, 2003. 137–43. Print.

Ko, Dorothy. *Teachers of the Inner Chambers: Women and Culture in Seventeenth-Century China*. Stanford: Stanford UP, 1994. Print.

Lee, Haiyan. *Revolution of the Heart: A Genealogy of Love in China, 1900–1950*. Stanford: Stanford UP, 2007. Print.

Leung, Hok-Sze Helen. "Thoughts on Lesbian Genders in Contemporary Chinese Cultures." *Journal of Lesbian Studies* 6:2 (2002): 123–133. Taylor & Francis Online. Web 15 Dec. 2012.

Li, Siu Leung. *Cross-Dressing in Chinese Opera*. Hong Kong: Hong Kong UP, 2003. Print.

Lim, Song Hwee. "How to Be Queer in Taiwan: Translation, Appropriation, and the Construction of a Queer Identity in Taiwan." Martin et al. 235–50.

Lin, Bai. "The Seat on the Verandah." Trans. Hu Ying. *The Mystified Boat: Postmodern Stories from China*. Ed. Frank Stewart. Honolulu: U of Hawai'i P, 2003. 83–109. Print.

Ling, Shuhua, "Once Upon a Time." *Writing Women in Modern China: The Revolutionary Years, 1936–1976*. Ed. and trans. Amy D. Dooling and Kristina M. Torgeson. New York: Columbia UP, 1998. 185–95. Print.

Liu, Renpeng, and Naifei Ding. "Reticent Poetics, Queer Politics." *Intra-Asian Cultural Studies* 6.1 (2005): 30–55. Print.

Martin, Fran, ed. *Angelwings: Contemporary Queer Fiction from Taiwan*. Honolulu: U of Hawai'i P, 2003.

  Backward Glances: Contemporary Chinese Cultures and the Female Homoerotic Imaginary. Durham: Duke UP, 2010. Print.

  Situating Sexualities: Queer Representation in Taiwanese Fiction, Film, and Public Culture. Hong Kong: Hong Kong UP, 2003. Print.

  "Stigmatic Bodies: The Corporeal Qiu Miaojin." *Embodied Modernities: Corporeality, Representation, and Chinese Cultures*. Ed. Fran Martin and Larissa Heinrich. Honolulu: U of Hawai'i P, 2006. 177–94. Print.

Martin, Fran, Peter A. Jackson, Mark McClelland, and Audrey Yue, eds. *AsiaPacifiQueer: Rethinking Genders and Sexualities*. Urbana: U of Illinois P, 2008. Print.

McMahon, Keith. *Misers, Shrews, and Polygamists: Sexuality and Male-Female Relations in Eighteenth-Century Chinese Fiction*. Durham: Duke UP, 1995. Print.

Qiu, Miaojin. "Platonic Hair." Martin, ed. *Angelwings* 51–74.

Sang, Tze-lan D. *The Emerging Lesbian: Female Same-Sex Desire in Modern China*. Chicago: U of Chicago P, 2003. Print.

Schaffer, Kay, and Xianlin Song. "Narrative, Trauma, and Memory: Chen Ran's *Private Life*, Tiananmen Square and Female Embodiment." *Asian Studies Review* 20.1 (2006): 161–73. EJC. Web. 10 Dec. 2012.

Sieber, Patricia. *Theaters of Desire: Authors, Readers, and the Reproduction of Early Chinese Song-Drama, 1300–2000*. New York: Palgrave, 2003. Print.

  ed. *Red is Not the Only Color: Contemporary Chinese Fiction on Love and Sex between Women, Collected Stories*. Lanham: Rowman, 2001. Print.

Silvio, Teri. "Lesbianism and Taiwanese Localism in *The Silent Thrush*." Martin et al. 217–34.

  "Reflexivity, Bodily Practice, and Identity in Taiwanese Opera." *GLQ* 4.5 (1999): 585–604. EJC. Web. 11 Dec. 2012.

Wang, Anyi. "Brothers." Trans. Jingyuan Zhang. Sieber, ed. 93–141.

Wang, Lingzhen. *Personal Matters: Women's Autobiographical Practice in Twentieth-Century China*. Stanford: Stanford UP, 2004. Print.

Widmer, Ellen. *The Beauty and the Book: Women and Fiction in Nineteenth-Century China*. Cambridge: Harvard U Asia Council, 2006. Print.

Wu Zao. *"Drinking Wine and Reading 'Encountering Sorrow': A Reflection in Disguise* by Wu Zao (1799–1862)." Trans. Sophie Volpp. *Under Confucian Eyes: Writings on Gender in Chinese History*. Ed. Susan Mann and Yu-Yin Cheng. Berkeley: U of California P, 2001. 239–50. Print.

Zheng, Yi. "'Personalized Writing' and Its Enthusiastic Critic: Women and Writing of the Chinese 'Post-New Era.'" *Tulsa Studies in Women's Literature* 23.1 (2004): 45–64. *JSTOR*. Web. 27 Jan. 2013.

Zhu, Yun. "Subjectification of the Female Body in Ding Ling's 'Summer Vacation.'" *Intertexts* 15.1 (2011): 39–59. Print.

29

Mesoamerican Mythmaking as Queer(ed) Visionary Hermeneutics

ANALOUISE KEATING

> The filth you relegate to Satan,
> I absorb. I convert.
> When I dance it burgeons out
> as song.
>
> I seek la diosa
> darkly awesome.
> In love with my own kind,
> I know you and inspirit you.
> All others flee from me.
>
> – Gloria Anzaldúa, "Canción de la diosa de la noche"

In these stanzas, Gloria Anzaldúa aligns herself with a pre-Conquest Mesoamerican creatrix figure; she rewrites the well-known cross-cultural story of feminine evil that casts women as dangerous nonhuman creatures whose unholy, terrifying powers must be contained and destroyed, transforming it into a celebration of her own "darkly awesome" queer nature. Like twentieth-century mainstream feminists, she reclaims her "Female/Elemental divinity" by replacing conventional religious images with earlier woman-identified metaphors for the divine.[1]

But by going partially outside Greco-Roman and Judeo-Christian traditions and identifying this "diosa" with Coatlicue, an all-powerful, gender-blurring earth god/dess in the Nahuatl cosmology, Anzaldúa deepens and expands her revisionary myth: she de-centers gender and includes innovative, culturally specific dimensions untapped by mainstream feminists. And, like mid-twentieth-century Chicano nationalists, Anzaldúa replaces Eurocentric stories about "American" identity with indigenous-inflected myths. But unlike these nationalists – who rely on heterosexualized, masculine metaphors – Anzaldúa explicitly queers her Mesoamerican narrative. Throughout her work, Anzaldúa selectively draws on and reinvents indigenous Mesoamerican (Toltec, Olmec, Nahuatl, Aztec, and so forth) imagery, philosophy, and belief systems. In them, she finds vehicles for self-affirmation; epistemological tools for resistance, intervention, and creation; and philosophical insights for new theories.

Anzaldúa is not alone in her feminist-inspired, queerly inflected revisionist Mesoamerican mythmaking. Cherríe Moraga, Ana Castillo, Chela Sandoval, and other mujeres-de-color borrow from, revise, and sometimes rewrite a variety of Mesoamerican stories, traditions, histories, and beliefs. Motivated at least partially by their own experiences of alienation both from the dominant U.S. culture and from the conservative Chicano movement of the mid-twentieth century, these writers use an array of Mesoamerican themes *selectively*, to (re)claim their indigenous connections and (re)invent alternative identities and theories. I bracket the prefixes to underscore the visionary, pragmatic nature of this enterprise. These authors do not return to a previously hidden past and discover authentic, empirically accurate pre-Conquest philosophies, traditions, and myths. Instead, they go "back" to go forward – mixing discovery with invention, developing new (although sometimes presented as ancient) narratives in which prehistorical, historical, and contemporary issues of gender, culture, sex, nationality, class, and worldview converge. Their revisionist mythmaking is strategic, subversive, and potentially transformative; it can serve multiple purposes including (but not limited to) the following: (1) critiquing contemporary homophobic, patriarchal, racist configurations of gendered sexual identity; (2) developing anti-patriarchal, anti-homophobic discourse redefining conventional forms of gender and sexuality; (3) inventing new theories and practices for social change; and (4) creating hybrid philosophies. In this Mesoamerican revisionist mythmaking, "queer" becomes a recursive gesture, a back-and-forth movement that synergistically combines elements of the present with (re)invented elements of the past. This frictional movement is intensely creative and facilitates the invention of new epistemologies, ontologies, and metaphysics.

But these (re)connections to Mesoamerican indigeneity have been highly contentious. According to some scholars, Chican@s' insistence on indigenous identities overlooks the ongoing existence and cultural specificity of contemporary indigenous (non-Chicano) peoples and oversimplifies (or entirely ignores) questions of land sovereignty. Josefina Saldaña-Portillo, for example, argues that Chican@ claims to indigenous identity represent a form of Mexican "indigenismo": a "state-sponsored policy" that "recuperat[es] and celebrat[es]" an indigenous past while, simultaneously, erasing contemporary Indian peoples and thus facilitating Mexican colonialism, including ownership of the land.[2] Sheila Contreras offers the most sustained criticism of this colonizing move, arguing that Anzaldúa and other Chicana feminists developed an "indigenist feminism" that relied on a Eurocentric "modernist primitiv-ism" that co-opts and obscures the identities and needs of real-life indigenous peoples.[3] While these critical views call readers' attention to important over-simplifications and omissions in some mujeres-de-color texts, they focus too exclusively on identity-related concerns (like individual and collective self-def-inition); ignore shifts in the authors' thinking; and overlook the visionary, uto-pian dimensions that revisionist mythmaking's queer recursivity opens up.

By going "back" to Mesoamerican-inflected worldviews, mujeres-de-color authors go forward, using their invented discoveries to combine social critique with the creation of innovative alternatives to the oppressive status quo. Their utopian hermeneutics are practical, designed to effect progressive change. I borrow the term "utopian hermeneutics" from José Esteban Muñoz. As Muñoz insists, utopian hermeneutics cannot be dismissed as escapist roman-ticized views of an impossible past. Rather, "utopian hermeneutics offers us a refined lens to view queerness, insofar as queerness, if it is indeed not quite here, is nonetheless intensely relational with the past. The present is not enough. It is impoverished and toxic for queers and other people who do not feel the privilege of majoritarian belonging, normative tastes, and 'rational' expectations" (27). For the authors in this analysis, Mesoamerican-inflected revisionist mythmaking offers an antidote to this toxicity, a healing ceremony of sorts – an epistemological, ontological tool with which to create viable pos-sibilities for an equitable future.

Although revisionist mythmaking was a common strategy for many twentieth-century U.S. feminist and ethnic-nationalist authors and activists, it has received relatively little scholarly attention. This limited attention is not surprising, given the restrictive definitions of "myth" – a word that, in the English language, has become almost synonymous with "falsehood" or "lie."[4] However, this dismissal of revisionist mythmaking, as well as the conflation of "myth" with "lies," is too simplistic and overlooks the crucial roles mythology plays in shaping psychic-material realities. Because mythic stories embody a culture's deep-seated (often hidden) assumptions, histories, and wounds, revi-sionist mythmaking offers an important tool for transformation on multiple levels: psychic lives, intellectual beliefs, social structures, and beyond. Applied to Mesoamerican history and worldviews, revisionist mythmaking functions as an innovative, transformational practice that queers normative stories in various ways: (1) retelling a well-known mythic story from different points of view; (2) rewriting the story by altering the plot and revising the story itself; (3) recovering alternative, previously lost, or forgotten versions of commonly accepted myths; and (4) writing new stories.[5] While Mesoamerican-inspired revisionist mythmaking often focuses on individual and collective identity-related issues (and thus opens itself to the previously mentioned criticisms), at its most innovative, these recursive uses of "Mesoamerica" produce new ontologies, epistemologies, aesthetics, metaphysics, and ethics. This chapter examines these philosophical contributions as they occur within three complex, recurring Mesoamerican-inflected themes: Aztlán, mestizaje, and cosmic mythic figures.

Aztlán

During the original peopling of the Americas, the first inhabitants migrated across the Bering Straits and walked south across the continent. The oldest evidence of humankind in the U.S. – the Chicanos' ancient Indian ancestors – was found in Texas and has been dated to 35,000 B.C. In the Southwest United States archeologists have found 20,000-year-old campsites of the Indians who migrated through, or permanently occupied, the Southwest, Aztlán – land of the herons, land of whiteness, the Edenic place of origin of the Azteca.
          – Gloria Anzaldúa, *Borderlands/La Frontera*

Geographically, Aztlán refers to the contemporary U.S. southwest. Mythically, Aztlán has functioned since the late 1960s to represent Mexican Americans' original home, thus authorizing their presence in the United States. Underscoring their ancient connection with the land, Chicano nationalists and some mujeres-de-color authors use Aztlán to rewrite the status quo story of U.S. westward expansion; by so doing, they generate self-esteem, challenge assimilation, and mobilize Mexican Americans for action.[6] These references to Aztlán have inspired a fierce nationalism but have distinct limitations, including a deeply embedded, although often invisible, masculine bias and the erasure of the Hopi, the Navajo, and other indigenous peoples. Although this erasure was generally overlooked, the masculinist bias was critiqued by early Chicana feminists, like Adelaida del Castillo, and by later feminists, like Anzaldúa and Moraga. Anzaldúa's *Borderlands/La Frontera* (1987) exemplifies this critique. In the first chapter she summarizes forty thousand years of migration as her ancestors, the "ancient Indians," cross the Bering Straits, move southward into and through what we now call Texas and Mexico, and then northward into the North American Southwest as enslaved Indians and mestizos, forced to participate in Spanish expeditions for gold. Like the earlier Chicano nationalists, Anzaldúa maintains that this doubled movement anchors U.S. Americans of Mexican ancestry in the land, "making Chicanos originally and secondarily indigenous to the Southwest" (27). However, Anzaldúa mixes affirmation with critique. Interweaving accounts of the racism, sexism, and classism she experienced growing up in south Texas with historical and mythic analyses of the successive Aztec and Spanish conquests of indigenous Mesoamerican gynecentric tribes, she exposes sexism and other forms of violence in Chicano nationalists' idealized Aztlán. Making a geographical-theoretical shift, Anzaldúa moves from Aztlán to the borderlands, developing her borderlands theory. For Anzaldúa, "borderlands" refers both to the literal boundary between Mexico and the United States *and* to a multilayered metaphor representing liminal, transformative opportunities. In her later work, Anzaldúa moves even further away from Aztlán (and its ethnic-specific nationalism), replacing borderlands with her multifaceted theory of nepantla. The Nahuatl word for "in-between space," nepantla, for Anzaldúa, represents liminality and potential transformation; she uses this term to theorize individual and collective identity formation, epistemological shifts, mediational identities, and aesthetic inspiration.[7]

Unlike Anzaldúa, who uses Aztlán as a critical point of departure for larger projects, Moraga adopts and reshapes this Chicano myth, retaining yet expanding its nationalistic underpinnings. She condemns the sexism and homophobia contained in Chicano nationalist versions without rejecting the myth of Aztlán itself. Rather than reject Aztlán's promise of community, Moraga redefines it more inclusively, to include women, queers, Native Americans, and the land. In "Queer Aztlán: The Re-formation of the Chicano Tribe," for example, she exposes the sexism, homophobia, and heteronormativity in Chicano references to Aztlán. As the title suggests, she does not entirely reject this Chicano origin story but instead queers it, calling for a decolonized but ethnic-specific nation: "The nationalism I seek is one that decolonizes the brown and female body as it decolonizes the brown and female earth. It is a new nationalism in which la Chicana Indígena stands at the center, and heterosexism and homophobia are no longer the cultural order of the day" (*Last* 150). Focusing on identity-related issues, Moraga centers "la Chicana Indígena," thus validating herself and other Chican@s.

Mestizaje

As a mestiza born to the lower strata, I am treated at best, as a second class citizen, at worst, as a non-entity. I am commonly perceived as a foreigner everywhere I go, including in the United States and in Mexico. This international perception is based on my color and features. I am neither black nor white. I am not light-skinned and cannot be mistaken for "white"; because my hair is so straight I cannot be mistaken for "black." And by U.S. standards and according to some North American Native Americans, I cannot make official claims to being india.   – Ana Castillo, *Massacre of the Dreamers*

The new mestiza queers have the ability, the flexibility, the malleability, the amorphous quality of being able to stretch this way and that way. We can add new labels, names, and identities as we mix with others.
                            – Gloria Anzaldúa, "To(o) Queer the Writer"

Conventionally, the terms "mestiza/o" and "mestizaje" refer to a biological/ cultural mixture, a hybrid identity of sorts. These terms originated with the Spanish conquest of Mesoamerican peoples and described the offspring (mestizos and mestizas) produced by the Spaniards' rape of indigenous women. "Mestizo" was pejorative, representing what Castillo describes as the permanent outsider – the "foreigner" or "second class citizen." Referencing Aztlán and an indigenous "Azteca" identity, Chicano nationalists redefined mestizaje in positive ways, reclaiming their indigenous ancestry while downplaying or entirely ignoring their European-Spanish roots.[8] No longer aliens, Chicanos became the original North Americans, making Euro-Americans the intruders. While this renaming was an important decolonizing strategy, it did not adequately distinguish between Chicanos/Latinos and contemporary indigenous southwestern peoples, thus dismissing issues of sovereignty and inadvertently negating the people themselves.

In *Borderlands/La Frontera*, Anzaldúa makes a radical break from these definitions of mestizaje, moving beyond biology and Mexicana culture and applying mestizaje to new contexts, like coalitional politics and philosophical thought. Drawing on her experiences of alienation in south Texas and her utopian inclusionary vision for systemic change, Anzaldúa creates her own mythic figure, the "new mestiza": a complex mixture of cultures, beliefs, experiences, and practices, Anzaldúa's mestiza exceeds biological classification. The product of two or more cultures and worldviews, the new mestiza lives in a "state of perpetual transition" as she attempts to reconcile, rather than reject, the warring voices in her head.[9] Anzaldúa queers conventional definitions of mestizaje in several ways. Feminizing the term "mestizo," she intervenes in twentieth-century male-dominated Chicano nationalism. Extending conventional definitions of biologically based mestizaje to encompass the experiences of non-Mexican, non-Indian peoples as well, she de-essentializes and pluralizes mestizajes' culturally specific identity component. Anzaldúa's queered mestizaje offers an alternative to conventional definitions of homosexuality that focus primarily on gender, sexual object choice, and sexual desire. Emphasizing multiple systems of difference and forms of desire simultaneously, Anzaldúa repositions sexuality as one component in a fluid identity constellation. As she explains in "To(o) Queer the Writer," "new mestiza queers" have "the ability, the flexibility, the amorphous quality of being able to stretch this way and that way. We can add new labels, names, and identities as we mix with others" (174).

Anzaldúa applies this queered mestizaje to epistemology and ethics. In her theory of knowledge, mestizaje functions metaphorically and experientially, facilitating her creation of a nonbinary epistemology and ethics, or what she calls "mestiza consciousness": a fluid transformational thinking process that breaks down rigid boundaries between apparently separate categories of meaning. Developed in *Borderlands/La Frontera*, mestiza consciousness is an innovative relational epistemology offering a genuine alternative to conventional Western Cartesian thought, with its either/or divisions. In her post-*Borderlands* work, Anzaldúa expands mestiza consciousness into ethics and aesthetics.[10]

However, as Moraga suggests, the use of these terms can be tricky. In her later work, Moraga questions these innovative uses of "mestizaje" and "mestiza," concerned that they reinforce U.S. imperialism:

> Although differently nuanced, both hybridity and mestizaje intend to address the cross-cultural collisions of multiple identities (queer, transnational, gender, etc.) requisite of a postmodern world. But as metaphors, are they brave enough to counter the insidiousness of the U.S. project of a global empire, whose cultural agenda is to erase our awareness of the bitter realities of social difference? Do the terms not assume and succumb to the loss of our aboriginality with no hope for recuperation. Could these words not reflect another attempt by the corporate academy, however furtively, to exploit the rhetoric of democratic multiculturalism and pluralism at home in order to engage our support and services for neocolonial profit abroad and southward?
>
> (*Xicana* 87–88)

Instead of focusing on mestizaje, which, she believes, concedes defeat (defined as "the loss of our aboriginality"), Moraga imaginatively reaches back, to a time prior to the Spanish Conquest; she borrows from indigenous Mesoamerican oral traditions in order to (re)claim her indigenous roots and authorize her work. She replaces "mestiza" with "Xicana Indígena." As this Nahuatl-inspired spelling of "Chicana" suggests, in her later work Moraga aligns herself almost entirely with her indigenous ancestry.[11] She creates a Mesoamerican-inflected aesthetics in her 2011 book, *A Xicana Codex of Changing Consciousness*, directly linking it with Mesoamerican traditions:

As Xicanas and Xicanos, one of our oldest written traditions resides on the indigenous ground of the spoken word, interpreted from the painted black marks of resin wept from trees onto a piece of amatl paper. MeXicanas and MeXicanos have always told stories aloud: as weapons against traiciones, as historical accounts and prophetic warnings, as preachers and teachers against wrongdoing, as songs of celebration, as exhalations of laughter, as prayer in the presence of the divine. And through this storytelling one's awareness of the world and its meanings grows and changes. (xvi)

Like Anzaldúa's Mesoamerican-inspired aesthetics, seen especially in her theory of "the Red and the Black Ink," Moraga's codex draws on indigenous theories of performative art, or what Anzaldúa describes in *Borderlands/La Frontera* as "invoked art" (89).

Despite the risks involved, other mujeres de color have embraced the terms "mestizaje" and "mestiza," repurposing them for innovative philosophical projects. In *Massacre of the Dreamers*, Castillo uses her mestiza identity to enact her queer hermeneutics (or what she calls "Xicanisma") and authorize a visionary theory of social change that can transform the world. While recognizing that centuries of conquest have erased any type of direct connections to indigenous knowledge, she maintains that her "genetic collective memory and ... life experience" empower her to develop a liberatory form of consciousness, a "mestiza conscientización" that draws on Mesamerican connections to offer a redemptive vision for planetary social change: "Our mestiza conscientización contains within itself the elements for an unthreatened planet; we can contribute that collective vision toward the development of an alternative social system" (220). This new consciousness can transform the world. Similarly, Sandoval takes mestizaje beyond exclusively biological, nationalistic categories and redefines it as an alternatively gendered, theoretical-practical tool for individual and collective change. In *Methodology of the Oppressed*, she names "radical *mestizaje*" as a "third gender category" composed of "an eccentric coalition of U.S. third world feminists" (46); an inclusionary mode of identity formation; and a decolonizing methodology. Like Anzaldúa and Castillo, she believes that this mestizaje-inspired innovation generates progressive social change.

Cosmic Mythic Figures

The male-dominated Azteca-Mexica culture drove the powerful female deities underground by giving them monstrous attributes and by substituting male deities in their place, thus splitting the female Self and the female deities. They divided her who had been complete, who possessed both upper

536

(light) and underworld (dark) aspects. *Coatlicue*, the serpent goddess, and her more sinister aspects, *Tlazolteotl* and *Cihuacoatl*, were "darkened" and disempowered much in the same manner as the Indian *Kali*.... After the Conquest, the Spaniards and their Church continued to split *Tonantsi/Guadalupe*. They desexed *Guadalupe*, taking *Coatlalopeuh*, the serpent/sexuality, out of her. They completed the split begun by the Nahuas by making *la Virgen de Guadalupe/Virgen María* into chaste virgins and *Tlazolteotl/Coatlicue/la Chingada* into *putas* [whores]. – Gloria Anzaldúa, *Borderlands/La Frontera*

It cost me a great deal to find their stories, but without my gods – Coatlicue, the mother of creation and destruction; Coyolxauhqui, her dismembered daughter; La Llorona, the inconsolable weeping woman – without these icons of collective MeXicana sedition, my criminal acts as a Xicana dyke writer would have no precedent, no history, and ultimately no consequence.
– Cherríe Moraga, *Xicana Codex of Changing Consciousness*

The cosmologies of the Maya, Toltecs, Olmecs, and other pre-Conquest Mesoamerican peoples were peopled by rich, complicated divinities who defy easy categorization: Toci/Tonan, Tonántzin, Cihuacoatl, Coatlicue, Coyolxauhqui, and others embodied an array of feminine, masculine, human, and nonhuman features in a dazzling synergistic complexity far exceeding Greek, Roman, or Judeo-Christian traditions. But as Anzaldúa notes, during successive conquests by the Aztec, Spaniards, and Anglos, these all-encompassing, highly potent mythic figures were drained of their cosmic energies and split into simplified representations of "good" (Tonántzin, la Virgen of Guadalupe) and "evil" (Coatlicue, Coyolxauhqui, Malinche, La Llorona); these shifts corresponded to, authorized, and enforced the decline in biological women's roles under the successive conquests.[12] This enforcement of conservative gender roles is particularly apparent in post-Conquest figures.

After the Spanish Conquest, Mesoamerican divinities were divided into three overly simplified representations of "good" and "evil" women, representations often functioning to subjugate real-life women: La Virgen Guadalupe, Malinche (also known as "la Chingada"), and La Llorona (the Wailing Woman). As Anzaldúa explains, "the true identity of all three has been subverted – Guadalupe to make us docile and enduring, la Chingada to make us ashamed of our Indian side, and la Llorona to make us long-suffering people. This obscuring has encouraged the *virgen/puta* (whore) dichotomy" (*Borderlands* 53).[13] Redefining and reclaiming these Mesoamerican figures, mujeres-de-color authors expose the limitations in contemporary sex-gender systems, develop self-affirming alternatives to conventional gender categories, and create innovative epistemologies and aesthetics.

Anzaldúa's work offers the most extensive (and, arguably, the most influential) demonstration of this complex multilayered queer hermeneutics. In *Borderlands/ La Frontera*, Anzaldúa draws from and (re)writes Toltec, Olmec, and other pre-Aztec cosmologies, in order to critique both the Chicano movement's sexism and the dominant U.S. culture's ethnocentrism; redefine female identity; and develop relational epistemologies, ontologies, and aesthetics that offer alternatives to binary Cartesian thought. Her revisions of Coatlicue and Coyolxauhqui illustrate this process. For pre-Aztec Nahuatl peoples, Coatlicue represented an ambiguously gendered creator figure preceding and containing all opposites, a chaotic creative energy or "primordial darkness" (71); for the Aztecs, Coatlicue is less complex and associated more exclusively with conventional female-gendered roles like motherhood. According to traditional (Aztec) versions of her story, Coatlicue miraculously becomes pregnant with Huitzilopochtli (the god of war). Her pregnancy horrifies her daughter, Coyolxauhqui, who incites her four hundred brothers to kill their mother. When Coyolxauhqui beheads Coatlicue, Huitzilopochtli (fully armed) jumps out of Coatlicue's body and kills Coyolxauhqui, beheading and dismembering her. In Aztec art, Coatlicue is generally depicted as a headless, monstrous figure.[14]

As Anzaldúa traces Coatlicue's descent from the pre-Aztec multigendered cosmic Source of all life into her demonic "Serpent Woman" status in the Aztec regime and La Llorona/Malinche in Mexican and Chicano thought, she charts the transition to increasingly male-dominated, hierarchical social structures that occurred during the Aztec and Spanish conquests. Stripped of her fierce cosmic powers, this creator was weakened, feminized, and split into two: as Tlazolteotl/Coatlicue/Malinche/Llorona, she became the embodiment of darkness, materiality, and female evil; and as Tontantsi/Guadalupe, she became purified, Christianized, "desexed," and transformed into the holy virgin mother (54). Retelling Coatlicue's story through her queer hermeneutics, Anzaldúa enacts a doubled gesture: First, she exposes the limitations in contemporary Western gender norms, Chicano celebrations of Aztlán, and the dichotomous epistemology on which conservative gender norms and masculinist nationalisms are based. Second – and simultaneously – she develops a posthumanist mythos that transforms Cartesian thought and its centralizing focus on the human.

Anzaldúa's Coatlicue is a queer figure indeed. Associating Coatlicue with "the animal, the alien, the sub- or suprahuman, the me that has something in common with the wind and the trees and the rocks" (*Borderlands* 72), Anzaldúa develops an animist-inflected subjectivity that anticipates twenty-first-century work in posthumanist studies. With her sometimes sexualized and highly erotic embrace of this nonhuman divinity, Anzaldúa redefines "human being" to underscore our porous boundaries and radical interconnectedness with all existence. This posthumanist subjectivity, in turn, inspires Anzaldúa to invent "the Coatlicue state," a multilayered theory introduced in *Borderlands/La Frontera* and developed in her later work. In various texts, the Coatlicue state represents the writing process, epistemological stasis, and the complicated resistance to oppression.[15] Building on Anzaldúa, Sandoval develops her own version of "the Coatlicue state," making it pivotal to her theory of resistance and transformation, which she names the "methodology of the oppressed" and "differential consciousness." A highly innovative approach to decolonization, Sandoval's differential consciousness theory redefines love as social praxis in revolutionary ways. Unlike conventional social justice movements, which become trapped in binary-oppositional thought, differential consciousness exceeds dichotomies by embracing contradiction. As she explains in *Methodology of the Oppressed*, "I define differential consciousness as a kind of anarchic activity (but with method), a form of ideological guerrilla warfare, and a new kind of ethical activity. . . . Inside this realm resides the only possible grounds for alliance across differences" (196). Representing an epistemological shift or "rupturing" in conventional modes of perception and practice, Sandoval's Coatlicue state is the nexus point from which this liberatory consciousness occurs.

In later essays like "now let us shift" and "Putting Coyolxauhqui Together," Anzaldúa expands her reinterpretation of Coatlicue to include Coyolxauhqui. Focusing especially on Coyolxauhqui's dismemberment, Anzaldúa borrows this story and develops a theory of curative writing and individual/collective identity (re)formation that she calls "the Coyolxauhqui imperative." Likening herself to this shattered god, Anzaldúa underscores her own sense of wounding as well as her desire to reconstitute herself and heal internal and external divisions. Just as Coyolxauhqui was beheaded and torn to pieces, so Anzaldúa feels fragmented. The Coyolxauhqui imperative represents both Anzaldúa's desire for healing and her attempts, through writing, to put herself together, to gather the fragmented pieces of her life and weave them into a complex, contradictory whole. As she explains in "now let us shift," Coyolxauhqui symbolizes "both the process of emotional psychical dismemberment, splitting body/mind/spirit/soul, and the creative work of putting all the pieces together in a new form, a partially unconscious work done in the night by the light of the moon, a labor of re-visioning and re-membering" (546). Significantly, Anzaldúa does not stop with this highly personal myth but also applies it more generally, to collective issues and historical events like the September 11, 2001 terrorist attacks and their aftermath. Lamenting both the visceral, reactionary anger expressed by many U.S. Americans and President Bush's hasty decision to bomb Afghanistan, she calls for thoughtful self-reflection to facilitate "the necessary process of dismemberment and fragmentation, ... reconstruction and reframing, ... putting the pieces together in a new way" ("Let us" 312).

For Moraga, Mesoamerican mythic figures offer empowering images of individual and collective gender and sexual identities, affirmation of her work as a "Xicana Indígena" author, and validation of her rebellion against male-dominated social structures. In *The Last Generation*, Moraga summarizes the traditional Aztec version of Coatlicue and Coyolxauhqui's story but reinterprets it through her lesbian-feminist beliefs. Unlike Anzaldúa and other mujeres-de-color authors, who generally avoid delving into the story's matricide, Moraga directly takes it on. In her interpretation, Coyolxauhqui has no alternative. Because her mother, Coatlicue, has aligned herself with her son, Huitzilopochtli, and thus with male-identified social structures and gender roles, Coyolxauhqui must kill her in order to mitigate patriarchal cultures' dangers. Her Coatlicue is passive and must be rescued:

> He [Huitzilopochtli] possesses the mother, holds her captive, because she cannot refuse any of her children, even her enemy son. Here, mother and daughter are pitted against each other and daughter must kill male-defined motherhood in order to save the culture from misogyny, war, and greed. But el hijo comes to the defense of patriarchal motherhood, kills la mujer rebelde, and female power is eclipsed by the rising light of the Sun/Son. This machista myth is enacted every day of our lives, every day that the sun (Huitzilopochtli) rises up from the horizon and the moon (Coyolxauhqui) is obliterated by his light.   (73–74)

Perhaps not surprising, Moraga aligns herself most closely to Coyolxauhqui, making her a role model and patron saint of sorts:

> I pray to the daughter, La Hija Rebelde. She who has been banished, the mutilated sister who transforms herself into the moon. She is la fuerza femenina, our attempt to pick up the fragments of our dismembered womanhood and reconstitute ourselves. She is the Chicana writer's words, the Chicana painter's canvas, the Chicana dancer's step. She is motherhood reclaimed and sisterhood honored. She is the female god we seek in our work, la Mechicana before the "fall."   (74)

While Coatlicue identified with the son and patriarchal culture, Coyolxauhqui rejects this patriarchal alliance, thus inspiring Moraga's devotion. Coyolxauhqui calls Moraga into battle, into continued struggles with the patriarchal status quo.

While the Catholic church and Chicano nationalists define La Virgen de Guadalupe as the archetypal good mother and passive, male-identified woman, Moraga, Anzaldúa, and other mujeres-de-color reinvent this figure. They revise her story by recovering her Mesoamerican antecedents and using these earlier stories to expose and condemn the misogyny and homophobia in Catholicism, the Chicano movement, and U.S. culture. Reconnecting Guadalupe with her ancient Mesoamerican roots, they redefine her as a powerful figure (Coatlicue, Tonantzín, and other versions of the "Serpent Woman") and focus their attention on these earlier, awe-inspiring gods rather than on La Virgin herself. Thus in her poem "Our Lady of the Cannery Workers," Moraga describes Guadalupe as "Mother Creator" (rather than mother *of* the creator) and calls her Tonantzín. Unlike conventional depictions of La Virgen as a docile, accepting woman, Moraga's Guadalupe is not passive; she does not accept the cannery women's current condition. She is furious, with "anger, righteous / and unforgiving," an anger that can inspire real-life women (*Last* 144).[16]

Malinche/Malintzin (also known as "La Chingada," "Malinalli," or "Doña Marina") represents both a historical figure and the mestizo nation's mythic "mother."[17] Conventional stories generally depict Malinche as an object, sold by her family into slavery and later given to Cortés, to whom she bore a son (the first mestizo). In these narratives, Malinche is a traitor and direct cause of her people's downfall: with her great linguistic skill, she translated for the Spanish, betraying Mesoamerican Indians and facilitating the Conquest. Indeed, betrayal is such a component of Malinche/Malintzin's identity that the term "Malinchistas" is used pejoratively to describe sellouts.[18] Women-of-color authors have retold Malinche's story from her point of view, describing her as a strong, brilliant woman whose family betrayed *her* by selling her into slavery. In these revisionist stories, Malinche chooses to assist Cortés in his conquest of the brutal Aztecs; she manipulates him to wreak vengeance against those who betrayed her. He is *her* tool. For example, Paula Gunn Allen (Laguna Pueblo/Sioux) retells the Conquest from Malinche's perspective in her poem, "Malinalli, La Malinche to Cortés, Conquistador," representing Cortés as a pawn used by Malinche and Cihuacoatl: "Ever I twisted you to my will, / oh great bringer of the goddess' wrath" (5). Unlike conventional depictions of Malinche as a weak-willed traitor, Allen's Malinche is a conscious agent of change who subversively uses the European colonizers to undermine patriarchal social structures. Chicanas and Native American women use revisionist mythmaking to redefine Malinche as an inspirational role model, a brilliant woman willing to defy the negative, patriarchal aspects of her cultura. As Inés Hernández-Ávila asserts, "We should consider the possibility that each

Mexicana/Chicana could become a Malinche in the sense of being a path-opener, a guide, a voice, a warrior woman, willing to go to the front to combat the injustices that our people suffer. In this way our indigenous mother will be revindicated and we will be revindicated as well" ("Open" 245). Anzaldúa and Moraga, among others, enact this willingness to identify with Malinche, claiming their autonomy and self-affirmation in the face of nationalist sexism and heteronormativity.[19]

Sometimes referred to as the "weeping woman," La Llorona is a central figure in Mexican, Mexican American, and Chican@ folklore, as well as an important presence in the writings of many mujeres de color. Her story, which precedes the Spanish Conquest of Mesoamerica, exists in many versions, but generally in post-Conquest literature, La Llorona represents the ghost of a beautiful young woman, seduced and abandoned by a man, who kills (usually by drowning) her children. Often found near bodies of water, she is destined to wander forever, crying for the children she murdered. The archetypal "bad mother," her story is used throughout the Southwest to frighten children into good behavior. These Llorona stories also function to control women, warning them of the deadly consequences for those who betray conventional gender expectations.

Mujeres-de-color authors use revisionist mythmaking to expose and reject these social injunctions. Going "back," to the pre-Conquest stories, they revise La Llorona, reconnecting her to her previous manifestations as earth goddesses like "Hungry Woman," who created the earth from her body, and Cihuacoatl, a warrior goddess of midwives and women who die in childbirth, whose wailing warned people of the Spanish Conquest. As Debra Blake notes, they create redemptive stories that reject conventional gender roles and challenge negative representations of woman. In the short story "La Llorona Loca: The Other Side," comedian Monica Palacios revises Llorona's story in tongue-in-cheek fashion, transforming her into "Caliente," a gorgeous 1970s Mexican lesbian, who is neither a mother nor a passive wife. Similarly, in her poem "The Postmodern Llorona," Anzaldúa renames this tragic figure "SERPENT WOMAN," a contemporary young woman who does not fear La Llorona but instead embraces her. Rejecting motherhood, Anzaldúa's postmodern Llorona is a student, a poet, and a lesbian:

> The dismembered missing children are not
> the issue of her womb – she has no children.
> She seeks the parts of herself
> she's lost along the way.

> ("Postmodern" 281)

In her children's book *Prietita and the Ghost Woman/Prietita y La Llorona*, Anzaldúa rewrites Llorona's story entirely, redefining her as loving guide. Moraga's play *The Hungry Woman: A Mexican Medea* offers the most extensive and "most complex retelling of the Llorona legend" (Blake 173). Merging the Greek myth of Medea with Chicano nationalist myths of Aztlán and the stories of Llorona and her pre-Conquest manifestations, Moraga's protagonist (the Mexican Medea of the title) is "a revolutionary woman warrior, who takes the form of a Mexican Medea and a rebellious Llorona, to represent the hope of a new nation-state where the expression of Chicana lesbian desire and Chicana/o and indigenous sovereignty is possible" (Blake 176).

As this brief foray through recent writings by mujeres de color indicates, Mesoamerican history and myth offer a rich source of potentially transformative material. Using revisionist mythmaking to develop their queer hermeneutics, Anzaldúa, Moraga, and other authors enact a recursive movement that synergistically mixes discovery with invention, producing new ontologies, epistemologies, aesthetics, metaphysics, and ethics that offer viable alternatives to conventional Eurocentric theories. While at times their Mesoamerican-inspired revisionist mythmaking focuses exclusively on identity-related issues and thus opens itself to the criticisms of appropriation described earlier, at its most innovative, these recursive uses of "Mesoamerica" respectfully draw on indigenous philosophies and worldviews to create visionary theories and praxes with the potential to transform social injustice.

Notes

1. The phrase is Mary Daly's (89). For examples of this revisionist work, which was widespread in the mainstream mid-twentieth-century U.S. women's movement, see Spretnak; Plaskow and Christ.
2. See Anzaldúa's "Speaking across the Divide" for thoughtful engagement with Saldaña-Portillo's critique. As Anzaldúa notes, Saldaña-Portillo focuses too narrowly on a small section of *Borderlands* and overlooks the ways Anzaldúa's views changed in her later work.
3. Both Saldaña-Portillo and Contreras focus especially on *Borderlands/La Frontera*, but their criticisms apply more generally (and perhaps more appropriately) to other mujeres-de-color writings. See also Soto's analysis of the "mestiza standpoint epistemology" in Castillo's novels: while Castillo tries to "queer the conquest in a manner that honors the indigenous female figure," she inadvertently romanticizes indigenous identity as "Aztec queens" (86). See also Ortiz's strong rejection of Chicano claims to indigeneity; and Hernández-Ávila, "Indigenous" for a discussion of this debate.

4. Twentieth-century poststructuralist criticism of cultural feminists' revisionist mythmaking also played a role in this rejection.
5. For a discussion of some of the positive and negative ways that cultural myths can impact our beliefs, see Cornell. For discussions of feminists' revisionist mythmaking, see DuPlessis. For discussions of gender and cultural revisionist mythmaking, see Bebout and Keating, *Women*.
6. See the 1969 *El Plan Espiritual de Aztlán*, adopted at the first National Chicano Youth Liberation Conference in Denver, Colorado. As Bebout notes, Aztlán has been and continues to be a key literary device in Chican@ nationalism and literature. Indeed, even the leading journal in Chican@ studies is titled *Aztlán: A Journal of Chicano Studies*. For a discussion of Aztlán as "myth of origin," see also Gaspar de Alba.
7. For discussions of the development of Anzaldúa's theory of nepantla, see Koshy and Keating, "Shifting."
8. As Hartley notes in "Chican@ Indigeneity," the African dimensions of this mestizaje were entirely ignored.
9. Anzaldúa develops her theory of the new mestiza throughout *Borderlands/La Frontera*; see especially the preface and Chapter 7.
10. For mestizaje's ethical components, see Anzaldúa's theories of "new tribalism" and conocimiento ("now") and Torres. For mestizaje's aesthetic dimensions, see Anzaldúa, "Haciendo."
11. As Luna notes, replacing "ch" with "x" serves – for Chicano nationalists and for contemporary writers – as "an act of Indigenous reclamation" (10).
12. Castillo also discusses these revisions in *Massacre of the Dreamers*. For additional scholarship on pre-Conquest Mesoamerican pantheons, see Hartley, "'Matriz'"; Blake; and Lara.
13. For discussions of these three figures, see Blake; and Lara. For a discussion of Anzaldúa's revisionist approach, see Perez.
14. There are many versions of Coatlicue-Coyolxauhqui's story. For two versions, see Blake. For a graphic description of Coatlicue, see Anzaldúa, *Borderlands* 69.
15. For the epistemological and compositional dimensions of the Coatlicue state, see Keating, *Women*; for the Coatlicue state's contributions to Anzaldúa's theory of resistance, see Lugones.
16. For additional examples of this shift from La Virgen to her earlier Mesoamerican forms, see Castillo's introduction to *Goddess of the Americas* and Anzaldúa's *Borderlands* ch. 3.
17. According to Chicana and Native American feminists, "Malintzin" is La Malinche's indigenous name. For an extensive discussion of this figure, see Alarcón, "Traduttora" and "Chicana's."
18. Twentieth-century Chicano nationalists ostracized Chicana feminists as "Malinchistas."

19. For Anzaldúa's discussion of La Malinche, see *Borderlands* 45–46. For Moraga's discussion, see "A Long Line of Vendidas" in *Loving*.

Works Cited

Alarcón, Norma. "Chicana's Feminist Literature: A Re-vision through Malintzin/or Malintzin: Putting Flesh Back on the Object." *This Bridge Called My Back*. Ed. Cherríe Moraga and Gloria Anzaldúa. New York: Kitchen Table, Women of Color P, 1983. 182–90. Print.

"Traduttora, Traditora: A Paradigmatic Figure of Chicana Feminism." *Scattered Hegemonies: Postmodernity and Transnational Feminist Practices*. Ed. Inderpal Grewal and Caren Kaplan. Minneapolis: U of Minnesota P, 1994. 110–33. Print.

Allen, Paula. "Malinalli, La Malinche to Cortés, Conquistador." *Life is a Fatal Disease: Collected Poems 1962–1995*. Albuquerque: West End P, 1997. 3–4. Print.

Anzaldúa, Gloria. *Borderlands/La Frontera: The New Mestiza*. 1987. 2nd ed. San Francisco: Aunt Lute, 1999. Print.

The Gloria Anzaldúa Reader. Ed. AnaLouise Keating. Durham: Duke UP, 2010. Print.

"Haciendo caras, una entrada." Introduction. *Making Face/Making Soul: Haciendo Caras: Creative and Critical Perspectives by Women of Color*. Ed. Gloria Anzaldúa. San Francisco: Aunt Lute, 1990. Xv–xxviii. Print.

"Let Us Be the Healing of the Wound." *Gloria Anzaldúa Reader* 313–17.

"Now Let Us Shift .... The Path of conocimiento .... Inner Work, Public Acts." *This Bridge We Call Home: Radical Visions for Transformation*. Ed. Gloria E. Anzaldúa and AnaLouise Keating. New York: Routledge, 2002. 540–78. Print.

"The Postmodern Llorona." *Gloria Anzaldúa Reader* 280–81.

Prietita and the Ghost Woman/ Prietita y La Llorona. San Francisco: Children's Book P, 1995. Print.

"Putting Coyolxauhqui Together, A Creative Process." *How We Work*. Ed. Marla Morris, Mary Aswell Doll, and William F. Pinar. New York: Lang, 1999. 241–59. Print.

"Speaking across the Divide." *Gloria Anzaldúa Reader* 282–94.

"To(o) Queer the Writer – Loca, escritora y chicana." *Gloria Anzaldúa Reader* 163–75.

Bebout, Lee. *Mythohistorical Interventions: The Chicano Movement and Its Legacies*. Minneapolis: U of Minnesota P, 2011. Print.

Blake, Debra J. *Chicana Sexuality and Gender: Cultural Refiguring in Literature, Oral History, and Art*. Durham: Duke UP, 2008. Print.

Castillo, Ana, ed. *Goddess of the Americas: Writings on the Virgin of Guadalupe*. New York: Riverhead, 1996. Print.

Massacre of the Dreamers: Essays on Xicanisma. Albuquerque: U of New Mexico P, 1994. Print.

Contreras, Sheila Maria. *Blood Lines: Myth, Indigenism, and Chicana/o Literature*. Austin: U of Texas P, 2008. Print.

Cornell, Drucilla. *Beyond Accommodation: Ethical Feminism, Deconstruction, and the Law*. New York: Routledge, 1991. Print.

Daly, Mary. *Pure Lust: Elemental Feminist Philosophy*. Boston: Beacon P, 1984. Print.

DuPlessis, Rachel Blau. *Writing beyond the Ending: Narrative Strategies of Twentieth-Century Women Writers*. Bloomington: Indiana UP, 1985. Print.

Gaspar de Alba, Alicia. "There's No Place Like Aztlán: Embodied Aesthetics in Chicana Art." *CR: The New Centennial Review* 4.2 (2004): 103–40. Print.

Hartley, George. "Chican@ Indigeneity, the Nation-State, and Colonialist Identity Formation." *Comparative Indigeneities of the Americas*. Ed. M. Bianet Castellanos, Lourdes Gutierrez Najera, and Arturo J. Aldama. Tucson: Arizona UP, 2012. 53–66. Print.

"'Matriz sin tumba': The Trash Goddess and the Healing Matrix of Gloria Anzaldúa's Reclaimed Womb." *MELUS* 35.1 (2010): 41–61. Print.

Hernández-Ávila, Inés. "Indigenous Intersections–Introduction." *Studies in American Indian Literatures* 15.3–4 (2003–04): 1–6. Print.

"An Open Letter to Chicanas: On the Power and Politics of Origin." *Reinventing the Enemy's Language: Contemporary Native Women's Writings of North America*. Ed. Joy Harjo and Gloria Bird. New York: Norton, 1997. 237–46. Print.

Keating, AnaLouise, ed. *EntreMundos/Among Worlds: New Perspectives on Gloria Anzaldúa*. New York: Palgrave, 2005. Print.

"Shifting Worlds, Una Entrada." *EntreMundos* 1–12.

Women Reading Women Writing: Self-Invention in Paula Gunn Allen, Gloria Anzaldúa, and Audre Lorde. Philadelphia: Temple UP, 1996. Print.

Koshy, Kavitha. "Nepantlera-Activism in the Transnational Moment: In Dialogue with Gloria Anzaldúa's Theorizing of Nepantla." *Human Architecture: Journal of the Sociology of Self-Knowledge* 4 (2006): 147–62. Print.

Lara, Irene. "Goddess of the Américas in the Decolonial Imaginary: Beyond the Virtuous Virgen/Pagan Puta Dichotomy." *Feminist Studies* 34.1–2 (2008): 99–130. Print.

Lugones, María. "On *Borderlands/La Frontera*: An Interpretive Essay." *Hypatia* 7 (1992): 31–38. Print.

Luna, Jennie M. "Building A Xicana Indígena Philosophical Base." *APA Newsletter on Hispanic/Latino Issues in Philosophy* 11.2 (2012): 10–16. Print.

Moraga, Cherríe. *The Hungry Woman: A Mexican Medea and Heart of the Earth: A Popul Vuh Story*. New Mexico: West End P, 2003. Print.

The Last Generation: Prose and Poetry. Boston: South End P, 1993. Print.

Loving in the War Years: lo que nunca pasó por sus labios. Boston: South End P, 1983. Print.

A Xicana Codex of Changing Consciousness: Writings, 2000–2010. Durham: Duke UP, 2011. Print.

Muñoz, José Esteban. *Cruising Utopia: The Then and There of Queer Futurity*. New York: New York UP, 2009. Print.

Ortiz, Simon. "E-mail Interview With Simon J. Ortiz." *Studies in American Indian Literatures* 15.3–4 (2003–04): 21–23. Print.

Palacios, Monica. "La Llorona Loca: The Other Side." *Living Chicana Theory*. Ed. Carla Trujillo. Berkeley: Third Woman P, 1998. Print.

Perez, Domino Renee. "Words, Worlds in Our Heads: Reclaiming La Llorona's Aztecan Antecedents in Gloria Anzaldúa's 'My Black *Angelos*.'" *Studies in American Indian Literatures* 15 (2003): 51–63. Print.

Plaskow, Judith, and Carol Christ, eds. *Weaving the Visions: New Patterns in Feminist Spirituality*. San Francisco: Harper, 1989. Print.

Saldaña-Portillo, Josefina. 2001. "Who's the Indian in Aztlán? Re-Writing Mestizaje, Indianism, and Chicanismo from the Lacandón." *The Latin American Subaltern Reader.* Ed. Ileana Rodríguez. Durham: Duke UP, 2001. 402–23. Print.

Sandoval, Chela. *Methodology of the Oppressed.* Minneapolis: U of Minnesota P, 2000. Print.

Soto, Sandy. *Reading Chican@ Like a Queer: The De-Mastery of Desire.* Austin: U of Texas P, 2010. Kindle.

Spretnak, Charlene, ed. *The Politics of Women's Spirituality: Essays on the Rise of Spiritual Power within the Feminist Movement.* New York: Doubleday, 1982. Print.

Torres, Mónica. "Doing Mestizaje: When Epistemology Becomes Ethics." Keating, *EntreMundos* 195–203.

30

Native American Literatures

LISA TATONETTI

The rise of a recognized body of queer Native American (U.S.) and Aboriginal (Canadian) literatures[1] occurs in the wake of two concurrent political moments rarely spoken of together – the post-Stonewall movement for gay rights and the Red Power era of Native activism. While these coeval political movements both enter public consciousness in the late 1960s and early 1970s, the recognition of gender variance in Indigenous communities in North America has a much longer history. I will return to the historical emergence of queer Native literature in the 1970s, but I begin with these nuanced Indigenous histories because such knowledge undergirds any attempt to map a genealogy of queer Native literatures.

Understandings of gender and sexuality in North American Indigenous communities differed significantly from those of the Spanish, French, and Anglo conquistadores, explorers, missionaries, travelers, settlers, and early anthropologists, whose documentations of encounter provide much of the written records of these historical periods. Many Indigenous communities recognized third and fourth genders and acknowledged roles for tribal members whose gender expression existed outside a naturalized male/female binary. Among the Zuni, for example, gender was considered an "acquired rather than an inborn trait" (Roscoe, *Zuni* 22). These complex gender roles and performances countered dominant European gender ideologies and thus, at times, explorers and settlers responded to such differences with horrifying violence. In one of the best-known early examples, when Vasco Núñez de Balboa encountered men dressed in women's clothes in Panama in 1513, he stripped the men naked and loosed his dogs to kill them. In 1540, Álvar Núñez Cabeza de Vaca described his time among the Karankawa Indians of Texas, saying, "In the time that I continued among them, I saw a most brutish and beastly custom, to wit, a man who was married to another, and these be certaine effeminate and impotent men who goe clothed and attired like women, and perform the office of a woman" (qtd. in Roscoe, *Changing* 4). Evidence

of the nuanced gender roles that scandalized Cabeza de Vaca does not exist
for every Native nation; however, anthropologist Will Roscoe argues, "alternative gender roles were among the most widely shared features of North
American societies," having "been documented in over 155 tribes" (*Changing*
7). The extant eighteenth- and nineteenth-century documentation demonstrates gender variance existed in every region of North America, crossing
geographical, national, and linguistic boundaries. These multiple gender roles
were as diverse as Native nations themselves. Sue-Ellen Jacobs explains that
the definitions of these roles may:

> encompass cross-sex, same-gender sexual relationships yet . . . may not include
> same-sex, cross-gender sex. The sexuality of individuals originally classified as
> [multiply gendered] turns out to be not exclusively homosexual, nor exclu-
> sively transgendered, nor transvestite. Some males were (and still are) classifi-
> catory women and some females were (and still are) classificatory men for life
> or for shorter, specified periods. ("Is" 29)

Such gender diversity reflects the complexity of Indigenous cosmologies.
The public decline of these complex gender systems relates directly to the
sustained settler assault on Indigenous traditions. As a result of physical and
psychological pressures from settlers, practices that once had been essential
components of daily life transformed into less visible, though still extant, ways
of being. Perhaps the best-known contemporary anthropological work on
Two-Spirit peoples in North America has been undertaken by Lakota anthropologist Bea Medicine, Navajo anthropologist Wesley Thomas, and, more
recently, Brian Joseph Gilley (Chickasaw/Cherokee), and Anglo anthropologists Jacobs, Sabine Lang, Roscoe, and Walter L. Williams.

While Native nations had tribally specific terms for those in gender variant positions, such as "winkte" among the Lakota and "nàdleehí" among the
Navajo, anthropologists historically used the term "berdache," which has connotations of sexual deviance. In 1990, at the third annual Native American/
First Nations gay and lesbian conference in Winnipeg, a group of Indigenous
scholars and activists instead coined the term "Two-Spirit." Jacobs, Thomas,
and Lang explain in their landmark collection *Two-Spirit People* that this decision responded to an anthropological history that situates Native people as
objects of study and to the troubling etymology of "berdache." More importantly, though, by coining "Two-Spirit," Indigenous people not only reclaimed
the power of self-definition, but also created a concept that evoked Indigenous,
rather than colonial, histories and cosmologies. At the same time, the transhistorical, pan-Indian term marked Native American and Aboriginal peoples'

desire to distance themselves from non-Native queer peoples. Qwo-Li Driskill (Cherokee), Chris Finley (Confederated Tribes of the Colville Reservation), Gilley, and Scott Lauria Morgensen argue that the "advent of the term *Two-Spirit* began a new era in the study of past and present Native American gender and sexual diversity" (11). While "Two-Spirit" has not been universally embraced, the term indexes an ideological shift that marks the inception of queer Indigenous studies.[2]

Expanding Literary Histories

Some of the earliest overtly queer Native literature has been, until recently, little known. In Native literary studies, this lack of visibility stems from two impulses in the field. The first hinges on a scholarly (and perhaps readerly) preoccupation with full-length fiction: attention was (and still is) paid to full-length fiction at the expense of short stories, memoir, nonfiction, drama, and, most important, poetry, which is by far the most common genre in Two-Spirit literature. The second source for this lack of visibility is a (mis)understanding of the Red Power era as inherently heteronormative, a time when, to borrow from prominent queer Creek/Cherokee scholar Craig Womack, "men were men and buffalo were scared" (*Red* 280). Thus, despite the establishment of the Gay American Indians (GAI), a political organization cofounded in 1975 by Barbara Cameron (Lakota) and Randy Burns (Paiute), during the Red Power era, queer Native people during this period were often represented as products of settler colonialism – Indigenous queerness was therefore crafted not as historical continuity but as a settler incursion into heteronormative Native cultures. However, rather than being inherently oppositional, the post-Stonewall movement for gay rights and the Red Power era of Native activism coalesce in the emergence of queer Native literature in the 1970s.

I turn here to Mohawk author Maurice Kenny's 1970s poetry to lay the groundwork for this claim. Although more queer Indigenous texts and authors will undoubtedly be reclaimed as we move further into the twenty-first century, Kenny is currently the first Native American writer to publish literature with overtly queer themes. Born in 1929 in Watertown, New York, Kenny began publishing poetry in the 1950s but did not publish work with Two-Spirit themes until the 1970s. The earliest collection of Kenny's poetry to include explicitly queer work is *Only as Far as Brooklyn*, published in 1979 by Good Gay Poets, a press that arose in the wake of the 1969 Stonewall Rebellion. Good Gay Poets emerged from the flourishing intellectual concerns of the Boston Gay Liberation Front as part of the queer literary renaissance, which included small publications and independent presses aimed at queer audiences.

The earliest of Kenny's work from these journals appears in the fall 1974 issue of *Fag Rag*, which contains "A Night, A Bridge, A River: (Beneath Brooklyn Bridge)" and "Greta Garbo." These poems center queer urbanity and gay male relationships rather than Indigeneity and depict Brooklyn Park, a space known for gay cruising, as a site of queer connection. By contrast, "Apache," which Kenny published in the June 1975 edition of *Mouth of the Dragon*, satirizes stereotypical expectations of Indigeneity. Thus, the titular Apache "warrior" rides not a horse, but a Yamaha motorcycle. Likewise, he "hotel[s]" in "wild Oakland" as opposed to lodging on a reservation, in a tribal village, or in the dusty west of the U.S. imaginary. Ultimately, Kenny's poems from the gay journals and newspapers of the queer renaissance destabilize dominant representations of Native identities in which Indigenous men are often depicted as hypermasculinized warriors ineluctably bound to the nineteenth century in affect and action.

If Kenny's work, as "Apache" demonstrates, includes themes seen throughout Native literature, it also indexes a concern specific to queer Native literature: the historical existence of same-sex desire in Indigenous cosmologies. A prime example of this focus can be seen in Kenny's best-known queer-themed poem, "Winkte," which was originally published in *ManRoot*'s spring-summer 1977 issue. "Winkte" calls for recognition of the accepted role Two-Spirit people had in their tribal nations. However, while "Winkte" casts queer sexuality and Indigeneity as intimately imbricated – Two-Spirit people, the speaker claims, strengthen rather than threaten their tribal nations – such was not the case in the literary history of the era during which these pieces were published. As a result, Kenny's little-known poetry from 1970s gay journals challenges not only dominant expectations of Native identities, but also the markedly heteronormative ethos of the Native newspapers, journals, and literary collections of the Red Power era.

Queer Indigenous Literature Anthologized

While Kenny's post-Stonewall poetry provides an important foundation for lesbian, gay, bisexual, transgender, transsexual, intersex, queer, and Two-Spirit (LGBTIQ2) Native literatures, the best-known early articulation of Two-Spirit concerns can be found in the influential women of color/queer of color anthologies that characterized the 1980s. As part of the rise of 1980s multiculturalism, these anthologies gave queer Native writers a visibility heretofore absent; however, while they signal the power of coalitional politics, they also, at times, threaten to subsume the specific concerns of Indigenous writers within a generic multiculturalism that elides tribal sovereignty. An overview of anthologies from the early 1980s to the present, then, provides a nuanced history of the field by mapping the central authors of the queer Native canon as well as the evolving concerns of this burgeoning field from these early years to the present day.

Latina authors/editors Gloria Anzaldúa and Cherríe Moraga's *This Bridge Called My Back* (1981) is the earliest of such collections. *This Bridge*'s significance stems not only from its status as the first compendium of literature by women of color, but also from its direct address of the imbricated relationships racism, poverty, and sexism have with homophobia. The anthology includes queer writers who identify either as Native or as Native and Latina.[3] These writers address concerns central to Native literature, such as stereotypical expectations about Native identities, violence against women, and the generational trauma of settler colonialism. Thus Barbara Cameron (Lakota) describes "the realities of being an Indian in South Dakota," where "Indians were open game for the white people, to kill, maim, beat up, insult, rape, cheat, or whatever atrocity the white people wanted to play with" (47). The writers in *This Bridge* also, however, engage concerns specific to queer Indigenous peoples, such as Max Wolf Valerio's (Blood/Chicana – then Anita Valerio) contention that "lesbianism" can function as "a barrier" to tribal affiliation (44). *This Bridge*, then, maps both the connections and disjunctions between Two-Spirit literature and other multiethnic literatures, as well as those between Two-Spirit and more canonical Native literature from this period, which did not overtly engage same-sex concerns.

Like *This Bridge*, Bay of Quinte Mohawk writer Beth Brant's important 1984 collection, *A Gathering of Spirit*, signaled the rise of 1980s women of color feminism. Although Brant's collection arose directly from such coalitions, its focus on Native women marked *A Gathering of Spirit* as significantly different from *This Bridge*. The collection originated as a 1983 special issue of *Sinister Wisdom*, a multicultural lesbian literature and arts journal edited by Michelle Cliff and Adrienne Rich. With their encouragement, Brant began soliciting work for the first anthology of Native women's writing edited by a Native woman. Ultimately, *A Gathering of Spirit* included among its sixty-plus contributors twelve women who identified as Native lesbians.[4] In Brant's collection, the words of established writers intermingle with those of women who are poor, imprisoned, and unknown in the literary world. Brant explains:

I wrote everywhere I thought there was a story to tell. I wanted to hear from the women yet unheard. I wanted voices traditionally silenced to be a part of this collection. So I wrote to prison organizations in the U.S. and Canada. I made contact with the anti-psychiatry network, Native women's health projects. I sent everywhere I could possibly think of and then looked for more.

(9)

As a result, *A Gathering of Spirit* powerfully illustrates how the realities of class, sexual violence, and incarceration must inform any understanding of Indigenous sexualities.

A landmark in the history of queer Native literature was the 1988 publication of the first anthology to focus solely on Two-Spirit texts: *Living the Spirit: A Gay American Indian Anthology*. *Living the Spirit* was compiled by the GAI in collaboration with white anthropologist Will Roscoe. All "decisions regarding contents, format, and publication arrangements were made by the GAI's board of directors" (Roscoe, *Zuni* xiv). Like Brant's *A Gathering of Spirit*, *Living the Spirit* carefully distinguished Indigenous concerns both from those of other people of color and from those of a white-identified queer community. For example, Burns's preface begins by differentiating queer Indigenous history from U.S. settler history:

When the U.S. Supreme Court cited "millennia of moral teaching" in support of Georgia's sodomy law and when the Vatican declared homosexuality "intrinsically evil," they must not have been thinking of American history and American morals. Because, throughout America, for centuries before and after the arrival of Europeans, gay and lesbian American Indians were recognized and valued members of tribal communities. As Mohawk author Maurice Kenny declares, "We were special!"

(1)

Comprised of fiction, poetry, memoir, interview, essay, photography, painting, and drawing, the anthology evidences both the GAI's growth as an organization and the talent of the many queer Native writers and artists of the period. The collection ranges from Kenny's and Anishinaabe writer Midnight Sun's insightful essays on Two-Spirit histories, to Menominee poet Chrystos's meditations on the psychic cost of racism, to Seminole/Muscogee/Dine visual artist Hulleah Tsinhnahjinnie's parody of a Lone Ranger and Tonto cartoon. Through these varied media and voices, *Living the Spirit* creates a continuum in which contemporary Indigenous artists build on the legacies of Native people who occupied diverse genders and sexualities to craft specifically Indigenous understandings of what it means to be queer and Native in the late twentieth century.

The power of coalition, whether between and among Two-Spirit people (*Living*), Native women (*Gathering*), or women of color more generally (*This Bridge*), undergirds many 1980s and early 1990s collections. In *Making Face, Making Soul* (1990), Anzaldúa continues this tradition with her second anthology by women of color writers. Her inclusion of queer Laguna Pueblo / Sioux writer Paula Gunn Allen, Brant, Chrystos, and Janice Gould (Koyangk'auwi Maidu) highlights their ongoing significance in the field, as these four authors are the most commonly anthologized queer Native writers of the 1980s and 1990s. The centrality of women of color feminist texts to the history of queer Native literature continues with Jamaican Canadian writer Makeda Silvera's 1991 *Piece of My Heart*, the first North American anthology specifically devoted to creative work by queer women of color.[5] In her introduction, Silvera discusses the anthology's history explaining that although the first submissions call went out in the mid-1980s, the project took five years to gain momentum. Silvera suggests perhaps lesbians of color "were not ready to put [their] lives on the line[,] ... not ready to come out, leave family – leave home in search of another home and family" (xiii). The rhetoric positing queerness as a barrier to familial connection, common for the time, is both reflected (in Valerio) and resisted by Two-Spirit writers. Rather than seeking a new home in non-Native queer communities, Native writers often address the need for retaining and/ or reinvigorating ties to Indigenous kinship networks. In Silvera's collection, the necessity of cultural / familial affiliation informs Brant's short story "Home Coming," while Eastern Cherokee author Victoria Lena Manyarrows's poem "the drum beats" suggests that Native lesbians become "whole and wise" through acts of cultural affirmation tied to Indigeneity (141).

Like the aforementioned women of color anthologies, collections of Native women's writing continue to serve as vehicles for queer Native writers from *Living the Spirit* to the present; however, not all of these collections directly engage Two-Spirit identities or same-sex desire, showing that, just as in the Red Power era, later Native-specific venues were not necessarily more reflective of Two-Spirit concerns than mainstream queer or queer of color coalitions. In fact, influential anthologies like Cherokee writer Rayna Green's *That's What She Said* (1984) and Allen's *Spider Woman's Granddaughters* (1989) omit reference to the intersectional concerns of queer Native people. Gould overtly addresses such silences in Cree lesbian poet Connie Fife's 1993 anthology *The Colour of Resistance*. In "A Maidu in the City of Gold," Gould contends, "Indian writers do not mince words. If we are being published now in greater numbers than ever before, still we face the actual potential of being silenced, especially if we are gay or lesbian writers" (238). The rise of 1980s and early 1990s anthologies often (but not always) countered such silences.

While more collections of Native women's, women of color, and queer of color writing would be published in the ensuing years, three twenty-first century anthologies – *This Bridge We Call Home* (2002), *Without Reservation: Indigenous Erotica* (2003), and *Sovereign Erotics* (2011) – mark the field's coming of age in their claims for Indigenous difference, erotic wholeness, and Two-Spirit diversity. The long-awaited sequel to *This Bridge Called My Back*, Anzaldúa and AnaLouise Keating's *This Bridge We Call Home*, like the first anthology, includes selections by Chrystos and Valerio. Valerio's autobiographical essay "'Now That You're White Man': Changing Sex in a Postmodern World – Being, Becoming, and Borders," expands the parameters of queer Native studies by centering transsexuality.[6] At the same time, *This Bridge We Call Home* also includes the most direct discussion to date about how Native women's concerns diverge from those of non-Native women of color when Ohlone/Costanoan-Esselen Nation/Chumash writer Deborah A. Miranda queries: "What do I ask of you, sisters of color? I ask, remember the differences between indigenous and diasporic; between indigenous and exile; between still-colonized native and freed slave; between *choosing* education as a way to speak, and having literacy shoved down your throat in a boarding school far from home, beaten into you" ("'What's'" 200). Thus, more than twenty years later, *This Bridge We Call Home* calls for the promises of *This Bridge Called My Back* to be fulfilled, not through a simplistic understanding of coalition, but through a rich and varied recognition of difference.

In another overtly political claim, First Nations Anishinaabe author Kateri Akiwenzie-Damm's edited collection, *Without Reservation*, returns the erotic to its historical place of importance in Native studies. The first anthology of Indigenous erotica, *Without Reservation* redresses what Akiwenzie-Damm identifies as "the utter lack" of "sex and sexuality" in Indigenous texts (xi), a concern of particular import to queer Indigenous studies. While Brant and Vickie Sears (Cherokee) published in Tee Corinne's 1991 collection of lesbian erotica, *Riding Desire*, those pieces are little known, indicative of the dearth of conversations about any form of Indigenous sexuality (much less queer ones).[7] Writing from queer Native writers in Akiwenzie-Damm's trans-Indigenous, pansexual collection includes Brant's "So Generously," which chronicles the steamy relationship between two poets, a range of Chrystos's poems such as "Hot My Hair Smells of Your Cunt," several poems by Samoan author Dan Taulapapa McMullin's about fa'afafine (Samoan Two-spirit people), as well as powerful poetry by First Nations authors Daniel David Moses (Delaware) and Gregory Scofield (Métis).

Fittingly, I conclude this section with the first collection of queer Native literature published since the GAI's *Living the Spirit*: the anthology *Sovereign Erotics*, edited by Qwo-Li Driskill (Cherokee), Daniel Heath Justice (Cherokee Nation), Deborah A. Miranda, and Lisa Tatonetti. Its expansive array of authors, genres, styles, and topics reflects both the continuity and change in the canon of queer Native literature. *Sovereign Erotics* begins with a nod to *Living the Spirit* in the form of Allen's poem "Some Like Indians Endure," the first piece in both texts. The collection includes recent work by Kenny and Gould, who were also in *Living*. Miranda's "Coyote Takes a Trip" echoes Brant's and Daniel-Harry Steward's revisions of the classic trickster narrative from *Living*, while pieces like Jaynie Lara's "Being Two-Spirit" mirror the first collection's explicit interest in defining Two-Spirit identities. *Sovereign Erotics* also marks the shifts in genre and content that occurred in the twenty-three-year gap between anthologies. Thus the collection contains Justice's fantasy fiction, Akwesasne Mohawk author James Thomas Stevens's lyric poems on English waterways, and short stories by Creek writers Janet McAdams and Chip Livingston that invoke the pounding beat of dance clubs. In the end, *Sovereign Erotics*, like the anthologies of the 1980s and 1990s, reaffirms the contemporary existence of Two-Spirit people and historical traditions of gender variance, while also demonstrating that writing by queer Native people cannot be confined to such parameters.

Queer Native Drama

Kenny's queer 1970s poetry and the anthologies of the 1980s mark two different sorts of beginnings for *overtly* queer Native literature; however, the work of the earliest recognized gay Native author, Oklahoma Cherokee Rollie Lynn Riggs (1899–1954), predates both those literary moments. Riggs was a prolific writer who composed some thirty-three plays, two poetry collections, numerous folk tunes, short stories, and an unfinished novel. Although Riggs, like most prominent artists of his time, was not open about his sexuality to the larger public, he was part of the queer literary community of the 1930s, '40s, and '50s. He worked with Aaron Copeland, who published several of Riggs's songs in *Old American Songs* (1950) and talked to him about turning his play *The Cherokee Night* (1936) into an opera. Riggs is best known for *Green Grow the Lilacs* (1931), which was adapted into the long-running Broadway hit *Oklahoma!* in 1943 (Weaver xii). Jace Weaver (Cherokee) resurrected Riggs's understudied plays in the late 1990s, while Womack offered the first serious analysis of Riggs's implicit depictions of queerness and Indigeneity in *Red on Red* (1999).

It would be more than thirty years after Riggs's death before another Native playwright, Cree dramatist Tomson Highway, would come to prominence. Highway's *The Rez Sisters*, which debuted in 1986 at the Friendship Center in Toronto, is considered one of the most influential plays in Native theatre and was the first Native production to tour Canada. Emily Dictionary, one of the seven "sisters" that populate the play (including blood sisters, sisters-in-laws, and adopted daughters), has butch characteristics and laments the loss of Rose, whom she "loved like no man has ever loved a woman" (*Rez* 97). Highway's *Dry Lips Oughta Move to Kapuskasing* (1989), which also takes place on the fictional Wasaychigan Hill Indian reserve, flips the script to center male characters. The trickster Nanabush appears in both plays, but changes gender from male in *Rez Sisters* to female in *Dry Lips* – functioning as a classic example of the long-standing tie between trickster figures and gender variance, a tradition invoked often in Two-Spirit literature as seen in the work of Brant, Gould, and Miranda. More recently, Highway published *Rose*, a third installation in what he has promised will be a seven-play cycle, as well as a stand-alone play, *Ernestine Shuswap Gets Her Trout* (2005), and Cree-language versions of his first two plays: *Iskooniguni Iskweewuk (Rez)* (2010) and *Paasteewitoon Kaapooskaysing Tageespichit (Dry Lips)* (2010).[8]

First Nations author Daniel David Moses (Delaware) began publishing in the same era as Highway, although his early work has no overtly queer content.[9] Moses's most overtly queer text is *The Indian Medicine Shows* (1995), which, interestingly enough, is also his first drama to center white characters. Comprised of two one-act plays – *The Moon and Dead Indians* and *Angel of the Medicine Show* – that both take place in the late nineteenth century, *The Indian Medicine Shows* examines the intersections of internalized homophobia and racialization. Since 2000, Moses has published a poetry collection, *Sixteen Jesuses* (2000), and several plays, including *Pursued by a Bear: Talks Monologues and Tales* (2005), *Kytopolis: A Play in Two Acts* (2008), and, most recently, a new book of poetry, *A Small Essay on the Largeness of Light and Other Poems* (2012). Moses continues to be an award-winning and prolific poet, playwright, and essayist.

The next generation of queer Native playwrights includes Highway's nephew, Bill Merasty, and Grassy Narrows First Nations playwright/performer Waawaate Fobister (Anishinaabe). Merasty, a noted Cree actor, has written two plays: *Fireweed* (1992) and *For Godly and Divinia / Godly's Divinia (A Love Story)*, an Aboriginal adaptation of *Romeo and Juliet* staged in 2000. Fobister's first play, *Agokwe*, which depicts the initial meeting and erotic attraction between two gay Aboriginal teens from different reserves, premiered in 2008 to much acclaim. An overview of queer Native drama thus highlights both the centrality of the First Nations literary canon to Two-Spirit studies and the movement of queerness from veiled allusion to central theme.

Queering Native Fiction

Queer Native fiction, like drama and the early women of color anthologies, emerges in the 1980s. Such fiction varies widely in its depiction of Indigenous experiences, ranging from tribal trickster narratives to representations of urban alienation; however, as we move toward the present day, a distinct focus on issues of sovereignty emerges. The first Native novel with a queer Indigenous protagonist is Allen's *The Woman Who Owned the Shadows* (1983). Allen's Ephanie Atencio shares a lesbian attraction with her childhood friend, Elena, and later recovers from abusive or ill-chosen heterosexual marriages through a same-sex relationship as an adult. Although most contemporary reviewers failed to mention the text's queer overtones, some fifteen years later, Allen's novel would be the focus of many of the first essay-length critical analyses of queer Native literature (see Tatonetti).

In 1985, Brant publishes *Mohawk Trail*, a collection of her own short stories, essays, and poetry. The specific traditions and landscape of the Bay of Quinte Mohawk ground the collection, which begins with a story of the Longhouse in a section called "Native Origins." Brant ends the section with "Coyote Learns a New Trick," in which the trickster "stuff[s] . . . diapers into her under-pants so it looked like she had a swell" (32) in order to fool Fox, a pretty female. By concluding the tribally grounded "Native Origins" section with this piece, Brant explicitly frames same-sex desire as part of, rather than apart from, long-standing Indigenous traditions. Here, Brant's writing aligns with Kenny's to claim a historical continuity for Two-Spirit erotics. But while Brant bases much of her fiction in specific Haudenosaunee tribal tradition, she also viv-idly describes the violence and alienation that characterizes the experiences of some LGBTIQ2 Native people. These nuanced considerations of queer Indigenous realities recur in Brant's 1991 short story collection *Food & Spirits* and her 1994 collection of personal essays, *Writing as Witness*. Throughout her work, Brant highlights how Two-Spirit ideologies help Native people heal from the ongoing reverberations of settler colonialism, a theme we see across queer Native literature and theory.

Vickie Sears, who often appeared alongside Brant, Chrystos, and Gould in the anthologies of the 1980s and early '90s, published her only monograph, *Simple Songs*, in 1990. Many of the characters in her fourteen short stories are children in the foster care system who grapple not only with the difficult realities of that life, which Sears knew well, but also with the experience of moving between Native and white communities. Together, these early queer Native women writers often consider issues of mixed-blood identity, gendered violence, and the healing power of writing.

While Pomo/Miwok author Greg Sarris's novels *Grand Avenue* (1994) and *Watermelon Nights* (1998) both contain queer characters, *The Woman Who Owned the Shadows* was the only novel with a queer Indigenous protagonist until Anishinaabe fiction writer Carole laFavor's 1996 *Along the Journey River*. LaFavor's Renee LaRoche, a lesbian detective on the Minnesota Red Earth Reservation, follows thieves, murderers, and Ojibwa traditions while juggling a steamy relationship with her white lover, Samantha Salisbury. *Evil Dead Center* (1997), laFavor's second book, continues the Renee LaRoche saga. LaFavor, an AIDS/HIV activist as well as a writer and woodcarver who died in 2011, pays close attention in both novels to the imbricated nature of tribal land, sovereignty, and sexuality. In fact, in many ways, laFavor's work can be read as a precursor to perhaps the best-known queer Native novel, Craig Womack's 2001 *Drowning in Fire*, which depicts Josh Henneha's coming of age as a gay Creek boy in 1970s rural Oklahoma. The contemporary sections of Womack's novel, set in 1993, layer the story of Josh's relationship with Jimmy Alexander, his former Creek schoolmate, together with a historical narrative of the Muscogee fight against U.S. government allotment policies. Four years after *Drowning in Fire*, Daniel Heath Justice published the first Native fantasy novel: *Kynship* (2005). Justice's fantasy trilogy – *Kynship*, *Wyrwood* (2006), and *Dreyd* (2007) – maps a third-gender tradition onto an allegorical retelling of the Cherokee Nation's fight to retain sovereignty. Together, laFavor, Womack, and Justice index the ties between tribal sovereignty and queer sexuality that have been vital to queer Indigenous literature since the 1970s publication of Kenny's "Winkte."

The Poetic Tradition in Queer Native Literature

Although fiction – especially full-length fiction – garners a lion's share of public attention, poetry functions as the cornerstone of the queer Native literary canon. Such prevalence is evidenced in the aforementioned anthologies as well as in the monographs of queer Native poetry that followed Kenny's *Only as Far as Brooklyn*. The early 1990s saw a significant rise in the publication of queer Native poets: by 1992, Chrystos, Gould, and Fife had all published their first collections, and Yuchi/Comanche poet Joe Dale Tate Nevaquaya's manuscript *Leaving Holes*, although not published until 2011, was the co-winner of the first Diane Decorah Memorial Award (today the Native Writer's Circle of America's First Book Award for Poetry).

The first collection to follow Kenny's was Chrystos's 1988 *Not Vanishing*, which was published the same year as *Living the Spirit*. One of the most important voices in queer Native literature, Chrystos's strong and often confrontational poems engage the intersections of poverty, oppression, erotic desire, dominant appropriation of Native images, and lesbianism. Her poetry regularly rejects conventional capitalization and punctuation to confront "300 years" of history in which "sacred beliefs have been made into pencils / names of cities gas stations" (7). At the same time, Chrystos calls the non-Native queer community to task for a legacy of racism while also crafting beautiful erotica in poems like "O Honeysuckle Woman." Chrystos highlights the imbricated nature of the political and the erotic throughout her subsequent work, from *Dream On* (1991) through *Red Rollercoaster* (2003).

The connections between and among the queer Native women writers of the 1980s and 1990s can be seen in the common themes and also, at times, style of their work. Like Chrystos and Brant, Gould explicitly ties Indigeneity to the erotic. Additionally, Chrystos, Gould, and Fife compare in their consistent turn toward autobiography. Consequently, Gould's poetry – *Beneath My Heart* (1990), *Earthquake Weather* (1996), and *Doubters and Dreamers* (2011) – chronicles the California history of her people, the Koyangk'auwi Maidu, and the personal history of her sometimes difficult relationship with her Native mother and white father (whose occasional crossdressing led to male-to-female transition), as well as offering powerful depictions of same-sex desire. Likewise, Fife's first collection, *Beneath the Naked Sun* (1992), parallels Chrystos's thematically by directly confronting settler colonialism as well as stylistically by largely eschewing punctuation and capitalization. In "the revolution of not vanishing," Fife says she is "ready to / follow the path" Chrystos "bulldozed" (49). Fife's later collections *Speaking through Jagged Rock* (1999) and *Poems for a New World* (2001) continue to map the connections among many of the writers referenced here, as well as acknowledging coalitions between international communities in poems like "Peace Is Not Genocide."

Also publishing his first book in the early 1990s was First Nations writer Gregory Scofield (Métis), who has since become one of the preeminent contemporary writers in Canada. Scofield's 1993 *The Gathering* begins with a Cree language story – "kaskitêw-maskwa osisima" ("Black Bear's Language") – and is subsequently divided into sections based on the four directions. Scofield terms his chronicles of urban experience "Survival Poetry":

> Raw, unflinching
> Watching your back in some skid row bar
> Down here
> Each line will give you a day – or make it your last
>
> (*Gathering* 34)

Native Canadiana / Songs From the Urban Rez (1996) similarly probes the relationship between Aboriginal identity and urbanity, as well as more overtly engaging queer sexuality. In *Love Medicine and One Song* (1997), Scofield dramatically shifts tone offering lyric poems, or "medicine songs," that emphasize the intersections of Cree images, Cree language, and the erotic. Scofield published paired books of poetry and memoir – *I Knew Two Métis Women* and *Thunder Through My Veins: Memories of a Métis Childhood* – in 1999. These texts not only craft Scofield's history but also emphasize his continued attention to the stories of women through his sensitive and often humorous snapshots of his mother and aunt. *Thunder Through My Veins* has since become a staple in Canadian universities. Scofield's feminism links his work to the anthologies of the 1980s and early 1990s, his representations of Two-Spirit urbanity situate his poetry alongside that of Kenny, Chrystos, Gould, and Fife, while his attention to Cree language ties his writing to Highway's.

Among the many queer Native American and Aboriginal writers who published their first books in the 1990s is poet/theorist/essayist Miranda, who, as mentioned previously, would also publish in later anthologies like *This Bridge We Call Home*. Like Gould's collections, Miranda's *Indian Cartography* (1999) refutes the history of erasure that claims California Indians disappeared in the face of Euro-American "progress," and investigates the contours of poverty, sexual abuse, strength, and love. Although *Indian Cartography*'s "Strawberries" and "Sometimes the Open Hand of Desire" have lesbian overtones, Miranda's earliest collection with overtly queer themes is *The Zen of La Llorona* (2005), which focuses on family history, the aftermath of her mother's death, and the possibilities of what Miranda calls the "indigenous erotic" (4). *Bad Indians* (2013), Miranda's most recent publication, combines history, poetry, primary documents, and personal photographs in a powerful tribal/personal memoir. In this way, Miranda, like Scofield, redefines traditional form to more effectively narrate Indigenous history.

While the connections between Indigenous peoples in North American have been evident for centuries in trade networks, familial relationships, and texts, global ties between Indigenous peoples, although also historical, have not always been visible to outsiders. These complex trans-Indigenous relationships are especially evident in the writing of lyric poet Stevens, who published his first book, *Tokinish*, in 1994. His next collection, *Combing the Snakes From His Hair* (2002), melds free verse poetry, drawings, and autobiography with formalist conventions and Iroquoian allusions. Stevens's 2006 collaboration with Samoan writer Caroline Sinavaiana, *Mohawk / Samoa: Transmigrations*, marks the transnational turn of contemporary Indigenous studies by pairing their Mohawk and Samoan cultures, art, and poetry. Likewise, Stevens's 2007 collection, *A Bridge Dead in Winter*, situates the Jesuit history in China alongside that of the Jesuit encroachment in Iroquoia.

Twenty-first-century queer Native poetry includes Sharron Proulx-Turner's (Métis) *What the Auntys Say* (2002) and her two 2008 texts: *She Is Reading with a Blanket in Her Hand*, a book of dedication poems, and *She Walks for Days Inside a Thousand Eyes: A Two-Spirit Story)*, a mixed-genre historical narrative. Additionally, Janet McAdams has not only published two collections of poetry, *The Island of Lost Luggage* (2000) and *Feral* (2007), but also began her work as the founding editor for the Salt Press Earthworks series on Native American poetry, which published Miranda, Stevens, and Driskill. Driskill's 2005 *Walking With Ghosts*, one of the earliest Earthworks offerings, melds embodied ruminations on Cherokee history with an exposure of the ongoing violence toward transsexuals. The continued expansion of the queer Native literary canon can be seen in the arc of work by writers like Abenaki poet Cheryl Savageau, whose early poetry collections – *Home Country* (1992), which she expanded into *Dirt Road Home* (1995) – center family relationships without directly addressing queerness. By contrast, Savageau's 2006 *Mother / Land* contains queer erotic themes in wonderfully steamy poems like "Where I Want Them" and "Red." The late 2000s continues to mark the increased production of work by queer Native poets with new work by established writers – including Kenny's *Connotations* (2008), Gould's *Doubters and Dreamers*, and Scofield's *Louis: The Heretic Poems*, as well as the publication of a new generation of authors. Chip Livingston's two gorgeous poetry collections, *Museum of False Starts* (2010) and *Crow-Blue, Crow-Black* (2012) and the many talented poets included in the 2010 international queer Indigenous issue of the journal *Yellow Medicine River*, edited by Ahimsa Timoteo Bodhrán, exemplify the vibrant nature of queer Indigenous literature in the current era.

Queer Indigenous Critiques

Many of the prominent creative writers in the field also theorize queer Indigeneity and, in fact, queer Native studies has come into being as a distinct field of inquiry in the twenty-first century. An early example of this trend is found in Kenny's essay "Tinselled Bucks" (1975/76). Kenny documents the prevalence of Two-Spirit (then still "berdache") traditions in historical sources, making an argument for the recovery of queer Native histories. Allen's groundbreaking 1981 essay "Beloved Women" follows Kenny's work to situate same-sex and multiple gender traditions as part of a continuum in Indigenous cultures. While Allen published a significant number of books of poetry and criticism, she is best known for her critical study *The Sacred Hoop* (1986), which identifies a genealogy for contemporary lesbians in Indigenous cultures. The book quickly became a staple in women's studies classes, where Allen's focus on the lives and literature of American Indian women filled a central gap in criticism and curriculum.

Brant's collection of personal essays, *Writing as Witness*, and Gould's 1994 essay "Disobedience (in Language) in Texts by Lesbian Native Americans" also expand this body of theoretical texts, while Womack's critical and creative work – *Red on Red* and *Drowning in Fire* – functions as a watershed moment in queer Native studies. Together, Kenny, Allen, Brant, Gould, and Womack mark a shift from literary criticism *about* queer Native and Aboriginal literatures to a Two-Spirit/queer Native *theory* undertaken *by and for* queer Indigenous peoples. Miranda's 2002 "Dildos, Hummingbirds, and Driving Her Crazy" and Driskill's 2004 "Stolen from Our Bodies" extend these interventions. Miranda argues that "if we want justice, we must work for the erotic" (14), while Driskill crafts a theory of the "Sovereign Erotic," "an erotic wholeness and/or healing from the historical trauma that First Nations people continue to survive, rooted within the histories, traditions and resistance struggles of [Indigenous] nations" (51). Such theoretical interventions can similarly be seen in Justice's, Highway's, and Scofield's pieces in Curve Lake First Nations Ojibway writer Drew Hayden Taylor's 2008 collection, *Me Sexy*; in the 2010 special issue of *GLQ*, "Sexuality, Nationality, Indigeneity," edited by Justice, Mark Rifkin, and Bethany Schneider; and in Driskill, Finley, Gilley, and Morgensen's *Queer Indigenous Studies* (2011), which was published as a companion to *Sovereign Erotics*. The early twenty-first century, then, constitutes a moment of renaissance in which the theories, literatures, and voices of queer Native American and Aboriginal peoples in North America proliferate. In the end, the breadth and depth of contemporary queer Native literature and theory claims and extends long-standing Indigenous histories while also presenting a decoloniz-ing challenge to U.S. and Canadian settler societies.

Notes

Thanks to the editors as well as Chadwick Allen, Qwo-Li Driskill, Brian Joseph Gilley, Daniel Heath Justice, Abby Knoblauch, Deborah Miranda, and Scott Morgensen for reading drafts and/or sharing expertise. Thanks, too, to the innumerable talented Two-Spirit writers referenced here – your work enriches my life and the world.

1. I employ common usage and collectively refer to Indigenous peoples in (what is now) the United States as "Native American" or "American Indian." For the Indigenous people of (what is now) Canada – First Nations, Inuit, and Métis – I use the collective term "Aboriginal." In my work, "Native" or "Indigenous" function as broader, transnational terms. Attempting to accurately address the similarities and differences between Native American and Aboriginal histories is inevitably complicated. For example, as markers of the dominant imaginary, the borders between these settler nations in some cases run directly through tribal nations. At the same time, however, Indigenous peoples in the United States and Canada, while sharing common experiences of settler colonial incursion, have disparate histories with U.S. and Canadian government poli-cies. U.S. Native studies scholarship has often elided these differences through the imposition of a U.S.-based conception of Native studies. I attempt to avoid those erasures here, but also recognize the limits of my understanding as a non-Native, U.S. scholar.

2. While some queer Native people employ "Two-Spirit," there also has been resistance to the term. "Two-Spirit" was quickly co-opted by the non-Native community and thus some see it as having New Age connotations that roman-ticize Indigenous identities. As the term's creators recognized, "Two-Spirit" is pantribal and lacks a relationship to a specific nation, gender role, or tribal practice. Finally, many Native people are simply more comfortable identifying as lesbian, gay, bisexual, trans, queer, and so forth. See the introductions to *Two-Spirit People* (ed. Jacobs, Thomas, and Lang), *Queer Indigenous Studies* (ed. Bodhrán), and *Sovereign Erotics* (ed. Driskill, Justice, et al.).

3. In addition to Cameron and Valerio, Jo Carrillo, Chrystos, and Naomi Littlebear Morena.

4. Paula Gunn Allen, Mary Bennett (Seneca), Brant, Cameron, Chrystos, Janice Gould, Elaine Hall (Creek), Terri Meyette (Yaqui), Mary Moran, Katei Sardella (Micmac), Vicki Sears, and Valerio.

5. The queer Native writers in Silvera's collection include Susan Beaver (Mohawk, Grand River Territory), Brant, Chrystos, Connie Fife, and Victoria Lena Manyarrows.

6. Valerio further engages transsexuality in his memoir *The Testosterone Files*.

7. Brant's poem "Language/Desire" (Corinne, *Riding*) describes a same-sex encounter with an explicitness heretofore absent in Native literature, while Sears's short story, "Baskets and Rugs" (in *Simple Songs*) intersperses memories of the first-person Native narrator's first sexual encounter with a white woman with her developing relationship with a Native woman.

8. Along with his plays, Highway published a semiautobiographical novel, *Kiss of the Fur Queen* (1998) that depicts the events and aftereffects of the Okimasis brothers' abuse at the hands of the head priest of a Residential School.

9. Like Kenny, Moses published a poetry collection, *Delicate Bodies* (1980), with a press that arose in the wake of Stonewall, blewointment. Moses followed with two 1988 plays, *Coyote City* and *The Dreaming Beauty*, before publishing another poetry collection, *The White Line* (1990), and a series of plays throughout the 1990s.

Works Cited

Akiwenzie-Damm, Kateri. "Erotica, Indigenous Style." *Without Reservation* xi–xii.
ed. *Without Reservation: Indigenous Erotica.* Wellington: Huia, 2003. Print.

Allen, Paula Gunn. "Beloved Women: Lesbians in American Indian Cultures." *Conditions* 7 (1981): 67–87. Print.
The Sacred Hoop: Recovering the Feminine in American Indian Traditions. Boston: Beacon P, 1986. Print.
Spider Woman's Granddaughters: Traditional Tales and Contemporary Writing by Native American Women. New York: Random, 1989. Print.
The Woman Who Owned the Shadows. San Francisco: Spinsters, 1983. Print.

Anzaldúa, Gloria, ed. *Making Face, Making Soul Haciendo Caras: Creative and Critical Perspectives by Women of Color.* San Francisco: Aunt Lute, 1990. Print.

Anzaldúa, Gloria, and AnaLouise Keating, eds. *This Bridge We Call Home: Radical Visions for Transformation.* New York: Routledge, 2002. Print.

Anzaldúa, Gloria, and Cherríe Moraga, ed. *This Bridge Called My Back: Writing by Radical Women of Color.* Watertown: Persephone P, 1981. Print.

Bodhrán, Ahimsa Timoteo, ed. *International Queer Indigenous Issue.* Spec. issue of *Yellow Medicine Review: A Journal of Indigenous Literature, Art, and Thought* (Fall 2010). Print.

Brant, Beth. *Food & Spirits.* Ithaca: Firebrand, 1991. Print.
ed. *A Gathering of Spirit: A Collection by North American Indian Women.* 1984. Ithaca: Firebrand, 1988. Print.
Mohawk Trail. Ithaca: Firebrand, 1985. Print.
Writing as Witness: Essay and Talk. Toronto: Women's P, 1994. Print.

Burns, Randy. Preface. Gay American Indians and Roscoe 1–5.

Chrystos. *Dream On.* Vancouver: Press Gang, 1991. Print.
Fire Power. Vancouver: Press Gang, 1995. Print.
Fugitive Colors. Cleveland: Cleveland State UP, 1995. Print.
In Her I Am. Vancouver: Press Gang, 1993. Print.
Not Vanishing. Vancouver: Press Gang, 1988. Print.
Red Rollercoaster. Flying Turtle P, 2003. Print.

Corinne, Tee, ed. *Riding Desire: An Anthology of Erotic Writing.* Austin: Banned, 1991. Print.

Driskill, Qwo-Li. "Stolen from Our Bodies: First Nations Two-Spirits/Queers and the Journey to a Sovereign Erotic." *SAIL* 16.2 (2004): 50–64. Print.

Walking with Ghosts. Cambridge: Salt P, 2005. Print.

Driskill, Qwo-Li, Daniel Heath Justice, Deborah Miranda, and Lisa Tatonetti, eds. *Sovereign Erotics: A Collection of Contemporary Two-Spirit Literature.* Tucson: U of Arizona P, 2011. Print.

Driskill, Qwo-Li, Chris Finley, Brian Joseph Gilley, and Scott Lauria Morgensen, eds. *Queer Indigenous Studies: Critical Interventions in Theory, Politics, and Literature.* Tucson: U of Arizona P, 2011. Print.

Fife, Connie, ed. *The Colour of Resistance: A Contemporary Collection of Writing by Aboriginal Women.* Toronto: Sister Vision P, 1993. Print.

Beneath the Naked Sun. Toronto: Sister Vision P, 1992. Print.

"Peace Is Not Genocide." *Poems* 50–51.

Poems for a New World. Vancouver: Ronsdale P, 2001. Print.

Speaking Through Jagged Rock. Fredericton: Broken Jaw P, 1999. Print.

"the revolution of not vanishing.' *Beneath* 49.

Gay American Indians and Will Roscoe, eds. *Living the Spirit: A Gay American Indian Anthology.* New York: St. Martin's, 1988. Print.

Gilley, Brian Joseph. *Becoming Two-Spirit: Gay Identity and Social Acceptance in Indian Country.* Lincoln: U of Nebraska P, 2006. Print.

Gould, Janice. *Beneath My Heart.* New York: Firebrand, 1990. Print.

"Disobedience (in Language) in Text by Lesbian Native Americans." *ARIEL: A Review of International English Literature* 25.1 (1994): 32–44. Print.

Doubters and Dreamers. Tucson: U Arizona P, 2011. Print.

Earthquake Weather. Tucson: U Arizona P, 1996. Print.

"A Maidu in the City of Gold: Some Thoughts on Censorship and American Indian Poetry." Fife, *Colour* 230–43.

Green, Rayna. *That's What She Said: Contemporary Poetry and Fiction by Native American Women.* Bloomington: Indiana UP, 1984. Print.

Highway, Tomson. *Dry Lips Oughta Move to Kapuskasing.* Saskatoon: Fifth House, 1989. Print.

Ernestine Shuswap Gets Her Trout: A "String Quartet" for Four Female Actors. Vancouver: Talonbooks, 2005. Print.

Iskooniguni Iskweewuk: Meetaweewin. Markham: Fifth House, 2010. Print.

Kiss of the Fur Queen. Norman: U of Oklahoma P, 1998. Print.

Paasteewitoon Kaapooskaysing Tageespichit: Meetaweewin. Markham: Fifth House, 2010. Print.

Rose: A Play. Vancouver: Talonbooks, 2003. Print.

The Rez Sisters: A Play in Two Acts. Saskatoon: Fifth House, 1988. Print.

Jacobs, Sue-Ellen. "Berdache: A Brief Review of Literature." *Colorado Anthropologist* 1.1 (1968): 25–40. Print.

"Is the 'North American Berdache' Merely a Phantom in the Imagination of Western Social Scientists?" Jacobs, Thomas, and Lang 21–43.

Jacobs, Sue-Ellen, Wesley Thomas, and Sabine Lang, eds. *Two-Spirit People: Native American Gender Identity, Sexuality, and Spirituality*. Urbana: U of Illinois P, 1997. Print.

Justice, Daniel Heath. *Dreyd: The Way of Thorn and Thunder, Book 3*. Ontario: Kegedonce P, 2007. Print.

Kynship: The Way of Thorn and Thunder. Ontario: Kegedonce P, 2005. Print.

Wyrwood: The Way of Thorn and Thunder, Book 2. Ontario: Kegedonce P, 2006. Print.

Justice, Daniel Heath, Mark Rifkin, and Bethany Schneider, eds. *Sexuality, Nationality, Indigeneity*. Spec. issue of *GLQ: A Journal of Lesbian and Gay Studies* 16.1–2 (2010). Print.

Kenny, Maurice. "Apache." *Mouth of the Dragon* 5 (1975): n.pag. Print.

Connotations: Poems. New York: White Pine P, 2008. Print.

"Greta Garbo." 1974. *Only* 19.

"A Night, A Bridge, A River (Beneath Brooklyn Bridge)" *Fag Rag* 10 (1974): 8. Print.

Only as Far as Brooklyn: Poems. Boston: Good Gay Poets, 1979. Print.

"Tinselled Bucks: An Historical Study in Indian Homosexuality." *Gay Sunshine* 26/27 (1975/76): 16–17, 15. Print.

"Winkte." *ManRoot* 11 (Spring/Summer 1977): 26. rpt. in *Only* 10–11.

LaFavor, Carole. *Along the Journey River: A Mystery*. Ann Arbor: Firebrand, 1996. Print.

Evil Dead Center: A Mystery. Ann Arbor: Firebrand, 1997. Print.

Livingston, Chip. *Crow-Blue, Crow-Black*. New York: NYQ, 2012. Print.

Museum of False Starts. Arlington: Gival P, 2010. Print.

Manyarrows, Victoria Lena. "the drum beats." Silvera 141.

McAdams, Janet. *Feral*. Cambridge: Salt, 2007. Print.

The Island of Lost Luggage. Tucson: U of Arizona P, 2000. Print.

Merasty, Billy, and Maggie Huculak. *Fireweed. Native Earth Performing Archives*. U of Guelph, Ontario: Conolly Theatre Archives, 1992. Print.

For Godly and Divinia / Godly's Divinia (A Love Story). Native Earth Performing Archives. U of Guelph, Ontario: Conolly Theatre Archives, 1990. Print.

Miranda, Deborah A. *Bad Indians: A Tribal Memoir*. Berkeley: Heyday, 2013. Print.

"Dildos, Hummingbirds, and Driving Her Crazy: Searching for American Indian Women's Love Poetry and Erotics." *Frontiers* 23.2 (2002): 135–49. Print.

Indian Cartography. Greenfield Center: Greenfield Review P, 1999. Print.

"'What's Wrong with a Little Fantasy?': Storytelling from the (Still) Ivory Tower." Anzaldúa and Keating 192–202.

The Zen of La Llorona. Cambridge: Salt, 2005. Print.

Moses, Daniel David. *Almighty Voice and His Wife: A Play in Two Acts*. Stratford: Williams-Wallace, 1992. Print.

Big Buck City: A Play in Two Acts. Toronto: Playwrights Union of Canada, 1991. Print.

Brebeuf's Ghost: A Tale of Horror in Three Acts. Toronto: Playwrights Guild of Canada, 1996. Print.

City of Shadows: A Play in One Act. Toronto: Playwrights Guild of Canada, 1995. Print.

Coyote City: A Play in Two Acts. Toronto: Playwrights Union of Canada, 1988. Print.

Delicate Bodies. Vancouver: Blewointment P, 1980. Print.

The Dreaming Beauty: A Play. Toronto: Playwrights Union of Canada, 1988. Print.

The Indian Medicine Shows: Two One-Act Plays. Toronto: Exile Editions, 1995. Print.

Kytopolis: A Play in Two Acts. Holstein: Exile Editions, 2008. Print.

Pursued by a Bear: Talks, Monologues, and Tales. Toronto: Exile Editions, 2005. Print.

Sixteen Jesuses. Toronto: Exile Editions, 2000. Print.

The White Line: Poems. Saskatoon: Fifth House, 1990. Print.

The Witch of Niagara: A Confabulation in One Act. Toronto: Playwrights Union of Canada, 1998. Print.

Nevaquaya, Joe Dale Tate. *Leaving Holes & Selected New Writings*. Norman: Mongrel Empire P, 2011. Print.

Proulx-Turner, Sharron. *She Is Reading with a Blanket in Her Hand*. Calgary: Frontenac House, 2008. Print.

She Walks for Days Inside a Thousand Eyes: A Two-Spirit Story. Winnipeg: Turnstone P, 2008. Print.

What the Auntys Say. Toronto: McGilligan, 2002. Print.

Riggs, Lynn. *The Cherokee Night and Other Plays*. Ed. Jace Weaver. Norman: U of Oklahoma P, 2003. Print.

Green Grow the Lilacs. 1931. *Cherokee.*

Roscoe, Will. *The Zuni Man-Woman*. Albuquerque: U of New Mexico P, 1991. Print.

Changing Ones: Third and Fourth Genders in Native North America. New York: St. Martins, 1998. Print.

Sarris, Greg. *Grand Avenue*. New York: Hyperion, 1994. Print.

Watermelon Nights. New York: Hyperion, 1998. Print.

Savageau, Cheryl. *Dirt Road Home*. Willimantic: Curbstone P, 1995. Print.

Home Country. Cambridge: Alice James, 1992. Print.

Mother/Land. Cambridge: Salt, 2006. Print.

Scofield, Gregory. *I Knew Two Metis Women: The Lives of Dorothy Scofield and Georgina Houle Young*. Victoria: Polestar, 1999. Print.

Love Medicine and One Song. Victoria: Polestar, 1997. Print.

Native Canadiana / Songs From the Urban Rez. Vancouver: Polestar, 1996. Print.

The Gathering: Stones for the Medicine Wheel. Vancouver: Polestar, 1993. 34. Print.

Thunder Through My Veins: Memories of a Métis Childhood. Toronto: Harper Flamingo Canada, 1999. Print.

Sears, Vickie. *Simple Songs*. Ithaca: Firebrand Books, 1990. Print.

Silvera, Makeda, ed. *Piece of My Heart: A Lesbian of Colour Anthology*. Toronto: Sister Vision P, 1991. Print.

Stevens, James Thomas. *A Bridge Dead in the Water*. Cambridge: Salt, 2007. Print.

Combing the Snakes from His Hair. East Lansing: Michigan State UP, 2002. Print.

dis(Orient). Long Beach: Palm P, 2005. Print.

Tokinish. New York: Intensity P, 1994. Print.

Stevens, James Thomas, and Caroline Sinavaiana. *Mohawk/Samoan Transmigrations*. Oakland: Subpress, 2005. Print.

Tatonetti, Lisa. "The Emergence and Importance of Queer American Indian Literatures, or, 'Help and Stories' in Thirty Years of *SAIL.*" *Studies in American Indian Literatures* 19.4 (2007): 143–70. Print.

Valerio, Anita. "It's In My Blood, My Face – My Mother's Voice, The Way I Sweat." Anzaldúa and Moraga 41–45.

Valerio, Max Wolf. "'Now That You're White Man': Changing Sex in a Postmodern World – Being, Becoming, and Borders." Anzaldúa and Keating 239–54.

The Testosterone Files: My Hormonal and Social Transformation from Female to Male. Emeryville: Seal P, 2006. Print.

Taylor, Drew Hayden. *Me Sexy: An Exploration of Native Sex and Sexuality.* Vancouver: Douglas & McIntyre, 2008. Print.

Weaver, Jace. Foreword. Riggs, *Cherokee* ix–xv.

William, Walter. *The Spirit and the Flesh.* Boston: Beacon P, 1986. Print.

Womack, Craig. *Drowning in Fire.* Tucson: U of Arizona P, 2001. Print.

Red on Red: Native American Literary Separatism. Minneapolis: U of Minnesota P, 1999. Print.

31

African American and African-Diasporic Writing, Post-1930

ROBERT REID-PHARR

Smoke and Fire

Is there some clear logic that would allow us to trace a path between work produced by black sexual minorities living in the early part of the twentieth century and those living in the early part of the twenty-first? How might writing produced by self-identified black sexual minorities be read in relation to those several traditions in which the figure of the black queer has been utilized to help produce narratives of African American and African diasporic culture and society? These questions are made more difficult still by the fact that LBGT identity formations as well as the meanings attached to those formations have been dynamic, ever changing, always up for debate. I turn, then, toward Richard Bruce Nugent's "Smoke, Lilies and Jade," a short story that appeared in the single, November 1926 issue of *Fire!!!: A Quarterly Devoted to Younger Negro Artists*, edited by Wallace Thurman. Nugent's text is believed to be the first explicit piece of black LBGT literature ever published. The work interests me here, however, because it demonstrates so clearly that from the Harlem Renaissance forward, the "known" black lesbian and gay subject whom an essay such as this should presumably hail has been a spectral figure, one who easily loses coherence when we examine the historical, ideological, and aesthetic contexts in which he has been produced.

What strikes one when reading "Smoke, Lilies and Jade" is not only how very muted the actual images of homosexual desire and intercourse actually are, but also the obvious self-consciousness that suffuses Nugent's opaque and difficult style. Very little happens in the text. Much of its effect is to leave its readers with a sense that modern sensibilities are marked by brooding and ever more complex practices of self-reflection. "He wanted to do something," Nugent writes. "[B]ut it was so comfortable just to lay there on the bed ...... his shoes off ... and think ... think of everything ... short disconnected thoughts – to wonder ... to remember ... to think and smoke" (33).[1]

Importantly, we find early in the story that its protagonist, Alex, came to New York shortly after the death of his father, yet "he *wasn't* like his father ... he couldn't sing ... he didn't want to sing ... he didn't want to sing" (33). Nugent disrupts expected narratives of patriarchal influence as well as distances his own art from those popular cultural forms (particularly music) with which African American life was so associated. Instead, Alex is a decidedly new character. He is still in the process of becoming. An out-of-work artist in New York City, he spends his days smoking, roaming the streets, reading Wilde, Freud, Boccacio, Schnitzler, and seeking the company of his many infamous friends.

Alex encounters Adrian, the character with whom he will initiate something just short of a homosexual affair, as he walks the streets in the early morning gloom: "perdone me senor tiene vd. fosforo [*sic*]," Alex hears. He "was glad to have been addressed in Spanish ... to have been asked for a match in English ... or to have been addressed in English at all ... would have been blasphemy just then" (36). Part of what becomes immediately apparent is that the nature of the desire being imaged here would be nearly impossible to describe within the narrative traditions that Nugent, Thurman, and the rest of the "younger Negro artists" whom they represent resist. Alex's aesthetic is structured by a self-conscious Modernism. It also reflects the jarring social and linguistic realities of New York such that regardless of one's ethnicity there are times when only the Spanish language will do.

The world that Alex inhabits and that Nugent describes is one in which desire has been loosed both from the expectation that it always will be directed in one direction versus another and that it only can be expressed in traditional forms. For Nugent, whose pacing, imagery, diction, and punctuation all point to a newly liberated prose style, the focus is on maintaining options and possibility:

> Beauty's lips touched his ... pressed hard ... cool ... opened slightly ... Alex opened his eyes ... into Beauty's ... parted his lips ... Dulce ... Beauty's breath was hot and short ... Alex ran his hand through Beauty's hair ... Beauty's lips pressed hard against his teeth ... Alex trembled ... could feel Beauty's body ... close against his ... hot ... tense ... white ... and soft ... soft ... soft ....
>
> (38)

I agree that the magic of this passage stems from the remarkable fact that Nugent was able to say so much, to say *that*, in 1926. What I want to reiterate, however, is that what Nugent has said may not line up as neatly with what many would take to be progressive narratives of black lesbian, gay, bisexual, and transgender liberation as one might hope. The body that is being so breathlessly celebrated here is, in fact, white. Moreover, it is not the only body in the story that receives Nugent's caressing attention. There is also Melva, Alex's other love. The tale ends with Alex's musings regarding the equivalence of the two in his affections. "Beauty ... Melva ... Beauty ... Melva" (39). Refusing to produce a cleanly evocative articulation of an emergent black gay sensibility, Nugent ends "Smoke, Lilies and Jade" in the same fugue of complex rumination with which it began: "one *can* love two at the same time ... Melva had kissed him ... one *can* ... and the street had been blue ... one *can* ... and the room was clouded with blue smoke" (39).

Lying in a hospital bed on New York's City Island, dying from the effects of tuberculosis and alcoholism, Nugent's friend and editor, Wallace Thurman, was in 1934 on the verge of ending a short life and career marked by incredible artistic ambition and a pronounced coyness surrounding the very open secret of his homosexuality. That Thurman was never "out" (he was briefly married to Louise Thompson, communist activist and cofounder of the Harlem Suitcase Theater) should not be taken as simply a product of the intense homophobia that he and other early twentieth-century homosexuals had to face. Instead, the sort of peek-a-boo aesthetic that Thurman developed was part of what made him valuable within the complex of relationships, institutions, and individuals that we now think of as the Harlem Renaissance. Indeed, it is exactly those aspects of Thurman's life and career that might today be read as confusing or contradictory that help to clarify not only some of the decisions that Thurman made as an intellectual but also the complex questions motivating this chapter. Or to jump perhaps a bit too quickly to one of my major arguments, the aesthetic concerns and procedures that we saw expressed in Nugent's "Smoke, Lilies and Jade" established not so much the trajectory of black LBGT literature in the twentieth and twenty-first centuries as the ideological contradictions that would continually bedevil black queer writers. The discursive and aesthetic complexity that many writers sought was often ill suited to the task of producing images of a clearly defined black lesbian and gay identity that might allow for the articulation of a coherent political and cultural community.

Moving to Harlem in 1925, Thurman became an editor of the socialist journal *The Messenger* in 1926. His play, *Harlem*, appeared on Broadway in 1929, the same year that he published his celebrated novel, *The Blacker the Berry: A Novel of Negro Life*. He followed this with the 1932 publication of both *The Interne* (written with Abraham Furman) and *Infants of the Spring*, a roman à clef in which he lampooned the group of artists and hangers-on who orbited "Niggerati Manor," the rooming house at 267 West 136th Street in Harlem, where Thurman once lived. What strikes one when reading *Infants* is just how uncertain Thurman seems to have been about the matter of how to name the complexity of yoking his political and artistic projects. If anything, the work reads as a decidedly bitter appraisal of what Thurman undoubtedly took as the foolhardiness underwriting the infinite sense of possibility that he and his peers had seen destroyed as the Harlem Renaissance came crashing down along with the country's stock markets in October 1929. Thurman is particularly scolding in his depiction of Paul Arbian, a character very closely modeled on the ever bohemian Nugent himself. "His face was the color of bleached saffron leaf," Thurman mocks. "His hair was wiry and untrained. It was his habit not to wear a necktie because he knew that his neck was too well modeled to be hidden from public gaze. "He wore no sox, either, nor underwear and those few clothes he did deign to affect were musty and disheveled" (8).

Paul is introduced through the scornful gaze of a narrator accustomed to – and a bit tired of – the figure of the tattered, self-obsessed artist. In his depiction of a type whose place in American society was increasingly tenuous as the country careened into the most bitter days of the Depression, Thurman seems to be asking how he and his compatriots could have been so naïve. It is almost as if writing at the end of his own very brief life, Thurman was forced to wonder if there was not some perversely intimate relation between his own ill health and the collapse of the dreams that sustained and motivated the Renaissance. Paul's articulation of the structure of his aesthetic is so stunningly close to that of Nugent's character, Alex, that it is easy to discern the bitterness directing Thurman's reassessment of the most notoriously queer aspects of the previous decades. Paul says without irony that "'I think that Oscar Wilde is the greatest man that ever lived. Huysmans's Des Esseintes is the greatest character in literature, and Baudelaire is the greatest poet. I also like Blake, Dowson, Verlaine, Rimbaud, Poe, and Whitman. And of course Whistler, Gauguin, Picasso, and Zuloaga'" (10). The point of course is that Paul is not only a modernist but, à la Wilde and Huysman, a decadent as well. The strain of the passage, the irritation that escapes Nugent only to infect his readers is built on the fact that Paul's tastes are simply a bit too obviously current and transgressive. He is a figure who for all of his modernist posturing is infinitely resistant to embracing the complexities of modernity. Paul Arbian (Arabian?) seems a bit too eager to remain aloof from that nationalist and Pan-Africanist intellectual impulse that may have been the most significant, most lasting product of the Harlem Renaissance. Instead, he cleaves to a perhaps more factually correct, but politically less useful understanding of himself as not only an artist resisting social convention, but also a multiracial figure descended from English, German, Indian, and African stock, stock for which he has no conscious affinity at all. And lest his readers miss Thurman's pointed critique, he ends the novel with Paul's suicide:

> Had Paul the debonair, Paul the poseur, Paul the irresponsible romanticist, finally faced reality and seen himself and the world as they actually were? Or was this merely another act, the final stanza in his drama of beautiful gestures? It was consonant with his character, this committing suicide. He had employed every other conceivable means to make himself stand out from the mob. Wooed the unusual, cultivated artificiality, defied all conventions of dress and conduct. Now perhaps he had decided that there was nothing left for him to do except execute self-murder in some bizarre manner. (184)

What stuns as one reads this passage is that it was one of the final pieces of published work by an author whose own reputation as an intellectual would be sustained by his association with the very type of cultivated artificiality that he decries. What seems obvious then is that Thurman seriously questioned the experimentation, artistic and social, that stood at the center of the Harlem Renaissance; indeed he may have suspected that the short trip from his own status as celebrated writer to an uncomfortable bed in a New York City charity hospital was itself an indication of a set of beliefs and practices that he and his peers were incapable of sustaining.

Of Modernism and Naturalism

Much of what I am attempting to do is to suture my discussion of writing by black sexual minorities to the history of African American and African diasporic writing more generally. In that regard, there is no way that we can proceed without taking into account the remarkable stature of Richard Wright in the history of black letters. Unlike previous black authors, Wright was not only able to support himself from his work alone (a trait he shared with Langston Hughes) but also with the publication of *Native Son* in 1940, a short eight years after the publication of Thurman's *Infants of the Spring*, he successfully turned the African American literary establishment away from the modernist experiments of the Renaissance and toward a focus on Naturalism that would dominate the field until at least the publication of James Baldwin's *Go Tell It on the Mountain* in 1953. It was the character of Bigger Thomas who did the heavy lifting for Wright. Bigger, a semiliterate youth living in a tenement on Chicago's South Side, represented the first time that an American author had the temerity to confront the most vicious stereotypes of black identity and to turn them toward his own ends. That Bigger kisses, suffocates, and then dismembers Mary, the daughter of his wealthy employer, Mr. Dalton, ultimately works to produce him as a profoundly modern character, one whose actions and psychology are produced in direct relation to the social environment into which he was born. Bigger lacks the ambiguity of either Alex or Paul. He only haltingly speaks during the course of the novel, whereas Alex and Paul seem voracious in their appetites for self-expression. Still, where Alex broods and Paul self-destructs, Bigger engages at an almost operatic level of action. After he murders and dismembers Mary Dalton, stuffing her remains into the family's furnace, he follows by smashing a brick against the head of his girl-friend, Bessie, then throwing her body down an air shaft. He then successfully misdirects the attentions of the police away from himself and toward Mary's boyfriend, Jan, until Mary's smoking ashes are found in the furnace.

What Wright achieves for black letters is nothing less than the articulation, however unstable, of a muscular black masculinity. In place of the opacity and equivocation of Uncle Tom, Uncle Remus, Alex, and Paul, Wright produces in Bigger a character composed entirely of reflective surfaces. The viciousness of white supremacy is tightly focused and directed back to its sources, disal-lowing all sentimentality, refusing the sympathetic tears of bankers' daughters (see Wright, "How" 454). At the same time, however, Wright's impressive prose and his own outsized presence in the intellectual apparatuses of the United States and Europe overshadowed the efforts of his peers, foreclosing alternative possibilities for the articulation of black identity.

Here I want to draw attention to the work of Wright's contemporary, Langston Hughes. Hughes, born six years before Wright in 1902 and dying seven years after him in 1967, is still understood primarily as either the major creative light of the Harlem Renaissance or as a blues poet who spoke to the everyday realities of African American individuals and communities. At the same time, much of the contemporary commentary on Hughes and his work centers around debating whether the historical record gives us enough infor-mation to prove his homosexuality. What too often gets left out, however, is both the matter of the author's radicalism and internationalism as well as the fact that his experiments with prose and poetry tended to model the ways our fetishization of certainty, our frenzied attempts to dismiss doubt can them-selves result in the production of tinny, one-dimensional depictions of human possibility that disable us in our efforts to name the complexity of human exis-tence. Recounting his experiences among Madrileña street walkers during the Spanish Civil War, Hughes writes:

> The darkness up and down the street would be pinpointed by the tiny flames of dozens and dozens of matches being lighted by soldiers to peer into the faces of the prostitutes walking in the dark. The black-out canyon of the

street danced with little flames of hope, burning briefly, then flung to the ground as some young soldier, lighting a match at the sound of a seductive voice, found himself peering into a broken-down witch's face. (331)

The now somewhat expected questions from the contemporary reader of this text would be, "What was Langston doing there? Was he hunting the prostitutes? The soldiers? Both?" These questions are fair as far as they go. What they miss, however, is the very clear way Hughes resists what I take to be the discipline of visibility and clarity that I argue became increasingly rigorous for black writers in the wake of Wright's success with *Native Son*. Indeed, the briefly burning hope that Hughes described is extinguished at precisely that moment when certainty is achieved. Seduction turns to disgust in the clarifying light of the recently scratched match.

One runs headfirst into a set of thorny issues that attend our attempts to define what is meant by black LBGT literature when many of the (black) individuals who have produced images of sexual minorities, black and otherwise, have never identified themselves as gay, while many purportedly gay writers have produced very little explicitly "queer" content. Literary historian Lawrence Jackson notes a romantic relationship during the mid-1930s between Dorothy West and Marian Minus. West is best known for having founded the journal *Challenge* in 1934 and publishing the novels *The Living Is Easy* (1948) and *The Wedding* (1995). Minus's essay "Present Trends of Negro Literature" (1937) laid the groundwork for Wright's much more influential piece, "Blueprint for Negro Writing" (1937). In both cases, however, these women's efforts were overshadowed by the much more hardboiled and male-focused efforts inspired by Wright (Jackson 7). Moreover, their status as forebears in a well-articulated tradition of black LBGT literature is tenuous at best.

Folk Ways and Politics

An even more vexing case in this regard is the life and work of Chester Himes.

Nowhere is the focus on toughness and hypermasculinism perfected by Wright more apparent than in the work of Himes, who would become best known for his detective novels featuring the black policemen Coffin Ed Johnson and Gravedigger Jones.[2] These works represented, however, only a part of Himes's considerable oeuvre. Although the detective fiction certainly demonstrates Himes's talent, their comedic elements are often much less effective than those in a novel like *Pinktoes* (1961); their expression of Himes's political commitment duller than in *The Lonely Crusade* (1947); and their depiction of the absurdly complex nature of the interplay of race and sex much less poignant than in *The End of a Primitive* (1955). Even more to the point, Himes's prison novel, *Cast the First Stone* (1952; reissued in 1999 as *Yesterday Will Make You Cry*), displays a stunning level of sensitivity not so much to the homosexuality of the prisoners, including the work's white protagonist, Jimmy Monroe, as to the complex human negotiations effected by incarcerated men as they confront the shocking levels of confusion, alienation, and violence of American prisons.

I would argue that one cannot truly appreciate Himes's work without reading it backward toward Claude McKay, the Jamaica-born radical author of *Home to Harlem* (1928), *Banjo* (1929), and *Banana Bottom* (1933).[3] Like Himes, McKay was keenly interested in the particular folk ways of black working-class and poor people as well as the codes of behavior expressed between men in sex-segregated environments. The controversy that greeted *Home to Harlem* upon its publication turned on its use of presumably foul language as well as its depiction of less than respectable aspects of New York's black culture, including gambling, drinking, prostitution, and homosexuality. Meanwhile, his novel *Banjo* is a classic modernist experiment in which he treats the distinctly working-class cosmopolitanism on display in the port of Marseilles.

Facing in the opposite direction, I would point out that although it is rarely noted, Himes's *Cast the First Stone* predated James Baldwin's groundbreaking novel *Giovanni's Room* (1956) by four years. In both cases, we see black authors turning to white characters to explore the ways that race and sexual desire are articulated in homosexual communities. In none of the aforementioned cases, however, is it possible to discern a clearly articulated desire to produce images of black LBGT individuals and communities that might be read as somehow distinct from the many overlapping identities and social formations that so intrigued these authors. Thus as we seek to produce histories of black LBGT identity, we would be wise to remember that evidence of queer sexual practice or affinity may not be sufficient to establish easy connections between current articulations of LBGT identity and those that come to us from earlier generations.

In making these arguments, I would point in the direction of the infinitely interesting figure of Lorraine Hansberry. The Chicago-born Hansberry was the fourth child of a middle-class family. Her father was a real estate broker, her mother a teacher. When the family bought a house in the Washington Park section of Chicago, thereby violating a restrictive racial covenant, they were challenged by angry white neighbors. The case went to trial, eventually being settled in the Hansberrys' favor in the Supreme Court's landmark 1940 decision, *Hansberry v. Lee*. Thus the environment in which Hansberry was reared was one that introduced her to the comforts of middle-class life while also encouraging her political and social radicalism. Moving to New York City in 1950, she began working with a group of communists and fellow travelers on Paul Robeson's newspaper, *Freedom*. She also began work on her play *A Raisin in the Sun*, loosely based on her family's experiences in Chicago. The play premiered on Broadway on March 11, 1959. It was eventually named the best play of 1959 by the New York Drama Critics' Circle and continued its run for nearly two years.

The thing one is immediately forced to wrestle with when examining the whole of Hansberry's life and career is the strange fact that she seems to have been a victim of her own success. Like Thurman, she died early, succumbing at age thirty-four to pancreatic cancer. Her ex-husband, Robert Nemiroff, then became executor of her unfinished manuscripts, collecting many of her writings into a play entitled *To Be Young, Gifted and Black*, which premiered on Broadway in 1968. This was followed by *Les Blancs* in 1970. In the process, Hansberry became largely known as a profoundly gifted African American playwright who created one of the most evocative and emotionally effective statements against racial segregation ever produced. What gets left out of this line of thought, however, is the very strong strain of radicalism and nonconformity underwriting Hansberry's aesthetic. I have mentioned already her association with the radical newspaper *Freedom*. I would add that her presumed lesbianism (she was a member of the Daughters of Bilitis, one of the first homophile organizations in the United States) ought to be understood not only as an expression of innate desire, but also as a continuation of her ongoing efforts around social justice and personal liberty. Writing in 1957 in the pages of the Daughters of Bilitis's magazine, *The Ladder*, she argued that "women, without wishing to foster any strict *separatist* notions, homo or hetero ... have a need for their own publications and organizations.... Women, like other oppressed groups of one kind or another, have particularly had to pay a price for the intellectual impoverishment that the second class status imposed on us for centuries created and sustained" (qtd. in Jackson 489).

A Queer Triangle

There is a sense in which all of the previous comments ought to be understood as a preamble to my discussion of the towering presence of James Baldwin. If there is, in fact, a tradition of black lesbian and gay writing it is undoubtedly at least in part due to the oversized position Baldwin held in the history of

American, African American, and LBGT letters. From the 1953 publication of his first novel, *Go Tell It on the Mountain*, in which he presented his protagonist, John Grimes, in a bildungsroman wholly saturated with never fully acknowledged homoeroticism, to his 1956 breakthrough novel, *Giovanni's Room*, where Baldwin laments the crushing fear that disrupts the ill-fated love affair between his protagonists, David and Giovanni, to the remarkable progression of his novels, plays, and essays, especially *Another Country* (1962), *Tell Me How Long the Train's Been Gone* (1968), and *Just above My Head* (1979), we witness the efforts of an intellectual seemingly intent on demonstrating not simply the vulgarities of race and sex in American and European cultures, but also, and importantly, possibilities for new forms of identity and affect lying just below the surface of often stunningly hidebound societies.

There is, however, another Baldwin to whom we should attend. Baldwin the critic, Baldwin the gadfly, Baldwin the individual who the evidence suggests could be difficult, petulant, ever spoiling comfortable assumptions and deeply held beliefs. In a now infamous November 1960 exchange between Wright and Baldwin at the Deux Magots café in Paris, Baldwin is reported to have accused Wright of producing in *Native Son* a work so capacious that it left no room for other African American authors. Thus as a creative intellectual, Baldwin had no choice but to destroy Wright. Also present at the event, Chester Himes reported that Baldwin claimed that "sons must slay their fathers," stressing the belief that the development of black literary culture is a process of continual destruction of old forms of style and address (Rowley 414–15; see also Baldwin 276–78). Producing a fun house reflection of the Deux Magots episode, Eldridge Cleaver turned the tables on his erstwhile mentor, Baldwin, writing in his 1968 collection *Soul on Ice* that "[t]he racial death-wish is manifested as the driving force in James Baldwin": "His hatred for blacks, even as he pleads what he conceives as their cause, makes him the apotheosis of the dilemma in the ethos of the black bourgeoisie who have completely rejected their African heritage, consider the loss irrevocable, and refuse to look again in that direction" (101).

Although each time I read these passages I chafe at Cleaver's homophobia, I am much more interested in what I take to be the generic implications of these statements. Cleaver accuses Baldwin of having turned his back on the ancestral African traditions that presumably bind together the various communities of the African diaspora. In doing so, however, he retreats to the same model of paternal disavowal that stands at the heart of the anxieties he names. For writers of Cleaver's generation, Baldwin represented a refreshingly destabilizing creative force that swept away the presumably clumsy, aloof, and overwrought productions of authors like Wright in order to make way for a new elegance of form as well as a reinvigorated commitment to radicalism. "It would have been a gas for me to sit on a pillow beneath the womb of Baldwin's type-writer and catch each newborn page as it entered this world of ours," Cleaver writes. "I was delighted that Baldwin, with those great big eyes of his, which one thought to be fixedly focused on the macrocosm, could also pierce the microcosm" (96).

Or to state the matter differently, Cleaver imagines Baldwin's creative practice as rather stunningly queer. In the place of the dominating father's phallus, one finds the "womb of Baldwin's typewriter," and most especially the piercing gaze of "those great big eyes of his." Indeed, to his credit Cleaver attempts to disrupt tiresome narratives of cultural production based on the reiteration of stale notions of heterosexual reproduction. Unfortunately, however, he seems unsettled by the very conceptual radicalism on display in this passage. Heaving a bit too close to the specters of old-fashioned rank-and-file homosexuals, he panics, retreating from his first timid efforts to rewrite narratives of African American literary influence through a fit of anti-gay expletives.

Although it is commonly acknowledged that Baldwin was forced through-out his career to address none-too-delicate homophobic attacks directed at him, I think that we would be wrong to assume that what was being dem-onstrated here was simply some version of free-floating, "natural" homo-phobia. Part of what the figure of the homosexual does in traditions of African and African American intellectualism, traditions that have been deeply marked by breaks with ancient structures of culture and society brought on by slavery, colonization, and forced migration, is to operate as a marker of those breaks, the very scar demonstrating the tear between what is and what was, as well as the place where that rupture has been not so much healed as naturalized. The black homosexual, particularly the black homosexual intellectual, stands at those locations where the traumas of the Middle Passage and white supremacy notwithstanding, black cultural life continues to thrive. Moreover, the tendency to treat the black "queer" sub-ject as at once the sign of rupture and of healing, indeed of renaissance, is a trope that developed with the self-conscious experimentation of the Harlem Renaissance and has continued more or less intact through nearly a century of black literature.

Understanding this matter allows us to construct better narratives of black literary history as well as to make sense of the many stunningly awkward "outbreaks" of homophobic discourse within black efforts to name and define our cultural traditions. In a May 1973 interview in *Playboy Magazine*, Huey Newton, cofounder of the Black Panther Party, makes a stunningly provocative set of claims about Cleaver's relationship to Baldwin:

> We met Baldwin shortly after he returned from Turkey, I guess in 1966 or the early part of '67. Eldridge had been invited to a party to meet him, and he asked me to go along. So we went over to San Francisco in his Volkswagen van and we got there first. Soon after, Baldwin arrived. Baldwin is a very small man in stature: I guess about five-one. Eldridge is about six-four, you know; at the time, he weighed about 250 pounds. Anyway, Baldwin just walked over to him and embraced him around the waist. And Eldridge leaned down from his full height and engaged Baldwin in a long passionate French kiss. They kissed each other on the mouth for a long time. When we left, Eldridge kept saying, "Don't tell anyone." I said all right. And I kept my word – until now. (84)

One has to suspend neither skepticism nor disbelief to appreciate not only how provocative Newton's claims are, but also, I would argue, how stabilizing and indeed comforting. Newton obviously means to slight Cleaver, to represent him as hypocritical and emotionally unstable: "I think Eldridge is so insecure that he has to assert his masculinity by destroying those he respects" (84). At the same time, however, he offers in this passage one of the richest images of the narratives of homoeroticism that underwrite African American literary culture that I have ever encountered. The tableau of Eldridge and Jimmy, six-four and burly, five-one and slight, locked in a rapturous embrace ultimately provides a certain unexpected aesthetic/ideological stability. The constant travel and alienation that presumably stands at the center of diasporic subjectivity is stalled for moment as the two meld. The longing between men that presumably structures much within modern art and culture is not mediated by a female cipher. Instead, as Newton suggests himself, the extreme pressure that attends African and African American subjectivity tends to obviate the need to deny the key role that the queer subject must necessarily play in the production and reproduction of culture. Indeed, the very presence of the African *American* individual proves not so much that African diasporic subjects have "rejected their African heritage," as Cleaver would claim, but that the connections are so tenuous, so clearly manmade, that the cultural practitioners responsible for fashioning them can never be thought to be exactly "straight."

Intersectionality and the Age of Anthology

Following Baldwin, there was in the 1970s and 1980s a flowering of work by black women writers, including lesbians, that was so provocative as to

permanently alter how we think about both African American and African
diasporic identity and community. Ann Shockley's 1970 *Loving Her* was the first
novel by a black writer with a lesbian protagonist. Following in her wake was a
group of black women writers intent on stressing the ways that race, gender,
and sexuality operated in every aspect of their lives. Thus perhaps the most
profound contribution of a figure like poet, essayist, and memoirist Audre
Lorde was her unblushing articulation of intersectionality, the idea that no
person can ever be thought to spring from a single source. Instead, each of us
might be best understood as a nodal point at which overlapping – and perhaps
even competing – discourses of race, gender, ethnicity, class, and sexuality
meet. In Lorde's case, it is important to note that although she was a consum-
mate New Yorker she was also of Caribbean descent, a fact to which she often
referred in the course of her writing. What strikes one when reading Lorde's
poetry, then, is not so much that she ignores questions of identity and origin,
but instead that she is always careful to never be overwhelmed by them:

> My face resembles your face
> less and less each day. When I was young
> no one mistook whose child I was.
> Features build coloring
> alone among my creamy fine-boned sisters
> marked me Byron's daughter.
>
> No sun set when you died, but a door
> opened onto my mother. After you left
> she grieved her crumpled world aloft
> an iron fist sweated with business symbols
> a printed blotter dwell in the house of Lord's
> your hollow voice changing down a hospital corridor
> > yea, though I walk through the valley
> > of the shadow of death
> > I will fear no evil.   (434)

In this aptly named poem, "Inheritance – His," Lorde hails the deceased ancestor, naming him and giving him leave to exist in the now that she inhabits.
At the same time, however, she refuses to relinquish knowledge of his essentially spectral nature. Her face is less and less like his. His voice is hollow, his
presence shadowed. Lorde reminds her readers that although she has lost full
contact with the traditions that sustain her, she will fear no evil. I would argue
then that what Lorde achieved in her career was a sort of conceptual/ideo-
logical reset. Not only did she invite black lesbian women to openly name
themselves, she also gave her students and followers necessary instruction in

how they might manage the complexities of their multiple, and multiplying, identities. With the 1982 publication of *Zami, A New Spelling of My Name: A Biomythography*, Lorde, like Baldwin before her, effectively bound together the two tendencies in African American letters that I have been at pains to describe. In this autobiographical text, the rich complexity of her prose, her turn toward myth, and her reliance on relentlessly clear detail produce a character who is challenging, experimental – and experimenting – while also thoroughly grounded in everyday reality.

I believe that it should come as no surprise that so much in contemporary black LBGT literature has appeared in collections and anthologies. In these multivoiced works one might see put into practice the belief that human identity is both grounded in tradition and marked by complexity and a need for constant change. In 1983, Barbara Smith edited the epoch-making collection *Homegirls: A Black Feminist Anthology*. Although the work was not exclusively lesbian, it was forthright in its recognition of the central roles that lesbians, particularly black lesbians, played in the development of feminist thought and culture. It also helped to bring feminist ideas surrounding overlapping identities and intersectionality to increasingly larger audiences.

Following the lead of lesbian writers, black gay men began in the 1980s to produce small literary magazines that provided room for emerging artists to experiment and develop their craft. Although many of these magazines were quite short lived there were others – such as *Blackheart: A Journal of Writing and Graphics by Black Gay Men*; *Black/Out: The Magazine of the National Coalition of Black Lesbians and Gays*; and *Other Countries* – that were published over several years. Building on this tradition, path-breaking editors pulled together several anthologies that acted as watersheds in the history of black LBGT cultural history. While *Black Men/White Men: A Gay Anthology*, edited by Michael J. Smith and published in 1983, represented an important statement of the gay interracialism, the 1986 publication of *In the Life: A Black Gay Anthology*, edited by Joseph Beam, was a first of its kind acknowledgment that there was a distinct and identifiable black gay community producing a literature of its own. This was quickly followed in 1987 by *Tongues Untied*, edited by Martin Humphries, a work published in London that brought together writers from the United States and the United Kingdom.

Most important of all, however, was the anthology *Brother to Brother: New Writings by Black Gay Men* (1991), edited by Essex Hemphill. This ambitious work had a number of key accomplishments. First, it introduced audiences to writing by Guy-Mark Foster, John Keene, David Frechette, Donald Woods, Assoto Saint, Melvin Dixon, Isaac Julien, Kobena Mercer, Ron

Simmons, Marlon Riggs, Charles Nero, and others who would prove to be key players in the development of contemporary black LBGT culture. The anthology also helped to articulate a long tradition of black gay writing that extended from the Harlem Renaissance to the tail end of the twentieth century. Among the authors listed in its bibliography were icons of black art and culture such as Nugent, Thurman, Baldwin, and Bayard Rustin, as well as contemporary authors like Samuel Delany and Randall Kenan, who were already developing astonishingly distinguished careers as novelists and critics. Perhaps even more importantly, however, the anthology helped to solidify the reputation of its editor, Essex Hemphill, whose collections *Conditions* (1986) and *Ceremonies* (1992) had become classics by the time of Hemphill's death in 1995.

In his 2004 encyclopedic study of African American fiction, *The Contemporary African American Novel*, Bernard Bell divides gay literature into essentially two camps. In the first he places the work of Larry Duplechan (*Eight Days a Week* [1985]; *Blackbird* [1986]; *Tangled Up in Blue* [1989]; and *Captain Swing* [1993]), novels that Bell claims focus on the difficulties that black gay men have in "coming out" within nonblack communities. He also includes in this group Samuel Delany's philosophical potboiler, *The Mad Man* (1994), a work that celebrates "extreme" forms of sexual practice and liberation from social conventions. Into the second group Bell places works such as Steven Corbin's *No Easy Place to Be* (1989), Melvin Dixon's *Trouble the Water* (1989), Randall Kenan's *Visitation of Spirits* (1989), and the novels of bestselling author E. Lynn Harris. Bell reads these as texts that are "[m]ore grounded in African American residual oral forms and generally less explicit sexually" (354).

Where I differ from Bell is in my contention that it is nearly impossible to divide black queer literature into such easily defined camps. Nor is it possible to weave together all of the threads of black queer cultural production into one harmonious whole. How the words of Jamaican writer Thomas Glave speak to those of Hilton Als, Darieck Scott, Gary Fisher, Sapphire, or Jewelle Gomez remains a perplexing matter even after we consider that all of these individuals are black sexual minorities. Nonetheless, the work that they produce can differ wildly. My challenge, then, is that we not take the label "black queer" as an opportunity to foreclose the difficulties we face when we attempt to discuss questions of tradition or continuity. Instead, a much more productive way to proceed would be to embrace that difficulty. In this way, I would invoke again the brooding, complex, not quite "right" figure of Alex from Nugent's "Smoke, Lilies and Jade." The slipperiness of this character, the way that he continually escapes our grasp, is, I believe, the great legacy left to us by

Nugent. With it we might announce our right to continually imagine who and what we are and how and why we write.

Notes

1. Here as below, the ellipses are Nugent's.
2. Titles in the classic series include: *A Rage in Harlem* (1957), *The Real Cool Killers* (1959), *The Crazy Kill* (1959), *All Shot Up* (1960), *The Big Gold Dream* (1960), *The Heat's On* (1966), and *Blind Man With a Pistol* (1969).
3. For a discussion of evidence suggesting McKay's homosexuality see Cooper; Holcomb.

Works Cited

Baldwin, James. "Alas, Poor Richard." 1961. *The Price of the Ticket: Collected Nonfiction, 1948–1985.* New York: St. Martin's P, 1985. 269–87. Print.

Bell, Bernard W. *The Contemporary African American Novel.* Amherst: U of Massachusetts P, 2004. Print.

Cleaver, Eldridge. *Soul on Ice.* New York: Dell, 1991. Print.

Cooper, Wayne F. *Claude McKay: Rebel Sojourner in the Harlem Renaissance, a Biography.* Baton Rouge: Louisiana State UP, 1996. Print.

Holcomb, Gary Edward. *Claude McKay, Code Name Sasha: Queer Black Marxism and the Harlem Renaissance.* Gainesville: UP of Florida, 2009. Print.

Hughes, Langston. *I Wonder as I Wander: An Autobiographical Journey.* New York: Hill, 1956. Print.

Jackson, Lawrence. *The Indignant Generation: A Narrative History of African American Writers and Critics, 1934–1960.* Princeton: Princeton UP, 2011. Print.

Lorde, Audre. "Inheritance – His." *The Collected Poems of Audre Lorde.* New York: Norton, 1997. 434–37. Print.

Newton, Huey. "Playboy Interview: Huey Newton, a Candid Conversation with the Embattled Leader of the Black Panther Party." By Lee Lockwood. *Playboy* 20.5 (1973): 73–90. Print.

Nugent, Richard Bruce. "Smoke, Lilies and Jade." *Fire: A Quarterly Devoted to Younger Negro Artists* 1.1 (1926): 33–39. Print.

Rowley, Hazel. *Richard Wright: The Life and Times.* New York: Holt, 2001. Print.

Thurman, Wallace. *Infants of the Spring.* 1932. London: Black Classics, 1998. Print.

Wright, Richard. "How 'Bigger' Was Born." 1941. *Native* 431–62.

Native Son. 1940. New York: HarperPerennial, 1998. Print.

32

Queer Poetry in the Long Twentieth Century

ERIC KEENAGHAN

Unlike members of ethnically structured minority groups, lesbian, gay, bisexual, and transgender (LGBT) individuals largely lack access to a continuous history passed on through biological families. Readymade narratives available through schools, media, and activist organizations are invaluable resources for disseminating gender and sexual minorities' historical sense. Cultural texts, including literature, have contributed crucially to the formation of those narratives. Michael Bronski reminds us that "entertainment in the broadest sense" – for example, "popular ballads, vaudeville, films, sculptures, plays, paintings, pornography, pulp novels" – has served both as "a primary mode of expression of LGBT identity" and as "one of the most effective means of social change" (xix). Cultural production is only one half of the equation, though; cultural reception is the other half. We "look to the past for something lacking in the present," David Halperin argues (23). Consequently, narratives of LGBT history are "necessarily and inevitably framed by contemporary preoccupations and investments," and are subject to revision (23). Our individual interpretations of, even identifications with, cultural texts preceding us – whether by decades or merely a year or two – guide us as we continually refashion our understandings of queer history, subjectivity, and community.

Poetry is one cultural form crucially facilitating such identifications. It records past manifestations of queer desire and subjectivity, informs a present moment's construction of LGBT identities and collectives, and opens spaces for reimagining future iterations of sexual and gender minority and difference. Consider "He Came to Read –" (1924), by Greek Alexandrian poet C.P. Cavafy. The poem depicts a reader who "is entirely devoted to books" (147). Cavafy himself often turned to antiquity to imagine a past when homoerotic expression was accepted. This youth is similarly attracted to "historians and poets," among whose "open" texts he naps (147). His having fallen asleep does not diminish his literary devotion; rather, his drowse allows the texts' "erotic fever" to suffuse his body, "with no silly modesty about the nature of the pleasure" (147). Together, history and poetry help Cavafy's ideal reader – as they do himself and his actual reader – overcome repressive moralistic codes.

Although this reading scene is solitary, others have imagined poetry as enabling historical identification on a collective scale. Among its consciousness-raising articles and political announcements, *COME OUT!*, the newspaper launched by New York City's Gay Liberation Front (GLF) after the 1969 Stonewall riots, regularly published original poetry celebrating gay and lesbian sexuality or condemning homophobia and heterosexism. In the inaugural issue, an unattributed one-page essay suggests the political significance for activists of reading past poetries, too. The anonymous author – later revealed to be John Lauritsen – praises sixteenth-century English poet and playwright Christopher Marlowe's *Hero and Leander* for the poem's "high camp" depiction of naked bathers in an "increasingly outrageous" scene, "a cross between Fire Island and Mardi Gras," that culminates in "[o]vertly Gay action" between Leander and Neptune (13). "All parts of the poem are exciting, and no matter what the action seems to be, *we* know what Marlowe *really* had in mind" (13). Winking at his readers, the unnamed GLF activist claims an epistemological privilege connecting him to this queer forebear. His anonymity invites readers also to connect with Marlowe, who, as the author notes, was a sexual outlaw and political rebel who avoided a sodomy trial only because of his untimely death in a bar fight. Recently mobilized by riots outside a local gay and transgender tavern, post-Stonewall outlaws would have identified with that biographical fact.

Whether inspiring individualized erotic freedom, as with Cavafy's youth, or a collective sense of politicized sexual liberation, as with the *COME OUT!* essay on Marlowe, poetry can motivate LGBT persons to reimagine and redefine sexual and gender difference. We should acknowledge the significance of such poetic identifications to avoid turning queer literary studies into the "paranoid project of exposure" Eve Kosofsky Sedgwick warns against (139). The characterization of LGBT literatures as only about the injured or maligned, she argues, produces teleological narratives pretending an impossible invulnerability to violence and oppression now. Those critical narratives also foreclose discoveries of unexpected connections with the past that might spur the imagination, thus inspiring change. In contrast, a "reparative" orientation toward literary history permits what Sedgwick unabashedly calls "hope" (146). "Because the reader has room to realize that the future may be different from the present," she argues, "it is also possible for her to entertain such profoundly painful, profoundly relieving, ethically crucial possibilities as that the past, in turn, could have happened differently from the way it actually did" (146).

If queer poetry allows us to imagine that history "could have happened differently," then its representations of LGBT historicity operate in the subjunctive mood. Subjunctivity accounts for historically actual conditions while also imagining what has not happened yet but could happen in the future.[1] Despite our awareness of our vulnerability and the precariousness of our historical being, we, as LGBT poets and readers, adapt and reimagine the past so as to redress present wrongs and look forward. Often affective and appealing to the emotional and imaginative faculties, poetry, as a cultural form, is particularly fit for fulfilling such cultural and subjective needs. Readers might see past poets as intimates and resources for self- and group construction, as Cavafy's youth and the GLF essayist do. Poets are themselves readers and therefore are prone to see their own audiences as potential collaborators, carrying out and realizing their visions for queer expression or future communality. In this way, queer history – poetically mediated and retold – is not a linear and progressive phenomenon, but instead is recursive, sustaining an active dialogue between past and present so as to enable LGBT subjects' agency, survival, and growth.

In this chapter, I attempt a reparative telling of queer poetic history. Concentrating on North American poetry from roughly the past 125 years, but also gesturing toward other global poetries, I trace how the genre has imagined, and has rendered imaginable, transformations of self and community. My history does not pretend to be comprehensive or totalizing. It would be impossible to trace all possible authors, poetic styles, or responses to social and political shifts in queer subjectivation and community building. Poetic history also does not unfold in a linear manner. Rather, it is rhizomatic, with multiple, sometimes conflicting, simultaneous trends. So, instead of a conventional linear narrative, I briefly touch on four topoi and representative poets that help illustrate poetry's subjunctive historicity: Queer Identification, Queer Influence, Queer Resistance, and Queer Horizons. When we read queer poetry through these themes, we can observe poets' responses to their respective historical contingencies as they anticipate future readers and speculatively gesture toward the horizon.

Queer Identification

Usually, one of the first questions LGBT readers ask when navigating the poetic past is, "Was this author gay, lesbian, bisexual, or transgender?" Identifying authors' sexuality or gender is important, but, as we shall see, by no means definitively qualifies or disqualifies a poem from the queer poetry archive. But for much of the long twentieth century, well before gay liberation (ca. 1969–75), many poets did self-identify as somehow queer. They even established poetic enclaves and networks presaging later understandings of sexual and gender difference as the basis for collective minority identity, rather than as symptoms of individuals' "deviance." From the 1890s through the 1930s, the circle of homosexual, though celibate, ephebes surrounding German neo-Romanticist Stefan George was among the earliest largely queer coteries. Through the Second World War, other avant-gardes emerged worldwide that counted self-identified LGBT poets as prominent members, such as Paris's Left Bank expatriate lesbian circle (Natalie Barney, Djuna Barnes), the Mexican avant-garde the Contemporáneos (Xavier Villaurrutia, Salvador Novo), the surrealist Spanish Generation of 1927 (Federico García Lorca, Vicente Aleixandre, Luis Cernuda), and the Cuban *Orígenes* group (José Rodríguez Feo, Gastón Baquero, José Lezama Lima). Whether writing of metaphysical eroticism or corporeal sex, these poets generated lexicons and styles influencing queer poetic expression for generations to come.

In the late 1940s, the example of the *George-Kreis* influenced Robert Duncan, Jack Spicer, and Robin Blaser's founding of the Berkeley Renaissance. Hoping to rejuvenate northern Californian literature, they promoted a similarly occultist and openly queer poetics. Not interested in personal celibacy and merely aesthetic eroticism, though, they also drew heavily on the overtly homosexual precedents of surrealists like Lorca and Jean Cocteau. Their local mission was executed by pursuing poetry's subjunctive possibility, drawing a past spirit of romance into a postwar and Cold War American present. As the group's members relocated in the mid-1950s, they contributed to a pre-Stonewall, North American network that brought queer poets into direct and indirect contact, in person and in the pages of little magazines – Stephen Jonas, Gerrit Lansing, and John Wieners from Spicer and Blaser's circle in Boston; Blaser's Canadian students George Stanley and Stan Persky; Black Mountain School poet Jonathan Williams and his one-time partner, later San Francisco transplant, Ronald Johnson; Bay Area film-poetry avant-gardist Kenneth Anger, poet and filmmaker James Broughton, and gay liberation publisher Paul Mariah. These individuals' paths crossed with other groups boasting queer members, including the Beats (Allen Ginsberg, Peter Orlovsky, Elise Cowen, Diane di Prima) and the New York School (Frank O'Hara, John Ashbery, James Schuyler, Kenward Elmslie).

Such poetic communities and networks facilitated the recognition of, even pride in, queer identities before LGBT minorities emerged as political entities. Yet, historical exigencies, such as repressive state regimes, rendered some LGBT subjects invisible or mute. For instance, Eugénio de Andrade started publishing during Portugal's oppressive New State (1932–74). He lyrically addresses lovers with the impersonal, nongendered second-person pronoun *tu*, which strategically overcomes his state-imposed silence by rendering his sexual orientation ambiguous. "Forbidden Words" (1951) is a rare instance when Andrade poignantly, though obliquely, registers the repressive conditions affecting his writing. "Water," "air," and even "the glow of fields of grain" cause him "hurt"; "this solitude of dark stone cuts me through," dividing him against himself and isolating him from his lover and the world (25). However, he persists in "sending you" these "forbidden words" (25). His transgressive communication is not explicitly queer, though; and Andrade connects the cause of his injury to natural, not political, causes.

In the postwar and Cold War United States, McCarthyism's repressive Lavender and Red Scares did not necessarily squelch queer poetic content. LGBT Beat, New York School, and Berkeley Renaissance poets wrote openly about same-sex love, thus risking censorship and literary blacklisting. However, those risks compelled some older or more established poets, such as Elizabeth Bishop, to suppress poetic mentions of their sexuality. "View of the Capitol from the Library of Congress," composed when Bishop was Consultant in Poetry at the Library of Congress (1949–50), is the unique instance of her criticism of the prohibitive federal government. At first, Washington, DC, seems grand. However, the Capitol's dome deflects the sunlight and the building "blankly stares" askance, "like a big white old wall-eyed horse" (69). This absurdity is augmented by flags' "limp stripes," whose detumescent impotence is doubled in an ineffective military band "playing hard and loud, but – queer – / the music doesn't quite come through" (69). Ironically, the state's "queer" obstruction of Bishop's perspective, desire, and aesthetic production open a space – however slight – for her to signal her hidden presence as a lesbian. Her poem offers a different kind of "music" that, unlike the nation's anthems, might "come through" to receptive readers.

Silenced or muffled expressions of queerness are not always attributable to state repression. When that is the case, we might do an injustice by forcibly identifying poets as LGBT. Yet, some *texts* still might be beneficially recovered as part of the queer poetry archive. Harlem Renaissance luminary Langston Hughes was infamously remiss to claim any orientation. Still, much of his work might be said to be queer because its interrogation of the intersectional reinforcement of gender, race, class, and sexual norms challenges the foundations of heteronormativity. Diasporic Filipino writer José Garcia Villa's poetry was similarly not forthcoming about his own possible same-sex attraction. Yet, his depiction of religious and aesthetic ecstasy are quite explicitly homoerotic, as in his invocation of "The Anchored Angel" (1954): "Through,whose,huge, discalced,arable,love, / Bloodblazes,oh,Christ's,gentle,egg: His,terrific,sperm" (138, Villa's punctuation). High modernist Marianne Moore, who Villa admired and befriended, also complicates the tendency to use biography for queer canon formation. Is hers a self-repressed lesbian poetry, or does it explore the eroticism of celibacy or a cross-gender identification with bachelorhood? Rather than engage in a paranoiac critical methodology looking for and outing supposedly repressed LGBT authors, we should extrapolate theorizations of poetic queerness out of the texts themselves. The past is not a passive receptacle on which we impose our critical frameworks and judgments. Instead, poetry speaks back to us, helping retheorize queer desire or past institutions' adverse effects on gender and sexual construction of *all* subjects.[2]

Such a subjunctive dialogue with poetry can help us achieve a fuller understanding of our own conceptual and ideological investments. Our interpretations of a text's queerness tell us more about our own historicity than about the author's biographical sexual or gender identification and expression, even if her sexuality is clearly established. Consider the expatriate high modernist Gertrude Stein. She was not closeted, per se, and her marriage to Alice B. Toklas is well known. Given these factors, we might read Stein's posthumously published "Lifting Belly" (1915–17) as a codified representation of her lesbianism, with the title phrase signifying cunnilingus and the repeated word *cow* serving as code for *orgasm*. Yet, this code is not clear in the poem, and the text defies easy deciphering. Consequently, some wonder if "Lifting Belly" is a lesbian poem or a poem registering an undefined "queer" eroticism, at the level of the signifier (see Holbrook; Scherr). Stein did characterize her relationship to composition and language in erotic terms: "Poetry is doing nothing but using losing refusing and pleasing and betraying and caressing nouns" (*Lectures* 231). But does a queer reading of her affective linguistic experimentalism diminish the scope of "Lifting Belly?" Indeed, the poem more overtly addresses the First World War – "A great many people are in the war" – than same-sex eroticism (*Writings* 413).[3] As Stein suggests, "Lifting belly is a language"; so, it might be best to approach the poem as a means for constructing her whole self, not only her sexuality ("Lifting belly means me") (*Writings* 422).

Nearly a century later, influenced by Stein, Juliana Spahr tackles issues of identification in a generically hybrid memoir about her *ménage* with two male poets. She self-reflexively characterizes her work as a:

> story of coming to an identity, coming to realize that they not only had a gender that was decided for them without their consent and by historical events that they had not even been alive to witness, but they also had a race and a

sexuality that was decided for them without their consent and by historical events that they had not been alive to witness and they just had to deal with this. So it is also a story of finding an ease in discomfort. And a catalogue of discomfort. (22)

Despite her unconventional family structure, Spahr, sensitive to encroaching on self-identified LGBT persons' and communities' political struggles, refuses to identify herself or her work as queer. Most important for her is the experimental, "discomforting" linguistic process of negotiating contemporary institutions that limit personal and political possibilities for identification, thus constituting a form of epistemological oppression that ideologically supports economic globalization and imperialist wars. Whether it is enough for Spahr's readers to refer to her poetics as deconstructive and disidentificatory remains to be seen; indeed, some might want or need to refer to her work as "queer."

Queer Influence

Poetry is a genealogical art, in which predecessors inform one's work. That dialogue is often conceived of as an intimate and interpersonal, though textually mediated, exchange. Indeed, a poem has a peculiar historical life: it is always belated, finding readers, on whom it depends to actualize its message or linguistic performance, after it has been written. Queer poets have been attracted to this quality, regarding it as enabling subjunctive, intergenerational collaborations rewriting self and community. Most famously, nineteenth-century U.S. poet Walt Whitman – whose deathbed edition of *Leaves of Grass* (1892) is an ur-text in my chapter's queer poetry archive – explicitly invites future writers in "Poets To Come" to use his poetry as a resource in their own transformative projects. "I myself but write one or two indicative words for the future," Whitman notes; and he "Leav[es] it to you to prove and define it [i.e., the future] / Expecting the main things from you" (14). Despite his ambition to include everything in his lifework, written and revised for nine editions published in nearly forty years' time, there was "Still something not told in poesy's voice or print – something lacking, / (Who knows? the best yet unexpress'd and lacking.)" ("The Unexpress'd" 467). Whitman believed that everyone succeeding him has a stake in trying to articulate that "unexpress'd" quantity.

LGBT poets have been particularly interested in taking up that call. Muriel Rukeyser, for one, claimed Whitman as "the poet of possibility" (83). "His discovery of himself is a discovery of America," she noted; to "Identify" is the chief means of realizing a collective possibility readers and writers, not the state, must continually recreate (75, 72). Allen Ginsberg's "A Supermarket in California" (1955) is a good example of the expression of new collective possibilities that Rukeyser believed Whitman inspired. The poem figures the nineteenth-century poet as a companion the Beat brings home. The two "stroll dreaming of the lost America of love," moving beyond suburbia and the titular supercenter of consumerist desire toward a new, more intimate – though still only dreamed of – American communality (Ginsberg 144). In the years leading up to Stonewall, Ronald Johnson's lyric series "Letters to Walt Whitman" (1967–69) similarly imagines gay men as finding their ways to an emergent gay community through *Leaves of Grass*: "There are Camerados, Walt – still, they come," and they will "whisper you / to the ears of others" (98).[4] American outsider Antler's labor epic "Factory" (1970) strives "to do for Continental Can Company / what Walt Whitman did for America" (25). In Antler's queer protest of industrial capitalism, sexuality and eroticism, though important, are secondary; most significant is Whitman's faith in futurity and the redefinition of all collective forms of life.

One of the poets most influenced by Whitman was American modernist Hart Crane, who "read the hints" in *Leaves of Grass* as clues to his forebear's gay desire and, in turn, presents his own writings as "the loud echoes of [Whitman's] songs" (Whitman, "Starting from Paumanok" 25). His epic *The Bridge* (1930) aims to rebuild the nation through his own queer embodied perspective, employing what Crane calls in "General Aims and Theories" (1925) "the implicit emotional dynamics of the [poetic] materials" to produce "a morality essentialized from experience directly" (221). *The Bridge* suggests stereotypically gay cruising scenarios on Manhattan's Bowery ("To Brooklyn Bridge") and in a bar populated by sailors ("Cutty Sark"). In the "Cape Hatteras" section, Crane explicitly invokes Whitman: "Walt, tell me, Walt Whitman, if infinity / Be the same as when you walked the beach / Near Paumanok" (89). Critical of his predecessor's "syllables of faith," Crane ponders his historical distance from Whitman and the consequential difference of his queer and national project from *Leaves*, which was written in "Not this our empire yet" (89). Nonetheless, he tries to overcome history, forcibly concluding *The Bridge* with the poem "Atlantis" and its vision of "Love" as "thine Everpresence, beyond time" that "bleeds infinity" (116, 117). Such ineffable eroticism heralds an all-encompassing unity Whitman's ongoing project resisted.

Whitman's influence is not limited to queer poetry originating within U.S. borders. As Robert Duncan remarks in "Changing Perspectives in Reading Whitman" (1970), poets often have understood Whitman as promoting a cosmopolitan promise, "a mystery of 'America' that belongs to dream and desire and the reawakening of earliest oneness with all peoples – at last, the nation of Mankind at large" (69). Responding to Whitman's characterization of *Leaves of Grass* as an intimate extension of himself, springing from his own embodied experience, gay male poets often interpret the core of that "mystery" as sexually expressive individualism. Whitman interpolates each of his readers as a companion and "follower," "a candidate for my affections" ("Whoever You Are Holding Me Now in Hand" 99). The reader is a "Passing stranger" who he "longingly" observes: "You must be he I was seeking, or she I was seeking, (it comes to me as of a dream,) / I have somewhere surely lived a life of joy with you" ("To a Stranger" 109). His parataxis does not just equate same-sex attraction with heterosexuality but actually prioritizes homosexuality in this erotic "dream," an imagined queer landscape of exchanges between poet and readers where anteriority and posterity share a common present. Such erotic images of embodied poetry have resonated with Whitman's answerers worldwide. In "Ode to Walt Whitman" (1930), Lorca addresses the Good Gray Bard as a "virile beauty" (157). Exemplifying *machismo*, Whitman's vision is compromised by modernity's ills: war, plague, fleeting time, even "urban faggots" whose effeminacy are "Always against" his ideal (Lorca 161). Although he doesn't explicitly invoke Whitman, Japanese poet Mutsuo Takahashi uses the Whitmanic devices of strophe, parataxis, enumeration, and blazon to render the gay male body sacrosanct and similarly virile in his long erotic poem "Ode" (1957), a paean to glory holes and anonymous sex. Like Whitman's "I Sing the Body Electric," Takahashi celebrates the male body's gritty realities – "Excreta, semen, tar of tobacco, sodden, rotting emotions" – for "From them, savage, rise perfumes" (72).

Each of the aforementioned poets drew from Whitman's example a different significance. However, none, not even Johnson, was invested in producing only an ethnically structured sexual minority. This is not merely because most of these authors were writing before gay liberation. Rather, as Duncan claims in his early, celebrated essay "The Homosexual in Society" (1944), a poet is above all "a human being seeking a creative life and expression, and that is a devotion to human freedom, toward the liberation of human love, human conflicts, human aspirations. To do this one must disown *all* the special groups (nations, churches, sexes, races) that would claim allegiance" (47). One arrives at "human freedom" by writing out of all of one's experience, including the pains of exclusion because of sexual difference; however, a poet cannot settle for a complete identification through sexual minority, or, for that matter, any exclusive identity rubric. To be a truly queer poet, one must write toward liberating all peoples and must strive for a stronger human collectivity, without ignoring one's own desires. That perhaps is Whitman's most valuable and influential lesson.

Queer Resistance

Allen Ginsberg's "Howl" (1955–56) epitomizes the lament of the experience of social injuries by the sexually marginalized. Written following the poet's state-mandated institutionalization for homosexuality, and dedicated to gay poet and fellow inmate Carl Solomon, "Howl" elegizes the oppression of gays and the rest of a "generation destroyed by madness" (Ginsberg 134). The seizure and censor-ship of *Howl and Other Poems* in 1957, and the subsequent highly publicized obscen-ity trial, resulted in Ginsberg's celebrity. So, some might be tempted to character-ize him and other queer outliers as merely embracing the role of the rebel to mark their difference from the mainstream. Romantic outlawry stretches back to French nineteenth-century visionary Arthur Rimbaud, who influenced later queer verse like that of sex worker and thief Jean Genet. Such queer poetic resis-tance need not be reduced to romantic individualism, though. Indeed, Genet's and Ginsberg's work serves as reminders that social and juridico-legal institutions mandate sexual and gender outliers' marginalization. Outlaws contend with those forces, from the social margins into which they have been pushed.

Imprisoned for sodomy in 1895, Irish author Oscar Wilde is another emi-nent gay outlaw. But his "Ballad of Reading Gaol" (1897) does not speak out against inequities faced only by homosexuals; rather, disturbed by another inmate's execution, he condemns "Man's grim Justice" and an overzealous state adversely affecting everyone:

> It slays the weak, it slays the strong,
> It has a deadly stride:
> With iron heel it slays the strong,
> The monstrous parricide!
>
> (180)

In the next century, around the world, queer poets incorporated homosexual content into their work as they raised their voices, as Wilde had, against repres-sive states and institutions, racism, and global capitalism. Algerian resistance fighter Jean Sénac, Italian communist and political critic Pier Paolo Pasolini, Cuban exile and former political prisoner Reinaldo Arenas, and Nuyorican ex-convict Miguel Piñero are but a few who carried on the Irishman's spirit in the sixties and seventies. Their poetry openly decries interrelated social injustices and exclusions.

Queer outlaws often have drawn on poetic forms' affective qualities to use their verse as consciousness-raising vehicles encouraging readers' politicized sympathy. Indeed, during U.S. gay liberation, poetry was a means of generating LGBT identification and broader coalitional opposition to a systemic oppression encompassing chauvinism, homophobia, heterosexism, imperialism, and white supremacism. Propagandist Allen Young noted that marginalized GLF activists were "outlaws" and "foreigners" in their own country because they opposed an exclusionary system of "sexism," wherein inflexible gender binaries were figured as the root of all sociopolitical inequities (13). Anti-sexist poetry appeared in liberation publications such as COME OUT!, Fag Rag, and The Furies, and gay presses such as Gay Sunshine and Out & Out published anthologies collecting agitprop verse, contemporary LGBT experimental poetry, and English-language or foreign-language queer predecessors' poetry.

Amidst this emerging and politicized queer literary market, Diane di Prima's work moves beyond identity-based liberation toward a whole-world transformation, thus exemplifying the conjunction of an avant-garde poetic sensibility and a politicized coalitional ethos. Her shamanistic epic Loba (1971–98) responds to Ginsberg's "Howl"; but di Prima envisions a matriarchal community to generate an ecological consciousness benefiting everyone. Like Loba, her Revolutionary Letters (ca. 1968–2003) is a continually expanded open series, published in five different versions. Begun before Stonewall, this series, even more than Loba, articulates a coalitional ethos informed by di Prima's New Left activism. Unlike her more highly regarded contemporaries such as Judy Grahn, Adrienne Rich, and Audre Lorde, she did not abandon that coalitional spirit, even temporarily, for lesbian separatism in the mid-1970s. Revolutionary Letters's early installments read like propaganda flyers, instructing readers how to take action against capitalism's imperialist war-machine. Early on, di Prima urges readers to "Free yourself"; for all – Native Americans, women, African Americans, gay men, even drug addicts – are "political prisoners" ("Revolutionary Letter #49" 63). Overcoming a shared internalized oppression ("killing / the white man in each of us, killing the desire / for brocade, for gold, for champagne brandy") lays the groundwork for "bring[ing] / back power" ("Revolutionary Letter #32" 45). One can only disidentify from oppressive forces, as di Prima writes decades later, through rewriting history and remembering what has been lost, "yr life" ("Revolutionary Letter #93: Memorial Day, 2003" 143). One must acknowledge one's erotic attachment to the entire world: "all you need to remember is what you love / Remember to Marry the World" (144). Amorously affirming belonging unites readers and poet and allows them to look together to the future: "we sit on shifting ground / at the edge of this ocean / ... & watch the hills flicker like dreamskin" ("Revolutionary Letter #58: Notes Toward an American History" 75).

Queer Horizons

The dream, memory, and futurity di Prima writes about are the building blocks of poetry's subjunctive history. Instead of disclosing a particular truth or prescribing a course of action, poetry trains readers to see the world differently, queerly. Although he was no revolutionist like di Prima, homosexual English émigré W.H. Auden similarly regarded poetry as crucial for survival. In the same Second World War-era poem famously announcing "poetry makes nothing happen," Auden still encourages poets to use their "unconstraining voice" to "Teach the free man how to praise" ("In Memory of W.B. Yeats" 248, 249). That "praise" is an ethical resource making human commonality imaginable.

In later generations, queer poets believed such ethical foundations motivate future political action. In the late eighties, Tim Dlugos, HIV-positive and concerned about American youths' political complacency, wrote of the need to attend a "light" whose "simple presence has / the power to destroy / the prisons we mistake for lives" ("The Sixties" 510). Dlugos arrived in New York City after Frank O'Hara's death, but the two shared a common faith in poetry's ability to spur the imagination and inspire action. Expressing solidarity with the anti-imperialist Negritude poets, O'Hara wrote in 1958 that the "the only truth is face to face, the poem whose words become your mouth / and dying in black and white we fight for what we love, not are" ("Ode: A Salute to the French Negro Poets" 305). Poetry's virtual "face to face" encounters mediate political action. A shared "fight," even self-sacrifice, results from empathic "love," not from potentially divisive identifications. Revisiting the past to mourn loss is another ethical means for poetry to facilitate change. One year after Stonewall, the Vietnam War still ongoing, gay liberation and proto-trans poet John Wieners implored the spirits of Jack Spicer and Stephen Jonas, his Boston cohort's departed "shining martyrs," to "tell us / what to do, read your poems" ("With Meaning" 127).[5] Wieners's elegy is deeply personal, but everyone stands to benefit from his friends' memory. "Rise and salvage our century," he commands (127). Poetry's "martyrs" cannot save the world, but reading their work does instruct readers how to *salvage* it, rebuilding from the detritus "With Meaning," as Wieners's title asserts.

Increasingly conscious of individuals' relationship to the whole world, many LGBT poets have not been invested in building identity-based minority enclaves. Today, especially, much queer poetry upholds the possibility that queer desire might be a viable means (though not the only one) of motivating *everyone* to move toward future horizons. For instance, Lebanon émigré Etel Adnan's long prose poem sequence "The Sea" (2012) comes to different terms with the past so as to remove us all from "the great slaughters consistently perpetrated throughout history," like those in her native Beirut that affected her firsthand, those in occupied North Africa she militated against while a student in France, and those now in the Middle East from which she is exiled (Adnan 37). Desire and language's currents pull us, like the sea's tides, into continuous movement, buoyed by sensuous thought and feeling. This fluid space is "permanent revelation; open revelation of itself, to itself" (35). Figured as a feminine erotic body through which Adnan moves, poetic language composes "the station of impermanence" and a queer dreamspace wherein she and her readers can "witness the junction of the past with the present" (13). The depths come to the surface, and then point to the future: "The horizon's perfection is due to its virtual reality. Alone in the midst of waves, the spirit pushes ahead" (30). Adnan's marine horizon denotes a subjunctive time-sense, regarding the past as a poetic resource for working through present traumas and global crises.

Such an idea of horizons might seem a soft note to end on, but I find it remarkable that, in light of poets' responses to the HIV / AIDS pandemic, some queer theorists abjure such future orientation and its significance for LGBT persons' survival and growth.[6] In his classic volume *Atlantis* (1995), Mark Doty, mourning the loss of his lover to AIDS, reclaims the "failing" New York cityscape as his "kingdom" ("Homo Will Not Inherit" 79). "My face" shares the same marks as "these walls," so "I'm not ashamed / to love Babylon's scrawl. How could I be?" (79). Finding a place in the present rectifies survivors' inability to share dreams' future-oriented space that his collection's title poem notes is the purview of children and the dying. How can one truly move on if "we don't even know where the living are, / / in this raddled and unraveling 'here'" ("Atlantis, Part 3" 56)? Possibility lies in recognizing that "the future's nothing / but this moment's gleaming rim," and a discovery of an ideal space "where it always was," "drenched, unchanged" ("Atlantis, Part 4" 58).

Queer horizons are not just the stuff of idyllic poeticism. They have grit, too. Witness Eileen Myles's searing volume *Not Me* (1991), about a Manhattan transformed by AIDS and related epidemics of junk and poverty, all exacerbated by a national culture overrun by the Moral Majority. "A public death," like the ones her seropositive friends suffered under the homophobic media's accusative gaze, "of course has no song" ("A Poem" 109). This predicament causes Myles to lament, "I have / no hope for / my culture now," a devastating pronouncement when broken up in such direct, short lines ("Hot Nights" 56). Passively hoping, inactively awaiting change, and generating a solipsistic confessional logorrhea are no solutions. Instead, Myles's meditative poetry offers a space of reflection, linguistic experiment, and self-exploration that points toward new agency. *Not Me* concludes with "a woman" – unnamed, seen only in dreams – leaving Myles's home. Whether a lover or some unknown side of herself, this figure takes a simple action that politically redefines the relationship between public and private spheres: she "stepped out of my / house and she opened the door" ("A Poem" 109). First she leaves, anonymously and thus controlling what she is (and is not), and *then* she "opened the door," thus allowing Myles to follow in that image's stead.

The HIV/AIDS crisis has proven formative for many queer writers' relationship to poetic possibility and a politicized ethos, but in the past decade transgender and genderqueer poets have led the way beyond strictures and injuries. They draw heavily on recent experimental work by the likes of such lesbian writers as late Chicana poet Gloria Anzaldúa and contemporary Québécois poet and novelist Nicole Brossard. Both outwardly wrestle with language, a medium exacting much pain and injury but also serving as a tool through which LGBT subjects can express desire and hope. Even if, as Brossard puts it, "language torments" and so prevents discovery of definitive and secure identities, linguistic struggles meaningfully can open momentarily restful spaces permitting renewal: "let's not touch silence / it is our reserve of hope / the renewed function of the future" ("Vertigo of the Present" 97). In the genre-queer experimentalist tradition of his compatriot Brossard, transgender poet Nathanaël's *We Press Ourselves Plainly* (2010) consists of narrative fragments, joined by ellipses, exploring "confinement" and "compression" acting on the "body, upon which the pressures of historical violence and its attendant catastrophes come to bear" (n.pag.).[7] Each ellipsis opens the text from within, offering, via a retrospective rewriting of the past, what the volume's last line calls "holes now" "where there were none" in the poet's original experience (Nathanaël 97). By seizing control of the very language system violently constraining him, marking and injuring his transgender body, Nathanaël finds opportunities for linguistic agency and freedom.

Late gender activist kari edwards's experimental long poem *obedience* (2005) also deals frankly with the pain of transgender persons' exclusion. The book subjects readers to the problem of "this language plague," the disenfranchisement reinforced, sometimes caused by, the very linguistic structures she attempts to unfix as "a body" working "to cure" her and our shared affliction (38). At discrete moments, edwards discovers:

> an operation in conjunction with the innumerable outside, outside walls of brute naming, or external objects bumped into doctrines of fixed limits, the discourse of lovers as the discourse of lovers, a constellation of objects, thick in layered shades, embroiled always dwellers, always close to obscure, dreaming merging lines on diverging edges, in the pleasure at midnight sharp, where action is the action taken, where the chains no longer imprison, where there is a constant period in time.
>
> (46)

Working to deliver herself and her readers to those intervals, though, necessitates traversing unbearable hurt. So, it is all the more striking that edwards concludes that process with one line, isolated from the rest: "let's begin again" (82). Even in the face of injury and death, her faith is in renewal.

Writing through his battle with terminal cancer, late African American and HIV-positive poet Reginald Shepherd reminds us, "Gods envy us because we die" ("Play Dead" 50). Queer poetry's power lays not in its bestowal of a kind of immortality on its authors; rather, its force owes to the fact that poetry allows writers and readers to move perpetually, through language and outside linear history. In appreciating such mobility, Shepherd makes life, not just death, more comprehensible. "The dead move fast, nowhere / to nowhere in no time at all" (50). Hearing Shepherd's voice in this posthumously published poem uncannily transports us, the readers who survive him, into that "nowhere" – a *utopia*, or no-place – where we might learn to appreciate our limited gift of life. From that space, in the company of others, queer poetry lets us mourn our dead, work through the present's pains, and reach into the horizon for transformative possibility.

Notes

1. I borrow the idea of literature's subjunctivity from Joanna Russ.
2. Reparative queer readings informing my brief discussion include Jarraway (68–97), Manry, and Vogel (104–31) on Hughes; Keenaghan ("Intimacy") on Hughes and Afro-Cuban poet Nicolás Guillén; Kahan, Leavell (35–76), and Levy (35–76) on Moore; Cruz and Ponce (58–88) on Villa.
3. Other war references in "Lifting Belly" include Dugny (419); "The king and the prince of Montenegro" (426); imperialist pasts beginning with Caesar (432–33); modern nationalism ("A great many people wish to salute" [424]); American patriotism ("Star spangled banner, story of Savannah" [434]); even peace ("Lifting belly is peaceable" [420]).
4. On Johnson and gay community, see Keenaghan, "World-Building."

5. Exemplary of a reparative and subjunctive rewriting of history, transgender poet Tim Trace Peterson recovers Wieners as a "trans or proto-trans" forebear (21). Wieners self-identified as gay yet cross-dressed occasionally and wrote openly about his femininity.

6. Edelman, Love, and Freeman theorize about the undesirability of queers' future orientation or about the difficulties of overcoming injurious pasts.

7. Poet Kazim Ali coins the term "genre-queer" to describe writing that hybridizes verse, prose, and narrative memoir and thus troubles heteronormativity and sexism, as well as imperialism. Such texts' "queerness" is not tied to authors' biographical sexuality; rather, it is an effect of the texts' formal disruption of ideologically laden conventions of narrating identity.

Works Cited

Adnan, Etel. *Sea and Fog*. Callicoon: Nightboat, 2012. Print.

Ali, Kazim. "Genre-queer: Notes against Generic Binaries." *Bending Genre: Notes on Creative Nonfiction*. Ed. Margot Singer and Nicole Walker. New York: Bloomsbury, 2013. 27–38. Print.

Anonymous [John Lauritsen]. "Christopher Marlowe." *COME OUT!* 1 (1969): 13. *Home Page of John Lauritsen*. Web. 22 July 2013. http://paganpressbooks.com/jpl/CO13.HTM.

Antler [Brad Burdick]. *The Selected Poems*. New York: Soft Skull, 2000. Print.

Auden, W.H. *Collected Poems*. Ed. Edward Mendelson. New York: Random, 1991. Print.

Bishop, Elizabeth. *The Complete Poems, 1927–1979*. New York: Farrar, 1983. Print.

Bronski, Michael. *A Queer History of the United States*. Boston: Beacon P, 2011. Print.

Brossard, Nicole. *Selections*. Berkeley: U of California P, 2010. Print.

Cavafy, C.P. *The Collected Poems*. Trans. Evangelos Sachperoglou. New York: Oxford UP, 2007. Print.

Crane, Hart. *The Complete Poems and Selected Letters and Prose of Hart Crane*. Ed. Brom Weber. Garden City: Doubleday, 1966. Print.

Cruz, Conchitina. "Queer Embodiment and the Question of National Identity in the *Ars Poetica* of José Garcia Villa." 2013. TS.

De Andrade, Eugénio. *Forbidden Words: Selected Poetry*. Trans. Alexis Levitin. New York: New Directions, 2003. Print.

Di Prima, Diane. *Loba*. New York: Penguin, 1998. Print.

———. *Revolutionary Letters*. San Francisco: Last Gasp, 2007. Print.

Dlugos, Tim. *A Fast Life: The Collected Poems*. Ed. David Trinidad. Callicoon: Nightboat, 2011. Print.

Doty, Mark. *Atlantis: Poems*. New York: Harper, 1995. Print.

Duncan, Robert. *A Selected Prose*. Ed. Robert J. Bertholf. New York: New Directions, 1995. Print.

Edelman, Lee. *No Future: Queer Theory and the Death Drive*. Durham: Duke UP, 2004. Print.

edwards, kari. *obedience*. n.p.: Factory School, 2005. Print.

Freeman, Elizabeth. *Time Binds: Queer Temporalities, Queer Histories*. Durham: Duke UP, 2010. Print.

García Lorca, Federico. *Poet in New York*. Ed. Christopher Maurer. Trans. Greg Simon and Steven F. White. New York: Farrar, 1988. Print.

Ginsberg, Allen. *Collected Poems, 1947–1997*. New York: Harper, 2006. Print.

Halperin, David M. *How To Do the History of Homosexuality*. Chicago: U of Chicago P, 2002. Print.

Holbrook, Susan. "Lifting Belly, Filling Petunias, and Making Meanings through the Trans-Poetic." *American Literature* 71.4 (1999): 751–71. Print.

Jarraway, David R. *Going the Distance: Dissident Subjectivity in Modernist American Literature*. Baton Rouge: Louisiana State UP, 2003. Print.

Johnson, Ronald. *Valley of the Many-Colored Grasses*. New York: Norton, 1969. Print.

Kahan, Benjamin. "The Viper's Traffic-Knot: Celibacy and Queerness in the 'Late' Marianne Moore." *GLQ: A Journal of Lesbian and Gay Studies* 14.4 (2008): 509–35. Print.

Keenaghan, Eric. "Intimacy and Injury: The Queer Transfiguration of Racialized Exclusion in Langston Hughes's Translations of Nicolás Guillén." *Translation Studies* 2.2 (2009): 163–77. Print.

"World-Building and Gay Identity: Ronald Johnson's Singularly Queer *Foundations*." *Ronald Johnson: Life and Works*. Ed. Eric Murphy Selinger and Joel Bettridge. Orono: National Poetry Foundation, 2008. 361–96. Print.

Leavell, Linda. "Marianne Moore, the James Family, and the Politics of Celibacy." *Twentieth-Century Literature* 49.2 (2003): 219–45. Print.

Levy, Ellen. *Criminal Ingenuity: Moore, Cornell, Ashbery, and the Struggle Between the Arts*. New York: Oxford UP, 2011. Print.

Love, Heather. *Feeling Backward: Loss and the Politics of Queer History*. Cambridge: Harvard UP, 2009. Print.

Manry, Jessica. "'See What *Vanity Fair* Says': Langston Hughes's Redefinition of Heteronormativity in the Revolutionary Erotic Poetics of 'Advertisement for the Waldorf-Astoria.'" 2013. TS.

Myles, Eileen. *Not Me*. New York: Semiotext(e), 1991. Print.

Nathanaël [Nathalie Stephens]. *We Press Ourselves Plainly*. Callicoon: Nightboat, 2010. Print.

O'Hara, Frank. *The Collected Poems*. Ed. Donald Allen. Berkeley: U of California P, 1995. Print.

Peterson, Tim Trace. "Being Unreadable and Being Unread: An Introduction." *Troubling the Line: Trans and Genderqueer Poetry and Poetics*. Ed. TC Tolbert and Tim Trace Peterson. Callicoon: Nightboat, 2013. 15–22. Print.

Ponce, Martin Joseph. *Beyond the Nation: Diasporic Filipino Literature and Queer Reading*. New York: New York UP, 2012. Print.

Rukeyser, Muriel. *The Life of Poetry*. 1949. Ashfield: Paris P, 1996. Print.

Russ, Joanna. "Speculations: The Subjunctivity of Science Fiction." 1973. *Essays in Feminism and Science Fiction*. Bloomington: Indiana UP, 1995. 15–25. Print.

Scherr, Rebecca. "Tactile Erotics: Gertrude Stein and the Erotics of Touch." *Literature Interpretation Theory* 18 (2007): 193–212. Print.

Sedgwick, Eve Kosofsky. *Touching Feeling: Affect, Pedagogy, Performativity*. Durham: Duke UP, 2003. Print.

Shepherd, Reginald. *Red Clay Weather*. Pittsburgh: U of Pittsburgh P, 2011. Print.

Spahr, Juliana. *The Transformation*. Berkeley: Atelos, 2007. Print.

Stein, Gertrude. *Lectures in America*. Boston: Beacon P, 1957. Print.

 Writings 1903–1932. Ed. Catharine R. Stimpson and Harriet Chessman. New York: Library of America, 1998. Print.

Takahashi, Mutsuo. *Poems of a Penisist*. Trans. Hiroaki Soto. Minneapolis: U of Minnesota P, 2012. Print.

Villa, José Garcia. *Doveglion: Collected Poems*. Ed. John Edwin Cowen. New York: Penguin, 2008. Print.

Vogel, Shane. *The Scene of Harlem Cabaret: Race, Sexuality, Performance*. Chicago: U of Chicago P, 2009. Print.

Whitman, Walt. *Leaves of Grass and Other Writings: A Norton Critical Edition*. Ed. Michael Moon. New York: Norton, 2002. Print.

Wieners, John. *Selected Poems, 1958–1984*. Ed. Raymond Foye. Santa Barbara: Black Sparrow, 1986. Print.

Wilde, Oscar. *The Soul of Man and Prison Writings*. Ed. Isobel Murray. New York: Oxford UP, 1990. Print.

Young, Allen. "Out of the Closets, into the Streets." *Out of the Closets: Voices of Gay Liberation*. Ed. Karla Jay and Allen Young. 1972. New York: New York UP, 1992. 6–31. Print.

33

Lesbian and Gay Drama

SARA WARNER

Performance plays an integral part in creating and sustaining queer public cultures, serving as a method of artistic inquiry, a mode of sexual expression, and a means of social protest. Sexual minorities have a rich legacy of entertaining audiences (straight and gay) in bars, cabarets, bathhouses, and "legitimate" theatres, but historically they have been most skilled in the art of crafting personas that enable them to survive the drama of compulsory heteronormativity. "All of us who are queer can loosely be described as solo performers," note David Román and Holly Hughes, "insofar as we have had to fashion identity around our gender and sexuality, drag being only one manifestation of this process" (6–7). Homosexuals learn to pass as straight to avoid insult, injury, and prosecution, often before they are old enough to be conscious of what they are doing or why. Unable to express deviant desires publicly, many lesbians and gays seek solace in the arts. The theatre has long been a haven for queers. It is a site of yearning and fantasy, a liminal world where almost anything is possible. Unconventional liaisons, aberrant behaviors, masquerade, and powerful emotions are the cornerstones of dramaturgy. Desire, including same-sex eroticism, motivates characters and audiences alike. Trafficking in magic and metamorphosis, glitter and glamour, which is to say in the possibility of transformation, the theatre provides both a respite and a resource for society's maligned and marginalized.

Because of the crowd theatre attracts and the representational power it wields, playhouses are prime targets for censorship. Seen as a danger – or, like prostitution, a necessary evil – theatre often is regulated and relegated to the physical margins of society. Legislation such as New York's Comstock Law of 1873 (which made it illegal to send obscene material through the mail) and The Wales Padlock Act of 1927 (which empowered police to close establishments and jail participants engaged in acts of "sexual degeneracy" and "perversion") dictated what forms of sexual expression could circulate freely in America. In the United Kingdom, the virulently homophobic Clause 28, enacted in 1988

---

and repealed in 2003, forbade "the promotion of homosexuality" by local authorities. Prior to this the Lord Chamberlain had, until 1968, the authority to prohibit the production or publication of any play he deemed threatening to the preservation of good manners and the public peace. Explicit depictions of homosexuality were allowed, provided queers were portrayed as deviant characters damned to a living hell and an early grave. Lesbians and gays were cast as predatory social pariahs engaged in a panoply of bad behaviors – alcoholism, drug addiction, and blackmail – whose pathetic lives ended in imprisonment, suicide, or some equally grisly form of death. The tortured fate and tragic demise of homosexuals are emplotted in some of the twentieth century's most well-known dramas: Lillian Hellman's *The Children's Hour* (1934); Terence Rattigan's *The Deep Blue Sea* (1952); and Tennessee Williams's *Suddenly, Last Summer* (1958), all of which were made into award-winning feature films.

Many writers and directors sought to evade censorship through the use of innuendo, subtext, and discursive sleights of hand. "Unable to be honest about their sexuality," observe Kim Marra and Robert Schanke, gay artists "used coded language, substituted straight for queer characters, and formed their plots in heterosexual contexts in order to gain acceptance and production of their plays" (3). Masters of the double entendre, lyricists Cole Porter, Lorenz Hart, and Stephen Sondheim penned campy, erotically charged songs that knowing audiences would discern. Musical theatre, contends D.A. Miller, made singing and dancing, activities typically associated with effeminacy in American culture, acceptable in a popular entertainment form that reified heterosexual romance, thereby enabling gay men not only to indulge in suspect behavior but garner favor for doing so. Lesbian spectators too delighted in what Stacy Wolf calls the "delicious queerness" of American musicals that feature strong female leads and flout gender expectations, such as *The Sound of Music, Gypsy,* and *Wicked* (205). Theatrical conventions enabled early and mid-twentieth-century queer dramatists like Noël Coward and William Inge to subsume same-sex desire into a play's subtext, to "vent their feelings in camouflaged form," in such a way that their art had immediate appeal to queer spectators (Kauffmann 93).

During the 1950s and 1960s, some theatre critics called for playwrights to stop peopling their productions with queers surreptitiously disguised as heterosexuals. One reviewer lambasted Edward Albee's *Who's Afraid of Virginia Woolf?* (1962) for its "morbidity and sexual perversity which," he claimed, "are there only to titillate an impotent and homosexual theater audience" (Bernstein 2). This sexual panic played an important part in the Cold War. Senator Joseph McCarthy's House Un-American Activities Committee (HUAC) blacklisted homosexuals along with communists on the grounds that queers posed a political and moral threat to the United States. Equating sexual deviants with political dissidents, HUAC cast queers as reprobates whose perverse desires endangered the nuclear family, the nation, and by extension, civilization itself, thereby ensuring, according to David Savran, that artists who identified as homosexuals ensconced themselves even further in the closet, cloaking their characters in shame and secrecy.

While homophobic policies had the effect of silencing queer playwrights, actors, and directors, especially those with commercial aspirations, they also had the unintended consequence of contributing to the politicizing of sexual identities and the proliferation of alternative performance venues. After World War II, sexual subcultures began to form in urban areas across the United States. Members of these enclaves began to view sexuality as an important rubric for understanding themselves as social subjects and as minority citizens in relationship to the dominant culture. Homosexuals created vast underground networks to develop and share work, which was often experimental in nature, among a supportive and adventurous sphere of artists and audiences. The most influential of these emergent spaces was Caffé Cino (1958–68), the birthplace of gay and lesbian theatre and the progenitor of the Off-Off-Broadway movement. This storefront coffeehouse on Cornelia Street in Greenwich Village offered its postage stamp-sized stage to aspiring playwrights of any sexual persuasion interested in pushing the boundaries of generic and social conventions.

Caffé Cino staged daring plays by and about gays, including Robert Patrick's *The Haunted Host* (1964), about a playwright who is visited by the ghost of an ex-lover, and Lanford Wilson's *The Madness of Lady Bright* (1964), which mesmerized audiences and critics alike with its disquieting portrait of an aging queen who is slowly losing her beauty and, along with it, her mind. The production ran for more than two hundred performances and earned Neil Flanagan an Obie Award. Doric Wilson's acclaimed *And He Made a Her* (1961), a satirical take on heterosexuality and monogamy in which Adam argues with three angels about why he has to share his life with Eve, transferred from Cino to the Cherry Lane Theater Off-Broadway. The night of the dress rehearsal Wilson was entrapped by an undercover cop and arrested on vice charges. After making bail, he ran directly to the safety of the Caffé, sat at a table, and penned *Now She Dances* (1961), an angry and sardonic take on the obscenity trials of Oscar Wilde.

In the 1950s and 1960s, queer performance developed in an array of spaces, including Jack Smith's loft apartment and Andy Warhol's Factory, where visual artists created camp extravaganzas featuring fierce transvestites and other flaming creatures in flamboyant theatrical spectacles. Warhol's film scenarist Ron Tavel joined forces with director John Vaccaro in 1966 to found the Playhouse of the Ridiculous. During rehearsals for *Conquest of the Universe*, aspiring actor and dramatist Charles Ludlam clashed so violently with Vaccaro that he was fired from his own play. Ludlam stormed off the set, dragging a cast of defectors with him, and formed The Ridiculous Theatrical Company, which flourished until his death from AIDS in 1987. The inaugural production was a competing version of *Conquest*, wryly titled *When Queens Collide*. A devoted scholar of both high art and popular culture, Ludlam brought incredible erudition to his craft, be it an adaptation of Shakespeare, a parody of Victorian Penny Dreadfuls, or sexy send-ups of science fiction. Ludlam was renowned for his female roles, namely the tubercular courtesan Marguerite Gautier and opera diva Maria Callas, which he played in low-cut dresses that exposed his hairy chest. The goal was not to pass as a woman but to seduce audiences into gradually forgetting he was a man.

While the theatre has sheltered many homosexuals and nurtured generations of gay artists, it has also perpetuated gross stereotypes that reinforce homophobic caricatures and reify social hierarchies of race, class, and gender. Mart Crowley's landmark play *The Boys in the Band* (1968), the first commercially successful drama to offer a sympathetic depiction of gay male sexuality, centers around a group of closeted and self-loathing upper-middle-class men. For their friend Harold's birthday, they rent a hustler, Cowboy, who is openly mocked by the affluent and intellectually superior college graduates who contract his services. While the party ends with every one of the boys being humiliated or abused, some to the extent that they want to kill themselves, they put on another record, mix another cocktail, and make it through another night. These seemingly frivolous "acts of gaiety" are what keep the protagonists alive (Warner). Unlike in most early plays about homosexuals, these characters are neither alone nor dead when the curtain falls. As Michael notes in the final scene, "It's not always the way it is in plays. Not all faggots bump themselves off at the end of the story!" (490). The members of *The Boys in the Band* may not be happy – they may not even be able to imagine themselves as happy ("show me a happy homosexual," says Michael, "and I'll show you a gay corpse") – but they manage, somehow, to be gay (516).

The Boys in the Band transferred to the Wyndham Theatre in London's West End, where ten years earlier Shelagh Delaney's *A Taste of Honey* (1959), about a working-class white girl who dates a black man and shares a flat with a homosexual acquaintance, revolutionized British theatre. Delaney paved the way for John Osborne's *A Patriot for Me* (1965), a tale of a McCarthy-style witch hunt in which two young men accused of being communists are tarred with the charge of homosexuality, and Charles Dyer's *Staircase* (1966), produced by the Royal Shakespeare Company, that features one of theatre's first gay male couples, albeit in a hostile, loveless relationship. Joe Orton, regarded as one of England's greatest comedic wits, was renowned for his "absolutely filthy" macabre comedies *Entertaining Mr. Sloane* (1964) and *Loot* (1966) (De Jongh 102). This working-class rebel and convicted felon's life was cut short when he was bludgeoned to death by his lover Kenneth Halliwell.

Martin Sherman's *Bent* (1979) dramatized the Nazi persecution of homosexuals at a time when there was scant awareness or historical evidence that gays were targeted as "undesirables" along with Jews, Gypsies, immigrants, the disabled, and criminals. Captured in a purge, lovers Rudy and Max are put on a train to Dachau. Max claims he is a Jew rather than a homosexual because he believes his chances of survival will be greater if he is assigned to wear the yellow star instead of the pink triangle. In an attempt to hide his sexuality, he beats Rudy to death in front of guards, who force Max to have sex with the corpse of a young girl to "prove" he is straight. At the camp, Max falls in love with another prisoner, Horst, who shows him that humanity lies in acknowledging his desire. The two make love to each other with words and their imagination under the glare of the guards. When Horst is shot, Max puts on his jacket with the pink triangle and commits suicide by falling on an electric fence.

Bent, like *The Boys in the Band*, was a watershed moment in gay and lesbian drama. Just a few months after the latter's premiere, some real-life queens staged their own revolutionary drama at the Stonewall Inn on Christopher Street. In the wee hours of June 28, 1969, a group of street hustlers and transgender patrons – many of them queers of color – fought back with righteous indignation when authorities raided the bar the night of Judy Garland's funeral. The riot police were called to restore order, and several members of the swelling crowd responded to this show of force by staging an impromptu chorus line. Locking arms and kicking up their heels, they sang: "We are the Village queens/We always wear blue jeans/We wear our hair in curls/Because we think we are girls" (Duberman 83). This spontaneous and highly self-conscious performance event spawned a national gay and lesbian liberation movement premised on the notion that sexual freedom is intimately linked to questions of citizenship and democracy.

In the wake of the Stonewall riots, political collectives such as the Gay Liberation Front (GLF), the Gay Activist Alliance (GAA), and the Radicalesbians staged arresting zap actions, highly performative nonviolent acts of guerrilla theatre combining physical comedy and symbolic costumes in brief, improvised skits designed to expose homophobia and catalyze public response to lesbian and gay issues. Doric Wilson, a participant in the uprising and a member of both GLF and GAA, wrote *Street Theatre* (1982), a satirical two-act play that cruises Christopher Street in the hours leading up to the riots. This Caffè Cino veteran cofounded The Other Side of Silence (TOSOS) (1974), the first professional gay theatre company in New York. TOSOS was the progenitor of queer theatre across North America and the United Kingdom, including London's Gay Sweatshop, Toronto's Buddies in Bad Times, Seattle's Alice B., and San Francisco's Theatre Rhinoceros.

Wowing Audiences: Lesbian Theatre at the Margins

Gay theatres provided increasing opportunities for male playwrights, but they were generally much less receptive to plays by and about lesbians. Valerie Solanas, author of the polemical political tract *SCUM Manifesto* (1967), tried in vain to find a producer for her play *Up Your Ass* (1965), an uproarious parody of heteronormativity, racial stereotypes, and sex roles. This experimental one-act chronicles the exploits of Bongi Perez, a self-described "vivacious, dynamic, single … queer," who cruises "real low-down funky broads, nasty bitchy hotshots" (*Up* 28). The protagonist, like the play's author, is a wiseass butch dyke who hustles for a living, panhandling and prostituting. Remarkable for its explicit portrayal of female desire, sexual subcultures, and urban street life, *Up Your Ass* features a multiracial cast of dueling drag queens, beatnik hipsters, hapless johns, a feces-obsessed femme fatale, and a homicidal housewife. Homosexuality is a given rather than a problem to be addressed, and degeneracy is redefined as a "scummy" virtue that enables social deviants and sexual minorities to escape a diseased patriarchal society.

The question of whether lesbian sexuality and dyke modes of humor can be made intelligible to broader audiences has preoccupied artists and activists since the earliest days of second wave feminism. The strategies for self-definition and self-promotion successfully employed by gay men to increase their visibility, political clout, and economic capital – namely camp, kitsch, and drag – have not been particularly efficacious for lesbians. The theatre world has done comparatively little to champion lesbians, in part because there were (and are) so few out dykes working as playwrights, directors, actors, or designers. Many bisexual and lesbian women, such as Lorraine Hansberry, María Irene Fornés, and Megan Terry, wrote plays with powerful female characters but not same-sex content. Why would they, given that there were so few places that would stage them? There was no lesbian equivalent of Caffé Cino until 1976 when two Cuban exiles, Ana Maria Simo and Magaly Alabau, founded Medusa's Revenge, a short-lived but influential performance space. Medusa's Revenge coexisted in time and space with TOSOS and Ridiculous, but they may as well have been on different planets, according to Simo, as they constituted completely different social worlds with distinct aesthetic practices, divergent political aims, and very little sense of solidarity around any shared notion of gay and lesbian theatre (Solomon and Minwalla 147–48).

Playwrights like Jane Chambers, who wrote plays with lesbian characters and who enjoyed a modicum of commercial success, tended to work in the realist vein, which meant that her protagonists died or were doomed to an onerous fate. Peopled with sympathetic, if stereotypical characters – brooding butches, doting femmes, closeted career women, and dykes who fall for straight women – Chambers's plays offer some of the first nuanced and tender portraits of lesbian communities. The Glines, a gay arts organization modeled on TOSOS, produced three of Chambers's plays: *Last Summer of Bluefish Cove* (1980), *My Blue Heaven* (1981), and *The Quintessential Image* (1989). The former chronicles a group of friends (many of them erstwhile lovers) who share summer holidays at the beach. The central protagonist, a womanizer named Lil, falls for a recent divorcee, Eva, whose coming out propels the plot. In a tragic twist of fate, Lil's happiness is cut short by her death from cancer. Her physical disease serves as symbolic punishment for the moral disease of lesbianism, but also of gender nonconformity and nonmonogamous sexuality.

Uninterested in perpetuating what Sue-Ellen Case and Jill Dolan have called the deadly dictates of realist drama, many dykes gravitated toward experimental forms, which they developed in agit-prop and avant-garde collectives. Roberta Sklar, Muriel Miguel, and Megan Terry left the Open Theater when it became apparent that the group had no interest in exploring issues related to women or lesbians. Partnering with Sondra Segal and Clare Coss, Sklar cofounded Women's Experimental Theatre (WET) in 1977. WET infused canonical texts with lesbian feminist perspectives on gender and sexuality. *The Daughter's Cycle Trilogy* (1977–80) offers a revisionist history of Greek drama from the perspective of the female characters. Many feminist collectives, such as It's All Right to Be Woman Theater and At the Foot of the Mountain, generated content through consciousness-raising sessions, and their productions created a public forum for the private issues that women suffered with in silence, including rape, abortion, and incest. Their productions were not devoid of humor, though they tended to be more solemn than silly. Abjuring the sober tone typically employed by other (predominantly white, middle-class) feminist collectives, Spiderwoman Theater revels in slapstick, burlesque, and bawdy humor to weave powerful social satires. This multicultural collective founded by Miguel and her two (heterosexual) sisters draws on the founders' cultural heritage as members of the Kuna and Rappahannock nations. Their first performance, a comedy titled *Women in Violence* (1975), addresses violence against women and among women, as well as self-inflicted abuse.

While touring Europe in the late 1970s, Spiderwoman lost their luggage and asked another troupe, a mixed-gender glam fab cabaret group called Hot Peaches, to borrow some costumes. When Lois Weaver met Peggy Shaw to pick up the costumes, it was love at first sight. Weaver and Shaw's personal and professional partnership, now in its fourth decade, has irrevocably altered the landscape of American theatre. In 1980, they cohosted an international theatre festival, WOW (Women's One World) in New York, and the event's success (thirty-six acts by artists from eight countries) led to the formation of WOW Café, a permanent performance space in the East Village. Comprised, in the words of Kate Davy, "of unabashed amateurs who [are] resolutely into chaos," the Café serves as a crucible for the production of lesbian feminist communities and radical artistic experimentation (96). Shaw and Weaver teamed with Deb Margolin, a queer-identified heterosexual, to form the Split Britches theatre company. Engaging in sex-radical role playing, this troupe exposes the systemic nature of compulsory heterosexuality, artfully subverting patriarchal constructions of gender, class, and desire with vaudeville shtick and a rough ("poor") performance aesthetic that defamiliarizes cultural myths. Split Britches lampoons sexual norms, theatrical conceits, and the conventions of lesbian subcultures in plays such as *Upwardly Mobile Home* (1984), *Little Women: The Tragedy* (1988), *Lesbians Who Kill* (1992), and the Obie Award-winning *Belle Reprieve*, a parody of Tennessee Williams's *Streetcar Named Desire* created with Bette Bourne and Paul "Precious Pearl" Shaw of Bloolips, an anarchic drag troupe from London. Shaw and Weaver form a dynamic butch-femme duo in *Anniversary Waltz* (1989), a celebration of their tenth year together. Their most recent collaboration is *Lost Lounge* (2009), a haunting meditation on memory, history, and the passing of time. Shaw is also an accomplished solo performer. Her poignant, autobiographical musings on butch life (*You're Just Like My Father* [1995], *Menopausal Gentleman* [1999], and *Ruff* [2012]) deal with issues of female masculinity, vitality and loss, aging and dying, health and queer life.

WOW is where Alina Troyano, a Cuban American performer and playwright, developed her performance alter egos Carmelita Tropicana, a Carmen Miranda-inspired spitfire, and Pingalito Betancourt, an archetypal macho

Latino man whose name is slang for penis. Both characters appear in the radiant *Milk of Amnesia – Leche de Amnesia* (1994). In this parody of Marcel Proust's *À la Recherche du temps perdu*, Tropicana journeys to the island her parents fled during the revolution, eats a pork sandwich, and falls into a CUMMA, a collective unconscious memory appropriation attack, a reaction to the economic devastation and human suffering inflicted by the U.S. trade embargo and the pain she has experienced as an immigrant forced to suppress various aspects of her Latina identity in order to assimilate into American culture. The recipient of a special citation Obie Award for sustained excellence in performance, Troyano collaborated on her most recent work, *Undocumented Gigolos/ Indocumentados*, with Marga Gomez, a queer Puerto Rican-Cuban-American humorist and playwright (*Memory Tricks* [1990], *Marga Gomez Is Pretty, Witty, and Gay* [1991], *Long Island Iced Latina* [2010]). Gomez and Troyano previously colluded on the perversely parodic *Single Wet Female* (2002).

One of Troyano's earliest roles at WOW was in Holly Hughes's *The Well of Horniness* (1983), a "dyke noir" that reimagines Radclyffe Hall's tortured tale of lesbian love, *The Well of Loneliness* (1928), as a screwball detective drama about a "lady dick" named Garnet McClit. Hughes was drawn to the anarchic, sex-positive atmosphere of WOW, where she developed several additional plays and solo pieces: *Dress Suits for Hire* (1987), performed by Shaw and Weaver; *World Without End* (1989), a wry meditation on relations with her mother; *Clit Notes* (1990), whose title could not be printed in most newspapers; and *Preaching to the Perverted* (2000), which details her experience as one of the NEA Four, a group of feminist and queer artists (Hughes, Karen Finley, Tim Miller, and John Fleck) whose grants were revoked by the National Endowment for the Arts in 1990 on the grounds that their work was offensive. The NEA Four sued the government for the reinstatement of their awards and won, but the Supreme Court overturned part of the ruling, and the NEA, pressured by Congress, instituted a decency clause and discontinued funding for individual artists.

The formal experimentation, political daring, and unbridled eroticism of the WOW Café gave birth to the Five Lesbian Brothers' decadent, politically incorrect sex comedies. Unorthodox in every imaginable way, *Voyage to Lesbos* (1990), *Brave Smiles . . . Another Lesbian Tragedy* (1992), *The Secretaries* (1994), and *Brides of the Moon* (1997) eviscerate stereotypes by lampooning social conventions of both heterosexual and homosexual cultures. The Brothers surprised fans with their realistic adaptation of Sophocles's tragedy titled *Oedipus at Palm Springs* (2005), told from the vantage point of Jocasta. The play, which premiered at the nearby New York Theatre Workshop, delivers a caustic critique of the mainstreaming of the LGBT movement, one that makes visible the emotional and political blind spots produced by a domesticated, depoliticized, and increasingly insular gay agenda dominated by same-sex marriage and the conservative rhetoric of "family values."

Two of the Brothers enjoy distinguished careers outside of the collective. Brother Angelos garnered rave reviews for her portrayal of lesbian novelist and cultural critic Susan Sontag in the Builders Association's *Sontag: Reborn* (2012). She starred, along with Troyano, in Hughes's *Let Them Eat Cake* (2010), a gay wedding in one act with confections, and in Half-Straddle's *In the Pony Palace/Football* (2011) at the Bushwick Starr in Brooklyn, the borough where many queer performers have migrated in search of more affordable rent. Brother Kron found success on the regional theatre circuit with a pair of autobiographical monologues, *101 Humiliating Stories* (1993) and the exquisite *2.5 Minute Ride* (1997), which juxtaposes a trip the artist took to Auschwitz with her father, a Holocaust survivor, and her family's annual vacation to an amusement park in Sandusky, Ohio. *Well* (2004), a "solo performance with other people in it," continues Kron's familial odyssey, this time mining the maternal for content (16). This work explores chronic illness in an effort to understand why some injuries, bodies, and histories heal, while others do not. In an extremely rare occurrence in the world of lesbian performance, *Well* moved to Broadway (Longacre Theatre 2006) and received two Tony nominations. In 2013, Kron, with composer Jeanine Tesori, adapted Alison Bechdel's acclaimed graphic novel *Fun Home* into a Pulitzer Prize-nominated musical about a lesbian daughter's quest to come to terms with her father's homosexuality and suicide that is bound for Broadway in 2015.

Acting Up: AIDS and Queer Theatres of Protest

Just as WOW Café and lesbian performance were flourishing, AIDS began to ravage gay male communities. Artists responded to the plague and the government's appalling apathy with a variety of theatrical interventions on an array of stages. *As Is* by Caffè Cino veteran William Hoffman and *The Normal Heart* by Larry Kramer, two early examples of what came to be known as "AIDS plays," premiered in 1985. Kramer was a founding member of Gay Men's Health Crisis and ACT UP, a direction action group committed to militant forms of civil disobedience and confrontational modes of public demonstrations, including zaps. Kramer's condemnation of casual sex – in *The Normal Heart* the autobiographical protagonist Ned Weeks urges his brothers to "fight for the right to get married instead of the right to legitimize promiscuity" – polarized the queer community and helped direct gay activism toward a more conservative, assimilationist agenda (78). Two award-winning revivals of *The Normal Heart* (2004, 2011) generated money and support for same-sex marriage referendums but failed to foment political outrage about the persistence of AIDS or its transformation into a global phenomenon that disproportionately affects people of color and the poor.

Another controversial AIDS drama, Jonathan Larson's Pulitzer Prize-winning rock opera *Rent* (1996), about artists struggling to survive in a gentrifying East Village, casts hipster heterosexuals at the center of the AIDS crisis, prompting charges that this adaptation of Puccini's *La Bohème* distorts history and whitewashes the issue of homophobia. Larson, who died unexpectedly the morning of *Rent*'s opening night Off-Broadway, was accused by Sarah Schulman of plagiarizing her novel *People in Trouble* (1990). Schulman, cofounder of the Lesbian Avengers, a direct action group committed to issues of dyke visibility, wanted to expose Larson's theft of her work as endemic of a widespread parasitic practice in which mainstream artists co-opt and capitalize on the ideas and aesthetics of minority culture workers. Rather than sue Larson's estate, she wrote *Stage Struck: Theatre, AIDS, and the Marketing of Gay America* (1998) to initiate a conversation about the ways *Rent* and projects like it enable heterosexual middle- and upper-middle-class audiences to explore multiculturalism and imagine themselves as tolerant without having to confront their privilege, prejudices, or actual people stigmatized by AIDS.

The first AIDS drama to win a Pulitzer Prize was Tony Kushner's epic two-part saga, *Angels in America: A Gay Fantasia on National Themes*. This daring theatrical experiment about life during the Reagan regime was one of the defining cultural events of the twentieth century. Part one, *Millennium Approaches*, was commissioned by the Mark Taper Forum and premiered at San Francisco's Eureka Theatre Company in 1991. Kushner wrote part two, *Perestroika*, as *Millennium Approaches* was being performed. The drama centers on Louis Ironson, a guilt-ridden Jewish idealist who abandons his lover, Prior Walter, when he shows symptoms of AIDS. Louis begins dating Joe Pitt, a closeted Mormon clerk at the U.S. Court of Appeals and the protégé of notorious McCarthyist Roy Cohn. Joe leaves his wife, Harper, a hysterical housewife with a Valium addiction, to explore his sexual identity. Cohn, himself deeply closeted, learns that he has AIDS and uses his influence to obtain an experimental drug, AZT. Belize, Cohn's nurse, steals the medicine to help Prior survive the plague. The play ends with Prior, Walter, Belize, and Hannah (Joe's mother) in Central Park, at the statue of the Angel of Bethesda, arguing about global politics. Prior breaks away from his friends and speaks directly to the audience, offering a message of hope for the future: "This disease will be the end of many of us, but not nearly all, and the dead will be commemorated and will struggle on with the living, and we are not going away. We won't die secret deaths anymore. The world only spins forward. We will be citizens. The time has come.... The Great Work Begins" (280). Kushner's subsequent work grapples with broad political issues, such as war, slavery, and terrorism, though not all of the plays explicitly foreground gay and lesbian issues. A collaboration with Jeanine Tesori, *Caroline or Change* (2002) – a musical about a Jewish family in Lake Charles, Louisiana and their black maid during the American Civil Rights movement – does not concern itself with sexual identity, but *The Intelligent Homosexual's Guide to Capitalism and Socialism with a Key to the Scriptures* (2009) insists on the centrality of sexuality to any analysis of economics, religion, the family, and the nation.

Performances such as Michael Kearns's *Intimacies* (1989) and Bill T. Jones's *Still/Here* (1994) provided a public forum for responding to and intervening in the AIDS crisis. With so many artists coming out in the context of the epidemic, the theatre has become a space where individuals can be openly and shamelessly queer. Homosexuals, and gay white men in particular, enjoy increasing success as out artists in mainstream, commercial, and not-for-profit theatres. American playwrights Richard Greenberg, Craig Lucas, Paul Rudnick, Harvey Fierstein, and Marc Shaiman, along with Britain's Peter Gill, Alan Bennett, and Mark Ravenhill and Canada's Michel Tremblay and Michel Marc Blanchard, produce wildly popular, critically acclaimed comedies, tragedies, and musicals with queer themes and characters. Terrence McNally has scored a string of hits that include *Lisbon Traviata* (1985); *Lips Together, Teeth Apart* (1991); *Kiss of the Spiderwoman* (1992); and *Love! Valor! Compassion!* (1995). The latter features several male couples who vacation annually at the home of a dancer named Gregory, whose pond creates ample opportunity for staged male nudity. This domestic setting enables McNally to focus on the intimate relationships of the protagonists, who seek solace, serenity, and the company of friends as they navigate personal, artistic, and health crises in this Tony award-winning play cum major Hollywood film. The broad appeal of *Love! Valor! Compassion!* stands in direct contrast to the controversy surrounding McNally's *Corpus Christi* (1997), a passion play that depicts Jesus and the Apostles as gay men living in contemporary Texas. Canceled before opening night because of boycotts and death threats against McNally, the play was eventually staged at Manhattan Theatre Club in 1998 (and later in England and Australia).

The violent protests delaying *Corpus Christi* meant that the play happened to open the day after the brutal death of college student Matthew Shepard in Wyoming, a national tragedy that inspired Moisés Kaufman and members of Tectonic Theater to create *The Laramie Project* (Denver Center for the Performing Arts 2000). A documentary drama based on interviews with inhabitants, newspaper reports, and the cast's personal reflections, *The Laramie Project* eschews realism in favor of a Brechtian-inflected dialectical approach intended to alienate spectators by thwarting absorption in theatrical spectacle and promoting instead a critical perspective on the action. Techniques designed to promote critical reflection include the use of eight actors to portray more than sixty characters in a series of short scenes that defy narrative cohesion, the decision not to represent Shepard on stage, and the conscious refusal to promote a single truth or moral to this story, thereby prompting the audience members to make sense of this complex situation for themselves.

Kaufman helped develop and directed Doug Wright's Pulitzer Prize-winning performance, *I Am My Own Wife* (2003), a one-man show based on conversations with Charlotte von Mahlsdorf, born Lothar Berfelde, a German antique dealer who, when she was a child, killed her Nazi father and survived psychiatric institutions, prison, and the war in East Berlin as an openly transgendered person. Queer documentary theatre, which dates back to Jonathan Katz's *Coming Out!* (1972) and Emily Mann's *Execution of Justice* (1974), about the assassination of Harvey Milk, uses archival materials to restage actual events in order to provoke questions about the veracity of the historical record, the (un)reliability of memory, and the problematic nature of concepts such as truth and justice (Bottoms). This genre of political performance seeks to catalyze social action beyond the theatre walls.

Stages of Progress: Lesbians, Queers of Color, and Transgender Artists' Quest for Parity

Tectonic Theater's Leigh Fondakowski created two extraordinary documentary theatre pieces, *I Think I Like Girls* (2002) and *Casa Cushman* (2010), about the immensely popular but largely forgotten nineteenth-century actress Charlotte Cushman, who challenged Victorian gender conventions with her portrayal of male characters, most notably Romeo. The success of these pieces pales in comparison to work by her gay male counterparts. While lesbians have gained prominence in television and film, dykes remain virtually invisible on Broadway and in regional theatres. Prior to Kron's *Well*, only a handful of productions by lesbians appeared on the Great White Way – Lily Tomlin's *Appearing Nightly* (1977) and *Search for Signs of Intelligent Life in the Universe* (1985, 2000); Sandra Bernhard's *Without You I'm Nothing* (1990) and *I'm*

Still Here ... Damn It! (1998); and Margaret Edson's *W;t* (1995) – though to call any of these productions dyke dramas would be an exaggeration. *W;t*, winner of the Pulitzer Prize (1999), explores the final hours in the life of an asexual spinster, English professor Vivian Bearing, who comes to the painful realization that her life's work, metaphysical poetry, provides little comfort as she faces death from ovarian cancer all alone. In true melodramatic fashion, this scholar learns too late that there's more to life than the quest for knowledge. Out actress Cynthia Nixon played the lead in the 2012 revival.

Paula Vogel was the first out lesbian to win the Pulitzer Prize for drama for *How I Learned to Drive* (1998). This controversial play explores the pedophilic relationship between L'il Bit and her Uncle Peck. Rejecting realism for a more presentational style, Vogel uses the metaphor of driving to stage a nuanced conversation about consent and coercion, pleasure and danger, control and manipulation. Her work employs humor and word play to deconstruct normative sexuality and the often absurd ideological dictates that script intimate encounters. *The Baltimore Waltz* (1992), directed by Anne Bogart and starring Cherry Jones, follows two siblings on a hedonistic trek through Europe in search of a cure for ATD (Acquired Toilet Disease), a communicable infection Anna contracts from the public bathroom where she teaches. The play is an elegy for Vogel's brother Carl who died of AIDS. Queer sexuality guides both *And Baby Makes Seven* (1984), an Albee-inspired drama of domestic dysfunction in which a lesbian couple and their gay male friend conceive a child, and *The Mineola Twins* (1996), a satirical look at the success and failures of the women's movement from the vantage point of twin sisters – one heterosexual and one homosexual, one radical and one conservative – played by a single actress. Despite Vogel's sustained success over three decades, she has never been produced on Broadway. Like the handful of lesbians who enjoy a significant degree of success in the theatre, she remains decidedly outside certain circuits of power, spheres of influence, and pockets of funding.

Lesbians, queers of color, and transgender artists often find themselves marginalized and lacking cultural capital, as racial distinctions and gender identifications continue to exert a profound effect on visibility and an artist's viability. Chicana dramatist Cherríe Moraga produces her plays primarily at feminist and queer theatres in the Bay Area. *Giving Up the Ghost* (1984), an assemblage of evocative monologues features three females: Marissa, a young butch dyke in her twenties; her younger self, Corky, whose male identification and rejection of traditional gender roles does not protect her from being raped; and Amalia, a heterosexual woman in her forties with a history of bad relationships. Both *Giving Up the Ghost* and *The Hungry Woman: A*

Mexican Medea (1995) re-envision the myth of La Malinche, the Aztec mistress of Cortes whose betrayal of her people earned her the nicknames La Vendida, "the sell-out," and La Chingada, "the fucked one," to deliver a pointed critique of sexism, racism, homophobia, and the masculinist politics of cultural nationalism. *Heroes and Saints* (1989) links the use of lethal pesticides in farming, and the utter disregard growers show for the health and safety of immigrant laborers, to the government's failure to intervene in the AIDS crisis in a stinging indictment of systemic discrimination. Though Moraga has been produced all over the globe, only one of her plays, *Heart of the Earth* (1994), has premiered in New York City. This adaptation of the Maya creation myth the Popul Vuh was commissioned by INTAR, the Hispanic American Arts Center, and produced at the Public Theater.

The roster of accomplished playwrights of color who have never appeared on Broadway includes Luis Alfaro (a MacArthur "genius" grant recipient) and Chay Yew (Artistic Director of Chicago's Victory Gardens Theatre), two men whose work takes up similar social and political themes as white dramatists McNally and Kushner with comparable verve and skill. Some artists are happily excluded from the mainstream and prefer playing for coterie audiences in small, not-for-profit theatres. Pomo Afro Homos (1991–95), a black gay male theatre collective, was born at Josie's Cabaret and Juice Joint in San Francisco's Castro District. With panache and piercing insight, Brian Freeman, Eric Gupton, and Djola Branner delivered, at the height of the AIDS crisis, edgy mosaics detailing the joys and conflicts, pleasures and contradictions of being queer and African American. *Fierce Love* and *Dark Fruit* challenge stereotypes and confront social stigmas by insisting that black men loving black men is a revolutionary act. Not content with simply "preaching to the converted" at gay venues, Pomo Afro Homo sought out a broad audience base (Miller and Román). Their in-yer-face performances of queer sexuality led to the group being banned from the 1991 National Black Theatre Festival. The issue of what it means to be gay, black, and militant in America structures Freeman's play *Civil Sex* (1997) about the life and legacy of openly gay Civil Rights activist Bayard Rustin, who planned the 1963 March on Washington despite Strom Thurmond's attempt to derail the event by branding him a communist and sexual pervert.

Pomo Afro Homo's Branner has performed in two performance pieces by gender-bending butch *griot* (a term, originating in precolonial West Africa, denoting a storyteller, praise singer, or poet) Sharon Bridgforth, *Blood Pudding* (Hyde Park Theatre, Austin 1998) and *Delta Dandy* (Fire and Ink Black Queer Writers Festival 2009). These gorgeous interdisciplinary works fuse poetry and polyphonic rhythms with ritual dance and dramatic interpretation in a theatrical jazz aesthetic to celebrate the history of African Americans and the range of gender expressions and sexualities within black communities. Haitian American performance artist Lenelle Möise tracks similar territory in *Expatriate* (Culture Project 2008). This work follows two friends, a budding lesbian Claudie and a straight femme fatale Alphine, in a trenchant exploration of desire, black female sexuality, and creative survival. These young women from a Boston housing project weather the scene of hopelessness in which they have been cast by engaging in fugitive dreams of escape and enchantment. Moving to New York, then Paris, they form a duo Black Venus, and, like generations of expatriate women of color before them, find both liberation and nefarious forms of discrimination on European stages. E. Patrick Johnson plays the *griot* in *Pouring Tea*, a documentary theatre piece based on the oral histories collected in his award-winning book *Sweet Tea: Black Gay Men of the South*. This one-man show, in which Johnston seamlessly inhabits a number of queer African American males aged nineteen to ninety-three talking about a range of topics – coming of age in the South, religion, sex, love, transgenderism, and coming out – premiered at About Face Theater in Chicago in 2010. He is currently at work on a companion piece, *Honeypot: Black Lesbians of the South*.

At its best, queer theatre drives a wedge between representation and reality, appearance and truth. Theatrical crossdressing can challenge gendered frameworks that constrain subjects, disrupt the contingent foundations of heteronormativity, and stage alternate arrangements of bodies and worlds. Drag extravaganzas *La Cage Aux Folles* (1983), *Vampire Lesbians of Sodom* (1985), and *Hairspray* (2002) are three of the longest-running shows in New York theatre history. Taylor Mac drags gender and species in audacious, metatheatrical orgies of delight. *Lily's Revenge* (2009; Obie Award), a four-hour spectacle incorporating vaudeville, Weimar cabaret, Japanese noh drama, "princess musicals," slam poetry, dream ballet, and *commedia dell'arte* features a thirty-plus-person cast. Mac plays the eponymous flower decked out in a bedazzled green garment and glittering makeup, a corolla of five white petals gracing his neck – one shy of a normal lily's bounty. Indeed, there is nothing normal about this potted protagonist who becomes a man in order to rescue a bride from marrying the wrong suitor. Inspired by anti-gay marriage advocates who use tradition and nostalgia as grounds for discrimination, *Lily's Revenge* deconstructs the stories that imprison us in the past, rearranging these fragments into new narratives. The production is less a paean for same-sex unions than it is a collective ritual of perversion in which Mac invites the actors and audience to marry everyone and everything, to solemnize our connection to each other and to the planet. Mac's epic events foster community building on a scale rarely seen in the theatre today. The success of Ru Paul's *Drag Race* franchise and the Tony Award-winning musical *Kinky Boots* (2013) speaks to the enduring appeal of male-to-female drag for both queer communities and mainstream audiences. Female-to-male drag, which flourished in the early twentieth century in Harlem cabarets and in drag king competitions in the 1990s, remains largely on the cultural periphery.

Generally speaking, transgender artists do not perform drag, though some genderqueer individuals such as Murray Hill (a.k.a. Betsey Gallagher, an entertainer who maintains a masculine persona in public and private) consciously enact and transform gender to expose its inherent theatricality. Kate Bornstein is a pioneer in the struggle for trans visibility and a tireless civil rights advocate. A male-to-female transgender lesbian writer and gender theorist, Bornstein narrates his transition from a biological man to a constructed female to a gender outlaw in *Hidden: A Gender* (1989, 2012). Ze has written and performed several shows about sexual preference, gender identity, and self-identification, including *Kate Bornstein Is a Queer and Pleasant Danger*; *Strangers in Paradox*; *The Opposite Sex Is Neither*; and *Virtually Yours*. Mx Justin Vivian Bond, who starred as Herculine Barbin, the intersexed teacher made famous by Foucault, in *Hidden: A Gender*, adapted Bornstein's short story "Dixie Belle: The Further Adventures of Huckleberry Finn" into a play titled *Christmas Spells* (2008). Featuring the drag-punk ensemble the Pixie Harlots, *Spells* casts Mark Twain's impish hero as a transgendered sex worker named Sassy Sarah in a Storyville brothel. Bond is best known as the gravel-throated geriatric chanteuse Kiki DuRane in the Tony-nominated cabaret duo Kiki and Herb (Kenny Mellman). Honing their act at gender transgressive clubs in San Francisco and New York, Kiki and Herb have thrilled audiences at Carnegie Hall and Broadway. John Cameron Mitchell developed *Hedwig and the Angry Inch* (Jane Street Theater 2000; Broadway's Belasco Theatre 2014), a rock opera about a botched sex reassignment surgery, at SqueezeBox, a punk-drag-sleaze party den, and genderqueer phenoms Vaginal Creme Davis, a multiracial intersex performance artist, and Jibz Cameron, a.k.a. Dynasty Handbag, crafted their personas at equally ambisexual milieus.

"The Great Work Begins"

Theatre is "the queerest art" not simply because it features queer content by queer authors but because it employs deconstructive strategies for exposing the processes by which identities are socially constructed (Solomon and Minwalla 9). Queer performance disrupts conventional ways of seeing and knowing, and for the past sixty years it has been a productive site for the generation, enjoyment, and study of furtive desires. Contemporary lesbian and gay theatre continues to expand the lexicon of sexuality and to amplify society's repertoire of imaginable subject positions. Today's artistic and social actors stage dramatic interventions as a means of expressing suspect longings, as a form of civic protest, and as a medium for imagining, if not living out, alternative ways of being in the world.

Queers have made incredible gains toward decriminalizing and de-pathologizing homosexuality. They have won hard-fought battles for the legalization of sodomy, domestic partner benefits, same-sex marriage, hate crime protections, and the end of the military's ban on openly gay troops. For better or worse, homosexuality is the new normal and gays – at least white, affluent, integrationist-oriented ones – are now America's model minority. As we celebrate hard-fought legal victories, we must recognize that the granting of LGBT liberties has accompanied the erosion of civil liberties for people of color and the passage of repressive legislation concerning women's reproductive health, immigrant rights, and the plight of the working poor. We must acknowledge the ways an increasingly narrow gay agenda, focused almost exclusively on a conservative "family values" platform, has contributed to increased racial animus and an amplification of class disparities. For queers of all stripes, the recently empowered and the yet excluded, performance remains a vital and creative force for personal growth and social change. Though we have made progress in the quest for a more perfect union, our most demanding challenges lie ahead. "The Great Work Begins."

Works Cited

Bernstein, Robin. *Cast Out: Queer Lives in Theater*. Ann Arbor: U of Michigan P, 2006. Print.

Bottoms, Stephen. "Putting the Document into Documentary: An Unwelcome Corrective?" *TDR* 50.3 (2006): 56–68. Print.

Case, Sue-Ellen. "Toward a Butch-Femme Aesthetic." *Making a Spectacle: Feminist Essays on Contemporary Women's Theatre*. Ed. Lynda Hart. Ann Arbor: U of Michigan P, 1989. 282–99. Print.

Davy, Kate. *Lady Dicks and Lesbian Brothers: Staging the Unimaginable at the WOW Café Theatre*. Ann Arbor: U of Michigan P, 2010. Print.

De Jongh, Nicholas. *Not in Front of the Audience: The Making of Gay Theatre*. New York: Routledge, 1992. Print.

Dolan, Jill. *Presence and Desire: Essays on Gender, Sexuality, Performance*. Ann Arbor: U of Michigan P, 1993. Print.

Duberman, Martin. *Stonewall*. New York: Dutton, 1993. Print.

Kauffmann, Stanley. "Homosexual Drama and Its Disguises." *New York Times* 23 Jan. 1966: 93. Print.

Kramer, Larry. *The Normal Heart and The Destiny of Me: Two Plays*. New York: Grove P, 2000. 78. Print.

Kron, Lisa. *Well*. New York: Theatre Communications Group, 2006. Print.

Kushner, Tony. *Angels in America: A Gay Fantasia on National Themes. Part Two: Perestroika*. New York: Theatre Communications Group, 1993. Print.

Marra, Kim, and Robert A. Schanke. *Staging Desire: Queer Readings of American Theater History*. Ann Arbor: U of Michigan P, 2002. Print.

Miller, D.A. *Place for Us: Essay on the Broadway Musical*. Cambridge: Harvard UP, 1998. Print.

Miller, Tim, and David Román. "Preaching to the Converted." *Theatre Journal* 47.2 (1995): 169–88. Print.

Román, David, and Holly Hughes, "*O Solo Homo*: An Introductory Conversation." *O Solo Homo: The New Queer Performance*. Ed. Holly Hughes and David Román. New York: Grove P, 1988. 1–16. Print.

Savran, David. *Communists, Cowboys and Queers: The Politics of Masculinity in the Work of Arthur Miller and Tennessee Williams*. Minneapolis: U of Minnesota P, 1992. Print.

Solanas, Valerie. *Up Your Ass, or From the Cradle to the Boat, or The Big Suck, or Up from the Slime and "A Young Girl's Primer on How to Attain the Leisure Class, a Non-Fictional Article Reprinted from Cavalier."* 1965. New York: SCUM, 1967. Print.

Solomon, Alisa, and Framji Minwalla, eds. *The Queerest Art: Essays on Lesbian and Gay Theater*. New York: New York UP, 2002. Print.

Warner, Sara. *Acts of Gaiety: LGBT Performance and the Politics of Pleasure*. Ann Arbor: U of Michigan P, 2012. Print.

Wolf, Stacy. *A Problem Like Maria: Gender and Sexuality in the American Musical*. Ann Arbor: U of Michigan P, 2002. Print.

34

Contemporary Gay and Lesbian Fiction in English

HUGH STEVENS

The Emergence of Gay and Lesbian Fiction as a Genre

Despite commonly held preconceptions about fiction before Stonewall, a number of British and American novels represented gay and lesbian lives during World War II and in the postwar period. Queer characters became increasingly visible in literary fiction, taking starring roles in novels by a range of writers, including Carson McCullers, Truman Capote, Angus Wilson, James Baldwin, Christopher Isherwood, Jane Rule, and Maureen Duffy.[1] Although academic literary criticism largely ignored contemporary fictional representations of homosexuality, many queer novels were reviewed in leading newspapers, receiving a range of positive and negative responses. And queer-themed pulp fiction sold in enormous numbers, revealing a huge popular demand for fictional representations of gay and lesbian lives. Paperback originals were freer to represent taboo topics than cinema, radio, and reputable hardcover books, and "more than two thousand lesbian-themed mass-market books were published between 1945 and 1970" (Stryker 61), as well as pulp titles dealing with male homosexuality, bisexuality, transvestism, and transsexualism.[2] Scholarly attention to this period has enabled a more nuanced account of gay and lesbian literature since 1970. Michael Bronski's refutation of the "myth that there were few (or no) books about homosexuality before Stonewall," and the "contradictory, but equally strong, myth that all of the pre-Stonewall novels had tragic endings" (11) enables us to see continuities in the development of queer writing across the postwar decades.

From the 1950s, a range of fiction and nonfiction books on queer subjects were available as cheap paperbacks. Paperback originals included sensationalist and lurid tragic tales of doomed homosexual passions, as well as more nuanced representations of lesbian life that showed the difficulties of being a dyke in the big city, usually New York, such as the best-selling *The Beebo Brinker*

Chronicles by Ann Bannon. There were also reprints of classics (marketed as lurid tragic tales in ways that belied their complexity) like Émile Zola's *Nana* (1880) and Radclyffe Hall's *The Well of Loneliness* (1928), and of a range of literary novels, originally published in hardback, which gave more positive or political representations of queer existence, such as Vidal's *The City and the Pillar* (1948) and Patricia Highsmith's *Carol* (first published pseudonymously in 1952 as *The Price of Salt*, by Claire Morgan), a romantic novel that shows a lesbian couple resolving to live together despite difficult circumstances.

After 1970, gay and lesbian fiction has been constituted, somewhat problematically, as a genre (or often as two distinct genres). The identification of genre in relation to the representation of sexuality – as opposed, say, to other thematic concerns such as nationality, race, and class, or formal divisions such as realism, modernism, and postmodernism – is restrictive in some ways, enabling in others. A gay novel can of course also be other kinds of novel – an Irish novel, a historical novel, an African American novel, for instance. The recognition of the genre of queer fiction allows critics and readers to ask a range of questions concerning the representation of queer life, and makes queer lives more visible in our culture. Nevertheless, some novelists who are gay or lesbian have rejected the label of gay and lesbian writing as limiting; others have written novels consciously constructed and marketed as politicized queer fiction, often published by specialist presses. Many writers have given qualified endorsements of the idea of gay and lesbian fiction, cautioning against excessive reliance on it.

When Alan Hollinghurst's *The Line of Beauty* won Britain's 2004 Booker Prize, debates about "gay fiction" circulated in the British press in ways that echoed decades of ambivalence toward the category on the part of queer readers, writers, and critics. In a *Guardian* interview, Hollinghurst was asked how he felt about headlines such as the *Daily Express*'s "Booker Won by Gay Sex" and the *Sun*'s "Gay Book Wins." His reply shrewdly foregrounded the limitations and possibilities of thinking about gay writing as a genre: "I only chafe at the 'gay writer' tag if it's thought to be what is most or only interesting about what I'm writing ... the books ... are actually about all sorts of other things as well – history, class, culture. . . . It's not just, as you would think if you read the headlines in the newspapers, about gay sex" (qtd. in Moss).

One might enlarge on Hollinghurst's position. It isn't surprising that gay and lesbian fiction has often been concerned with sexual questions, but queer novels have never been "just" about sex and sexuality. Their representation of sexuality has been varied and complex, and they cannot be seen as constructing a uniform and consensual position on queer sexual behavior and politics.

Many fiction writers (including Pat Califia, Dennis Cooper, Samuel Delany, and Jane DeLynn) show characters enjoying transgressive sex in urban subcultural spaces, whereas others (Isabel Miller, David Leavitt) show characters with little interest in urban queer scenes. Gay and lesbian fiction since 1970 has concerned itself not only with gay sex, history, class, culture, and the very question of queer identity itself (to what extent does homosexuality constitute an identity?), but also with gay relationships, relationships of queer protagonists with their families, the nature of life in gay and lesbian subcultures, and living with HIV / AIDS. These themes have been explored in relation to a range of explicitly political questions, such as the treatment of queers by the culture at large, as well as debates within queer culture about queer identity, lifestyle, race and ethnicity, and the identification of homosexuality as necessarily dissident, virtually normal, or somewhere in between these pole positions. The development of contemporary queer fiction has paralleled the development of queer cultures, which have enabled the recognition of what Matt, the butch lesbian character central to one of the most important and most accomplished of lesbian novels written before Stonewall, Maureen Duffy's *The Microcosm* (1966), presciently identified as "dozens of ways of being queer" (273). Queer fiction since Stonewall, in its heterogeneity, has reflected the heterogeneity of queer identities, culture, and politics.

If writers were canonized according to what we might call, after Joni Mitchell, the "star-maker machinery" behind the successful literary novel, a machinery that depends on four kinds of celestial identification – sales figures (the reward of the marketplace), book reviews (the approval of the press), literary prizes (the arbitrary seals of approval awarded by distinguished jurors), and academic literary criticism (institutional beatification) – then our canon of gay and lesbian English-language fiction might include Edmund White, Alan Hollinghurst, Jeanette Winterson, Alice Walker, Colm Tóibín, Sarah Waters, and ... who else? One can think of many writers who might get one star – but how many earn two or three? There is no agreed corpus of contemporary queer fiction that can be recognized as the best and most worthy, and readers who are keen to explore contemporary queer fiction will discover that there are as many ways of writing LGBT-themed fiction as there are ways of being queer. The narrator of Edmund White's *The Farewell Symphony* (1997) recalls that many of the many men he had sex with in the late sixties would also tell him "their stories, as though the main pressure behind cruising were narrative rather than sexual.... The silence imposed on homosexuals had finally been broken, and we were all talking at once" (47). Gay and lesbian fiction might be thought of as a large room, or a library, full of such stories, in which case the literary historian's attempt to narrate their history will only be another story, subject to revision and objections. Although mainstream gay and radical queer politics and theory since 1970 have often brought lesbian and gay male concerns together, lesbian and gay male fiction have followed different trajectories, in some ways crossing, in others diverging.

Post-Stonewall Lesbian Fiction

Gay liberation and lesbian feminism enabled the development of a new and radical lesbian fiction, which was not content with telling stories of lesbians accommodating to prejudices and the pressure to remain closeted to society at large, unable to live openly outside an enclosed community. In *The Microcosm*, a large cast of lesbian narrators tells us their stories, all of which show the pressures of living in the "microcosm," namely "the gay world as a universe in little" (286–87). Duffy's novel begins in despair – its opening scene describes the burial of the butch Carol, or Carl, who has gassed herself – and ends in tentative hope. Many of the lesbians in the House of Shades (based on London's most important lesbian club in this period, the Gateway Club, which ran from 1930 to 1985) are butches or femmes, and at the end of the novel Matt (who refers to himself as "he") is wanting to break out of this subcultural world. He rejects the idea that he should continue to live in "the gay world as a universe ... a microcosm if you like," and decides instead that queers should "learn to live in the world," which "should live with us and make use of us, not as scapegoats ... but as who we are" (286–87).

Matt's decision might be seen as typical of a pre-Stonewall political formation – the politics of the homophile movement – in which the task of the lesbian or gay man is to adapt to the world, while working to make the world a more tolerant place.[3] Lesbian feminism and gay liberation, however, rejected liberal agitation in favor of a more radical, transformational politics expressed through revolutionary activism. Lesbian feminists of the early seventies aimed for nothing less than a wholesale remaking of the world, or the creation of a "lesbian nation" apart from the world, a world of "women-identified women."[4]

The emergence of a new radical lesbian fiction, which did not conform to the demands of the mass fiction market, was enabled by the formation of feminist and women's presses in the 1970s and 1980s.[5] New independent presses, including Daughters, Inc., Naiad Press, and Seal Press in the United States, and The Women's Press, Onlywomen Press, and Virago in the United Kingdom, began publishing lesbian writing in a range of genres, including fiction, poetry, and historical and political writing.[6] The highly politicized fiction that emerged from these presses worked in tandem with a range of nonfiction titles appearing in the early 1970s that advanced a radical theory and politics, including Del Martin and Phyllis Lyon's *Lesbian/Woman* (1972), Sydney Abbott and Barbara Love's *Sappho Was a Right-on Woman* (1972), and Karla Jay and Allen Young's *Out of the Closets: Voices of Gay Liberation* (1972). These titles helped form a political consciousness for numerous readers, including remarkable genre-crossing and gender-crossing cartoonist Alison Bechdel, born in 1960. In her graphic memoir *Fun Home: A Family Tragicomic*, Bechdel shows herself devouring these political works at college alongside a range of queer fiction, in an extraordinary reading odyssey that began when she was nineteen. In one of her illustrated memories, she is reading seventy-seven-year-old Elsa's account of her lesbian identity in Nancy and Casey Adair's *Word Is Out: Stories of Some of Our Lives* (1978), a book of interviews of lesbians and gay men who had, Bechdel notes, "completely cast aside their own qualms" about their sexuality (74). Reading titles like these, she recalls, helped her realize that she was a lesbian "in a manner consistent with my bookish upbringing"; this revelation was "not of the flesh, but of the mind" (74). But of course her reading was extracurricular: in the early 1980s, lesbian and gay literature was not part of the university syllabus. In retrospect, she wishes she had called it an "independent reading," noting that "'Contemporary and Historical Perspectives on Homosexuality' would have had quite a legitimate ring" (205).

Lesbian fiction of the 1970s and 1980s is wide-ranging and defies easy classification. The independent presses published serious "literary fiction" alongside innovative genre fiction. Lesbian feminist utopian and science fiction novels by writers such as Joanna Russ (*The Female Man* [1975]) and Sally Gearhart (*The Wanderground* [1978]) began to explore the possibility of separatist female communities.[7] Since the 1980s, many writers have written entertaining and political lesbian crime fiction: these include Barbara Wilson (*Murder in the Collective* [1984]), Mary Wings (*She Came Too Late* [1986], and other novels featuring detective Emma Victor, who investigates crime in lesbian and gay communities in Boston and San Francisco), and Katherine V. Forrest (*Amateur City* [1984] and other Kate Delafield mysteries).[8] The best-selling lesbian novel of the decade, Rita Mae Brown's *Rubyfruit Jungle* – first published by Daughters, Inc in 1973, and subsequently released as a mass market paperback by Bantam in 1977 – is often seen as definitive of fiction of this period. Its coming-of-age narrative of a feisty lesbian protagonist who moves from provincial origins – when the novel opens Molly Bolt is a seven-year-old girl living in "Coffee Hollow, a rural dot outside of York, Pennsylvania" (3) – to the metropolitan destiny of New York's queer community is certainly a prototypical "coming-out" story, but the realist bildungsroman was only one of many kinds of lesbian novel published since 1970.[9] Only a few of the novels from this period portray queer childhoods, and those that have adult lesbian protagonists often tell stories of lesbians who are already out when the novel begins.

In any case, the marketing of fiction as "lesbian fiction" freed the novelist from the requirement making the establishment of the protagonist's queerness an integral part of the narrative. *Sister Gin*, June Arnold's comic novel about a book review editor, Su, radicalizing herself at the age of fifty, is stylishly confident in its representation of lesbian relationships and desires. "Su was [Bettina's] queen of scarves" (4), we are told at the beginning of this novel about a group of (mostly lesbian) genteel women living in Wilmington, North Carolina. Bettina and Su regularly have dinner as a couple with Luz, Bettina's mother, and their friends include seventy-seven-year-old Mamie Carter, lesbian grandmother and vigilante radical (Mamie's bridge-playing friends, under the name of the "Shirley Temple Emeritae," deal out appropriate punishments to Wilmington's rapists). *Sister Gin* does engage with the politics of "coming out": Su comes out to her mother, who responds by thinking that "that word" (lesbian) "isn't a nice word," that "people don't care what you think as long as you don't tell them about it" (82). And Su keeps her job at Wilmington's (ironically named) *Commercial-Appeal* by avoiding reviewing books with lesbian content. But coming out is only one concern in Arnold's stylish novel, alongside aging, menopause, sexual politics, and race relations, and (as the title indicates) the temptation to drink too much gin.

The most challenging of 1970s lesbian novels, Bertha Harris's *Lover* (1976), assembles a fantastical cast of magical women and sets them loose in a genre-bending and gender-bending performance incorporating opera, drama, Hollywood movies, and saints' narratives. *Lover* suggests the modernism of Virginia Woolf (its playful collapsing of the boundaries between fact and fiction, history and invention, biography and novel are reminiscent of *Orlando*) and Djuna Barnes (it shares with *Nightwood* a fascination with the carnivalesque, the burlesque, and popular entertainment such as vaudeville and the circus).[10] It shows as well a sharp and original appropriation of postmodern fiction. Its celebration of lesbian eroticism and love between women and its playful depictions of gender-crossing and drag work paradoxically to "denaturalize" the very sign of lesbian. Its postmodernity, magic realism, and self-reflexiveness show Harris conversant with avant-garde fiction of the sixties and seventies – her narrative innovations bring to mind a range of novelists writing after World War II, including Donald Barthelme, Angela Carter, and Thomas

Pynchon. What makes *Lover* unique is the fun with which it portrays one of its characters, Veronica, as the lesbian novelist within the novel creating the lesbian novel that it is our pleasure to read. *Lover* opens with a synopsis of Richard Strauss's *Der Rosenkavalier*, so "the first thing we see" is the Marschallin in bed with her young man Octavian, "played by a very young woman" (3). It then segues to Saint Lucy, who has gouged out her own eyes, being visited by Saint Agatha (whose breasts, as we learn a few pages later, were cut off when she spurned the advances of Quintian). Agatha tells Lucy (in one of many erotically charged encounters between female saints in the novel): "Thou art light" (5). The next fluid move is to the births of Samaria, Daisy, and Flynn, three generations of lovers, and then Veronica, the novel's novelist and forger of Old Masters, whose lover gives her "an old silver cigarette case, with the initials *BH* engraved in one corner of the lid" (6). The novel collages together fragments in a manner that is at first bewildering as the reader negotiates switches from third-person narration to a range of first-person segments with different narrators, sometimes identifiable as one of the novel's characters, and sometimes anonymous. One of the narrators, the novel teases, might be Bertha Harris herself, whose identity often seems indistinguishable from that of Veronica, just as "Veronica's veil took the face [of Christ] on itself and afterwards no one could tell which was the real face and which was the face on the veil" (58). But postmodern playfulness does not prevent the novel giving a seductive account of New York lesbian life in the early seventies. In her introduction to the novel, Harris describes it as "the pleasure dome" she imagined for the "intellectually gifted, visionary, creative and sexually subversive women" she had met in the "women's liberation movement" (xx–xxi), and *Lover* inventively merges politics with pleasure, making "the lesbian" visible while also acknowledging (in ways that anticipate 1990s queer theory) the provisional, fragmentary, and performative nature of lesbian identity.

The close interface between fiction and politics has remained visible in some but not all lesbian fiction that has emerged since the 1980s. The most politically engaged lesbian novelist in this period is New Yorker Sarah Schulman, who after many years as a member of ACT UP (the AIDS Coalition To Unleash Power) became a founding member, in 1992, of activist organization Lesbian Avengers.[11] Schulman depicts New York's gay and lesbian subculture – in particular the bars and clubs of the Lower East Side – and the political struggles of the 1980s and 1990s in a range of savvy, witty, and irreverent postmodern novels, which often interact with and deconstruct other genres. Her first novel, *The Sophie Horowitz Story* (1984), parodies the detective novel, with its eponymous heroine, a journalist trying to unravel what has happened to radical lesbian feminists Germaine Covington and Laura Wolfe, who have vanished after robbing a bank. *People in Trouble* (1990) and *Rat Bohemia* (1995) portray the new queer radicalism of 1980s New Yorkers struggling with the ravages of the AIDS epidemic.

The best-known lesbian novelist to emerge in the 1980s, however, is Jeanette Winterson, whose fictions create romantic myths of lesbian desire that aren't explicitly tied to any communitarian politics. Her hugely popular first novel, *Oranges Are Not the Only Fruit* (1985), an autobiographical bildungsroman, portrays a young girl – also called Jeanette – in a working-class Lancashire town realizing her lesbian identity in the most unpromising and hostile family environment. Jeanette's adoptive mother – an Elim Pentecostalist – is convinced that Jeanette, a talented child preacher, has ahead of her a promising career as a missionary, but these plans come up against an insurmountable obstacle when Jeanette falls in love with her friend Melanie. The church does not agree with Jeanette's view that "Melanie is a gift from the Lord, and it would be ungrateful not to appreciate her" (102). The novel is marvelously comic and upbeat, despite its painful depictions of the cruel treatment Jeanette receives at the hands of Pastor Spratt and the church elders. They condemn her as "impure" and "unnatural" and attempt to exorcise her of her lesbian demon (which returns "sevenfold").

The prose of *Oranges*, brimming with echoes of scripture, biblical cadences, and the prophetic utterances of Jeanette's mother, is highly original. The novel creatively interweaves realism based on vivid evocations of events and sharp specification of concrete detail with postmodern fables, many of them based on the Grail legend, paralleling Jeanette's ordeal with Perceval's quest for the "Holy Grail covered with white samite" (161). Winterson's subsequent novels abandon realism for her own original hybrid of postmodernism, magic realism, parody, and fantasy, which makes problematic any straightforward understanding of her fiction as "lesbian." *The Passion* (1987) and *Sexing the Cherry* (1989), with their fantastical characters such as the bisexual, androgynous, cross-dressing Villanelle and the monstrous giantess the Dog Woman, have been read by some critics as lesbian postmodern subversions of the normal and the natural, and criticized by others as evading material and political realities.[12] *Written on the Body* (1993) has proved easier to interpret as a lesbian novel, despite the fact that its narrator is unnamed and never (explicitly) reveals her gender. The love of the "I" of the novel for a married woman, Louise, is figured as a grand romantic passion. While the plot of the novel is (self-consciously) melodramatic, sentimental, and implausible – "I" leaves Louise so that her husband, a leading cancer researcher, can give her the best treatment available – these "Operatic heroics and a tragic end" (187) move "I" to celebrate "the cells, tissues, systems and cavities" of Louise's deteriorating body in a series of erotic and devotional prose poems or arias. Here is "I" singing the praises of Louise's "cavities":

> Let me penetrate you. I am the archaeologist of tombs. I would devote my life to marking your passageways, the entrances and exits of that impressive mausoleum, your body. How tight and secret are the funnels and wells of youth and health. A wriggling finger can hardly detect the start of an ante-chamber, much less push through to the wide aqueous halls that hide womb, gut and brain. (119)

Critics have compared the novel's textual erotics with Monique Wittig's *The Lesbian Body* (1973) and Roland Barthes's *The Lover's Discourse* (1977), as well as with other lesbian novels of rapturous love. "Engulfment is a moment of hypnosis," writes Barthes; here we see Winterson, like Barthes, endlessly sustaining "the discourse of the beloved's absence" (11, 15).

The Erotic City of Gay Male Fiction

More than any other novel of the period between the end of World War II and Stonewall, Vidal's *The City and the Pillar* (1948) anticipates the many gay novels of the late twentieth century that explore gay identity in relation to a gay subculture. The novel gave remarkably candid accounts of what it describes as the "abnormal underworld" of Hollywood, which is "closer to the surface than anywhere else in America," the "homosexual bars" of New Orleans, and the "well-organized homosexual world in New York," which drew "thousands" from "all over the country," where they "had nothing to lose by being free and reasonably open in their behaviour" (67, 82, 152–53). Just as important, the novel's articulation of the significance of coming out of the closet anticipates the politics of the 1970s gay liberation movement. When the novel's hero, Jim Willard, travels from New York, where he enjoys "four or five" sexual encounters a week with the men he meets in gay bars, back to his hometown in Virginia to visit friends and family, he finds himself "impatient of the masquerade" (157, 173). His desire to "come out and tell them what he was and defy them" (173) echoes a striking argument made by his friend Paul Sullivan in a gay bar in New Orleans. Paul argues that homosexuals "must declare ourselves, become known; allow the world to discover this subterranean life of ours which connects kings and farm boys, artists and clerks" (84).[13]

This "subterranean life" surfaced in explicit detail in an explosion of gay fiction that began in the late 1970s. If heterosexuality was associated by gay liberation with the monogamous couple, this new gay fiction showed homo-sexual men enjoying sex with a range of different partners not only in bed-rooms but also in cruising areas, bars, sex clubs, and bathhouses. 1978, often described as a key year for gay fiction, saw the publication of Larry Kramer's *Faggots*, Andrew Holleran's *Dancer from the Dance*, and the first of Armistead Maupin's popular and entertaining *Tales of the City* novels, set in San Francisco. Kramer's novel, a comic satire often criticized for its sensationalism, form-lessness, and wooden writing, is a moralistic attack on gay promiscuity in New York, showing characters with names like Randy Dildough and Jack Humpstone frequenting such locales as the Toilet Bowl and the Everhard Baths. The novel's hero, Fred Lemish, rather implausibly hopes to find his perfect match in this heartless world. *Dancer*, by contrast, offers a rapturous celebration of the same urban ghetto: its men, "bound together by a common love of a certain kind of music, physical beauty, and style," danced with "the ecstasy of saints receiving the stigmata" (38). The beautiful face of its hero, Anthony Malone, glows with "radiant exhilaration" when he dances, which makes others think that he "took speed, when he didn't. It was his joy that there were men who loved other men" (230).

Over the next two decades American gay male fiction transformed itself from a field of isolated figures to a crowded scene.[14] The most comprehensive fictional account of postwar gay history sees gay lives through the lens of an individual, the unnamed protagonist and narrator of Edmund White's trilogy of autobiographical novels, which collectively portray American gay men as a group "oppressed in the fifties, freed in the sixties, exalted in the seventies and wiped out in the eighties" (*Farewell* 405). The fortunes of White's narrator – let's call him "Ed" for ease of reference – are closely related to the trials, tribu-lations, triumphs, and sorrows of the group, even though he spends many years trying not to become a member of it. The boy of *A Boy's Own Story* (1982), growing up in the Midwest in the 1940s and 1950s, is "sunk into a cross-eyed, nose-picking turpitude of shame and self-loathing," is aware of himself as "a sissy" who would flunk any "quiz for masculinity," and is appalled at his own homosexuality because he "never doubted that homosexuality was a sickness" (126, 9, 118). *The Beautiful Room Is Empty* (1988) takes Ed from the mid-fifties, remembered as a time when "[t]he three most heinous crimes known to man were Communism, heroin addiction and homosexuality," and ends with his ambivalent participation in the Stonewall riots, torn between an urge "to be responsible and disperse the crowd peacefully" – a feeling that it is only foolish to protest "[o]ur right to our 'pathetic malady'" – and a "wild exhila-ration" that he sees as a "gleeful counterpart" to rage (7, 182). White's prose in this novel is often gorgeous, ornate, and baroque with the "goldest fili-gree" (150) of a young girl's blond hair illuminated by the evening sun passing through it. But the stories he tells – such as that of his lover Lou, the heroin addict who has damaged his digestive tract by biting through a thermometer and swallowing "all the broken glass and the mercury too" (111), so that when he shoots up he requires a "'high colonic irrigation'" (116) – are appalling in their intensity, shot through with the same "self-hatred" that consumes Ed the undergraduate every time he looks for anonymous sexual encounters in the Student Union toilets (59).

While White's autobiographical fiction explores his childhood and youth, much fiction of the 1980s continues to describe contemporary gay life in urban centers. The exhilaration of *Dancer*, however, was to change utterly with the arrival of the AIDS epidemic. Toward the end of *Nights of Aruba* (1983), Andrew Holleran's second novel, Paul, the main character and narrator of the tale, mentions that "[c]elebrities of our sexual demimonde were dying of bizarre cancers" (232). The "cancer," Paul's friend Mister Friel informs him, "has everyone so frightened now that they won't just sleep with anyone that moves"; Mister Friel is seeing a young man "interested in knowing a person before he sleeps with him. He told me so! He wants to put sex after intimacy, rather than the other way around" (233). It is notable that this early mention in fiction of AIDS (although Holleran does not yet have a name for it) already connects it with anxiety about sexual intimacy. Fictional celebrations of sexual pleasure, nonetheless, proliferated in the 1980s and 1990s, but this same fiction also registered what British author Adam Mars-Jones called "The Changes of Those Terrible Years" (227). These changes are sometimes only hinted at in 1980s fiction. William Beckwith, the protagonist of Alan Hollinghurst's won-derfully assured first novel, *The Swimming-Pool Library* (1988), recalls his erotic adventures in London in 1983; AIDS, nowhere mentioned in the novel, is only the "faint flicker of calamity, like flames around a photograph, something seen out of the corner of the eye" as he enjoys "the last summer of its kind there was ever to be ... my *belle époque*" (3). Will's erotic peregrinations bring him in contact with the elderly Charles Nantwich, and through his friend-ship with Charles he becomes increasingly aware of queer lives of the past. Historical and political awareness temporarily shatter his leisurely pleasure dome, but at the end of the novel he sees "a suntanned young lad in pale blue trunks that I rather liked the look of" (288).

In much gay fiction since the late 1980s, however, the terrible changes are faced directly. Many of the best novels about AIDS contrast life before and after the epidemic. In the third novel of White's trilogy, *The Farewell Symphony*, the beautiful room is crowded with men enjoying the erotic life of post-Stonewall United States, though the novel ends with many of them departing, just as the musicians leave the stage in Haydn's playful symphony that gives the novel its title. The first ten chapters register the wondrous changes in New York's gay scene from 1968 to the end of the 1970s, a period in which Ed believed "that the couple would disappear and be replaced by new, polyvalent molecules of affection or Whitmanesque adhesiveness," in which gay men "wanted sexual friends, loving comrades, multiple husbands in a whole polyandry of desire. Exclusivity was a form of death – worse, old hat" (341, 246). The reader familiar with gay culture and gay fiction will not be surprised that the last, eleventh chapter begins by recalling that "Somebody at my gym became ill" (364), but familiarity makes the ending of White's symphony no less sad or terrifying. The novel is an elegy not just for friends, sexual partners, and lovers, but for a way of life.

Some fiction by novelists who were HIV-positive and died before the introduction of antiretroviral therapies captured the realities of living with AIDS with painful immediacy.[15] British novelist Oscar Moore's *A Matter of Life and Sex* (1991) shows its protagonist, Hugo, continuing to look for sex "even in the jaws of the disease, even as the cities he played in were turning to funeral parlours" (145). That Moore was exploring his own life (he had been HIV-positive since he was twenty-three, and died at the age of thirty-six in 1996) is brilliantly hinted at in the pseudonym under which he first published the novel: Alec F. Moran is an anagram of *roman à clef*. In Christopher Coe's *Such Times*, published in 1993, one year before he died, Timothy's descriptions of his present life – he is writing in the summer of 1992, has recently lost his lover Jasper, and his friend Dominic is seriously ill – are interspersed with memories of his first meeting Jasper eighteen years ago, in New York's Continental Baths, and of the intervening years. Autobiography merges movingly with fiction in David Feinberg's accounts of the adventures of his alter ego B. J. Rosenthal in *Eighty-Sixed* (1989) and *Spontaneous Combustion* (1991). Everyday life is recorded in sharp particularity, as if in a journal. Feinberg and Coe exploit the openness and fluidity of the novel form to write highly politicized yet entertaining biographical fiction, preoccupied with time and mortality. The first part of *Eighty-Sixed*, "1980: Ancient History," shows B. J. enjoying visits to the St. Mark's Baths, and evenings at bars and clubs such as the Flamingo, 12 West, the Stud, and the Spike. The second half of the novel, "1986: Learning How to Cry," moves subtly and chillingly from past-tense to present-tense narration. It opens with a prologue giving statistics of HIV infection in January 1986: "At present there is no cure for AIDS," B. J. tells us, as he calculates the odds that he is infected. In this "age of anxiety," gay men are going to the gym "to keep out of trouble," and intimacy with others has been replaced by time spent "home with the VCR, watching porno, 'Masterbates Theatre'" (201). *Eighty-Sixed* describes a world in which AIDS permeates everyday existence: obituaries proliferate in the gay press, telephone conversations are filled with tales of disease and dying, and the only weapon to ward off despair is mordant humor. In *Spontaneous Combustion*, B. J. tests positive, joins ACT UP, and hopes for "some sort of cure in the future" (80). An appendix to the novel imagines "hundreds of thousands of ecstatic fags and dykes" celebrating the cure for AIDS, but doesn't tell us if B. J. has survived to join them (223). B. J.'s creator died on November 2, 1994, aged thirty-seven.

Fiction after Queer Radicalism

"Saffron said she would buy the flowers herself. Anything to get away from Mummy and Meredith." The novel with a young straight but queer Goth protagonist, her piercings and tats disapproved of by her suburban Tory lesbian parents (married, of course), hasn't quite been written: the so-called mainstreaming of gay and lesbian identities has been conspicuous in its absence in recent gay and lesbian fiction. But in Michael Cunningham's Pulitzer Prize-winning novel *The Hours* (1998), Clarissa Vaughan regrets "the lovely little black dress she can't buy for her daughter because Julia is in thrall to a queer theorist and insists on T-shirts and combat boots" (21). This "almost scandalously privileged" lesbian mother struggles to get on with her daughter's friend Mary, who also wears butch boots and hates shopping as "such a waste of time" (10, 159). Although queer fiction isn't overpopulated by same-sex couples with children, in many gay and lesbian novels written in the past few decades, by writers like Cunningham and David Leavitt, homosexuality and familial life are by no means antithetical.

In many recent gay and lesbian novels, the lines connecting queer identity and radical politics are occasionally redrawn, and at times are missing altogether. Queer identities are accommodated in a world more tolerant than that portrayed in radical fiction of the post-Stonewall period. Colm Tóibín's *The Blackwater Lightship* (1999), with its cast of three women (grandmother, mother, and daughter Helen), and three men (Helen's brother Declan, and his gay friends Larry and Paul), all trying to look after Declan, who is dying of AIDS, confronts familial and provincial Ireland with the confident and sad energies of the queer metropolis. The scene queens in Alan Hollinghurst's comic novel *The Spell* (1998), on the other hand, live in an almost hermetically sealed gay male world, although Robin once knew a woman named Jane who provided him with a son, young Danny, whose love of casual sex and drugs and clubs doesn't prevent him becoming amorously entangled with Alex, the ex of his father's younger lover Justin. Justin, an unemployed actor who doesn't lack financial resources, likes shopping. One hot summer afternoon he takes a taxi from Harvey Nichols to Issey Miyake, where he spends more than £3,000 on a suit and shirt, then returns to the Musgrove Hotel, where he pays "large vague sums of money" to be urinated on by Carlo the "Italian hunk," a rent boy whose size is twenty-five, "in centimetri, of course" (194). Other things happen as well in this novel, which is ironic, perhaps, in its portrayal of wealthy homosexuals discriminating among the pleasures of alcohol, ecstasy, cocaine, and marijuana. But if their behavior is at times mildly transgressive, no one seems to mind, although Justin gets in a tiff when he finds his lover Robin has paid for sex with Terry, an odd job man always on the lookout for opportunities. Justin expresses his displeasure by placing some of Terry's bent black pubic hairs on the breakfast plates, then wonders if the plates are by Lucy Rie, and how much Robin paid for them.

The Spell was less than ecstatically received. Hollinghurst's next novel, *The Line of Beauty* (2004), returns to the 1980s of *The Swimming-Pool Library*, but the decade has become a site of memory. Recalling many earlier novels about AIDS, it takes its hero Nick Guest through the 1980s, and remembers the hypocrisies of a homophobic Conservative government presided over by Margaret Thatcher. Hollinghurst's turn to the past is emblematic of the rise of the historical novel as a new dominant genre in lesbian and gay fiction: his most recent novel, *The Stranger's Child* (2011), is a historical saga stretching from 1913 to 2008.

Many realist novels imagining queer lives in the past have appeared since Sarah Waters's first novel, *Tipping the Velvet* (1998), thrillingly imagined lesbian experience in the sexual underworld of Victorian London. The picaresque adventures of heroine Nan Astley, who reinvents herself first as male impersonator Nan King, a star of the Victorian music halls, and then makes money as a rent boy, sharing the streets with London's "Mary-Anns," breathed new life into a genre perceived as fusty. More recently Edmund White (*Hotel de Dream* [2007]), Colm Tóibín (*The Master* [2004]), and Emma Donoghue (*The Sealed Letter* [2008]) have all set novels in the nineteenth century, reflecting our abiding interest in Victorian lesbian and gay subcultures, and Jamie O'Neill's *At Swim, Two Boys* (2001) shows two adolescents in love in Dublin in the period leading up to the 1916 Easter Rising. Two important precursors to these historical novels are Isabel Miller's *Patience and Sarah* (1969), about two women living together on a farm in nineteenth-century New England, and Mark Merlis's *American Studies* (1994), based on the life of literary critic F. O. Matthiessen, who committed suicide in 1950.

Unlike Winterson's postmodernist *The Passion* and *Sexing the Cherry*, these novels recreate particular periods in great detail, and while they do not pretend to be objective historical documents, their verisimilitude and coherence allow the reader to imagine queer identities and desires in a time when same-sex love was still the love that dared not speak its name. Victorian fiction's shy allusions to queer criminality are supplemented by recent fiction's free representations of the "other Victorians" who populated the queer underworld of nineteenth-century London and New York. Nineteenth-century writing about queer subcultures was privately published and circulated. On the other hand, both *Tipping the Velvet* – complete with lesbian dildoes and aristocratic orgies – and Waters's *Fingersmith* (2002), a lesbian reworking of Victorian sensation fiction, became popular BBC television dramas. This popularity is not surprising. Although the queer historical novel is always implicitly political, its primary impulse is to tell exciting, emotionally complex stories, in which dramatic tension depends on the criminal status of the sexual underground, the coded and furtive nature of queer double lives.

Notes

1. See, for example, McCullers, *Reflections in a Golden Eye* (1941); Capote, *Other Voices, Other Rooms* (1948); Wilson, *Hemlock and After* (1952); Baldwin, *Giovanni's Room* (1956); Isherwood, *A Single Man* (1964); Rule, *Desert of the Heart* (1964); Duffy, *The Microcosm* (1966).
2. Stryker and Bronski give useful overviews of the paperback market's representation of queer lives in postwar America.
3. For an excellent reading of *The Microcosm*, and an account of how Duffy "incurred the almost universal opprobrium of key figures" in American lesbian literary circles of the 1970s, see Smith 144–55.
4. See "The Woman-Identified Woman," an influential 1970 radical lesbian manifesto, in Jay and Young 172–77.
5. See Pollack and Knight for essays on American lesbian novelists of this period. The best monograph on lesbian fiction in the two decades after Stonewall is Zimmerman's.
6. Murray gives a full account of how the women's presses promoted "writing by women from minority groups marginalised by early second-wave feminism: black women, women from ethnic minorities, working-class women, lesbians and disabled women" (73).

7. See Zimmerman 143–63 and Andermahr for analyses of lesbian utopian and science fiction.

8. For a full overview of lesbian and gay male detective fiction, see Markowitz.

9. Although *Rubyfruit Jungle* was the best-selling novel of the 1970s, gay and lesbian critics have been unenthusiastic about its political and literary merits. See Emery 105–26 for a critical discussion of the novel's politics.

10. For an account of the novel's "erotics of reading" in relation to Barnes, see Allen 1–10.

11. Schulman's essays on lesbian and gay politics, on the AIDS crisis, and excerpts from the Lesbian Avengers Handbook are collected in *My American History*.

12. Makinen, with her summaries of the extensive critical writing on eight of Winterson's novels, traces debates about the relationship between lesbianism and postmodernism in Winterson's fiction.

13. All citations are from the 1950 Bantam paperback edition of the novel, an abridgement of the 1948 first edition. Vidal cut out much of the most interesting political material when he revised it for publication (as *The City and the Pillar Revised*) in 1965. Current editions follow the less interesting 1965 text.

14. See Nelson for short essays, with bibliographies, on American gay novelists; for critical accounts of post-Stonewall fiction see McRuer, Woodhouse, Brookes, and Davidson.

15. See Canning, as well as Dean and Ruszczycky in this volume, for surveys of AIDS literature and critical writing about AIDS.

Works Cited

Allen, Carolyn. *Following Djuna: Women Lovers and the Erotics of Loss*. Bloomington: Indiana UP, 1996. Print.

Andermahr, Sonya. "The Politics of Separatism and Lesbian Utopian Fiction." *New Lesbian Criticism: Literary and Cultural Readings*. Ed. Sally Munt. New York: Harvester, 1992. 133–52. Print.

Arnold, June. *Sister Gin*. 1975. New York: Feminist P, 1989. Print.

Barthes, Roland. *A Lover's Discourse: Fragments*. 1977. New York: Hill, 1978. Print.

Bechdel, Alison. *Fun Home: A Family Tragicomic*. London: Jonathan Cape, 2006. Print.

Bronski, Michael, ed. *Pulp Friction: Uncovering the Golden Age of Gay Male Pulps*. New York: St. Martin's, 2003. Print.

Brookes, Les. *Gay Male Fiction since Stonewall: Ideology, Conflict, and Aesthetics*. New York: Routledge, 2009. Print.

Brown, Rita Mae. *Rubyfruit Jungle*. 1973. New York: Bantam, 1977. Print.

Canning, Richard. "The Literature of AIDS." *The Cambridge Companion to Gay and Lesbian Writing*. Ed. Hugh Stevens. Cambridge: Cambridge UP, 2011. 132–47. Print.

Cunningham, Michael. *The Hours*. 1998. London: Fourth Estate, 1999. Print.

Davidson, Guy. *Queer Commodities: Contemporary US Fiction, Consumer Capitalism, and Gay and Lesbian Subcultures*. New York: Palgrave, 2012. Print.

Duffy, Maureen. *The Microcosm*. 1966. London: Virago, 1989. Print.

Emery, Kim. *The Lesbian Index: Pragmatism and Lesbian Subjectivity in the Twentieth-Century United States*. Albany: State U of New York P, 2002. Print.

Feinberg, David. *Eighty-Sixed*. New York: Penguin, 1989. Print.

Spontaneous Combustion. New York: Penguin, 1991. Print.

Harris, Bertha. *Lover*. 1976. New York: New York UP, 1993. Print.

Holleran, Andrew. *Dancer from the Dance*. 1978. New York: Plume, 1986. Print.

Nights in Aruba. 1983. New York: Plume, 1984. Print.

Hollinghurst, Alan. *The Swimming-Pool Library*. London: Chatto, 1988. Print.

The Spell. London: Chatto, 1998. Print.

The Line of Beauty. London: Picador, 2004. Print.

Jay, Karla, and Allen Young, eds. *Out of the Closets: Voices of Gay Liberation*. 1972. Twentieth anniversary ed. New York: New York UP, 1992. Print.

Makinen, Merja. *The Novels of Jeanette Winterson*. Houndmills: Palgrave, 2005. Print.

Markowitz, Judith A. *The Gay Detective Novel: Lesbian and Gay Main Characters and Themes in Mystery Fiction*. Jefferson: McFarland, 2004. Print.

Mars-Jones, Adam. *Monopolies of Loss*. London: Faber, 1992. Print.

McRuer, Robert. *The Queer Renaissance: Contemporary American Literature and the Reinvention of Lesbian and Gay Identities*. New York: New York UP, 1997. Print.

Moore, Oscar. *A Matter of Life and Sex*. 1991. London: Penguin, 1992. Print.

Moss, Stephen. "I don't make moral judgements." *The Guardian*. 20 October 2004. Web. 15 Nov. 2012.

Murray, Simone. *Mixed Media: Feminist Presses and Publishing Politics*. London: Pluto, 2004. Print.

Nelson, Emmanuel S., ed. *Contemporary Gay American Novelists: A Bio-Bibliographical Critical Sourcebook*. Westport: Greenwood P, 1993. Print.

Pollack, Sandra, and Denise D. Knight, eds. *Contemporary Lesbian Writers of the United States: A Bio-Bibliographical Critical Sourcebook*. Westport: Greenwood P, 1993. Print.

Schulman, Sarah. *My American History: Lesbian and Gay Life during the Reagan/Bush Years*. New York: Routledge, 1994. Print.

Smith, Patricia Juliana. *Lesbian Panic: Homoeroticism in British Women's Fiction*. New York: Columbia UP, 1997. Print.

Stryker, Susan. *Queer Pulp: Perverted Passions from the Golden Age of the Paperback*. San Francisco: Chronicle, 2001. Print.

Vidal, Gore. *The City and the Pillar*. 1948. New York: Bantam, 1950. Print.

White, Edmund. *The Beautiful Room Is Empty*. London: Picador, 1988. Print.

A Boy's Own Story. 1982. London: Picador, 1983. Print.

The Farewell Symphony. 1997. New York: Vintage, 1998. Print.

Winterson, Jeanette. *Oranges Are Not the Only Fruit*. 1985. London: Vintage, 1991. Print.

Written on the Body. 1992. London: Vintage, 1993. Print.

Woodhouse, Reed. *Unlimited Embrace: A Canon of Gay Fiction, 1945–1995*. Amherst: U of Massachusetts P, 1998. Print.

Zimmerman, Bonnie. *The Safe Sea of Women: Lesbian Fiction 1969–1989*. Boston: Beacon P, 1990. Print.

35

Autobiography

DAVID BERGMAN

Beginnings

The first explicitly same-sex autobiographies published in English appeared as case studies in Havelock Ellis's *Sexual Inversion* (1897), a groundbreaking medical book. Often Ellis would summarize these case studies, but it is significant how he would also let these men and women speak for themselves, reprinting their communications in full. If autobiography in general began as religious confession, queer autobiography began as medical evidence. Even in French, among the earliest examples, Herculine Barbin's memoir was published as part of *Question médico-légale de l'identité* (1872). On the one hand, these works are written for outsiders to arouse sympathy and understanding from heterosexuals; on the other hand, they are written for insiders to lift the spirits of fellow "sufferers." Consequently, queer autobiography often changes rhetorical stances to accommodate these two different audiences. I want to distinguish these queer autobiographies from a work such as Gertrude Stein's *Autobiography of Alice B. Toklas* (1933). Stein neither addresses her sexuality nor allows the reader to become an insider to the text. Like Ellis's gallery of portraits, Stein allows no formula to stereotype her subjects. The very nature of chapters such as this one tends to flatten differences and force similarities. I hope by the number of titles mentioned and the various subgenres represented to minimize the flattening.

One can see the rhetorical tensions of straight and gay audiences played out in the earliest American same-sex autobiographies. The title page of Claude Hartland's *The Story of a Life* (1901) announces that it is "[f]or the consideration of the Medical Fraternity," but the preface indicates that it was "a means by which similar sufferers may be reached and relieved" (n.pag.). Hartland is careful to present himself as a comforting figure, both victim of psychic and social forces beyond his control and survivor, who has retained his moral and emotional bearings. Mary Casal's *The Stone Wall* (1930), perhaps the earliest lesbian autobiography in America, was also intended for both heterosexual and lesbian readers. Unlike Hartland, Casal does not ask for help from the medical profession (or from anyone) to cure her homosexuality, rather she believes that the relation between women "is the highest and most complete union of two human beings" (165). The lesson she wishes to teach (and she was a schoolmistress) is the need to understand troubled youngsters who suffer from sexual repression. Children must not be frightened about sex; their desires must be treated with gentleness.

Journals and Diaries

Because early gay and lesbian memoir (and I shall use the terms *autobiography* and *memoir* interchangeably) is shaped by the need to justify and defend homosexuals, they are less useful in giving a picture of the lives of gay men and lesbians than their journals. To be sure, journals often obscure or transform events to suit their authors, but because they are written over long periods, they are less likely to be shaped by overarching concerns. Among the most astonishing documents is Anne Lister's journal, which runs four million words. Lister (1791–1840) was born into a wealthy, Yorkshire landowning family. Unlike Jane Austen, with whom she is roughly contemporary, she inherited the family estate, Shibden Hall, which left her time to seduce, with surprising luck, various women of the neighborhood and pen her diary, whose erotic portion she rendered in a code of her own devising.

Yet another remarkable document is the diary published as *Jeb and Dash*. Ina Russell, the editor, went to great lengths to disguises the names of her uncle Carter Newman Bealer (Jeb) and his longtime friend Isham W. Perkins (Dash), even though they were dead for nearly thirty years. What makes this diary particularly interesting is that, unlike most of the journals that have survived, *Jeb and Dash* is not by a famous person or literary figure. Bealer was a low-level clerk in a government office who for long stretches lived in the YMCA. He presents the life of the average gay Washingtonian.

The same cannot be said of Christopher Isherwood (1904–86), whose diaries start in 1939, and so far run to four long volumes and host a panoply of Hollywood celebrities and cultural figures. They cover much of the same territory as his novels and memoirs, combining an exuberant sex life with artistic striving and spiritual commitment. An even earlier and more detailed journal is by Claude Fredericks (1923–2012), who counted Anaïs Nin, May Sarton, and James Merrill among his friends. His journal begins in 1932 and takes forty-three hundred pages to get only as far as 1943. Fredericks continues writing in his journal until his death, and it gives the most detailed account of a gay man's life that we have. Through its pages, we discover a gay underground in Springfield, Missouri in the late 1930s, and the rather open romancing of Harvard undergraduates in the early forties. British painter Keith Vaughn died with his pen in his hand in the midst of writing an entry. Donald Vining (1917–98) published five volumes of A Gay Diary (1979–93), which starts in the mid-thirties and presents the lives of gay men at the fringe of Broadway. Perhaps the most renowned diarist is composer Ned Rorem (1923–). Tart, unsparing, and explicit, Rorem's diaries – collected in many volumes – were shocking to readers in 1966 when they began to be published. Adding to the shock was that he wrote about events only ten years in the past and about people still alive. One of Rorem's lovers was bisexual novelist, poet, playwright, and essayist Paul Goodman (1911–72), whose own journal Five Years (1966) remains a fascinating work. Fredericks, Vaughn, Vining, Rorem, and Goodman all saw their journals into print. Their diaries were never meant to be secret.

Death sometimes ends the hide-and-seek element in people's lives. Susan Sontag (1933–2004), for instance, refused to acknowledge her lesbianism during her life although the truth was widely known. Only after her death did her son, David Reiff, publish Reborn (2008), her journals and notebooks from the years 1947–63, which show that the most sophisticated intellectuals can produce emotional lives as messy as anyone's. Among the finest journals are those of May Sarton (1912–95), and they may be of more lasting significance than her novels and poetry. Her first Journal of a Solitude (1973), written when she was already sixty, reduces the beloved's name to a letter – Sarton is not completely open about being a lesbian – but the context makes it clear that the beloved is a woman. Journal of a Solitude was followed by five more volumes that are quietly unflinching in their observation and self-assessment. Doris Grumbach's diaries also should be mentioned for their warmth and wisdom though they, too, are less than explicit.

Gay Liberation

From the late sixties through the 1970s, a number of autobiographies appeared that either advanced or were made possible by the gay liberation movement. Perhaps the finest gay autobiography written is J.R. Ackerley's My Father and Myself (1968), which juxtaposes Ackerley's life as a gay man with the no-less-unconventional life of his father, who kept a secret second family as well as, perhaps, a history of having been a male prostitute. Tennessee Williams's Memoirs (1975) was met with harsh critical reactions because of its explicitness.

One critic wrote, "if he has not exactly opened his heart, he has opened his fly" (qtd. in Hale 253). Williams saw himself within the gay liberation movement, which he calls a "serious crusade to assert ... a free position in society" (50). The most famous of these gay liberation period autobiographies was Quentin Crisp's *The Naked Civil Servant* (1968). Crisp (1908–99) decided early in life to appear unabashedly as he was – a homosexual. He was a one-man liberation army *avant la lettre*.

A number of men directly involved in the gay liberation movement wrote memoirs. *I Have More Fun with You than Anyone* (1972) and *Roommates Can't Always Be Lovers* (1974) by Lige Clark (1942–75) and Jack Nichols (1938–2005) articulate the early gay liberationist belief that meaningful relations cannot be drawn from the marriage model. Clark was murdered in Mexico while in his thirties; Nichols had a distinguished career as a journalist. Arthur Bell (1939–84) wrote a lively early account of the Gay Activist Alliance (GAA) in *Dancing the Gay Lib Blues* (1971). Arnie Kantrowitz (1940–) describes how his closeted life was changed by the GAA in *Under the Rainbow* (1977). Perhaps the most popular autobiography of the period, a book that has been in print ever since, is *The Best Little Boy in the World* (1973) by Andrew Tobias (1947–) under the name of John Reid. The book, written in "the breezy but informed approach that has become his trademark" (v), is about a highly neurotic and lustful student who is both hampered and energized by the need to compensate for being gay by achieving everything else his parents wanted of him. Two autobiographies from religious figures were also of significance. In *The Lord Is My Shepherd & He Knows I'm Gay*, Reverend Troy D. Perry, the founder of the Metropolitan Community Church, articulates how Christianity – even evangelical Christianity – can be joined with homosexuality. Malcolm Boyd (1923–), who had become famous for his work in civil rights, published *Take off the Masks* (1978).

Only a dozen years separate the Stonewall riots in 1969, the symbolic beginning of the gay revolution, and the first announcements of what would become AIDS, but there have been a number of chroniclers of that generation. Felice Picano (1946–) is one of the most assiduous, producing a tetralogy of memoirs, starting with *Ambidextrous* (1985) that begins with him at eleven and concluding with *Art & Sex in Greenwich Village* (2007), when he is a successful writer and publisher. Michael Rumaker (1932–), who was educated at Black Mountain, wrote a controversial book in its time, *A Day and a Night at the Baths* (1979), celebrating the exercise of sexual freedom. Here we may place the work of Edmund White (1940–), the most famous author of this generation of gay writers. Much of his fiction is autobiographical, but his two memoirs are particularly fine. *City Boy* (2009) is a chronological account of gay life in New York during the sixties and seventies. *My Lives* (2005) covers his childhood through his sixties in such chapters as "My Blonds" and "My Hustlers."

AIDS Memoirs

The AIDS epidemic has produced some of the finest writing by both men and women. Rebecca Brown wrote *The Gift of the Body*, an extraordinary fictional memoir of her experiences as an AIDS healthcare worker, told with a tenderness increased by its linguistic restraint. Mark Doty (1953–) has written lyrically and with great psychological precision a remarkable account of the death of his partner Wally Roberts, *Heaven's Coast* (1996). Both Brown and Doty write of AIDS from the point of view of those who had not contracted the disease. Those stricken with AIDS wrote with an understandable urgency and anger. One of the finest works of this period is *Close to the Knives: A Memoir of Disintegration* (1991) by David Wojnarowicz (1954–92), who was also a painter, photographer, and performance artist. Wojnarowicz's father terrorized his family, throwing them down until blood flowed from their ears (152). At sixteen, he escaped to hustle on the street. But it was AIDS that alerted him to the political dimensions of suffering. *Before Night Falls* (1993) by Reinaldo Arenas (1943–90) tells how an escape from Castro's Cuba ends in tragedy in New York. Perhaps the best-known work on AIDS is Paul Monette's *Borrowed Time* (1988). At first Monette (1945–95), a successful writer, shares a privileged, glamorous life in Los Angeles with his partner, Roger Horwitz (1941–86), a highly successful Hollywood lawyer. But soon Horwitz gets ill, and Monette discovers that he also is infected with HIV. The disease tests their love for one another. Hervé Guibert created a furor in France with his memoir *To The Friend Who Did Not Save My Life* (1990) with its indictment of Michel Foucault. By far the angriest (and the funniest) memoirs of AIDS are by David B. Feinberg (1956–94). Feinberg was a dedicated member of the direct action group ACT UP, and he gives witness to the terrible changes in the lives of the gay community. Since the advances in AIDS treatment, there have been fewer AIDS memoirs, but two deserve note. Douglas Wright (1956–), a New Zealand dancer and choreographer, has written *Ghost Dance* (2004) and *Terra Incognito* (2006) that record a life in extended time.

African American men are disproportionally affected by HIV / AIDS, but they have left relatively few accounts. Archbishop Carl Bean (1944–) devotes a good portion of his memoir *I Was Born This Way* (2010) to founding the Minority AIDS Project (MAP) that cares especially for people of color. Another noteworthy example is Gary Fisher, whose diary, filled with sadomasochistic encounters, registers the anger, frustration, and despair of an educated black man stricken with a terminal disease. Glenn Burke's autobiography *Out at Home* (1995) is more about his promising career in the major leagues where he played for the LA Dodgers under famed coach Tommy Lasorda. But when Burke (1952–95) started palling around with Spunky Lasorda, Tommy's rather flamboyantly gay son, he was abruptly traded. His career ruined, Burke drinks heavily, takes drugs, contracts AIDS, and finds himself for short periods living on the street. Burke's faith, however, remains. "I'll soon be in Heaven with the Lord," he writes, "And I'll be rejoining so many of my friends" (117).

Military Memoirs

Lesbian and gay autobiographies are written from or about social institutions to which queers have been placed or denied admission. The subgenres of gay and lesbian memoir are often defined by these social institutions and cultural practices. For example, queers have often been assigned to medical institutions and prisons; their memoirs are often about freeing themselves from such places. Other memoirs about professional athletics or the military are about returning to places from which they have been rejected or reconciling themselves to their exclusion.

Before the recent change in policy (September 2011), the military was one of the major institutions from which queer people were barred. Time will tell whether this subgenre will disappear now that homosexuals are allowed in the military. Joseph Steffan (1964–) tells in *Honor Bound* (1992) of being denied both a degree and a commission in the Navy when just before graduation as a top midshipman from the Naval Academy in Annapolis, he announced that he was homosexual. One of the most moving testimonies is Margarethe Cammermeyer's *Serving in Silence* (1994), which was made into a motion picture. With more than a quarter of a century of service, Cammermeyer (1942–) was a much honored Vietnam veteran and on her way to being Chief Nurse of the National Guard, for which she needed top secret clearance. When asked about her sexual orientation, she answered honestly, and her honesty brought the end of her military career. Don't Ask/Don't Tell and the various Middle East wars have also brought accounts by Reichen Lehmkuhl, Bronson Lemur, and Jeffrey McCowen.

There are very few gay memoirs of World War II, but one of the most extraordinary is *The Cage* (1949), an account of life in an Italian prisoner of war camp and published remarkably in the forties. Written by Dan Billany and

David Dowie, it tells of Billany's passionate attachment to Dowie. The two escaped from the prison and finished the book while hiding in a farmhouse whose owner, true to his word, sent the manuscript as promised to Billany's family after the war. Unfortunately, Billany and Dowie, after leaving the farmhouse, were never seen again. Myles Hildyard's *It Is Bliss Here* (2005) is a rare combination of letters and journals from a war hero. James Lord's *My Queer War* (2010) was published posthumously.

Prison Memoirs

With changes in the law, we forget how frequently prisons were a specter of queer memoir. In fact, the entire genre of gay autobiography may be said to have sprung from Oscar Wilde's *De Profundis* (1905), his letter from Reading Gaol, where he was sent after his conviction for committing acts of "gross indecency." *De Profundis* is more a spiritual autobiography than a narrative of specific events. To get a sense of how men were treated in England after being found guilty of homosexuality, one should read Peter Wildeblood's *Against the Law* or Rupert Croft-Cook's *A Verdict of You All*, both published in 1955. In fact, Wildeblood's case spurred the creation of the Wolfenden Committee, whose report in 1957 recommended to Parliament the abolition of laws criminalizing sex between consenting adults.

The prison has been the site of two of the most brilliantly written books. The most famous is Jean Genet's *A Thief's Journal* (1964), which, like all of Genet's work, records not only his love for crime, but for "the handsomest criminals" (12). It takes place not in prison for the most part, but the penitentiary hovers above the action, casting its long shadow. Less known but extraordinarily well written is James Blake's *The Joint* (1971), a collection of letters written between 1951 and 1964. Blake was hailed as a writer by such figures as Nelson Algren, Simone de Beauvoir, and Jean Paul Sartre, who translated some of his work into French. Like *A Thief's Journal*, *The Joint* is a love story in which Blake, a pianist, meets Dan, an ostensibly heterosexual drummer, in prison. Dan protects Blake as his "boy," a role Blake assumed with other men. Blake gets Dan off of drugs; Dan pushes Blake as a musician. But out of jail, their relationship falls apart. Despite their efforts to keep free of prison, they both return, although separated, behind bars.

A third, more recent book is worth noting, J.T. Parsell's *Fish: A Memoir of a Boy in a Man's Prison* (2006). At seventeen, Tim Parsell (1960–) goes to prison, where he is immediately raped. He finds "protection" from Slip Slide, a ruthless drug dealer, but gentle and affectionate lover. *Fish* does an excellent job of presenting the pecking order of prison. According to the prison system, Tim is neither a drag queen nor a "man." He cannot be *gay*, because it is a category unrecognized in the prison system. He can only be a *boy*, and as such, he is required to service men sexually.

Women are less likely than men to be placed in prison, and there are very few first-person accounts of their lives behind bars. An exception is *Grace after Midnight* (2007) by Felicia "Snoop" Pearson, who achieved some fame as the transgender enforcer in the television series *The Wire*. With a crack-addicted mother and no father, she is placed in a foster family as an infant. She found mentors in two men who dealt drugs. But none of these protectors could save her from rape and violence. As she writes, "Death lived on our street" (35). At thirteen she murdered a woman and was sentenced to ten years in prison.

Holocaust Narratives

Even the grimmest prison, however, cannot compete with the horror of Nazi concentration camps. The earliest of these accounts is Heinz Heger's *The Men with the Pink Triangle* (1980). From a well-to-do Viennese family, Heger (1917–94) fell in love with "Fred," who unfortunately was the son of a high-ranking Nazi official. Fred's father sent Heger first to prison and then to concentration camp. A more searing account is *I, Pierre Seel, Deported Homosexual* (1994). Seel (1923–2005) was only seventeen when he was sent to the camp in Schirmech-Vorbrück for rehabilitation. He was experimented on and starved. But the worst punishment, which caused him to wake up fifty years later "howling in the middle of the night," was watching his lover, whom he hoped had escaped capture, being dragged into the middle of the camp, stripped naked, a tin pail placed over his head, and attacked by guard dogs who "first bit into his groin and thighs, then devoured him right in front of us" (43).

Gad Beck (1923– 2012), a gay Jew, escaped the concentration camps by disappearing into Berlin. His memoir, *An Underground Life* (2000), is a remarkable account distinguished by Beck's exuberance. Not only does Beck go underground but he takes care of others hiding in Berlin. Beck finds places for them to stay, gets them food, and brings them mail. And despite all of his work, he still has time for lots of sex. Although Beck was old when he wrote the memoir, the book sparkles with a teenager's delight in getting away scot free right under the enemy's nose.

What is astounding is that all these narratives end in hope. Gays were to be excluded from the military, worked to death in concentration camps, and forced to perform as sex workers in prisons. Yet these are fundamentally tales of survival. The authors, with the exception of James Blake, are writing from outside the institutions to which they have been confined or with hopes of reentering the one from which they have been excluded. Of course, for the most part, it is the survivors who get to write autobiographies just as history is written by the victors.

Sport Memoirs

One of the most contested cultural places for queer folk is the sports arena. They generally express pride in having found a way into a world that would exclude them. Dying of AIDS, Glenn Burke (1952–95) ends *Out at Home* (1995) not with anger or self-recrimination, but with a joke. After saying he has no regrets, he admits to one: "I should have been a basketball player!" (117). Esera Tuaolo (1968–), a nose guard for the Green Bay Packers, is raped as a child, has difficulty in school, and for long periods is separated from his family. Yet his autobiography *Alone in the Trenches* (206) ends with falling in love and adopting two children.

There are exceptions, of course. Roy Simmons's *Out of Bounds* is a terrifying picture of self-destruction. Like Burke, Simmons (1956–2014) is African American and grew up in a fatherless home. But Simmons suffered much more trauma. He was raped repeatedly by his next-door neighbor. As a college football star, he began drinking heavily and living a double life because if "the stigma of homosexuality among young black men is three to four times greater than it is for young white men," how much greater it must be for black football players (68). By the time he reaches the NFL, his partying is out of control. He goes to prison, spends time on the street, and contracts AIDS. "You cry out for help in all the wrong ways when the words won't come out right," he confesses at the end of the book and apologizes to a host of those he let down.

Other gay athletes who have written about their lives include diver Greg Louganis in *Breaking the Surface* (1995); Dave Kopay (1942–), a football player, in *The Dave Kopay Story* (1977); Billy Bean, a baseball player, in *Going the Other Way* (2003); and John Amaechi, the black English basketball player in *Man in the Middle* (2007). But among the earliest gay sports memoirs is Martina Navratilova's *Martina* (1985). Writing at the height of her fame, Navratilova seems less disturbed by being bisexual than by her difficulties focusing on tennis. "I'm not a one-sex person, and yet I hate the term *bisexual*. It sounds creepy to me, and I don't think I'm creepy – There are times when I feel downright romantic" (173). Twenty-five years ago these were daring words, especially from one of the world's finest tennis players.

One of Navratilova's best moves was hiring Renée Richards, a male-to-female (MTF) transsexual, as her coach. Renée Richards has written two autobiographies: *Second Serve: The Renée Richards Story* (1983) and *No Way Renée* (2007). The first is penned in the heat of controversy, the second in the quiet of a life richly experienced. They are unlike any transgender autobiography because Richards fought in three spheres: as a patient, as a physician, and as a tennis player. Only someone with extreme needs would have dared to confront such obstacles. Her memoirs are unusual for other reasons: as the child of two doctors and as a doctor herself, she is able to write with a clinical distance not to be found in any other transgender autobiography, and as a septuagenarian, she speaks in *No Way Renée* from a rare perspective. *No Way Renée* ends on a much more valedictory note than *Second Serve*. In it, Richards regrets not her sex change operation or becoming a woman but "that circumstances turned me into a transsexual, whether through nature or nurture" (286).

Transgender Memoirs

Renée Richards's memoirs were not the first transgender personal accounts. That distinction goes to *Man into Woman* (1933, ed. Hoyer) constructed from the extensive notes left by Lili Elbe (1882–1931), who was born as Einar Wegener, a Danish painter. Perhaps the most famous MTF (male to female) transsexual was Christine Jorgensen (1929–89), whose sweet and simple "personal autobiography" was published in 1967. Many consider *Conundrum* (1974) to be the best written account of transgender experience. Jan Morris (1926–), the author, had made a distinguished reputation as a journalist and travel writer before changing sex. Three more recent MTF autobiographies of note are Jennifer Finney Boylan's *She's Not There: A Life in Two Genders* (2003), and Joy Ladin's *Through the Door of Life: A Jewish Journey between Genders* (2012), and Kate Bornstein's *A Queer and Pleasant Danger* (2012). Richards, Boylan, Morris, Bornstein, and Ladin's stories all have similar features. Morris starts her memoir addressing her "conundrum" directly: "I was three or perhaps four years old when I realized that I had been born into the wrong body, and should really be a girl. I remember the moment well, and it is the earliest memory of my life" (1). All of the MTFs have similar early perceptions of being placed into the wrong body. They manage this problem in a variety of ways. Boylan (1958–) "was rarely depressed and reacted to [his] awful life with joy, with humor, and with light" (31). Other descended into depression. Each hoped to find a solution in marriage, and they all fathered children. It is surprising how often wives were understanding or at least tolerant of their husbands as they made the transition to womanhood. Their children also seem to adjust (particularly when the wife makes her peace with the alteration in the relationship). Of these authors, Joy Ladin (1961–) is the most philosophical. She approaches the problem as an orthodox Jew (three of the four authors are Jewish), and she is troubled by how the spiritual sense of being a woman needs to be translated into the highly material realm of eyeliner and earrings, skirts and panty hose.

One of the more interesting MTF transgender autobiographies is Charlotte von Mahlsdorf's *I Am My Own Woman* (1995). Mahlsdorf (1928–2002) was born in Germany. Fearing for her life, she used a rolling pin to kill her father, a man so violent that he "got to be too much even for the Nazis" (20). Released from prison at the end of the war, she began what would become the Grüderzeit Museum, the museum of everyday things, which she kept open through the communist dictatorship.

Female-to-male (FTM) transsexuals follow a very different path if one can generalize from three popular books – Jamison Green's *Becoming a Visible Man* (2004), Nick Krieger's *Nina Here nor There: My Journey beyond Gender* (2011), and Chaz Bono's *Transition: The Story of How I Became a Man* (2011). None of these three had the feeling that they were boys trapped in girls' bodies although they each felt, as Chaz Bono (1969–) puts it, "like a boy" (13). Unlike MTF stories in which the men first get married, the FTM narrative includes a period of lesbianism. To be sure, MTF trans-women often have homosexual experience. Kate Bornstein (1948) haunted the male cruising areas as a boy looking to fellate whomever he encountered. Jan Morris speaks matter of factly of her homosexual relations with men. But in both cases homosexual relations were merely episodes in a predominantly heterosexual orientation. However, "the majority of the trans-men that I have known," Chas Bono informs us, "at some point in their lives, identified as lesbians" (42). Green (1948–) puts it this way: "I ... determined that since I had a female body and I was attracted to female-bodied people, I must be a lesbian" (17). What they discover is a deep discomfort in lesbian relationship. Having sex with another female-bodied person reminds them of having female bodies themselves. Nick Krieger stops making love with his girlfriend because "[t]here's [*sic*] just so many tits in the bedroom. Four of them" (105). He found it "too painful to link myself to women" (132). Jamison Green runs an FTM support group that becomes rife with dissention because trans-men "from our group decided that there were too many gay-identified guys joining up, that too many people who looked like lesbians were coming to the meetings" (77).

One element that unites FTM and MTF autobiographies is that they often culminate in a sex reassignment therapy, including hormone therapy and/

or surgery. In so doing, the transautobiography returns at least in part to the medical origins of queer autobiography. FTM autobiographies are often concerned with how much surgery to perform; whether they would feel comfortable with just a "top job" or would they also need a "bottom job." The narratives of trans-women are rife with legal, familial, and financial obstacles to surgery; both Morris and Richards travel to Morocco to circumvent bureaucratic resistance. Perhaps because of the obstacles and the length of time reassignment takes, MTFs tend to see their surgeons as wizards who transform them with one swoop of the scalpel. In contrast, trans-men by and large view their doctors as highly trained technicians. The MTF autobiographies emphasize how surgery brings their bodies into harmony with their deepest sense of themselves; FTM autobiographies emphasize the operation as a means of presenting the trans-man as he wishes to be seen.

The fluidity of gender is the subject of several autobiographies. Justin Vivian Bond (1963–) presents the artist as the transgendered child in his *Tango: My Childhood, Backwards and in High Heels* (2011). As a boy, Bond is not so much a sissy as an Eve Arden, career woman, tough, sly, and romantically hopeful.

Sissies and Tomboys: Enduring Stereotypes

Despite the fluidity of gender, two intermediate figures appear in many autobiographies – the tomboy and the sissy. *Tomboy* is a fairly old term, stretching back to the sixteenth century; *sissy*, however, is an Americanism that goes back only as far as the end of the nineteenth century. The difference in longevity of the terms may be the reason that the tomboy is more accepted than the sissy. More likely, however, the tomboy is more accepted because it does honor to masculinity and is not viewed as a determined step toward homosexuality. In American mythology, the tomboy can be transformed into the prom queen, but the sissy is always a queer.

"I was a tomboy who liked to go hunting with my dad and play quarterback in tackle football games with my brother and his friends," admits Chely Wright (1970–), although she is careful to point out that she also enjoyed dresses and dolls (19). The tomboy is related to independence and assertiveness, two qualities valued in America. In one of the best recent memoirs, *Mean Little Deaf Queer* (2009), Terry Galloway shakes her fists at the stars and shouts at the heavens, "Just you try!" She comments: "I had looked the bully of the intimidating universe right in the eye and stared it down. . . . If that were true, that I could be as fearlessly arrogant as my cowboy idols, as recklessly resolute and bad, then I knew those stars were as much mine as anyone's. I had a real shot at becoming, at the very least, the hero of my own story" (70). For lesbians, the tomboy stage may be especially helpful in developing the courage and strength to act on their sexuality.

Claude Hartland, who wrote the first gay autobiography, was a sissy. By the age of five, he was "sensitive to the extreme and shrank from horror from causing any one [*sic*] or anything pain" (7). Rigoberto González (1970–) tells us in his exquisite memoir *Butterfly Boy* (2006) about growing up in a Mexican American family in which he suffered from poverty and homophobia. "Effeminate and demure," he is beaten by his ailing and much loved mother as a way to protect his father from having to confront his son's budding sexuality (88). As he recounts in his memoir, *What Becomes of the Brokenhearted* (2004), E. Lynn Harris (1955–2009) was beaten by his father so many times he attempted suicide. A recurrent topic of African American gay autobiography is how the sissy boy is a provocation to black men requiring violence or sex or both. "When I was between the ages of nine and fourteen," Carl Bean (1944–) recalls in *Was Born This Way* (2010), "more than a few older men had their way with me.... They saw me as a soft, chubby boy with round buttocks and full breasts. There was no hiding the fact that I was gay. This excited their aggression" (47). The sissy is especially a figure of Southern culture, where he is particularly stigmatized. In *Mississippi Sissy* (2007), Kevin Sessums (1956–) quotes Flannery O'Connor: "When I am asked why Southern writers particularly have a penchant for writing about freaks, I say it's because we are still able to recognize one" (3).

Post-Gay Autobiographies

David Sedaris (1956–) is a pivotal writer. On the one hand, he is openly and unapologetically gay. His sexuality is a given for many of his personal essays. On the other hand, the focus of his work is usually not about being gay. His most famous work, "The SantaLand Diaries," which could never have been written by a heterosexual writer, maintains its focus on the institution of Christmas and its demeaning commercialism. Sedaris is a precursor of what might be called post-gay autobiographies in which the authors' homosexuality is neither the central focus nor the crucial factor in their lives. These writers were born in the sixties and later.

A particularly touching example of post-gay autobiography is *Red Dust Road* (2010) by Scottish poet Jackie Kay (1961–), who was adopted by two extraordinary parents – both committed communists – who wished to bring up a mixed race baby. The bulk of the book is about her search for and relationship with her birthmother, who was from the Highlands, and her birthfather, who was a botanist from Nigeria. One of the most gripping lesbian memoirs is Staceyann Chin's *The Other Side of Paradise* (2009). Like Kay, Chin (1971–) is of mixed race, Chinese and African, and like Kay, she grew up without her birth parents. The focus of her memoir is surviving as a mouthy, intelligent, and rambunctious youngster barely tolerated by the relatives who for a time give her shelter. A very different book is *Unbearable Lightness* (2010) by actress Portia de Rossi (1973–) who married Ellen Degeneres. Being a lesbian has been less of a problem in her life than being anorexic and bulimic. She acknowledges that sexuality and eating disorders may be connected, but the narrative she unfolds is far more about the problems of body image than anything else. One of the happier post-gay memoirs is Josh Kilmer-Purcell's *The Bucolic Plague* (2010), in which Kilmer-Purcell (1969–) and his partner, Dr. Brent Ridge, try to bring to life the abandoned Beekman Farm estate in Sharon Springs, New York. Two much darker works fall under the heading of post-gay autobiography. The first is Bill Clegg's *Portrait of an Addict as a Young Man* (2010), in which Clegg (1970–) loses his job, his friends, his money, and his lover to satisfy his addiction for crack cocaine. Clegg's is a portrait of an obsession that leaves no room for anything else, neither pleasure, nor joy, nor human connection. Clegg has followed up *Portrait* with *Ninety Days* (2012), about his slow recovery from addiction. The last work is Augusten Burroughs's best-seller *Running with Scissors* (2002), which was made into a motion picture.

Many gay books have featured mad and controlling psychotherapists. Reneé Richards (1934–) went to famous analyst Robert C. Bok. Martin Duberman (1930–) wrote *Cures* (1991), his devastating history of psychotherapy. But no one comes close to Augusten Burroughs's Dr. Finch, who reads divine intervention into the shape and direction of his turds. But not all therapists are monsters. Alison Bechdel (1960–) has celebrated two therapists in her recent graphic-memoir, *Are You My Mother?* (2012). In its dense pages studded with quotes from Freud, D.W. Winnicott, and Melanie Klein, we return to the earliest scenes of queer autobiography, though not to explain homosexuality, but to illuminate mother-daughter relations.

We read autobiographies to learn about lives very different from our own, or to find solace in lives that are like our own, or to delight in the pleasures of the text. As same-sex relations become less stigmatized and homosexual orientations become a part of the fabric of life, LGBT autobiographies will be read increasingly for their literary rather than for their medical or sociological value. Solace will give way to curiosity and shock to delight. Yet there is a ways to go. We are just beginning to hear from such authors as Abdellah Taïa and Rachid O., who can provide both solace and pleasure from the postcolonial world.

Works Cited

Ackerley, J.R. *My Father and Myself.* London: Bodley Head, 1968. Print.

Amaechi, John, and Chris Bull. *Man in the Middle.* New York: ESPN Books, 2007. Print.

Arenas, Reinaldo. *Before Night Falls.* New York: Viking, 1994. Print.

Bean, Billy. *Going the Other Way: Lessons from a Life in and out of Major-League Baseball.* New York: Marlowe, 2003. Print.

Bean, Carl, and David Ritz. *I Was Born This Way: A Gay Preacher's Journey through Gospel Music, Disco Stardom, and a Ministry in Christ.* New York: Simon, 2010. Print.

Barbin, Herculine, and Michel Foucault. *Herculine Barbin: Being the Recently Discovered Memoirs of a Nineteenth-Century French Hermaphrodite.* New York: Vintage, 1980. Print.

Bechdel, Alison. *Are You My Mother?: A Comic Drama.* Boston: Houghton, 2012. Print.

Beck, Gad. *An Underground Life: Memoirs of a Gay Jew in Nazi Germany.* Madison: U of Wisconsin P, 2000. Print.

Bell, Arthur. *Dancing the Gay Lib Blues: A Year in the Homosexual Liberation Movement.* New York: Simon, 1971. Print.

Billany, Dan, and David Dowie. *The Cage.* London: Longmans, 1949. Print.

Blake, James. *The Joint.* Garden City: Doubleday, 1971. Print.

Bond, Justin Vivian. *Tango: My Childhood, Backward and in High Heels.* New York: Feminist P, 2011. Print.

Bono, Chaz. *Transition: The Story of How I Became a Man.* New York: Dutton, 2011. Print.

Bornstein, Kate. *A Queer and Pleasant Danger.* Boston: Beacon P, 2012. Print.

Boyd, Malcolm. *Take off the Masks.* Garden City: Doubleday, 1978. Print.

Boylan, Jennifer Finney. *She's Not There: A Life in Two Genders.* New York: Broadway, 2003. Print.

Brown, Rebecca. *The Gifts of the Body.* New York: HarperCollins, 1994. Print.

Burke, Glenn, and Erik Sherman. *Out at Home: The Glenn Burke Story.* New York: Excel P, 1995. Print.

Burroughs, Augusten. *Running with Scissors.* New York: St. Martin's, 2002. Print.

Cammermeyer, Margarethe, and Chris Fisher. *Serving in Silence.* New York: Viking, 1994. Print.

Casal, Mary, *The Stone Wall: An Autobiography.* New York: Arno P, 1975. Print.

Chin, Staceyann. *The Other Side of Paradise: A Memoir.* New York: Scribner, 2009. Print.

Clark, Lige, and Jack Nichols. *I Have More Fun with You than Anyone.* New York: St. Martin's, 1972. Print.

Clark, Lige. *Roommates Can't Always Be Lovers.* New York: St. Martin's, 1974. Print.

Clegg, Bill. *Ninety Days: A Memoir of Recovery.* Boston: Little Brown, 2012. Print.

 Portrait of the Addict as a Young Man. Boston: Little Brown, 2010. Print.

Crisp, Quentin. *The Naked Civil Servant.* New York: Holt, 1968. Print.

Croft-Cooke, Rupert. *The Verdict of You All.* London: Secker, 1955. Print.

De Rossi, Portia. *Unbearable Lightness: A Story of Loss and Gain.* New York: Atria, 2010. Print.

Doty, Mark. *Heaven's Coast: A Memoir*. New York: Harper, 1996. Print.

Duberman, Martin. *Cures: A Gay Man's Odyssey*. New York: Dutton, 1991. Print.

Ellis, Havelock, and J.A. Symonds. *Sexual Inversion*, 1897. New York: Arno P, 1975. Print.

Feinberg, David B. *Queer and Loathing: Rants and Raves of a Raging AIDS Clone*. New York: Viking, 1994. Print.

Fisher, Gary. *Gary in Your Pocket: Stories and Notebooks of Gary Fisher*. Ed. Eve Kosofsky Sedgwick. Durham: Duke UP, 1996. Print.

Fredericks, Claude. *The Journal of Claude Fredericks*. 3 vols. Xlibris, 2011. Print.

Genet, Jean. *The Thief's Journal*. 1964. Trans. Bernard Frechtman. New York: Grove P, 1964. Print.

Galloway, Terry. *Mean Little Deaf Queer: A Memoir*. Boston: Beacon P, 2009. Print.

González, Rigoberto. *Butterfly Boy: Memories of a Chicano Mariposa*. Madison: U of Wisconsin P, 2006. Print.

Goodman, Paul. *Five Years: Thoughts during a Useless Time*. New York: Brussel, 1966. Print.

Green, Jamison. *Becoming a Visible Man*. Nashville: Vanderbilt UP, 2004. Print.

Guibert, Herve, *To the Friend Who Did Not Save My Life*. Trans. Linda Coverdale. New York: Atheneum, 1990. Print.

Hale, Allean. "A Few Notes and Corrections." Afterword. Williams 253–54.

Harris, E. Lynn. *What Becomes of the Brokenhearted*. New York: Anchor, 2004. Print.

Hartland, Claude. *The Story of a Life: For the Medical Fraternity*. 1905. Bolinas: Grey Fox P, 1985. Print.

Hildyard, Myles. *It Is Bliss Here: Letters Home, 1939–1945*. London: Bloomsbury, 2005. Print.

Heger, Heinz. *The Men with the Pink Triangle: The True Life and Death Story of Homosexuals in the Nazi Death Camps*. Trans. David Fernbach. New York: Alyson, 1980. Print.

Hoyer, Niels, ed. *Man into Woman*. London: Jarrolds, 1933. Print.

Jorgensen, Christine. *Christine Jorgensen: A Personal Autobiography*. New York: R.S. Eriksson, 1967. Print.

Kantrowitz, Arnie. *Under the Rainbow: Growing Up Gay*. New York: Morrow, 1977. Print.

Kay, Jackie. *Red Dust Road: An Autobiographical Journey*. New York: Atlas, 2010. Print.

Kilmer-Purcell, Josh. *The Bucolic Plague: How Two Manhattanites Became Gentlemen Farmers: An Unconventional Memoir*. New York: Harper, 2010. Print.

Kopay, David. *The David Kopay Story: An Extraordinary Self-Revelation*. Westminster: Arbor House, 1977. Print.

Krieger, Nick. *Nina Here nor There: My Journey beyond Gender*. Boston: Beacon P, 2011. Print.

Ladin, Joy. *Through the Door of Life: A Jewish Journey between Genders*. Madison: U of Wisconsin P, 2012. Print.

Lister, Anne. *I Know My Own Heart: The Diaries of Anne Lister, 1791–1840*. Ed. Helena Whitbread. New York: New York UP, 1988. Print.

Lord, James. *My Queer War*. New York: Farrar, 2010. Print.

Louganis, Greg, and Eric Marcus. *Breaking the Surface*. New York: Random, 1995. Print.

Mahlsdorf, Charlotte von. *I Am My Own Woman: The Outlaw Life of Charlotte Von Mahlsdorf*. Pittsburgh: Cleis, 1995. Print.

Monette, Paul. *Borrowed Time: An AIDS Memoir*. San Diego: Harcourt, 1988. Print.

Morris, Jan. *Conundrum*. New York: Harcourt, 1974. Print.

Navratilova, Martina, and George Vecsey. *Martina*. New York: Knopf, 1985. Print.

Parsell, T. J. *Fish: A Memoir of a Boy in a Man's Prison*. New York: Carroll, 2006. Print.

Pearson, Felicia "Snoop," and David Ritz. *Grace after Midnight*. New York: Grand Central, 2007. Print.

Perry, Troy D. *The Lord Is My Shepherd & He Knows I'm Gay*. Los Angeles: Universal Fellowship P, 1972. Print.

Picano, Felice. *Ambidextrous: The Secret Life of Children*. New York: Gay Presses of New York, 1985. Print.

  Art and Sex in Greenwich Village: Gay Literary Life after Stonewall. New York: Carroll, 2007. Print.

Richards, Renée, and John Ames. *No Way Renée: The Second Half of My Notorious Life*. New York: Simon, 2007. Print.

  Second Serve: The Renée Richards Story. New York: Stein, 1983. Print.

Rumaker, Michael. *A Day and a Night at the Baths*. Bolinas: Grey Fox P, 1979. Print.

Russell, Ina, ed. *Jeb and Dash: A Diary of Gay Culture, 1918–1945*. Boston: Faber, 1994. Print.

Sarton, May. *Journal of a Solitude*. New York: Norton, 1973. Print.

Sedaris, David. *SantaLand Diaries*. New York: Abacus, 2008. Print.

Seel, Pierre. *I, Pierre Seel, Deported Homosexual: A Memoir of Nazi Terror*. New York: Basic, 1994. Print.

Sessums, Kevin. *Mississippi Sissy*. New York: St. Martin's, 2007. Print.

Simmons, Roy, and Damon DiMarco. *Out of Bounds: Coming Out of Sexual Abuse, Addiction, and My Life of Lies in the NFL Closet*. New York: Carroll, 2006. Print.

Sontag, Susan. *Reborn: Journals and Notebooks 1947–1963*. Ed. David Rieff. New York: Farrar, 2008. Print.

Steffan, Joseph. *Honor Bound: A Gay Naval Midshipman Fights to Serve His Country*. New York: Avon, 1993. Print.

Stein, Gertrude. *The Autobiography of Alice B. Toklas*. New York: Harcourt, 1933. Print.

Tobias, Andrew. *The Best Little Boy in the World*. New York: Modern Library, 1998. Print.

Tuaolo, Esera, and John Rosengren. *Alone in the Trenches: My Life as a Gay Man in the NFL*. Naperville: Sourcebooks, 2006. Print.

Vining, Donald. *A Gay Diary: 1946–1982*. 5 vols. New York: Pepys, 1980–93. Print.

White, Edmund. *City Boy*. New York: Bloomsbury, 2009. Print.

  My Lives. New York: Bloomsbury, 2005. Print.

Wilde, Oscar. *De Profundis*. London: Methuen, 1905. Print.

Wildeblood, Peter. *Against the Law*. London: Weidenfeld, 1955. Print.

Williams, Tennessee. *Memoirs*. Garden City: Doubleday, 1975. Print.

Wojnarowicz, David. *Close to the Knives: A Memoir of Disintegration*. New York: Vintage, 1991. Print.

Wright, Chely. *Like Me: Confessions of a Heartland Country Singer*. Milwaukee: Hal Leonard, 2011. Print.

Wright, Douglas. *Ghost Dance*. Auckland: Penguin, 2004. Print.

  Terra Incognito. Aukland: Penguin, 2006. Print.

36

The Literature of "What If . . . ?"

DARIECK SCOTT

What is the worth of reading fiction about characters and events that aren't real and couldn't be real? Dismissal of fiction that doesn't fit easily under the rubric of realism – *prejudice* against nonrealism or beyond-realism, in other words – partakes of a political project that underpins the study of literatures in the Anglo American academy. This project's fundamental assumption is that literature worthy of criticism must present a kind of illuminating mirror of some portion of "the truth about" human life, and it should do so in order to give readers a kind of knowledge supplementary to what we would otherwise glean from histories, journalism, philosophy, and the sciences. The purpose of a literature, from this point of view, is to function as the primary texts of a secular religion – hence the importation of the term "canon" into literary criticism. The texts that thus earn the adjective *literary* provide a common set of referents for the moral or political compass of the educated class of a given nation, who, in the absence of such a canon, and given the inability of the Bible to command the full attention of every reader everywhere as it once did in the golden age of limited literacy (so the argument goes), might dangerously fail to see themselves as a nation or people at all, and so Rome will fall again. Fictional works in which elves or the disintegration of galactic empires figure prominently must by such criteria earn no better than a withering critical glance, and may be lucky to avoid a backhanded clout.

But what counts as "real" is, in many complex ways, often enough simply a designation of, or reinforcement for, the status quo. Thus adherence to the "real" seamlessly supports those who benefit from social and economic arrangements remaining just as they are, with all the extant injustices and inequalities that have so far not failed to define every human society above the scale of hunter-gatherer clan in one fashion or another. While works of sci-fi/fantasy may of course reinforce the status quo in their own ways, a genre that starts from a question of "what if" is empowered to *question* and reimagine what we assume to be reality – for example, the reality of clear demarcations between gay and straight sexualities, or between gay and straight identities. Thus, sci-fi/fantasy is a fruitful mode for imagining *possibility* – especially where possibilities seem most constrained in what we helplessly persist in reestablishing as our (often dreadful) common reality: What if "woman" and "man" did not mean what we live them as meaning? What if most people expressed their sexualities, or chose their sexual and romantic partners, without regard to a notion of "the opposite sex," if sexuality were lived not under a set of heterosexual or homosexual or even bisexual assumptions, but occurred most pleasurably with a partner of a third, androgynous "gender"? What if a society didn't ascribe different sexual stereotypes to different racial groupings – or if the sexual stereotypes we are taught to ascribe to black or brown people were ascribed to white people, or bisque-colored people?

The questions invited by sci-fi/fantasy's generic posture, then, seem rather useful even as a means by which to tell "the truth about" our "real" world. This is to say nothing of serious value of the *pleasure* provided by what gets dismissed as "escape" – the dismissal of escapism being something that ought to always raise the question of what exactly readers or audiences desire to escape from, and why that escape is needed.

Sci-fi/fantasy's fundamental "what if" suits the genre well to *queer* representation. One of the avenues open to achieve otherwise suppressed or repressed representations is to elude the strictures of the "real." From the point of view of the normative, paradox, unspeakability, and unreality attend what it is to live a lesbian or gay or transgender or queer reality – and thus, precisely in their being barred or only intermittently counted in the mainstream or in the norm, such realities might most readily be represented under the rubric of the speculative, the fantastic, or the horrific.[1] This may be why the devices of the unreal are at the center of two of the earliest treatments of modern queer sexuality by canonical writers in literature written in English: Oscar Wilde's *The Picture of Dorian Gray* (1890), in which the beautiful effeminate young Gray, desired and admired by all the men and the women in his midst, preserves his beauty by means of an unexplained act of supernatural will so that all the physical costs of his many sins and debaucheries (including decodable hints of homosexual activity) are reflected in a painted portrait of him rather than in the aging or deterioration of his own body; and Virginia Woolf's *Orlando* (1928), where immortality that seems to be associated with the ability to change genders (and a skill at crossdressing) enables Orlando, whom we first see as a young Elizabethan nobleman, to thrive over four centuries and in a host of richly imagined adventures, and to conclude the novel as a married woman in 1928. The possibility for both writers to represent in their fiction nonnormative romantic attachments and sexualities (and perhaps, to speak their own "unspeakable" queerness) seems either to require or to be encouraged by a turn to devices of unreality. Wilde's and Woolf's works are arguably precursors to the contemporary genre(s) of science fiction and fantasy.

A great part of LGBTQ science fiction and fantasy literature's significance in our world is its invention of alternative worlds that render thinkable what might have been unthinkable, its provision of templates for a kind of collective practice of fantasizing (publicly distributed, individually consumed, publicly reanimated in fandom): this is the *work* it does – on our minds as readers, in seeding readers' imaginations, and, through those readers acting almost as viral vectors, thus sowing those seeds with potential political effect in the sum total of the imaginations of our popular cultures. It is also the *pleasure* the literature provides. This chapter aims to investigate the forms of *work* fantasy and sci-fi do on how we imagine gender and sexuality – the work of queering our perception of the possible – and to suggest the *pleasures* of such imaginings. The latter aim must remain suggestive because only reading the texts surveyed here (and the many deserving others I'll fail even to mention) would fully achieve it; here it's not possible to go much further than to offer the sweet tortures of Tantalus. The standard prophylactic applies also: this is absolutely not a comprehensive discussion of LGBTQ sci-fi and fantasy, nor is it intended to identify a canon of the very best; rather, it is an idiosyncratic collage of such works.[2]

The literary works here surveyed, and the literature of which I'm claiming these works are exemplary, reimagine our human (and sometimes animal) histories – but especially the histories of the Mediterranean, Europe and the Americas, south and eastern Asia, and less frequently of Africa – often in the form of inventing the histories of civilizations and cultures on other planets, or of species at once like and fundamentally unlike humans, or in the form of reimagining mythic traditions and fairy tales. Such newly minted histories produce characters for whom the male-female gender polarity we live as fundamental, with its concomitant masculine-feminine binary (a common enough, though perhaps still distressingly too-specialized word for this phenomenon is, of course, sexism), and the general marginalization, suppression, or repression of homosexual or nonheterosexual desire and sexuality (a fancy word for which is heterosexism), constitutes a center that does not hold: and the rough beast born of such histories, which tends rather to strut than to slouch, is an array of sparkling worlds in which male and female hold different meanings, or have no meaning, and sexuality takes on at least a bisexual if not a multiplicity of forms, which Freudians might, rubbing their hands with glee, refer to as polymorphously perverse. Such reinvented histories and worlds, such rearrangements of our most tectonic assumptions, of course suggest and sometimes strive to reveal to us that our reality is imaginary.

The Queer "Pattern" of Octavia Butler

LGBTQ science fiction and fantasy has been described as a "tiny field" (Berman 5). This may be an accurate accounting given the general marginality of sci-fi/fantasy to what is published and read as literature (an art form that is itself diminished, compared to forms in other media). But if tiny, it is perhaps a kind of small rhizome, with long branching tendrils appearing unexpectedly in a variety of places. Octavia E. Butler's *Wild Seed* (1980) is a part of her Patternist series, comprised of five novels telling a recognizably mainstream sci-fi/fantasy kind of story: a future earth transformed by an extraterrestrial plague is the battleground for telepaths and persons of immense paranormal powers. The story begins in seventeenth-century west Africa, with the protagonist, Anyanwu, a centuries-old Ibo woman who can reshape her body "down to the smallest living part" (Butler, *Wild* 219) and thus can even mimic at the genetic level any human or animal of whose flesh she's acquired a sample. Anyanwu is discovered concealing her abilities by the nomadic Doro, an east African Nubian, who is also a mutant but has lived nearly four millennia, and whose "ability" is that he must transfer his consciousness from one body to another; each body Doro occupies eventually debilitates, and when he is forced to or chooses to transfer into another body, the previous host dies. Anyanwu and Doro are each in their own way profoundly lonely people, seeking through different means to build communities of persons who, like them, are outcasts – Anyanwu by literally giving birth to successive generations and thus mothering her own lineage, Doro by establishing communities of people with paranormal talents all over the world, the inhabitants of which he terrorizes or cozens into having sexual partners whom he designates, in order to produce ever more talented and powerful progeny. Doro seduces Anyanwu to join him on his ship – a ship full of other people he's purchased as part of the African slave trade, but which travels the dreaded Middle Passage in high comfort – to his American colony. Doro's long attempt to gain control over Anyanwu and her shape-changing and DNA-manipulating healing abilities can obviously be read, and frequently is read, as a reimagining of, and commentary on, African slavery in the Americas. The battle between Anyanwu and Doro is also, as it develops, at one level a classic battle of the (most traditionally conceived) sexes, pitting a murderous, tyrannical male with eugenic fantasies against a nurturing, naturally healing woman who sacrifices her own freedom to protect her children and descendants.

The novel nonetheless has a pronounced queer element, even if it is not often categorized among LGBTQ fiction in the genre(s).[3] Butler plots the novel so that the seemingly sexist conception of its principals as well as both characters' apparently heterosexist concerns (they are chiefly interested in having children via sexual reproduction) are hollowed out and reshaped, and Anyanwu and Doro are driven to form what can (and I think should) be seen as queer communities. Anyanwu first proves her shape-changing power to Doro by, at his request, changing from an older woman to a younger woman to an animal, and finally to a young male. He verifies her ability by stripping aside the momentarily male Anyanwu's clothing to inspect her male genitals, as though witnessing the previous metamorphoses were insufficient evidence. Doro then proposes to take Anyanwu to a place where they can have children that will not die – which she misinterprets according to her Ibo norms as a proposal of marriage – and their new union is sealed when they have sex: the first sign that Anyanwu has given her assent is that her male body grows breasts. Their union is normalized, both through Anyanwu's own conception of it and through the author's apparent fulfillment of readers' normative expectations of heterosexual sex; but clearly in a world of shape-changers, gender and heterosexuality are already in this initial encounter in flux.

Not long after, while Anyanwu is still deceived as to Doro's intentions (he plans to mate her with a telekinetic of European, Native American, and African descent he's fathered in one of his host bodies), the two have a discussion about their sexual lives. Anyanwu has been having sex with Doro in at least a couple of different male bodies, but she reveals to him that she reshapes her own body when they have sex, implying that she reforms her vaginal canal for him:

[Doro:] "What are you saying, woman? What have you been doing?" . . .

[Anyanwu:] "Only giving you pleasure. You have told me how well I please you." . . .

"Someday," he murmured, vaguely preoccupied, "we will both change. I will become a woman and find out whether you make an especially talented man."

"*No!*" She jerked away from him. . . . "We will *not* do such a thing!" . . . "Doro, we will not do it!" . . .

"All right," he said agreeably. "It was only a suggestion. You might enjoy it." . . .

"It would be a vile thing," she whispered. "Surely an abomination." . . . She looked to see whether he was still smiling, and he was. For an instant, she wondered herself what such a switch might be like. She knew she could become an adequate man, but could this strange being ever be truly womanly? What if ...? No! (100, last ellipsis in original)

The ellipsis can be completed in a number of ways, which Butler portrays Anyanwu as fearing to make fully conscious, and Butler perhaps expects her sci-fi/fantasy readers to shy away from as well. What if Doro *really* "is" a woman? What would it even mean for him to "really" be a woman, when he occupies female bodies at will and has done so before? What if it gave Anyanwu pleasure to have a male body and have sex with Doro as a woman (i.e., what would that mean about who she is in terms of her sexuality)? What if she remained a woman and Doro became a woman and they had sex in those bodies? Doro is positioned as the villain for much of the novel, constraining the choices of those he encounters to suit his will – like any enslaver. But here it is Anyanwu who is constrained by her own assumptions and by her determination to constrict Doro's sexuality.

Anyanwu's vehement, repeated refusals are clear echoes of an earlier moment in the novel, when one of Doro's merely human agents, Daly, discovers that Anyanwu, like Doro, can be either gender. Daly, who's presented to us as even more villainous than Doro (he's a greedy slave trader indifferent to the suffering of the Africans he helps kidnap for Doro's breeding program), calls Anyanwu a "monster," and scoffs, "'I suppose now you will breed creatures who don't know whether to piss standing or squatting.... Such things should be burned. They are against God!'" Doro is as amused by Daly as he is by Anyanwu's condemnation of "abomination," for Doro knows what Daly himself knows but refuses to acknowledge, that "the slaver [Daly] longed to be one of Doro's monstrosities" (46). Anyanwu, too, desires to be free of the cultural and religious strictures defining gender roles and heterosexuality and even humanity that she passionately defends, but which her powers already undermine and render rather obsolete – she has in fact already in her three centuries lived as a man for a time, and fathered children – and Doro knows this. Accordingly, Anyanwu goes on to do what she abominates: When she escapes from Doro and founds her own community in Louisiana in the nineteenth century, she gathers paranormally gifted individuals from among black, white, and mixed folk in the area, shaping herself as necessary into a white man who can own property and slaves. At one point, she meets Denice, a clairvoyant white woman who instantly penetrates Anyanwu's "false" white male body to find the true consciousness within, and the two fall in love, marry, and have children:

[Doro:] "Why did she marry you?"

[Anyanwu:] "Because I believed her [that she had telepathic powers]. . . . Because I was not afraid or ridiculing. And because after a while, we started to want each other."

"Even though she knew you were a woman and black?"

"Even so." Anyanwu . . . [remembered] that lovely, fearful courting.

They had been as fearful of marrying each other as they had been of losing each other.   (218)

In truth, Anyanwu's denials and cries of abomination at the moment Doro makes his proposal that they switch genders do not actually describe her true affective ties or sexual life. The Anyanwu-Denice relationship appears to be heterosexual, and perhaps sexually is so, but in terms of consciousness and how the two identify themselves and each other, it is not. In *Wild Seed*, neither Anyanwu's nor Doro's desired notion of family or affective community – Anyanwu's traditional west African kinship network of extended family, and Doro's segregated eugenics enclave, both of which require a subordination if not a condemnation of sexual and romantic choices not consonant with the commandment of reproduction above all else – ultimately obtains. The compromise community they build becomes a planetary network of telepathically connected "different" people, the disembodied (or all-bodied) "pattern" after which the series is named. And the novel, which is a novel "about" shape-changers and telepaths in a war for political power, and about chattel slavery and the cultural metamorphoses Africans and Europeans had to achieve in order to remake their shared world in the Americas, is also an LGBTQ sci-fi/fantasy novel – one of the precious few to really consider race in contiguity with gender and sexuality.

Reimagining and Unimagining Gender

In the queer worlds of science fiction and fantasy, we find many reimaginings of gender and gender roles. And even in worlds where gender categories are defined much as we pretend they are in our own world, we find a surprising number of characters with same-sex loves and lusts.

Pathbreakers in the former regard are Ursula Le Guin and Joanna Russ. Le Guin's 1969 novel *The Left Hand of Darkness* follows Genly Ai, an ethnologist from the spacefaring Hainish – originally humans of Earth – whose studies take him to Winter, a planet where the inhabitants have no gender, except during a short monthly gender-cycle. Though Genly finds it difficult to trust a person with no settled gender, he eventually develops a nonsexual love for one of Winter's high political officials. The narration generally refers to Winter's inhabitants as "he," a misleading linguistic reflection – and thus analysis – of our equation of "man" with "human." The Hainish are at it again reporting about the peculiarities of particular planetary cultures' organizations of gender, and thereby revealing the peculiarity of our own, in a later Le Guin story, "The Matter of Seggri" (1994). There, agents specializing in first contact with non-spacefaring species find that on Seggri women and men live separately, with boys ritually taken from their mothers at age eleven to live in guarded castles, while the women, who are the vast majority of the population, go about the business of running the Seggri civilization. On Seggri, women are educated, skilled in all manner of labor and creativity, serve as the world's political leaders, and marry each other, often taking on third partners or more, and raise families. The men consider themselves superior because of their prowess in a rugby-like sport and in sex – the most successful athletes are also prime choices in popular "fuckeries," lively entertainment brothels where women pay men for pleasure and for impregnation. Female homosexuality is a matter of course – it's what the marriages are partly about – but male homosexuality is frowned on and sometimes actively persecuted (by the men), unless it functions as humiliation necessary to establish the pecking order in the men's petty hierarchical castle-politics, which occupy them endlessly. Depicting a number of different perspectives including an imagined short story within Le Guin's story ostensibly written by one of Seggri's artists, "The Matter of Seggri" addresses the dissatisfactions, profound cruelties, and tragic waste that mark the everyday existences of people in a culture where social esteem and life-possibilities are distributed according to gender.

Joanna Russ's *The Female Man* (1975) gives us narratives of four women in what appear to be separate times and universes, who find themselves transported or visible to each other's worlds, and eventually become participants in a war being fought between women and men on a futurist earth. One of the principal characters is Joanna, a 1970s woman attempting to gain respect in academia, who feels that she must actually *become* a man in order to do so – "a female man, of course," she explains, "my body and soul were exactly the same" (5). Another is Jeannine, a 1940s-like husband-hunter in a world where the Great Depression did not end. The other two are the conventionally heroic, admirable Janet, a police officer with a wife (though no one on her world, we are told, marries monogamously) and daughter on the world Whileaway, where a mysterious plague (it seems) has done away altogether with the male of the species, but the female survivors have, among their many acts of technological virtuosity, devised ways to reproduce solely with ova; and the combative Jael, fighting a violent war against men. The novel ends looking forward to the day when the accounts in *The Female Man* will not be deemed speculative, or indeed relevant. "For on that day, we will be free," declares the narrator (presumably Joanna). "Remember: we will all be changed. In a moment, in the twinkling of an eye, we will all be free" (214, 213).

Elizabeth A. Lynn's short story "The Man Who Was Pregnant" (1977) and Butler's "Bloodchild" (1984) also speculate on how we might experience the shattering of our assumptions about biological destiny. Lynn's story, inspired, she says, by little more than seeing a man on a San Francisco bus wearing an androgynous caftan, details some nine months in the life of a man who becomes pregnant, mysteriously (he speculates that his male lover, Sandy, is responsible because the woman he's dating, Louise, "could clearly have had nothing to do with the event" [124]). As the baby comes to term the narrator's breasts grow and his penis shrinks ("making a pathway for the baby" [125]), but these bodily transformations are matched and even surpassed by changes in how he's treated – patronizingly if not contemptuously by his doctors, distantly by his soon-to-be former lovers, and with loving but sometimes stormy support by his sisters. In Butler's "Bloodchild," a group of humans fleeing from war and the threat of enslavement on earth has established a colony, which has existed for generations, on an extrasolar world dominated by an intelligent insectoid species. The Tlic reproduce parasitically, gestating their young in the flesh of warm-blooded creatures, and so the humans are perfect surrogate mothers for them. An arrangement between the two species allows the humans to have refuge on the planet in exchange for selected humans serving as surrogates (a painful process wherein the larva eats the body it is implanted in, unless it is surgically removed in time). Men are the Tlic's customary choice of mother, because women are needed to maintain the population and give birth to more mother-surrogates for the Tlic. Though it is often read, like *Wild Seed*, as a commentary about slavery, the suspenseful story, in which young Gan, the male protagonist, contemplates suicide but eventually chooses to bear "his" Tlic sponsor/owner's young – in part because he loves her – is Butler's recasting of pregnancy in the unexpected light of parasitism.

Male authors generally have been less trenchant in their exposure of the gender system and its differential privileges. An exception is Samuel R. Delany, whose *Trouble on Triton* (1976) depicts a utopian human colony on one of Saturn's moons, where procedures to easily change genders (and sexual orientations) are available to all citizens, and they do so according to whim, fashion, or desire – but rarely because they identify one gender or another with them*selves*. This is especially troubling for Bron Helstrom, an immigrant who, like the Hainish ethnologist in *The Left Hand of Darkness*, is resistant to the notion and practice of gender as flexible rather than fundamental. Bron, assured that he is male and heterosexual, searches for love, thinks he finds it in a (currently) female director named the Spike, and, when this relationship fails (in part because he insists it follow his idea of male-female heterosexuality), he changes into a woman who prefers men, in order to be what he desires the Spike to be. This, too, fails to satisfy Bron, especially when, at the novel's end, she-Bron encounters a man who's been altered (apparently) to look exactly like Bron did as a man. Bron is horrified, crying out in what feels to her to be a compelled but deeply false performance – and in what is perhaps a childish railing against the empty incongruity between gender and identity – "'I shall destroy *you* – as you destroyed *me!*'" (Delany, *Trouble* 276).

Another exception is Clive Barker: his gorgeously rendered *Imajica* (1991), the story of travelers between five dimensions, featuring magical creatures, an imprisoned goddess, and the slaying of a tyrannical God, has as a central character, almost the message-bearer or angelic figure of the tale, a being named Pie 'oh' pah, a "mystif" who changes shape and gender according to the desires or expectations of its admirer (which are sometimes its victims because Pie 'oh' pah is also an assassin). Pie 'oh' pah was in one of its guises the servant of the protagonist, Gentle, a son of the imprisoned goddess, who is unaware of his heritage or his powers, until Pie 'oh' pah arrives on the scene; and in the course of their adventures Gentle and Pie 'oh' pah fall in love and marry.

Queer Romances

Same-sex love, lust, and attachment can be found in an array of sci-fi/fantasy titles that, unlike the works discussed earlier, do not spin gender in the particle accelerator and measure what happens to it under pressure. In these worlds, what is queer is the unremarked but highly visible presence, or sometimes the centrality, of gay romance. In many of the following texts the authors have conceived social contexts and histories where heterosexuality is predominant as it is in "reality," but doesn't brandish truncheons and issue citations the way our normative heterosexuality does.

Elizabeth Lynn's *Watchtower* (1978), *The Dancers of Arun* (1979), and *The Northern Girl* (1980) imagine a feudal, seemingly European society (the routine choice of setting in fantasy fiction, given the long, productive shadow of J. R. R. Tolkien's androcentric and mostly sexuality-devoid Middle-earth) with the kind of attention to realist detail for which the popular George R. R.

Martin, author of the ongoing *Game of Thrones* series, is critically vaunted. But whereas in Martin's vast canvas of characters, some of whom are quite explicitly lusty, only three or four appear to have same-sex attractions or liaisons, and these mostly appear in the form of guesses and gossip, Lynn's primary characters – traditional warriors, princes, farmers, and bastard children of aristocracy – frequently are in (or desire to be in) homosexual relationships, including a pair of kick-ass female assassins and messengers-for-hire whom many believe to be of a nonhuman androgynous race. *The Chronicles of Tornor*, as the trilogy is called, tracks the development of a mystical martial arts cult that challenges the old male-centered, war-glorifying culture of Lynn's world, and the most ardent practitioners of the new cult seem to be same-sex pairs (or triples) as well as heterosexual couples, all bound together as fighting units like the Sacred Band of Thebes. Lynn's diptych, *Dragon's Winter* (1998) and *Dragon's Treasure* (2003), featuring a conflict between a king who is a kind of were-dragon and an evil sorcerer, also centers same-sex love, as does her story "The Woman Who Fell in Love with the Moon" (1979), which in fairytale style describes three magnificently beautiful warrior sisters and their contests of weaponry against the avatar of the moon-goddess, with whom one sister begins a passionate sexual and romantic affair.

Jim Grimsley's *Kirith Kirin* (2000) is probably undervalued as a work of sci-fi/fantasy, despite chronicling an epic battle waged between good and evil witches in a Tolkienesque world and featuring one of the most convincingly imagined systems for the explanation of magic (based on quantum physics). Perhaps it flies beneath the radar of the genre's classics because the familiar boy-who-becomes-a-great-wizard trope is reworked in *Kirith* through Jessex, a boy who loves, and, in tender scenes sleeps with, an immortal king. Grimsley, otherwise known for his literary fiction, continues his series at much later points in the imagined history of his universe in *The Ordinary* (2004) and *The Last Green Tree* (2006), where the role of nigh-omnipotent witch ruler of the realm is held by an immortal woman who falls in love with a woman of the human-descended, spacefaring Hormling species. *Kirith*'s Jessex also tries to outsmart the creator of his world, YY-Mother, a goddess (despite the chromosomal allusion of her name) who slays him in the as-yet uncompleted series.

Tilting against the deities, which also characterizes *Imajica*, and which we might begin to read as a device that some of these texts, especially those written by gay men, use to figure their protest against the undergirding rules of the gender/sexuality system that Le Guin and Russ try more explicitly to reimagine, also features in Hal Duncan's kaleidoscopic *Vellum* (2006) and *Ink* (2007). This diptych involves a war among angels, demons, and gods, and the quest for a "book" that contains the map of reality. The story splinters across a number of alternate dimensions and different historical epochs, and among several main characters tracks a troop of fey bad-boy sodomite terrorist revolutionaries with names like Puck and Jumpin' Jack Flash who fight against the (often angelic, demonic, or divine) powers-that-be in the novels' various realities, including 1999 and the Great War. Some of the same characters – and the same action – appears in the provocative story "The Last Straw" (2007), where the bad boys try to assassinate all the cloned copies of government official Jack Straw in a fascist Britain ruled by Tony Blair and patrolled by blackshirts and Royal Highland Falangists. Such references, along with Duncan's style, which is as caffeinated as a textualization of a *Matrix* film fight sequence, suggest the debt Duncan and others owe to another canonical writer who used sci-fi/ fantasy devices to tell his stories, but who is not generally accounted a genre writer: William Burroughs, whose hallucinatory mythos in *Wild Boys* (1971) and *Port of Saints* (1975) (to name but two of Burroughs's novels that make use of the "wild boys") imagines a kind of all-male utopia in the form of a dystopia, with the men busy shooting guns while fondling their bulging jockstraps and fucking each other, all in the service of a revolution waged via time travel against history's injustices, in the midst of plague and catastrophe.

In this chapter I can only glance across the bow, in no particular order, of a host of same-sex heroes in the alternative-world adventures of: Ellen Kushner's (sometimes joined by partner Delia Sherman) elegant *Swordspoint* (1989), *The Fall of the Kings* (2002), and *The Privilege of the Sword* (2006), where mostly male duelists, scholars, and lordlings in a shabby, vaguely eighteenth- or nineteenth-century European urban setting ply their trades and become embroiled in aristocratic politics while taking various, mostly male, lovers; Storm Constantine's *Wraethu* series (beginning 1993), chronicling a future where psychically and physically powerful vampiric quasi-humans, hermaphroditic but largely male-appearing, dominate the earth; Marion Zimmer Bradley, whose *Darkover* series (beginning 1976) features a planet where humans and aliens have interbred, one result being the Free Amazons, a number of whom have lesbian relationships; Mercedes Lackey's *Herald Mage* series (beginning 1989), where the greatest of the mages, Vanyel, is in love with another man; Elizabeth Bear, who imagines Christopher Marlowe coming to after his fatal tavern brawl in the land of Faerie and becoming a lover of a Faerie prince (*Ink and Steel* [2008] and *Hell and Earth* [2008]), and rewrites the Norse gods' Ragnarok with Fenris as the feral lover of a male Valkyrie-like warrior (*All the Windwracked Stars* [2008] and *By the Mountain Bound* [2009]); Melissa Scott's and Lisa A. Barnett's *Point of Hopes* (1995), *Point of Dreams* (2001), and *Point of Knives* (2012), where police-procedural work using magic in an alternate-universe medieval/ Renaissance-era urban setting takes place against the backdrop of heroes Nicholas and Philip's relationship; and Lynn Flewelling's popular *Nightrunner* series (beginning 1996), where a somewhat Marlovian (albeit of Faerie descent) thief/intelligencer in a tenuously Elizabethan royal court adopts as apprentice and then lover a provincial young man he rescues from a dungeon – and startles him by showing him to the brothel district in the big city, where brothels for men who want men and women who want women are just as numerous as those for heterosexual women and men. Of note also is Jacqueline Carey, the author of several series of novels beginning with *Kushiel's Dart* (2001), where Phèdre, a young courtesan preternaturally gifted as a sexual masochist – pain and submission for her are ecstatic gifts, and pathways to knowledge and even power – is trained as an intelligence agent in Terre d'Ange, an alternative Renaissance-era France peopled by the descendants of rebellious angels and Elua, the offspring of an alternative Jesus named Yeshua and the maternal goddess of earth. Elua's Aleister-Crowley-esque commandment to his followers is "Love as thou wilt." Carey's heroines have primary relationships with men, but Phèdre as well as a later female character both enjoy their most passionate attachments with women; the denizens of Terre d'Ange are known to have multiple lovers of both sexes, and numerous same-sex liaisons appear casually in the stories.

Some of these works are written by authors like Delany and Russ who self-represent as LGBTQ; many others are by authors who self-represent as straight, like Le Guin. Taking in the whole of the works by these prolific and mostly popular writers, many of whose books are sold as mainstream sci-fi/ fantasy, the field does not appear to be tiny. It is possible to randomly pick up a book like N. K. Jemison's *The Hundred Thousand Kingdoms* (2010), where characters struggle against a repressive political empire ruled by magic, and find that the empire's dominance results from an ancient conflict between a triumvirate of deities, two of whom are male lovers. This is in addition to the less numerous, harder to find publications of Steve Berman's Lethe Press, his *Icarus: The Magazine of Gay Speculative Fiction*, and his excellent anthologies like *So Fey: Queer Fairy Fiction* (2007). And then at the outer edge of our literature – or perhaps encircling it, like a great sea – lies the vast digital trove of fan fiction and slash fiction based on television, movies, and popular books like the Harry Potter novels, in which authors – frequently women, mostly self-identified as straight insofar as they are sexually identified at all – concoct episodes for their beloved characters (like Harry Potter and Draco Malfoy) to become romantic and sexual partners in scenarios rarely imagined or hinted at in the original creations. Counted thus, the incidence of gay romantic attachments in sci-fi/fantasy seems to me comparatively high, higher certainly than in literary fiction. The analogy would be if a significant number of your favorite TV shows centrally starred actors of color, but the shows weren't marketed as "black" or "Latino" and didn't only appear on just one or two channels. The overall sense, then, is that over time the genre has become notably inclusive of LGBTQ representation. Authors, publishers, and readers have created a thriving, established mode of collective fantasizing, a world that is both "real" (in that it manifests a part of human consumption of art in our shared reality) and alternative (in that LGBTQ presence is arguably more pronounced, and more likely, than in many other arenas of our shared reality).

Sexual Possibilities

Inclusiveness takes one step, albeit an important one, toward the realization of the genre's greatest promise. This promise is approached as the work and pleasure of reimagination reaches to the very foundation stones of the "real," and the vertigo of "What if . . . ?" makes us so dizzy that the familiar reorientation back into our politically constrained reality at the close of the book becomes elusive. LGBTQ sci-fi/fantasy has made strides in reimagining gender roles and the episteme of gender itself, and in imagining worlds of diminished or absent heterosexism. But there has arguably been less in terms of speculating about how sexuality itself can be alternatively conceived. (This proposition, however, is tricky because gender by some analytics is a modality of sexuality, or vice versa; and certainly there are no scissors with fine enough blades to entirely pare one from the other.) Part of the relative paucity of such reimagining must be owed to the toll of another genre-label that functions as a dismissal: explicit or sustained attention to sexuality and how we have sex or think about sex almost always gets designated, sneeringly, as pornography. Given this prejudice, it might be a double blow to the aim of being read seriously (and to the prospect of being published) to double speculative alternative unrealities with pornography. (The slash fiction folks do it all the time – and aren't taken seriously.)

There are important exceptions to the relative lack of reimagining the sexual. Butler's *Dawn* (1987), *Adulthood Rites* (1988), and *Imago* (1989) posit an earth devastated by nuclear war, where aliens called the Oankali have arrived to rescue the survivors and heal the planet. The price they demand is that the surviving humans reproduce with them, for the Oankali are gene-traders, traveling the stars and remaking their species with each new encounter. The

Oankali find humans fascinating, but humans are repulsed by the tentacled beings. (We can see, in the parallel here with the Tlic in "Bloodchild," how Butler uses human-alien sexuality to dramatize the overweening fear of difference that dominates human life.) But the rescued humans have been altered by the Oankali and cannot reproduce without their aid. The survivors learn to have sex with the Oankali, who stimulate the humans' brain and nervous centers directly to give them sexual pleasure – while the Oankali empathically experience and amplify the same sensations – and then collect the sperm and ova produced to create children, who also bear Oankali genetic material. The humans are of course quite resistant to this new arrangement, but one consequence of their first sexual encounter with an Oankali present to amplify their pleasure is that they become temporarily repulsed by the touch of other humans, unless the Oankali neuter assists them. Families consist of offspring, a male-female human pair of parents, and a male-female-neuter Oankali triad of parents (the neuter is the chief facilitator of the gene trading).

Delany's four novel-length collection of tales, the Nevèrÿon series (1979–87), is set in a civilization, probably in Africa and / or Asia, circa 5000 BCE, where slavery is pervasive, and the slaveholders are usually brown-skinned, the slaves fair-skinned. Among Delany's speculative portraits of this world is an extended fictive meditation, threaded through many of the tales, on the prehistory of human sexuality. The series dramatizes Delany's insight that diversifying sexual practices and the process of building a civilization arise together. "[T]he reason cities grow," Delany notes, "is that people in the provinces universally believe sex is more available there. . . . Individuals leave tribes for cities because of sex and the talk of sex – in a tribal context where, because of food, sex must be fairly carefully controlled" (Delany, "Sword" 135). Prominent among the tales' characters is Gorgik, who as a young boy in the city observes a young man wearing a slave collar and marked with spectacular scars that Gorgik realizes must come from a whipping. Fascinated with everything about the young man, Gorgik is inexplicably aroused to see the man remove the slave collar – which, if he is a slave, is not supposed to come off. Gorgik never unravels the mystery of the young man, and subsequently is himself enslaved in a mine, then as the sex slave of a noblewoman, and then becomes a liberator, freeing slaves throughout the empire, until he eventually becomes a minister in the imperial government overseeing the emancipation of the empire's slaves. Gorgik's early witnessing of the young man with the collar marks him powerfully, however: in his relationships with the men who become his partners, he insists that he or his partner wear a slave collar during sex. "'We are both free men,'" Gorgik explains. "'For the boy the collar is symbolic – of our mutual affection.... For myself, it is sexual – a necessary part in the pattern that allows both action and orgasm to manifest themselves within the single circle of desire'" (*Tales* 238). Here, Delany experiments within the setting of an imaginary prehistoric past with the Foucauldian insight that what we think of or speak of as our "natural" "sexuality" is in fact a production and function of the discourse of modernity. Gorgik's sexual desire is instantiated, incited, by a relation to a sign, a symbol – what might otherwise be designated as "the talk of sex" for which individuals leave their tribes for the cities, and which is just as substantial as, or is largely the substance of, the sexual acts. Sex here is revealed as not sex with a body, or not only with a body; rather, it refers to sexual acts with a *meaning* of the sign on the body, or for which the body serves as an extension or materialization.

Sex with a sign – with a meaning one makes, with bodies transformed by new meanings – and thus sex with the effect of offering pleasurable and even freeing mutations of what it is to be human: this might serve as a good metaphor for the enterprise of reimagining gender and sexuality in textual form, which is part of the promise, the work and the pleasure, of LGBTQ science fiction and fantasy.

Notes

1. Regarding the "unspeakable" in this context, see Delany, "Pornography."
2. For the purposes of this chapter I refer to science fiction and fantasy as though they were a single genre, which is obviously not how they are marketed, and sometimes – perhaps often – not how the writers of these works conceive them, or their readers read them. But especially where queerness with its definitive defiance of boundary is concerned, it will, I hope, prove useful and proper to discuss these texts with nary a nod to which side of the dividing line they fall on. On the question of sci-fi and fantasy, see Le Guin.
3. *Wild Seed* is noted as part of the Patternist series, but not discussed at all in Garber and Paleo's excellent bibliography of LGBTQ science fiction, fantasy, and horror. The novel was, however, shortlisted among the "retrospective winners" of the James A. Tiptree Award, an annual literary prize first awarded in 1991 for sci-fi and fantasy works that explore or expand readers' notions about gender.

Works Cited

Barker, Clive. *Imajica*. London: HarperCollins, 1991. Print.
Berman, Steve. "Welcome to Icarus 13." *Icarus* 13 (Summer 2012): 5. Print.
Butler, Octavia. "Bloodchild." *Bloodchild and Other Stories*. New York: Four Walls Eight Windows, 1984. 1–32. Print.

Wild Seed. New York: Warner, 1980. Print.

Delany, Samuel R. *Tales of Nevèrÿon*. 1979. Hanover: Wesleyan UP, 1993. Print.

"Pornography and Censorship." *Shorter Views: Queer Thoughts and the Politics of the Paraliterary*. Hanover: Wesleyan UP, 1999. 292–97. Print.

"Sword & Sorcery, S/M, and the Economics of Inadequation: The *Camera Obscura* Interview." *Silent Interviews: On Language, Race, Sex, Science Fiction, and Some Comics*. Hanover: Wesleyan UP, 1994. 127–63. Print.

Trouble on Triton. 1976. Hanover: Wesleyan UP, 1996. Print.

Garber, Eric, and Lyn Paleo. *Uranian Worlds: A Guide to Alternative Sexuality in Science Fiction, Fantasy, and Horror*. Boston: Hall, 1990. Print.

Le Guin, Ursula K. *The Left Hand of Darkness*. New York: Walker, 1969. Print.

"The Matter of Seggri." *The Unreal and the Real: Selected Stories of Ursula K. Le Guin Volume 2: Outer Space, Inner Space*. Easthampton: Small Beer P, 2012. Print.

Lynn, Elizabeth A. *The Woman Who Loved the Moon and Other Stories*. New York: Berkley Books, 1981. Print.

Russ, Joanna. *The Female Man*. 1975. Boston: Beacon P, 1986. Print.

37

Gay Male and Lesbian Pulp Fiction
and Mass Culture

MICHAEL BRONSKI

A Prehistory of Pulp Fiction

The term "pulp fiction" is used indiscriminately in twentieth-century American culture, less as an accurate description of a mid-century commercial literary genre, but rather to locate and pinpoint what Susan Sontag, in her essay "Notes on 'Camp,'" calls a "sensibility." Sontag equates the concept of a "sensibility" with personal taste – that is, a preference for a type of person, object, or idea – but she comes closer to defining it when she writes directly about "camp" as "a way of seeing the world as an aesthetic phenomenon" (277). "Pulp fiction" is understood by most Americans as specific way of seeing the world as a place of heightened emotions, violent actions, and eroticized behaviors, all of which take place in a demi-mode, often criminal, social milieu that is firmly outside of middle-class stability and respectability. Quentin Tarantino's titling his 1994 film *Pulp Fiction* is a prime example of how the term immediately conveys an atmosphere of lurid images and sensationalist emotions.

In gay male and lesbian culture the idea of "pulp fiction" originates in the publication, and wide circulation, of lesbian- and gay-themed paperback novels in the 1950s. These novels are remembered today less for their content – although this has an influence as well – than for their covers. Their "pulp" content was displayed through cover images that were slightly exaggerated, highly dramatized, illuminated with vibrant color, and hovered between a tradition of strict realism and the cartoon. Almost all covers, in addition to the title and author, contained a "shocking" banner headline that made a descriptive, often moralistic statement: "She Dared Enter a Lesbian World" (Fletcher Flora's *Strange Sister* [1954]); "The Novel of a Love Society Forbids" (Clair Morgan's [pseudonym of Patricia Highsmith] *The Price of Salt* [1953]); "A Strange Relationship in a Small Southern Town" (Thomas Hal Phillips's *The Bitterweed Path* [1950]); "The Powerful Story of a Man's Conflicting Love" (Charles Jackson's *The Fall of Valor* [1946]). Because "pulp fiction" is a way of "seeing the world," these covers play an enormous part in defining a "pulp" sensibility within gay male and lesbian culture, and their impact resonates, in various ways, today.

The revolutionary impact of these novels, as well as a subset of gay male publications – particularly, the physique magazine – and more specifically, the impact of a "pulp" sensibility on today's world of LGBTQ literature and culture is enormous. They are simultaneously viewed as an important key to an unexplored gay male and lesbian historical past, a template for contemporary narratives of LGBTQ life, and a point of origin for racial and class inequities and prejudices that exist in the community today. While there is no stable meaning for gay male and lesbian pulps today – just as there is no stable meaning of any "sensibility," its ways of seeing the world open to broad interpretation – their role, after more than half a century, in today's LGBTQ culture is indisputable.

Understanding the place of gay male and lesbian pulp novels in the broader cultures of the postwar 1950s requires some rudimentary knowledge of how, in previous decades, the publishing industry dealt with both sexual and erotic materials as well as how changing technologies allowed, even economically mandated, changes in both printing and distribution. All U.S. publishing, from colonial times to the early 1960s – when the Supreme Court radically changed the definition of obscenity and essentially the censorship laws – had to grapple with the threat and reality of both legal and extralegal censorship. This affected not only any materials related to LGBTQ content, but also descriptions of heterosexual sex, information about birth control, and even, at certain points, scientific knowledge of reproduction. And censorship of fiction was not restricted to pornography or explicitly erotic writing, but was often aimed at literary work as well. James Joyce's *Ulysses* was not legally available nationally until 1933; D. H. Lawrence's *Lady Chatterley's Lover* was deemed not obscene by the U.S. Supreme Court in 1959. Such restrictions made it even more surprising that gay male and lesbian material was even available in the 1950s, but did ensure that only a very specific narrative could be told in books published by both mainstream and more alternative publishers.

The battle for publishing and distributing both literary and nonliterary erotic material was fought on several fronts. Established publishers such Alfred and Blanch Knopf, founders, in 1915, of Alfred Knopf Inc., shied away from titles that might bring them into trouble with the law. They were interested in publishing Radclyffe Hall's lesbian-themed 1928 *The Well of Loneliness* (which had already been banned in the United Kingdom), but declined when it became clear that it could be judged legally obscene. More adventurous, younger publishers such as Albert and Charles Boni, Horace Liveright, Pascal Corvici, Donald Fried, and others were willing to fight government and social censors (Gertzman 145). (The firm Corvici-Fried published *The Well of Loneliness*, won the court battle, and sold one hundred thousand copies the first year.)

Simultaneously, other publishers took a more underground approach and printed a wide range of erotic materials – John Cleland's classic erotic 1748 novel *Memoirs of a Woman of Pleasure* (also known as *Fanny Hill*); Daniel Defoe's *Moll Flanders* with erotic illustrations; Frank Harris's *My Life and Loves*; Boccaccio's *Decameron* with erotic illustrations; Pierre Louys's *Aphrodite*; and J. G. Bertram's fictional erotic flagellation memoir *The Merry Order of St. Bridget* – which they peddled surreptitiously to bookstores, via personal subscription sales (which avoided prosecution for the public sale of obscenity), and through mail order catalogues. Men such as Samuel Roth, Esar Levin, and Benjamin Rebhuhns published and distributed, from the early 1920s to the 1940s, under such imprints as Panurge Press, Falstaff Press, Golden Hind Press, and Rarity Press. This thriving, enormously lucrative alternative to mainstream publishing essentially formed the template for the publication of much lesbian and gay male material over the next decades. Although the "bookleggers" and "smutmongers" dealt mainly in heterosexual erotica, some lesbian and gay male content was often also available, and often only available, through them (Gertzman 223, 160–61). Because obscenity laws were intended to prohibit all materials that might tend to "deprave and corrupt," often any lesbian or gay male content could render a book obscene. Titles such as *The Well of Loneliness*, *Oscar Wilde Three Times Tried* (transcripts of Wilde's trial; 1910), Theophile Gautier's *Mademoiselle de Maupin* (1835), and George Eekhoud's *Strange Love: The Story of an Abnormal Passion* (1900) were of great interest to lesbians and gay men, and were bought and read by heterosexuals as well. These were the precursors, in many ways, to the advent of LGBTQ pulp fiction in the years after World War II.

The explosion of postwar gay male and lesbian pulps must be placed in another, more contemporary context as well. This context, equally important in framing gay and lesbian pulp fiction, was the mass production of pictorial magazines – usually called physique or physical culture magazines – aimed at a gay male audience that featured the male body in idealized, muscular poses. Publications such as *Physique Pictorial*, *Tomorrow's Man*, *Vim*, and *Body Beautiful* were sold openly on newsstands. As with lesbian and gay male pulp novels, the physique magazines had roots that were decades old.

While idealization of the male body is clearly evident in the sculptures of Attic Greece and the neoclassical work of Italian Renaissance artists such as

Michelangelo – both of whom British Victorian homosexuals used as emblematic of male homoerotic desire – the commercialization of the muscular male form began at the turn of the century with the advent of a physical culture movement in both the United Kingdom and the United States. Eugen Sandow, a Prussian strong man and circus performer in the 1890s, gained a name for himself in London's music halls and on the American vaudeville circuit for his feats of strength and displaying his perfect body. A great deal of Sandow's fame was generated from photographs of him in "classical" poses nearly nude. These studio photographs, sold in stores and at shows, were enormously popular. In 1897, he opened his Institute of Physical Culture, and by 1901 began publishing *Sandow's Magazine of Physical Culture and British Sport*. Within a decade, his Institutes open in other countries, he started a line of fitness equipment as well as food supplements (Chapman 100–28).

The display of Sandow's body was twofold. It was a symbol of the perfect white male body – his poses as Hercules and Greek statues reinforced the idea that he was the epitome of Western masculinity and racial purity – in a world in which the British Empire was beginning to crumble (Kasson 54). It was also, simultaneously, the overt object of sexual desire for both women and men. There are accounts of homosexual men in London collecting his photographs. This commercialization of the male body as a sex object was a turning point in Anglo and American culture. As John Kasson notes, "Sandow revealed the erotics of the male body could be broadly exposed precisely because it was never explicitly mentioned" (76).

The United States was dealing with its own crisis in race and masculinity – economic shifts had moved many men from jobs of physical labor to office work and the 1909 formation of the NAACP greatly advanced the civil rights movement. Physical culture magazines drew a larger readership, beginning with Bernarr Macfadden's *Physical Culture*. With its slogan "Weakness Is a Crime; Don't Be a Criminal," the magazine began publication in 1899 and folded in 1955. Macfadden was an ardent nationalist and anti-immigrant, worried about race suicide, and often inveighed against homosexuality. *Physical Culture* generated a host of imitations over the ensuing decades, increasing after World War II, including *Health and Strength*, *American Manhood*, and *Iron Man*. These magazines – offering tips on body building, exercise, and weight lifting – promoted a highly racialized idea of American heterosexual masculinity even as they were predicated on displaying the nearly naked male body in objectified, eroticized poses.

With these cultural, economic, and publishing preconditions in place – each of which were responsible for substantive shifts in how America conceptualized and grappled with sexuality and gender – all that the lesbian and gay male pulp and physique magazine revolution needed to occur was a decisive spark. That spark was World War II, which radically altered how sex and gender were conceptualized and enacted in American culture. It also helped create new social and political opportunities for LGBTQ people.

Impact of World War II

On December 7, 1941, the United States entered World War II, which had been ongoing since September 1939. The draft and enlistment entailed the massive relocation of men into the armed forces. By 1945, more than sixteen million United States citizens and residents had joined the armed forces. The majority of the men were white. Seven hundred thousand, or 4 percent of the military, were African Americans; the military also included three hundred fifty thousand Mexican Americans. The majority of men in all branches were in their twenties; 35 percent of those who enlisted in the Navy during the war years were teenagers. For the first time, women were allowed to enlist, finding social status and respect not offered by civilian life. More than two hundred ninety thousand women served in the war in the Women Auxiliary Army Corps (WAAC) and other branches of the armed forces. Military work allowed women to be viewed as strong, competent, and skilled professionals.

With men at war, civilian job opportunities were open to women. Before 1941, women comprised less than 25 percent of the U.S. workforce; about twelve million workers. By 1945 they were a full third of the workforce, more than eighteen million. Before the war, not all women were expected to work; married middle-class women were often supported by their husbands. These new work opportunities were a boon to lesbians and other single women who did not rely on male support. These workplace shifts substantially altered perceptions of gender roles and women workers were now regarded as independent and strong. World War II also radically challenged ideas about private and public, broadening the parameter of social permissibility. It was now permissible for men to show deeply felt personal emotions in public. Displays of sexual passion were now acceptable public behaviors as illustrated by Alfred Eisenstaedt's famous photograph, *V–J day in Times Square*, in which a sailor is passionately kissing a nurse in the broad daylight. Such behavior, unthinkable before the war, was now acceptable.

The female body was now a fortified body that built ships and defended democracy. Images of women in the popular press portrayed them as strong – Rosie the Riveter was a national hero – and competent. *Making WAVES: Navy*

Women of World War II, a collection of photographs the U.S. Navy commissioned to document women's naval wartime experience, displays how female gender roles were altered during these years. This was in sharp contrast to the bodies of men at war. Images of fighting men in the popular press were a jarring combination of extraordinarily valiant and extraordinarily fragile. Men were often pictured shirtless on battleships or in trenches; dirty, sweaty, and vulnerable. *At Ease: Navy Men of World War II* documents these changes in representing the male body. These new national standards of valorized, fragile masculinity and strong women radically altered U.S. ideas about gender (Vettel-Becker).

This was also the first time in American history that large-scale, highly organized, single-sex social arrangements were considered vital to national security. Men on battleships and battlefields lived together in close quarters with little privacy. This physical intimacy and stressful conditions often led to emotional and sexual intimacy. Servicemen turned to their fellow troops for emotional and psychological support. Without men in their everyday lives, female armed forces members formed emotional friendships in a more open culture that encouraged awareness of sexual possibilities.

Wartime conditions produced social systems appealing to homosexuals. Single-sex environments encouraged homosocial relationships. Lesbians living economically and socially independent of men found the military a haven. Homosexual men could now avoid their families' heterosexual expectations. In many fundamental ways, the national stage was being set for the emergence not only of wider representation of gay men and lesbians in the national media, including paperback novels, but, as we will see, in the broader world of politics as well. The new representations of gay men and lesbians could not happen with traditional technologies or methods of distribution of materials. Just as social and cultural ideas about homosexuality were changing during these years, so were the ways materials were printed and brought to an ever-increasing public. Paperbound (soon to be called paperbacks) books began to circulate and quickly found an eager audience. They were cheaper to produce, cheaper to buy, easy to carry if you were traveling (one of the first imprints was called Pocket Books), and because they were not sold in bookstores but with magazines and newspapers, they reached a wider market.

During and after World War II, new publishing companies emerged, magazine publishers branched out, and even more traditional publishers began to produce the new paperback. At first these companies relied on reprinting titles, often classics, that were in the public domain, and then previously published fiction and nonfiction. But as the market quickly grew – sales figures for a popular title could reach into the millions – publishers developed a new approach. In 1950, Fawcett Books decided to produce paperback originals, which had the advantages of costing less to acquire as there was no need to pay a fee to the original publisher and authors would get a small advance and relay on royalties. The other advantage was that these books could quickly address contemporary, often explosive, issues such as juvenile delinquency, urban crime, and all forms of licit and illicit sex. As the market grew and became competitive, the cover art on these books began to change and become more vivid and eye catching, often to the point of being lurid. This was, to a large degree, because the cover images were taken from oil paintings commissioned by the publishers, so that colors, framing, and details were both bold and authoritative: erotic without being cheap or sleazy. This aesthetic is what we now associate with the idea of pulp fiction (Zimet). These books were not distributed through the traditional vendors that stocked bookstores, but by companies that supplied magazines to highly trafficked locations such as train and bus stations, newsstands, drugstores, and stationary stores; they were displayed on racks rather than shelves and sold for between twenty-five and fifty cents.

Postwar Mass Culture

All of these preconditions were important in setting the stage for the advent of lesbian and gay pulp novels, but they were also indicative of even larger changes in 1950s culture. The accepted myth is that the 1950s was a time of great sexual repression and that homosexuality was largely unspoken and unseen. Nothing could be further from the truth. While there was certainly a social mandate for sexual conservatism during these postwar years, this was in stark contrast to the many ways that the United States was obsessed with sexuality and with homosexuality in particular. We can see this in a number of ways in popular culture. While *Father Knows Best* and *I Love Lucy* were popular television shows that embraced a domesticated view of the decade's family life, Marilyn Monroe and Jayne Mansfield (and a host of imitators) – perhaps a cultural response to the less sexualized working woman of the war years – glorified the eroticized female body. Hollywood's star-making machinery turned out numerous highly sexualized male stars such as Rock Hudson, Tab Hunter, Guy Williams, Troy Donahue, Anthony Perkins, Rory Calhoun, and Ty Hardin, who appeared shirtless in provocative, sexualized studio photographs – quickly named beefcake – that portrayed the male body in new ways that were remarkably similar to the valorized, vulnerable, exposed bodies of the men in World War II photos and those in the physique magazines.

These visual manifestations of sexuality, while culturally pervasive, were only one indicator of a national preoccupation with sexuality. The enormous, almost frenzied, interest in the publication of Alfred Kinsey's *Sexual Behavior in the Human Male* in 1948 and *Sexual Behavior in the Human Female* in 1953 is a prime example of how pervasive, and public, postwar interest in sexuality was. Both volumes were national best sellers (although probably went mostly unread as they were composed mainly of statistical charts accompanied by scientific explanations), but more important, both generated a wealth of popular analysis (published in the newly available paperback format), newspaper reporting, editorials, opinion pieces, magazines articles, cartoons, jokes, and even LP comedy records (Butt). The American public was especially fascinated and shocked by Kinsey's findings on homosexual behavior. Relying on face-to-face interviews and a sophisticated statistical analysis, Kinsey reported that, between their teen years and old age, 37 percent of all males had some form of homosexual contact and of those who remained single until the age of thirty-five, 50 percent had overt homosexual experience to orgasm. Even more surprising was that 10 percent of males were more or less exclusively homosexual for at least three years between the ages of sixteen and fifty-five, and 4 percent of males were exclusively homosexual throughout their lives. Five years later, in the companion volume, Kinsey stated that homosexual behavior among women was half of what he discovered in men, but that female orgasm was far more prevalent in homosexual couplings than heterosexual. The idea that homosexual activity was commonplace in America was shocking to many readers, but not necessarily a new one. Philip Wylie, in his hugely popular 1942 critique of American culture, *A Generation of Vipers*, explicitly detailed the hypocrisy of the American male discomfort with homosexuals, when same-sex behavior was so prevent in all-male institutions such as the military.

This very public discussion about homosexuality (and sexuality in general) was also fueled by a national preoccupation with psychoanalysis and its relationship to human behavior, particularly sexual behavior. Popularized psychoanalytic case studies included books such as Robert Lindner's 1955 *The Fifty Minute Hour* and Corbett H. Thigpen and Hervey M. Cleckley's 1957 examination of a split personality, *The Three Faces of Eve*, which was made into an award-winning Hollywood film later that year. Homosexuality was a perfect subject for psychoanalytic writers who could write about it professionally, yet not, as Kinsey did, abstractly. Books such as A. M. Krich's 1954 *The Homosexuals: As Seen by Themselves and Thirty Authorities*, Edmund Berger's 1956 *Homosexuality: Disease or Way of Life*, and Richard C. Robertiello's 1959 *Voyage from Lesbos: The Psychoanalysis of a Female Homosexual* were all popular studies of homosexuality. While the Bergler and Robertielo studies treat homosexuality as a serious psychological illness, this was true of many, but not all, psychoanalysts. Robert Lindner, in his very popular 1956 *Must You Conform?*, viewed homosexuality not merely as a clear deviation from a conventional Freudian psychosexual development, but also as an important attempt to assert individuality in an increasingly conformist American culture.

In this vibrant mix of cultural, social, political, and medical discussion, the homophile movement was born. The Mattachine Society, the first gay male political group in the United States, was founded in Los Angeles in 1950 by Harry Hay, a political organizer, along with a small group of other men (D'Emilio; Hay and Roscoe). The Daughters of Bilitis (DOB), the first lesbian political organization, was founded in San Francisco in 1955 by Del Martin and Phyllis Lyon, a couple looking to form a social support group for other lesbians. Neither group had a direct connection to the discussion of gay and lesbian issues in the press or books, nor did they have a connection to the explosion of pulp fiction that was just beginning (Gallo). However, it was this national social and political context that allowed, and helped, each group form, and it was the publishing culture of pulp fiction that supported their continuing, by helping to create and sustain gay male and lesbian communities.

The conflation of the social and political factors at this period of U.S. history made the emergence of lesbian and gay male pulps almost inevitable. They were – as a sensibility – the perfect material manifestation of national preoccupations with sex, gender, and outsider status as well as a materialization of newly emerging homosexual communities within this culture. It is important, however, to make very clear distinctions between the lesbian and gay male pulp genres as each is distinct and reflective not only of a very specific literary history, but of the differences between the actual communities themselves.

Lesbian Pulps

The genre of lesbian pulp was a direct result of the paperback original revolution started by Fawcett Books in 1950. Tereska Torrès's *Women's Barracks* was published shortly after Fawcett started its Gold Medal line. At the age of twenty, Paris-born Torrès, who was Jewish, fled France when the Nazis invaded and served in the French Free Forces during the war. In 1948, at the urging of her husband, novelist Myer Levin, she submitted her diaries of her military experience to Fawcett for publication. With its sexy cover (by Barye Phillips) of women soldiers in undergarments dressing – and the cover banner

"The Frank Autobiography of a French Girl Soldier" – the book was an immediate hit and sold more than two million copies in five years. (By 2012 it had sold four million copies [Fox n.pag.].) Ironically, *Women's Barracks* has only minimal lesbian content. In a 2010 interview, Torrès stated: "There are five main characters. Only one and a half of them could be considered lesbian. I don't see why it is considered a lesbian classic" (Litchfield n.pag.). Torrès's comment missed the point – the popularity of *Women's Barracks* occurred because there was already huge desire in the American book-buying public to read about lesbians. Moreover, given the liminal position of homosexuality in American culture – it was discussed and highly visible, yet remained to some degree unspeakable and forbidden – *Women's Barracks* was perfect to bring the topic of lesbianism to the mass market paperback: it was lesbian, but not too lesbian; it was European, not American; it placed female desires in the context of World War II, but not in the American armed forces, and it was based on actual events, but presented as fiction. The sales of the book were so strong that Fawcett decided to publish more original fiction with lesbian themes.

In 1951, Dick Carroll, an editor at Fawcett, commissioned Marijane Meaker, a lesbian who had only published a few stories at this point, to write a lesbian novel. Under the gender-ambiguous name Vin Packer, Fawcett released *Spring Fire* about the love of two college girls, Leda and Mitch, in a college sorority. On her editor's insistence, because of worries about censorship, the novel had an unhappy ending although the narrative itself was completely sympathetic. As with *Women's Barracks*, the cover art (again by Barye Phillips) displayed women in undergarments; here slips, not bras and panties), which helped sell the book. In the first year, *Spring Fire* sold a million and a half copies (Forrest x). *Spring Fire* was Meaker's only lesbian pulp novel. Her later work for Gold Medal under Vin Parker were crime novels, often based on true events such as the noted Fredan-Wepman murder case (*Whisper His Sin* [1954]), the murder of Emmet Till (*Dark Don't Catch Me* [1956] and *3-Day Terror* [1957]), the New Zealand Parker-Hulme murder case (*The Evil Friendship* [1958]), as well as exposés of juvenile delinquency and suburban adultery, which, because of their sympathetic views, took on the role of social advocacy. Meaker continued to write on lesbian themes for Gold Medal under the name of Ann Aldrich, and published sociological observations on lesbian life such as *We Walk Alone* (1955) and *We, Too, Must Love* (1958). In this context, it is possible to view *Spring Fire* – as well as all of the lesbian pulps – as not simply novels, but sociological texts that exposed and explored the lives of homosexuals, and the homosexual milieu, for a broader audience. Given the enormous sales that these books garnered, it may be safely assumed that their readership included not only lesbians, and probably some gay men, but a huge number of hetero-sexual women who may have identified with the characters, and heterosexual men who were intrigued or sexually excited by the stories.

The sociological impact of these books is evident not only in the sales fig-ures but in the number of them published. While Fawcett was responsible for many of the most literary titles – almost all by lesbian authors such as Ann Bannon, *Odd Girl Out* (1957), *I Am a Woman* (1959); Valerie Taylor, *The Girls in 3-B* (1959); Paula Christian, *Edge of Twilight* (1959) – there were hundreds and hundreds of other lesbian-themed titles published by a variety of companies. Jaye Zimet, in *Strange Sisters: The Art of Lesbian Pulp Fiction, 1949–1969*, repro-duces four hundred covers of the most famous, and there are many more. Some of these were reprints of earlier literary works – such as Radclyffe Hall's 1928 *The Well of Loneliness* (reprinted by Perma with new editions in 1951, 1955, and 1960), Gale Wilhelm's *We Too Are Drifting* (1935) (reprinted by Lion in 1951), Elizabeth Craigin's *Either Is Love* (1937) (republished by Lion in 1956) – but most were paperback originals. Publishing houses such as Pocket Books, Avon, and Fawcett favored titles that were, if not literary, at least literate, but as the paperback industry grew, newer companies such as Midwood and Beacon released titles with no discernable literary merit, such as Don King's *The Bitter Love* (1959), Kay Addams's *Warped Desires* (1960), and Arthur Adlon's *By Love Depraved* (1961).

The bulk of the lesbian-themed pulps (from the earliest titles to the later ones published in the late 1950s and early 1960s) were presumably written by men; pseudonymous males were the main writers in the industry. These were frankly exploitative and not particularly sympathetic to homosexuality. Their cover art was increasingly less artistic, often relying on crude, cartoonish cari-catures of voluptuous, half-dressed women. It is important to separate these two categories of pulps – the sympathetic titles mostly written by lesbians and the exploitative titles written by (probably) heterosexual men – because they are not only essentially different genres, but because their impact on popular and LGBTQ cultures differed as well. The lesbian-written pulps were concerned with a series of personal and domestic issues from discovering a lesbian sexuality, coming out, entering the lesbian social scene, finding love, and navigating relationships. Even when they ended in failed relationships (which many did), they were often life-guidebooks for the lesbian. As such, they were in many ways the basis for early post-Stonewall lesbian literature such as the novels of Rita Mae Brown, Jane Rule, and Ann-Allen Shockley. The second category of pulps focused almost entirely on the, mostly unrealistic, sexual exploits of their characters. Increasingly as national censorship laws were weakened by court challenges, their sexual content reaffirmed and made more sexually explicit the previously existing stereotype of the oversexed lesbian that has become a staple of both popular fiction and pornography.

Yet the impact of all of these titles over more than a decade was tremendous in bringing the topic of lesbianism into the continuing, larger public conversation about sexuality and gender roles that began in the mid-1940s. This was especially true within the larger contexts of the psychoanalytically influenced discussions that were occurring in both the scientific and popular press at the time. While the lesbian pulp phenomenon was incredibly important for the lesbian community, it was as important to heterosexuals who were attempting to make sense of their own sexual lives and desires that had been thrown from their traditional underpinnings during and after the war. While heterosexual male readers of lesbian pulps may have found them titillating they were also being given new understandings – at least in the best of the pulps – of alternatives for not only female desire, but human relationships.

Gay-Themed Popular Fiction

In the popular imagination, lesbian pulp novels are often categorized alongside, or simply lumped together with, gay male-themed novels. While there are some similarities, particularly in regard to production, distribution, and community formation, there are also many decisive differences. The main difference is the genesis of the material as well as the larger readership.

Lesbian pulp novels were a direct result of the innovation of the paperback original that revolutionized publishing in the late 1940s. While there were some previously published literary novels with lesbian themes – Gale Welheim's *Torchlight to Valhalla* (1938), Anna Elizabet Weirauch's *The Scorpion* (1932), and Dorothy Bussy's *Olivia* (1948) – which were released with "pulp" covers in the 1950s, there were many more gay male-themed literary novels that were first published in cloth by prestigious publishing houses. Many of these were by (closeted) gay male writers. Some of these received glowing critical attention – Charles Jackson's *The Lost Weekend* (1944) and his *The Fall of Valor* (1946), William Maxwell's *The Folded Leaf* (1945), Truman Capote's *Other Voices, Other Rooms* (1948), and James Baldwin's *Giovanni's Room* (1956) – while others, such as Nial Kent's *The Divided Path* (1949), Michael de Forrest's *The Gay Year* (1949), James Barr's *Quatrefoil* (1950), and Jay Little's *Somewhere between the Two* (1956), were published in cloth by reputable houses, but probably intended for a primarily gay male audience. There were also numerous novels with openly gay male characters and themes written by women during this time: Carson McCullers's *Reflections in a Golden Eye* (1941), Isabel Bolton's *A Christmas Tree* (1949), Grace Zaring Stone's *The Grotto* (1951), and Marguerite Yourcenar's *Memoirs of Hadrian* (1951 French edition, 1954 English edition).

The publication of gay male-themed literary titles was so prevalent that there were probably close to three hundred titles published between 1940 and 1969, the year of the Stonewall riots. Why was there such an enormous disparity in the quantity of lesbian-themed and gay male-themed literary fiction? This was a reflection of two realities. The first is undoubtedly the greater male access to publishing that was predicated on gender, not sexual orientation. The second was a national preoccupation with masculinity, especially about gender roles and sexuality, that emerged after World War II. As with the lesbian pulps, these depictions of various types of male gender performance as well as sexual identities were placed securely within the discussions of psychiatry and psychoanalysis of the 1950s. This public discussion about gender roles, with implications about sexual orientation, was culturally vibrant for both women and men and is evident in popular Hollywood films such as *All About Eve* (1950), *Rebel Without a Cause* (1955), *The Strange One* (1957), and *Imitation of Life* (1959).

But the main difference between the lesbian pulps and the gay male pulps was that almost all of the novels published in paper by companies such as Avon, Popular, Fawcett, and Pocket Books with gay male content were reissues of previously released cloth editions, and almost all were literary novels, many of which had been reviewed in the mainstream press. These literary novels, when they were issued in paperback, were given a similar visual marketing approach as the lesbian pulps. Harrison Dowd's well-received *The Night Air* (1950) featured a striking painting of a distraught-looking man with the banner "A Homosexual Looks at Himself"; Fritz Peters's critically noted *Finistère* (1951) portrays a young, unhappy-looking gay man, with a heterosexual couple behind him with the banner "A Powerful Novel of a Tragic Love." These cover designs and copy were misleading on both the (early lesbian-authored) lesbian and gay male pulps. While they may not have ended happily (often because of the homophobia the characters faced), the stories were generally sympathetic to the characters and never as "tragic," "twisted," or "strange" as the covers indicated. These deceptive covers were in part a marketing technique to position the books as condemning homosexuality, but they were also for the publisher's self-protection to ensure that no censors would accuse them of promoting homosexuality.

These gay male-themed pulps were, as was the case with Vin Packer, Ann Bannon, and Valerie Taylor, part of the first wave of the genre. As more companies began to publish pulp novels, the tenor and the tone of the novels began to change. As with the lesbian pulps, there were some blatantly homophobic titles published, but they were relatively few as heterosexual male readers were not titillated by sensational exposés of male homosexuality. When the newer companies began to publish more sexually explicit gay male pulps, they were usually written by gay men and usually were erotic, humorous, or both. Publishers such as Greenleaf, Classical Publications, and Barclay Books were releasing gay male-themed erotica in 1965, and many other companies were to follow. By the late 1980s, close to forty-five hundred titles had been released (Norman). Most of these companies, many based on the West Coast, had very little relationship to traditional publishing companies (most of which were in New York) and saw these books simply as product to be written, released, and sold as quickly as possible. Culturally, the gay male pulp had, at this point in time, evolved into erotica or soft-core pornography.

The bulk of these books were badly written, generated by writing factories of freelance writers who were paid by the manuscript and given no copyright or royalty. Books were barely edited, and proofreading was haphazard. This was a very different arrangement than the first wave of publishers who were part of a traditional publishing industry. Like the earlier pulps, these books were not usually sold in traditional bookstores, but because of their more explicit content and cover were often not sold on display racks in bus stations. They were most often sold in "adult bookstores." These stores sold erotic literature (and later sometimes sex toys and erotic clothing, and frequently they sold drug paraphernalia found in "head shops"). They had existed as early as the 1930s, growing more prevalent in the later 1950s and 1960s, but with the relaxing of censorship laws in the later 1960s they became ubiquitous, along with the advent of the "adult theatre" that showed erotic films in many urban areas.

Despite the strictly commercial conditions in which these novels were written, there were some authors and publishers that produced quality, even literary products. Richard Amory's romantic gay Western trilogy *Song of the Loon* (1966), *Aaron's Song* (1966), and *Listen, The Loon Sings* (1968) were very well written and extraordinarily popular. Later editions of *Loon* claimed that it had sold more than one hundred thousand copies. While this is probably a marketing exaggeration, the book was common enough to produce a parody sequel, *Fruit of the Loon* (1968), as well as a feature film, and later a pornographic version. Greenleaf, under the editorial direction of Earl Kemp, was one of the only erotica houses that cared about quality (Banis and Cleto). Along with the Amory titles, they also published a series of novels by Victor Banis (under the name Don Holliday), in particular *The Man from C.A.M.P.* series, a witty take on James Bond thrillers, as well as Chris Davidson and Phil Andros (the pseudonym for Samuel Stewart; see Spring).

Pulps' Influence on Lesbian and Gay Life

What were the immediate and lasting effects of the pulp revolution on lesbian and gay male life, communities, and cultures? The answers to both of these questions are complicated. For lesbian and gay men who were teens or adults in the 1950s and 1960s, these books were often the first, and in some cases the only, connection they had to a concept that there was a larger homosexual world in the United States. The fact that these novels were easily available in bus stations and newsstands gave homosexuality a particular visibility because these were fictional works that could stir the individual imagination. Critics have noted that lesbian and gay male pulps worked to simply reinforce the existing negative, homophobic cultural stereotypes of the times. This is true for some of the novels in some of the time periods, but completely false as a general statement. Many of the lesbian-themed pulps, mostly written by men, published after the first wave of Gold Medal imprints, were misogynist and homophobic. But the earlier pulps – by Vin Packer, Ann Bannon, Valerie Taylor, and March Hastings – were for the most part complex in their approach to lesbian life. While happy endings were elusive, although not impossible, these books are more accurately read not as products of homophobia, but rather as complicated answers to homophobia. Not only were these authors constrained by publishing conventions (unhappy ending, sensational cover art, moralistic banner language on the covers) but they were, in some sense, using the books to deal with their own complicated relationships to their sexuality. The lesbian readers of the time (and later) may well have not been responding negatively to the unhappy circumstances of the narratives, but using them to understand their own emotions and sexuality.

It is a slightly different situation with the gay male-themed pulps. Many of these novels were already in print and part of a national conversation about masculinity and sexuality, which was still dealing with the effects of World War II on American masculinity. A preponderance of these novels dealt with homosexual themes during the war, such as John Horne Burns's *The Gallery* (1947), Loren Whal's *The Invisible Glass* (1950), and Lonnie Coleman's *Ship's Company* (1955). Even more novels, such as Charles Jackson's *The Fall of Valor* (1946), Gore Vidal's *The City and the Pillar* (1949), and James Barr's *Quatrefoil* (1950), examined the after effects of the war on the men who had fought. Like the physique magazines, these novels were cultural discussions and negotiations about appropriate postwar gender affect, behavior, and sexual desire. As with the lesbian-themed pulps, many of these stories did not have happy endings, but to critique them for this is, given the time period, beside the point. To a large degree, the famous "unhappy ending" of the gay male and lesbian pulp is overstated. Aside from the fact that many of these novels are sympathetic to the characters and their plights, in many cases the "unhappy ending" is clearly a result of the social homophobia that the characters face. For example Peters's *Finistère*, often held up as a prime example of the "sad young man" novel, can easily be read as a chilling exposé of how familial and cultural homophobia causes the death of a teenage boy (Bronski, introduction 17). While the later waves of lesbian-themed books were clearly homophobic, this is not true for the later gay male-themed books that were written by gay men and overwhelmingly positive about reaffirming gay male sexuality and life.

Whatever personal reaction to these books occurred, there is great evidence that for many lesbians and gay men, they worked as stepping stones to finding and entering a homosexual community. Katherine Forrest writes of the importance of finding and reading Ann Bannon's *Odd Girl Out* in a Detroit drug store in 1957: "I found it when I was eighteen years old. It opened the door to my soul and told me who I was. It led me to other books that told me who some of us were, and how some of us lived" (ix). This is a common testimonial for lesbian and gay men born in the later 1930s and the 1940s. Forrest's eloquence here is powerful, but does not address the specifics of how these books concretely aided community building. This happened in a number of ways. The narratives in some books – Ann Bannon's series, Michael deForrest's *The Gay Year*, Harrison's Dowd's *The Night Air* – were located in real neighborhoods where lesbian and gay men lived: in all of these cases, Greenwich Village. As such they actually give specific geographic locations for homosexuals throughout the country to know where to find other lesbian and gay men. Other books such as Lonnie Coleman's *Sam* (1959) could give an inexperienced gay man insight into the proper etiquette for navigating a bathhouse or a gay bar. Often books, in describing homes in which homosexuals lived, would give the novice a sense of how to identify others like him. For example, reproductions and visual images of Michelangelo's David were very common in pre-Stonewall gay male life decor and used by men as a coded way to safely identify common sexual interests. It was also ubiquitous in the physique magazines as well as the male homophile publications (Butt 63). Many novels, such as March Hasting's *Three Women* (1958), are filled with descriptions of what lesbians wore – particularly in relationship to butch/femme roles – and how they looked. Such information was available nowhere else for the novice lesbian.

The legacy of these books on the LGBTQ community today is clear. Most of these novels were rejected by the young women and men coming out right after the Stonewall riots and involved in the gay liberation and gay rights movements. After such a decisive political and cultural break, these narratives were seen as pessimistic, self-hating, and filled with negative images. Gay liberation, in its fervent desire to move quickly into the future, did not understand the importance or the complexity of the past. A decade later, many of these titles were reclaimed by younger lesbians and gay men. In the early 1980s, Naiad Press, under the editorial direction of Barbara Grier (who had been an editor and book reviewer for *The Ladder* throughout the 1960s and 1970s), reprinted the novels of Ann Bannon, Paula Christian, and Valerie Taylor. By the end of the decade, critical work was being done in the academy on the literary and cultural impact of these novels. During this time, gay male collectors began buying and selling both early and later pulps – for their cover art and for insight into gay male history. Critical and social evaluations came when Arsenal Pulp Press began publishing their Little Sisters Classics series, which republished *Finistère* and Armory's *Song of the Loon*. Literary critics also began examining the historical importance of these works as well (Bronski, *Pulp*; Young).

A lasting effect of this dichotomy was that a genre, or tradition, of gay male-themed fiction began, and has remained a firm fixture of the American literary canon. Today, many gay male-themed writers such as Gore Vidal, Christopher Isherwood, Edmund White, Alan Hollinghurst, and Andrew Holleran, among others, have had relatively little difficulty entering the mainstream of American political letters, but as Sarah Schulman and others have noted, lesbian-themed work has a far, far more difficult time getting published, and openly lesbian writers are routinely excluded from non-LGBTQ specific literary awards, artistic support venues, and foundation grants.

Works Cited

Bachner, Evan. *At Ease: Navy Men of World War II*. New York: Abrams, 2004. Print.

Making WAVES: Navy Women of World War II. New York: Abrams, 2008. Print.

Banis, Victor J., and Fabio Cleto. *Spine Intact, Some Creases: Remembrances of a Paperback Writer*. Genova: ECIG, 2004. Print.

Bronski, Michael. "Introduction." *Finistère*. By Fritz Peters. 1952. Vancouver: Arsenal Pulp P, 2006. 9–25. Print.

Pulp Friction: Uncovering the Golden Age of Gay Male Pulps. New York: St. Martin's, 2002. Print.

Butt, Gavin. *Between You and Me: Queer Disclosures in the New York Art World, 1948–1963.* Durham: Duke UP, 2005. Print.

Chapman, David L. *Sandow the Magnificent: Eugen Sandow and the Beginnings of Bodybuilding.* Urbana: U of Illinois P, 1994. Print.

D'Emilio, John. *Sexual Politics, Sexual Communities: The Making of a Homosexual Minority in the United States, 1940–1970.* Chicago: U of Chicago P, 1983. Print.

Forrest, Katherine V. *Lesbian Pulp Fiction: The Sexually Intrepid World of Lesbian Paperback Novels, 1950–1965.* San Francisco: Cleis P, 2005. Print.

Fox, Margalit. "Tereska Torrès, 92, Writer of Lesbian Fiction, Dies." *New York Times* 24 Sept. 2012. Web. 27 Dec. 2013.

Gallo, Marcia M. *Different Daughters: A History of the Daughters of Bilitis and the Rise of the Lesbian Rights Movement.* New York: Carroll & Graf, 2006. Print.

Gertzman, Jay A. *Bookleggers and Smuthounds: The Trade in Erotica, 1920–1940.* Philadelphia: U of Pennsylvania P, 1999. Print.

Hay, Harry, and Will Roscoe. *Radically Gay: Gay Liberation in the Words of Its Founder.* Boston: Beacon, 1996. Print.

Kasson, John F. *Houdini, Tarzan, and the Perfect Man: The White Male Body and the Challenge of Modernity in America.* New York: Hill, 2001. Print.

Litchfield, Joan. "Tereska Torrès: The Reluctant Queen of Lesbian Literature." *The Independent* 5 Feb. 2010. Web. 31 Jan. 2014.

Norman, Tom. *American Gay Erotic Paperbacks: A Bibliography.* Burbank: n.pag., 1994. Print.

Sontag, Susan. "Notes on 'Camp.'" *Against Interpretation, and Other Essays.* New York: Farrar, 1966. 275–92. Print.

Spring, Justin. *Secret Historian: The Life and Times of Samuel Steward, Professor, Tattoo Artist, and Sexual Renegade.* New York: Farrar, 2010. Print.

Vettel-Becker, Patricia. *Shooting from the Hip: Photography, Masculinity, and Postwar America.* Minneapolis: U of Minnesota P, 2005. Print.

Wylie, Philip. *Generation of Vipers.* New York: Farrar, 1942. Print.

Young, Ian. *Out in Paperback: A Visual History of Gay Pulps.* Toronto: LMB, 2007. Print.

Zimet, Jaye. *Strange Sisters: The Art of Lesbian Pulp Fiction, 1949–1969.* New York: Viking Studio, 1999. Print.

38

Childhood Studies: Children's and Young Adult Literatures

ERIC L. TRIBUNELLA

Childhood and Sexuality

Children, childhood, and children's culture are central to the construction and enactment of gender and sexuality. In his foundational history, Michel Foucault identifies the child as one of the privileged objects around which the discourse of sexuality has developed since the eighteenth century. The child links parents and relatives, teachers and administrators, healthcare workers and child experts, and whole communities of citizens in a broad web of relations across which power operates. Because children occupy these intersections between the family and the state, childhood sexuality proves especially useful as a strategic site of knowledge and power (Foucault 103–05). The sense that children are prone to sexual pleasure but must refrain from sexual activity further conspires to make child sex a problem. At stake in this proliferation of discourse about the problem of child sex, according to Foucault, is not the regulation or repression of sexuality, but its very production (105). The child is therefore critical to modern hetero / homosexual definition and the construction of sexuality more generally, which includes affectional, romantic, and sexual desires, pleasures, and relations. The notion of childhood sexuality as a problem remains the dominant framework by which it is conceptualized and figured, including in children's literature and culture.

Much of the early discourse on the sexual health and morality of children that emerged in the West during the nineteenth century focused on schoolboys. John Chandos documents campaigns to eliminate "immorality" and "vice" from schools in nineteenth-century England: "In the interval dividing the early and mid-century a feverish anxiety, especially in the middle classes, to prevent or abridge sexual experience in the young grew to the dimensions of a collective neurosis" (287). Michael Stolberg credits the anonymous publication of *Onania, or The Heinous Sin of Self-Pollution* (1716) with igniting the Euro-American obsession with the physical and moral dangers of the "solitary vice" (37). According to Stolberg, "masturbation was believed to be particularly prevalent among the young, whose careful moral and religious education was increasingly considered a principal task to which parents and school, from early on, were to turn all their attention" (47). Adults also feared the possibility of same-sex relations between boys. In his *Sexual Inversion* (1897), considered the first book-length study of homosexuality in English, Havelock Ellis notes the prevalence of homosexuality in elite British boarding schools: "The institution which presents these phenomena to us in the most marked and the most important manner is, naturally the school, in England especially the public school" (44). Over the course of the nineteenth century, adults developed elaborate practices to prevent boys from experimenting sexually.

Adults also worried about the sexual knowledge and experiences of girls, especially the sexual exploitation of young girls by older men and the sex work of adolescents. Christine Stansell argues that much of the anxiety about prostitution in the mid-nineteenth century actually centered on children. "It was in large part the involvement of young girls," she writes, "that brought prostitution to public attention in the 1850s" (89). The concern about girlhood prostitution was linked to other fears about the reproductive sexuality and economic mobility of working-class and immigrant girls in the United States (Stansell 90). In England, journalist W.T. Stead created an international scandal in 1885 by publishing a series of investigative reports describing in lurid detail the world of child prostitution. To illustrate the ease with which girl prostitutes could be acquired, Stead arranged to purchase thirteen-year-old Eliza Armstrong from her alcoholic mother for £5, an act for which he was later tried and convicted. The outcry over Stead's reports pressured Parliament to pass the Criminal Law Amendment Act of 1885 raising the age of consent for girls from thirteen to sixteen (Odem 12).

Though these cases indicate that Sigmund Freud was not the first to acknowledge the sexual lives of children, Freud did work to counter the widespread belief that childhood sexuality was unnatural or aberrant. As he wrote in 1905, "It is true that in the literature of the subject one occasionally comes across remarks upon precocious sexual activity in small children – upon erections, masturbation and even activities resembling coitus. But these are always quoted only as exceptional events, as oddities or as horrifying instances of precocious depravity" (39). Freud revolutionized thinking about childhood sexuality by noting that it usually takes forms unlike those of adult sexuality, and he cited thumb sucking and the holding back of stool as examples of physical activities in which children engage for pleasure. That pleasure, he claims, results more from the nature of the stimulus than from the body part involved, and any part of the body can be manipulated to cause sensual, and hence sexual, pleasure. For Freud, sexual activity is not limited to the stimulation of the genitals. Moreover, children only gradually construct what Freud refers to as the mental dams that direct the sexual aim to culturally sanctioned objects. Prior to this process, the child maintains a polymorphously perverse disposition in which sexual pleasure can be found in a wide array of activities and objects (100, 105).

The Queerness of Children and Childhood

Children and depictions of children usually do not conform to expectations of normative, heterosexual, dyadic, genital relations, and the sexual categories and identities that are operative in adult culture typically do not apply to children and can even obscure the desires, pleasures, and possibilities of childhood. Studying childhood sexuality in children's literature involves considering elements that might not initially appear sexual – perhaps because they do not involve genital activity or even human relationships – but that nonetheless constitute objects of desire or sources of pleasure. Children's affinities for or pleasurable experiences with food, siblings or parents, animal companions, inanimate objects such as blankets or toys, scenarios of capture and concealment, rough-and-tumble play, or their own bodies represent some of the possibilities that could be understood in terms of childhood sexuality. Activities or pleasures that are sometimes considered perversions in adulthood may be the more common expressions of desire and pleasure in childhood. The ways childhood sexualities defy expectations of adult sexualities point to what some critics have described as the queerness of children.

Steven Bruhm and Natasha Hurley describe the queer child as one "whose play confirms neither the comfortable stories of child (a)sexuality nor the supposedly blissful promises of adult heteronormativity" (ix). Bruhm and Hurley argue that the adult focus on what children can or will become "opens up a space for childhood queerness – creating space for the figure of the child to be queer as long as the queerness can be rationalized as a series of mistakes or misplaced desire" (xiv). Such is the case in works like John Knowles's *A Separate Peace* (1959), in which Gene refuses to acknowledge his homoerotic attachment to Finny and becomes responsible for his friend's death, or like Katherine Paterson's *Bridge to Terabithia* (1977), in which the tomboyish Leslie perishes and her sensitive friend Jesse becomes more conventionally boyish as a result of her influence (see Tribunella). Debates about whether Gene and Finny are really gay, or questions about whether Jesse and Leslie would be, are not the point. Adult sexual identities and practices do not always fit children and adolescents comfortably. While the children or adolescents in these books do not identify as gay, and we cannot know whether they are proto-gay, their queerness is signaled by same-sex desires or unconventional gender expressions.

Bruhm and Hurley point to the very queerness of childhood and of any sexual expression by children, who are barred from being sexual at all. According to Kathryn Bond Stockton, all children are queer: "the child, from the standpoint of 'normal' adults, is always queer: either 'homosexual' ... or 'not-yet-straight,' merely approaching the official destination of straight couplehood" ("Growing" 283). For the child who is supposed to be sexually ignorant and even asexual, "sex itself seems shockingly queer" (296). Similarly for Tison Pugh, even heterosexuality in the context of children's culture can be queer. Pugh notes that while heterosexuality is ubiquitous in children's literature, the presumed heterosexuality of children remains at odds with the imperative that children be and remain sexually inexperienced (4–5).

The paradoxical position of children in relation to sexuality complicates identification and terminology. For Kenneth Kidd, "the genital test is useless" in identifying childhood (homo)sexuality (115). His claim is supported by James Howe's contemporary children's novel *Totally Joe* (2005), in which the twelve-year-old protagonist ultimately identifies as gay and "likes" other boys, but certainly cannot imagine kissing them, let alone engaging in genital sexual relations with them: "I mean, bumping elbows is one thing, and holding hands is awesome, but actually putting your mouth on somebody else's mouth and exchanging saliva? ☺ *Ewww!*" (89). Joe adapts gay identity to fit the current form of his childhood desire: he "likes" boys but still thinks of kissing and sex as gross, so his sense of himself as gay does not include genital-sexual desire.

In *The Queer Child* (2009), Stockton argues against using terms like "gay" or "homosexual" to describe children: "For this queer child, whatever its conscious grasp of itself, has not been able to present itself according to the category 'gay' or 'homosexual' – categories culturally deemed too adult, since they are sexual, though we do presume every child to be straight" (7). I argue that the problem with the categories "gay" and "homosexual" may not be that they are sexual ones, but that they are sexual in adult ways, as Howe's *Totally Joe* suggests. The character of Joe offers insight into how the gay child is not simply a miniature or younger gay adult; rather, gay children must be understood on their own terms. If there is a danger in employing a vocabulary devised by and for adults to describe children, it is in the ways such language can obscure the distinct sexualities of children.

The focus on adult identity categories can obscure the ways children's play, or their punishments, reflect bodily pleasures and sexual possibilities. For instance, in Louisa May Alcott's *Little Men* (1871), Jo recalls running away as a girl to show off a new pair of shoes and falling asleep curled up with a dog. Marmee later punishes Jo by tying her to a bedpost. Now an adult herself, Jo punishes the ten-year-old Nan for running off by tying her to the sofa: "'I'd just as lief [gladly] be tied up as not – I like to play dog,' and Nan put on a don't-care face, and began to growl and grovel on the floor" (218). When the younger Rob finds Nan, he is "so charmed with the new punishment, that he got a jump rope and tethered himself to the other end of the sofa in the most social manner" (219). The protagonists in Rudyard Kipling's "The Moral Reformers," one of the stories in *Stalky and Co.* (1899), tie up and beat two other boys under the ruse of playing a game. These are scenes of childhood pleasure in various objects or practices: a new pair of shoes, being tied up, falling asleep with a dog, physically abusing other youths.

While these unremarkable incidents of childhood play or punishment may seem unrelated to sexual matters, they resonate remarkably with what nineteenth-century sexologist Richard von Krafft-Ebing describes as examples of childhood sexuality. In one case, he refers to a thirty-four-year-old man who developed a fetish for women's shoes at the age of seven (131), and one thirty-five-year-old woman reports fantasizing at the age of six or eight about being whipped by her female friends (139). Others of his adult patients report childhood pleasure in stroking fur (183) or playing with domestic pets (406–07). Whether we understand sexuality in children's literature as always queer or not, writing for youth illustrates that desires, pleasures, and relations are typical features of the child's fictional landscape, despite the common misperception that children's books are devoid of sexuality or sexual knowledge.

Same-Sex Desire and Gender Variance in Classic Children's Literature

Children's texts have long included representations of same-sex desires and pleasures, even as they appear distinct to childhood. Though fairy tales are popularly associated with heteronormative outcomes, some include or even center on same-sex relationships. The Grimm Brothers' version of "The Frog King" (1812) ends not with the marriage of the princess to her transformed prince, but on the love of the Frog King's servant, Faithful Heinrich, for his master: "Faithful Heinrich had been so saddened by the transformation of his master into a frog that he had to have three hoops placed around his heart to keep it from bursting with pain and sorrow" (Grimm and Grimm 50). Even queerer is the brief love between the statue of a prince and a male swallow in Oscar Wilde's "The Happy Prince" (1888). As the swallow prepares to die, the prince asks him for a kiss on the lips, and the prince's lead heart breaks when the swallow falls dead. Christina Rossetti's "Goblin Market" (1862), a fairy tale in verse, describes a girl who is seduced by goblin fruit and nears death when she cannot obtain more. She is rescued when her companion braves the goblins to acquire the fruit and bring the juice to the dying girl: "Come and kiss me. / Never mind my bruises, / Hug me, kiss me, suck my juices" (13). Rossetti's poem joins other fairy tales like "The Frog King" and "The Happy Prince" in demonstrating queer desires or relations.

Before the more explicit depiction of gay identity emerged in children's and young adult literature during the last few decades of the twentieth century, a key expression of same-sex desire could be found in intimate and romantic friendships between boys. These friendships are typically critical to the maturation of boys into men and to their initiation into traditionally homosocial institutions of commerce, government, empire, and the military. Thomas Hughes's *Tom Brown's Schooldays* (1857), the most prominent nineteenth-century school story for boys, focuses on the intimate friendship between the eponymous protagonist and a younger boy named George Arthur. Both youths benefit from their friendship, with Tom's developing a sense of responsibility and avoiding expulsion and Arthur's acquiring some of Tom's pluck and athleticism. The novel implies the possibility of boyhood homosexuality by distinguishing between "noble friendships," such as the one between Tom and Arthur, and ignoble ones in which the younger boys are "petted and pampered" and therefore "ruined" by older youths (233). Frederic Farrar's *Eric, or Little by Little* (1858) presents a more sentimental and ominous picture of romantic friendships, which contribute to the main character's being corrupted and ultimately expelled. Other genres, such as adventure fiction, similarly depict romantic friendships. In R.M. Ballantyne's *The Coral Island* (1858), which relates the experiences of three boy castaways, Ralph recalls "embracing [his friends] indiscriminately in [their] dripping garments, and giving utterance to incoherent rhapsodies" (272). The three friends are ultimately caught up in events that involve the colonization of the Fijian Islands, linking their homosocial experience as castaways to the expansion of the British Empire. Michael Moon describes Horatio Alger's classic American story of upward mobility *Ragged Dick* (1869) as a "homoerotic romance" between Dick and his fellow bootblack Fosdick, and he argues that the patronage of boys by men ensures the reproduction of capitalist systems (88). Homoerotic or homoaffectional friendships continued to be the main expression of same-sex desire in children's and young adult literature through the mid-twentieth century.

Girls' books have also included romantic friendships as a key feature of girl-hood and domestic life. Sue Sims suggests that Susan Coolidge's girls' school story *What Katy Did at School* (1873) helped reshape the genre as less moralistic and more pleasurable (5–6). In Coolidge's novel, Katy and her sister Clover are sent to a New England boarding school where they develop intimate friend-ships with other girls. The narrator describes one relationship between two girls who are so "utterly unlike, that Katy thought it odd they should have chosen to be together" (Coolidge 36). She discovers, however, that "Rose liked to protect, and Mary to be protected."

Critics have noted the same-sex eroticism of other classic domestic novels about girls. Roberta Seelinger Trites observes that Jo's love for her mother and sisters in *Little Women* (1868) is expressed "too firmly in the language of passionate love to pass for simple expressions of familial love" (37). Marah Gubar describes the relationship between Anne and Diana in Lucy Maud Montgomery's *Anne of Green Gables* (1908) as "love at first sight" (54), and she argues that Montgomery repeatedly delays heterosexual unions in the Anne series, thereby making "room for passionate relationships between women that prove far more romantic than traditional marriages" (47). Laura Robinson goes even further, identifying the lesbian subtext of later books in the Anne series, which she reads in the context of Montgomery's response to an obses-sive female fan. As with boys' books, girls' fiction often emphasizes intimate, homosocial, and even homoerotic relationships between girls.

Many of the classic children's works noted earlier include gender-non-conforming children as characters, often sensitive boys and tomboyish girls. George Arthur in *Tom Brown* is a sickly, saintly boy who needs the protection of the more robust Tom to thrive. Thomas Bailey Aldrich's *The Story of a Bad Boy* (1869) explicitly references Hughes's novel and also includes a small, timid boy, Binny, who is abused by bullies and later drowns. In *Little Women*, the boy next door, Laurie, is described as "not very strong" and as having "pretty manners" (53), in contrast with the tomboyish Jo, who announces, "I hate to think I've got to grow up, and be Miss March, and wear long gowns, and look as prim as a China aster! It's bad enough to be a girl, anyway, when I like boys' games and work and manners!" (5). Katy's insistence on outside play and her refusal to be a "good" girl in Coolidge's *What Katy Did* result in the accident that paralyzes her, which occasions her transformation into a more domes-tic young lady. Though not unsympathetic characters, sissies and tomboys in classic children's literature typically experience severe trials and either perish or reform into more conventional young men and women.

Possibly the first works for children actually described by their author as "homosexual" are the two boys' adventure novels of Edward Prime-Stevenson: *White Cockades: An Incident of the "Forty-Five"* (1887) and *Left to Themselves: Being the Ordeal of Philip and Gerald* (1891). Prime-Stevenson is best known for writing one of the first explicitly homosexual American novels for adults, *Imre* (1906). "Fiction for young people that has uranian hints naturally is thought the last sort for circulating among British boys and girls," Prime-Stevenson writes in 1908 (*Intersexes* 366). He identifies his own children's books as "homosexual in essence" and offers them as rare contributions to homosexual children's literature (368). Prime-Stevenson sets *White Cockades* during the 1745 Jacobite uprising, when Charles Stuart, the grandson of King James II, fought in Scotland to regain the throne. A sympathetic Scottish man and his sixteen-year-old son, Andrew, hide the prince from English soldiers, and Prince Stuart and Andrew develop an immediate and intense mutual affection. At the conclusion of the novel, the prince announces, "Whither I go, shall he go; and where I lodge, shall he lodge" (210). The narrator adds that "he and his gallant looking protégé seemed inseparable even in private" (214). Prime-Stevenson describes *Left to Themselves* as a more explicit depiction of "Uranian adolescence," calling it "a romantic story in which a youth in his latter teens is irresistibly attracted to a much younger lad, and becomes, *con amore* responsible for the latter's personal safety, in a series of events that throw them together – for life" (*Intersexes* 368). Philip and Gerald experience various adventures on their journey from New York to Nova Scotia, and after triumphing over their antagonist, the youths remain lifelong companions. Prime-Stevenson's work represents an important landmark in the history of gay children's fiction and long predates the emergence of more explicit LGBT literature for children and young adults during the mid-twentieth century.

Contemporary LGBT Children's and Young Adult Literature

Critics usually identify John Donovan's *I'll Get There. It Better Be Worth the Trip* (1969) as the first explicitly gay children's novel because it is likely the first to depict a sexual experience between boys. Though Davy and Altschuler, who are about fourteen, do not identify as gay, they kiss and share an unspecified sexual encounter. Davy is raised by his grandmother until her death, after which he moves to New York City with his beloved dog, Fred, to live with his alcoholic and unstable mother. Although Davy initially seems undisturbed by his experience with Altschuler and even initiates their second kiss, he later rejects his feelings when Fred is struck by a car and dies shortly after the boys are found together by Davy's mother. Davy perceives Fred's death as punishment for his homosexual experience, and at the conclusion of the novel, he tells Altschuler that they can never be intimate again and should pursue relationships with girls. Altschuler's response indicates that he thinks differently and may accept his feelings for Davy: "If you think it's dirty or something like that, I wouldn't do it again. If I were you" (157). Though Davy appears to reject his homosexuality, the novel leaves the future ambiguous, with Davy's noting that he "respected" his beloved Fred and could "respect" Altschuler, and Altschuler's responding that he "respected" his dead friend Larry Wilkins, about whom Altschuler may have had feelings before Davy. "Respect" appears to serve as a temporary placeholder for love and points to the possibility that Davy will embrace his queer potential.

I'll Get There exemplifies some of the queer possibilities that constitute childhood sexuality, including relationships with nonhuman objects. Although *I'll Get There* is known for its depiction of same-sex eroticism, Davy's first significant love and intimate companion is his dog. He thinks, "who can keep a big lover like Fred at a distance? He goes crazy just to give me a kiss whenever I come home" (10). Over the course of the novel, Davy repeatedly describes the exchange of physical pleasure with Fred: the dog nuzzles him and humps his leg, and Davy strokes and coddles him in return. Davy insists that Fred is his closest companion and speaks about their relationships in the most passionate of terms, and his mother even refers to the relationship between boy and dog as a "love affair" (92). Early in the novel, Davy falls asleep with his arms around Fred, which parallels the later scene between Davy and Altschuler when Davy's mother discovers them together. Because Fred's death follows shortly after Davy and Altschuler's sexual experience, Altschuler appears to replace Fred, retroactively reinforcing the importance of Fred to Davy and the dog's equivalence with a human love object. Davy and Fred's relationship may sound like the mundane affection of boy and dog, but understanding childhood sexuality means taking children seriously when they express love or communicate desire that departs from traditional adult expressions.

Rosa Guy's *Ruby* (1976) is the first novel for youth to feature an explicitly romantic and sexual relationship between girls, and it depicts adolescent sexuality as fluid and exploratory. Ruby, originally from the West Indies, lives in Harlem with her father and sister and develops a relationship with high school classmate Daphne, an African American girl. Guy, herself an immigrant from

Trinidad, focuses both on Ruby's attempt to remedy her loneliness through her relationship with Daphne, and on the young women's distinct perspectives on race that emerge from their different national origins. Daphne thinks Ruby too conciliatory with white people and refers to her as an "Uncle Tom," and Ruby replies that she cannot hate in the same way because she is not American (Guy 47, 49). Despite their personal and political differences, Ruby thinks that she has found "a likeness of herself" in Daphne (55), and Guy refers to their kissing (55) and lovemaking (147). Still, both characters remain interested in men, with Daphne's setting her mind on "going straight" (216) and Ruby's returning to her ex-boyfriend at the conclusion of the novel.

After *I'll Get There* and *Ruby*, LGBT youth literature developed in two main bodies: picture books for younger readers focusing on gender-variant children or children with gay parents, and young adult (YA) fiction about LGBT teens or their relatives. Gay YA fiction has tended to focus on traditional features of contemporary queer adolescence: understanding and naming romantic and sexual feelings, constructing an identity as LGBT, coming out, accepting gay family members, and dealing with homophobia. Many of the early young adult novels about homosexuality involve characters determining whether their same-sex attractions are situational or permanent. Chuck struggles to understand his feelings for his tutor, Justin, in Isabel Holland's *The Man Without a Face* (1972), and Chloe and Val wonder whether their feelings for each other mean they are lesbians or experiencing a temporary crush in Deborah Hautzig's *Hello, Dollface* (1978). Early lesbian and gay fiction for teens frequently links homosexuality with tragedy. Justin dies of a heart attack in Holland's novel, and in Sandra Scoppetone's *Happy Endings Are All Alike* (1978), a lesbian teenager, Jaret, is discovered having sex with her girlfriend and later raped by the boy who had seen her. Michael Cart and Christine Jenkins refer to Aiden Chambers's *Dance on My Grave* (1982) as "the first literary novel about homosexuality" for teens, though it, too, ends tragically when the protagonist's love interest is killed in a motorcycle accident (67). Nancy Garden's *Annie on My Mind* (1982) offers a similarly sophisticated and enduring depiction of lesbian adolescence and coming out. Liza, who attends an expensive private school, develops a relationship with working-class Annie after meeting at the Metropolitan Museum of Art. The girls slowly identify as "gay," and their reading of classic works of gay literature, which they find at their lesbian teachers' apartment, helps them clarify their feelings. Though Liza faces persecution and near expulsion from school, the novel concludes with the girls' reaffirmation of their mutual love. Both M.E. Kerr's *Deliver Us from Evie* (1994) and Jacqueline Woodson's *From the Notebooks of Melanin Sun*

(1995) reflect on the experiences of teens with gay family members: Parr's older sister comes out as a lesbian in the small farming community of Kerr's novel, and Brooklynite teen Melanin struggles to accept both his mother's lesbianism and her interracial relationship with a white woman in Woodson's book. *Melanin Sun*, like *Ruby*, is one of the few young adult novels to address both sexuality and race.

Some LGBT fiction for young adults has understandably assumed didactic and consciousness-raising tones, with homosexuality in the context of het-eronormative culture constructed as a problem. The dominance of realism in young adult literature, or what is called New Realism, emerged in the late 1960s and gave rise to the problem novel, in which the narrative is restricted to a singular issue in order to provide lessons to readers through the experiences of fictional characters. The impulse to instruct can interfere with literary innova-tion and expression, and in the context of LGBT fiction, it sometimes reinforces the notion of same-sex desire or gender variance as a problem. Alex Sanchez's *Rainbow Boys* (2001) and its sequels use the narrative techniques of fiction to teach readers about coming out, safe sex, the dangers of Internet cruising, and services available to gay teens. The adolescents in Bret Hartinger's *Geography Club* (2003), who eventually form a Gay-Straight Alliance, learn that kids from different cliques can come together for a common purpose. The tone of these works is often instructional and their style straightforward. They describe the quotidian details of adolescent life and focus on plot and information rather than character or language. In both works, young adults deal with coming out and the homophobic responses of classmates and family members, and the gay experience for adolescents is depicted as a struggle, usefully reflecting reality for many young people but also reinforcing the notion of being gay as difficult and painful.

While realist problem novels serve important functions for young read-ers by providing representations of gay lives, some authors have taken more experimental approaches to LGBT issues and characters, encouraging readers to imagine alternative possibilities for life and art. Francesca Lia Block's *Weetzie Bat* (1989), set in 1980s Los Angeles, describes the adventures of Weetzie and her friend Dirk, who is gay. Exhibiting qualities of magical realism, this short novel is marketed as a postmodern fairy tale in which characters encounter genies and fairy godmothers. *Weetzie Bat* avoids making Dirk's sexuality a problem and deals with his sexual experiences and search for a boyfriend as ordinary and even exciting features of adolescent life, though it also deals seriously with the issue of HIV/AIDS. A prequel, *Baby Bebop* (1995), focuses on Dirk's initial coming out and his experience with being gay-bashed, but it artfully weaves his story together with the history of Dirk's family and his dream-visions of the Holocaust. David Levithan's *Boy Meets Boy* (2003) also rejects strict realism. It focuses on a town in which homosexuality or queerness is completely normalized, protagonist Paul has been proudly out since kindergarten, and the quarterback of the high school football team is a transgender youth named Infinite Darlene, who is also the homecoming queen.

Still other texts navigate between providing information or instructions to readers and making use of language and narrative to render LGBT issues artfully. M.E. Kerr's *Night Kites* (1986), for instance, is the first young adult novel to deal with HIV/AIDS. Teen-aged Erick confronts the fact that his older brother is gay and HIV-positive, and the family must deal with both their own shock at this news and the bigotry of their community. Kerr is also one of the first to treat bisexuality as valid and possible and not just as a sign of adolescent uncertainty in *"Hello, I Lied"* (1997). After coming out as gay, sixteen-year-old Lang falls in love with a French girl named Huegette while his boyfriend is away. He never identifies as bisexual and insists that he does not want to "analyze it, explain it, or name it," but neither does he reject his period of love for Huegette, even after his boyfriend returns and the two resume their relationship (166). Julie Anne Peters's *Luna* (2004), while not the first YA novel to include a transgender character, is the first to focus on the experience of being a transgender teen. Though Peters represents transgenderism as a problem for Luna and her family, she represents the full complexity of Luna's experience through both the use of language and the structure of the narrative.

While the body of lesbian and gay literature for young adults continues to expand, works for younger readers with gay characters remain rare, as Kenneth Kidd has observed (114). Alex Sanchez's *So Hard to Say* (2004) and Lisa Jahn-Clough's *Country Girl, City Girl* (2004) are among the few works to be published for or about gay preteen or preadolescent characters. Jahn-Clough's novel describes the vastly different worlds of thirteen-year-old farm girl Phoebe and worldly fourteen-year-old New Yorker Melita. A clash of cultures also figures in Sanchez's *So Hard*, in which eighth-grader Frederick moves from Wisconsin to California, where he befriends a thirteen-year-old girl named Xio and slowly realizes that he cannot reciprocate her feelings for him because he prefers boys.

LGBT Picture Books

Works that have been described as gay children's literature include picture books about children with lesbian or gay parents, such as Jane Severance and

Tea Schook's *When Megan Went Away* (1979), about a girl whose two mommies split up, or Johnny Valentine and Melody Sarecki's *One Dad, Two Dads, Brown Dad, Blue Dads* (2004), which presents a variety of different kinds of fathers. Such works are usually designed to teach young children that different family arrangements are available and legitimate, and they tend to avoid explicit depictions of same-sex intimacy or romance. For instance, while the original edition of Lesléa Newman and Diana Souza's *Heather Has Two Mommies* (1989) describes both the budding relationship between Heather's future mommies and their visit to a fertility doctor, the tenth- and twentieth-anniversary editions omit these pages to minimize controversy and increase their potential use in schools, according to Newman (n.pag.). Michael Willhoite's *Daddy's Roommate* (1990), in contrast, shows the unnamed protagonist's father and his partner embracing and cuddling, and in the United States, *Daddy's Roommate* was the second most frequently challenged book of the 1990s, according to the American Library Association.

Other picture books depict gender-variant or transgender children, such as Oliver in Tomie DePaola's *Oliver Button Is a Sissy* (1979), Georgia from Sharon Wyeth's *Tomboy Trouble* (1998), and Bailey in Marcus Ewert and Rex Ray's *10,000 Dresses* (2008). As with books about gay parents, most works about gender variance appear designed to teach readers, including adult readers, not to bully or persecute sissies and tomboys. Teasing by peers and scolding by parents are common features. Oliver Button is called a sissy because he likes to tap dance, and eight-year-old Georgia is bullied for having short hair and liking sports. The narrator of *10,000 Dresses* refers to Bailey with feminine pronouns, but Bailey is scolded by her mother for liking dresses, saying, "You're a boy. Boys don't wear dresses!" (n.pag.). Works about gender-variant children sometimes reflect anxieties about homosexuality. As Michelle Abate notes, Charlotte Zolotow and William Pene Du Bois's *William's Doll* (1985) allays fears that William will grow up gay by having his grandmother explain to his father that playing with a doll will make good practice for being a father (Abate 41).

Some LGBT picture books feature anthropomorphic animals as same-sex parents or gender-variant beasts. Animal characters can be used to invoke the sense of tradition or wisdom associated with fairy tales and animal fables or to deflect controversy by appearing fantastical or cute. Harvey Fierstein and Henry Cole's *The Sissy Duckling* (2002) recasts the tale of the ugly duckling to address childhood gender, and Justin Richardson and Peter Parnell's *And Tango Makes Three* (2005) describes two male penguins who make a nest and raise a chick together. *Tango* has failed to avoid controversy, however, having become one of the most frequently challenged children's books in recent years.

Rarely do children's picture books feature same-sex loving children. Linda de Haan and Stern Nijland's *King and King* (2003) depicts a prince who prefers his own sex and refuses to marry a princess, but the protagonist appears to be a young man rather than a child. More commonly, picture books allude to the queer pleasures of childhood sexuality, even if accidentally. Though Kevin Henkes's Caldecott Honor book and Phoenix Award winner *Owen* (1993) has not been described as LGBT children's literature, it does point to the polymorphously perverse possibilities of children. Owen, a young anthropomorphic mouse, is strongly attached to his yellow blanket, which goes everywhere with him. The blanket can be described as a transitional object, which D.W. Winnicott theorizes as a bridge between an infant's autoerotic period and later childhood when one recognizes the boundaries between self and other. For adults, inseparability from or pleasure in a piece of cloth might be recognized as a fetish, and we can understand children's pleasurable attachments to inanimate objects or nonhuman beings as suggestive of childhood sexuality.

The work of Maurice Sendak, one of the most celebrated picture book author-illustrators, often depicts the sensual desires and pleasures of childhood. Sendak has described the trilogy composed of *Where the Wild Things Are* (1963), *In the Night Kitchen* (1970), and *Outside Over There* (1981) as "all variations on the same theme: how children master various feelings" (Lanes 227). Max's threat to "eat up!" his mother and his ecstatic "rumpus" with the Wild Things, Mickey's naked play in a pan of cake batter and his promise to provide the bakers with "milk," and the kidnapping of Ida's baby sister by goblins for a wedding and "kidnap honeymoon" all invoke the complex inner lives and bodily pleasures of children. In not approaching sexual matters directly, these works may come closer to depicting the queer possibilities of child sexuality.

The Queer Possibilities of Children

Both Freud and Foucault demonstrated in different ways how the "problem" of child sex has been central to the structures or discourses of sexuality more broadly. The fascination with origins in both scientific and popular culture, part of the "problem" of sexuality, reinforces the idea of the child as an object of scrutiny for those seeking to discover the "causes" of same-sex desires and pleasures or variant expressions of gender. Many LGBT adults are similarly invested in origins, in pinpointing the moment or period of discovery, or in understanding the feelings of "difference" experienced by their younger selves (even if feelings of difference are actually endemic to childhood more generally). Childhood is often set aside as a time and space for socialization and education, especially with regards to gender and sexuality, and the fact that the child is imagined as the embodiment of species survival and ideological reproduction positions children at the nexus of cultural battles over sexual matters. Children are compelled and coerced to assimilate and perform sexual norms, and gender-variant and (proto)gay children are often objects of intense rhetorical and physical violence, which further attaches to childhood an affective density that makes many people, and perhaps LGBT and queer adults in particular, concerned with childhood. Rather than innocent or devoid of sexual matters, childhood and children's culture are everywhere marked by gender and sexuality.

To the extent that gay studies and queer theory trace their genealogies in part to Freud and Foucault, and for the many reasons just cited, the figure of the gay or queer child has always been a focal point for queer scholars. Eve Kosofsky Sedgwick, Michael Moon, James Kincaid, Lee Edelman, and others have all considered permutations of the queer child or the queerness of children, and some of the most nuanced explorations of childhood sexuality can be found in studies of children's literature, like those collected in Abate and Kidd's *Over the Rainbow: Queer Children's and Young Adult Literature* (2011). Children's literature reflects the full complexity of childhood sexuality as experienced by child characters, as constructed in literary representations, and as presented to child readers, from the most normative of imperatives to the queerest of possibilities. The conception of child sexuality as a problem still dominates the most explicit depictions of nonnormative desires and pleasures in children's literature and culture, but the more accidental allusions to children's queer or perverse pleasures provide opportunities to examine how childhood sexualities differ from those of adults.

Works Cited

Abate, Michelle. "Trans/Forming Girlhood: Transgenderism, the Tomboy Formula, and Gender Identity Disorder in Sharon Dennis Wyeth's *Tomboy Trouble*." *The Lion and the Unicorn* 32.1 (2008): 40–60. Print.

Abate, Michelle, and Kenneth B. Kidd, eds. *Over the Rainbow: Queer Children's and Young Adult Literature*. Ann Arbor: U of Michigan P, 2011. Print.

Alcott, Louisa May. *Little Men*. 1871. New York: Grosset, 1947. Print.

    Little Women. 1868. New York: Signet Classic, 2004. Print.

Alger, Horatio. *Ragged Dick; or, Street Life in New York with the Boot-Blacks*. Boston: Loring, 1868. Print.

Ballantyne, R.M. *The Coral Island*. 1858. Oxford: Oxford World's Classics, 1990. Print.

Bruhm, Steven, and Natasha Hurley, eds. *Curiouser: On the Queerness of Children*. Minneapolis: U of Minnesota P, 2004. Print.

Cart, Michael, and Christine Jenkins. *The Heart Has Its Reasons: Young Adult Literature with Gay/Lesbian/Queer Content, 1969–2004*. Lanham: Scarecrow P, 2006. Print.

Chandos, John. *Boys Together: English Public Schools, 1800–1864*. New Haven: Yale UP, 1984. Print.

Coolidge, Susan. *What Katy Did: A Story*. Boston: Roberts Brothers, 1873. Print.

Donovan, John. *I'll Get There. It Better Be Worth the Trip*. New York: Dell, 1969. Print.

Edelman, Lee. *No Future: Queer Theory and the Death Drive*. Durham: Duke UP, 2004. Print.

Ellis, Havelock. *Sexual Inversion (Studies in the Psychology of Sex)*. 1897. Philadelphia: F. A. Davis, 1901. Web. 24 Jan. 2014.

Foucault, Michel. *The History of Sexuality, Volume I: An Introduction*. 1976. Trans. Robert Hurley. New York: Vintage, 1990. Print.

Freud, Sigmund. *Three Essays in the Theory of Sexuality*. 1905. Trans. James Strachey. New York: Basic, 2000. Print.

Grimm, Wilhelm, and Jacob Grimm. "The Frog King, or Iron Heinrich." *The Classic Fairy Tales*. Ed. Maria Tatar. New York: Norton, 1999. 47–49. Print.

Gubar, Marah. "'Where Is the Boy?': The Pleasures of Postponement in the *Anne of Green Gables* Series." *The Lion and the Unicorn* 25.1 (2001): 47–69. *Project Muse*. Web. 24 Jan. 2014.

Guy, Rosa. *Ruby*. 1976. New York: Just Us, 2005. Print.

Howe, James. *Totally Joe*. 2005. New York: Atheneum, 2007.

Hughes, Thomas. *Tom Brown's Schooldays*. 1857. Oxford: Oxford World Classics, 1999. Print.

Kerr, M.E. *"Hello, I Lied."* 1997. New York: Harper Teen, 1998. Print.

Kidd, Kenneth B. Introduction. *Lesbian/Gay Literature for Children and Young Adults*. Spec. issue of *Children's Literature Association Quarterly* 23.3 (1998): 114–19. Print.

Kincaid, James R. *Child-Loving: The Erotic Child and Victorian Culture*. New York: Routledge, 1992. Print.

Krafft-Ebing, Richard von. *Psychopathia Sexualis, with Especial Reference to Contrary Sexual Instinct: A Medico-Legal Study*. 1892. Trans. Charles Gilbert Chaddock. Philadelphia: Davis, 1894. Web. 24 Jan. 2014.

Lanes, Selma G. *The Art of Maurice Sendak*. New York: Abrams, 1980. Print.

Moon, Michael. "'The Gentle Boy from the Dangerous Classes': Pederasty, Domesticity, and Capitalism in Horatio Alger." *Representations* 19.3 (1987): 87–110. Print.

Newman, Lesléa, and Diana Souza. *Heather Has Two Mommies: Twentieth Anniversary Edition*. New York: Alyson, 2009. Print.

Odem, Mary E. *Delinquent Daughters: Protecting and Policing Adolescent Female Sexuality in the United States, 1885–1920*. Chapel Hill: U of North Carolina P, 1995. Print.

Prime-Stevenson, Edward [Xavier Mayne]. *The Intersexes: A History of Similisexualism as a Problem in Social Life*. 1908. New York: Arno P, 1975. Print.

———. *White Cockades: An Incident of the "Forty-Five."* New York: Scribner's, 1887. Print.

Pugh, Tison. *Innocence, Heterosexuality, and the Queerness of Children's Literature*. New York: Routledge, 2011. Print.

Robinson, Laura. "Bosom Friends: Lesbian Desire in L. M. Montgomery's Anne Books." *Canadian Literature* 180 (Spring 2004): 12–30. Print.

Rossetti, Christina. *Goblin Market and Other Poems*. 1862. Mineola: Dover, 1994. Print.

Sedgwick, Eve Kosofsky. "How to Bring Your Kids Up Gay." *Social Text* 29 (1991): 18–27. Print.

Sims, Sue. Introduction. *The Encyclopaedia of Girls' School Stories*. Eds. Sue Sims and Hilary Clare. London: Ashgate, 2000. 1–18. Print.

Stansell, Christine. "Women on the Town: Sexual Exchange and Prostitution." *The Girls' History and Culture Reader: The Nineteenth Century*. Ed. Miriam Forman-Brunell and Leslie Paris. Champaign: U of Illinois P, 2011. 80–103. Print.

Stockton, Kathryn Bond. "Growing Sideways, or Versions of the Queer Child: The Ghost, the Homosexual, the Freudian, the Innocent, and the Interval of the Animal." Bruhm and Hurley 277–316.

The Queer Child, or Growing Sideways in the Twentieth Century. Durham: Duke UP, 2009. Print.

Stolberg, Michael. "Self-Pollution, Moral Reform, and the Venereal Trade: Notes on the Sources and Historical Context of *Onania* (1716)." *Journal of the History of Sexuality* 9.1–2 (2000): 37–61. Print.

Tribunella, Eric. *Melancholia and Maturation: The Use of Trauma in American Children's Literature*. Knoxville: U of Tennessee P, 2010. Print.

Trites, Roberta Seelinger. "Queer Performances: Lesbian Politics in *Little Women*." Abate and Kidd 33–58.

Winnicott, D.W. *Playing and Reality*. New York: Routledge, 2005. Print.

39

AIDS Literatures

TIM DEAN AND STEVEN RUSZCZYCKY

AIDS transformed gay writing by confronting it with death on a scale hitherto unknown. When, in 1981, gay men started dying from what we now call AIDS, nobody knew how it was transmitted or how infectious it might be. The ensuing social panic around this new disease spawned a representational matrix that was designed primarily to insulate the uninfected from those who were sick. As historian Sander Gilman has shown, images of disease are meant to contain it, while new diseases tend to be represented in the iconography employed to quarantine older ones. The discursive desire for containment, born of fear and ignorance, dominated early representations of the epidemic. As a result, much of what is considered AIDS literature responds not only to the experience of living with HIV but also to the phobic, stigmatizing discourses that have overwritten that experience from the start. People with HIV/AIDS have to fight a potentially fatal viral infection, but they also must combat the overwhelmingly hostile social perceptions of their disease. It is from within this battle fought on two fronts simultaneously – the biomedical and the sociocultural – that the literatures of AIDS have been forged.

Our metaphors of battle and combat are neither incidental nor innocent. In *AIDS and Its Metaphors*, Susan Sontag claimed that "military metaphors contribute to the stigmatizing of certain illnesses and, by extension, of those who are ill" (11). Nevertheless, for gay men the early years of the epidemic – during which virtually an entire generation was struck down – felt like a war zone. In the Western world, especially the United States, even gay men who remained uninfected were deeply scarred by the epidemic, emerging as long-term casualties of its horrors (as psychologist Walt Odets has shown). The literature of AIDS bears comparison with the literature of war, not only because of the staggering mortalities involved but also because of the traumatic suddenness with which people were plunged into extreme conditions characterized by life-and-death stakes.[1] Nothing had prepared us for AIDS and, to begin with, the primary resources for dealing with it were discursive. A trauma that was at

once physiological and social, AIDS posed an immense challenge to representation – it is easy to forget the early uncertainty over what to name the virus
or the syndrome – even as it also unleashed what critic Paula Treichler called
"an epidemic of signification." Trauma, by defying linguistic containment,
paradoxically provokes repeated attempts to symbolize the gash it rips open in
the fabric of everyday life.

Understood as a response to trauma, the literature of AIDS may be more
akin to war literature or Holocaust literature than to other kinds of gay and
lesbian writing.[2] If AIDS qualifies as more than one gay literary theme among
others, then this is because it prompts fundamental questions concerning the
politics and ethics of representation. How should one bear witness to a community's trauma, suffering, and death? How memorialize those who die from
AIDS? How write about a subject whose conflation of sex and death provokes
terrors of contamination? How combat the intense stigma that conduces to
silence? As Andrew Holleran, one of the most articulate early writers on the
epidemic, put it, "How could one write at all, in fact, when the only work
that mattered was that of the men organizing social services, taking care of
friends, trying to find a microbiological solution to a microbiological horror...?" (*Ground* 15). In the early years, when the sense of crisis was at its height,
writing about the epidemic seemed both an indefensible distraction, on one
hand, and an absolutely necessary response to trauma, on the other.

A motivated refusal to write about AIDS – as in *The New York Times*'s uncon-
scionably long silence on the subject – undergirds the epidemic's complex
politics of representation. President Ronald Reagan's refusal to mention AIDS
publicly until late in 1987, by which point it had killed more than twenty-five
thousand U.S. citizens, exemplified a tendency, still present today, to shroud
the disease in silence and denial. It is as if, by not mentioning it, AIDS might
become more distant, less threatening. Silence generates the illusion of safety.
This discursive strategy seeks to protect those who are (or who imagine themselves to be) HIV-negative by quarantining those living with HIV/AIDS in
a kind of unreality, where their lives and deaths barely register. In response
to this strategy of silencing, the activist group ACT UP (AIDS Coalition to
Unleash Power) adopted as its motto "Silence = Death," a slogan that made it
politically imperative to create counter-discourses about the epidemic. These
counter-discourses, along with the activism they sparked, form an essential
component of the literature of AIDS – and not just because ACT UP was
cofounded (in New York in 1987) by writer Larry Kramer, whose play *The
Normal Heart* (1985) condemned more vociferously than anyone *The New York
Times*'s silence on AIDS.

The category of "AIDS literatures" thus encompasses not only imaginative writing but also performance, activism, and documentary, along with scientific, journalistic, and bureaucratic discourses surrounding the epidemic.
Given this discursive proliferation, it is crucial to resist the impulse to bifurcate
AIDS literatures into dominant versus counter-discourses. Such bifurcations –
of mainstream versus marginal, straight versus gay, or HIV-positive versus
HIV-negative – unhelpfully reproduce the paranoid logic of us-versus-them
that organized public discourse about the epidemic from its inception. While
it is useful to assess how much of the epidemic's literary production qualifies as counter-discursive, it is equally necessary to appreciate the complexity
of counter-discourse, including its range of ambition, strategy, context, and
genre. Because it would be impossible, in a single chapter, to do justice to
the wealth of material or the multiplicity of experiences of living with HIV /
AIDS, we have chosen to focus on writing by gay men in the disparate genres
of memoir, poetry, drama, and pornography. Thanks to its indelible association with sex, AIDS maintains a strong connection with that most explicit
genre of gay representation – pornography. This connection has received scant
attention in the extensive scholarship on AIDS literatures, for reasons that we
explain toward the end of this chapter. We also will discuss why, although the
epidemic continues, with an estimated fifty thousand new infections per year
in the United States alone, the literature of AIDS no longer seems contemporary. AIDS literatures have begun to look like historical artifacts, relics of a
time that is not our own.

Writing in 1985, from the midst of what he called "Ground Zero," Holleran
observed, "Someday – not just yet – there will be novels about all of this, but
they will face the problem writing about it stumbles against now: how to
include the individual stories, the astonishingly various ways in which people
have behaved" (*Ground* 27). Even among North American, middle-class gay
men (falsely assumed to be a homogeneous category), there was considerable
diversity of experience in the epidemic, let alone among different geographical, racial, and sexual populations. The problem of how to include, in a single
textual compass, a sufficiently diverse range of individual experience is, as
Holleran implies, a representational problem that perennially confronts the
realist novel. It is a problem of genre, a question of what novelistic representation may accomplish; but it is also an ideological problem, a question of
inclusive representation or *representativeness*.

The issue of representativeness has bedeviled AIDS discourse from the
beginning, insofar as those most directly affected have struggled to make
themselves heard amid the cacophony of expert voices speaking about them.

This problem, endemic to the history of homosexuality, sharpened gay men's resolve to represent themselves. Although AIDS never has been an exclusively "gay disease," in the Western world gay men represent its most visible demographic and disproportionately its writers. That the literature of AIDS does not adequately represent the diversity of populations affected by it has to do, in part, with gay men's presence in publishing and the arts, as well as their willingness not only to challenge but also to embrace the stigma of what is seen as a sexually transmitted disease. Thus, we focus here on specifically *gay* AIDS literatures, recognizing that our selection of authors and texts is neither representative nor comprehensive.[3]

Aides mémoire

Editor Stephen Greco records in his journal a conversation with novelist Robert Ferro, who said in 1987, "writers with AIDS just don't live long enough to make a book out of their experiences, or are too exhausted or preoccupied to work efficiently on one" (qtd. in Greco 115). The rapidity with which people died in the epidemic's early years discouraged many from undertaking large-scale projects, such as novels, in favor of more modest literary forms, such as stories, poems, memoirs, and diaries. The challenge for writers working in these forms lay in how to capture a life affected by illness, without simply inscribing it in the stereotypical narrative arc of irreversible decline and death furnished by mainstream accounts of AIDS. Fiction writers Adam Mars-Jones and Edmund White, collaborating transatlantically on *The Darker Proof* (1987), a book of short stories about living with HIV, explained how they "chose the story as a form, rather than the novel, because the novel has an inevitable trajectory to it. That is, you begin healthy and end sick and dead. We wanted to get into and out of the subject matter in a more angular and less predictable way" (qtd. in Canning 141). If mainstream accounts tended to picture HIV-positive people all dying from AIDS in the same helpless manner, then gay writers would shift the emphasis by representing people who were actively, and in manifold ways, living with HIV/AIDS.

The genre of memoir, considered as an intimate form of testimony to experience, is well suited to this enterprise. Rather than a steady progression toward death, AIDS memoirists such as Mark Doty, Paul Monette, or David Wojnarowicz describe oscillations between periods of sickness and recovery, along with the sudden appearance or disappearance of symptoms. Resisting the totalizing narrative of irreversible decline, gay AIDS memoirs unfold vignettes that often are plotted in nonlinear form to suggest how foreshortened time amplifies the life of every moment. For example, Wojnarowicz's *Close to the Knives: A Memoir of Disintegration* (1991) eschews linear narrative in favor of a series of fragmented portraits, brief essays, and diary entries, composed in long, sparsely punctuated sentences that mix together depictions of street violence, hospital room visits, urban and rural panoramas, calls to political action, and anonymous sexual encounters. This memoir's structure evokes the associative quality of images, memories, and dreams, with the affects of lust and rage providing the energy that links one scene or idea to the next. In a section devoted to the impending death of an unnamed lover, for instance, the author's touching of his own body provokes memories of sex that splinter into further associations with anonymous bodies and body parts (78–79).

In a subsequent section, these associative energies furnish a strategy for drawing more overtly political links between the epidemic and other forms of suffering:

> Outside my windows there are thousands of people without homes who are trying to deal with having AIDS. If I think *my* life at times has a nightmarish quality about it … think for a moment what it would be like to be facing winter winds and shit menus at the limited shelters, and the rampant T.B., and the rapes, muggings, stabbings in those shelters…. So picture yourself with a couple of the three hundred and fifty opportunistic infections unable to respond physiologically to the few drugs released by the foot-dragging deal-making FDA and having to maintain a junk habit; or even having to try and kick that habit without any clinical help while keeping yourself alive seven years to get a drug that you need immediately. (118–19)

In the spirit of his work as a graphic artist, Wojnarowicz emphasizes the visual, urging readers to "picture" the conditions facing the homeless and injection drug users, those who comprise part of this "nightmarish" epidemic but lack ready access to the means of representation whereby they could portray their plight. *Close to the Knives* draws together various fragments according to what scholar Tom Roach calls Wojnarowicz's "politics of shared estrangement," rooted in "the absolute singularity and radical common-ness of finitude" (139).

If AIDS decimated the gay community, it also prompted the creation of new kinds of connection and community among the sick. AIDS memoirs make vivid in quite different ways that death is what is shared: my death is never mine alone, especially in an epidemic. Another visual artist, Hervé Guibert, made this connection when, in *To the Friend Who Did Not Save My Life* (1990), he composed a fictionalized account, written in the form of a journal, of the illness and death of Michel Foucault (who is given the pseudonym Muzil).

The intimate friendship shared by Foucault and Guibert, men of different generations, afforded the latter many opportunities to record the former's final days, despite an acute awareness that he was doing so against the philosopher's wishes. "What right did I have to record all that? What right did I have to use friendship in such a mean fashion? And with someone I adored with all my heart?" Guibert's narrator asks himself (91). The answer comes in a flash: "I was completely entitled to do this since it wasn't so much my friend's last agony I was describing as it was my own, which was waiting for me and would be just like his, for it was now clear that besides being bound by friendship, we would share the same fate in death" (91). According to this logic, one writes of the other's death from AIDS as a way of coming to terms with his own (Foucault died in 1984, Guibert in 1991). Mourning the other, one performs also the impossible task of mourning oneself.

Because *To the Friend Who Did Not Save My Life* narrated Foucault's illness and death against his wishes, the book raised a host of ethical questions, sparking intense controversy in France upon publication. However, writing a memoir about someone else's death from AIDS is conventionally understood as an act of mourning, of commemoration, and of witnessing. It represents a way of keeping the beloved alive posthumously. Hence, for example, Mark Doty observes in *Heaven's Coast* (1996), a memoir of his lover's battle with AIDS: "Now sometimes I feel as if his memories are mine; when one loses a lover, the pact becomes intensified, in a way: who else will keep these stories?" (153). If Guibert betrayed a pact with Foucault, then conversely Doty keeps faith with the memory of Wally Roberts (1951–94) by describing the final years of his life. *Heaven's Coast* adopts the convolutions of memory in its nonlinear structure, allowing past, present, and future to revise each other repeatedly as the narrative progresses. "Death requires a new negotiation with memory," Doty notes (40). Remembrance is not only a major theme of *Heaven's Coast* but also helps to shape the memoir's narrative form.

Doty describes how Wally's illness changes the quality of their relationship, transforming lovers into strangers and then back into lovers. The corporeal and emotional effects of AIDS prompt a new way of understanding intimacy in terms of impermanence. For Doty, AIDS functioned "as a kind of intensifier, something which makes things more firmly, deeply themselves" (*Heaven's* 3). This perspective counters the conventional association of AIDS with physical wasting and subjective diminishment because even as illness reduces the body it simultaneously intensifies an impersonal essence. When Doty reflects on his inability to recognize Wally's physical features – "I'm starting to feel I can't remember what Wally was like before he was sick; it seems so long now that I can't visualize the old face, hear the old voice" (251) – he realizes that, with so much stripped away, the "quality which is most essentially Wally" emerges more clearly: "Its characteristics are wonder and humor, delight in things, a tender regard" (253). As both the beloved's body and the writer's memory vanish, something else comes shining through, which Doty aspires to capture in memoir and, especially, in poetry.

The AIDS Lyric

Along with Rafael Campo, Tory Dent, Thom Gunn, and D. A. Powell, Doty is widely recognized as one of the preeminent poets of the epidemic. Poetry, particularly in the form of elegy, offers an occasion for commemorating the dead, and there has been no shortage of occasional lyrics about ailing or deceased individuals by poets of all sexualities, genders, races, and abilities.[4] It is necessary to acknowledge, however, that some of the writing produced in response to AIDS remains unequal in its literary execution to its strength of feeling. For example, Paul Monette, a significant voice early in the epidemic, published not only two memoirs of living with AIDS but also a slim volume of elegies for his partner Roger Horowitz, *Love Alone: 18 Elegies for Rog* (1988). What distinguishes the work of poets such as Doty, Gunn, and Powell (whom we concentrate on here) is that their poetry about AIDS moves beyond the elegiac or sentimental, even as they draw on the powerful memorial resources of verse. We leave aside, for a separate occasion, the extraordinary work of Tory Dent, who in three volumes of challenging, allusive poems charted her physical and emotional experience of living with AIDS for seventeen years, until her death in 2005.

"I thought your illness a kind of solvent / dissolving the future a little at a time," Doty writes in the title poem of *Atlantis* (1995), a volume that reads as the companion text to *Heaven's Coast* (*Atlantis* 57). Never named directly, AIDS is described as:

> not even a real word
> but an acronym, a vacant
> four-letter cipher
>
> that draws meanings into itself,
> reconstitutes the world. (50)

This reconstituting of the world – not only by illness but, just as significantly, by the poetic imagination – represents one of Doty's principal subjects. The world needs reconstituting because it is ceaselessly falling apart, whether as a consequence of AIDS or of other forces. Doty pays special attention to the intensification of life manifested by people and objects in decline or decay. "My art," the speaker of "Two Ruined Boats" declares, "could only articulate the sheen, / or chronicle the fashion in which / / the world gains luster as it falls apart" (*Atlantis* 89). He is a poet of the unmaking and remaking of the world, and of its shifting luminosity throughout decomposition and recreation.

Doty's originality lies in his making AIDS part of his poetic perspective, rather than treating it as just an object of description or reflection. Regarding his involvement in the epidemic, the poet explains, "AIDS is no longer something I write about, but is part of the way I see or speak" ("Letter"). This transformation of perspective infuses poems that ostensibly do not concern AIDS or gay sexuality with a vision that is shaped by the pressure of accelerated mortality. For example, the opening poem of *My Alexandria* (1993), "Demolition," describes the destruction of an old New England rooming house; by the end of this volume a reader grasps how the demolition or disappearance of urban landscapes is connected to the bodily disintegrations caused by illness. Virtually all of the poems in *My Alexandria* were composed in the wake of learning that Wally had tested HIV-positive, though they are not primarily elegiac. Instead, exercising a supremely American impulse to "make it new," Doty reinvents the ancient poetic topos of mutability in response to postmodern, specifically gay conditions of mortality.[5]

By stretching the lyric to incorporate the voices and words of friends living with HIV / AIDS, Doty's poetry preserves something of those whose earthly lives are coming to a close. And by remaining open to the broken, the contingent, the uninterpretable, his writing succeeds in capturing what the final poem in *Atlantis* calls "the silken undulation / between this life and the next" (101). In a comparable gesture, Thom Gunn, in *The Man with Night Sweats* (1992), extends the capacity of the AIDS lyric by encompassing within it the comic as well as the elegiac, and eros along with thanatos. For example, his poem "In Time of Plague" forthrightly articulates the erotic potential of sharing needles:

> My thoughts are crowded with death
> and it draws so oddly on the sexual
> that I am confused
> confused to be attracted
> by, in effect, my own annihilation.
> Who are these two, these fiercely attractive men
> who want me to stick their needle in my arm? (59)

Here, sex and death are "confused," melded together, as the speaker's fate would be melded with that of "these fiercely attractive men" if he accepted their invitation. To acknowledge the sexual allure of needle sharing goes against everything we have been told in the official, pedagogical discourses surrounding the epidemic. Gunn shows how poetry not only confers a kind of life in the face of death but also offers a means for speaking the unspeakable.

Poetry's potential in the fight against AIDS is the ultimate subject of *The Man with Night Sweats*. In "Memory Unsettled" – a poem that, according to Gunn's notes, remembers Charlie Hinkle (also the subject of "To a Dead Graduate Student") – the speaker conjures this potential in the starkest terms:

> When near your death a friend
> Asked you what he could do,
> "Remember me," you said.
> We will remember you.   (76)

The stanza performs its promise of remembrance in several ways: by preserving Charlie Hinkle's words, his elementary dying wish ("'Remember me'"), and by utilizing the capacity of monosyllabic rhyme, together with a simple rhythm, to make an utterance memorable. In its effort to preserve memory against the depredations of time, the stanza enfolds temporality by unobtrusively including locutions in past, present, and future tenses.

"Time's // not the enemy," claims Doty's speaker in the final poem of *Atlantis* (100). Yet for centuries the losses occasioned by time's passing have been regarded as precisely the poet's enemy, and increasingly so in the age of AIDS. Poetry combats time and loss through memorializations of verbal form and by transfiguring individual particularities into the generality of myth. This is how Gunn's reference to *the* man with night sweats transforms ordinary men with AIDS-related symptoms into a mythic figure, one who stands for a whole generation of men in San Francisco, where the British expatriate poet lived for more than four decades. *The Man with Night Sweats* was Gunn's first volume of poetry in a decade – the decade that we now know as the epidemic's worst, at least in Europe and North America. By the late 1990s, drug treatments became available that made an HIV-positive diagnosis no longer an inevitable death sentence. That changed people's lives and it altered, too, how gay men wrote about the epidemic. Without the pressure of imminent mortality as its subject, poetry confronts different questions and requires new forms of invention. *Cocktails* (2004), a volume of experimental verses by D. A. Powell, exemplifies lyric invention in the wake of antiretrovirals.

The poems in *Cocktails* make evident that its title carries a triple meaning, referring at once to mixed drinks imbibed at gay bars, to the combination of antiretroviral drugs that keep HIV-positive folks alive, and, punningly, to "cock tales" that gay men circulate when discussing their erotic experience. In other words, the book's title archly evokes sex, drugs, and booze – with the emphasis on the new drug regimens that initially required many medications daily, before the availability of the now ubiquitous one-a-day pills. In a poem subtitled *"a song of the last supper,"* Powell's speaker names the drugs:

> *use it up wear it out: ain't nothing left in this old world I care about*
> a damasked table surrounded by bachelors.   some already parted
> regimens of azt, d4t, cryxivan, viracept and early slumber   (54)

The "bachelors" at this last supper include protease inhibitors in their meal, as Powell mixes sacred and profane, popular and literary in his poem, combining disco lyrics with an epigraph from Sir Philip Sidney, "All love is dead, infected / With plague of deep disdain" – lines that signify quite differently in the context of HIV medications.

One of the most striking contexts in *Cocktails* involves the religious imagery with which Powell intensifies his poems' erotics. In a poem subtitled *"a song of Mary the mother,"* he compares having HIV to pregnancy through immaculate conception ("would that a potion could blot out the host inside me" [44]), thus suggesting, via this carefully elaborated sacrilegious metaphor, a radically different perspective on the nonhuman life growing inside his body. Like others writing about HIV / AIDS, Powell deploys Christian imagery not as redemptive but in rebuttal to the moralistic condemnations of gay sex and people with AIDS spouted by the religious right (particularly during the first decade of the epidemic in the United States); and, like Gunn, he invokes the religious ecstasies of poets such as Richard Crashaw and John Donne to do so. That is to say, Powell draws on specifically poetic resources in his contribution to the struggle against HIV / AIDS.

Performing AIDS

The poetry of Doty, Gunn, and Powell succeeds partly by inviting into the ostensibly univocal space of lyric many voices besides the poet's own. One hears, in the best of their poems, not a solitary singer but a choir, in which the dissonance among voices is as vital as the harmony. When that dissonance reaches a certain pitch, however, you have not a poem but a play, with different voices assigned to individuated characters and the dramatic possibilities opened up by live bodies interacting in physical space. The presence of live bodies, whether on stage or on the street, was especially crucial during the epidemic's early years, when people with AIDS were being treated systematically as invisible or already dead. In that context, every verbal and embodied performance that publicly invoked HIV / AIDS bore an activist resonance. Such performances registered, in public space, the vivid presence of people with HIV / AIDS.

As critic David Román observes, however, the theatre of AIDS, more than other kinds of performance, challenges literary and cultural history because so often AIDS performances generated significant local effects without leaving reliable documentary traces. Performers died and their performances were not always recorded or preserved in scripts: fatal illness exacerbates the ephemerality of physical presence. If the literature of AIDS aspires to combat bodily evanescence, then nowhere is this ambition more palpable than in plays whose drama is set in motion by the revelation of diagnosis. Early AIDS plays, such as William Hoffman's *As Is* (1985) and Larry Kramer's *The Normal Heart* (1985), were staged during the same year as the first blood test for HIV became available; their drama revolves around characters who receive a death sentence that they then must impart to others. The desperate social and biomedical context of the 1980s helps to account for what may appear to audiences today as these plays' excessive sentimentality or didacticism.

When it comes to writing and performance around an urgent issue such as AIDS, it may be misleading to evaluate work in terms of criteria not its own. The goals of activist art and theatre differ from those of nonactivist writing or performance. As Douglas Crimp and Adam Rolston argue, in their discussion of the graphics and performances of ACT UP, "The aesthetic values of the traditional art world are of little consequence to AIDS activists. What counts in activist art is its propaganda effect" (15).[6] The "propaganda effect" depends on a particular message reaching as broad an audience as possible, with minimal room for ambiguity or interpretation. For example, the work of Pomo Afro Homos, a trio of black performers, inflects a long tradition of political theatre with African American oral traditions, in order to intervene in the epidemic's politics of race and sexuality. As Román notes in his account of Pomo Afro Homos' performances, their three-man show *Fierce Love* played against the public backdrop of basketball star Magic Johnson's announcement, in November 1991, of his HIV-positive diagnosis – an event that drew national attention to the incidence of HIV / AIDS in the African-American community while nonetheless maintaining the comparative invisibility of black gay men (154–76).

In another performance, *Dark Fruit*, the Pomo Afro Homos took on what they saw as the stereotyping of black gay men in contemporary theatre. *Dark Fruit* opens with each of the trio performing a gay black character from another play – Jacob from Harvey Fierstein's *La Cage aux Folles*, Paul from John Guare's *Six Degrees of Separation*, and Belize from Tony Kushner's Pulitzer Prize-winning *Angels in America*. This scene of black actors appropriating others' dramatic characters puts the Pomo Afro Homos in dialogue with the most prominent theatrical production to emerge from the epidemic. *Angels in America* (1992) itself confronts, among other charged issues, the U.S. politics of race through exchanges between black gay and Jewish gay characters, as when Louis blurts out to Belize:

> It's – look, race, yes, but ultimately race here is a political question, right? Racists just try to use race here as a tool in a political struggle. It's not really about race. Like the spiritualists try to use that stuff, are you enlightened, are you centered, channeled, whatever, this reaching out for a spiritual past in a country where no indigenous spirits exist – only the Indians, I mean Native American spirits and we killed them off so now, there are no gods here, no ghosts and spirits in America, there are no angels in America, no spiritual past, no racial past, there's only the political .... (*Millennium* 92)

Louis's denial of the spiritual past no less than of the racial past is spectacularly given the lie, in *Angels in America*, by the antirealist appearance of both ghosts and angels, as well as by his sounding suspiciously like the character of Roy Cohn, the closeted prosecutor of McCarthyism whose ostentatious power-mongering was of little use when he too was dying from AIDS.

It is not only because *Angels in America* features historical characters, such as Roy Cohn or Ethel Rosenberg, among its fictional ones that it should be understood as a play about history and its losses. Kushner's play connects the 1950s with the 1980s, perceiving in governmental neglect of people with AIDS a reanimation of the national homophobia that energized McCarthyism three decades earlier. But *Angels in America*, while in some sense about history, also manifests a political philosophy *of* history through its figure of the angel, who apocalyptically appears to the protagonist-with-AIDS, Prior Walter, at the end of Part One, *Millennium Approaches*. This is Walter Benjamin's angel of history, whose imminence is announced in the play by the ghost of Ethel Rosenberg: "History is about to crack wide open. Millennium approaches" (112). A version of this angel appears also in "The Wings," the magnificent long poem at the center of Doty's *My Alexandria*, which describes the angel as "that form / / between us and the unthinkable"

(49). Confronting the limits of representation, the most ambitious imaginative writing about AIDS turned repeatedly, during the 1990s, to angels as figures of historical crisis.

The critical and commercial success of *Angels in America*, coinciding as it did with the transition from twelve dark years of Republican presidency to the start of the Clinton administration, helped to nudge AIDS onto the scene of national public debate. However, in registering that shift in the national conversation about AIDS, we should not forget the extent to which activist struggle laid the groundwork for the success of Kushner's play. Activist performance, community theatre, and popular gay discourse surrounding the epidemic all contributed to the literary works that have been canonized as "AIDS Literature." Writing the history of AIDS entails a perpetual struggle not to forget the lesser players and ordinary voices that too easily vanish from the historical record. Acknowledging that, we wish to conclude by examining the popular genre of pornography, a cultural form that holds special significance for gay men and that endeavored to come to terms, in various ways, with the epidemic's impact on gay sexual practice.

Pornography Confronts AIDS

Despite the fact that both pornographers and AIDS activists turned to sexually explicit forms of representation in an effort to alter gay men's sexual practices during the epidemic, pornography usually is omitted from histories of the epidemic's literature. Historians' and critics' ambivalence about pornography is matched by pornography's uncertainty over how to represent safer sex practices without compromising its primary function of arousal. The ethics of representation was debated not only in rarefied cultural contexts but also among pornographers, who argued about whether porn had a responsibility to educate as well as to entertain. Some, such as the editors of popular gay kink magazine *Drummer*, drew a clear distinction between writing that promoted HIV prevention and escapist, pornographic fiction that contravened safer sex guidelines.[7] Others, working closely with HIV prevention activists, saw in pornography significant potential for promoting safer sex practices. According to John Preston, writing in 1985, pornography would show its consumers that "sex is not over with" (12).

The latter approach is exemplified in *Autopornography* (1997), a fascinating memoir by gay porn performer Scott O'Hara, who provides an exceptionally articulate account of living with HIV long term while nonetheless pursuing a very active sex life. O'Hara discusses his effort to reconcile the conflict between what he identifies as "the two most important things in my life: sperm and HIV" (128). In 1994, he followed the lead of Seattle tattoo artist Lamar VanDyke and had "HIV+" inked on his left bicep as a way of communicating his serostatus to potential lovers. "AIDS has been an undeniable blessing," O'Hara writes; "it woke me up to what was important; it let me know that NOW was the time to do it" (129). Like other AIDS memoirs, *Autopornography* expresses a desire to rethink the temporalities of illness by reevaluating present action. In keeping with the memoirists discussed earlier, O'Hara explores the implications of finitude, but he recasts this question explicitly within the domain of erotic practice.[8]

O'Hara often is regarded as the progenitor of "barebacking," or condomless anal sex, a practice that has divided the porn industry and the gay community. By the end of the 1980s, producers of moving image porn, responding to the pressure to represent safer sex, began showing condom usage on screen. Precautions that began as an attempt to protect performers from HIV infection were subsequently used to "educate [viewers'] desire" (Escoffier 197). Similar precautions were employed by producers of print pornography, which has no live performers to protect. For instance, Alyson Publications compelled Pat Califia to revise previously published stories in conformity with the press's "policy against eroticizing high-risk sex," before they could be published in his 1988 collection, *Macho Sluts* (Califia 61). In his introduction to the book, Califia reports begrudgingly revising his fiction, including writing condom use into stories depicting penetrative anal and oral sex that had not previously mentioned it. Other writers worked with Alyson Publications to produce material that actively promoted safer sex practices. John Preston's anthology *Hot Living* and Max Exander's *Safestud*, both published in 1985, suggest how safer sex pornography sometimes involved a collaborative effort among writers, activists, and publishers. For example, the stories collected in *Hot Living* sought to promote a range of "safer" sexual practices by following available medical guidelines about what constituted acceptable behavior for men having sex with men. These books manifest a commitment to recovering gay erotic life through the use of responsible pornographic representation.

Published nearly a decade after these forms of activist pornography, Samuel R. Delany's novel *The Mad Man* (1994) – which the author has described as a "serious work of pornography" (Delany and Long 133) – explores how such attempts to contain the epidemic had lost their sensitivity to the heterogeneity of gay sexual experience. By the early 1990s, guidelines for "safer sex" exhibited a narrow-minded focus on "the condom code," or the use of condoms for penetrative anal sex. This shift in AIDS education resulted as much from assumptions that linked anal sex to post-Stonewall gay identity as from epidemiological research. What legal scholar David Chambers calls "the hegemony of anal intercourse" obscured the wide range of gay sexual practices for which there was no accurate data on HIV transmission probabilities (358). Delany's novel explores this problem via a narrator who eschews penetrative anal sex in favor of oral intercourse, racialized BDSM scenarios, group masturbation, foot fetishism, fisting, bestiality, and the rapturous consumption of an astonishing range of bodily fluids that many readers likely find disgusting. In a "Disclaimer" that prefaces the novel, Delany writes:

> *The Mad Man* is not a book about "safe sex." Rather it is specifically a book about various sexual acts whose status as vectors of HIV contagion we have no hard-edged knowledge of because the monitored studies that would give statistical portraits of the relation between such acts and Seroconversion (from HIV- to HIV+) have not been done. Reprinted as an appendix is the last large-scale such study to be made widely and publicly available, back in 1987, in the British journal *The Lancet*. (xiii)

Delany's startling novel employs pornographic representation along with scientific studies to dramatize just how much remains unknown about HIV transmission routes. By drawing attention to unconventional sex acts, *The Mad Man* examines how gaps in knowledge about HIV vectors often intensified the sexual risk of those whose race or poverty posed a barrier to identification with well-connected communities of urban, white gay men. Yet, in ways that resonate with Wojnarowicz's *Close to the Knives*, Delany's novel suggests that sex can build unexpected solidarities in finitude, as when an African American graduate student becomes both friend and lover to a group of homeless men and hustlers living on the fringes of New York City.

A few years after Delany explored these issues, the availability of effective antiretroviral drugs transformed the literature of AIDS, gay pornography, and gay men's sexual practices. Bareback sex, bareback porn, and – at least in France – bareback fiction all have risen to prominence over the past decade or so.[9] Many critics and activists have interpreted these developments as a sign that the tragic lessons of the epidemic's first decade have been forgotten, as if barebacking represented simply another loss. Yet AIDS literatures suggest that gay men's relation to history and to time is more complex than a narrative of pure loss is willing to acknowledge. Even Holleran, preparing *Ground Zero*, his landmark collection of essays, for republication two decades later, in 2008, admits that he has forgotten much of the epidemic's first decade: "I realized I had forgotten life in New York in the eighties when I began looking through *Ground Zero*. In fact, what struck me immediately as I leafed through its pages ... was that New York in 1983 seemed as exotic as ancient Egypt" (*Chronicle* 2). Writing about AIDS may function not only as remembrance but also as a means of forgetting its horrors through mourning.

"How difficult it is to say goodbye / to scourge," writes AIDS doctor Rafael Campo in a poem titled "Elegy for the AIDS virus," pointing with no small degree of irony to the challenges entailed in relinquishing loss (*Diva* 46).[10] "[E]ven the business of dying must be set aside occasionally," says the speaker of one of Powell's poems in *Chronic* (2009), a volume of lyrics that redescribes living with HIV in terms explicitly of its temporal effects (25). This recent poem ends by hearkening back to the time immediately before AIDS appeared on the horizon:

> touch: that sensation I'd almost lost.   or how to curl into another's body
>> hermit-crab style
> the grouchy old man in my mirror said "bare terror."   said "who's sharing
>> your towels?"
> go away, you bitter cuss.   it's still 1980 somewhere, some corner of your dark
>> apartment
> where the mystery of the lyric hasn't faded.   and love is in the chorus waiting
>> to be born   (25)

There is more than just nostalgia in these lines that pair the promise of lyric with the possibilities of love, because Powell is reflecting on the imbrication not only of variant temporalities but also of disjunctive relations to time. The experience of time before AIDS is overlaid with fear in the time of AIDS, and both are re-experienced, in the poem, during a time when HIV/AIDS has become "chronic," ongoing rather than fatal. Those earlier times, like the literature that documented them, have not vanished, but they look and feel radically different from the perspective of our present. Still with us, AIDS is no longer what it once was.

Notes

1. See Sherry for an excellent analysis, more nuanced than Sontag's, of the language of war in AIDS discourses.
2. See Kramer, *Reports*, for the Holocaust analogy. For theorizations of literature as testimony and as a distinctive response to trauma, see Caruth; Felman and Laub. AIDS literature has been discussed as a form of testimonial witnessing by R. Chambers in *Facing It* and *Untimely Interventions*.

3. For a survey of AIDS literature that aspires to representativeness, see Canning. Literary scholarship on AIDS exploded in the early 1990s, with three volumes of critical essays: see Nelson; Murphy and Poirier; and Pastore; see also the somewhat later monograph by Kruger. What might be called the lesbian literary response to AIDS is represented best by the fiction of Brown, Schulman (*People*; *Rat*), and Sontag (Sontag and Hodgkin).

4. See, for example, the remarkable collection compiled by Klein. In *Unending Dialogue*, Hadas assembled and contextualized poetry from a workshop she directed for people with AIDS at Gay Men's Health Crisis in New York City.

5. For an extended account of this aspect of Doty's poetry, see Dean, "Strange."

6. Out of the large volume of cultural criticism responding to the epidemic, Douglas Crimp's is among the most notable (see *AIDS*; *Melancholia*).

7. In 1986, the editors began including a disclaimer that sought to defend the sexual practices represented in *Drummer*'s stories as escapist fantasy. "In other than fictional pieces," they wrote, "we will emphasize safe sex with respect to contagious diseases and safe and sane behavior with respect to all activities" ("CAUTION" 2).

8. O'Hara's memoir bears comparison with the writing of Gary Fisher, an African American graduate student at Berkeley, whose journal combines literary meditations with pornographic descriptions of anonymous, mostly condomless, mostly interracial sex and reflections on his experience of HIV.

9. On bareback sex as the basis for a subculture, see Dean, *Unlimited*. For notable instances of bareback fiction, see Dustan (*In My Room*; *LXiR*) and Rémès (*Je bande*; *Serial*).

10. It is strange to hear a physician referring to "the AIDS virus" because, as activists have insisted for decades, this locution conflates the medical syndrome AIDS with the human immunodeficiency virus, thereby suggesting that HIV infection is infection with AIDS. Despite this qualification, we want to stress that Campo's prose about caring for the sick, in *The Poetry of Healing*, is among his best writing.

Works Cited

Benjamin, Walter. "Theses on the Philosophy of History." *Illuminations*. Ed. Hannah Arendt. Trans. Harry Zohn. New York: Schocken, 1969. 252–64. Print.

Brown, Rebecca. *The Gifts of the Body*. New York: Harper, 1994. Print.

Califia, Patrick. *Macho Sluts*. Vancouver: Arsenal Pulp P, 2009. Print.

Campo, Rafael. *Diva*. Durham: Duke UP, 1999. Print.

The Poetry of Healing: A Doctor's Education in Empathy, Identity, and Desire. New York: Norton, 1997. Print.

What the Body Told. Durham: Duke UP, 1996. Print.

Canning, Richard. "The Literature of AIDS." *The Cambridge Companion to Gay and Lesbian Writing*. Ed. Hugh Stevens. Cambridge: Cambridge UP, 2011. 132–47. Print.

Caruth, Cathy. *Unclaimed Experience: Trauma, Narrative, History*. Baltimore: Johns Hopkins UP, 1996. Print.

"CAUTION." *Drummer* 100 (Oct. 1986): 2. Print.

Chambers, David L. "Gay Men, AIDS, and the Code of the Condom." *Harvard Civil-Rights Liberties Law Review* 29 (1994): 353–85. Print.

Chambers, Ross. *Facing It: AIDS Diaries and the Death of the Author*. Ann Arbor: U of Michigan P, 1998. Print.

   Untimely Interventions: AIDS Writing, Testimonial, and the Rhetoric of Haunting. Ann Arbor: U of Michigan P, 2004. Print.

Crimp, Douglas, ed. *AIDS: Cultural Analysis / Cultural Activism*. Cambridge: MIT P, 1988. Print.

   Melancholia and Moralism: Essays on AIDS and Queer Politics. Cambridge: MIT P, 2002. Print.

Crimp, Douglas, and Adam Rolston. *AIDS Demo Graphics*. Seattle: Bay P, 1990. Print.

Dean, Tim. "Strange Paradise: An Essay on Mark Doty" *Modern American Poetry*. U of Illinois. Web. 24 Jan. 2014.

   Unlimited Intimacy: Reflections on the Subculture of Barebacking. Chicago: U of Chicago P, 2009. Print.

Delany, Samuel R. *The Mad Man*. New York: Richard Kasak, 1994. Print.

Delany, Samuel R., and Thomas L. Long. "The Thomas L. Long Interview." *Shorter Views: Queer Thoughts and the Politics of the Paraliterary*. Hanover: Wesleyan UP, 1999: 123–38. Print.

Dent, Tory. *Black Milk: Poems*. Riverdale-on-Hudson: Sheep Meadow P, 2005. Print.

   HIV, Mon Amour: Poems. Riverdale-on-Hudson: Sheep Meadow P, 1999. Print.

   What Silence Equals: Poems. New York: Persea, 1993. Print.

Doty, Mark. *Atlantis: Poems*. New York: Harper, 1995. Print.

   Heaven's Coast: A Memoir. New York: Harper, 1996. Print.

   Letter to Tim Dean. 22 March 1994. TS.

   My Alexandria: Poems. Urbana: U of Illinois P, 1993. Print.

Dustan, Guillaume. *In My Room*. Trans. Brad Rumph. London: Serpent's Tail, 1998. Print.

   LXiR. Paris: Balland, 2002. Print.

Escoffier, Jeffrey. *Bigger than Life: The History of Gay Porn Cinema from Beefcake to Hardcore*. Philadelphia: Running P, 2009. Print.

Exander, Max. *Safestud: The Safesex Chronicles of Max Exander*. Boston: Alyson, 1985. Print.

Felman, Shoshana, and Dori Laub. *Testimony: Crises of Witnessing in Literature, Psychoanalysis, and History*. New York: Routledge, 1992. Print.

Fisher, Gary. *Gary in Your Pocket: Stories and Notebooks of Gary Fisher*. Ed. Eve Kosofsky Sedgwick. Durham: Duke UP, 1996. Print.

Gilman, Sander L. *Disease and Representation: Images of Illness from Madness to AIDS*. Ithaca: Cornell UP, 1988. Print.

Greco, Stephen. "Excerpts from a Journal." *Personal Dispatches: Writers Confront AIDS*. Ed. John Preston. New York: St. Martin's, 1989. 114–23. Print.

Guibert, Hervé. *To the Friend Who Did Not Save My Life*. 1990. Trans. Linda Coverdale. New York: High Risk, 1994. Print.

Gunn, Thom. *The Man with Night Sweats*. New York: Farrar, 1992. Print.

Hadas, Rachel. *Unending Dialogue: Voices from an AIDS Poetry Workshop*. Boston: Faber and Faber, 1993. Print.

Hoffman, William M. *As Is: A Play*. New York: Random, 1985. Print.

Holleran, Andrew. *Chronicle of a Plague, Revisited: AIDS and Its Aftermath*. New York: Da Capo P, 2008. Print.

——. *Ground Zero*. New York: Morrow, 1988. Print.

Klein, Michael, ed. *Poets for Life: Seventy-Six Poets Respond to AIDS*. New York: Crown, 1989. Print.

Kramer, Larry. *Reports from the Holocaust: The Making of an AIDS Activist*. New York: St. Martin's, 1989. Print.

——. *The Normal Heart*. New York: Plume, 1985. Print.

Kruger, Steven F. *AIDS Narratives: Gender and Sexuality, Fiction and Science*. New York: Garland, 1996. Print.

Kushner, Tony. *Angels in America: A Gay Fantasia on National Themes*. Part 1: *Millennium Approaches*. New York: Theatre Communications Group, 1993. Print.

——. *Angels in America: A Gay Fantasia on National Themes*. Part 2: *Perestroika*. New York: Theatre Communications Group, 1993. Print.

Mars-Jones, Adam, and Edmund White. *The Darker Proof: Stories from a Crisis*. London: Faber, 1987. Print.

Monette, Paul. *Love Alone: 18 Elegies for Rog*. New York: St. Martin's, 1988. Print.

Murphy, Timothy, and Suzanne Poirier. *Writing AIDS: Gay Literature, Language, and Analysis*. New York: Columbia UP, 1993. Print.

Nelson, Emmanuel S., ed. *AIDS: The Literary Response*. New York: Twayne, 1992. Print.

Odets, Walt. *In the Shadow of the Epidemic: Being HIV-Negative in the Age of AIDS*. Durham: Duke UP, 1995. Print.

O'Hara, Scott. *Autopornography: A Memoir of Life in the Lust Lane*. New York: Harrington Park P, 1997. Print.

Pastore, Judith Laurence, ed. *Confronting AIDS through Literature: The Responsibilities of Representation*. Urbana: U of Illinois P, 1993. Print.

Pomo Afro Homos. *Dark Fruit. Staging Gay Lives: An Anthology of Contemporary Gay Theatre*. Ed. John Clum. Boulder: Westview P, 1996. 319–43. Print.

——. *Fierce Love: Stories from Black Gay Life. Colored Contradictions: An Anthology of Contemporary African-American Plays*. Ed. Harry J. Elam, Jr. and Robert Alexander. New York: Plume, 1996. 255–85. Print.

Powell, D. A. *Cocktails*. Saint Paul: Graywolf P, 2004. Print.

——. *Chronic*. Saint Paul: Graywolf P, 2009. Print.

Preston, John, ed. *Hot Living: Erotic Stories about Safer Sex*. Boston: Alyson, 1985. Print.

Rémès, Érik. *Je bande donc je suis*. Paris: Blanche, 2004. Print.

——. *Serial Fucker: Journal d'un barebacker*. Paris: Blanche, 2003. Print.

Roach, Tom. *Friendship as a Way of Life: Foucault, AIDS, and the Politics of Shared Estrangement*. Albany: State U of New York P, 2012. Print.

Román, David. *Acts of Intervention: Performance, Gay Culture, and AIDS*. Bloomington: Indiana UP, 1998. Print.

Schulman, Sarah. *People in Trouble*. New York: Dutton, 1990. Print.

——. *Rat Bohemia*. New York: Dutton, 1995. Print.

Sherry, Michael S. "The Language of War in AIDS Discourse." *Writing AIDS: Gay Literature, Language, and Analysis*. Murphy and Poirier, 39–53.

Sontag, Susan. *AIDS and Its Metaphors*. New York: Farrar, 1988. Print.

Sontag, Susan, and Howard Hodgkin. *The Way We Live Now*. London: Cape, 1991. Print.

Treichler, Paula A. "AIDS, Homophobia, and Biomedical Discourse: An Epidemic of Signification." Crimp, *AIDS* 31–70.

Wojnarowicz, David. *Close to the Knives: A Memoir of Disintegration*. New York: Vintage, 1991. Print.

Index

Mars-Jones, Adam, 636, 715
Martial (M. Valerius Martialis), 79–80
Martin, Del, 27–28, 629–30, 685
Martin, George R.R., 669–70
Marx, Karl, 247
Mattachine Society, 685
Matthiessen, F. O., 639–40
Maugham, W. Somerset, 411
Maupin, Armistead, 634–35
Maxwell, William, 688–89
Mayoral, Marina, 440
McAdams, Janet, 556, 562
McCowen, Jeffrey, 648
McCullers, Carson, 626, 688–89
McKay, Claude, 316, 577
McMullin, Dan Taulapapa, 555–56
McNally, Terrence, 618, 621–22
Meaker, Marijane, 686–87
Medieval femininity, 90–91
Medieval gender, 90
Medieval Iberia, poetry in, 99
Medieval masculinity, 90
Meduasa's Revenge, 613
Mehta, Deepa, 506–07
Meiners, Christoph, 258–59
Melville, Herman, 47, 289, 293–94, 295–97
memoirs, AIDS, 647–48, 715–18
 See also autobiographies, same-sex
Mendicutti, Eduardo, 439
Merasty, Bill, 557–58
Merchant, Hoshang, 504, 505
Merlis, Mark, 639–40
Merrill, James, 644–45
Merzliakov, Aleksei, 422–23
Mesoamerican mythmaking
 cosmic figures, 536–43
 introduction, 529–32
 mestizaje, 533–36
mestizaje, 533–36
metonym, 275
Michaelis, Johann David, 256
Middle Ages
 gender and sexuality in, 89
 lives of saints and mystical visions in, 99–101
 passionate friendships in, 96–98
 poetry of same-sex desire in, 98–99
Miguel, Muriel, 613–14
military memoirs, 648–49
Milk, Harvey, 619
Mill, John Stuart, 403–04
Millay, Edna St. Vincent, 379–80, 391–92
Miller, D. A., 608

Miller, Isabel, 628, 639–40
Miller, James E., 387–88
Mills, Florence, 318–19
Milton, John, 174–76, 177
mime, Roman, 71–72
Miranda, Deborah A., 555, 556, 561, 563
Mirror, The, 135–36
Mitchell, Joni, 628–29
Moby Dick (Melville), 293–94
modernism. *See* literary modernism
modernist poetry, queer approaches
 to, 379
Mogutin, Yaroslav, 435–36
Moix, Ana María, 449, 451–52, 453–54
Monette, Paul, 647, 715–16, 718
Monk, The (Lewis), 276–80
Montesquiou-Fezensac, Count Robert de, 335
Mooise, Lenelle, 363
Moon, Michael, 700–01, 709
Moore, Marianne, 594
Moore, Oscar, 637–38
Mootoo, Shani, 363
Mopeli-Paulus, A. S., 481
Moraga, Cherríe, 530, 532, 533, 535, 540, 552, 620–21
Moran, Alec F., 637–38
Morell, Maurice, 19–20
Morris, Jan, 652, 654
Mortiz, Karl Philipp, 265–66
Moses, Daniel David, 555–56, 557
Mpoyi-Buatu, Thomas, 482–83, 485–86
Muñoz, José Esteban, 531
musical theater, 608
Musonius Rufus, 70
My Beautiful Laundrette (film), 506
Myles, Eileen, 601–02
mystics, medieval, 100–01

Nagrodskaia, Evdokia, 431
Naiad Press, 629–30, 693
Namjoshi, Sunit, 506
Nashe, Thomas, 221
nationality
 history of modern, 245
 imagining, 244–47
 racial violence and, 249–51
 sexual meaning and, 251–52
 volatility and, 247–49
Native American literatures
 gender and, 548–50
 poetic tradition in queer, 559–62
 queer critiques, 563–64
 queer drama, 556–58